Applications = Code + Markup:

A Guide to the Microsoft® Windows® Presentation Foundation

Charles Petzold

PUBLISHED BY
Microsoft Press
A Division of Microsoft Corporation
One Microsoft Way
Redmond, Washington 98052-6399

Library of Congress Control Number 2006928845

978-0-7356-1957-9
0-7356-1957-3

Printed and bound in the United States of America.

2 3 4 5 6 7 8 9   QWT   1 0 9 8 7 6

Distributed in Canada by H.B. Fenn and Company Ltd.

A CIP catalogue record for this book is available from the British Library.

Microsoft Press books are available through booksellers and distributors worldwide. For further information about international editions, contact your local Microsoft Corporation office or contact Microsoft Press International directly at fax (425) 936-7329. Visit our Web site at www.microsoft.com/mspress. Send comments to mspinput@microsoft.com.

Acquisitions Editor: Ben Ryan
Project Editor: Valerie Woolley
Technical Editor: Kenn Scribner
Copy Editor: Becka McKay
Indexer: William Meyers

Body Part No. X12-41747

The modern digital computer was invented and intended
as a device that should facilitate and speed up complicated
and time-consuming computations. In the majority of
applications its capability to store and access large amounts
of information plays the dominant part and is considered to
be its primary characteristic, and its ability to compute,
i.e., to calculate, to perform arithmetic, has in many cases
become almost irrelevant.

– *Niklaus Wirth,* Algorithms + Data Structures = Programs *(1976)*

I am going a long way. . .
To the island valley of Avilion;
Where falls not hail, or rain, or any snow
Nor ever wind blows loudly, but it lies
Deep-meadow'd, happy, fair with orchard lawns
And bowery hollows crown'd with summer sea,
Where I will heal me of my grievous wound.

— *Tennyson,* Idylls of the King

Table of Contents

Introduction

This book shows you how to use the Microsoft Windows Presentation Foundation (WPF) to write programs that run under Microsoft Windows. These programs can be either regular stand-alone Windows applications (which are now often called *client* applications) or front ends for distributed applications. The WPF is considered to be the primary application programming interface (API) for Microsoft Windows Vista, but you can also run WPF applications under Microsoft Windows XP with Service Pack 2 or Windows Server 2003 after you have installed Microsoft .NET Framework 3.0.

Although you use the WPF for writing what are sometimes called "regular type Windows apps," these are definitely not your parents' Windows programs. The WPF includes a new look, a new philosophy concerning control customization, new graphics facilities (including animation and 3D), and a new programming interface.

The WPF actually has *two* interrelated programming interfaces. You can write WPF programs entirely using C# or any other programming language that complies with the .NET Common Language Specification (CLS). In addition, the WPF includes an exciting new XML-based markup language called the Extensible Application Markup Language (or XAML, pronounced "zammel"), and in some cases you can write entire programs in XAML. Generally, however, you will build your applications from both code *and* markup (as the title of this book implies). You'll use XAML for defining the user interface and visuals of your application—including graphics and animation—and you'll write code for handling user input events.

Your Background

In writing this book, I have assumed that you already have experience with the C# programming language and previous versions of the .NET Framework. If that is not the case, please refer to my short book titled *.NET Book Zero: What the C or C++ Programmer Needs to Know about C# and the .NET Framework*. This book is free and is available for reading or downloading from the following page of my Web site:

http://www.charlespetzold.com/dotnet

If you are a beginning programmer, I recommend that you learn C# first by writing console programs, which are character-mode programs that run in a Command Prompt window. My book *Programming in the Key of C#: A Primer for Aspiring Programmers* (Microsoft Press, 2003) takes this approach.

This Book

I have been writing programs for Windows since 1985, and the WPF is the most exciting development in Windows programming that I've experienced. But because it supports two very different programming interfaces, the WPF has also presented great challenges for me in writing this book. After giving the matter much thought, I decided that every WPF programmer should have a solid foundation in writing WPF applications entirely in code. For that reason, Part I of this book shows you how to write complete WPF programs using C#.

Several features of the WPF required enhancements to .NET properties and events, and it's important to understand these enhancements, particularly when you're working with XAML. For this reason, I have devoted chapters in Part I specifically to the new concepts of dependency properties and routed input events.

Part II of this book focuses on XAML. I show how to create small XAML-only applications and also how to combine XAML with C# code in creating larger, more sophisticated applications. One of the first jobs I take on in Part II is to create a programming tool called XAML Cruncher that has helped me a lot in learning XAML, and which I hope will help you as well. Because XAML is used primarily to create the visuals of an application, most of the graphics coverage in this book is found in Part II.

In the long run, most of the XAML that gets written in this world will probably be generated by interactive designers and other programming tools. I'm sure that you will eventually use these designers and tools yourself to facilitate the development of your applications. However, I think it's vital for every WPF programmer to be able to write XAML "manually," and that's what I show you how to do in this book. If you're like me, you'll discover that programming in XAML—particularly when you're using a tool such as XAML Cruncher—can be great fun as an end in itself.

My books are tutorials more than references. Readers of my previous books have found the books most useful when they begin reading Chapter 1 and continue sequentially. Getting your fingers accustomed to typing C# and XAML is essential. Like learning to juggle or playing the oboe, programming is not something you can learn just from reading a book. Generally people learn a programming interface more quickly and deeply when they actually type in the code themselves. Particularly in the early chapters, try doing this, and don't hesitate to experiment with variations in the code. In the early chapters I have suggested many such experiments.

Windows and Programming

Microsoft released the first version of Windows in the fall of 1985. Since then, Windows has been progressively updated and enhanced, most dramatically in Microsoft Windows NT (1993) and Windows 95 (1995), when Windows moved from a 16-bit architecture to a 32-bit architecture.

When Windows was first released, there was really only one way to write a Windows application, and that was by using the C programming language to access the Windows API. Over the years, many other languages have been adapted for doing Windows programming, including Microsoft Visual Basic and C++. For C-based languages, Microsoft currently offers four approaches to writing Windows applications, as detailed in the following table.

How to Write a Windows Application Using a C-Based Language (Microsoft-Centric View)

Year Introduced	Language	Interface
1985	C	Windows application programming interface
1992	C++	Microsoft Foundation Class (MFC) library
2001	C# or C++	Windows Forms (part of the .NET Framework 1.0)
2006	C# or C++	Windows Presentation Foundation (WPF)

It's not my job to tell you what language or interface you should use to write Windows applications. That's a decision only you can make based on your particular programming job and the resources available to you.

If you want to learn more about the Windows API, many people have found my book *Programming Windows* (fifth edition, Microsoft Press, 1998) to be valuable. Although I never cared for MFC, historically it has been one of the most popular approaches to Windows programming. A good place to learn about MFC is the book *Programming Windows with MFC* (second edition, Microsoft Press, 1999) by Jeff Prosise and, for advanced programmers, *Programming Applications for Microsoft Windows* (Microsoft Press, 1999) by Jeffrey Richter.

If you'd rather engage in more modern Windows programming (this is, after all, the twenty-first century), .NET is really the way to go. Programs written for .NET are generally compiled into an intermediate code (the Microsoft Intermediate Language, or MSIL), which is then compiled into native code when the application is run. This managed code helps protect the operating system from errant programs that might damage the user's system, and it also lets .NET programs be potentially platform independent.

It might seem odd that Microsoft has released two distinct .NET platforms for writing Windows client applications. I believe that Windows Forms still has a strong role to play in Windows application development. Particularly with the enhancements in the .NET Framework 2.0, Windows Forms has a greater array of powerful controls and standard dialog boxes than the WPF, and in many ways it's the easier programming platform. I've written two books on Windows Forms. *Programming Windows with C#* (Microsoft Press, 2001) is large and comprehensive, and it covers the first version of Windows Forms in detail. *Programming Microsoft Windows Forms* (Microsoft Press, 2005) is short and streamlined. It supplements the earlier book with coverage of Windows Forms 2.0 features, and by itself it can help a beginning Windows Forms programmer get quickly up to speed.

Whereas the WPF may not yet have the range of controls or standard dialog boxes supported in Windows Forms, it lays a strong foundation for an extensive future. In particular, if you need to do a lot of control customization or graphics, the WPF is the way to go.

System Requirements

To use this book, you'll need:

- Windows Vista, Windows XP with Service Pack 2, or Windows Server 2003.
- Microsoft Visual Studio 2005 Standard Edition, Visual Studio 2005 Professional Edition, Microsoft Visual C# 2005 Express Edition, or a later edition of Visual Studio. (Visual C# 2005 Express Edition does not include a collection of the bitmaps and icons I've used in this book.)
- The .NET Framework 3.0 (included as part of Windows Vista).
- The .NET Framework 3.0 Software Development Kit (SDK).
- A computer capable of running this software.

All versions of the .NET Framework and software development kits are available from the Microsoft Web site:

http://msdn.microsoft.com/netframework/downloads/updates

In theory, you don't need Visual Studio to compile and run WPF applications. The SDK includes a command-line program named MSBuild that can build WPF applications from C# project (.csproj) files. However, Visual Studio certainly makes WPF development easier, and some would argue that in this day and age, it's really essential.

Prerelease Software

This book was reviewed and tested against the June 2006 Community Technology Preview (CTP) of the .NET Framework 3.0. I expect this book to be fully compatible with the final release of the .NET Framework 3.0 and SDK, but if there are any changes or corrections, they will be collected in the Microsoft Knowledge Base article cited in the "Support for This Book" section of this introduction.

Code Samples

All the code samples discussed in this book can be downloaded from the book's companion content page at the following Web address:

http://www.microsoft.com/mspress/companion/0-7356-1957-3

Support for This Book

Every effort has been made to ensure the accuracy of this book and the companion content. As corrections or changes are collected, they will be added to a Microsoft Knowledge Base article.

Microsoft Press provides support for books and companion content at the following Web site:

http://www.microsoft.com/learning/support/books

Questions and Comments

If you have comments, questions, or ideas regarding this book or the companion content, or if you have questions that are not answered by visiting the sites previously mentioned, please send them to Microsoft Press via e-mail at:

mspinput@microsoft.com

or via postal mail at:

Microsoft Press
Attn: Applications = Code + Markup *Editor*
One Microsoft Way
Redmond, WA 98052-6399

Please note that Microsoft software product support is not offered through these addresses.

Author's Web Site

Information specific to this book can also be found on this page of my Web site:

http://www.charlespetzold.com/wpf

Information about my other books, as well as a blog and miscellaneous articles, can be accessed from the home page of my Web site.

Special Thanks

For helping put this book together, I want to thank my agent, Claudette Moore of the Moore Literary Agency, and my editors at Microsoft Press: Valerie Woolley (project editor), Kenn Scribner (technical editor), and the other folks listed on the copyright page of this book who have tried their best to polish my prose and correct my misconceptions.

I've also benefited greatly from a community of bloggers—many but not all of whom work at Microsoft—who have written about WPF programming and indirectly contributed to this book, and people who have emailed me with pointers. The most prominent are (in alphabetical order) Chris Anderson, Pete Blois, Aaron Cornelius at *www.wiredprairie.us*, Pablo Fernicola, Jessica Fosler, Henry Hahn, Karsten Januszewski, Chuck Jazdzewski, Nick Kramer, Rahul Patil, Rob Relyea, Greg Schechter, Tim Sneath, David Teitlebaum, and Shawn Van Ness.

Of course, even with this lineup of impeccable guidance, I am perfectly capable of blundering, and any errors or bugs that might still remain in this book are entirely my responsibility.

Most of all, I want to thank Deirdre, who offers words of wisdom, sentences of sympathy, paragraphs of patience, chapters of charity, and a big long book of love.

Charles Petzold
New York City and Roscoe, New York
September 2005–June 2006

Part I
Code

Chapter 1
The Application and the Window

An application written for the Microsoft Windows Presentation Foundation (WPF) generally begins its seconds or hours on the Windows desktop by creating objects of type *Application* and *Window*. A simple WPF program looks like this:

```
SayHello.cs
//-------------------------------------------
// SayHello.cs (c) 2006 by Charles Petzold
//-------------------------------------------
using System;
using System.Windows;

namespace Petzold.SayHello
{
    class SayHello
    {
        [STAThread]
        public static void Main()
        {
            Window win = new Window();
            win.Title = "Say Hello";
            win.Show();

            Application app = new Application();
            app.Run();
        }
    }
}
```

You're familiar with the *System* namespace, I assume. (If not, you should probably read my online book *.NET Book Zero* available on my Web site at *www.charlespetzold.com*.) The SayHello program also includes a *using* directive for *System.Windows*, which is the namespace that includes all the basic WPF classes, structures, interfaces, delegates, and enumerations, including the classes *Application* and *Window*. Other WPF namespaces begin with the preface *System.Windows*, such as *System.Windows.Controls*, *System.Windows.Input*, and *System.Windows.Media*. A notable exception is the namespace *System.Windows.Forms*, which is the primary Windows Forms namespace. All namespaces that begin with *System.Windows.Forms* are also Windows Forms namespaces, except for *System.Windows.Forms.Integration*, which includes classes that can help you integrate Windows Forms and WPF code.

The sample programs shown in this book have a consistent naming scheme. Each program is associated with a Microsoft Visual Studio project. All code in the project is enclosed in a namespace definition. The namespace always consists of my last name followed by the name of the project. For this first example, the project name is SayHello and the namespace is then *Petzold.SayHello*. Each class in the project is given a separate source code file, and the name of the file generally matches the name of the class. If the project consists of only one class, which is the case for this first example, that class is usually given the same name as the project.

In any WPF program, the *[STAThread]* attribute must precede *Main* or the C# compiler will complain. This attribute directs the threading model of the initial application thread to be a single-threaded apartment, which is required for interoperability with the Component Object Model (COM). "Single-threaded apartment" is an old COM-era, pre-.NET programming term, but for our purposes you could imagine it to mean our application won't be using multiple threads originating from the runtime environment.

In the SayHello program, *Main* begins by creating an object of type *Window*, which is the class you use for creating a standard application window. The *Title* property indicates the text that will appear in the window's caption bar, and the *Show* method displays the window on the screen.

The final important step is to call the *Run* method of a new *Application* object. In Windows programming parlance, this method creates the message loop that allows the application to receive user input from the keyboard and mouse. If the program is running on a Tablet PC, the application also receives input from the stylus.

You'll probably use Visual Studio 2005 to create, compile, and run applications written for the Windows Presentation Foundation. If so, you can re-create the SayHello program by following these steps:

1. Select New Project from the File menu.

2. In the New Project dialog, select Visual C#, Windows Presentation Foundation, and Empty Project. Find a good home for the project and give it the name SayHello. Uncheck the Create Directory For Solution option. Click OK.

3. In the Solution Explorer on the right, the References section must include PresentationCore, PresentationFramework, System, and WindowsBase. If the References section doesn't include these DLLs, add them. Right-click References and select Add Reference. (Or, select Add Reference from the Project menu.) In the Add Reference dialog, click the .NET tab and select the required DLLs. Click OK.

4. In the Solution Explorer on the right, right-click the SayHello project name and then select New Item from the Add menu. (Or, select Add New Item from the Project menu.) In the Add New Item dialog, select Code File. Type in the file name SayHello.cs. Click OK.

5. Type the program shown earlier in the chapter into the SayHello.cs file.

6. Select Start Without Debugging from the Debug menu (or press Ctrl+F5) to compile and run the program.

For most of the example programs shown in Part I of this book, the process of creating projects will follow basically the same steps, except that some projects (including one in this chapter) have multiple source code files.

When you close the window created by SayHello, you'll discover that a console window has also been running. The presence of this console window is governed entirely by a compiler flag that you can control in the project's properties. Right-click the project name at the right and select Properties from the menu. (Or, select Properties from the Project menu.) Now you can explore or alter aspects of the project. Note that the Output Type is set to Console Application. Obviously this setting hasn't affected the program's ability to go far beyond the console in creating a window. Change the Output Type to Windows Application, and the program will run as before but without the console window. I personally find the console window very useful in program development. I use it for displaying textual information while the program is running, and for debugging. If a program is so buggy that it doesn't even display a window, or if it displays a window but enters an infinite loop, it's easy to terminate the application by typing Ctrl+C in the console window.

The *Window* and *Application* classes used in SayHello both derive from *DispatcherObject*, but *Window* has a much longer pedigree, as shown in the class hierarchy:

Object
> *DispatcherObject* (abstract)
>> *Application*
>> *DependencyObject*
>>> *Visual* (abstract)
>>>> *UIElement*
>>>>> *FrameworkElement*
>>>>>> *Control*
>>>>>>> *ContentControl*
>>>>>>>> *Window*

Of course, it's not necessary to be intimately familiar with the class hierarchy just yet, but as you make your way through the Windows Presentation Foundation, you'll encounter these classes again and again.

A program can create only one *Application* object, which exists as a constant anchor for the rest of the program. The *Application* object is invisible; the *Window* object is not—it appears on the screen in all its glory as a standard Windows window. It has a caption bar displaying the text indicated in the *Title* property. The caption bar has a system menu icon on the left, and minimize, maximize, and close icons on the right. The window has a sizing border, and it has a client area occupying the vast interior of the window.

Within limits, you can mix up the order of the statements in the *Main* method of the SayHello program and the program will still work. For example, you can set the *Title* property after calling *Show*. In theory, that change causes the window to be displayed initially without a title in its caption bar, but the change will probably happen too quickly to see.

You can create the *Application* object before creating the *Window* object, but the call to *Run* must be last. The *Run* method does not return until the window is closed. At that point, the *Main* method ends and Windows cleans up after your program. If you remove the call to *Run*, the *Window* object is still created and displayed, but it's immediately destroyed when *Main* ends.

Instead of calling the *Show* method of the *Window* object, you can pass the *Window* object as an argument to the *Run* method:

```
app.Run(win);
```

In this case, the *Run* method takes the responsibility of calling *Show* for the *Window* object.

A program doesn't really get started until it calls the *Run* method. Only then can the *Window* object respond to user input. When the user closes the window and the *Run* method returns, the program is ready to terminate. Thus, the program spends almost all of its existence deep within the *Run* call. But how can the program do anything if it is spending all its time in *Run*?

Following initialization, virtually everything a program does is in response to an *event*. These events usually indicate keyboard, mouse, or stylus input from the user. The *UIElement* class (which refers to the user interface, of course) defines a number of keyboard-, mouse-, and stylus-related events; the *Window* class inherits all those events. One of those events is named *MouseDown*. A window's *MouseDown* event occurs whenever the user clicks the client area of the window with the mouse.

Here's a program that mixes up the order of the statements in *Main* a bit, and also installs an event handler for the *MouseDown* event of the window:

HandleAnEvent.cs

```
//------------------------------------------------
// HandleAnEvent.cs (c) 2006 by Charles Petzold
//------------------------------------------------
using System;
using System.Windows;
using System.Windows.Input;
```

```
namespace Petzold.HandleAnEvent
{
    class HandleAnEvent
    {
        [STAThread]
        public static void Main()
        {
            Application app = new Application();

            Window win = new Window();
            win.Title = "Handle An Event";
            win.MouseDown += WindowOnMouseDown;

            app.Run(win);
        }
        static void WindowOnMouseDown(object sender, MouseButtonEventArgs args)
        {
            Window win = sender as Window;
            string strMessage =
                string.Format("Window clicked with {0} button at point ({1})",
                              args.ChangedButton, args.GetPosition(win));
            MessageBox.Show(strMessage, win.Title);
        }
    }
}
```

I like to give my event handlers names that begin with the class or object responsible for the event, followed by the word *On*, followed by the event name itself (hence *WindowOnMouse-Down*). But you can name your event handlers whatever you want.

The *MouseDown* event is documented as requiring an event handler defined in accordance with the *MouseButtonEventHandler* delegate, which has a first argument of type *object*, and a second argument of type *MouseButtonEventArgs*. That class is defined in the *System.Windows.Input* namespace, so the program includes another *using* directive. This program must define the event handler as *static* because the handler is referred to from the *static* method *Main*.

Most subsequent programs in this book will include a *using* directive for *System.Windows.Input* even if they don't need it.

The *MouseDown* event is fired whenever the user clicks the client area of the window with any mouse button. The first argument to the event handler is the object firing the event, which is the *Window* object. The event handler can safely cast that object to an object of type *Window*.

The event handler in the *HandleTheEvent* needs the *Window* object for two purposes: First, it uses the *Window* object as an argument to the *GetPosition* method defined by the *MouseButtonEventArgs* class. This method returns an object of type *Point* (a structure defined in *System.Windows*) with the mouse coordinates relative to the top-left corner of the *GetPosition* argument. Second, the event handler accesses the *Title* property of the *Window* object and uses that property as the title of the message box.

The *MessageBox* class is defined in the *System.Windows* namespace as well. It contains 12 over-loads of the static *Show* method that allow lots of options for displaying buttons and images. By default, only an OK button appears.

The message box in the HandleAnEvent program displays the position of the mouse cursor relative to the upper-left corner of the client area. You may have naturally assumed that those coordinates were pixels. They are not. They are device-independent units of 1/96 inch. I'll have more to say about this odd coordinate system later in this chapter.

The event handler in HandleAnEvent casts the *sender* argument to an object of type *Window*, but there are other ways for the event handler to obtain this *Window* object. The *Window* object created in *Main* could have been saved as a static field and the event handler could have used that. Or, the event handler could have taken advantage of some properties of the *Application* class. *Application* has a static property named *Current* that returns the *Application* object created by the program. (As I mentioned, a program can create only one *Application* object.) *Application* also includes an instance property named *MainWindow* that returns a *Window* object. So the event handler could have set a local *Window* variable like this:

```
Window win = Application.Current.MainWindow;
```

If the only purpose for obtaining the *Window* object in this event handler was to access the *Title* text for the message box, the *MessageBox.Show* method could have included an argument of *Application.Current.MainWindow.Title*.

The *Application* class defines several events that may be useful. As is customary in .NET, most of these events are associated with protected methods that generally have the responsibility for firing the event. The *Startup* event defined by *Application* is fired from the protected *OnStartup* method and occurs soon after the program calls the *Run* method of the *Application* object. A call to the *OnExit* method (and the firing of the corresponding *Exit* event) occurs when the *Run* method is about to return. You can use these two occasions to perform application-wide initialization or cleanup.

The *OnSessionEnding* method and *SessionEnding* event indicate that the user has chosen to log off the Windows session or shut down the computer. This event is delivered with an argument of type *SessionEndingCancelEventArgs*, a class that derives from *CancelEventArgs* and which includes a property named *Cancel*. If your application wants to prevent Windows from shutting down, set that property to *true*. This event is only received if you compile your program as a Windows Application rather than as a Console Application.

If your program needs to handle some events of the *Application* class, it can install event handlers for those events, but it is most convenient to define a class that inherits from *Application*, such as the class in this next example, *InheritTheApp*. A class that inherits from *Application* can simply override the underlying methods responsible for firing the events.

```
InheritTheApp.cs
//------------------------------------------------
// InheritTheApp.cs (c) 2006 by Charles Petzold
//------------------------------------------------
using System;
using System.Windows;
using System.Windows.Input;

namespace Petzold.InheritTheApp
{
    class InheritTheApp : Application
    {
        [STAThread]
        public static void Main()
        {
            InheritTheApp app = new InheritTheApp();
            app.Run();
        }
        protected override void OnStartup(StartupEventArgs args)
        {
            base.OnStartup(args);

            Window win = new Window();
            win.Title = "Inherit the App";
            win.Show();
        }
        protected override void OnSessionEnding(SessionEndingCancelEventArgs args)
        {
            base.OnSessionEnding(args);

            MessageBoxResult result =
                MessageBox.Show("Do you want to save your data?",
                                MainWindow.Title, MessageBoxButton.YesNoCancel,
                                MessageBoxImage.Question, MessageBoxResult.Yes);

            args.Cancel = (result == MessageBoxResult.Cancel);
        }
    }
}
```

The *InheritTheApp* class derives from *Application* and overrides the *OnStartup* and *OnSession-Ending* methods defined by the *Application* class. In this program, the *Main* method doesn't create an object of type *Application*, but rather an object of type *InheritTheApp*. Yet *Main* is a member of this very class. It may seem a little odd that *Main* creates an instance of a class to which it belongs, but it's perfectly legitimate because *Main* is defined as static. The *Main* method exists even if no *InheritTheApp* object has yet been created.

InheritTheApp overrides both the *OnStartup* method (which is called soon after the program calls *Run*) and *OnSessionEnding*. It is during the *OnStartup* method that the program takes the opportunity to create a *Window* object and show it. The *InheritTheApp* class could alternatively have performed this task in its constructor.

In the *OnSessionEnding* override, the program displays a message box with Yes, No, and Cancel buttons. Notice that the title of the message box is set to *MainWindow.Title*. Because this is an instance method of a class that derives from *Application*, the simple reference to *MainWindow* obtains the value of that property for this instance. You could preface *MainWindow* with the *this* keyword to make it more explicit that *MainWindow* is a property of *Application*.

Of course, the program has no data to save, so it ignores the Yes and No responses and allows the application to shut down and Windows to continue terminating the user session. If the response is Cancel, it sets the *Cancel* flag of the *SessionEndingCancelEventArgs* object to *true*. This, in turn, prevents Windows from shutting down or logging off at this time. You can tell which action is specified, shutdown or logoff, by accessing the *ReasonSessionEnding* property of *SessionEndingCancelEventArgs*. *ReasonSessionEnding* provides you with an enumerated value, which is either *ReasonSessionEnding.Logoff* or *ReasonSessionEnding.Shutdown*.

Both *OnStartup* and *OnSessionEnding* in the program begin by calling the method in the base classes. These calls are not strictly needed in these cases, but they can't hurt. It's generally wise, however, to call the base class method unless you have specific reasons for not doing so.

As you know, you can run programs from the Command Prompt window, and in doing so you can give command-line arguments to the program. Windows programs are no different. To process command-line arguments, you must define the *Main* method a little differently:

```
public static void Main(string[] args)
```

Any command-line arguments are passed to *Main* as an array of strings. This array of strings can also be accessed in the *OnStartup* method as the *Args* property of the StartupEventArgs argument.

The fact that *Application* has a property named *MainWindow* suggests that a program can have multiple windows. This is certainly true. Typically, many of these extra windows take the form of transitory dialog boxes, but dialog boxes are basically additional *Window* objects with just a few differences in the way they're displayed and the way they interact with the user.

Here's a program that throws a party by inviting several more windows to the desktop:

ThrowWindowParty.cs

```
//-------------------------------------------------
// ThrowWindowParty.cs (c) 2006 by Charles Petzold
//-------------------------------------------------
using System;
using System.Windows;
using System.Windows.Input;
```

```
namespace Petzold.ThrowWindowParty
{
    class ThrowWindowParty: Application
    {
        [STAThread]
        public static void Main()
        {
            ThrowWindowParty app = new ThrowWindowParty();
            app.Run();
        }
        protected override void OnStartup(StartupEventArgs args)
        {
            Window winMain = new Window();
            winMain.Title = "Main Window";
            winMain.MouseDown += WindowOnMouseDown;
            winMain.Show();

            for (int i = 0; i < 2; i++)
            {
                Window win = new Window();
                win.Title = "Extra Window No. " + (i + 1);
                win.Show();
            }
        }
        void WindowOnMouseDown(object sender, MouseButtonEventArgs args)
        {
            Window win = new Window();
            win.Title = "Modal Dialog Box";
            win.ShowDialog();
        }
    }
}
```

Like the *InheritTheApp* class, the *ThrowWindowParty* class inherits from *Application* and creates a *Window* object in the override of its *OnStartup* method. It then creates two more *Window* objects and shows them as well. (I'll discuss what goes on in the *MouseDown* event handler shortly.)

The first thing you'll notice is that the three windows created in the *OnStartup* override are equal citizens in this application. You can click any window and that window will come to the foreground. You can close them in any order, and only when the last window is closed will the program terminate. If one of the windows did not have the caption "Main Window," you'd be hard-pressed to identify it.

However, if your program were to examine the *MainWindow* property of the *Application* object, it would find that the first window for which *Show* was called is considered the main window of the application (at least initially).

The *Application* class also includes a property named *Windows* (notice the plural) that is of type *WindowCollection*. The *WindowCollection* class is a typical .NET collection class that implements the *ICollection* and *IEnumerable* interfaces and (as the name implies) stores multiple *Window* objects. The class includes a property named *Count* and an indexer that lets you obtain all the individual *Window* objects that your program has called *Show* for and that still exist. At the end of the *OnStartup* override, the *Windows.Count* property would return 3, and *Windows[0]* would be the window with the caption "Main Window."

One of the oddities of this program is that all three windows show up in the Windows taskbar, which (if you're like most users) sits at the bottom of your Windows screen. It is considered very uncool for programs to occupy multiple slots in the Windows taskbar. To suppress the display of those extra windows, you'll want to include the following statement in the *for* loop:

```
win.ShowInTaskbar = false;
```

But now something else is peculiar. If you close the window labeled "Main Window" first, you'll see the taskbar entry disappear—but the program is obviously still running and still displaying two windows!

A program generally chooses to terminate when the *Run* method returns, and by default, the *Run* method returns when the user closes the last window. This behavior is governed by the *ShutdownMode* property of *Application*, which you set to a member of the *ShutdownMode* enumeration. Besides the default *ShutdownMode.OnLastWindowClose* member, you can specify *ShutdownMode.OnMainWindowClose*. Try inserting the following statement right before the call to *Run*:

```
app.ShutdownMode = ShutdownMode.OnMainWindowClose;
```

Or, try inserting the following statement anywhere in the *OnStartup* override. (In *Main*, you must preface the property with the name of the *Application* object; in the *OnStartup* method, you just specify the property and optionally preface it with the keyword *this*.)

```
ShutdownMode = ShutdownMode.OnMainWindowClose;
```

Now *Run* returns and the program terminates whenever the main window is closed.

Without removing the change to the *Shutdown* property, try inserting this statement in the *for* loop:

```
MainWindow = win;
```

MainWindow is, you'll recall, a property of the *Application* class. This is how your program can specify which window you choose as the main window. At the conclusion of the *for* loop, the window labeled "Extra Window No. 2" will be considered the main window, and that's the window you must close to terminate the program.

There's a third option for *ShutdownMode*: You can set the property to the enumeration member *ShutdownMode.OnExplicitShutdown*, in which case *Run* returns only when the program explicitly calls the *Shutdown* method of *Application*.

Now remove any code you've inserted involving the *ShutdownMode* and *MainWindow* properties of the *Application* class. There's another way to establish a hierarchy among multiple windows, and that's by using the *Owner* property defined by the *Window* class. By default, this property is *null*, which means that the window has no owner. You can set the *Owner* property to and other *Window* object in the application (with the exception that ownership cannot be circular). For example, try inserting this code in the *for* loop:

```
win.Owner = winMain;
```

Now the two extra windows are owned by the main window. You can still switch back and forth between all three windows, but as you do so you'll see that the owned windows always appear in the foreground of their owner. When you minimize the owner, the owned windows disappear from the screen, and when you close the owner, the owned windows are also automatically closed. These two extra windows have become *modeless* dialog boxes.

Modeless dialogs are the less common of the two main categories of dialog boxes. Much more common is the *modal* dialog box. You can see an example of a modal dialog box by clicking the client area of the *ThrowWindowParty* main window with the mouse. The *WindowOnMouseDown* method creates another *Window* object and gives it a *Title* property, but instead of calling *Show* it calls *ShowDialog*. Unlike *Show*, *ShowDialog* doesn't immediately return, and the modal dialog box it displays doesn't let you switch to other windows in the program. (It will allow you to switch to other programs running under *Windows*, however.) Only when you close the modal dialog box does the call to *ShowDialog* return.

Modeless dialog boxes, on the other hand, *do* allow you to work with the main application with the dialog window in place. A good example of a modeless dialog is the Quick Find dialog in Visual Studio. It allows you to find strings in your source code, but yet also allows you to edit the source file with the Quick Find dialog still active. Modal dialogs capture user input to the application and force you to dismiss the dialog before you can work with other application windows. Modeless dialog boxes do not.

Try this. Go back to the first example program, SayHello, and in the source code change *Show* to *ShowDialog* and comment out all references to the *Application* object. The program still works because *ShowDialog* implements its own message loop to handle input events. Modal dialog boxes become modal by not participating in the message loop of the application and hence not allowing the application to obtain user input events.

The previous two programs defined a class that inherited from *Application*. It is possible (and quite common) for a program to define a class that inherits from *Window*. The following program contains three classes and three source code files. To add additional empty source code files to an existing project in Visual Studio 2005, right-click the project name in the Solution Explorer and then select Add New Item from the shortcut menu. Or, select Add New Item from the Project menu. In either case, the item you want to add is a Code File, which is initially empty.

The project name is InheritAppAndWindow, which is also the name of a class that contains only *Main*:

InheritAppAndWindow.cs

```
//----------------------------------------------------
// InheritAppAndWindow.cs (c) 2006 by Charles Petzold
//----------------------------------------------------
using System;
using System.Windows;
using System.Windows.Input;

namespace Petzold.InheritAppAndWindow
{
    class InheritAppAndWindow
    {
        [STAThread]
        public static void Main()
        {
            MyApplication app = new MyApplication();
            app.Run();
        }
    }
}
```

Main creates an object of type *MyApplication* and calls *Run* on that object. The *MyApplication* class derives from *Application* and is defined like this:

MyApplication.cs

```
//---------------------------------------------------
// MyApplication.cs (c) 2006 by Charles Petzold
//---------------------------------------------------
using System;
using System.Windows;
using System.Windows.Input;

namespace Petzold.InheritAppAndWindow
{
    class MyApplication : Application
    {
        protected override void OnStartup(StartupEventArgs args)
        {
            base.OnStartup(args);

            MyWindow win = new MyWindow();
            win.Show();
        }
    }
}
```

In the override of the *OnStartup* method, the class creates an object of type *MyWindow*, which is the third class in the project and derives from *Window*:

```
MyWindow.cs
//-------------------------------------------
// MyWindow.cs (c) 2006 by Charles Petzold
//-------------------------------------------
using System;
using System.Windows;
using System.Windows.Input;

namespace Petzold.InheritAppAndWindow
{
    public class MyWindow : Window
    {
        public MyWindow()
        {
            Title = "Inherit App & Window";
        }
        protected override void OnMouseDown(MouseButtonEventArgs args)
        {
            base.OnMouseDown(args);

            string strMessage =
                string.Format("Window clicked with {0} button at point ({1})",
                            args.ChangedButton, args.GetPosition(this));
            MessageBox.Show(strMessage, Title);
        }
    }
}
```

Classes that derive from *Window* generally use the constructor of the class to initialize themselves. The only custom initialization this particular window performs is setting the *Title* property. Notice that the property need not be prefaced with any object name because *MyWindow* inherits that property from *Window*. You can optionally preface the property with the keyword *this*:

```
this.Title = "Inherit App & Window";
```

Rather than installing an event handler for the *MouseDown* event, the class can override the *OnMouseDown* method. Because *OnMouseDown* is an instance method, it can pass the keyword *this* to the *GetPosition* method to refer to the *Window* object, and it can refer to the *Title* property directly.

Although there's nothing wrong with the program just shown, it's somewhat more common (and easier) in a code-only WPF program to define a class that inherits from *Window*, but not a class that inherits from *Application*. Here's a typical single-file program:

```
InheritTheWin.cs
//-----------------------------------------------
// InheritTheWin.cs (c) 2006 by Charles Petzold
//-----------------------------------------------
using System;
using System.Windows;
using System.Windows.Input;

namespace Petzold.InheritTheWin
{
    class InheritTheWin : Window
    {
        [STAThread]
        public static void Main()
        {
            Application app = new Application();
            app.Run(new InheritTheWin());
        }
        public InheritTheWin()
        {
            Title = "Inherit the Win";
        }
    }
}
```

This is the structure I'll use for many of the sample programs in Part I of this book. It's fairly short, as you can see, and if you really wanted to strip the *Main* method down, you could cram all its functionality into a single statement:

```
new Application().Run(new InheritTheWin());
```

Let's play around with this program. I'll make some suggestions for how to change the program, and you can either follow along or (even better) try some others on your own.

The window is positioned and sized on the screen by the Windows operating system itself, but you can override that behavior. The *Window* class inherits *Width* and *Height* properties from *FrameworkElement*, and you can set those properties in the constructor:

```
Width = 288;
Height = 192;
```

In setting these two properties, you aren't limited to integers. The properties are defined as *double* values, so you can set them like so:

```
Width = 100 * Math.PI;
Height = 100 * Math.E;
```

The *Width* and *Height* properties are initially undefined, and if your program never sets them, they remain undefined, which means they have values of NaN, the abbreviation immortalized by the IEEE (Institute of Electrical and Electronics Engineers, Inc.) floating-point standard for "not a number."

So if you ever need to obtain the actual size of the window, don't use the *Width* and *Height* properties. Use the read-only properties *ActualWidth* and *ActualHeight* instead. However, these latter two properties will equal 0 in the constructor of the window; they only become applicable when the window is displayed on the screen.

It may have seemed like I chose two numbers at random when I showed these two statements earlier:

```
Width = 288;
Height = 192;
```

These numbers are not pixels. If the *Width* and *Height* properties were specified in units of pixels, they wouldn't have to be defined as double-precision floating-point values. The units in which you specify all dimensions and locations in Windows Presentation Foundation are sometimes called *device-independent pixels* or *logical pixels* but it's probably best not to refer to pixels at all. I will call them *device-independent units*. Each unit is 1/96 inch, so those values of 288 and 192 actually indicate that the window is to be 3 inches wide by 2 inches tall.

If you take a ruler to your monitor, you probably won't measure precisely those dimensions, however. The relationship between pixels and inches is established by Windows and changeable by the user. Right-click your Windows screen and select Properties from the drop-down menu. Click the Settings tab and then click the Advanced button, and then click the General tab if you have a choice.

By default, Windows establishes a display resolution of 96 dots per inch, and if that's the case on your machine, the *Width* and *Height* values of 288 and 192 correspond precisely to pixels.

However, if you have your video display set to 120 DPI (a common alternative among users born before the first release of *Star Wars*) and a WPF program sets window *Width* and *Height* properties of 288 and 192, the pixel width of the window will be 360, and the height will be 240, consistently implying a window size of 3 inches by 2 inches.

As monitors become available in the future with much higher resolutions than we're accustomed to now, WPF programs should be able to run without change. For example, suppose you have a monitor that achieves approximately 200 pixels to the inch. To avoid everything becoming very tiny on the screen, users will need to use Display Properties to set a commensurate resolution, perhaps 192 DPI. When a WPF program sets a *Width* and *Height* of 288 and 192 device-independent units, those dimensions now become 576 pixels and 384 pixels—still 3 inches by 2 inches.

The use of these device-independent units is pervasive throughout the Windows Presentation Foundation. For example, some programs shown earlier in this chapter used a message box to display the location of a mouse click relative to the upper-left corner of the client area. That location was not in units of pixels, but rather in device-independent units of 1/96 inch.

If you experiment with very small values of *Width* and *Height*, you'll discover that the window always displays at least part of the caption bar. These minimum dimensions of the window— again in device-independent units of 1/96 inch—can be obtained from the static read-only properties *SystemParameters.MinimumWindowWidth* and *SystemParameters.MinimumWindowHeight*. The *SystemParameters* class has a number of static properties with information like this.

If you'd like to position your window at a particular location of the screen, you can do that as well by setting the *Left* and *Top* properties defined by the *Window* class:

```
Left = 500;
Top = 250;
```

These two properties specify the location of the top-left corner of the window relative to the top-left corner of the screen. Again, these are *double* values in device-independent units, and if your program does not set these properties, they remain values of NaN. The *Window* class does not define *Right* and *Bottom* properties. The right and bottom location of the window is implied by the *Left* and *Top* properties and the size of the window.

Suppose your video adapter and monitor are capable of displaying 1600 pixels horizontally and 1200 pixels vertically, and that's what you've set as your display resolution in the Display Properties dialog. Suppose you examine the values returned from the static properties *System-Parameters.PrimaryScreenWidth* and *SystemParameters.PrimaryScreenHeight*. Will these values be 1600 and 1200? Only if your screen DPI setting is 96. In that case, you've expressed a wish that your display be 16-2/3 inches by 12-1/2 inches.

However, if you've set your assumed screen DPI as 120, *SystemParameters.PrimaryScreenWidth* and *SystemParameters.PrimaryScreenHeight* return values of 1280 by 960 device-independent units, implying a metrical size of 13-1/3 inches by 10 inches.

Because *SystemParameters* reports nearly all dimensions in device-independent units— exceptions are the *SystemParameters* properties *SmallIconWidth* and *SmallIconHeight*, which are in units of pixels—you can safely use most values in calculations without any conversions. For example, you can position a window at the lower-right corner of the screen using the following code:

```
Left = SystemParameters.PrimaryScreenWidth - Width;
Top = SystemParameters.PrimaryScreenHeight - Height;
```

This code implies that you've already set the *Width* and *Height* properties. But you may not like the results. If you have a taskbar at the bottom of your screen, it will obscure the bottom part of your window. You might prefer to position your window instead at the lower-right corner of the *work area*, which is that area of the screen not occupied by any application desktop toolbars (of which the Windows taskbar is the most common example).

The *SystemParameters.WorkArea* property returns an object of type *Rect*, a structure that defines a rectangle in terms of the coordinate location of its upper-left corner and its size. This *WorkArea* property must be defined as a *Rect* rather than just a width and height because the user can put the taskbar at the left of the screen. In that case, the *Left* property of the *Rect* structure will be non-zero, and the *Width* property will equal the screen width minus the *Left* value.

Here's code to position your window in the lower-right corner of the work area:

```
Left = SystemParameters.WorkArea.Width - Width;
Top = SystemParameters.WorkArea.Height - Height;
```

And here's code that positions your window in the *center* of the work area:

```
Left = (SystemParameters.WorkArea.Width - Width) / 2 +
            SystemParameters.WorkArea.Left;
Top = (SystemParameters.WorkArea.Height - Height) / 2 +
            SystemParameters.WorkArea.Top;
```

As an alternative to this code, you can use the *WindowStartupLocation* property defined by the *Window* class. You set this property to a member of the *WindowStartupLocation* enumeration. The default value is *WindowStartupLocation.Manual*, which means that either the program or the Windows operating system manually positions the window. You can set the property to *WindowStartupLocation.CenterScreen* to center the window. Despite the name of this enumeration member, the window is centered in the work area rather than on the screen. (The third option is *WindowStartupLocation.CenterOwner*, which you use with modal dialog boxes to set them in the center of their owners.)

Here's a little program that positions itself in the center of the work area and lets you change its size by 10 percent with each press of the up or down arrow key:

GrowAndShrink.cs

```
//------------------------------------------------
// GrowAndShrink.cs (c) 2006 by Charles Petzold
//------------------------------------------------
using System;
using System.Windows;
using System.Windows.Input;

namespace Petzold.GrowAndShrink
{
    public class GrowAndShrink : Window
    {
        [STAThread]
```

```
    public static void Main()
    {
        Application app = new Application();
        app.Run(new GrowAndShrink());
    }
    public GrowAndShrink()
    {
        Title = "Grow & Shrink";
        WindowStartupLocation = WindowStartupLocation.CenterScreen;
        Width = 192;
        Height = 192;
    }
    protected override void OnKeyDown(KeyEventArgs args)
    {
        base.OnKeyDown(args);

        if (args.Key == Key.Up)
        {
            Left -= 0.05 * Width;
            Top -= 0.05 * Height;
            Width *= 1.1;
            Height *= 1.1;
        }
        else if (args.Key == Key.Down)
        {
            Left += 0.05 * (Width /= 1.1);
            Top += 0.05 * (Height /= 1.1);
        }
    }
}
}
```

The *OnKeyDown* method (and the related *KeyDown* event) report on keystrokes. Each time you press and release a key on the keyboard, the *OnKeyDown* and *OnKeyUp* methods are called. You can process keys by overriding the methods. The *Key* property of the *KeyEventArgs* object is a member of the large *Key* enumeration and tells you what key is involved. Because the *Left*, *Top*, *Width*, and *Height* properties are all floating-point values, no information is lost as you increase and decrease the size of the window. You'll reach certain minimums and maximums imposed by Windows, but the properties still keep their calculated values.

The *OnKeyDown* and *OnKeyUp* methods are useful for obtaining keystrokes of the cursor movement keys and function keys, but for obtaining actual Unicode characters from the keyboard you should override the *OnTextInput* method. The *Text* property of the *TextComposition-EventArgs* argument is a string of Unicode characters. In general, the string will be just one character, but speech and handwriting input can also generate calls to *OnTextInput*, and the string might be longer.

The following program doesn't set a *Title* property. Instead, you can type your own.

```
TypeYourTitle.cs
//-----------------------------------------------
// TypeYourTitle.cs (c) 2006 by Charles Petzold
//-----------------------------------------------
using System;
using System.Windows;
using System.Windows.Input;

namespace Petzold.TypeYourTitle
{
    public class TypeYourTitle : Window
    {
        [STAThread]
        public static void Main()
        {
            Application app = new Application();
            app.Run(new TypeYourTitle());
        }
        protected override void OnTextInput(TextCompositionEventArgs args)
        {
            base.OnTextInput(args);

            if (args.Text == "\b" && Title.Length > 0)
                Title = Title.Substring(0, Title.Length - 1);

            else if (args.Text.Length > 0 && !Char.IsControl(args.Text[0]))
                Title += args.Text;
        }
    }
}
```

The only control character that the method allows is a backspace ('\b') and then only when the *Title* is at least one character in length. Otherwise, the method simply appends text typed from the keyboard to the *Title* property.

The *Window* class defines other properties that affect the appearance and behavior of the window. You can set the *WindowStyle* property to a member of the *WindowStyle* enumeration. The default is *WindowStyle.SingleBorderWindow*. The *WindowStyle.ThreeDBorderWindow* is a little fancier, but actually decreases the size of the client area a smidgen. You generally use *WindowStyle.ToolWindow* for dialog boxes. The caption bar is a little shorter, and the window has a close button but no minimize and maximize buttons. However, you can still minimize and maximize the window by pressing Alt+Spacebar to invoke the system menu. You can also resize the tool window. The *WindowStyle.None* also has a sizing border but doesn't even display a caption bar. You can still invoke the system menu by typing Alt+Spacebar. The *Title* property is not displayed by the window but it does appear in the task bar.

The presence or absence of the sizing border is governed by the *ResizeMode* property, which you set to a member of the *ResizeMode* enumeration. The default is *ResizeMode.CanResize*, which lets the user resize the window, minimize it, or maximize it. You can display a little grip in the lower-left corner of the client area with *ResizeMode.CanResizeWithGrip*. The option *ResizeMode.CanMinimize* suppresses the sizing border and disables the maximize box, but still allows the window to be minimized. This option is useful for windows that have a fixed size. Finally, *ResizeMode.NoResize* suppresses the minimize and maximize buttons as well as the sizing border.

You can set the *WindowState* property to a member of the *WindowState* enumeration to govern how your window is initially displayed. The options are *WindowState.Normal*, *WindowState.Minimized*, or *WindowState.Maximized*.

Set the *Topmost* property to *true* to make your window appear in the foreground of all other windows. (You should use this with discretion, and only with windows for which this feature serves a purpose. Of course, give the user an option to turn it off.)

Another important property of the *Window* class is *Background*. This is a property that *Window* inherits from *Control* and it governs the color of the client area. Yet *color* is far too mild a term for what you can actually do with that *Background* property. The *Background* property is an object of type *Brush*, and the types of brushes you can use to color the background of your window include gradient brushes, and brushes based on bitmaps and other images. Brushes play such an important role in the Windows Presentation Foundation that two chapters in this book are devoted to them. The first of those two chapters is the next chapter, so let's plunge into it.

Chapter 2
Basic Brushes

The vast interior of the standard window is referred to as the window's *client area*. This is the part of the window in which your program displays text, graphics, and controls, and through which it receives user input.

The client areas of the windows created in the previous chapter were probably colored white, but that's only because white is the default color for the background of window client areas. You may have used Microsoft Windows Control Panel to set your system colors to non-default values for aesthetic reasons or to flaunt your eccentric individuality. More seriously, you might be someone who sees the screen better when the background of the window is black and foreground objects (such as text) are white. If so, you probably wish that more developers were aware of your needs and treated your desired screen colors with respect.

Color in the Windows Presentation Foundation is encapsulated in the *Color* structure defined in the *System.Windows.Media* namespace. As is customary with graphics environments, the *Color* structure uses levels of red, green, and blue primaries to represent color. These three primaries are generally referred to as R, G, and B, and the three-dimensional space defined by these three primaries is known as an RGB color space.

The *Color* structure contains three read/write properties of type *byte* named simply R, G, and B. The values of these three properties range from 0 through 255. When all three properties are 0, the color is black. When all three properties are 255, the color is white.

To these three primaries, the *Color* structure adds an alpha channel denoted by the property named A. The alpha channel governs the opacity of the color, where a value of 0 means that the color is entirely transparent and 255 means opaque, and values in between denote degrees of transparency.

Like all structures, *Color* has a parameterless constructor, but this constructor creates a color with the A, R, G, and B properties all set to 0—a color that is both black and entirely transparent. To make this a visible color, your program can manually set the four *Color* properties, as shown in the following example:

```
Color clr = new Color();
clr.A = 255;
clr.R = 255;
clr.G = 0;
clr.B = 255;
```

The resultant color is an opaque magenta.

The *Color* structure also includes several static methods that let you create *Color* objects with a single line of code. This method requires three arguments of type *byte*:

```
Color clr = Color.FromRgb(r, g, b)
```

The resultant color has an *A* value of 255. You can also specify the alpha value directly in this static method:

```
Color clr = Color.FromArgb(a, r, g, b)
```

The RGB color space implied by byte values of red, green, and blue primaries is sometimes known as the sRGB color space, where *s* stands for *standard*. The sRGB space formalizes common practices in displaying bitmapped images from scanners and digital cameras on computer monitors. When used to display colors on the video display, the values of the sRGB primaries are generally directly proportional to the voltages of the electrical signals sent from the video display board to the monitor.

However, sRGB is clearly inadequate for representing color on other output devices. For example, if a particular printer is capable of a greener green than a typical computer monitor, how can that level of green be represented when the maximum value of 255 represents the monitor green?

To meet these concerns, other RGB color spaces have been defined. The *Color* structure in the Windows Presentation Foundation supports one of these alternatives, the scRGB color space, which was formerly known as sRGB64 because the primaries are represented by 64-bit values. In the *Color* structure, the scRGB primaries are actually stored as single-precision *float* values. To accommodate the scRGB color space, the *Color* structure contains four properties of type *float* named *ScA*, *ScR*, *ScG*, and *ScB*. These properties are *not* independent of the *A*, *R*, *G*, and *B* properties. Changing the *G* property also changes the *ScG* property and vice versa.

When the *G* property is 0, the *ScG* property is also 0. When the *G* property is 255, the *ScG* property is 1. Within this range, the relationship is not linear, as shown in the following table.

scG	G
<= 0	0
0.1	89
0.2	124
0.3	149
0.4	170
0.5	188
0.6	203
0.7	218
0.8	231
0.9	243
>= 1.0	255

The relationship between scR and R—and between scB and B—is the same as that between scG and G. The values of scG can be less than 0 or greater than 1 to accommodate colors that are beyond the gamut of the video display and the numerical range of sRGB.

Cathode ray tubes in common use today do not display light in a linear fashion. The light intensity (I) is related to the voltages (V) sent to the display in the following power relationship:

$$I = V^\gamma$$

where the gamma exponent is a value that is characteristic of the display and ambient light, but for commonly used monitors and viewing conditions is generally between 2.2 and 2.5. (The sRGB standard assumes 2.2.)

Human visual perception to light intensity is nonlinear as well—approximately proportional to the light intensity to the 1/3 power. Fortunately, the nonlinearity of human perception and the nonlinearity of the CRT tend to offset each other, so that the sRGB primaries (which are proportional to the display voltages) are roughly perceptually linear. That is, an RGB value of 80-80-80 (in hexadecimal) roughly corresponds to what a person might categorize as "medium gray." This is part of what makes sRGB such a compelling standard.

The scRGB primaries, however, are designed to be linear in relationship to light intensity, so the relationship between scG and G is

$$scG \cong \left(\frac{G}{255} \right)^{2.2}$$

where the exponent of 2.2 is the value of gamma assumed in the sRGB standard. Notice that this relationship is approximate. It is least accurate in the low values. The transparency channel has a simpler relationship:

$$scA = \frac{A}{255}$$

You can create a *Color* object based on scRGB primaries using this static method:

```
Color clr = Color.FromScRgb(a, r, g, b);
```

The arguments are *float* values, and can be less than 0 or greater than 1.

System.Windows.Media also includes a class named *Colors* (notice the plural) that contains 141 static read-only properties whose names begin alphabetically with *AliceBlue* and *AntiqueWhite* and conclude with *Yellow* and *YellowGreen*. For example:

```
Color clr = Colors.PapayaWhip;
```

All but one of these color names are the same as those commonly supported by Web browsers. The exception is the *Transparent* property, which returns a *Color* value with an alpha value of 0. The other 140 properties in the *Colors* class return a *Color* object based on preset sRGB values with an alpha level of 255.

Your program can change the background color of the client area by setting the *Background* property, a property that *Window* inherits from *Control*. However, you don't set *Background* to a *Color* object; you set *Background* to a much more versatile object of type *Brush*.

Brushes are used so extensively in the WPF that they demand early attention in this book. *Brush* itself is actually an abstract class, as shown in the following class hierarchy:

Object
    DispatcherObject (abstract)
        DependencyObject
            Freezable (abstract)
                Animatable (abstract)
                    Brush (abstract)
                        GradientBrush (abstract)
                            LinearGradientBrush
                            RadialGradientBrush
                      SolidColorBrush
                      TileBrush (abstract)
                        DrawingBrush
                        ImageBrush
                        VisualBrush

What you actually use to set the *Background* property of the *Window* object is an instance of one of the nonabstract classes that inherit from *Brush*. All *Brush*-related classes are part of the *System.Windows.Media* namespace. In this chapter I will discuss *SolidColorBrush* and the two classes that inherit from *GradientBrush*.

As the name may suggest, the simplest type of brush is *SolidColorBrush*, which is a brush based on a single color. In one of the later programs in Chapter 1, you can set the color of the client area after including a *using* directive for *System.Windows.Media* and putting code like the following in the constructor for the *Window* class:

```
Color clr = Color.FromRgb(0, 255, 255);
SolidColorBrush brush = new SolidColorBrush(clr);
Background = brush;
```

This causes the background to appear as the color cyan. Of course, you can do the whole thing in one line of code, like this:

```
Background = new SolidColorBrush(Color.FromRgb(0, 255, 255));
```

SolidColorBrush also has a parameterless constructor and a property named *Color* that lets you set or alter the color of the brush after the object has been created. For example:

```
SolidColorBrush brush = new SolidColorBrush();
brush.Color = Color.FromRgb(128, 0, 128);
```

The following program varies the background color of the client area based on the proximity of the mouse pointer to the window's center. This program includes a *using* directive for *System.Windows.Media*, as will most future programs in this book.

VaryTheBackground.cs

```
//----------------------------------------------------
// VaryTheBackground.cs (c) 2006 by Charles Petzold
//----------------------------------------------------
using System;
using System.Windows;
using System.Windows.Input;
using System.Windows.Media;

namespace Petzold.VaryTheBackground
{
    public class VaryTheBackground : Window
    {
        SolidColorBrush brush = new SolidColorBrush(Colors.Black);

        [STAThread]
        public static void Main()
        {
            Application app = new Application();
            app.Run(new VaryTheBackground());
        }
        public VaryTheBackground()
        {
            Title = "Vary the Background";
            Width = 384;
            Height = 384;
            Background = brush;
        }
        protected override void OnMouseMove(MouseEventArgs args)
        {
            double width = ActualWidth
                - 2 * SystemParameters.ResizeFrameVerticalBorderWidth;
            double height = ActualHeight
                - 2 * SystemParameters.ResizeFrameHorizontalBorderHeight
                - SystemParameters.CaptionHeight;

            Point ptMouse = args.GetPosition(this);
            Point ptCenter = new Point(width / 2, height / 2);
```

```
                  Vector vectMouse = ptMouse - ptCenter;
                  double angle = Math.Atan2(vectMouse.Y, vectMouse.X);
                  Vector vectEllipse = new Vector(width / 2 * Math.Cos(angle),
                                                  height / 2 * Math.Sin(angle));
                  Byte byLevel = (byte) (255 * (1 - Math.Min(1, vectMouse.Length /
                                                          vectEllipse.Length)));
                  Color clr = brush.Color;
                  clr.R = clr.G = clr.B = byLevel;
                  brush.Color = clr;
              }
          }
      }
```

As you move the mouse toward the center of the client area, the background changes to lighter shades of gray. The background becomes black when the mouse is beyond an imaginary ellipse that fills the client area.

All the action happens in the overridden *OnMouseMove* method, which is called whenever the mouse is moved over the program's client area. The method is a little complex for a couple reasons. The method must first calculate the size of the client area, but unless there's something actually *in* the client area, there's no good way to determine its size. The method begins by using the *ActualWidth* and *ActualHeight* properties of the window and then subtracting the dimensions of the sizing border and caption bar as obtained from static properties of the *SystemParameters* class.

The method obtains the mouse pointer's location by calling the *GetPosition* method in the *MouseEventArgs* class, and saves that *Point* object in *ptMouse*. This location is a certain distance from the center of the client area, which is the *Point* structure named *ptCenter*. The method then subtracts *ptCenter* from *ptMouse*. If you examine the documentation of the *Point* structure, you'll find that subtracting one *Point* from another results in an object of type *Vector*, which this method saves as *vectMouse*. Mathematically, a vector is a magnitude and a direction. The magnitude of *vectMouse* is the distance between *ptCenter* and *ptMouse*, and it's provided by the *Length* property of the *Vector* structure. The direction of a *Vector* object is provided by its *X* and *Y* properties, which represent a direction from the origin—the point (0, 0)—to the point (*X*, *Y*). In this particular case, *vectMouse.X* equals *ptMouse.X* minus *ptCenter.X* and similarly for *Y*.

The direction of a *Vector* object can also be represented as an angle. The *Vector* structure includes a static method named *AngleBetween* that calculates the angle between two *Vector* objects. The *OnMouseMove* method in the VaryTheBackground program shows a direct calculation of the angle of *vectMouse* based on the inverse tangent of the ratio of its *Y* and *X* properties. This angle is in radians measured clockwise from the horizontal axis. The method then uses that angle to calculate another *Vector* object that represents the distance from the center of the client area to a point on an ellipse that fills the client area. The level of gray is simply proportional to the ratio of the two vectors.

The *OnMouseMove* method obtains the *Color* object associated with the *SolidColorBrush* originally created as a field of the class, sets the three primaries to the gray level, and then sets the *Color* property of the brush to this new value.

That this program works at all may astonish you. Obviously somebody is redrawing the client area every time the brush changes, but it's all happening behind the scenes. This dynamic response is possible because *Brush* derives from the *Freezable* class, which implements an event named *Changed*. This event is fired whenever any changes are made to the *Brush* object, and this is how the background can be redrawn whenever a change occurs in the brush.

This *Changed* event and similar mechanisms are used extensively behind the scenes in the implementation of animation and other features in the Windows Presentation Foundation.

Just as the *Colors* class provides a collection of 141 static read-only properties with all the named colors, a class named *Brushes* (again, notice the plural) provides 141 static read-only properties with the same names as those in *Colors* but which return objects of type *Solid-ColorBrush*. Instead of setting the *Background* property like this:

```
Background = new SolidColorBrush(Colors.PaleGoldenrod);
```

you can use this:

```
Background = Brushes.PaleGoldenrod;
```

Although these two statements will certainly color your window background with the same color, there is a difference between the two approaches that reveals itself in a program like VaryTheBackground. In that program try replacing the following field definition:

```
SolidColorBrush brush = new SolidColorBrush(Colors.Black);
```

with

```
SolidColorBrush brush = Brushes.Black;
```

Recompile and run. Now you get an Invalid Operation Exception that states "Cannot set a property on object '#FF000000' because it is in a read-only state." The problem is the very last statement in the *OnMouseMove* method, which attempts to set the *Color* property of the brush. (The hexadecimal number quoted in the exception is the current value of the *Color* property.)

The *SolidColorBrush* objects returned from the *Brushes* class are in a *frozen* state, which means they can no longer be altered. Like the *Changed* event, freezing is implemented in the *Freezable* class, from which *Brush* inherits. If the *CanFreeze* property of a *Freezable* object is *true*, it's possible to call the *Freeze* method to render the object frozen and unchangeable. The *IsFrozen* property indicates this state by becoming *true*. Freezing objects can improve performance because they no longer need to be monitored for changes. A frozen *Freezable* object can also be shared across threads, while an unfrozen *Freezable* object cannot. Although you cannot unfreeze a frozen object, you can make an unfrozen copy of it. The following code *will* work as a field definition of VaryTheBackground:

```
SolidColorBrush brush = Brushes.Black.Clone();
```

If you'd like to see these 141 brushes rendered on the window's client area, the FlipThrough-TheBrushes program lets you use the up and down arrow keys to flip through them.

```
FlipThroughTheBrushes.cs
//-------------------------------------------------------
// FlipThroughTheBrushes.cs (c) 2006 by Charles Petzold
//-------------------------------------------------------
using System;
using System.Reflection;
using System.Windows;
using System.Windows.Input;
using System.Windows.Media;

namespace Petzold.FlipThroughTheBrushes
{
    public class FlipThroughTheBrushes : Window
    {
        int index = 0;
        PropertyInfo[] props;

        [STAThread]
        public static void Main()
        {
            Application app = new Application();
            app.Run(new FlipThroughTheBrushes());
        }
        public FlipThroughTheBrushes()
        {
            props = typeof(Brushes).GetProperties(BindingFlags.Public |
                                                  BindingFlags.Static);
            SetTitleAndBackground();
        }
        protected override void OnKeyDown(KeyEventArgs args)
        {
            if (args.Key == Key.Down || args.Key == Key.Up)
            {
                index += args.Key == Key.Up ? 1 : props.Length - 1;
                index %= props.Length;
                SetTitleAndBackground();
            }
            base.OnKeyDown(args);
        }
        void SetTitleAndBackground()
        {
            Title = "Flip Through the Brushes - " + props[index].Name;
            Background = (Brush) props[index].GetValue(null, null);
        }
    }
}
```

This program uses reflection to obtain the members of the *Brushes* class. The first line of the constructor uses the expression *typeof(Brushes)* to obtain an object of type *Type*. The *Type* class defines a method named *GetProperties* that returns an array of *PropertyInfo* objects, each one corresponding to one of the properties of the class. You'll notice that the program explicitly restricts itself to the public and static properties from the *Brushes* class using a *BindingFlags* argument to *GetProperties*. That restriction isn't necessary in this case because all the properties of *Brushes* are public and static, but it can't hurt.

Both in the constructor and in the *OnKeyDown* override, the program calls *SetTitleAndBackground* to set the *Title* property and the *Background* property to one of the members of the *Brushes* class. The expression *props[0].Name* returns a string with the name of the first property in the class, which is the string "AliceBlue". The expression *props[0].GetValue(null, null)* returns the actual *SolidColorBrush* object. *GetValue* requires two *null* arguments for this job. Normally, the first argument would be the object you're obtaining the property value from. Since *Brushes* is a static property, there is no object. The second argument is used only if the property is an indexer.

The *System.Windows* namespace has a *SystemColors* class that is similar to both *Colors* and *Brushes* in that it contains only static read-only properties that return *Color* values and *Solid-ColorBrush* objects. This class provides the current user's color preferences as stored in the Windows registry. *SystemColors.WindowColor*, for example, indicates the user's preference for the background of the client area, while *SystemColors.WindowTextColor* is the user's preferred color for text in the client area. *SystemColors.WindowBrush* and *SystemColors.WindowTextBrush* return *SolidColorBrush* objects created with these same colors. For most real-world applications, you should use these colors for most simple text and monochromatic graphics.

The brush objects returned from *SystemColors* are frozen. Your program can change this brush:

```
Brush brush = new SystemColorBrush(SystemColors.WindowColor);
```

but it cannot change this brush:

```
Brush brush = SystemColors.WindowBrush;
```

Only objects based on classes that derive from *Freezable* can be frozen. There is no such thing as a frozen *Color* object, because *Color* is a structure.

One alternative to a solid-color brush is a gradient brush, which displays a gradually changing mix of two or more colors. Normally, gradient brushes would be an advanced programming topic, but they are easy to create in the Windows Presentation Foundation, and they are quite popular in modern color schemes.

In its simplest form, the *LinearGradientBrush* requires two *Color* objects (let's call them *clr1* and *clr2*) and two *Point* objects (*pt1* and *pt2*). The point *pt1* is colored with *clr1*, and *pt2* is colored with *clr2*. The line connecting *pt1* and *pt2* is colored with a mix of *clr1* and *clr2*, so that the midpoint is the average of *clr1* and *clr2*. Every line perpendicular to the line connecting *pt1* and *pt2* is colored uniformly with a proportion of the two colors. I'll discuss shortly what happens on the other side of *pt1* and *pt2*.

Now here's the really good news: Normally you would have to specify the two points in units of pixels or (in the case of the Windows Presentation Foundation) device-independent units, and if you wanted to apply a gradient to a window background you would have to re-specify the points whenever the window size changed.

The WPF gradient brush includes a feature that makes it unnecessary to recreate or modify the brush based on the size of the window. By default, you specify the two points relative to the surface that the gradient brush is coloring, where the surface is considered to be 1 unit wide and 1 unit high. The upper-left corner of the surface is the point (0, 0). The lower-right corner is the point (1, 1).

For example, if you want red at the upper-left corner of your client area and blue at the lower-right corner, and a linear gradient between them, use the following constructor, which lets you specify two colors and two points:

```
LinearGradientBrush brush = new LinearGradientBrush(Colors.Red, Colors.Blue,
                                    new Point(0, 0), new Point(1, 1));
```

Here's a program that does precisely that:

```
GradiateTheBrush.cs
//-------------------------------------------------
// GradiateTheBrush.cs (c) 2006 by Charles Petzold
//-------------------------------------------------
using System;
using System.Windows;
using System.Windows.Input;
using System.Windows.Media;

namespace Petzold.GradiateTheBrush
{
    public class GradiateTheBrush : Window
    {
        [STAThread]
        public static void Main()
        {
            Application app = new Application();
            app.Run(new GradiateTheBrush());
        }
        public GradiateTheBrush()
        {
            Title = "Gradiate the Brush";

            LinearGradientBrush brush =
                new LinearGradientBrush(Colors.Red, Colors.Blue,
                                    new Point(0, 0), new Point(1, 1));
            Background = brush;
        }
    }
}
```

As you change the size of the client area, this gradient brush changes behind the scenes. Again, the *Change* event implemented by the *Freezable* class makes this possible.

Although it's often convenient to set points using this relative coordinate system, it isn't the only option. The *GradientBrush* class defines a *MappingMode* property that you set to a member of the *BrushMappingMode* enumeration. The only members are *RelativeToBoundingBox*, which is the default, and *Absolute*, which lets you use device-independent units.

In hexadecimal RGB terms, the color at the upper-left corner of the client area in Gradiate-TheBrush is FF-00-00 and the color at the lower right is 00-00-FF. You would expect the color midway between those two to be either 7F-00-7F or 80-00-80, depending solely on rounding, and that is certainly the case, because the default *ColorInterpolationMode* property is the enumeration value *ColorInterpolationMode.SRgbLinearInterpolation*. The alternative is *ColorInterpolationMode.ScRgbLinearInterpolation*, which causes the midway color to be the scRGB value 0.5-0-0.5, which is the sRGB value BC-00-BC.

If you just need to create a horizontal or vertical gradient, it's easier to use this constructor of *LinearGradientBrush*:

```
new LinearGradientBrush(clr1, clr2, angle);
```

Specify *angle* in degrees. A value of 0 is a horizontal gradient with *clr1* on the left, equivalent to

```
new LinearGradientBrush(clr1, clr2, new Point(0, 0), new Point(1, 0));
```

A value of 90 creates a vertical gradient with *clr1* on the top, equivalent to

```
new LinearGradientBrush(clr1, clr2, new Point(0, 0), new Point(0, 1));
```

Other angle values may be trickier to use. In the general case, the first point is always the origin, while the second point is computed like so:

```
new Point(cos(angle), sin(angle))
```

For an angle of 45 degrees, for example, the second point is approximately (0.707, 0.707). Keep in mind that this is relative to the client area, so if the client area isn't square (which is often the case), the line between the two points is not actually at 45 degrees. Also, a good chunk of the lower-right corner of the window is beyond this point. What happens there? By default, it's colored with the second color. This behavior is governed by the *SpreadMethod* property, which is set to a member of the *GradientSpreadMethod* enumeration. The default is *Pad*, which means that the color at the end is just continued as long as it's needed. Other possibilities are *Reflect* and *Repeat*. You might want to try the following code in GradiateTheBrush:

```
LinearGradientBrush brush =
    new LinearGradientBrush(Colors.Red, Colors.Blue,
                        new Point(0, 0), new Point(0.25, 0.25));

brush.SpreadMethod = GradientSpreadMethod.Reflect;
```

This brush displays a gradient from red to blue between the points (0, 0) and (0.25, 0.25), then from blue to red between (0.25, 0.25) and (0.5, 0.5), then red to blue from (0.5, 0.5) to (0.75, 0.75), and finally blue to red from (0.75, 0.75) to (1, 1).

If you make the window very narrow or very short to exaggerate the difference between the horizontal and vertical dimensions, the uniformly colored lines become nearly vertical or nearly horizontal. You may prefer that a gradient between two opposite corners have a uniformly colored line between the other two corners.

Will a diagram help? Here's the GradiateTheBrush client area when stretched to oblong dimensions:

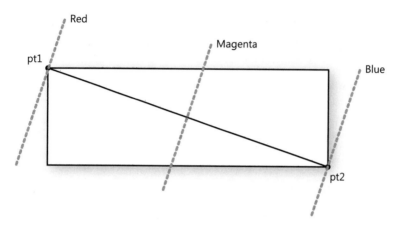

The dashed lines represent the uniformly colored areas, which are always perpendicular to the line connecting *pt1* and *pt2*. You might prefer a gradient that instead looks like this:

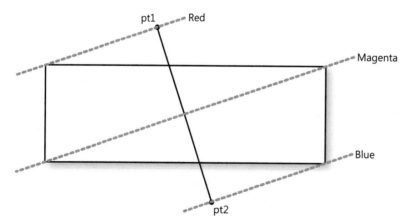

Now the area colored with magenta extends between the two corners. The problem is that we need to calculate *pt1* and *pt2* so that the line connecting those two points is perpendicular to the line connecting the bottom-left and top-right corners.

It can be shown (my passive-voice inner mathematician says) that the length of the lines from the center of the rectangle to *pt1* and *pt2* (which I'll call *L*) can be calculated like this:

$$L = \frac{W \cdot H}{\sqrt{W^2 + H^2}}$$

where *W* is the width of the window and *H* is the height. Let me convince you. Here's the same view of the client area with some additional lines and labels:

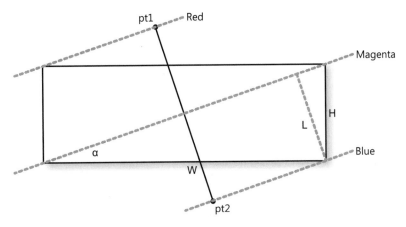

Notice that the line labeled L is parallel to the line connecting *pt1* and *pt2*. The sine of the angle α can be calculated in two ways. First, it's *H* divided by the length of the diagonal of the rectangle:

$$\sin(\alpha) = \frac{H}{\sqrt{W^2 + H^2}}$$

Or, *W* can be a hypotenuse if *L* is the opposite side:

$$\sin(\alpha) = \frac{L}{W}$$

Combine these two equations and solve for L.

The following program creates a *LinearGradientBrush* with a *MappingMode* of *Absolute* in its constructor, but not with the intention of using that brush without modification. The constructor also installs a handler for the *SizeChanged* event, which is triggered whenever the size of the window changes.

```
AdjustTheGradient.cs
//------------------------------------------------
// AdjustTheGradient.cs (c) 2006 by Charles Petzold
//------------------------------------------------
using System;
```

```
using System.Windows;
using System.Windows.Input;
using System.Windows.Media;

namespace Petzold.AdjustTheGradient
{
    class AdjustTheGradient: Window
    {
        LinearGradientBrush brush;

        [STAThread]
        public static void Main()
        {
            Application app = new Application();
            app.Run(new AdjustTheGradient());
        }
        public AdjustTheGradient()
        {
            Title = "Adjust the Gradient";
            SizeChanged += WindowOnSizeChanged;

            brush = new LinearGradientBrush(Colors.Red, Colors.Blue, 0);
            brush.MappingMode = BrushMappingMode.Absolute;
            Background = brush;
        }
        void WindowOnSizeChanged(object sender, SizeChangedEventArgs args)
        {
            double width = ActualWidth
                - 2 * SystemParameters.ResizeFrameVerticalBorderWidth;
            double height = ActualHeight
                - 2 * SystemParameters.ResizeFrameHorizontalBorderHeight
                - SystemParameters.CaptionHeight;

            Point ptCenter = new Point(width / 2, height / 2);
            Vector vectDiag = new Vector(width, -height);
            Vector vectPerp = new Vector(vectDiag.Y, -vectDiag.X);

            vectPerp.Normalize();
            vectPerp *= width * height / vectDiag.Length;

            brush.StartPoint = ptCenter + vectPerp;
            brush.EndPoint = ptCenter - vectPerp;
        }
    }
}
```

The event handler begins by calculating the width and height of the client area, just as in the VaryTheBackground program earlier in this chapter. The *Vector* object *vectDiag* is a vector representing the diagonal from the lower-left to the upper-right corner. This can alternatively be calculated by subtracting the coordinate of the lower-left corner from the upper-right corner:

```
vectDiag = new Point(width, 0) - new Point(0, height);
```

The *vectPerp* object is perpendicular to the diagonal. Perpendicular vectors are easily created by swapping the *X* and *Y* properties and making one of them negative. The *Normalize* method divides the *X* and *Y* properties by the *Length* property so that the *Length* property becomes 1. The event handler then multiplies *vectPerp* by the length I referred to earlier as L.

The final step is to set the *StartPoint* and *EndPoint* properties of the *LinearGradientBrush*. These properties are normally set through one of the brush constructors, and they are the only two properties that *LinearGradientBrush* defines itself. (The brush also inherits some properties from the abstract *GradientBrush* class.)

Again, notice that it's only necessary for the program to change a property of the *LinearGradientBrush* for the window to update itself with the updated brush. That's the "magic" of the *Changed* event defined by the *Freezable* class (and similar WPF features).

The *LinearGradientBrush* is actually more versatile than the two programs presented so far. The brush can also create a gradient between multiple colors. To take advantage of this feature, it's necessary to make use of the *GradientStops* property defined by *GradientBrush*.

The *GradientStops* property is an object of type *GradientStopCollection*, which is a collection of *GradientStop* objects. *GradientStop* defines two properties named *Color* and *Offset*, and a constructor that includes these two properties:

```
new GradientStop(clr, offset)
```

The value of the *Offset* property is normally between 0 and 1 and represents a relative distance between *StartPoint* and *EndPoint*. For example, if *StartPoint* is (70, 50) and *EndPoint* is (150, 90), an *Offset* property of 0.25 refers to the point one-quarter of the distance from *StartPoint* to *EndPoint*, or (90, 60). Of course, if your *StartPoint* is (0, 0) and your *EndPoint* is (0, 1) or (1, 0) or (1, 1), the point corresponding to the *Offset* is much easier to determine.

Here's a program that creates a horizontal *LinearGradientBrush* and sets seven *GradientStop* objects corresponding to the seven traditional colors of the rainbow. Each *GradientStop* is 1/6 of the window width further to the right.

FollowTheRainbow.cs

```
//--------------------------------------------------
// FollowTheRainbow.cs (c) 2006 by Charles Petzold
//--------------------------------------------------
using System;
using System.Windows;
using System.Windows.Input;
using System.Windows.Media;

namespace Petzold.FollowTheRainbow
{
    class FollowTheRainbow: Window
    {
        [STAThread]
```

```
        public static void Main()
        {
            Application app = new Application();
            app.Run(new FollowTheRainbow());
        }
        public FollowTheRainbow()
        {
            Title = "Follow the Rainbow";

            LinearGradientBrush brush = new LinearGradientBrush();
            brush.StartPoint = new Point(0, 0);
            brush.EndPoint = new Point(1, 0);
            Background = brush;

            // Rainbow mnemonic is the name Roy G. Biv.
            brush.GradientStops.Add(new GradientStop(Colors.Red, 0));
            brush.GradientStops.Add(new GradientStop(Colors.Orange, .17));
            brush.GradientStops.Add(new GradientStop(Colors.Yellow, .33));
            brush.GradientStops.Add(new GradientStop(Colors.Green, .5));
            brush.GradientStops.Add(new GradientStop(Colors.Blue, .67));
            brush.GradientStops.Add(new GradientStop(Colors.Indigo, .84));
            brush.GradientStops.Add(new GradientStop(Colors.Violet, 1));
        }
    }
}
```

From here, it's a short leap from the *LinearGradientBrush* to the *RadialGradientBrush*. All that's required is changing the name of the class used for the brush and removing the *StartPoint* and *EndPoint* assignments:

CircleTheRainbow.cs

```
//------------------------------------------------
// CircleTheRainbow.cs (c) 2006 by Charles Petzold
//------------------------------------------------
using System;
using System.Windows;
using System.Windows.Input;
using System.Windows.Media;

namespace Petzold.CircleTheRainbow
{
    public class CircleTheRainbow : Window
    {
        [STAThread]
        public static void Main()
        {
            Application app = new Application();
            app.Run(new CircleTheRainbow());
        }
        public CircleTheRainbow()
        {
```

```
            Title = "Circle the Rainbow";

            RadialGradientBrush brush = new RadialGradientBrush();
            Background = brush;

            // Rainbow mnemonic is the name Roy G. Biv.
            brush.GradientStops.Add(new GradientStop(Colors.Red, 0));
            brush.GradientStops.Add(new GradientStop(Colors.Orange, .17));
            brush.GradientStops.Add(new GradientStop(Colors.Yellow, .33));
            brush.GradientStops.Add(new GradientStop(Colors.Green, .5));
            brush.GradientStops.Add(new GradientStop(Colors.Blue, .67));
            brush.GradientStops.Add(new GradientStop(Colors.Indigo, .84));
            brush.GradientStops.Add(new GradientStop(Colors.Violet, 1));
        }
    }
}
```

Now the brush starts in the center of the client area with red, and then goes through the colors until violet defines an ellipse that fills the client area. Beyond the ellipse in the corners of the client area, violet continues because the default *SpreadMethod* is *Fill*.

Obviously, the *RadialGradientBrush* class defines several properties with useful default values. Three of these properties define an ellipse: The *Center* property is a *Point* object of default value (0.5, 0.5), which is the center of the area that the brush covers. The *RadiusX* and *RadiusY* properties are two *double* values that govern the horizontal and vertical radii of the ellipse. The default values are 0.5, so both horizontally and vertically the ellipse reaches the edges of the area filled by the brush.

The perimeter of the ellipse defined by the *Center*, *RadiusX*, and *RadiusY* properties is set to the color that has an *Offset* property of 1. (In CircleTheRainbow, that color is violet.)

A fourth property is named *GradientOrigin*, and like the *Center* property, it is a *Point* object with a default value of (0.5, 0.5). As the name implies, the *GradientOrigin* is the point at which the gradient begins. It is the point at which you'll see the color that has an *Offset* of 0. (In CircleTheRainbow, that's red.)

The gradient occurs between *GradientOrigin* and the circumference of the ellipse. If *GradientOrigin* equals *Center* (the default case), the gradient occurs from the center of the ellipse to its perimeter. If *GradientOrigin* is offset somewhat from *Center*, the gradient will be more compressed where *GradientOrigin* is closest to the ellipse perimeter, and more spread out where *GradientOrigin* is farther away. To see this effect, insert the following statement into CircleTheRainbow:

```
brush.GradientOrigin = new Point(0.75, 0.75);
```

You may want to experiment with the relationship between the *Center* and *GradientOrigin* properties; the ClickTheGradientCenter program lets you do so. It uses a two-argument constructor for *RadialGradientBrush* that defines the color at *GradientOrigin* and the color on the perimeter of the ellipse. However, the program sets the *RadiusX* and *RadiusY* properties to

0.10, and the *SpreadMethod* to *Repeat* so that the brush appears as a series of concentric gradient circles.

ClickTheGradientCenter.cs

```
//--------------------------------------------------------
// ClickTheGradientCenter.cs (c) 2006 by Charles Petzold
//--------------------------------------------------------
using System;
using System.Windows;
using System.Windows.Input;
using System.Windows.Media;

namespace Petzold.ClickTheGradientCenter
{
    class ClickTheRadientCenter : Window
    {
        RadialGradientBrush brush;

        [STAThread]
        public static void Main()
        {
            Application app = new Application();
            app.Run(new ClickTheRadientCenter());
        }
        public ClickTheRadientCenter()
        {
            Title = "Click the Gradient Center";
            brush = new RadialGradientBrush(Colors.White, Colors.Red);
            brush.RadiusX = brush.RadiusY = 0.10;
            brush.SpreadMethod = GradientSpreadMethod.Repeat;
            Background = brush;
        }
        protected override void OnMouseDown(MouseButtonEventArgs args)
        {
            double width = ActualWidth
                - 2 * SystemParameters.ResizeFrameVerticalBorderWidth;
            double height = ActualHeight
                - 2 * SystemParameters.ResizeFrameHorizontalBorderHeight
                - SystemParameters.CaptionHeight;

            Point ptMouse = args.GetPosition(this);
            ptMouse.X /= width;
            ptMouse.Y /= height;

            if (args.ChangedButton == MouseButton.Left)
            {
                brush.Center = ptMouse;
                brush.GradientOrigin = ptMouse;
            }
            else if (args.ChangedButton == MouseButton.Right)
                brush.GradientOrigin = ptMouse;
        }
    }
}
```

The program overrides *OnMouseDown* so that you can also click the client area. The left mouse button changes both the *Center* and *GradientOrigin* properties to the same value. You'll see that the whole brush is simply shifted from the center of the client area. A click of the right mouse button changes only the *GradientOrigin*. You'll probably want to keep fairly close to the *Center* point, and at least within the inner circle. Now you can see how the gradient is compressed on one side and expanded on the other.

The effect was so interesting that I decided to animate it. The following program, RotateThe-GradientOrigin, does *not* use any of the animation features built into the Windows Presentation Foundation. Instead, it uses a simple timer to change the *GradientOrigin* property.

There are at least four timer classes in .NET, and three of them are named *Timer*. The *Timer* classes in *System.Threading* and *System.Timers* can't be used in this particular program because the timer events occur in a different thread, and *Freezable* objects must be changed in the same thread in which they're created. The *Timer* class in *System.Windows.Forms* is an encapsulation of the standard Windows timer, but using it would require adding the System.Windows.Forms.dll assembly as an additional reference.

The *DispatcherTimer* class located in the *System.Windows.Threading* namespace is the one to use in WPF programs if you need the events to occur in the application thread. You set an *Interval* property from a *TimeSpan* property, but you can't get more frequent "ticks" than once every 10 milliseconds.

The program creates a 4-inch-square window so that it doesn't eat up *too* much processing time.

```
RotateTheGradientOrigin.cs
//-----------------------------------------------------------
// RotateTheGradientOrigin.cs (c) 2006 by Charles Petzold
//-----------------------------------------------------------
using System;
using System.Windows;
using System.Windows.Input;
using System.Windows.Media;
using System.Windows.Threading;

namespace Petzold.RotateTheGradientOrigin
{
    public class RotateTheGradientOrigin : Window
    {
        RadialGradientBrush brush;
        double angle;

        [STAThread]
        public static void Main()
        {
            Application app = new Application();
            app.Run(new RotateTheGradientOrigin());
        }
```

```
        public RotateTheGradientOrigin()
        {
            Title = "Rotate the Gradient Origin";
            WindowStartupLocation = WindowStartupLocation.CenterScreen;
            Width = 384;          // ie, 4 inches
            Height = 384;

            brush = new RadialGradientBrush(Colors.White, Colors.Blue);
            brush.Center = brush.GradientOrigin = new Point(0.5, 0.5);
            brush.RadiusX = brush.RadiusY = 0.10;
            brush.SpreadMethod = GradientSpreadMethod.Repeat;
            Background = brush;

            DispatcherTimer tmr = new DispatcherTimer();
            tmr.Interval = TimeSpan.FromMilliseconds(100);
            tmr.Tick += TimerOnTick;
            tmr.Start();
        }
        void TimerOnTick(object sender, EventArgs args)
        {
            Point pt = new Point(0.5 + 0.05 * Math.Cos(angle),
                                 0.5 + 0.05 * Math.Sin(angle));
            brush.GradientOrigin = pt;
            angle += Math.PI / 6;      // ie, 30 degrees
        }
    }
}
```

I've been focusing on the *Background* property of *Window* in this chapter, but three other properties of *Window* are also of type *Brush*. One of these is *OpacityMask*, a property that *Window* inherits from *UIElement*, but this is best discussed in context with bitmaps in Chapter 31.

Window inherits the other two *Brush* properties from *Control*. The first is *BorderBrush*, which draws a border around the perimeter of the client area. Try inserting this code in a recent program from this chapter:

```
BorderBrush = Brushes.SaddleBrown;
BorderThickness = new Thickness(25, 50, 75, 100);
```

The *Thickness* structure has four properties named *Left*, *Top*, *Right*, and *Bottom*, and the four-argument constructor sets those properties in that order. These are device-independent units that indicate the width of the border on the four sides of the client area. If you want the same border width on all four sides, you can use the single-argument constructor:

```
BorderThickness = new Thickness(50);
```

Of course, you can use a gradient brush for the border:

```
BorderBrush = new GradientBrush(Colors.Red, Colors.Blue,
                                new Point(0, 0), new Point(1, 1));
```

This looks a lot like a gradient brush that fills the client area—you'll see red at the top-left corner and blue at the bottom-right corner—except that the brush only appears around the perimeter of the client area. The *BorderBrush* detracts from the size of the client area, as is easy to determine when you include a *BorderBrush* and set the *Background* property with a gradient brush. If both *BorderBrush* and the *Background* have the same gradient brush, the two brushes don't blend in with each other:

```
Background = new GradientBrush(Colors.Red, Colors.Blue,
                    new Point(0, 0), new Point(1, 1));
```

The background brush appears complete within the area not covered by the border brush.

The only other property of *Window* that is of type *Brush* is *Foreground*, but for that property to do anything, we need to put some *content* in the window. Content comes in many different forms, from plain text to graphical images to controls, and this is what you'll begin exploring in the next chapter.

Chapter 3
The Concept of Content

The *Window* class has more than 100 public properties, and some of them—such as the *Title* property that identifies the window—are quite important. But by far the most important property of *Window* is the *Content* property. You set the *Content* property of the window to the object you want in the window's client area.

You can set the *Content* property to a string, you can set it to a bitmap, you can set it to a drawing, and you can set it to a button, or a scrollbar, or any one of 50-odd controls supported by the Windows Presentation Foundation. You can set the *Content* property to just about anything. But there's only one little problem:

You can only set the *Content* property to *one* object.

This restriction is apt to be a bit frustrating in the early stages of working with content. Eventually, of course, you'll see how to set the *Content* property to an object that can play host to multiple other objects. For now, working with a single content object will keep us busy enough.

The *Window* class inherits the *Content* property from *ContentControl*, a class that derives from *Control* and from which *Window* immediately descends. The *ContentControl* class exists almost solely to define this *Content* property and a few related properties and methods.

The *Content* property is defined as type *object*, which suggests that it can be set to *any* object, and that's just about true. I say "just about" because you cannot set the *Content* property to another object of type *Window*. You'll get a run-time exception that indicates that *Window* must be the "root of a tree," not a branch of another *Window* object.

You can set the *Content* property to a text string, for example:

```
DisplaySomeText.cs
//-------------------------------------------------
// DisplaySomeText.cs (c) 2006 by Charles Petzold
//-------------------------------------------------
using System;
using System.Windows;
using System.Windows.Input;
using System.Windows.Media;

namespace Petzold.DisplaySomeText
{
    public class DisplaySomeText : Window
    {
        [STAThread]
```

```
        public static void Main()
        {
            Application app = new Application();
            app.Run(new DisplaySomeText());
        }
        public DisplaySomeText()
        {
            Title = "Display Some Text";
            Content = "Content can be simple text!";
        }
    }
}
```

This program displays the text "Content can be simple text!" in the upper-left corner of the client area. If you make the window too narrow to fit all the text, you'll find that the text is truncated rather than automatically wrapped (alas), but you can insert line breaks in the text using the carriage return character ("\r") or a line feed ("\n"), or both: "\r\n".

The program includes a *using* directive for the *System.Windows.Media* namespace so that you can experiment with properties that affect the color and font of the text. These properties are all defined by the *Control* class from which *Window* derives.

Nothing except good taste will prevent you from setting the font used to display text in the client area like so:

```
FontFamily = new FontFamily("Comic Sans MS");
FontSize = 48;
```

This code can go anywhere in the constructor of the class.

There is no such thing as a *Font* class in the WPF. The first line of this code makes reference to a *FontFamily* object. A font family (also known as a type family) is a collection of related typefaces. Under Windows, font families have familiar names such as Courier New, Times New Roman, Arial, Palatino Linotype, Verdana, and, of course, Comic Sans MS.

A *typeface* (also known as a face name) is the combination of a font family and a possible variation, such as Times New Roman Bold, Times New Roman Italic, and Times New Roman Bold Italic. Not every variation is available in every font family, and some font families have variations that affect the widths of individual characters, such as Arial Narrow.

The term *font* is generally used to denote a combination of a particular typeface with a particular size. The common measurement of fonts is the *em size*. (The term comes from the size of the square piece of metal type used in olden days for the capital M.) The em size is commonly described as the height of the characters in the Latin alphabet—the uppercase and lowercase letters A through Z without diacritical marks—from the very top of the ascenders to the bottom of the descenders. However, the em size is not a metrical concept. It is a typographical design concept. The actual size of characters in a particular font could be somewhat greater than or less than what the em size implies.

Commonly, the em size is specified in a unit of measurement known as the *point*. In traditional typography, a point is 0.01384 inch, but in computer typography, the point is assumed to be exactly 1/72 inch. Thus, a 36-point em size (often abbreviated as a *36-point font*) refers to characters that are about 1/2 inch tall.

In the Windows Presentation Foundation, you set the em size you want by using the *FontSize* property. But you don't use points. Like every measurement in the WPF, you specify the *FontSize* in device-independent units, which are 1/96 inch. Setting the *FontSize* property to 48 results in an em size of 1/2 inch, which is equivalent to 36 points.

If you're accustomed to specifying em sizes in points, just multiply the point size by 4/3 (or divide by 0.75) when setting the *FontSize* property. If you're not accustomed to specifying em sizes in points, you should get accustomed to it, and just multiply the point size by 4/3 when setting the *FontSize* property.

The default *FontSize* property is 11, which is 8.25 points. Much of *The New York Times* is printed in an 8-point type. *Newsweek* uses a 9-point type. This book has 10-point type.

You can use a full typeface name in the *FontFamily* constructor:

```
FontFamily = new FontFamily("Times New Roman Bold Italic");
FontSize = 32;
```

That's a 24-point Times New Roman Bold Italic font. However, it's more common to use the family name in the *FontFamily* constructor and indicate bold and italic by setting the *FontStyle* and *FontWeight* properties:

```
FontFamily = new FontFamily("Times New Roman");
FontSize = 32;
FontStyle = FontStyles.Italic;
FontWeight = FontWeights.Bold;
```

Notice that the *FontStyle* and *FontWeight* properties are set to static read-only properties of the *FontStyles* (plural) and *FontWeights* (plural) classes. These static properties return objects of type *FontStyle* and *FontWeight*, which are structures that have limited use by themselves.

Here's an interesting little variation:

```
FontStyle = FontStyles.Oblique;
```

An italic typeface is often stylistically a bit different from the non-italic (or *roman*) typeface. Look at the lowercase "a" to see the difference. But an oblique typeface simply slants all the letters of the roman typeface to the right. For some font families, you can set a *FontStretch* property to a static property of the *FontStretches* class.

You're already familiar with the *Background* property that colors the background of the client area. The *Foreground* property colors the text itself. Try this:

```
Brush brush = new LinearGradientBrush(Colors.Black, Colors.White,
                                 new Point(0, 0), new Point(1, 1));
Background = brush;
Foreground = brush;
```

Both the foreground and background are now colored with the same brush, which you might fear would potentially render the foreground text invisible. This doesn't happen, however. As you discovered in Chapter 2, gradient brushes used for coloring the background are by default automatically adjusted to the size of the client area. Similarly, the foreground brush is automatically adjusted to the size of the *content*—the actual text string. Changing the size of the window does not affect that foreground brush. But when you make the client area exactly the same size as the size of the text, the two brushes coincide and the text disappears.

Now try this:

```
SizeToContent = SizeToContent.WidthAndHeight;
```

The *SizeToContent* property defined by the *Window* class causes the window to adjust itself to be just as big as the size of its content. If you're still using the same *LinearGradientBrush* for foreground and background, you won't be able to see the text. You set the *SizeToContent* property to a member of the *SizeToContent* enumeration: *Manual* (which is the default), *Width*, *Height*, or *WidthAndHeight*. With the latter three, the window adjusts its width, height, or both the size of its contents. This is a very handy property that you'll often use when designing dialog boxes or other forms. When setting a window to the size of its content, you'll often want to suppress the sizing border with the following:

```
ResizeMode = ResizeMode.CanMinimize;
```

or

```
ResizeMode = ResizeMode.NoResize;
```

You can add a border inside the client area with the code shown at the end of Chapter 2:

```
BorderBrush = Brushes.SaddleBrown;
BorderThickness = new Thickness(25, 50, 75, 100);
```

You'll see that both the foreground brush and *SizeToContent* take account of this border. The content always appears inside this border.

The display of a text string by the DisplaySomeText program is actually much more generalized than it may at first appear. As you know, all objects have a *ToString* method that's supposed to return a string representation of the object. The window uses the *ToString* method to display the object. You can convince yourself of this by setting the *Content* property to something other than a string:

```
Content = Math.PI;
```

Or try this:

```
Content = DateTime.Now;
```

In both cases, what the window displays is identical to the string returned from *ToString*. If the object is based on a class that doesn't override *ToString*, the default *ToString* method just displays the fully qualified class name. For example:

```
Content = EventArgs.Empty;
```

That displays the string "System.EventArgs". The only exception I've found is for arrays. If you do something like this

```
Content = new int[57];
```

the window displays the text string "Int32[] Array" while the *ToString* method returns "System.Int32[]".

Here's a program that sets the *Content* property to an empty text string, but then adds characters to this text string based on input from the keyboard. It's similar to the TypeYourTitle program from the first chapter, but this one also lets you enter carriage returns and tabs.

RecordKeystrokes.cs
```
//-------------------------------------------------
// RecordKeystrokes.cs (c) 2006 by Charles Petzold
//-------------------------------------------------
using System;
using System.Windows;
using System.Windows.Input;
using System.Windows.Media;

namespace Petzold.RecordKeystrokes
{
    public class RecordKeystrokes : Window
    {
        [STAThread]
        public static void Main()
        {
            Application app = new Application();
            app.Run(new RecordKeystrokes());
        }
        public RecordKeystrokes()
        {
            Title = "Record Keystrokes";
            Content = "";
        }
        protected override void OnTextInput(TextCompositionEventArgs args)
        {
            base.OnTextInput(args);
            string str = Content as string;

            if (args.Text == "\b")
            {
```

```
                if (str.Length > 0)
                    str = str.Substring(0, str.Length - 1);
            }
            else
            {
                str += args.Text;
            }
            Content = str;
        }
    }
}
```

The RecordKeystrokes program works only because the *Content* property is changing with each keystroke, and the *Window* class is responding to this change by redrawing the client area. It is very easy to make a little variation of this program that won't work at all. For example, define an empty string as a field:

```
string str = "";
```

Set the *Content* property to this variable in the constructor:

```
Content = str;
```

Remove that same statement from the *OnTextInput* override, and also remove the definition of *str*. Now the program doesn't work. Take a look at the compound assignment statement in *OnTextInput*:

```
str += args.Text;
```

It's equivalent to the following statement:

```
str = str + args.Text;
```

The problem with both statements is that the *string* object returned from the concatenation operation is not the same *string* object that entered it. Strings, remember, are immutable. The concatenation operation creates a new string, but the *Content* property is still set to the original string.

Now try something a little different. You'll need a *using* directive for *System.Text* for this. Define a *StringBuilder* object as a field:

```
StringBuilder build = new StringBuilder("text");
```

In the program's constructor, set *Content* equal to that object:

```
Content = build;
```

You should be confident (and you would be correct) in assuming that the window will display "text" because the *ToString* method of the *StringBuilder* object returns the string that it has built.

Replace the code in the *OnTextInput* method with this:

```
if (args.Text == "\b")
{
    if (build.Length > 0)
        build.Remove(build.Length - 1, 1);
}
else
{
    build.Append(args.Text);
}
```

And, again the code doesn't work. Although there's only one *StringBuilder* object in this program, the window has no way of knowing when the string stored by this *StringBuilder* object changes, so it doesn't update the window with the new text string.

I'm pointing out these cases because sometimes objects in the Windows Presentation Foundation seem to update themselves as if by magic. It may seem like magic, but it's not. There's always some method of notification in the form of an event. Being aware of what's going on (or not going on) can help you better understand the environment. The revised RecordKeystrokes program with the *StringBuilder* object won't even work if you insert the following statement

```
Content = build;
```

at the bottom of the *OnTextInput* override. The window is smart enough to know that you're assigning the same object to *Content* that you've already set to *Content*, so no update is necessary. But try these statements:

```
Content = null;
Content = build;
```

That code works.

We've seen that window content can be plain text. But the purpose of the *Content* property is *not* to display simple unformatted text. No, no, no, no, no. What the *Content* property really wants is something more *graphical* in nature, and that's an instance of any class that derives from *UIElement*.

UIElement is an *extremely* important class in the Windows Presentation Foundation. This is the class that implements keyboard, mouse, and stylus handling. The *UIElement* class also contains an important method named *OnRender*. The *OnRender* method is invoked to obtain the graphical representation of an object. (You'll see an example at the end of this chapter.)

As far as the *Content* property goes, the world is divided into two groups of objects: Those that derive from *UIElement* and those that do not. In the latter group, the object is displayed with *ToString*; in the former group, it's displayed with *OnRender*. Classes that derive from *UIElement* (and their instantiated objects) are often referred to collectively as *elements*.

The only class that inherits directly from *UIElement* is *FrameworkElement*, and all the elements you'll encounter in the Windows Presentation Foundation derive from *FrameworkElement*. In theory, *UIElement* provides the necessary structure of user interface events and screen rendering that can support various programming frameworks. The Windows Presentation Foundation is one such framework and consists of all the classes that derive from *FrameworkElement*. In a practical sense, you probably won't make much of a distinction between the properties, methods, and events defined by *UIElement* and those defined by *FrameworkElement*.

One popular class that inherits from *FrameworkElement* is *Image*. Here's the class hierarchy:

Object

> *DispatcherObject* (abstract)

>> *DependencyObject*

>>> *Visual* (abstract)

>>>> *UIElement*

>>>>> *FrameworkElement*

>>>>>> *Image*

The *Image* class lets you easily include an image in a document or an application. Here's a program that pulls a bitmap from my Web site and displays it in the window:

```
ShowMyFace.cs
//------------------------------------------
// ShowMyFace.cs (c) 2006 by Charles Petzold
//------------------------------------------
using System;
using System.Windows;
using System.Windows.Controls;
using System.Windows.Input;
using System.Windows.Media;
using System.Windows.Media.Imaging;

namespace Petzold.ShowMyFace
{
    class ShowMyFace : Window
    {
        [STAThread]
        public static void Main()
        {
            Application app = new Application();
            app.Run(new ShowMyFace());
        }
```

```
        public ShowMyFace()
        {
            Title = "Show My Face";

            Uri uri = new Uri("http://www.charlespetzold.com/PetzoldTattoo.jpg");
            BitmapImage bitmap = new BitmapImage(uri);
            Image img = new Image();
            img.Source = bitmap;
            Content = img;
        }
    }
}
```

A couple of steps are required to display an image. The program first creates an object of *Uri* that indicates the location of the bitmap. This is passed to the *BitmapImage* constructor, which actually loads the image into memory. (Many popular formats are supported, including GIF, TIFF, JPEG, and PNG.) The *Image* class displays the image in the window. It is an instance of the *Image* class that you set to the *Content* property of the window.

You can find the *Image* class in the *System.Windows.Controls* namespace. Strictly speaking, *Image* is not considered a control and does not derive from the *Control* class. But the *System.Windows.Controls* namespace is so important that I'll include it in most programs from here on. The *BitmapImage* class is located in the *System.Windows.Media.Imaging* namespace, which is certainly an important namespace if you're working with bitmaps. However, I won't generally include a *using* directive for this namespace unless the program requires it.

Alternatively, you can load an image file from a local disk drive. You'll need a fully qualified file name as the argument in the *Uri* constructor, or you'll need to preface the relative file name with "file://". Here's some replacement code that retrieves the image of the fly fisherman scooping up a yummy trout:

```
Uri uri = new Uri(
    System.IO.Path.Combine(
        Environment.GetEnvironmentVariable("windir"),"Gone Fishing.bmp"));
```

The *Environment.GetEnvironmentVariable* method retrieves the "*windir*" environment variable, which is a string like "C:\WINDOWS". The *Path.Combine* method combines that path name with the file name of the desired bitmap so that I (the lazy programmer) don't have to worry about inserting slashes correctly. You can either preface the *Path* class with *System.IO* (as I've done) or include a *using* directive for that namespace.

Rather than passing the *Uri* object to the *BitmapImage* constructor, you can set the *Uri* object to the *UriSource* property of *BitmapImage*. However, it's recommended that you surround the setting of this property with calls to the *BeginInit* and *EndInit* methods in *BitmapImage*:

```
bitmap.BeginInit();
bitmap.UriSource = uri;
bitmap.EndInit();
```

As you know, bitmaps have a pixel width and a pixel height, which is to the number of picture elements actually encoded in the file. The *BitmapImage* class inherits integer read-only *Pixel-Width* and *PixelHeight* properties from *BitmapSource* that reveals this information. Bitmaps often (but not always) have embedded resolution information. Sometimes this resolution information is important (a scan of a rare postage stamp) and sometimes it's not (a photo of your postal carrier). The resolution information in dots per inch is available from the read-only *double* values *DpiX* and *DpiY*. The *BitmapImage* class also includes read-only *double* properties named *Width* and *Height*. These values are calculated with the following formulas:

$$Width = \frac{96 \cdot PixelWidth}{DpiX}$$

$$Height = \frac{96 \cdot PixelWidth}{DpiY}$$

Without the value of 96 in the numerator, these formulas would give a width and height of the image in inches. The 96 converts inches into device-independent units. The *Height* and *Width* properties constitute the metrical size of the bitmap in device-independent units. *BitmapImage* also inherits from *BitmapSource* a *Format* property that provides the color format of the bitmap; for those bitmaps that have a color table, the *Palette* property gives access to that.

Regardless of whether the ShowMyFace program is displaying my face, or the trout fisherman, or an image of your choice, you'll notice that the image is displayed as large as possible within the confines of the window, but without distortion. Unless the aspect ratio of the client area is exactly that of the window, you'll see some of the client window background on either the top and bottom sides or the left and right sides of the image.

The size of the image within the window is governed by several properties of *Image*, one of which is *Stretch*. By default, the *Stretch* property equals the enumeration value *Stretch.Uniform*, which means that the image is increased or decreased in size uniformly (that is, the same in both the horizontal and vertical directions) to fill the client area.

You can alternatively set the *Stretch* property to *Stretch.Fill*:

```
img.Stretch = Stretch.Fill;
```

This setting causes the image to fill up the entire window, generally distorting the image by increasing or decreasing it by different amounts horizontally or vertically. The *Stretch.UniformToFill* option stretches the image uniformly, but also completely fills the client area. It performs this amazing feat by truncating the image on one side.

The *Stretch.None* option causes the image to be displayed in its metrical size, which is obtainable from the *Width* and *Height* properties of the *BitmapSource*.

If you use a *Stretch* option other than *Stretch.None*, you can also set the *StretchDirection* property of *Image*. The default is the enumeration value *StretchDirection.Both*, which means that the image can be stretched greater than or less than its metrical size. With *StretchDirection.DownOnly*, the image is never larger than its metrical size, and with *StretchDirection.UpOnly*, the image is never smaller than its metrical size.

Regardless of how you size the image, the image is always (except for *Stretch.UniformToFill*) positioned in the center of the window. You can change that by setting the *Horizontal-Alignment* and *VerticalAlignment* properties that *Image* inherits from *FrameworkElement*. For example, this code moves the image to the upper right of the client area:

```
img.HorizontalAlignment = HorizontalAlignment.Right;
img.VerticalAlignment = VerticalAlignment.Top;
```

The *HorizontalAlignment* and *VerticalAlignment* properties have a surprisingly important role in layout in the Windows Presentation Foundation. You'll encounter these properties again and again. If you'd prefer the *Image* object to be in the upper-right corner, but not flush against the edges, you can set a margin around the *Image* object:

```
img.Margin = new Thickness(10);
```

Margin is defined in *FrameworkElement* and often used to insert a little breathing room around elements. You can use the *Thickness* structure to define either the same margin on all four sides (in this case 10/96 inch or about 0.1 inches) or different margins on all four sides. As you'll recall, the four-argument constructor of *Thickness* sets the fields in left-top-right-bottom order:

```
img.Margin = new Thickness(192, 96, 48, 0);
```

Now the margin is 2 inches on the left, 1 inch on the top, 1/2 inch on the right, and nothing on the bottom. You can see how the margins are respected when you make the window too small for both the image and the margins: The image disappears before the margins do.

The *Image* object also has *Width* and *Height* properties that it inherits from *FrameworkElement*. These are read/write *double* values, and if you check their values, you'll see that they are unde-fined, which is indicated by values of "not a number," or NaN. (It's the same as with the *Window* object.) You can also set a precise *Width* and *Height* of the *Image* object, although these may not be consistent with some *Stretch* settings.

You can also size the window to the metrical size of the image:

```
SizeToContent = SizeToContent.WidthAndHeight;
```

Setting the *Foreground* property of the *Window* object has no effect on the display of the image; the *Foreground* property only comes into play when the window content is text or (as we'll see) another type of element that displays text.

Normally, setting the *Background* property of the *Window* object only has an effect in the areas of the client area not covered by the image. But try this:

```
img.Opacity = 0.5;
Background = new LinearGradientBrush(Colors.Red, Colors.Blue,
                            new Point(0, 0), new Point(1, 1));
```

Now the brush shows through the image. The *Opacity* property (which *Image* inherits from *UIElement*) is 1 by default, but you can set it to any value between 0 and 1 to make an element transparent. (It won't work with the *Window* object itself, however.)

A full discussion of graphics transforms awaits us in Chapter 29 of this book, but for now you can see how easy it is to rotate a bitmap:

```
img.LayoutTransform = new RotateTransform(45);
```

The *Image* class does not have its own *Background* and *Foreground* properties because those properties are defined by the *Control* class and *Image* is not derived from *Control*. The distinction may be a little confusing at first. In earlier Windows application programming interfaces, virtually everything on the screen was considered a control. That is obviously not the case here. A control is really just another visual object, and is characterized mostly by giving feedback to user input. Elements like *Image* can obtain user input, of course, because all the keyboard, mouse, and stylus input events are defined by *UIElement*.

Take a look at the namespace *System.Windows.Shapes*, which contains an abstract class named *Shape* and six other classes that derive from it. These classes also derive from *UIElement* by way of *FrameworkElement*:

Object

    DispatcherObject (abstract)

        DependencyObject

            Visual (abstract)

                UIElement

                    FrameworkElement

                        Shape (abstract)

                            Ellipse

                            Line

                            Path

                            Polygon

                            Polyline

                            Rectangle

While *Image* is the standard way to display raster images, these *Shape* classes implement simple two-dimensional vector graphics. Here's a program that creates an object of type *Ellipse*:

```
ShapeAnEllipse.cs
//---------------------------------------------------
// ShapeAnEllipse.cs (c) 2006 by Charles Petzold
//---------------------------------------------------
using System;
using System.Windows;
using System.Windows.Controls;
using System.Windows.Input;
using System.Windows.Media;
using System.Windows.Shapes;

namespace Petzold.ShapeAnEllipse
{
    class ShapeAnEllipse : Window
    {
        [STAThread]
        public static void Main()
        {
            Application app = new Application();
            app.Run(new ShapeAnEllipse());
        }
        public ShapeAnEllipse()
        {
            Title = "Shape an Ellipse";

            Ellipse elips = new Ellipse();
            elips.Fill = Brushes.AliceBlue;
            elips.StrokeThickness = 24;      // 1/4 inch
            elips.Stroke =
                new LinearGradientBrush(Colors.CadetBlue, Colors.Chocolate,
                                        new Point(1, 0), new Point(0, 1));
            Content = elips;
        }
    }
}
```

The ellipse fills the client area. The circumference is a quarter-inch thick and is colored with a gradient brush. The interior is filled with an Alice Blue brush, the only color named after a daughter of Teddy Roosevelt.

Neither the *Shape* class nor the *Ellipse* class defines any properties to set a size of the ellipse, but the *Ellipse* class inherits *Width* and *Height* properties from *FrameworkElement*, and these do just fine:

```
elips.Width = 300;
elips.Height = 300;
```

Just as with *Image*, you can now use the *HorizontalAlignment* and *VerticalAlignment* properties to position the ellipse in the center, horizontally to the left or right, or vertically at the top or bottom:

```
elips.HorizontalAlignment = HorizontalAlignment.Left;
elips.VerticalAlignment = VerticalAlignment.Bottom;
```

Both the *HorizontalAlignment* and *VerticalAlignment* enumerations have members named *Center*, but they also have members named *Stretch*, and for many elements, *Stretch* is the default. *Stretch* is the default for *Ellipse*, and that's why the *Ellipse* initially fills the client area. The element stretches to the boundaries of its container. In fact, if you set *HorizontalAlignment* and *VerticalAlignment* to anything other than *Stretch* without also setting explicit *Width* and *Height* properties, the ellipse collapses into a quarter-inch ball with only its perimeter showing.

If you don't set the *Width* and *Height* properties, however, you can set any or all of the *Min-Width*, *MaxWidth*, *MinHeight*, and *MaxHeight* properties (all inherited from *Framework-Element*) to restrict the ellipse to a particular range of sizes. By default, all these properties are undefined. At any time (except in the constructor of the window), the program can obtain the actual size of the ellipse from the read-only *ActualWidth* and *ActualHeight* properties.

If I seem a bit obsessive about the size of elements set as the content of a window, it's only because this is an important issue. You are probably accustomed to assigning specific sizes to controls and other graphical objects, but the Windows Presentation Foundation doesn't require that, and it is vital that you get a good feel for the way in which visual objects are sized.

What you won't find in the *Ellipse* class are any properties that allow you to position the ellipse at a particular location in the client area of the window. The closest you can come at this point is through setting the *HorizontalAlignment* and *VerticalAlignment* properties.

Earlier I showed you how to set the *Content* property of the *Window* to any text string, and also how to set the font of that text. However, text that you set directly to the *Content* property of the window must have uniform formatting. You can't specify that particular words are bold or italic, for example.

If you need to do that, instead of setting the *Content* property of your window to a *string*, you can set it to an object of type *TextBlock*:

FormatTheText.cs
```
//-----------------------------------------------
// FormatTheText.cs (c) 2006 by Charles Petzold
//-----------------------------------------------
using System;
using System.Windows;
using System.Windows.Controls;
using System.Windows.Input;
using System.Windows.Media;
using System.Windows.Documents;
```

```
namespace Petzold.FormatTheText
{
    class FormatTheText : Window
    {
        [STAThread]
        public static void Main()
        {
            Application app = new Application();
            app.Run(new FormatTheText());
        }
        public FormatTheText()
        {
            Title = "Format the Text";

            TextBlock txt = new TextBlock();
            txt.FontSize = 32;                  // 24 points
            txt.Inlines.Add("This is some ");
            txt.Inlines.Add(new Italic(new Run("italic")));
            txt.Inlines.Add(" text, and this is some ");
            txt.Inlines.Add(new Bold(new Run("bold")));
            txt.Inlines.Add(" text, and let's cap it off with some ");
            txt.Inlines.Add(new Bold(new Italic(new Run("bold italic"))));
            txt.Inlines.Add(" text.");
            txt.TextWrapping = TextWrapping.Wrap;

            Content = txt;
        }
    }
}
```

Although this is the first program in this book that explicitly creates a *TextBlock* object, you've actually seen one before. If you set the *Content* property to a string, *ContentControl* (from which *Window* derives) creates an object of type *TextBlock* to actually display the string. The *TextBlock* class derives directly from *FrameworkElement*. It defines a property named *Inlines*, which is of type *InlineCollection*, which is a collection of *Inline* objects.

TextBlock itself is included in the *System.Windows.Controls* namespace but *Inline* is part of *System.Windows.Documents*, and it doesn't even derive from *UIElement*. Here's a partial class hierarchy showing *Inline* and some of its descendents:

Object

    DispatcherObject (abstract)

        DependencyObject

            ContentElement

                FrameworkContentElement

                    TextElement (abstract)

> *Inline* (abstract)
>
> > *Run*
> >
> > *Span*
> >
> > > *Bold*
> > >
> > > *Hyperlink*
> > >
> > > *Italic*
> > >
> > > *Underline*

You might notice a somewhat parallel structure in this class hierarchy with the earlier ones. The *ContentElement* and *FrameworkContentElement* classes are analogous to the *UIElement* and *FrameworkElement* classes. However, the *ContentElement* class contains no *OnRender* method. Objects based on classes that derive from *ContentElement* do not draw themselves on the screen. Instead, they achieve a visual representation on the screen only through a class that drives from *UIElement,* which provides the necessary *OnRender* method.

More specifically, objects of the types *Bold* and *Italic* do not draw themselves. In the Format-TheText program, these *Bold* and *Italic* objects are rendered by the *TextBlock* object.

Don't confuse the *ContentElement* class with *ContentControl*. A *ContentControl* is a control, such as *Window*, which contains a property named *Content*. The *ContentControl* object renders itself on the screen even if its *Content* property is *null*. But a *ContentElement* object must be part (that is, content) of some other element to be rendered.

The bulk of the FormatTheText program is devoted to assembling the *Inlines* collection of the *TextBlock*. The *InlineCollection* class implements *Add* methods for objects of *string, Inline*, and *UIElement* (the last of which lets you embed other elements in the *TextBlock*). However, the *Bold* and *Italic* constructors accept only *Inline* objects and not string objects, so the program uses a *Run* constructor first for each *Bold* or *Italic* object.

The program sets the *FontSize* property of the *TextBlock*:

```
txt.FontSize = 32;
```

However, the program works the same way if it sets the *FontSize* property of the window instead:

```
FontSize = 32;
```

Similarly, the program can set the *Foreground* property of the window and the *TextBlock* text appears in that color:

```
Foreground = Brushes.CornflowerBlue;
```

Elements on the screen exist in a tree of parent-child hierarchies. The window is parent to the *TextBlock*, which is parent to a number of *Inline* elements. These elements inherit the values of the *Foreground* property and all font-related properties from their parent elements unless these properties are explicitly set on the children. You'll see how this works in Chapter 8.

Like the *UIElement* class, the *ContentElement* class defines many user-input events. It is possible to attach event handlers to the individual *Inline* elements that make up the text displayed by *TextBlock*, and the following program demonstrates this technique.

ToggleBoldAndItalic.cs

```
//-------------------------------------------------------
// ToggleBoldAndItalic.cs (c) 2006 by Charles Petzold
//-------------------------------------------------------
using System;
using System.Windows;
using System.Windows.Controls;
using System.Windows.Documents;
using System.Windows.Input;
using System.Windows.Media;

namespace Petzold.ToggleBoldAndItalic
{
    public class ToggleBoldAndItalic : Window
    {
        [STAThread]
        public static void Main()
        {
            Application app = new Application();
            app.Run(new ToggleBoldAndItalic());
        }
        public ToggleBoldAndItalic()
        {
            Title = "Toggle Bold & Italic";

            TextBlock text = new TextBlock();
            text.FontSize = 32;
            text.HorizontalAlignment = HorizontalAlignment.Center;
            text.VerticalAlignment = VerticalAlignment.Center;
            Content = text;

            string strQuote = "To be, or not to be, that is the question";
            string[] strWords = strQuote.Split();

            foreach (string str in strWords)
            {
                Run run = new Run(str);
                run.MouseDown += RunOnMouseDown;
                text.Inlines.Add(run);
                text.Inlines.Add(" ");
            }
        }
```

```
        void RunOnMouseDown(object sender, MouseButtonEventArgs args)
        {
            Run run = sender as Run;

            if (args.ChangedButton == MouseButton.Left)
                run.FontStyle = run.FontStyle == FontStyles.Italic ?
                    FontStyles.Normal : FontStyles.Italic;

            if (args.ChangedButton == MouseButton.Right)
                run.FontWeight = run.FontWeight == FontWeights.Bold ?
                    FontWeights.Normal : FontWeights.Bold;
        }
    }
}
```

The constructor breaks up a famous quotation from *Hamlet* into words, and then creates a *Run* object based on each word and puts the words back together into the *Inlines* collection of the *TextBlock* object. During this process the program also attaches the *RunOnMouseDown* handler to the *MouseDown* event of each *Run* object.

The *Run* class inherits *FontStyle* and *FontWeight* properties from the *TextElement* class, and the event handler changes these properties based on which mouse button was clicked. For the left mouse button, if the *FontStyle* property is currently *FontStyles.Italic*, the event handler sets the property to *FontStyles.Normal*. If the property is currently *FontStyles.Normal*, the handler changes it to *FontStyles.Italic*. Similarly, the *FontWeight* property is toggled between *FontWeights.Normal* and *FontWeights.Bold*.

I mentioned earlier that the *Content* property of the window really wants an instance of a class that derives from *UIElement*, because that class defines a method named *OnRender* that visually renders the object on the screen. The last program in this chapter is named RenderTheGraphic and has two source code files. The first file is a class that defines a custom element. The second file sets an instance of that class as its window content. The following class derives from *FrameworkElement*, which is the sole class that directly derives from *UIElement*. It overrides the crucial *OnRender* method to obtain a *DrawingContext* object that it uses to draw an ellipse with the *DrawEllipse* method. The class is a simple imitation of the *Ellipse* class found in the *System.Windows.Shapes* namespace.

SimpleEllipse.cs
```
//---------------------------------------------
// SimpleEllipse.cs (c) 2006 by Charles Petzold
//---------------------------------------------
using System;
using System.Windows;
using System.Windows.Media;

namespace Petzold.RenderTheGraphic
{
    class SimpleEllipse : FrameworkElement
    {
```

```
        protected override void OnRender(DrawingContext dc)
        {
            dc.DrawEllipse(Brushes.Blue, new Pen(Brushes.Red, 24),
                new Point(RenderSize.Width / 2, RenderSize.Height / 2),
                RenderSize.Width / 2, RenderSize.Height / 2);
        }
    }
}
```

The *RenderSize* property is determined before *OnRender* is called based on possible *Width* and *Height* settings, and negotiations between this class and the container in which it will appear.

If you have earlier experience with Windows programming (and even if you don't) you might assume that this method draws an ellipse directly on the screen. It does not. The *DrawEllipse* arguments are retained to render the ellipse on the screen at a later time. This "later time" may be right away, but only by retaining graphics from different sources and compositing them on the screen can the WPF achieve much of its graphical magic.

Here's a program that creates an object of *SimpleEllipse* and sets its *Content* property to that object:

RenderTheGraphic.cs

```
//-------------------------------------------------
// RenderTheGraphic.cs (c) 2006 by Charles Petzold
//-------------------------------------------------
using System;
using System.Windows;

namespace Petzold.RenderTheGraphic
{
    class RenderTheGraphic : Window
    {
        [STAThread]
        public static void Main()
        {
            Application app = new Application();
            app.Run(new ReplaceMainWindow());
        }
        public ReplaceMainWindow()
        {
            Title = "Render the Graphic";

            SimpleEllipse elips = new SimpleEllipse();
            Content = elips;
        }
    }
}
```

The ellipse fills the client area. Of course, you'll want to experiment with setting the *Width* and *Height* properties of *SimpleEllipse* and with setting the *HorizontalAlignment* and *VerticalAlignment* properties.

Although this chapter has made use of elements found in the *System.Windows.Controls* namespace, it hasn't made use of any classes that derive from *Control* (except for *Window* itself, of course). Controls are designed to obtain input from users and put that input to work. You'll see how in the next chapter.

Chapter 4
Buttons and Other Controls

In the Windows Presentation Foundation, the term *control* is somewhat more specialized than in earlier Windows programming interfaces. In Windows Forms, for example, everything that appears on the screen is considered a control of some sort. In the WPF, the term is reserved for elements that are *user interactive*, which means that they generally provide some kind of feedback to the user when they are prodded with the mouse or triggered by a keystroke. The *TextBlock, Image,* and *Shape* elements discussed in Chapter 3 all receive keyboard, mouse, and stylus input, but they choose to ignore it. Controls actively monitor and process user input.

The *Control* class descends directly from *FrameworkElement*:

Object

    DispatcherObject (abstract)

        DependencyObject

           Visual (abstract)

               UIElement

                  FrameworkElement

                     Control

Window derives from *Control* by way of *ContentControl*, so you've already seen some of the properties that *Control* adds to *FrameworkElement*. Properties defined by *Control* include *Background, Foreground, BorderBrush, BorderThickness,* and font-related properties, such as *FontWeight* and *FontStretch*. (Although *TextBlock* also has a bunch of font properties, *TextBlock* does not derive from *Control*. *TextBlock* defines those properties itself.)

From *Control* descend more than 50 other classes, providing programmers with favorites such as buttons, list boxes, scroll bars, edit fields, menus, and toolbars. The classes implementing these controls can all be found in the *System.Windows.Controls* and *System.Windows.Controls .Primitives* namespaces, along with other classes that do not derive from *Control*.

The archetypal control is the button, represented in the WPF by the *Button* class. The *Button* class has a property named *Content* and an event named *Click* that is triggered when the user presses the button with the mouse or keyboard.

The following program creates a *Button* object and installs a handler for the *Click* event to display a message box in response to button clicks.

ClickTheButton.cs

```
//-------------------------------------------------
// ClickTheButton.cs (c) 2006 by Charles Petzold
//-------------------------------------------------
using System;
using System.Windows;
using System.Windows.Controls;
using System.Windows.Input;
using System.Windows.Media;

namespace Petzold.ClickTheButton
{
    public class ClickTheButton : Window
    {
        [STAThread]
        public static void Main()
        {
            Application app = new Application();
            app.Run(new ClickTheButton());
        }
        public ClickTheButton()
        {
            Title = "Click the Button";

            Button btn = new Button();
            btn.Content = "_Click me, please!";
            btn.Click += ButtonOnClick;

            Content = btn;
        }
        void ButtonOnClick(object sender, RoutedEventArgs args)
        {
            MessageBox.Show("The button has been clicked and all is well.",
                            Title);
        }
    }
}
```

The *Content* property of the *Button* object is assigned a text string, and the *Button* object itself is set to the *Content* property of the *Window*. Don't worry about the exact order of these statements: You can set button properties and attach the event handler either before or after the button is made part of the window.

That fact that *Button* has a *Content* property just like *Window* is no coincidence. Both of these classes (and a few more) derive from *ContentControl*, and that's where the *Content* property is defined. Here's a partial class hierarchy starting with *Control*:

Control

　　ContentControl

　　　　ButtonBase (abstract)

Button

Window

That both *Window* and *ButtonBase* have the same *Content* property has a profound implication: All the varieties of objects that you can use as the content of a window can also be used as the content of a button. A button can display a bitmap, a *Shape* object, and formatted text. In fact, you can even set the *Content* property of one *Button* object to another *Button* object.

By now, you may not be surprised to see the button occupying the entire interior of the window's client area, and to see the button change its size accordingly as you change the size of the window.

The button initially does not have input focus, which means that it doesn't receive keystrokes typed from the keyboard. If you run the program and press the space bar, nothing will happen. However, even if the button does not have input focus, you can trigger the button by pressing Alt+C. If you watch closely, you'll even see the first letter of "Click me, please!" become underlined when you press the Alt key. Such a keyboard shortcut is provided when you precede a letter in the text string that you set to the *Content* property with an underline character. This feature is used more often for menu items than for buttons, but when used with buttons and other controls, it can give dialog boxes a more extensive keyboard interface.

You can give the button input focus by pressing the Tab key or clicking the button with the left mouse button. You'll notice a dotted line within the button border that indicates it has input focus. Thereafter, you can trigger the button by pressing the space bar or the Enter key.

You can programmatically give the button input focus by including the following statement in the window class's constructor:

```
btn.Focus();
```

Even if the button does not have input focus, it can respond to presses of the Enter key if you make the button a "default" button:

```
btn.IsDefault = true;
```

Or, you can make it respond to the Escape key by virtue of this property:

```
btn.IsCancel = true;
```

These two properties are generally used for the OK and Cancel buttons in dialog boxes. You can set both properties for the same button—a technique commonly used in "About" dialogs that contain only a single OK button.

Look closely and you'll notice that the border around the button changes a bit when the mouse passes over the button. The button also changes its background color when you click it. This feedback is part of what distinguishes controls from other elements.

ButtonBase defines a property named *ClickMode* that you can set to a member of the *ClickMode* enumeration to govern how the button responds to mouse clicks. The default is *Click-Mode.Release*, which means that the *Click* event is not fired until the mouse button is released. You can alternatively set the property to *ClickMode.Press* or *ClickMode.Hover*; the latter fires the event when the mouse cursor is simply passed over the button.

I know I've been ignoring an elephant in the room, which is the enormousness of the button as it fills the window's client area. As you discovered in the previous chapter, *FrameworkEle-ment* defines a property named *Margin*, which you can use to give an element a little space around its exterior:

```
btn.Margin = new Thickness(96);
```

Insert that statement, recompile, and now the button is surrounded by an inch of space on all sides. The button is still pretty big, of course, but let's take advantage of that by altering the button internals somewhat. The content of the button—the text string—is currently hovering in the center. We can instead put it down in the lower-left corner with the following two statements:

```
btn.HorizontalContentAlignment = HorizontalAlignment.Left;
btn.VerticalContentAlignment = VerticalAlignment.Bottom;
```

In the previous chapter, I discussed the *HorizontalAlignment* and *VerticalAlignment* properties. Look closely and you'll see that the properties in these two lines of code have the word *Content* in the middle, and because of this, they refer to what's going on inside the button. By now you know that *HorizontalAlignment* is an enumeration with four members: *Center*, *Left*, *Right*, and *Stretch*, and that *VerticalAlignment* is also an enumeration with the four fields: *Center*, *Top*, *Bottom*, and *Stretch*. (The use of the *Stretch* members in this context have the same effect as *Left* and *Top*.)

It is also possible to add a little padding to the inside of the button. You use the same *Thickness* structure as the *Margin* property:

```
btn.Padding = new Thickness(96);
```

Now there's about an inch of space between the interior of the button and the button's content.

The *Margin* property (defined by *FrameworkElement*) affects the exterior of the button; the *Padding* property (defined by *Control*) affects the interior of the button.

Just as the *HorizontalContentAlignment* and *VerticalContentAlignment* properties defined by *Control* affect the positioning of the button's content within the button, the *HorizontalAlign-ment* and *VerticalAlignment* properties affect the positioning of the button within its container (the client area). For a button, these two properties are set to *HorizontalAlignment.Stretch* and

VerticalAlignment.Stretch by default, which is why the button is stretched to fill the client area of the window. Let's set both values to *Center*:

```
btn.HorizontalAlignment = HorizontalAlignment.Center;
btn.VerticalAlignment = VerticalAlignment.Center;
```

Now the button's size is affected solely by the content of the button, including the padding. Although it's not immediately obvious, the *Margin* is still respected as well. This is more evident if you make the margin different on the four sides:

```
btn.Margin = new Thickness(96, 192, 192, 96);
```

If you set the *HorizontalAlignment* and *VerticalAlignment* to something other than *Center*, you also see how the *Margin* property is observed:

```
btn.HorizontalAlignment = HorizontalAlignment.Left;
btn.VerticalAlignment = VerticalAlignment.Top;
```

With a margin of 0, the button would sit in the corner of the client area. With a larger margin, the button is displaced from the corner. The margin plays such an important role in positioning the button that if you make the window smaller than what the margin requires, the button itself will start to disappear!

Now let's remove all the experimental code except for two statements that set *HorizontalAlignment* and *VerticalAlignment* to *Center*:

```
btn.HorizontalAlignment = HorizontalAlignment.Center;
btn.VerticalAlignment = VerticalAlignment.Center;
```

The button should now be properly sized to its content and sitting in the center of the window. The button will accommodate itself to the size of its content, even if the size of that content changes after the button has been displayed. You can also put in line breaks. And if you really need to, you can give the button an explicit size:

```
btn.Width = 96;
btn.Height = 96;
```

Of course, the less explicitly you set the sizes of controls, the happier you'll be. Remember that WPF will try to size the content to fit the individual user's screen resolution. Setting sizes of controls to specific values countermands this.

If you eliminate all the code you've added, there's still another approach to making the button a proper size. This is by setting the *SizeToContent* property of the window:

```
SizeToContent = SizeToContent.WidthAndHeight;
```

Now the window is sized to fit a normal-sized button. Any *Margin* set on the *Button* will be honored.

By default, the font that appears in a button is Tahoma with an em size of 11. (That's 8¼ points.) You can change the em size easily, as well as the font family:

```
btn.FontSize = 48;
btn.FontFamily = new FontFamily("Times New Roman");
```

You can alternatively set the *FontSize* and *FontFamily* of the *Window* and the button will inherit those values. (But they won't take precedence over values set specifically for the *Button*.) And, of course, you can change the colors:

```
btn.Background = Brushes.AliceBlue;
btn.Foreground = Brushes.DarkSalmon;
btn.BorderBrush = Brushes.Magenta;
```

The *BorderThickness* property has no effect on buttons. Changing the button background is not altogether satisfactory because the button no longer provides feedback when it's being clicked.

On the other hand, you might want to give the user additional feedback, perhaps when the mouse enters the airspace above the button. Here's a program that uses a *TextBlock* to display formatted text in the button, but changes the color in response to *MouseEnter* and *MouseLeave* events:

```
FormatTheButton.cs
//-------------------------------------------------
// FormatTheButton.cs (c) 2006 by Charles Petzold
//-------------------------------------------------
using System;
using System.Windows;
using System.Windows.Controls;
using System.Windows.Documents;
using System.Windows.Input;
using System.Windows.Media;

namespace Petzold.FormatTheButton
{
    public class FormatTheButton : Window
    {
        Run runButton;

        [STAThread]
        public static void Main()
        {
            Application app = new Application();
            app.Run(new FormatTheButton());
        }
        public FormatTheButton()
        {
            Title = "Format the Button";
```

```
            // Create the Button and set as window content.
            Button btn = new Button();
            btn.HorizontalAlignment = HorizontalAlignment.Center;
            btn.VerticalAlignment = VerticalAlignment.Center;
            btn.MouseEnter += ButtonOnMouseEnter;
            btn.MouseLeave += ButtonOnMouseLeave;
            Content = btn;

            // Create the TextBlock and set as button content.
            TextBlock txtblk = new TextBlock();
            txtblk.FontSize = 24;
            txtblk.TextAlignment = TextAlignment.Center;
            btn.Content = txtblk;

            // Add formatted text to the TextBlock.
            txtblk.Inlines.Add(new Italic(new Run("Click")));
            txtblk.Inlines.Add(" the ");
            txtblk.Inlines.Add(runButton = new Run("button"));
            txtblk.Inlines.Add(new LineBreak());
            txtblk.Inlines.Add("to launch the ");
            txtblk.Inlines.Add(new Bold(new Run("rocket")));
        }
        void ButtonOnMouseEnter(object sender, MouseEventArgs args)
        {
            runButton.Foreground = Brushes.Red;
        }
        void ButtonOnMouseLeave(object sender, MouseEventArgs args)
        {
            runButton.Foreground = SystemColors.ControlTextBrush;
        }
    }
}
```

Notice that the *Run* object containing the word *button* is stored as a field named *runButton*. When the mouse cursor enters the button, that *Run* object's *Foreground* property is colored red. When the cursor leaves the button, the color is restored to the default control text color obtained from *SystemColors.ControlTextBrush*.

The next program displays a button with an image instead of text, and rather than load the image over the Internet or rely on an image in a file, the image has actually been embedded into the executable file as a *resource*. This word *resource* is used in a couple different ways in the Windows Presentation Foundation. The type of resource I'll show you here can be differentiated as an *assembly resource*. The resource is a file (generally a binary file) that is made part of the project in Visual Studio and becomes part of an executable or a dynamic-link library.

If you have a bitmap that you'd like to make part of a Visual Studio project, right-click the project name in the Solution Explorer and select Add Existing Item. (Or, select Add Existing Item from the Project menu in Visual Studio.) In the dialog box, navigate to the item and click the Add button. The file should then show up in the list of project files. Right-click the item and select Properties. Make sure that the Build Action is set for Resource.

In your program, you can gain access to that file using the *Uri* constructor, where *filename* is the name of the file:

```
Uri uri = new Uri("pack://application:,,/filename");
```

Notice the two commas and the forward slash in front of the file name.

If you have a bunch of image files in your project, you may want to keep them in a separate directory of the project. You would first right-click the project name in the Solution Explorer and select Add New Folder. (Or, select New Folder from the Project menu in Visual Studio.) Give the folder a name like *Images*. Then you can right-click that folder name to add the image files to that folder. When you need to load the images into your program, use the following syntax:

```
Uri uri = new Uri("pack://application:,,/Images/filename");
```

Notice that there's a forward slash in front of the directory name.

Here's a project that includes a file named *munch.png* of the famous screaming man from Edvard Munch's etching *The Scream*. Perhaps you could use this image on a button you really don't want the user to press.

ImageTheButton.cs
```
//-------------------------------------------------
// ImageTheButton.cs (c) 2006 by Charles Petzold
//-------------------------------------------------
using System;
using System.Windows;
using System.Windows.Controls;
using System.Windows.Input;
using System.Windows.Media;
using System.Windows.Media.Imaging;

namespace Petzold.ImageTheButton
{
    public class ImageTheButton : Window
    {
        [STAThread]
        public static void Main()
        {
            Application app = new Application();
            app.Run(new ImageTheButton());
        }
        public ImageTheButton()
        {
            Title = "Image the Button";

            Uri uri = new Uri("pack://application:,,/munch.png");
            BitmapImage bitmap = new BitmapImage(uri);
```

```
        Image img = new Image();
        img.Source = bitmap;
        img.Stretch = Stretch.None;

        Button btn = new Button();
        btn.Content = img;
        btn.HorizontalAlignment = HorizontalAlignment.Center;
        btn.VerticalAlignment = VerticalAlignment.Center;

        Content = btn;
      }
   }
}
```

If you have an image file that has some transparency, you might want to try using that one in this program: You'll see the normal *Button* background through the transparent parts.

Now, wouldn't it be nice to have both an image *and* text in a button? Yes, it certainly would. But we're stuck with the same problem we had in putting multiple objects in a window: The *Content* property can be set to only one object. I'm sure this is annoying, but it won't be long before a solution will be at hand.

Installing a handler for the button's *Click* event is certainly the most traditional way for a program to be notified when the user clicks a button. However, it could be that a particular operation in your program can be triggered through several sources—perhaps a menu item, a toolbar item, and a button. Perhaps you even implement a scripting language that can trigger this same operation. It might make more sense to route all these controls through a single point.

This is the idea behind a property named *Command*, which is defined by the *ButtonBase* class and some other classes, including *MenuItem*. For common commands, you set the *Command* property of the *Button* object equal to a static property of the classes *ApplicationCommands*, *ComponentCommands*, *MediaCommands*, *NavigationCommands*, or *EditingCommands*. The first four of these classes are located in the *System.Windows.Input* namespace; the last is in *System.Windows.Documents*. The static properties of these classes are all of type *RoutedUI-Command*. You can also create your own objects of type *RoutedUICommand* (as Chapter 14 demonstrates).

For example, if you wanted a particular button to perform a clipboard Paste command, you would set the *Command* property like so:

```
btn.Command = ApplicationCommands.Paste;
```

It's not required, but you may also want to set the button text to the standard text for that command:

```
btn.Content = ApplicationCommands.Paste.Text;
```

The other step is to associate this particular Paste command with event handlers. This association is called a *binding*, and it's one of several types of bindings you'll find in the Windows Presentation Foundation. The *UIElement* class defines (and the *Control* and *Window* classes inherit) a property named *CommandBindings*, which is a collection of *CommandBinding* objects. You'll probably use the *CommandBindings* collection of the window, so the statement looks something like this:

```
CommandBindings.Add(new CommandBinding(ApplicationCommands.Paste,
                          PasteOnExecute, PasteCanExecute));
```

PasteOnExecute and *PasteCanExecute* are two event handlers that are located in your program. (You can name them whatever you want.) In the *PasteOnExecute* handler, you carry out the Paste command. Sometimes, however, your program can't carry out a Paste command because the clipboard doesn't contain data in the format you want. That's the purpose of the *PasteCanExecute* handler. This handler checks the clipboard for data of the proper format. If the data isn't available, the handler can set a flag and the *Button* will automatically be disabled.

If this same program also has a menu item for Paste, you just need to assign the *Command* property of the menu item to *ApplicationCommands.Paste*, and the same binding will apply.

Here's a simple program that demonstrates command bindings:

```
CommandTheButton.cs
//-----------------------------------------------
// CommandTheButton.cs (c) 2006 by Charles Petzold
//-----------------------------------------------
using System;
using System.Windows;
using System.Windows.Controls;
using System.Windows.Input;
using System.Windows.Media;

namespace Petzold.CommandTheButton
{
    public class CommandTheButton : Window
    {
        [STAThread]
        public static void Main()
        {
            Application app = new Application();
            app.Run(new CommandTheButton());
        }
        public CommandTheButton()
        {
            Title = "Command the Button";

            // Create the Button and set as window content.
            Button btn = new Button();
            btn.HorizontalAlignment = HorizontalAlignment.Center;
            btn.VerticalAlignment = VerticalAlignment.Center;
```

```
        btn.Command = ApplicationCommands.Paste;
        btn.Content = ApplicationCommands.Paste.Text;
        Content = btn;

        // Bind the command to the event handlers.
        CommandBindings.Add(new CommandBinding(ApplicationCommands.Paste,
                        PasteOnExecute, PasteCanExecute));
    }
    void PasteOnExecute(object sender, ExecutedRoutedEventArgs args)
    {
        Title = Clipboard.GetText();
    }
    void PasteCanExecute(object sender, CanExecuteRoutedEventArgs args)
    {
        args.CanExecute = Clipboard.ContainsText();
    }
    protected override void OnMouseDown(MouseButtonEventArgs args)
    {
        base.OnMouseDown(args);
        Title = "Command the Button";
    }
  }
}
```

The constructor of the window assigns *ApplicationCommands.Paste* to the *Command* property of the *Button* object. The constructor concludes by creating a *CommandBinding* object that associates *ApplicationCommands.Paste* with the event handlers *PasteOnExecute* and *PasteCan-Execute*. This *CommandBinding* object is made a part of the window's *CommandBindings* collection.

The two event handlers *PasteOnExecute* and *PasteCanExecute* use static methods from the *Clipboard* class (located in *System.Windows*). The static *GetText* and *ContainsText* methods both exist in overloaded versions that allow you to be specific about the type of text you want—including comma-separated format, HTML, RTF, Unicode, or XAML—but this program doesn't use those text types. The text it gets from the clipboard is just used to set the window's *Title* property. Since you may want to experiment with this program a bit, the last method in the program lets you click anywhere in the window to restore the *Title* text.

Before running the program, you might want to copy some text to the clipboard from Notepad or another text-based application (even Visual Studio) just so the program has something to work with. You'll discover that the button responds not only to the normal keyboard and mouse input, but also to Ctrl+V, the standard keyboard shortcut for Paste. That's one of the benefits of using a command binding rather than just handling the *Click* event.

Now copy a bitmap into the clipboard. No need to run Paint or PhotoShop! Just press the Print Screen key to copy the screen image into the clipboard. Whenever there's a change in the clipboard, any bound can-execute event handlers (such as *PasteCanExecute*) are called so that the handler has the opportunity to properly set the *CanExecute* property of the event arguments. The button is immediately disabled. Now copy some text into the clipboard. The button is enabled again. Behind the scenes, the command binding changes the *IsEnabled* property that *Button* inherits from *UIElement*.

While the most common buttons carry out commands either through *Click* event handlers or command bindings, other types of buttons indicate options. A *CheckBox* control consists of a square box generally followed by some text. The box can be checked or unchecked to indicate a particular program option. For example, a font-selection dialog might have *CheckBox* controls for Bold, Italic, and Underline.

RadioButton controls are generally used to display a group of mutually exclusive items. (The term comes from the buttons commonly found on car radios for selecting preset stations.)

Both *CheckBox* and *RadioButton* are considered types of "toggle" buttons, as is clear from a complete view of the classes that descend from *ButtonBase*:

Control

> *ContentControl*

>> *ButtonBase* (abstract)

>>> *Button*

>>> *GridViewColumnHeader*

>>> *RepeatButton*

>>> *ToggleButton*

>>>> *CheckBox*

>>> *RadioButton*

ToggleButton is not abstract, so you can also create an object of type *ToggleButton*, which looks just like a regular button except that it toggles on and off. The *ToggleButton* in the following program changes the *ResizeMode* property of the window.

```
ToggleTheButton.cs
//-------------------------------------------------
// ToggleTheButton.cs (c) 2006 by Charles Petzold
//-------------------------------------------------
using System;
using System.Windows;
using System.Windows.Controls;
using System.Windows.Controls.Primitives;
using System.Windows.Input;
using System.Windows.Media;

namespace Petzold.ToggleTheButton
{
```

```
public class ToggleTheButton : Window
{
    [STAThread]
    public static void Main()
    {
        Application app = new Application();
        app.Run(new ToggleTheButton());
    }
    public ToggleTheButton()
    {
        Title = "Toggle the Button";

        ToggleButton btn = new ToggleButton();
        btn.Content = "Can _Resize";
        btn.HorizontalAlignment = HorizontalAlignment.Center;
        btn.VerticalAlignment = VerticalAlignment.Center;
        btn.IsChecked = (ResizeMode == ResizeMode.CanResize);
        btn.Checked += ButtonOnChecked;
        btn.Unchecked += ButtonOnChecked;
        Content = btn;
    }
    void ButtonOnChecked(object sender, RoutedEventArgs args)
    {
        ToggleButton btn = sender as ToggleButton;
        ResizeMode =
            (bool)btn.IsChecked ? ResizeMode.CanResize : ResizeMode.NoResize;
    }
}
```

ToggleTheButton uses the button to switch the *ResizeMode* property of the window between *ResizeMode.CanResize* and *ResizeMode.NoResize*. The button automatically toggles itself on and off as the user clicks it. The *IsChecked* property indicates the current setting. Notice that the program initializes *IsChecked* to *true* if *ResizeMode* is initially *ResizeMode.CanResize* and *false* otherwise. Two events named *Checked* and *Unchecked* are triggered as the button is checked and unchecked. You can attach the same event handler to both events and simply use the *IsChecked* property to distinguish them, which is exactly what ToggleTheButton does.

Notice that the *IsChecked* property must be cast to a *bool* before being used in the C# conditional operator. The *IsChecked* property is actually a nullable *bool*, and can take on values of *true*, *false*, and *null*. If you set the *IsThreeState* property of *ToggleButton* to *true*, you can set *IsChecked* to *null* to display a third, "indeterminate" state of the button. For example, an Italic button in a word processing program might use this indeterminate state if the currently selected text has a mix of both italic and non-italic characters. (However, if the currently selected text is in a font that doesn't allow italics, the program would disable the Italic button by setting its *IsEnabled* property to *false*.)

The *CheckBox* class adds almost nothing to *ToggleButton*. You can create a *CheckBox* in this program just by replacing the button creation code with this:

```
CheckBox btn = new CheckBox();
```

You don't need to change the event handler. The program works the same except that the button looks different. You could also change ToggleTheButton's button to a *RadioButton*, but the program wouldn't work properly. You cannot uncheck a radio button by manually clicking it.

Because a *ToggleButton* or a *CheckBox* essentially represents the value of a Boolean, it makes sense that a particular toggle button be associated with a Boolean property of some object. This is called *data binding*, and it is such an important part of the Windows Presentation Foundation that Chapter 23 is devoted to the topic.

A *ToggleButton* used with data binding doesn't need to have its *IsChecked* property initialized, or have handlers installed for the *Checked* and *Unchecked* events. What's required instead is a call to the *SetBinding* method, which the button inherits from the *FrameworkElement* class. For a *ToggleButton* or *CheckBox* object, the call is typically something like this:

```
btn.SetBinding(ToggleButton.IsCheckedProperty, "SomeProperty");
```

where the second argument is a string with the name of a property you want associated with the *IsChecked* state of the button. You specify the object that "SomeProperty" belongs to with the *DataContext* property of *Button*.

The first argument to the *SetBinding* method probably looks even stranger than the second argument. It refers *not* to the *IsChecked* property of a *ToggleButton* object, but instead to something called *IsCheckedProperty* that appears to be a static member of the *ToggleButton* class.

ToggleButton does indeed define a static field named *IsCheckedProperty* that is an object of type *DependencyProperty*. Chapter 8 is devoted in its entirety to dependency properties. For now, think of it just as a convenient way to refer to a particular property defined by *ToggleButton*.

So, to what Boolean property do we want to bind the *ToggleButton*? One convenient Boolean is the *Topmost* property of the window. As you'll recall, if *Topmost* is set to *true*, the window always appears in the foreground of other windows. The *SetBinding* call looks like this:

```
btn.SetBinding(ToggleButton.IsCheckedProperty, "Topmost");
```

The data binding won't try to guess which object in the program is the one whose *Topmost* property you're referring to, so you need to specify that object by setting the *DataContext* property of the button to the window object:

```
btn.DataContext = this;
```

Here's the complete program:

```
BindTheButton.cs
//-----------------------------------------------
// BindTheButton.cs (c) 2006 by Charles Petzold
//-----------------------------------------------
using System;
using System.Windows;
```

```
using System.Windows.Controls;
using System.Windows.Controls.Primitives;
using System.Windows.Input;
using System.Windows.Media;

namespace Petzold.BindTheButton
{
    public class BindTheButton : Window
    {
        [STAThread]
        public static void Main()
        {
            Application app = new Application();
            app.Run(new BindTheButton());
        }
        public BindTheButton()
        {
            Title = "Bind theButton";

            ToggleButton btn = new ToggleButton();
            btn.Content = "Make _Topmost";
            btn.HorizontalAlignment = HorizontalAlignment.Center;
            btn.VerticalAlignment = VerticalAlignment.Center;
            btn.SetBinding(ToggleButton.IsCheckedProperty, "Topmost");
            btn.DataContext = this;
            Content = btn;

            ToolTip tip = new ToolTip();
            tip.Content = "Toggle the button on to make " +
                          "the window topmost on the desktop";
            btn.ToolTip = tip;
        }
    }
}
```

When you run this program, the button will be automatically initialized to the current state of the *Topmost* property of the window. As you click the button on and off, that property will be changed.

The *System.Windows.Data* namespace includes a class named *Binding* that you can alternatively use to create and set a data binding. This code can replace the statements that call *SetBinding* and set the *DataContext* property in the BindTheButton program:

```
Binding bind = new Binding("Topmost");
bind.Source = this;
btn.SetBinding(ToggleButton.IsCheckedProperty, bind);
```

The Binding class gives you more options in defining the data binding, as you'll discover in Chapter 23.

The BindTheButton program also includes a *ToolTip* object that is set to the *ToolTip* property of the *Button*. The text appears when the mouse cursor pauses over the button. The *ToolTip* property is defined by *FrameworkElement*, so you can attach a tooltip to other elements as well as controls. Like *ButtonBase* and *Windows*, *ToolTip* derives from *ContentControl*, so you can use formatted text in the *ToolTip*, and even pictures if you really want to mess with the heads of your users.

If you'd like to see a *ToolTip* with an image, go back to the ImageTheButton program and insert the following four lines at the end of the constructor:

```
btn.Content = "Don't Click Me!";
ToolTip tip = new ToolTip();
tip.Content = img;
btn.ToolTip = tip;
```

The *Button* gets some text to display, but the *ToolTip* gets *The Scream*.

Another simple control that derives from *ContentControl* is *Label*. Traditionally the *Label* control has been the standard way to display short text strings in forms and dialog boxes. For example, here's a label that might appear in a File Open dialog:

```
Label lbl = new Label();
lbl.Content = "File _name:";
```

With versatile elements such as *TextBlock*, the *Label* control would seem to be obsolete, but it's really not, and the key to its longevity is the ability to use underscores in text that you assign to the *Content* property. In a File Open dialog box, pressing Alt+N shifts the input focus not to the label—because labels are commonly non-focusable—but to the control after the label, which is probably a *TextBox* control that lets the user enter and edit text. Thus, labels continue to maintain their role as assistants in keyboard navigation.

Speaking of the *TextBox* control, the Windows Presentation Foundation supports the two we've come to expect:

Control

    TextBoxBase (abstract)

        TextBox

        RichTextBox

Although the *TextBox* has content, it is not considered a *ContentControl* because the content is always text. Instead it has a *Text* property that lets you set an initial string or obtain the string that the user typed.

Because *TextBox* derives from *Control*, you can specify the background and foreground brushes used in the control, as well as the font. However, at any time, all the text that appears in a particular *TextBox* will always be the same color and use the same font. The *RichTextBox* control lets the program (and the user) apply various character and paragraph formatting to different parts of the text. The difference between *TextBox* and *RichTextBox* is the same as the difference between Windows Notepad and Windows WordPad.

By default, a *TextBox* control allows entry of a single line of text. Here is the first dialog box to appear in this book. It contains a single *TextBox* control.

UriDialog.cs

```
//----------------------------------------
// UriDialog.cs (c) 2006 by Charles Petzold
//----------------------------------------
using System;
using System.Windows;
using System.Windows.Controls;
using System.Windows.Input;
using System.Windows.Media;

namespace Petzold.NavigateTheWeb
{
    class UriDialog : Window
    {
        TextBox txtbox;

        public UriDialog()
        {
            Title = "Enter a URI";
            ShowInTaskbar = false;
            SizeToContent = SizeToContent.WidthAndHeight;
            WindowStyle = WindowStyle.ToolWindow;
            WindowStartupLocation = WindowStartupLocation.CenterOwner;

            txtbox = new TextBox();
            txtbox.Margin = new Thickness(48);
            Content = txtbox;

            txtbox.Focus();
        }
        public string Text
        {
            set
            {
                txtbox.Text = value;
                txtbox.SelectionStart = txtbox.Text.Length;
            }
            get
            {
                return txtbox.Text;
            }
        }
        protected override void OnKeyDown(KeyEventArgs args)
        {
            if (args.Key == Key.Enter)
                Close();
        }
    }
}
```

This *UriDialog* class inherits from *Window* but it doesn't include a *Main* method (that method will be in the class for the main window of this program) and it sets several properties at the top of the constructor. Dialog boxes shouldn't appear in the taskbar; they usually are sized to their content, and they often get a *WindowStyle* of *ToolWindow*. (The *ToolWindow* style allows a dialog to be resizable but not to have minimize or maximize buttons.) The *WindowStartup-Location* property specifies that the dialog is to be positioned in the center of its owner (a window we haven't met yet).

The *Title* says "Enter a URI" and a *TextBox* sits in the middle of the client area, ready for the user to type something in. The class also has a public property named *Text*. Dialog box classes almost always contain public properties. That's how a program interacts with the dialog. This *Text* property simply provides public access to the *Text* property of the *TextBox* control. Notice also that the *set* accessor uses the *SelectionStart* property of the *TextBox* to position the cursor at the end of whatever text is set. The user can close the dialog by clicking the Close icon or pressing the Enter key, a feature that the *OnKeyDown* override provides.

Here's the program that uses the *UriDialog*. This program sets the *Content* property of its window to an object of type *Frame*. *Frame* also inherits from *ContentControl*, but this program sets the *Source* property of *Frame* rather than the *Content* property.

```
NavigateTheWeb.cs
//----------------------------------------------
// NavigateTheWeb.cs (c) 2006 by Charles Petzold
//----------------------------------------------
using System;
using System.Windows;
using System.Windows.Controls;
using System.Windows.Input;
using System.Windows.Media;

namespace Petzold.NavigateTheWeb
{
    public class NavigateTheWeb : Window
    {
        Frame frm;

        [STAThread]
        public static void Main()
        {
            Application app = new Application();
            app.Run(new NavigateTheWeb());
        }
        public NavigateTheWeb()
        {
            Title = "Navigate the Web";

            frm = new Frame();
            Content = frm;

            Loaded += OnWindowLoaded;
        }
```

```
void OnWindowLoaded(object sender, RoutedEventArgs args)
{
    UriDialog dlg = new UriDialog();
    dlg.Owner = this;
    dlg.Text = "http://";
    dlg.ShowDialog();

    try
    {
        frm.Source = new Uri(dlg.Text);
    }
    catch (Exception exc)
    {
        MessageBox.Show(exc.Message, Title);
    }
}
}
}
```

The program sets an event handler for the *Loaded* event. By the time *OnWindowLoaded* is called, the main window is already displayed on the screen. That's when the window creates an object of type *UriDialog*, assigns its *Owner*, and assigns the *Text* property the string "http://". The call to *ShowDialog* displays the modal dialog and doesn't return until the user closes the dialog. With any luck, the user will type a valid URI of a Web site. Notice that the dialog box expands in width if the URI is too long to fit in the text box. The *TextBox* expands to fit the text, and the *Window* follows.

When *ShowDialog* returns, the program sets the *Source* property of the *Frame* control and the result is an instant Web browser! Of course, you don't have a row of navigation buttons, but the Backspace key functions as the browser's Back button, and you have a few other options (including printing) by right-clicking the Web page.

The *UriDialog* box is able to close itself when the user presses the Enter key because by default the *TextBox* isn't interested in the Enter key. If you set

```
txtbox.AcceptsReturn = true;
```

the single-line edit control becomes a multiline edit control and now handles carriage returns. Here's a program that contains a *TextBox* control that fills the window's client area. Perhaps it's the beginning of a Notepad clone. But rather than use a File menu for loading and saving files, this program uses a file with a fixed name and location. The program could be used for taking random notes and preserving them between Windows sessions.

EditSomeText.cs

```
//-------------------------------------------------
// EditSomeText.cs (c) 2006 by Charles Petzold
//-------------------------------------------------
using System;
using System.ComponentModel;            // for CancelEventArgs
```

```
using System.IO;
using System.Windows;
using System.Windows.Controls;
using System.Windows.Input;
using System.Windows.Media;

namespace Petzold.EditSomeText
{
    class EditSomeText : Window
    {
        static string strFileName = Path.Combine(
            Environment.GetFolderPath(
                Environment.SpecialFolder.LocalApplicationData),
                    "Petzold\\EditSomeText\\EditSomeText.txt");

        TextBox txtbox;

        [STAThread]
        public static void Main()
        {
            Application app = new Application();
            app.Run(new EditSomeText());
        }
        public EditSomeText()
        {
            Title = "Edit Some Text";

            // Create the text box.
            txtbox = new TextBox();
            txtbox.AcceptsReturn = true;
            txtbox.TextWrapping = TextWrapping.Wrap;
            txtbox.VerticalScrollBarVisibility = ScrollBarVisibility.Auto;
            txtbox.KeyDown += TextBoxOnKeyDown;
            Content = txtbox;

            // Load the text file.
            try
            {
                txtbox.Text = File.ReadAllText(strFileName);
            }
            catch
            {
            }

            // Set the text box caret and input focus.
            txtbox.CaretIndex = txtbox.Text.Length;
            txtbox.Focus();
        }
        protected override void OnClosing(CancelEventArgs args)
        {
            try
            {
                Directory.CreateDirectory(Path.GetDirectoryName(strFileName));
                File.WriteAllText(strFileName, txtbox.Text);
            }
        }
```

```
        catch (Exception exc)
        {
            MessageBoxResult result =
                MessageBox.Show("File could not be saved: " + exc.Message +
                                "\nClose program anyway?", Title,
                                MessageBoxButton.YesNo,
                                MessageBoxImage.Exclamation);

            args.Cancel = (result == MessageBoxResult.No);
        }
    }
    void TextBoxOnKeyDown(object sender, KeyEventArgs args)
    {
        if (args.Key == Key.F5)
        {
            txtbox.SelectedText = DateTime.Now.ToString();
            txtbox.CaretIndex = txtbox.SelectionStart +
                                        txtbox.SelectionLength;
        }
    }
}
}
```

The program defines a location and name for the file in the area known as *local isolated storage*. The static *File.ReadAllText* method attempts to load the file in the window's constructor, and the static *File.WriteAllText* method saves the file. The program also installs an event handler for the *KeyDown* event so that it can insert the date and time into the file when the user presses F5.

The *RichTextBox* is much more complex than the *TextBox* because it stores text that could have a variety of different character and paragraph formatting. If you're familiar with previous Windows controls similar to *RichTextBox*, you might naturally assume that the control stores text in the Rich Text Format (RTF), a file format that dates from the mid-1980s and which was intended to provide an interchange format among word processing programs. The WPF version of *RichTextBox* certainly supports RTF (and plain text as well) but it also supports an XML-based file format that is a subset of the Extensible Application Markup Language (XAML) supported by WPF.

The following program uses the standard File Open and File Save dialog boxes that can be found in the *Microsoft.Win32* namespace. The program doesn't have a menu, so the dialog boxes are invoked when you press Ctrl+O and Ctrl+S. This feature presented a problem: The *RichTextBox* likes to see all the keystrokes. If you attach a handler to the control's *KeyDown* event, you won't get anything.

The solution is a technique I'll discuss more in Chapter 9. Keyboard, mouse, and stylus events actually occur first in the window, in the form of *preview* events. So, to examine keystrokes before they get to the *RichTextBox*, the following program overrides the window's *OnPreviewKeyDown* method. When the override encounters a Ctrl+O or Ctrl+S, it displays the proper dialog box and sets the *Handled* property of the event arguments to *true*, indicating that the particular event has been taken care of, and the keystroke should *not* go to the *RichTextBox*.

Because there are no menus or toolbars in this program, text formatting is limited to the built-in commands Ctrl+I, Ctrl+U, and Ctrl+B for italics, underline, and bold.

EditSomeRichText.cs

```
//--------------------------------------------------
// EditSomeRichText.cs (c) 2006 by Charles Petzold
//--------------------------------------------------
using Microsoft.Win32;
using System;
using System.IO;
using System.Windows;
using System.Windows.Controls;
using System.Windows.Documents;
using System.Windows.Input;
using System.Windows.Media;

namespace Petzold.EditSomeRichText
{
    public class EditSomeRichText : Window
    {
        RichTextBox txtbox;
        string strFilter =
            "Document Files(*.xaml)|*.xaml|All files (*.*)|*.*";

        [STAThread]
        public static void Main()
        {
            Application app = new Application();
            app.Run(new EditSomeRichText());
        }
        public EditSomeRichText()
        {
            Title = "Edit Some Rich Text";

            txtbox = new RichTextBox();
            txtbox.VerticalScrollBarVisibility = ScrollBarVisibility.Auto;
            Content = txtbox;

            txtbox.Focus();
        }
        protected override void OnPreviewTextInput(TextCompositionEventArgs args)
        {
            if (args.ControlText.Length > 0 && args.ControlText[0] == '\x0F')
            {
                OpenFileDialog dlg = new OpenFileDialog();
                dlg.CheckFileExists = true;
                dlg.Filter = strFilter;

                if ((bool)dlg.ShowDialog(this))
                {
                    FlowDocument flow = txtbox.Document;
```

```
                    TextRange range = new TextRange(flow.ContentStart,
                                                    flow.ContentEnd);
                    Stream strm = null;

                    try
                    {
                        strm = new FileStream(dlg.FileName, FileMode.Open);
                        range.Load(strm, DataFormats.Xaml);
                    }
                    catch (Exception exc)
                    {
                        MessageBox.Show(exc.Message, Title);
                    }
                    finally
                    {
                        if (strm != null)
                            strm.Close();
                    }
                }

                args.Handled = true;
            }
            if (args.ControlText.Length > 0 && args.ControlText[0] == '\x13')
            {
                SaveFileDialog dlg = new SaveFileDialog();
                dlg.Filter = strFilter;

                if ((bool)dlg.ShowDialog(this))
                {
                    FlowDocument flow = txtbox.Document;
                    TextRange range = new TextRange(flow.ContentStart,
                                                    flow.ContentEnd);
                    Stream strm = null;

                    try
                    {
                        strm = new FileStream(dlg.FileName, FileMode.Create);
                        range.Save(strm, DataFormats.Xaml);
                    }
                    catch (Exception exc)
                    {
                        MessageBox.Show(exc.Message, Title);
                    }
                    finally
                    {
                        if (strm != null)
                            strm.Close();
                    }
                }
                args.Handled = true;
            }
            base.OnPreviewTextInput(args);
        }
    }
}
```

Formatted text gets into and out of the *RichTextBox* through the *Document* property. This *Document* property is of type *FlowDocument*, and the following code creates a *TextRange* object that encompasses the entire document:

```
TextRange range = new TextRange(flow.ContentStart, flow.ContentEnd);
```

The *TextRange* class defines two methods named *Load* and *Save*. The first argument is a *Stream*; the second is a string describing the desired data format. For this second argument it's easiest to get those strings from static members of the *DataFormats* class. With the *RichTextBox*, you can use *DataFormats.Text*, *DataFormats.Rtf*, *DataFormats.Xaml*, and *DataFormats.XamlPackage*, which is actually a ZIP file that contains binary resources the document might require. This program is hard-coded to use *DataFormats.Xaml*. (The program can't load any arbitrary XAML file, however.) You may want to look at these files to get a glimpse of the format of documents under the Windows Presentation Foundation.

I'm sure there are many other marvelous and useful programs we could write with a window that hosts just a single object, but I can't think of any more. And that is why we really need to figure out how to put multiple controls in a window.

Chapter 5
Stack and Wrap

Controls that derive from the *ContentControl* class (such as *Window*, *Button*, *Label*, and *Tool-Tip*) have a property named *Content* that you can set to almost any object. Commonly, this object is either a *string* or an instance of a class that derives from *UIElement*. The problem is you can set *Content* to only *one* object, which may be satisfactory for simple buttons, but is clearly inadequate for a window.

Fortunately, the Windows Presentation Foundation includes several classes designed specifically to alleviate this problem. These are collectively known as *panels*, and the art and science of putting controls and other elements on the panel is known as *layout*.

Panels derive from the *Panel* class. This partial class hierarchy shows the most important derivatives of *Panel*:

UIElement

    FrameworkElement

        Panel (abstract)

            Canvas

            DockPanel

            Grid

            StackPanel

            UniformGrid

            WrapPanel

The panel is a relatively recent concept in graphical windowing environments. Traditionally, a Windows program populated its windows and dialog boxes with controls by specifying their precise size and location. The Windows Presentation Foundation, however, has a strong commitment to *dynamic layout* (also known as *automatic layout*). The panels themselves are responsible for sizing and positioning elements based on different layout models. That's why a variety of classes derive from *Panel*: Each supports a different type of layout.

Panel defines a property named *Children* used to store the child elements. The *Children* property is an object of type *UIElementCollection*, which is a collection of *UIElement* objects. Thus, the children of a panel can be *Image* objects, *Shape* objects, *TextBlock* objects, and *Control* objects, just to mention the most popular candidates. The children of a panel can also include other panels. Just as you use a panel to host multiple elements in a window, you use a panel to host multiple elements in a button or any other *ContentControl* object.

In this chapter I'll discuss the *StackPanel*, which arranges child elements in a vertical or horizontal stack, and the *WrapPanel*, which is similar to the *StackPanel* except that child elements can wrap to the next column or row.

The next chapter will focus on the *DockPanel*, which automates the positioning of elements against the inside edges of their parents, and the *Grid*, which hosts children in a grid of rows and columns. The *UniformGrid* is similar to the *Grid* except that all the rows are equal height and all the columns are equal width.

It will then be time to look at the *Canvas*, which allows you to arrange elements by specifying their precise coordinate locations. Of course, the *Canvas* panel is closest to traditional layout and consequently is probably used least of these five options.

Although automatic layout is a crucial feature in the Windows Presentation Foundation, you can't use it in a carefree way. Almost always, you'll have to use your own aesthetic sense in tweaking certain properties of the elements, most commonly *HorizontalAligment*, *VerticalAlignment*, *Margin*, and *Padding*.

The following program sets the *Content* property of its window to a *StackPanel* and then creates 10 buttons that become children of the panel.

StackTenButtons.cs

```
//--------------------------------------------------
// StackTenButtons.cs (c) 2006 by Charles Petzold
//--------------------------------------------------
using System;
using System.Windows;
using System.Windows.Controls;
using System.Windows.Input;
using System.Windows.Media;

namespace Petzold.StackTenButtons
{
    class StackTenButtons : Window
    {
        [STAThread]
        public static void Main()
        {
            Application app = new Application();
            app.Run(new StackTenButtons());
        }
        public StackTenButtons()
        {
            Title = "Stack Ten Buttons";

            StackPanel stack = new StackPanel();
            Content = stack;
```

```
            Random rand = new Random();

            for (int i = 0; i < 10; i++)
            {
                Button btn = new Button();
                btn.Name = ((char)('A' + i)).ToString();
                btn.FontSize += rand.Next(10);
                btn.Content = "Button " + btn.Name + " says 'Click me'";
                btn.Click += ButtonOnClick;

                stack.Children.Add(btn);
            }
        }
        void ButtonOnClick(object sender, RoutedEventArgs args)
        {
            Button btn = args.Source as Button;

            MessageBox.Show("Button " + btn.Name + " has been clicked",
                            "Button Click");
        }
    }
}
```

Notice that the program creates an object of type *Random* and then increases the *FontSize* property of each button with a small random number. Each button is added to the *Children* collection of the *StackPanel* with the following statement:

```
stack.Children.Add(btn);
```

I've given each button a slightly different *FontSize* to demonstrate how the *StackPanel* works with elements of different sizes. When you run the program, you'll see the buttons arranged from the top down in the order they were added to the *Children* collection. Each button gets a height that is suitable for displaying its content. The width of each button, however, extends to the width of the *StackPanel*, which itself fills the client area of the window.

When experimenting with this program, you may want to give the *StackPanel* a non-default *Background* brush so that you can see exactly how big it is:

```
stack.Background = Brushes.Aquamarine;
```

By default, the *StackPanel* arranges its children vertically. You can alter that behavior by setting the *Orientation* property:

```
stack.Orientation = Orientation.Horizontal;
```

Now you see that each button has a width that reflects its content, but the button heights extend to the full height of the panel. Depending on the width of your monitor size, you may or may not notice that the window will mercilessly truncate the display of some buttons if the window isn't large enough to fit them all.

For the remainder of this experiment, let's go back to a vertical orientation and just keep in mind that the following discussion applies to both orientations, with all references to *horizontal* and *vertical* swapped, of course.

It is unlikely that you want buttons extending the full width of the window. You can make them less wide by setting the *HorizontalAlignment* property of each button in the *for* loop of the program:

```
btn.HorizontalAlignment = HorizontalAlignment.Center;
```

The *StackPanel* still occupies the full width of the client area, but now each button is made a proper size. Alternatively, you can set the *HorizontalAlignment* of the *StackPanel* itself:

```
stack.HorizontalAlignment = HorizontalAlignment.Center;
```

Now the *StackPanel* becomes only large enough to fit the maximum width of the buttons.

The background color of the *StackPanel* illustrates a subtle difference between setting the horizontal alignment of the buttons and the panel: When you set the *HorizontalAlignment* of each button to *Center*, each button is made wide enough to fit its content. When you alternatively set the *HorizontalAlignment* property of the *StackPanel* to *Center*, the panel is made large enough to fit the widest button. Each button still has a *HorizontalAlignment* property of *Stretch*, so each button stretches to the width of the *StackPanel*. Result: All the buttons are the same width.

Perhaps the most satisfying solution is to forgo setting the *HorizontalAlignment* properties on either the panel or the buttons, and just size the window to the content:

```
SizeToContent = SizeToContent.WidthAndHeight;
ResizeMode = ResizeMode.CanMinimize;
```

Now the window is exactly the size of its content, which is the size of the *StackPanel*, which now reflects the width of the widest button. You may like to have all the buttons the same width, or you may want the width of each button to reflect its particular content. That's an aesthetic decision, and you can impose your verdict by the way you set the *HorizontalAlignment* property of each button.

What you probably do *not* want, however, is for all the buttons to be jammed up against each other as they've been so far. You'll want to set a margin around each button:

```
btn.Margin = new Thickness(5);
```

This is much, much better. Each button now has a margin of five device-independent units (about 1/20 inch) on each side. Still, some sticklers (like me) may not be entirely satisfied. Because each button has about 1/20-inch margin on all sides, the distance between adjacent buttons is 1/10 inch. However, the margin between the buttons and the border of the window is still only 1/20 inch. You can fix that by setting a margin on the panel itself:

```
stack.Margin = new Thickness(5);
```

You can now remove the background brush for the *StackPanel* and you have a nice, attractive (albeit do-nothing) program.

You may have noticed that when giving each *Button* some *Content* text, I first assigned the *Name* property of the *Button* to the short text string "A", "B", "C", and so forth. You can use these *Name* strings to later obtain the objects they're associated with by calling the *FindName* property defined by *FrameworkElement*. For example, in some event handler or other method in the window class you can have the following code:

```
Button btn = FindName("E") as Button;
```

Although you're calling the *FindName* method of *Window*, the method will search recursively through the window *Content* and then the *StackPanel*.

You can also index the *Children* property of the panel. For example, the following expression returns the sixth element added to the *Children* collection:

```
stack.Children[5]
```

The *UIElementCollection* class has several methods that can help you deal with the child elements. If *el* is an element in the collection, the expression

```
stack.Children.IndexOf(el)
```

returns the index of that element in the collection, or −1 if the element is not part of the collection. The *UIElementCollection* also has methods to insert an element into the location at a particular index and to remove elements from the collection.

Event handlers—such as *ButtonOnClick* in StackTenButtons—must often obtain the object that generated the event. The technique I've been using so far is the traditional .NET approach. The first argument to the event handler (typically named *sender*) is cast to an object of the correct type:

```
Button btn = sender as Button;
```

However, the StackTenButtons program ignores the sender argument and instead uses a property of the *RoutedEventArgs* object, which is the second argument to the event handler:

```
Button btn = args.Source as Button;
```

In this particular program, it doesn't matter which technique is used. The source of the *Click* event obtained from the *Source* property of *RoutedEventArgs* is the same as the object sending the event: the object to which the event handler is attached and which is obtained from the *sender* argument. When an event handler is attached to the element originating the event, these two values are the same.

However, an alternative event-handling scenario causes these two values to be different. You can try this alternative by commenting out the statement in the *for* loop that assigns the handler to the *Click* event of each button and then inserting the following statement at the very end of the constructor outside of the *for* loop:

```
stack.AddHandler(Button.ClickEvent, new RoutedEventHandler(ButtonOnClick));
```

The *AddHandler* method is defined by *UIElement*. The first argument must be an object of type *RoutedEvent*, and it is. *ClickEvent* is a static read-only field of type *RoutedEvent* that is defined by *ButtonBase* and inherited by *Button*. The second argument indicates the event handler that you want to attach to this event. It must be specified in the form of a constructor of the delegate type of the event handler, in this case *RoutedEventHandler*.

The call to *AddHandler* instructs the *StackPanel* to monitor all its children for events of type *Button.ClickEvent*, and to use *ButtonOnClick* as the handler for those events. After you recompile, the program works the same except that slightly different information is coming through the event handler. The *Source* property of *RoutedEventArgs* still identifies the *Button* object, but the *sender* argument is now the *StackPanel* object.

You don't need to call *AddHandler* for the *StackPanel*. You could instead call *AddHandler* for the window itself:

```
AddHandler(Button.ClickEvent, new RoutedEventHandler(ButtonOnClick));
```

Now the same event handler will apply to all *Button* objects that are anywhere in the tree that descends from the window. The *sender* argument to the event handler is now the *Window* object.

I'll have more to say about routed events in Chapter 9.

Panels can be nested. Here's a program that displays 30 buttons in 3 columns of 10 buttons each. Four *StackPanel* objects are involved.

StackThirtyButtons.cs
```
//---------------------------------------------------
// StackThirtyButtons.cs (c) 2006 by Charles Petzold
//---------------------------------------------------
using System;
using System.Windows;
using System.Windows.Controls;
using System.Windows.Input;
using System.Windows.Media;

namespace Petzold.StackThirtyButtons
{
    class StackThirtyButtons : Window
    {
        [STAThread]
        public static void Main()
        {
            Application app = new Application();
            app.Run(new StackThirtyButtons());
        }
```

```
        public StackThirtyButtons()
        {
            Title = "Stack Thirty Buttons";
            SizeToContent = SizeToContent.WidthAndHeight;
            ResizeMode = ResizeMode.CanMinimize;
            AddHandler(Button.ClickEvent, new RoutedEventHandler(ButtonOnClick));

            StackPanel stackMain = new StackPanel();
            stackMain.Orientation = Orientation.Horizontal;
            stackMain.Margin = new Thickness(5);
            Content = stackMain;

            for (int i = 0; i < 3; i++)
            {
                StackPanel stackChild = new StackPanel();
                stackMain.Children.Add(stackChild);

                for (int j = 0; j < 10; j++)
                {
                    Button btn = new Button();
                    btn.Content = "Button No. " + (10 * i + j + 1);
                    btn.Margin = new Thickness(5);
                    stackChild.Children.Add(btn);
                }
            }
        }
        void ButtonOnClick(object sender, RoutedEventArgs args)
        {
            MessageBox.Show("You clicked the button labeled " +
                        (args.Source as Button).Content);
        }
    }
}
```

Notice the *AddHandler* call near the top of the constructor. All the buttons share the same *Click* event handler. The constructor creates one *StackPanel* with a horizontal orientation that fills the client area. This *StackPanel* is parent to 3 other *StackPanel* objects, each of which has a vertical orientation and is parent to 10 buttons. The buttons and the first *StackPanel* are given a *Margin* of five device-independent units, and the window is sized to fit the result.

Keep adding more and more buttons, and pretty soon you're going to cry, "Yikes, I have so many buttons they won't even fit on my screen." And at that point you need a scroll bar or two.

Rather than a scroll bar, you'd be better off in this instance with the *ScrollViewer* class. Like *Window* and *ButtonBase*, *ScrollViewer* inherits from *ContentControl*. The difference is that if the content of the *ScrollViewer* is too large to be displayed within the size of the control, *Scroll-Viewer* lets you scroll it.

Here's a program that sets the *Content* property of its window to an object of type *ScrollViewer* and sets the *Content* property of the *ScrollViewer* to a *StackPanel* that contains 50 buttons.

ScrollFiftyButtons.cs

```
//-------------------------------------------------
// ScrollFiftyButtons.cs (c) 2006 by Charles Petzold
//-------------------------------------------------
using System;
using System.Windows;
using System.Windows.Controls;
using System.Windows.Input;
using System.Windows.Media;

namespace Petzold.ScrollFiftyButtons
{
    class ScrollFiftyButtons : Window
    {
        [STAThread]
        public static void Main()
        {
            Application app = new Application();
            app.Run(new ScrollFiftyButtons());
        }
        public ScrollFiftyButtons()
        {
            Title = "Scroll Fifty Buttons";
            SizeToContent = SizeToContent.Width;
            AddHandler(Button.ClickEvent, new RoutedEventHandler(ButtonOnClick));

            ScrollViewer scroll = new ScrollViewer();
            Content = scroll;

            StackPanel stack = new StackPanel();
            stack.Margin = new Thickness(5);
            scroll.Content = stack;

            for (int i = 0; i < 50; i++)
            {
                Button btn = new Button();
                btn.Name = "Button" + (i + 1);
                btn.Content = btn.Name + " says 'Click me'";
                btn.Margin = new Thickness(5);

                stack.Children.Add(btn);
            }
        }
        void ButtonOnClick(object sender, RoutedEventArgs args)
        {
            Button btn = args.Source as Button;

            if (btn != null)
                MessageBox.Show(btn.Name + " has been clicked",
                                "Button Click");
        }
    }
}
```

If the window (or your monitor) isn't large enough to display 50 buttons, you can use the vertical scroll bar to scroll the lower buttons into view.

The *ScrollViewer* has two properties that govern the visibility of the vertical and horizontal scroll bars. By default, the *VerticalScrollBarVisibility* property is the enumeration member *ScrollBarVisibility.Visible*, which means that the scroll bar is always visible, but it's inactive when it's not needed.

The default setting of the *HorizontalScrollBarVisibility* property is *ScrollBarVisibility.Disabled*, which means that the scroll bar is never visible.

Another option is *ScrollBarVisibility.Auto*, which means that the scroll bar appears only when it's needed. You might try setting the *VerticalScrollBar* property to this member and also decrease the number of buttons to something that can fit on your screen. As you make the window tall enough for the vertical scroll bar to disappear, you'll notice that all the buttons get wider because they have additional space in which to stretch! (Of course, you can avoid that effect by setting the *HorizontalAlignment* property of the buttons to *HorizontalAlignment.Center*.)

You can set the *HorizontalScrollBarVisibility* property to *ScrollBarVisibility.Visible* or *ScrollBarVisibility.Auto*. Now when you make the window too narrow for the buttons, a horizontal scroll bar lets you scroll the right sides into view. Without a horizontal scroll bar, when you make the window narrow, the *ScrollViewer* gives the *StackPanel* a narrower width. A very narrow *StackPanel* makes the buttons less wide, and button content is truncated. With a horizontal scroll bar, the *StackPanel* gets the width it needs.

You'll notice that the program sets the *Margin* property of each *Button* to five units on all four sides, and uses the same margin for the *StackPanel*. The *Margin* property on the *ScrollViewer* is not set, however, because it would cause the scroll bar to be offset from the edges of the window, which would look very strange.

Toward the beginning of the constructor, the *SizeToContent* property is set so that only the width of the window is sized to its content:

```
SizeToContent = SizeToContent.Width;
```

The customary setting of *SizeToContent.WidthAndHeight* causes the window to be sized to display all 50 buttons, so that doesn't make much sense. Moreover, the constructor doesn't set the *ResizeMode* property to *ResizeMode.CanMinimize* as I've often shown with windows that have been sized to their content. That option suppresses the sizing border and doesn't let you experiment with changing the width and height of the window.

You'll notice something a little different in the *Click* event handler. After casting the *Source* property of *RoutedEventArgs* to a *Button* object, the code checks if the result is *null*. The result will be null if *Source* is not actually a *Button* object. How can this be? Try it: comment out the *if* statement, recompile the program, and then click one of the arrows at the end of the scroll bar. The program bombs out with a Null Reference Exception.

If you investigate the problem, you'll find that the problem occurs when the *Source* property of *RoutedEventArgs* refers to the *ScrollBar* object. An object of type *ScrollBar* cannot be cast to an object of type *Button*. But if you look at the documentation for the *ScrollBar* control, you'll find that it doesn't even implement a *Click* event. So why is an object of type *ScrollBar* even showing up in this event handler?

The answer is revealed if you check another property of the *RoutedEventArgs* named *Original-Source*. Sometimes controls are built up of other controls, and the *ScrollBar* is a good example. The two arrows at the ends are *RepeatButton* objects, and these objects generate *Click* events. The *OriginalSource* property of *RoutedEventArgs* indeed reveals an object of type *RepeatButton*.

Keep this example in mind when you attach event handlers to a parent object. You may need to perform some additional checks in the event handler. Another solution in this particular program is to call *AddHandler* for the *StackPanel* rather than for the window.

Scrollbars represent the traditional solution for fitting more elements than space allows. The Windows Presentation Foundation offers another solution called the *Viewbox*. To try it out, first comment out the three lines of code in ScrollFiftyButtons that deal with the *ScrollViewer*. Instead, create an object of type *Viewbox* and set its *Child* property to the *StackPanel*:

```
Viewbox view = new Viewbox();
Content = view;
view.Child = stack;
```

Now the entire *StackPanel* and its fifty buttons are reduced in size to fit in the window. While this is not quite the best solution for buttons with text on them, keep it in mind for other space problems.

I've been focusing on getting multiple buttons in a window. The *StackPanel* is also useful in putting multiple elements *into* buttons. The following program creates a single button, but the button contains a *StackPanel* that has four children: an *Image*, a *Label*, and two *Polyline* objects. (*Polyline* inherits from *Shape*.)

DesignAButton.cs
```
//-------------------------------------------------
// DesignAButton.cs (c) 2006 by Charles Petzold
//-------------------------------------------------
using System;
using System.Windows;
using System.Windows.Controls;
using System.Windows.Input;
using System.Windows.Media;
using System.Windows.Media.Imaging;
using System.Windows.Shapes;

namespace Petzold.DesignAButton
{
    public class DesignAButton : Window
```

```
{
    [STAThread]
    public static void Main()
    {
        Application app = new Application();
        app.Run(new DesignAButton());
    }
    public DesignAButton()
    {
        Title = "Design a Button";

        // Create a Button as content of the Window.
        Button btn = new Button();
        btn.HorizontalAlignment = HorizontalAlignment.Center;
        btn.VerticalAlignment = VerticalAlignment.Center;
        btn.Click += ButtonOnClick;
        Content = btn;

        // Create a StackPanel as content of the Button.
        StackPanel stack = new StackPanel();
        btn.Content = stack;

        // Add a Polyline to the StackPanel.
        stack.Children.Add(ZigZag(10));

        // Add an Image to the StackPanel.
        Uri uri = new Uri("pack://application:,,/BOOK06.ICO");  // 32-pixels
        BitmapImage bitmap = new BitmapImage(uri);
        Image img = new Image();
        img.Margin = new Thickness(0, 10, 0, 0);
        img.Source = bitmap;
        img.Stretch = Stretch.None;
        stack.Children.Add(img);

        // Add a Label to the StackPanel.
        Label lbl = new Label();
        lbl.Content = "_Read books!";
        lbl.HorizontalContentAlignment = HorizontalAlignment.Center;
        stack.Children.Add(lbl);

        // Add another Polyline to the StackPanel.
        stack.Children.Add(ZigZag(0));
    }
    Polyline ZigZag(int offset)
    {
        Polyline poly = new Polyline();
        poly.Stroke = SystemColors.ControlTextBrush;
        poly.Points = new PointCollection();

        for (int x = 0; x <= 100; x += 10)
            poly.Points.Add(new Point(x, (x + offset) % 20));

        return poly;
    }
```

```
        void ButtonOnClick(object sender, RoutedEventArgs args)
        {
            MessageBox.Show("The button has been clicked", Title);
        }
    }
}
```

The two *Polyline* objects are created in the *ZigZag* method. These are the same images (a jagged line) except that the second is inverted. The *Image* element is a little picture of a book that I found in the collection of icons and bitmaps distributed with Visual Studio 2005. I gave the *Image* element a *Margin* of 10 units, but only on the top to prevent it from being jammed against the *Polyline*.

The *Label* control contains the text "Read books!"; notice the underline character preceding the letter *R*. Even though this *Label* control is one of four elements on the button, and it isn't even the first one, this underline on its text content is enough to enable an Alt+R keyboard interface for the button.

Although you may have been skeptical that you'd ever create a stack of 50, 30, or even 10 buttons, there's one type of button that almost always appears in a stack, and that's the radio button.

Traditionally, a group of mutually exclusive radio buttons are children of a group box, which is a control with a simple outline border and a text heading. In the Windows Presentation Foundation, this is the *GroupBox* control, which is one of three classes that descend from *HeaderedContentControl*:

Control

    ContentControl

        HeaderedContentControl

            Expander

            GroupBox

            TabItem

Because *HeaderedContentControl* derives from *ContentControl*, these controls have a *Content* property. The controls also have a *Header* property, which (like *Content*) is of type *object*. *GroupBox* adds nothing to *HeaderedContentControl*. Use the *Header* property to set the heading at the top of the *GroupBox*. Although this heading is customarily text, you can really make it whatever you want. Use *Content* for the interior of the *GroupBox*. You'll probably want to put a *StackPanel* in there.

TuneTheRadio shows how to put four radio buttons in a group box by way of a *StackPanel*. The radio buttons let you dynamically change the *WindowStyle* property of the window.

TuneTheRadio.cs

```csharp
//---------------------------------------------
// TuneTheRadio.cs (c) 2006 by Charles Petzold
//---------------------------------------------
using System;
using System.Windows;
using System.Windows.Controls;
using System.Windows.Input;
using System.Windows.Media;

namespace Petzold.TuneTheRadio
{
    public class TuneTheRadio : Window
    {
        [STAThread]
        public static void Main()
        {
            Application app = new Application();
            app.Run(new TuneTheRadio());
        }
        public TuneTheRadio()
        {
            Title = "Tune the Radio";
            SizeToContent = SizeToContent.WidthAndHeight;

            GroupBox group = new GroupBox();
            group.Header = "Window Style";
            group.Margin = new Thickness(96);
            group.Padding = new Thickness(5);
            Content = group;

            StackPanel stack = new StackPanel();
            group.Content = stack;

            stack.Children.Add(
                CreateRadioButton("No border or caption",
                            WindowStyle.None));
            stack.Children.Add(
                CreateRadioButton("Single-border window",
                            WindowStyle.SingleBorderWindow));
            stack.Children.Add(
                CreateRadioButton("3D-border window",
                            WindowStyle.ThreeDBorderWindow));
            stack.Children.Add(
                CreateRadioButton("Tool window",
                            WindowStyle.ToolWindow));

            AddHandler(RadioButton.CheckedEvent,
                    new RoutedEventHandler(RadioOnChecked));
        }
        RadioButton CreateRadioButton(string strText, WindowStyle winstyle)
        {
            RadioButton radio = new RadioButton();
            radio.Content = strText;
```

```
                radio.Tag = winstyle;
                radio.Margin = new Thickness(5);
                radio.IsChecked = (winstyle == WindowStyle);

                return radio;
            }
        void RadioOnChecked(object sender, RoutedEventArgs args)
        {
                RadioButton radio = args.Source as RadioButton;
                WindowStyle = (WindowStyle)radio.Tag;
        }
    }
}
```

I gave the *GroupBox* a 1-inch margin so that it stands out a bit more from the window background. *GroupBox* is also given a padding of about 1/20 inch, which is the same value used for the margin of each radio button. (Alternatively, you can set the *Margin* property of the interior *StackPanel* to the same value.) The radio buttons are then separated from each other and the inside of the *GroupBox* by 1/10 inch. The *CreateRadioButton* method gives the *Content* of each button a text string and assigns the *Tag* property the corresponding member of the *Window-Style* enumeration. Notice that *CreateRadioButton* also sets the *IsChecked* property of the radio button that corresponds to the current setting of the window's *WindowStyle* property.

The checking and unchecking of sibling radio buttons happens automatically from either the mouse or keyboard. When you're using the keyboard, the cursor movement keys change the input focus among the sibling radio buttons. The space bar checks the currently focused button. All the program needs to do is monitor which button is being checked. (Some programs might also need to know when a button is losing its check mark.) It is usually most convenient to use the same event handler for sibling radio buttons. When writing code for the event handler, keep in mind that the *IsChecked* property has already been set.

It could be that you have a bunch of sibling radio buttons that comprise two or more mutually exclusive groups. To distinguish between these groups, use the *GroupName* property defined by *RadioButton*. Set *GroupName* to a unique string for each group of mutually exclusive buttons, and the multiple groups will be automatically checked and unchecked correctly. You can use the same *GroupName* property in your event handler to determine which group of buttons is affected.

The panel most similar to *StackPanel* is *WrapPanel*. During the years that the Windows Presentation Foundation was being designed and created, the *WrapPanel* actually preceded the *Stack-Panel*. The *WrapPanel* displays rows or columns of elements and automatically wraps to the next row (or column) if there's not enough room. It sounds quite useful, but it turned out that developers were mostly using *WrapPanel* without the wrapping. These developers didn't know it at the time, but they really wanted a *StackPanel*.

WrapPanel is useful when you need to display an unknown number of items in a two-dimensional area. (Think of it as Windows Explorer in non-detail view.) It's likely that all these items will be the same size. *WrapPanel* doesn't require that, but it has *ItemHeight* and *ItemWidth* properties that you can use to enforce uniform height or width. The only other property that *WrapPanel* defines is *Orientation*, which you use the same way as for *StackPanel*.

It is difficult to imagine an application of *WrapPanel* that doesn't also involve *ScrollViewer*. Let's use *WrapPanel* and *ScrollViewer* and some buttons to build a crude imitation of the right side of Windows Explorer. The program is called ExploreDirectories and it has two classes. Here's the first.

```
ExploreDirectories.cs
//-------------------------------------------------
// ExploreDirectories.cs (c) 2006 by Charles Petzold
//-------------------------------------------------
using System;
using System.Windows;
using System.Windows.Controls;
using System.Windows.Input;
using System.Windows.Media;

namespace Petzold.ExploreDirectories
{
    public class ExploreDirectories : Window
    {
        [STAThread]
        public static void Main()
        {
            Application app = new Application();
            app.Run(new ExploreDirectories());
        }
        public ExploreDirectories()
        {
            Title = "Explore Directories";

            ScrollViewer scroll = new ScrollViewer();
            Content = scroll;

            WrapPanel wrap = new WrapPanel();
            scroll.Content = wrap;

            wrap.Children.Add(new FileSystemInfoButton());
        }
    }
}
```

Well, isn't this simple? The content of the window is a *ScrollViewer*, and the content of the *ScrollViewer* is a *WrapPanel*, and *WrapPanel* has one child—an object of type *FileSystemInfo-Button*. Apparently this button is really hot stuff.

I named *FileSystemInfoButton* for the *FileSystemInfo* object in *System.IO*. The two classes that derive from *FileSystemInfo* are *FileInfo* and *DirectoryInfo*. If you have a particular object of type

FileSystemInfo, you can determine whether it refers to a file or to a directory by using the *is* operator.

The *FileSystemInfoButton* class derives from *Button* and stores a *FileSystemInfo* object as a field. The class has three constructors. The single-argument constructor is the one used most. It requires an argument of type *FileSystemInfo*, which it stores as a field. The constructor sets the button's *Content* to the *Name* property of this object. That's either the name of a directory or the name of a file. If this object is a *DirectoryInfo*, the text is bolded.

The parameterless constructor is used only when the program starts up and the window adds the first child to the *WrapPanel*. The parameterless constructor passes a *DirectoryInfo* object for the My Documents directory to the single-argument constructor.

```
FileSystemInfoButton.cs
//------------------------------------------------------
// FileSystemInfoButton.cs (c) 2006 by Charles Petzold
//------------------------------------------------------
using System;
using System.Diagnostics;        // For the Process class
using System.IO;
using System.Windows;
using System.Windows.Controls;
using System.Windows.Input;
using System.Windows.Media;

namespace Petzold.ExploreDirectories
{
    public class FileSystemInfoButton : Button
    {
        FileSystemInfo info;

        // Parameterless constructor make "My Documents" button.
        public FileSystemInfoButton()
            :
            this(new DirectoryInfo(
                Environment.GetFolderPath(Environment.SpecialFolder.MyDocuments)))
        {
        }

        // Single-argument constructor makes directory or file button.
        public FileSystemInfoButton(FileSystemInfo info)
        {
            this.info = info;
            Content = info.Name;
            if (info is DirectoryInfo)
                FontWeight = FontWeights.Bold;
            Margin = new Thickness(10);
        }

        // Two-argument constructor makes "Parent Directory" button.
        public FileSystemInfoButton(FileSystemInfo info, string str)
            :
            this(info)
```

```
    {
        Content = str;
    }

    // OnClick override does everything else.
    protected override void OnClick()
    {
        if (info is FileInfo)
        {
            Process.Start(info.FullName);
        }
        else if (info is DirectoryInfo)
        {
            DirectoryInfo dir = info as DirectoryInfo;
            Application.Current.MainWindow.Title = dir.FullName;

            Panel pnl = Parent as Panel;
            pnl.Children.Clear();

            if (dir.Parent != null)
                pnl.Children.Add(new FileSystemInfoButton(dir.Parent, ".."));

            foreach (FileSystemInfo inf in dir.GetFileSystemInfos())
                pnl.Children.Add(new FileSystemInfoButton(inf));
        }
        base.OnClick();
    }
}
```

When you run the program, you'll see a single button labeled My Documents. You can click that button to see the contents of that directory. If you click a button showing the name of a file, the application associated with that file is launched. Most directories listed after the first will also contain a button with two periods ("..") that you can use to navigate to the parent directory. When that button doesn't appear, you're at the root of the disk drive and you can't go back any further.

The *OnClick* override handles all of this logic. It first checks whether the *info* object stored as a field is an object of type *FileInfo*. If so, it uses the static *Process.Start* method (located in the *System.Diagnostics* namespace) to launch the application.

If the *info* object refers to a directory, the new directory name is displayed as the window *Title*. The *OnClick* method then clears the current children from the *WrapPanel*. If the new directory has a parent, the two-element constructor creates the button with two periods. The *OnClick* method concludes by obtaining the contents of the directory from *GetFileSystemInfos* and creating *FileSystemInfoButton* objects for each.

Of course, you'll want to experiment with navigating to a directory containing many files and examining how the *ScrollViewer* scrolls the rest of the *WrapPanel* into view.

Chapter 6

The Dock and the Grid

A traditional Windows program has a fairly standard layout. An application's menu almost always sits at the top of the main window's client area and extends to the full width of the window. The menu is said to be *docked* at the top of the client area. If the program has a toolbar, that too is docked at the top of the client area, but obviously only one control can be docked at the very edge. If the program has a status bar, it is docked at the bottom of the client area.

A program such as Windows Explorer displays a directory tree in a control docked at the left side of the client area. But the menu, toolbar, and status bar all have priority over the tree-view control because they extend to the full width of the client area while the tree-view control extends vertically only in the space left over by the other controls.

The Windows Presentation Foundation includes a *DockPanel* class to accommodate your docking needs. You create a *DockPanel* like so:

```
DockPanel dock = new DockPanel();
```

If you're creating this *DockPanel* in the constructor of a *Window* object, you'll probably set it to the window's *Content* property:

```
Content = dock;
```

It is fairly common for window layout to begin with *DockPanel* and then (if necessary) for other types of panels to be children of the *DockPanel*. You add a particular control (named, perhaps, *ctrl*) or other element to the *DockPanel* using the same syntax as with other panels:

```
dock.Children.Add(ctrl);
```

But now it gets a little strange, for you must indicate on which side of the *DockPanel* you want *ctrl* docked. To dock *ctrl* on the right side of the client area, for example, the code is:

```
DockPanel.SetDock(ctrl, Dock.Right);
```

Don't misread this statement: it does *not* refer at all to the *DockPanel* object you've just created named *dock*. Instead, *SetDock* is a static method of the *DockPanel* class. The two arguments are the control (or element) you're docking, and a member of the *Dock* enumeration, either *Dock.Left*, *Dock.Top*, *Dock.Right*, or *Dock.Bottom*.

It doesn't matter if you call this *DockPanel.SetDock* method before or after you add the control to the *Children* collection of the *DockPanel* object. In fact, you can call *DockPanel.SetDock* for a particular control even if you've never created a *DockPanel* object and have no intention of ever doing so!

This strange *SetDock* call makes use of an *attached property*, which is something I'll discuss in more detail in Chapter 8. For now, you can perhaps get a better grasp of what's going on by knowing that the static *SetDock* call above is equivalent to the following code:

```
ctrl.SetValue(DockPanel.DockProperty, Dock.Right);
```

The *SetValue* method is defined by the *DependencyObject* class (from which much of the Windows Presentation Foundation descends) and *DockPanel.DockProperty* is a static read-only field. This is the attached property, and this attached property and its setting (*Dock.Right*) are actually stored by the control. When performing layout, the *DockPanel* object can obtain the *Dock* setting of the control by calling:

```
Dock dck = DockPanel.GetDock(ctrl);
```

which is actually equivalent to:

```
Dock dck = (Dock) ctrl.GetValue(DockPanel.DockProperty);
```

The following program creates a *DockPanel* and 17 buttons as children of this *DockPanel*.

```
DockAroundTheBlock.cs
//-------------------------------------------------
// DockAroundTheBlock.cs (c) 2006 by Charles Petzold
//-------------------------------------------------
using System;
using System.Windows;
using System.Windows.Controls;
using System.Windows.Input;
using System.Windows.Media;

namespace Petzold.DockAroundTheBlock
{
    class DockAroundTheBlock : Window
    {
        [STAThread]
        public static void Main()
        {
            Application app = new Application();
            app.Run(new DockAroundTheBlock());
        }
        public DockAroundTheBlock()
        {
            Title = "Dock Around the Block";

            DockPanel dock = new DockPanel();
            Content = dock;
```

```
        for (int i = 0; i < 17; i++)
        {
            Button btn = new Button();
            btn.Content = "Button No. " + (i + 1);
            dock.Children.Add(btn);
            btn.SetValue(DockPanel.DockProperty, (Dock)(i % 4));
        }
    }
  }
}
```

In this program, the following statement

```
DockPanel.SetDock(btn, (Dock)(i % 4));
```

cleverly assigns each button a member of the *Dock* enumeration in a cycle: *Dock.Left, Dock.Top, Dock.Right,* and *Dock.Bottom,* which have the numeric values 0, 1, 2, and 3. You can easily see how the controls added earliest have priority in hugging the side of the *DockPanel* over those added latest. Each button has a content-appropriate size in one direction and is stretched in the other direction.

The control added last (which displays the string "Button No. 17") is not docked at all but occupies the leftover interior space. This behavior is by virtue of the default *true* setting of the *DockPanel* property *LastChildFill.* Although the program calls *DockPanel.SetDock* for that last button, the value is ignored. Try adding the statement

```
dock.LastChildFill = false;
```

any time after the *DockPanel* is created to see the last button docked as well and the leftover space unfilled.

So, when using a *DockPanel,* you work from the outside in. The first children get priority against the edge of the parent; the subsequent children are further toward the center.

Children of the *DockPanel* normally expand to fill the full width (or height) of the panel because the *HorizontalAlignment* and *VerticalAlignment* properties of the children are both *Stretch* by default. Try inserting the following statement to see something strange:

```
btn.HorizontalAlignment = HorizontalAlignment.Center;
```

The buttons docked on the top and bottom (as well as the last button in the center) are all reduced in width. Obviously, this is not standard user interface practice. Neither is setting a *Margin* property on docked controls.

Here's a program that uses a *DockPanel* in a more conventional way. It creates a *Menu, ToolBar, StatusBar, ListBox,* and *TextBox* controls, but because these controls are covered in more detail in later chapters, they remain mere skeletons of their potential. The *TextBox* is the last child, so it fills the space not required by the other controls.

MeetTheDockers.cs

```
//-----------------------------------------------
// MeetTheDockers.cs (c) 2006 by Charles Petzold
//-----------------------------------------------
using System;
using System.Windows;
using System.Windows.Controls;
using System.Windows.Controls.Primitives;
using System.Windows.Input;
using System.Windows.Media;

namespace Petzold.MeetTheDockers
{
    public class MeetTheDockers : Window
    {
        [STAThread]
        public static void Main()
        {
            Application app = new Application();
            app.Run(new MeetTheDockers());
        }
        public MeetTheDockers()
        {
            Title = "Meet the Dockers";

            DockPanel dock = new DockPanel();
            Content = dock;

            // Create menu.
            Menu menu = new Menu();
            MenuItem item = new MenuItem();
            item.Header = "Menu";
            menu.Items.Add(item);

            // Dock menu at top of panel.
            DockPanel.SetDock(menu, Dock.Top);
            dock.Children.Add(menu);

            // Create tool bar.
            ToolBar tool = new ToolBar();
            tool.Header = "Toolbar";

            // Dock tool bar at top of panel.
            DockPanel.SetDock(tool, Dock.Top);
            dock.Children.Add(tool);

            // Create status bar.
            StatusBar status = new StatusBar();
            StatusBarItem statitem = new StatusBarItem();
            statitem.Content = "Status";
            status.Items.Add(statitem);

            // Dock status bar at bottom of panel.
            DockPanel.SetDock(status, Dock.Bottom);
            dock.Children.Add(status);
```

```
            // Create list box.
            ListBox lstbox = new ListBox();
            lstbox.Items.Add("List Box Item");

            // Dock list box at left of panel.
            DockPanel.SetDock(lstbox, Dock.Left);
            dock.Children.Add(lstbox);

            // Create text box.
            TextBox txtbox = new TextBox();
            txtbox.AcceptsReturn = true;

            // Add text box to panel & give it input focus.
            dock.Children.Add(txtbox);
            txtbox.Focus();
        }
    }
}
```

This program is woefully incomplete, of course, because none of these controls actually does anything, but you may also feel that it's incomplete in a less obvious way. There should really be a splitter between the *ListBox* and the *TextBox* so that you can allocate the space between these two controls.

A splitter is implemented in the *Grid* panel, but that's not the only reason to use a *Grid*. The *Grid* panel displays its children in a collection of cells organized as rows and columns. It may at first seem possible to achieve rows and columns of controls by using a technique similar to the StackThirtyButtons program in the previous chapter. However, often when you arrange controls in rows and columns you want them to line up both horizontally and vertically. Each row of three buttons in StackThirtyButtons would not have lined up correctly if the buttons were of various sizes.

The *Grid* is perhaps the most useful layout panel, but it is also the most complex. Although it's possible to make *Grid* your single, all-purpose layout solution, you should probably be more flexible. The Windows Presentation Foundation supports different types of panels for a reason.

With that in mind, however, you start by creating an object of type *Grid*:

```
Grid grid = new Grid();
```

When experimenting with the *Grid*, you may want to display lines between the cells:

```
grid.ShowGridLines = true;
```

Setting this property to *true* causes dotted lines to appear between the cells. There is no way to change the style or color or width of these lines. If you want lots of control over the lines between your rows and columns in a way that might be suitable in a printed document, you probably want to use a *Table* rather a *Grid*. The *Table* (defined in the *System.Windows.Documents* namespace) is more like a table you might find in HTML or a word processor. The *Grid* is strictly for layout.

You need to tell the *Grid* how many rows and columns you want, and how these rows and columns should be sized. The height of each row can be one of the following options:

- Fixed in device-independent units
- Based on the tallest child of that row
- Based on leftover space (perhaps apportioned among other rows)

Similarly, the width of each column can also be one of these three options. These three options correspond to three members of the *GridUnitType* enumeration: *Pixel*, *Auto*, and *Star*. (The term *star* comes from the use of an asterisk in HTML tables to apportion leftover space.)

You specify the height of rows and the width of columns using a class named *GridLength*. Two constructors are available. If you just specify a value:

```
new GridLength(100)
```

the value is assumed to be a dimension in device-independent units. That constructor is equivalent to:

```
new GridLength(100, GridUnitType.Pixel)
```

You can also specify a value with the enumeration member *GridUnitType.Star*:

```
new GridLength(50, GridUnitType.Star)
```

The value you specify is used for apportioning leftover space, but the numeric value has meaning only when taken in combination with other rows or columns that use *GridUnitType.Star*. You can also specify *GridUnitType.Auto* in a constructor:

```
new GridLength(0, GridUnitType.Auto)
```

However, in this case, the numeric value is ignored, and you can alternatively use the static property

```
GridLength.Auto
```

which returns an object of type *GridLength*.

Grid has two properties named *RowDefinitions* and *ColumnDefinitions*. These properties are of type *RowDefinitionCollection* and *ColumnDefinitionCollection*, which are collections of *RowDefinition* and *ColumnDefinition* objects.

You create a *RowDefinition* object for every row of the *Grid*. The crucial property is *Height*, which you set to a *GridLength* object. (*RowDefinition* also has *MinHeight* and *MaxHeight* properties that you can use to constrain the height, but these are optional.) The crucial property of *ColumnDefinition* is *Width*, which you also set to a *GridLength* object. *ColumnDefinition* also includes *MinWidth* and *MaxWidth* properties.

Unfortunately, the code to set the *RowDefinitions* and *ColumnDefinitions* collections is rather wordy. This code sets four rows:

```
RowDefinition rowdef = new RowDefinition();
rowdef.Height = GridLength.Auto;
grid.RowDefinitions.Add(rowdef);

rowdef = new RowDefinition();
rowdef.Height = new GridLength(33, GridUnitType.Star);
grid.RowDefinitions.Add(rowdef);

rowdef = new RowDefinition();
rowdef.Height = new GridLength(150);
grid.RowDefinitions.Add(rowdef);

rowdef = new RowDefinition();
rowdef.Height = new GridLength(67, GridUnitType.Star);
grid.RowDefinitions.Add(rowdef);
```

The height of the first row is based on the tallest element in that row. The height of the third row is 150 device-independent units. Depending on the height of the *Grid* itself, there may be some space left over. If so, that space is apportioned 33 percent to the second row and 67 percent for the forth row. Those values don't have to be specified in percentages, although the code is certainly clearer when they are. The *Grid* control simply adds up all the *GridUnitType.Star* values, and then divides each value by that sum to determine the allocation of space.

Column definitions are similar, except that you set the *Width* property. With any luck, you may be able to put some of them in a *for* loop.

The default *Height* and *Width* properties are *GridUnitType.Star* with a value of 1, so if you want to distribute space among the rows and columns equally, you can use these defaults. But you still need to add *RowDefinition* and *ColumnDefinition* objects to the collections for every row and column you want. The code reduces to statements like this:

```
grid.RowDefinitions.Add(new RowDefinition());
```

If you need only a single-column *Grid*, you don't need to add a *ColumnDefinition*. You won't need a *RowDefinition* for a single-row *Grid*, and you won't need either for a single-cell *Grid*.

You add a control to the *Grid* just as with any other panel:

```
grid.Children.Add(ctrl);
```

You then need to specify a zero-based row and column where this control is to appear by using the static *SetRow* and *SetColumn* methods:

```
Grid.SetRow(ctrl, 2);
Grid.SetColumn(ctrl, 5);
```

That's the third row and the sixth column (the indices are zero-based). As with *DockPanel* .*SetDock*, these calls make use of attached properties. The defaults are rows and columns of 0.

Multiple objects can go into a single cell, but often you won't see them all. If you don't see something you know you put in the grid, it's likely it received the same row and column as something else.

The *HorizontalAlignment* and *VerticalAlignment* properties of the element affect how the element is positioned within the cell. In general, if the cell is not sized to the element, the element will be sized to the cell.

The following program creates a *Grid* that occupies the entire client area. The window sizes itself to the size of the *Grid* and suppresses the window sizing border. The program gives the *Grid* three rows and two columns, all using *GridLength.Auto*. In the cells of this *Grid* the program positions four *Label* controls and two *TextBox* controls, into which you can enter dates. The program calculates a difference between the two dates.

I originally wrote a Win32 version of this program for a friend who was researching family genealogy and needed to calculate the years, months, and days between birth dates and death dates. I was able to use the DATETIMEPICK_CLASS for that program. Unfortunately, the initial release of the Windows Presentation Foundation has no equivalent control, so this program uses the static *DateTime.TryParse* method to convert text strings into a date. I also changed the names and labels when I realized most readers of this book will probably use the program to determine how long they've lived so far.

CalculateYourLife.cs

```
//---------------------------------------------------
// CalculateYourLife.cs (c) 2006 by Charles Petzold
//---------------------------------------------------
using System;
using System.Windows;
using System.Windows.Controls;
using System.Windows.Input;
using System.Windows.Media;

namespace Petzold.CalculateYourLife
{
    class CalculateYourLife : Window
    {
        TextBox txtboxBegin, txtboxEnd;
        Label lblLifeYears;

        [STAThread]
        public static void Main()
        {
            Application app = new Application();
            app.Run(new CalculateYourLife());
        }
        public CalculateYourLife()
        {
            Title = "Calculate Your Life";
            SizeToContent = SizeToContent.WidthAndHeight;
            ResizeMode = ResizeMode.CanMinimize;
```

```csharp
// Create the grid.
Grid grid = new Grid();
Content = grid;

// Row and column definitions.
for (int i = 0; i < 3; i++)
{
    RowDefinition rowdef = new RowDefinition();
    rowdef.Height = GridLength.Auto;
    grid.RowDefinitions.Add(rowdef);
}

for (int i = 0; i < 2; i++)
{
    ColumnDefinition coldef = new ColumnDefinition();
    coldef.Width = GridLength.Auto;
    grid.ColumnDefinitions.Add(coldef);
}

// First label.
Label lbl = new Label();
lbl.Content = "Begin Date: ";
grid.Children.Add(lbl);
Grid.SetRow(lbl, 0);
Grid.SetColumn(lbl, 0);

// First TextBox.
txtboxBegin = new TextBox();
txtboxBegin.Text = new DateTime(1980, 1, 1).ToShortDateString();
txtboxBegin.TextChanged += TextBoxOnTextChanged;
grid.Children.Add(txtboxBegin);
Grid.SetRow(txtboxBegin, 0);
Grid.SetColumn(txtboxBegin, 1);

// Second label.
lbl = new Label();
lbl.Content = "End Date: ";
grid.Children.Add(lbl);
Grid.SetRow(lbl, 1);
Grid.SetColumn(lbl, 0);

// Second TextBox.
txtboxEnd = new TextBox();
txtboxEnd.TextChanged += TextBoxOnTextChanged;
grid.Children.Add(txtboxEnd);
Grid.SetRow(txtboxEnd, 1);
Grid.SetColumn(txtboxEnd, 1);

// Third label.
lbl = new Label();
lbl.Content = "Life Years: ";
grid.Children.Add(lbl);
Grid.SetRow(lbl, 2);
Grid.SetColumn(lbl, 0);
```

```
            // Label for calculated result.
            lblLifeYears = new Label();
            grid.Children.Add(lblLifeYears);
            Grid.SetRow(lblLifeYears, 2);
            Grid.SetColumn(lblLifeYears, 1);

            // Set margin for everybody.
            Thickness thick = new Thickness(5); // ~1/20 inch.
            grid.Margin = thick;

            foreach (Control ctrl in grid.Children)
                ctrl.Margin = thick;

            // Set focus and trigger the event handler.
            txtboxBegin.Focus();
            txtboxEnd.Text = DateTime.Now.ToShortDateString();
        }
        void TextBoxOnTextChanged(object sender, TextChangedEventArgs args)
        {
            DateTime dtBeg, dtEnd;

            if (DateTime.TryParse(txtboxBegin.Text, out dtBeg) &&
                DateTime.TryParse(txtboxEnd.Text, out dtEnd))
            {
                int iYears = dtEnd.Year - dtBeg.Year;
                int iMonths = dtEnd.Month - dtBeg.Month;
                int iDays = dtEnd.Day - dtBeg.Day;

                if (iDays < 0)
                {
                    iDays += DateTime.DaysInMonth(dtEnd.Year,
                                        1 + (dtEnd.Month + 10) % 12);
                    iMonths -= 1;
                }
                if (iMonths < 0)
                {
                    iMonths += 12;
                    iYears -= 1;
                }
                lblLifeYears.Content =
                    String.Format("{0} year{1}, {2} month{3}, {4} day{5}",
                                  iYears, iYears == 1 ? "" : "s",
                                  iMonths, iMonths == 1 ? "" : "s",
                                  iDays, iDays == 1 ? "" : "s");
            }
            else
            {
                lblLifeYears.Content = "";
            }
        }
    }
}
```

The program installs event handlers for the *TextChanged* events of the two *TextBox* controls. As the name suggests, this event is fired whenever the text changes. After converting the text strings to *DateTime* objects, the event handler calculates the difference between the two dates. Normally, if you subtract one *DateTime* object from another, you'll get a *TimeSpan* object, but that wasn't quite adequate. I wanted the program to calculate the difference between two dates much like a person would. For example, if the start date is the fifth day of the month, and the end date is the twentieth day of the same month or a different month, I wanted the difference to be 15 days.

If the start date is the twentieth day of the month (May, for example), and the end date is the fifth day of a month (such as September), I wanted the program to tally three full months from May 20 to August 20, and then a number of days from August 20 to September 5. That last calculation required taking into account the number of days in the month preceding the end date. The static *DaysInMonth* method of *DateTime* and some modulo arithmetic did the trick.

Let's look at another layout example using the *Grid*. Here's a layout that might be found in a data-entry form. The program creates two *Grid* panels as children of a *StackPanel*. The first *Grid* panel has two columns and five rows for labels and *TextBox* controls. The second *Grid* has one row and two columns for the OK and Cancel buttons.

EnterTheGrid.cs

```
//-------------------------------------------------
// EnterTheGrid.cs (c) 2006 by Charles Petzold
//-------------------------------------------------
using System;
using System.Windows;
using System.Windows.Controls;
using System.Windows.Input;
using System.Windows.Media;

namespace Petzold.EnterTheGrid
{
    public class EnterTheGrid : Window
    {
        [STAThread]
        public static void Main()
        {
            Application app = new Application();
            app.Run(new EnterTheGrid());
        }
        public EnterTheGrid()
        {
            Title = "Enter the Grid";
            MinWidth = 300;
            SizeToContent = SizeToContent.WidthAndHeight;

            // Create StackPanel for window content.
            StackPanel stack = new StackPanel();
            Content = stack;
```

```
// Create Grid and add to StackPanel.
Grid grid1 = new Grid();
grid1.Margin = new Thickness(5);
stack.Children.Add(grid1);

// Set row definitions.
for (int i = 0; i < 5; i++)
{
    RowDefinition rowdef = new RowDefinition();
    rowdef.Height = GridLength.Auto;
    grid1.RowDefinitions.Add(rowdef);
}

// Set column definitions.
ColumnDefinition coldef = new ColumnDefinition();
coldef.Width = GridLength.Auto;
grid1.ColumnDefinitions.Add(coldef);

coldef = new ColumnDefinition();
coldef.Width = new GridLength(100, GridUnitType.Star);
grid1.ColumnDefinitions.Add(coldef);

// Create labels and text boxes.
string[] strLabels = { "_First name:", "_Last name:",
                       "_Social security number:",
                       "_Credit card number:",
                       "_Other personal stuff:" };

for(int i = 0; i < strLabels.Length; i++)
{
    Label lbl = new Label();
    lbl.Content = strLabels[i];
    lbl.VerticalContentAlignment = VerticalAlignment.Center;
    grid1.Children.Add(lbl);
    Grid.SetRow(lbl, i);
    Grid.SetColumn(lbl, 0);

    TextBox txtbox = new TextBox();
    txtbox.Margin = new Thickness(5);
    grid1.Children.Add(txtbox);
    Grid.SetRow(txtbox, i);
    Grid.SetColumn(txtbox, 1);
}

// Create second Grid and add to StackPanel.
Grid grid2 = new Grid();
grid2.Margin = new Thickness(10);
stack.Children.Add(grid2);

// No row definitions needed for single row.
// Default column definitions are "star".
grid2.ColumnDefinitions.Add(new ColumnDefinition());
grid2.ColumnDefinitions.Add(new ColumnDefinition());
```

```
        // Create buttons.
        Button btn = new Button();
        btn.Content = "Submit";
        btn.HorizontalAlignment = HorizontalAlignment.Center;
        btn.IsDefault = true;
        btn.Click += delegate { Close(); };
        grid2.Children.Add(btn);     // Row & column are 0.

        btn = new Button();
        btn.Content = "Cancel";
        btn.HorizontalAlignment = HorizontalAlignment.Center;
        btn.IsCancel = true;
        btn.Click += delegate { Close(); };
        grid2.Children.Add(btn);
        Grid.SetColumn(btn, 1);      // Row is 0.

        // Set focus to first text box.
        (stack.Children[0] as Panel).Children[1].Focus();
    }
  }
}
```

This program relies on the default behavior of elements to fill their parents. The *StackPanel* occupies the full width of the window, as do the two *Grid* panels. In the top *Grid* panel, the first column (containing the labels) has a width of *GridLength.Auto* while the second column (with the *TextBox* controls) has a width of *GridUnitType.Star*, which means that they occupy all the remaining available space. The result: When you make the window wider, the *TextBox* controls expand in width. The *TextBox* controls (and the window) also expand when you type text in the control that exceeds its initial width. The window is given a minimum width of 300 units to prevent the TextBox controls from looking a little too small when the program starts up.

The height of the first five rows is based on the height of the *TextBox* controls. To force the *Label* controls to line up attractively with each *TextBox*, the program sets the *VerticalContentAlignment* property of each *Label* to *Center*.

The program could have used a horizontal *StackPanel* rather than a single-row *Grid* for the OK and Cancel buttons, but notice that the column widths both are *GridUnitType.Star*, so the buttons maintain the same relative spacing as the window becomes wider.

It is possible for an element in a *Grid* to occupy multiple adjacent columns or multiple adjacent rows, or both. You specify the number of columns or rows you want an element to occupy through use of the static *Grid.SetRowSpan* and *Grid.SetColumnSpan* methods. Here's some sample code:

```
grid.Children.Add(ctrl);
Grid.SetRow(ctrl, 3);
Grid.SetRowSpan(ctrl, 2);
Grid.SetColumn(ctrl, 5);
Grid.SetColumnSpan(ctrl, 3);
```

The control named *ctrl* will occupy the area encompassed by the six cells in zero-based rows 3 and 4, and columns 5, 6, and 7.

The following program has roughly the same layout of controls as EnterTheGrid but uses just one *Grid* panel with six rows and four columns. The first five rows contain the labels and text boxes; the last row has the buttons. The first column is for the labels. The rightmost two columns are for the buttons. The text boxes span the second, third, and fourth columns.

```
SpanTheCells.cs
//-------------------------------------------
// SpanTheCells.cs (c) 2006 by Charles Petzold
//-------------------------------------------
using System;
using System.Windows;
using System.Windows.Controls;
using System.Windows.Input;
using System.Windows.Media;

namespace Petzold.SpanTheCells
{
    public class SpanTheCells : Window
    {
        [STAThread]
        public static void Main()
        {
            Application app = new Application();
            app.Run(new SpanTheCells());
        }
        public SpanTheCells()
        {
            Title = "Span the Cells";
            SizeToContent = SizeToContent.WidthAndHeight;

            // Create Grid.
            Grid grid = new Grid();
            grid.Margin = new Thickness(5);
            Content = grid;

            // Set row definitions.
            for (int i = 0; i < 6; i++)
            {
                RowDefinition rowdef = new RowDefinition();
                rowdef.Height = GridLength.Auto;
                grid.RowDefinitions.Add(rowdef);
            }

            // Set column definitions.
            for (int i = 0; i < 4; i++)
            {
                ColumnDefinition coldef = new ColumnDefinition();

                if (i == 1)
                    coldef.Width = new GridLength(100, GridUnitType.Star);
```

```
                else
                    coldef.Width = GridLength.Auto;

            grid.ColumnDefinitions.Add(coldef);
        }

        // Create labels and text boxes.
        string[] astrLabel = { "_First name:", "_Last name:",
                               "_Social security number:",
                               "_Credit card number:",
                               "_Other personal stuff:" };

        for(int i = 0; i < astrLabel.Length; i++)
        {
            Label lbl = new Label();
            lbl.Content = astrLabel[i];
            lbl.VerticalContentAlignment = VerticalAlignment.Center;
            grid.Children.Add(lbl);
            Grid.SetRow(lbl, i);
            Grid.SetColumn(lbl, 0);

            TextBox txtbox = new TextBox();
            txtbox.Margin = new Thickness(5);
            grid.Children.Add(txtbox);
            Grid.SetRow(txtbox, i);
            Grid.SetColumn(txtbox, 1);
            Grid.SetColumnSpan(txtbox, 3);
        }

        // Create buttons.
        Button btn = new Button();
        btn.Content = "Submit";
        btn.Margin = new Thickness(5);
        btn.IsDefault = true;
        btn.Click += delegate { Close(); };
        grid.Children.Add(btn);
        Grid.SetRow(btn, 5);
        Grid.SetColumn(btn, 2);

        btn = new Button();
        btn.Content = "Cancel";
        btn.Margin = new Thickness(5);
        btn.IsCancel = true;
        btn.Click += delegate { Close(); };
        grid.Children.Add(btn);
        Grid.SetRow(btn, 5);
        Grid.SetColumn(btn, 3);

        // Set focus to first text box.
        grid.Children[1].Focus();
    }
  }
}
```

Notice that the program gives all six rows heights of *GridLength.Auto*, and all four columns except the second heights of *GridLength.Auto*. The second column has a *GridLengthType.Star*, so it uses all leftover space.

As you make the window wider, the text boxes expand to fill the space because one of the columns they occupy is set for *GridLengthType.Star*. The two buttons maintain their positions at the far right of the window. Also, the window automatically expands as the user types long text into the text boxes.

The *Grid* panel also comes to the rescue when you need a horizontal or vertical *splitter*, which is a thin bar the user can move to apportion space between two areas of the window.

The *GridSplitter* class derives from *Control* by way of the *Thumb* class. The *GridSplitter* must be a child of a *Grid* panel, and a program assigns the *GridSplitter* row and column positions (and optional cell spanning) just like any other child of *Grid*:

```
GridSplitter split = new GridSplitter();
split.Width = 6;
grid.Children.Add(split);
Grid.SetRow(split, 3);
Grid.SetColumn(split, 2);
```

One oddity, however: The *GridSplitter* can share a cell with another element, and it's possible that the *GridSplitter* will partially obscure the element in that cell or the element in that cell will completely obscure the *GridSplitter*. If you want *GridSplitter* to share a cell with another element, you can avoid these problems by giving the element in the cell a little margin where the *GridSplitter* appears, or adding the *GridSplitter* to the child collection *after* the element in that cell so that it appears in the foreground.

By default, the *GridSplitter* has a *HorizontalAlignment* of *Right* and a *VerticalAlignment* of *Stretch*, which causes the splitter to appear as a vertical bar at the right edge of the cell. The default width of a GridSplitter is 0, so assign the Width property to a small amount (perhaps 1/16th inch or 6 units). You can then move the splitter back and forth to change the width of the column the splitter is in, and the width of the column to the right of the splitter. Here's a small program that creates nine buttons in a 3 × 3 grid, and puts a splitter in the center cell:

```
SplitNine.cs
//-------------------------------------------
// SplitNine.cs (c) 2006 by Charles Petzold
//-------------------------------------------
using System;
using System.Windows;
using System.Windows.Controls;
using System.Windows.Input;
using System.Windows.Media;

namespace Petzold.SplitNine
{
    public class SplitNine : Window
    {
        [STAThread]
```

```
    public static void Main()
    {
        Application app = new Application();
        app.Run(new SplitNine());
    }
    public SplitNine()
    {
        Title = "Split Nine";

        Grid grid = new Grid();
        Content = grid;

        // Set row and column definitions.
        for (int i = 0; i < 3; i++)
        {
            grid.ColumnDefinitions.Add(new ColumnDefinition());
            grid.RowDefinitions.Add(new RowDefinition());
        }

        // Create 9 buttons.
        for (int x = 0; x < 3; x++)
            for (int y = 0; y < 3; y++)
            {
                Button btn = new Button();
                btn.Content = "Row " + y + " and Column " + x;
                grid.Children.Add(btn);
                Grid.SetRow(btn, y);
                Grid.SetColumn(btn, x);
            }

        // Create splitter.
        GridSplitter split = new GridSplitter();
        split.Width = 6;
        grid.Children.Add(split);
        Grid.SetRow(split, 1);
        Grid.SetColumn(split, 1);
    }
}
```

When you run this program, you'll see the splitter on the right side of the center cell, obscuring the right edge of the button. You can give the buttons a little margin to make the splitter stand out:

```
btn.Margin = new Thickness(10);
```

But that looks a little odd as well.

Of course, even if the splitter appears in just one cell, the column widths in all the rows change as you move the splitter. It would make more sense for the splitter to span the full height of the grid:

```
Grid.SetRow(split, 0);
Grid.SetColumn(split, 1);
Grid.SetRowSpan(split, 3);
```

But let's keep the splitter in one cell for experimental purposes. The crucial properties for the *GridSplitter* are *HorizontalAlignment* and *VerticalAlignment*. These properties govern whether the splitter is horizontal or vertical, where the splitter appears in the cell, and what rows or columns are affected. With default settings (*HorizontalAlignment* of *Right* and *VerticalAlignment* of *Stretch*) the *GridSplitter* sits on the right edge of the cell. Moving the splitter changes the apportionment of width between the column the splitter is in and the column to the right of the splitter.

You can change *HorizontalAlignment* to *Left* by inserting the following code:

```
split.HorizontalAlignment = HorizontalAlignment.Left;
```

Now the splitter apportions space between the column that it's in and the column to the left of the splitter column. Try this:

```
split.HorizontalAlignment = HorizontalAlignment.Center:
```

Now the splitter sits in the center of the middle button, and moving it affects not the width of the center column, but the widths of the two columns on either side of the splitter. This may seem like the most bizarre use of a splitter ever, but it's actually key to using *GridSplitter* sanely. If the cells in that center column were actually empty of buttons, and the width of that cell was set to *GridLength.Auto*, the splitter would look and act with some degree of normalcy.

You have just seen how the splitter can affect the widths of two different pairs of column depending on the *HorizontalAlignment* setting of *Right* (the default), *Left*, or *Center*. You can override that behavior with the *ResizeBehavior* property of *GridSplitter*. You set this property to a member of the *GridResizeBehavior* enumeration. The members of this enumeration refer to which columns are affected by the splitter, referring to the column the splitter is located in as *current*. The members are *CurrentAndNext* (the behavior normally encountered when the splitter is right-aligned), *PreviousAndCurrent* (which happens when the splitter is left-aligned), and *PreviousAndNext* (when the splitter is centered). The fourth member of the *GridResizeBehavior* enumeration is the default: *BasedOnAlignment*, which doesn't override the behavior normally associated with the alignment of the splitter.

You can make the splitter horizontal by setting the *HorizontalAlignment* to *Stretch* and the *VerticalAlignment* to *Top*, *Center*, or *Bottom*. These settings cause the splitter to appear at the top of the cell:

```
split.HorizontalAlignment = HorizontalAlignment.Stretch;
split.VerticalAlignment = VerticalAlignment.Top;
split.Height = 6;
```

As you move the splitter, you apportion space between the row in which the splitter appears and the row above it.

As you've seen, the *GridSplitter* is vertical if *VerticalAlignment* is set to *Stretch* and horizontal if *HorizontalAlignment* is set to *Stretch*. A vertical splitter affects column widths; a horizontal splitter affects row heights. You can change this particular association between the appearance of the splitter and its functionality with the *ResizeDirection* property. You set it to a member of the *GridResizeDirection* enumeration: either *Columns*, *Rows*, or *Auto* (the default). Try this:

```
split.HorizontalAlignment = HorizontalAlignment.Stretch;
split.VerticalAlignment = VerticalAlignment.Top;
split.ResizeDirection = GridResizeDirection.Columns;
```

Now the splitter is horizontal but you can't move it up and down. You can only move it back and forth to change the column widths.

The *GridSplitter* is even more versatile than that. You can set both *HorizontalAlignment* and *VerticalAlignment* to *Stretch* to make the splitter fill the cell . (Don't set *Width* or *Height*.) Or, you can avoid using *Stretch* with either *HorizontalAlignment* or *VerticalAlignment* and make the splitter appear as a box whose size is governed by *Width* and *Height*.

My recommendations are simple: Don't put a *GridSplitter* in a cell occupied by another element, and devote an entire *Grid* to splitting functionality. If you want a vertical splitter, create a *Grid* with three columns. Give the middle column a *Width* of *GridLength.Auto*, and put the splitter in that column. If you want a horizontal splitter, create a *Grid* with three rows. Give the middle row a *Height* of *GridLength.Auto*, and put the splitter in that row. In either case, you can put whatever you want in the two outer columns or rows, including other *Grid* panels.

Here's a program that creates a three-column *Grid* that hosts a button, a vertical splitter, and a three-row *Grid*. The three-row *Grid* has another button, a horizontal splitter, and a third button.

```
SplitTheClient.cs
//-----------------------------------------------
// SplitTheClient.cs (c) 2006 by Charles Petzold
//-----------------------------------------------
using System;
using System.Windows;
using System.Windows.Controls;
using System.Windows.Input;
using System.Windows.Media;

class SplitTheClient : Window
{
    [STAThread]
    public static void Main()
    {
        Application app = new Application();
        app.Run(new SplitTheClient());
    }
    public SplitTheClient()
    {
        Title = "Split the Client";

        // Grid with vertical splitter.
        Grid grid1 = new Grid();
        grid1.ColumnDefinitions.Add(new ColumnDefinition());
        grid1.ColumnDefinitions.Add(new ColumnDefinition());
        grid1.ColumnDefinitions.Add(new ColumnDefinition());
```

```
        grid1.ColumnDefinitions[1].Width = GridLength.Auto;
        Content = grid1;

        // Button at left of vertical splitter.
        Button btn = new Button();
        btn.Content = "Button No. 1";
        grid1.Children.Add(btn);
        Grid.SetRow(btn, 0);
        Grid.SetColumn(btn, 0);

        // Vertical splitter.
        GridSplitter split = new GridSplitter();
        split.ShowsPreview = true;
        split.HorizontalAlignment = HorizontalAlignment.Center;
        split.VerticalAlignment = VerticalAlignment.Stretch;
        split.Width = 6;
        grid1.Children.Add(split);
        Grid.SetRow(split, 0);
        Grid.SetColumn(split, 1);

        // Grid with horizontal splitter.
        Grid grid2 = new Grid();
        grid2.RowDefinitions.Add(new RowDefinition());
        grid2.RowDefinitions.Add(new RowDefinition());
        grid2.RowDefinitions.Add(new RowDefinition());
        grid2.RowDefinitions[1].Height = GridLength.Auto;
        grid1.Children.Add(grid2);
        Grid.SetRow(grid2, 0);
        Grid.SetColumn(grid2, 2);

        // Button at top of horizontal splitter.
        btn = new Button();
        btn.Content = "Button No. 2";
        grid2.Children.Add(btn);
        Grid.SetRow(btn, 0);
        Grid.SetColumn(btn, 0);

        // Horizontal splitter.
        split = new GridSplitter();
        split.ShowsPreview = true;
        split.HorizontalAlignment = HorizontalAlignment.Stretch;
        split.VerticalAlignment = VerticalAlignment.Center;
        split.Height = 6;
        grid2.Children.Add(split);
        Grid.SetRow(split, 1);
        Grid.SetColumn(split, 0);

        // Bottom at bottom of horizontal splitter.
        btn = new Button();
        btn.Content = "Button No. 3";
        grid2.Children.Add(btn);
        Grid.SetRow(btn, 2);
        Grid.SetColumn(btn, 0);
    }
}
```

This program sets the *ShowsPreview* property of *GridSplitter* to *true*. When you move the splitter, the cells don't actually change in size until you release the mouse button. Notice that you can use the Tab key to give the splitter input focus and move it with the cursor keys. If the response is not to your liking, check out the *KeyboardIncrement* property.

As you may have noticed, when you changed the size of the SplitNine or SplitTheClient windows, the row heights and column heights changed proportionally. It's possible you may want one row or column to remain fixed in size while the other one changes. (You can see this behavior in Windows Explorer: As you change the size of the window, the left side of the splitter remains fixed in size.) The equal redistribution of space occurs when the rows or columns have a *Height* or *Width* of *GridLengthType.Star*. To keep a row or column fixed as you change the size of the window, use *GridLengthType.Pixel* or (undoubtedly more commonly) *GridLength.Auto*.

The next program demonstrates this technique and a few others. I wrote the first version of this program for Windows 1.0 and it appeared in the May 1987 issue of *Microsoft Systems Journal*. In retrospect, the program was a pioneering study in automatic layout. The original program consisted of six labels and three scrollbars that let you select levels of red, green, and blue primaries to see the result. As you made the program window larger or smaller, the program resized and relocated the labels and scrollbars within the window. Calculations were involved, and ugly ones at that.

The Windows Presentation Foundation *ScrollBar* derives from *Control* by way of *RangeBase*. (*RangeBase* is an abstract class that is also parent to *ProgressBar* and *Slider*.) Scrollbars can be positioned vertically or horizontally based on the setting of the *Orientation* property. The *Value* property can range from the value of the *Minimum* property to the *Maximum* property. Clicking the arrows on the ends of the scrollbar change *Value* by the amount specified in the *SmallChange* property. Clicking the area on the side of the thumbs changes the value by *LargeChange*. All these numbers are *double* values.

Let me repeat that: All these properties of the *ScrollBar* are *double* values, including the *Value* property itself, and don't be surprised to see it take on non-integral values. If you need integral values, convert what the *ScrollBar* hands you.

The *ScrollBar* class inherits a *ValueChanged* event from *RangeBase* and defines a *Scroll* event as well. The *Scroll* event is delivered with additional information in the form of a member of the *ScrollEventType* enumeration that lets you know what part of the scrollbar the user was manipulating. For example, if your program can't keep up with thumb movement, it might ignore all events of type *ScrollEventType.ThumbTrack* and get a final thumb location in the event of type *ScrollEventType.EndScroll*.

The ScrollCustomColors program creates two *Grid* panels. The first (called gridMain) exists solely to implement a vertical splitter. The first cell contains a second *Grid* panel (simply called grid) that contains the six labels and three scrollbars. The center cell of *GridMain* contains the *GridSplitter* and the last cell contains a *StackPanel* used solely to display its *Background* color.

This program sets the initial size of the window to 500 device-independent units. When defining the three columns of *gridMain*, it gives the cell containing the scrollbars and labels a width of 200 units, while the cell containing the *StackPanel* has a width based on *GridUnitType.Star*. When you make the window wider or small, only the size of the *StackPanel* is affected.

ScrollCustomColors.cs

```
//----------------------------------------------------
// ScrollCustomColors.cs (c) 2006 by Charles Petzold
//----------------------------------------------------
using System;
using System.Windows;
using System.Windows.Controls;
using System.Windows.Controls.Primitives;
using System.Windows.Media;

class ColorScroll : Window
{
    ScrollBar[] scrolls = new ScrollBar[3];
    TextBlock[] txtValue = new TextBlock[3];
    Panel pnlColor;

    [STAThread]
    public static void Main()
    {
        Application app = new Application();
        app.Run(new ColorScroll());
    }
    public ColorScroll()
    {
        Title = "Color Scroll";
        Width = 500;
        Height = 300;

        // GridMain contains a vertical splitter.
        Grid gridMain = new Grid();
        Content = gridMain;

        // GridMain column definitions.
        ColumnDefinition coldef = new ColumnDefinition();
        coldef.Width = new GridLength(200, GridUnitType.Pixel);
        gridMain.ColumnDefinitions.Add(coldef);

        coldef = new ColumnDefinition();
        coldef.Width = GridLength.Auto;
        gridMain.ColumnDefinitions.Add(coldef);

        coldef = new ColumnDefinition();
        coldef.Width = new GridLength(100, GridUnitType.Star);
        gridMain.ColumnDefinitions.Add(coldef);

        // Vertical splitter.
        GridSplitter split = new GridSplitter();
        split.HorizontalAlignment = HorizontalAlignment.Center;
```

```
split.VerticalAlignment = VerticalAlignment.Stretch;
split.Width = 6;
gridMain.Children.Add(split);
Grid.SetRow(split, 0);
Grid.SetColumn(split, 1);

// Panel on right side of splitter to display color.
pnlColor = new StackPanel();
pnlColor.Background = new SolidColorBrush(SystemColors.WindowColor);
gridMain.Children.Add(pnlColor);
Grid.SetRow(pnlColor, 0);
Grid.SetColumn(pnlColor, 2);

// Secondary grid at left of splitter.
Grid grid = new Grid();
gridMain.Children.Add(grid);
Grid.SetRow(grid, 0);
Grid.SetColumn(grid, 0);

// Three rows for label, scroll, and label.
RowDefinition rowdef = new RowDefinition();
rowdef.Height = GridLength.Auto;
grid.RowDefinitions.Add(rowdef);

rowdef = new RowDefinition();
rowdef.Height = new GridLength(100, GridUnitType.Star);
grid.RowDefinitions.Add(rowdef);

rowdef = new RowDefinition();
rowdef.Height = GridLength.Auto;
grid.RowDefinitions.Add(rowdef);

// Three columns for Red, Green, and Blue.
for (int i = 0; i < 3; i++)
{
    coldef = new ColumnDefinition();
    coldef.Width = new GridLength(33, GridUnitType.Star);
    grid.ColumnDefinitions.Add(coldef);
}

for (int i = 0; i < 3; i++)
{
    Label lbl = new Label();
    lbl.Content = new string[] { "Red", "Green", "Blue" }[i];
    lbl.HorizontalAlignment = HorizontalAlignment.Center;
    grid.Children.Add(lbl);
    Grid.SetRow(lbl, 0);
    Grid.SetColumn(lbl, i);

    scrolls[i] = new ScrollBar();
    scrolls[i].Focusable = true;
    scrolls[i].Orientation = Orientation.Vertical;
    scrolls[i].Minimum = 0;
    scrolls[i].Maximum = 255;
    scrolls[i].SmallChange = 1;
```

```
            scrolls[i].LargeChange = 16;
            scrolls[i].ValueChanged += ScrollOnValueChanged;
            grid.Children.Add(scrolls[i]);
            Grid.SetRow(scrolls[i], 1);
            Grid.SetColumn(scrolls[i], i);

            txtValue[i] = new TextBlock();
            txtValue[i].TextAlignment = TextAlignment.Center;
            txtValue[i].HorizontalAlignment = HorizontalAlignment.Center;
            txtValue[i].Margin = new Thickness(5);
            grid.Children.Add(txtValue[i]);
            Grid.SetRow(txtValue[i], 2);
            Grid.SetColumn(txtValue[i], i);
        }

        // Initialize scroll bars.
        Color clr = (pnlColor.Background as SolidColorBrush).Color;
        scrolls[0].Value = clr.R;
        scrolls[1].Value = clr.G;
        scrolls[2].Value = clr.B;

        // Set initial focus.
        scrolls[0].Focus();
    }
    void ScrollOnValueChanged(object sender, RoutedEventArgs args)
    {
        ScrollBar scroll = sender as ScrollBar;
        Panel pnl = scroll.Parent as Panel;
        TextBlock txt = pnl.Children[1 +
                            pnl.Children.IndexOf(scroll)] as TextBlock;

        txt.Text = String.Format("{0}\n0x{0:X2}", (int)scroll.Value);
        pnlColor.Background =
            new SolidColorBrush(
                Color.FromRgb((byte) scrolls[0].Value,
                        (byte) scrolls[1].Value,(byte) scrolls[2].Value));
    }
}
```

The *ValueChanged* event handler updates the *TextBlock* associated with the *ScrollBar* whose value has changed, and then recalculates a new *Color* based on the settings of all three scrollbars.

Similar to the *Grid* panel is the *UniformGrid*, a grid whose columns are always the same width and rows are always the same height. There are no *RowDefinition* or *ColumnDefinition* objects associated with a *UniformGrid*. Instead, you simply specify the number of rows and columns with the *Rows* and *Columns* properties. There are no attached properties, either. As you add children to the *UniformGrid*, they sequentially occupy the cells in the first row, then the second row, and so forth. One or both of the *Rows* and *Columns* properties can be zero, and the *UniformGrid* will figure out a suitable value from the number of children.

You'll see an example of *UniformGrid* in the next chapter, where I use it to implement the famous 14-15 puzzle, otherwise known as *Jeu de Tacquin*.

Chapter 7

Canvas

The *Canvas* panel is the layout option closest to traditional graphical environments. You specify where elements go using coordinate positions. As with the rest of the Windows Presentation Foundation, these coordinates are device-independent units of 1/96 inch relative to the upper-left corner.

You may have noticed that elements themselves have no *X* or *Y* or *Left* or *Top* property. When using a *Canvas* panel, you specify the location of child elements with the static methods *Canvas.SetLeft* and *Canvas.SetTop*. Like the *SetDock* method defined by *DockPanel*—and the *SetRow*, *SetColumn*, *SetRowSpan*, and *SetColumnSpan* methods defined by *Grid*—*SetLeft* and *SetTop* are associated with attached properties defined by the *Canvas* class. If you'd like, you can alternatively use *Canvas.SetRight* or *Canvas.SetBottom*, to specify the location of the right or bottom of the child element relative to the right or bottom of the *Canvas*.

Some of the *Shapes* classes—specifically, *Line*, *Path*, *Polygon*, and *Polyline*—already contain coordinate data. If you add these elements to the *Children* collection of a *Canvas* panel and don't set any coordinates, they will be positioned based on the coordinate data of the element. Any explicit coordinate position that you set with *SetLeft* or *SetTop* is added to the coordinate data of the element.

Many elements, such as controls, will properly size themselves on a *Canvas*. However, some elements will not (for example, the *Rectangle* and *Ellipse* classes), and for those you must assign explicit *Width* and *Height* values. It is also common to assign the *Width* and *Height* properties of the *Canvas* panel itself.

It's also possible—and often desirable—to overlap elements on a *Canvas* panel. As you've seen, you can put multiple elements into the cells of a *Grid*, but the effect is often difficult to control. With *Canvas*, the layering of elements is easy to control and predict. The elements added to the *Children* collection earlier are covered by those added later.

For example, suppose you want a button to display a blue 1.5-inch-square background with rounded corners and a yellow star one inch in diameter centered within the square. Here's the code:

```
PaintTheButton.cs
//-------------------------------------------------
// PaintTheButton.cs (c) 2006 by Charles Petzold
//-------------------------------------------------
using System;
using System.Windows;
using System.Windows.Controls;
using System.Windows.Input;
using System.Windows.Media;
using System.Windows.Shapes;
```

```
namespace Petzold.PaintTheButton
{
    public class PaintTheButton : Window
    {
        [STAThread]
        public static void Main()
        {
            Application app = new Application();
            app.Run(new PaintTheButton());
        }
        public PaintTheButton()
        {
            Title = "Paint the Button";

            // Create the Button as content of the window.
            Button btn = new Button();
            btn.HorizontalAlignment = HorizontalAlignment.Center;
            btn.VerticalAlignment = VerticalAlignment.Center;
            Content = btn;

            // Create the Canvas as content of the button.
            Canvas canv = new Canvas();
            canv.Width = 144;
            canv.Height = 144;
            btn.Content = canv;

            // Create Rectangle as child of canvas.
            Rectangle rect = new Rectangle();
            rect.Width = canv.Width;
            rect.Height = canv.Height;
            rect.RadiusX = 24;
            rect.RadiusY = 24;
            rect.Fill = Brushes.Blue;
            canv.Children.Add(rect);
            Canvas.SetLeft(rect, 0);
            Canvas.SetRight(rect, 0);

            // Create Polygon as child of canvas.
            Polygon poly = new Polygon();
            poly.Fill = Brushes.Yellow;
            poly.Points = new PointCollection();

            for (int i = 0; i < 5; i++)
            {
                double angle = i * 4 * Math.PI / 5;
                Point pt = new Point(48 * Math.Sin(angle),
                                    -48 * Math.Cos(angle));
                poly.Points.Add(pt);
            }
            canv.Children.Add(poly);
            Canvas.SetLeft(poly, canv.Width / 2);
            Canvas.SetTop(poly, canv.Height / 2);
        }
    }
}
```

The program creates a *Button* and makes that the content of the window. It then creates a *Canvas* 1.5 inches square and makes that the content of the button. Because the *HorizontalAlignment* and *VerticalAlignment* properties of the button have been set to *Center*, the button will size itself to the size of the *Canvas* panel.

The program then creates a *Rectangle* shape and assigns its *Width* and *Height* properties to be the same as the *Canvas*. The *Rectangle* is added to the *Canvas* children collection in the same way as other panels:

```
canv.Children.Add(rect);
```

The following code ensures that the *Rectangle* is positioned at the top-left corner of the *Canvas*:

```
Canvas.SetLeft(rect, 0);
Canvas.SetRight(rect, 0);
```

Strictly speaking, these two statements are not required because the default settings are 0.

The next step involves a *Polygon* shape. The *Polygon* class defines a property named *Points* of type *PointCollection* to store the points of the polygon. However, the *Points* property in a newly created *Polygon* object is *null*. You must explicitly create an object of type *PointCollection* and assign it to the *Points* property. The PaintTheButton program shows one way of doing this that involves the parameterless constructor of *PointCollection*. Each point is then added to the collection with the *Add* method.

PointCollection also defines a constructor that requires an argument of type *IEnumerable<Point>*. An array of *Point* objects is acceptable here, as well as a *List<Point>* collection.

The code in the *for* loop calculates the points of the star. These points will have X and Y coordinates that range from −48 to 48, with the center of the ellipse at the point (0, 0). To center the ellipse within the *Canvas*, the following code offsets all points in the polygon by half the width and height of the *Canvas*:

```
Canvas.SetLeft(poly, canv.Width / 2);
Canvas.SetTop(poly, canv.Height / 2);
```

You'll notice that the interior pentagon of the star is not filled. That's a result of the default setting of the *FillRule* property defined by *Polygon*. The enumeration value *FillRule.EvenOdd* implements an algorithm based on the lines of the polygon that separate a particular enclosed area from infinity. An area is filled only if the number of lines going in one direction minus the number of lines going in the opposite direction is odd. Set *FillRule* to *FillRule.NonZero* to fill the center of the star as well.

Although you can certainly use *Canvas* for laying out controls in your window, you'll probably find it more of a hindrance than a help in that job. *Canvas* is good for displaying graphics (as you'll see in Part 2 of this book), and doing mouse-driven drawing (shown in Chapter 9, coming up soon) but avoid it for general layout jobs.

The following class actually derives from *Canvas* to implement a tile used in a game. The class defines a constant named SIZE that defines a size of 2/3-inch square for the tile, and another constant named BORD that defines a 1/16-inch-wide border. This border is shaded to give the appearance of three-dimensionality. By convention, objects on the computer screen are shaded to mimic a light source at the upper-left corner. The border consists of two *Polygon* objects colored with *SystemColors.ControlLightLightBrush* (for the top and left edges) and *SystemColors.ControlDarkBrush* for the shadow at the right and bottom edges. The interior of the tile thus appears to be raised.

Tile.cs
```
//-------------------------------------
// Tile.cs (c) 2006 by Charles Petzold
//-------------------------------------
using System;
using System.Windows;
using System.Windows.Controls;
using System.Windows.Input;
using System.Windows.Media;
using System.Windows.Shapes;

namespace Petzold.PlayJeuDeTacquin
{
    public class Tile : Canvas
    {
        const int SIZE = 64;      // 2/3 inch
        const int BORD = 6;       // 1/16 inch
        TextBlock txtblk;

        public Tile()
        {
            Width = SIZE;
            Height = SIZE;

            // Upper-left shadowed border.
            Polygon poly = new Polygon();
            poly.Points = new PointCollection(new Point[]
                {
                    new Point(0, 0), new Point(SIZE, 0),
                    new Point(SIZE-BORD, BORD),
                    new Point(BORD, BORD),
                    new Point(BORD, SIZE-BORD), new Point(0, SIZE)
                });
            poly.Fill = SystemColors.ControlLightLightBrush;
            Children.Add(poly);

            // Lower-right shadowed border.
            poly = new Polygon();
            poly.Points = new PointCollection(new Point[]
                {
                    new Point(SIZE, SIZE), new Point(SIZE, 0),
                    new Point(SIZE-BORD, BORD),
```

```
                    new Point(SIZE-BORD, SIZE-BORD),
                    new Point(BORD, SIZE-BORD), new Point(0, SIZE)
            });
        poly.Fill = SystemColors.ControlDarkBrush;
        Children.Add(poly);

        // Host for centered text.
        Border bord = new Border();
        bord.Width = SIZE - 2 * BORD;
        bord.Height = SIZE - 2 * BORD;
        bord.Background = SystemColors.ControlBrush;
        Children.Add(bord);
        SetLeft(bord, BORD);
        SetTop(bord, BORD);

        // Display of text.
        txtblk = new TextBlock();
        txtblk.FontSize = 32;
        txtblk.Foreground = SystemColors.ControlTextBrush;
        txtblk.HorizontalAlignment = HorizontalAlignment.Center;
        txtblk.VerticalAlignment = VerticalAlignment.Center;
        bord.Child = txtblk;
    }
    // Public property to set text.
    public string Text
    {
        set { txtblk.Text = value; }
        get { return txtblk.Text; }
    }
  }
}
```

Notice the way in which the program sets the *Points* collection of the *Polygon* objects: The entire *Point* array is defined in the *PointCollection* constructor!

The *Tile* class must also display some text in the center of the tile. Rather than trying to figure out the actual size of the *TextBlock* element and centering it on the *Canvas*, the class takes an easy way out. After creating its own border from two polygons, the *Tile* class then creates an actual object of type *Border*, which is a class that derives from *FrameworkElement* by way of *Decorator*. This *Border* element is positioned in the center of the tile. *Decorator* defines (and *Border* inherits) a property named *Child* that can hold a single instance of *UIElement*, and that's the *TextBlock*. The *TextBlock* sets its *HorizontalAlignment* and *Vertical-Alignment* properties to *Center* to sit in the center of the *Border* object. The *Border* object can display a border of a solid color (and with rounded edges), but *Tile* doesn't require that feature.

The *Tile* class is for a puzzle called *Jeu de Tacquin*—the teasing game—or in English, the 14-15 Puzzle. The puzzle was probably invented in the 1870s by American puzzle-maker Sam Loyd (1841–1911). In its classic form, the game consists of 15 numbered squares in a 4 × 4 grid, leaving one blank cell so that you can move the squares around. Here's the class for the blank cell:

```
Empty.cs
//-------------------------------------
// Empty.cs (c) 2006 by Charles Petzold
//-------------------------------------

namespace Petzold.PlayJeuDeTacquin
{
    class Empty : System.Windows.FrameworkElement
    {
    }
}
```

In its original form, the numbered squares were arranged in numeric order except with the 14 and 15 swapped. Sam Loyd offered $1000 to anyone who could find a way to shift the squares to correct the numeric order. A solution is impossible, as was first disclosed in an 1879 article in the *American Journal of Mathematics*. An analysis appears in volume 4 of *The World Of Mathematics* (Simon and Schuster, 1956).

In computer form, *Jeu de Tacquin* was one of the first game programs created for the Apple Macintosh, where it was called PUZZLE, and it also made an appearance in early versions of the Microsoft Windows Software Development Kit (renamed MUZZLE) as the only sample program coded in Microsoft Pascal rather than C.

Both the Macintosh and Windows versions of the puzzle displayed the cells in correct order with a menu option to scramble the cells. My version has a *Button* for scrambling the cells, and it creates a *DispatcherTimer* for the job so that you can watch the scrambling action.

The layout begins with a *StackPanel* with two children: the scramble button and another *Border* object. The *Border* object here is strictly for aesthetic purposes: It draws a thin line to separate the *Button* from the content of the *Border*. The *Child* property of the *Border* is a *UniformGrid* panel, which holds the 15 *Tile* objects and the one *Empty*.

```
PlayJeuDeTacquin.cs
//------------------------------------------------
// PlayJeuDeTacquin.cs (c) 2006 by Charles Petzold
//------------------------------------------------
using System;
using System.Windows;
using System.Windows.Controls;
using System.Windows.Controls.Primitives;
using System.Windows.Input;
using System.Windows.Media;
using System.Windows.Threading;

namespace Petzold.PlayJeuDeTacquin
```

```
{
    public class PlayJeuDeTacquin : Window
    {
        const int NumberRows = 4;
        const int NumberCols = 4;

        UniformGrid unigrid;
        int xEmpty, yEmpty, iCounter;
        Key[] keys = { Key.Left, Key.Right, Key.Up, Key.Down };
        Random rand;
        UIElement elEmptySpare = new Empty();

        [STAThread]
        public static void Main()
        {
            Application app = new Application();
            app.Run(new PlayJeuDeTacquin());
        }
        public PlayJeuDeTacquin()
        {
            Title = "Jeu de Tacquin";
            SizeToContent = SizeToContent.WidthAndHeight;
            ResizeMode = ResizeMode.CanMinimize;
            Background = SystemColors.ControlBrush;

            // Create StackPanel as content of window.
            StackPanel stack = new StackPanel();
            Content = stack;

            // Create Button at top of window.
            Button btn = new Button();
            btn.Content = "_Scramble";
            btn.Margin = new Thickness(10);
            btn.HorizontalAlignment = HorizontalAlignment.Center;
            btn.Click += ScrambleOnClick;
            stack.Children.Add(btn);

            // Create Border for aesthetic purposes.
            Border bord = new Border();
            bord.BorderBrush = SystemColors.ControlDarkDarkBrush;
            bord.BorderThickness = new Thickness(1);
            stack.Children.Add(bord);

            // Create Unigrid as Child of Border.
            unigrid = new UniformGrid();
            unigrid.Rows = NumberRows;
            unigrid.Columns = NumberCols;
            bord.Child = unigrid;

            // Create Tile objects to fill all but one cell.
            for (int i = 0; i < NumberRows * NumberCols - 1; i++)
            {
                Tile tile = new Tile();
                tile.Text = (i + 1).ToString();
```

```
                tile.MouseLeftButtonDown += TileOnMouseLeftButtonDown;
                unigrid.Children.Add(tile);
        }
        // Create Empty object to fill the last cell.
        unigrid.Children.Add(new Empty());
        xEmpty = NumberCols - 1;
        yEmpty = NumberRows - 1;
    }
    void TileOnMouseLeftButtonDown(object sender, MouseButtonEventArgs args)
    {
        Tile tile = sender as Tile;

        int iMove = unigrid.Children.IndexOf(tile);
        int xMove = iMove % NumberCols;
        int yMove = iMove / NumberCols;

        if (xMove == xEmpty)
            while (yMove != yEmpty)
                MoveTile(xMove, yEmpty + (yMove - yEmpty) /
                                    Math.Abs(yMove - yEmpty));
        if (yMove == yEmpty)
            while (xMove != xEmpty)
                MoveTile(xEmpty + (xMove - xEmpty) /
                                    Math.Abs(xMove - xEmpty), yMove);
    }
    protected override void OnKeyDown(KeyEventArgs args)
    {
        base.OnKeyDown(args);

        switch (args.Key)
        {
            case Key.Right: MoveTile(xEmpty - 1, yEmpty);  break;
            case Key.Left:  MoveTile(xEmpty + 1, yEmpty);  break;
            case Key.Down:  MoveTile(xEmpty, yEmpty - 1);  break;
            case Key.Up:    MoveTile(xEmpty, yEmpty + 1);  break;
        }
    }
    void ScrambleOnClick(object sender, RoutedEventArgs args)
    {
        rand = new Random();
        iCounter = 16 * NumberCols * NumberRows;

        DispatcherTimer tmr = new DispatcherTimer();
        tmr.Interval = TimeSpan.FromMilliseconds(10);
        tmr.Tick += TimerOnTick;
        tmr.Start();
    }
    void TimerOnTick(object sender, EventArgs args)
    {
        for (int i = 0; i < 5; i++)
        {
            MoveTile(xEmpty, yEmpty + rand.Next(3) - 1);
            MoveTile(xEmpty + rand.Next(3) - 1, yEmpty);
        }
```

```
        if (0 == iCounter--)
            (sender as DispatcherTimer).Stop();
    }
    void MoveTile(int xTile, int yTile)
    {
        if ((xTile == xEmpty && yTile == yEmpty) ||
            xTile < 0 || xTile >= NumberCols ||
            yTile < 0 || yTile >= NumberRows)
            return;

        int iTile = NumberCols * yTile + xTile;
        int iEmpty = NumberCols * yEmpty + xEmpty;

        UIElement elTile = unigrid.Children[iTile];
        UIElement elEmpty = unigrid.Children[iEmpty];

        unigrid.Children.RemoveAt(iTile);
        unigrid.Children.Insert(iTile, elEmptySpare);
        unigrid.Children.RemoveAt(iEmpty);
        unigrid.Children.Insert(iEmpty, elTile);

        xEmpty = xTile;
        yEmpty = yTile;
        elEmptySpare = elEmpty;
    }
}
}
```

The program handles all movement of the *Tile* objects by manipulating the *Children* collection of the *UniformGrid*, and that happens in the *MoveTile* method at the very bottom of the file. The two arguments to *MoveTile* are the horizontal and vertical grid coordinates of the tile to be moved. There's no ambiguity about where that tile is to be moved because it can only be moved into the cell currently occupied by the *Empty* object. Notice that the *MoveTile* code first obtains the two elements being swapped by indexing the *Children* collection, and then performs a pair of *RemoveAt* and *Insert* calls to exchange their places. Watch out for the order of statements like this: Any time you remove or insert a child element, the indices of all the child elements after it change.

The program has both a keyboard and a mouse interface. The mouse interface is in the form of an event handler for the *MouseLeftButtonDown* event of the *Tile* object. The particular *Tile* object being clicked is easily obtainable by casting the first argument of the event handler. The user can move multiple tiles with a single mouse click, and that's the purpose of the *while* loop.

The keyboard interface is in the form of an override to the window's *OnKeyDown* method. The cursor up, down, left, and right keys move a tile adjoining the empty cell into the empty cell.

The number of rows and columns in the PlayJeuDeTacquin program are indicated by two fields. You can change those to whatever you want, although the display of numbers in the tiles doesn't quite work when it gets into the 4-digit range, and the scrambling operation may go on for awhile.

Chapter 8
Dependency Properties

Here's a program that contains six buttons in a two-row, three-column *Grid*. Each button lets you change the *FontSize* property to a value identified by the button text. However, the three buttons in the top row change the *FontSize* property of the window, while the three buttons in the bottom row change the *FontSize* property of the clicked button.

SetFontSizeProperty.cs

```
//-------------------------------------------------------
// SetFontSizeProperty.cs (c) 2006 by Charles Petzold
//-------------------------------------------------------
using System;
using System.Windows;
using System.Windows.Controls;
using System.Windows.Documents;
using System.Windows.Input;
using System.Windows.Media;

namespace Petzold.SetFontSizeProperty
{
    public class SetFontSizeProperty : Window
    {
        [STAThread]
        public static void Main()
        {
            Application app = new Application();
            app.Run(new SetFontSizeProperty());
        }
        public SetFontSizeProperty()
        {
            Title = "Set FontSize Property";
            SizeToContent = SizeToContent.WidthAndHeight;
            ResizeMode = ResizeMode.CanMinimize;
            FontSize = 16;
            double[] fntsizes = { 8, 16, 32 };

            // Create Grid panel.
            Grid grid = new Grid();
            Content = grid;

            // Define row and columns.
            for (int i = 0; i < 2; i++)
            {
                RowDefinition row = new RowDefinition();
                row.Height = GridLength.Auto;
                grid.RowDefinitions.Add(row);
            }
```

```
            for (int i = 0; i < fntsizes.Length; i++)
            {
                ColumnDefinition col = new ColumnDefinition();
                col.Width = GridLength.Auto;
                grid.ColumnDefinitions.Add(col);
            }

            // Create six buttons.
            for (int i = 0; i < fntsizes.Length; i++)
            {
                Button btn = new Button();
                btn.Content = new TextBlock(
                    new Run("Set window FontSize to " + fntsizes[i]));
                btn.Tag = fntsizes[i];
                btn.HorizontalAlignment = HorizontalAlignment.Center;
                btn.VerticalAlignment = VerticalAlignment.Center;
                btn.Click += WindowFontSizeOnClick;
                grid.Children.Add(btn);
                Grid.SetRow(btn, 0);
                Grid.SetColumn(btn, i);

                btn = new Button();
                btn.Content = new TextBlock(
                    new Run("Set button FontSize to " + fntsizes[i]));
                btn.Tag = fntsizes[i];
                btn.HorizontalAlignment = HorizontalAlignment.Center;
                btn.VerticalAlignment = VerticalAlignment.Center;
                btn.Click += ButtonFontSizeOnClick;
                grid.Children.Add(btn);
                Grid.SetRow(btn, 1);
                Grid.SetColumn(btn, i);
            }
        }
        void WindowFontSizeOnClick(object sender, RoutedEventArgs args)
        {
            Button btn = args.Source as Button;
            FontSize = (double)btn.Tag;
        }
        void ButtonFontSizeOnClick(object sender, RoutedEventArgs args)
        {
            Button btn = args.Source as Button;
            btn.FontSize = (double)btn.Tag;
        }
    }
}
```

The window constructor initializes its *FontSize* property to 16 device-independent units. The window creates a *Grid* and populates it with six buttons. All buttons display content with a *TextBlock*. (The program works the same if the *Content* property of each *Button* is set to a string.) The three buttons on the top row change the *FontSize* property of the *Window* object to 8, 16, or 32 units. The three buttons on the bottom row change the *FontSize* property of the individual button being pressed.

When the program starts running, all the buttons display text in a 16-unit-tall font. This initial *FontSize* property set for the window seems to filter through the *Grid* and the buttons to affect the *TextBlock* element. As you click each of the buttons in the top row, all the buttons change to reflect the new *FontSize* set for the window.

When you click a button in the bottom row, however, only that button changes because the event handler sets the *FontSize* property only for the button being clicked. But now click a button on the top row. Any button on which you individually set the *FontSize* no longer changes in response to changes in the window *FontSize*. A *FontSize* set specifically for the *Button* seems to have priority over a *FontSize* that the *Button* inherits from the *Window*.

The *Window*, the *Grid*, the six *Button* objects, and the six *TextBlock* objects form an element tree that can be visualized like this:

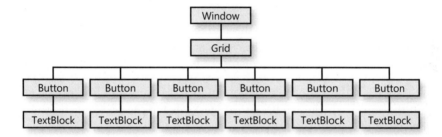

This element tree consists of all the visual objects explicitly created by the program. By *visual object* I mean those objects we can actually see on the screen, even if we only have the potential of seeing them. For example, if the *TextBlock* had no text or the *Grid* had no children, they would still be considered visual objects. More formally, I mean those objects based on classes that descend from the *Visual* class, generally by way of *UIElement* and *FrameworkElement*.

This little tree is *not* the tree known as the *logical tree* in the Windows Presentation Foundation documentation. In this program, the logical tree also includes the *RowDefinition* and *Column-Definition* objects associated with the *Grid*, and the *Run* objects associated with the *TextBlock*. These objects are not visual objects. They are instead based on classes that derive from *ContentElement* by way of *FrameworkContentElement*.

This little tree is also not the tree known in WPF documentation as the *visual tree*, although it's close. The visual tree may include visual objects that the program does not explicitly create. For example, to display its border and background, the *Button* object creates an object of type *ButtonChrome* (defined in the *Microsoft.Windows.Themes* namespace), and *ButtonChrome* derives from *Visual*, *UIElement*, and *FrameworkElement* by way of *Decorator*. Objects of type *ButtonChrome* are part of the visual tree, and there are probably others that we don't even know about.

Still, the tree shown on the previous page is a useful simplification for understanding how properties such as *FontSize* are handled. When a program explicitly sets the *FontSize* property of an object in a visual tree, all of the objects that are lower in the tree also get that same *FontSize*. These lower objects in the tree are said to "inherit" the property from their parent (but don't confuse this notion of inheritance with class inheritance). However, if a particular object had previously had its *FontSize* property explicitly set, it is not subject to this inheritance process.

So, when you click one of the buttons in the top row, the event handler in the program sets the *FontSize* property for the window, and there's obviously some additional work done behind the scenes so that the same *FontSize* property is set for all the window's descendents, except that any descendent that has previously had its own *FontSize* property set rejects this inherited value.

One interesting aspect of all this is that *Grid* doesn't even have a *FontSize* property. Obviously, the propagation of the *FontSize* property through the tree is somewhat more sophisticated than a simple parent-to-child handoff. The *Grid* lets its children get the new *FontSize* even though the *Grid* itself has no *FontSize* property.

When you click one of the buttons in the bottom row, the event handler sets the *FontSize* property for the *Button*, which then passes this new value to the *TextBlock*. If you happened to insert two lines like this:

```
(btn.Content as TextBlock).FontSize = 12;
```

in the *for* loop (after each *Content* property has been set), the whole program would stop working. After *TextBlock* receives an explicit *FontSize* setting, it rejects any values passed down through inheritance.

If the *FontSize* property is never explicitly set by the program, objects that have this property get a default value (which happens to be 11 units).

It is possible to formulate some generalizations about the *FontSize* property. There is a default value of *FontSize*, but that default is low in priority. A value inherited from an ancestor in an element tree is higher in priority than the default, and a value explicitly set on the object has the highest priority.

FontSize isn't the only property that works like this. *UIElement* defines four properties (*AllowDrop*, *IsEnabled*, *IsVisible*, and *SnapToDevicePixels*) that are inherited through the element tree. The *CultureInfo*, *FlowDirection*, and *InputScope* properties defined by *FrameworkElement* also propagate through the tree, as well as the *FontFamily*, *FontSize*, *FontStretch*, *FontStyles*, *FontWeight*, and *Foreground* properties defined by *Control*. (The *Background* property is not inherited through the tree, but the default is *null*, which is rendered as transparent, so visual children may seem to inherit the *Background* set on their parents.)

Imagine for a moment you are designing a system like the Windows Presentation Foundation and you wanted to implement a process for properties to be inherited through an element tree. You'd probably seek a way to do it in a consistent manner with a minimum of duplicated code.

As you click buttons in the SetFontSizeProperty program, you witness them dynamically changing size to accommodate the new *FontSize* values, and this change in button size also affects the *Grid* and the *Window* itself. Obviously, changes in the *FontSize* property cause the *Grid* to revise its initial layout. As a hypothetical designer of the WPF, you'd probably want changes in the *FontFamily* and the other font properties to affect the program in the same way. However, you wouldn't want changes to *Foreground* to force *Grid* to revise its layout. All that's necessary with a change in the *Foreground* is for buttons to get redrawn.

In previous chapters, you saw how instances of classes such as *Brush* and *Shapes* can be made to dynamically respond to changes in their properties. This concept forms the basis of the animation system of the WPF. In Chapter 4, you saw how a button could be bound to a property of the window, and you'll discover in later chapters of this book that properties of objects can also be subject to templates and styles. If you were designing a system like the WPF, you'd probably want to handle all these features in a consistent manner.

Perhaps as a hypothetical designer of the WPF, you might even stumble upon the concept of *dependency properties*—so called because they are properties that depend on a number of other properties and outside influences, sometimes in an extensive and intricate manner.

In conventional .NET programming, the value of an object's font size would be stored by the class in a private field, perhaps initialized with a default value:

```
double fntsize = 11;
```

This private field would be publicly visible as the *FontSize* property:

```
public double FontSize
{
    get
    {
        return fntsize;
    }
    set
    {
        fntsize = value;
        ...
    }
}
```

The ellipsis in the *set* accessor indicates that there's probably more code that needs to be executed here. Perhaps the control needs to change its size or at least be repainted. Perhaps a *FontSizeChanged* event needs to be fired. Or perhaps descendents in the element tree need to be enumerated for *FontSize* inheritance.

In the Windows Presentation Foundation, the use of dependency properties allows much of this notification work to occur automatically in common scenarios. The *Control* class defines a *FontSize* property of type *double* (as we'll see) but it also defines an associated field named *FontSizeProperty* of type *DependencyProperty*:

```
public class Control: FrameworkElement
{
    ...
    public static readonly DependencyProperty FontSizeProperty;
    ...
}
```

This field is known as a dependency property. It's public and it's static, which means that the field is referenced with the class name rather than an object name. A static read-only field can only be set in the field definition itself or in a static constructor. Generally, a class creates an object of type *DependencyProperty* by a call to the static *DependencyProperty.Register* method, which may look something like this:

```
FontSizeProperty = DependencyProperty.Register("FontSize", typeof(double),
                                        typeof(Control));
```

The arguments are the text name of the property associated with the dependency property, the data type of the property, and the class type registering the property. In actuality, there's usually some more code involved. The *DependencyProperty* object often includes metadata that describes some crucial aspects of the property. The following code is probably much closer to how the *FontSizeProperty* is actually registered in the *Control* class:

```
public class Control: FrameworkElement
{
    ...
    public static readonly DependencyProperty FontSizeProperty;
    ...
    static Control()
    {
        FrameworkPropertyMetadata metadata = new FrameworkPropertyMetadata();
        metadata.DefaultValue = 11;
        metadata.AffectsMeasure = true;
        metadata.Inherits = true;
        metadata.IsDataBindingAllowed = true;
        metadata.DefaultUpdateSourceTrigger = UpdateSourceTrigger.PropertyChanged;

        FontSizeProperty =
            DependencyProperty.Register("FontSize", typeof(double),
                typeof(Control), metadata, ValidateFontSize);
    }
    static bool ValidateFontSize(object obj)
    {
        double dFontSize = (double) obj;
        return dFontSize > 0 && dFontSize <= 35791;
    }
    ...
}
```

This metadata indicates a default value of 11. The *FontSize* property affects the size of the element, so *AffectsMeasure* is set to *true*. The property (as we've seen) is also inherited through the element tree, a characteristic indicated by the *Inherits* property. Data binding is allowed, and the *DefaultUpdateSourceTrigger* indicates how data-binding is to work. (I'll get deeper into data-binding in Chapter 23.) In addition, the *DependencyProperty.Register* call includes the metadata as an argument, and also a method provided by the *Control* class to validate *FontSize* values. The method returns *true* if the value is greater than zero and less than a certain maximum. (I've determined by experimentation that there's an upper limit of 35,791 logical units for the *FontSize*.)

All this preliminary work pays off when it comes time to define the actual *FontSize* property. Here's how the *Control* class probably does it:

```
public class Control: FrameworkElement
{
    ...
        public double FontSize
        {
            set
            {
                SetValue(FontSizeProperty, value);
            }
            get
            {
                return (double) GetValue(FontSizeProperty);
            }
        }
    ...
}
```

Where do the *SetValue* and *GetValue* methods come from? These methods are defined in the *DependencyObject* class from which much of the WPF descends:

Object

> *DispatcherObject* (abstract)

>> *DependencyObject*

>>> *Visual* (abstract)

>>>> *UIElement*

>>>>> *FrameworkElement*

>>>>>> *Control*

Watch out for similar names: Both *DependencyObject* and *DependencyProperty* are classes. Many classes in the WPF descend from *DependencyObject* and thus have *SetValue* and *GetValue* methods. These methods work with fields defined as static *DependencyProperty* objects.

Even though the *DependencyProperty* object passed to the *SetValue* and *GetValue* methods is static, *SetValue* and *GetValue* are instance methods, and they are setting and obtaining values associated with the particular instance. The *DependencyObject* is maintaining the current value, and handling all the routine stuff as well. For example, if *SetValue* hasn't yet been called for the particular *Control* instance, *GetValue* returns the value of the *DefaultValue* property associated with the metadata of *FontSizeProperty*.

When a program such as SetFontSizeProperty sets the *FontSize* property, the *SetValue* method has some work to do. The method must call the validation method to determine if the value is proper. If not, it throws an exception. Because the *AffectsMeasure* flag is set for *FontSize-Property*, the *SetValue* method must cause a recalculation in the size of the control, which also requires the control to be redrawn. That redrawing logic uses the new *FontSize* in displaying text. (For a property like *Foreground*, the *AffectsMeasure* flag is *false* but the *AffectsRender* flag is *true*. The control isn't resized, but it is redrawn.) The *SetValue* method must also pass the new value down through the tree as a result of the *Inherits* flag. Elements in the tree can accept that new value for themselves, or reject it if their own *FontSize* property has been explicitly set.

Although examining how the *FontSize* property works is certainly helpful in understanding dependency properties, the lessons are hammered home only when you define a dependency property on your own.

The class that follows inherits from *Button* but includes a new dependency property. This class is called *SpaceButton*, and before you get ideas about launching buttons into orbit, you should know that the *SpaceButton* merely displays text with spaces inserted between each letter. *SpaceButton* adds two properties to those found in the normal *Button* class: *Text* and *Space*. For contrast, the class implements the *Text* property as a traditional .NET property, while the *Space* property is implemented in conjunction with a dependency property. The *SpaceButton* sets its *Content* property to the *Text* string with spaces inserted as indicated by the value of the *Space* property.

```
SpaceButton.cs
//-------------------------------------------
// SpaceButton.cs (c) 2006 by Charles Petzold
//-------------------------------------------
using System;
using System.Text;
using System.Windows;
using System.Windows.Controls;
using System.Windows.Input;
using System.Windows.Media;

namespace Petzold.SetSpaceProperty
{
    public class SpaceButton : Button
    {
        // A traditional .NET private field and public property.
        string txt;

        public string Text
        {
```

```
        set
        {
            txt = value;
            Content = SpaceOutText(txt);
        }
        get
        {
            return txt;
        }
    }


    // A DependencyProperty and public property.
    public static readonly DependencyProperty SpaceProperty;

    public int Space
    {
        set
        {
            SetValue(SpaceProperty, value);
        }
        get
        {
            return (int)GetValue(SpaceProperty);
        }
    }

    // Static constructor.
    static SpaceButton()
    {
        // Define the metadata.
        FrameworkPropertyMetadata metadata = new FrameworkPropertyMetadata();
        metadata.DefaultValue = 1;
        metadata.AffectsMeasure = true;
        metadata.Inherits = true;
        metadata.PropertyChangedCallback += OnSpacePropertyChanged;

        // Register the DependencyProperty.
        SpaceProperty =
            DependencyProperty.Register("Space", typeof(int),
                                       typeof(SpaceButton), metadata,
                                       ValidateSpaceValue);
    }

    // Callback method for value validation.
    static bool ValidateSpaceValue(object obj)
    {
        int i = (int)obj;
        return i >= 0;
    }

    // Callback method for property changed.
    static void OnSpacePropertyChanged(DependencyObject obj,
                            DependencyPropertyChangedEventArgs args)
```

```
    {
        SpaceButton btn = obj as SpaceButton;
        btn.Content = btn.SpaceOutText(btn.txt);
    }

    // Method to insert spaces in the text.
    string SpaceOutText(string str)
    {
        if (str == null)
            return null;

        StringBuilder build = new StringBuilder();

        foreach (char ch in str)
            build.Append(ch + new string(' ', Space));

        return build.ToString();
    }
    }
  }
}
```

The program begins with the traditionally coded *Text* property. The string itself is stored in a private field named *txt*. Traditional .NET properties often need to include code in the *set* accessor so that the class actually does something with the new property. This *Text* property calls the *SpaceOutText* method to insert spaces in the text and then sets the *Content* property from that.

The rest of the file is the overhead for the *Space* property. The class defines a public static readonly field named *SpaceProperty* and implements the *Space* property *set* and *get* accessors with the *SetValue* and *GetValue* calls defined by *DependencyObject*. The *Space* property has nothing more to do.

The static constructor of the class sets up the metadata and registers the dependency property. Notice the two callback methods involved with this property. The *ValidateSpaceValue* property returns *true* if the value is acceptable. A negative number of spaces wouldn't make sense, so *ValidateSpaceValue* returns *false* for negative values.

The *OnSpacePropertyChanged* method will be called whenever the property changes. Like the *set* accessor for the *Text* property, this method sets the button *Content* property from the return value of *SpaceOutText*. The *SpaceOutText* method refers to the *Space* property to obtain the number of desired spaces.

Both callback methods must be defined as *static*. That's not a big deal for the *ValidateSpaceValue* method, but *OnSpacePropertyChanged* needs to cast the first argument to a *SpaceButton* and use that to reference everything in the object it needs. But it basically does the same thing that the *set* accessor of the *Text* property does.

Notice that the *SpaceButton* class sets the *AffectsMeasure* and *Inherits* properties of the metadata to *true*, but includes no other code to implement these features. It's all automatic.

The *FontSize* property that we were examining earlier is defined in *Control* and inherited by both *Button* and *Window*. This new *Space* property I've added to *Button* is supposed to be inherited through the element tree, but it's not defined anywhere else. I want to demonstrate property inheritance, so let's make a class named *SpaceWindow* that implements this same dependency property. *SpaceWindow* doesn't do anything itself with the property, so the class is rather shorter than *SpaceButton*.

SpaceWindow.cs

```
//------------------------------------------------
// SpaceWindow.cs (c) 2006 by Charles Petzold
//------------------------------------------------
using System;
using System.Windows;
using System.Windows.Controls;
using System.Windows.Input;
using System.Windows.Media;

namespace Petzold.SetSpaceProperty
{
    public class SpaceWindow : Window
    {
        // DependencyProperty and property.
        public static readonly DependencyProperty SpaceProperty;

        public int Space
        {
            set
            {
                SetValue(SpaceProperty, value);
            }
            get
            {
                return (int)GetValue(SpaceProperty);
            }
        }

        // Static constructor.
        static SpaceWindow()
        {
            // Define metadata.
            FrameworkPropertyMetadata metadata = new FrameworkPropertyMetadata();
            metadata.Inherits = true;

            // Add owner to SpaceProperty and override metadata.
            SpaceProperty =
                SpaceButton.SpaceProperty.AddOwner(typeof(SpaceWindow));
            SpaceProperty.OverrideMetadata(typeof(SpaceWindow), metadata);
        }
    }
}
```

Just as in *SpaceButton*, this class defines both the *SpaceProperty* field and the *Space* property itself. The static constructor doesn't register a new *Space* property, however. Instead, it adds another owner to the *Space* property registered by the *SpaceButton* class. When a class adds a new owner to a previously registered dependency property, the original metadata isn't applied, and the class must create its own metadata. Because *SpaceWindow* doesn't do much with this *Space* property, it only needs to ensure that the *Inherits* flag is set.

The final class in this project is very similar to *SetFontSizeProperty* and is called *SetSpaceProperty*:

```
SetSpaceProperty.cs
//-------------------------------------------------
// SetSpaceProperty.cs (c) 2006 by Charles Petzold
//-------------------------------------------------
using System;
using System.Windows;
using System.Windows.Controls;
using System.Windows.Input;
using System.Windows.Media;

namespace Petzold.SetSpaceProperty
{
    public class SetSpaceProperty : SpaceWindow
    {
        [STAThread]
        public static void Main()
        {
            Application app = new Application();
            app.Run(new SetSpaceProperty());
        }
        public SetSpaceProperty()
        {
            Title = "Set Space Property";
            SizeToContent = SizeToContent.WidthAndHeight;
            ResizeMode = ResizeMode.CanMinimize;
            int[] iSpaces = { 0, 1, 2 };

            Grid grid = new Grid();
            Content = grid;

            for (int i = 0; i < 2; i++)
            {
                RowDefinition row = new RowDefinition();
                row.Height = GridLength.Auto;
                grid.RowDefinitions.Add(row);
            }
            for (int i = 0; i < iSpaces.Length; i++)
            {
                ColumnDefinition col = new ColumnDefinition();
                col.Width = GridLength.Auto;
                grid.ColumnDefinitions.Add(col);
            }
```

```
            for (int i = 0; i < iSpaces.Length; i++)
            {
                SpaceButton btn = new SpaceButton();
                btn.Text = "Set window Space to " + iSpaces[i];
                btn.Tag = iSpaces[i];
                btn.HorizontalAlignment = HorizontalAlignment.Center;
                btn.VerticalAlignment = VerticalAlignment.Center;
                btn.Click += WindowPropertyOnClick;
                grid.Children.Add(btn);
                Grid.SetRow(btn, 0);
                Grid.SetColumn(btn, i);

                btn = new SpaceButton();
                btn.Text = "Set button Space to " + iSpaces[i];
                btn.Tag = iSpaces[i];
                btn.HorizontalAlignment = HorizontalAlignment.Center;
                btn.VerticalAlignment = VerticalAlignment.Center;
                btn.Click += ButtonPropertyOnClick;
                grid.Children.Add(btn);
                Grid.SetRow(btn, 1);
                Grid.SetColumn(btn, i);
            }
        }
        void WindowPropertyOnClick(object sender, RoutedEventArgs args)
        {
            SpaceButton btn = args.Source as SpaceButton;
            Space = (int)btn.Tag;
        }
        void ButtonPropertyOnClick(object sender, RoutedEventArgs args)
        {
            SpaceButton btn = args.Source as SpaceButton;
            btn.Space = (int)btn.Tag;
        }
    }
}
```

Notice that this class inherits from *SpaceWindow* rather than *Window*. Just as in the earlier program, it creates six buttons but these buttons are of type *SpaceButton*. These buttons show up with text that contains one space between each character because that's what the default is. Just as in the previous program, when you click a button in the top row, all the buttons change, but when you click a button in the bottom row, only that button changes and remains unchangeable thereafter. By implementing a dependency property, the *SpaceButton* class is now ready for data binding, styling, animation, and all kinds of craziness.

Another mystery is now about to be solved. Chapter 5 introduced the *DockPanel* and with it static methods named *SetDock* and *GetDock*. Subsequently, similar properties were encountered with *Grid* and *Canvas*. The *SetDock* property certainly has an odd syntax:

```
DockPanel.SetDock(ctrl, Dock.Right);
```

Alternatively, perhaps it would have been possible for *UIElement* to define a *Dock* property so that the property could be set like this:

```
ctrl.Dock = Dock.Right; // Not the way it's done in WPF.
```

That's how it's done in Windows Forms. But in the WPF, this *Dock* property would come into play only when the control is a child of a *DockPanel*. There might be other panels—even ones that you create—that might require other properties, and it doesn't make sense to burden *UIElement* with all these properties for all the different types of panels.

Another possibility would be to have an expanded *Add* method of the *Children* property:

```
dock.Children.Add(ctrl, Dock.Right); // Not the way it's done in WPF.
```

But that *Children* property is actually an object of type *UIElementCollection*, and it's used for all panels, not just the *DockPanel*. Another possibility would involve an instance property of *DockPanel* named *SetDock*:

```
dock.SetDock(ctrl, Dock.Right); // Not the way it's done in WPF.
```

This would work, of course, but the *DockPanel* would have to maintain a second collection of controls with their associated *Dock* members. While performing layout, the *DockPanel* would enumerate all the elements in its *Children* collection and then search the second collection for a matching element for the *Dock* member. You might have assumed that the actual syntax:

```
DockPanel.SetDock(ctrl, Dock.Right);
```

involved storing the control and the associated *Dock* value in some kind of collection. But the *SetDock* and *GetDock* properties of *DockPanel* are actually implemented like this:

```
public class DockPanel : Panel
{
    ...
    public static readonly DependencyProperty DockProperty;
    ...
    public static void SetDock(UIElement el, Dock dck)
    {
        el.SetValue(DockProperty, dck);
    }
    public static Dock GetDock(UIElement el)
    {
        return (Dock) el.GetValue(DockProperty);
    }
}
```

DockProperty is defined as a *DependencyProperty* but it is registered with a *DependencyProperty* .*RegisterAttached* method, so it's called an *attached property*. If it were a normal dependency property, *DockProperty* would be associated with a property named *Dock* with calls to *SetValue* and *GetValue*. There is no property named *Dock*. Instead, *DockProperty* is referred to in two static methods defined by *DockPanel* named *SetDock* and *GetDock*. These methods call *SetValue* and *GetValue* for the element (or control) passed as an argument to the methods. These are the same *SetValue* and *GetValue* methods defined by *DependencyObject* and used in connection with dependency properties. (However, notice that the class implementing the attached property doesn't call its own *SetValue* and *GetValue* methods. For that reason, a class implementing an attached property doesn't need to derive from *DependencyObject*.)

Here's the call to *SetDock* again as it might be encountered in a typical program:

```
DockPanel.SetDock(ctrl, Dock.Right);
```

That call is exactly equivalent to this call:

```
ctrl.SetValue(DockPanel.DockProperty, Dock.Right);
```

You can verify this for yourself by replacing calls to *SetDock* with equivalent calls to *SetValue*.

When that *ctrl* object gets a call to its *SetValue* method with an initial argument of *DockPanel.DockProperty*, it probably stores the property and the value in a collection of some sort. But this collection is part of the child element, and not part of the *DockPanel* object.

When the *DockPanel* object is laying out the elements, it can obtain the *Dock* value associated with the control by calling its static *GetDock* method:

```
Dock dck = DockPanel.GetDock(ctrl);
```

This call is equivalent to:

```
Dock dck = (Dock) ctrl.GetValue(DockPanel.DockProperty);
```

Attached properties are much less common than ordinary dependency properties, and you've already encountered many of the most important ones.

If you are now exploring the Fields section of the class documentation, you've also seen static fields named (for example) *KeyDownEvent* of type *RoutedEvent*. The role of those fields will become apparent in the next chapter.

Chapter 9
Routed Input Events

Under the Windows Presentation Foundation, the three primary forms of user input are the keyboard, the mouse, and the stylus. (Stylus input is available on Tablet PCs and through digitizing tablets.) Previous chapters have shown code that installed event handlers for some keyboard and mouse events, but this chapter examines input events more comprehensively.

Input events are defined with delegates whose second argument is a type that descends from *RoutedEventArgs* by way of *InputEventArgs*. The following class hierarchy is complete from *InputEventArgs* on down.

Object

    EventArgs

        RoutedEventArgs

            InputEventArgs

                KeyboardEventArgs

                    KeyboardFocusChangedEventArgs

                    KeyEventArgs

                MouseEventArgs

                    MouseButtonEventArgs

                    MouseWheelEventArgs

                    QueryCursorEventArgs

                StylusEventArgs

                    StylusButtonEventArgs

                    StylusDownEventArgs

                    StylusSystemGestureEventArgs

                TextCompositionEventArgs

RoutedEventArgs is used extensively in the Windows Presentation Foundation as part of the support for event routing, which is a mechanism that allows elements to process events in a very flexible manner. Events are said to be *routed* when they travel up and down the element tree.

The user clicks the mouse button. Who gets the event? The traditional answer is "the visible and enabled control most in the foreground under the mouse pointer." If a button is on a window and the user clicks the button, the button gets the event. Very simple.

But under the Windows Presentation Foundation, this simple approach doesn't work very well. A button is not just a button. A button has content, and this content can consist of a panel that in turn contains shapes and images and text blocks. Each of these elements is capable of receiving mouse events. Sometimes it's proper for these individual elements to process their own mouse events, but not always. If these elements decorate the surface of a button, it makes the most sense for the button to handle the events. It would help if there existed a mechanism to route the events through the shapes, images, text blocks, and panels to the button.

The user presses a key on the keyboard. Who gets the event? The traditional answer is "the control that has the input focus." If a window contains multiple text boxes, for example, only one has the input focus and that's the one that gets the event.

But wouldn't it be nice if there existed a mechanism that allowed the window to examine the keyboard events first? Perhaps the window could decide if the event was something it was interested in processing before the event even got to the text box. (The EditSomeRichText program in Chapter 4 does precisely that to display file dialog boxes when the user types Ctrl+O or Ctrl+S.)

Event routing in the WPF allows both scenarios. There is always an element that is considered the "source" of an event. For mouse and stylus events, the source of the event is generally the element most in the foreground underneath the mouse pointer or stylus. This element must be both visible and enabled. (That is, the element's *Visibility* property must equal the enumeration member *Visibility.Visible*, and the *IsEnabled* property must be *true*.) If the element is not visible and enabled, the source of the event is the topmost underlying element that *is* enabled and visible.

The source of a keyboard event is the element that has the input focus. For both keyboard and mouse events, only one element is the source of any particular event, but all ancestors of the source element in the element tree also potentially have access to that event.

The *UIElement* class defines most of the user-input events. In the Events section of *UIElement* documentation, you'll see, for example, the *MouseDown* event, which signals when the user clicks any mouse button. In the Methods section of the documentation of *UIElement*, you'll see *OnMouseDown*, which is the protected virtual method that corresponds to that event. Any class that derives from *UIElement* can override the *OnMouseDown* method rather than install a *MouseDown* event handler. The two approaches are functionally identical, but the *OnMouseDown* call occurs before the *MouseDown* event is fired.

When overriding a virtual method such as *OnMouseDown*, it is common to call the method in the base class:

```
protected override void OnMouseDown(MouseEventArgs args)
{
    base.OnMouseDown(args);
    ...
}
```

In Windows Forms, calling the *OnMouseDown* method in the base class was very important because that's where the base class fired the *MouseDown* event. The *OnMouseDown* method as implemented in the *Control* class in Windows Forms probably looks something like this:

```
// This is Windows Forms, not the Windows Presentation Foundation!
protected virtual void OnMouseDown(MouseEventArgs args)
{
    ...
    if (MouseDown != null)
        MouseDown(this, args)
    ...
}
```

In Windows Forms, a class called *MyControl* could derive from *Control* and override *OnMouseDown* without calling the method in the base class. This is usually not good, because if the program then created an object of type *MyControl* and attached a *MouseDown* event handler to that object, that handler would never get any events.

In the Windows Presentation Foundation, this is not an issue. The firing of the *MouseDown* event occurs outside of the call to *OnMouseDown*. As the documentation for *OnMouseDown* in the *UIElement* class states, "This method has no default implementation." In other words, the body of the *OnMouseDown* method in *UIElement* is empty. In a class that inherits directly from *UIElement*, you can safely override *OnMouseDown* without calling the method in the base class and inflict no bad side effects on any class that inherits from your class or instantiates your class. You'll see the same statement about "no default implementation" in the other input-related virtual methods in *UIElement*.

The WPF documentation indicates not only when a class defines a virtual method, but also when a class overrides that method. Look at the list of methods in *FrameworkElement*, the class that inherits directly from *UIElement*. Do you see *OnMouseDown*? No, *FrameworkElement* does not override *OnMouseDown*. Now check *Control*, which inherits directly from *Framework-Element*. Once again, *OnMouseDown* is not listed. Now check *ButtonBase*. There you will see an override not of *OnMouseDown*, but of *OnMouseLeftButtonDown*, which is a related method that *ButtonBase* uses to generate its *Click* event. The *OnMouseLeftButtonDown* method in *ButtonBase* is not responsible for firing the *MouseLeftButtonDown* event, but it is responsible for firing the *Click* event. If you derive a class from *ButtonBase*, and if you override *OnMouseLeftButtonDown* without calling the method in the base class, you will effectively disable the *Click* event. The documentation for *OnMouseLeftButtonDown* in *ButtonBase* does *not* say that the "method has no default implementation."

Although *UIElement* does not fire its events in the corresponding *On* methods, other classes may take a different approach. For example, the *ButtonBase* class defines an *OnClick* method. The *OnMouseLeftButtonDown* override in *ButtonBase* almost certainly calls *OnClick*, and the *OnClick* method is responsible for firing the *Click* event. As with the *OnMouseLeftButtonDown* method, if you derive from *ButtonBase* and override *OnClick* without calling the method in the base class, you will disable the *Click* event for any object based on your class.

As a general rule, it's a good idea whenever you override a virtual method to call the method in the base class unless you have a specific reason for not doing so. I tend to do that even for methods where it is documented as unnecessary.

The *MouseDown* event and the *OnMouseDown* virtual protected method are joined by other related members of the *UIElement* class. In the Fields section of the *UIElement* documentation, you'll also see a static read-only field of type *RoutedEvent* named *MouseDownEvent*. As you'll discover in this chapter, these *RoutedEvent* objects have a role similar to that of dependency properties. *MouseDownEvent* provides an easy way to refer to the *MouseDown* event in some method calls, and the *RoutedEvent* class encapsulates information that governs how the event is routed to other elements in the element tree.

In the *UIElement* documentation, you'll also find an event named *PreviewMouseDown*, a method named *OnPreviewMouseDown*, and a field named *PreviewMouseDownEvent*. This pattern of names is pervasive throughout most of the user input events defined by *UIElement*. You'll see shortly how these two sets of events work.

The class hierarchy shown at the beginning of this chapter suggests that *RoutedEventArgs* is an important class in WPF user events, and many other classes besides *InputEventArgs* inherit from *RoutedEventArgs*.

RoutedEventArgs defines just four properties that are often useful in event handling. One of these properties is named *RoutedEvent*, and it's an object of type *RoutedEvent*. The *RoutedEvent* property of *RoutedEventArgs* identifies the event itself. For a *MouseDown* event, for example, this property will be equal to *MouseDownEvent*, which is the static field defined in *UIElement*. You could use the same event handler for different types of events and identify the events with code like this:

```
if (args.RoutedEvent == MouseDownEvent)
{
    ...
}
else if (args.RoutedEvent == MouseUpEvent)
{
    ...
}
```

The *Source* and *OriginalSource* properties of *RoutedEventArgs* are both of type *object* and indicate (as the names imply) the element that is the source of the event. In general, the *Source* property is *very* important, but in some cases you might also need to look at the *OriginalSource* property.

The *Handled* property of *RoutedEventArgs* is initially *false*, but may be set to *true* to prevent future routing of the event. The EditSomeRichText program in Chapter 4 used this property to prevent the Ctrl+O and Ctrl+S keystrokes from going to the *RichTextBox* itself.

To the properties defined by *RoutedEventArgs*, *InputEventArgs* adds a *Device* property of type *InputDevice* to identify the input device, and a *TimeStamp* property of type *int*.

Let's examine some actual routed events. The program below is called ExamineRoutedEvents, and the first thing you should know is that it inherits from *Application* rather than *Window*, and then creates an object of type *Window* and several other elements as well. The original version of the program defined a class named *ExamineRoutedEvents* that inherited from *Window*, but (as you'll see) the program displays text with class names such as "TextBlock" and "Button" and "Grid" and it was just too confusing for the program to display a class named "ExamineRoutedEvents" rather than a class simply named "Window."

ExamineRoutedEvents.cs
```
//-------------------------------------------------------
// ExamineRoutedEvents.cs (c) 2006 by Charles Petzold
//-------------------------------------------------------
using System;
using System.Windows;
using System.Windows.Controls;
using System.Windows.Documents;
using System.Windows.Input;
using System.Windows.Media;

namespace Petzold.ExamineRoutedEvents
{
    public class ExamineRoutedEvents: Application
    {
        static readonly FontFamily fontfam = new FontFamily("Lucida Console");
        const string strFormat = "{0,-30} {1,-15} {2,-15} {3,-15}";
        StackPanel stackOutput;
        DateTime dtLast;

        [STAThread]
        public static void Main()
        {
            ExamineRoutedEvents app = new ExamineRoutedEvents();
            app.Run();
        }
        protected override void OnStartup(StartupEventArgs args)
        {
            base.OnStartup(args);

            // Create the Window.
            Window win = new Window();
            win.Title = "Examine Routed Events";
```

```
// Create the Grid and make it Window content.
Grid grid = new Grid();
win.Content = grid;

// Make three rows.
RowDefinition rowdef = new RowDefinition();
rowdef.Height = GridLength.Auto;
grid.RowDefinitions.Add(rowdef);

rowdef = new RowDefinition();
rowdef.Height = GridLength.Auto;
grid.RowDefinitions.Add(rowdef);

rowdef = new RowDefinition();
rowdef.Height = new GridLength(100, GridUnitType.Star);
grid.RowDefinitions.Add(rowdef);

// Create the Button & add it to the Grid.
Button btn = new Button();
btn.HorizontalAlignment = HorizontalAlignment.Center;
btn.Margin = new Thickness(24);
btn.Padding = new Thickness(24);
grid.Children.Add(btn);

// Create the TextBlock & add it to the Button.
TextBlock text = new TextBlock();
text.FontSize = 24;
text.Text = win.Title;
btn.Content = text;

// Create headings to display above the ScrollViewer.
TextBlock textHeadings = new TextBlock();
textHeadings.FontFamily = fontfam;
textHeadings.Inlines.Add(new Underline(new Run(
    String.Format(strFormat,
    "Routed Event", "sender", "Source", "OriginalSource"))));
grid.Children.Add(textHeadings);
Grid.SetRow(textHeadings, 1);

// Create the ScrollViewer.
ScrollViewer scroll = new ScrollViewer();
grid.Children.Add(scroll);
Grid.SetRow(scroll, 2);

// Create the StackPanel for displaying events.
stackOutput = new StackPanel();
scroll.Content = stackOutput;

// Add event handlers.
UIElement[] els = { win, grid, btn, text };

foreach (UIElement el in els)
{
    // Keyboard
    el.PreviewKeyDown += AllPurposeEventHandler;
```

```
                   el.PreviewKeyUp += AllPurposeEventHandler;
                   el.PreviewTextInput += AllPurposeEventHandler;
                   el.KeyDown += AllPurposeEventHandler;
                   el.KeyUp += AllPurposeEventHandler;
                   el.TextInput += AllPurposeEventHandler;

                   // Mouse
                   el.MouseDown += AllPurposeEventHandler;
                   el.MouseUp += AllPurposeEventHandler;
                   el.PreviewMouseDown += AllPurposeEventHandler;
                   el.PreviewMouseUp += AllPurposeEventHandler;

                   // Stylus
                   el.StylusDown += AllPurposeEventHandler;
                   el.StylusUp += AllPurposeEventHandler;
                   el.PreviewStylusDown += AllPurposeEventHandler;
                   el.PreviewStylusUp += AllPurposeEventHandler;

                   // Click
                   el.AddHandler(Button.ClickEvent,
                       new RoutedEventHandler(AllPurposeEventHandler));
               }
               // Show the window.
               win.Show();
           }
           void AllPurposeEventHandler(object sender, RoutedEventArgs args)
           {
               // Add blank line if there's been a time gap.
               DateTime dtNow = DateTime.Now;
               if (dtNow - dtLast > TimeSpan.FromMilliseconds(100))
                   stackOutput.Children.Add(new TextBlock(new Run(" ")));
               dtLast = dtNow;

               // Display event information.
               TextBlock text = new TextBlock();
               text.FontFamily = fontfam;
               text.Text = String.Format(strFormat,
                               args.RoutedEvent.Name,
                               TypeWithoutNamespace(sender),
                               TypeWithoutNamespace(args.Source),
                               TypeWithoutNamespace(args.OriginalSource));
               stackOutput.Children.Add(text);
               (stackOutput.Parent as ScrollViewer).ScrollToBottom();
           }
           string TypeWithoutNamespace(object obj)
           {
               string[] astr = obj.GetType().ToString().Split('.');
               return astr[astr.Length - 1];
           }
       }
   }
}
```

This program creates elements that it assembles into the following tree:

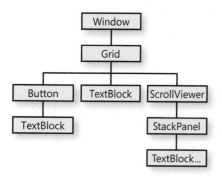

The *Window* object is considered the "root" of the tree. (Yes, I know—if the *Window* is the root of the tree, the tree is upside-down. But this is a special kind of tree.) From the *Window*, all the other elements are considered to be "down" from that root. From the perspective of one of the *TextBlock* elements, the *Window* is considered to be "up" in the tree.

The ExamineRoutedEvents program installs various event handlers for the *Window*, *Grid*, and *Button* elements, and also for the *TextBlock* content of the *Button*. These event handlers encompass several common keyboard, mouse, and stylus events but all share the same method, *AllPurposeEventHandler*.

Whenever the *AllPurposeEventHandler* receives a new event, it creates a new *TextBlock* object (corresponding to the *TextBlock* with the ellipsis shown in the tree diagram). This *TextBlock* object displays information about the event, including the first argument to the event handler (typically called *sender*) as well as the *RoutedEvent*, *Source*, and *OriginalSource* properties of the *RoutedEventArgs* argument. The event handler then adds that *TextBlock* to a *StackPanel* that is the content of a *ScrollViewer*. The *TextBlock* element in the center of the tree diagram simply provides headings for the information the program displays.

To help you read the output, the *AllPurposeEventHandler* attempts to insert a blank line whenever an event follows another by at least 100 milliseconds. Just be aware that this feature doesn't always work flawlessly if your fingers are very fast or the events are delayed for some reason.

When you run the program, you'll see a big button at the top with the text "Examine Routed Events." I want you to click the text in that button with the *right* mouse button. You should see the sequence of events listed in the following table:

RoutedEvent	sender	Source	OriginalSource
PreviewMouseDown	Window	TextBlock	TextBlock
PreviewMouseDown	Grid	TextBlock	TextBlock
PreviewMouseDown	Button	TextBlock	TextBlock
PreviewMouseDown	TextBlock	TextBlock	TextBlock

RoutedEvent	sender	Source	OriginalSource
MouseDown	TextBlock	TextBlock	TextBlock
MouseDown	Button	TextBlock	TextBlock
MouseDown	Grid	TextBlock	TextBlock
MouseDown	Window	TextBlock	TextBlock

This sequence is followed by a similar pattern for the *PreviewMouseUp* event and then for the *MouseUp* event. (If you see an *OriginalSource* of *ButtonChrome*, you didn't right-click the text in the button.)

The first argument to the event handler—typically called *sender*—is always the object on which you attached the event handler. This argument indicates the object that is sending the event to your application. The *Source* property of *RoutedEventArgs* is the element that actually raised the event.

The sequence shown in the table is the essence of event routing. The *PreviewMouseDown* event is an example of a *tunneling* event. The event begins at the root of the visual tree and "tunnels down" to the element directly underneath the mouse cursor. The *MouseDown* event is a *bubbling* event. The event "bubbles up" through visual parents to the root element. (This terminology of "down" and "up" depends on the tree being visualized with its root at the top.)

Event routing provides an extremely flexible way to handle events. If any element higher in the tree wants first dibs on the mouse-down action, it can do so by handling the *PreviewMouseDown* event. If any of these elements wants only those mouse-down events ignored by elements lower in the tree, it can receive those as well by handling *MouseDown*.

Now move the mouse cursor slightly away from the button text but still within the confines of the button and click again with the *right* mouse button. Here's what you'll see:

RoutedEvent	sender	Source	OriginalSource
PreviewMouseDown	Window	Button	ButtonChrome
PreviewMouseDown	Grid	Button	ButtonChrome
PreviewMouseDown	Button	Button	ButtonChrome
MouseDown	Button	Button	ButtonChrome
MouseDown	Grid	Button	ButtonChrome
MouseDown	Window	Button	ButtonChrome

You'll also see an identical pattern for *PreviewMouseUp* and *MouseUp*. The *TextBlock* is not involved in this event because it's no longer under the mouse pointer. Instead, the *Button* object is raising the event as indicated by the *Source* property, but the *OriginalSource* property indicates that the foreground object actually underneath the mouse pointer is an object of type *ButtonChrome*. Have you ever heard of *ButtonChrome*? Neither did I before I wrote and ran this program. *ButtonChrome* inherits from *Decorator* (which in turn derives from *FrameworkElement*) and can be found in the *Microsoft.Windows.Themes* namespace. *Button* uses *ButtonChrome* to draw its surface.

The lesson here is simple: The *OriginalSource* property is often something you can safely ignore. You'll usually focus on the *Source* property. (However, if *Source* is not giving you what you want and *OriginalSource* is, then obviously use that instead.)

I've been telling you to click the button with the *right* mouse button. There's a reason for that. If you click the button *TextBlock* with the left mouse button, you'll see the following sequence:

RoutedEvent	sender	Source	OriginalSource
PreviewMouseDown	Window	TextBlock	TextBlock
PreviewMouseDown	Grid	TextBlock	TextBlock
PreviewMouseDown	Button	TextBlock	TextBlock
PreviewMouseDown	TextBlock	TextBlock	TextBlock
MouseDown	TextBlock	TextBlock	TextBlock

And then the *MouseDown* events end. There are no more. What happened to them?

The *Button* class happens to be *very* interested in the left mouse button, because that's what it uses to generate *Click* events. As I mentioned earlier, *ButtonBase* overrides the *OnMouseLeftButtonDown* method. When that method is called, *ButtonBase* begins the work that will eventually result in a *Click* event. Because *ButtonBase* is, in effect, handling the left mouse button and putting it to work, it sets the *Handled* flag of *RoutedEventArgs* to *true*. That flag halts a call to the *MouseDown* event handlers, as well as all further routing of the event through the tree.

As you release the left mouse button, you'll see the following sequence of events:

RoutedEvent	sender	Source	OriginalSource
PreviewMouseUp	Window	Button	Button
PreviewMouseUp	Grid	Button	Button
PreviewMouseUp	Button	Button	Button
Click	Button	Button	Button
Click	Grid	Button	Button
Click	Window	Button	Button

The *TextBlock* is no longer involved. The *Button* has "captured the mouse" (a technique I'll discuss shortly) and has become the source of this event. During the call to the *OnLeftMouseButtonUp* method, *ButtonBase* sets the *Handled* property of the event arguments to *true*, and generates a *Click* event, which continues through the tree back up to the window. (The *Click* event exists only in a bubbling version. There is no tunneling *PreviewClick* event.)

The *Click* event is defined by *ButtonBase* and inherited by *Button*. The *Window* class knows nothing about *Click* events and neither does *Grid*. It would normally be impossible to install a *Click* event handler on a *Window* or *Grid* object. But *UIElement* defines an *AddHandler* method (and a corresponding *RemoveHandler* method) that accepts a first argument of type

RoutedEvent and lets you install an event handler for any routed event of any other element in the same tree. Here's how the ExamineRoutedEvents program uses *AddHandler* to install a *Click* event handler on the other elements:

```
el.AddHandler(Button.ClickEvent,
    new RoutedEventHandler(AllPurposeEventHandler));
```

Installing a handler on a panel (for example) is a very useful technique for consolidating the handling of particular events coming from a number of child elements.

If you run this program on a Tablet PC, you'll want to tap the program's button with the stylus. First you'll see a *PreviewStylusDown* event tunnel down the tree from *Window* to *Grid* to *Button* to *TextBlock*, and then you'll see the *StylusDown* event bubble up the tree from *TextBlock* to *Button* to *Grid* to *Window*. At that point, *PreviewMouseDown* and *MouseDown* events are generated just as if you had clicked with the left mouse button. When you release the stylus from the screen, the *PreviewStylusUp* event tunnels down from the Window to the *Button* and the *StylusUp* event bubbles up from the *Button* to the *Window*. (The *TextBlock* is out of the picture.) Then, *PreviewMouseUp* and *MouseUp* events are generated. The stylus always generates mouse events as well as stylus events.

Because you've been clicking the button with the mouse or stylus, it has the input focus. Press a function key. You'll see a *PreviewKeyDown* event tunnel down the tree from the *Window* to the *Grid* to the *Button*, and then a *KeyDown* event bubble up the tree from the *Button* to the *Grid* to the *Window*. Obviously the *Button* has the input focus and not the *TextBlock*. As you release the key you'll see a *PreviewKeyUp* tunnel down the tree and *KeyUp* events bubble up the tree in the same pattern.

Now press any letter key. You'll see three *PreviewKeyDown* events and three *KeyDown* events, followed by three *PreviewTextInput* events and three *TextInput* events. The *TextInput* events indicate actual text input generated from the keyboard. As you release the key, you'll see three *PreviewKeyUp* events and three *KeyUp* events.

Now press the spacebar. As with the left mouse button, the *Button* control is very interested in the spacebar. Here's what you'll see:

RoutedEvent	sender	Source	OriginalSource
PreviewKeyDown	Window	Button	Button
PreviewKeyDown	Grid	Button	Button
PreviewKeyDown	Button	Button	Button
PreviewKeyUp	Window	Button	Button
PreviewKeyUp	Grid	Button	Button
PreviewKeyUp	Button	Button	Button
Click	Button	Button	Button
Click	Grid	Button	Button
Click	Window	Button	Button

The *Button* stops further processing of the *KeyDown* event and then turns the *KeyUp* event into a *Click*. You'll see something similar for the Enter key.

Defining a routed event in your own class is similar to defining a dependency property. Suppose you have a control in which you need a *Click*-like event that you'd rather call *Knock*. You first define a static read-only field of type *RoutedEvent* for *Knock* (and optionally *PreviewKnock*):

```
public static readonly RoutedEvent KnockEvent;
public static readonly RoutedEvent PreviewKnockEvent;
```

By convention, the field names consist of the name of the event followed by the word *Event*.

In the field definition itself or in a static constructor, you call the static *EventManager.Register-RoutedEvent* method. The first argument is the text name of the event:

```
KnockEvent =
    EventManager.RegisterRoutedEvent("Knock", RoutingStrategy.Bubble,
        typeof(RoutedEventHandler), typeof(YourClass));

PreviewKnockEvent =
    EventManager.RegisterRoutedEvent("PreviewKnock", RoutingStrategy.Tunnel,
        typeof(RoutedEventHandler), typeof(YourClass));
```

Notice that the second argument is *RoutingStrategy.Bubble* for the *Knock* event and *Routing-Strategy.Tunnel* for *PreviewKnock*. The only other member of the *RoutingStrategy* enumeration is *Direct*, in which case the event is not routed. The third argument is shown as *RoutedEventHandler* here, but it can be any delegate with an argument of *RoutedEventArgs* or a descendent. The fourth argument is the type of the class in which you're defining this event.

You must also define the actual *Knock* and *PreviewKnock* events. The first line of this block of code looks similar to the way you define a regular .NET event using the *event* keyword and the delegate associated with the event:

```
public event RoutedEventHandler Knock
{
    add { AddHandler(KnockEvent, value); }
    remove { RemoveHandler(KnockEvent, value); }
}
```

But this event definition also includes *add* and *remove* accessors that refer to the static routed event. *AddHandler* and *RemoveHandler* are defined by *DependencyObject*. The *value* argument is the event handler. An *event* definition for *PreviewKnock* would be similar but refer to the *PreviewKnockEvent* event.

When it comes time for your class to actually raise these events (most likely in the *OnMouseUp* method), you create an object of type *RoutedEventArgs* (or a descendent):

```
RoutedEventArgs argsEvent = new RoutedEventArgs();
argsEvent.RoutedEvent = YourClass.PreviewKnockEvent;
argsEvent.Source = this;
RaiseEvent(argsEvent);
```

```
argsEvent = new RoutedEventArgs();
argsEvent.RoutedEvent = YourClass.KnockEvent;
argsEvent.Source = this;
RaiseEvent(argsEvent);
```

You'll recognize the *RoutedEvent* and *Source* properties of *RoutedEventArgs*, of course. *Routed-EventArgs* also defines a constructor that accepts these two values. If you don't explicitly set *OriginalSource*, the *OriginalSource* is set by default from *Source*. The *RaiseEvent* method is defined by *UIElement*. Notice that you call *RaiseEvent* for the tunneling event first, followed by the bubbling event.

A complete program using the *Knock* and *PreviewKnock* events is presented in Chapter 10.

Although I've been discussing user input events as implemented in the *UIElement* class, these events are implemented in *ContentElement* as well. This is the class from which *TextElement*, *FixedDocument*, and *FlowDocument* derive. The *ContentElement* objects are elements that cannot render themselves on the screen, but are rendered by other elements. Both *UIElement* and *ContentElement* implement the *IInputElement* interface, which also includes most (but not all) of the user input events defined by *UIElement* and *ContentElement*.

Both *UIElement* and *ContentElement* define 10 events that begin with the word *Mouse* and 8 that begin with *PreviewMouse*.

Event handlers for the *MouseMove*, *PreviewMouseMove*, *MouseEnter*, and *MouseLeave* events are all of type *MouseEventHandler*, and the event is accompanied by an object of type *MouseEventArgs*. (There are no *PreviewMouseEnter* or *PreviewMouseLeave* events.) The *MouseMove* event occurs a multitude of times when the mouse cursor is moved across the surface of an element. The *MouseEnter* and *MouseLeave* events occur when the mouse cursor enters and leaves the area occupied by the element. *UIElement* and *ContentElement* also define two related read-only properties. *IsMouseOver* is *true* if the mouse cursor is anywhere over the element. *IsMouseDirectlyOver* is *true* if the mouse cursor is over the element but not over any child elements.

When handling a *MouseMove*, *MouseEnter*, or *MouseLeave* event, you might want to know which mouse buttons, if any, are currently pressed. *MouseEventArgs* has separate read-only properties for all the types of buttons found on a mouse: *LeftButton*, *MiddleButton,* and *RightButton*, as well as the two extended buttons, *XButton1* and *XButton2*. Each of these properties is set to a member of the *MouseButtonState* enumeration, which has just two members: *Pressed* and *Released*.

Particularly for a *MouseMove* event, your program may need to know the location of the mouse cursor. The *GetPosition* method defined by *MouseEventArgs* requires an argument of any type that implements the *IInputElement* interface and returns a *Point* object in device-independent coordinates relative to the upper-left corner of that element.

The *MouseDown*, *MouseUp*, *PreviewMouseDown*, and *PreviewMouseUp* events occur when the user presses and releases a mouse button over an element in your program. These events are accompanied by objects of type *MouseButtonEventArgs*. You can identify what button triggered the event by examining the *ChangedButton* property. This is a member of the *MouseButton* enumeration, which has members *Left*, *Middle*, *Right*, *XButton1*, and *XButton2*. If the user presses two buttons simultaneously, each generates its own *MouseDown* event. The *MouseButtonEventArgs* class also defines a property named *ButtonState*, which is a member of the *MouseButtonState* enumeration. Obviously, for a *MouseDown* event, the *ButtonState* property will equal *MouseButtonState.Pressed*, and for a *MouseUp* event, it will be *MouseButtonState.Released*, but the presence of this property lets you distinguish the two events if you use the same event handler for both *MouseDown* and *MouseUp*.

The *UIElement* and *ContentElement* classes also define events specifically for the left and right mouse buttons named *MouseLeftButtonDown*, *MouseRightButtonDown*, *MouseLeftButtonUp*, and *MouseRightButtonUp*, all with *Preview* versions. Think of these as "convenience" events. There is really no difference between processing a *MouseLeftButtonDown* event and processing a *MouseDown* event by enclosing your logic in an *if* statement:

```
if (args.ChangedButton == MouseButton.Left)
{
    ...
}
```

Just to get an idea of how these left button and right button events fit in with everything else, you may want to insert the following code in the *foreach* loop in ExamineRoutedEvents:

```
el.MouseLeftButtonDown += AllPurposeEventHandler;
el.MouseLeftButtonUp += AllPurposeEventHandler;
el.PreviewMouseLeftButtonDown += AllPurposeEventHandler;
el.PreviewMouseLeftButtonUp += AllPurposeEventHandler;

el.MouseRightButtonDown += AllPurposeEventHandler;
el.MouseRightButtonUp += AllPurposeEventHandler;
el.PreviewMouseRightButtonDown += AllPurposeEventHandler;
el.PreviewMouseRightButtonUp += AllPurposeEventHandler;
```

You'll see these events interleaved between the "down" and "up" events. Each element in the tree generates either a *MouseLeftButtonUp* or *MouseRightButtonUp* event just prior to the *MouseUp* event, and similarly for the "down" and "preview" versions.

The *MouseWheel* and *PreviewMouseWheel* events report on turns of the wheel located on some modern mouse devices. The wheel doesn't turn smoothly but has tactile (and sometimes audible) ticks. Today's wheel mouse devices associate a value of 120 with each tick. Perhaps wheel mouse devices of the future will have finer ticks and be associated with smaller numbers, but for now the *Delta* property of *MouseWheelEventArgs* is 120 per tick if the wheel is turned away from the user, and –120 if the wheel is turned toward the user. A program can determine if a mouse wheel is present by the *SystemParameters.IsMouseWheelPresent* value.

A program can also get information about the current mouse position and the state of mouse buttons through static properties in the *Mouse* class. This class also has static methods to attach and remove mouse event handlers. The *MouseDevice* class has instance methods for mouse position and button state.

The *Control* class defines an additional mouse event named *MouseDoubleClick* and a corresponding *OnMouseDoubleClick* method that are accompanied by objects of type *MouseButtonEventHandler*.

The mouse is represented on screen by a bitmap called the mouse cursor. In the Windows Presentation Foundation, this is an object of type *Cursor*, most conveniently made available in the *Cursors* class. To associate a particular cursor with an element, you can set the *Cursor* object to the *Cursor* property defined by *FrameworkElement*. Or, for more flexibility, you can attach a handler for the *QueryCursor* event (or override the *OnQueryCursor* method). This event is triggered whenever the mouse is moved. The *QueryCursorEventArgs* object that accompanies this event includes a property named *Cursor* that you set to the appropriate *Cursor* object.

It is tempting to believe that *MouseDown* and *MouseUp* events occur in pairs. From the perspective of your application, they definitely do not. For example, suppose the user moves the mouse cursor to your application's window and presses a button. Your window gets a *MouseDown* event. Now, with the button still pressed, the user moves the cursor away from your window and releases the button. Your application's window has no knowledge of that event.

Sometimes this normal mouse behavior is not desirable. Sometimes it is convenient for a program to know what's happening with the mouse outside of its window. For example, consider a drawing program where the user presses the mouse to begin drawing a graphical object, and then the mouse drifts outside the window, perhaps only momentarily. It would be preferable for the application to keep receiving *MouseMove* events during the time the mouse is outside the borders of the window.

Or look at a standard *Button* control. The *Button* generates a *Click* event when the left mouse button is released, but the processing preceding that *Click* event is obviously more complex: If you press the left mouse button while the mouse is positioned over the button, the button surface turns darker to indicate that it's been depressed. Now, with the mouse button still pressed, move the mouse pointer away from the *Button* object. You'll see the surface turn normal again. If you release the mouse button and then move the pointer back to the button, the *Button* knows that the mouse button has been released.

This behavior is possible through a process called *capturing the mouse*. To capture the mouse, an element calls the *CaptureMouse* method defined by *UIElement* or *ContentElement* (or the static *Capture* method of the *Mouse* class). The method returns *bool* if the capture is successful. It's not a good idea to try to capture the mouse other than during a *MouseDown* event. It might confuse the user and it's just not very useful.

After an element calls *CaptureMouse*, it will continue to receive *MouseMove* and *MouseUp* events even if the mouse pointer is moved away from the element. The read-only *IsMouseCaptured* property will be *true* to indicate the capture. When the element gets a *MouseUp* event, it is proper to release the mouse capture with a call to *ReleaseMouseCapture* or to the static *Mouse.Capture* method with a *null* argument.

Mouse capturing can potentially interfere with the proper operation of Windows. For that reason, Windows can unilaterally free the mouse from your program's capture. If you don't release the mouse on receipt of a *MouseUp* event, and the user clicks another window, your program will lose the mouse capture. Even if your program abides by all the rules and Windows suddenly needs to put a system-modal dialog on the screen, your program will lose the mouse capture.

If you have a need to capture the mouse, you should also install an event handler for the *LostMouseCapture* event, and use that occasion to perform any necessary clean-up. The *LostMouseCapture* event is also triggered when your program calls *Mouse.Capture* with a *null* argument, so you may need to distinguish between a normal loss of mouse capture and one that's being imposed on you.

Mouse capturing and many of the mouse events are demonstrated in the DrawCircles program. You may want to try using the program before you look at the source code. Press the left mouse button over the window and drag the mouse to draw circles in the window's client area. The initial point that you click becomes the circle's center. When you release the left mouse button, the circle is drawn with a blue perimeter and a red interior.

If you press the right mouse button over one of the circles, you can drag it to a new location. If you click the middle mouse button over a circle, you can toggle the interior brush between red and transparent. Pressing the Escape key aborts any drawing or dragging operation.

DrawCircles.cs

```
//-----------------------------------------
// DrawCircles.cs (c) 2006 by Charles Petzold
//-----------------------------------------
using System;
using System.Windows;
using System.Windows.Controls;
using System.Windows.Input;
using System.Windows.Media;
using System.Windows.Shapes;

namespace Petzold.DrawCircles
{
    public class DrawCircles : Window
    {
        Canvas canv;

        // Drawing-Related fields.
        bool isDrawing;
        Ellipse elips;
        Point ptCenter;
```

```
// Dragging-Related fields.
bool isDragging;
FrameworkElement elDragging;
Point ptMouseStart, ptElementStart;

[STAThread]
public static void Main()
{
    Application app = new Application();
    app.Run(new DrawCircles());
}
public DrawCircles()
{
    Title = "Draw Circles";
    Content = canv = new Canvas();
}
protected override void OnMouseLeftButtonDown(MouseButtonEventArgs args)
{
    base.OnMouseLeftButtonDown(args);

    if (isDragging)
        return;

    // Create a new Ellipse object and add it to canvas.
    ptCenter = args.GetPosition(canv);
    elips = new Ellipse();
    elips.Stroke = SystemColors.WindowTextBrush;
    elips.StrokeThickness = 1;
    elips.Width = 0;
    elips.Height = 0;
    canv.Children.Add(elips);
    Canvas.SetLeft(elips, ptCenter.X);
    Canvas.SetTop(elips, ptCenter.Y);

    // Capture the mouse and prepare for future events.
    CaptureMouse();
    isDrawing = true;
}
protected override void OnMouseRightButtonDown(MouseButtonEventArgs args)
{
    base.OnMouseRightButtonDown(args);

    if (isDrawing)
        return;

    // Get the clicked element and prepare for future events.
    ptMouseStart = args.GetPosition(canv);
    elDragging = canv.InputHitTest(ptMouseStart) as FrameworkElement;

    if (elDragging != null)
    {
        ptElementStart = new Point(Canvas.GetLeft(elDragging),
                                   Canvas.GetTop(elDragging));
        isDragging = true;
    }
```

```
    }
    protected override void OnMouseDown(MouseButtonEventArgs args)
    {
        base.OnMouseDown(args);

        if (args.ChangedButton == MouseButton.Middle)
        {
            Shape shape = canv.InputHitTest(args.GetPosition(canv)) as Shape;

            if (shape != null)
                shape.Fill = (shape.Fill == Brushes.Red ?
                                    Brushes.Transparent : Brushes.Red);
        }
    }
    protected override void OnMouseMove(MouseEventArgs args)
    {
        base.OnMouseMove(args);
        Point ptMouse = args.GetPosition(canv);

        // Move and resize the Ellipse.
        if (isDrawing)
        {
            double dRadius = Math.Sqrt(Math.Pow(ptCenter.X - ptMouse.X, 2) +
                                    Math.Pow(ptCenter.Y - ptMouse.Y, 2));

            Canvas.SetLeft(elips, ptCenter.X - dRadius);
            Canvas.SetTop(elips, ptCenter.Y - dRadius);
            elips.Width = 2 * dRadius;
            elips.Height = 2 * dRadius;
        }
        // Move the Ellipse.
        else if (isDragging)
        {
            Canvas.SetLeft(elDragging,
                ptElementStart.X + ptMouse.X - ptMouseStart.X);
            Canvas.SetTop(elDragging,
                ptElementStart.Y + ptMouse.Y - ptMouseStart.Y);
        }
    }
    protected override void OnMouseUp(MouseButtonEventArgs args)
    {
        base.OnMouseUp(args);

        // End the drawing operation.
        if (isDrawing && args.ChangedButton == MouseButton.Left)
        {
            elips.Stroke = Brushes.Blue;
            elips.StrokeThickness = Math.Min(24, elips.Width / 2);
            elips.Fill = Brushes.Red;

            isDrawing = false;
            ReleaseMouseCapture();
        }
        // End the capture operation.
```

```
                else if (isDragging && args.ChangedButton == MouseButton.Right)
                {
                    isDragging = false;
                }
        }
        protected override void OnTextInput(TextCompositionEventArgs args)
        {
            base.OnTextInput(args);

            // End drawing or dragging with press of Escape key.
            if (args.Text.IndexOf('\x1B') != -1)
            {
                if (isDrawing)
                    ReleaseMouseCapture();

                else if (isDragging)
                {
                    Canvas.SetLeft(elDragging, ptElementStart.X);
                    Canvas.SetTop(elDragging, ptElementStart.Y);
                    isDragging = false;
                }
            }
        }
        protected override void OnLostMouseCapture(MouseEventArgs args)
        {
            base.OnLostMouseCapture(args);

            // Abnormal end of drawing: Remove child Ellipse.
            if (isDrawing)
            {
                canv.Children.Remove(elips);
                isDrawing = false;
            }
        }
    }
}
```

The window covers its client area with a *Canvas* panel. Almost always when you're drawing based on mouse input, you want to use *Canvas*. Rather than installing event handlers, the window class overrides seven mouse-related methods. DrawCircles strives less for consistency than for demonstrating different mouse-handling techniques. For example, the program has separate *OnLeftMouseButtonDown* and *OnRightMouseButtonDown* methods for initiating drawing and dragging, but combines the end of these operations in a single *OnMouseUp* method. The window captures the mouse for drawing, but not for dragging.

During the *OnLeftMouseButtonDown* method, the program creates an *Ellipse* object, adds it to the *Canvas* child collection, and captures the mouse. The method also sets the *isDrawing* field to *true* so that all future event handlers know exactly what's going on.

Further processing occurs during the *OnMouseMove* override. I wanted the original mouse click to indicate the center of the circle, and for the perimeter to track the mouse cursor position as it's moved. This required recalculating the *Width* and *Height* properties as well as the *Canvas.LeftProperty* and *Canvas.RightProperty* attached properties. An alternative—more suitable for a rectangle than for a circle—would have been to assign the initial mouse position to one corner of the bounding rectangle and the current mouse position to the opposite corner. These are not necessarily the upper-left and lower-right corners because the user could move the mouse above or to the left of the original position.

In the *OnMouseUp* override, the first section applies to the drawing operation. The method now gives the ellipse a blue perimeter and a red interior. It sets *isDrawing* to *false* and releases the mouse capture. Releasing the mouse capture generates a call to the *OnLostMouseCapture*, but because *isDrawing* is already *false*, no further work is done here. But notice the *OnTextInput* override. If the user presses the Escape key and *isDrawing* is *true*, the method calls *ReleaseMouseCapture*. The resultant call to *OnLostMouseCapture* now has a little cleanup work to do in removing the *Ellipse* object from the *Canvas* child collection.

Pressing the right mouse button initiates a dragging operation. The *OnRightMouseButtonDown* method calls *InputHitTest* on the *Canvas* object to determine which element (if any) is underneath the mouse cursor. The method saves the mouse position and that element's position in fields. During subsequent calls to *OnMouseMove*, the program moves the ellipse. Because the mouse is not captured during this operation, if you move the mouse outside the window, the ellipse will stop moving. You can then release the mouse button and move the mouse back into the window, and the ellipse will resume following the mouse around even though the button is not pressed. It's not a serious problem, however. All you need to do is click with the right mouse button and the dragging operation concludes. In a real-world application, you'll want to capture the mouse during such a dragging operation.

Finally, clicking the middle button toggles the interior brush between *Brushes.Red* and *Brushes.Transparent*. I originally wrote this logic to set the *Fill* property of the *Ellipse* to *null* rather than *Brushes.Transparent*. The default *Fill* value is *null* anyway, so I knew it wouldn't cause a problem. However, with a *null* interior, you need to click the ellipse on the perimeter to get it to respond. You can no longer click in the interior to move it or even subsequently toggle the *Fill* brush.

This program is a good example of why it was necessary for the designers of the Windows Presentation Foundation to implement routed event handling. When you first start using the program, you're actually triggering events from the *Canvas* rather than from the *Window*. While it would have been easy enough to install event handlers for the *Canvas*, what happens after you've drawn a few circles? If you click an existing circle, the *Ellipse* object is now the source of the mouse event. In a nonrouted system, you'd need to force mouse events to the canvas, perhaps by setting the *IsEnabled* flag of the *Ellipse* to *false*. Routed events give you much more flexibility in how you structure your program.

If you're using a Tablet PC, all stylus input is converted to mouse events, so you can use the stylus with the DrawCircles program. But you may want to write code specifically for the Tablet PC. There are three general programming interfaces you can use.

The highest-level WPF programming interface to the Tablet PC is the *InkCanvas*, which sounds like a type of panel, but it's not. *InkCanvas* inherits from *FrameworkElement*, and implements ink rendering and retention. I mentioned earlier that stylus input is always converted to mouse input. *InkCanvas* goes in the other direction as well: It will respond to mouse input and treat it like stylus input. When you draw in the *InkCanvas* using the stylus or mouse, the *InkCanvas* draws the actual lines on its surface and saves them in its *Strokes* property as a collection of *Stroke* objects, which are basically polylines with drawing attributes attached. Each stroke consists of touching the stylus to the screen, moving it, and lifting the stylus from the screen. With the mouse, each stroke begins when the left mouse button is pressed and ends when the button is released. Chapter 22 has a sample program using *InkCanvas*.

The lowest-level WPF programming interface to the Tablet PC can be found in the *System-Windows.Input.StylusPlugins* namespace. Stylus plug-ins are classes that you write to render, modify, or store stylus input.

Between these two extremes is a collection of events defined by *UIElement* and *ContentElement* that begin with *Stylus* and *PreviewStylus*. These events are very similar to the mouse events, although the actual activity with the input device may be a little different. For example, a *MouseDown* event occurs when you press a mouse button; a *StylusDown* event occurs when you touch the stylus to the screen. The *StylusButtonDown* event refers not to pressing the stylus to the screen, but to the button on the side of the stylus that you press to change the meaning of the *StylusDown* event. (Perhaps with the stylus button depressed the stylus invokes a context menu.)

Here's a program that runs on the Tablet PC only. It creates two objects of type *Polyline* on receipt of a *StylusDown* event and adds these polylines to the *Canvas* child collection. (Like *Ellipse*, *Polyline* inherits from the *Shape* class.) The program captures the stylus and adds additional points to each of the two polylines during *StylusMove* events. The lines are terminated with a *StylusUp* event or a press of the Escape key.

The gimmick in this program is that the second polyline is drawn at an offset from the first one, resulting in a real-time drop-shadow effect. Notice that the *Points* collection of the foreground polyline always gets *ptStylus* while the shadow polyline gets *ptStylus* plus *vectShadow*.

ShadowTheStylus.cs

```
//-----------------------------------------------
// ShadowTheStylus.cs (c) 2006 by Charles Petzold
//-----------------------------------------------
using System;
using System.Windows;
using System.Windows.Controls;
using System.Windows.Input;
using System.Windows.Media;
using System.Windows.Shapes;
```

```
namespace Petzold.ShadowTheStylus
{
    public class ShadowTheStylus : Window
    {
        // Define some constants for the stylus polylines.
        static readonly SolidColorBrush brushStylus = Brushes.Blue;
        static readonly SolidColorBrush brushShadow = Brushes.LightBlue;
        static readonly double widthStroke = 96 / 2.54;        // 1 cm
        static readonly Vector vectShadow =
                        new Vector(widthStroke / 4, widthStroke / 4);

        // More fields for stylus-move operations.
        Canvas canv;
        Polyline polyStylus, polyShadow;
        bool isDrawing;

        [STAThread]
        public static void Main()
        {
            Application app = new Application();
            app.Run(new ShadowTheStylus());
        }
        public ShadowTheStylus()
        {
            Title = "Shadow the Stylus";

            // Create a Canvas for window content.
            canv = new Canvas();
            Content = canv;
        }
        protected override void OnStylusDown(StylusDownEventArgs args)
        {
            base.OnStylusDown(args);
            Point ptStylus = args.GetPosition(canv);

            // Create a Polyline with rounded ends and joins for the foreground.
            polyStylus = new Polyline();
            polyStylus.Stroke = brushStylus;
            polyStylus.StrokeThickness = widthStroke;
            polyStylus.StrokeStartLineCap = PenLineCap.Round;
            polyStylus.StrokeEndLineCap = PenLineCap.Round;
            polyStylus.StrokeLineJoin = PenLineJoin.Round;
            polyStylus.Points = new PointCollection();
            polyStylus.Points.Add(ptStylus);

            // Another Polyline for the shadow.
            polyShadow = new Polyline();
            polyShadow.Stroke = brushShadow;
            polyShadow.StrokeThickness = widthStroke;
            polyShadow.StrokeStartLineCap = PenLineCap.Round;
```

```
        polyShadow.StrokeEndLineCap = PenLineCap.Round;
        polyShadow.StrokeLineJoin = PenLineJoin.Round;
        polyShadow.Points = new PointCollection();
        polyShadow.Points.Add(ptStylus + vectShadow);

        // Insert shadow before all foreground polylines.
        canv.Children.Insert(canv.Children.Count / 2, polyShadow);

        // Foreground can go at end.
        canv.Children.Add(polyStylus);

        CaptureStylus();
        isDrawing = true;
        args.Handled = true;
    }
    protected override void OnStylusMove(StylusEventArgs args)
    {
        base.OnStylusMove(args);

        if (isDrawing)
        {
            Point ptStylus = args.GetPosition(canv);
            polyStylus.Points.Add(ptStylus);
            polyShadow.Points.Add(ptStylus + vectShadow);
            args.Handled = true;
        }
    }
    protected override void OnStylusUp(StylusEventArgs args)
    {
        base.OnStylusUp(args);

        if (isDrawing)
        {
            isDrawing = false;
            ReleaseStylusCapture();
            args.Handled = true;
        }
    }
    protected override void OnTextInput(TextCompositionEventArgs args)
    {
        base.OnTextInput(args);

        // End drawing with press of Escape key.
        if (isDrawing && args.Text.IndexOf('\x1B') != -1)
        {
            ReleaseStylusCapture();
            args.Handled = true;
        }
    }
    protected override void OnLostStylusCapture(StylusEventArgs args)
    {
        base.OnLostStylusCapture(args);
```

```
          // Abnormal end of drawing: Remove child shapes.
          if (isDrawing)
          {
              canv.Children.Remove(polyStylus);
              canv.Children.Remove(polyShadow);
              isDrawing = false;
          }
      }
    }
}
```

One of the key statements in this program occurs towards the end of the *OnStylusDown* method when the shadow polyline is added in the middle of the *Children* collection of the *Canvas*:

```
canv.Children.Insert(canv.Children.Count / 2, polyShadow);
```

In contrast, the foreground polyline is just added at the end:

```
canv.Children.Add(polyStylus);
```

Keep in mind that the *Children* collection is rendered in order, so that all the shadows are drawn first, followed by all the foreground lines. This is an excellent example of the convenience of retained graphics. Readers interested in how programmers managed similar jobs back in the dark ages of Windows Forms and the Tablet PC API might want to look at my online article "In Search of the Real-Time Drop Shadow" (*http://www.charlespetzold.com/etc/ RealTimeDropShadow*).

If you want to handle both mouse and stylus events such as *InkCanvas*, you'll probably need to distinguish whether a mouse event comes from actual mouse activity or is generated from the stylus. *MouseEventArgs* has a property named *StylusDevice*. If this property is *null*, the event came from the mouse. If it's an object of type *StylusDevice*, the event was generated by the stylus. *StylusEventArgs* has an identical property, so you can even identify a particular stylus device if the computer has more than one.

Much routine keyboard handling in a Windows Presentation Foundation application will probably be relegated to the *TextBox* and *RichTextBox* controls, or to controls such as *Scroll-Viewer* that can respond to some cursor movement keys. But there will be times when you'll need to look at keyboard input yourself.

An element or control is the source of a keyboard input event only if it has keyboard focus—that is, the *IsKeyboardFocused* property is *true*. Keyboard events are routed events, so all the ancestors in the tree of the focused element can participate in keyboard input. For these elements, the *IsKeyboardFocusedWithin* property is *true*.

To obtain keyboard focus, an element must have its *Focusable* property set to *true*. (Unlike the other keyboard-related properties, methods, and events, *Focusable* is defined by the *FrameworkElement* class.) The shift of input focus through the element tree is generally governed by the user clicking with the mouse or pressing the Tab or cursor-movement keys. (The *Control* class defines *IsTabStop* and *TabIndex* properties in connection with Tab navigation.) A program can set focus to a particular element by calling the *Focus* method for that element. A program can get more involved with focus navigation with the *MoveFocus* method defined by *FrameworkElement*.

When elements gain and lose keyboard focus, they generate *GotKeyboardFocus* and *LostKeyboardFocus* events. These are routed events, and both events also come in tunneling versions (*PreviewGotKeyboardFocus* and *PreviewLostKeyboardFocus*) so that all elements up the tree can become aware of a change in focus. The *Source* property of the event arguments always indicates the element gaining or losing the keyboard focus. The *KeyboardFocusedChangedEventArgs* class also defines two properties of type *IInputElement* named *OldFocus* and *NewFocus*.

Keyboard input is associated with three types of events that generally occur in this order:

- *KeyDown*: event arguments of type *KeyEventArgs*
- *TextInput*: event arguments of type *TextCompositionEventArgs*
- *KeyUp*: event argument of type *KeyEventArgs*

If you press a shift key or a function key or a cursor movement key, no *TextInput* event is generated. If you type a capital A by pressing the Shift key and then the A key, you'll get two *KeyDown* events, a *TextInput* event, and two more *KeyUp* events as you lift your fingers from the keys.

KeyEventArgs includes a property named *Key* that identifies the key involved in the event. *Key* is a member of the massive *Key* enumeration, which contains more than 200 members, many of them referring to keys I've never seen and hope to never see.

The following program can help you understand keyboard events by displaying the properties of the event arguments accompanying *KeyDown*, *TextInput*, and *KeyUp*.

```
ExamineKeystrokes.cs
//-----------------------------------------------
// ExamineKeystrokes.cs (c) 2006 by Charles Petzold
//-----------------------------------------------
using System;
using System.Windows;
using System.Windows.Controls;
using System.Windows.Input;
using System.Windows.Media;

namespace Petzold.ExamineKeystrokes
{
    class ExamineKeystrokes : Window
    {
        StackPanel stack;
        ScrollViewer scroll;
```

```
    string strHeader = "Event       Key                  Sys-Key   Text      " +
                       "Ctrl-Text Sys-Text  Ime           KeyStates       " +
                       "IsDown   IsUp    IsToggled IsRepeat ";
    string strFormatKey = "{0,-10}{1,-20}{2,-10}                           " +
                       "    {3,-10}{4,-15}{5,-8}{6,-7}{7,-10}{8,-10}";
    string strFormatText = "{0,-10}                                        " +
                       "{1,-10}{2,-10}{3,-10}";
    [STAThread]
    public static void Main()
    {
        Application app = new Application();
        app.Run(new ExamineKeystrokes());
    }
    public ExamineKeystrokes()
    {
        Title = "Examine Keystrokes";
        FontFamily = new FontFamily("Courier New");

        Grid grid = new Grid();
        Content = grid;

        // Make one row "auto" and the other fill the remaining space.
        RowDefinition rowdef = new RowDefinition();
        rowdef.Height = GridLength.Auto;
        grid.RowDefinitions.Add(rowdef);
        grid.RowDefinitions.Add(new RowDefinition());

        // Display header text.
        TextBlock textHeader = new TextBlock();
        textHeader.FontWeight = FontWeights.Bold;
        textHeader.Text = strHeader;
        grid.Children.Add(textHeader);

        // Create StackPanel as child of ScrollViewer for displaying events.
        scroll = new ScrollViewer();
        grid.Children.Add(scroll);
        Grid.SetRow(scroll, 1);

        stack = new StackPanel();
        scroll.Content = stack;
    }
    protected override void OnKeyDown(KeyEventArgs args)
    {
        base.OnKeyDown(args);
        DisplayKeyInfo(args);
    }
    protected override void OnKeyUp(KeyEventArgs args)
    {
        base.OnKeyUp(args);
        DisplayKeyInfo(args);
    }
    protected override void OnTextInput(TextCompositionEventArgs args)
    {
        base.OnTextInput(args);
```

```
            string str =
                String.Format(strFormatText, args.RoutedEvent.Name, args.Text,
                                    args.ControlText, args.SystemText);
            DisplayInfo(str);
        }
        void DisplayKeyInfo(KeyEventArgs args)
        {
            string str =
                String.Format(strFormatKey, args.RoutedEvent.Name, args.Key,
                        args.SystemKey, args.ImeProcessedKey, args.KeyStates,
                        args.IsDown, args.IsUp, args.IsToggled, args.IsRepeat);
            DisplayInfo(str);
        }
        void DisplayInfo(string str)
        {
            TextBlock text = new TextBlock();
            text.Text = str;
            stack.Children.Add(text);
            scroll.ScrollToBottom();
        }
    }
}
```

It's also possible to get keyboard information apart from the events. The *Keyboard* class has a static property named *PrimaryDevice* that is of type *KeyboardDevice*, and *KeyboardDevice* has methods to get the state of every key on the keyboard.

Several of the programs in the following two chapters show keyboard and mouse handling in the context of actual classes. The *MedievalButton* class in Chapter 10 and the *RoundedButton* class in Chapter 11 mimic the handling of mouse and keyboard input in normal buttons. The CalculateInHex program and *ColorGrid* control in Chapter 11 both illustrate common keyboard and mouse handling.

Chapter 10
Custom Elements

Normally a chapter such as this would be titled "Custom Controls," but in the Windows Presentation Foundation the distinction between elements and controls is rather amorphous. Even if you mostly create custom controls rather than elements, you'll probably also be using custom elements in constructing those controls. This chapter and the next two show mostly those techniques for creating custom elements and controls that are best suited for procedural code such as C#. In Part 2 of this book, you'll learn about alternative ways to create custom controls using XAML, and also about styling and template features that can help you customize controls.

When creating a custom element, you'll almost certainly be inheriting from *Framework-Element*, just like *Image*, *Panel*, *TextBlock*, and *Shape* do. (You could alternatively inherit from *UIElement*, but the process is somewhat different than what I'll be describing.) When creating a custom control, you'll probably inherit from *Control* or (if you're lucky) from one of the classes that derive from *Control* such as *ContentControl*.

When faced with the job of designing a new element, the question poses itself: Should you inherit from *FrameworkElement* or *Control*? Object-oriented design philosophy suggests that you should inherit from the lowest class in the hierarchy that provides what you need. For some classes, that will obviously be *FrameworkElement*. However, the *Control* class adds several important properties to *FrameworkElement* that you might want: These properties include *Background*, *Foreground*, and all the font-related properties. Certainly if you'll be displaying text, these properties are very handy. But *Control* also adds some properties that you might prefer to ignore but which you'll probably feel obligated to implement: *HorizontalContentAlignment*, *VerticalContentAlignment*, *BorderBrush*, *BorderThickness*, and *Padding*. For example, if you inherit from *Control*, and if horizontal and vertical content alignment potentially make a difference in how you display the contents of the control, you should probably do something with the *HorizontalContentAlignment* and *VerticalContent-Alignment* properties.

The property that offers the biggest hint concerning the difference between elements and controls is *Focusable*. Although *FrameworkElement* defines this property, the default value is *false*. The *Control* class redefines the default to *true*, strongly suggesting that controls are elements that can receive keyboard input focus. Although you can certainly inherit from *FrameworkElement* and set *Focusable* to *true*, or inherit from *Control* and set *Focusable* to *false* (as several controls do), it's an interesting and convenient way to distinguish elements and controls.

At the end of Chapter 3, I presented a program called RenderTheGraphic that included a class that inherited from *FrameworkElement*. Here's that class:

```
SimpleEllipse.cs
//---------------------------------------------------
// SimpleEllipse.cs (c) 2006 by Charles Petzold
//---------------------------------------------------
using System;
using System.Windows;
using System.Windows.Media;

namespace Petzold.RenderTheGraphic
{
    class SimpleEllipse : FrameworkElement
    {
        protected override void OnRender(DrawingContext dc)
        {
            dc.DrawEllipse(Brushes.Blue, new Pen(Brushes.Red, 24),
                new Point(RenderSize.Width / 2, RenderSize.Height / 2),
                RenderSize.Width / 2, RenderSize.Height / 2);
        }
    }
}
```

The virtual *OnRender* method is defined by *UIElement*. The single argument is an object of type *DrawingContext*. (Old-time Windows programmers like me will find it hard to resist naming this object *dc* in honor of the Device Context used for drawing in Win16 and Win32 programs. Both DCs serve similar purposes, although they are certainly not functionally equivalent.) The *DrawingContext* class defines a collection of drawing methods that represent the lowest-level drawing you can do and still call your code a "pure WPF application." I'll discuss a couple of these methods in the next two chapters but use others later in this book.

Code in the *OnRender* method should assume a drawing surface that has an origin of (0,0) with a width and height given by the dimensions of the *RenderSize* property (also defined by *UIElement*). In the *OnRender* method in the *SimpleEllipse* class, the first argument to *Draw-Ellipse* is a blue brush to fill the interior of the ellipse and the second argument is a 24-unit-wide (quarter inch) red pen used to stroke the perimeter of the ellipse. The third argument is a *Point* object indicating the center of the ellipse, and the final two arguments are the horizontal and vertical radii.

Of course, what a program draws in its *OnRender* method does not go directly to the screen. The graphical object defined in *OnRender* is retained by the WPF graphics system and displayed along with other visual objects in a composition. The graphical object is retained until a subsequent call to *OnRender* replaces it. Calls to *OnRender* can occur any time the system detects a need to update the visual rendition of the element. This generally happens much less often than WM_PAINT messages in Win32 or *Paint* events in Windows Forms programs, however, because the graphics are retained. *OnRender* needn't be called when a visual object is exposed while moving another window, for example. But *OnRender* is called if the element size changes. An explicit call to the *InvalidateVisual* method (defined by *UIElement*) can also force a call to *OnRender*.

The graphical object that *OnRender* draws also plays a role in the processing of mouse events. For example, if you draw an ellipse with a *null* interior brush, the interior will not respond to the mouse.

An *OnRender* method typically uses the *RenderSize* property for drawing, or at least to determine the dimensions in which to draw. Where does this property come from? As you'll see in more detail in this chapter and the next, *RenderSize* is calculated by *UIElement* based on a number of factors. The dimensions of *RenderSize* are duplicated in the protected *ActualWidth* and *ActualHeight* properties of the element.

If you go back and experiment with the RenderTheGraphic program—or recall much of the experimentation with element size in the early chapters—you'll see that *RenderSize* is most obviously related to the size of the container in which the element appears. In the RenderThe-Graphic program, this container is the client area of the window. But other factors can affect *RenderSize*. If you set the *Margin* property for the ellipse, *RenderSize* is reduced by the margin values.

If a program explicitly sets the *Width* or *Height* properties for the element, these properties take priority over the container size in the calculation of *RenderSize*. If *Width* is set to a value other than NaN (not a number), *RenderSize.Width* will equal *Width*, and that's the width *OnRender* uses to draw the ellipse. If the container is then made narrower than *Width*, part of the ellipse is truncated. If a program sets *MinWidth*, *MaxWidth*, *MinHeight*, or *MaxHeight*, the element is displayed with the *MaxWidth* or *MaxHeight* dimensions if the container is larger than those dimensions. If the container is smaller than *MaxWidth* or *MaxHeight*, the container size governs the element size. But if the container gets smaller than *MinWidth* or *MinHeight*, the ellipse stops decreasing in size and part of it is truncated.

The size of elements is also influenced by their *HorizontalAlignment* and *VerticalAlignment* properties. Try setting these properties in RenderTheGraphic:

```
elips.HorizontalAlignment = HorizontalAlignment.Center;
elips.VerticalAlignment = VerticalAlignment.Center;
```

You'll see the ellipse collapse into a tiny ball a quarter inch in diameter. What's happened here is that *RenderSize* now has *Width* and *Height* properties of zero, and the only thing visible is part of the quarter-inch-thick perimeter around the ellipse.

Despite zero dimensions, the figure is still somewhat visible because of the logic *DrawEllipse* uses to render the line drawn as the perimeter around the ellipse. This line is geometrically positioned based on the center and radius values passed to the *DrawEllipse* method. However, if this perimeter has a width of 24 units, the quarter-inch-wide line around the ellipse actually straddles the geometric circumference of the ellipse. Half the line falls inside the geometric circumference of the ellipse and half falls outside. You can see this in a couple of ways. If you remove all extra code from RenderTheGraphic, you'll see that half the perimeter is cut off on the four sides of the client area. Now try setting the size of the ellipse like this:

```
elips.Width = 26;
elips.Height = 26;
```

The ellipse you'll see will have a tiny dot in the center and a 24-unit-wide red perimeter. The actual displayed size of the ellipse is 50 units wide and 50 units high—the 26 specified in the *Width* and *Height* properties plus 12 more on each side for the line around the perimeter.

This *SimpleEllipse* class is perhaps a first step in creating something very much like the *Ellipse* class from the Shapes library. What more would need to be done in such a class?

Most important, you'd need to define some dependency properties for the brushes used for filling and stroking the ellipse, and for the thickness of the perimeter. You might also consider making some adjustments so that the display of the ellipse more closely mimics the actual *Ellipse* method. You can analyze that behavior by going back to the ShapeTheEllipse program, also presented in Chapter 3. Here's what you'll find:

- When the ellipse occupies the full size of the client area, none of the perimeter is clipped.

- To get the same type of image you saw when you set the *Width* and *Height* properties of *SimpleEllipse* to 26 in RenderTheGraphic, you need to set both the *Width* and *Height* properties of the regular *Ellipse* equal to 50.

- However, when you set *HorizontalAlignment* and *VerticalAlignment* of the ellipse to *Center*, the regular *Ellipse* object collapses into a quarter-inch ball—exactly the same size as *SimpleEllipse*.

It is very common for elements to provide some indication of their preferred size, but this is something that *SimpleEllipse* isn't doing, and that's somewhat unusual. Almost always, an element needs a particular minimum size in which to display itself. *TextBlock*, for example, needs to be able to display its text. An element's minimum preferred size is sometimes known as a *desired size*.

A custom element class should *not* use any of the public properties to define its own desired size. A custom element class should *not* set its *Width*, *Height*, *MinWidth*, *MaxWidth*, *MinHeight*, or *MaxHeight* properties. These properties are for use by *consumers* of the class—classes that instantiate your custom element class—and you should let those consumers do what they want with these properties.

Instead, a custom element class declares its desired size by overriding the *MeasureOverride* method defined by *FrameworkElement*. The *MeasureOverride* method surely has a peculiar name, and there's a reason for it. *MeasureOverride* is similar to a method defined by *UIElement* named *MeasureCore*. *FrameworkElement* redefines *MeasureCore* as sealed, which means that classes that inherit from *FrameworkElement* cannot override it. *FrameworkElement* instead defines *MeasureOverride* as a substitute for *MeasureCore*. *FrameworkElement* requires a different approach to element sizing than *UIElement* because of the inclusion of the *Margin* property. The element requires space for its margin but doesn't actually use that space for itself.

A class that inherits from *FrameworkElement* overrides *MeasureOverride* like so:

```
protected override Size MeasureOverride(Size sizeAvailable)
{
    Size sizeDesired;
    ...
    return sizeDesired;
}
```

A call to *MeasureOverride* always precedes the first call to *OnRender*. Thereafter, there may be additional calls to *OnRender* if the element needs to be refreshed but nothing has happened to affect the element's size. A program can force a call to *MeasureOverride* by calling *Invalidate-Measure* for the element.

The *sizeAvailable* argument indicates the size being made available to the element. The *Width* and *Height* dimensions of this *Size* object can range from 0 to positive infinity.

For example, in a window that just sets its *Content* property to the element, *sizeAvailable* is simply the client size of the window. However, if the window sets its *SizeToContent* property equal to *SizeToContent.WidthAndHeight*, the *sizeAvailable* argument will have a *Width* and *Height* set to *Double.PositiveInfinity* under the assumption that the window can grow to whatever size the element needs. If a window has *SizeToContent* set to *SizeToContent.Width* (for example), *sizeAvailable.Width* will equal infinity, and *sizeAvailable.Height* will be the height of the client area. (However, if the user then changes the size of the window by dragging the sizing border, *sizeAvailable* reverts to the actual client area size.)

Suppose the element is a child of a *StackPanel* with a default vertical orientation. In that case, *sizeAvailable.Width* will be the width of the *StackPanel* (which, of course, will normally be the width of its container) and *sizeAvailable.Height* will be infinity.

Suppose the element is a child of a *Grid*, and the element is in a column that has a *GridLength* of 300 pixels. Then *sizeAvailable.Width* will equal 300. If the width of the column has been set to *GridLength.Auto*, *sizeAvailable.Width* will be infinity because the column will grow in size to accommodate the element. If the width is a *GridLength* of *GridUnitType.Star*, *sizeAvailable.Width* will indicate some portion of the leftover width being made available to this column.

If the *Margin* property of the element has been set, some space is required for that margin and less size is available to the element itself. The *sizeAvailable.Width* property is reduced by the sum of the *Left* and *Right* properties of the margin, and *sizeAvailable.Height* is reduced by the sum of the *Top* and *Bottom* properties. Of course, dimensions that start out as infinity will remain infinite regardless of the margins. The dimensions of *sizeAvailable* will always be non-negative.

Everything I've said in the past four paragraphs has to be modified if any of the following properties of the element have been set: *Width, MinWidth, MaxWidth, Height, MinHeight, MaxHeight*. These are properties being imposed on the element by a consumer of the element. Recall that these properties have default values of NaN. Only if a program sets these properties will they have some effect on the sizing and layout of the element.

If *Width* is set, the *sizeAvailable.Width* argument will equal *Width*, and similarly for *Height*. Alternatively, if *MinWidth* is set, *sizeAvailable.Width* will be greater than or equal to *MinWidth* (which means that it could still be infinity). If *MaxWidth* is set, *sizeAvailable.Width* will be less than or equal to *MaxWidth*.

The class should use its override of the *MeasureOverride* method to indicate an appropriate "natural" size of the element. Such a natural size is most obvious in the case of *TextBlock* or an *Image* element displaying a bitmap in its metrical size. If there is no natural size for the element, the element should return its minimum acceptable size. This minimum acceptable size could well be zero, or it could be something quite small.

If you don't override *MeasureOverride*, the base implementation in *FrameworkElement* returns zero. Returning zero from *MeasureOverride* does not mean that your element will be rendered at that size! This should be obvious from the RenderTheEllipse program, which displays a satisfactory ellipse in most cases even though *SimpleEllipse* doesn't override *MeasureOverride* and lets the base implementation return zero.

What mostly prevents elements from being rendered with a zero size are the default *Horizontal-Alignment* and *VerticalAlignment* settings of *Stretch*. The *sizeAvailable* argument to *Measure-Override* does not reflect any alignment settings, but the calculation of the *RenderSize* property takes account of them.

If you're defining just a simple element without children—as you'll see in the next chapter, everything changes when you have children—your *MeasureOverride* method quite possibly doesn't even need to examine the *sizeAvailable* argument. An exception is when your element needs to maintain a particular aspect ratio. For example, the *Image* class returns a value from *MeasureOverride* based on the size of the bitmap it needs to display and its *Stretch* property, which indicates how the bitmap is to be displayed. If *Stretch* equals *Stretch.None, MeasureOverride* in *Image* returns the metrical size of the bitmap. For *Stretch.Uniform* (the default setting), *MeasureOverride* uses the *sizeAvailable* argument to calculate a size that maintains the correct aspect ratio but has one dimension equaling either the *Width* or *Height* dimension of *sizeAvailable*. If one of the dimensions of *sizeAvailable* is *Infinity*, it uses the other dimension of *sizeAvailable* to compute a displayed size of the image. If both are infinity, *MeasureOverride* returns the metrical size of the bitmap. For *Stretch.Fill, MeasureOverride* simply returns the *sizeAvailable* argument unless one or both of the properties are infinity, in which case it falls back on the logic in *Stretch.Uniform*.

But *Image* is really an exception. Most elements that don't have a natural size should return zero or a small value. *MeasureOverride* must not return a *Size* object with a dimension of infinity even if the argument to *MeasureOverride* has an infinite dimension or two. (When I tried it, the *InvalidOperationException* message said exactly that: the element "should not return PositiveInfinity as its DesiredSize, even if Infinity is passed in as available size. Please fix the implementation of this override.")

An element should not attempt to take account of its *Width* and *Height* (and related properties) while processing the *MeasureOverride* method. These properties have already been taken into account when *MeasureOverride* is called. As I mentioned earlier, an element should not set its own *Width* and *Height* properties. These properties are for consumers of the element.

The regular *Ellipse* class from the Shapes library (or, more accurately, the *Shape* class from which *Ellipse* derives) processes the *MeasureOverride* method by returning a *Size* object with its dimensions set to the value of its *Thickness* property, which is usually a small number.

Here's a class that comes much closer to the behavior of *Ellipse*.

BetterEllipse.cs

```
//-----------------------------------------------
// BetterEllipse.cs (c) 2006 by Charles Petzold
//-----------------------------------------------
using System;
using System.Windows;
using System.Windows.Controls;
using System.Windows.Input;
using System.Windows.Media;

namespace Petzold.RenderTheBetterEllipse
{
    public class BetterEllipse : FrameworkElement
    {
        // Dependency properties.
        public static readonly DependencyProperty FillProperty;
        public static readonly DependencyProperty StrokeProperty;

        // Public interfaces to dependency properties.
        public Brush Fill
        {
            set { SetValue(FillProperty, value); }
            get { return (Brush)GetValue(FillProperty); }
        }
        public Pen Stroke
        {
            set { SetValue(StrokeProperty, value); }
            get { return (Pen)GetValue(StrokeProperty); }
        }
        // Static constructor.
        static BetterEllipse()
        {
            FillProperty =
                DependencyProperty.Register("Fill", typeof(Brush),
                    typeof(BetterEllipse), new FrameworkPropertyMetadata(null,
                        FrameworkPropertyMetadataOptions.AffectsRender));
```

```
            StrokeProperty =
                DependencyProperty.Register("Stroke", typeof(Pen),
                        typeof(BetterEllipse), new FrameworkPropertyMetadata(null,
                                FrameworkPropertyMetadataOptions.AffectsMeasure));
    }
    // Override of MeasureOverride.
    protected override Size MeasureOverride(Size sizeAvailable)
    {
        Size sizeDesired = base.MeasureOverride(sizeAvailable);

        if (Stroke != null)
            sizeDesired = new Size(Stroke.Thickness, Stroke.Thickness);

        return sizeDesired;
    }
    // Override of OnRender.
    protected override void OnRender(DrawingContext dc)
    {
        Size size = RenderSize;

        // Adjust rendering size for width of Pen.
        if (Stroke != null)
        {
            size.Width = Math.Max(0, size.Width - Stroke.Thickness);
            size.Height = Math.Max(0, size.Height - Stroke.Thickness);
        }

        // Draw the ellipse.
        dc.DrawEllipse(Fill, Stroke,
            new Point(RenderSize.Width / 2, RenderSize.Height / 2),
            size.Width / 2, size.Height / 2);
    }
  }
}
```

If you examine the regular *Shape* class, you'll see that it defines a bunch of properties begin-ning with the word *Stroke* that govern the appearance of lines such as the *Ellipse* perimeter. Rather than implement all these various *Stroke* properties in my class, I decided to define just one property named *Stroke* of type *Pen*, because the *Pen* class basically encapsulates all the properties that *Shape* explicitly defines. Notice that *MeasureOverride* returns a size based on the thickness of the *Pen* object (but only if the *Pen* actually exists), and *OnRender* decreases the size of the ellipse radii by the *Thickness* property.

I decided that *Fill* and *Stroke* should be backed with the dependency properties *FillProperty* and *StrokeProperty* so that the class would be ready for animation. Notice the definition of the *FrameworkPropertyMetadata* in the static constructor: The *Fill* property has a flag of *AffectsRender* and the *Stroke* property has a flag of *AffectsMeasure*. When the *Fill* property is changed, the *InvalidateVisual* method is effectively called, which generates a new call to *OnRender*. But a change to the *Stroke* property effectively causes *InvalidateMeasure* to be called, which generates a call to *MeasureOverride*, which is then followed by a call to *OnRender*. The difference is that the size of the element as indicated in *MeasureOverride* is affected by the *Pen* but not by the *Brush*.

As you'll see when you run the RenderTheBetterEllipse program, the ellipse perimeter fits entirely in the window's client area.

```
RenderTheBetterEllipse.cs
//----------------------------------------------------------
// RenderTheBetterEllipse.cs (c) 2006 by Charles Petzold
//----------------------------------------------------------
using System;
using System.Windows;
using System.Windows.Controls;
using System.Windows.Input;
using System.Windows.Media;

namespace Petzold.RenderTheBetterEllipse
{
    public class RenderTheBetterEllipse : Window
    {
        [STAThread]
        public static void Main()
        {
            Application app = new Application();
            app.Run(new RenderTheBetterEllipse());
        }
        public RenderTheBetterEllipse()
        {
            Title = "Render the Better Ellipse";

            BetterEllipse elips = new BetterEllipse();
            elips.Fill = Brushes.AliceBlue;
            elips.Stroke = new Pen(
                new LinearGradientBrush(Colors.CadetBlue, Colors.Chocolate,
                                        new Point(1, 0), new Point(0, 1)),
                24);        // 1/4 inch

            Content = elips;
        }
    }
}
```

Now suppose you want to add code to *BetterEllipse* to display some text centered within the element. Because you've already implemented the *MeasureOverride* and *OnRender* methods, you might feel inclined to simply add some code to the *OnRender* method to call the *DrawText* method of *DrawingContext*. By itself, the *DrawText* method looks fairly simple:

```
dc.DrawText(formtxt, pt);
```

The second argument is a *Point* where the text is to begin. (By default, the text origin for English and other western languages is the upper-left corner of the text.) However, the first argument to *DrawText* is an object of type *FormattedText*, and that one's a real doozy. The simplest of its two constructors has six arguments. The first argument is a text string, and the arguments go on to include information about the display characteristics of this string. One of these arguments is a *Typeface* object, which you can create like this:

```
new Typeface(new FontFamily("Times New Roman"), FontStyles.Italic,
             FontWeights.Normal, FontStretches.Normal)
```

Or like this, which is somewhat easier:

```
new Typeface("Times New Roman Italic");
```

But *FormattedText* is more versatile than the constructors imply. The *FormattedText* object is capable of having different formatting applied to different parts of the text. Methods defined by *FormattedText*, such as *SetFontSize* and *SetFontStyle*, have versions to specify an offset into the text string and a number of characters to apply the formatting.

At any rate, you could add a little text to the *BetterEllipse* method by inserting the following code at the end of the *OnRender* method:

```
FormattedText formtxt =
    new FormattedText("Hello, ellipse!", CultureInfo.CurrentCulture, FlowDirection,
                      new Typeface("Times New Roman Italic"), 24,
                      Brushes.DarkBlue);

Point ptText = new Point((RenderSize.Width - formtxt.Width) / 2,
                         (RenderSize.Height - formtxt.Height) / 2);

dc.DrawText(formtxt, ptText);
```

You'll need a *using* directive for *System.Globalization* to reference the static *CultureInfo.Current-Culture* property. Conveniently, *FlowDirection* is a property of *FrameworkElement*. The calculations involved in *ptText* determine the upper-left corner of the text, assuming that it is positioned in the center of the ellipse.

You'll certainly want to make sure this code goes *after* the *DrawEllipse* call. Otherwise the ellipse will be visually on top of the text and at least part of the text will be hidden behind the ellipse. Even if the text is in the foreground, there are problems when you give the ellipse a small size:

```
elips.Width = 50;
```

In this case it's likely the text will exceed the dimensions of the ellipse. As you'll note if you actually add this code and try it out, *OnRender* will not clip the text to the dimensions of *RenderSize*. *OnRender* only performs clipping if either dimension of the *sizeDesired* return value from *MeasureOverride* exceeds the corresponding dimension of the *sizeAvailable* argument to *MeasureOverride*. Clipping is based on *sizeAvailable*. If an *OnRender* method itself wants to prevent graphics from spilling over the dimensions of *RenderSize*, it can set a clipping region for the *DrawingContext*:

```
dc.PushClip(new RectangleGeometry(new Rect(new Point(0, 0), RenderSize)));
```

But what the class really needs to be doing is determining *FormattedText* before or during the *MeasureOverride* call. *MeasureOverride* can then take account of the text size in determining the desired size of the element.

Of course, in creating this hypothetical "ellipse with embedded text" class, measuring the string is just the first step. You'll probably want to define properties not only for the text, but also for all the font properties required by *FormattedText*.

Rather than trying to stuff text into an ellipse, however, let's instead put text inside something a little more conventional, like a button. A class that inherits from *Control* (as a button probably will) has access to all the font properties defined by *Control*. These can be passed directly to the *FormattedText* constructor.

Here's a class named *MedievalButton* that inherits from *Control* to define a button that displays text. The class includes a *Text* property so a program can set the text that the button displays, and the property is backed by the dependency property *TextProperty*. The class also defines two *Click*-like routed events named *Knock* and *PreviewKnock*. (The code I showed in Chapter 9 for the *Knock* and *PreviewKnock* events originated in this code.)

Although this class may seem very modern in its implementation of a dependency property and routed input events, I call this class a *medieval* button because it draws itself entirely in its *OnRender* method. As you'll see, better techniques exist for defining custom and controls.

MedievalButton.cs

```
//------------------------------------------------
// MedievalButton.cs (c) 2006 by Charles Petzold
//------------------------------------------------
using System;
using System.Globalization;
using System.Windows;
using System.Windows.Controls;
using System.Windows.Input;
using System.Windows.Media;

namespace Petzold.GetMedieval
{
    public class MedievalButton : Control
    {
        // Just two private fields.
        FormattedText formtxt;
        bool isMouseReallyOver;

        // Static readonly fields.
        public static readonly DependencyProperty TextProperty;
        public static readonly RoutedEvent KnockEvent;
        public static readonly RoutedEvent PreviewKnockEvent;

        // Static constructor.
        static MedievalButton()
        {
```

```
        // Register dependency property.
        TextProperty =
            DependencyProperty.Register("Text", typeof(string),
                                        typeof(MedievalButton),
                new FrameworkPropertyMetadata(" ",
                        FrameworkPropertyMetadataOptions.AffectsMeasure));

        // Register routed events.
        KnockEvent =
            EventManager.RegisterRoutedEvent("Knock", RoutingStrategy.Bubble,
                    typeof(RoutedEventHandler), typeof(MedievalButton));

        PreviewKnockEvent =
            EventManager.RegisterRoutedEvent("PreviewKnock",
                    RoutingStrategy.Tunnel,
                    typeof(RoutedEventHandler), typeof(MedievalButton));
    }
    // Public interface to dependency property.
    public string Text
    {
        set { SetValue(TextProperty, value == null ? " " : value); }
        get { return (string)GetValue(TextProperty); }
    }
    // Public interface to routed events.
    public event RoutedEventHandler Knock
    {
        add { AddHandler(KnockEvent, value); }
        remove { RemoveHandler(KnockEvent, value); }
    }
    public event RoutedEventHandler PreviewKnock
    {
        add { AddHandler(PreviewKnockEvent, value); }
        remove { RemoveHandler(PreviewKnockEvent, value); }
    }
    // MeasureOverride called whenever the size of the button might change.
    protected override Size MeasureOverride(Size sizeAvailable)
    {
        formtxt = new FormattedText(
                Text, CultureInfo.CurrentCulture, FlowDirection,
                new Typeface(FontFamily, FontStyle, FontWeight, FontStretch),
                FontSize, Foreground);

        // Take account of Padding when calculating the size.
        Size sizeDesired = new Size(Math.Max(48, formtxt.Width) + 4,
                                            formtxt.Height + 4);
        sizeDesired.Width += Padding.Left + Padding.Right;
        sizeDesired.Height += Padding.Top + Padding.Bottom;

        return sizeDesired;
    }
    // OnRender called to redraw the button.
    protected override void OnRender(DrawingContext dc)
    {
        // Determine background color.
        Brush brushBackground = SystemColors.ControlBrush;
```

```
        if (isMouseReallyOver && IsMouseCaptured)
            brushBackground = SystemColors.ControlDarkBrush;

        // Determine pen width.
        Pen pen = new Pen(Foreground, IsMouseOver ? 2 : 1);

        // Draw filled rounded rectangle.
        dc.DrawRoundedRectangle(brushBackground, pen,
                              new Rect(new Point(0, 0), RenderSize), 4, 4);

        // Determine foreground color.
        formtxt.SetForegroundBrush(
                IsEnabled ? Foreground : SystemColors.ControlDarkBrush);

        // Determine start point of text.
        Point ptText = new Point(2, 2);

        switch (HorizontalContentAlignment)
        {
            case HorizontalAlignment.Left:
                ptText.X += Padding.Left;
                break;

            case HorizontalAlignment.Right:
                ptText.X += RenderSize.Width - formtxt.Width - Padding.Right;
                break;

            case HorizontalAlignment.Center:
            case HorizontalAlignment.Stretch:
                ptText.X += (RenderSize.Width - formtxt.Width -
                        Padding.Left - Padding.Right) / 2;
                break;
        }
        switch (VerticalContentAlignment)
        {
            case VerticalAlignment.Top:
                ptText.Y += Padding.Top;
                break;

            case VerticalAlignment.Bottom:
                ptText.Y +=
                    RenderSize.Height - formtxt.Height - Padding.Bottom;
                break;

            case VerticalAlignment.Center:
            case VerticalAlignment.Stretch:
                ptText.Y += (RenderSize.Height - formtxt.Height -
                        Padding.Top - Padding.Bottom) / 2;
                break;
        }
        // Draw the text.
        dc.DrawText(formtxt, ptText);
}
// Mouse events that affect the visual look of the button.
protected override void OnMouseEnter(MouseEventArgs args)
```

```csharp
        {
            base.OnMouseEnter(args);
            InvalidateVisual();
        }
        protected override void OnMouseLeave(MouseEventArgs args)
        {
            base.OnMouseLeave(args);
            InvalidateVisual();
        }
        protected override void OnMouseMove(MouseEventArgs args)
        {
            base.OnMouseMove(args);

            // Determine if mouse has really moved inside or out.
            Point pt = args.GetPosition(this);
            bool isReallyOverNow = (pt.X >= 0 && pt.X < ActualWidth &&
                                    pt.Y >= 0 && pt.Y < ActualHeight);
            if (isReallyOverNow != isMouseReallyOver)
            {
                isMouseReallyOver = isReallyOverNow;
                InvalidateVisual();
            }
        }
        // This is the start of how 'Knock' events are triggered.
        protected override void OnMouseLeftButtonDown(MouseButtonEventArgs args)
        {
            base.OnMouseLeftButtonDown(args);
            CaptureMouse();
            InvalidateVisual();
            args.Handled = true;
        }
        // This event actually triggers the 'Knock' event.
        protected override void OnMouseLeftButtonUp(MouseButtonEventArgs args)
        {
            base.OnMouseLeftButtonUp(args);

            if (IsMouseCaptured)
            {
                if (isMouseReallyOver)
                {
                    OnPreviewKnock();
                    OnKnock();
                }
                args.Handled = true;
                Mouse.Capture(null);
            }
        }
        // If lose mouse capture (either internally or externally), redraw.
        protected override void OnLostMouseCapture(MouseEventArgs args)
        {
            base.OnLostMouseCapture(args);
            InvalidateVisual();
        }
        // The keyboard Space key or Enter also triggers the button.
        protected override void OnKeyDown(KeyEventArgs args)
```

```
    {
        base.OnKeyDown(args);
        if (args.Key == Key.Space || args.Key == Key.Enter)
            args.Handled = true;
    }
    protected override void OnKeyUp(KeyEventArgs args)
    {
        base.OnKeyUp(args);
        if (args.Key == Key.Space || args.Key == Key.Enter)
        {
            OnPreviewKnock();
            OnKnock();
            args.Handled = true;
        }
    }
    // OnKnock method raises the 'Knock' event.
    protected virtual void OnKnock()
    {
        RoutedEventArgs argsEvent = new RoutedEventArgs();
        argsEvent.RoutedEvent = MedievalButton.PreviewKnockEvent;
        argsEvent.Source = this;
        RaiseEvent(argsEvent);
    }
    // OnPreviewKnock method raises the 'PreviewKnock' event.
    protected virtual void OnPreviewKnock()
    {
        RoutedEventArgs argsEvent = new RoutedEventArgs();
        argsEvent.RoutedEvent = MedievalButton.KnockEvent;
        argsEvent.Source = this;
        RaiseEvent(argsEvent);
    }
}
}
```

Although this class surely has many methods (most of which are overrides of methods defined in *UIElement* or *FrameworkElement*), not much in this class should be new to you. The static constructor registers the *Text* dependency property and the *Knock* and *PreviewKnock* routed events, and public properties and events are defined immediately following the static constructor.

The *MeasureOverride* method creates an object of type *FormattedText* and stores it as a field. Notice that almost every argument to *FormattedText*—and to the *Typeface* constructor that is the fourth argument to *FormattedText*—is a property defined by *FrameworkElement*, *Control*, or (in the case of the *Text* property) *MedievalButton* itself. The *FormattedText* constructor may look scary, but it's easy to fill up in a class that inherits from *Control*.

The *MeasureOverride* method concludes by calculating a desired size of the button. This size is the width and height of the formatted text, plus 4 units to accommodate a border. To prevent a short text string from resulting in a tiny button, the button width is minimized at a half inch. The *MeasureOverride* method concludes by taking account of the *Padding* property defined by *Control*.

The *MeasureOverride* method should not try to account for the element's *Margin* property, *HorizontalAlignment*, or *VerticalAlignment*. If the control wishes to implement its *BorderBrush* and *BorderThickness* properties, it can do so, but these properties have no effect otherwise. A control that implements these properties would probably treat the *BorderThickness* dimensions the same way I've treated the border thickness in *MedievalButton*.

OnRender draws the button. The only two drawing calls are *DrawRoundedRectangle* to draw the button border and background, and *DrawText* to display the text inside the button, but much preliminary work needs to be done to determine the actual colors and locations of these items.

The background of the brush should be a little darker when the button has been pressed and the mouse pointer is still positioned over the button. The outline of the button should be a little thicker (I decided) when the mouse pointer is over the button. The text normally has a color based on the *Foreground* property defined by *Control*, but it should be different if the button is disabled. The two *switch* statements calculate a starting position of the text based on *HorizontalContentAlignment*, *VerticalContentAlignment*, and *Padding*. Notice that the *Point* object named *ptText* is initialized to the point (2, 2) to allow room for the border drawn by the *Rectangle* call.

The remainder of the class handles input events. For *OnMouseEnter* and *OnMouseLeave*, all that's necessary is a call to *InvalidateVisual* so that the button is redrawn. I had originally intended for *OnRender* to use the *IsMouseOver* property to determine if the mouse was positioned over the button. However, if the mouse is captured, *IsMouseOver* returns *true* regardless of the position of the mouse. To allow *OnRender* to correctly color the button background, the *OnMouseMove* override calculates the value of a field I called *isMouseReallyOver*.

During the *OnMouseLeftButtonDown* call, the class captures the mouse, invalidates the appearance of the button, and sets the *Handled* property of *MouseButtonEventArgs* to *true*. Setting *Handled* to *true* prevents the *MouseLeftButtonDown* event from bubbling back up the visual tree to the window. It's consistent with the way that the regular *Button* class handles *Click* events.

The *OnMouseLeftButtonUp* call effectively fires the *PreviewKnock* and *Knock* events in that order by calling *OnPreviewKnock* and *OnKnock*. I patterned these two latter methods on the protected virtual parameterless *OnClick* method implemented by *Button*. The *OnKeyDown* and *OnKeyUp* overrides similarly fire the *PreviewKnock* and *Knock* events when the user presses the spacebar or the Enter key.

Here's a program named GetMedieval that creates an instance of *MedievalButton*.

```
GetMedieval.cs
//----------------------------------------------
// GetMedieval.cs (c) 2006 by Charles Petzold
//----------------------------------------------
using System;
using System.Windows;
using System.Windows.Controls;
```

```
using System.Windows.Input;
using System.Windows.Media;

namespace Petzold.GetMedieval
{
    public class GetMedieval : Window
    {
        [STAThread]
        public static void Main()
        {
            Application app = new Application();
            app.Run(new GetMedieval());
        }
        public GetMedieval()
        {
            Title = "Get Medieval";

            MedievalButton btn = new MedievalButton();
            btn.Text = "Click this button";
            btn.FontSize = 24;
            btn.HorizontalAlignment = HorizontalAlignment.Center;
            btn.VerticalAlignment = VerticalAlignment.Center;
            btn.Padding = new Thickness(5, 20, 5, 20);
            btn.Knock += ButtonOnKnock;

            Content = btn;
        }
        void ButtonOnKnock(object sender, RoutedEventArgs args)
        {
            MedievalButton btn = args.Source as MedievalButton;
            MessageBox.Show("The button labeled \"" + btn.Text +
                            "\" has been knocked.", Title);
        }
    }
}
```

You can experiment with the button's *HorizontalAlignment*, *VerticalAlignment*, *Horizontal-ContentAlignment*, *VerticalContentAlignment*, *Margin*, and *Padding* properties to assure yourself that this button behaves pretty much the same as the normal *Button*. However, if you explicitly make the *MedievalButton* very narrow

```
btn.Width = 50;
```

you'll see the right side of the button truncated. You may want your button to always display an outline regardless of how small it gets. You can do this by returning a size from *Measure-Override* that is always less than or equal to the *sizeAvailable* argument:

```
sizeDesired.Width = Math.Min(sizeDesired.Width, sizeAvailable.Width);
sizeDesired.Height = Math.Min(sizeDesired.Height, sizeAvailable.Height);
```

However, *OnRender* will not perform clipping unless either dimension of the *sizeDesired* return value *exceeds* the corresponding dimension in *sizeAvailable*. (With the code using *Math.Min*, the dimensions of *sizeDesired* will always be less than or equal to the dimensions of *sizeAvailable.*) Long text that exceeds the bounds of the button will still be displayed. You can force clipping to kick in by adding a small amount to the dimensions of *sizeDesired* (just 0.1 will work) or by beginning *OnRender* with code to set a clipping region based on *RenderSize*:

```
dc.PushClip(new RectangleGeometry(new Rect(new Point(0, 0), RenderSize)));
```

To examine the implementation of routed events in *MedievalButton*, you can include the MedievalButton.cs file in the *ExamineRoutedEvents* project from Chapter 9, and you can substitute *MedievalButton* for *Button* in the program. You'll need to include a *using* directive for *Petzold .GetMedieval*, and make several other changes. Replace the following statement:

```
btn.Content = text;
```

with

```
btn.Text = text.Text;
```

Also, change the statement referring to *Button.ClickEvent* so that it refers to *MedievalButton.KnockEvent*. If you want to observe the *PreviewKnock* events, you can insert another *AddHandler* statement for that event.

Suppose you rather like using the *MedievalButton* class rather than *Button*, but sometimes you prefer that a word or two in the button text be italicized. Fortunately, the *FormattedText* class includes methods such as *SetFontStyle* and *SetFontWeight* that let you apply formatting to a subset of the text. So, you can replace the *Text* property of *MedievalButton* with a *FormattedText* property and just give the button a preformatted *FormattedText* object to display.

And then, of course, one day you'll need *MedievalButton* to display a bitmap. Perhaps by this time you've observed that *DrawingContext* has a *DrawImage* method that accepts an argument of type *ImageSource*—the same type of object you use with the *Image* element—so you can include a new property in *MedievalButton* named *ImageSource* and put a *DrawImage* call in *OnRender*. But now you need to decide if you want the bitmap to replace the text or to be displayed along with the text, and possibly include different placement options.

Of course, you know there's a better way because the regular *Button* class simply has a property named *Content*, and *Content* can be any object whatsoever. If you look at the documentation of *Button* and *ButtonBase* you'll see that these classes do not themselves override *OnRender*. These classes are relegating the actual rendering to other classes. In the ExamineRoutedEvents program in the previous chapter, you probably got a sense that a *Button* was really a *ButtonChrome* object and whatever element happened to be the content of the button (in that case a *TextBlock*).

Structurally, the *SimpleEllipse*, *BetterEllipse*, and *MedievalButton* classes illustrate the simplest way in which a class can inherit from *FrameworkElement* or *Control*. All that's really necessary is overriding *OnRender*, possibly accompanied by an override of *MeasureOverride*. (Of course, the *OnRender* and *MeasureOverride* methods might themselves be somewhat complex but the overall structure is simple.) However, it is more common for elements to have *children*. These children complicate the structure of the element, but make it much more versatile.

Chapter 11
Single-Child Elements

Many classes that inherit from *FrameworkElement* or *Control* have children, and to accommodate these children the class usually overrides one property and four methods. These five overrides are:

1. *VisualChildrenCount*. This read-only property is defined by the *Visual* class from which *UIElement* inherits. A class that derives from *FrameworkElement* overrides this property so that the element can indicate the number of children that the element maintains. The override of *VisualChildrenCount* in your class will probably look something like this:

   ```
   protected override int VisualChildrenCount
   {
       get
       {
           ...
       }
   }
   ```

2. *GetVisualChild*. This method is also defined by *Visual*. The parameter is an index from 0 to one less than the value returned from *VisualChildrenCount*. The class must override this method so that the element can return the child corresponding to that index:

   ```
   protected override Visual GetVisualChild(int index)
   {
       ...
   }
   ```

   The documentation states that this method should never return *null*. If the index is incorrect, the method should raise an exception.

3. *MeasureOverride*. You've seen this one before. An element calculates its desired size during this method and returns that size:

   ```
   protected override Size MeasureOverride(Size sizeAvailable)
   {
       ...
       return sizeDesired;
   }
   ```

   But an element with children must also take into account the sizes required by the children. It does this by calling the *Measure* method for each child, and then examining the *DesiredSize* property of that child. *Measure* is a public method defined by *UIElement*.

4. *ArrangeOverride*. This method is defined by *FrameworkElement* to replace the *ArrangeCore* method defined by *UIElement*. The method receives a *Size* object indicating the final layout size for the element. During the *ArrangeOverride* call the element

arranges its children on its surface by calling *Arrange* for each child. *Arrange* is a public method defined by *UIElement*. The single argument to *Arrange* is a *Rect* object that indicates the location and size of the child relative to the parent. The *ArrangeOverride* method generally returns the same *Size* object it received:

```
protected override Size ArrangeOverride(Size sizeFinal)
{
    ...
    return sizeFinal;
}
```

5. *OnRender*. This method allows an element to draw itself. An element's children draw themselves in their own *OnRender* methods. The children will appear on top of whatever the element draws during the element's *OnRender* method:

```
protected override void OnRender(DrawingContext dc)
{
    ...
}
```

The calls to *MeasureOverride*, *ArrangeOverride*, and *OnRender* occur in sequence. A call to *MeasureOverride* is always followed by a call to *ArrangeOverride*, which is always followed by a call to *OnRender*. However, subsequent *OnRender* calls might occur without being preceded by a call to *ArrangeOverride*, and subsequent *ArrangeOverride* calls might occur without being preceded by a call to *MeasureOverride*.

In this chapter, I will focus on elements that have just one child. Elements with multiple children are commonly categorized as *panels*, and I'll discuss those in the next chapter.

Here's a class named *EllipseWithChild* that inherits from *BetterEllipse* from Chapter 10 (just so it doesn't have to duplicate the *Brush* and *Fill* properties) but includes another property named *Child* of type *UIElement*.

EllipseWithChild.cs
```
//-----------------------------------------------
// EllipseWithChild.cs (c) 2006 by Charles Petzold
//-----------------------------------------------
using System;
using System.Windows;
using System.Windows.Controls;
using System.Windows.Input;
using System.Windows.Media;

namespace Petzold.EncloseElementInEllipse
{
    public class EllipseWithChild : Petzold.RenderTheBetterEllipse.BetterEllipse
    {
        UIElement child;

        // Public Child property.
        public UIElement Child
```

```
    {
        set
        {
            if (child != null)
            {
                RemoveVisualChild(child);
                RemoveLogicalChild(child);
            }
            if ((child = value) != null)
            {
                AddVisualChild(child);
                AddLogicalChild(child);
            }
        }
        get
        {
            return child;
        }
    }
    // Override of VisualChildrenCount returns 1 if Child is non-null.
    protected override int VisualChildrenCount
    {
        get
        {
            return Child != null ? 1 : 0;
        }
    }
    // Override of GetVisualChildren returns Child.
    protected override Visual GetVisualChild(int index)
    {
        if (index > 0 || Child == null)
            throw new ArgumentOutOfRangeException("index");

        return Child;
    }
    // Override of MeasureOverride calls child's Measure method.
    protected override Size MeasureOverride(Size sizeAvailable)
    {
        Size sizeDesired = new Size(0, 0);

        if (Stroke != null)
        {
            sizeDesired.Width += 2 * Stroke.Thickness;
            sizeDesired.Height += 2 * Stroke.Thickness;

            sizeAvailable.Width =
                Math.Max(0, sizeAvailable.Width - 2 * Stroke.Thickness);
            sizeAvailable.Height =
                Math.Max(0, sizeAvailable.Height - 2 * Stroke.Thickness);
        }
        if (Child != null)
        {
            Child.Measure(sizeAvailable);
```

```
                sizeDesired.Width += Child.DesiredSize.Width;
                sizeDesired.Height += Child.DesiredSize.Height;
            }
            return sizeDesired;
        }
        // Override of ArrangeOverride calls child's Arrange method.
        protected override Size ArrangeOverride(Size sizeFinal)
        {
            if (Child != null)
            {
                Rect rect = new Rect(
                    new Point((sizeFinal.Width - Child.DesiredSize.Width) / 2,
                              (sizeFinal.Height - Child.DesiredSize.Height) / 2),
                              Child.DesiredSize);
                Child.Arrange(rect);
            }
            return sizeFinal;
        }
    }
}
```

The private *child* field is accessible through the public *Child* property. Although it's unlikely that a child of this element will derive from *UIElement* but not from *FrameworkElement*, it's common to assume that element children are *UIElement* objects, and that's the type of this field and property.

Notice that the *set* accessor of the *Child* property calls the methods *AddVisualChild* and *AddLogicalChild* when setting the *child* field to a non-*null* element, and *RemoveVisualChild* and *RemoveLogicalChild* if *child* has previously been set to a non-*null* element. It is the responsibility of a class that maintains child elements to call these methods to maintain a proper visual and logical element tree. The visual and logical trees are necessary for the proper operation of property inheritance and event routing.

The override of *VisualChildrenCount* in this class returns 1 if *Child* is non-null and 0 otherwise. The override of *GetVisualChild* returns the *Child* property, and raises an exception if it's not available.

You may wonder about the necessity of overriding *GetVisualChild*. Because the *set* accessor of the *Child* property calls *AddVisualChild*, isn't it reasonable to assume that the default implementation of *GetVisualChild* returns that element? Whether it's reasonable or not, it doesn't work that way. Implementing *VisualChildrenCount* and *GetVisualChild* is your responsibility in any class that derives from *FrameworkElement* and maintains its own child collection.

As in any class that derives from *FrameworkElement*, the argument to *MeasureOverride* is an available size that can range from 0 to infinity. The method calculates a desired size and returns it the method. In *EllipseWithChild* the method begins with a *sizeDesired* object of zero dimensions and then adds to *sizeDesired* twice the width of the perimeter of the ellipse. The method is indicating that it wants to display at least the entire perimeter. These widths and heights are then subtracted from the *sizeAvailable* argument, but with logic that prevents zero values.

If the *Child* property is non-*null*, *MeasureOverride* continues by calling the *Measure* method of the child with the adjusted *sizeAvailable*. This *Measure* method of the child eventually calls the child's *MeasureOverride* method, and that method potentially calls the *Measure* methods of the child's children. This is how an entire tree of child elements is measured. The *Measure* method is basically responsible for updating the element's *DesiredSize* property.

The *Measure* method of the child does not return a value, but *MeasureOverride* can now examine the *DesiredSize* property of the child and take that size into account when determining its own *sizeDesired*. This is what the *EllipseWithChild* class returns from *MeasureOverride*.

What is this *DesiredSize* property? Of course, the immediate impulse is to identify it with the return value from *MeasureOverride*. It's similar, but it's not quite the same. The big difference is that *DesiredSize* includes any *Margin* set on the element. I'll discuss the calculations that go on behind the scenes shortly.

The *ArrangeOverride* method gives an element the opportunity to arrange its child elements on its surface. The argument to *ArrangeOverride* is a final layout size. The *ArrangeOverride* method is responsible for calling the *Arrange* method of all its children. *Arrange* has a *Rect* argument indicating the location and size of the child: The *Left* and *Top* properties must be relative to the upper-left corner of the parent. The *Width* and *Height* properties are generally extracted from the *DesiredSize* property of the child. The *Arrange* method assumes that the *Width* and *Height* properties of the *Rect* parameter include the child's *Margin*, which is why *DesiredSize* (which includes the child's *Margin*) is the proper choice for setting these properties.

The *Arrange* method in the child eventually calls the child's *ArrangeOverride* method with an argument that excludes the *Margin*, which potentially calls its children's *Arrange* methods, and so forth.

Here's a program that creates an *EllipseWithChild* object and assigns the *Child* property a *TextBlock* object. It could just as well assign the *Child* property an *Image* object or any other element.

```
EncloseElementInEllipse.cs
//------------------------------------------------------
// EncloseElementInEllipse.cs (c) 2006 by Charles Petzold
//------------------------------------------------------
using System;
using System.Windows;
using System.Windows.Controls;
using System.Windows.Input;
using System.Windows.Media;

namespace Petzold.EncloseElementInEllipse
{
    public class EncloseElementInEllipse : Window
```

```
    {
        [STAThread]
        public static void Main()
        {
            Application app = new Application();
            app.Run(new EncloseElementInEllipse());
        }
        public EncloseElementInEllipse()
        {
            Title = "Enclose Element in Ellipse";

            EllipseWithChild elips = new EllipseWithChild();
            elips.Fill = Brushes.ForestGreen;
            elips.Stroke = new Pen(Brushes.Magenta, 48);
            Content = elips;

            TextBlock text = new TextBlock();
            text.FontFamily = new FontFamily("Times New Roman");
            text.FontSize = 48;
            text.Text = "Text inside ellipse";

            // Set Child property of EllipseWithChild to TextBlock.
            elips.Child = text;
        }
    }
}
```

As you can see from experimenting with this program, the *TextBlock* element is always enclosed within the ellipse perimeter except when the ellipse is so small that the curvature of the perimeter causes the *MeasureOverride* logic to break down. If not enough space is available for the entire text, the text is clipped. The *TextBlock* element probably uses one of the techniques discussed in Chapter 10 to make sure its text doesn't spill out beyond the boundaries of the element.

It should now be fairly clear that layout in the Windows Presentation Foundation is a two-pass process that begins with a root element and works downward through the element tree. The root element is an object of type *Window*. This object has a single visual child of type *Border*. (That's the sizing border around the window.) The border has a visual child of type *Grid*. The grid has two children: an *AdornerDecorator* and a *ResizeGrip* (the latter of which only optionally appears in the window). The *AdornerDecorator* has one visual child of type *ContentPresenter*, which is responsible for hosting the *Content* property of the window. In the preceding program, the single visual child of the *ContentPresenter* is an *EllipseWithChild*, and its single visual child is a *TextBlock*. (I obtained information about the visual tree of this program through static methods of the *VisualTreeHelper* class.)

Each of these elements processes the *MeasureOverride* method by calling *Measure* on each of its children. (In most cases, that's just one child.) The *Measure* method of the child element calls the child element's *MeasureOverride* method, which then calls *Measure* on each of the child's children, and so on. A similar process occurs with *ArrangeOverride* and *Arrange*.

Here's the general logic behind these methods:

The argument to *MeasureOverride* (which is commonly called *sizeAvailable*) is generally the size of the element's container minus the element's *Margin* property. This argument can range from 0 to positive infinity. It is infinite if the container can size itself to the size of its children. However, if the element's *Height* property has been set to something other than NaN, *sizeAvailable.Height* will equal that property. If *MinHeight* or *MaxHeight* has been set, *sizeAvailable.Height* will reflect those constraints, and similarly for width.

MeasureOverride is responsible for calling *Measure* for each of its children. If an element has one child and the child is to occupy the entire surface of the element, the argument to *Measure* can be the same *sizeAvailable* parameter to *MeasureOverride*. Most commonly, the argument to *Measure* is a size based on *sizeAvailable* but somewhat less than that size. For example, *Ellipse-WithChild* offers its child a size from which the ellipse's own border has been subtracted.

The *Measure* method in the child calls the child's *MeasureOverride* method and uses the return value of *MeasureOverride* to calculate its own *DesiredSize* property. This calculation can be conceived as occurring in several steps. Here's how *DesiredSize.Width* is calculated. (The other dimension is calculated identically.)

1. If the element's *Width* property is NaN, *DesiredSize.Width* is the return value from *MeasureOverride*. Otherwise, *DesiredSize.Width* equals the element's *Width*.

2. *DesiredSize.Width* is adjusted by adding the *Left* and *Right* properties of the *Margin*.

3. *DesiredSize.Width* is adjusted so that it is not larger than the width of the container.

So, *DesiredSize* is basically the layout size required of the element including the element's margin, but not larger than the container. It is not very useful for an element to examine its own *DesiredSize*, but the *DesiredSize* properties of the element's children are very useful. After calling *Measure* on each of its children, an element can examine the children's *DesiredSize* properties to determine how much space each child needs and then calculate its own return value from the *MeasureOverride* method.

The parameter to *ArrangeOverride* (commonly called *sizeFinal*) is calculated from the original parameter to *MeasureOverride* and the return value from *MeasureOverride*, with a couple of other factors. Here's how *sizeFinal.Width* is calculated:

If *Width*, *MinWidth*, and *MaxWidth* are all NaN and the *HorizontalAlignment* property of the element is set to *Center*, *Left*, or *Right*, *sizeFinal.Width* equals the return value from *Measure-Override*. If *HorizontalAlignment* is set to *Stretch*, *sizeFinal.Width* equals the maximum of the *sizeAvailable* argument to *MeasureOverride* and the return value from *MeasureOverride*. If the *Width* property has been set to something other than NaN, *sizeFinal.Width* is the maximum of the *Width* property and the return value from *MeasureOverride*.

The job of the *ArrangeOverride* method is to lay out its children. Conceptually, the parent element needs to arrange its children in a rectangle whose upper-left corner is the point (0, 0) and whose size is the *sizeFinal* argument to *ArrangeOverride*. Commonly, *ArrangeOverride* uses the *sizeFinal* argument and the *DesiredSize* property of the child to calculate a *Rect* object for that child that indicates the upper-left corner and size of the child. The parent passes this *Rect* object to the *Arrange* method of each child. This is how the children get positioned on the surface of the parent.

After calling *Arrange* on its children, *ArrangeOverride* generally returns its *sizeFinal* parameter. (The base implementation of *ArrangeOverride* does precisely that.) However, it could return something different. Whatever *ArrangeOverride* returns becomes *RenderSize*.

In general, controls and elements are built up of other elements. Often, a control begins with some kind of *Decorator* object. *Decorator* inherits from *FrameworkElement* and defines a *Child* property of type *UIElement*. For example, the *Border* class inherits from *Decorator* to define properties *Background*, *BorderBrush*, *BorderThickness*, *CornerRadius* (for rounded corners), and *Padding*. The *ButtonChrome* class (in the *Microsoft.Windows.Themes* namespace) also inherits from *Decorator* and provides the look of the standard *Button*. The *Button* is basically a *ButtonChrome* object and a *ContentPresenter* object that is a child of the *ButtonChrome* object.

Here is a decorator for something I call a rounded button. The class implements its *OnRender* method by calling *DrawRoundedRectangle*. The horizontal and vertical radii of the corners are set to half the button's height so that the left and right sides of the button are circular.

RoundedButtonDecorator.cs

```
//-------------------------------------------------------
// RoundedButtonDecorator.cs (c) 2006 by Charles Petzold
//-------------------------------------------------------
using System;
using System.Windows;
using System.Windows.Controls;
using System.Windows.Input;
using System.Windows.Media;

namespace Petzold.CalculateInHex
{
    public class RoundedButtonDecorator : Decorator
    {
        // Public dependency property.
        public static readonly DependencyProperty IsPressedProperty;

        // Static constructor.
        static RoundedButtonDecorator()
        {
            IsPressedProperty =
                DependencyProperty.Register("IsPressed", typeof(bool),
                        typeof(RoundedButtonDecorator),
                        new FrameworkPropertyMetadata(false,
                                FrameworkPropertyMetadataOptions.AffectsRender));
        }
```

```
            // Public property.
            public bool IsPressed
            {
                set { SetValue(IsPressedProperty, value); }
                get { return (bool)GetValue(IsPressedProperty); }
            }


            // Override of MeasureOverride.
            protected override Size MeasureOverride(Size sizeAvailable)
            {
                Size szDesired = new Size(2, 2);
                sizeAvailable.Width -= 2;
                sizeAvailable.Height -= 2;

                if (Child != null)
                {
                    Child.Measure(sizeAvailable);
                    szDesired.Width += Child.DesiredSize.Width;
                    szDesired.Height += Child.DesiredSize.Height;
                }
                return szDesired;
            }
            // Override of ArrangeOverride.
            protected override Size ArrangeOverride(Size sizeArrange)
            {
                if (Child != null)
                {
                    Point ptChild =
                        new Point(Math.Max(1, (sizeArrange.Width -
                                                 Child.DesiredSize.Width) / 2),
                                  Math.Max(1, (sizeArrange.Height -
                                                 Child.DesiredSize.Height) / 2));

                    Child.Arrange(new Rect(ptChild, Child.DesiredSize));
                }
                return sizeArrange;
            }
            // Override of OnRender.
            protected override void OnRender(DrawingContext dc)
            {
                RadialGradientBrush brush = new RadialGradientBrush(
                        IsPressed ? SystemColors.ControlDarkColor :
                                    SystemColors.ControlLightLightColor,
                        SystemColors.ControlColor);

                brush.GradientOrigin = IsPressed ? new Point(0.75, 0.75) :
                                                   new Point(0.25, 0.25);
                dc.DrawRoundedRectangle(brush,
                        new Pen(SystemColors.ControlDarkDarkBrush, 1),
                        new Rect(new Point(0, 0), RenderSize),
                                RenderSize.Height / 2, RenderSize.Height / 2);
            }
        }
    }
}
```

The class doesn't explicitly define a *Child* property because it inherits that property from *Decorator*. The class defines one additional property named *IsPressed* that it uses for the radial gradient brush created in the *OnRender* method. To indicate a pressed button, *OnRender* uses a darker center and shifts the gradient origin.

The *RoundedButton* class shown next uses its constructor to create an object of type *Rounded-ButtonDecorator* and then calls *AddVisualChild* and *AddLogicalChild* to make that decorator a child. *RoundedButton* defines its own *Child* property but simply transfers any child set from this property to the decorator. The class returns 1 from its override of the *VisualChildCount* property and returns the *RoundedButtonDecorator* object from *GetVisualChild*.

RoundedButton thus doesn't need to do any drawing and is solely responsible for processing user input. The input logic is very similar to *MedievalButton* in Chapter 10, except that Rounded-Button defines a *Click* event to signal that the button has been pressed. The *IsPressed* property in *RoundedButton* provides direct access to the same property in *RoundedButtonDecorator*. A program using *RoundedButton* can simulate a button being pressed and released by setting this property.

RoundedButton.cs

```
//-----------------------------------------
// RoundedButton.cs (c) 2006 by Charles Petzold
//-----------------------------------------
using System;
using System.Windows;
using System.Windows.Controls;
using System.Windows.Input;
using System.Windows.Media;

namespace Petzold.CalculateInHex
{
    public class RoundedButton : Control
    {
        // Private field.
        RoundedButtonDecorator decorator;

        // Public static ClickEvent.
        public static readonly RoutedEvent ClickEvent;

        // Static Constructor.
        static RoundedButton()
        {
            ClickEvent =
                EventManager.RegisterRoutedEvent("Click", RoutingStrategy.Bubble,
                    typeof(RoutedEventHandler), typeof(RoundedButton));
        }
        // Constructor.
        public RoundedButton()
        {
            decorator = new RoundedButtonDecorator();
            AddVisualChild(decorator);
            AddLogicalChild(decorator);
        }
```

```
// Public properties.
public UIElement Child
{
    set { decorator.Child = value; }
    get { return decorator.Child; }
}
public bool IsPressed
{
    set { decorator.IsPressed = value; }
    get { return decorator.IsPressed; }
}
// Public event.
public event RoutedEventHandler Click
{
    add { AddHandler(ClickEvent, value); }
    remove { RemoveHandler(ClickEvent, value); }
}
// Overridden property and methods.
protected override int VisualChildrenCount
{
    get { return 1; }
}
protected override Visual GetVisualChild(int index)
{
    if (index > 0)
        throw new ArgumentOutOfRangeException("index");

    return decorator;
}
protected override Size MeasureOverride(Size sizeAvailable)
{
    decorator.Measure(sizeAvailable);
    return decorator.DesiredSize;
}
protected override Size ArrangeOverride(Size sizeArrange)
{
    decorator.Arrange(new Rect(new Point(0, 0), sizeArrange));
    return sizeArrange;
}
protected override void OnMouseMove(MouseEventArgs args)
{
    base.OnMouseMove(args);

    if (IsMouseCaptured)
        IsPressed = IsMouseReallyOver;
}
protected override void OnMouseLeftButtonDown(MouseButtonEventArgs args)
{
    base.OnMouseLeftButtonDown(args);
    CaptureMouse();
    IsPressed = true;
    args.Handled = true;
}
protected override void OnMouseLeftButtonUp(MouseButtonEventArgs args)
```

```
        {
            base.OnMouseRightButtonUp(args);

            if (IsMouseCaptured)
            {
                if (IsMouseReallyOver)
                    OnClick();

                Mouse.Capture(null);
                IsPressed = false;
                args.Handled = true;
            }
        }
        bool IsMouseReallyOver
        {
            get
            {
                Point pt = Mouse.GetPosition(this);
                return (pt.X >= 0 && pt.X < ActualWidth &&
                        pt.Y >= 0 && pt.Y < ActualHeight);
            }
        }
        // Method to fire Click event.
        protected virtual void OnClick()
        {
            RoutedEventArgs argsEvent = new RoutedEventArgs();
            argsEvent.RoutedEvent = RoundedButton.ClickEvent;
            argsEvent.Source = this;
            RaiseEvent(argsEvent);
        }
    }
}
```

The CalculateInHex program creates 29 instances of *RoundedButton* to make a hexadecimal calculator. The buttons are laid out in a *Grid* panel, and three of the buttons require some special handling in the window's constructor to make them span multiple columns.

CalculateInHex.cs

```
//-----------------------------------------------
// CalculateInHex.cs (c) 2006 by Charles Petzold
//-----------------------------------------------
using System;
using System.Windows;
using System.Windows.Controls;
using System.Windows.Input;
using System.Windows.Media;
using System.Windows.Threading;

namespace Petzold.CalculateInHex
{
    public class CalculateInHex : Window
    {
```

```
// Private fields.
RoundedButton btnDisplay;
ulong numDisplay;
ulong numFirst;
bool bNewNumber = true;
char chOperation = '=';

[STAThread]
public static void Main()
{
    Application app = new Application();
    app.Run(new CalculateInHex());
}
// Constructor.
public CalculateInHex()
{
    Title = "Calculate in Hex";
    SizeToContent = SizeToContent.WidthAndHeight;
    ResizeMode = ResizeMode.CanMinimize;

    // Create Grid as content of window.
    Grid grid = new Grid();
    grid.Margin = new Thickness(4);
    Content = grid;

    // Create five columns.
    for (int i = 0; i < 5; i++)
    {
        ColumnDefinition col = new ColumnDefinition();
        col.Width = GridLength.Auto;
        grid.ColumnDefinitions.Add(col);
    }

    // Create seven rows.
    for (int i = 0; i < 7; i++)
    {
        RowDefinition row = new RowDefinition();
        row.Height = GridLength.Auto;
        grid.RowDefinitions.Add(row);
    }

    // Text to appear in buttons.
    string[] strButtons = { "0",
                            "D", "E", "F", "+", "&",
                            "A", "B", "C", "-", "|",
                            "7", "8", "9", "*", "^",
                            "4", "5", "6", "/", "<<",
                            "1", "2", "3", "%", ">>",
                            "0", "Back", "Equals" };
    int iRow = 0, iCol = 0;

    // Create the buttons.
    foreach (string str in strButtons)
```

```
        {
            // Create RoundedButton.
            RoundedButton btn = new RoundedButton();
            btn.Focusable = false;
            btn.Height = 32;
            btn.Margin = new Thickness(4);
            btn.Click += ButtonOnClick;

            // Create TextBlock for Child of RoundedButton.
            TextBlock txt = new TextBlock();
            txt.Text = str;
            btn.Child = txt;

            // Add RoundedButton to Grid.
            grid.Children.Add(btn);
            Grid.SetRow(btn, iRow);
            Grid.SetColumn(btn, iCol);

            // Make an exception for the Display button.
            if (iRow == 0 && iCol == 0)
            {
                btnDisplay = btn;
                btn.Margin = new Thickness(4, 4, 4, 6);
                Grid.SetColumnSpan(btn, 5);
                iRow = 1;
            }

            // Also for Back and Equals.
            else if (iRow == 6 && iCol > 0)
            {
                Grid.SetColumnSpan(btn, 2);
                iCol += 2;
            }

            // For all other buttons.
            else
            {
                btn.Width = 32;
                if (0 == (iCol = (iCol + 1) % 5))
                    iRow++;
            }
        }
    }
}
// Click event handler.
void ButtonOnClick(object sender, RoutedEventArgs args)
{
    // Get the clicked button.
    RoundedButton btn = args.Source as RoundedButton;

    if (btn == null)
        return;

    // Get the button text and the first character.
    string strButton = (btn.Child as TextBlock).Text;
    char chButton = strButton[0];
```

```
                 // Some special cases.
                 if (strButton == "Equals")
                     chButton = '=';

                 if (btn == btnDisplay)
                     numDisplay = 0;

                 else if (strButton == "Back")
                     numDisplay /= 16;

                 // Hexadecimal digits.
                 else if (Char.IsLetterOrDigit(chButton))
                 {
                     if (bNewNumber)
                     {
                         numFirst = numDisplay;
                         numDisplay = 0;
                         bNewNumber = false;
                     }
                     if (numDisplay <= ulong.MaxValue >> 4)
                         numDisplay = 16 * numDisplay + (ulong)(chButton -
                                     (Char.IsDigit(chButton) ? '0' : 'A' - 10));
                 }
                 // Operation.
                 else
                 {
                     if (!bNewNumber)
                     {
                         switch (chOperation)
                         {
                             case '=': break;
                             case '+': numDisplay = numFirst + numDisplay; break;
                             case '-': numDisplay = numFirst - numDisplay; break;
                             case '*': numDisplay = numFirst * numDisplay; break;
                             case '&': numDisplay = numFirst & numDisplay; break;
                             case '|': numDisplay = numFirst | numDisplay; break;
                             case '^': numDisplay = numFirst ^ numDisplay; break;
                             case '<': numDisplay = numFirst << (int)numDisplay; break;
                             case '>': numDisplay = numFirst >> (int)numDisplay; break;
                             case '/':
                                 numDisplay =
                                     numDisplay != 0 ? numFirst / numDisplay :
                                                       ulong.MaxValue;
                                 break;
                             case '%':
                                 numDisplay =
                                     numDisplay != 0 ? numFirst % numDisplay :
                                                       ulong.MaxValue;
                                 break;
                             default: numDisplay = 0; break;
                         }
                     }
                     bNewNumber = true;
                     chOperation = chButton;
                 }
```

```
            // Format display.
            TextBlock text = new TextBlock();
            text.Text = String.Format("{0:X}", numDisplay);
            btnDisplay.Child = text;
    }
    protected override void OnTextInput(TextCompositionEventArgs args)
    {
            base.OnTextInput(args);

            if (args.Text.Length == 0)
                return;

            // Get character input.
            char chKey = Char.ToUpper(args.Text[0]);

            // Loop through buttons.
            foreach (UIElement child in (Content as Grid).Children)
            {
                RoundedButton btn = child as RoundedButton;
                string strButton = (btn.Child as TextBlock).Text;

                // Messy logic to check for matching button.
                if ((chKey == strButton[0] && btn != btnDisplay &&
                        strButton != "Equals" && strButton != "Back") ||
                    (chKey == '=' && strButton == "Equals") ||
                    (chKey == '\r' && strButton == "Equals") ||
                    (chKey == '\b' && strButton == "Back") ||
                    (chKey == '\x1B' && btn == btnDisplay))
                {
                    // Simulate Click event to process keystroke.
                    RoutedEventArgs argsClick =
                        new RoutedEventArgs(RoundedButton.ClickEvent, btn);
                    btn.RaiseEvent(argsClick);

                    // Make the button appear as if it's pressed.
                    btn.IsPressed = true;

                    // Set timer to unpress button.
                    DispatcherTimer tmr = new DispatcherTimer();
                    tmr.Interval = TimeSpan.FromMilliseconds(100);
                    tmr.Tag = btn;
                    tmr.Tick += TimerOnTick;
                    tmr.Start();

                    args.Handled = true;
                }
            }
    }
    void TimerOnTick(object sender, EventArgs args)
    {
        // Unpress button.
        DispatcherTimer tmr = sender as DispatcherTimer;
        RoundedButton btn = tmr.Tag as RoundedButton;
        btn.IsPressed = false;
```

```
            // Turn off time and remove event handler.
            tmr.Stop();
            tmr.Tick -= TimerOnTick;
        }
    }
}
```

Most of the logic for the calculator is concentrated in the *ButtonOnClick* method used for handling *Click* events from all the buttons. However, the button also has a keyboard interface, and that's handled in the *OnTextInput* override. The method identifies the button that corresponds to the key being pressed and then raises the *Click* event on that button by calling the *RaiseEvent* method of a *RoutedEventArgs* object. The *OnTextInput* method concludes by making the button appear as if it has been pressed by setting the *IsPressed* property to *true*. Of course, this property must be reset to *false* at some point, so a *DispatcherTimer* is created for that express purpose.

Besides overriding *FrameworkElement* and *Control*, there is another approach to creating custom controls that is used much more in XAML than in procedural code. This is through the definition of a *template*. I'll be discussing this technique in more detail in Chapter 25, but you might like to see how it's done in procedural code first.

The key property of *Control* that allows this approach is *Template*, which is of type *Control-Template*. This *Template* property essentially defines the look and feel of the control. As you know by now, a normal *Button* is basically a *ButtonChrome* object and a *ContentPresenter* object. The *ButtonChrome* object gives the button the look of its background and border, while the *ContentPresenter* is responsible for hosting whatever you've set to the button's *Content* property. The template defines the links between these elements as well as "triggers" that cause the control to react to certain changes in element properties.

To create a custom template for a control, first create an object of type *ControlTemplate*:

```
ControlTemplate template = new ControlTemplate();
```

The *ControlTemplate* class inherits a property named *VisualTree* from *FrameworkTemplate*. This is the property that defines which elements make up the control. The syntax of the code that goes into constructing the template is likely to look rather strange because it's necessary to define certain elements and their properties without actually creating those elements. This is accomplished through a class named *FrameworkElementFactory*. You create a *Framework-ElementFactory* object for each element in the visual tree. For example:

```
FrameworkElementFactory factoryBorder =
            new FrameworkElementFactory(typeof(Border));
```

You can also specify properties and attach event handlers for that element. You refer to properties and events using *DependencyProperty* and *RoutedEvent* fields defined or inherited by the element. Here's an example of setting a property:

```
factoryBorder.SetValue(Border.BorderBrushProperty, Brushes.Red);
```

You can also establish a parent-child relationship with multiple *FactoryElementFactory* objects:

```
factoryBorder.AppendChild(factoryContent);
```

But keep in mind that the elements are not created until the control is ready to be rendered.

The *ControlTemplate* also defines a property named *Triggers*, which is a collection of *Trigger* objects that define how the control changes as a result of certain changes in properties. The *Trigger* class has a property named *Property* of type *DependencyProperty* that indicates the property to monitor, and a *Value* property for the value of that property. For example:

```
Trigger trig = new Trigger();
trig.Property = UIElement.IsMouseOverProperty;
trig.Value = true;
```

When the *IsMouseOver* property becomes *true*, something happens, and that something is indicated by one or more *Setter* objects. For example, you might want the *FontStyle* property to change to italics:

```
Setter set = new Setter();
set.Property = Control.FontStyleProperty;
set.Value = FontStyles.Italic;
```

The *Setter* is associated with the *Trigger* by becoming part of the trigger's *Setters* collection:

```
trig.Setters.Add(set);
```

And the *Trigger* becomes part of the *ControlTemplate*:

```
template.Triggers.Add(trig);
```

Now you're ready to create a button and give it this template:

```
Button btn = new Button();
btn.Template = template;
```

And now the button has a whole new look, but it otherwise generates *Click* events as before. Here's a program that assembles a *ControlTemplate* for a *Button* in code:

BuildButtonFactory.cs
```
//----------------------------------------------------
// BuildButtonFactory.cs (c) 2006 by Charles Petzold
//----------------------------------------------------
using System;
using System.Windows;
using System.Windows.Controls;
using System.Windows.Input;
using System.Windows.Media;

namespace Petzold.BuildButtonFactory
{
```

```
public class BuildButtonFactory : Window
{
    [STAThread]
    public static void Main()
    {
        Application app = new Application();
        app.Run(new BuildButtonFactory());
    }
    public BuildButtonFactory()
    {
        Title = "Build Button Factory";

        // Create a ControlTemplate intended for a Button object.
        ControlTemplate template = new ControlTemplate(typeof(Button));

        // Create a FrameworkElementFactory for the Border class.
        FrameworkElementFactory factoryBorder =
            new FrameworkElementFactory(typeof(Border));

        // Give it a name to refer to it later.
        factoryBorder.Name = "border";

        // Set certain default properties.
        factoryBorder.SetValue(Border.BorderBrushProperty, Brushes.Red);
        factoryBorder.SetValue(Border.BorderThicknessProperty,
                                new Thickness(3));
        factoryBorder.SetValue(Border.BackgroundProperty,
                                SystemColors.ControlLightBrush);

        // Create a FrameworkElementFactory for the
        // ContentPresenter class.
        FrameworkElementFactory factoryContent =
            new FrameworkElementFactory(typeof(ContentPresenter));

        // Give it a name to refer to it later.
        factoryContent.Name = "content";

        // Bind some ContentPresenter properties to Button properties.
        factoryContent.SetValue(ContentPresenter.ContentProperty,
            new TemplateBindingExtension(Button.ContentProperty));

        // Notice that the button's Padding is the content's Margin!
        factoryContent.SetValue(ContentPresenter.MarginProperty,
            new TemplateBindingExtension(Button.PaddingProperty));

        // Make the ContentPresenter a child of the Border.
        factoryBorder.AppendChild(factoryContent);

        // Make the Border the root element of the visual tree.
        template.VisualTree = factoryBorder;

        // Define a new Trigger when IsMouseOver is true.
        Trigger trig = new Trigger();
        trig.Property = UIElement.IsMouseOverProperty;
        trig.Value = true;
```

```csharp
    // Associate a Setter with that Trigger to change the
    //  CornerRadius property of the "border" element.
    Setter set = new Setter();
    set.Property = Border.CornerRadiusProperty;
    set.Value = new CornerRadius(24);
    set.TargetName = "border";

    // Add the Setter to the Setters collection of the Trigger.
    trig.Setters.Add(set);

    // Similarly, define a Setter to change the FontStyle.
    // (No TargetName is needed because it's the button's property.)
    set = new Setter();
    set.Property = Control.FontStyleProperty;
    set.Value = FontStyles.Italic;

    // Add it to the same trigger's Setters collection as before.
    trig.Setters.Add(set);

    // Add the Trigger to the template.
    template.Triggers.Add(trig);

    // Similarly, define a Trigger for IsPressed.
    trig = new Trigger();
    trig.Property = Button.IsPressedProperty;
    trig.Value = true;

    set = new Setter();
    set.Property = Border.BackgroundProperty;
    set.Value = SystemColors.ControlDarkBrush;
    set.TargetName = "border";

    // Add the Setter to the trigger's Setters collection.
    trig.Setters.Add(set);

    // Add the Trigger to the template.
    template.Triggers.Add(trig);

    // Finally, create a Button.
    Button btn = new Button();

    // Give it the template.
    btn.Template = template;

    // Define other properties normally.
    btn.Content = "Button with Custom Template";
    btn.Padding = new Thickness(20);
    btn.FontSize = 48;
    btn.HorizontalAlignment = HorizontalAlignment.Center;
    btn.VerticalAlignment = VerticalAlignment.Center;
    btn.Click += ButtonOnClick;

    Content = btn;
}
```

```
        void ButtonOnClick(object sender, RoutedEventArgs args)
        {
            MessageBox.Show("You clicked the button", Title);
        }
    }
}
```

The *Template* property is defined by the *Control* class, so you can use this technique with your own custom controls. In fact, you can entirely define custom controls using this approach, and you'll see XAML examples in Part II of this book.

You may have noticed that the *Measure* and *Arrange* methods are defined by the *UIElement* class, but that *VisualChildrenCount* and *GetVisualChild* are defined by the *Visual* class. Let's look at the class hierarchy from *Object* to *Control* once again:

Object

> *DispatcherObject* (abstract)

>> *DependencyObject*

>>> *Visual* (abstract)

>>>> *UIElement*

>>>>> *FrameworkElement*

>>>>>> *Control*

The children of an element are generally other elements, but some or all of the children may actually be visuals—an instance of any class that descends from *Visual*. These visuals are what constitute the visual tree.

The following class hierarchy shows all the descendants of *Visual* except for the descendents of *FrameworkElement*:

Object

> *DispatcherObject* (abstract)

>> *DependencyObject*

>>> *Visual* (abstract)

>>>> *ContainerVisual*

>>>>> *DrawingVisual*

>>>>> *HostVisual*

Viewport3DVisual

UIElement

FrameworkElement

Of particular interest here is *DrawingVisual*. As you've seen, a class that derives from *UIElement* can override the *OnRender* method and obtain a *DrawingContext* to draw graphical objects on the screen. The only other place you can get a *DrawingContent* object is from *DrawingVisual*. Here's how:

```
DrawingVisual drawvis = new DrawingVisual();
DrawingContext dc = drawvis.RenderOpen();
// draw on dc
...
dc.Close();
```

Following the execution of this code you are now a proud owner of a *DrawingVisual* object—in other words, a "visual" that stores a particular image. The parameters to the drawing functions of the *DrawingContext* that you called gave this visual a specific location and size. That location is relative to some parent element that may not yet exist. To display this visual on the screen, a particular element must indicate the existence of the child visual with the return value of *VisualChildrenCount* and *GetVisualChild*. That's it. You can't call *Measure* or *Arrange* on this visual because those methods are defined by *UIElement*. The visual is displayed relative to its parent element and visibly on top of anything the element draws during *OnRender*. The order with respect to other children of the element depends on the order established by *GetVisual-Child*: Later visuals will appear in the foreground of earlier visuals.

If you want this visual to participate in event routing (which probably means that you want mouse events to be routed to the parent element of the visual), you should also call *AddVisual-Child* to add the visual to the visual tree of the element.

Here's a class called *ColorCell* that derives from *FrameworkElement*. This class is responsible for rendering an element that is always 20 device-independent units square. In the center of this element is a 12-unit-square color. That little rectangle is an object of type *DrawingVisual* created during the class's constructor—notice that the constructor has a *Color* parameter—and stored as a field.

ColorCell.cs
```
//-------------------------------------------
// ColorCell.cs (c) 2006 by Charles Petzold
//-------------------------------------------
using System;
using System.Windows;
using System.Windows.Media;
```

```
namespace Petzold.SelectColor
{
    class ColorCell : FrameworkElement
    {
        // Private fields.
        static readonly Size sizeCell = new Size(20, 20);
        DrawingVisual visColor;
        Brush brush;

        // Dependency properties.
        public static readonly DependencyProperty IsSelectedProperty;
        public static readonly DependencyProperty IsHighlightedProperty;

        static ColorCell()
        {
            IsSelectedProperty =
                DependencyProperty.Register("IsSelected", typeof(bool),
                        typeof(ColorCell), new FrameworkPropertyMetadata(false,
                                FrameworkPropertyMetadataOptions.AffectsRender));

            IsHighlightedProperty =
                DependencyProperty.Register("IsHighlighted", typeof(bool),
                        typeof(ColorCell), new FrameworkPropertyMetadata(false,
                                FrameworkPropertyMetadataOptions.AffectsRender));
        }
        // Properties.
        public bool IsSelected
        {
            set { SetValue(IsSelectedProperty, value); }
            get { return (bool)GetValue(IsSelectedProperty); }
        }
        public bool IsHighlighted
        {
            set { SetValue(IsHighlightedProperty, value); }
            get { return (bool)GetValue(IsHighlightedProperty); }
        }
        public Brush Brush
        {
            get { return brush; }
        }
        // Constructor requires Color argument.
        public ColorCell(Color clr)
        {
            // Create a new DrawingVisual and store as field.
            visColor = new DrawingVisual();
            DrawingContext dc = visColor.RenderOpen();

            // Draw a rectangle with the color argument.
            Rect rect = new Rect(new Point(0, 0), sizeCell);
            rect.Inflate(-4, -4);
            Pen pen = new Pen(SystemColors.ControlTextBrush, 1);
            brush = new SolidColorBrush(clr);
            dc.DrawRectangle(brush, pen, rect);
            dc.Close();
```

```
            // AddVisualChild is necessary for event routing!
            AddVisualChild(visColor);
            AddLogicalChild(visColor);
        }


        // Override protected properties and methods for visual child.
        protected override int VisualChildrenCount
        {
            get
            {
                return 1;
            }
        }
        protected override Visual GetVisualChild(int index)
        {
            if (index > 0)
                throw new ArgumentOutOfRangeException("index");

            return visColor;
        }


        // Override protected methods for size and rendering of element.
        protected override Size MeasureOverride(Size sizeAvailable)
        {
            return sizeCell;
        }
        protected override void OnRender(DrawingContext dc)
        {
            Rect rect = new Rect(new Point(0, 0), RenderSize);
            rect.Inflate(-1, -1);
            Pen pen = new Pen(SystemColors.HighlightBrush, 1);

            if (IsHighlighted)
                dc.DrawRectangle(SystemColors.ControlDarkBrush, pen, rect);
            else if (IsSelected)
                dc.DrawRectangle(SystemColors.ControlLightBrush, pen, rect);
            else
                dc.DrawRectangle(Brushes.Transparent, null, rect);
        }
    }
}
```

The *VisualChildrenCount* property returns 1 to indicate the presence of this visual, and *GetVisualChild* returns the visual itself. *MeasureOverride* simply returns the size of the total element. *OnRender* displays a rectangle that appears underneath the visual. The brush that *DrawRectangle* uses is based on two properties named *IsSelected* and *IsHighlighted* that are backed with dependency properties.

Forty *ColorCell* objects are part of a control I've called *ColorGrid*. *ColorGrid* overrides *VisualChildrenCount* to return 1 and *GetVisualChild* to return an object of type *Border*. By that time, the *Child* property of this *Border* object has been assigned a *UniformGrid* panel, and the *UniformGrid* panel has been filled with 40 instances of *ColorCell*, each with a different color.

ColorGrid.cs

```
//-------------------------------------------
// ColorGrid.cs (c) 2006 by Charles Petzold
//-------------------------------------------
using System;
using System.Windows;
using System.Windows.Controls;
using System.Windows.Controls.Primitives;
using System.Windows.Input;
using System.Windows.Media;
using System.Windows.Shapes;

namespace Petzold.SelectColor
{
    class ColorGrid : Control
    {
        // Number of rows and columns.
        const int yNum = 5;
        const int xNum = 8;

        // The colors to be displayed.
        string[,] strColors = new string[yNum, xNum]
        {
            { "Black", "Brown", "DarkGreen", "MidnightBlue",
                "Navy", "DarkBlue", "Indigo", "DimGray" },
            { "DarkRed", "OrangeRed", "Olive", "Green",
                "Teal", "Blue", "SlateGray", "Gray" },
            { "Red", "Orange", "YellowGreen", "SeaGreen",
                "Aqua", "LightBlue", "Violet", "DarkGray" },
            { "Pink", "Gold", "Yellow", "Lime",
                "Turquoise", "SkyBlue", "Plum", "LightGray" },
            { "LightPink", "Tan", "LightYellow", "LightGreen",
                "LightCyan", "LightSkyBlue", "Lavender", "White" }
        };

        // The ColorCell objects to be created.
        ColorCell[,] cells = new ColorCell[yNum, xNum];
        ColorCell cellSelected;
        ColorCell cellHighlighted;

        // Elements that comprise this control.
        Border bord;
        UniformGrid unigrid;

        // Currently selected color.
        Color clrSelected = Colors.Black;

        // Public "Changed" event.
        public event EventHandler SelectedColorChanged;

        // Public constructor.
        public ColorGrid()
        {
            // Create a Border for the control.
            bord = new Border();
```

```
            bord.BorderBrush = SystemColors.ControlDarkDarkBrush;
            bord.BorderThickness = new Thickness(1);
            AddVisualChild(bord);  // necessary for event routing.
            AddLogicalChild(bord);

            // Create a UniformGrid as a child of the Border.
            unigrid = new UniformGrid();
            unigrid.Background = SystemColors.WindowBrush;
            unigrid.Columns = xNum;
            bord.Child = unigrid;

            // Fill up the UniformGrid with ColorCell objects.
            for (int y = 0; y < yNum; y++)
            for (int x = 0; x < xNum; x++)
            {
                Color clr = (Color) typeof(Colors).
                    GetProperty(strColors[y, x]).GetValue(null, null);

                cells[y, x] = new ColorCell(clr);
                unigrid.Children.Add(cells[y, x]);

                if (clr == SelectedColor)
                {
                    cellSelected = cells[y, x];
                    cells[y, x].IsSelected = true;
                }

                ToolTip tip = new ToolTip();
                tip.Content = strColors[y, x];
                cells[y, x].ToolTip = tip;
            }
        }
        // Public get-only SelectedColor property.
        public Color SelectedColor
        {
            get { return clrSelected; }
        }

        // Override of VisualChildrenCount.
        protected override int VisualChildrenCount
        {
            get { return 1; }
        }
        // Override of GetVisualChild.
        protected override Visual GetVisualChild(int index)
        {
            if (index > 0)
                throw new ArgumentOutOfRangeException("index");

            return bord;

        }
        // Override of MeasureOverride.
        protected override Size MeasureOverride(Size sizeAvailable)
        {
```

```
        bord.Measure(sizeAvailable);
        return bord.DesiredSize;
}
// Override of ArrangeOverride.
protected override Size ArrangeOverride(Size sizeFinal)
{
        bord.Arrange(new Rect(new Point(0, 0), sizeFinal));
        return sizeFinal;
}
// Mouse event handling.
protected override void OnMouseEnter(MouseEventArgs args)
{
        base.OnMouseEnter(args);

        if (cellHighlighted != null)
        {
            cellHighlighted.IsHighlighted = false;
            cellHighlighted = null;
        }
}
protected override void OnMouseMove(MouseEventArgs args)
{
        base.OnMouseMove(args);
        ColorCell cell = args.Source as ColorCell;

        if (cell != null)
        {
            if (cellHighlighted != null)
                cellHighlighted.IsHighlighted = false;

            cellHighlighted = cell;
            cellHighlighted.IsHighlighted = true;
        }
}
protected override void OnMouseLeave(MouseEventArgs args)
{
        base.OnMouseLeave(args);

        if (cellHighlighted != null)
        {
            cellHighlighted.IsHighlighted = false;
            cellHighlighted = null;
        }
}
protected override void OnMouseDown(MouseButtonEventArgs args)
{
        base.OnMouseDown(args);

        ColorCell cell = args.Source as ColorCell;

        if (cell != null)
        {
            if (cellHighlighted != null)
                cellHighlighted.IsSelected = false;
```

```
            cellHighlighted = cell;
            cellHighlighted.IsSelected = true;
        }
        Focus();
    }
    protected override void OnMouseUp(MouseButtonEventArgs args)
    {
        base.OnMouseUp(args);
        ColorCell cell = args.Source as ColorCell;

        if (cell != null)
        {
            if (cellSelected != null)
                cellSelected.IsSelected = false;

            cellSelected = cell;
            cellSelected.IsSelected = true;

            clrSelected = (cellSelected.Brush as SolidColorBrush).Color;
            OnSelectedColorChanged(EventArgs.Empty);
        }
    }
    // Keyboard event handling.
    protected override void OnGotKeyboardFocus(
                            KeyboardFocusChangedEventArgs args)
    {
        base.OnGotKeyboardFocus(args);

        if (cellHighlighted == null)
        {
            if (cellSelected != null)
                cellHighlighted = cellSelected;
            else
                cellHighlighted = cells[0, 0];

            cellHighlighted.IsHighlighted = true;
        }
    }
    protected override void OnLostKeyboardFocus(
                            KeyboardFocusChangedEventArgs args)
    {
        base.OnGotKeyboardFocus(args);

        if (cellHighlighted != null)
        {
            cellHighlighted.IsHighlighted = false;
            cellHighlighted = null;
        }
    }
    protected override void OnKeyDown(KeyEventArgs args)
    {
        base.OnKeyDown(args);
```

```
int index = unigrid.Children.IndexOf(cellHighlighted);
int y = index / xNum;
int x = index % xNum;

switch (args.Key)
{
    case Key.Home:
        y = 0;
        x = 0;
        break;

    case Key.End:
        y = yNum - 1;
        x = xNum + 1;
        break;

    case Key.Down:
        if ((y = (y + 1) % yNum) == 0)
            x++;
        break;

    case Key.Up:
        if ((y = (y + yNum - 1) % yNum) == yNum - 1)
            x--;
        break;

    case Key.Right:
        if ((x = (x + 1) % xNum) == 0)
            y++;
        break;

    case Key.Left:
        if ((x = (x + xNum - 1) % xNum) == xNum - 1)
            y--;
        break;

    case Key.Enter:
    case Key.Space:
        if (cellSelected != null)
            cellSelected.IsSelected = false;

        cellSelected = cellHighlighted;
        cellSelected.IsSelected = true;
        clrSelected = (cellSelected.Brush as SolidColorBrush).Color;
        OnSelectedColorChanged(EventArgs.Empty);
        break;

    default:
        return;
}
if (x >= xNum || y >= yNum)
    MoveFocus(new TraversalRequest(
                    FocusNavigationDirection.Next));
```

```
                  else if (x < 0 || y < 0)
                      MoveFocus(new TraversalRequest(
                                  FocusNavigationDirection.Previous));
                  else
                  {
                      cellHighlighted.IsHighlighted = false;
                      cellHighlighted = cells[y, x];
                      cellHighlighted.IsHighlighted = true;
                  }
                  args.Handled = true;
              }
              // Protected method to fire SelectedColorChanged event.
              protected virtual void OnSelectedColorChanged(EventArgs args)
              {
                  if (SelectedColorChanged != null)
                      SelectedColorChanged(this, args);
              }
          }
      }
```

I patterned *ColorGrid* after a control in Microsoft Word. You may have seen it on the Format Background menu or emerging from the Font Color button on the Formatting toolbar. There is always one cell that is "selected." This corresponds to the color obtained through the read-only *SelectedColor* property. (I made this property read-only because the control is not able to accept arbitrary colors not in its grid.) The selected color is indicated by a lighter background rectangle. You can change the selected color using the mouse.

When *ColorGrid* has input focus, there is also a "highlighted" cell, indicated by a darker background rectangle. You can change which cell is highlighted using the cursor movement keys. When you get to the beginning or end of the grid, the *MoveFocus* method shifts input focus to the previous or next control. The highlighted cell can become the selected cell with a tap of the spacebar or the Enter key.

Whenever the selected color changes, the control makes a call to its *OnSelectedColorChanged* method, which then fires its *SelectedColorChanged* event.

Here's a program that creates an object of type *ColorGrid* and puts it between two do-nothing buttons so that you can see how the input focus works. The window installs an event handler for the *SelectedColorChanged* event and changes the window background based on the *SelectedColor* property of the control.

SelectColor.cs

```
//-------------------------------------------
// SelectColor.cs (c) 2006 by Charles Petzold
//-------------------------------------------
using System;
using System.Windows;
using System.Windows.Controls;
```

```
using System.Windows.Input;
using System.Windows.Media;

namespace Petzold.SelectColor
{
    public class SelectColor : Window
    {
        [STAThread]
        public static void Main()
        {
            Application app = new Application();
            app.Run(new SelectColor());
        }
        public SelectColor()
        {
            Title = "Select Color";
            SizeToContent = SizeToContent.WidthAndHeight;

            // Create StackPanel as content of window.
            StackPanel stack = new StackPanel();
            stack.Orientation = Orientation.Horizontal;
            Content = stack;

            // Create do-nothing button to test tabbing.
            Button btn = new Button();
            btn.Content = "Do-nothing button\nto test tabbing";
            btn.Margin = new Thickness(24);
            btn.HorizontalAlignment = HorizontalAlignment.Center;
            btn.VerticalAlignment = VerticalAlignment.Center;
            stack.Children.Add(btn);

            // Create ColorGrid control.
            ColorGrid clrgrid = new ColorGrid();
            clrgrid.Margin = new Thickness(24);
            clrgrid.HorizontalAlignment = HorizontalAlignment.Center;
            clrgrid.VerticalAlignment = VerticalAlignment.Center;
            clrgrid.SelectedColorChanged += ColorGridOnSelectedColorChanged;
            stack.Children.Add(clrgrid);

            // Create another do-nothing button.
            btn = new Button();
            btn.Content = "Do-nothing button\nto test tabbing";
            btn.Margin = new Thickness(24);
            btn.HorizontalAlignment = HorizontalAlignment.Center;
            btn.VerticalAlignment = VerticalAlignment.Center;
            stack.Children.Add(btn);
        }
        void ColorGridOnSelectedColorChanged(object sender, EventArgs args)
        {
            ColorGrid clrgrid = sender as ColorGrid;
            Background = new SolidColorBrush(clrgrid.SelectedColor);
        }
    }
}
```

I assume you're familiar with the *ListBox* control, which is a control that displays multiple items (generally text items) in a vertical list and let the user select one. Does *ColorGrid* look anything like a *ListBox* to you? It doesn't really look like one to me, but consider the two controls more abstractly. Both let you choose an item from a collection of multiple items.

In Chapter 13, you'll see how to create a control very similar to *ColorGrid* by using most of the keyboard, mouse, and selection logic already built into *ListBox*.

Chapter 12
Custom Panels

Some descendants of *FrameworkElement* have children and some do not. Those that don't include *Image* and all the *Shape* descendants. Other descendants of *FrameworkElement*—such as everything that derives from *ContentControl* and *Decorator*—have the capability to support a single child, although often the child can also have a nested child. A class that inherits from *FrameworkElement* can also support multiple children, and the descendants of *Panel* are one important category of such elements. But it's not necessary to inherit from *Panel* to host multiple children. For example, *InkCanvas* inherits directly from *FrameworkElement* and maintains a collection of multiple children.

In this chapter I will show you how to inherit from *Panel* and how to support multiple children without inheriting from *Panel*, and you'll probably understand why inheriting from *Panel* is easier. The big gift of *Panel* is the definition of the *Children* property for storing the children. This property is of type *UIElementCollection*, and that collection itself handles the calling of *AddVisualChild*, *AddLogicalChild*, *RemoveVisualChild*, and *RemoveLogicalChild* when children are added to or removed from the collection. *UIElementCollection* is able to perform this feat because it has knowledge of the parent element. The sole constructor of *UIElementCollection* requires two arguments: a visual parent of type *UIElement* and a logical parent of type *FrameworkElement*. The two arguments can be identical, and usually are.

As you can determine from examining the documentation of *Panel*, the *Panel* class overrides *VisualChildrenCount* and *GetVisualChild* and handles these for you. When inheriting from *Panel* it is usually not necessary to override *OnRender*, either. The *Panel* class defines a *Background* property and undoubtedly simply calls *DrawRectangle* with the background brush during its *OnRender* override.

That leaves *MeasureOverride* and *ArrangeOverride*—the two essential methods you must implement in your panel class. The *Panel* documentation gives you some advice on implementing these methods: It recommends that you use *InternalChildren* rather than *Children* to obtain the collection of children. The *InternalChildren* property (also an object of type *UIElementCollection*) includes everything in the normal *Children* collection plus children added through data binding.

Perhaps the simplest type of panel is the *UniformGrid*. This grid contains a number of rows that have the same height, and columns that have the same width. To illustrate what's involved in implementing a panel, the following *UniformGridAlmost* class attempts to duplicate the functionality of *UniformGrid*. The class defines a property named *Columns* backed by a dependency property that indicates a default value of 1. *UniformGridAlmost* does not attempt to figure out the number of columns and rows based on the number of children. It requires that the *Columns* property be set explicitly, and then determines the number of rows based on the number of children. This calculated *Rows* value is available as a read-only property. *UniformGridAlmost* doesn't include a *FirstColumn* property, either. (That's why I named it *Almost*.)

UniformGridAlmost.cs

```
// UniformGridAlmost.cs (c) 2006 by Charles Petzold

using System;
using System.Windows;
using System.Windows.Input;
using System.Windows.Controls;
using System.Windows.Media;

namespace Petzold.DuplicateUniformGrid
{
    class UniformGridAlmost : Panel
    {
        // Public static readonly dependency properties.
        public static readonly DependencyProperty ColumnsProperty;

        // Static constructor to create dependency property.
        static UniformGridAlmost()
        {
            ColumnsProperty =
                DependencyProperty.Register(
                    "Columns", typeof(int), typeof(UniformGridAlmost),
                    new FrameworkPropertyMetadata(1,
                        FrameworkPropertyMetadataOptions.AffectsMeasure));
        }
        // Columns property.
        public int Columns
        {
            set { SetValue(ColumnsProperty, value); }
            get { return (int)GetValue(ColumnsProperty); }
        }
        // Read-Only Rows property.
        public int Rows
        {
            get { return (InternalChildren.Count + Columns - 1) / Columns; }
        }
        // Override of MeasureOverride apportions space.
        protected override Size MeasureOverride(Size sizeAvailable)
        {
            // Calculate a child size based on uniform rows and columns.
            Size sizeChild = new Size(sizeAvailable.Width / Columns,
                                      sizeAvailable.Height / Rows);
```

```
        // Variables to accumulate maximum widths and heights.
        double maxwidth = 0;
        double maxheight = 0;

        foreach (UIElement child in InternalChildren)
        {
            // Call Measure for each child ...
            child.Measure(sizeChild);

            // ... and then examine DesiredSize property of child.
            maxwidth = Math.Max(maxwidth, child.DesiredSize.Width);
            maxheight = Math.Max(maxheight, child.DesiredSize.Height);
        }
        // Now calculate a desired size for the grid itself.
        return new Size(Columns * maxwidth, Rows * maxheight);
    }
    // Override of ArrangeOverride positions children.
    protected override Size ArrangeOverride(Size sizeFinal)
    {
        // Calculate a child size based on uniform rows and columns.
        Size sizeChild = new Size(sizeFinal.Width / Columns,
                                  sizeFinal.Height / Rows);

        for (int index = 0; index < InternalChildren.Count; index++)
        {
            int row = index / Columns;
            int col = index % Columns;

            // Calculate a rectangle for each child within sizeFinal ...
            Rect rectChild =
                new Rect(new Point(col * sizeChild.Width,
                                   row * sizeChild.Height),
                         sizeChild);

            // ... and call Arrange for that child.
            InternalChildren[index].Arrange(rectChild);
        }
        return sizeFinal;
    }
}
}
```

For *MeasureOverride*, the class first calculates an available size for each child, assuming that the area is divided by equal rows and columns. (Keep in mind that *sizeAvailable* could be infinite in one or both dimensions, in which case *sizeChild* will also have an infinite dimension or two.) The method calls *Measure* for each child and then examines *DesiredSize*, keeping a running accumulation of the width of the widest element and the height of the tallest element in the grid. Preferably, the grid should be large enough so that every cell is this width and height.

The *ArrangeOverride* method gives the panel the opportunity to arrange all the children in a grid. From the argument to the method, it's easy to calculate the width and height of each cell and the position of each child. The method calls *Arrange* for each child and then returns.

The *UniformGridAlmost* class and the following *DuplicateUniformGrid* class comprise the
DuplicateUniformGrid project.

```
DuplicateUniformGrid.cs
//-----------------------------------------------------
// DuplicateUniformGrid.cs (c) 2006 by Charles Petzold
//-----------------------------------------------------
using System;
using System.Windows;
using System.Windows.Controls;
using System.Windows.Input;
using System.Windows.Media;

namespace Petzold.DuplicateUniformGrid
{
    public class DuplicateUniformGrid : Window
    {
        [STAThread]
        public static void Main()
        {
            Application app = new Application();
            app.Run(new DuplicateUniformGrid());
        }
        public DuplicateUniformGrid()
        {
            Title = "Duplicate Uniform Grid";

            // Create UniformGridAlmost as content of window.
            UniformGridAlmost unigrid = new UniformGridAlmost();
            unigrid.Columns = 5;
            Content = unigrid;

            // Fill UniformGridAlmost with randomly-sized buttons.
            Random rand = new Random();

            for (int index = 0; index < 48; index++)
            {
                Button btn = new Button();
                btn.Name = "Button" + index;
                btn.Content = btn.Name;
                btn.FontSize += rand.Next(10);
                unigrid.Children.Add(btn);
            }
            AddHandler(Button.ClickEvent, new RoutedEventHandler(ButtonOnClick));
        }
        void ButtonOnClick(object sender, RoutedEventArgs args)
        {
            Button btn = args.Source as Button;
            MessageBox.Show(btn.Name + " has been clicked", Title);
        }
    }
}
```

The program creates a *UniformGridAlmost* object, sets 5 columns, and then fills it with 48 buttons of various sizes. Here are several experiments you'll want to try:

- Set *SizeToContent* of the window to *SizeToContent.WidthAndHeight*. The window and the grid now collapse so that all cells are the size of the largest button.

- Set *HorizontalAlignment* and *VerticalAlignment* of the grid to *Center*. Now the window remains a default size but grid collapses so that all cells are the size of the largest button.

- Set *HorizontalAlignment* and *VerticalAlignment* of each button to *Center*. Now the grid remains the same size as the client area, and each cell of the grid is a uniform size, but the buttons are all sized to their content.

- Set *Height* and *Width* properties of the grid to values inadequate for all the buttons. Now the grid tries to fit all the buttons in the grid, but part of the grid is truncated.

In other words, the grid is behaving as we might hope and expect. To further test it, dig out the *ColorGrid* control from the last chapter and replace *UniformGrid* with *UniformGridAlmost*.

Usually, you will first encounter the concept of *attached* properties with panels. *DockPanel*, *Grid*, and *Canvas* all have attached properties. As you recall, when you add an element to a *Canvas*, you also set two attached properties that apply to the element:

```
canv.Children.Add(el);
Canvas.SetLeft(el, 100);
Canvas.SetTop(el, 150);
```

When I first introduced attached properties, I mentioned that the panels used these attached properties when laying out their children. It is now time to examine how this is done.

The *CanvasClone* class shown here is very much like *Canvas* except that it implements only the *Left* and *Top* attached properties and doesn't bother with *Right* and *Bottom*.

```
CanvasClone.cs
//---------------------------------------------
// CanvasClone.cs (c) 2006 by Charles Petzold
//---------------------------------------------
using System;
using System.Windows;
using System.Windows.Controls;
using System.Windows.Input;
using System.Windows.Media;

namespace Petzold.PaintOnCanvasClone
{
    public class CanvasClone : Panel
    {
        // Define two dependency properties.
```

```
        public static readonly DependencyProperty LeftProperty;
        public static readonly DependencyProperty TopProperty;

        static CanvasClone()
        {
            // Register the dependency properties as attached properties.
            // Default value is 0 and any change invalidates parent's arrange.
            LeftProperty = DependencyProperty.RegisterAttached("Left",
                    typeof(double), typeof(CanvasClone),
                    new FrameworkPropertyMetadata(0.0,
                        FrameworkPropertyMetadataOptions.AffectsParentArrange));

            TopProperty = DependencyProperty.RegisterAttached("Top",
                    typeof(double), typeof(CanvasClone),
                    new FrameworkPropertyMetadata(0.0,
                        FrameworkPropertyMetadataOptions.AffectsParentArrange));
        }
        // Static methods to set and get attached properties.
        public static void SetLeft(DependencyObject obj, double value)
        {
            obj.SetValue(LeftProperty, value);
        }
        public static double GetLeft(DependencyObject obj)
        {
            return (double)obj.GetValue(LeftProperty);
        }
        public static void SetTop(DependencyObject obj, double value)
        {
            obj.SetValue(TopProperty, value);
        }
        public static double GetTop(DependencyObject obj)
        {
            return (double)obj.GetValue(TopProperty);
        }
        // Override of MeasureOverride just calls Measure on children.
        protected override Size MeasureOverride(Size sizeAvailable)
        {
            foreach (UIElement child in InternalChildren)
                child.Measure(new Size(Double.PositiveInfinity,
                                       Double.PositiveInfinity));

            // Return default value (0, 0).
            return base.MeasureOverride(sizeAvailable);
        }
        // Override of ArrangeOverride positions children.
        protected override Size ArrangeOverride(Size sizeFinal)
        {
            foreach (UIElement child in InternalChildren)
                child.Arrange(new Rect(
                    new Point(GetLeft(child), GetTop(child)), child.DesiredSize));

            return sizeFinal;
        }
    }
}
```

There is actually *nothing* in the class that is named *Left* or *Top*. The static read-only fields *Left-Property* and *TopProperty* are defined exactly like regular dependency properties. The static constructor, however, registers these properties with the static method *DependencyProperty.RegisterAttached*. Take careful note of the metadata option *FrameworkPropertyMetadataOptions.AffectsParentArrange*. These attached properties are always attached to a child of the canvas, so whenever the property changes, it affects the *parent's* arrangement—that is, the canvas's arrangement—because the canvas is responsible for positioning its children. There is a similar flag named *AffectsParentMeasure* to use when a change in an attached property affects the size of the parent and not just the layout.

The class next defines four static methods for setting and getting these attached properties. When these methods are called, the first argument will probably be a child of the canvas, or an element that is soon to be a child of the canvas. Notice that the *Set* methods call the child's *SetValue* method so that the property is stored with the child.

All *MeasureOverride* does is call *Measure* for each of its children with an infinite size. This is consistent with *Canvas*. Generally, elements placed on a canvas are given an explicit size, or otherwise have a size that is fairly fixed (such as a bitmap image or a polyline). The call to *Measure* is necessary to allow the child to calculate its *DesiredSize* property, which is used during *ArrangeOverride*. *MeasureOverride* returns the value from the base class implementation of the method, which is the size (0, 0).

The *ArrangeOverride* method simply calls *Arrange* on each of its children, positioning the child at the location obtained from the *GetLeft* and *GetTop* methods. These methods call *GetValue* on the child. (At this point, an interesting distinction between classes that define dependency properties and those that define only attached properties becomes evident. A class that defines dependency properties must derive from *DependencyObject* because the class calls the *SetValue* and *GetValue* methods that it inherits from *DependencyObject*. However, a class that defines attached properties need *not* derive from *DependencyObject*, because it doesn't need to call its own *SetValue* and *GetValue* methods.)

Here's a simple program that demonstrates that *CanvasClone* can actually position elements on its surface:

```
PaintOnCanvasClone.cs
//----------------------------------------------------
// PaintOnCanvasClone.cs (c) 2006 by Charles Petzold
//----------------------------------------------------
using System;
using System.Windows;
using System.Windows.Controls;
using System.Windows.Input;
using System.Windows.Media;
using System.Windows.Shapes;

namespace Petzold.PaintOnCanvasClone
{
```

```
public class PaintOnCanvasClone : Window
{
    [STAThread]
    public static void Main()
    {
        Application app = new Application();
        app.Run(new PaintOnCanvasClone());
    }
    public PaintOnCanvasClone()
    {
        Title = "Paint on Canvas Clone";

        Canvas canv = new Canvas();
        Content = canv;

        SolidColorBrush[] brushes =
            { Brushes.Red, Brushes.Green, Brushes.Blue };

        for (int i = 0; i < brushes.Length; i++)
        {
            Rectangle rect = new Rectangle();
            rect.Fill = brushes[i];
            rect.Width = 200;
            rect.Height = 200;
            canv.Children.Add(rect);
            Canvas.SetLeft(rect, 100 * (i + 1));
            Canvas.SetTop(rect, 100 * (i + 1));
        }
    }
}
```

To really give *CanvasClone* a workout, however, you'll want to include it in the DrawCircles program from Chapter 9. (It was only after I tried *CanvasClone* in DrawCircles that I realized the importance of the *AffectsParentArrange* flag on the attached property metadata.) Be sure to change every mention of *Canvas* in that program to *Petzold.PaintOnCanvasClone.CanvasClone*. Several methods in the program deal with the *Left* and *Top* attached properties, and those must all be changed to use *CanvasClone*. Unfortunately, you won't get any kind of error if the program sets or gets an attached property for a nonexistent *Canvas* class. But the program will only work if you set and get the attached properties for *CanvasClone*.

If you create a class that supports multiple children but doesn't inherit from *Panel*, you'll probably want to define a property named *Children* of type *UIElementCollection*, and also a *Background* property of type *Brush*. That approach comes closest to *Panel* itself.

On the other hand, it's also instructive to create a panel-like element by inheriting directly from *FrameworkElement* and implementing a custom child collection that is not an object of type *UIElementCollection* (if only to see what the problems are).

It is tempting to implement this child collection by first defining a private field like so:

```
List<UIElement> children = new List<UIElement>();
```

And then to expose this collection through a public property:

```
public List<UIElement> Children
{
    get { return children; }
}
```

That way, you could add children to this collection in the same way you add children to one of the regular panels:

```
pnl.children.Add(btn);
```

But something is missing. The class that defines this *children* field and *Children* property has no way of knowing when something is added to or removed from the collection. The class needs to know exactly what's going into the collection and what's being removed so that it can properly call *AddVisualChild*, *AddLogicalChild*, *RemoveVisualChild*, and *RemoveLogicalChild*.

One possible solution is to write a class somewhat similar to *UIElementCollection* that either performs these jobs itself, or notifies the panel class when a child has entered or left the collection.

Or, you could keep the simple private *children* field and instead define methods like this:

```
public void Add(UIElement el)
{
    children.Add(el);
    AddVisualChild(el);
    AddLogicalChild(el);
}
```

and like this:

```
public void Remove(UIElement el)
{
    children.Remove(el);
    RemoveVisualChild(el);
    RemoveLogicalChild(el);
}
```

So instead of adding a child element to the panel like this:

```
pnl.children.Add(btn);
```

you do it like this:

```
pnl.Add(btn);
```

How many of these methods you want to write is up to you. The *Add* is essential, of course. *Remove*, *IndexOf*, *Count*, and perhaps an indexer are optional, depending on the application.

Here's a class that inherits from *FrameworkElement*, maintains its own collection of children, and arranges the children in a diagonal pattern from upper left to lower right.

DiagonalPanel.cs

```
//---------------------------------------------
// DiagonalButton.cs (c) 2006 by Charles Petzold
//---------------------------------------------
using System;
using System.Collections.Generic;
using System.Windows;
using System.Windows.Controls;
using System.Windows.Input;
using System.Windows.Media;

namespace Petzold.DiagonalizeTheButtons
{
    class DiagonalPanel : FrameworkElement
    {
        // Private children collection.
        List<UIElement> children = new List<UIElement>();

        // Private field.
        Size sizeChildrenTotal;

        // Dependency Property.
        public static readonly DependencyProperty BackgroundProperty;

        // Static constructor to create Background dependency property.
        static DiagonalPanel()
        {
            BackgroundProperty =
                DependencyProperty.Register(
                    "Background", typeof(Brush), typeof(DiagonalPanel),
                    new FrameworkPropertyMetadata(null,
                        FrameworkPropertyMetadataOptions.AffectsRender));
        }
        // Background property.
        public Brush Background
        {
            set { SetValue(BackgroundProperty, value); }
            get { return (Brush)GetValue(BackgroundProperty); }
        }
        // Methods to access child collection.
        public void Add(UIElement el)
        {
            children.Add(el);
            AddVisualChild(el);
            AddLogicalChild(el);
            InvalidateMeasure();
        }
```

```csharp
public void Remove(UIElement el)
{
    children.Remove(el);
    RemoveVisualChild(el);
    RemoveLogicalChild(el);
    InvalidateMeasure();
}
public int IndexOf(UIElement el)
{
    return children.IndexOf(el);
}

// Overridden properties and methods
protected override int VisualChildrenCount
{
    get { return children.Count; }
}
protected override Visual GetVisualChild(int index)
{
    if (index >= children.Count)
        throw new ArgumentOutOfRangeException("index");

    return children[index];
}
protected override Size MeasureOverride(Size sizeAvailable)
{
    sizeChildrenTotal = new Size(0, 0);

    foreach (UIElement child in children)
    {
        // Call Measure for each child ...
        child.Measure(new Size(Double.PositiveInfinity,
                               Double.PositiveInfinity));

        // ... and then examine DesiredSize property of child.
        sizeChildrenTotal.Width += child.DesiredSize.Width;
        sizeChildrenTotal.Height += child.DesiredSize.Height;
    }
    return sizeChildrenTotal;
}
protected override Size ArrangeOverride(Size sizeFinal)
{
    Point ptChild = new Point(0, 0);

    foreach (UIElement child in children)
    {
        Size sizeChild = new Size(0, 0);

        sizeChild.Width = child.DesiredSize.Width *
                          (sizeFinal.Width / sizeChildrenTotal.Width);
        sizeChild.Height = child.DesiredSize.Height *
                          (sizeFinal.Height / sizeChildrenTotal.Height);

        child.Arrange(new Rect(ptChild, sizeChild));
```

```
                    ptChild.X += sizeChild.Width;
                    ptChild.Y += sizeChild.Height;
            }
            return sizeFinal;
        }
        protected override void OnRender(DrawingContext dc)
        {
            dc.DrawRectangle(Background, null,
                            new Rect(new Point(0, 0), RenderSize));
        }
    }
}
```

The class defines a *Background* property (backed by a dependency property) and implements *OnRender* simply by drawing this background brush over its entire surface. The class implements the *Add* and *Remove* methods I showed earlier, as well as an *IndexOf* method. The class also has very simple overrides of *VisualChildrenCount* and *GetVisualChild*.

It wasn't immediately obvious to me what *Size* values I should pass to the children's *Measure* methods during *MeasureOverride*. I first thought it should be similar to *UniformGridAlmost*: If the panel had seven children, the argument to *Measure* should be 1/7 of the *sizeAvailable* parameter to *MeasureOverride*. But that's not right: If one child is much larger than the other, that child should get more space. I then decided that the entire *sizeAvailable* parameter should be passed to the *Measure* method of each child, and then convinced myself that wasn't right either. It would be wrong if a child assumed that it had exclusive use of all that space.

The only alternative was to give *Measure* a *Size* argument of infinite dimensions, and let the child determine its size without any prompting. It's exactly the same as if you created a *Grid* and gave each of its rows and columns a *GridLength* of *Auto*, and then put children in the diagonal cells.

In *ArrangeOverride*, however, I decided to do something a little different. The class retains the *sizeChildrenTotal* value calculated during *MeasureOverride* as a field, and then uses that—together with the *sizeFinal* parameter to *ArrangeOverride* and the *DesiredSize* property of each child—to scale the children up to the final size of the panel. Remember: A call to *MeasureOverride* is always followed by a call to *ArrangeOverride*, so that anything you calculate during *MeasureOverride* (such as *sizeChildrenTotal*) you can later use in *ArrangeOverride*.

The DiagonalizeTheButtons program creates a panel of type *DiagonalPanel* and puts five buttons in it of various sizes. The panel is always at least the size necessary to fit all five buttons, but the buttons become bigger if the panel is larger than that size.

DiagonalizeTheButtons.cs

```
//-------------------------------------------------------
// DiagonalizeTheButtons.cs (c) 2006 by Charles Petzold
//-------------------------------------------------------
using System;
using System.Windows;
using System.Windows.Controls;
```

```
using System.Windows.Input;
using System.Windows.Media;

namespace Petzold.DiagonalizeTheButtons
{
    public class DiagonalizeTheButtons : Window
    {
        [STAThread]
        public static void Main()
        {
            Application app = new Application();
            app.Run(new DiagonalizeTheButtons());
        }
        public DiagonalizeTheButtons()
        {
            Title = "Diagonalize the Buttons";

            DiagonalPanel pnl = new DiagonalPanel();
            Content = pnl;

            Random rand = new Random();

            for (int i = 0; i < 5; i++)
            {
                Button btn = new Button();
                btn.Content = "Button Number " + (i + 1);
                btn.FontSize += rand.Next(20);
                pnl.Add(btn);
            }
        }
    }
}
```

The final example in this chapter is a radial panel—that is, a panel that arranges its children in a circle. But before you start coding such a panel, you really need to nail down some conceptual issues.

A circle can be divided into pie slice wedges, and probably the most straightforward approach to arranging elements in a circle is to position each element in its own wedge. To take maximum advantage of the space available in the wedge, the element must snugly fit within the circumference of the circle at the outer part of the wedge, as shown here:

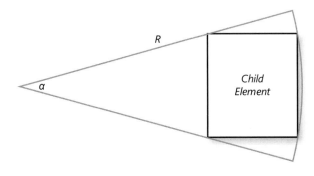

This particular wedge happens to be located at the far right part of the total circle, so the element is oriented normally. That's certainly convenient, but for other wedges, the element must be rotated so that it fits in the wedge in the same way.

The panel width and height equals twice the radius R, and all the angles α total 360 degrees. For a particular child element size, the larger the radius, the smaller the angle. There are two general ways to go about apportioning space for the children: If the size of the panel is fixed, angles can be apportioned based on the size of each element. This approach is best if you expect the children to vary widely in size.

However, if you expect all the children to be about the same size, it makes more sense to give each element the same angle, so α equals 360 degrees divided by the number of children. The radius R can then be calculated based on the largest child. This is the approach that I took.

It is fairly straightforward to calculate a radius R based on a fixed angle α and a width (W) and height (H) of a child element. First, construct a line A that bisects angle α and extends to the inner edge of the child:

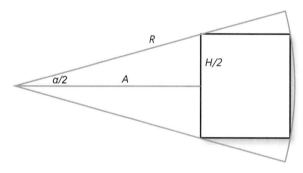

You can calculate the length of A like so:

$$A = \frac{H/2}{\tan(\alpha/2)}$$

In the code coming up for the radial panel, this length A is called *innerEdgeFromCenter*, referring to the inner edge of the element and the center of the circle. The program also calculates *outerEdgeFromCenter*, which is *innerEdgeFromCenter* plus the width W of the element, as shown here:

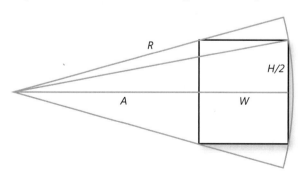

Notice the other line drawn from the center to the top-right corner of the element. That too is a radius. It is now possible to use the Pythagorean theorem to calculate the length of that line:

$$R = \sqrt{(A+W)^2 + \left(\frac{H}{2}\right)^2}$$

The diagrams of the pie wedge show an element that is nearly square, but many elements (such as buttons or text blocks) are wider than they are high. Both the width and the height play a role in determining the radius, but the orientation shown in the diagrams suggests that the element's height dominates, and that a collection of elements will be arranged on the panel like so:

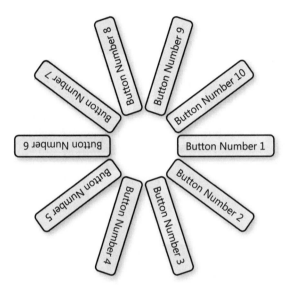

It is also possible to orient the buttons so that the width dominates the calculation:

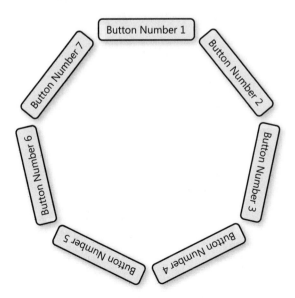

I call these two possibilities *ByHeight* and *ByWidth*, and they are represented as two members of an enumeration:

RadialPanelOrientation.cs
```
//------------------------------------------------------
// RadialPanelOrientation.cs (c) 2006 by Charles Petzold
//------------------------------------------------------
namespace Petzold.CircleTheButtons
{
    public enum RadialPanelOrientation
    {
        ByWidth,
        ByHeight
    }
}
```

The *RadialPanel* class defines a property named *Orientation* of type *RadialPanelOrientation* backed by a dependency property that indicates a default value of *ByWidth* (corresponding to the second of the two diagrams of buttons arranged in a circle). The class inherits from *Panel*, so it can take advantage of the *Children* and *InternalChildren* collections as well as the *Background* property. (It has enough to do without worrying about the routine stuff!)

RadialPanel also defines another property named *ShowPieLines* that is similar to the *ShowGridLines* property of *Grid*. It is intended solely for experimentation.

RadialPanel.cs
```
//---------------------------------------------
// RadialPanel.cs (c) 2006 by Charles Petzold
//---------------------------------------------
using System;
using System.Windows;
using System.Windows.Controls;
using System.Windows.Input;
using System.Windows.Media;

namespace Petzold.CircleTheButtons
{
    public class RadialPanel : Panel
    {
        // Dependency Property.
        public static readonly DependencyProperty OrientationProperty;

        // Private fields.
        bool showPieLines;
        double angleEach;          // angle for each child
        Size sizeLargest;          // size of largest child
        double radius;             // radius of circle
        double outerEdgeFromCenter;
        double innerEdgeFromCenter;

        // Static constructor to create Orientation dependency property.
        static RadialPanel()
```

```
{
    OrientationProperty =
        DependencyProperty.Register("Orientation",
            typeof(RadialPanelOrientation), typeof(RadialPanel),
            new FrameworkPropertyMetadata(RadialPanelOrientation.ByWidth,
                FrameworkPropertyMetadataOptions.AffectsMeasure));
}
// Orientation property.
public RadialPanelOrientation Orientation
{
    set { SetValue(OrientationProperty, value); }
    get { return (RadialPanelOrientation)GetValue(OrientationProperty); }
}
// ShowPieLines property.
public bool ShowPieLines
{
    set
    {
        if (value != showPieLines)
            InvalidateVisual();

        showPieLines = value;
    }
    get
    {
        return showPieLines;
    }
}
// Override of MeasureOverride.
protected override Size MeasureOverride(Size sizeAvailable)
{
    if (InternalChildren.Count == 0)
        return new Size(0, 0);

    angleEach = 360.0 / InternalChildren.Count;
    sizeLargest = new Size(0, 0);

    foreach (UIElement child in InternalChildren)
    {
        // Call Measure for each child ...
        child.Measure(new Size(Double.PositiveInfinity,
                               Double.PositiveInfinity));

        // ... and then examine DesiredSize property of child.
        sizeLargest.Width = Math.Max(sizeLargest.Width,
                                     child.DesiredSize.Width);

        sizeLargest.Height = Math.Max(sizeLargest.Height,
                                      child.DesiredSize.Height);
    }
    if (Orientation == RadialPanelOrientation.ByWidth)
    {
        // Calculate the distance from the center to element edges.
        innerEdgeFromCenter = sizeLargest.Width / 2 /
                            Math.Tan(Math.PI * angleEach / 360);
        outerEdgeFromCenter = innerEdgeFromCenter + sizeLargest.Height;
```

```
                // Calculate the radius of the circle based on the largest child.
                radius = Math.Sqrt(Math.Pow(sizeLargest.Width / 2, 2) +
                                Math.Pow(outerEdgeFromCenter, 2));
        }
        else
        {
            // Calculate the distance from the center to element edges.
            innerEdgeFromCenter = sizeLargest.Height / 2 /
                                    Math.Tan(Math.PI * angleEach / 360);
            outerEdgeFromCenter = innerEdgeFromCenter + sizeLargest.Width;

            // Calculate the radius of the circle based on the largest child.
            radius = Math.Sqrt(Math.Pow(sizeLargest.Height / 2, 2) +
                            Math.Pow(outerEdgeFromCenter, 2));
        }
        // Return the size of that circle.
        return new Size(2 * radius, 2 * radius);
    }
    // Override of ArrangeOverride.
    protected override Size ArrangeOverride(Size sizeFinal)
    {
        double angleChild = 0;
        Point ptCenter = new Point(sizeFinal.Width / 2, sizeFinal.Height / 2);
        double multiplier = Math.Min(sizeFinal.Width / (2 * radius),
                                sizeFinal.Height / (2 * radius));

        foreach (UIElement child in InternalChildren)
        {
            // Reset RenderTransform.
            child.RenderTransform = Transform.Identity;

            if (Orientation == RadialPanelOrientation.ByWidth)
            {
                // Position the child at the top.
                child.Arrange(
                    new Rect(ptCenter.X - multiplier * sizeLargest.Width / 2,
                            ptCenter.Y - multiplier * outerEdgeFromCenter,
                            multiplier * sizeLargest.Width,
                            multiplier * sizeLargest.Height));
            }
            else
            {
                // Position the child at the right.
                child.Arrange(
                    new Rect(ptCenter.X + multiplier * innerEdgeFromCenter,
                            ptCenter.Y - multiplier * sizeLargest.Height / 2,
                            multiplier * sizeLargest.Width,
                            multiplier * sizeLargest.Height));
            }
            // Rotate the child around the center (relative to the child).
            Point pt = TranslatePoint(ptCenter, child);
            child.RenderTransform =
                        new RotateTransform(angleChild, pt.X, pt.Y);
```

```
                    // Increment the angle.
                    angleChild += angleEach;
            }
        return sizeFinal;
    }
    // Override OnRender to display optional pie lines.
    protected override void OnRender(DrawingContext dc)
    {
        base.OnRender(dc);

        if (ShowPieLines)
        {
            Point ptCenter =
                new Point(RenderSize.Width / 2, RenderSize.Height / 2);
            double multiplier = Math.Min(RenderSize.Width / (2 * radius),
                                    RenderSize.Height / (2 * radius));
            Pen pen = new Pen(SystemColors.WindowTextBrush, 1);
            pen.DashStyle = DashStyles.Dash;

            // Display circle.
            dc.DrawEllipse(null, pen, ptCenter, multiplier * radius,
                                            multiplier * radius);
            // Initialize angle.
            double angleChild = -angleEach / 2;

            if (Orientation == RadialPanelOrientation.ByWidth)
                angleChild += 90;

            // Loop through each child to draw radial lines from center.
            foreach (UIElement child in InternalChildren)
            {
                dc.DrawLine(pen, ptCenter,
                    new Point(ptCenter.X + multiplier * radius *
                            Math.Cos(2 * Math.PI * angleChild / 360),
                        ptCenter.Y + multiplier * radius *
                            Math.Sin(2 * Math.PI * angleChild / 360)));
                angleChild += angleEach;
            }
        }
    }
}
}
```

The *MeasureOverride* method calculates an *angleEach* by simply dividing 360 by the total number of children. It then loops through all the children and calls *Measure* with an infinite size. The *foreach* loop examines the size of each child and finds the largest width and height of all the children. It stores this in the variable *sizeLargestChild*.

The remainder of the *MeasureOverride* method depending on the orientation. The method calculates the two fields *innerEdgeFromCenter* and *outerEdgeFromCenter*, and then the radius of the circle. The size that *MeasureOverride* returns is a square with dimensions that are double the calculated radius.

ArrangeOverride begins by calculating a center point of *sizeFinal* and a factor I call *multiplier*. This is a multiplicative factor that can be applied to items calculated during *MeasureOverride* (specifically, *sizeLargest*, *innerEdgeFromCenter*, and *outerEdgeFromCenter*) to expand the circle to the dimensions of *sizeFinal*. For *RadialPanelOrientation.ByWidth*, the *Arrange* method arranges every child at the top of the circle. For *ByHeight*, the *Arrange* method puts each child at the position on the far right. The *RenderTransform* method then rotates the child around the center of *sizeFinal* by *angleChild* degrees. (Notice that *angleChild* begins at 0 and increases by *angleEach* for each child.) The second and third arguments to *RenderTransform* indicate the center of *sizeFinal* relative to the child.

RenderTransform is one of two different graphics transforms supported by *FrameworkElement*. I demonstrated *LayoutTransform* in Chapter 3. As the name implies, *LayoutTransform* affects layout because it causes different *DesiredSize* values to be calculated by the *Measure* method. For example, suppose an element normally calculates a *DesiredSize* of 100 units wide by 25 units high. If *LayoutTransform* is set for a 90-degree rotation, *DesiredSize* will be 25 units wide and 100 units high.

RenderTransform, however, is intended mostly for transforms that should not affect layout. As the documentation suggests, *RenderTransform* is "typically intended for animating or applying a temporary effect to an element." Obviously, the *RadialPanel* class is using *RenderTransform* for a far more profound effect, but it's also very clear that something that affects element size (such as *LayoutTransform*) shouldn't be messed with during layout.

And here's a program to experiment with *RadialPanel*. It's set up to arrange 10 buttons of somewhat varying size with a *ByWidth* orientation.

```
CircleTheButtons.cs
//-------------------------------------------------
// CircleTheButtons.cs (c) 2006 by Charles Petzold
//-------------------------------------------------
using System;
using System.Windows;
using System.Windows.Controls;
using System.Windows.Input;
using System.Windows.Media;

namespace Petzold.CircleTheButtons
{
    public class CircleTheButtons : Window
    {
        [STAThread]
        public static void Main()
        {
            Application app = new Application();
            app.Run(new CircleTheButtons());
        }
        public CircleTheButtons()
        {
            Title = "Circle the Buttons";
```

```
            RadialPanel pnl = new RadialPanel();
            pnl.Orientation = RadialPanelOrientation.ByWidth;
            pnl.ShowPieLines = true;
            Content = pnl;

            Random rand = new Random();

            for (int i = 0; i < 10; i++)
            {
                Button btn = new Button();
                btn.Content = "Button Number " + (i + 1);
                btn.FontSize += rand.Next(10);
                pnl.Children.Add(btn);
            }
        }
    }
}
```

As a result of the *multiplier* factor in the *ArrangeOverride* method in *RadialPanel*, as the panel expands to the size of its container, the buttons expand proportionally. (You can set *multiplier* to 1 to prevent this expansion of buttons.) You might want to try the typical experiments: If you set *SizeToContent* of the window to *WidthAndHeight*, or if you set the *HorizontalAlignment* and *VerticalAlignment* properties of the panel to something other than *Stretch*, every button will be the size of the largest button, and the panel will be just as large as it needs to be. You can also try setting a non-zero *Margin* for each button, or setting the *HorizontalAlignment* or *VerticalAlignment* of the buttons to something besides *Stretch*.

And, of course, you can set the *RadialPanel* orientation to *ByWidth* and change the number of buttons to 40 or so.

Although panels are used most obviously for laying out windows and dialog boxes, they can also play roles in layout *within* controls. You saw an example of this in the *ColorGrid* control from the previous chapter. But consider a more general-purpose control, such as a *ListBox*. A *ListBox* basically begins with a *Border*, and the *Border* has a child of *ScrollViewer*, and the *ScrollViewer* has a child of a *StackPanel*, and the items listed by the *ListBox* are children of the *StackPanel*.

What do you suppose might happen if it was possible to substitute the *StackPanel* in a *ListBox* with some other kind of panel, such as the *RadialPanel*? The *ListBox* would look completely different, but it would still work in much the same way. The next chapter will take on this challenge and conclude with a radial list box.

Chapter 13
ListBox Selection

Many of the controls presented so far in this book have derived from *ContentControl*. These controls include *Window*, *Label*, *Button*, *ScrollViewer*, and *ToolTip*. All these controls have a *Content* property that you set to a string or to another element. If you set the *Content* property to a panel, you can put multiple elements on that panel.

The *GroupBox*—commonly used to hold radio buttons—also derives from *ContentControl* but by way of *HeaderedContentControl*. The *GroupBox* has a *Content* property, and it also has a *Header* property for the text (or whatever) that appears at the top of the box.

The *TextBox* and *RichTextBox* controls do *not* derive from *ContentControl*. These controls derive from the abstract class *TextBoxBase* and allow the user to enter and edit text. The *ScrollBar* class also does not derive from *ContentControl*. It inherits from the abstract *RangeBase* class, a class characterized by maintaining a *Value* property of type *double* that ranges between *Minimum* and *Maximum* properties.

Beginning with this chapter, you will be introduced to another major branch of the *Control* hierarchy: The *ItemsControl* class, which derives directly from *Control*. Controls that derive from *ItemsControl* display multiple items, generally of the same sort, either in a hierarchy or a list. These controls include menus, toolbars, status bars, tree views, and list views.

This particular chapter focuses mostly on *ListBox*, which is one of three controls that derive from *ItemsControl* by way of *Selector*:

Control

    ItemsControl

        Selector (abstract)

            ComboBox

            ListBox

            TabControl

Considered abstractly, a *ListBox* allows the user to select one item (or, optionally, multiple items) from a collection of items. In its default form, the *ListBox* is plain and austere. The items are presented in a vertical list and scroll bars are automatically provided if the list is too long or the items too wide. The *ListBox* highlights the selected item and provides a keyboard and mouse interface. (The *ComboBox* is similar to the *ListBox* but the list of items is not permanently displayed. I'll discuss *ComboBox* in Chapter 15.)

The crucial property of *ListBox* is *Items*, which the class inherits from *ItemsControl*. *Items* is of type *ItemCollection*, which is a collection of items of type *object*, which implies that just about any object can go into a *ListBox*. Although a *ListBoxItem* class exists specifically for list box items, you aren't required to use it. The simplest approach involves putting strings in the *ListBox*.

A program creates a *ListBox* object in the expected manner:

```
ListBox lstbox = new ListBox();
```

The *ListBox* is a collection of items, and these items must be added to the *Items* collection in a process called "filling the *ListBox*":

```
lstbox.Items.Add("Sunday");
lstbox.Items.Add("Monday");
lstbox.Items.Add("Tuesday");
lstbox.Items.Add("Wednesday");
...
```

Of course, list boxes are almost never filled with individual *Add* statements. Very often an array is involved:

```
string[] strDayNames = { "Sunday", "Monday", "Tuesday", "Wednesday",
                         "Thursday", "Friday", "Saturday" };

foreach(string str in strDayNames)
    list.Items.Add(str);
```

And it's always nice to find a class like *DateTimeFormatInfo* in the *System.Globalization* namespace that provides these names for you in the user's own language:

```
string[] strDayNames = DateTimeFormatInfo.CurrentInfo.DayNames;
```

or a "culture-independent" language (that is, English):

```
string[] strDayNames = DateTimeFormatInfo.InvariantInfo.DayNames;
```

Another way to fill up the *ListBox* is by setting the *ItemsSource* property defined by *Items-Control*. You can set *ItemsSource* to any object that implements the *IEnumerable* interface, which means that you can set *ItemsSource* to any collection that you might also use with *foreach*. For example:

```
lstbox.ItemsSource = DateTimeFormatInfo.CurrentInfo.DayNames;
```

These two approaches to filling the *ListBox*—adding items through the *Add* method of the *Items* property and setting *ItemsSource*—are mutually exclusive.

Both the *Items* and *ItemsSource* properties are defined by the *ItemsControl* class. Two other useful *ListBox* properties are defined by *Selector*. These are *SelectedIndex* and *SelectedItem*, which indicate the item currently selected in the *ListBox* and which the *ListBox* displays with a special colored background (by default, blue).

By default, *SelectedIndex* equals −1 and *SelectedItem* equals *null*, which means that no item is selected. The *ListBox* doesn't automatically decide that a particular item from the *Items* collection should be selected. If your program doesn't deliberately set a selected item, *SelectedIndex* remains −1 and *SelectedItem* remains *null* until the user gets hold of the control.

If your program wants to set a selected item before the user sees the *ListBox*, it can do so by setting either *SelectedIndex* or *SelectedItem*. For example,

```
lstbox.SelectedItem = 5;
```

selects the sixth item in the *Items* collection. *SelectedIndex* must be an integer ranging from −1 to one less than the number of items in the *Items* collection. If an item is selected, then

```
lstbox.SelectedItem
```

is equivalent to

```
lstbox.Items[lstbox.SelectedIndex]
```

When the selection changes, the *ListBox* fires the *SelectionChanged* event defined by *Selector*.

As a case study, let's try to design a *ListBox* that lets the user choose a color. This is a fairly common example, but certainly a useful one. (Someday, someone will write a book entitled *A Brief History of Color Selection Controls* and it will be 1,700 pages long.)

As you already know, the *System.Windows.Media* namespace has a class named *Colors* that contains 141 static properties with names that range from *AliceBlue* to *YellowGreen*. These static properties return objects of type *Color*. You could define an array like this and then fill up the list box from this array:

```
Color[] clrs = { Colors.AliceBlue, Colors.AntiqueWhite, ... };
```

But before you type 141 color names, there's a better approach, made possible by reflection. As you learned in Chapter 2, a program can use reflection to obtain all the *Color* objects defined in *Colors*. The expression *typeof(Colors)* returns an object of type *Type*, which defines a method named *GetProperties* that returns an array of *PropertyInfo* objects, each one corresponding to a property of the *Colors* class. You can then use the *Name* property of *PropertyInfo* to obtain the name of the property and the *GetValue* method to obtain the actual *Color* value.

The eventual goal here is to display the actual colors in the *ListBox* in some fashion. But let's start out simply with just the color names.

ListColorNames.cs

```
//------------------------------------------------
// ListColorNames.cs (c) 2006 by Charles Petzold
//------------------------------------------------
using System;
using System.Reflection;
using System.Windows;
```

```
using System.Windows.Controls;
using System.Windows.Input;
using System.Windows.Media;

namespace Petzold.ListColorNames
{
    class ListColorNames : Window
    {
        [STAThread]
        public static void Main()
        {
            Application app = new Application();
            app.Run(new ListColorNames());
        }
        public ListColorNames()
        {
            Title = "List Color Names";

            // Create ListBox as content of window.
            ListBox lstbox = new ListBox();
            lstbox.Width = 150;
            lstbox.Height = 150;
            lstbox.SelectionChanged += ListBoxOnSelectionChanged;
            Content = lstbox;

            // Fill ListBox with Color names.
            PropertyInfo[] props = typeof(Colors).GetProperties();

            foreach (PropertyInfo prop in props)
                lstbox.Items.Add(prop.Name);
        }
        void ListBoxOnSelectionChanged(object sender,
                                SelectionChangedEventArgs args)
        {
            ListBox lstbox = sender as ListBox;
            string str = lstbox.SelectedItem as string;

            if (str != null)
            {
                Color clr =
                    (Color)typeof(Colors).GetProperty(str).GetValue(null, null);
                Background = new SolidColorBrush(clr);
            }
        }
    }
}
```

You might benefit from getting a feel for the user interface of the *ListBox* before exploring the programmatic interface.

This program does not set input focus to the *ListBox*, and there is no initially selected item. You can fix that by clicking one of the items in the *ListBox* with the mouse. The background of the window changes to that color. You can continue to use the mouse to click different items. You can scroll the items by clicking the scroll bar. The currently selected *ListBox* item is always displayed with a special background color (blue by default). Notice also that the color of the text of the selected item changes from black to white to contrast with that blue background.

Of course, you can control the *ListBox* entirely from the keyboard. When you first run the program, press the Tab key to give the *ListBox* input focus. You'll see a dotted *focus rectangle* surrounding the first item. At this point, there is no selected item. You can press the spacebar to select the item indicated by the focus rectangle. Press the Up or Down arrow key to change the selected item. The *ListBox* also responds to Page Up, Page Down, Home, and End. You can type letters to move to items that begin with that letter.

If you hold the Ctrl key down and click the currently selected item with the mouse, the item will become unselected. (The color of the window background remains the same because the program is ignoring that little anomaly.) If you hold the Ctrl key down while pressing the Up and Down arrow keys, you can move the focus rectangle without changing the selection. You can then select an item or clear a selection with the spacebar. Again, it is possible to put the *ListBox* into a state where no item is currently selected.

Let's look at the code. The window constructor begins by creating a *ListBox* and giving it an explicit size in device-independent units. It is common to give a *ListBox* a specific size. The dimensions you choose will depend on the contents of the *ListBox* and its context.

If you don't give the *ListBox* a specific size, the control will fill the entire space allowed for it. If you instead set *HorizontalAlignment* and *VerticalAlignment* to *Center*, the *ListBox* will still stretch itself vertically to display as many items as possible, and the width will be based on the currently visible items. As you scroll through the items, it's possible that you will then witness the *ListBox* becoming narrower and wider depending on the particular items it displays.

The program fills the *ListBox* with color names and sets a handler for the *SelectionChanged* event. The event handler obtains the selected item from the *ListBox* using the *SelectedItem* property. (Notice that the event handler checks for a *null* value indicating no currently selected item and doesn't do anything in that case.) In this program, the *ListBox* item is a string, so it needs to be converted into a *Color* object. Again, reflection comes to the rescue. The *GetProperty* call obtains the *PropertyInfo* object associated with the static property in *Colors*, and *GetValue* obtains the *Color* object.

If you'd prefer that the *ListBox* have input focus and display a selection when the program starts up, you can add code to the bottom of the window constructor like this:

```
lstbox.SelectedItem = "Magenta";
lstbox.ScrollIntoView(lstbox.SelectedItem);
lstbox.Focus();
```

Notice the *ScrollIntoView* call to scroll the *ListBox* so that the selected item is visible.

Although the *Selector* class implements only single-selection logic, the *ListBox* class itself allows the selection of multiple items. You set the *SelectionMode* property to a member of the *SelectionMode* enumeration: *Single*, *Extended*, or *Multiple*.

With *SelectionMode.Multiple*, you select and clear individual items with a click of the left mouse button. Or, you can use the arrow keys to move a focus rectangle and select or clear individual items with the spacebar.

With *SelectionMode.Extended*, you can select and clear individual items with the mouse only when the Ctrl key is pressed. Or, you can select a range of items by holding down the Shift key and clicking each item. If neither the Shift key nor the Ctrl key is down, a mouse click causes all previous selections to be unselected. When using the keyboard rather than the mouse, you must hold the Ctrl key to move the focus rectangle, and you select individual items with the spacebar. Or you can hold down the Shift key and use the arrow keys to select a group of consecutive items.

When using *ListBox* in a multiple-selection mode, you'll make use of the *SelectedItems* property (notice the plural), which is a collection of multiple items. Although the *ListBox* class has the necessary support of multiple-selection boxes, the *SelectionChanged* event defined by the *Selector* class also helps out. This event comes with an object of type *SelectionChangedEventArgs* with two properties named *AddedItems* and *RemovedItems*. These are both lists of items that have been added to or removed from the collection of selected items. If you're working with a single-selection *ListBox*, you usually don't need to bother with these properties.

The *Items* collection of *ListBox* is a collection of objects of type *object*, so it's possible to put *Color* objects directly in the *ListBox*. Let's try that.

```
ListColorValues.cs
//-------------------------------------------------
// ListColorValues.cs (c) 2006 by Charles Petzold
//-------------------------------------------------
using System;
using System.Reflection;
using System.Windows;
using System.Windows.Input;
using System.Windows.Controls;
using System.Windows.Media;

namespace Petzold.ListColorValues
{
    class ListColorValues : Window
    {
        [STAThread]
        public static void Main()
        {
            Application app = new Application();
            app.Run(new ListColorValues());
        }
        public ListColorValues()
```

```
        {
            Title = "List Color Values";

            // Create ListBox as content of window.
            ListBox lstbox = new ListBox();
            lstbox.Width = 150;
            lstbox.Height = 150;
            lstbox.SelectionChanged += ListBoxOnSelectionChanged;
            Content = lstbox;

            // Fill ListBox with Color values.
            PropertyInfo[] props = typeof(Colors).GetProperties();

            foreach (PropertyInfo prop in props)
                lstbox.Items.Add(prop.GetValue(null, null));
        }
        void ListBoxOnSelectionChanged(object sender,
                                     SelectionChangedEventArgs args)
        {
            ListBox lstbox = sender as ListBox;

            if (lstbox.SelectedIndex != -1)
            {
                Color clr = (Color)lstbox.SelectedItem;
                Background = new SolidColorBrush(clr);
            }
        }
    }
}
```

This approach simplifies the event handler because the *SelectedItem* need only be cast to an object of type *Color*. Otherwise, it's a disaster. The *ListBox* displays the string returned from the *ToString* method of *Color*, and that turns out to be strings like "#FFF0F8FF." Even programmers with eight fingers on each hand don't like seeing hexadecimal color values in list boxes. The problem is that the *Color* structure knows nothing about the names in the *Colors* class. I wouldn't be surprised if the entire *Colors* class was implemented with properties like this:

```
public static Color AliceBlue
{
    get { return Color.FromRgb(0xF0, 0xF8, 0xFF); }
}
```

That's my guess, anyway.

Color is not the most conducive type of object to go into a *ListBox*. Much better are those objects that have a *ToString* method that returns exactly what you want to display to the user. Of course, that's not always possible, and there are some who would argue that *ToString* should return a string representation that might be human-readable, but which is primarily formatted for easy computer readability. Regardless, in the case of *Color*, major changes would need to be made so that *ToString* returned the color name.

Here's a class called *NamedColor* that illustrates a somewhat more desirable definition of a
class you might use with a *ListBox*.

NamedColor.cs

```
//---------------------------------------------
// NamedColor.cs (c) 2006 by Charles Petzold
//---------------------------------------------
using System;
using System.Reflection;
using System.Windows.Media;

namespace Petzold.ListNamedColors
{
    class NamedColor
    {
        static NamedColor[] nclrs;
        Color clr;
        string str;

        // Static constructor.
        static NamedColor()
        {
            PropertyInfo[] props = typeof(Colors).GetProperties();
            nclrs = new NamedColor[props.Length];

            for (int i = 0; i < props.Length; i++)
                nclrs[i] = new NamedColor(props[i].Name,
                                    (Color)props[i].GetValue(null, null));
        }

        // Private constructor.
        private NamedColor(string str, Color clr)
        {
            this.str = str;
            this.clr = clr;
        }

        // Static read-only property.
        public static NamedColor[] All
        {
            get { return nclrs; }
        }

        // Read-only properties.
        public Color Color
        {
            get { return clr; }
        }
        public string Name
        {
            get
            {
                string strSpaced = str[0].ToString();
```

```
                        for (int i = 1; i < str.Length; i++)
                            strSpaced += (char.IsUpper(str[i]) ? " " : "") +
                                                str[i].ToString();
                        return strSpaced;
                    }
                }

                // Override of ToString method.
                public override string ToString()
                {
                    return str;
                }
            }
        }
```

The *NamedColor* class has two private instance fields named *clr* and *str* that store a *Color* value and a string with the color name (such as "AliceBlue"). These fields are set in the private *NamedColor* constructor. The fields are accessible from the public *Color* property and the override of the *ToString* property.

The *Name* property is similar to *ToString* except that it inserts spaces into the color names to make them actual words. For example, "AliceBlue" becomes "Alice Blue".

The static constructor is crucial to the functionality of this class. This static constructor uses reflection to access the *Colors* class. For each property in that class, the static *NamedColor* constructor uses the private instance constructor to create an object of type *NamedColor*. The array of resultant *NamedColor* objects is stored as a field and is publicly accessible through the static *All* method.

So, we could use this class instead of *Colors* to fill up a *ListBox* with code as simple as this:

```
foreach (NamedColor nclr in NamedColor.All)
    lstbox.Items.Add(nclr);
```

The *ListBox* uses the string returned from *ToString* to display the items. In the event handler you'd cast the *SelectedItem* to an object of type *NamedColor* and then access the *Color* property:

```
Color clr = (lstbox.SelectedItem as NamedColor).Color;
```

That's one way to do it, but there's an easier alternative. Rather than filling up the *ListBox* with a *foreach* loop, you can instead pass the array of *NamedColor* values directly to the *ItemsSource* property of the *ListBox*:

```
lstbox.ItemsSource = NamedColor.All;
```

This statement replaces the *foreach* loop, and the program works the same way.

Regardless of whether you use the *foreach* loop or *ItemsSource*, all the items in the *ListBox* are of the same type, and that type is *NamedColor*. This little fact allows you to use three other *ListBox* properties: *DisplayMemberPath*, *SelectedValuePath*, and *SelectedValue*.

The *DisplayMemberPath* property is defined by *ItemsControl*. You optionally set this property to a string containing the name of a property that you want the *ListBox* to use to display the items. For items of type *NamedColor*, that property is *Name*:

```
lstbox.DisplayMemberPath = "Name";
```

Now, instead of using *ToString* to display each item, the *ListBox* will use the *Name* property of each item and the colors will appear as "Alice Blue" rather than "AliceBlue".

The other two properties you can use are defined by the *Selector* class and are related. You use the *SelectedValuePath* property to indicate the name of the property that represents the value of the item. For the *NamedColor* class, that property is *Color*, so you can set *SelectedValuePath* like this:

```
lstbox.SelectedValuePath = "Color";
```

Now, rather than using *SelectedIndex* or *SelectedItem* in your event handler to obtain the currently selected item, you can instead use *SelectedValue*. The *SelectedValue* property returns the *Color* property of the selected item. Casting is still required but the code is definitely simpler:

```
Color clr = (Color) lstbox.SelectedValue;
```

In summary, the strings you assign to *DisplayMemberPath* and *SelectedValuePath* must be the names of properties defined by the class (or structure) of the type of the *ListBox* items. *DisplayMemberPath* tells the *ListBox* which property to use for displaying the items in the *ListBox*. *SelectedValuePath* tells the *ListBox* which property to use for returning a value from *SelectedValue*. (*DisplayMemberPath* and *SelectedValuePath* are "paths" because the properties could be nested in other properties, and you would specify the entire path by separating the property names with periods.)

Here's a complete program that uses the *NamedColor* class to fill its *ListBox*.

```
ListNamedColors.cs
//-------------------------------------------------
// ListNamedColors.cs (c) 2006 by Charles Petzold
//-------------------------------------------------
using System;
using System.Windows;
using System.Windows.Controls;
using System.Windows.Input;
using System.Windows.Media;
```

```
namespace Petzold.ListNamedColors
{
    class ListNamedColors : Window
    {
        [STAThread]
        public static void Main()
        {
            Application app = new Application();
            app.Run(new ListNamedColors());
        }
        public ListNamedColors()
        {
            Title = "List Named Colors";

            // Create ListBox as content of window.
            ListBox lstbox = new ListBox();
            lstbox.Width = 150;
            lstbox.Height = 150;
            lstbox.SelectionChanged += ListBoxOnSelectionChanged;
            Content = lstbox;

            // Set the items and the property paths.
            lstbox.ItemsSource = NamedColor.All;
            lstbox.DisplayMemberPath = "Name";
            lstbox.SelectedValuePath = "Color";
        }
        void ListBoxOnSelectionChanged(object sender,
                                        SelectionChangedEventArgs args)
        {
            ListBox lstbox = sender as ListBox;

            if (lstbox.SelectedValue != null)
            {
                Color clr = (Color)lstbox.SelectedValue;
                Background = new SolidColorBrush(clr);
            }
        }
    }
}
```

Creating a whole class solely for filling a *ListBox* may seem excessive, but as you can see, the code that uses that class is cleaned up considerably.

But can we clean it up even more? Well, it's too bad that the *ListBox* is returning a *SelectedValue* of type *Color*, when what we really need to set the *Background* property of the window is an object of type *Brush*. If *ListBox* were instead storing objects with a *Brush* property, we could actually bind the *SelectedValue* property of the *ListBox* with the *Background* property of the window.

Let's try it. This class is virtually identical to *NamedColor* except that it replaces references to *Color* and *Colors* with *Brush* and *Brushes*.

NamedBrush.cs

```
//------------------------------------------
// NamedBrush.cs (c) 2006 by Charles Petzold
//------------------------------------------
using System;
using System.Reflection;
using System.Windows.Media;

namespace Petzold.ListNamedBrushes
{
    public class NamedBrush
    {
        static NamedBrush[] nbrushes;
        Brush brush;
        string str;

        // Static constructor.
        static NamedBrush()
        {
            PropertyInfo[] props = typeof(Brushes).GetProperties();
            nbrushes = new NamedBrush[props.Length];

            for (int i = 0; i < props.Length; i++)
                nbrushes[i] = new NamedBrush(props[i].Name,
                                    (Brush)props[i].GetValue(null, null));
        }

        // Private constructor.
        private NamedBrush(string str, Brush brush)
        {
            this.str = str;
            this.brush = brush;
        }

        // Static read-only property.
        public static NamedBrush[] All
        {
            get { return nbrushes; }
        }

        // Read-only properties.
        public Brush Brush
        {
            get { return brush; }
        }
        public string Name
        {
            get
            {
                string strSpaced = str[0].ToString();
```

```
                    for (int i = 1; i < str.Length; i++)
                        strSpaced += (char.IsUpper(str[i]) ? " " : "") +
                                            str[i].ToString();
                    return strSpaced;
                }
            }

            // Override of ToString method.
            public override string ToString()
            {
                return str;
            }
        }
    }
}
```

If you put *NamedBrush* objects in a *ListBox*, you'll set *SelectedValuePath* to "Brush". If you choose to have an event handler, you could set the *Background* property from the *SelectedValue* simply with a little casting:

```
Background = (Brush)lstbox.SelectedValue;
```

However, when the event handler gets this easy, it can be dispensed with altogether and replaced with a data binding:

```
lstbox.SetBinding(ListBox.SelectedValueProperty, "Background");
lstbox.DataContext = this;
```

This binding indicates that the *SelectedValue* property of the *ListBox* object is to be bound with the *Background* property of the object *this* (which is the window). Here's the complete program that uses *NamedBrush*:

ListNamedBrushes.cs
```
//-------------------------------------------------
// ListNamedBrushes.cs (c) 2006 by Charles Petzold
//-------------------------------------------------
using System;
using System.Windows;
using System.Windows.Controls;
using System.Windows.Input;
using System.Windows.Media;

namespace Petzold.ListNamedBrushes
{
    public class ListNamedBrushes : Window
    {
        [STAThread]
        public static void Main()
        {
            Application app = new Application();
            app.Run(new ListNamedBrushes());
        }
```

```
        public ListNamedBrushes()
        {
            Title = "List Named Brushes";

            // Create ListBox as content of window.
            ListBox lstbox = new ListBox();
            lstbox.Width = 150;
            lstbox.Height = 150;
            Content = lstbox;

            // Set the items and the property paths.
            lstbox.ItemsSource = NamedBrush.All;
            lstbox.DisplayMemberPath = "Name";
            lstbox.SelectedValuePath = "Brush";

            // Bind the SelectedValue to window Background.
            lstbox.SetBinding(ListBox.SelectedValueProperty, "Background");
            lstbox.DataContext = this;
        }
    }
}
```

What's nice about this program is that it no longer has any event handlers. I always think of event handlers as moving parts in a machine. Get rid of them, and you're coding with no moving parts. (Of course, there are moving parts behind the scenes, but those aren't our problem.)

Fortunately, if you put the *ListBox* in a state where there is no selected item, the window doesn't care if the *Background* property is set to *null*. It just turns the client area black and awaits further instruction.

I want to focus now on showing actual colors in the *ListBox*. It will be preferable to show both the color *and* the name, but we'll look at some simpler alternatives first. So far, the only objects appearing as *ListBox* items have been text strings. It is possible to put *Shape* objects into the *ListBox* instead. This program shows how.

ListColorShapes.cs

```
//---------------------------------------------
// ListColorShapes.cs (c) 2006 by Charles Petzold
//---------------------------------------------
using System;
using System.Reflection;
using System.Windows;
using System.Windows.Controls;
using System.Windows.Input;
using System.Windows.Media;
using System.Windows.Shapes;

namespace Petzold.ListColorShapes
{
```

```
class ListColorShapes : Window
{
    [STAThread]
    public static void Main()
    {
        Application app = new Application();
        app.Run(new ListColorShapes());
    }
    public ListColorShapes()
    {
        Title = "List Color Shapes";

        // Create ListBox as content of window.
        ListBox lstbox = new ListBox();
        lstbox.Width = 150;
        lstbox.Height = 150;
        lstbox.SelectionChanged += ListBoxOnSelectionChanged;
        Content = lstbox;

        // Fill ListBox with Ellipse objects.
        PropertyInfo[] props = typeof(Brushes).GetProperties();
        foreach (PropertyInfo prop in props)
        {
            Ellipse ellip = new Ellipse();
            ellip.Width = 100;
            ellip.Height = 25;
            ellip.Margin = new Thickness(10, 5, 0, 5);
            ellip.Fill = prop.GetValue(null, null) as Brush;
            lstbox.Items.Add(ellip);
        }
    }
    void ListBoxOnSelectionChanged(object sender,
                            SelectionChangedEventArgs args)
    {
        ListBox lstbox = sender as ListBox;

        if (lstbox.SelectedIndex != -1)
            Background = (lstbox.SelectedItem as Shape).Fill;
    }
}
}
```

The constructor of the window creates an *Ellipse* object for each property of the *Brushes* class, and assigns that *Brush* object to the *Fill* property of the shape. The event handler is fairly simple: The *Fill* property of the *SelectedItem* is simply assigned to the *Background* property of the window.

When you run this program, you'll see why I used *Ellipse* rather than *Rectangle*, and why I gave each item a healthy margin. *ListBox* denotes the currently selected item with a background color (blue by default), and this technique relies on the items themselves not entirely obscuring the background.

You can also use binding with this program. Rather than attaching an event handler, you could specify that the selected value should be the *Fill* property of the item, and that this selected value should be bound to the *Background* property of the window:

```
lstbox.SelectedValuePath = "Fill";
lstbox.SetBinding(ListBox.SelectedValueProperty, "Background");
lstbox.DataContext = this;
```

What if we want a color *and* a name? One approach is to use *Label* controls as the *ListBox* items. The *Label* text could provide the color name and the background of the label could provide the color. Of course, we'll need to make sure that the foreground color of the text displayed by the label does not blend in with the background, and that there's a sufficient margin around the label so that the *ListBox* can display the selection color.

ListColoredLabels.cs
```
//-------------------------------------------------
// ListColoredLabels.cs (c) 2006 by Charles Petzold
//-------------------------------------------------
using System;
using System.Reflection;
using System.Windows;
using System.Windows.Controls;
using System.Windows.Input;
using System.Windows.Media;

namespace Petzold.ListColoredLabels
{
    class ListColoredLabels : Window
    {
        [STAThread]
        public static void Main()
        {
            Application app = new Application();
            app.Run(new ListColoredLabels());
        }
        public ListColoredLabels()
        {
            Title = "List Colored Labels";

            // Create ListBox as content of window.
            ListBox lstbox = new ListBox();
            lstbox.Height = 150;
            lstbox.Width = 150;
            lstbox.SelectionChanged += ListBoxOnSelectionChanged;
            Content = lstbox;

            // Fill ListBox with label controls.
            PropertyInfo[] props = typeof(Colors).GetProperties();

            foreach (PropertyInfo prop in props)
            {
                Color clr = (Color)prop.GetValue(null, null);
                bool isBlack = .222 * clr.R + .707 * clr.G + .071 * clr.B > 128;
```

```
                    Label lbl = new Label();
                    lbl.Content = prop.Name;
                    lbl.Background = new SolidColorBrush(clr);
                    lbl.Foreground = isBlack ? Brushes.Black : Brushes.White;
                    lbl.Width = 100;
                    lbl.Margin = new Thickness(15, 0, 0, 0);
                    lbl.Tag = clr;
                    lstbox.Items.Add(lbl);
                }
            }
            void ListBoxOnSelectionChanged(object sender,
                                    SelectionChangedEventArgs args)
            {
                ListBox lstbox = sender as ListBox;
                Label lbl = lstbox.SelectedItem as Label;

                if (lbl != null)
                {
                    Color clr = (Color)lbl.Tag;
                    Background = new SolidColorBrush(clr);
                }
            }
        }
    }
}
```

Notice that the program calculates the Boolean *isBlack* value based on the luminance of the color, which is a standard weighted average of the three primaries. This value determines whether the text is displayed in white or black against the colored background.

The event handler could have set the window *Background* brush from the *Background* property of the *Label*, but I decided to use the *Tag* property instead just for a little variety. (The program could alternatively set the *SelectedValuePath* to "Background" and set the window *Background* from the *SelectedValue*, or use binding.)

This program works, but I'm sure you'll agree that it doesn't look very good. To show the blue highlight, the labels are given a width of 100, with a margin of 15 on the left, and some extra space on the right from the width of the *ListBox* itself. It's not quite as elegant as it might be.

I mentioned earlier in this chapter that there exists a class named *ListBoxItem* that derives from *ContentControl*. Obviously, you're not required to use that class in your list boxes, as has been well demonstrated. And if you substitute *ListBoxItem* for *Label* in the previous program, you'll get something that becomes very awkward. The *ListBox* uses the Background property of the *ListBoxItem* for highlighting the selected item, so the selection doesn't stand out as it should.

Still, who says we need to use standard highlighting? We could come up with an alternative for indicating the selected item. The following program takes a rather unconventional approach. It uses *ListBoxItem* objects under the assumption that something more is needed to highlight the selected item.

ListWithListBoxItems.cs

```
//----------------------------------------------------
// ListWithListBoxItems.cs (c) 2006 by Charles Petzold
//----------------------------------------------------
using System;
using System.Reflection;
using System.Windows;
using System.Windows.Controls;
using System.Windows.Input;
using System.Windows.Media;

class ListWithListBoxItems : Window
{
    [STAThread]
    public static void Main()
    {
        Application app = new Application();
        app.Run(new ListWithListBoxItems());
    }
    public ListWithListBoxItems()
    {
        Title = "List with ListBoxItem";

        // Create ListBox as content of window.
        ListBox lstbox = new ListBox();
        lstbox.Height = 150;
        lstbox.Width = 150;
        lstbox.SelectionChanged += ListBoxOnSelectionChanged;
        Content = lstbox;

        // Fill ListBox with ListBoxItem objects.
        PropertyInfo[] props = typeof(Colors).GetProperties();

        foreach (PropertyInfo prop in props)
        {
            Color clr = (Color)prop.GetValue(null, null);
            bool isBlack = .222 * clr.R + .707 * clr.G + .071 * clr.B > 128;

            ListBoxItem item = new ListBoxItem();
            item.Content = prop.Name;
            item.Background = new SolidColorBrush(clr);
            item.Foreground = isBlack ? Brushes.Black : Brushes.White;
            item.HorizontalContentAlignment = HorizontalAlignment.Center;
            item.Padding = new Thickness(2);
            lstbox.Items.Add(item);
        }
    }
    void ListBoxOnSelectionChanged(object sender, SelectionChangedEventArgs args)
    {
        ListBox lstbox = sender as ListBox;
        ListBoxItem item;
```

```
        if (args.RemovedItems.Count > 0)
        {
            item = args.RemovedItems[0] as ListBoxItem;
            String str = item.Content as String;
            item.Content = str.Substring(2, str.Length - 4);
            item.FontWeight = FontWeights.Regular;
        }
        if (args.AddedItems.Count > 0)
        {
            item = args.AddedItems[0] as ListBoxItem;
            String str = item.Content as String;
            item.Content = "[ " + str + " ]";
            item.FontWeight = FontWeights.Bold;
        }

        item = lstbox.SelectedItem as ListBoxItem;

        if (item != null)
            Background = item.Background;
    }
}
```

The *SelectionChanged* event handler not only sets the window *Background* brush from the *Background* of the selected *ListBoxItem*, but also alters the text in that item. It surrounds the text with square brackets and gives it a bolded font. Of course, every item becoming unselected has to be undone. The item that has just been selected and the item that is unselected are both available from the *AddedItems* and *RemovedItems* properties of *SelectionChangedEventArgs*. (These two properties are plural to account for multiple-selection list boxes.)

If giving the selected item a bolded font and brackets isn't enough to make it stand out, you could use the actual font size. Add the following statement to the *AddedItem* sections:

```
item.FontSize *= 2;
```

Undo the increase with this statement in the *RemovedItems* section:

```
item.FontSize = lstbox.FontSize;
```

You'll want to make the *ListBox* itself wider to allow for this increase in item font sizes.

ListBoxItem itself has two events named *Selected* and *Unselected*, and two methods named *OnSelected* and *OnUnselected*. A class that inherits from *ListBoxItem* could override these methods to implement the text-changing and font-changing logic a bit more smoothly.

The following class inherits from *ListBoxItem* and overrides the *OnSelected* and *OnUnselected* methods. But what it really demonstrates is the use of a *StackPanel* to display both a *Rectangle* object colored with the color and a *TextBlock* object with the color name.

ColorListBoxItem.cs

```csharp
//------------------------------------------------
// ColorListBoxItem.cs (c) 2006 by Charles Petzold
//------------------------------------------------
using System;
using System.Windows;
using System.Windows.Controls;
using System.Windows.Input;
using System.Windows.Media;
using System.Windows.Shapes;

namespace Petzold.ListColorsElegantly
{
    class ColorListBoxItem : ListBoxItem
    {
        string str;
        Rectangle rect;
        TextBlock text;

        public ColorListBoxItem()
        {
            // Create StackPanel for Rectangle and TextBlock.
            StackPanel stack = new StackPanel();
            stack.Orientation = Orientation.Horizontal;
            Content = stack;

            // Create Rectangle to display color.
            rect = new Rectangle();
            rect.Width = 16;
            rect.Height = 16;
            rect.Margin = new Thickness(2);
            rect.Stroke = SystemColors.WindowTextBrush;
            stack.Children.Add(rect);

            // Create TextBlock to display color name.
            text = new TextBlock();
            text.VerticalAlignment = VerticalAlignment.Center;
            stack.Children.Add(text);
        }
        // Text property becomes Text property of TextBlock.
        public string Text
        {
            set
            {
                str = value;
                string strSpaced = str[0].ToString();

                for (int i = 1; i < str.Length; i++)
                    strSpaced += (char.IsUpper(str[i]) ? " " : "") +
                                 str[i].ToString();
                text.Text = strSpaced;
            }
            get { return str; }
        }
```

```
            // Color property becomes Brush property of Rectangle.
            public Color Color
            {
                set { rect.Fill = new SolidColorBrush(value); }
                get
                {
                    SolidColorBrush brush = rect.Fill as SolidColorBrush;
                    return brush == null ? Colors.Transparent : brush.Color;
                }
            }
            // Make font bold when item is selected.
            protected override void OnSelected(RoutedEventArgs args)
            {
                base.OnSelected(args);
                text.FontWeight = FontWeights.Bold;
            }
            protected override void OnUnselected(RoutedEventArgs args)
            {
                base.OnUnselected(args);
                text.FontWeight = FontWeights.Regular;
            }
            // Implement ToString for keyboard letter interface.
            public override string ToString()
            {
                return str;
            }
        }
    }
```

The *ColorListBoxItem* class creates the *StackPanel* (with a horizontal orientation), *Rectangle*, and *TextBlock* in its constructor. The class defines a *Text* property that sets the *Text* property of the *TextBlock*, and a *Color* property associated with the *Brush* used for the *Rectangle*. The class overrides the *OnSelected* and *OnUnselected* methods to make the text of the selected item bold.

The *ColorListBox* class inherits from *ListBox* and uses reflection to fill itself with objects of type *ColorListBoxItem*. It also defines a new property named *SelectedColor* that simply refers to *SelectedValue*.

ColorListBox.cs
```
//----------------------------------------------
// ColorListBox.cs (c) 2006 by Charles Petzold
//----------------------------------------------
using System;
using System.Reflection;
using System.Windows;
using System.Windows.Controls;
using System.Windows.Input;
using System.Windows.Media;

namespace Petzold.ListColorsElegantly
{
    class ColorListBox : ListBox
```

```
    {
        public ColorListBox()
        {
            PropertyInfo[] props = typeof(Colors).GetProperties();

            foreach (PropertyInfo prop in props)
            {
                ColorListBoxItem item = new ColorListBoxItem();
                item.Text = prop.Name;
                item.Color = (Color)prop.GetValue(null, null);
                Items.Add(item);
            }
            SelectedValuePath = "Color";
        }
        public Color SelectedColor
        {
            set { SelectedValue = value; }
            get { return (Color)SelectedValue; }
        }
    }
}
```

Once the *ColorListBoxItem* and *ColorListBox* classes are defined, the code to create such a *ListBox* becomes very straightforward and elegant. Elegant too is the display of the colored rectangles and text string in the *ListBox*.

ListColorsElegantly.cs

```
//-------------------------------------------------
// ListColorsElegantly.cs (c) 2006 by Charles Petzold
//-------------------------------------------------
using System;
using System.Windows;
using System.Windows.Controls;
using System.Windows.Input;
using System.Windows.Media;

namespace Petzold.ListColorsElegantly
{
    public class ListColorsElegantly : Window
    {
        [STAThread]
        public static void Main()
        {
            Application app = new Application();
            app.Run(new ListColorsElegantly());
        }
        public ListColorsElegantly()
        {
            Title = "List Colors Elegantly";

            ColorListBox lstbox = new ColorListBox();
            lstbox.Height = 150;
            lstbox.Width = 150;
```

```
                lstbox.SelectionChanged += ListBoxOnSelectionChanged;
                Content = lstbox;

                // Initialize SelectedColor.
                lstbox.SelectedColor = SystemColors.WindowColor;
            }
            void ListBoxOnSelectionChanged(object sender,
                                        SelectionChangedEventArgs args)
            {
                ColorListBox lstbox = sender as ColorListBox;
                Background = new SolidColorBrush(lstbox.SelectedColor);
            }
        }
    }
}
```

But still the question nags: With the Windows Presentation Foundation, is it possible to do something similar even elegantlier?

Yes, it is. You probably recall the BuildButtonFactory program in Chapter 11 that redefined the look of the button by setting the *Template* property defined by *Control*. The *ListBox* inherits that property, but *ItemsControl* also defines two more template-related properties: The *ItemTemplate* property (of type *DataTemplate*) lets you define the appearance of the items and bindings between the properties of the items and the data source. The *ItemsPanel* property (of type *ItemsPanelTemplate*) lets you substitute a different panel for displaying the items.

The ListColorsEvenElegantlier program demonstrates the use of the *ItemTemplate* property. The program also requires the *NamedBrush* class presented earlier in this chapter.

ListColorsEvenElegantlier.cs

```
//------------------------------------------------------------
// ListColorsEvenElegantlier.cs (c) 2006 by Charles Petzold
//------------------------------------------------------------
using Petzold.ListNamedBrushes;
using System;
using System.Windows;
using System.Windows.Controls;
using System.Windows.Data;
using System.Windows.Input;
using System.Windows.Media;
using System.Windows.Shapes;

namespace Petzold.ListColorsEvenElegantlier
{
    public class ListColorsEvenElegantlier : Window
    {
        [STAThread]
        public static void Main()
        {
            Application app = new Application();
            app.Run(new ListColorsEvenElegantlier());
        }
```

```
public ListColorsEvenElegantlier()
{
    Title = "List Colors Even Elegantlier";

    // Create a DataTemplate for the items.
    DataTemplate template = new DataTemplate(typeof(NamedBrush));

    // Create a FrameworkElementFactory based on StackPanel.
    FrameworkElementFactory factoryStack =
                    new FrameworkElementFactory(typeof(StackPanel));
    factoryStack.SetValue(StackPanel.OrientationProperty,
                                    Orientation.Horizontal);

    // Make that the root of the DataTemplate visual tree.
    template.VisualTree = factoryStack;

    // Create a FrameworkElementFactory based on Rectangle.
    FrameworkElementFactory factoryRectangle =
                    new FrameworkElementFactory(typeof(Rectangle));
    factoryRectangle.SetValue(Rectangle.WidthProperty, 16.0);
    factoryRectangle.SetValue(Rectangle.HeightProperty, 16.0);
    factoryRectangle.SetValue(Rectangle.MarginProperty, new Thickness(2));
    factoryRectangle.SetValue(Rectangle.StrokeProperty,
                                    SystemColors.WindowTextBrush);
    factoryRectangle.SetBinding(Rectangle.FillProperty,
                                    new Binding("Brush"));
    // Add it to the StackPanel.
    factoryStack.AppendChild(factoryRectangle);

    // Create a FrameworkElementFactory based on TextBlock.
    FrameworkElementFactory factoryTextBlock =
                    new FrameworkElementFactory(typeof(TextBlock));
    factoryTextBlock.SetValue(TextBlock.VerticalAlignmentProperty,
                                    VerticalAlignment.Center);
    factoryTextBlock.SetValue(TextBlock.TextProperty,
                                    new Binding("Name"));
    // Add it to the StackPanel.
    factoryStack.AppendChild(factoryTextBlock);

    // Create ListBox as content of window.
    ListBox lstbox = new ListBox();
    lstbox.Width = 150;
    lstbox.Height = 150;
    Content = lstbox;

    // Set the ItemTemplate property to the template created above.
    lstbox.ItemTemplate = template;

    // Set the ItemsSource to the array of NamedBrush objects.
    lstbox.ItemsSource = NamedBrush.All;

    // Bind the SelectedValue to window Background.
    lstbox.SelectedValuePath = "Brush";
```

```
            lstbox.SetBinding(ListBox.SelectedValueProperty, "Background");
            lstbox.DataContext = this;
        }
    }
}
```

The window constructor begins by creating an object of type *DataTemplate*. (Towards the end of the constructor, this object is assigned to the *ItemTemplate* property of a *ListBox*.) Notice that the *DataTemplate* constructor is passed the type of the *NamedBrush* class, indicating that the *ListBox* will be filled with items of type *NamedBrush*.

The program next proceeds to construct a visual tree to display these items. At the root of the visual tree is a *StackPanel*. A *FrameworkElementFactory* object for a *StackPanel* is assigned to the *VisualTree* property of the *DataTemplate*. Next are created two more *FrameworkElementFactory* objects for *Rectangle* and *TextBlock*, and these are added to the children collection of the *FrameworkElementFactory* object for the *StackPanel*. Notice that the *Fill* property of the *Rectangle* element is bound to the *Brush* property of *NamedBrush* and the *Text* property of the *TextBlock* element is bound to the *Name* property of *NamedBrush*.

It is now time to create the *ListBox*. The code that concludes the program should look familiar, except for the assignment of the *DataTemplate* object just created to the *ItemTemplate* property of *ListBox*. *ListBox* will now display *NamedBrush* items with the visual tree of this template.

The constructor wraps up by filling the list box using *ItemsSource* and the static *All* property of *NamedBrush*. The *SelectedValuePath* is the *Brush* property of the *NamedBrush* item, and this is bound with the *Background* property of the window.

I said at the outset of this chapter that *ListBox* is a control for selecting one item out of many. Back in Chapter 11, the *ColorGrid* control displayed 40 *ColorCell* elements on a *UniformGrid* and supplied an extensive keyboard and mouse interface for selecting a color from this grid.

It is possible to use a *ListBox* for this control and avoid duplicating a lot of keyboard and mouse code already in *ListBox*. All that's really necessary is to persuade *ListBox* to use a *UniformGrid* rather than a *StackPanel* for presenting the items, and that is accomplished in the following class with three statements. The *ColorGridBox* class inherits from *ListBox* and nearly achieves the full functionality of the *ColorGrid* control from Chapter 11. (And what it doesn't duplicate is fairly minor.)

ColorGridBox.cs

```
//-------------------------------------------
// ColorGridBox.cs (c) 2006 by Charles Petzold
//-------------------------------------------
using System;
using System.Windows;
using System.Windows.Controls;
using System.Windows.Controls.Primitives;
```

```
using System.Windows.Data;
using System.Windows.Input;
using System.Windows.Media;
using System.Windows.Shapes;

namespace Petzold.SelectColorFromGrid
{
    class ColorGridBox : ListBox
    {
        // The colors to be displayed.
        string[] strColors =
        {
            "Black", "Brown", "DarkGreen", "MidnightBlue",
                "Navy", "DarkBlue", "Indigo", "DimGray",
            "DarkRed", "OrangeRed", "Olive", "Green",
                "Teal", "Blue", "SlateGray", "Gray",
            "Red", "Orange", "YellowGreen", "SeaGreen",
                "Aqua", "LightBlue", "Violet", "DarkGray",
            "Pink", "Gold", "Yellow", "Lime",
                "Turquoise", "SkyBlue", "Plum", "LightGray",
            "LightPink", "Tan", "LightYellow", "LightGreen",
                "LightCyan", "LightSkyBlue", "Lavender", "White"
        };

        public ColorGridBox()
        {
            // Define the ItemsPanel template.
            FrameworkElementFactory factoryUnigrid =
                        new FrameworkElementFactory(typeof(UniformGrid));
            factoryUnigrid.SetValue(UniformGrid.ColumnsProperty, 8);
            ItemsPanel = new ItemsPanelTemplate(factoryUnigrid);

            // Add items to the ListBox.
            foreach (string strColor in strColors)
            {
                // Create Rectangle and add to ListBox.
                Rectangle rect = new Rectangle();
                rect.Width = 12;
                rect.Height = 12;
                rect.Margin = new Thickness(4);
                rect.Fill = (Brush)
                    typeof(Brushes).GetProperty(strColor).GetValue(null, null);
                Items.Add(rect);

                // Create ToolTip for Rectangle.
                ToolTip tip = new ToolTip();
                tip.Content = strColor;
                rect.ToolTip = tip;
            }

            // Indicate that SelectedValue is Fill property of Rectangle item.
            SelectedValuePath = "Fill";
        }
    }
}
```

The constructor begins by creating a *FrameworkElementFactory* object for the *UniformGrid* panel, and assigning the *Columns* property a value of 8. The *ItemsPanelTemplate* constructor accepts this factory directly, and the *ItemsPanelTemplate* object is assigned to the *ItemsPanel* property of the *ListBox*. That's all that's necessary to get a *ListBox* to use an alternative to *StackPanel*.

Most of the rest of the constructor is devoted to filling up the *ListBox* with *Rectangle* objects, each with a *ToolTip* indicating the name of the color. The constructor concludes by assigning the *SelectedValuePath* property of the *ListBox* to the *Fill* property of the *ListBox* items, which refers to the *Fill* property of the *Rectangle*.

The SelectColorFromGrid program is very similar to the SelectColor program used in Chapter 11 to test the new control, except that this program binds the *SelectedValue* property of the *Color-GridBox* control with the *Background* property of the window.

```
SelectColorFromGrid.cs
//-----------------------------------------------------
// SelectColorFromGrid.cs (c) 2006 by Charles Petzold
//-----------------------------------------------------
using System;
using System.Windows;
using System.Windows.Controls;
using System.Windows.Input;
using System.Windows.Media;

namespace Petzold.SelectColorFromGrid
{
    public class SelectColorFromGrid : Window
    {
        [STAThread]
        public static void Main()
        {
            Application app = new Application();
            app.Run(new SelectColorFromGrid());
        }
        public SelectColorFromGrid()
        {
            Title = "Select Color from Grid";
            SizeToContent = SizeToContent.WidthAndHeight;

            // Create StackPanel as content of window.
            StackPanel stack = new StackPanel();
            stack.Orientation = Orientation.Horizontal;
            Content = stack;

            // Create do-nothing button to test tabbing.
            Button btn = new Button();
            btn.Content = "Do-nothing button\nto test tabbing";
            btn.Margin = new Thickness(24);
            btn.HorizontalAlignment = HorizontalAlignment.Center;
```

```
        btn.VerticalAlignment = VerticalAlignment.Center;
        stack.Children.Add(btn);

        // Create ColorGridBox control.
        ColorGridBox clrgrid = new ColorGridBox();
        clrgrid.Margin = new Thickness(24);
        clrgrid.HorizontalAlignment = HorizontalAlignment.Center;
        clrgrid.VerticalAlignment = VerticalAlignment.Center;
        stack.Children.Add(clrgrid);

        // Bind Background of window to selected value of ColorGridBox.
        clrgrid.SetBinding(ColorGridBox.SelectedValueProperty, "Background");
        clrgrid.DataContext = this;

        // Create another do-nothing button.
        btn = new Button();
        btn.Content = "Do-nothing button\nto test tabbing";
        btn.Margin = new Thickness(24);
        btn.HorizontalAlignment = HorizontalAlignment.Center;
        btn.VerticalAlignment = VerticalAlignment.Center;
        stack.Children.Add(btn);
    }
  }
}
```

In particular, I want you to test the keyboard interface of *ColorGridBox*. You can navigate horizontally with the Left and Right arrow keys, and vertically with the Up and Down arrow keys. (Unlike the custom *ColorGrid* control, *ColorGridBox* does not wrap from one column or row to another. Nor does it jump to the next control when it gets to the beginning or the end. These are minor concerns, I think.) Page Up and Page Down go to the top and bottom of a column. Home goes to the first item, and End to the last.

I am convinced that *ListBox* implements a generalized keyboard navigation logic that is based on the relative position of items as they are displayed on the screen. This becomes more evident in the following program, which substitutes the *RadialPanel* from Chapter 12 in the *ListBox* and uses it to display *Rectangle* elements for all 141 colors in the *Brushes* class.

This class is similar to *ColorGridBox* in that it inherits from *ListBox*, and the constructor begins by setting the *ItemsPanel* property of *ListBox* to an *ItemsPanelTemplate* based on a *Framework-ElementFactory* for an alternative panel.

ColorWheel.cs
```
//-------------------------------------------
// ColorWheel.cs (c) 2006 by Charles Petzold
//-------------------------------------------
using Petzold.CircleTheButtons;
using System;
using System.Reflection;
using System.Windows;
using System.Windows.Controls;
```

```
using System.Windows.Data;
using System.Windows.Input;
using System.Windows.Media;
using System.Windows.Shapes;

namespace Petzold.SelectColorFromWheel
{
    class ColorWheel : ListBox
    {
        public ColorWheel()
        {
            // Define the ItemsPanel template.
            FrameworkElementFactory factoryRadialPanel =
                        new FrameworkElementFactory(typeof(RadialPanel));
            ItemsPanel = new ItemsPanelTemplate(factoryRadialPanel);

            // Create the DataTemplate for the items.
            DataTemplate template = new DataTemplate(typeof(Brush));
            ItemTemplate = template;

            // Create a FrameworkElementFactory based on Rectangle.
            FrameworkElementFactory elRectangle =
                        new FrameworkElementFactory(typeof(Rectangle));
            elRectangle.SetValue(Rectangle.WidthProperty, 4.0);
            elRectangle.SetValue(Rectangle.HeightProperty, 12.0);
            elRectangle.SetValue(Rectangle.MarginProperty,
                                    new Thickness(1, 8, 1, 8));
            elRectangle.SetBinding(Rectangle.FillProperty, new Binding(""));

            // Use that factory for the visual tree.
            template.VisualTree = elRectangle;

            // Set the items in the ListBox.
            PropertyInfo[] props = typeof(Brushes).GetProperties();

            foreach (PropertyInfo prop in props)
                Items.Add((Brush)prop.GetValue(null, null));
        }
    }
}
```

After setting the *ItemsPanel* property, the constructor then goes on to define a *DataTemplate* object that it assigns to the *ItemTemplate* property of *Listbox*. The *DataTemplate* indicates that the *ListBox* items are of type *Brush*. The visual tree consists of a single element of type *Rectangle*, and the *Fill* property is bound with the item itself (indicated by an empty string argument to the *Binding* constructor).

The constructor concludes by filling up the *ListBox* with all the static properties of the *Brushes* class. It is not necessary to set *SelectedValuePath* for the *ListBox* because the items in the *ListBox* are actually *Brush* items. Without the custom *ItemTemplate*, they would be displayed as hexadecimal RGB values.

The SelectColorFromWheel program, which is almost identical to SelectColorFromGrid, lets you experiment with the *ColorWheel* control.

SelectColorFromWheel.cs

```
//-----------------------------------------------------
// SelectColorFromWheel.cs (c) 2006 by Charles Petzold
//-----------------------------------------------------
using System;
using System.Windows;
using System.Windows.Controls;
using System.Windows.Input;
using System.Windows.Media;

namespace Petzold.SelectColorFromWheel
{
    public class SelectColorFromWheel : Window
    {
        [STAThread]
        public static void Main()
        {
            Application app = new Application();
            app.Run(new SelectColorFromWheel());
        }
        public SelectColorFromWheel()
        {
            Title = "Select Color from Wheel";
            SizeToContent = SizeToContent.WidthAndHeight;

            // Create StackPanel as content of window.
            StackPanel stack = new StackPanel();
            stack.Orientation = Orientation.Horizontal;
            Content = stack;

            // Create do-nothing button to test tabbing.
            Button btn = new Button();
            btn.Content = "Do-nothing button\nto test tabbing";
            btn.Margin = new Thickness(24);
            btn.HorizontalAlignment = HorizontalAlignment.Center;
            btn.VerticalAlignment = VerticalAlignment.Center;
            stack.Children.Add(btn);

            // Create ColorWheel control.
            ColorWheel clrwheel = new ColorWheel();
            clrwheel.Margin = new Thickness(24);
            clrwheel.HorizontalAlignment = HorizontalAlignment.Center;
            clrwheel.VerticalAlignment = VerticalAlignment.Center;
            stack.Children.Add(clrwheel);

            // Bind Background of window to selected value of ColorWheel.
            clrwheel.SetBinding(ColorWheel.SelectedValueProperty, "Background");
            clrwheel.DataContext = this;
```

```
            // Create another do-nothing button.
            btn = new Button();
            btn.Content = "Do-nothing button\nto test tabbing";
            btn.Margin = new Thickness(24);
            btn.HorizontalAlignment = HorizontalAlignment.Center;
            btn.VerticalAlignment = VerticalAlignment.Center;
            stack.Children.Add(btn);
        }
    }
}
```

The keyboard interface is very interesting. The Up and Down arrow keys only move the selected color on the left half or the right half of the circle. They can't move the selected color from one side to the other. Similarly, the Left and Right arrow keys work only on the top half or the bottom half. To move the selected color all the way around (clockwise, for example), you need to switch from the Right arrow to the Down arrow in the upper-right quadrant, and then from the Down arrow to the Left arrow on the lower-right quadrant, and so forth.

Giving a *ListBox* a whole new look is a very powerful technique. It is why you should think of *ListBox* any time you need the user to select one item out of many. Think first of that abstract nature of the *ListBox* and then how you can alter the control to make it look and behave exactly the way you want.

Chapter 14
The Menu Hierarchy

The traditional focus of the user interface in a Windows application is the menu. The menu occupies prime real estate at the top of the application window, right under the caption bar and extending the full width of the window. In repose, the menu is commonly a horizontal list of text items. Clicking an item on this top-level menu generally displays a boxed list of other items, called a drop-down menu or a submenu. Each submenu contains other menu items that can either trigger commands or invoke other nested submenus.

In short, the menu is a hierarchy. Every item on the menu is an object of type *MenuItem*. The menu itself is an object of type *Menu*. To understand where these two controls fit into the other Windows Presentation Foundation controls, it is helpful to examine the following partial class hierarchy:

Control

    ContentControl

        HeaderedContentControl

    ItemsControl

        HeaderedItemsControl

These four classes that derive from *Control* encompass many familiar controls:

- Controls that derive from *ContentControl* are characterized by a property named *Content*. These controls include buttons, labels, tool tips, the scroll viewer, list box items, and the window itself.

- The *HeaderedContentControl* derives from *ContentControl* and adds a *Header* property. The group box falls under this category.

- *ItemsControl* defines a property named *Items* that is a collection of other objects. This category includes the list box and combo box.

- *HeaderedItemsControls* adds a *Header* property to the properties it inherits from *Items-Control*. A menu item is one such control.

The *Header* property of the *MenuItem* object is the visual representation of the item itself, usually a short text string that is optionally accompanied by a small bitmap. Each menu item also potentially contains a collection of items that appear in a submenu. These submenu items are collected in the *Items* property. For menu items that invoke commands directly, the *Items* collection is empty.

For example, the first item on the top-level menu is typically File. This is a *MenuItem* object. The *Header* property is the text string "File" and the *Items* collection includes the *MenuItem* objects for New, Open, Save, and so forth.

The only part of the menu that doesn't follow this pattern is the top-level menu itself. The top-level menu certainly is a collection of items (File, Edit, View, and Help, for example) but there is no header associated with this collection. For that reason, the top-level menu is an object of type *Menu*, which derives from *ItemsControl*. This partial class hierarchy shows the menu-related classes:

Control

    ItemsControl

        HeaderItemsControl

            MenuItem

            MenuBase (abstract)

                ContextMenu

                Menu

      Separator

The *Separator* control simply displays a horizontal or vertical line (depending on its context) that's often used on submenus to separate menu items into functional categories.

The items in the menu can actually be objects of almost any type, but you'll generally use *MenuItem* because it defines several properties and events commonly associated with menu items. Like *ButtonBase*, *MenuItem* defines a *Click* event and a *Command* property. Your program can handle many menu items just as if they were buttons.

MenuItem also defines a property named *Icon* that lets you put a little picture in the menu item in a standard location. Interestingly, the *Icon* property is of type *Object*, which means you can easily use an element from the Shapes library (as I'll demonstrate in this chapter).

Menu items can be checked, either to denote on/off options or to indicate one item selected from a group of mutually exclusive items. *MenuItem* includes a Boolean *IsChecked* property to turn checkmarks on and off, and an *IsCheckable* property to automate the toggling of checkmarks. The *Checked* event is fired when the *IsChecked* property changes from *false* to *true*. The *Unchecked* event indicates when *IsChecked* changes from *true* to *false*.

Sometimes it's necessary for a program to disable certain items on a submenu. For example, the Save option on the File menu should be disabled if the program currently has no document to save. It is often most convenient to disable menu items when the submenu is being displayed. *MenuItem* defines a *SubmenuOpened* event to help out.

Constructing a menu generally begins at the top and proceeds downward. You first create an object of type *Menu*:

```
Menu menu = new Menu();
```

Commonly, the first item is File:

```
MenuItem itemFile = new MenuItem();
itemFile.Header = "_File";
```

As in other controls, the underline character facilitates navigation with the keyboard. When the user presses the Alt key, the *F* in "File" becomes underlined, and pressing the F key then opens the File submenu. On the top-level menu, and in each submenu, underlined letters should be unique.

You make the File item part of the top-level menu by adding it to the *Items* collection of the *Menu* object:

```
menu.Items.Add(itemFile);
```

The first item on the File menu is often New:

```
MenuItem itemNew = new MenuItem();
itemNew.Header = "_New";
itemNew.Click += NewOnClick;
itemFile.Items.Add(itemNew);
```

This New item is a command, so assign the *Click* event a handler to process that command. Add the New item to the *File* collection:

```
itemFile.Items.Add(itemNew);
```

And so forth.

Here's a program that displays a little text in its client area and constructs a menu. Only one of the File items is implemented, but the menu includes a top-level Window item containing four checkable items that let you change the properties of the window.

PeruseTheMenu.cs

```
//-----------------------------------------------
// PeruseTheMenu.cs (c) 2006 by Charles Petzold
//-----------------------------------------------
using System;
using System.Windows;
using System.Windows.Controls;
using System.Windows.Input;
using System.Windows.Media;

namespace Petzold.PeruseTheMenu
{
    public class PeruseTheMenu : Window
```

```
    {
        [STAThread]
        public static void Main()
        {
            Application app = new Application();
            app.Run(new PeruseTheMenu());
        }
        public PeruseTheMenu()
        {
            Title = "Peruse the Menu";

            // Create DockPanel.
            DockPanel dock = new DockPanel();
            Content = dock;

            // Create Menu docked at top.
            Menu menu = new Menu();
            dock.Children.Add(menu);
            DockPanel.SetDock(menu, Dock.Top);

            // Create TextBlock filling the rest.
            TextBlock text = new TextBlock();
            text.Text = Title;
            text.FontSize = 32;        // ie, 24 points.
            text.TextAlignment = TextAlignment.Center;
            dock.Children.Add(text);

            // Create File menu.
            MenuItem itemFile = new MenuItem();
            itemFile.Header = "_File";
            menu.Items.Add(itemFile);

            MenuItem itemNew = new MenuItem();
            itemNew.Header = "_New";
            itemNew.Click += UnimplementedOnClick;
            itemFile.Items.Add(itemNew);

            MenuItem itemOpen = new MenuItem();
            itemOpen.Header = "_Open";
            itemOpen.Click += UnimplementedOnClick;
            itemFile.Items.Add(itemOpen);

            MenuItem itemSave = new MenuItem();
            itemSave.Header = "_Save";
            itemSave.Click += UnimplementedOnClick;
            itemFile.Items.Add(itemSave);

            itemFile.Items.Add(new Separator());

            MenuItem itemExit = new MenuItem();
            itemExit.Header = "E_xit";
            itemExit.Click += ExitOnClick;
            itemFile.Items.Add(itemExit);
```

```
        // Create Window menu.
        MenuItem itemWindow = new MenuItem();
        itemWindow.Header = "_Window";
        menu.Items.Add(itemWindow);

        MenuItem itemTaskbar = new MenuItem();
        itemTaskbar.Header = "_Show in Taskbar";
        itemTaskbar.IsCheckable = true;
        itemTaskbar.IsChecked = ShowInTaskbar;
        itemTaskbar.Click += TaskbarOnClick;
        itemWindow.Items.Add(itemTaskbar);

        MenuItem itemSize = new MenuItem();
        itemSize.Header = "Size to _Content";
        itemSize.IsCheckable = true;
        itemSize.IsChecked = SizeToContent == SizeToContent.WidthAndHeight;
        itemSize.Checked += SizeOnCheck;
        itemSize.Unchecked += SizeOnCheck;
        itemWindow.Items.Add(itemSize);

        MenuItem itemResize = new MenuItem();
        itemResize.Header = "_Resizable";
        itemResize.IsCheckable = true;
        itemResize.IsChecked = ResizeMode == ResizeMode.CanResize;
        itemResize.Click += ResizeOnClick;
        itemWindow.Items.Add(itemResize);

        MenuItem itemTopmost = new MenuItem();
        itemTopmost.Header = "_Topmost";
        itemTopmost.IsCheckable = true;
        itemTopmost.IsChecked = Topmost;
        itemTopmost.Checked += TopmostOnCheck;
        itemTopmost.Unchecked += TopmostOnCheck;
        itemWindow.Items.Add(itemTopmost);
}
void UnimplementedOnClick(object sender, RoutedEventArgs args)
{
        MenuItem item = sender as MenuItem;
        string strItem = item.Header.ToString().Replace("_", "");
        MessageBox.Show("The " + strItem +
                        " option has not yet been implemented", Title);
}
void ExitOnClick(object sender, RoutedEventArgs args)
{
        Close();
}
void TaskbarOnClick(object sender, RoutedEventArgs args)
{
        MenuItem item = sender as MenuItem;
        ShowInTaskbar = item.IsChecked;
}
void SizeOnCheck(object sender, RoutedEventArgs args)
```

```
        {
            MenuItem item = sender as MenuItem;
            SizeToContent = item.IsChecked ? SizeToContent.WidthAndHeight :
                                             SizeToContent.Manual;
        }
        void ResizeOnClick(object sender, RoutedEventArgs args)
        {
            MenuItem item = sender as MenuItem;
            ResizeMode = item.IsChecked ? ResizeMode.CanResize :
                                          ResizeMode.NoResize;
        }
        void TopmostOnCheck(object sender, RoutedEventArgs args)
        {
            MenuItem item = sender as MenuItem;
            Topmost = item.IsChecked;
        }
    }
}
```

Notice that the constructor begins by creating a *DockPanel*. Customarily the menu is docked on the top of the client area, and unless you want to baffle users, your menus will appear there as well. The *DockPanel* is the standard base panel for windows that have menus, toolbars, or status bars. You can get the same effect with a *StackPanel* or *Grid*, but the *DockPanel* is standard.

The *UnimplementedOnClick* method handles the *Click* events for the New, Open, and Save items. The *Click* handler for the Exit item calls *Close* on the *Window* object to end the program. A *Separator* separates the Exit item from the others, as is common.

The four items on the Window menu all have their *IsCheckable* property set to *true* to enable automatic toggling of the checkmark. The *IsChecked* property indicates whether a checkmark currently appears or not. For the first and third items, the program installs a handler for the *Click* event. For the second and fourth items, the program installs the same handler for the *Checked* and *Unchecked* events. It doesn't really matter which approach you use. Potentially installing separate *Checked* and *Unchecked* handlers lets you perform actions without explicitly examining the *IsChecked* property. In this program, the *Click*, *Checked*, and *Unchecked* event handlers all merely use the *IsChecked* property to set certain properties of the window.

Try commenting out the following two lines of code:

```
itemTaskbar.IsChecked = ShowInTaskbar;
itemTaskbar.Click += TaskbarOnClick;
```

And replace them with these:

```
itemTaskbar.SetBinding(MenuItem.IsCheckedProperty, "ShowInTaskbar");
itemTaskbar.DataContext = this;
```

You can also get rid of the entire *TaskbarOnClick* method, and the program will work the same. This is a little taste of data binding. Basically you're telling the *MenuItem* that the *IsChecked* property should always be the same value as the *ShowInTaskbar* property of the *this* object (the window). You can set such a data binding with the *Topmost* menu item as well, but you can't do it with the other two because the properties aren't Booleans.

If you want a menu item to have a checkmark, and you don't set the *IsCheckable* property to *true*, you'll need to handle *Click* events and manually check and uncheck the item using the *IsChecked* property. This approach is necessary when you use the menu to display a group of mutually exclusive items, where checking any item causes the previously checked item to become unchecked (much like a group of radio buttons). With a group of mutually exclusive checked items, you'll leave the *IsCheckable* property in its default *false* setting so that there's no automatic toggling, and you'll probably set the *IsChecked* property on one of the items when initially creating the items. You'll also handle all the checking and unchecking logic yourself in the *Click* event handlers. Often it's easiest to share a single *Click* handler for all the items in a mutually exclusive group.

To keep track of the currently checked item in any mutually exclusive group, you'll probably maintain a field of type *MenuItem* named (for example) *itemChecked*:

```
MenuItem itemChecked;
```

You initialize this field in the window's constructor. If you use a single *Click* event handler for the whole group of mutually exclusive items, the *Click* event handler begins by unchecking the currently checked item:

```
itemChecked.IsChecked = false;
```

The handler then saves the item being clicked as the new value of *itemChecked*, and checks that item:

```
itemChecked = args.Source as MenuItem;
itemChecked.IsChecked = true;
```

The event handler can then do whatever specifically needs to be done for these items. Here's a program similar to the TuneTheRadio program in Chapter 5 that lets you change the *WindowStyle* property of the window:

```
CheckTheWindowStyle.cs
//-------------------------------------------------
// CheckTheWindowStyle.cs (c) 2006 by Charles Petzold
//-------------------------------------------------
using System;
using System.Windows;
using System.Windows.Controls;
using System.Windows.Input;
using System.Windows.Media;
```

```
namespace Petzold.CheckTheWindowStyle
{
    public class CheckTheWindowStyle : Window
    {
        MenuItem itemChecked;

        [STAThread]
        public static void Main()
        {
            Application app = new Application();
            app.Run(new CheckTheWindowStyle());
        }
        public CheckTheWindowStyle()
        {
            Title = "Check the Window Style";

            // Create DockPanel.
            DockPanel dock = new DockPanel();
            Content = dock;

            // Create Menu docked at top.
            Menu menu = new Menu();
            dock.Children.Add(menu);
            DockPanel.SetDock(menu, Dock.Top);

            // Create TextBlock filling the rest.
            TextBlock text = new TextBlock();
            text.Text = Title;
            text.FontSize = 32;
            text.TextAlignment = TextAlignment.Center;
            dock.Children.Add(text);

            // Create MenuItem objects to change WindowStyle.
            MenuItem itemStyle = new MenuItem();
            itemStyle.Header = "_Style";
            menu.Items.Add(itemStyle);

            itemStyle.Items.Add(
                CreateMenuItem("_No border or caption", WindowStyle.None));

            itemStyle.Items.Add(
                CreateMenuItem("_Single-border window",
                            WindowStyle.SingleBorderWindow));

            itemStyle.Items.Add(
                CreateMenuItem("3_D-border window",
                            WindowStyle.ThreeDBorderWindow));
            itemStyle.Items.Add(
                CreateMenuItem("_Tool window",
                            WindowStyle.ToolWindow));
        }
        MenuItem CreateMenuItem(string str, WindowStyle style)
        {
            MenuItem item = new MenuItem();
            item.Header = str;
            item.Tag = style;
```

```
            item.IsChecked = (style == WindowStyle);
            item.Click += StyleOnClick;

            if (item.IsChecked)
                itemChecked = item;

            return item;
        }
        void StyleOnClick(object sender, RoutedEventArgs args)
        {
            itemChecked.IsChecked = false;
            itemChecked = args.Source as MenuItem;
            itemChecked.IsChecked = true;

            WindowStyle = (WindowStyle)itemChecked.Tag;
        }
    }
}
```

Because the four items that appear on the Style menu are rather similar and share the same *Click* event handler, the program defines a little method named *CreateMenuItem* specifically to create these items. Each item has a text string describing a particular member of the *Window-Style* enumeration. The ever-handy *Tag* property of the *MenuItem* object gets the enumeration member itself. If the particular *WindowStyle* enumeration member is the same as the window's *WindowStyle* property, the method sets the *IsChecked* property to *true* and also sets the *item-Checked* field to that item.

The *Click* event handler unchecks the *itemChecked* item, sets *itemChecked* to the clicked item, and concludes by setting the *WindowStyle* property of the window based on the *Tag* property of the clicked item.

If you think about it, the CheckTheWindowStyle program doesn't really need to maintain the *itemChecked* field. That's simply for convenience. The program can always determine which item is currently checked by searching through the *Items* collection of the Style item, or even by examining the *WindowStyle* property of the window.

It's not even necessary to check and uncheck the items in the *Click* event handler. Instead, the program can prepare the submenu for viewing during the *SubmenuOpened* event and check the correct item at that time. The following program demonstrates an alternative approach to checking and unchecking menu items. Two menu items let you change the foreground and background brushes of a *TextBlock* element.

CheckTheColor.cs
```
//-------------------------------------------------
// CheckTheColor.cs (c) 2006 by Charles Petzold
//-------------------------------------------------
using System;
using System.Reflection;
using System.Windows;
```

```
using System.Windows.Controls;
using System.Windows.Input;
using System.Windows.Media;
using System.Windows.Shapes;

namespace Petzold.CheckTheColor
{
    public class CheckTheColor : Window
    {
        TextBlock text;

        [STAThread]
        public static void Main()
        {
            Application app = new Application();
            app.Run(new CheckTheColor());
        }
        public CheckTheColor()
        {
            Title = "Check the Color";

            // Create DockPanel.
            DockPanel dock = new DockPanel();
            Content = dock;

            // Create Menu docked at top.
            Menu menu = new Menu();
            dock.Children.Add(menu);
            DockPanel.SetDock(menu, Dock.Top);

            // Create TextBlock filling the rest.
            text = new TextBlock();
            text.Text = Title;
            text.TextAlignment = TextAlignment.Center;
            text.FontSize = 32;
            text.Background = SystemColors.WindowBrush;
            text.Foreground = SystemColors.WindowTextBrush;
            dock.Children.Add(text);

            // Create menu items.
            MenuItem itemColor = new MenuItem();
            itemColor.Header = "_Color";
            menu.Items.Add(itemColor);

            MenuItem itemForeground = new MenuItem();
            itemForeground.Header = "_Foreground";
            itemForeground.SubmenuOpened += ForegroundOnOpened;
            itemColor.Items.Add(itemForeground);

            FillWithColors(itemForeground, ForegroundOnClick);

            MenuItem itemBackground = new MenuItem();
            itemBackground.Header = "_Background";
            itemBackground.SubmenuOpened += BackgroundOnOpened;
            itemColor.Items.Add(itemBackground);
```

```
                FillWithColors(itemBackground, BackgroundOnClick);
        }
        void FillWithColors(MenuItem itemParent, RoutedEventHandler handler)
        {
            foreach (PropertyInfo prop in typeof(Colors).GetProperties())
            {
                Color clr = (Color)prop.GetValue(null, null);
                int iCount = 0;

                iCount += clr.R == 0 || clr.R == 255 ? 1 : 0;
                iCount += clr.G == 0 || clr.G == 255 ? 1 : 0;
                iCount += clr.B == 0 || clr.B == 255 ? 1 : 0;

                if (clr.A == 255 && iCount > 1)
                {
                    MenuItem item = new MenuItem();
                    item.Header = "_" + prop.Name;
                    item.Tag = clr;
                    item.Click += handler;
                    itemParent.Items.Add(item);
                }
            }
        }
        void ForegroundOnOpened(object sender, RoutedEventArgs args)
        {
            MenuItem itemParent = sender as MenuItem;

            foreach (MenuItem item in itemParent.Items)
                item.IsChecked =
                    ((text.Foreground as SolidColorBrush).Color == (Color)item.Tag);
        }
        void BackgroundOnOpened(object sender, RoutedEventArgs args)
        {
            MenuItem itemParent = sender as MenuItem;

            foreach (MenuItem item in itemParent.Items)
                item.IsChecked =
                    ((text.Background as SolidColorBrush).Color == (Color)item.Tag);
        }
        void ForegroundOnClick(object sender, RoutedEventArgs args)
        {
            MenuItem item = sender as MenuItem;
            Color clr = (Color)item.Tag;
            text.Foreground = new SolidColorBrush(clr);
        }
        void BackgroundOnClick(object sender, RoutedEventArgs args)
        {
            MenuItem item = sender as MenuItem;
            Color clr = (Color)item.Tag;
            text.Background = new SolidColorBrush(clr);
        }
    }
}
```

The program creates a top-level menu item of Color and a submenu containing the two items Foreground and Background. For each of these items, the *FillWithColors* method adds individual color items to the nested submenu. The logic is a little elaborate because it restricts the menu to only those colors where at least two of the Red, Green, and Blue primaries are either 0 or 255. (Remove that logic if you want to see how a large menu is handled under the Windows Presentation Foundation.)

For the Foreground menu item, the *ForegroundOnOpened* method handles the *SubmenuOpened* event, while the *ForegroundOnClick* method handles the *Click* events for each of the colors on the Foreground submenu. (The Background menu works similarly.) The *ForegroundOnOpened* handler loops through the items in the *Items* property and sets the value of the *IsChecked* property to *true* if the item corresponds to the current foreground color of the *TextBlock*, and *false* otherwise. The *ForegroundOnClick* method doesn't have to bother with checking and unchecking and needs only to create a new brush for the *TextBlock*.

Can we get the actual colors into the menu? Yes, of course, and the *MenuItem* class has an *Icon* property intended for little pictures (or whatever) at the left side of the item. In the *if* block in the *FillWithColors* method, any time after the *MenuItem* has been created, add the following code. I've already provided the *using* directive for *System.Windows.Shapes*.

```
Rectangle rect = new Rectangle();
rect.Fill = new SolidColorBrush(clr);
rect.Width = 2 * (rect.Height = 12);
item.Icon = rect;
```

The checkmarks share the space with any *Icon* property that may be set.

You'll probably recall the *ColorGrid* control from Chapter 11 and the similar (but simpler) *ColorGridBox* control from Chapter 13. You can use these controls as menu items, and the following program shows how. This project requires a link to the ColorGridBox.cs file. Notice that this program contains a *using* directive for that project.

SelectColorFromMenuGrid.cs

```
//---------------------------------------------------------
// SelectColorFromMenuGrid.cs (c) 2006 by Charles Petzold
//---------------------------------------------------------
using Petzold.SelectColorFromGrid;
using System;
using System.Windows;
using System.Windows.Controls;
using System.Windows.Input;
using System.Windows.Media;

namespace Petzold.SelectColorFromMenuGrid
{
    public class SelectColorFromMenuGrid : Window
    {
        [STAThread]
        public static void Main()
```

```
    {
        Application app = new Application();
        app.Run(new SelectColorFromMenuGrid());
    }
    public SelectColorFromMenuGrid()
    {
        Title = "Select Color from Menu Grid";

        // Create DockPanel.
        DockPanel dock = new DockPanel();
        Content = dock;

        // Create Menu docked at top.
        Menu menu = new Menu();
        dock.Children.Add(menu);
        DockPanel.SetDock(menu, Dock.Top);

        // Create TextBlock filling the rest.
        TextBlock text = new TextBlock();
        text.Text = Title;
        text.FontSize = 32;
        text.TextAlignment = TextAlignment.Center;
        dock.Children.Add(text);

        // Add items to menu.
        MenuItem itemColor = new MenuItem();
        itemColor.Header = "_Color";
        menu.Items.Add(itemColor);

        MenuItem itemForeground = new MenuItem();
        itemForeground.Header = "_Foreground";
        itemColor.Items.Add(itemForeground);

        // Create ColorGridBox and bind with Foreground of window.
        ColorGridBox clrbox = new ColorGridBox();
        clrbox.SetBinding(ColorGridBox.SelectedValueProperty, "Foreground");
        clrbox.DataContext = this;
        itemForeground.Items.Add(clrbox);

        MenuItem itemBackground = new MenuItem();
        itemBackground.Header = "_Background";
        itemColor.Items.Add(itemBackground);

        // Create ColorGridBox and bind with Background of window.
        clrbox = new ColorGridBox();
        clrbox.SetBinding(ColorGridBox.SelectedValueProperty, "Background");
        clrbox.DataContext = this;
        itemBackground.Items.Add(clrbox);
    }
}
```

As in the previous program, this program creates a top-level item of Color with Foreground and Background items in the Color submenu. Instead of adding multiple items to the

Foreground and Background submenus, the program adds just one item to each—an object of type *ColorGridBox*. Because *ColorGridBox* was written so that the *SelectedValue* property is an object of type *Brush*, it is possible to avoid event handlers entirely and simply provide bindings between the *SelectedValueProperty* dependency property of the *ColorGridBox* and the *Foreground* and *Background* properties of the window.

You've seen how handling the *SubmenuOpen* event can be useful for checking items on the menu. Handling this event is particularly common in programs that need to disable certain menu items. The Edit menu is one common example. A program that has the ability to transfer text in and out of the clipboard shouldn't enable the Paste item unless the clipboard actually contains text. The Cut, Copy, and Delete options should be enabled only if the program is able to copy something to the clipboard.

The following program does nothing but implement an Edit menu that lets you Cut, Copy, Paste, and Delete the text in a *TextBlock* element. The project also includes four bitmaps as application resources that it uses to create *Image* elements that it sets to the *Icon* property of each menu item. (I obtained these images from the library shipped with Microsoft Visual Studio; however, these images originally had resolutions of 72 dots per inch so I changed them to 96 DPI.)

CutCopyAndPaste.cs

```
//-------------------------------------------------
// CutCopyAndPaste.cs (c) 2006 by Charles Petzold
//-------------------------------------------------
using System;
using System.Windows;
using System.Windows.Controls;
using System.Windows.Input;
using System.Windows.Media;
using System.Windows.Media.Imaging;

namespace Petzold.CutCopyAndPaste
{
    public class CutCopyAndPaste : Window
    {
        TextBlock text;
        protected MenuItem itemCut, itemCopy, itemPaste, itemDelete;

        [STAThread]
        public static void Main()
        {
            Application app = new Application();
            app.Run(new CutCopyAndPaste());
        }
        public CutCopyAndPaste()
        {
            Title = "Cut, Copy, and Paste";
```

```
// Create DockPanel.
DockPanel dock = new DockPanel();
Content = dock;

// Create Menu docked at top.
Menu menu = new Menu();
dock.Children.Add(menu);
DockPanel.SetDock(menu, Dock.Top);

// Create TextBlock filling the rest.
text = new TextBlock();
text.Text = "Sample clipboard text";
text.HorizontalAlignment = HorizontalAlignment.Center;
text.VerticalAlignment = VerticalAlignment.Center;
text.FontSize = 32;
text.TextWrapping = TextWrapping.Wrap;
dock.Children.Add(text);

// Create Edit menu.
MenuItem itemEdit = new MenuItem();
itemEdit.Header = "_Edit";
itemEdit.SubmenuOpened += EditOnOpened;
menu.Items.Add(itemEdit);

// Create items on Edit menu.
itemCut = new MenuItem();
itemCut.Header = "Cu_t";
itemCut.Click += CutOnClick;
Image img = new Image();
img.Source = new BitmapImage(
                new Uri("pack://application:,,/Images/CutHS.png"));
itemCut.Icon = img;
itemEdit.Items.Add(itemCut);

itemCopy = new MenuItem();
itemCopy.Header = "_Copy";
itemCopy.Click += CopyOnClick;
img = new Image();
img.Source = new BitmapImage(
                new Uri("pack://application:,,/Images/CopyHS.png"));
itemCopy.Icon = img;
itemEdit.Items.Add(itemCopy);

itemPaste = new MenuItem();
itemPaste.Header = "_Paste";
itemPaste.Click += PasteOnClick;
img = new Image();
img.Source = new BitmapImage(
                new Uri("pack://application:,,/Images/PasteHS.png"));
itemPaste.Icon = img;
itemEdit.Items.Add(itemPaste);
```

```
            itemDelete = new MenuItem();
            itemDelete.Header = "_Delete";
            itemDelete.Click += DeleteOnClick;
            img = new Image();
            img.Source = new BitmapImage(
                        new Uri("pack://application:,,/Images/DeleteHS.png"));
            itemDelete.Icon = img;
            itemEdit.Items.Add(itemDelete);
        }
        void EditOnOpened(object sender, RoutedEventArgs args)
        {
            itemCut.IsEnabled =
            itemCopy.IsEnabled =
            itemDelete.IsEnabled = text.Text != null && text.Text.Length > 0;
            itemPaste.IsEnabled = Clipboard.ContainsText();
        }
        protected void CutOnClick(object sender, RoutedEventArgs args)
        {
            CopyOnClick(sender, args);
            DeleteOnClick(sender, args);
        }
        protected void CopyOnClick(object sender, RoutedEventArgs args)
        {
            if (text.Text != null && text.Text.Length > 0)
                Clipboard.SetText(text.Text);
        }
        protected void PasteOnClick(object sender, RoutedEventArgs args)
        {
            if (Clipboard.ContainsText())
                text.Text = Clipboard.GetText();
        }
        protected void DeleteOnClick(object sender, RoutedEventArgs args)
        {
            text.Text = null;
        }
    }
}
```

The program stores the Cut, Copy, Paste, and Delete *MenuItem* objects as fields and accesses them during the *EditOnOpened* event handler. The handler enables Cut, Copy, and Delete only if the *TextBlock* contains at least one character of text. To enable the Paste item, the handler uses the return value from the static *Clipboard.ContainsText* method.

The *PasteOnClick* method uses the static *Clipboard.GetText* method to copy text from the clipboard. Similarly, *CopyOnClick* calls *Clipboard.SetText*. The Delete command doesn't need to access the clipboard and simply sets the *Text* property of the *TextBlock* element to *null*. The *CutOnClick* event handler take advantage of the fact that a Cut is simply a Copy followed by a Delete by calling *CopyOnClick* and *DeleteOnClick*.

The CutCopyAndPaste program has the standard underlined characters for the Edit menu. A user can trigger the Paste command by pressing Alt, E, P for example. However, these edit commands also have standard keyboard shortcuts called *accelerators*: Ctrl+X for Cut, Ctrl+C for Copy, Ctrl+V for Paste, and the Delete key for Delete. You'll notice that these aren't implemented in the CutCopyAndPaste program.

It's fairly easy to get the text "Ctrl+X" displayed alongside the Cut item. Just set the *Input-GestureText* property of the menu item:

```
itemCut.InputGestureText = "Ctrl+X";
```

However, actually triggering a Cut command when the user types Ctrl+X is something else entirely. It does not happen automatically and you have two options to make it happen: You can handle the keyboard input on your own (which I'll show shortly) or you can use command bindings (which I'll show after that).

If you decide to handle the keyboard input on your own, you should treat that input as high priority. In other words, you want to examine keyboard input for possible menu accelerators before anybody else gets hold of that input, and that means you'll probably override the *OnPreviewKeyDown* method of the window. If a keystroke corresponds to an enabled menu item, carry out the command and set the *Handled* property of the event arguments to *true*.

The job of handling keyboard input to trigger menu items is eased somewhat by the *Key-Gesture* class. You can define an object of type *KeyGesture* for Ctrl+X like this:

```
KeyGesture gestCut = new KeyGesture(Key.X, ModifierKeys.Control);
```

This class doesn't include much, and the only reason to use it is to make use of the *Matches* method that accepts an *InputEventArgs* argument. You can call the *Matches* method during the *OnPreviewKeyDown* override using the *KeyEventArgs* argument delivered with that event. (*KeyEventArgs* derives from *InputEventArgs*.) The *Matches* method will recognize that its argument is actually a *KeyEventArgs*, and returns *true* if the key being pressed is the same as the key defined in the *KeyGesture* object. The processing in your *OnPreviewKeyDown* override might look like this:

```
if (gestCut.Matches(null, args))
{
    CutOnClick(this, args);
    args.Handled = true;
}
```

You can pass the *KeyEventArgs* object directly to *CutOnClick* because *KeyEventArgs* derives from *RoutedEventArgs*. However, this code doesn't check whether a Cut item is actually valid before calling the Click handler. One simple approach you might consider is checking whether the *itemCut* menu item is enabled. But that won't work because *itemCut* is enabled and disabled only when the drop-down menu is displayed.

Fortunately, you'll notice that the *CopyOnClick* and *PasteOnClick* methods in the CutCopyAnd-Paste program don't actually perform the Copy and Paste operations unless the commands are valid. Those checks allow the following program to inherit from CutCopyAndPaste to implement the standard keyboard accelerators for the Edit menu. This project requires a link to the CutCopyAndPaste.cs source code file. There's no *using* directive for that project's namespace; instead, the *class* definition refers to the fully qualified name of the *CutCopyAndPaste* class.

ControlXCV.cs

```
//-------------------------------------------
// ControlXCV.cs (c) 2006 by Charles Petzold
//-------------------------------------------
using System;
using System.Windows;
using System.Windows.Controls;
using System.Windows.Input;
using System.Windows.Media;

namespace Petzold.ControlXCV
{
    public class ControlXCV : Petzold.CutCopyAndPaste.CutCopyAndPaste
    {
        KeyGesture gestCut = new KeyGesture(Key.X, ModifierKeys.Control);
        KeyGesture gestCopy = new KeyGesture(Key.C, ModifierKeys.Control);
        KeyGesture gestPaste = new KeyGesture(Key.V, ModifierKeys.Control);
        KeyGesture gestDelete = new KeyGesture(Key.Delete);

        [STAThread]
        public new static void Main()
        {
            Application app = new Application();
            app.Run(new ControlXCV());
        }
        public ControlXCV()
        {
            Title = "Control X, C, and V";

            itemCut.InputGestureText = "Ctrl+X";
            itemCopy.InputGestureText = "Ctrl+C";
            itemPaste.InputGestureText = "Ctrl+V";
            itemDelete.InputGestureText = "Delete";
        }
        protected override void OnPreviewKeyDown(KeyEventArgs args)
        {
            base.OnKeyDown(args);
            args.Handled = true;

            if (gestCut.Matches(null, args))
                CutOnClick(this, args);

            else if (gestCopy.Matches(null, args))
                CopyOnClick(this, args);

            else if (gestPaste.Matches(null, args))
                PasteOnClick(this, args);
```

```
            else if (gestDelete.Matches(null, args))
                DeleteOnClick(this, args);

            else
                args.Handled = false;
        }
    }
}
```

Whenever you inherit from a class that defines a *Main* method (as the *CutCopyAndPaste* class does) and you supply a new *Main* method (as the *ControlXCV* class does) you need to tell Visual Studio which *Main* method is the true entry point to the program. Select Project Properties and change Startup Object to the class with the *Main* method you want to use.

The program defines and sets the four *KeyGesture* objects as fields, and also needs to set the *InputGestureText* property of each *MenuItem* to the corresponding string. (Unfortunately, *KeyGesture* itself doesn't provide that information through its *ToString* method or otherwise.) The *OnPreviewKeyDown* method begins by setting the *Handled* property of its event arguments to *true*, and then resets it to *false* if the key doesn't match one of the define gestures.

If you have more than just a few *KeyGesture* objects floating around, you'll probably want to store them in a collection. You can define a field that creates a generic *Dictionary* like this:

```
Dictionary<KeyGesture, RoutedEventHandler> gests =
                        new Dictionary<KeyGesture, RoutedEventHandler>();
```

The constructor of your window can fill it up with the *KeyGesture* objects and their associated event handlers:

```
gests.Add(new KeyGesture(Key.X, ModifierKeys.Control), CutOnClick);
gests.Add(new KeyGesture(Key.C, ModifierKeys.Control), CopyOnClick);
gests.Add(new KeyGesture(Key.V, ModifierKeys.Control), PasteOnClick);
gests.Add(new KeyGesture(Key.Delete), DeleteOnClick);
```

The *OnPreviewKeyDown* method can then search for a match and call the corresponding event handler by looping through the dictionary:

```
foreach (KeyGesture gest in gests.Keys)
    if (gest.Matches(null, args))
    {
        gests[gest](this, args);
        args.Handled = true;
    }
```

The first statement in the *if* block line indexes the *Dictionary* object named *gests* with the matching *KeyGesture* object named *gest*. The result is the *RoutedEventHandler* object, which the statement calls by passing arguments of *this* and the *KeyEventArgs* object.

If you'd rather not call the *Click* event handlers directly, you could instead define a *Dictionary* with the *MenuItem* as the *Value*:

```
Dictionary<KeyGesture, MenuItem> gests =
                        new Dictionary<KeyGesture, MenuItem>();
```

You add entries to this dictionary like so:

```
gests.Add(new KeyGesture(Key.X, ModifierKeys.Control), itemCut);
```

And now the *OnKeyDown* processing looks like this:

```
foreach (KeyGesture gest in gests.Keys)
    if (gest.Matches(null, args))
        gests[gest].RaiseEvent(
            new RoutedEventArgs(MenuItem.ClickEvent, gests[gest]));
```

By this time you may have concluded that command bindings probably provide a simpler approach, and they certainly do. The CommandTheButton program in Chapter 4 showed how to use command bindings with a button. Using them with menu items is quite similar. Generally you'll be using static properties of type *RoutedUICommand* from the *Application-Commands* class and (for more esoteric applications) from the *ComponentCommands*, *Editing-Commands*, *MediaCommands*, and *NavigationCommands* classes, but you can also make your own, as I'll demonstrate.

To use one of the predefined static properties, you set the *Command* property of the *MenuItem* like this:

```
itemCut.Command = ApplicationCommands.Cut;
```

If you don't set the *Header* property of the *MenuItem*, it will use the *Text* property of the *Routed-UICommand*, which is *almost* OK except there's no preceding underline. Regardless, the *MenuItem* automatically adds the "Ctrl+X" text to the menu item.

The other crucial step is creating a command binding based on the *RoutedUICommand* object, and adding it to the *CommandBindings* collection of the window:

```
CommandBindings.Add(new CommandBinding(ApplicationCommands.Cut,
                            CutOnExecute, CutCanExecute));
```

This command binding automatically provides for keyboard handling of the standard accelerators associated with the commands. As you'll see, the accelerator is defined within the *RoutedUICommand* object. The command binding associates the command with the *CommandBinding* events *CanExecute* and *Executed*. When using *RoutedUICommand* objects, there is no need to provide an event handler specifically to enable and disable the items on the Edit menu. The enabling and disabling occurs via the *CanExecute* handlers by setting the *CanExecute* property of the *CanExecuteRoutedEventArgs* to *true* or *false*. You can share *CanExecute* handlers among several menu items if appropriate.

Here's a program that implements command bindings for the four standard items on the Edit menu.

```
CommandTheMenu.cs
//-------------------------------------------------
// CommandTheMenu.cs (c) 2006 by Charles Petzold
//-------------------------------------------------
using System;
using System.Windows;
using System.Windows.Controls;
using System.Windows.Input;
using System.Windows.Media;

namespace Petzold.CommandTheMenu
{
    public class CommandTheMenu : Window
    {
        TextBlock text;

        [STAThread]
        public static void Main()
        {
            Application app = new Application();
            app.Run(new CommandTheMenu());
        }
        public CommandTheMenu()
        {
            Title = "Command the Menu";

            // Create DockPanel.
            DockPanel dock = new DockPanel();
            Content = dock;

            // Create Menu docked at top.
            Menu menu = new Menu();
            dock.Children.Add(menu);
            DockPanel.SetDock(menu, Dock.Top);

            // Create TextBlock filling the rest.
            text = new TextBlock();
            text.Text = "Sample clipboard text";
            text.HorizontalAlignment = HorizontalAlignment.Center;
            text.VerticalAlignment = VerticalAlignment.Center;
            text.FontSize = 32;      // ie, 24 points
            text.TextWrapping = TextWrapping.Wrap;
            dock.Children.Add(text);

            // Create Edit menu.
            MenuItem itemEdit = new MenuItem();
            itemEdit.Header = "_Edit";
            menu.Items.Add(itemEdit);
```

```
        // Create items on Edit menu.
        MenuItem itemCut = new MenuItem();
        itemCut.Header = "Cu_t";
        itemCut.Command = ApplicationCommands.Cut;
        itemEdit.Items.Add(itemCut);

        MenuItem itemCopy = new MenuItem();
        itemCopy.Header = "_Copy";
        itemCopy.Command = ApplicationCommands.Copy;
        itemEdit.Items.Add(itemCopy);

        MenuItem itemPaste = new MenuItem();
        itemPaste.Header = "_Paste";
        itemPaste.Command = ApplicationCommands.Paste;
        itemEdit.Items.Add(itemPaste);

        MenuItem itemDelete = new MenuItem();
        itemDelete.Header = "_Delete";
        itemDelete.Command = ApplicationCommands.Delete;
        itemEdit.Items.Add(itemDelete);

        // Add command bindings to window collection.
        CommandBindings.Add(new CommandBinding(ApplicationCommands.Cut,
                            CutOnExecute, CutCanExecute));
        CommandBindings.Add(new CommandBinding(ApplicationCommands.Copy,
                            CopyOnExecute, CutCanExecute));
        CommandBindings.Add(new CommandBinding(ApplicationCommands.Paste,
                            PasteOnExecute, PasteCanExecute));
        CommandBindings.Add(new CommandBinding(ApplicationCommands.Delete,
                            DeleteOnExecute, CutCanExecute));
    }
    void CutCanExecute(object sender, CanExecuteRoutedEventArgs args)
    {
        args.CanExecute = text.Text != null && text.Text.Length > 0;
    }
    void PasteCanExecute(object sender, CanExecuteRoutedEventArgs args)
    {
        args.CanExecute = Clipboard.ContainsText();
    }
    void CutOnExecute(object sender, ExecutedRoutedEventArgs args)
    {
        ApplicationCommands.Copy.Execute(null, this);
        ApplicationCommands.Delete.Execute(null, this);
    }
    void CopyOnExecute(object sender, ExecutedRoutedEventArgs args)
    {
        Clipboard.SetText(text.Text);
    }
    void PasteOnExecute(object sender, ExecutedRoutedEventArgs args)
    {
        text.Text = Clipboard.GetText();
    }
    void DeleteOnExecute(object sender, ExecutedRoutedEventArgs args)
```

```
        {
            text.Text = null;
        }
    }
}
```

Notice that Cut, Copy, and Delete all share the same *CanExecute* handler.

Although it's nice to implement the standard Edit items with command bindings, it's even more fun to create new ones. You can add this code to the CommandTheMenu program at the end of the constructor. The object here is to create a new command called Restore that restores the *TextBlock* to its original text. The Restore command has a keyboard shortcut of Ctrl+R.

Because a particular *RoutedUICommand* can be associated with multiple key gestures, a collection must be defined even if you want only one gesture:

```
InputGestureCollection collGestures = new InputGestureCollection();
```

Add the appropriate *KeyGesture* to this collection:

```
collGestures.Add(new KeyGesture(Key.R, ModifierKeys.Control));
```

And then create a *RoutedUICommand*:

```
RoutedUICommand commRestore =
    new RoutedUICommand("_Restore", "Restore", GetType(), collGestures);
```

The first argument to the constructor becomes the *Text* property and the second is the *Name* property. (Notice that I've added an underline to the *Text* property.) The third argument is the owner (which can be simply the *Window* object) and the fourth argument is a collection of keyboard gestures.

Now the *MenuItem* can be defined and added to the menu:

```
MenuItem itemRestore = new MenuItem();
itemRestore.Header = "_Restore";
itemRestore.Command = commRestore;
itemEdit.Items.Add(itemRestore);
```

Setting the *Header* property isn't required because it picks up the *Text* property from the *RoutedUICommand*. The command must also be added to the window's command collection. Here's where event handlers are specified:

```
CommandBindings.Add(new CommandBinding(commRestore, RestoreOnExecute));
```

The *RestoreOnExecute* handler simply restores the *TextBlock* text to its original value:

```
void RestoreOnExecute(object sender, ExecutedRoutedEventArgs args)
{
    text.Text = "Sample clipboard text";
}
```

The programs so far in this chapter have dealt with the *Menu* control that normally sits near the top of the window. The Windows Presentation Foundation also includes a *ContextMenu* control, customarily invoked in response to a click of the right mouse button.

Like *ToolTip*, *ContextMenu* is a property as well as a class. And like *ToolTip* again, a *Context-Menu* property is defined by both *FrameworkElement* and *FrameworkContentElement*. If you'd like, you can define a *ContextMenu* object that is associated with a particular element, and then assign that *ContextMenu* object to the *ContextMenu* property of the element. The context menu then opens whenever the user right-clicks that element. You can install event handlers to initialize the menu when it opens, and to be notified of clicks and checks.

If you don't set the *ContextMenu* object to the *ContextMenu* property of some element, you need to open the context menu "manually"—probably in response to a *MouseRightButtonUp* event. Fortunately, opening the context menu is as easy as setting the *IsOpen* property to *true*. By default, the context menu appears at the location of the mouse pointer.

The following program is similar to the ToggleBoldAndItalic program from Chapter 3. It displays a famous quotation and lets you right-click each word with the mouse. A context menu is displayed that lists formatting options Bold, Italic, Underline, Overline, Strikethrough, and Baseline. The program creates only one *ContextMenu* object for use with all the words of the text, and doesn't attempt to keep track of the formatting of each word. Instead, whenever the context menu is displayed, it is initialized with the formatting of the particular word being clicked.

PopupContextMenu.cs

```
//-------------------------------------------------
// PopupContextMenu.cs (c) 2006 by Charles Petzold
//-------------------------------------------------
using System;
using System.Windows;
using System.Windows.Controls;
using System.Windows.Documents;
using System.Windows.Input;
using System.Windows.Media;

namespace Petzold.PopupContextMenu
{
    public class PopupContextMenu : Window
    {
        ContextMenu menu;
        MenuItem itemBold, itemItalic;
        MenuItem[] itemDecor;
        Inline inlClicked;

        [STAThread]
        public static void Main()
        {
            Application app = new Application();
            app.Run(new PopupContextMenu());
        }
```

```
public PopupContextMenu()
{
    Title = "Popup Context Menu";

    // Create ContextMenu.
    menu = new ContextMenu();

    // Add an item for "Bold".
    itemBold = new MenuItem();
    itemBold.Header = "Bold";
    menu.Items.Add(itemBold);

    // Add an item for "Italic".
    itemItalic = new MenuItem();
    itemItalic.Header = "Italic";
    menu.Items.Add(itemItalic);

    // Get all the TextDecorationLocation members.
    TextDecorationLocation[] locs =
        (TextDecorationLocation[])
            Enum.GetValues(typeof(TextDecorationLocation));

    // Create an array of MenuItem objects and fill them up.
    itemDecor = new MenuItem[locs.Length];

    for (int i = 0; i < locs.Length; i++)
    {
        TextDecoration decor = new TextDecoration();
        decor.Location = locs[i];

        itemDecor[i] = new MenuItem();
        itemDecor[i].Header = locs[i].ToString();
        itemDecor[i].Tag = decor;
        menu.Items.Add(itemDecor[i]);
    }

    // Use one handler for the entire context menu.
    menu.AddHandler(MenuItem.ClickEvent,
                new RoutedEventHandler(MenuOnClick));

    // Create a TextBlock as content of the window.
    TextBlock text = new TextBlock();
    text.FontSize = 32;
    text.HorizontalAlignment = HorizontalAlignment.Center;
    text.VerticalAlignment = VerticalAlignment.Center;
    Content = text;

    // Break a famous quotation up into words.
    string strQuote = "To be, or not to be, that is the question";
    string[] strWords = strQuote.Split();

    // Make each word a Run, and add to the TextBlock.
    foreach (string str in strWords)
    {
        Run run = new Run(str);
```

```
                    // Make sure that TextDecorations is an actual collection!
                    run.TextDecorations = new TextDecorationCollection();
                    text.Inlines.Add(run);
                    text.Inlines.Add(" ");
                }
            }
            protected override void OnMouseRightButtonUp(MouseButtonEventArgs args)
            {
                base.OnMouseRightButtonUp(args);

                if ((inlClicked = args.Source as Inline) != null)
                {
                    // Check the menu items according to properties of the InLine.
                    itemBold.IsChecked = (inlClicked.FontWeight == FontWeights.Bold);
                    itemItalic.IsChecked = (inlClicked.FontStyle == FontStyles.Italic);

                    foreach (MenuItem item in itemDecor)
                        item.IsChecked = (inlClicked.TextDecorations.Contains
                            (item.Tag as TextDecoration));

                    // Display context menu.
                    menu.IsOpen = true;
                    args.Handled = true;
                }
            }
            void MenuOnClick(object sender, RoutedEventArgs args)
            {
                MenuItem item = args.Source as MenuItem;

                item.IsChecked ^= true;

                // Change the Inline based on the checked or unchecked item.
                if (item == itemBold)
                    inlClicked.FontWeight =
                        (item.IsChecked ? FontWeights.Bold : FontWeights.Normal);

                else if (item == itemItalic)
                    inlClicked.FontStyle =
                        (item.IsChecked ? FontStyles.Italic : FontStyles.Normal);

                else
                {
                    if (item.IsChecked)
                        inlClicked.TextDecorations.Add(item.Tag as TextDecoration);
                    else
                        inlClicked.TextDecorations.Remove(item.Tag as TextDecoration);
                }
                (inlClicked.Parent as TextBlock).InvalidateVisual();
            }
        }
    }
}
```

The first part of the window constructor is devoted to creating the *ContextMenu* object. After adding Bold and Italic items to the menu, the window constructor obtains the members of the *TextDecorationLocation* enumeration. These members are *Underline*, *Overline*, *Strikethrough*, and *Baseline*. The constructor uses the *AddHandler* method of the *ContextMenu* to assign a single *Click* handler for all the menu items.

The *Split* method of the *String* class divides the quotation into words. These are made into objects of type *Run* and patched together into a single *TextBlock* object. Notice that a *TextDecorationCollection* is explicitly created for each *Run* object. This collection does not exist by default and the *TextDecorations* property is normally *null*.

Although the *OnMouseRightButtonUp* method seemingly obtains mouse events to the window, event routing provides that if an *Inline* object is clicked, the *Source* property of the event arguments will indicate that object. (Recall that *Run* derives from *Inline*.) The event handler can then initialize the menu based on the properties of the clicked word.

The *MenuOnClick* manually toggles the *IsChecked* property of the clicked item. This isn't really necessary because the menu disappears when it's clicked, but the event handler uses the new value of this *IsChecked* property to determine how to change the formatting of the clicked *Inline* object.

I began this chapter by noting that the menu occupies a regal position near the top of the window. As you know, directly below the menu is often a toolbar, and (sometimes almost as important) a status bar often sits at the bottom of a window. These are the subjects of the next chapter.

Chapter 15
Toolbars and Status Bars

Not very long ago, menus and toolbars were easy to distinguish. Menus consisted of a hierarchical collection of text items, while toolbars consisted of a row of bitmapped buttons. But once icons and controls began appearing on menus, and drop-down menus sprouted from toolbars, the differences became less obvious. Traditionally, toolbars are positioned near the top of the window right under the menu, but toolbars can actually appear on any side of the window. If they're at the bottom, they should appear above the status bar (if there is one).

ToolBar is a descendant of *HeaderedItemsControl*, just like *MenuItem* and (as you'll see in the next chapter) *TreeViewItem*. This means that *ToolBar* has an *Items* collection, which consists of the items (buttons and so forth) displayed on the toolbar. *ToolBar* also has a *Header* property, but it's not cusomarily used on horizontal toolbars. It makes more sense on vertical toolbars as a title.

There is no *ToolBarItem* class. You put the same elements and controls on the toolbar that you put on your windows and panels. Buttons are very popular, of course, generally displaying small bitmaps. The *ToggleButton* is commonly used to display on/off options. The *ComboBox* is very useful on toolbars, and a single-line *TextBox* is also possible. You can even put a *MenuItem* on the toolbar to have drop-down options, perhaps containing other controls. Use *Separator* to frame items into functional groups. Because toolbars tend to have more graphics and less text than windows and dialog boxes, it is considered quite rude not to use tooltips with toolbar items. Because toolbar items often duplicate menu items, it is common for them to share command bindings.

Here is a rather nonfunctional program that creates a *ToolBar* and populates it with eight buttons. The program defines an array of eight static properties from the *ApplicationCommands* class (of type *RoutedUICommand*) and a corresponding array of eight file names of bitmaps located in the Images directory of the project. Each button's *Command* property is assigned one of these *RoutedUICommand* objects and gets a bitmapped image.

CraftTheToolbar.cs
```
//------------------------------------------------
// CraftTheToolbar.cs (c) 2006 by Charles Petzold
//------------------------------------------------
using System;
using System.Windows;
using System.Windows.Controls;
using System.Windows.Input;
using System.Windows.Media;
using System.Windows.Media.Imaging;
```

```
namespace Petzold.CraftTheToolbar
{
    public class CraftTheToolbar : Window
    {
        [STAThread]
        public static void Main()
        {
            Application app = new Application();
            app.Run(new CraftTheToolbar());
        }
        public CraftTheToolbar()
        {
            Title = "Craft the Toolbar";

            RoutedUICommand[] comm =
                {
                    ApplicationCommands.New, ApplicationCommands.Open,
                    ApplicationCommands.Save, ApplicationCommands.Print,
                    ApplicationCommands.Cut, ApplicationCommands.Copy,
                    ApplicationCommands.Paste, ApplicationCommands.Delete
                };

            string[] strImages =
                {
                    "NewDocumentHS.png", "openHS.png", "saveHS.png",
                    "PrintHS.png", "CutHS.png", "CopyHS.png",
                    "PasteHS.png", "DeleteHS.png"
                };

            // Create DockPanel as content of window.
            DockPanel dock = new DockPanel();
            dock.LastChildFill = false;
            Content = dock;

            // Create Toolbar docked at top of window.
            ToolBar toolbar = new ToolBar();
            dock.Children.Add(toolbar);
            DockPanel.SetDock(toolbar, Dock.Top);

            // Create the Toolbar buttons.
            for (int i = 0; i < 8; i++)
            {
                if (i == 4)
                    toolbar.Items.Add(new Separator());

                // Create the Button.
                Button btn = new Button();
                btn.Command = comm[i];
                toolbar.Items.Add(btn);

                // Create an Image as content of the Button.
                Image img = new Image();
                img.Source = new BitmapImage(
                    new Uri("pack://application:,,/Images/" + strImages[i]));
                img.Stretch = Stretch.None;
                btn.Content = img;
```

```
                    // Create a ToolTip based on the UICommand text.
                    ToolTip tip = new ToolTip();
                    tip.Content = comm[i].Text;
                    btn.ToolTip = tip;

                    // Add the UICommand to the window command bindings.
                    CommandBindings.Add(
                        new CommandBinding(comm[i], ToolBarButtonOnClick));
                }
            }
            // Do-nothing command handler for button.
            void ToolBarButtonOnClick(object sender, ExecutedRoutedEventArgs args)
            {
                RoutedUICommand comm = args.Command as RoutedUICommand;
                MessageBox.Show(comm.Name +
                                " command not yet implemented", Title);
            }
        }
    }
}
```

Clicking any of the buttons causes a message box to pop up from the *ToolBarButtonOnClick* event handler. This event handler becomes associated with each of the *RoutedUICommand* objects when the commands are added to the window's command bindings collection in the last statement of the *for* loop. Notice that the *Text* property of each *RoutedUICommand* plays a role in the creation of the *ToolTip* control associated with each button.

A very nice byproduct of these command bindings is a keyboard interface. Typing Ctrl+N, Ctrl+O, Ctrl+S, Ctrl+P, Ctrl+X, Ctrl+C, Ctrl+V, or the Delete key will also bring up the message box.

The images are from the library shipped with Microsoft Visual Studio 2005. They are 16 pixels square. In some cases, I had to use an image-editing program to change the resolution of the image to 96 dots per inch. In the context of the Windows Presentation Manager, that means that the images are really 1/6 inch square, about the height of 12-point type. On higher-resolution displays these images should remain about the same physical size, although they may not be quite as sharp.

Here's an interesting experiment. Remove the statement that prevents the toolbar from filling the client area:

```
dock.LastChildFill = false;
```

Now add a *RichTextBox* control to the *DockPanel*. This code can go right before the *for* loop:

```
RichTextBox txtbox = new RichTextBox();
dock.Children.Add(txtbox);
```

Also for this experiment it is important to set the keyboard input focus to the *RichTextBox* at the very close of the window constructor:

```
txtbox.Focus();
```

As you may know, *RichTextBox* processes Ctrl+X, Ctrl+C, and Ctrl+V to implement Cut, Copy, and Paste. (You can also see these three commands on a little context menu when you right-click the *RichTextBox*.) But the command bindings that *RichTextBox* implements interact with the window's command bindings in very desirable ways: If there is no text selected in the *RichTextBox*, the Cut and Copy buttons are disabled! If you select some text and you click one of these buttons, it performs the operation rather than displaying the message box. (However, if the buttons are disabled and you type Ctrl+X or Ctrl+C, the *RichTextBox* ignores the keystrokes and the program displays the message box.)

Even without this help from *RichTextBox*, a program that implements a Paste button needs to enable and disable the button based on the contents of the clipboard. If a program chooses *not* to use the standard *RoutedUICommand* objects, it will need to set a timer to check the contents of the clipboard (perhaps every tenth second) and enable the button based on what it finds. Using the standard *RoutedUICommand* objects is usually easier because calls are made to the *CanExecute* handler associated with the command binding whenever the contents of the clipboard change.

Some programs (such as Microsoft Internet Explorer) display some text along with toolbar buttons for those buttons whose meaning might not be so obvious. You can easily do this with a WPF toolbar by using a *StackPanel* on the button. First, comment out this statement from the *if* loop:

```
btn.Content = img;
```

Add the following code right after that statement:

```
StackPanel stack = new StackPanel();
stack.Orientation = Orientation.Horizontal;
btn.Content = stack;

TextBlock txtblk = new TextBlock();
txtblk.Text = comm[i].Text;

stack.Children.Add(img);
stack.Children.Add(txtblk);
```

Now each button displays text to the right of the image. You can move the text below the image simply by changing the *Orientation* of the *StackPanel* to *Vertical*. You can change the order of the *Image* and *TextBlock* simply by swapping the statements that add them to the *StackPanel* children collection.

You may have noticed a little grip-like image at the far left of the toolbar. If you pass your mouse over the grip, you'll see the mouse cursor change to *Cursors.SizeAll* (the four-directional arrow cursor), but despite the visual cues, you won't be able to budge the toolbar. (I'll show you how to get that to work shortly.) If you set the *Header* property of the *ToolBar* object, that text string (or whatever) appears between the grip and the first item on the toolbar.

If you make the window too narrow to fit the entire toolbar, a little button at the far right becomes enabled. Clicking that button causes the other buttons on the toolbar to appear as a little popup. What you are looking at here is an object of type *ToolBarOverflowPanel*. In addition, the *ToolBar* uses a class named *ToolBarPanel* to arrange the items on itself. It is unlikely you'll need to use *ToolBarPanel* or *ToolBarOverflowPanel* yourself. The following class hierarchy shows all *ToolBar*-related classes:

FrameworkElement

    Control

        ItemsControl

            HeaderedItemsControl

                ToolBar

    Panel (abstract)

        StackPanel

        ToolBarPanel

      ToolBarOverflowPanel

    ToolBarTray

Although *ToolBarPanel* and *ToolBarOverflowPanel* work behind the scenes, the *ToolBarTray* class becomes important if you're implementing multiple toolbars or you want vertical toolbars.

The MoveTheToolbar program demonstrates the use of the *ToolBarTray*. It creates two of them, one docked at the top of the client area and the other docked to the left. Within each *ToolBarTray*, the program creates three *ToolBar* controls with a header (just for identification) and six buttons containing letters as content.

MoveTheToolbar.cs

```
//--------------------------------------------------
// MoveTheToolbar.cs (c) 2006 by Charles Petzold
//--------------------------------------------------
using System;
using System.Windows;
using System.Windows.Controls;
using System.Windows.Input;
using System.Windows.Media;

namespace Petzold.MoveTheToolbar
{
    public class MoveTheToolbar : Window
    {
        [STAThread]
```

```
    public static void Main()
    {
        Application app = new Application();
        app.Run(new MoveTheToolbar());
    }
    public MoveTheToolbar()
    {
        Title = "Move the Toolbar";

        // Create DockPanel as content of window.
        DockPanel dock = new DockPanel();
        Content = dock;

        // Create ToolBarTray at top and left of window.
        ToolBarTray trayTop = new ToolBarTray();
        dock.Children.Add(trayTop);
        DockPanel.SetDock(trayTop, Dock.Top);

        ToolBarTray trayLeft = new ToolBarTray();
        trayLeft.Orientation = Orientation.Vertical;
        dock.Children.Add(trayLeft);
        DockPanel.SetDock(trayLeft, Dock.Left);

        // Create TextBox to fill rest of client area.
        TextBox txtbox = new TextBox();
        dock.Children.Add(txtbox);

        // Create six Toolbars...
        for (int i = 0; i < 6; i++)
        {
            ToolBar toolbar = new ToolBar();
            toolbar.Header = "Toolbar " + (i + 1);

            if (i < 3)
                trayTop.ToolBars.Add(toolbar);
            else
                trayLeft.ToolBars.Add(toolbar);

            // ... with six buttons each.
            for (int j = 0; j < 6; j++)
            {
                Button btn = new Button();
                btn.FontSize = 16;
                btn.Content = (char)('A' + j);
                toolbar.Items.Add(btn);
            }
        }
    }
}
```

Notice that the *ToolBarTray* docked at the left of the client area is given an *Orientation* of *Vertical*. Any *ToolBar* controls that are part of that tray display their items vertically. The program sets the *Header* property of each *ToolBar* to a number. The toolbars numbered 1, 2, and 3 are in the top *ToolBarTray*. Those numbered 4, 5, and 6 are in the left *ToolBarTray*.

Within each tray you can move the toolbars so that they follow one another horizontally across the top or vertically on the left (this is the default arrangement) or you can move them into multiple rows (on the top) or multiple columns (on the left). You cannot move a *ToolBar* from one *ToolBarTray* to another.

If you want to initialize the positions of the toolbars within the tray, or you want to save the arrangment preferred by the user, you use two integer properties of *ToolBar* named *Band* and *BandIndex*. For a horizontal *ToolBar*, the *Band* indicates the row the *ToolBar* occupies. The *BandIndex* is a position in that row, starting from the left. For a vertical *ToolBar*, the *Band* indicates the column the *ToolBar* occupies, and the *BandIndex* is a position in that column from the top. By default, all toolbars have a *Band* of 0 and a *BandIndex* numbered beginning at 0 and increasing based on the order in which they're added to the *ToolBarTray*.

For the remainder of this chapter, I'd like to show toolbars in a more "real-life" application. The FormatRichText program that I'll be assembling has no menu, but it does have four toolbars and one status bar. The four toolbars are devoted to handling file I/O, the clipboard, character formatting, and paragraph formatting.

As usual, the *FormatRichText* class that is the bulk of this program inherits from *Window*. But I wanted to keep the source code files reasonably small and to group related pieces of code, so I've split the *FormatRichText* class into six parts using the *partial* keyword. Each part of this class is in a different file. The first file is named FormatRichText.cs, but the file that contains the code related to opening and saving files is located in FormatRichText.File.cs. This project also requires a link to the ColorGridBox.cs file from Chapter 11.

Here's the first file.

FormatRichText.cs

```
//--------------------------------------------------
// FormatRichText.cs (c) 2006 by Charles Petzold
//--------------------------------------------------
using System;
using System.Windows;
using System.Windows.Controls;
using System.Windows.Input;
using System.Windows.Media;

namespace Petzold.FormatRichText
{
    public partial class FormatRichText : Window
    {
        RichTextBox txtbox;
```

```
[STAThread]
public static void Main()
{
    Application app = new Application();
    app.Run(new FormatRichText());
}
public FormatRichText()
{
    Title = "Format Rich Text";

    // Create DockPanel as content of window.
    DockPanel dock = new DockPanel();
    Content = dock;

    // Create ToolBarTray docked at top of client area.
    ToolBarTray tray = new ToolBarTray();
    dock.Children.Add(tray);
    DockPanel.SetDock(tray, Dock.Top);

    // Create RichTextBox.
    txtbox = new RichTextBox();
    txtbox.VerticalScrollBarVisibility = ScrollBarVisibility.Auto;

    // Call methods in other files.
    AddFileToolBar(tray, 0, 0);
    AddEditToolBar(tray, 1, 0);
    AddCharToolBar(tray, 2, 0);
    AddParaToolBar(tray, 2, 1);
    AddStatusBar(dock);

    // Fill rest of client area with RichTextBox and give it focus.
    dock.Children.Add(txtbox);
    txtbox.Focus();
}
}
}
```

The constructor creates a *DockPanel*, *ToolBarTray*, and a *RichTextBox*. Notice that the *RichText-Box* is stored as a field to be accessible to the other parts of the *FormatRichText* class. The constructor then calls five methods (*AddFileToolBar* and so forth), each of which is in a separate file. The second and third arguments to these methods are the desired *Band* and *BandIndex* properties of the *ToolBar* control.

The second file of the FormatRichText project is named FormatRichText.File.cs and is devoted to loading and saving files. A *RichTextBox* control is capable of loading and saving files in four different formats. These four formats correspond to four static read-only fields in the *DataFormats* class. They are *DataFormats.Text*, *DataFormats.Rtf* (Rich Text Format), *DataFormats.Xaml*, and *DataFormats.XamlPackage* (which is actually a ZIP file containing other files that contribute to a complete document). These formats are listed in an array defined as a field near the top of this file. Notice that *DataFormats.Text* is repeated at the end to make a total of five. These correspond to the five sections of the *strFilter*, which is required by the *OpenFileDialog* and *SaveFileDialog* classes to show the different file types and extensions in the dialog boxes.

FormatRichText.File.cs

```
//----------------------------------------------------
// FormatRichText.File.cs (c) 2006 by Charles Petzold
//----------------------------------------------------
using Microsoft.Win32;
using System;
using System.IO;
using System.Windows;
using System.Windows.Controls;
using System.Windows.Documents;
using System.Windows.Input;
using System.Windows.Media;
using System.Windows.Media.Imaging;

namespace Petzold.FormatRichText
{
    public partial class FormatRichText : Window
    {
        string[] formats =
            {
                DataFormats.Xaml, DataFormats.XamlPackage, DataFormats.Rtf,
                DataFormats.Text, DataFormats.Text
            };

        string strFilter =
            "XAML Document Files (*.xaml)|*.xaml|" +
            "XAML Package Files (*.zip)|*.zip|" +
            "Rich Text Format Files (*.rtf)|*.rtf|" +
            "Text Files (*.txt)|*.txt|" +
            "All files (*.*)|*.*";

        void AddFileToolBar(ToolBarTray tray, int band, int index)
        {
            // Create the ToolBar.
            ToolBar toolbar = new ToolBar();
            toolbar.Band = band;
            toolbar.BandIndex = index;
            tray.ToolBars.Add(toolbar);

            RoutedUICommand[] comm =
                {
                    ApplicationCommands.New, ApplicationCommands.Open,
                    ApplicationCommands.Save
                };

            string[] strImages =
                {
                    "NewDocumentHS.png", "openHS.png", "saveHS.png"
                };

            // Create buttons for the ToolBar.
            for (int i = 0; i < 3; i++)
            {
                Button btn = new Button();
                btn.Command = comm[i];
                toolbar.Items.Add(btn);
```

```
                    Image img = new Image();
                    img.Source = new BitmapImage(
                            new Uri("pack://application:,,/Images/" +
                                    strImages[i]));

                    img.Stretch = Stretch.None;
                    btn.Content = img;

                    ToolTip tip = new ToolTip();
                     tip.Content = comm[i].Text;
                    btn.ToolTip = tip;
                }


            // Add the command bindings.
            CommandBindings.Add(
                new CommandBinding(ApplicationCommands.New, OnNew));
            CommandBindings.Add(
                new CommandBinding(ApplicationCommands.Open, OnOpen));
            CommandBindings.Add(
                new CommandBinding(ApplicationCommands.Save, OnSave));
        }


        // New: Set content to an empty string.
        void OnNew(object sender, ExecutedRoutedEventArgs args)
        {
            FlowDocument flow = txtbox.Document;
            TextRange range = new TextRange(flow.ContentStart,
                                            flow.ContentEnd);
            range.Text = "";
        }


        // Open: Display dialog box and load file.
        void OnOpen(object sender, ExecutedRoutedEventArgs args)
        {
            OpenFileDialog dlg = new OpenFileDialog();
            dlg.CheckFileExists = true;
            dlg.Filter = strFilter;

            if ((bool)dlg.ShowDialog(this))
            {
                FlowDocument flow = txtbox.Document;
                TextRange range = new TextRange(flow.ContentStart,
                                                flow.ContentEnd);
                FileStream strm = null;

                try
                {
                    strm = new FileStream(dlg.FileName, FileMode.Open);
                    range.Load(strm, formats[dlg.FilterIndex - 1]);
                }
                catch (Exception exc)
                {
                    MessageBox.Show(exc.Message, Title);
                }
```

```
            finally
            {
                if (strm != null)
                    strm.Close();
            }
        }
    }

    // Save: Display dialog box and save file.
    void OnSave(object sender, ExecutedRoutedEventArgs args)
    {
        SaveFileDialog dlg = new SaveFileDialog();
        dlg.Filter = strFilter;

        if ((bool)dlg.ShowDialog(this))
        {
            FlowDocument flow = txtbox.Document;
            TextRange range = new TextRange(flow.ContentStart,
                                            flow.ContentEnd);

            FileStream strm = null;

            try
            {
                strm = new FileStream(dlg.FileName, FileMode.Create);
                range.Save(strm, formats[dlg.FilterIndex - 1]);
            }
            catch (Exception exc)
            {
                MessageBox.Show(exc.Message, Title);
            }
            finally
            {
                if (strm != null)
                    strm.Close();
            }
        }
    }
}
```

The *AddFileToolBar* method creates a *ToolBar* object and then creates three *Button* objects corresponding to the standard commands *ApplicationCommands.New*, *ApplicationCommands .Open*, and *ApplicationCommands.Save*. (You'll notice that the FormatRichText program responds to Ctrl+N, Ctrl+O, and Ctrl+S, the standard keyboard accelerators for these commands.)

To keep this program simple, I've omitted some amenities. The program doesn't retain a file name, so it can't implement Save by simply saving the file under that name. Nor does it warn you about files that you've modified but haven't yet saved. These features are missing here but they are implemented in the NotepadClone program in Chapter 18.

The *OnOpen* and *OnSave* methods are fairly similar to each other. They both display a dialog box and, if the user presses the Open or Save button, the method obtains a *FlowDocument* object from the *RichTextBox*, and then creates a *TextRange* object corresponding to the entire content of the document. The *TextRange* class has *Load* and *Save* methods; the first argument is a *Stream*, the second is a field from *DataFormats*. The methods index the *formats* array using the *FilterIndex* property of the dialog box. This property indicates the part of *strFilter* that the user had selected prior to pressing the Open or Save button. (Notice that 1 is subtracted from *FilterIndex* because the property is 1-based rather than 0-based.)

The next file handles the commands normally found on the Edit menu. Experimentation with the CraftTheToolbar program at the beginning of this chapter revealed that command bindings added to the window become connected to command bindings for the child with input focus—that is, the *RichTextBox*. The code in this file creates the buttons and command bindings, and adds the command bindings to the window's collection, but most of them are unimplemented. The *RichTextBox* itself handles most of the clipboard logic.

FormatRichText.Edit.cs

```
//---------------------------------------------------
// FormatRichText.Edit.cs (c) 2006 by Charles Petzold
//---------------------------------------------------
using System;
using System.Windows;
using System.Windows.Controls;
using System.Windows.Input;
using System.Windows.Media;
using System.Windows.Media.Imaging;

namespace Petzold.FormatRichText
{
    public partial class FormatRichText : Window
    {
        void AddEditToolBar(ToolBarTray tray, int band, int index)
        {
            // Create Toolbar.
            ToolBar toolbar = new ToolBar();
            toolbar.Band = band;
            toolbar.BandIndex = index;
            tray.ToolBars.Add(toolbar);

            RoutedUICommand[] comm =
                {
                    ApplicationCommands.Cut, ApplicationCommands.Copy,
                    ApplicationCommands.Paste, ApplicationCommands.Delete,
                    ApplicationCommands.Undo, ApplicationCommands.Redo
                };

            string[] strImages =
                {
                    "CutHS.png", "CopyHS.png",
                    "PasteHS.png", "DeleteHS.png",
                    "Edit_UndoHS.png", "Edit_RedoHS.png"
                };
```

```
        for (int i = 0; i < 6; i++)
        {
            if (i == 4)
                toolbar.Items.Add(new Separator());

            Button btn = new Button();
            btn.Command = comm[i];
            toolbar.Items.Add(btn);

            Image img = new Image();
            img.Source = new BitmapImage(
                    new Uri("pack://application:,,/Images/" + strImages[i]));
            img.Stretch = Stretch.None;
            btn.Content = img;

            ToolTip tip = new ToolTip();
            tip.Content = comm[i].Text;
            btn.ToolTip = tip;
        }

        CommandBindings.Add(new CommandBinding(ApplicationCommands.Cut));
        CommandBindings.Add(new CommandBinding(ApplicationCommands.Copy));
        CommandBindings.Add(new CommandBinding(ApplicationCommands.Paste));
        CommandBindings.Add(new CommandBinding(
                    ApplicationCommands.Delete, OnDelete, CanDelete));

        CommandBindings.Add(new CommandBinding(ApplicationCommands.Undo));
        CommandBindings.Add(new CommandBinding(ApplicationCommands.Redo));
    }
    void CanDelete(object sender, CanExecuteRoutedEventArgs args)
    {
        args.CanExecute = !txtbox.Selection.IsEmpty;
    }
    void OnDelete(object sender, ExecutedRoutedEventArgs args)
    {
        txtbox.Selection.Text = "";
    }
}
}
```

The only button that didn't seem to work right was Delete, so I added *CanExecute* and *Executed* handlers for that command. The *RichTextBox* keeps the Undo and Redo buttons enabled all the time, which is not quite right, but when I tried to implement *CanExecute* handlers for those commands by calling the *CanUndo* and *CanRedo* methods of *RichTextBox*, I discovered that those methods always return *true* as well!

It's with the next file that things start to get interesting. This is the *ToolBar* that handles character formatting, which includes the font family, font size, bold and italic, foreground color, and background color.

The controls in this toolbar must display the font family and other character formatting associated with the currently selected text or (if there's no selection) the text insertion point. You obtain the currently selected text in the *RichTextBox* with the *Selection* property. This property is of type *TextSelection*, which is basically a *TextRange* object. *TextRange* defines two methods named *GetPropertyValue* and *ApplyPropertyValue*. The first argument to both methods is a dependency property involved with formatting.

For example, here's how to get the *FontFamily* associated with the currently selected text of a *RichTextBox* named *txtbox*:

```
txtbox.Selection.GetPropertyValue(FlowDocument.FontFamilyProperty);
```

Notice that you're obtaining a property of the *FlowDocument*, which is what the *RichTextBox* stores. What happens when the current selection encompasses multiple font families (or other character or paragraph properties) is not well documented. You should check for a return value of *null* and also that the type of the return value is what you need. To set a new *FontFamily* (named *fontfam*, for example) to the current selection (or insertion point), you call:

```
txtbox.Selection.ApplyPropertyValue(FlowDocument.FontFamilyProperty, fontfam);
```

To keep the controls in the toolbar updated, you must attach a handler for the *Selection-Changed* event of the *RichTextBox*.

The character-formatting *ToolBar* uses *ComboBox* controls for the font family and font size. The *ComboBox* is a combination of a *TextBox* and a *ListBox*, and you can control whether it's more like one or the other.

ComboBox derives from *Selector*, just like *ListBox*. You fill the *ComboBox* with items using either the *Items* collection or the *ItemsSource* property. *ComboBox* inherits *SelectedIndex*, *SelectedItem*, and *SelectedValue* properties from *Selector*. Unlike *ListBox*, the *ComboBox* does not have a multiple-selection mode.

In its normal resting state, the *ComboBox* displays just one line of text, which is settable and accessible through the *Text* property. A button at the far right of the *ComboBox* causes the actual list of items to be displayed. The part of the *ComboBox* displaying the list of items is known as the "drop-down." *ComboBox* defines read-write properties *MaxDropDownHeight* and *IsDropDownOpen*, and two events *DropDownOpen* and *DropDownClosed*.

ComboBox defines an important property named *IsEditable* that has a default value of *false*. In this non-editable mode, the top part of the *ComboBox* displays the selected item (if there is one). If the user clicks on that display, the drop-down is unfurled or retracted. The user cannot type anything into that field, but pressing a letter might cause an item to be selected that begins with that letter. A program can obtain a text representation of the selected item or set the selected item through the *Text* property, but it's probably safer to use *SelectedItem*. If a program attempts to set the *Text* property to something that doesn't correspond to an item in the *ComboBox*, no item is selected.

If a program sets *IsEditable* to *true*, the top part of the *ComboBox* changes to a *TextBox*, and the user can type something into that field. However, there is no event to indicate when this text is changing.

The *ComboBox* has a third mode that has limited use: If a program sets *IsEditable* to *true*, it can also set *IsReadOnly* to *true*. In that case, the user cannot change the item in the *EditBox*, but the item can be selected for copying to the clipboard. *IsReadOnly* has no effect when *IsEditable* is *false*.

Combo boxes can be tricky in actual use, even when—like the *ComboBox* for the font family—the *IsEditable* property keeps its default setting of *false*. (It makes no sense for a user to type a font family that does not exist in the list.) It is tempting to just attach a handler for the *Selection-Changed* event of the *ComboBox*, and to conclude processing with a call to shift input focus back to the *RichTextBox*, and that is how I've implemented the *ComboBox* for the *FontFamily*. If the user just clicks the arrow on the *ComboBox*, and then clicks a font family, that works fine. It also works fine if the user clicks the arrow on the *ComboBox* and then uses the keyboard to scroll through the list, pressing Enter to select an item or Escape to abandon the whole process.

However, there are some flaws with this simple approach: Suppose a user clicks the text part of the *ComboBox* and then clicks it again so that the list retracts. The *ComboBox* should still have input focus. The user can now press the up and down arrow keys to scroll through the list. Should the selected text in the *RichTextBox* change to reflect the selected font family? Probably, and I think the *ComboBox* should retain input focus during this process. However, suppose the user next presses Escape. The selected text in the *RichTextBox* should revert back to the font family it had before the *ComboBox* was invoked, and keyboard input focus should then shift from the *ComboBox* back to the *RichTextBox*. Keyboard input focus should also shift back to the *RichTextBox* when the user presses the Enter key, but in that case the current selection in the *ComboBox* should be applied to the selected text in the *RichTextBox*. Implementing this logic—the sadistic teacher says—is an exercise left to the reader.

The *ComboBox* for the font size is even worse. Traditionally, such a *ComboBox* must list a bunch of common font sizes, but it should also allow the user to type something else. The *ComboBox* must have its *IsEditable* property set to *true*. But how do you know when the user has finished typing something? A user should be able to leave the *ComboBox* by pressing Tab (in which case keyboard focus moves to the next control in the *ToolBar*), Enter (in which case focus goes to the *RichTextBox*), or Escape (in which case focus goes to the *RichTextBox* but the *ComboBox* value is restored to what it was before editing). The user can also get out of the *ComboBox* by clicking the mouse somewhere else. All of these involve a loss of input focus, so the following code installs an event handler for the *LostKeyboardFocus* event of the *ComboBox*. It is this event handler that contains the *Double.TryParse* code to convert the text entered by the user into a number. If that conversion fails, the text is restored to its original value. Saving that original value required a handler for the *GotKeyboardFocus* event. The job also required a handler for *PreviewKeyDown* to process the Enter and Escape keys.

```
FormatRichText.Char.cs
//-----------------------------------------------------------
// FormatRichText.Char.cs (c) 2006 by Charles Petzold
//-----------------------------------------------------------
using Petzold.SelectColorFromGrid;      // for ColorGridBox
using System;
using System.Windows;
```

```
using System.Windows.Controls;
using System.Windows.Controls.Primitives;
using System.Windows.Documents;
using System.Windows.Input;
using System.Windows.Media;
using System.Windows.Media.Imaging;

namespace Petzold.FormatRichText
{
    public partial class FormatRichText : Window
    {
        ComboBox comboFamily, comboSize;
        ToggleButton btnBold, btnItalic;
        ColorGridBox clrboxBackground, clrboxForeground;

        void AddCharToolBar(ToolBarTray tray, int band, int index)
        {
            // Create ToolBar and add to ToolBarTray.
            ToolBar toolbar = new ToolBar();
            toolbar.Band = band;
            toolbar.BandIndex = index;
            tray.ToolBars.Add(toolbar);

            // Create ComboBox for font families.
            comboFamily = new ComboBox();
            comboFamily.Width = 144;
            comboFamily.ItemsSource = Fonts.SystemFontFamilies;
            comboFamily.SelectedItem = txtbox.FontFamily;
            comboFamily.SelectionChanged += FamilyComboOnSelection;
            toolbar.Items.Add(comboFamily);

            ToolTip tip = new ToolTip();
            tip.Content = "Font Family";
            comboFamily.ToolTip = tip;

            // Create ComboBox for font size.
            comboSize = new ComboBox();
            comboSize.Width = 48;
            comboSize.IsEditable = true;
            comboSize.Text = (0.75 * txtbox.FontSize).ToString();
            comboSize.ItemsSource = new double[]
                {
                    8, 9, 10, 11, 12, 14, 16, 18,
                    20, 22, 24, 26, 28, 36, 48, 72
                };
            comboSize.SelectionChanged += SizeComboOnSelection;
            comboSize.GotKeyboardFocus += SizeComboOnGotFocus;
            comboSize.LostKeyboardFocus += SizeComboOnLostFocus;
            comboSize.PreviewKeyDown += SizeComboOnKeyDown;
            toolbar.Items.Add(comboSize);

            tip = new ToolTip();
            tip.Content = "Font Size";
            comboSize.ToolTip = tip;
```

```
// Create Bold button.
btnBold = new ToggleButton();
btnBold.Checked += BoldButtonOnChecked;
btnBold.Unchecked += BoldButtonOnChecked;
toolbar.Items.Add(btnBold);

Image img = new Image();
img.Source = new BitmapImage(
        new Uri("pack://application:,,/Images/boldhs.png"));
img.Stretch = Stretch.None;
btnBold.Content = img;

tip = new ToolTip();
tip.Content = "Bold";
btnBold.ToolTip = tip;

// Create Italic button.
btnItalic = new ToggleButton();
btnItalic.Checked += ItalicButtonOnChecked;
btnItalic.Unchecked += ItalicButtonOnChecked;
toolbar.Items.Add(btnItalic);

img = new Image();
img.Source = new BitmapImage(
        new Uri("pack://application:,,/Images/ItalicHS.png"));
img.Stretch = Stretch.None;
btnItalic.Content = img;

tip = new ToolTip();
tip.Content = "Italic";
btnItalic.ToolTip = tip;

toolbar.Items.Add(new Separator());

// Create Background and Foreground color menu.
Menu menu = new Menu();
toolbar.Items.Add(menu);

// Create Background menu item.
MenuItem item = new MenuItem();
menu.Items.Add(item);

img = new Image();
img.Source = new BitmapImage(
        new Uri("pack://application:,,/Images/ColorHS.png"));
img.Stretch = Stretch.None;

item.Header = img;

clrboxBackground = new ColorGridBox();
clrboxBackground.SelectionChanged += BackgroundOnSelectionChanged;
item.Items.Add(clrboxBackground);
```

```
        tip = new ToolTip();
        tip.Content = "Background Color";
        item.ToolTip = tip;

        // Create Foreground menu item.
        item = new MenuItem();
        menu.Items.Add(item);

        img = new Image();
        img.Source = new BitmapImage(
                new Uri("pack://application:,,/Images/Color_fontHS.png"));
        img.Stretch = Stretch.None;
        item.Header = img;

        clrboxForeground = new ColorGridBox();
        clrboxForeground.SelectionChanged += ForegroundOnSelectionChanged;
        item.Items.Add(clrboxForeground);

        tip = new ToolTip();
        tip.Content = "Foreground Color";
        item.ToolTip = tip;

        // Install handler for RichTextBox SelectionChanged event.
        txtbox.SelectionChanged += TextBoxOnSelectionChanged;
    }

    // Handler for RichTextBox SelectionChanged event.
    void TextBoxOnSelectionChanged(object sender, RoutedEventArgs args)
    {
        // Obtain FontFamily of currently selected text...
        object obj = txtbox.Selection.GetPropertyValue(
                                        FlowDocument.FontFamilyProperty);
        // ... and set it in the ComboBox.
        if (obj is FontFamily)
            comboFamily.SelectedItem = (FontFamily)obj;
        else
            comboFamily.SelectedIndex = -1;

        // Obtain FontSize of currently selected text...
        obj = txtbox.Selection.GetPropertyValue(
                                        FlowDocument.FontSizeProperty);
        // ... and set it in the ComboBox.
        if (obj is double)
            comboSize.Text = (0.75 * (double)obj).ToString();
        else
            comboSize.SelectedIndex = -1;

        // Obtain FontWeight of currently selected text...
        obj = txtbox.Selection.GetPropertyValue(
                                        FlowDocument.FontWeightProperty);
        // .. and set the ToggleButton.
        if (obj is FontWeight)
            btnBold.IsChecked = (FontWeight)obj == FontWeights.Bold;
```

```
        // Obtain FontStyle of currently selected text...
        obj = txtbox.Selection.GetPropertyValue(
                                      FlowDocument.FontStyleProperty);
        // .. and set the ToggleButton.
        if (obj is FontStyle)
            btnItalic.IsChecked = (FontStyle)obj == FontStyles.Italic;

        // Obtain colors and set the ColorGridBox controls.
        obj = txtbox.Selection.GetPropertyValue(
                                      FlowDocument.BackgroundProperty);
        if (obj != null && obj is Brush)
            clrboxBackground.SelectedValue = (Brush)obj;

        obj = txtbox.Selection.GetPropertyValue(
                                      FlowDocument.ForegroundProperty);
        if (obj != null && obj is Brush)
            clrboxForeground.SelectedValue = (Brush)obj;
}

// Handler for FontFamily ComboBox SelectionChanged.
void FamilyComboOnSelection(object sender, SelectionChangedEventArgs args)
{
    // Obtain selected FontFamily.
    ComboBox combo = args.Source as ComboBox;
    FontFamily family = combo.SelectedItem as FontFamily;

    // Set it on selected text.
    if (family != null)
        txtbox.Selection.ApplyPropertyValue(
                    FlowDocument.FontFamilyProperty, family);

    // Set focus back to TextBox.
    txtbox.Focus();
}

// Handlers for FontSize ComboBox.
string strOriginal;

void SizeComboOnGotFocus(object sender, KeyboardFocusChangedEventArgs args)
{
    strOriginal = (sender as ComboBox).Text;
}
void SizeComboOnLostFocus(object sender, KeyboardFocusChangedEventArgs args)
{
    double size;

    if (Double.TryParse((sender as ComboBox).Text, out size))
        txtbox.Selection.ApplyPropertyValue(
                FlowDocument.FontSizeProperty, size / 0.75);
    else
        (sender as ComboBox).Text = strOriginal;
}
```

```
        void SizeComboOnKeyDown(object sender, KeyEventArgs args)
        {
            if (args.Key == Key.Escape)
            {
                (sender as ComboBox).Text = strOriginal;
                args.Handled = true;
                txtbox.Focus();
            }
            else if (args.Key == Key.Enter)
            {
                args.Handled = true;
                txtbox.Focus();
            }
        }
        void SizeComboOnSelection(object sender, SelectionChangedEventArgs args)
        {
            ComboBox combo = args.Source as ComboBox;

            if (combo.SelectedIndex != -1)
            {
                double size = (double) combo.SelectedValue;
                txtbox.Selection.ApplyPropertyValue(
                        FlowDocument.FontSizeProperty, size / 0.75);

                txtbox.Focus();
            }
        }

        // Handler for Bold button.
        void BoldButtonOnChecked(object sender, RoutedEventArgs args)
        {
            ToggleButton btn = args.Source as ToggleButton;

            txtbox.Selection.ApplyPropertyValue(FlowDocument.FontWeightProperty,
                (bool)btn.IsChecked ? FontWeights.Bold : FontWeights.Normal);
        }

        // Handler for Italic button.
        void ItalicButtonOnChecked(object sender, RoutedEventArgs args)
        {
            ToggleButton btn = args.Source as ToggleButton;

            txtbox.Selection.ApplyPropertyValue(FlowDocument.FontStyleProperty,
                (bool)btn.IsChecked ? FontStyles.Italic : FontStyles.Normal);
        }
        // Handler for Background color changed.
        void BackgroundOnSelectionChanged(object sender,
                                          SelectionChangedEventArgs args)
        {
            ColorGridBox clrbox = args.Source as ColorGridBox;
            txtbox.Selection.ApplyPropertyValue(FlowDocument.BackgroundProperty,
                                      clrbox.SelectedValue);
        }
```

```
        // Handler for Foreground color changed.
        void ForegroundOnSelectionChanged(object sender,
                                            SelectionChangedEventArgs args)
        {
            ColorGridBox clrbox = args.Source as ColorGridBox;
            txtbox.Selection.ApplyPropertyValue(FlowDocument.ForegroundProperty,
                                            clrbox.SelectedValue);
        }
    }
}
```

The remainder of this file is straightforward by comparison. The *AddCharToolBar* method also creates two *ToggleButton* objects for Bold and Italic, and a menu for background and foreground colors. Yes, the toolbar contains an entire menu, but it consists of just two items. Each of these two *MenuItem* objects has its *Header* set to a bitmap to represent the background or foreground color, and has an *Items* collection that contains just a *ColorGridBox* control.

Following the character-formatting toolbar, the paragraph-formatting toolbar should be a snap, since it contains only four images for alignment: Left, Right, Center, and Justified. However, I couldn't find adequate images, so I had to create them right in the code. The *CreateButton* method puts a 16-unit-square *Canvas* on a *ToggleButton* and draws 5 lines that represent the various types of alignment.

FormatRichText.Para.cs

```
//-------------------------------------------------
// FormatRichText.Para.cs (c) 2006 by Charles Petzold
//-------------------------------------------------
using System;
using System.Windows;
using System.Windows.Controls;
using System.Windows.Controls.Primitives;
using System.Windows.Documents;
using System.Windows.Input;
using System.Windows.Media;
using System.Windows.Shapes;

namespace Petzold.FormatRichText
{
    public partial class FormatRichText : Window
    {
        ToggleButton[] btnAlignment = new ToggleButton[4];

        void AddParaToolBar(ToolBarTray tray, int band, int index)
        {
            // Create ToolBar and add to tray.
            ToolBar toolbar = new ToolBar();
            toolbar.Band = band;
            toolbar.BandIndex = index;
            tray.ToolBars.Add(toolbar);
```

```
            // Create ToolBar items.
            toolbar.Items.Add(btnAlignment[0] =
                CreateButton(TextAlignment.Left, "Align Left", 0, 4));
            toolbar.Items.Add(btnAlignment[1] =
                CreateButton(TextAlignment.Center, "Center", 2, 2));
            toolbar.Items.Add(btnAlignment[2] =
                CreateButton(TextAlignment.Right, "Align Right", 4, 0));
            toolbar.Items.Add(btnAlignment[3] =
                CreateButton(TextAlignment.Justify, "Justify", 0, 0));

            // Attach another event handler for SelectionChanged.
            txtbox.SelectionChanged += TextBoxOnSelectionChanged2;
        }
        ToggleButton CreateButton(TextAlignment align, string strToolTip,
                                  int offsetLeft, int offsetRight)
        {
            // Create ToggleButton.
            ToggleButton btn = new ToggleButton();
            btn.Tag = align;
            btn.Click += ButtonOnClick;

            // Set Content as Canvas.
            Canvas canv = new Canvas();
            canv.Width = 16;
            canv.Height = 16;
            btn.Content = canv;

            // Draw lines on the Canvas.
            for (int i = 0; i < 5; i++)
            {
                Polyline poly = new Polyline();
                poly.Stroke = SystemColors.WindowTextBrush;
                poly.StrokeThickness = 1;

                if ((i & 1) == 0)
                    poly.Points = new PointCollection(new Point[]
                        {
                            new Point(2, 2 + 3 * i), new Point(14, 2 + 3 * i)
                        });
                else
                    poly.Points = new PointCollection(new Point[]
                        {
                            new Point(2 + offsetLeft, 2 + 3 * i),
                            new Point(14 - offsetRight, 2 + 3 * i)
                        });

                canv.Children.Add(poly);
            }

            // Create a ToolTip.
            ToolTip tip = new ToolTip();
            tip.Content = strToolTip;
            btn.ToolTip = tip;

            return btn;
        }
```

```
        // Handler for TextBox SelectionChanged event.
        void TextBoxOnSelectionChanged2(object sender, RoutedEventArgs args)
        {
            // Obtain the current TextAlignment.
            object obj = txtbox.Selection.GetPropertyValue(
                                    Paragraph.TextAlignmentProperty);
            // Set the buttons.
            if (obj != null && obj is TextAlignment)
            {
                TextAlignment align = (TextAlignment)obj;

                foreach (ToggleButton btn in btnAlignment)
                    btn.IsChecked = (align == (TextAlignment)btn.Tag);
            }
            else
            {
                foreach (ToggleButton btn in btnAlignment)
                    btn.IsChecked = false;
            }
        }
        // Handler for Button Click event.
        void ButtonOnClick(object sender, RoutedEventArgs args)
        {
            ToggleButton btn = args.Source as ToggleButton;

            foreach (ToggleButton btnAlign in btnAlignment)
                btnAlign.IsChecked = (btn == btnAlign);

            // Set the new TextAlignment.
            TextAlignment align = (TextAlignment) btn.Tag;
            txtbox.Selection.ApplyPropertyValue(Paragraph.TextAlignmentProperty,
                                    align);
        }
    }
}
```

That concludes the toolbar logic. The FormatRichText program also includes a status bar. In this program, the *StatusBar* is an *ItemsControl* (much like *Menu*) and the *StatusBarItem* is a *ContentControl* (just like *MenuItem*), as this partial class hierarchy shows:

Control

   ContentControl

      StatusBarItem

  ItemsControl

    StatusBar

Status bars are customarily docked at the bottom of the client area. In practice, status bars usually only contain text and the occasional *ProgressBar* when a large file needs to be loaded or saved (or some other lengthy job takes place). Internally, a *StatusBar* uses a *DockPanel* for layout, so if your status bar contains multiple items, you can call *DockPanel. SetDock* to position them. The last item fills the remaining interior space of the status bar, so you can use *Horizontal-Alignment* to position it. For status bars containing only one item, use *HorizontalAlignment* to position the item. The *StatusBar* in this program merely displays the current date and time.

FormatRichText.Status.cs
```csharp
//------------------------------------------------------
// FormatRichText.Status.cs (c) 2006 by Charles Petzold
//------------------------------------------------------
using System;
using System.Windows;
using System.Windows.Controls;
using System.Windows.Controls.Primitives;
using System.Windows.Input;
using System.Windows.Media;
using System.Windows.Threading;

namespace Petzold.FormatRichText
{
    public partial class FormatRichText : Window
    {
        StatusBarItem itemDateTime;

        void AddStatusBar(DockPanel dock)
        {
            // Create StatusBar docked at bottom of client area.
            StatusBar status = new StatusBar();
            dock.Children.Add(status);
            DockPanel.SetDock(status, Dock.Bottom);

            // Create StatusBarItem.
            itemDateTime = new StatusBarItem();
            itemDateTime.HorizontalAlignment = HorizontalAlignment.Right;
            status.Items.Add(itemDateTime);

            // Create timer to update StatusBarItem.
            DispatcherTimer tmr = new DispatcherTimer();
            tmr.Interval = TimeSpan.FromSeconds(1);
            tmr.Tick += TimerOnTick;
            tmr.Start();
        }
        void TimerOnTick(object sender, EventArgs args)
        {
            DateTime dt = DateTime.Now;
            itemDateTime.Content = dt.ToLongDateString() + " " +
                                    dt.ToLongTimeString();
        }
    }
}
```

FormatRichText is well on its way to mimicking much of the functionality of the Windows WordPad program, but I'm not going to pursue that. Instead, Chapter 18 features a clone of Windows Notepad, admittedly a much easier goal, but one that pays off when it is adapted in Chapter 20 to become a valuable programming tool called XamlCruncher.

Chapter 16
TreeView and ListView

The *TreeView* control displays hierarchical data. Perhaps the most prominent tree view of all time is the left side of Windows Explorer, where all the user's disk drives and directories are displayed. A tree view also shows up in the left side of the Microsoft Document Viewer used to display Microsoft Visual Studio and .NET documentation. The tree view in the Document Viewer shows all the .NET namespaces, followed by nested classes and structures, and then methods and properties, among other information.

Each item on the Windows Presentation Foundation *TreeView* control is an object of type *TreeViewItem*. A *TreeViewItem* is usually identified by a short text string but also contains a collection of nested *TreeViewItem* objects. In this way, *TreeView* is very similar to *Menu*, and *TreeViewItem* is very similar to *MenuItem*, as you can see from the following selected class hierarchy showing all major controls covered in the previous two chapters:

Control

    ItemsControl

        HeaderedItemsControl

            MenuItem

            ToolBar

            TreeViewItem

        MenuBase (abstract)

            ContextMenu

            Menu

        StatusBar

        TreeView

As you'll recall, *ItemsControl* is also the parent class of *Selector*, which is the parent class of *List-Box* and *ComboBox*. *ItemsControl* contains an important property named *Items*, which is a collection of the items that appear listed in the control. To *ItemsControl* the *HeaderedItemsControl* adds a property named *Header*. Although this *Header* property is of type *Object*, very often it's just a text string.

Just as *Menu* is a collection of the top-level *MenuItem* objects—and hence has no *Header* property itself—*TreeView* is a collection of top-level *TreeViewItem* objects and also has no *Header* property.

The following program populates a *TreeView* control "manually"—that is, with explicit hard-coded items.

```
ManuallyPopulateTreeView.cs
//-----------------------------------------------------------
// ManuallyPopulateTreeView.cs (c) 2006 by Charles Petzold
//-----------------------------------------------------------
using System;
using System.Windows;
using System.Windows.Controls;
using System.Windows.Input;
using System.Windows.Media;

namespace Petzold.ManuallyPopulateTreeView
{
    public class ManuallyPopulateTreeView : Window
    {
        [STAThread]
        public static void Main()
        {
            Application app = new Application();
            app.Run(new ManuallyPopulateTreeView());
        }
        public ManuallyPopulateTreeView()
        {
            Title = "Manually Populate TreeView";

            TreeView tree = new TreeView();
            Content = tree;

            TreeViewItem itemAnimal = new TreeViewItem();
            itemAnimal.Header = "Animal";
            tree.Items.Add(itemAnimal);

            TreeViewItem itemDog = new TreeViewItem();
            itemDog.Header = "Dog";
            itemDog.Items.Add("Poodle");
            itemDog.Items.Add("Irish Setter");
            itemDog.Items.Add("German Shepherd");
            itemAnimal.Items.Add(itemDog);

            TreeViewItem itemCat = new TreeViewItem();
            itemCat.Header = "Cat";
            itemCat.Items.Add("Calico");

            TreeViewItem item = new TreeViewItem();
            item.Header = "Alley Cat";
            itemCat.Items.Add(item);
```

```
            Button btn = new Button();
            btn.Content = "Noodles";
            itemCat.Items.Add(btn);

            itemCat.Items.Add("Siamese");
            itemAnimal.Items.Add(itemCat);

            TreeViewItem itemPrimate = new TreeViewItem();
            itemPrimate.Header = "Primate";
            itemPrimate.Items.Add("Chimpanzee");
            itemPrimate.Items.Add("Bonobo");
            itemPrimate.Items.Add("Human");
            itemAnimal.Items.Add(itemPrimate);

            TreeViewItem itemMineral = new TreeViewItem();
            itemMineral.Header = "Mineral";
            itemMineral.Items.Add("Calcium");
            itemMineral.Items.Add("Zinc");
            itemMineral.Items.Add("Iron");
            tree.Items.Add(itemMineral);

            TreeViewItem itemVegetable = new TreeViewItem();
            itemVegetable.Header = "Vegetable";
            itemVegetable.Items.Add("Carrot");
            itemVegetable.Items.Add("Asparagus");
            itemVegetable.Items.Add("Broccoli");
            tree.Items.Add(itemVegetable);
        }
    }
}
```

The program shows two different ways to add *TreeViewItem* objects to a parent item. You can explicitly create an object of type *TreeViewItem* and add that to the *ItemCollection* object referenced by the *Items* property. This approach is necessary if the item has child items. However, if the item has no children, a much simpler approach is to pass a text string to the *Add* method of the *Items* collection. You'll even notice that one of the items (for the type of cat known as Noodles) is actually a *Button* control because Noodles is, well, a very special cat.

This program gives you an opportunity to explore the user interface of *TreeView*. You can click a plus sign to expand an item and click the minus sign to collapse it. The *TreeView* also has a complete keyboard interface based around the arrow keys.

Other than that, the program doesn't show any useful generalized techniques for programming the *TreeView*. Although it's common to populate a *Menu* control by manually adding items and subitems, populating a *TreeView* control in this way is probably quite rare in real-life applications. It's much more common to populate a *TreeView* control based on some database or other information external to the program.

For example, a *TreeView* control that displays disk drives and directories uses classes from the *System.IO* namespace to populate the *TreeView*. Here's a program that assembles a *TreeView* control showing all the directories on the current system drive. (The system drive is usually drive C, of course, but if a drive has multiple bootable partitions, the system drive could be something else.)

Let the name of this program be a warning to you: This program shows the *wrong* way to populate a *TreeView* with a directory tree!

```
RecurseDirectoriesInefficiently.cs
//-----------------------------------------------------------------
// RecurseDirectoriesInefficiently.cs (c) 2006 by Charles Petzold
//-----------------------------------------------------------------
using System;
using System.IO;
using System.Windows;
using System.Windows.Controls;
using System.Windows.Input;
using System.Windows.Media;

namespace Petzold.RecurseDirectoriesInefficiently
{
    public class RecurseDirectoriesInefficiently : Window
    {

        [STAThread]
        public static void Main()
        {
            Application app = new Application();
            app.Run(new RecurseDirectoriesInefficiently());
        }
        public RecurseDirectoriesInefficiently()
        {
            Title = "Recurse Directories Inefficiently";

            TreeView tree = new TreeView();
            Content = tree;

            // Create TreeViewItem based on system drive.
            TreeViewItem item = new TreeViewItem();
            item.Header = Path.GetPathRoot(Environment.SystemDirectory);
            item.Tag = new DirectoryInfo(item.Header as string);
            tree.Items.Add(item);

            // Fill recursively.
            GetSubdirectories(item);
        }
        void GetSubdirectories(TreeViewItem item)
        {
            DirectoryInfo dir = item.Tag as DirectoryInfo;
            DirectoryInfo[] subdirs;

            try
            {
                // Get subdirectories.
                subdirs = dir.GetDirectories();
            }
```

```
            catch
            {
                return;
            }


            // Loop through subdirectories.
            foreach (DirectoryInfo subdir in subdirs)
            {
                // Create a new TreeViewItem for each directory.
                TreeViewItem subitem = new TreeViewItem();
                subitem.Header = subdir.Name;
                subitem.Tag = subdir;
                item.Items.Add(subitem);

                // Recursively obtain subdirectories.
                GetSubdirectories(subitem);
            }
        }
    }
}
```

In theory, the program looks fine. The window constructor creates the *TreeView* control and creates the first *TreeViewItem*. This item's *Header* property is assigned the path root of the current system drive (for example, a text string like "C:\") and the *Tag* property gets a *DirectoryInfo* object based on that same string. The constructor then passes this *TreeViewItem* object to *GetSubdirectories*.

GetSubdirectories is a recursive method. It uses the *GetDirectories* method of *DirectoryInfo* to obtain all the child subdirectories. (A *try-catch* block is necessary in case it encounters a directory where access is forbidden.) For each subdirectory, the method creates a new *TreeViewItem* object and then calls *GetSubdirectories* with that new item. Structurally, this is precisely the way we once wrote command-line utilities to display directory trees.

Of course, what's fine for the command line is *terrible* for a graphical environment. If you dare to run this program, you'll discover that it spends a long time grinding through the disk before displaying the window. Not only is the time delay a problem, but the program is doing much more than it needs to. It's highly unlikely the user needs to see every single directory the program is adding to the *TreeView*. The program may even be exercising parts of the hard drive that haven't been touched since the machine left the factory!

A much better *TreeView* for displaying a directory tree obtains subdirectories only when they're required—for example, when the user clicks the plus sign next to a directory. Actually, that's a little too late. The plus sign is displayed only if the item has child items, so the program has to be one step ahead of the user. For each item that is displayed, the subitems need to be present, but the *sub*-subitems don't need to be immediately included.

When you delay loading data, such as I've described, you're using a technique known as "lazy loading." To do *TreeView* lazy loading properly, you need to be familiar with *TreeViewItem* events, of which there are four. The *Expanded* event signals when a user clicks a plus sign to display child items, or when a program manually sets the *IsExpanded* property to *true*. The *Collapse* event signals the opposite: Child items are being hidden. The *Selected* and *Unselected* events indicate that an item is being selected by the user or the *IsSelected* property has changed. All four events have accompanying *On* methods.

In addition, the *TreeView* itself has a *SelectedItemChanged* event. However, the *SelectedItem* property of *TreeView* is read-only, so if you want to programmatically set an initial selected item in a *TreeView*, set the *IsSelected* property of the actual *TreeViewItem*.

Let's see if we can use these events to implement a directory *TreeView* that actually works well. To make this exercise even more fun, let's display a list of files when a directory is selected. And to make it even *more* fun than that, let's use little bitmaps in the *TreeView*. These bitmaps, obtained from the *outline\16color_nomask* directory of the Visual Studio image library, require a white background. I modified some of them to make the device resolution 96 DPI. The images I used are 35Floppy.bmp, Cddrive.bmp, Clsdfold.bmp ("closed folder"), Drive.bmp, and Openfold.bmp. As in Windows Explorer, the folder image changes from closed to open when a directory is selected.

In a nod towards reusability, this project begins with a class that inherits from *TreeViewItem* called *ImagedTreeViewItem*.

```
ImagedTreeViewItem.cs
//-------------------------------------------------
// ImagedTreeViewItem.cs (c) 2006 by Charles Petzold
//-------------------------------------------------
using System;
using System.Windows;
using System.Windows.Controls;
using System.Windows.Input;
using System.Windows.Media;

namespace Petzold.RecurseDirectoriesIncrementally
{
    public class ImagedTreeViewItem : TreeViewItem
    {
        TextBlock text;
        Image img;
        ImageSource srcSelected, srcUnselected;

        // Constructor makes stack with image and text.
        public ImagedTreeViewItem()
        {
            StackPanel stack = new StackPanel();
            stack.Orientation = Orientation.Horizontal;
            Header = stack;

            img = new Image();
            img.VerticalAlignment = VerticalAlignment.Center;
            img.Margin = new Thickness(0, 0, 2, 0);
            stack.Children.Add(img);
```

```
                text = new TextBlock();
                text.VerticalAlignment = VerticalAlignment.Center;
                stack.Children.Add(text);
        }
        // Public properties for text and images.
        public string Text
        {
                set { text.Text = value; }
                get { return text.Text; }
        }
        public ImageSource SelectedImage
        {
                set
                {
                    srcSelected = value;

                    if (IsSelected)
                        img.Source = srcSelected;
                }
                get { return srcSelected; }
        }
        public ImageSource UnselectedImage
        {
                set
                {
                    srcUnselected = value;

                    if (!IsSelected)
                        img.Source = srcUnselected;
                }
                get { return srcUnselected; }
        }
        // Event overrides to set image.
        protected override void OnSelected(RoutedEventArgs args)
        {
                base.OnSelected(args);
                img.Source = srcSelected;
        }
        protected override void OnUnselected(RoutedEventArgs args)
        {
                base.OnUnselected(args);
                img.Source = srcUnselected;
        }
    }
}
```

The *ImagedTreeViewItem* class sets the *Header* property it inherits from *TreeViewItem* to a *Stack-Panel*. The *StackPanel* children are an *Image* object and a *TextBlock*. A public property named *Text* lets a consumer of this control set the *Text* property of the *TextBlock*. The two other public properties are both of type *ImageSource* and are named *SelectedImage*—the image that is to appear when the item is selected—and *UnselectedImage*, the image that appears otherwise. Overrides of the *OnSelected* and *OnUnselected* methods are responsible for setting the *Source* property of the *Image* object to the proper *ImageSource*.

The *DirectoryTreeViewItem* class inherits from *ImagedTreeViewItem* and supplies the two images that its base class requires. The constructor of this class has a *DirectoryInfo* parameter that it saves as a field and exposes through its public *DirectoryInfo* property. (Another way to think about this is that *DirectoryTreeViewItem* is a visual wrapper around a *DirectoryInfo* object.) Notice that the constructor also sets the *Text* property that *ImagedTreeViewItem* defines.

DirectoryTreeViewItem.cs

```
//-----------------------------------------------------
// DirectoryTreeViewItem.cs (c) 2006 by Charles Petzold
//-----------------------------------------------------
using System;
using System.IO;
using System.Windows;
using System.Windows.Controls;
using System.Windows.Input;
using System.Windows.Media;
using System.Windows.Media.Imaging;

namespace Petzold.RecurseDirectoriesIncrementally
{
    public class DirectoryTreeViewItem: ImagedTreeViewItem
    {
        DirectoryInfo dir;

        // Constructor requires DirectoryInfo object.
        public DirectoryTreeViewItem(DirectoryInfo dir)
        {
            this.dir = dir;
            Text = dir.Name;

            SelectedImage = new BitmapImage(
                new Uri("pack://application:,,/Images/OPENFOLD.BMP"));

            UnselectedImage = new BitmapImage(
                new Uri("pack://application:,,/Images/CLSDFOLD.BMP"));
        }
        // Public property to obtain DirectoryInfo object.
        public DirectoryInfo DirectoryInfo
        {
            get { return dir; }
        }
        // Public method to populate with items.
        public void Populate()
        {
            DirectoryInfo[] dirs;

            try
            {
                dirs = dir.GetDirectories();
            }
            catch
            {
                return;
            }
```

```
                    foreach (DirectoryInfo dirChild in dirs)
                        Items.Add(new DirectoryTreeViewItem(dirChild));
                }
                // Event override to populate subitems.
                protected override void OnExpanded(RoutedEventArgs args)
                {
                    base.OnExpanded(args);

                    foreach (object obj in Items)
                    {
                        DirectoryTreeViewItem item = obj as DirectoryTreeViewItem;
                        item.Populate();
                    }
                }
            }
        }
    }
```

The public *Populate* method obtains all the subdirectories of the *DirectoryInfo* object associated with the item, and creates new *DirectoryTreeViewItem* objects that are children of this item. Originally, I defined *Populate* as a private method that was called from the constructor. You'll see shortly why I had to make it public and not called by default.

The class also overrides the *OnExpanded* method. The *OnExpanded* method essentially brings into view all the child subdirectories. At this time, all these child subdirectories need to be populated with their own subdirectories so that they properly display plus signs (or not). That's the job of the *OnExpanded* method.

The *DirectoryTreeView* class derives from *TreeView*. This is the class responsible for obtaining all the disk drives and beginning the process of creating *DirectoryTreeViewItem* objects.

DirectoryTreeView.cs
```
//---------------------------------------------------
// DirectoryTreeView.cs (c) 2006 by Charles Petzold
//---------------------------------------------------
using System;
using System.IO;
using System.Windows;
using System.Windows.Controls;
using System.Windows.Input;
using System.Windows.Media;
using System.Windows.Media.Imaging;

namespace Petzold.RecurseDirectoriesIncrementally
{
    public class DirectoryTreeView : TreeView
    {
        // Constructor builds partial directory tree.
        public DirectoryTreeView()
        {
            RefreshTree();
        }
```

```
public void RefreshTree()
{
    BeginInit();
    Items.Clear();

    // Obtain the disk drives.
    DriveInfo[] drives = DriveInfo.GetDrives();

    foreach (DriveInfo drive in drives)
    {
        char chDrive = drive.Name.ToUpper()[0];
        DirectoryTreeViewItem item =
                new DirectoryTreeViewItem(drive.RootDirectory);

        // Display VolumeLabel if drive ready; otherwise just DriveType.
        if (chDrive != 'A' && chDrive != 'B' &&
                drive.IsReady && drive.VolumeLabel.Length > 0)
            item.Text = String.Format("{0} ({1})", drive.VolumeLabel,
                                                   drive.Name);
        else
            item.Text = String.Format("{0} ({1})", drive.DriveType,
                                                   drive.Name);

        // Determine proper bitmap for drive.
        if (chDrive == 'A' || chDrive == 'B')
            item.SelectedImage = item.UnselectedImage = new BitmapImage(
                new Uri("pack://application:,,/Images/35FLOPPY.BMP"));

        else if (drive.DriveType == DriveType.CDRom)
            item.SelectedImage = item.UnselectedImage = new BitmapImage(
                new Uri("pack://application:,,/Images/CDDRIVE.BMP"));
        else
            item.SelectedImage = item.UnselectedImage = new BitmapImage(
                new Uri("pack://application:,,/Images/DRIVE.BMP"));

        Items.Add(item);

        // Populate the drive with directories.
        if (chDrive != 'A' && chDrive != 'B' && drive.IsReady)
            item.Populate();
    }
    EndInit();
}
```

Although not used in this project, I gave *DirectoryTreeView* a public *RefreshTree* method. This might be called from a Refresh menu item. Here it's just called from the constructor. The *RefreshTree* method goes into an initialization block by calling *BeginInit*, deletes all its items, and recreates them. After *BeginInit* is called, the *TreeView* won't attempt to keep itself visually updated because that could slow down the construction of the tree.

The *RefreshTree* method obtains an array of *DriveInfo* objects describing all the drives on the machine. The *RootDirectory* property of *DriveInfo* is an object of type *DirectoryInfo*, so it's easy to create a *DirectoryTreeViewItem* from it. However, the A and B drives have to be handled with kid gloves. The next-to-last thing you want when initializing a *TreeView* control is for a floppy disk drive to start spinning. The very last thing you want is for a message box to pop up complaining that there's no disk in the drive! That's why this code doesn't touch the *IsReady* property of *DriveInfo* for floppy drives. Also, notice that the method calls *Populate* for the drive only if the drive is not a floppy disk and the *IsReady* property is *true*.

The final class in the RecurseDirectoriesIncrementally project is a class with that name that inherits from *Window*.

```
RecurseDirectoriesIncrementally.cs
//------------------------------------------------------------------
// RecurseDirectoriesIncrementally.cs (c) 2006 by Charles Petzold
//------------------------------------------------------------------
using System;
using System.IO;
using System.Windows;
using System.Windows.Controls;
using System.Windows.Input;
using System.Windows.Media;

namespace Petzold.RecurseDirectoriesIncrementally
{
    class RecurseDirectoriesIncrementally : Window
    {
        StackPanel stack;

        [STAThread]
        public static void Main()
        {
            Application app = new Application();
            app.Run(new RecurseDirectoriesIncrementally());
        }
        public RecurseDirectoriesIncrementally()
        {
            Title = "Recurse Directories Incrementally";

            // Create Grid as content of window.
            Grid grid = new Grid();
            Content = grid;

            // Define ColumnDefinition objects.
            ColumnDefinition coldef = new ColumnDefinition();
            coldef.Width = new GridLength(50, GridUnitType.Star);
            grid.ColumnDefinitions.Add(coldef);

            coldef = new ColumnDefinition();
            coldef.Width = GridLength.Auto;
            grid.ColumnDefinitions.Add(coldef);
```

```
            coldef = new ColumnDefinition();
            coldef.Width = new GridLength(50, GridUnitType.Star);
            grid.ColumnDefinitions.Add(coldef);

            // Put DirectoryTreeView at left.
            DirectoryTreeView tree = new DirectoryTreeView();
            tree.SelectedItemChanged += TreeViewOnSelectedItemChanged;
            grid.Children.Add(tree);
            Grid.SetColumn(tree, 0);

            // Put GridSplitter in center.
            GridSplitter split = new GridSplitter();
            split.Width = 6;
            split.ResizeBehavior = GridResizeBehavior.PreviousAndNext;
            grid.Children.Add(split);
            Grid.SetColumn(split, 1);

            // Put scrolled StackPanel at right.
            ScrollViewer scroll = new ScrollViewer();
            grid.Children.Add(scroll);
            Grid.SetColumn(scroll, 2);

            stack = new StackPanel();
            scroll.Content = stack;
        }
        void TreeViewOnSelectedItemChanged(object sender,
                    RoutedPropertyChangedEventArgs<object> args)
        {
            // Get selected item.
            DirectoryTreeViewItem item = args.NewValue as DirectoryTreeViewItem;

            // Clear out the DockPanel.
            stack.Children.Clear();

            // Fill it up again.
            FileInfo[] infos;

            try
            {
                infos = item.DirectoryInfo.GetFiles();
            }
            catch
            {
                return;
            }

            foreach (FileInfo info in infos)
            {
                TextBlock text = new TextBlock();
                text.Text = info.Name;
                stack.Children.Add(text);
            }
        }
    }
}
```

The constructor creates a *Grid* with three columns—one for the *DirectoryTreeView*, one for the *GridSplitter*, and the third for a *ScrollViewer* that contains a *StackPanel*. This is where files are displayed.

The constructor sets an event handler for the *SelectedItemChanged* event and processes that event by clearing all child elements from the *StackPanel* and then filling it up again with all the files in the selected directory. Of course, you can't *do* anything with these files, but you're well on your way to writing a clone of Windows Explorer.

You might recall the *ItemTemplate* property of *ListBox*. In Chapter 13, "ListBox Selection," I showed you how to define a *DataTemplate* object that you can set to the *ItemTemplate* property. This *DataTemplate* includes a *VisualTree* that describes how items are to be visually represented in the *ListBox*.

That *ItemTemplate* property is defined by *ItemsControl*, so it's inherited by *TreeView*. Moreover, a class named *HierarchicalDataTemplate* derives from *DataTemplate*, and this class is ideal for describing hierarchical data from which a *TreeView* is built. To use this facility, you'll want to begin by defining a class that describes the hierarchical data you want the *TreeView* to display.

Here is such a class, named *DiskDirectory*, that is basically a wrapper around a *DirectoryInfo* object. In fact, if *DirectoryInfo* were not sealed, I would have derived *DiskDirectory* from *DirectoryInfo* and the class would have been simplified a bit. I wouldn't have needed the constructor or the *Name* property, for example.

DiskDirectory.cs

```
//-----------------------------------------------
// DiskDirectory.cs (c) 2006 by Charles Petzold
//-----------------------------------------------
using System;
using System.Collections.Generic;
using System.IO;

namespace Petzold.TemplateTheTree
{
    public class DiskDirectory
    {
        DirectoryInfo dirinfo;

        // Constructor requires DirectoryInfo object.
        public DiskDirectory(DirectoryInfo dirinfo)
        {
            this.dirinfo = dirinfo;
        }

        // Name property returns directory name.
        public string Name
        {
            get { return dirinfo.Name; }
        }
```

```
        // Subdirectories property returns collection of DiskDirectory objects.
        public List<DiskDirectory> Subdirectories
        {
            get
            {
                List<DiskDirectory> dirs = new List<DiskDirectory>();
                DirectoryInfo[] subdirs;

                try
                {
                    subdirs = dirinfo.GetDirectories();
                }
                catch
                {
                    return dirs;
                }

                foreach (DirectoryInfo subdir in subdirs)
                    dirs.Add(new DiskDirectory(subdir));

                return dirs;
            }
        }
    }
}
```

The crucial property here is *Subdirectories*, which basically calls *GetDirectories* and then creates a *DiskDirectory* object for each subdirectory and adds that to a *List* collection. This *List* object is what it returns from the property.

The TemplateTheTree program makes use of the *DiskDirectory* class in defining a data template for a *TreeView*.

TemplateTheTree.cs
```
//-------------------------------------------------
// TemplateTheTree.cs (c) 2006 by Charles Petzold
//-------------------------------------------------
using System;
using System.IO;
using System.Windows;
using System.Windows.Controls;
using System.Windows.Data;
using System.Windows.Input;
using System.Windows.Media;

namespace Petzold.TemplateTheTree
{
    public class TemplateTheTree : Window
    {
        [STAThread]
        public static void Main()
```

```
        {
            Application app = new Application();
            app.Run(new TemplateTheTree());
        }
    public TemplateTheTree()
    {
        Title = "Template the Tree";

        // Create TreeView and set as content of window.
        TreeView treevue = new TreeView();
        Content = treevue;

        // Create HierarchicalDataTemplate based on DiskDirectory.
        HierarchicalDataTemplate template =
                new HierarchicalDataTemplate(typeof(DiskDirectory));

        // Set Subdirectories property as ItemsSource.
        template.ItemsSource = new Binding("Subdirectories");

        // Create FrameworkElementFactory for TextBlock.
        FrameworkElementFactory factoryTextBlock =
                new FrameworkElementFactory(typeof(TextBlock));

        // Bind Text property with Name property from DiskDirectory.
        factoryTextBlock.SetBinding(TextBlock.TextProperty,
                                new Binding("Name"));

        // Set this Textblock as the VisualTree of the template.
        template.VisualTree = factoryTextBlock;

        // Create a DiskDirectory object for the system drive.
        DiskDirectory dir = new DiskDirectory(
            new DirectoryInfo(
                Path.GetPathRoot(Environment.SystemDirectory)));

        // Create a root TreeViewItem and set its properties.
        TreeViewItem item = new TreeViewItem();
        item.Header = dir.Name;
        item.ItemsSource = dir.Subdirectories;
        item.ItemTemplate = template;

        // Add TreeViewItem to TreeView.
        treevue.Items.Add(item);
        item.IsExpanded = true;
    }
    }
}
```

The *HierarchicalDataTemplate* object created here is based on the *DiskDirectory* class. This template will be associated with a *TreeViewItem* object, which essentially displays a *DiskDirectory* object. *HierarchicalDataTemplate* has an *ItemsSource* property for the source of its *Items* collection. This is the *Subdirectories* property of *DiskDirectory*.

The next step is to build a visual tree based on *FrameworkElementFactory* objects. To keep this example simple, the visual tree for the *TreeViewItem* is merely a *TextBlock*. The *Text* property of this *TextBlock* is bound with the *Name* property from *DiskDirectory*.

The constructor continues by creating an object of type *DiskDirectory* for the system drive. (Again, I'm keeping the example simple by not getting all the drives.) A single *TreeViewItem* is created with its *Header* property set to the *Name* property of the *DiskDirectory* object, its *Items-Source* property set to the *Subdirectories* property of the *DiskDirectory* object, and its *ItemTemplate* property set to the *HierarchicalDataTemplate* we've just created. Thus, children of this root *TreeViewItem* will be based on the *Subdirectories* property of the created *DiskDirectory* object, but these children will be displayed using the *HierarchicalDataTemplate*, and this template describes where all future items come from and how they are displayed. The *TreeView* displays a directory tree efficiently with no event handler.

Although this program shows how to use this technique when every *TreeViewItem* is the same sort of object, it's also possible to use it with tree views where parent and child items may be different types. I show more template examples in Chapter 25.

The final *TreeView* example in this chapter uses the control to display all the Windows Presentation Foundation public classes that descend from *DispatcherObject*. The *TreeView* is ideal for this job because the items can be shown in a visual hierarchy that parallels the inheritance hierarchy. Although the program displays names of classes, let's make the code somewhat generalized by writing a class that displays the name associated with any *Type* object. The *TypeTreeViewItem* class inherits from *TreeViewItem* and includes a property named *Type*. Of course, the type of the *Type* property is *Type*.

```
TypeTreeViewItem.cs
//---------------------------------------------------
// TypeTreeViewItem.cs (c) 2006 by Charles Petzold
//---------------------------------------------------
using System;
using System.Windows;
using System.Windows.Controls;

namespace Petzold.ShowClassHierarchy
{
    class TypeTreeViewItem : TreeViewItem
    {
        Type typ;

        // Two constructors.
        public TypeTreeViewItem()
        {
        }
        public TypeTreeViewItem(Type typ)
        {
            Type = typ;
        }
```

```
        // Public Type property of type Type.
        public Type Type
        {
            set
            {
                typ = value;

                if (typ.IsAbstract)
                    Header = typ.Name + " (abstract)";
                else
                    Header = typ.Name;
            }
            get
            {
                return typ;
            }
        }
    }
}
```

The program has two constructors to let you set the *Type* property when creating the object or later. Notice that the *set* accessor of the *Type* property sets the *Header* property of the *TreeViewItem* to the *Name* property of the *Type* object, possibly with the word *abstract* in parentheses. For example, you could create an object of *TypeTreeViewItem* and set the *Type* property like this:

```
TypeTreeViewItem item = new TypeTreeViewItem();
item.Type = typeof(Button);
```

The item displays the simple text "Button", but the actual *Type* object associated with this item would still be available from the *Type* property. (The *set* accessor of the *Type* property could have set *Header* to the *Type* object itself, but in that case the *Type* object would have been displayed using the *ToString* method of the *Type* class, and *ToString* returns the fully-qualified name—for example, "System.Windows.Controls.Button".)

The next step in creating this program is defining a class named *ClassHierarchyTreeView* that inherits from *TreeView*.

```
ClassHierarchyTreeView.cs
//-------------------------------------------------------
// ClassHierarchyTreeView (c) 2006 by Charles Petzold
//-------------------------------------------------------
using System;
using System.Collections.Generic;
using System.Reflection;
using System.Windows;
using System.Windows.Controls;
```

```
namespace Petzold.ShowClassHierarchy
{
    public class ClassHierarchyTreeView : TreeView
    {
        public ClassHierarchyTreeView(Type typeRoot)
        {
            // Make sure PresentationCore is loaded.
            UIElement dummy = new UIElement();

            // Put all the referenced assemblies in a List.
            List<Assembly> assemblies = new List<Assembly>();

            // Get all referenced assemblies.
            AssemblyName[] anames =
                    Assembly.GetExecutingAssembly().GetReferencedAssemblies();

            // Add to assemblies list.
            foreach (AssemblyName aname in anames)
                assemblies.Add(Assembly.Load(aname));

            // Store descendants of typeRoot in a sorted list.
            SortedList<string, Type> classes = new SortedList<string, Type>();
            classes.Add(typeRoot.Name, typeRoot);

            // Get all the types in the assembly.
            foreach (Assembly assembly in assemblies)
                foreach (Type typ in assembly.GetTypes())
                    if (typ.IsPublic && typ.IsSubclassOf(typeRoot))
                        classes.Add(typ.Name, typ);

            // Create root item.
            TypeTreeViewItem item = new TypeTreeViewItem(typeRoot);
            Items.Add(item);

            // Call recursive method.
            CreateLinkedItems(item, classes);
        }
        void CreateLinkedItems(TypeTreeViewItem itemBase,
                               SortedList<string, Type> list)
        {
            foreach (KeyValuePair<string, Type> kvp in list)
                if (kvp.Value.BaseType == itemBase.Type)
                {
                    TypeTreeViewItem item = new TypeTreeViewItem(kvp.Value);
                    itemBase.Items.Add(item);
                    CreateLinkedItems(item, list);
                }
        }
    }
}
```

Everything happens in the constructor of this class. The constructor requires a root *Type* that begins the hierarchy. It first creates a *List* object for storing all the *AssemblyName* objects referenced by the program, and then loads these assemblies to make *Assembly* objects.

The constructor then creates a *SortedList* object to store the *Type* objects representing those classes that derive from *typeRoot*. These *Type* objects are sorted by the *Name* property of the type. The constructor simply loops through all the *Assembly* objects and the *Type* objects in each assembly searching for these classes.

Once all the classes are accumulated in the *SortedList*, the constructor must create a *TypeTree-ViewItem* for each of these classes. That's the job of the recursive *CreateLinkedItems* method. The first argument is *TypeTreeViewItem* associated with a particular class. The method simply loops through all the classes in the *SortedList* and finds those whose base type is that class. The method creates a new *TypeTreeViewItem* for each of them and adds it to the collection of the base class.

The previous two source code files and the next one are all part of the ShowClassHierarchy project. The constructor sets the window content to an object of type *ClassHierarchyTreeView* with a root class of *DispatcherObject*.

ShowClassHierarchy.cs

```
//----------------------------------------------------
// ShowClassHierarchy.cs (c) 2006 by Charles Petzold
//----------------------------------------------------
using System;
using System.Collections.Generic;
using System.Reflection;
using System.Windows;
using System.Windows.Controls;

namespace Petzold.ShowClassHierarchy
{
    class ShowClassHierarchy : Window
    {
        [STAThread]
        public static void Main()
        {
            Application app = new Application();
            app.Run(new ShowClassHierarchy());
        }
        public ShowClassHierarchy()
        {
            Title = "Show Class Hierarchy";

            // Create ClassHierarchyTreeView.
            ClassHierarchyTreeView treevue =
                new ClassHierarchyTreeView(
                    typeof(System.Windows.Threading.DispatcherObject));

            Content = treevue;
        }
    }
}
```

You might be tempted to replace the reference to *DispatcherObject* with *typeof(Object)* to get an even bigger class hierarchy, but the logic in *ClassHierarchyTreeView* breaks down when two classes in different namespaces have the same name, which is the case when you begin with *Object*.

If the *TreeView* control resembles the left side of Windows Explorer, the *ListView* control comes closest to resembling the right side. In Windows Explorer, you can choose different views: Icons, Tiles, List, Thumbnails, or Details. You've already seen in Chapter 13 how you can define a template for the *ListBox* and display objects in different formats, so for many displays of objects you can use a *ListBox* with a custom template. The tough one, however, is the Details view, because that requires multiple columns and column headings. That's where *ListView* comes to the rescue.

The *ListView* control derives directly from *ListBox*. (Also, *ListViewItem* derives directly from *ListBoxItem*.) Just like *ListBox*, *ListView* has a property named *Items* that stores the objects displayed by the control. *ListView* also has an *ItemsSource* property that you can set to an array or other collection of objects. *ListView* adds just one additional property to *ListBox*, a property named *View* of type *ViewBase*. If *View* is null, *ListView* basically functions just like *ListBox*.

Currently only one class derives from *ViewBase*, and that's *GridView*, which displays objects in multiple columns with column headings. The crucial property of *GridView* is *Columns*, an object of type *GridViewColumnCollection*. For each column you want displayed, you'll create an object of type *GridViewColumn* and add it to the *Columns* collection. The *GridViewColumn* object indicates the column heading, the column width, and the property of the item you want displayed in that column.

For example, suppose you've set the *Items* collection of your *ListView* control to objects of type *Personnel*, a class that has properties named *FirstName*, *LastName*, *EmailAddress*, and so forth. In defining each column of the *ListView*, you indicate the particular property of *Personnel* (*FirstName*, *LastName*, or whatever) you want displayed in that column. You identify the property with a binding.

The first program I want to show you displays all the properties and values from the *System-Parameters* class. The *SystemParameters* class has numerous static properties such as *Menu-BarHeight* and *IsMouseWheelPresent*. These particular properties indicate the default height of the application menu and whether or not the mouse attached to the computer has a mouse wheel.

The first step in displaying information in a *GridView* is to define a class describing the items you want to display. I want two columns in the *GridView*: the first for the name of the property and the second for the value. The class for storing each item I named *SystemParams*.

```
SystemParam.cs
//-------------------------------------------
// SystemParam.cs (c) 2006 by Charles Petzold
//-------------------------------------------

namespace Petzold.ListSystemParameters
{
    public class SystemParam
```

```
    {
        string strName;
        object objValue;

        public string Name
        {
            set { strName = value; }
            get { return strName; }
        }
        public object Value
        {
            set { objValue = value; }
            get { return objValue; }
        }
        public override string ToString()
        {
            return Name + "=" + Value;
        }
    }
}
```

The *ListSystemParameters* class inherits from *Window* and creates a *ListView* control that fills its client area. It then creates a *GridView* object and sets that to the *View* property of the *ListView*.

ListSystemParameters.cs

```
//----------------------------------------------------
// ListSystemParameters.cs (c) 2006 by Charles Petzold
//----------------------------------------------------
using System;
using System.Collections.Generic;        // for experimentation
using System.ComponentModel;             // for experimentation
using System.Reflection;
using System.Windows;
using System.Windows.Data;
using System.Windows.Input;
using System.Windows.Controls;
using System.Windows.Media;

namespace Petzold.ListSystemParameters
{
    class ListSystemParameters : Window
    {
        [STAThread]
        public static void Main()
        {
            Application app = new Application();
            app.Run(new ListSystemParameters());
        }
        public ListSystemParameters()
        {
            Title = "List System Parameters";
```

```
                // Create a ListView as content of the window.
                ListView lstvue = new ListView();
                Content = lstvue;

                // Create a GridView as the View of the ListView.
                GridView grdvue = new GridView();
                lstvue.View = grdvue;

                // Create two GridView columns.
                GridViewColumn col = new GridViewColumn();
                col.Header = "Property Name";
                col.Width = 200;
                col.DisplayMemberBinding = new Binding("Name");
                grdvue.Columns.Add(col);

                col = new GridViewColumn();
                col.Header = "Value";
                col.Width = 200;
                col.DisplayMemberBinding = new Binding("Value");
                grdvue.Columns.Add(col);

                // Get all the system parameters in one handy array.
                PropertyInfo[] props = typeof(SystemParameters).GetProperties();

                // Add the items to the ListView.
                foreach (PropertyInfo prop in props)
                    if (prop.PropertyType != typeof(ResourceKey))
                    {
                        SystemParam sysparam = new SystemParam();
                        sysparam.Name = prop.Name;
                        sysparam.Value = prop.GetValue(null, null);
                        lstvue.Items.Add(sysparam);
                    }
        }
    }
}
```

The first *GridViewColumn* is for displaying the property names of the *SystemParameters* class. The *Header* property is "Property Name" and the *Width* property is 200 device-independent units. The *DisplayMemberBinding* property of *GridViewColumn* must be set to a binding indicating the property of the data to display, in this case a property of *SystemParam*. This column should display the *Name* property of *SystemParam*, so:

```
col.DisplayMemberBinding = new Binding("Name");
```

Similarly, the second column is given a *Header* property of "Value" and bound with the *Value* property of *SystemParams*.

So far, the *ListView* has no items. The constructor concludes by using reflection to obtain an array of *PropertyInfo* objects from *SystemParameters*. For each property, the program creates an object of type *SystemParam* and assigns the *Name* property from the *Name* property of

PropertyInfo and the *Value* property from the *GetValue* method of *PropertyInfo*. Each item is added to the *Items* collection.

Notice that the logic skips all properties in *SystemParameters* of type *ResourceKey*. Each property in the class exists in two forms. For example, *MenuBarHeight* is of type *double*, and *MenuBarHeightKey* is of type *ResourceKey*. The properties of type *ResourceKey* are mostly for use in XAML, as you'll discover in Chapter 21.

If you delete the program statement

```
lstvue.View = grdvue;
```

the *View* property remains at its default *null* value and the *ListView* behaves just a *ListBox*. The items are displayed with strings from the *ToString* method of *SystemParem,* which certainly gives you all the information but not very attractively.

One problem with the *ListSystemParameters* program is that the items are not sorted. There are a couple ways to fix that problem. One approach is to sort the *PropertyInfo* array before the *foreach* loop. For this job you'll need a small class that implements the *IComparer* interface and has a *Compare* method to compare two *PropertyInfo* items. Here's a simple implementation of such a class:

```
class PropertyInfoCompare : IComparer<PropertyInfo>
{
    public int Compare(PropertyInfo prop1, PropertyInfo prop2)
    {
        return string.Compare(prop1.Name, prop2.Name);
    }
}
```

The ListSystemParameters.cs file already includes a *using* directive for *System.Collections .Generic*. To sort the *PropertyInfo* array using the *PropertyInfoCompare* class, you simply call:

```
Array.Sort(props, new PropertyInfoCompare());
```

A second approach requires a *using* directive for the *System.ComponentModel* namespace (which ListSystemParameters.cs already has). You create a *SortDescription* object referencing a property of the items you want sorted, and add it to the *SortDescriptions* collection defined by *ItemCollection*:

```
lstvue.Items.SortDescriptions.Add(
    new SortDescription("Name", ListSortDirection.Ascending));
```

A third approach involves a *SortedList* collection. This approach is shown in the next version of the program. It defines a *SortedList* with *string* objects as keys and *SystemParam* objects as values:

```
SortedList<string, SystemParam> sortlist = new SortedList<string, SystemParam>();
```

The program then fills up this *SortedList* from the *PropertyInfo* array:

```
foreach (PropertyInfo prop in props)
    if (prop.PropertyType != typeof(ResourceKey))
    {
        SystemParam sysparam = new SystemParam();
        sysparam.Name = prop.Name;
        sysparam.Value = prop.GetValue(null, null);
        sortlist.Add(prop.Name, sysparam);
    }
```

Notice that the property name is also the key name of the *SortedList*, and hence the item used for sorting. The final step is to just set the *Values* collection of the *SortedList* to the *ItemsSource* property of the *ListView*:

```
lstvue.ItemsSource = sortlist.Values;
```

The *Values* property of the *SortedList* is the collection of sorted *SystemParam* objects.

This second version of the program also corrects a little problem with the second column. Because it's displaying various values, it makes more sense to right-justify the contents. There are no alignment settings on the columns. Instead, a more generalized solution involves templates.

This version of the program creates a *DataTemplate*, initializes it with a visual tree consisting of a right-justified *TextBlock*, and then sets it to the *CellTemplate* property of the second *GridViewColumn*:

```
ListSortedSystemParameters.cs
//-----------------------------------------------------------
// ListSortedSystemParameters.cs (c) 2006 by Charles Petzold
//-----------------------------------------------------------
using Petzold.ListSystemParameters;          // for SystemParam
using System;
using System.Collections.Generic;
using System.Reflection;
using System.Windows;
using System.Windows.Controls;
using System.Windows.Data;
using System.Windows.Input;
using System.Windows.Media;

namespace Petzold.ListSortedSystemParameters
{
    public class ListSortedSystemParameters : Window
    {
        [STAThread]
        public static void Main()
        {
            Application app = new Application();
            app.Run(new ListSortedSystemParameters());
        }
        public ListSortedSystemParameters()
        {
            Title = "List Sorted System Parameters";
```

```csharp
            // Create a ListView as content of the window.
            ListView lstvue = new ListView();
            Content = lstvue;

            // Create a GridView as the View of the ListView.
            GridView grdvue = new GridView();
            lstvue.View = grdvue;

            // Create two GridView columns.
            GridViewColumn col = new GridViewColumn();
            col.Header = "Property Name";
            col.Width = 200;
            col.DisplayMemberBinding = new Binding("Name");
            grdvue.Columns.Add(col);

            col = new GridViewColumn();
            col.Header = "Value";
            col.Width = 200;
            grdvue.Columns.Add(col);

            // Create DataTemplate for second column.
            DataTemplate template = new DataTemplate(typeof(string));
            FrameworkElementFactory factoryTextBlock =
                new FrameworkElementFactory(typeof(TextBlock));
            factoryTextBlock.SetValue(TextBlock.HorizontalAlignmentProperty,
                                HorizontalAlignment.Right);
            factoryTextBlock.SetBinding(TextBlock.TextProperty,
                                new Binding("Value"));
            template.VisualTree = factoryTextBlock;
            col.CellTemplate = template;

            // Get all the system parameters in one handy array.
            PropertyInfo[] props = typeof(SystemParameters).GetProperties();

            // Create a SortedList to hold the SystemParam objects.
            SortedList<string, SystemParam> sortlist =
                                new SortedList<string, SystemParam>();

            // Fill up the SortedList from the PropertyInfo array.
            foreach (PropertyInfo prop in props)
                if (prop.PropertyType != typeof(ResourceKey))
                {
                    SystemParam sysparam = new SystemParam();
                    sysparam.Name = prop.Name;
                    sysparam.Value = prop.GetValue(null, null);
                    sortlist.Add(prop.Name, sysparam);
                }

            // Set the ItemsSource property of the ListView.
            lstvue.ItemsSource = sortlist.Values;
        }
    }
}
```

Notice that the *Text* property of the *TextBlock* is bound to the *Value* property of *SystemParam*, so the normal *DisplayMemberBinding* is no longer allowed.

When I was exploring dependency properties for Chapter 8, I wrote a small console program for myself that used reflection to obtain information about the dependency properties that some WPF classes defined. But I wanted something more generalized, and that was the origin of the *ClassHierarchyTreeView* (described earlier in this chapter) and the *DependencyPropertyListView* (coming up). The final program in this chapter is named ExploreDependencyProperties and it unites these two controls in a single window separated by a splitter. When you select a class from the *ClassHierarchyTreeView*, the *DependencyPropertyListView* shows the dependency properties defined by that class, including the *FrameworkMetadata* flags, if any.

DependencyPropertyListView inherits from *ListView* and displays a collection of objects of type *DependencyProperty*. Each column is bound to a particular property of *DependencyProperty*. For example, the first column is bound to the *Name* property, and the second to the *OwnerType* property.

But here the problems begin. If you just bind a column in the *ListView* to the *OwnerType* property of *DependencyProperty*, you'll see strings like "System.Windows.Controls.Button." That's hard to read. Instead, I wanted the column to contain just "Button." Fortunately, there's a way to do this. When you define a *DataTemplate* object for the *CellTemplate* property of the *GridViewColumn* object, you also define a *Binding* that links the property you want to display with the element that displays it. The *Binding* class defines a property named *Converter* that can convert this bound data to a desired format. This *Converter* property is of type *IValueConverter*, which is an interface with just two methods: *Convert* and *ConvertBack*.

So, we need a class that implements the *IValueConverter* interface that converts a *Type* object (such as *System.Windows.Controls.Button*) to a *string* ("Button"), and here it is.

TypeToString.cs

```
//-------------------------------------------
// TypeToString.cs (c) 2006 by Charles Petzold
//-------------------------------------------
using System;
using System.Globalization;
using System.Windows.Data;

namespace Petzold.ExploreDependencyProperties
{
    class TypeToString : IValueConverter
    {
        public object Convert(object obj, Type type, object param,
                        CultureInfo culture)
        {

            // This is the class name without this namespace.
            return (obj as Name).Type;
```

```
        }
        public object ConvertBack(object obj, Type type, object param,
                                  CultureInfo culture)
        {
            return null;
        }
    }
}
```

The object to be converted enters the *Convert* method through the first parameter. In the usage of this class, this object will be of type *Type*. It's cast to a Type object and then the Name property provides the name without the namespace. In my application, the ConvertBack method is never used, so it can simply return null. This conversion is also good for displaying the *PropertyType* property of *DependencyProperty*.

As you may recall, *DependencyProperty* defines a property named *DefaultMetadata* of type *PropertyMetadata*. This *PropertyMetadata* object has some useful information in it, particularly the *DefaultValue* property. However, many elements define their metadata by using an object of type *FrameworkPropertyMetadata*, which has the essential properties *AffectsMeasure*, *Affects-Arrange*, *AffectsRender*, and others. These metadata properties are often set through a constructor using a *FrameworkPropertyMetadataOptions* enumeration, and this is what I focused on. I didn't want to devote a whole bunch of columns showing Boolean values of *AffectsMeasure*, *AffectsArrange*, and so on. I wanted one column that would show all the *FrameworkProperty-MetadataOptions* members used to create the metadata in the first place.

That's the purpose of this conversion class. The *Convert* method converts an object of the enumeration type *FrameworkPropertyMetadata* to an object of type *FrameworkPropertyMeta-dataOptions*.

MetadataToFlags.cs

```
//-----------------------------------------------
// MetadataToFlags.cs (c) 2006 by Charles Petzold
//-----------------------------------------------
using System;
using System.Globalization;
using System.Windows;
using System.Windows.Data;

namespace Petzold.ExploreDependencyProperties
{
    class MetadataToFlags : IValueConverter
    {
        public object Convert(object obj, Type type, object param,
                              CultureInfo culture)
        {
            FrameworkPropertyMetadataOptions flags = 0;
            FrameworkPropertyMetadata metadata =
                                    obj as FrameworkPropertyMetadata;
```

```
                if (metadata == null)
                    return null;

                if (metadata.AffectsMeasure)
                    flags |= FrameworkPropertyMetadataOptions.AffectsMeasure;

                if (metadata.AffectsArrange)
                    flags |= FrameworkPropertyMetadataOptions.AffectsArrange;

                if (metadata.AffectsParentMeasure)
                    flags |= FrameworkPropertyMetadataOptions.AffectsParentMeasure;

                if (metadata.AffectsParentArrange)
                    flags |= FrameworkPropertyMetadataOptions.AffectsParentArrange;

                if (metadata.AffectsRender)
                    flags |= FrameworkPropertyMetadataOptions.AffectsRender;

                if (metadata.Inherits)
                    flags |= FrameworkPropertyMetadataOptions.Inherits;

                if (metadata.OverridesInheritanceBehavior)
                    flags |= FrameworkPropertyMetadataOptions.
                                              OverridesInheritanceBehavior;

                if (metadata.IsNotDataBindable)
                    flags |= FrameworkPropertyMetadataOptions.NotDataBindable;

                if (metadata.BindsTwoWayByDefault)
                    flags |= FrameworkPropertyMetadataOptions.BindsTwoWayByDefault;

                if (metadata.Journal)
                    flags |= FrameworkPropertyMetadataOptions.Journal;

                return flags;
            }
            public object ConvertBack(object obj, Type type, object param,
                            CultureInfo culture)
            {
                return new FrameworkPropertyMetadata(null,
                            (FrameworkPropertyMetadataOptions)obj);
            }
        }
    }
}
```

When this converted item is actually displayed, the *ToString* method defined by the *Enum* structure formats the enumeration into readable comma-separated members.

It's now time to look at *DependencyPropertyListView*. The class derives from *ListView* and defines a property named *Type*, backed by the dependency property *TypeProperty*. Set the *Type* property of this *ListView* and the control displays all the *DependencyProperty* objects defined by that *Type*. The *OnTypePropertyChanged* method is responsible for using reflection to obtain all the *DependencyProperty* objects and putting them in a *SortedList* collection that it uses to set the *ItemsSource* property of *ListView*.

DependencyPropertyListView.cs

```
//------------------------------------------------------------
// DependencyPropertyListView.cs (c) 2006 by Charles Petzold
//------------------------------------------------------------
using System;
using System.Collections.Generic;
using System.Reflection;
using System.Windows;
using System.Windows.Controls;
using System.Windows.Data;

namespace Petzold.ExploreDependencyProperties
{
    public class DependencyPropertyListView : ListView
    {
        // Define dependency property for Type.
        public static DependencyProperty TypeProperty;

        // Register dependency property in static constructor.
        static DependencyPropertyListView()
        {
            TypeProperty = DependencyProperty.Register("Type", typeof(Type),
                    typeof(DependencyPropertyListView),
                    new PropertyMetadata(null,
                        new PropertyChangedCallback(OnTypePropertyChanged)));
        }
        // Static method called when TypeProperty changes.
        static void OnTypePropertyChanged(DependencyObject obj,
                                DependencyPropertyChangedEventArgs args)
        {
            // Get the ListView object involved.
            DependencyPropertyListView lstvue = obj as DependencyPropertyListView;

            // Get the new value of the Type property.
            Type type = args.NewValue as Type;

            // Get rid of all the items currently stored by the ListView.
            lstvue.ItemsSource = null;

            // Get all the DependencyProperty fields in the Type object.
            if (type != null)
            {
                SortedList<string, DependencyProperty> list =
                                new SortedList<string, DependencyProperty>();
                FieldInfo[] infos = type.GetFields();

                foreach (FieldInfo info in infos)
                    if (info.FieldType == typeof(DependencyProperty))
                        list.Add(info.Name,
                                (DependencyProperty)info.GetValue(null));
```

```csharp
                // Set the ItemsSource to the list.
                lstvue.ItemsSource = list.Values;
        }
    }
    // Public Type property.
    public Type Type
    {
        set { SetValue(TypeProperty, value); }
        get { return (Type)GetValue(TypeProperty); }
    }
    // Constructor.
    public DependencyPropertyListView()
    {
        // Create a GridView and set to View property.
        GridView grdvue = new GridView();
        this.View = grdvue;

        // First column displays the 'Name' property of DependencyProperty.
        GridViewColumn col = new GridViewColumn();
        col.Header = "Name";
        col.Width = 150;
        col.DisplayMemberBinding = new Binding("Name");
        grdvue.Columns.Add(col);

        // Second column is labeled 'Owner'.
        col = new GridViewColumn();
        col.Header = "Owner";
        col.Width = 100;
        grdvue.Columns.Add(col);

        // Second column displays 'OwnerType' of DependencyProperty.
        // This one requires a data template.
        DataTemplate template = new DataTemplate();
        col.CellTemplate = template;

        // A TextBlock will display the data.
        FrameworkElementFactory elTextBlock =
                    new FrameworkElementFactory(typeof(TextBlock));
        template.VisualTree = elTextBlock;

        // Bind the 'OwnerType' property of DependencyProperty
        //   with the Text property of the TextBlock
        //   using a converter of TypeToString.
        Binding bind = new Binding("OwnerType");
        bind.Converter = new TypeToString();
        elTextBlock.SetBinding(TextBlock.TextProperty, bind);

        // Third column is labeled 'Type'.
        col = new GridViewColumn();
        col.Header = "Type";
        col.Width = 100;
        grdvue.Columns.Add(col);
```

```
                // This one requires a similar template to bind with 'PropertyType'.
                template = new DataTemplate();
                col.CellTemplate = template;
                elTextBlock = new FrameworkElementFactory(typeof(TextBlock));
                template.VisualTree = elTextBlock;
                bind = new Binding("PropertyType");
                bind.Converter = new TypeToString();
                elTextBlock.SetBinding(TextBlock.TextProperty, bind);

                // Fourth column labeled 'Default' displays
                //   DefaultMetadata.DefaultValue.
                col = new GridViewColumn();
                col.Header = "Default";
                col.Width = 75;
                col.DisplayMemberBinding =
                            new Binding("DefaultMetadata.DefaultValue");
                grdvue.Columns.Add(col);

                // Fifth column is similar.
                col = new GridViewColumn();
                col.Header = "Read-Only";
                col.Width = 75;
                col.DisplayMemberBinding = new Binding("DefaultMetadata.ReadOnly");
                grdvue.Columns.Add(col);

                // Sixth column, ditto.
                col = new GridViewColumn();
                col.Header = "Usage";
                col.Width = 75;
                col.DisplayMemberBinding =
                            new Binding("DefaultMetadata.AttachedPropertyUsage");
                grdvue.Columns.Add(col);

                // Seventh column displays metadata flags.
                col = new GridViewColumn();
                col.Header = "Flags";
                col.Width = 250;
                grdvue.Columns.Add(col);

                // A template is required to convert using MetadataToFlags.
                template = new DataTemplate();
                col.CellTemplate = template;
                elTextBlock = new FrameworkElementFactory(typeof(TextBlock));
                template.VisualTree = elTextBlock;
                bind = new Binding("DefaultMetadata");
                bind.Converter = new MetadataToFlags();
                elTextBlock.SetBinding(TextBlock.TextProperty, bind);
            }
        }
    }
```

This class's constructor is mainly responsible for defining all the columns. Some of them are simple, and some involve the two converters I discussed.

Finally, the *ExploreDependencyProperties* class puts it all together. It creates a *ClassHierarchy-TreeView* and a *DependencyPropertyListView* and puts a *GridSplitter* in between.

ExploreDependencyProperties.cs

```
//------------------------------------------------------------
// ExploreDependencyProperties.cs (c) 2006 by Charles Petzold
//------------------------------------------------------------
using Petzold.ShowClassHierarchy;        // for ClassHierarchyTreeView
using System;
using System.Windows;
using System.Windows.Controls;
using System.Windows.Input;
using System.Windows.Media;

namespace Petzold.ExploreDependencyProperties
{
    public class ExploreDependencyProperties : Window
    {
        [STAThread]
        public static void Main()
        {
            Application app = new Application();
            app.Run(new ExploreDependencyProperties());
        }
        public ExploreDependencyProperties()
        {
            Title = "Explore Dependency Properties";

            // Create Grid as content of window.
            Grid grid = new Grid();
            Content = grid;

            // Three column definitions for Grid.
            ColumnDefinition col = new ColumnDefinition();
            col.Width = new GridLength(1, GridUnitType.Star);
            grid.ColumnDefinitions.Add(new ColumnDefinition());

            col = new ColumnDefinition();
            col.Width = GridLength.Auto;
            grid.ColumnDefinitions.Add(col);

            col = new ColumnDefinition();
            col.Width = new GridLength(3, GridUnitType.Star);
            grid.ColumnDefinitions.Add(col);

            // ClassHierarchyTreeView goes on left side.
            ClassHierarchyTreeView treevue =
                        new ClassHierarchyTreeView(typeof(DependencyObject));
            grid.Children.Add(treevue);
            Grid.SetColumn(treevue, 0);

            // GridSplitter goes in the center cell.
            GridSplitter split = new GridSplitter();
            split.HorizontalAlignment = HorizontalAlignment.Center;
```

```
            split.VerticalAlignment = VerticalAlignment.Stretch;
            split.Width = 6;
            grid.Children.Add(split);
            Grid.SetColumn(split, 1);

            // DependencyPropertyListView goes on right side.
            DependencyPropertyListView lstvue = new DependencyPropertyListView();
            grid.Children.Add(lstvue);
            Grid.SetColumn(lstvue, 2);

            // Set a binding between TreeView and ListView.
            lstvue.SetBinding(DependencyPropertyListView.TypeProperty,
                        "SelectedItem.Type");
            lstvue.DataContext = treevue;
        }
    }
}
```

The last two statements of the constructor set a binding between the *Type* property of the *DependencyPropertyListView* control and the *Type* property of the *SelectedItem* property of *ClassHierarchyTreeView*. That *SelectedItem* property is actually an object of type *TypeTreeView-Item* that conveniently defines a property named *Type*. The simplicity of this binding justifies all the previous work (almost).

Chapter 17
Printing and Dialog Boxes

If you want a good scare, try browsing the *System.Printing* namespace. You'll see classes related to printer drivers, printer queues, print servers, and printer jobs. The good news about printing is that for most applications you can safely ignore much of the stuff in *System.Printing*. Most of your printing logic will probably center around the *PrintDialog* class defined in the *System.Windows.Controls* namespace.

The major class you'll need from *System.Printing* is named *PrintTicket*. Your projects will also need a reference to the ReachFramework.dll assembly to use that class. It's also useful for programs that print to maintain a field of type *PrintQueue*. That class can also be found in the *System.Printing* namespace, but it's from the System.Printing.dll assembly. Other printing-related classes are defined in *System.Windows.Documents*.

The *PrintDialog* class displays a dialog box, of course, but the class also includes methods to print a single page or to print a multi-page document. In both cases, what you print on the page is an object of type *Visual*. As you know by now, one important class that inherits from *Visual* is *UIElement*, which means that you can print an instance of any class that derives from *FrameworkElement*, including panels, controls, and other elements. For example, you could create a *Canvas* or other panel; put a bunch of child controls, elements, or shapes on it; and then print it.

Although printing a panel seems to offer a great deal of flexibility, a more straighforward approach to printing takes advantage of the *DrawingVisual* class, which also derives from *Visual*. I demonstrated *DrawingVisual* in the *ColorCell* class that's part of the *SelectColor* project in Chapter 11. The *DrawingVisual* class has a method named *RenderOpen* that returns an object of type *DrawingContext*. You call methods in *DrawingContext* (concluding with a call to *Close*) to store graphics in the *DrawingVisual* object.

The following program, PrintEllipse, is just about the simplest printing program imaginable. A printing program should have something that initiates printing. In this case, it's a button. When you click the button, the program creates an object of type *PrintDialog* and displays it. In this dialog box, you might choose a printer (if you have more than one) and possibly change some printer settings. Then you click the Print button to dismiss the *PrintDialog*, and the program begins preparing to print.

PrintEllipse.cs

```
//-------------------------------------------------
// PrintEllipse.cs (c) 2006 by Charles Petzold
//-------------------------------------------------
using System;
using System.Windows;
using System.Windows.Controls;
using System.Windows.Input;
```

```
using System.Windows.Media;

namespace Petzold.PrintEllipse
{
    public class PrintEllipse : Window
    {
        [STAThread]
        public static void Main()
        {
            Application app = new Application();
            app.Run(new PrintEllipse());
        }
        public PrintEllipse()
        {
            Title = "Print Ellipse";
            FontSize = 24;

            // Create StackPanel as content of Window.
            StackPanel stack = new StackPanel();
            Content = stack;

            // Create Button for printing.
            Button btn = new Button();
            btn.Content = "_Print...";
            btn.HorizontalAlignment = HorizontalAlignment.Center;
            btn.Margin = new Thickness(24);
            btn.Click += PrintOnClick;
            stack.Children.Add(btn);
        }
        void PrintOnClick(object sender, RoutedEventArgs args)
        {
            PrintDialog dlg = new PrintDialog();

            if ((bool)dlg.ShowDialog().GetValueOrDefault())
            {
                // Create DrawingVisual and open DrawingContext.
                DrawingVisual vis = new DrawingVisual();
                DrawingContext dc = vis.RenderOpen();

                // Draw ellipse.
                dc.DrawEllipse(Brushes.LightGray, new Pen(Brushes.Black, 3),
                            new Point(dlg.PrintableAreaWidth / 2,
                                    dlg.PrintableAreaHeight / 2),
                            dlg.PrintableAreaWidth / 2,
                            dlg.PrintableAreaHeight / 2);

                // Close DrawingContext.
                dc.Close();

                // Finally, print the page.
                dlg.PrintVisual(vis, "My first print job");
            }
        }
    }
}
```

ShowDialog is defined as returning a nullable *bool*. For this particular dialog box, *ShowDialog* returns *true* if the user clicks the Print button, *false* if the user clicks Cancel, and *null* if the dialog box is closed by clicking the red Close button at the far right of the title bar. The *GetValueOrDefault* call converts the *null* return to *false* so that the result can be safely cast to a *bool* for the *if* statement.

If the *ShowDialog* method returns *true*, the program creates an object of type *DrawingVisual*, calls *RenderOpen* to return a *DrawingContext* object, and then calls both *DrawEllipse* and *Close* on the *DrawingContext*. Finally, the *DrawingVisual* is passed to the *PrintVisual* method of *PrintDialog* with a text string that identifies the print job in the printer queue.

Notice that the *DrawEllipse* arguments reference two properties defined by *PrintDialog* named (somewhat incorrectly) *PrintableAreaWidth* and *PrintableAreaHeight*. When the page printed by the PrintEllipse program comes out of your printer, you'll probably see that parts of the ellipse are truncated because they fall in unprintable areas of the page. The *PrintableAreaWidth* and *PrintableAreaHeight* properties do *not* refer to the printable area of the page, but instead indicate the total physical size of the page in device-independent units (1/96 inch).

Toward the bottom of the Print dialog are four radio buttons labeled All, Selection, Current Page, and Pages that indicate what part of the document the user wants printed: the entire document, the current selection, the current page, or a range of pages specified by the user. All radio buttons except the first are disabled by default. The Selection and Current Page buttons cannot be enabled in the initial release of the Windows Presentation Foundation. You can enable the Pages buttons by setting the *UserPageRangeEnabled* property to *true*.

You can initialize the radio button that's checked and later obtain the user's choice through the *PageRangeSelection* property, which is a member of the *PageRangeSelection* enumeration: *AllPages* or *UserPages*. If the *PageRangeSelection* property equals *PageRangeSelection.UserPages* (corresponding to the radio button labeled Pages), the *PageRanges* property of *PrintDialog* is a collection of objects of type *PageRange*, which is a structure with *PageFrom* and *PageTo* properties.

The Print dialog also includes a Number of Copies field. Enter a number greater than 1 in this field and the *PrintVisual* method prints multiple copies.

The Print dialog has a button labeled Printer Preferences that you click to invoke the printer-specific property pages. If you select a different page size on those pages, you'll notice by what the program prints that the page size is obviously reflected in the *PrintableAreaWidth* and *PrintableAreaHeight* properties. You can also switch the page orientation to landscape, but the effect is not quite noticeable in this program.

The user's requested page orientation, number of copies, and much other information is collected in a property of *PrintDialog* named *PrintTicket* of type *PrintTicket*, a class defined in the *System.Printing* namespace and stored in the ReachFramework assembly. To use *Print-Ticket*, you'll need a reference to ReachFramework.dll.

If you invoke the *PrintDialog* in the PrintEllipse program, change a setting (such as the page orientation), print, and then invoke the *PrintDialog* again, you'll see that the setting has reverted back to its default. These days, polite programs usually preserve user selections such as page orientation between print jobs. To do this, you can define a field of type *PrintTicket*.

```
PrintTicket prntkt;
```

Of course, *prntkt* is initially *null*. When you create an object of type *PrintDialog* in preparation for displaying the dialog box, you set the dialog's *PrintTicket* from this field, but only if the field is not *null*:

```
PrintDialog dlg = new PrintDialog();

if (prntkt != null)
    dlg.PrintTicket = prntkt;
```

If the user clicks the Print button in the dialog, you want to save the *PrintTicket* from the dialog box to the field:

```
if (dlg.ShowDialog().GetValueOrDefault())
{
    prntkt = dlg.PrintTicket;
    ...
}
```

This setting and getting of the *PrintTicket* ensures that user choices are preserved. If the user opens the Print dialog, sets page orientation to Landscape, clicks OK, and then opens the Print dialog again, the orientation will still be displayed as Landscape.

If the user has multiple printers, these show up in a *ComboBox* at the top of each of the Print dialog. If the user selects a non-default printer in the Print dialog, you probably want to bring up the Print dialog the next time showing that same printer. You can do this by saving the *PrintQueue* property of the dialog box as a field of type *PrintQueue*, and setting that property from the field when the dialog box is displayed. You'll need a reference to the System.Printing assembly to use *PrintQueue*.

One part of the print equation that's missing from the *PrintDialog* is a facility for the user to select page margins, so for that job let's create a dialog box specifically for that purpose. Dialog box classes derive from *Window* and are very similar to other *Window*-based classes. But there are a few differences.

The constructor of a dialog box class should set the *ShowInTaskbar* property to *false*. Very often the dialog box is sized to its contents and the *ResizeMode* is set to *NoResize*. You can set the *WindowStyle* to either *SingleBorderWindow* or *ToolWindow*, whichever you prefer. It is no longer considered proper to display a dialog box without a title bar.

The easy way to position a dialog box relative to its owner is by setting the *WindowStartupLocation* to *CenterOwner*. Even if you just leave the *WindowStartupLocation* property at its default setting (which lets Windows itself position the dialog), the *Owner* property of the dialog box must still be set to the *Window* object that invoked the dialog. Usually the code looks something like this:

```
MyDialog dlg = new MyDialog();
dlg.Owner = this;
```

If a dialog box with a *null* owner is displayed and the user switches to another application, the dialog box could end up *behind* the window that invoked it, but the application's window would still be prohibited from receiving input. It's not a pretty situation.

The *CommonDialog* class defined in the *Microsoft.Win32* namespace (and from which *OpenFileDialog* and *SaveFileDialog* are derived) defines a *ShowDialog* method that requires an *Owner* argument That's one way to do it. Or, the constructor of the dialog box class could require an *Owner* argument. If you do that, you have a bit more flexibility in positioning the dialog box. For example, suppose you want to position the dialog box offset one inch from the top left corner of the application window. The constructor code is simply

```
public MyDialog(Window owner)
{
    Left = 96 + owner.Left;
    Top = 96 + owner.Top;
    ...
}
```

Almost always, a dialog box defines at least one public property for the information that the dialog box obtains from the user and provides to the application. You might even want to define a class or structure specifically to contain all the information that a particular dialog box provides. In the definition of this property, the *set* accessor initializes the dialog box controls from the value of the property. The *get* accessor obtains the properties from the controls.

A dialog box contains OK and Cancel buttons, although the OK button might actually be labeled Open, Save, or Print. The OK button has its *IsDefault* property set to *true* so that the button is clicked if the user presses the Enter key anywhere within the dialog box. The Cancel button has its *IsCancel* property set to *true*, so the button is clicked if the user presses the Escape key.

You don't need to provide a *Click* handler for the Cancel button. The dialog box is terminated automatically as a result of the *true* setting of the *IsCancel* property. The *Click* handler for the OK button need only set the *DialogResult* property to *true*. That terminates the dialog box and causes *ShowDialog* to return *true*.

The *PageMarginsDialog* class contains four *TextBox* controls to let the user enter left, right, top, and bottom page margins in inches. The class defines a single public property named *PageMargins* of type *Thickness* that converts between inches and device-independent units. The *get* accessor of the *PageMargins* property can call *Double.Parse* to convert the contents of the four *TextBox* controls to numbers without fear because the class disables the OK button until all fields contain valid values.

PageMarginsDialog.cs

```
//-------------------------------------------------
// PageMarginsDialog.cs (c) 2006 by Charles Petzold
//-------------------------------------------------
using System;
using System.Windows;
using System.Windows.Controls;
using System.Windows.Controls.Primitives;

namespace Petzold.PrintWithMargins
{
    class PageMarginsDialog : Window
    {
        // Internal enumeration to refer to the paper sides.
        enum Side
        {
            Left, Right, Top, Bottom
        }

        // Four TextBox controls for numeric input.
        TextBox[] txtbox = new TextBox[4];
        Button btnOk;

        // Public property of type Thickness for page margins.
        public Thickness PageMargins
        {
            set
            {
                txtbox[(int)Side.Left].Text = (value.Left / 96).ToString("F3");
                txtbox[(int)Side.Right].Text =
                                        (value.Right / 96).ToString("F3");
                txtbox[(int)Side.Top].Text = (value.Top / 96).ToString("F3");
                txtbox[(int)Side.Bottom].Text =
                                        (value.Bottom / 96).ToString("F3");
            }
            get
            {
                return new Thickness(
                        Double.Parse(txtbox[(int)Side.Left].Text) * 96,
                        Double.Parse(txtbox[(int)Side.Top].Text) * 96,
                        Double.Parse(txtbox[(int)Side.Right].Text) * 96,
                        Double.Parse(txtbox[(int)Side.Bottom].Text) * 96);
            }
        }
    }
```

```
// Constructor.
public PageMarginsDialog()
{
    // Standard settings for dialog boxes.
    Title = "Page Setup";
    ShowInTaskbar = false;
    WindowStyle = WindowStyle.ToolWindow;
    WindowStartupLocation = WindowStartupLocation.CenterOwner;
    SizeToContent = SizeToContent.WidthAndHeight;
    ResizeMode = ResizeMode.NoResize;

    // Make StackPanel content of Window.
    StackPanel stack = new StackPanel();
    Content = stack;

    // Make GroupBox a child of StackPanel.
    GroupBox grpbox = new GroupBox();
    grpbox.Header = "Margins (inches)";
    grpbox.Margin = new Thickness(12);
    stack.Children.Add(grpbox);

    // Make Grid the content of the GroupBox.
    Grid grid = new Grid();
    grid.Margin = new Thickness(6);
    grpbox.Content = grid;

    // Two rows and four columns.
    for (int i = 0; i < 2; i++)
    {
        RowDefinition rowdef = new RowDefinition();
        rowdef.Height = GridLength.Auto;
        grid.RowDefinitions.Add(rowdef);
    }

    for (int i = 0; i < 4; i++)
    {
        ColumnDefinition coldef = new ColumnDefinition();
        coldef.Width = GridLength.Auto;
        grid.ColumnDefinitions.Add(coldef);
    }

    // Put Label and TextBox controls in Grid.
    for (int i = 0; i < 4; i++)
    {
        Label lbl = new Label();
        lbl.Content = "_" + Enum.GetName(typeof(Side), i) + ":";
        lbl.Margin = new Thickness(6);
        lbl.VerticalAlignment = VerticalAlignment.Center;
        grid.Children.Add(lbl);
        Grid.SetRow(lbl, i / 2);
        Grid.SetColumn(lbl, 2 * (i % 2));

        txtbox[i] = new TextBox();
        txtbox[i].TextChanged += TextBoxOnTextChanged;
        txtbox[i].MinWidth = 48;
```

```
        txtbox[i].Margin = new Thickness(6);
        grid.Children.Add(txtbox[i]);
        Grid.SetRow(txtbox[i], i / 2);
        Grid.SetColumn(txtbox[i], 2 * (i % 2) + 1);
    }

    // Use UniformGrid for OK and Cancel buttons.
    UniformGrid unigrid = new UniformGrid();
    unigrid.Rows = 1;
    unigrid.Columns = 2;
    stack.Children.Add(unigrid);

    btnOk = new Button();
    btnOk.Content = "OK";
    btnOk.IsDefault = true;
    btnOk.IsEnabled = false;
    btnOk.MinWidth = 60;
    btnOk.Margin = new Thickness(12);
    btnOk.HorizontalAlignment = HorizontalAlignment.Center;
    btnOk.Click += OkButtonOnClick;
    unigrid.Children.Add(btnOk);

    Button btnCancel = new Button();
    btnCancel.Content = "Cancel";
    btnCancel.IsCancel = true;
    btnCancel.MinWidth = 60;
    btnCancel.Margin = new Thickness(12);
    btnCancel.HorizontalAlignment = HorizontalAlignment.Center;
    unigrid.Children.Add(btnCancel);
}
// Enable OK button only if the TextBox controls have numeric values.
void TextBoxOnTextChanged(object sender, TextChangedEventArgs args)
{
    double result;
    btnOk.IsEnabled =
        Double.TryParse(txtbox[(int)Side.Left].Text, out result) &&
        Double.TryParse(txtbox[(int)Side.Right].Text, out result) &&
        Double.TryParse(txtbox[(int)Side.Top].Text, out result) &&
        Double.TryParse(txtbox[(int)Side.Bottom].Text, out result);
}
// Dismiss dialog on OK click.
void OkButtonOnClick(object sender, RoutedEventArgs args)
{
    DialogResult = true;
}
    }
}
```

The *PageMarginsDialog* class is part of the PrintWithMargins project, which also includes the following file. This program demonstrates using *PrintQueue* and *PrintTicket* objects to save and transfer settings between multiple invocations of the dialog box. The *PageMarginsDialog* is displayed when you click the button labeled Page Setup.

PrintWithMargins.cs

```csharp
//-------------------------------------------------
// PrintWithMargins.cs (c) 2006 by Charles Petzold
//-------------------------------------------------
using System;
using System.Globalization;
using System.Windows;
using System.Windows.Controls;
using System.Windows.Input;
using System.Windows.Media;
using System.Printing;

namespace Petzold.PrintWithMargins
{
    public class PrintWithMargins : Window
    {
        // Private fields to save information from PrintDialog.
        PrintQueue prnqueue;
        PrintTicket prntkt;
        Thickness marginPage = new Thickness(96);

        [STAThread]
        public static void Main()
        {
            Application app = new Application();
            app.Run(new PrintWithMargins());
        }
        public PrintWithMargins()
        {
            Title = "Print with Margins";
            FontSize = 24;

            // Create StackPanel as content of window.
            StackPanel stack = new StackPanel();
            Content = stack;

            // Create button for Page Setup.
            Button btn = new Button();
            btn.Content = "Page Set_up...";
            btn.HorizontalAlignment = HorizontalAlignment.Center;
            btn.Margin = new Thickness(24);
            btn.Click += SetupOnClick;
            stack.Children.Add(btn);

            // Create Print button.
            btn = new Button();
            btn.Content = "_Print...";
            btn.HorizontalAlignment = HorizontalAlignment.Center;
            btn.Margin = new Thickness(24);
            btn.Click += PrintOnClick;
            stack.Children.Add(btn);
        }
        // Page Setup button: Invoke PageMarginsDialog.
        void SetupOnClick(object sender, RoutedEventArgs args)
```

```
        {
            // Create dialog and initialize PageMargins property.
            PageMarginsDialog dlg = new PageMarginsDialog();
            dlg.Owner = this;
            dlg.PageMargins = marginPage;

            if (dlg.ShowDialog().GetValueOrDefault())
            {
                // Save page margins from dialog box.
                marginPage = dlg.PageMargins;
            }
        }
        // Print button: Invoke PrintDialog.
        void PrintOnClick(object sender, RoutedEventArgs args)
        {
            PrintDialog dlg = new PrintDialog();

            // Set PrintQueue and PrintTicket from fields.
            if (prnqueue != null)
                dlg.PrintQueue = prnqueue;

            if (prntkt != null)
                dlg.PrintTicket = prntkt;

            if (dlg.ShowDialog().GetValueOrDefault())
            {
                // Save PrintQueue and PrintTicket from dialog box.
                prnqueue = dlg.PrintQueue;
                prntkt = dlg.PrintTicket;

                // Create DrawingVisual and open DrawingContext.
                DrawingVisual vis = new DrawingVisual();
                DrawingContext dc = vis.RenderOpen();
                Pen pn = new Pen(Brushes.Black, 1);

                // Rectangle describes page minus margins.
                Rect rectPage = new Rect(marginPage.Left, marginPage.Top,
                            dlg.PrintableAreaWidth -
                                (marginPage.Left + marginPage.Right),
                            dlg.PrintableAreaHeight -
                                (marginPage.Top + marginPage.Bottom));

                // Draw rectangle to reflect user's margins.
                dc.DrawRectangle(null, pn, rectPage);

                // Create formatted text object showing PrintableArea properties.
                FormattedText formtxt = new FormattedText(
                    String.Format("Hello, Printer! {0} x {1}",
                                dlg.PrintableAreaWidth / 96,
                                dlg.PrintableAreaHeight / 96),
                    CultureInfo.CurrentCulture,
                    FlowDirection.LeftToRight,
                    new Typeface(new FontFamily("Times New Roman"),
                                FontStyles.Italic, FontWeights.Normal,
                                FontStretches.Normal),
                    48, Brushes.Black);
```

```
                        // Get physical size of formatted text string.
                        Size sizeText = new Size(formtxt.Width, formtxt.Height);

                        // Calculate point to center text within margins.
                        Point ptText =
                            new Point(rectPage.Left +
                                          (rectPage.Width - formtxt.Width) / 2,
                                      rectPage.Top +
                                          (rectPage.Height - formtxt.Height) / 2);

                        // Draw text and surrounding rectangle.
                        dc.DrawText(formtxt, ptText);
                        dc.DrawRectangle(null, pn, new Rect(ptText, sizeText));

                        // Close DrawingContext.
                        dc.Close();

                        // Finally, print the page(s).
                        dlg.PrintVisual(vis, Title);
                    }
                }
            }
        }
```

This program prints a rectangle based on the page margins selected by the user and centers some text within the margins, also surrounded by a rectangle. The text contains the words "Hello, Printer!" followed by the dimensions of the page in inches.

Because *PrintVisual* prints an object of type *Visual*, you can put together a page by arranging elements and controls on a panel, such as a *Canvas*. You can extend this technique into graphics with the Shapes library and you can use *TextBlock* for displaying text.

Here's a program named PrintaBunchaButtons that prints a *Grid* panel with a gradient brush background and 25 buttons of various sizes arranged on it.

PrintaBunchaButtons.cs

```
//-------------------------------------------------
// PrintaBunchaButtons.cs (c) 2006 by Charles Petzold
//-------------------------------------------------
using System;
using System.Windows;
using System.Windows.Controls;
using System.Windows.Input;
using System.Windows.Media;

namespace Petzold.PrintaBunchaButtons
{
    public class PrintaBunchaButtons : Window
    {
        [STAThread]
        public static void Main()
        {
            Application app = new Application();
            app.Run(new PrintaBunchaButtons());
        }
```

```
public PrintaBunchaButtons()
{
    Title = "Print a Bunch of Buttons";
    SizeToContent = SizeToContent.WidthAndHeight;
    ResizeMode = ResizeMode.CanMinimize;

    // Create 'Print' button.
    Button btn = new Button();
    btn.FontSize = 24;
    btn.Content = "Print ...";
    btn.Padding = new Thickness(12);
    btn.Margin = new Thickness(96);
    btn.Click += PrintOnClick;
    Content = btn;
}
void PrintOnClick(object sender, RoutedEventArgs args)
{
    PrintDialog dlg = new PrintDialog();

    if ((bool)dlg.ShowDialog().GetValueOrDefault())
    {
        // Create Grid panel.
        Grid grid = new Grid();

        // Define five auto-sized rows and columns.
        for (int i = 0; i < 5; i++)
        {
            ColumnDefinition coldef = new ColumnDefinition();
            coldef.Width = GridLength.Auto;
            grid.ColumnDefinitions.Add(coldef);

            RowDefinition rowdef = new RowDefinition();
            rowdef.Height = GridLength.Auto;
            grid.RowDefinitions.Add(rowdef);
        }

        // Give the Grid a gradient brush.
        grid.Background =
            new LinearGradientBrush(Colors.Gray, Colors.White,
                            new Point(0, 0), new Point(1, 1));

        // Every program needs a bit of randomness.
        Random rand = new Random();

        // Fill the Grid with 25 buttons.
        for (int i = 0; i < 25; i++)
        {
            Button btn = new Button();
            btn.FontSize = 12 + rand.Next(8);
            btn.Content = "Button No. " + (i + 1);
            btn.HorizontalAlignment = HorizontalAlignment.Center;
            btn.VerticalAlignment = VerticalAlignment.Center;
            btn.Margin = new Thickness(6);
            grid.Children.Add(btn);
            Grid.SetRow(btn, i % 5);
            Grid.SetColumn(btn, i / 5);
        }
```

```
                          // Size the Grid.
                          grid.Measure(new Size(Double.PositiveInfinity,
                                                Double.PositiveInfinity));

                          Size sizeGrid = grid.DesiredSize;

                          // Determine point for centering Grid on page.
                          Point ptGrid =
                              new Point((dlg.PrintableAreaWidth - sizeGrid.Width) / 2,
                                        (dlg.PrintableAreaHeight - sizeGrid.Height) / 2);
                          // Layout pass.
                          grid.Arrange(new Rect(ptGrid, sizeGrid));

                          // Now print it.
                          dlg.PrintVisual(grid, Title);
                      }
                  }
              }
          }
```

To illustrate this technique most clearly, the program doesn't have some of the features of the previous program—such as defining margins or saving settings with *PrintTicket* and *PrintQueue*.

When a program prints an instance of a class derived from *UIElement*, a crucial step is required: You must subject the element to layout, which means you must call *Measure* and *Arrange* on the object. Otherwise, the object will have a zero dimension and won't show up on the page. The PrintaBunchaButtons program uses infinite dimensions when calling *Measure* on the *Grid* object; the alternative is basing the dimensions on the size of the page. When calling *Arrange*, the program obtains the size of the *Grid* from its *DesiredSize* property, calculates a point that puts the *Grid* in the center of the page, and then calls *Arrange* with that point and size. Now the *Grid* is ready to pass to *PrintVisual*.

You could print a multi-page document by making multiple calls to *PrintVisual*, but each page would be considered a different print job. To better print a multi-page document, a program calls the *PrintDocument* method defined by *PrintDialog*. The arguments to *PrintDocument* are an instance of a class derived from *DocumentPaginator* and a text string for the print queue describing the document.

DocumentPaginator is an abstract class defined in *System.Windows.Documents*. You must define a class that inherits from *DocumentPaginator* and you must override several properties and methods that *DocumentPaginator* defines as abstract. One of these methods is *GetPage*, which returns an object of type *DocumentPage*. You can easily create a *DocumentPage* object from a *Visual*, which means that multi-page printing isn't all that different from single-page printing. Each page of the document is a *Visual*.

Your *DocumentPaginator* derivative must override the Boolean read-only *IsPageCountValid* property, the read-only *PageCount* property, a read-write *PageSize* property, the *GetPage* method (which has a zero-based page number argument and returns an object of type *DocumentPage*), and the *Source* property, which can return *null*.

A *DocumentPaginator* derivative probably also defines some properties on its own. For example, suppose you want to write a program that prints a banner. Banner programs once printed on continuous stretches of fanfold paper, but these days banner printer programs print one big letter per page. The class that derives from *DocumentPaginator* probably needs a property of type *Text*, which a program sets to something like "Happy Birthday to the Greatest Mom in All the World, and Probably Other Planets as Well." The *DocumentPaginator* derivative should also have a property to specify the font. An approach that doesn't require a bunch of properties involves consolidating most of the font information into an object of type *Typeface*.

However, if you want to keep your *DocumentPaginator* derivative a bit simpler, you can probably dispense with the custom properties and instead just define a constructor that accepts this information. The *DocumentPaginator* object is usually not around long enough to make a difference in which approach you use. You'll probably create the object in response to a click of Print button in *PrintDialog*, and abandon it after calling *PrintDocument*.

Here's a class named *BannerDocumentPaginator* that defines two properties named *Text* and *Typeface*.

```
BannerDocumentPaginator.cs
//-------------------------------------------------------
// BannerDocumentPaginator.cs (c) 2006 by Charles Petzold
//-------------------------------------------------------
using System;
using System.Globalization;
using System.Windows;
using System.Windows.Controls;
using System.Windows.Documents;
using System.Windows.Media;

namespace Petzold.PrintBanner
{
    public class BannerDocumentPaginator : DocumentPaginator
    {
        string txt = "";
        Typeface face = new Typeface("");
        Size sizePage;
        Size sizeMax = new Size(0, 0);

        // Public properties specific to this DocumentPaginator.
        public string Text
        {
            set { txt = value; }
            get { return txt; }
        }
        public Typeface Typeface
        {
            set { face = value; }
            get { return face; }
        }
    }
```

```
    // Private function to create FormattedText object.
    FormattedText GetFormattedText(char ch, Typeface face, double em)
    {
        return new FormattedText(ch.ToString(), CultureInfo.CurrentCulture,
                        FlowDirection.LeftToRight, face, em, Brushes.Black);
    }
    // Necessary overrides.
    public override bool IsPageCountValid
    {
        get
        {
            // Determine maximum size of characters based on em size of 100.
            foreach (char ch in txt)
            {
                FormattedText formtxt = GetFormattedText(ch, face, 100);
                sizeMax.Width = Math.Max(sizeMax.Width, formtxt.Width);
                sizeMax.Height = Math.Max(sizeMax.Height, formtxt.Height);
            }
            return true;
        }
    }
    public override int PageCount
    {
        get { return txt == null ? 0 : txt.Length; }
    }
    public override Size PageSize
    {
        set { sizePage = value; }
        get { return sizePage; }
    }
    public override DocumentPage GetPage(int numPage)
    {
        DrawingVisual vis = new DrawingVisual();
        DrawingContext dc = vis.RenderOpen();

        // Assume half-inch margins when calculating em size factor.
        double factor = Math.Min((PageSize.Width - 96) / sizeMax.Width,
                            (PageSize.Height - 96) / sizeMax.Height);

        FormattedText formtxt = GetFormattedText(txt[numPage], face,
                                        factor * 100);
        // Find point to center character in page.
        Point ptText = new Point((PageSize.Width - formtxt.Width) / 2,
                            (PageSize.Height - formtxt.Height) / 2);

        dc.DrawText(formtxt, ptText);
        dc.Close();

        return new DocumentPage(vis);
    }
    public override IDocumentPaginatorSource Source
    {
        get { return null; }
    }
  }
}
```

As the name *DocumentPaginator* suggests, the class needs to paginate a document. It must determine how many pages the document has and what goes on each page. For this paginator, the page count is simple: It's the number of characters in the text string. However, this paginator must also determine how large these characters should be. This job requires constructing objects of type *FormattedText* for each letter to determine the height of the letters and the maximum character width.

If you define a constructor that has arguments with all the information the class needs to perform a pagination, the constructor could also contain the pagination logic. Otherwise, if you define properties, you must find another place for the pagination to occur. It seems reasonable to me that the *IsPageCountValid* property is a good spot because that property is called before anything else. In its *IsPageCountValid* property, therefore, *BannerDocumentPaginator* creates *FormattedText* objects for every character in the text string based on the *Typeface* property and an em size of 100, and saves the largest size it encounters.

The *GetPage* method is responsible for returning objects of type *DocumentPage*, which can be created from an object of type *Visual*. The method creates a *DrawingVisual*, opens a *DrawingContext*, and calculates a multiplicative factor based on the largest character size and the size of the page minus half-inch margins. The method constructs a new *FormattedText* object and centers it on the page with a call to *DrawText*. This *DrawingVisual* is passed to the *DocumentPage* constructor and *GetPage* returns the resultant object.

The user interface for the banner program is fairly straightforward:

PrintBanner.cs

```
//-------------------------------------------
// PrintBanner.cs (c) 2006 by Charles Petzold
//-------------------------------------------
using System;
using System.Printing;
using System.Windows;
using System.Windows.Controls;
using System.Windows.Input;
using System.Windows.Media;

namespace Petzold.PrintBanner
{
    public class PrintBanner : Window
    {
        TextBox txtbox;

        [STAThread]
        public static void Main()
        {
            Application app = new Application();
            app.Run(new PrintBanner());
        }
        public PrintBanner()
```

```
        {
            Title = "Print Banner";
            SizeToContent = SizeToContent.WidthAndHeight;

            // Make StackPanel content of window.
            StackPanel stack = new StackPanel();
            Content = stack;

            // Create TextBox.
            txtbox = new TextBox();
            txtbox.Width = 250;
            txtbox.Margin = new Thickness(12);
            stack.Children.Add(txtbox);

            // Create Button.
            Button btn = new Button();
            btn.Content = "_Print...";
            btn.Margin = new Thickness(12);
            btn.Click += PrintOnClick;
            btn.HorizontalAlignment = HorizontalAlignment.Center;
            stack.Children.Add(btn);

            txtbox.Focus();
        }
        void PrintOnClick(object sender, RoutedEventArgs args)
        {
            PrintDialog dlg = new PrintDialog();

            if (dlg.ShowDialog().GetValueOrDefault())
            {
                // Make sure orientation is Portrait.
                PrintTicket prntkt = dlg.PrintTicket;
                prntkt.PageOrientation = PageOrientation.Portrait;
                dlg.PrintTicket = prntkt;

                // Create new BannerDocumentPaginator object.
                BannerDocumentPaginator paginator = new BannerDocumentPaginator();

                // Set Text property from TextBox.
                paginator.Text = txtbox.Text;

                // Give it a PageSize property based on the paper dimensions.
                paginator.PageSize = new Size(dlg.PrintableAreaWidth,
                                              dlg.PrintableAreaHeight);

                // Call PrintDocument to print the document.
                dlg.PrintDocument(paginator, "Banner: " + txtbox.Text);
            }
        }
    }
}
```

A banner program really works best with a Portrait page orientation, so even if the user selects Landscape, the *PrintOnClick* method changes it back to Portrait. The method then creates an object of type *BannerDocumentPaginator* and sets the *Text* and *PageSize* properties. The method concludes by passing the initialized *BannerDocumentPaginator* object to *PrintDocument*, which does the rest.

Notice that the PrintBanner program doesn't give *BannerDocumentPaginator* a custom *Typeface* object. What this program really needs is a font dialog, but unfortunately, the first version of the Windows Presentation Foundation doesn't include one. That leaves me to do the job. I really didn't want to write a font dialog, but I had to.

Font dialogs are generally built from combo boxes with list portions that are always visible. Unfortunately, the *ComboBox* class in the first version of the Windows Presentation Foundation doesn't support this mode, and my first attempt to mimic such a combo box with an *TextBox* and a *ListBox* didn't work very well. I wanted input focus to always stay with the *TextBox*, but I found it difficult to prevent the *ListBox* from getting input focus. I then realized that the job must really begin with a simple non-focusable control that looked and acted like a *ListBox* that I called *Lister*. This is the first file of the ChooseFont project.

```
Lister.cs
//---------------------------------------
// Lister.cs (c) 2006 by Charles Petzold
//---------------------------------------
using System;
using System.Collections;
using System.Windows;
using System.Windows.Controls;
using System.Windows.Input;
using System.Windows.Media;

namespace Petzold.ChooseFont
{
    class Lister : ContentControl
    {
        ScrollViewer scroll;
        StackPanel stack;
        ArrayList list = new ArrayList();
        int indexSelected = -1;

        // Public event.
        public event EventHandler SelectionChanged;

        // Constructor.
        public Lister()
        {
            Focusable = false;

            // Make Border the content of the ContentControl.
            Border bord = new Border();
            bord.BorderThickness = new Thickness(1);
            bord.BorderBrush = SystemColors.ActiveBorderBrush;
            bord.Background = SystemColors.WindowBrush;
            Content = bord;
```

```
        // Make ScrollViewer the child of the border.
        scroll = new ScrollViewer();
        scroll.Focusable = false;
        scroll.Padding = new Thickness(2, 0, 0, 0);
        bord.Child = scroll;

        // Make StackPanel the content of the ScrollViewer.
        stack = new StackPanel();
        scroll.Content = stack;

        // Install a handler for the mouse left button down.
        AddHandler(TextBlock.MouseLeftButtonDownEvent,
            new MouseButtonEventHandler(TextBlockOnMouseLeftButtonDown));

        Loaded += OnLoaded;
    }
    void OnLoaded(object sender, RoutedEventArgs args)
    {
        // Scroll the selected item into view when Lister is first displayed.
        ScrollIntoView();
    }

    // Public methods to add, insert, etc, items in Lister.
    public void Add(object obj)
    {
        list.Add(obj);
        TextBlock txtblk = new TextBlock();
        txtblk.Text = obj.ToString();
        stack.Children.Add(txtblk);
    }
    public void Insert(int index, object obj)
    {
        list.Insert(index, obj);
        TextBlock txtblk = new TextBlock();
        txtblk.Text = obj.ToString();
        stack.Children.Insert(index, txtblk);
    }
    public void Clear()
    {
        SelectedIndex = -1;
        stack.Children.Clear();
        list.Clear();
    }
    public bool Contains(object obj)
    {
        return list.Contains(obj);
    }
    public int Count
    {
        get { return list.Count; }
    }

    // This method is called to select an item based on a typed letter.
    public void GoToLetter(char ch)
```

```
    {
        int offset = SelectedIndex + 1;

        for (int i = 0; i < Count; i++)
        {
            int index = (i + offset) % Count;

            if (Char.ToUpper(ch) == Char.ToUpper(list[index].ToString()[0]))
            {
                SelectedIndex = index;
                break;
            }
        }
    }

    // SelectedIndex property is responsible for displaying selection bar.
    public int SelectedIndex
    {
        set
        {
            if (value < -1 || value >= Count)
                throw new ArgumentOutOfRangeException("SelectedIndex");
            if (value == indexSelected)
                return;

            if (indexSelected != -1)
            {
                TextBlock txtblk = stack.Children[indexSelected] as TextBlock;
                txtblk.Background = SystemColors.WindowBrush;
                txtblk.Foreground = SystemColors.WindowTextBrush;
            }

            indexSelected = value;

            if (indexSelected > -1)
            {
                TextBlock txtblk = stack.Children[indexSelected] as TextBlock;
                txtblk.Background = SystemColors.HighlightBrush;
                txtblk.Foreground = SystemColors.HighlightTextBrush;
            }
            ScrollIntoView();

            // Trigger SelectionChanged event.
            OnSelectionChanged(EventArgs.Empty);
        }
        get
        {
            return indexSelected;
        }
    }
    // SelectedItem property makes use of SelectedIndex.
    public object SelectedItem
    {
        set
        {
            SelectedIndex = list.IndexOf(value);
        }
```

```csharp
        get
        {
            if (SelectedIndex > -1)
                return list[SelectedIndex];

            return null;
        }
    }

    // Public methods to page up and down through the list.
    public void PageUp()
    {
        if (SelectedIndex == -1 || Count == 0)
            return;
        int index = SelectedIndex - (int)(Count *
                        scroll.ViewportHeight / scroll.ExtentHeight);
        if (index < 0)
            index = 0;

        SelectedIndex = index;
    }
    public void PageDown()
    {
        if (SelectedIndex == -1 || Count == 0)
            return;

        int index = SelectedIndex + (int)(Count *
                        scroll.ViewportHeight / scroll.ExtentHeight);
        if (index > Count - 1)
            index = Count - 1;
        SelectedIndex = index;
    }

    // Private method to scroll selected item into view.
    void ScrollIntoView()
    {
        if (Count == 0 || SelectedIndex == -1 ||
                        scroll.ViewportHeight > scroll.ExtentHeight)
            return;

        double heightPerItem = scroll.ExtentHeight / Count;
        double offsetItemTop = SelectedIndex * heightPerItem;
        double offsetItemBot = (SelectedIndex + 1) * heightPerItem;

        if (offsetItemTop < scroll.VerticalOffset)
            scroll.ScrollToVerticalOffset(offsetItemTop);

        else if (offsetItemBot > scroll.VerticalOffset + scroll.ViewportHeight)
            scroll.ScrollToVerticalOffset(scroll.VerticalOffset +
                offsetItemBot - scroll.VerticalOffset - scroll.ViewportHeight);
    }

    // Event handler and trigger.
    void TextBlockOnMouseLeftButtonDown(object sender,
                                MouseButtonEventArgs args)
```

```
        {
            if (args.Source is TextBlock)
                SelectedIndex = stack.Children.IndexOf(args.Source as TextBlock);
        }

        protected virtual void OnSelectionChanged(EventArgs args)
        {
            if (SelectionChanged != null)
                SelectionChanged(this, args);
        }
    }
}
```

Lister is a *ContentControl* with a *Border* containing a *ScrollViewer* containing a *StackPanel* containing multiple *TextBlock* items. Near the bottom of the file is a *TextBlockOnMouseLeft-ButtonDown* method that sets the *SelectedIndex* property to the index of the clicked *TextBlock*. The *SelectedIndex* property is responsible for maintaining the foreground and background colors of the *TextBlock* items to indicate which item is currently selected, and to trigger the *SelectionChanged* event by calling *OnSelectionChanged*.

The keyboard interface for changing the selected item is handled external to the *Lister* control in the next class. The *TextBoxWithLister* class also derives from *ContentControl* and contains a *DockPanel* with a *TextBox* control and a *Lister* element. The class overrides the *OnPreviewKeyDown* method to change the selected item based on the cursor movement keys.

TextBoxWithLister.cs
```
//------------------------------------------------
// TextBoxWithLister.cs (c) 2006 by Charles Petzold
//------------------------------------------------
using System;
using System.Collections;
using System.Windows;
using System.Windows.Controls;
using System.Windows.Input;
using System.Windows.Media;

namespace Petzold.ChooseFont
{
    class TextBoxWithLister : ContentControl
    {
        TextBox txtbox;
        Lister lister;
        bool isReadOnly;

        // Public events.
        public event EventHandler SelectionChanged;
        public event TextChangedEventHandler TextChanged;

        // Constructor.
```

```
public TextBoxWithLister()
{
    // Create DockPanel as content of control.
    DockPanel dock = new DockPanel();
    Content = dock;

    // TextBox is docked at top.
    txtbox = new TextBox();
    txtbox.TextChanged += TextBoxOnTextChanged;
    dock.Children.Add(txtbox);
    DockPanel.SetDock(txtbox, Dock.Top);

    // Lister fills remainder of DockPanel.
    lister = new Lister();
    lister.SelectionChanged += ListerOnSelectionChanged;
    dock.Children.Add(lister);
}
// Public properties involving the TextBox item.
public string Text
{
    get { return txtbox.Text; }
    set { txtbox.Text = value; }
}
public bool IsReadOnly
{
    set { isReadOnly = value; }
    get { return isReadOnly; }
}

// Other public properties interface with Lister element.
public object SelectedItem
{
    set
    {
        lister.SelectedItem = value;

        if (lister.SelectedItem != null)
            txtbox.Text = lister.SelectedItem.ToString();
        else
            txtbox.Text = "";
    }
    get
    {
        return lister.SelectedItem;
    }
}
public int SelectedIndex
{
    set
    {
        lister.SelectedIndex = value;
        if (lister.SelectedIndex == -1)
            txtbox.Text = "";
        else
            txtbox.Text = lister.SelectedItem.ToString();
```

```
        }
        get
        {
            return lister.SelectedIndex;
        }
    }
    public void Add(object obj)
    {
        lister.Add(obj);
    }
    public void Insert(int index, object obj)
    {
        lister.Insert(index, obj);
    }
    public void Clear()
    {
        lister.Clear();
    }
    public bool Contains(object obj)
    {
        return lister.Contains(obj);
    }


    // On a mouse click, set the keyboard focus.
    protected override void OnMouseDown(MouseButtonEventArgs args)
    {
        base.OnMouseDown(args);
        Focus();
    }
    // When the keyboard focus comes, pass it to the TextBox.
    protected override void OnGotKeyboardFocus(
                                    KeyboardFocusChangedEventArgs args)
    {
        base.OnGotKeyboardFocus(args);

        if (args.NewFocus == this)
        {
            txtbox.Focus();
            if (SelectedIndex == -1 && lister.Count > 0)
                SelectedIndex = 0;
        }
    }


    // When a letter key is typed, pass it to GoToLetter method of Lister.
    protected override void OnPreviewTextInput(TextCompositionEventArgs args)
    {
        base.OnPreviewTextInput(args);

        if (IsReadOnly)
        {
            lister.GoToLetter(args.Text[0]);
            args.Handled = true;
        }
    }
```

```
// Handling of cursor movement keys to change selected item.
protected override void OnPreviewKeyDown(KeyEventArgs args)
{
    base.OnKeyDown(args);

    if (SelectedIndex == -1)
        return;
    switch (args.Key)
    {
        case Key.Home:
            if (lister.Count > 0)
                SelectedIndex = 0;
            break;

        case Key.End:
            if (lister.Count > 0)
                SelectedIndex = lister.Count - 1;
            break;

        case Key.Up:
            if (SelectedIndex > 0)
                SelectedIndex--;
            break;

        case Key.Down:
            if (SelectedIndex < lister.Count - 1)
                SelectedIndex++;
            break;

        case Key.PageUp:
            lister.PageUp();
            break;

        case Key.PageDown:
            lister.PageDown();
            break;

        default:
            return;
    }
    args.Handled = true;
}
// Event handlers and triggers.
void ListerOnSelectionChanged(object sender, EventArgs args)
{
    if (SelectedIndex == -1)
        txtbox.Text = "";
    else
        txtbox.Text = lister.SelectedItem.ToString();

    OnSelectionChanged(args);
}
void TextBoxOnTextChanged(object sender, TextChangedEventArgs args)
```

```
        {
            if (TextChanged != null)
                TextChanged(this, args);
        }
        protected virtual void OnSelectionChanged(EventArgs args)
        {
            if (SelectionChanged != null)
                SelectionChanged(this, args);
        }
    }
}
```

This class has two modes that are governed by the *IsReadOnly* property. If the setting is *false*, the user is free to type anything into the *TextBox*, and the program that makes use of this control obtains the user's selection from this *TextBox*. This is the mode that the *FontDialog* uses for the font size. The list part of the control should present a bunch of common font sizes, but the user should be allowed to enter anything else.

If *IsReadOnly* is *true*, the *TextBox* always displays the selected item and nothing can be manually entered. Any press of a letter on the keyboard is passed to the *GoToLetter* method of *Lister*, which attempts to select the next item beginning with that letter. This mode is good for the font family, font style, font weight, and font stretch boxes that *FontDialog* displays. To keep this dialog box as simple as possible, I decided that the user shouldn't be able to select or enter anything that's not actually available.

Despite the setting of the *IsReadOnly* property, the *TextBox* always maintains the keyboard input focus. The control is notified through an event handler when the user has clicked an item in the list section, but the list section doesn't get the input focus from that action. The *OnPreviewKeyDown* override provides much of the keyboard interface for the control by handling all the cursor movement keys.

The *FontDialog* class itself has five *TextBoxWithLister* controls (to display the font families, styles, weights, stretches, and sizes), five labels identifying those controls, another *Label* for displaying sample text, and OK and Cancel buttons, but the real complexity comes from the dynamic content of the controls.

The first *TextBoxWithLister* control displays all the available font families. These are obtained from the static *Fonts.SystemFontFamilies* method and this control is filled with those families toward the end of the constructor. However, every font family has different available font styles, weights, and stretches. Whenever the user selects a different font family, the *FamilyOnSelectionChanged* handler in the *FontDialog* class must clear out three *TextBoxWithLister* controls and fill them up again based on the *FamilyTypeface* objects available from the *FamilyTypefaces* property of the selected *FontFamily* object.

FontDialog defines just two public properties: A *Typeface* property encapsulates the *FontFamily*, *FontStyle*, *FontWeight*, and *FontStretch* properties, and the *FaceSize* property (of type *double*) is for the size of the font. (I couldn't call this latter property *FontSize* because *FontDialog* itself inherits a *FontSize* property that governs the size of the font used in controls within the dialog box!)

FontDialog.cs

```
//-------------------------------------------
// FontDialog.cs (c) 2006 by Charles Petzold
//-------------------------------------------
using System;
using System.Collections.Generic;
using System.Windows;
using System.Windows.Controls;
using System.Windows.Input;
using System.Windows.Media;

namespace Petzold.ChooseFont
{
    public class FontDialog : Window
    {
        TextBoxWithLister boxFamily, boxStyle, boxWeight, boxStretch, boxSize;
        Label lblDisplay;
        bool isUpdateSuppressed = true;
        // Public properties.

        public Typeface Typeface
        {
            set
            {
                if (boxFamily.Contains(value.FontFamily))
                    boxFamily.SelectedItem = value.FontFamily;
                else
                    boxFamily.SelectedIndex = 0;

                if (boxStyle.Contains(value.Style))
                    boxStyle.SelectedItem = value.Style;
                else
                    boxStyle.SelectedIndex = 0;

                if (boxWeight.Contains(value.Weight))
                    boxWeight.SelectedItem = value.Weight;
                else
                    boxWeight.SelectedIndex = 0;

                if (boxStretch.Contains(value.Stretch))
                    boxStretch.SelectedItem = value.Stretch;
                else
                    boxStretch.SelectedIndex = 0;
            }
            get
            {
                return new Typeface((FontFamily)boxFamily.SelectedItem,
                                    (FontStyle)boxStyle.SelectedItem,
                                    (FontWeight)boxWeight.SelectedItem,
                                    (FontStretch)boxStretch.SelectedItem);
            }
        }
    }
```

```csharp
    public double FaceSize
    {
        set
        {
            double size = 0.75 * value;
            boxSize.Text = size.ToString();

            if (!boxSize.Contains(size))
                boxSize.Insert(0, size);

            boxSize.SelectedItem = size;
        }
        get
        {
            double size;

            if (!Double.TryParse(boxSize.Text, out size))
                size = 8.25;

            return size / 0.75;
        }
    }

    // Constructor.
    public FontDialog()
    {
        Title = "Font";
        ShowInTaskbar = false;
        WindowStyle = WindowStyle.ToolWindow;
        WindowStartupLocation = WindowStartupLocation.CenterOwner;
        SizeToContent = SizeToContent.WidthAndHeight;
        ResizeMode = ResizeMode.NoResize;

        // Create three-row Grid as content of window.
        Grid gridMain = new Grid();
        Content = gridMain;

        // This row is for the TextBoxWithLister controls.
        RowDefinition rowdef = new RowDefinition();
        rowdef.Height = new GridLength(200, GridUnitType.Pixel);
        gridMain.RowDefinitions.Add(rowdef);

        // This row is for the sample text.
        rowdef = new RowDefinition();
        rowdef.Height = new GridLength(150, GridUnitType.Pixel);
        gridMain.RowDefinitions.Add(rowdef);

        // This row is for the buttons.
        rowdef = new RowDefinition();
        rowdef.Height = GridLength.Auto;
        gridMain.RowDefinitions.Add(rowdef);

        // One column in main Grid.
        ColumnDefinition coldef = new ColumnDefinition();
        coldef.Width = new GridLength(650, GridUnitType.Pixel);
        gridMain.ColumnDefinitions.Add(coldef);
```

```
// Create two-row, five-column Grid for TextBoxWithLister controls.
Grid gridBoxes = new Grid();
gridMain.Children.Add(gridBoxes);

// This row is for the labels.
rowdef = new RowDefinition();
rowdef.Height = GridLength.Auto;
gridBoxes.RowDefinitions.Add(rowdef);

// This row is for the EditBoxWithLister controls.
rowdef = new RowDefinition();
rowdef.Height = new GridLength(100, GridUnitType.Star);
gridBoxes.RowDefinitions.Add(rowdef);

// First column is FontFamily.
coldef = new ColumnDefinition();
coldef.Width = new GridLength(175, GridUnitType.Star);
gridBoxes.ColumnDefinitions.Add(coldef);

// Second column is FontStyle.
coldef = new ColumnDefinition();
coldef.Width = new GridLength(100, GridUnitType.Star);
gridBoxes.ColumnDefinitions.Add(coldef);

// Third column is FontWeight.
coldef = new ColumnDefinition();
coldef.Width = new GridLength(100, GridUnitType.Star);
gridBoxes.ColumnDefinitions.Add(coldef);

// Fourth column is FontStretch.
coldef = new ColumnDefinition();
coldef.Width = new GridLength(100, GridUnitType.Star);
gridBoxes.ColumnDefinitions.Add(coldef);

// Fifth column is Size.
coldef = new ColumnDefinition();
coldef.Width = new GridLength(75, GridUnitType.Star);
gridBoxes.ColumnDefinitions.Add(coldef);

// Create FontFamily labels and TextBoxWithLister controls.
Label lbl = new Label();
lbl.Content = "Font Family";
lbl.Margin = new Thickness(12, 12, 12, 0);
gridBoxes.Children.Add(lbl);
Grid.SetRow(lbl, 0);
Grid.SetColumn(lbl, 0);

boxFamily = new TextBoxWithLister();
boxFamily.IsReadOnly = true;
boxFamily.Margin = new Thickness(12, 0, 12, 12);
gridBoxes.Children.Add(boxFamily);
Grid.SetRow(boxFamily, 1);
Grid.SetColumn(boxFamily, 0);

// Create FontStyle labels and TextBoxWithLister controls.
lbl = new Label();
lbl.Content = "Style";
```

```
lbl.Margin = new Thickness(12, 12, 12, 0);
gridBoxes.Children.Add(lbl);
Grid.SetRow(lbl, 0);
Grid.SetColumn(lbl, 1);

boxStyle = new TextBoxWithLister();
boxStyle.IsReadOnly = true;
boxStyle.Margin = new Thickness(12, 0, 12, 12);
gridBoxes.Children.Add(boxStyle);
Grid.SetRow(boxStyle, 1);
Grid.SetColumn(boxStyle, 1);

// Create FontWeight labels and TextBoxWithLister controls.
lbl = new Label();
lbl.Content = "Weight";
lbl.Margin = new Thickness(12, 12, 12, 0);
gridBoxes.Children.Add(lbl);
Grid.SetRow(lbl, 0);
Grid.SetColumn(lbl, 2);

boxWeight = new TextBoxWithLister();
boxWeight.IsReadOnly = true;
boxWeight.Margin = new Thickness(12, 0, 12, 12);
gridBoxes.Children.Add(boxWeight);
Grid.SetRow(boxWeight, 1);
Grid.SetColumn(boxWeight, 2);

// Create FontStretch labels and TextBoxWithLister controls.
lbl = new Label();
lbl.Content = "Stretch";
lbl.Margin = new Thickness(12, 12, 12, 0);
gridBoxes.Children.Add(lbl);
Grid.SetRow(lbl, 0);
Grid.SetColumn(lbl, 3);

boxStretch = new TextBoxWithLister();
boxStretch.IsReadOnly = true;
boxStretch.Margin = new Thickness(12, 0, 12, 12);
gridBoxes.Children.Add(boxStretch);
Grid.SetRow(boxStretch, 1);
Grid.SetColumn(boxStretch, 3);

// Create Size labels and TextBoxWithLister controls.
lbl = new Label();
lbl.Content = "Size";
lbl.Margin = new Thickness(12, 12, 12, 0);
gridBoxes.Children.Add(lbl);
Grid.SetRow(lbl, 0);
Grid.SetColumn(lbl, 4);

boxSize = new TextBoxWithLister();
boxSize.Margin = new Thickness(12, 0, 12, 12);
gridBoxes.Children.Add(boxSize);
Grid.SetRow(boxSize, 1);
Grid.SetColumn(boxSize, 4);
```

```
// Create Label to display sample text.
lblDisplay = new Label();
lblDisplay.Content = "AaBbCc XxYzZz 012345";
lblDisplay.HorizontalContentAlignment = HorizontalAlignment.Center;
lblDisplay.VerticalContentAlignment = VerticalAlignment.Center;
gridMain.Children.Add(lblDisplay);
Grid.SetRow(lblDisplay, 1);

// Create five-column Grid for Buttons.
Grid gridButtons = new Grid();
gridMain.Children.Add(gridButtons);
Grid.SetRow(gridButtons, 2);

for (int i = 0; i < 5; i++)
    gridButtons.ColumnDefinitions.Add(new ColumnDefinition());

// OK button.
Button btn = new Button();
btn.Content = "OK";
btn.IsDefault = true;
btn.HorizontalAlignment = HorizontalAlignment.Center;
btn.MinWidth = 60;
btn.Margin = new Thickness(12);
btn.Click += OkOnClick;
gridButtons.Children.Add(btn);
Grid.SetColumn(btn, 1);

// Cancel button.
btn = new Button();
btn.Content = "Cancel";
btn.IsCancel = true;
btn.HorizontalAlignment = HorizontalAlignment.Center;
btn.MinWidth = 60;
btn.Margin = new Thickness(12);
gridButtons.Children.Add(btn);
Grid.SetColumn(btn, 3);

// Initialize FontFamily box with system font families.
foreach (FontFamily fam in Fonts.SystemFontFamilies)
        boxFamily.Add(fam);

// Initialize FontSize box.
double[] ptsizes = new double[] { 8, 9, 10, 11, 12, 14, 16, 18,
                                20, 22, 24, 26, 28, 36, 48, 72 };
foreach (double ptsize in ptsizes)
    boxSize.Add(ptsize);

// Set event handlers.
boxFamily.SelectionChanged += FamilyOnSelectionChanged;
boxStyle.SelectionChanged += StyleOnSelectionChanged;
boxWeight.SelectionChanged += StyleOnSelectionChanged;
boxStretch.SelectionChanged += StyleOnSelectionChanged;
boxSize.TextChanged += SizeOnTextChanged;
```

```
                // Initialize selected values based on window properties.
                // (These will probably be overridden when properties are set.)
                Typeface = new Typeface(FontFamily, FontStyle,
                                        FontWeight, FontStretch);
                FaceSize = FontSize;

                // Set keyboard focus.
                boxFamily.Focus();
                // Allow updates to the sample text.
                isUpdateSuppressed = false;
                UpdateSample();
            }

            // Event handler for SelectionChanged in FontFamily box.
            void FamilyOnSelectionChanged(object sender, EventArgs args)
            {
                // Get selected FontFamily.
                FontFamily fntfam = (FontFamily)boxFamily.SelectedItem;

                // Save previous Style, Weight, Stretch.
                // These should only be null when this method is called for the
                //   first time.
                FontStyle? fntstyPrevious = (FontStyle?)boxStyle.SelectedItem;
                FontWeight? fntwtPrevious = (FontWeight?) boxWeight.SelectedItem;
                FontStretch? fntstrPrevious = (FontStretch?)boxStretch.SelectedItem;

                // Turn off Sample display.
                isUpdateSuppressed = true;

                // Clear Style, Weight, and Stretch boxes.
                boxStyle.Clear();
                boxWeight.Clear();
                boxStretch.Clear();

                // Loop through typefaces in selected FontFamily.
                foreach (FamilyTypeface ftf in fntfam.FamilyTypefaces)
                {
                    // Put Style in boxStyle (Normal always at top).
                    if (!boxStyle.Contains(ftf.Style))
                    {
                        if (ftf.Style == FontStyles.Normal)
                            boxStyle.Insert(0, ftf.Style);
                        else
                            boxStyle.Add(ftf.Style);
                    }
                    // Put Weight in boxWeight (Normal always at top).
                    if (!boxWeight.Contains(ftf.Weight))
                    {
                        if (ftf.Weight == FontWeights.Normal)
                            boxWeight.Insert(0, ftf.Weight);
                        else
                            boxWeight.Add(ftf.Weight);
                    }
                    // Put Stretch in boxStretch (Normal always at top).
                    if (!boxStretch.Contains(ftf.Stretch))
```

```
            {
                if (ftf.Stretch == FontStretches.Normal)
                    boxStretch.Insert(0, ftf.Stretch);
                else
                    boxStretch.Add(ftf.Stretch);
            }
        }

        // Set selected item in boxStyle.
        if (boxStyle.Contains(fntstyPrevious))
            boxStyle.SelectedItem = fntstyPrevious;
        else
            boxStyle.SelectedIndex = 0;

        // Set selected item in boxWeight.
        if (boxWeight.Contains(fntwtPrevious))
            boxWeight.SelectedItem = fntwtPrevious;
        else
            boxWeight.SelectedIndex = 0;

        // Set selected item in boxStretch.
        if (boxStretch.Contains(fntstrPrevious))
            boxStretch.SelectedItem = fntstrPrevious;
        else
            boxStretch.SelectedIndex = 0;

        // Resume Sample update and update the Sample.
        isUpdateSuppressed = false;
        UpdateSample();
    }

    // Event handler for SelectionChanged in Style, Weight, Stretch boxes.
    void StyleOnSelectionChanged(object sender, EventArgs args)
    {
        UpdateSample();
    }

    // Event handler for TextChanged in Size box.
    void SizeOnTextChanged(object sender, TextChangedEventArgs args)
    {
        UpdateSample();
    }

    // Update the Sample text.
    void UpdateSample()
    {
        if (isUpdateSuppressed)
            return;
        lblDisplay.FontFamily = (FontFamily)boxFamily.SelectedItem;
        lblDisplay.FontStyle = (FontStyle)boxStyle.SelectedItem;
        lblDisplay.FontWeight = (FontWeight)boxWeight.SelectedItem;
        lblDisplay.FontStretch = (FontStretch)boxStretch.SelectedItem;

        double size;
```

```
                    if (!Double.TryParse(boxSize.Text, out size))
                        size = 8.25;
                    lblDisplay.FontSize = size / 0.75;
                }

                // OK button terminates dialog box.
                void OkOnClick(object sender, RoutedEventArgs args)
                {
                    DialogResult = true;
                }
            }
        }
    }
```

To test out the *FontDialog*, this *ChooseFont* program simply creates a *Button* in the middle of its client area and invokes the dialog whenever the button is clicked. If the user clicks OK, the program sets the window's font properties to those from the dialog box and, of course, the button inherits those properties.

ChooseFont.cs

```
//-------------------------------------------
// ChooseFont.cs (c) 2006 by Charles Petzold
//-------------------------------------------
using System;
using System.Windows;
using System.Windows.Controls;
using System.Windows.Input;
using System.Windows.Media;

namespace Petzold.ChooseFont
{
    public class ChooseFont : Window
    {
        [STAThread]
        public static void Main()
        {
            Application app = new Application();
            app.Run(new ChooseFont());
        }
        public ChooseFont()
        {
            Title = "Choose Font";
            Button btn = new Button();
            btn.Content = Title;
            btn.HorizontalAlignment = HorizontalAlignment.Center;
            btn.VerticalAlignment = VerticalAlignment.Center;
            btn.Click += ButtonOnClick;
            Content = btn;
        }
        void ButtonOnClick(object sender, RoutedEventArgs args)
        {
            FontDialog dlg = new FontDialog();
            dlg.Owner = this;
```

```
                    // Set FontDialog properties from Window.
                    dlg.Typeface = new Typeface(FontFamily, FontStyle,
                                                FontWeight, FontStretch);
                    dlg.FaceSize = FontSize;

                    if (dlg.ShowDialog().GetValueOrDefault())
                    {
                        // Set Window properties from FontDialog.
                        FontFamily = dlg.Typeface.FontFamily;
                        FontStyle = dlg.Typeface.Style;
                        FontWeight = dlg.Typeface.Weight;
                        FontStretch = dlg.Typeface.Stretch;
                        FontSize = dlg.FaceSize;
                    }
                }
            }
        }
    }
```

Without further ado, here is a better version of the banner printer program. This project requires links to the BannerDocumentPaginator.cs file and the three files used for the *Font-Dialog* class: Lister.cs, TextBoxWithLister.cs, and FontDialog.cs. This new version of the program has a Font button that displays the *FontDialog*. The typeface you specify there is just transferred to the *BannerDocumentPaginator*. The size you request is ignored, of course, because the *BannerDocumentPaginator* calculates its own font size based on the size of the page.

PrintBetterBanner.cs

```
//----------------------------------------------------
// PrintBetterBanner.cs (c) 2006 by Charles Petzold
//----------------------------------------------------
using Petzold.ChooseFont;
using Petzold.PrintBanner;
using System;
using System.Printing;
using System.Windows;
using System.Windows.Controls;
using System.Windows.Input;
using System.Windows.Media;

namespace Petzold.PrintBetterBanner
{
    public class PrintBetterBanner : Window
    {
        TextBox txtbox;
        Typeface face;

        [STAThread]
        public static void Main()
        {
            Application app = new Application();
            app.Run(new PrintBetterBanner());
        }
```

```
public PrintBetterBanner()
{
    Title = "Print Better Banner";
    SizeToContent = SizeToContent.WidthAndHeight;
    // Make StackPanel content of window.
    StackPanel stack = new StackPanel();
    Content = stack;

    // Create TextBox.
    txtbox = new TextBox();
    txtbox.Width = 250;
    txtbox.Margin = new Thickness(12);
    stack.Children.Add(txtbox);

    // Create Font Button.
    Button btn = new Button();
    btn.Content = "_Font...";
    btn.Margin = new Thickness(12);
    btn.Click += FontOnClick;
    btn.HorizontalAlignment = HorizontalAlignment.Center;
    stack.Children.Add(btn);

    // Create Print Button.
    btn = new Button();
    btn.Content = "_Print...";
    btn.Margin = new Thickness(12);
    btn.Click += PrintOnClick;
    btn.HorizontalAlignment = HorizontalAlignment.Center;
    stack.Children.Add(btn);

    // Initialize Facename field.
    face = new Typeface(FontFamily, FontStyle, FontWeight, FontStretch);
    txtbox.Focus();
}
void FontOnClick(object sender, RoutedEventArgs args)
{
    FontDialog dlg = new FontDialog();
    dlg.Owner = this;
    dlg.Typeface = face;

    if (dlg.ShowDialog().GetValueOrDefault())
    {
        face = dlg.Typeface;
    }
}
void PrintOnClick(object sender, RoutedEventArgs args)
{
    PrintDialog dlg = new PrintDialog();

    if (dlg.ShowDialog().GetValueOrDefault())
    {

        // Make sure orientation is Portrait.
        PrintTicket prntkt = dlg.PrintTicket;
        prntkt.PageOrientation = PageOrientation.Portrait;
        dlg.PrintTicket = prntkt;
```

```
                    // Create new DocumentPaginator object.
                    BannerDocumentPaginator paginator = new BannerDocumentPaginator();

                    // Set Text property from TextBox.
                    paginator.Text = txtbox.Text;

                    // Set Typeface property from field.
                    paginator.Typeface = face;

                    // Give it a PageSize property based on the paper dimensions.
                    paginator.PageSize = new Size(dlg.PrintableAreaWidth,
                                                  dlg.PrintableAreaHeight);
                    // Call PrintDocument to print the document.
                    dlg.PrintDocument(paginator, "Banner: " + txtbox.Text);
                }
            }
        }
    }
```

A banner paginator might serve a purpose in illustrating the basics of printing multiple pages; it's not nearly as useful as a program that arranges text into pages. Such a paginator can be quite complex when multiple typefaces are involved, but even a paginator that handles plain text with a uniform font isn't trivial.

Despite the difficulties, the Notepad Clone presented in the next chapter requires a paginator that handles plain text and word wrapping, and the *PlainTextDocumentPaginator* class (also in the next chapter) is a significant part of that project.

Chapter 18

The Notepad Clone

In the course of learning a new operating system or programming interface, there comes a time when the programmer looks at a common application and says, "I could write that program." To prove it, the programmer might even take a stab at coding a clone of the application. Perhaps "clone" is not quite the right word, for the new program isn't anywhere close to a genetic copy. The objective is to mimic the user interface and functionality as close as possible *without* duplicating copyrighted code!

The Notepad Clone presented in this chapter is very close to the look, feel, and functionality of the Microsoft Windows Notepad program. The only major feature I left out was the Help window. (I'll demonstrate how to implement application Help information in Chapter 25.) Notepad Clone has file I/O, printing, search and replace, a font dialog, and it saves user preferences between sessions.

The Notepad Clone project requires links to the PrintMarginDialog.cs file from the previous chapter and the three files that contribute to the *FontDialog*: FontDialog.cs, Lister.cs, and TextBoxWithLister.cs. All the other files that comprise Notepad Clone are in this chapter.

Of course, the world hardly needs another plain text editor, but the benefit of writing a Notepad Clone is not purely academic. In Chapter 20 I will add a few files to those shown in this file and create another program named XAML Cruncher. You'll find XAML Cruncher to be a powerful tool for learning and experimenting with Extended Application Markup Language (XAML) throughout Part II of this book. Because two classes in the XAML Cruncher program derive from classes in the Notepad Clone program, Notepad Clone sometimes makes itself more amenable to inheritance with somewhat roundabout code. I'll point out when that's the case.

The first file of the Notepad Clone project is simply a series of C# attribute statements that result in the creation of metadata in the NotepadClone.exe file. This metadata identifies the program, including a copyright notice and version information. You should include such a file in any "real-life" application.

```
NotepadCloneAssemblyInfo.cs
//-------------------------------------------------------------
// NotepadCloneAssemblyInfo.cs (c) 2006 by Charles Petzold
//-------------------------------------------------------------
using System.Reflection;

[assembly: AssemblyTitle("Notepad Clone")]
[assembly: AssemblyProduct("NotepadClone")]
[assembly: AssemblyDescription("Functionally Similar to Windows Notepad")]
[assembly: AssemblyCompany("www.charlespetzold.com")]
```

```
[assembly: AssemblyCopyright("\x00A9 2006 by Charles Petzold")]
[assembly: AssemblyVersion("1.0.*")]
[assembly: AssemblyFileVersion("1.0.0.0")]
```

You don't have to treat this file any differently than you treat the other C# source code files in the project. It's compiled along with everything else. This file is the *only* file in the Notepad Clone program that is not also in the XAML Cruncher project. XAML Cruncher has its own assembly information file.

I mentioned that Notepad Clone saves user preferences between sessions. These days, XML is the standard format for saving settings. Generally, applications store per-user program settings in the area of isolated storage known as "user application data." For a program named NotepadClone distributed by a company named Petzold and installed by a user named Deirdre, the program settings would be saved in this directory:

\Documents and Settings\Deirdre\Application Data\Petzold\NotepadClone

However, the XAML Cruncher program is downloadable from my Web site using the ClickOnce application installation, and for that type of installation it's recommended that program settings go in the area known as "local user application data":

\Documents and Settings\Deirdre\Local Settings\Application Data\Petzold\NotepadClone

Although both of these areas are specific to the particular user, the regular user application data is intended for roaming—that is, when the user logs on to a different computer—whereas the local user application data is specific to a particular user on the particular computer.

It's handy to define user preference as public fields or properties in a class specific to this purpose. You can then use the *XmlSerializer* class to automatically save and load the information in XML format. The first step to saving or loading the file is to create an *XmlSerializer* object based on the class you want to serialize:

```
XmlSerializer xml = new XmlSerializer(typeof(MyClass));
```

You can then save an object of type *MyClass* in XML by calling the *Serialize* method. To specify the file, you'll need an object of type *Stream*, *XmlWriter*, or *TextWriter* (from which *StreamWriter* descends). The *Deserialize* method of *XmlSerializer* converts XML into an object of the type you specified in the *XmlSerializer* constructor. The *Deserialize* method returns an object of type *object* that you can cast into the correct type.

As you might guess, the *XmlSerializer* class uses reflection to look inside the class you specify in the *XmlSerializer* constructor and examine its members. According to the documentation, *XmlSerializer* actually generates code that is executed outside your execution space. For that reason, any class you want serialized must be defined as *public*. *XmlSerializer* serializes and deserializes only fields and properties that are defined as *public*, and it ignores any read-only or write-only members. When deserializing, *XmlSerializer* creates an object of the proper type using the class's parameterless constructor and then sets the object's properties from the XML elements. *XmlSerializer* won't work with a class that has no parameterless constructor.

If any serializable members of the class are complex data types, those classes and structures must also be *public* and must also have parameterless constructors. The *XmlSerializer* will treat the public read/write properties and fields of these other classes and structures as nested elements. *XmlSerializer* can also handle properties that are arrays and *List* objects.

Here is the *NotepadCloneSettings* class. For convenience and to save space, I've defined the public members as fields rather than properties.

```
NotepadCloneSettings.cs
//----------------------------------------------------
// NotepadCloneSettings.cs (c) 2006 by Charles Petzold
//----------------------------------------------------
using System;
using System.IO;
using System.Windows;
using System.Windows.Media;
using System.Xml.Serialization;

namespace Petzold.NotepadClone
{
    public class NotepadCloneSettings
    {
        // Default Settings.
        public WindowState WindowState = WindowState.Normal;
        public Rect RestoreBounds = Rect.Empty;
        public TextWrapping TextWrapping = TextWrapping.NoWrap;
        public string FontFamily = "";
        public string FontStyle =
            new FontStyleConverter().ConvertToString(FontStyles.Normal);
        public string FontWeight =
            new FontWeightConverter().ConvertToString(FontWeights.Normal);
        public string FontStretch =
            new FontStretchConverter().ConvertToString(FontStretches.Normal);
        public double FontSize = 11;

        // Save settings to file.
        public virtual bool Save(string strAppData)
        {
            try
            {
                Directory.CreateDirectory(Path.GetDirectoryName(strAppData));
                StreamWriter write = new StreamWriter(strAppData);
                XmlSerializer xml = new XmlSerializer(GetType());
                xml.Serialize(write, this);
                write.Close();
            }
            catch
            {
                return false;
            }
            return true;
        }
```

```
    // Load settings from file.
    public static object Load(Type type, string strAppData)
    {
        StreamReader reader;
        object settings;
        XmlSerializer xml = new XmlSerializer(type);

        try
        {
            reader = new StreamReader(strAppData);
            settings = xml.Deserialize(reader);
            reader.Close();
        }
        catch
        {
            settings =
                type.GetConstructor(System.Type.EmptyTypes).Invoke(null);
        }
        return settings;
    }
}
}
```

The class contains two methods. The *Save* method requires a fully qualified file name and creates *StreamWriter* and *XmlSerializer* objects for writing out the fields. The *Load* method is static because it's responsible for creating an object of type *NotepadCloneSettings*, either by calling *Deserialize* or (if the settings file does not yet exist) by using the class's constructor.

The *Load* method is more complex than it needs to be because I reuse this file and derive from it in the XAML Cruncher project. If I didn't need to reuse the class, the *Type* parameter to *Load* wouldn't be required, and the argument to the *XmlSerializer* constructor would instead be *typeof(NotepadCloneSettings)*. Rather than using reflection to invoke the class's constructor in the *catch* block, a simple *new NotepadCloneSettings()* would suffice.

As you can see, the first three fields are two enumerations and a structure. These serialize and deserialize fine. However, most of the font-related properties weren't quite so agreeable. *FontStyle*, for example, is a structure with no public fields or properties. I explicitly defined these font-related fields in *NotepadCloneSettings* as *string* objects, and then initialized them from various classes (such as *FontStyleConverter*) that are most often used in parsing XAML.

The NotepadClone.cs file is next, and if you think this file looks a little small to be the main file of the project, you're absolutely right. As is normal, my *NotepadClone* class derives from *Window*, but I have divided the source code for this class into seven files using the *partial* keyword. The different files roughly correspond to the top-level menu items. For example, the code in the NotepadClone.Edit.cs file is also part of the *NotepadClone* class but it handles the creation and event handling of the Edit menu.

It is helpful to keep in mind that these seven files are all part of the same class and have direct access to the methods and fields defined in other files. In particular, the *TextBox* control that dominates the program's client area is stored in a field named *txtbox*. Lots of different methods need access to that object.

The NotepadClone.cs file contains the *NotepadClone* constructor, which begins by accessing some of the assembly metadata defined in the NotepadCloneAssemblyInfo.cs file to obtain the program title (the string "Notepad Clone") and to construct a file path to store the settings. The program uses this approach to make it hospitable to inheritance. The constructor then proceeds by laying out the window with a *DockPanel*, *Menu*, *StatusBar*, and *TextBox*. Virtually all of the menu construction is relegated to other files.

NotepadClone.cs

```
//-------------------------------------------
// NotepadClone.cs (c) 2006 by Charles Petzold
//-------------------------------------------
using System;
using System.ComponentModel;
using System.IO;
using System.Reflection;
using System.Windows;
using System.Windows.Controls;
using System.Windows.Controls.Primitives;
using System.Windows.Input;
using System.Windows.Media;

namespace Petzold.NotepadClone
{
    public partial class NotepadClone : Window
    {
        protected string strAppTitle;       // Name of program for title bar.
        protected string strAppData;        // Full file name of settings file.
        protected NotepadCloneSettings settings;    // Settings.
        protected bool isFileDirty = false; // Flag for file save prompt.

        // Controls used in main window.
        protected Menu menu;
        protected TextBox txtbox;
        protected StatusBar status;

        string strLoadedFile;               // Fully qualified loaded file name.
        StatusBarItem statLineCol;          // Line and column status.

        [STAThread]
        public static void Main()
        {
            Application app = new Application();
            app.ShutdownMode = ShutdownMode.OnMainWindowClose;
            app.Run(new NotepadClone());
        }
        public NotepadClone()
        {
            // Get this executing assembly to access attributes.
            Assembly asmbly = Assembly.GetExecutingAssembly();
```

```
// Get the AssemblyTitle attribute for the strAppTitle field.
AssemblyTitleAttribute title = (AssemblyTitleAttribute)asmbly.
    GetCustomAttributes(typeof(AssemblyTitleAttribute), false)[0];
strAppTitle = title.Title;
// Get the AssemblyProduct attribute for the strAppData file name.
AssemblyProductAttribute product = (AssemblyProductAttribute)asmbly.
    GetCustomAttributes(typeof(AssemblyProductAttribute), false)[0];
strAppData = Path.Combine(
    Environment.GetFolderPath(
        Environment.SpecialFolder.LocalApplicationData),
            "Petzold\\" + product.Product + "\\" +
            product.Product + ".Settings.xml");

// Create DockPanel as content of window.
DockPanel dock = new DockPanel();
Content = dock;

// Create Menu docked at top.
menu = new Menu();
dock.Children.Add(menu);
DockPanel.SetDock(menu, Dock.Top);

// Create StatusBar docked at bottom.
status = new StatusBar();
dock.Children.Add(status);
DockPanel.SetDock(status, Dock.Bottom);

// Create StatusBarItem to display line and column.
statLineCol = new StatusBarItem();
statLineCol.HorizontalAlignment = HorizontalAlignment.Right;
status.Items.Add(statLineCol);
DockPanel.SetDock(statLineCol, Dock.Right);

// Create TextBox to fill remainder of client area.
txtbox = new TextBox();
txtbox.AcceptsReturn = true;
txtbox.AcceptsTab = true;
txtbox.VerticalScrollBarVisibility = ScrollBarVisibility.Auto;
txtbox.HorizontalScrollBarVisibility = ScrollBarVisibility.Auto;
txtbox.TextChanged += TextBoxOnTextChanged;
txtbox.SelectionChanged += TextBoxOnSelectionChanged;
dock.Children.Add(txtbox);

// Create all the top-level menu items.
AddFileMenu(menu);              // in NotepadClone.File.cs
AddEditMenu(menu);              // in NotepadClone.Edit.cs
AddFormatMenu(menu);            // in NotepadClone.Format.cs
AddViewMenu(menu);             // in NotepadClone.View.cs
AddHelpMenu(menu);             // in NotepadClone.Help.cs

// Load settings saved from previous run.
settings = (NotepadCloneSettings) LoadSettings();

// Apply saved settings.
WindowState = settings.WindowState;
```

```csharp
        if (settings.RestoreBounds != Rect.Empty)
        {
            Left = settings.RestoreBounds.Left;
            Top = settings.RestoreBounds.Top;
            Width = settings.RestoreBounds.Width;
            Height = settings.RestoreBounds.Height;
        }

        txtbox.TextWrapping = settings.TextWrapping;
        txtbox.FontFamily = new FontFamily(settings.FontFamily);
        txtbox.FontStyle = (FontStyle) new FontStyleConverter().
                        ConvertFromString(settings.FontStyle);
        txtbox.FontWeight = (FontWeight) new FontWeightConverter().
                        ConvertFromString(settings.FontWeight);
        txtbox.FontStretch = (FontStretch) new FontStretchConverter().
                        ConvertFromString(settings.FontStretch);
        txtbox.FontSize = settings.FontSize;

        // Install handler for Loaded event.
        Loaded += WindowOnLoaded;

        // Set focus to TextBox.
        txtbox.Focus();
}
// Overridable method to load settings, called from constructor.
protected virtual object LoadSettings()
{
        return NotepadCloneSettings.Load(typeof(NotepadCloneSettings),
                                strAppData);
}
// Event handler for Loaded event: Simulates New command &
//   possibly loads command-line file.
void WindowOnLoaded(object sender, RoutedEventArgs args)
{
        ApplicationCommands.New.Execute(null, this);

        // Get command-line arguments.
        string[] strArgs = Environment.GetCommandLineArgs();

        if (strArgs.Length > 1) // First argument is program name!
        {
            if (File.Exists(strArgs[1]))
            {
                LoadFile(strArgs[1]);
            }
            else
            {
                MessageBoxResult result =
                    MessageBox.Show("Cannot find the " +
                        Path.GetFileName(strArgs[1]) + " file.\r\n\r\n" +
                        "Do you want to create a new file?",
                        strAppTitle, MessageBoxButton.YesNoCancel,
                        MessageBoxImage.Question);
```

```
                // Close the window if the user clicks "Cancel".
                if (result == MessageBoxResult.Cancel)
                    Close();

                // Create and close file for "Yes".
                else if (result == MessageBoxResult.Yes)
                {
                    try
                    {
                        File.Create(strLoadedFile = strArgs[1]).Close();
                    }
                    catch (Exception exc)
                    {
                        MessageBox.Show("Error on File Creation: " +
                                        exc.Message, strAppTitle,
                            MessageBoxButton.OK, MessageBoxImage.Asterisk);
                        return;
                    }
                    UpdateTitle();
                }
                // No action for "No".
            }
        }
    }
    // OnClosing event: See if it's OK to trash the file.
    protected override void OnClosing(CancelEventArgs args)
    {
        base.OnClosing(args);
        args.Cancel = !OkToTrash();
        settings.RestoreBounds = RestoreBounds;
    }
    // OnClosed event: Set fields of 'settings' and call SaveSettings.
    protected override void OnClosed(EventArgs args)
    {
        base.OnClosed(args);
        settings.WindowState = WindowState;
        settings.TextWrapping = txtbox.TextWrapping;

        settings.FontFamily = txtbox.FontFamily.ToString();
        settings.FontStyle =
            new FontStyleConverter().ConvertToString(txtbox.FontStyle);
        settings.FontWeight =
            new FontWeightConverter().ConvertToString(txtbox.FontWeight);
        settings.FontStretch =
            new FontStretchConverter().ConvertToString(txtbox.FontStretch);
        settings.FontSize = txtbox.FontSize;

        SaveSettings();
    }
    // Overridable method to call Save in the 'settings' object.
    protected virtual void SaveSettings()
    {
        settings.Save(strAppData);
    }
```

```
    // UpdateTitle displays file name or "Untitled".
    protected void UpdateTitle()
    {
        if (strLoadedFile == null)
            Title = "Untitled - " + strAppTitle;
        else
            Title = Path.GetFileName(strLoadedFile) + " - " + strAppTitle;
    }
    // When the TextBox text changes, just set isFileDirty.
    void TextBoxOnTextChanged(object sender, RoutedEventArgs args)
    {
        isFileDirty = true;
    }
    // When the selection changes, update the status bar.
    void TextBoxOnSelectionChanged(object sender, RoutedEventArgs args)
    {
        int iChar = txtbox.SelectionStart;
        int iLine = txtbox.GetLineIndexFromCharacterIndex(iChar);

        // Check for error that may be a bug.
        if (iLine == -1)
        {
            statLineCol.Content = "";
            return;
        }

        int iCol = iChar - txtbox.GetCharacterIndexFromLineIndex(iLine);
        string str = String.Format("Line {0} Col {1}", iLine + 1, iCol + 1);

        if (txtbox.SelectionLength > 0)
        {
            iChar += txtbox.SelectionLength;
            iLine = txtbox.GetLineIndexFromCharacterIndex(iChar);
            iCol = iChar - txtbox.GetCharacterIndexFromLineIndex(iLine);
            str += String.Format(" - Line {0} Col {1}", iLine + 1, iCol + 1);
        }
        statLineCol.Content = str;
    }
}
}
```

Towards the end of the constructor, the *NotepadClone* class calls a virtual method named *LoadSettings* to load the settings file, and also installs a handler for the *Loaded* event. The *Loaded* event handler is responsible for checking command-line arguments and possibly loading a file. All file-related methods are located in the NotepadClone.File.cs file (coming up).

The NotepadClone.cs file concludes with event handlers for the *TextChanged* and *Selection-Changed* events of the *TextBox*. The *TextChanged* handler simply sets the *isFileDirty* flag to *true* so that the program properly prompts the user to save the file if it's been altered. The *Selection-Changed* handler is responsible for displaying the line and column numbers of the caret or selection in the status bar.

The *AddFileMenu* method in the NotepadClone.File.cs file is responsible for assembling the File menu and handling all file-related commands. Many of the items on the File menu have corresponding static properties in the *ApplicationCommands* class. These items can be handled with command bindings.

NotepadClone.File.cs

```
//-------------------------------------------------
// NotepadClone.File.cs (c) 2006 by Charles Petzold
//-------------------------------------------------
using Microsoft.Win32;
using System;
using System.IO;
using System.Windows;
using System.Windows.Controls;
using System.Windows.Input;
using System.Windows.Media;
using System.Printing;

namespace Petzold.NotepadClone
{
    public partial class NotepadClone : Window
    {
        // Filter for File Open and Save dialog boxes.
        protected string strFilter =
                    "Text Documents(*.txt)|*.txt|All Files(*.*)|*.*";

        void AddFileMenu(Menu menu)
        {
            // Create top-level File item.
            MenuItem itemFile = new MenuItem();
            itemFile.Header = "_File";
            menu.Items.Add(itemFile);

            // New menu item.
            MenuItem itemNew = new MenuItem();
            itemNew.Header = "_New";
            itemNew.Command = ApplicationCommands.New;
            itemFile.Items.Add(itemNew);
            CommandBindings.Add(
                new CommandBinding(ApplicationCommands.New, NewOnExecute));

            // Open menu item.
            MenuItem itemOpen = new MenuItem();
            itemOpen.Header = "_Open...";
            itemOpen.Command = ApplicationCommands.Open;
            itemFile.Items.Add(itemOpen);
            CommandBindings.Add(
                new CommandBinding(ApplicationCommands.Open, OpenOnExecute));

            // Save menu item.
            MenuItem itemSave = new MenuItem();
            itemSave.Header = "_Save";
            itemSave.Command = ApplicationCommands.Save;
```

```
        itemFile.Items.Add(itemSave);
        CommandBindings.Add(
            new CommandBinding(ApplicationCommands.Save, SaveOnExecute));

        // Save As menu item.
        MenuItem itemSaveAs = new MenuItem();
        itemSaveAs.Header = "Save _As...";
        itemSaveAs.Command = ApplicationCommands.SaveAs;
        itemFile.Items.Add(itemSaveAs);
        CommandBindings.Add(
            new CommandBinding(ApplicationCommands.SaveAs, SaveAsOnExecute));

        // Separators and printing items.
        itemFile.Items.Add(new Separator());
        AddPrintMenuItems(itemFile);
        itemFile.Items.Add(new Separator());

        // Exit menu item.
        MenuItem itemExit = new MenuItem();
        itemExit.Header = "E_xit";
        itemExit.Click += ExitOnClick;
        itemFile.Items.Add(itemExit);
    }
    // File New command: Start with empty TextBox.
    protected virtual void NewOnExecute(object sender,
                                        ExecutedRoutedEventArgs args)
    {
        if (!OkToTrash())
            return;

        txtbox.Text = "";
        strLoadedFile = null;
        isFileDirty = false;
        UpdateTitle();
    }
    // File Open command: Display dialog box and load file.
    void OpenOnExecute(object sender, ExecutedRoutedEventArgs args)
    {
        if (!OkToTrash())
            return;
        OpenFileDialog dlg = new OpenFileDialog();
        dlg.Filter = strFilter;

        if ((bool)dlg.ShowDialog(this))
        {
            LoadFile(dlg.FileName);
        }
    }
    // File Save command: Possibly execute SaveAsExecute.
    void SaveOnExecute(object sender, ExecutedRoutedEventArgs args)
    {
        if (strLoadedFile == null || strLoadedFile.Length == 0)
            DisplaySaveDialog("");
        else
            SaveFile(strLoadedFile);
    }
```

```
    // File Save As command; display dialog box and save file.
    void SaveAsOnExecute(object sender, ExecutedRoutedEventArgs args)
    {
        DisplaySaveDialog(strLoadedFile);
    }
    // Display Save dialog box and return true if file is saved.
    bool DisplaySaveDialog(string strFileName)
    {
        SaveFileDialog dlg = new SaveFileDialog();
        dlg.Filter = strFilter;
        dlg.FileName = strFileName;

        if ((bool)dlg.ShowDialog(this))
        {
            SaveFile(dlg.FileName);
            return true;
        }
        return false;              // for OkToTrash.
    }
    // File Exit command: Just close the window.
    void ExitOnClick(object sender, RoutedEventArgs args)
    {
        Close();
    }
    // OkToTrash returns true if the TextBox contents need not be saved.
    bool OkToTrash()
    {
        if (!isFileDirty)
            return true;

        MessageBoxResult result =
            MessageBox.Show("The text in the file " + strLoadedFile +
                            " has changed\n\n" +
                            "Do you want to save the changes?",
                            strAppTitle,
                            MessageBoxButton.YesNoCancel,
                            MessageBoxImage.Question,
                            MessageBoxResult.Yes);

        if (result == MessageBoxResult.Cancel)
            return false;

        else if (result == MessageBoxResult.No)
            return true;

        else // result == MessageBoxResult.Yes
        {
            if (strLoadedFile != null && strLoadedFile.Length > 0)
                return SaveFile(strLoadedFile);

            return DisplaySaveDialog("");
        }
    }
    // LoadFile method possibly displays message box if error.
    void LoadFile(string strFileName)
```

```
    {
        try
        {
            txtbox.Text = File.ReadAllText(strFileName);
        }
        catch (Exception exc)
        {
            MessageBox.Show("Error on File Open: " + exc.Message, strAppTitle,
                        MessageBoxButton.OK, MessageBoxImage.Asterisk);
            return;
        }
        strLoadedFile = strFileName;
        UpdateTitle();
        txtbox.SelectionStart = 0;
        txtbox.SelectionLength = 0;
        isFileDirty = false;
    }
    // SaveFile method possibly displays message box if error.
    bool SaveFile(string strFileName)
    {
        try
        {
            File.WriteAllText(strFileName, txtbox.Text);
        }
        catch (Exception exc)
        {
            MessageBox.Show("Error on File Save" + exc.Message, strAppTitle,
                        MessageBoxButton.OK, MessageBoxImage.Asterisk);
            return false;
        }
        strLoadedFile = strFileName;
        UpdateTitle();
        isFileDirty = false;
        return true;
    }
}
}
```

This file also contains the all-important *OkToTrash* method, which interrogates the user to determine if it's all right to abandon a file that has some changes made but which hasn't yet been saved.

The two printing-related items on the File menu are handled in the next source code file, NotepadClone.Print.cs. The logic in this file should look fairly similar to the printing code from the previous chapter. The big difference here is that this file uses a class named *PlainTextDocumentPaginator*, which has several properties, such as *Typeface* and *FaceSize*, that are similar to those in *FontDialog* and which the code here gets from the *TextBox*. Another *PlainTextDocumentPaginator* property is *TextWrapping*, which is the *TextBox* property that controls how text is wrapped (or not).

NotepadClone.Print.cs

```
//----------------------------------------------------
// NotepadClone.Print.cs (c) 2006 by Charles Petzold
//----------------------------------------------------
using Petzold.PrintWithMargins;     // for PageMarginsDialog.
using System;
using System.Windows;
using System.Windows.Controls;
using System.Windows.Input;
using System.Windows.Media;
using System.Printing;

namespace Petzold.NotepadClone
{
    public partial class NotepadClone : Window
    {
        // Fields for printing.
        PrintQueue prnqueue;
        PrintTicket prntkt;
        Thickness marginPage = new Thickness(96);
        void AddPrintMenuItems(MenuItem itemFile)
        {
            // Page Setup menu item.
            MenuItem itemSetup = new MenuItem();
            itemSetup.Header = "Page Set_up...";
            itemSetup.Click += PageSetupOnClick;
            itemFile.Items.Add(itemSetup);

            // Print menu item.
            MenuItem itemPrint = new MenuItem();
            itemPrint.Header = "_Print...";
            itemPrint.Command = ApplicationCommands.Print;
            itemFile.Items.Add(itemPrint);
            CommandBindings.Add(
                new CommandBinding(ApplicationCommands.Print, PrintOnExecuted));
        }
        void PageSetupOnClick(object sender, RoutedEventArgs args)
        {
            // Create dialog and initialize PageMargins property.
            PageMarginsDialog dlg = new PageMarginsDialog();
            dlg.Owner = this;
            dlg.PageMargins = marginPage;

            if (dlg.ShowDialog().GetValueOrDefault())
            {
                // Save page margins from dialog box.
                marginPage = dlg.PageMargins;
            }
        }
        void PrintOnExecuted(object sender, ExecutedRoutedEventArgs args)
        {
            PrintDialog dlg = new PrintDialog();
```

```
                    // Get the PrintQueue and PrintTicket from previous invocations.
                    if (prnqueue != null)
                        dlg.PrintQueue = prnqueue;

                    if (prntkt != null)
                        prntkt = dlg.PrintTicket;

                    if (dlg.ShowDialog().GetValueOrDefault())
                    {
                        // Save PrintQueue and PrintTicket from dialog box.
                        prnqueue = dlg.PrintQueue;
                        prntkt = dlg.PrintTicket;

                        // Create a PlainTextDocumentPaginator object.
                        PlainTextDocumentPaginator paginator =
                            new PlainTextDocumentPaginator();

                        // Set the paginator properties.
                        paginator.PrintTicket = prntkt;
                        paginator.Text = txtbox.Text;
                        paginator.Header = strLoadedFile;
                        paginator.Typeface =
                            new Typeface(txtbox.FontFamily, txtbox.FontStyle,
                                         txtbox.FontWeight, txtbox.FontStretch);
                        paginator.FaceSize = txtbox.FontSize;
                        paginator.TextWrapping = txtbox.TextWrapping;
                        paginator.Margins = marginPage;
                        paginator.PageSize = new Size(dlg.PrintableAreaWidth,
                                                      dlg.PrintableAreaHeight);
                        // Print the document.
                        dlg.PrintDocument(paginator, Title);
                    }
                }
            }
        }
    }
```

The *PlainTextDocumentPaginator* obviously does most of the grunt work. I gave the class a text property named *Header* that Notepad Clone sets to the file name of the loaded file. I also wanted the paginator to print a footer consisting of the page number and the total number of pages, for example, "Page 5 of 15."

The basic formatting occurs in the *Format* method of *PlainTextDocumentPaginator*. The method loops through each line of text in the file. (Keep in mind that when wrapping is in effect, each line of text is basically a paragraph.) Each line is passed to the *ProcessLine* method, which takes wrapping into account to break the text line into one or more printable lines. Each printable line is stored as a *PrintLine* object in a *List* collection. After all the *PrintLine* objects are accumulated, it is easy to determine the number of pages based on the size of the page, the margins, and the total numbers of lines. The *Format* method concludes by drawing text on the page using *DrawText* calls.

PlainTextDocumentPaginator.cs

```
//----------------------------------------------------------
// PlainTextDocumentPaginator.cs (c) 2006 by Charles Petzold
//----------------------------------------------------------
using System;
using System.Collections.Generic;
using System.Globalization;
using System.IO;
using System.Printing;
using System.Windows;
using System.Windows.Controls;
using System.Windows.Documents;
using System.Windows.Media;

namespace Petzold.NotepadClone
{
    public class PlainTextDocumentPaginator : DocumentPaginator
    {
        // Private fields, including those associated with public properties.
        char[] charsBreak = new char[] { ' ', '-' };
        string txt = "";
        string txtHeader = null;
        Typeface face = new Typeface("");
        double em = 11;
        Size sizePage = new Size(8.5 * 96, 11 * 96);
        Size sizeMax = new Size(0, 0);
        Thickness margins = new Thickness(96);
        PrintTicket prntkt = new PrintTicket();
        TextWrapping txtwrap = TextWrapping.Wrap;

        // Stores each page as a DocumentPage object.
        List<DocumentPage> listPages;

        // Public properties.
        public string Text
        {
            set { txt = value; }
            get { return txt; }
        }
        public TextWrapping TextWrapping
        {
            set { txtwrap = value; }
            get { return txtwrap; }
        }
        public Thickness Margins
        {
            set { margins = value; }
            get { return margins; }
        }
        public Typeface Typeface
        {
            set { face = value; }
```

```
        get { return face; }
    }
    public double FaceSize
    {
        set { em = value; }
        get { return em; }
    }
    public PrintTicket PrintTicket
    {
        set { prntkt = value; }
        get { return prntkt; }
    }
    public string Header
    {
        set { txtHeader = value; }
        get { return txtHeader; }
    }


    // Required overrides.
    public override bool IsPageCountValid
    {
        get
        {
            if (listPages == null)
                Format();

            return true;
        }
    }
    public override int PageCount
    {
        get
        {
            if (listPages == null)
                return 0;

            return listPages.Count;
        }
    }
    public override Size PageSize
    {
        set { sizePage = value; }
        get { return sizePage; }
    }
    public override DocumentPage GetPage(int numPage)
    {
        return listPages[numPage];
    }
    public override IDocumentPaginatorSource Source
    {
        get { return null; }
    }
```

```
// An internal class to indicate if an arrow is to be printed at the
//   end of the line of text.
class PrintLine
{
    public string String;
    public bool Flag;

    public PrintLine(string str, bool flag)
    {
        String = str;
        Flag = flag;
    }
}

// Formats entire document into pages.
void Format()
{
    // Store each line of the document as with LineWithFlag object.
    List<PrintLine> listLines = new List<PrintLine>();
    // Use this for some basic calculations.
    FormattedText formtxtSample = GetFormattedText("W");

    // Width of printed line.
    double width = PageSize.Width - Margins.Left - Margins.Right;

    // Serious problem: Abandon ship.
    if (width < formtxtSample.Width)
        return;

    string strLine;
    Pen pn = new Pen(Brushes.Black, 2);
    StringReader reader = new StringReader(txt);

    // Call ProcessLine to store each line in listLines.
    while (null != (strLine = reader.ReadLine()))
        ProcessLine(strLine, width, listLines);
    reader.Close();

    // Now start getting ready to print pages.
    double heightLine = formtxtSample.LineHeight + formtxtSample.Height;
    double height = PageSize.Height - Margins.Top - Margins.Bottom;
    int linesPerPage = (int)(height / heightLine);

    // Serious problem: Abandon ship.
    if (linesPerPage < 1)
        return;

    int numPages = (listLines.Count + linesPerPage - 1) / linesPerPage;
    double xStart = Margins.Left;
    double yStart = Margins.Top;

    // Create the List to store each DocumentPage object.
    listPages = new List<DocumentPage>();
```

```
for (int iPage = 0, iLine = 0; iPage < numPages; iPage++)
{
    // Create the DrawingVisual and open the DrawingContext.
    DrawingVisual vis = new DrawingVisual();
    DrawingContext dc = vis.RenderOpen();

    // Display header at top of page.
    if (Header != null && Header.Length > 0)
    {
        FormattedText formtxt = GetFormattedText(Header);
        formtxt.SetFontWeight(FontWeights.Bold);
        Point ptText = new Point(xStart, yStart - 2 * formtxt.Height);
        dc.DrawText(formtxt, ptText);
    }
    // Display footer at bottom of page.
    if (numPages > 1)
    {
        FormattedText formtxt =
            GetFormattedText("Page " + (iPage+1) + " of " + numPages);
        formtxt.SetFontWeight(FontWeights.Bold);
        Point ptText = new Point(
            (PageSize.Width + Margins.Left -
                                Margins.Right - formtxt.Width) / 2,
            PageSize.Height - Margins.Bottom + formtxt.Height);
        dc.DrawText(formtxt, ptText);
    }
    // Look through the lines on the page.
    for (int i = 0; i < linesPerPage; i++, iLine++)
    {
        if (iLine == listLines.Count)
            break;

        // Set up information to display the text of the line.
        string str = listLines[iLine].String;
        FormattedText formtxt = GetFormattedText(str);
        Point ptText = new Point(xStart, yStart + i * heightLine);
        dc.DrawText(formtxt, ptText);

        // Possibly display the little arrow flag.
        if (listLines[iLine].Flag)
        {
            double x = xStart + width + 6;
            double y = yStart + i * heightLine + formtxt.Baseline;
            double len = face.CapsHeight * em;
            dc.DrawLine(pn, new Point(x, y),
                            new Point(x + len, y - len));
            dc.DrawLine(pn, new Point(x, y),
                            new Point(x, y - len / 2));
            dc.DrawLine(pn, new Point(x, y),
                            new Point(x + len / 2, y));
        }
    }
    dc.Close();
```

```
                // Create DocumentPage object based on visual.
                DocumentPage page = new DocumentPage(vis);
                listPages.Add(page);
            }
        reader.Close();
    }

    // Process each line of text into multiple printed lines.
    void ProcessLine(string str, double width, List<PrintLine> list)
    {
        str = str.TrimEnd(' ');

        // TextWrapping == TextWrapping.NoWrap.
        // ----------------------------------
        if (TextWrapping == TextWrapping.NoWrap)
        {
            do
            {
                int length = str.Length;

                while (GetFormattedText(str.Substring(0, length)).Width >
                                                                      width)
                    length--;
                list.Add(new PrintLine(str.Substring(0, length),
                                            length < str.Length));
                str = str.Substring(length);
            }
            while (str.Length > 0);
        }
        // TextWrapping == TextWrapping.Wrap or TextWrapping.WrapWithOverflow.
        // ------------------------------------------------------------------
        else
        {
            do
            {
                int length = str.Length;
                bool flag = false;

                while (GetFormattedText(str.Substring(0, length)).Width > width)
                {
                    int index = str.LastIndexOfAny(charsBreak, length - 2);

                    if (index != -1)
                        length = index + 1; // Include trailing space or dash.
                    else
                    {
                        // At this point, we know that the next possible
                        //   space or dash break is beyond the allowable
                        //   width. Check if there's *any* space or dash break.
                        index = str.IndexOfAny(charsBreak);

                        if (index != -1)
                            length = index + 1;
                        // If TextWrapping.WrapWithOverflow, just display the
                        //   line. If TextWrapping.Wrap, break it with a flag.
```

```
                                      if (TextWrapping == TextWrapping.Wrap)
                                      {
                                          while (GetFormattedText(str.Substring(0, length)).
                                                                               Width > width)
                                              length--;
                                          flag = true;
                                      }
                                      break;  // out of while loop.
                                  }
                              }

                              list.Add(new PrintLine(str.Substring(0, length), flag));
                              str = str.Substring(length);
                          }
                          while (str.Length > 0);
                      }
                  }
                  // Private method to create FormattedText object.
                  FormattedText GetFormattedText(string str)
                  {
                      return new FormattedText(str, CultureInfo.CurrentCulture,
                              FlowDirection.LeftToRight, face, em, Brushes.Black);
                  }
              }
          }
      }
```

The trickiest part of this class is obviously the *ProcessLine* method that breaks each line of text into multiple printable lines. This method must potentially break lines into pieces based on the presence of spaces or dashes in the text and the current word-wrap option.

In previous incarnations of editing controls similar to the *TextBox*, word wrapping was either on or off. Either the editing control wrapped long lines within the borders of the control, or it truncated long lines at the right margin.

In the WPF version of the *TextBox*, word wrapping is represented by the *TextWrapping* property, which is set to a member of the *TextWrapping* enumeration. The members are *NoWrap*, *Wrap*, and *WrapWithOverflow*. This new scheme is attempting to solve a little problem. What happens if the user wants wrapping but a particular word is too long to fit within the *TextBox* width? With the *TextWrapping.Wrap* option, as much of the word is displayed as possible, and then the rest of the word is displayed on the next line. With the *TextWrapping.WrapWithOverflow* option, the long word is not split. In effect, the word overflows into the margin. You can't see it on the screen, but it was my feeling that this last option should let long words spill over into the margin of the page.

Although the difference between *Wrap* and *WrapWithOverflow* obviously caused some minor coding headaches, I was more interested in doing something sensible with the *NoWrap* option. Because this paginator is also a part of XAML Cruncher, I wanted printed output of source code to more closely resemble pages that come out of Visual Studio. If a line is too long for one line, Visual Studio lets it spill over the next line, and draws a little arrow in the margin to indicate the continued line.

That is why *PlainTextDocumentPaginator* stores each printable line as an object of type *PrintLine*. The *PrintLine* class includes a Boolean *Flag* field that indicates if the little arrow should be drawn at the end of the line. These arrows occur for long lines when the *TextWrapping* option is *NoWrap*, but also when the option is *Wrap* and a long word must be split between two lines.

Interestingly enough, the Windows Notepad program uses the same wrapping logic when printing documents regardless of the current word-wrap setting. After I spent the time doing separate printing logic for the three word-wrap settings, I can only characterize Notepad's approach as "lazy."

Let's move on to the Edit menu, which is a combination of easy stuff and hard stuff. The easy stuff consists of all the clipboard-related commands, which should be familiar to you by now.

NotepadClone.Edit.cs

```
//-------------------------------------------------
// NotepadClone.Edit.cs (c) 2006 by Charles Petzold
//-------------------------------------------------
using System;
using System.Windows;
using System.Windows.Controls;
using System.Windows.Input;

namespace Petzold.NotepadClone
{
    public partial class NotepadClone
    {
        void AddEditMenu(Menu menu)
        {
            // Top-level Edit menu.
            MenuItem itemEdit = new MenuItem();
            itemEdit.Header = "_Edit";
            menu.Items.Add(itemEdit);
            // Undo menu item.
            MenuItem itemUndo = new MenuItem();
            itemUndo.Header = "_Undo";
            itemUndo.Command = ApplicationCommands.Undo;
            itemEdit.Items.Add(itemUndo);
            CommandBindings.Add(new CommandBinding(
                ApplicationCommands.Undo, UndoOnExecute, UndoCanExecute));
            // Redo menu item.
            MenuItem itemRedo = new MenuItem();
            itemRedo.Header = "_Redo";
            itemRedo.Command = ApplicationCommands.Redo;
            itemEdit.Items.Add(itemRedo);
            CommandBindings.Add(new CommandBinding(
                ApplicationCommands.Redo, RedoOnExecute, RedoCanExecute));

            itemEdit.Items.Add(new Separator());

            // Cut, Copy, Paste, and Delete menu items.
            MenuItem itemCut = new MenuItem();
            itemCut.Header = "Cu_t";
            itemCut.Command = ApplicationCommands.Cut;
```

```
    itemEdit.Items.Add(itemCut);
    CommandBindings.Add(new CommandBinding(
        ApplicationCommands.Cut, CutOnExecute, CutCanExecute));

    MenuItem itemCopy = new MenuItem();
    itemCopy.Header = "_Copy";
    itemCopy.Command = ApplicationCommands.Copy;
    itemEdit.Items.Add(itemCopy);
    CommandBindings.Add(new CommandBinding(
        ApplicationCommands.Copy, CopyOnExecute, CutCanExecute));

    MenuItem itemPaste = new MenuItem();
    itemPaste.Header = "_Paste";
    itemPaste.Command = ApplicationCommands.Paste;
    itemEdit.Items.Add(itemPaste);
    CommandBindings.Add(new CommandBinding(
        ApplicationCommands.Paste, PasteOnExecute, PasteCanExecute));

    MenuItem itemDel = new MenuItem();
    itemDel.Header = "De_lete";
    itemDel.Command = ApplicationCommands.Delete;
    itemEdit.Items.Add(itemDel);
    CommandBindings.Add(new CommandBinding(
        ApplicationCommands.Delete, DeleteOnExecute, CutCanExecute));

    itemEdit.Items.Add(new Separator());

    // Separate method adds Find, FindNext, and Replace.
    AddFindMenuItems(itemEdit);

    itemEdit.Items.Add(new Separator());

    // Select All menu item.
    MenuItem itemAll = new MenuItem();
    itemAll.Header = "Select _All";
    itemAll.Command = ApplicationCommands.SelectAll;
    itemEdit.Items.Add(itemAll);
    CommandBindings.Add(new CommandBinding(
        ApplicationCommands.SelectAll, SelectAllOnExecute));

    // The Time/Date item requires a custom RoutedUICommand.
    InputGestureCollection coll = new InputGestureCollection();
    coll.Add(new KeyGesture(Key.F5));
    RoutedUICommand commTimeDate =
        new RoutedUICommand("Time/_Date", "TimeDate", GetType(), coll);
    MenuItem itemDate = new MenuItem();
    itemDate.Command = commTimeDate;
    itemEdit.Items.Add(itemDate);
    CommandBindings.Add(
        new CommandBinding(commTimeDate, TimeDateOnExecute));
}
// Redo event handlers.
void RedoCanExecute(object sender, CanExecuteRoutedEventArgs args)
{
    args.CanExecute = txtbox.CanRedo;
}
```

```
    void RedoOnExecute(object sender, ExecutedRoutedEventArgs args)
    {
        txtbox.Redo();
    }
    // Undo event handlers.
    void UndoCanExecute(object sender, CanExecuteRoutedEventArgs args)
    {
        args.CanExecute = txtbox.CanUndo;
    }
    void UndoOnExecute(object sender, ExecutedRoutedEventArgs args)
    {
        txtbox.Undo();
    }
    // Cut event handlers.
    void CutCanExecute(object sender, CanExecuteRoutedEventArgs args)
    {
        args.CanExecute = txtbox.SelectedText.Length > 0;
    }
    void CutOnExecute(object sender, ExecutedRoutedEventArgs args)
    {
        txtbox.Cut();
    }
    // Copy and Delete event handlers.
    void CopyOnExecute(object sender, ExecutedRoutedEventArgs args)
    {
        txtbox.Copy();
    }
    void DeleteOnExecute(object sender, ExecutedRoutedEventArgs args)
    {
        txtbox.SelectedText = "";
    }
    // Paste event handlers.
    void PasteCanExecute(object sender, CanExecuteRoutedEventArgs args)
    {
        args.CanExecute = Clipboard.ContainsText();
    }
    void PasteOnExecute(object sender, ExecutedRoutedEventArgs args)
    {
        txtbox.Paste();
    }
    // SelectAll event handler.
    void SelectAllOnExecute(object sender, ExecutedRoutedEventArgs args)
    {
        txtbox.SelectAll();
    }
    // Time/Date event handler.
    void TimeDateOnExecute(object sender, ExecutedRoutedEventArgs args)
    {
        txtbox.SelectedText = DateTime.Now.ToString();
    }
  }
}
```

By comparison, the hard part of the Edit menu involves the commands Find, Find Next, and Replace. These commands involve modeless dialog boxes. The Find and Replace dialog boxes are so similar that I first wrote an abstract class named *FindReplaceDialog* that contained all the controls common to both the Find and Replace dialogs. The class isn't very complex, and the code is mostly devoted to laying out the controls in a *Grid* on the surface of the dialog. Because this is a modeless dialog box, it looks a little different from other classes that derive from *Window*. The dialog box contains a Cancel button, but that's not necessarily required in a modeless dialog box because the user can terminate the dialog by closing the window. Consequently, all the Cancel button does is call *Close*.

What modeless dialog boxes almost always require are public events. The three events that *FindReplaceDialog* defines (at the very top of the class) are called *FindNext*, *Replace*, and *ReplaceAll*, and they correspond to the three other buttons in the dialog. These events provide a way for the modeless dialog to notify its owner window that the user has pressed one of these buttons and is expecting something to happen.

```
FindReplaceDialog.cs
//---------------------------------------------------
// FindReplaceDialog.cs (c) 2006 by Charles Petzold
//---------------------------------------------------
using System;
using System.Windows;
using System.Windows.Controls;

namespace Petzold.NotepadClone
{
    abstract class FindReplaceDialog : Window
    {
        // Public events.
        public event EventHandler FindNext;
        public event EventHandler Replace;
        public event EventHandler ReplaceAll;

        // Protected fields.
        protected Label lblReplace;
        protected TextBox txtboxFind, txtboxReplace;
        protected CheckBox checkMatch;
        protected GroupBox groupDirection;
        protected RadioButton radioDown, radioUp;
        protected Button btnFind, btnReplace, btnAll;

        // Public properties.
        public string FindWhat
        {
            set { txtboxFind.Text = value; }
            get { return txtboxFind.Text; }
        }
        public string ReplaceWith
        {
            set { txtboxReplace.Text = value; }
            get { return txtboxReplace.Text; }
        }
```

```csharp
    public bool MatchCase
    {
        set { checkMatch.IsChecked = value; }
        get { return (bool)checkMatch.IsChecked; }
    }
    public Direction Direction
    {
        set
        {
            if (value == Direction.Down)
                radioDown.IsChecked = true;
            else
                radioUp.IsChecked = true;
        }
        get
        {
            return (bool)radioDown.IsChecked ? Direction.Down : Direction.Up;
        }
    }

    // Protected constructor (because class is abstract).
    protected FindReplaceDialog(Window owner)
    {
        // Set common dialog box properties.
        ShowInTaskbar = false;
        WindowStyle = WindowStyle.ToolWindow;
        SizeToContent = SizeToContent.WidthAndHeight;
        WindowStartupLocation = WindowStartupLocation.CenterOwner;
        Owner = owner;

        // Create Grid with three auto-sized rows and columns.
        Grid grid = new Grid();
        Content = grid;

        for (int i = 0; i < 3; i++)
        {
            RowDefinition rowdef = new RowDefinition();
            rowdef.Height = GridLength.Auto;
            grid.RowDefinitions.Add(rowdef);

            ColumnDefinition coldef = new ColumnDefinition();
            coldef.Width = GridLength.Auto;
            grid.ColumnDefinitions.Add(coldef);
        }

        // Find what: Label and TextBox.
        Label lbl = new Label();
        lbl.Content = "Fi_nd what:";
        lbl.VerticalAlignment = VerticalAlignment.Center;
        lbl.Margin = new Thickness(12);
        grid.Children.Add(lbl);
        Grid.SetRow(lbl, 0);
        Grid.SetColumn(lbl, 0);
```

```
txtboxFind = new TextBox();
txtboxFind.Margin = new Thickness(12);
txtboxFind.TextChanged += FindTextBoxOnTextChanged;
grid.Children.Add(txtboxFind);
Grid.SetRow(txtboxFind, 0);
Grid.SetColumn(txtboxFind, 1);

// Replace with: Label and TextBox.
lblReplace = new Label();
lblReplace.Content = "Re_place with:";
lblReplace.VerticalAlignment = VerticalAlignment.Center;
lblReplace.Margin = new Thickness(12);
grid.Children.Add(lblReplace);
Grid.SetRow(lblReplace, 1);
Grid.SetColumn(lblReplace, 0);

txtboxReplace = new TextBox();
txtboxReplace.Margin = new Thickness(12);
grid.Children.Add(txtboxReplace);
Grid.SetRow(txtboxReplace, 1);
Grid.SetColumn(txtboxReplace, 1);

// Match Case CheckBox.
checkMatch = new CheckBox();
checkMatch.Content = "Match _case";
checkMatch.VerticalAlignment = VerticalAlignment.Center;
checkMatch.Margin = new Thickness(12);
grid.Children.Add(checkMatch);
Grid.SetRow(checkMatch, 2);
Grid.SetColumn(checkMatch, 0);

// Direction GroupBox and two RadioButtons.
groupDirection = new GroupBox();
groupDirection.Header = "Direction";
groupDirection.Margin = new Thickness(12);
groupDirection.HorizontalAlignment = HorizontalAlignment.Left;
grid.Children.Add(groupDirection);
Grid.SetRow(groupDirection, 2);
Grid.SetColumn(groupDirection, 1);

StackPanel stack = new StackPanel();
stack.Orientation = Orientation.Horizontal;
groupDirection.Content = stack;

radioUp = new RadioButton();
radioUp.Content = "_Up";
radioUp.Margin = new Thickness(6);
stack.Children.Add(radioUp);

radioDown = new RadioButton();
radioDown.Content = "_Down";
radioDown.Margin = new Thickness(6);
stack.Children.Add(radioDown);
```

```
        // Create StackPanel for the buttons.
        stack = new StackPanel();
        stack.Margin = new Thickness(6);
        grid.Children.Add(stack);

        Grid.SetRow(stack, 0);
        Grid.SetColumn(stack, 2);
        Grid.SetRowSpan(stack, 3);

        // Four buttons.
        btnFind = new Button();
        btnFind.Content = "_Find Next";
        btnFind.Margin = new Thickness(6);
        btnFind.IsDefault = true;
        btnFind.Click += FindNextOnClick;
        stack.Children.Add(btnFind);

        btnReplace = new Button();
        btnReplace.Content = "_Replace";
        btnReplace.Margin = new Thickness(6);
        btnReplace.Click += ReplaceOnClick;
        stack.Children.Add(btnReplace);

        btnAll = new Button();
        btnAll.Content = "Replace _All";
        btnAll.Margin = new Thickness(6);
        btnAll.Click += ReplaceAllOnClick;
        stack.Children.Add(btnAll);

        Button btn = new Button();
        btn.Content = "Cancel";
        btn.Margin = new Thickness(6);
        btn.IsCancel = true;
        btn.Click += CancelOnClick;
        stack.Children.Add(btn);

        txtboxFind.Focus();
    }
    // Enable the first three buttons only if there's some text to find.
    void FindTextBoxOnTextChanged(object sender, TextChangedEventArgs args)
    {
        TextBox txtbox = args.Source as TextBox;
        btnFind.IsEnabled =
        btnReplace.IsEnabled =
        btnAll.IsEnabled = (txtbox.Text.Length > 0);
    }
    // The FindNextOnClick method calls the OnFindNext method,
    //      which fires the FindNext event.
    void FindNextOnClick(object sender, RoutedEventArgs args)
    {
        OnFindNext(new EventArgs());
    }
    protected virtual void OnFindNext(EventArgs args)
    {
        if (FindNext != null)
            FindNext(this, args);
    }
```

```
        // The ReplaceOnClick method calls the OnReplace method,
        //      which fires the Replace event.
        void ReplaceOnClick(object sender, RoutedEventArgs args)
        {
            OnReplace(new EventArgs());
        }
        protected virtual void OnReplace(EventArgs args)
        {
            if (Replace != null)
                Replace(this, args);
        }
        // The ReplaceAllOnClick method calls the OnReplaceAll method,
        //      which fires the ReplaceAll event.
        void ReplaceAllOnClick(object sender, RoutedEventArgs args)
        {
            OnReplaceAll(new EventArgs());
        }
        protected virtual void OnReplaceAll(EventArgs args)
        {
            if (ReplaceAll != null)
                ReplaceAll(this, args);
        }
        // The Cancel button just closes the dialog box.
        void CancelOnClick(object sender, RoutedEventArgs args)
        {
            Close();
        }
    }
}
```

The three events defined by *FindReplaceDialog* are standard, old-fashioned .NET events. Each event is associated with a protected virtual method whose name begins with the word *On* followed by the event name. These *On* methods are responsible for triggering the actual events. In this program, each *On* method is called by the *Click* event handler of the button associated with the event. These *On* methods aren't required, but they are available to override for any class that cares to inherit from *FindReplaceDialog*.

The *FindDialog* class derives from *FindReplaceDialog* and simply hides those controls that don't belong.

FindDialog.cs
```
//-----------------------------------------
// FindDialog.cs (c) 2006 by Charles Petzold
//-----------------------------------------
using System;
using System.Windows;
using System.Windows.Controls;

namespace Petzold.NotepadClone
{
    class FindDialog : FindReplaceDialog
    {
```

```
        public FindDialog(Window owner): base(owner)
        {
            Title = "Find";

            // Hide some controls.
            lblReplace.Visibility = Visibility.Collapsed;
            txtboxReplace.Visibility = Visibility.Collapsed;
            btnReplace.Visibility = Visibility.Collapsed;
            btnAll.Visibility = Visibility.Collapsed;
        }
    }
}
```

The *ReplaceDialog* class could potentially do more than simply assign its own *Title* property, but that's all it does here:.

ReplaceDialog.cs
```
//--------------------------------------------------
// ReplaceDialog.cs (c) 2006 by Charles Petzold
//--------------------------------------------------
using System;
using System.Windows;
using System.Windows.Controls;

namespace Petzold.NotepadClone
{
    class ReplaceDialog : FindReplaceDialog
    {
        public ReplaceDialog(Window owner): base(owner)
        {
            Title = "Replace";
        }
    }
}
```

The *FindReplaceDialog* class also makes use of this enumeration for searching down or up through the text:

Direction.cs
```
namespace Petzold.NotepadClone
{
    enum Direction
    {
        Down,
        Up
    }
}
```

The NotepadClone.Find.cs file is responsible for creating the three find and replace *MenuItem* objects for the Edit menu. The *Click* event handlers for Find and Replace create objects of type

FindDialog and *ReplaceDialog* respectively, and install event handlers for one or more of the custom events defined by the *FindReplaceDialog* class. This is how the program is notified when the user clicks one of the buttons on the dialog.

```
NotepadClone.Find.cs
//---------------------------------------------------
// NotepadClone.Find.cs (c) 2006 by Charles Petzold
//---------------------------------------------------
using System;
using System.Windows;
using System.Windows.Controls;
using System.Windows.Input;

namespace Petzold.NotepadClone
{
    public partial class NotepadClone
    {
        string strFindWhat = "", strReplaceWith = "";
        StringComparison strcomp = StringComparison.OrdinalIgnoreCase;
        Direction dirFind = Direction.Down;
        void AddFindMenuItems(MenuItem itemEdit)
        {
            // Find menu item
            MenuItem itemFind = new MenuItem();
            itemFind.Header = "_Find...";
            itemFind.Command = ApplicationCommands.Find;
            itemEdit.Items.Add(itemFind);
            CommandBindings.Add(new CommandBinding(
                ApplicationCommands.Find, FindOnExecute, FindCanExecute));

            // The Find Next item requires a custom RoutedUICommand.
            InputGestureCollection coll = new InputGestureCollection();
            coll.Add(new KeyGesture(Key.F3));
            RoutedUICommand commFindNext =
                new RoutedUICommand("Find _Next", "FindNext", GetType(), coll);

            MenuItem itemNext = new MenuItem();
            itemNext.Command = commFindNext;
            itemEdit.Items.Add(itemNext);
            CommandBindings.Add(
                new CommandBinding(commFindNext, FindNextOnExecute,
                                                FindNextCanExecute));
            MenuItem itemReplace = new MenuItem();
            itemReplace.Header = "_Replace...";
            itemReplace.Command = ApplicationCommands.Replace;
            itemEdit.Items.Add(itemReplace);
            CommandBindings.Add(new CommandBinding(
                ApplicationCommands.Replace, ReplaceOnExecute, FindCanExecute));
        }
        // CanExecute method for Find and Replace.
        void FindCanExecute(object sender, CanExecuteRoutedEventArgs args)
        {
            args.CanExecute = (txtbox.Text.Length > 0 && OwnedWindows.Count == 0);
        }
```

```
        void FindNextCanExecute(object sender, CanExecuteRoutedEventArgs args)
        {
            args.CanExecute = (txtbox.Text.Length > 0 && strFindWhat.Length > 0);
        }
        // Event handler for Find menu item.
        void FindOnExecute(object sender, ExecutedRoutedEventArgs args)
        {
            // Create dialog box.
            FindDialog dlg = new FindDialog(this);

            // Initialize properties.
            dlg.FindWhat = strFindWhat;
            dlg.MatchCase = strcomp == StringComparison.Ordinal;
            dlg.Direction = dirFind;

            // Install event handler and show dialog.
            dlg.FindNext += FindDialogOnFindNext;
            dlg.Show();
        }
        // Event handler for Find Next menu item.
        // F3 key invokes dialog box if there's no string to find yet.
        void FindNextOnExecute(object sender, ExecutedRoutedEventArgs args)
        {
            if (strFindWhat == null || strFindWhat.Length == 0)
                FindOnExecute(sender, args);
            else
                FindNext();
        }
        // Event handler for Replace menu item.
        void ReplaceOnExecute(object sender, ExecutedRoutedEventArgs args)
        {
            ReplaceDialog dlg = new ReplaceDialog(this);

            dlg.FindWhat = strFindWhat;
            dlg.ReplaceWith = strReplaceWith;
            dlg.MatchCase = strcomp == StringComparison.Ordinal;
            dlg.Direction = dirFind;

            // Install event handlers.
            dlg.FindNext += FindDialogOnFindNext;
            dlg.Replace += ReplaceDialogOnReplace;
            dlg.ReplaceAll += ReplaceDialogOnReplaceAll;

            dlg.Show();
        }


        // Event handler installed for Find/Replace dialog box "Find Next" button.
        void FindDialogOnFindNext(object sender, EventArgs args)
        {
            FindReplaceDialog dlg = sender as FindReplaceDialog;

            // Get properties from dialog box.
            strFindWhat = dlg.FindWhat;
            strcomp = dlg.MatchCase ? StringComparison.Ordinal :
                            StringComparison.OrdinalIgnoreCase;
            dirFind = dlg.Direction;
```

```
            // Call FindNext to do the actual find.
        FindNext();
    }

// Event handler installed for Replace dialog box "Replace" button.
void ReplaceDialogOnReplace(object sender, EventArgs args)
{
    ReplaceDialog dlg = sender as ReplaceDialog;
    // Get properties from dialog box.
    strFindWhat = dlg.FindWhat;
    strReplaceWith = dlg.ReplaceWith;
    strcomp = dlg.MatchCase ? StringComparison.Ordinal :

                        StringComparison.OrdinalIgnoreCase;
    if (strFindWhat.Equals(txtbox.SelectedText, strcomp))
        txtbox.SelectedText = strReplaceWith;
    FindNext();
}

// Event handler installed for Replace dialog box "Replace All" button.
void ReplaceDialogOnReplaceAll(object sender, EventArgs args)
{
    ReplaceDialog dlg = sender as ReplaceDialog;
    string str = txtbox.Text;
    strFindWhat = dlg.FindWhat;
    strReplaceWith = dlg.ReplaceWith;
    strcomp = dlg.MatchCase ? StringComparison.Ordinal :
                    StringComparison.OrdinalIgnoreCase;
    int index = 0;
    while (index + strFindWhat.Length < str.Length)
    {

        index = str.IndexOf(strFindWhat, index, strcomp);

        if (index != -1)
        {
            str = str.Remove(index, strFindWhat.Length);
            str = str.Insert(index, strReplaceWith);
            index += strReplaceWith.Length;
        }
        else
            break;
    }
    txtbox.Text = str;
}

// General FindNext method.
void FindNext()
{
    int indexStart, indexFind;

    // The starting position of the search and the direction of the search
    //      are determined by the dirFind variable.
    if (dirFind == Direction.Down)
```

```
        {
            indexStart = txtbox.SelectionStart + txtbox.SelectionLength;
            indexFind = txtbox.Text.IndexOf(strFindWhat, indexStart, strcomp);
        }
        else
        {
            indexStart = txtbox.SelectionStart;
            indexFind = txtbox.Text.LastIndexOf(strFindWhat, indexStart, strcomp);
        }
        // If IndexOf (or LastIndexOf) does not return -1, select the found text.
        // Otherwise, display a message box.
        if (indexFind != -1)
        {
            txtbox.Select(indexFind, strFindWhat.Length);
            txtbox.Focus();
        }
        else
            MessageBox.Show("Cannot find \"" + strFindWhat + "\"", Title,
                        MessageBoxButton.OK, MessageBoxImage.Information);
    }
  }
}
```

The Format menu contains two menu items: Word Wrap and Font. In the standard Windows Notepad, the Word Wrap option is checked or unchecked. But in my Notepad Clone, I wanted to expose the three options (*TextWrapping.NoWrap*, *TextWrapping.Wrap*, and *TextWrapping.Wrap-WithOverflow*), if only to test the printing logic in the *PlainTextDocumentPaginator* class.

The following class derives from *MenuItem* and is named *WordWrapMenuItem*. This is the item that will appear in the Format menu. The *Header* property is the text "Word Wrap" and *Items* collection contains three items in a submenu that correspond to the three members of the *TextWrapping* enumeration. Notice that each of these three items has its *Tag* property set to one of the *TextWrapping* members.

WordWrapMenuItem.cs

```
//-----------------------------------------------
// WordWrapMenuItem.cs (c) 2006 by Charles Petzold
//-----------------------------------------------
using System;
using System.Windows;
using System.Windows.Controls;
using System.Windows.Controls.Primitives;
namespace Petzold.NotepadClone
{
    public class WordWrapMenuItem : MenuItem
    {
        // Register WordWrap dependency property.
        public static DependencyProperty WordWrapProperty =
                DependencyProperty.Register("WordWrap", typeof(TextWrapping),
                                    typeof(WordWrapMenuItem));
        // Define WordWrap property.
```

```
        public TextWrapping WordWrap
        {
            set { SetValue(WordWrapProperty, value); }
            get { return (TextWrapping)GetValue(WordWrapProperty); }
        }
        // Constructor creates Word Wrap menu item.
        public WordWrapMenuItem()
        {
            Header = "_Word Wrap";

            MenuItem item = new MenuItem();
            item.Header = "_No Wrap";
            item.Tag = TextWrapping.NoWrap;
            item.Click += MenuItemOnClick;
            Items.Add(item);

            item = new MenuItem();
            item.Header = "_Wrap";
            item.Tag = TextWrapping.Wrap;
            item.Click += MenuItemOnClick;
            Items.Add(item);

            item = new MenuItem();
            item.Header = "Wrap with _Overflow";
            item.Tag = TextWrapping.WrapWithOverflow;
            item.Click += MenuItemOnClick;
            Items.Add(item);
        }
        // Set checked item from current WordWrap property.
        protected override void OnSubmenuOpened(RoutedEventArgs args)
        {
            base.OnSubmenuOpened(args);

            foreach (MenuItem item in Items)
                item.IsChecked = ((TextWrapping)item.Tag == WordWrap);
        }
        // Set WordWrap property from clicked item.
        void MenuItemOnClick(object sender, RoutedEventArgs args)
        {
            WordWrap = (TextWrapping)(args.Source as MenuItem).Tag;
        }
    }
}
```

This class defines a dependency property named *WordWrapProperty* as the basis for a public *WordWrap* property. The class references this *WordWrap* property in its two event handlers. The *OnSubmenuOpened* method applies a checkmark to the item whose *Tag* property equals the current value of the *WordWrap* property. The *MenuItemOnClick* method sets the *WordWrap* property to the *Tag* property of the clicked item.

Notice that the *WordWrapMenuItem* class contains no reference to the *TextBox*. Apart from the public constructor, the public *WordWrap* property, and the public *WordWrapProperty* field, the class appears to be rather self-contained. How does it interact with the *TextWrapping* property of the *TextBox*?

The answer is data binding, as the next installment of the *NotepadClone* class demonstrates.

NotepadClone.Format.cs

```
//----------------------------------------------------
// NotepadClone.Format.cs (c) 2006 by Charles Petzold
//----------------------------------------------------
using Petzold.ChooseFont;
using System;
using System.Windows;
using System.Windows.Controls;
using System.Windows.Data;
using System.Windows.Media;

namespace Petzold.NotepadClone
{
    public partial class NotepadClone
    {
        void AddFormatMenu(Menu menu)
        {
            // Create top-level Format item.
            MenuItem itemFormat = new MenuItem();
            itemFormat.Header = "F_ormat";
            menu.Items.Add(itemFormat);

            // Create Word Wrap menu item.
            WordWrapMenuItem itemWrap = new WordWrapMenuItem();
            itemFormat.Items.Add(itemWrap);

            // Bind item to TextWrapping property of TextBox.
            Binding bind = new Binding();
            bind.Path = new PropertyPath(TextBox.TextWrappingProperty);
            bind.Source = txtbox;
            bind.Mode = BindingMode.TwoWay;
            itemWrap.SetBinding(WordWrapMenuItem.WordWrapProperty, bind);

            // Create Font menu item.
            MenuItem itemFont = new MenuItem();
            itemFont.Header = "_Font...";
            itemFont.Click += FontOnClick;
            itemFormat.Items.Add(itemFont);
        }
        // Font item event handler.
        void FontOnClick(object sender, RoutedEventArgs args)
        {
            FontDialog dlg = new FontDialog();
            dlg.Owner = this;
            // Set TextBox properties in FontDialog.
            dlg.Typeface = new Typeface(txtbox.FontFamily, txtbox.FontStyle,
                                    txtbox.FontWeight, txtbox.FontStretch);
            dlg.FaceSize = txtbox.FontSize;
```

```
            if (dlg.ShowDialog().GetValueOrDefault())
            {
                // Set FontDialog properties in TextBox.
                txtbox.FontFamily = dlg.Typeface.FontFamily;
                txtbox.FontSize = dlg.FaceSize;
                txtbox.FontStyle = dlg.Typeface.Style;
                txtbox.FontWeight = dlg.Typeface.Weight;
                txtbox.FontStretch = dlg.Typeface.Stretch;
            }
        }
    }
}
```

After creating a *WordWrapMenuItem* object and adding it to the Format item, the program creates a *Binding* object to bind the *TextWrapping* property of the *TextBox* with the *WordWrap* property of *WordWrapMenuItem*:

```
Binding bind = new Binding();
bind.Path = new PropertyPath(TextBox.TextWrappingProperty);
bind.Source = txtbox;
bind.Mode = BindingMode.TwoWay;
itemWrap.SetBinding(WordWrapMenuItem.WordWrapProperty, bind);
```

This is not the only way to define this data binding. In the code shown, the *TextBox* is considered the source of the data and the *WordWrapMenuItem* is the target of the data. The binding mode is set to *TwoWay* so that changes in the target are also reflected in the source (which is the normal way that the data changes are reflected). But it's easy to switch around the source and target:

```
Binding bind = new Binding();
bind.Path = new PropertyPath(WordWrapMenuItem.WordWrapProperty);
bind.Source = itemWrap;
bind.Mode = BindingMode.TwoWay;
txtbox.SetBinding(TextBox.TextWrappingProperty, bind);
```

Notice that the last statement now calls the *SetBinding* method of the *TextBox* rather than the *WordWrapMenuItem*.

The easy part of the Format menu is the Font item. (Well, it's easy if you have the *FontDialog* class from the previous chapter available!) The *Click* event handler creates a *FontDialog* object, initializes the *Typeface* and *FaceSize* properties from the *TextBox*, and then updates the *TextBox* properties if the user clicks OK.

The View menu is fairly trivial. It contains a single Status Bar item that displays or hides the program's status bar. All it needs to do is toggle the *Visibility* property of the *StatusBar* between *Visibility.Visible* and *Visibility.Collapsed*.

NotepadClone.View.cs

```
//-------------------------------------------------
// NotepadClone.View.cs (c) 2006 by Charles Petzold
//-------------------------------------------------
using System;
using System.Windows;
using System.Windows.Controls;

namespace Petzold.NotepadClone
{
    public partial class NotepadClone
    {
        MenuItem itemStatus;

        void AddViewMenu(Menu menu)
        {
            // Create top-level View item.
            MenuItem itemView = new MenuItem();
            itemView.Header = "_View";
            itemView.SubmenuOpened += ViewOnOpen;
            menu.Items.Add(itemView);

            // Create Status Bar item on View menu.
            itemStatus = new MenuItem();
            itemStatus.Header = "_Status Bar";
            itemStatus.IsCheckable = true;
            itemStatus.Checked += StatusOnCheck;
            itemStatus.Unchecked += StatusOnCheck;
            itemView.Items.Add(itemStatus);
        }
        void ViewOnOpen(object sender, RoutedEventArgs args)
        {
            itemStatus.IsChecked = (status.Visibility == Visibility.Visible);
        }
        void StatusOnCheck(object sender, RoutedEventArgs args)
        {
            MenuItem item = sender as MenuItem;
            status.Visibility =
                item.IsChecked ? Visibility.Visible : Visibility.Collapsed;
        }
    }
}
```

We're in the home stretch now. The final item on the top-level menu is Help, but I'm not going to implement the Help Topics item. I'll show you how to create a Help file in Chapter 25. This Help menu displays a single menu item with the text "About Notepad Clone..." and invokes the *AboutDialog* class when the item is clicked.

NotepadClone.Help.cs

```
//-------------------------------------------------
// NotepadClone.Help.cs (c) 2006 by Charles Petzold
//-------------------------------------------------
using System;

using System.Reflection;

using System.Windows;
using System.Windows.Controls;

namespace Petzold.NotepadClone
{
    public partial class NotepadClone
    {
        void AddHelpMenu(Menu menu)
        {
            MenuItem itemHelp = new MenuItem();
            itemHelp.Header = "_Help";
            itemHelp.SubmenuOpened += ViewOnOpen;
            menu.Items.Add(itemHelp);

            MenuItem itemAbout = new MenuItem();
            itemAbout.Header = "_About " + strAppTitle + "...";
            itemAbout.Click += AboutOnClick;
            itemHelp.Items.Add(itemAbout);
        }
        void AboutOnClick(object sender, RoutedEventArgs args)
        {
            AboutDialog dlg = new AboutDialog(this);
            dlg.ShowDialog();
        }
    }
}
```

The constructor in the following *AboutDialog* class begins by accessing the assembly to fish out several attributes that it uses for constructing *TextBlock* objects. The only part of this file that's hard-coded is the URL of my Web site, which is displayed by a *Hyperlink* text element, and which is passed to the static *Process.Start* method to launch your Web browser.

AboutDialog.cs

```
//-------------------------------------------
// AboutDialog.cs (c) 2006 by Charles Petzold
//-------------------------------------------
using System;
using System.Diagnostics;        // for Process class
using System.Reflection;
using System.Windows;
using System.Windows.Controls;
using System.Windows.Documents;
using System.Windows.Media;
namespace Petzold.NotepadClone
```

```csharp
{
    class AboutDialog : Window
    {
        public AboutDialog(Window owner)
        {
            // Get attributes from assembly.
            // Get this executing assembly to access attributes.
            Assembly asmbly = Assembly.GetExecutingAssembly();
            // Get the AssemblyTitle attribute for the program name.
            AssemblyTitleAttribute title =
                (AssemblyTitleAttribute)asmbly.GetCustomAttributes(
                    typeof(AssemblyTitleAttribute), false)[0];
            string strTitle = title.Title;

            // Get the AssemblyFileVersion attribute.
            AssemblyFileVersionAttribute version =
                (AssemblyFileVersionAttribute)asmbly.GetCustomAttributes(
                    typeof(AssemblyFileVersionAttribute), false)[0];
            string strVersion = version.Version.Substring(0, 3);
            // Get the AssemblyCopyright attribute.
            AssemblyCopyrightAttribute copy =
                (AssemblyCopyrightAttribute)asmbly.GetCustomAttributes(
                    typeof(AssemblyCopyrightAttribute), false)[0];
            string strCopyright = copy.Copyright;

            // Standard window properties for dialog boxes.
            Title = "About " + strTitle;
            ShowInTaskbar = false;
            SizeToContent = SizeToContent.WidthAndHeight;
            ResizeMode = ResizeMode.NoResize;
            Left = owner.Left + 96;
            Top = owner.Top + 96;

            // Create StackPanel as content of window.
            StackPanel stackMain = new StackPanel();
            Content = stackMain;

            // Create TextBlock for program name.
            TextBlock txtblk = new TextBlock();
            txtblk.Text = strTitle + " Version " + strVersion;
            txtblk.FontFamily = new FontFamily("Times New Roman");
            txtblk.FontSize = 32;          // 24 points
            txtblk.FontStyle = FontStyles.Italic;
            txtblk.Margin = new Thickness(24);
            txtblk.HorizontalAlignment = HorizontalAlignment.Center;
            stackMain.Children.Add(txtblk);

            // Create TextBlock for copyright.
            txtblk = new TextBlock();
            txtblk.Text = strCopyright;
            txtblk.FontSize = 20;          // 15 points.
            txtblk.HorizontalAlignment = HorizontalAlignment.Center;
            stackMain.Children.Add(txtblk);
            // Create TextBlock for Web site link.
            Run run = new Run("www.charlespetzold.com");
```

```
            Hyperlink link = new Hyperlink(run);
            link.Click += LinkOnClick;
            txtblk = new TextBlock(link);
            txtblk.FontSize = 20;
            txtblk.HorizontalAlignment = HorizontalAlignment.Center;
            stackMain.Children.Add(txtblk);

            // Create OK button.
            Button btn = new Button();
            btn.Content = "OK";
            btn.IsDefault = true;
            btn.IsCancel = true;
            btn.HorizontalAlignment = HorizontalAlignment.Center;
            btn.Margin = new Thickness(24);
            btn.Click += OkOnClick;
            stackMain.Children.Add(btn);

            btn.Focus();
        }
        // Event handlers.
        void LinkOnClick(object sender, RoutedEventArgs args)
        {
            Process.Start("http://www.charlespetzold.com");
        }
        void OkOnClick(object sender, RoutedEventArgs args)
        {
            DialogResult = true;
        }
    }
}
```

The OK button has both its *IsDefault* and *IsCancel* properties set to *true* to allow the user to dismiss the dialog with either the Enter key or the Escape key.

With this file, the Notepad Clone project is complete. As I've already promised, at the beginning of Chapter 20 I'm going to resurrect this project, add a couple of files to it, and turn it into a programming tool named XAML Cruncher. The purpose of the next chapter is to introduce you to XAML and convince you that XAML Cruncher is a valuable tool to have.

Part II
Markup

Chapter 19
XAML (Rhymes with Camel)

This is a valid snippet of Extensible Markup Language (XML):

```
<Button Foreground="LightSeaGreen" FontSize="24pt">
    Hello, XAML!
</Button>
```

These three lines comprise a single XML element: a start tag, an end tag, and content between the two tags. The element type is *Button*. The start tag includes two attribute specifications with attribute names of *Foreground* and *FontSize*. These are assigned attribute values, which XML requires to be enclosed in single or double quotation marks. Between the start tag and end tag is the element content, which in this case is some character data (to use the XML terminology).

XML was designed as a general-purpose markup language that would have a wide range of applications, and the Extensible Application Markup Language (or XAML) is one of those applications.

XAML (pronounced "zammel") is a supplementary programming interface for the Window Presentation Foundation. As you may have surmised, that snippet of XML is also a valid snippet of XAML. *Button* is a class defined in the *System.Windows.Controls* namespace, and *Foreground* and *FontSize* are properties of that class. The text "Hello, XAML!" is the text that you would normally assign to the *Content* property of the *Button* object.

XAML is designed mostly for object creation and initialization. The XAML snippet shown above corresponds to the following equivalent (but somewhat wordier) C# code:

```
Button btn = new Button();
btn.Foreground = Brushes.LightSeaGreen;
btn.FontSize = 32;
btn.Content = "Hello, XAML!"
```

Notice that the XAML does not require that *LightSeaGreen* be explicitly identified as a member of the *Brushes* class, and that the string "24pt" is acceptable as an expression of 24 points. A typographical point is 1/72 inch, so 24 points corresponds to 32 device-independent units. Although XML can often be somewhat verbose (and XAML increases the verbosity in some respects), XAML is often more concise than the equivalent procedural code.

The layout of a program's window is often a hierarchy of panels, controls, and other elements. This hierarchy is paralleled by nested elements in XAML:

```
<StackPanel>
    <Button Foreground="LightSeaGreen" FontSize="24pt">
        Hello, XAML!
    </Button>
```

```
    <Ellipse Fill="Brown" Width="200" Height="100" />

    <Button>
        <Image Source="http://www.charlespetzold.com/PetzoldTattoo.jpg"
               Stretch="None" />
    </Button>
</StackPanel>
```

In this snippet of XAML, the *StackPanel* has three children: a *Button*, an *Ellipse*, and another *Button*. The first *Button* has text content. The other *Button* has an *Image* for its content. Notice that the *Ellipse* and *Image* elements have no content, so the elements can be written with the special XML empty-element syntax, where the end tag is replaced by a slash before the closing angle bracket of the start tag. Also notice that the *Stretch* attribute of the *Image* element is assigned a member of the *Stretch* enumeration simply by referring to the member name.

A XAML file can often replace an entire constructor of a class that derives from *Window*, which is the part of the class that generally performs layout and attaches event handlers. The event handlers themselves must be written in procedural code such as C#. However, if you can replace an event handler with a data binding, that binding can usually go right into the XAML.

The use of XAML separates the visual appearance of an application from its functionality. This separation allows designers to work with XAML files to create an attractive user interface, while the programmers focus more on the run-time interactions among the elements and controls. Design tools that generate XAML are already becoming available.

Even for programmers who don't have access to a graphics design artist conveniently occupying an adjacent cubicle, Visual Studio has its own built-in designer that generates XAML. Obviously a designer that generates XML is much preferred to a designer that generates C# code, as was the case with the Visual Studio designer for Windows Forms. A designer that generates procedural code must later read that generated code, and it often relies on the code being in a particular format. For that reason, the human programmer isn't allowed to mess with it. XML, however, was specifically designed to be editable by both computer and human. As long as each editor leaves the XAML in a syntactically correct state, there should be no problem.

Despite the availability of designers that generate XAML, you as a programmer will benefit greatly by learning the syntax of XAML, and the best way to learn is by doing. I believe that every WPF programmer should be fluent in XAML and adept at coding XAML by hand, and that's what I'm going to show you how to do.

Although the snippets of XAML shown so far in this chapter might be found in the context of some larger XAML document, they are not ready to stand by themselves. A certain ambiguity exists. What is that *Button* element? Could it be a *shirt* button? An *electrical* button? A *campaign* button? It is very desirable that XML documents not be ambiguous. If two XML documents use the same element name for different purposes, something should clearly distinguish the two documents.

For this reason, the XML *namespace* was devised. A XAML document created by a WPF programmer has a different namespace than XML documents created by a manufacturer of shirt buttons.

You declare a default XML namespace in the document with an attribute of *xmlns*. The namespace applies to the element in which the namespace declaration appears, along with all child elements. XML namespace names must be unique and persistent, and it is very common to use URLs for this purpose. For the XAML used in Windows Presentation Foundation programs, the URL is:

http://schemas.microsoft.com/winfx/2006/xaml/presentation

Don't bother going to your Web browser to look at that location. There's nothing there. It's just a namespace name that Microsoft has devised to uniquely identify XAML elements such as *Button* and *StackPanel* and *Image*.

The snippet of XAML shown at the beginning of this chapter can become a full-fledged XAML document by adding the *xmlns* attribute and the proper namespace:

```
<Button xmlns="http://schemas.microsoft.com/winfx/2006/xaml/presentation"
        Foreground="LightSeaGreen" FontSize="24pt">
    Hello, XAML!
</Button>
```

That XAML is now ready to be put into a little file, perhaps created with Notepad or Notepad-Clone, and perhaps with an XML comment at the top to identify the file. You can save the following file to your hard drive.

XamlButton.xaml
```
<!-- ==============================================
        XamlButton.xaml (c) 2006 by Charles Petzold
     ============================================== -->
<Button xmlns="http://schemas.microsoft.com/winfx/2006/xaml/presentation"
        Foreground="LightSeaGreen" FontSize="24pt">
    Hello, XAML!
</Button>
```

The shaded background of this file listing means that the file is among the source code for this book that you can download from the Microsoft Press Web site. If you don't feel like typing it in, you'll find this file in the *Chapter 19* directory.

However you obtain the file, if you have the WinFx extensions to .NET installed or you're running Microsoft Vista, you can launch the file just like a program by double-clicking the file name in Windows Explorer or, if you're so inclined, by running it off the command-line prompt. You'll see Microsoft Internet Explorer come up, and the button will fill the bulk of Internet Explorer's client area except for a couple of navigation buttons below the Address Bar. The navigation buttons will be disabled because there's no place for them to go from here.

(If you're running Microsoft Vista, the navigation buttons will not appear in the client area; their functionality is subsumed by Internet Explorer's own navigation buttons.)

A file such as XamlButton.xaml is known as "loose" XAML or "stand-alone" XAML. The .xaml file name extension is associated with a program named PresentationHost.exe. Launching the XAML causes PresentationHost.exe to run, and this program is responsible for creating an object of type *Page* (a class derived from *FrameworkElement* but somewhat similar to *Window*), which can then be hosted by Internet Explorer. The PresentationHost.exe program also converts the loaded XAML into an actual *Button* object, and sets that object to the *Content* property of the *Page*.

If there's an error in the XAML, Internet Explorer will let you know, and you can click a "More information" button in Internet Explorer that reveals the presence of PresentationHost.exe and also shows a stack trace. Among references to many other methods in the stack trace, you can spot a particular static method named *XamlReader.Load* in the *System.Windows.Markup* namespace. This is the method that converts XAML into objects, and I'll show you how to use it shortly.

Besides running XamlButton.xaml from your hard drive, you can also put the file on your Web site and launch it from there. You might need to register the MIME type of the .xaml file name extension, however. On some servers, this is accomplished by adding the following line to a file named .htaccess:

```
AddType application/xaml+xml xaml
```

Here's another "stand-alone" XAML file that creates a *StackPanel* with three children: a *Button*, an *Ellipse*, and a *ListBox*.

```
XamlStackPanel.xaml
<!-- =============================================
       XamlStackPanel.xaml (c) 2006 by Charles Petzold
     ============================================= -->
<StackPanel xmlns="http://schemas.microsoft.com/winfx/2006/xaml/presentation">

    <Button HorizontalAlignment="Center" Margin="24">
        Hello, XAML!
    </Button>

    <Ellipse Width="200" Height="100" Margin="24"
             Stroke="Red" StrokeThickness="10" />

    <ListBox Width="100" Height="100" Margin="24">
        <ListBoxItem>Sunday</ListBoxItem>
        <ListBoxItem>Monday</ListBoxItem>
        <ListBoxItem>Tuesday</ListBoxItem>
        <ListBoxItem>Wednesday</ListBoxItem>
        <ListBoxItem>Thursday</ListBoxItem>
        <ListBoxItem>Friday</ListBoxItem>
        <ListBoxItem>Saturday</ListBoxItem>
    </ListBox>

</StackPanel>
```

XML files are required to have only one root element, and in this file that root element is a *StackPanel*. Between the *StackPanel* start tags and end tags is the content of the *StackPanel*—its three children. The *Button* element looks pretty similar to the one you've already seen. The *Ellipse* element includes five attributes (corresponding to properties of the *Ellipse* class) but no content, so it uses the empty-element syntax. The *ListBox* element has seven children, which are *ListBoxItem* elements. The content of each *ListBoxItem* is a text string.

In general, XAML files represent an entire element tree. When PresentationHost.exe loads a XAML file, not only is each element in the tree created and initialized, but the elements are also assembled into the visual tree.

When launching these stand-alone XAML files, you may have noticed that the title bar of Internet Explorer displays the path name of the file. In a real-life application, you probably want to control the text that appears there. You can do that by making the root element a *Page*, setting the *WindowTitle* property, and making the *StackPanel* a child of *Page*, as in this stand-alone XAML file.

```
XamlPage.xaml

<!-- =======================================
        XamlPage.xaml (c) 2006 by Charles Petzold
     ======================================= -->
<Page xmlns="http://schemas.microsoft.com/winfx/2006/xaml/presentation"
      WindowTitle="Xaml Page">
    <StackPanel>

        <Button HorizontalAlignment="Center" Margin="24">
            Hello, XAML!
        </Button>

        <Ellipse Width="200" Height="100" Margin="24"
                 Stroke="Red" StrokeThickness="10" />

        <ListBox Width="100" Height="100" Margin="24">
            <ListBoxItem>Sunday</ListBoxItem>
            <ListBoxItem>Monday</ListBoxItem>
            <ListBoxItem>Tuesday</ListBoxItem>
            <ListBoxItem>Wednesday</ListBoxItem>
            <ListBoxItem>Thursday</ListBoxItem>
            <ListBoxItem>Friday</ListBoxItem>
            <ListBoxItem>Saturday</ListBoxItem>
        </ListBox>

    </StackPanel>
</Page>
```

You might be inclined to try a stand-alone XAML file with a root element of *Window*. That won't work, because PresentationHost.exe wants to make the root element a child of something, and a *Window* object can't be a child of anything. The root element of a stand-alone XAML file can be anything that derives from *FrameworkElement* except for *Window*.

Suppose you have a C# program that defines a string variable (named *strXaml*, for example) containing a small but complete XAML document:

```
string strXaml =
    "<Button xmlns='http://schemas.microsoft.com/winfx/2006/presentation'" +
    "        Foreground='LightSeaGreen' FontSize='24pt'>" +
    "   Click me!" +
    "</Button>";
```

To make the string more readable, I've used single quotes rather than double quotes on the attributes. Could you write a program that parses this string to create and initialize a *Button* object? You'd certainly be using reflection a lot, and making certain assumptions regarding the data used to set the *Foreground* and *FontSize* properties. It's entirely conceivable that such a parser would be possible, so it will be no surprise that one already exists. The *System.Windows.Markup* namespace contains a class named *XamlReader* with a static method named *Load* that can parse XAML and turn it into an initialized object. (In addition, the static *XamlWriter.Save* method goes in the opposite direction. It generates XAML from objects.)

A Windows Presentation Foundation program can use *XamlReader.Load* to convert a chunk of XAML into an object. If the root element of the XAML has child elements, those elements are converted as well and put together in the visual tree implied by the hierarchy of the XAML.

To use *XamlReader.Load*, you'll want a *using* directive for *System.Windows.Markup*, of course, but you'll also need a reference to the System.Xml.dll assembly, which contains XML-related classes that *XamlReader.Load* obviously requires. Unfortunately, *XamlReader.Load* can't directly accept a string argument. Otherwise, you could just pass some XAML directly to the method and cast the result to an object of the desired type:

```
Button btn = (Button) XamlReader.Load(strXaml);    // Won't work!
```

XamlReader.Load requires either a *Stream* object or an *XmlReader* object. Here's one approach I've seen that uses a *MemoryStream* object for the job. (You'll need a *using* directive for the *System.IO* namespace for this code.) A *StreamWriter* writes the string into a *MemoryStream*, and that *MemoryStream* is passed to *XamlReader.Load*:

```
MemoryStream memory = new MemoryStream(strXaml.Length);
StreamWriter writer = new StreamWriter(memory);
writer.Write(strXaml);
writer.Flush();
memory.Seek(0, SeekOrigin.Begin);
object obj = XamlReader.Load(memory);
```

Here's a somewhat smoother approach that requires *using* directives for both *System.Xml* and *System.IO*:

```
StringReader strreader = new StringReader(strXaml);
XmlTextReader xmlreader = new XmlTextReader(strreader);
object obj = XamlReader.Load(xmlreader);
```

You could actually use this approach with one almost-unreadable statement:

```
object obj = XamlReader.Load(new XmlTextReader(new StringReader(strXaml)));
```

The following program defines the *strXaml* string as shown above, converts that short XAML document into an object, and sets it to the *Content* property of the window:

```
LoadEmbeddedXaml.cs
//-------------------------------------------------
// LoadEmbeddedXaml.cs (c) 2006 by Charles Petzold
//-------------------------------------------------
using System;
using System.IO;
using System.Windows;
using System.Windows.Controls;
using System.Windows.Markup;
using System.Xml;

namespace Petzold.LoadEmbeddedXaml
{
    public class LoadEmbeddedXaml : Window
    {
        [STAThread]
        public static void Main()
        {
            Application app = new Application();
            app.Run(new LoadEmbeddedXaml());
        }
        public LoadEmbeddedXaml()
        {
            Title = "Load Embedded Xaml";

            string strXaml =
                "<Button xmlns='http://schemas.microsoft.com/" +
                                "winfx/2006/xaml/presentation'" +
                "       Foreground='LightSeaGreen' FontSize='24pt'>" +
                "   Click me!" +
                "</Button>";

            StringReader strreader = new StringReader(strXaml);
            XmlTextReader xmlreader = new XmlTextReader(strreader);
            object obj = XamlReader.Load(xmlreader);

            Content = obj;
        }
    }
}
```

Because this program happens to know that the object returned from *XamlReader.Load* is actually a *Button* object, the program could cast it to a *Button*:

```
Button btn = (Button) XamlReader.Load(xmlreader);
```

The program could then attach an event handler if you had one in the code:

```
btn.Click += ButtonOnClick;
```

You could do anything with this *Button* that you could do if your program contained explicit code to create and initialize it.

Of course, defining some XAML as a string variable is a little awkward. Perhaps a better approach to converting a chunk of XAML into an object at run time is loading the XAML as a resource stored in the executable file of the program.

Let's begin with an empty project as usual, perhaps named LoadXamlResource. Add a reference to the System.Xml assembly along with the other WPF assemblies. Select Add New Item from the Project menu (or right-click the project name and select Add New Item). Select a template of XML File and a file name of LoadXamlResource.xml. (What I'm going to show you here is somewhat easier if you give this file an extension of .xml rather than .xaml. If you use the .xaml extension, Visual Studio will want to load the XAML designer and make certain assumptions about the file that aren't quite appropriate yet.) Here's the XML file.

LoadXamlResource.xml

```xml
<!-- ================================================
        LoadXamlResource.xml (c) 2006 by Charles Petzold
     ================================================ -->
<StackPanel xmlns="http://schemas.microsoft.com/winfx/2006/xaml/presentation">

    <Button Name="MyButton"
            HorizontalAlignment="Center"
            Margin="24">
        Hello, XAML!
    </Button>

    <Ellipse Width="200"
             Height="100"
             Margin="24"
             Stroke="Red"
             StrokeThickness="10" />

    <ListBox Width="100"
             Height="100"
             Margin="24">
        <ListBoxItem>Sunday</ListBoxItem>
        <ListBoxItem>Monday</ListBoxItem>
        <ListBoxItem>Tuesday</ListBoxItem>
        <ListBoxItem>Wednesday</ListBoxItem>
        <ListBoxItem>Thursday</ListBoxItem>
        <ListBoxItem>Friday</ListBoxItem>
        <ListBoxItem>Saturday</ListBoxItem>
    </ListBox>

</StackPanel>
```

As you can see, this file is very similar to the stand-alone XamlStack.xaml file. The big difference is that I've also included a *Name* attribute for the *Button* object. The *Name* property is defined by *FrameworkElement*.

Very important: Right-click the LoadXamlResource.xml file in Visual Studio and select Properties. Make sure the Build Action is set to Resource or the program won't be able to load it as a resource.

The LoadXamlResource project also contains a rather normal-looking C# file with a class that inherits from *Window*.

```
LoadXamlResource.cs
//-------------------------------------------------
// LoadXamlResource.cs (c) 2006 by Charles Petzold
//-------------------------------------------------
using System;
using System.IO;
using System.Windows;
using System.Windows.Controls;
using System.Windows.Markup;

namespace Petzold.LoadXamlResource
{
    public class LoadXamlResource : Window
    {
        [STAThread]
        public static void Main()
        {
            Application app = new Application();
            app.Run(new LoadXamlResource());
        }
        public LoadXamlResource()
        {
            Title = "Load Xaml Resource";

            Uri uri = new Uri("pack://application:,,,/LoadXamlResource.xml");
            Stream stream = Application.GetResourceStream(uri).Stream;
            FrameworkElement el = XamlReader.Load(stream) as FrameworkElement;
            Content = el;

            Button btn = el.FindName("MyButton") as Button;

            if (btn != null)
                btn.Click += ButtonOnClick;
        }
        void ButtonOnClick(object sender, RoutedEventArgs args)
        {
            MessageBox.Show("The button labeled '" +
                        (args.Source as Button).Content +
                        "' has been clicked");
        }
    }
}
```

The constructor creates a *Uri* object for the XML resource, and uses the static *Application .GetResourceStream* property to return a *StreamResourceInfo* object. *StreamResourceInfo* includes a property named *Stream* that returns a *Stream* object for the resource. This *Stream* object becomes the argument to *XamlReader.Load*, and the object that property returns (an object of type *StackPanel*) is assigned to the *Content* property of the window.

Once the object converted from the XAML has become part of the visual tree of the window, it is possible to use the *FindName* method to locate an element in the tree with the specified name. This is the *Button*. The program can then attach an event handler, or do something else with the element. This is perhaps the most straightforward way in which a program can connect event handlers to XAML loaded at run time.

Here's a little variation. The project is named LoadXamlWindow, and like the previous project, this XML file must have a Build Action of Resource:

```
LoadXamlWindow.xml
<!-- =================================================
        LoadXamlWindow.xml (c) 2006 by Charles Petzold
     ================================================= -->
<Window xmlns="http://schemas.microsoft.com/winfx/2006/xaml/presentation"
        Title="Load Xaml Window"
        SizeToContent="WidthAndHeight"
        ResizeMode="CanMinimize">
    <StackPanel>

        <Button HorizontalAlignment="Center"
                Margin="24">
            Hello, XAML!
        </Button>

        <Ellipse Width="200"
                 Height="100"
                 Margin="24"
                 Stroke="Red"
                 StrokeThickness="10" />

        <ListBox Width="100"
                 Height="100"
                 Margin="24">
            <ListBoxItem>Sunday</ListBoxItem>
            <ListBoxItem>Monday</ListBoxItem>
            <ListBoxItem>Tuesday</ListBoxItem>
            <ListBoxItem>Wednesday</ListBoxItem>
            <ListBoxItem>Thursday</ListBoxItem>
            <ListBoxItem>Friday</ListBoxItem>
            <ListBoxItem>Saturday</ListBoxItem>
        </ListBox>

    </StackPanel>
</Window>
```

This XAML has a root element of *Window*. Notice that the attributes on the *Window* start tag include *Title*, *SizeToContent*, and *ResizeMode*. The latter two are assigned members from the enumeration associated with each property.

A root element of *Window* isn't allowed for stand-alone XAML files because Presentation-Host.exe wants to make the converted XAML a child of something. Fortunately, the following program knows that the XAML resource is a *Window* object, so it doesn't inherit from *Window* or directly create a *Window* object itself.

LoadXamlWindow.cs

```
//----------------------------------------------
// LoadXamlWindow.cs (c) 2006 by Charles Petzold
//----------------------------------------------
using System;
using System.IO;
using System.Windows;
using System.Windows.Controls;
using System.Windows.Markup;

namespace Petzold.LoadXamlWindow
{
    public class LoadXamlWindow
    {
        [STAThread]
        public static void Main()
        {
            Application app = new Application();

            Uri uri = new Uri("pack://application:,,,/LoadXamlWindow.xml");
            Stream stream = Application.GetResourceStream(uri).Stream;
            Window win = XamlReader.Load(stream) as Window;

            win.AddHandler(Button.ClickEvent,
                        new RoutedEventHandler(ButtonOnClick));

            app.Run(win);
        }
        static void ButtonOnClick(object sender, RoutedEventArgs args)
        {
            MessageBox.Show("The button labeled '" +
                        (args.Source as Button).Content +
                        "' has been clicked");
        }
    }
}
```

The *Main* method creates an *Application* object, loads the XAML, and casts the return value of *XamlReader.Load* to a *Window* object. The program installs an event handler for the button's *Click* event not by finding the button in the visual tree, but by calling the *AddHandler* method on the window. Finally the *Main* method passes the *Window* object to the *Run* method of *Application*.

Here's a program that includes an Open File dialog box that lets you load a XAML file from disk. You can use this program to load any of the XAML files shown in this chapter so far, including those with a file name extension of .xml.

```
LoadXamlFile.cs
//-------------------------------------------
// LoadXamlFile.cs (c) 2006 by Charles Petzold
//-------------------------------------------
using Microsoft.Win32;
using System;
using System.IO;
using System.Windows;
using System.Windows.Controls;
using System.Windows.Markup;
using System.Xml;

namespace Petzold.LoadXamlFile
{
    public class LoadXamlFile : Window
    {
        Frame frame;

        [STAThread]
        public static void Main()
        {
            Application app = new Application();
            app.Run(new LoadXamlFile());
        }
        public LoadXamlFile()
        {
            Title = "Load XAML File";

            DockPanel dock = new DockPanel();
            Content = dock;

            // Create button for Open File dialog.
            Button btn = new Button();
            btn.Content = "Open File...";
            btn.Margin = new Thickness(12);
            btn.HorizontalAlignment = HorizontalAlignment.Left;
            btn.Click += ButtonOnClick;
            dock.Children.Add(btn);
            DockPanel.SetDock(btn, Dock.Top);

            // Create Frame for hosting loaded XAML.
            frame = new Frame();
            dock.Children.Add(frame);
        }
        void ButtonOnClick(object sender, RoutedEventArgs args)
        {
            OpenFileDialog dlg = new OpenFileDialog();
            dlg.Filter = "XAML Files (*.xaml)|*.xaml|All files (*.*)|*.*";
```

```
        if ((bool)dlg.ShowDialog())
        {
            try
            {
                // Read file with XmlTextReader.
                XmlTextReader xmlreader = new XmlTextReader(dlg.FileName);

                // Convert XAML to object.
                object obj = XamlReader.Load(xmlreader);

                // If it's a Window, call Show.
                if (obj is Window)
                {
                    Window win = obj as Window;
                    win.Owner = this;
                    win.Show();
                }

                // Otherwise, set as Content of Frame.
                else
                    frame.Content = obj;
            }
            catch (Exception exc)
            {
                MessageBox.Show(exc.Message, Title);
            }
        }
    }
}
```

As you can see in the *ButtonOnClick* method, getting a file name from *OpenFileDialog* makes
the XAML loading a bit easier than in the programs that loaded XAML as resources. The file
name can be passed directly to the *XmlTextReader* constructor, and that object is accepted by
XamlReader.Load.

The method has some special logic if the object returned from *XamlReader.Load* is a *Window.*
It sets the *Owner* property of the *Window* object to itself and then calls *Show* as if the loaded
window were a modeless dialog box. (I added the code to set the *Owner* property after I discovered that I could close the main application window, but the window loaded from XAML
would still hang around, preventing the application from terminating. That didn't seem quite
proper to me. An alternative solution is setting the *ShutdownMode* property of the *Application*
object to *ShutdownMode.OnMainWindowClose*, which is the approach taken by the XAML
Cruncher program in the next chapter.)

You have now seen a couple of different approaches to loading a XAML element tree at run
time, and you've even gotten a feel for how the code that loads the XAML can locate various
elements in the tree and attach event handlers to them.

However, in real-life applications, it's much more common to compile the XAML along with
the rest of your source code. It's more efficient, certainly, and there are certain desirable things

you can do by compiling the XAML that simply cannot be done in stand-alone XAML. One of these desirable things is specifying the name of an event handler right in the XAML. Generally this event handler itself is located in a procedural code file, but you can also embed some C# code right in the XAML. This is possible only when you compile the XAML with the rest of your project. Generally your project will contain one XAML file for every page or window in the application (including dialog boxes), and a code file associated with each XAML file (often called a *code behind* file). But you can use as little or as much XAML as you want in your projects.

All the XAML you've seen so far has used classes and properties that are part of the Windows Presentation Foundation. But XAML is not a WPF-specific markup language. It is more correct to think of WPF as one possible application of XAML. XAML could be used with other application frameworks that are not WPF at all. (For example, another application that uses XAML is the Windows Workflow Foundation.)

The XAML specification defines several elements and attributes that you can use in any XAML application, including WPF. These elements and attributes are associated with an XML namespace different from the WPF namespace, and if you want to use the XAML-specific elements and attributes (and you will) you need to include a second namespace declaration in your XAML files. This second namespace declaration refers to this URL:

http://schemas.microsoft.com/winfx/2006/xaml

It's the same as the URL for WPF except without the additional path of *presentation*, which refers to the Windows *Presentation* Foundation. The WPF namespace declaration will continue to appear in all the XAML files in this book:

```
xmlns="http://schemas.microsoft.com/winfx/2006/xaml/presentation"
```

The namespace for XAML-specific elements and attributes is customarily declared with a prefix of *x*:

```
xmlns:x="http://schemas.microsoft.com/winfx/2006/xaml"
```

You can use whatever prefix you want, of course (as long as it doesn't begin with the letters *XML*), but *x* has already become entrenched as the convention in many XAML files.

(In theory, it might make more sense for the default namespace in a XAML file to be the namespace associated with XAML itself, and then to use a second namespace declaration for the WPF elements. However, the elements and attributes defined by XAML are very few, so to avoid a lot of "hair" in the XAML, it makes the most practical sense for the default namespace to be the one associated with the WPF elements.)

In this chapter, you'll see examples of the *Class* attribute and the *Code* element, both of which belong to the XAML namespace rather than the WPF namespace. Because the XAML namespace is customarily associated with a prefix of *x*, the *Class* attribute and *Code* element usually appear in XAML files as *x:Class* and *x:Code*, and that's how I'll refer to them.

The *x:Class* attribute can only appear in the root element of a XAML file. This attribute is only allowed with XAML that you compile as part of your project. It cannot appear in loose XAML or XAML loaded by a program at run time. The *x:Class* attribute looks something like this:

```
x:Class="MyNamespace.MyClassName"
```

Very often, this *x:Class* attribute will appear in a root element of *Window*, so the XAML file might have an overall structure like this:

```
<Window xmlns="http://schemas.microsoft.com/winfx/2006/xaml/presentation"
        xmlns:x="http://schemas.microsoft.com/winfx/2006/xaml"
        x:Class="MyNamespace.MyClassName"
        ... >
  ...
</Window>
```

The "MyNamespace" namespace referred to here is the .NET namespace (also called the common language runtime, or CLR, namespace) associated with the application project. Very often you will have a corresponding *Window* class written in C# that has the same namespace and class name, and which is defined with the *partial* keyword:

```
public namespace MyNamespace
{
    public partial class MyClassName: Window
    {
        ...
    }
}
```

This is the code-behind file because it contains code—very often event handlers but possibly some initialization code as well—that supports the controls and elements defined in the XAML file. The XAML file and the code-behind file are essentially each part of the same class, and that's often a class of type *Window*.

Once again, let's begin with an empty project. Let's call this one CompileXamlWindow. This project will have two files, a XAML file named CompileXamlWindow.xaml and a C# file named CompileXamlWindow.cs. Both files will effectively be part of the same class, which has a fully qualified name of *Petzold.CompileXamlWindow.CompileXamlWindow*.

Let's create the XAML file first. In the empty project, add a new item of type XML File, and specify the name of the file as CompileXamlWindow.xaml. Visual Studio will load a designer, but try to avoid it. In the lower left corner of the source window, click the Xaml tab rather than the Design tab.

If you check the Properties for the CompileXamlWindow.xaml file, the Build Action should be Page. If not, set it to Page. (Earlier in the LoadXamlResource and the LoadXamlWindow projects, I specified that you should use a file name extension of .xml for the XAML files, and now I'm telling you to use a .xaml extension. It really doesn't matter what extension you use. What matters is the Build Action. In the previous project, we wanted the file to become a resource of the executable. In this current project, we want the file to be compiled, and that's what the Build Action of Page enables.)

The CompileXamlWindow.xaml file is somewhat similar to the LoadXamlWindow.xml file. The first big difference is that this file includes a second namespace declaration for the *x* prefix, and an *x:Class* attribute appears in the root element. What we are defining here is a class that inherits from *Window* with the fully qualified class name of *Petzold.CompileXamlWindow* *.CompileXamlWindow*.

CompileXamlWindow.xaml

```xml
<!-- ================================================
        CompileXamlWindow.xaml (c) 2006 by Charles Petzold
     ================================================ -->
<Window xmlns="http://schemas.microsoft.com/winfx/2006/xaml/presentation"
        xmlns:x="http://schemas.microsoft.com/winfx/2006/xaml"
        x:Class="Petzold.CompileXamlWindow.CompileXamlWindow"
        Title="Compile XAML Window"
        SizeToContent="WidthAndHeight"
        ResizeMode="CanMinimize">
    <StackPanel>

        <Button HorizontalAlignment="Center"
                Margin="24"
                Click="ButtonOnClick">
            Click the Button
        </Button>

        <Ellipse Name="elips"
                Width="200"
                Height="100"
                Margin="24"
                Stroke="Black"/>

        <ListBox Name="lstbox"
                Width="150"
                Height="150"
                Margin="24"
                SelectionChanged="ListBoxOnSelection" />

    </StackPanel>
</Window>
```

In effect—and, as you'll see, in actuality—this XAML document defines a class that in C# syntax looks something like this:

```csharp
namespace Petzold.CompileXamlWindow
{
    public partial class CompileXamlWindow: Window
    {
        ...
    }
}
```

The *partial* keyword implies that the *CompileXamlWindow* class has additional code somewhere else. That's the code in the C# code-behind file.

Notice also that the XAML element for the button includes the *Click* event as another attribute and assigns the event to a handler named *ButtonOnClick*. Where is this event handler? It will be in the C# part of the *CompileXamlWindow* class. The *ListBox* also requires a handler for the *SelectionChanged* event.

Also, both the *Ellipse* and *ListBox* include *Name* attributes with values of *elips* and *lstbox*, respectively. You saw earlier how a program can locate these elements in a tree using the *Find-Name* method. When you compile XAML in the project, the *Name* attributes play an extremely important role. They become fields of the class, so the class created from the XAML during compilation is more like this:

```
namespace Petzold.CompileXamlWindow
{
    public partial class CompileXamlWindow: Window
    {
        Ellipse elips;
        ListBox lstbox;
        ...
    }
}
```

In the part of the *CompileXamlWindow* class that you write in C#, you can refer to these fields directly. Here's the code-behind file that contains the rest of the *CompileXamlWindow* class:

```
CompileXamlWindow.cs
//----------------------------------------------------
// CompileXamlWindow.cs (c) 2006 by Charles Petzold
//----------------------------------------------------
using System;
using System.Reflection;
using System.Windows;
using System.Windows.Controls;
using System.Windows.Input;
using System.Windows.Media;

namespace Petzold.CompileXamlWindow
{
    public partial class CompileXamlWindow : Window
    {
        [STAThread]
        public static void Main()
        {
            Application app = new Application();
            app.Run(new CompileXamlWindow());
        }
        public CompileXamlWindow()
        {
            // Required method call to hook up event handlers and
```

```
        // initialize fields.
        InitializeComponent();

        // Fill up the ListBox with brush names.
        foreach (PropertyInfo prop in typeof(Brushes).GetProperties())
            lstbox.Items.Add(prop.Name);
    }
    // Button event handler just displays MessageBox.
    void ButtonOnClick(object sender, RoutedEventArgs args)
    {
        Button btn = sender as Button;
        MessageBox.Show("The button labled '" + btn.Content +
                    "' has been clicked.");
    }
    // ListBox event handler changes Fill property of Ellipse.
    void ListBoxOnSelection(object sender, SelectionChangedEventArgs args)
    {
        ListBox lstbox = sender as ListBox;
        string strItem = lstbox.SelectedItem as string;
        PropertyInfo prop = typeof(Brushes).GetProperty(strItem);
        elips.Fill = (Brush)prop.GetValue(null, null);
    }
  }
 }
```

The class *CompileXamlWindow* derives from *Window*, as is normal, but the declaration also contains the *partial* keyword. The class has a static *Main* method, as usual. The constructor for *CompileXamlWindow*, however, begins by calling *InitializeComponent*. This method appears to be part of the *CompileXamlWindow* class, but it's nowhere to be seen. You will actually see this method shortly. For now you should know that it performs some vital functions, such as set-ting the fields named *lstbox* and *elips* to the *ListBox* and *Ellipse* elements created from the XAML, as well as attaching the event handlers to the *Button* and *ListBox* controls.

The constructor of *CompileXamlWindow* doesn't set the *Title* property or any content of the window because that's all done in the XAML. But it does need to fill up the list box. The remainder of the code is devoted to the two event handlers. The *ButtonOnClick* handler simply displays the *MessageBox* that you're probably tired of by now. The handler for the *Selection-Changed* event handler of *ListBox* changes the *Fill* property of the *Ellipse* object. Although this event handler obtains the *ListBox* object from the *sender* argument to the handler, it could also simply access the *lstbox* field. You can delete the first statement in the event handler and the program will work just the same.

When you compile and run the project, you'll see that it works, which is the important objec-tive, of course, but at this point you might also crave a few insights into *how* it works.

Take a look at the *obj* subdirectory of the project, and either the *Release* or *Debug* subdirectory of *obj* (depending how you've compiled the project). You'll see a file with the name CompileXaml-Window.baml. That file name extension stands for *Binary XAML*, and yes, it's pronounced "bammel." That's the XAML file, already parsed and tokenized, and converted to a binary form. That file becomes part of the executable as an application resource.

You'll also see a file with the name CompileXamlWindow.g.cs. That's the code generated from the XAML file. (The g stands for *generated*.) Open it up in Notepad or another text viewer. This is the other part of the *CompileXamlWindow* class, and it is compiled along with the Compile-XamlWindow.cs file. Near the top of the class you'll see two fields declared and named *lstbox* and *elips*. You'll also see the *InitializeComponent* method that loads the BAML file at run time and converts it into the element tree. At the bottom of the file you'll see the method that sets the *lstbox* and *elips* fields and attaches the event handlers. (Sometimes Visual Studio will display compilation error messages concerning these generated files. That's something you need to handle without editing the generated code.)

When the constructor of the *CompileXamlWindow* class begins execution, the *Content* property of the window is *null* and all the window properties (such as *Title*, *SizeToWindow*, and *ResizeMode*) have default values. Following the call to *InitializeComponent*, the *Content* is the *StackPanel* and the other properties have been set to values indicated in the XAML file.

The types of connections between XAML and C# code illustrated in the CompileXamlWindow program—sharing a single class, specifying event handlers, and setting fields—are possible only when you compile the XAML along with the code. When you load the XAML at run time by directly (or indirectly) calling *XamlReader.Load*, your options are more limited. You have access to the objects created by the XAML, but it's not quite as easy to set event handlers, or to save the objects as fields.

One of the first questions programmers often have about XAML is "Can I use my own classes in it?" Yes, you can. To use a custom class defined in a C# file that is compiled along with the rest of your project, all you need in the XAML is another namespace declaration.

Suppose you have a custom control named *MyControl* in a C# file with a CLR namespace of *MyNamespace*. You include this C# file as part of the project. In the XAML file, you must associate this CLR namespace with a prefix—for example, *stuff*, using a namespace declaration like this:

```
xmlns:stuff="clr-namespace:MyNamespace"
```

The text "clr-namespace" must be written in lowercase and followed by a colon. (It resembles the *http*: part of a common XML namespace declaration. In the next chapter, I'll discuss the more enhanced syntax you use when referring to a namespace in an external dynamic-link library.) This namespace declaration must appear before the first reference to *MyControl*, or as an attribute in the *MyControl* element. The *MyControl* element requires the prefix *stuff* in front of it:

```
<stuff:MyControl ... >
```

What prefix should you use? (I'm assuming you've already rejected "stuff" as a general-purpose solution.) Short prefixes are customary, but certainly not required. If your project contains source code from multiple CLR namespaces, you'll need a prefix for each of these namespaces, so the prefix should probably resemble the name of the CLR namespace to avoid confusion. If all the custom classes you need are in one namespace, the prefix *src* (meaning *source code*) is often seen.

Let's create a new project named UseCustomClass. This project contains a link to the Color-GridBox.cs file from the SelectColorFromGrid project in Chapter 13, "ListBox Selection." The *ColorGridBox* class is in the namespace *Petzold.SelectColorFromGrid*, so to use this class in a XAML file, you'll need a namespace declaration like this:

```
xmlns:src="clr-namespace:Petzold.SelectColorFromGrid"
```

Here's the UseCustomClass.xaml file that contains that namespace declaration to enable the file to reference the *ColorGridBox* control with a prefix of *src*.

UseCustomClass.xaml

```
<!-- ================================================
        UseCustomClass.xaml (c) 2006 by Charles Petzold
     ================================================ -->
<Window xmlns="http://schemas.microsoft.com/winfx/2006/xaml/presentation"
        xmlns:x="http://schemas.microsoft.com/winfx/2006/xaml"
        xmlns:src="clr-namespace:Petzold.SelectColorFromGrid"
        x:Class="Petzold.UseCustomClass.UseCustomClass"
        Title="Use Custom Class"
        SizeToContent="WidthAndHeight"
        ResizeMode="CanMinimize">
    <StackPanel Orientation="Horizontal">
        <Button HorizontalAlignment="Center"
                VerticalAlignment="Center"
                Margin="24">
            Do-nothing button to test tabbing
        </Button>

        <src:ColorGridBox HorizontalAlignment="Center"
                          VerticalAlignment="Center"
                          Margin="24"
                          SelectionChanged="ColorGridBoxOnSelectionChanged" />

        <Button HorizontalAlignment="Center"
                VerticalAlignment="Center"
                Margin="24">
            Do-nothing button to test tabbing
        </Button>
    </StackPanel>
</Window>
```

The code-behind file contains *Main*, a call to *InitializeComponent*, and the *SelectionChanged* event handler for the *ColorGridBox* control.

UseCustomClass.cs

```
//------------------------------------------------
// UseCustomClass.cs (c) 2006 by Charles Petzold
//------------------------------------------------
using Petzold.SelectColorFromGrid;
using System;
using System.Windows;
using System.Windows.Controls;
using System.Windows.Input;
using System.Windows.Media;

namespace Petzold.UseCustomClass
{
    public partial class UseCustomClass : Window
    {
        [STAThread]
        public static void Main()
        {
            Application app = new Application();
            app.Run(new UseCustomClass());
        }
        public UseCustomClass()
        {
            InitializeComponent();
        }
        void ColorGridBoxOnSelectionChanged(object sender,
                                        SelectionChangedEventArgs args)
        {
            ColorGridBox clrbox = args.Source as ColorGridBox;
            Background = (Brush) clrbox.SelectedValue;
        }
    }
}
```

The UseCustomClass.cs file requires a *using* directive for the namespace *Petzold.SelectColor-FromGrid* because the event handler refers to the *ColorGridBox* class. You could change that reference to just *ListBox* (from which *ColorGridBox* derives) and leave out the *using* directive. It is possible to dispense with the *SelectionChanged* event handler entirely by defining a data binding right in the XAML, but the syntax is a bit unusual and I'm afraid you'll have to wait until Chapter 23 to see how it's done.

I mentioned earlier that you'll generally have a XAML file and a corresponding code-behind file for every window and dialog box in your application. But don't fall into the trap of believing that XAML files can't be used for elements other than *Window*. The following project, UseCustomXamlClass, defines a custom class derived from *Button* (albeit a very simple one) entirely in XAML. You define a custom class in XAML using the *x:Class* attribute on the root element, which is the only place the attribute can appear. The following XAML file defines this *Button* derivative as the class *CenteredButton*. The XAML sets the *HorizontalAlignment* and *VerticalAlignment* properties to *Center*, and gives the button a little margin.

```
CenteredButton.xaml
<!-- ===================================================
        CenteredButton.xaml (c) 2006 by Charles Petzold
     =================================================== -->
<Button xmlns="http://schemas.microsoft.com/winfx/2006/xaml/presentation"
        xmlns:x="http://schemas.microsoft.com/winfx/2006/xaml"
        x:Class="Petzold.UseCustomXamlClass.CenteredButton"
        HorizontalAlignment="Center"
        VerticalAlignment="Center"
        Margin="12" />
```

The code-behind file is a partial class for *CenteredButton* that is so simple that no *using* directives are required.

```
CenteredButton.cs
//----------------------------------------------
// CenteredButton.cs (c) 2006 by Charles Petzold
//----------------------------------------------

namespace Petzold.UseCustomXamlClass
{
    public partial class CenteredButton
    {
        public CenteredButton()
        {
            InitializeComponent();
        }
    }
}
```

The project also contains a XAML file for a class that derives from *Window*. Besides the normal *x:Class* attribute, this file also contains an XML namespace declaration for the project's namespace so that a *StackPanel* can include five instances of the *CenteredButton* class.

```
UseCustomXamlClass.xaml
<!-- ===================================================
        UseCustomXamlClass.xaml (c) 2006 by Charles Petzold
     =================================================== -->
<Window xmlns="http://schemas.microsoft.com/winfx/2006/xaml/presentation"
        xmlns:x="http://schemas.microsoft.com/winfx/2006/xaml"
        xmlns:src="clr-namespace:Petzold.UseCustomXamlClass"
        x:Class="Petzold.UseCustomXamlClass.UseCustomXamlClass"
        Title = "Use Custom XAML Class">
    <StackPanel Name="stack">
        <src:CenteredButton>Button A</src:CenteredButton>
        <src:CenteredButton>Button B</src:CenteredButton>
        <src:CenteredButton>Button C</src:CenteredButton>
        <src:CenteredButton>Button D</src:CenteredButton>
        <src:CenteredButton>Button E</src:CenteredButton>
    </StackPanel>
</Window>
```

Notice that the *StackPanel* has a *Name* attribute with the value of *stack*. The code-behind file can simply use that name to add five additional buttons (ten total) to the *StackPanel*.

```
UseCustomXamlClass.cs
//----------------------------------------------------
// UseCustomXamlClass.cs (c) 2006 by Charles Petzold
//----------------------------------------------------
using System;
using System.Windows;
using System.Windows.Controls;
using System.Windows.Input;
using System.Windows.Media;

namespace Petzold.UseCustomXamlClass
{
    public partial class UseCustomXamlClass : Window
    {
        [STAThread]
        public static void Main()
        {
            Application app = new Application();
            app.Run(new UseCustomXamlClass());
        }
        public UseCustomXamlClass()
        {
            InitializeComponent();

            for (int i = 0; i < 5; i++)
            {
                CenteredButton btn = new CenteredButton();
                btn.Content = "Button No. " + (i + 1);
                stack.Children.Add(btn);
            }
        }
    }
}
```

Besides having XAML files for *Window* and perhaps other elements and controls, it is also common for a project to have a XAML file for the *Application* object. One interesting outcome of doing this is that your program no longer requires an explicit *Main* method.

Let's try it. This project is called IncludeApplicationDefinition. It has two XAML files (one for *Application* and one for *Window*) and two corresponding code-behind files. The XAML file for *Window* contains only a button so it's very short:

```
MyWindow.xaml
<!-- =========================================
        MyWindow.xaml (c) 2006 by Charles Petzold
     ========================================= -->
<Window xmlns="http://schemas.microsoft.com/winfx/2006/xaml/presentation"
        xmlns:x="http://schemas.microsoft.com/winfx/2006/xaml"
        x:Class="Petzold.IncludeApplicationDefinition.MyWindow"
        Title="Include Application Definition"
```

```
            SizeToContent="WidthAndHeight"
            ResizeMode="CanMinimize">
        <Button HorizontalAlignment="Center"
                VerticalAlignment="Center"
                Margin="1.5in"
                Click="ButtonOnClick">
            Click the Button
        </Button>
    </Window>
```

This XAML shares a namespace of *Petzold.IncludeApplicationDefinition* and a class name of *MyWindow* with the partial class derived from *Window* and defined in MyWindow.cs. The class's constructor calls *InitializeComponent* and also includes an event handler for the *Click* event of the *Button*.

MyWindow.cs

```
//----------------------------------------
// MyWindow.cs (c) 2006 by Charles Petzold
//----------------------------------------
using System;
using System.Windows;
using System.Windows.Controls;
using System.Windows.Input;

namespace Petzold.IncludeApplicationDefinition
{
    public partial class MyWindow : Window
    {
        public MyWindow()
        {
            InitializeComponent();
        }
        void ButtonOnClick(object sender, RoutedEventArgs args)
        {
            Button btn = sender as Button;
            MessageBox.Show("The button labled '" + btn.Content +
                            "' has been clicked.");
        }
    }
}
```

The second XAML file is for the *Application* object. The namespace is still *Petzold.Include-ApplicationDefinition*, but the class is *MyApplication*.

MyApplication.xaml

```
<!-- ===============================================
        MyApplication.xaml (c) 2006 by Charles Petzold
     =============================================== -->
<Application xmlns="http://schemas.microsoft.com/winfx/2006/xaml/presentation"
             xmlns:x="http://schemas.microsoft.com/winfx/2006/xaml"
             x:Class="Petzold.IncludeApplicationDefinition.MyApplication"
             StartupUri="MyWindow.xaml" />
```

The Build Action of the MyApplication.xaml file must be ApplicationDefinition. Watch out: Visual Studio might change that Build Action under certain circumstances (such as renaming the file). If you ever use a XAML file to define an *Application* object and you get an error message about no *Main* method in the project, check the Build Action of the XAML file for the *Application* object.

Notice the final attribute of *StartupUri*, which refers to the MyWindow.xaml file. Of course, by the time the application runs, the MyWindow.xaml file will have been compiled into the MyWindow.baml file and made an application resource, but it's still the initial window that you want the application to display. The *StartupUri* attribute here takes the place of the *Run* method normally called in *Main*.

Finally, here's MyApplication.cs, which doesn't do anything at all. In some applications it might have some event handlers for the *Application* object, if these were defined by attributes in the MyApplication.xaml file.

```
MyApplication.cs
//--------------------------------------------
// MyApplication.cs (c) 2006 by Charles Petzold
//--------------------------------------------
using System;
using System.Windows;

namespace Petzold.IncludeApplicationDefinition
{
    public partial class MyApplication : Application
    {
    }
}
```

That's the whole project. There's obviously no *Main* method, but after you compile the program, you can look at the generated file MyApplication.g.cs, and that's where you'll find *Main*.

The MyApplication.cs file is so inconsequential that you can delete it entirely from the project, and the project will compile and run just as before. (In fact, when I was first putting this project together I accidentally used a different class name in MyApplication.xaml and MyApplication.cs, and that project compiled and ran fine as well!)

It is also possible (although unlikely for many applications) that the project can include only XAML files and no code files. Such a no-code project makes more sense when the controls actually have some data bindings defined in the XAML, or when you use some XAML animation. This project is named CompileXamlOnly and it has two files. The first is the *Application* file:

```
XamlOnlyApp.xaml
<!-- =============================================
        XamlOnlyApp.xaml (c) 2006 by Charles Petzold
     ============================================= -->
<Application xmlns="http://schemas.microsoft.com/winfx/2006/xaml/presentation"
             StartupUri="XamlOnlyWindow.xaml" />
```

As I mentioned earlier, this *Application* file must have a Build Action of ApplicationDefinition, or nothing will work. Notice that the *StartupUri* is the XamlOnlyWindow.xaml file, which is this one:

```
XamlOnlyWindow.xaml
<!-- =============================================
        XamlOnlyWindow.xaml (c) 2006 by Charles Petzold
        ============================================= -->
<Window xmlns="http://schemas.microsoft.com/winfx/2006/xaml/presentation"
        Title="Compile XAML Only"
        SizeToContent="WidthAndHeight"
        ResizeMode="CanMinimize">
    <StackPanel>

        <Button HorizontalAlignment="Center"
                Margin="24">
            Just a Button
        </Button>

        <Ellipse Width="200"
                 Height="100"
                 Margin="24"
                 Stroke="Red"
                 StrokeThickness="10" />

        <ListBox Width="100"
                 Height="100"
                 Margin="24">
            <ListBoxItem>Sunday</ListBoxItem>
            <ListBoxItem>Monday</ListBoxItem>
            <ListBoxItem>Tuesday</ListBoxItem>
            <ListBoxItem>Wednesday</ListBoxItem>
            <ListBoxItem>Thursday</ListBoxItem>
            <ListBoxItem>Friday</ListBoxItem>
            <ListBoxItem>Saturday</ListBoxItem>
        </ListBox>

    </StackPanel>
</Window>
```

Notice that neither file defines a class name. If you check, you'll discover that Visual Studio generates code for only the *Application* XAML file and gives it a class name of *Application__*. The generated file includes the *Main* method. There is no generated code file for the *Window* XAML file, but Visual Studio compiles the *Window* into a BAML file, so the whole setup is similar to projects that include explicit code. No BAML file is required for the *Application* class because it doesn't define an element tree or anything else required during execution.

Suppose you start out with a XAML-only application, and then you decide that the application really needs some C# code. But you'd rather not create a whole new C# file just for that code. I don't know why. (Maybe you can tell *me*. It's *your* project!) Fortunately for you, it is entirely possible to embed C# code into a XAML file. It's not pretty, but it works.

This project is called EmbedCodeInXaml, and the first file is the *Application* class:

EmbeddedCodeApp.xaml

```
<!-- =================================================
        EmbeddedCodeApp.xaml (c) 2006 by Charles Petzold
     ================================================= -->
<Application xmlns="http://schemas.microsoft.com/winfx/2006/xaml/presentation"
             StartupUri="EmbeddedCodeWindow.xaml" />
```

The *StartupUri* refers to the EmbeddedCodeWindow.xaml file, which has a *Button*, *Ellipse*, and *ListBox* and also some embedded C# code.

EmbeddedCodeWindow.xaml

```
<!-- =================================================
        EmbeddedCodeWindow.xaml (c) 2006 by Charles Petzold
     ================================================= -->
<Window xmlns="http://schemas.microsoft.com/winfx/2006/xaml/presentation"
        xmlns:x="http://schemas.microsoft.com/winfx/2006/xaml"
        x:Class="Petzold.CompileXamlOnly.EmbeddedCodeWindow"
        Title="Embed Code in XAML"
        SizeToContent="WidthAndHeight"
        ResizeMode="CanMinimize"
        Loaded="WindowOnLoaded">
    <StackPanel>

        <Button HorizontalAlignment="Center"
                Margin="24"
                Click="ButtonOnClick">
            Click the Button
        </Button>

        <Ellipse Name="elips"
                 Width="200"
                 Height="100"
                 Margin="24"
                 Stroke="Red"
                 StrokeThickness="10" />

        <ListBox Name="lstbox"
                 Width="150"
                 Height="150"
                 Margin="24"
                 SelectionChanged="ListBoxOnSelection" />

        <x:Code>
            <![CDATA[
        void WindowOnLoaded(object sender, RoutedEventArgs args)
        {
            foreach (System.Reflection.PropertyInfo prop in
                                    typeof(Brushes).GetProperties())
                lstbox.Items.Add(prop.Name);
        }
```

```
        void ButtonOnClick(object sender, RoutedEventArgs args)
        {
            Button btn = sender as Button;
            MessageBox.Show("The button labeled '" +
                            btn.Content +
                            "' has been clicked.");
        }
        void ListBoxOnSelection(object sender, SelectionChangedEventArgs args)
        {
            string strItem = lstbox.SelectedItem as string;
            System.Reflection.PropertyInfo prop =
                            typeof(Brushes).GetProperty(strItem);
            elips.Fill = (Brush)prop.GetValue(null, null);
        }
        ]]>
    </x:Code>

    </StackPanel>
</Window>
```

Embedded code requires using the *x:Code* element and a CDATA section within the *x:Code* element. The XML specification defines CDATA (which stands for "character data") as a section in an XML file for "blocks of text containing characters which would otherwise be recognized as markup," which is certainly the case for symbols used in C# and other programming languages.

The CDATA section always begins with the string "<![CDATA[" and always ends with the string "]]>". Within the CDATA section, the characters "]]>" must not appear under any circumstances. That may actually be a problem if you write C# code that looks like this:

```
if (array1[array2[i]]>5)
```

Simply insert a little white space somewhere within that inadvertent CDATA delimiter and all will be well.

During compilation of this project, the C# code is transferred into the EmbeddedCode-Window.g.cs file. This embedded code cannot define fields. The embedded code might require fully qualified namespace names if the generated code file does not automatically include *using* directives for those namespaces. Notice that the embedded code in Embedded-CodeWindow.xaml file needs to fully qualify classes in the *System.Reflection* namespace.

Although embedding C# code in a XAML file is sometimes convenient, it is much too ugly and awkward as a general-purpose solution. You'll probably have a happier, longer, and more fulfilling life if you never use embedded code in your XAML files and forget you ever saw it.

Perhaps you remember the DesignAButton program from Chapter 5, "Stack and Wrap." That program assigned a *StackPanel* to the *Content* property of a *Button*, and then decorated the *StackPanel* with two *Polyline* objects, a *Label*, and an *Image* showing an icon named BOOK06.ICO that I obtained from the image library included with Visual Studio. Let's try to mimic that program with a XAML-only project—or rather, a project that includes only XAML and the icon file.

The icon file must have a Build Action of Resource. The following DesignXamlButtonApp.xaml file must have a Build Action of Application Definition.

DesignXamlButtonApp.xaml

```
<!-- =======================================================
      DesignXamlButtonApp.xaml (c) 2006 by Charles Petzold
     ======================================================= -->
<Application xmlns="http://schemas.microsoft.com/winfx/2006/xaml/presentation"
             StartupUri="DesignXamlButtonWindow.xaml" />
```

The final part of the project is the XAML file for the *Window* with a Build Action of Page.

DesignXamlButtonWindow.xaml

```
<!-- =======================================================
      DesignXamlButtonWindow.xaml (c) 2006 by Charles Petzold
     ======================================================= -->
<Window xmlns="http://schemas.microsoft.com/winfx/2006/xaml/presentation"
        Title="Design XAML Button"
        SizeToContent="WidthAndHeight"
        ResizeMode="CanMinimize">
    <Button HorizontalAlignment="Center"
            VerticalAlignment="Center"
            Margin="24">
        <StackPanel>
            <Polyline Stroke="Black"
                      Points="0 10,10 0,20 10,30 0,40 10,50 0,
                      60 10,70 0,80 10,90 0,100 10" />

            <Image Margin="0,10,0,0"
                   Source="BOOK06.ICO"
                   Stretch="None" />

            <Label HorizontalAlignment="Center">
                _Read Books!
            </Label>

            <Polyline Stroke="Black"
                      Points="0 0,10 10,20 0,30 10,40 0,50 10,
                      60 0,70 10,80 0,90 10,100 0" />
        </StackPanel>
    </Button>
</Window>
```

This window contains only a *Button*, but the *Button* contains a *StackPanel*, and the *StackPanel* contains four other elements. The two *Polyline* elements specify a series of eleven points each as *X* and *Y* pairs. Notice that commas separate the points. You can alternatively use spaces to separate the points and commas to separate the *X* and *Y* coordinates of each point. Or you can use spaces for both purposes or commas for both purposes.

The XAML *Image* element is very elegant as well. Rather than defining a *Uri* object and then creating a *BitmapImage* from that *Uri*, and then assigning the *BitmapImage* object to the *Source* property of *Image*—all of which is required in C# code and which you can examine in the original DesignAButton.cs file—you can simply set the *Source* property to the name of the icon file. If you want, you can use the entire URI that references the icon resource ("pack://application:,,/ BOOK06.ICO") but I think just the file name looks a lot cleaner.

XAML includes many little shortcuts like these, and I'll begin exploring them in the next chapter. But first we need a program that lets us interactively experiment with XAML and explore its syntax to the fullest extent possible.

Chapter 20
Properties and Attributes

The *XamlReader.Load* method that you encountered in the last chapter might have suggested a handy programming tool to you. Suppose you have a *TextBox* and you attach a handler for the *TextChanged* event. As you type XAML into that *TextBox*, the *TextChanged* event handler could try passing that XAML to the *XamlReader.Load* method and display the resultant object. You'd need to put the call to *XamlReader.Load* in a *try* block because most of the time the XAML will be invalid while it's being entered, but such a programming tool would potentially allow immediate feedback of your experimentations with XAML. It would be a great tool for learning XAML and fun as well.

That's the premise behind the XAML Cruncher program. It's certainly not the first program of its type, and it won't be the last. XAML Cruncher is build on Notepad Clone. As you'll see, XAML Cruncher replaces the *TextBox* that fills Notepad Clone's client area with a *Grid*. The *Grid* contains the *TextBox* in one cell and a *Frame* control in another with a *GridSplitter* in between. When the XAML you type into the *TextBox* is successfully converted into an object by *XamlReader.Load*, that object is made the *Content* of the *Frame*.

The XamlCruncher project includes every file in the NotepadClone project except for NotepadCloneAssemblyInfo.cs. That file is replaced with this one:

```
XamlCruncherAssemblyInfo.cs
//--------------------------------------------------------
// XamlCruncherAssemblyInfo.cs (c) 2006 by Charles Petzold
//--------------------------------------------------------
using System.Reflection;

[assembly: AssemblyTitle("XAML Cruncher")]
[assembly: AssemblyProduct("XamlCruncher")]
[assembly: AssemblyDescription("Programming Tool Using XamlReader.Load")]
[assembly: AssemblyCompany("www.charlespetzold.com")]
[assembly: AssemblyCopyright("\x00A9 2006 by Charles Petzold")]
[assembly: AssemblyVersion("1.0.*")]
[assembly: AssemblyFileVersion("1.0.0.0")]
```

As you'll recall, the *NotepadCloneSettings* class contained several items saved as user preferences. The *XamlCruncherSettings* class inherits from *NotepadCloneSettings* and adds just three items. The first is named *Orientation* and it governs the orientation of the *TextBox* and the *Frame*. XAML Cruncher has a menu item that lets you put one on top of the other or have them side by side. Also, XAML overrides the normal *TextBox* handling of the Tab key and inserts spaces instead. The second user preference is the number of spaces inserted when you press the Tab key.

The third user preference is a string containing some simple XAML that shows up in the *Text-Box* when you first run the program or when you select New from the File command. A menu item lets you set the current contents of the *TextBox* as this startup document item.

```
XamlCruncherSettings.cs
//----------------------------------------------------
// XamlCruncherSettings.cs (c) 2006 by Charles Petzold
//----------------------------------------------------
using System;
using System.Windows;
using System.Windows.Controls;
using System.Windows.Media;

namespace Petzold.XamlCruncher
{
    public class XamlCruncherSettings : Petzold.NotepadClone.NotepadCloneSettings
    {
        // Default settings of user preferences.
        public Dock Orientation = Dock.Left;
        public int TabSpaces = 4;
        public string StartupDocument =
            "<Button xmlns=\"http://schemas.microsoft.com/winfx" +
                    "/2006/xaml/presentation\"\r\n" +
            "        xmlns:x=\"http://schemas.microsoft.com/winfx" +
                    "/2006/xaml\">\r\n" +
            "    Hello, XAML!\r\n" +
            "</Button>\r\n";

        // Constructor to initialize default settings in NotepadCloneSettings.
        public XamlCruncherSettings()
        {
            FontFamily = "Lucida Console";
            FontSize = 10 / 0.75;
        }
    }
}
```

In addition, the *XamlCruncherSettings* constructor changes the default font to a 10-point, fixed-pitch, Lucida Console. Of course, once you run XAML Cruncher, you can change the font to whatever you want.

Here's the *XamlCruncher* class that derives from the *NotepadClone* class. This class is responsible for creating the *Grid* that becomes the new content of the *Window*, as well as for creating the top-level menu item labeled "Xaml" and the six items on its submenu.

```
XamlCruncher.cs
//--------------------------------------------
// XamlCruncher.cs (c) 2006 by Charles Petzold
//--------------------------------------------
using System;
using System.IO;                        // for StringReader
```

```
using System.Text;                          // for StringBuilder
using System.Windows;
using System.Windows.Controls;
using System.Windows.Controls.Primitives;   // for StatusBarItem
using System.Windows.Input;
using System.Windows.Markup;                // for XamlReader.Load
using System.Windows.Media;
using System.Windows.Threading;             // for DispatcherUnhandledExceptionEventArgs
using System.Xml;                           // for XmlTextReader

namespace Petzold.XamlCruncher
{
    class XamlCruncher : Petzold.NotepadClone.NotepadClone
    {
        Frame frameParent;              // To display object created by XAML.
        Window win;                     // Window created from XAML.
        StatusBarItem statusParse;      // Displays parsing error or OK.
        int tabspaces = 4;              // When Tab key pressed.

        // Loaded settings.
        XamlCruncherSettings settingsXaml;

        // Menu maintenance.
        XamlOrientationMenuItem itemOrientation;
        bool isSuspendParsing = false;

        [STAThread]
        public new static void Main()
        {
            Application app = new Application();
            app.ShutdownMode = ShutdownMode.OnMainWindowClose;
            app.Run(new XamlCruncher());
        }
        // Public property for menu item to suspend parsing.
        public bool IsSuspendParsing
        {
            set { isSuspendParsing = value; }
            get { return isSuspendParsing; }
        }
        // Constructor.
        public XamlCruncher()
        {
            // New filter for File Open and Save dialog boxes.
            strFilter = "XAML Files(*.xaml)|*.xaml|All Files(*.*)|*.*";

            // Find the DockPanel and remove the TextBox from it.
            DockPanel dock = txtbox.Parent as DockPanel;
            dock.Children.Remove(txtbox);

            // Create a Grid with three rows and columns, all 0 pixels.
            Grid grid = new Grid();
            dock.Children.Add(grid);

            for (int i = 0; i < 3; i++)
            {
                RowDefinition rowdef = new RowDefinition();
```

```
      rowdef.Height = new GridLength(0);
      grid.RowDefinitions.Add(rowdef);

      ColumnDefinition coldef = new ColumnDefinition();
      coldef.Width = new GridLength(0);
      grid.ColumnDefinitions.Add(coldef);
}

// Initialize the first row and column to 100*.
grid.RowDefinitions[0].Height =
            new GridLength(100, GridUnitType.Star);
grid.ColumnDefinitions[0].Width =
            new GridLength(100, GridUnitType.Star);

// Add two GridSplitter controls to the Grid.
GridSplitter split = new GridSplitter();
split.HorizontalAlignment = HorizontalAlignment.Stretch;
split.VerticalAlignment = VerticalAlignment.Center;
split.Height = 6;
grid.Children.Add(split);
Grid.SetRow(split, 1);
Grid.SetColumn(split, 0);
Grid.SetColumnSpan(split, 3);

split = new GridSplitter();
split.HorizontalAlignment = HorizontalAlignment.Center;
split.VerticalAlignment = VerticalAlignment.Stretch;
split.Height = 6;
grid.Children.Add(split);
Grid.SetRow(split, 0);
Grid.SetColumn(split, 1);
Grid.SetRowSpan(split, 3);

// Create a Frame for displaying XAML object.
frameParent = new Frame();
frameParent.NavigationUIVisibility = NavigationUIVisibility.Hidden;
grid.Children.Add(frameParent);

// Put the TextBox in the Grid.
txtbox.TextChanged += TextBoxOnTextChanged;
grid.Children.Add(txtbox);

// Case the loaded settings to XamlCruncherSettings.
settingsXaml = (XamlCruncherSettings)settings;

// Insert "Xaml" item on top-level menu.
MenuItem itemXaml = new MenuItem();
itemXaml.Header = "_Xaml";
menu.Items.Insert(menu.Items.Count - 1, itemXaml);

// Create XamlOrientationMenuItem & add to menu.
itemOrientation =
    new XamlOrientationMenuItem(grid, txtbox, frameParent);
itemOrientation.Orientation = settingsXaml.Orientation;
itemXaml.Items.Add(itemOrientation);
```

```
// Menu item to set tab spaces.
MenuItem itemTabs = new MenuItem();
itemTabs.Header = "_Tab Spaces...";
itemTabs.Click += TabSpacesOnClick;
itemXaml.Items.Add(itemTabs);

// Menu item to suppress parsing.
MenuItem itemNoParse = new MenuItem();
itemNoParse.Header = "_Suspend Parsing";
itemNoParse.IsCheckable = true;
itemNoParse.SetBinding(MenuItem.IsCheckedProperty,
                              "IsSuspendParsing");
itemNoParse.DataContext = this;
itemXaml.Items.Add(itemNoParse);

// Command to reparse.
InputGestureCollection collGest = new InputGestureCollection();
collGest.Add(new KeyGesture(Key.F6));
RoutedUICommand commReparse =
    new RoutedUICommand("_Reparse", "Reparse",
                          GetType(), collGest);

// Menu item to reparse.
MenuItem itemReparse = new MenuItem();
itemReparse.Command = commReparse;
itemXaml.Items.Add(itemReparse);

// Command binding to reparse.
CommandBindings.Add(new CommandBinding(commReparse,
                      ReparseOnExecuted));

// Command to show window.
InputGestureCollection collGest = new InputGestureCollection();
collGest.Add(new KeyGesture(Key.F7));
RoutedUICommand commShowWin =
    new RoutedUICommand("Show _Window", "ShowWindow",
                          GetType(), collGest);

// Menu item to show window.
MenuItem itemShowWin = new MenuItem();
itemShowWin.Command = commShowWin;
itemXaml.Items.Add(itemShowWin);

// Command binding to show window.
CommandBindings.Add(new CommandBinding(commShowWin,
                ShowWindowOnExecuted, ShowWindowCanExecute));

// Menu item to save as new startup document.
MenuItem itemTemplate = new MenuItem();
itemTemplate.Header = "Save as Startup _Document";
itemTemplate.Click += NewStartupOnClick;
itemXaml.Items.Add(itemTemplate);

// Insert Help on Help menu.
MenuItem itemXamlHelp = new MenuItem();
itemXamlHelp.Header = "_Help...";
```

```
        itemXamlHelp.Click += HelpOnClick;
        MenuItem itemHelp = (MenuItem)menu.Items[menu.Items.Count - 1];
        itemHelp.Items.Insert(0, itemXamlHelp);

        // New StatusBar item.
        statusParse = new StatusBarItem();
        status.Items.Insert(0, statusParse);
        status.Visibility = Visibility.Visible;

        // Install handler for unhandled exception.
        // Comment out this code when experimenting with new features
        //    or changes to the program!
        Dispatcher.UnhandledException += DispatcherOnUnhandledException;

    }
    // Override of NewOnExecute handler puts StartupDocument in TextBox.
    protected override void NewOnExecute(object sender,
                                        ExecutedRoutedEventArgs args)
    {
        base.NewOnExecute(sender, args);
        string str = ((XamlCruncherSettings)settings).StartupDocument;

        // Make sure the next Replace doesn't add too much.
        str = str.Replace("\r\n", "\n");

        // Replace line feeds with carriage return/line feeds.
        str = str.Replace("\n", "\r\n");
        txtbox.Text = str;          isFileDirty = false;
    }
    // Override of LoadSettings loads XamlCruncherSettings.
    protected override object LoadSettings()
    {
        return XamlCruncherSettings.Load(typeof(XamlCruncherSettings),
                                         strAppData);
    }
    // Override of OnClosed saves Orientation from menu item.
    protected override void OnClosed(EventArgs args)
    {
        settingsXaml.Orientation = itemOrientation.Orientation;
        base.OnClosed(args);
    }
    // Override of SaveSettings saves XamlCruncherSettings object.
    protected override void SaveSettings()
    {
        ((XamlCruncherSettings)settings).Save(strAppData);
    }
    // Handler for Tab Spaces menu item.
    void TabSpacesOnClick(object sender, RoutedEventArgs args)
    {
        XamlTabSpacesDialog dlg = new XamlTabSpacesDialog();
        dlg.Owner = this;
        dlg.TabSpaces = settingsXaml.TabSpaces;
```

```
        if ((bool)dlg.ShowDialog().GetValueOrDefault())
        {
            settingsXaml.TabSpaces = dlg.TabSpaces;
        }
    }
    // Handler for Reparse menu item.
    void ReparseOnExecuted(object sender, ExecutedRoutedEventArgs args)
    {
        Parse();
    }
    // Handlers for Show Window menu item.
    void ShowWindowCanExecute(object sender, CanExecuteRoutedEventArgs args)
    {
        args.CanExecute = (win != null);
    }
    void ShowWindowOnExecuted(object sender, ExecutedRoutedEventArgs args)
    {
        if (win != null)
            win.Show();
    }
    // Handler for Save as New Startup Document menu item.
    void NewStartupOnClick(object sender, RoutedEventArgs args)
    {
        ((XamlCruncherSettings)settings).StartupDocument = txtbox.Text;
    }
    // Help menu item.
    void HelpOnClick(object sender, RoutedEventArgs args)
    {
        Uri uri = new Uri("pack://application:,,,/XamlCruncherHelp.xaml");
        Stream stream = Application.GetResourceStream(uri).Stream;

        Window win = new Window();
        win.Title = "XAML Cruncher Help";
        win.Content = XamlReader.Load(stream);
        win.Show();
    }
    // OnPreviewKeyDown substitutes spaces for Tab key.
    protected override void OnPreviewKeyDown(KeyEventArgs args)
    {
        base.OnPreviewKeyDown(args);

        if (args.Source == txtbox && args.Key == Key.Tab)
        {
            string strInsert = new string(' ', tabspaces);
            int iChar = txtbox.SelectionStart;
            int iLine = txtbox.GetLineIndexFromCharacterIndex(iChar);

            if (iLine != -1)
            {
                int iCol = iChar - txtbox.GetCharacterIndexFromLineIndex(iLine);
                strInsert = new string(' ',
                    settingsXaml.TabSpaces - iCol % settingsXaml.TabSpaces);
            }
```

```
                txtbox.SelectedText = strInsert;
                txtbox.CaretIndex = txtbox.SelectionStart + txtbox.SelectionLength;
                args.Handled = true;
            }
        }
        // TextBoxOnTextChanged attempts to parse XAML.
        void TextBoxOnTextChanged(object sender, TextChangedEventArgs args)
        {
            if (IsSuspendParsing)
                txtbox.Foreground = SystemColors.WindowTextBrush;
            else
                Parse();
        }

        // General Parse method also called for Reparse menu item.
        void Parse()
        {
            StringReader strreader = new StringReader(txtbox.Text);
            XmlTextReader xmlreader = new XmlTextReader(strreader);

            try
            {
                object obj = XamlReader.Load(xmlreader);
                txtbox.Foreground = SystemColors.WindowTextBrush;

                if (obj is Window)
                {
                    win = obj as Window;
                    statusParse.Content = "Press F7 to display Window";
                }
                else
                {
                    win = null;
                    frameParent.Content = obj;
                    statusParse.Content = "OK";
                }
            }
            catch (Exception exc)
            {
                txtbox.Foreground = Brushes.Red;
                statusParse.Content = exc.Message;
            }
        }
        // UnhandledException handler required if XAML object throws exception.
        void DispatcherOnUnhandledException(object sender,
                                DispatcherUnhandledExceptionEventArgs args)
        {
            statusParse.Content = "Unhandled Exception: " + args.Exception.Message;
            args.Handled = true;
        }
    }
}
```

The *Parse* method toward the bottom of the class is responsible for parsing the XAML. If *XamlReader.Load* raises an exception, the handler turns the text of the *TextBox* red and displays the exception message in the status bar. Otherwise, it sets the object to the *Content* of the *Frame* control. Special handling exists for an object of type *Window*. That's saved as a field to await the pressing of F7 to launch it as a separate window.

Sometimes something in the element tree created from the XAML throws an exception. Because the object created from the XAML is part of the application, this exception could cause XAML Cruncher itself to be terminated through no fault of its own. For that reason, the program installs an *UnhandledException* event handler and processes the event by displaying the message in the status bar. In general, programs shouldn't install this event handler unless (like XAML Cruncher) they may encounter exceptions that are not related to buggy program code.

The menu item that lets you change the number of tab spaces displays a small dialog box. The layout of this dialog box is a XAML file.

```xml
XamlTabSpacesDialog.xaml
<!-- ========================================================
     XamlTabSpacesDialog.xaml (c) 2006 by Charles Petzold
     ======================================================== -->
<Window xmlns="http://schemas.microsoft.com/winfx/2006/xaml/presentation"
        xmlns:x="http://schemas.microsoft.com/winfx/2006/xaml"
        x:Class="Petzold.XamlCruncher.XamlTabSpacesDialog"
        Title="Tab Spaces"
        WindowStyle="ToolWindow"
        SizeToContent="WidthAndHeight"
        ResizeMode="NoResize"
        WindowStartupLocation="CenterOwner">
    <StackPanel>
        <StackPanel Orientation="Horizontal">
            <Label Margin="12,12,6,12">
                _Tab spaces (1-10):
            </Label>
            <TextBox Name="txtbox"
                     TextChanged="TextBoxOnTextChanged"
                     Margin="6,12,12,12"/>
        </StackPanel>
        <StackPanel Orientation="Horizontal">
            <Button Name="btnOk"
                    Click="OkOnClick"
                    IsDefault="True"
                    IsEnabled="False"
                    Margin="12">
                OK
            </Button>
            <Button IsCancel="True"
                    Margin="12">
                Cancel
            </Button>
        </StackPanel>
    </StackPanel>
</Window>
```

This XAML file shouldn't contain any surprises if you've assimilated the contents of the previous chapter. The code-behind file defines the public *TabSpaces* property and two event handlers.

```
XamlTabSpacesDialog.cs
//--------------------------------------------------
// XamlTabSpacesDialog.cs (c) 2006 by Charles Petzold
//--------------------------------------------------
using System;
using System.Windows;
using System.Windows.Controls;

namespace Petzold.XamlCruncher
{
    public partial class XamlTabSpacesDialog
    {
        public XamlTabSpacesDialog()
        {
            InitializeComponent();
            txtbox.Focus();
        }
        public int TabSpaces
        {
            set { txtbox.Text = value.ToString(); }
            get { return Int32.Parse(txtbox.Text); }
        }
        void TextBoxOnTextChanged(object sender, TextChangedEventArgs args)
        {
            int result;
            btnOk.IsEnabled = (Int32.TryParse(txtbox.Text, out result) &&
                               result > 0 && result < 11);
        }
        void OkOnClick(object sender, RoutedEventArgs args)
        {
            DialogResult = true;
        }
    }
}
```

The class defines a property named *TabSpaces* that directly accesses the *Text* property of the *TextBox*. You'll notice that the *get* accessor calls the static *Parse* method of the *Int32* structure with full confidence that it won't raise an exception. That confidence is a result of the *Text-Changed* event handler, which doesn't enable the OK button until the static *TryParse* returns *true* and the entered number isn't less than 1 or greater than 10.

The *XamlCruncher* class invokes this dialog box when the user selects the Tab Spaces item from the menu. Here are the entire contents of the *Click* event handler for that menu item:

```
XamlTabSpacesDialog dlg = new XamlTabSpacesDialog();
dlg.Owner = this;
dlg.TabSpaces = settingsXaml.TabSpaces;
```

```
if ((bool)dlg.ShowDialog().GetValueOrDefault())
{
    settingsXaml.TabSpaces = dlg.TabSpaces;
}
```

Setting the *Owner* property ensures that the *WindowStartupLocation* specified in the XAML file works. This is one dialog box where it's problematic if the *TabSpaces* property is accessed when the user dismisses the dialog box by clicking the Cancel button. The *TabSpaces* property is only guaranteed not to raise an exception if the user clicks the OK button.

The menu item to change the orientation of the *TextBox* and the *Frame* has its own class that symbolizes the four available orientations with little pictures. The class must also rearrange the elements on the *Grid* when the user selects a new orientation.

XamlOrientationMenuItem.cs

```
//-----------------------------------------------------------
// XamlOrientationMenuItem.cs (c) 2006 by Charles Petzold
//-----------------------------------------------------------
using System;
using System.Globalization;
using System.Windows;
using System.Windows.Controls;
using System.Windows.Media;

namespace Petzold.XamlCruncher
{
    class XamlOrientationMenuItem : MenuItem
    {
        MenuItem itemChecked;
        Grid grid;
        TextBox txtbox;
        Frame frame;

        // Orientation public property of type Dock.
        public Dock Orientation
        {
            set
            {
                foreach (MenuItem item in Items)
                    if (item.IsChecked = (value == (Dock)item.Tag))
                        itemChecked = item;
            }
            get
            {
                return (Dock)itemChecked.Tag;
            }
        }

        // Constructor requires three arguments.
        public XamlOrientationMenuItem(Grid grid, TextBox txtbox, Frame frame)
        {
            this.grid = grid;
            this.txtbox = txtbox;
            this.frame = frame;
```

```
        Header = "_Orientation";

        for (int i = 0; i < 4; i++)
            Items.Add(CreateItem((Dock)i));

        (itemChecked = (MenuItem) Items[0]).IsChecked = true;
}
// Create each menu item based on Dock setting.
MenuItem CreateItem(Dock dock)
{
    MenuItem item = new MenuItem();
    item.Tag = dock;
    item.Click += ItemOnClick;
    item.Checked += ItemOnCheck;

    // Two text strings that appear in menu item.
    FormattedText formtxt1 = CreateFormattedText("Edit");
    FormattedText formtxt2 = CreateFormattedText("Display");
    double widthMax = Math.Max(formtxt1.Width, formtxt2.Width);

    // Create a DrawingVisual and a DrawingContext.
    DrawingVisual vis = new DrawingVisual();
    DrawingContext dc = vis.RenderOpen();

    // Draw boxed text on the visual.
    switch (dock)
    {
        case Dock.Left:        // Edit on left, display on right.
            BoxText(dc, formtxt1, formtxt1.Width, new Point(0, 0));
            BoxText(dc, formtxt2, formtxt2.Width,
                    new Point(formtxt1.Width + 4, 0));
            break;

        case Dock.Top:         // Edit on top, display on bottom.
            BoxText(dc, formtxt1, widthMax, new Point(0, 0));
            BoxText(dc, formtxt2, widthMax,
                    new Point(0, formtxt1.Height + 4));
            break;

        case Dock.Right:       // Edit on right, display on left.
            BoxText(dc, formtxt2, formtxt2.Width, new Point(0, 0));
            BoxText(dc, formtxt1, formtxt1.Width,
                    new Point(formtxt2.Width + 4, 0));
            break;

        case Dock.Bottom:      // Edit on bottom, display on top.
            BoxText(dc, formtxt2, widthMax, new Point(0, 0));
            BoxText(dc, formtxt1, widthMax,
                    new Point(0, formtxt2.Height + 4));
            break;
    }

    dc.Close();
```

```
        // Create Image object based on Drawing from visual.
        DrawingImage drawimg = new DrawingImage(vis.Drawing);
        Image img = new Image();
        img.Source = drawimg;

        // Set the Header of the menu item to the Image object.
        item.Header = img;

        return item;
}
// Handles the hairy FormattedText arguments.
FormattedText CreateFormattedText(string str)
{
    return new FormattedText(str, CultureInfo.CurrentCulture,
        FlowDirection.LeftToRight,
        new Typeface(SystemFonts.MenuFontFamily, SystemFonts.MenuFontStyle,
                    SystemFonts.MenuFontWeight, FontStretches.Normal),
        SystemFonts.MenuFontSize, SystemColors.MenuTextBrush);
}
// Draws text surrounded by a rectangle.
void BoxText(DrawingContext dc, FormattedText formtxt,
                                double width, Point pt)
{
    Pen pen = new Pen(SystemColors.MenuTextBrush, 1);

    dc.DrawRectangle(null, pen,
        new Rect(pt.X, pt.Y, width + 4, formtxt.Height + 4));
    double X = pt.X + (width - formtxt.Width) / 2;
    dc.DrawText(formtxt, new Point(X + 2, pt.Y + 2));
}
// Check and uncheck items when clicked.
void ItemOnClick(object sender, RoutedEventArgs args)
{
    itemChecked.IsChecked = false;
    itemChecked = args.Source as MenuItem;
    itemChecked.IsChecked = true;
}
// Change the orientation based on the checked item.
void ItemOnCheck(object sender, RoutedEventArgs args)
{
    MenuItem itemChecked = args.Source as MenuItem;

    // Initialize the 2nd and 3rd rows and columns to zero.
    for (int i = 1; i < 3; i++)
    {
        grid.RowDefinitions[i].Height = new GridLength(0);
        grid.ColumnDefinitions[i].Width = new GridLength(0);
    }

    // Initialize the cell of the TextBox and Frame to zero.
    Grid.SetRow(txtbox, 0);
    Grid.SetColumn(txtbox, 0);
    Grid.SetRow(frame, 0);
    Grid.SetColumn(frame, 0);
```

```
            // Set row and columns based on the orientation setting.
            switch ((Dock)itemChecked.Tag)
            {
                case Dock.Left:              // Edit on left, display on right.
                    grid.ColumnDefinitions[1].Width = GridLength.Auto;
                    grid.ColumnDefinitions[2].Width =
                            new GridLength(100, GridUnitType.Star);
                    Grid.SetColumn(frame, 2);
                    break;

                case Dock.Top:              // Edit on top, display on bottom.
                    grid.RowDefinitions[1].Height = GridLength.Auto;
                    grid.RowDefinitions[2].Height =
                            new GridLength(100, GridUnitType.Star);
                    Grid.SetRow(frame, 2);
                    break;

                case Dock.Right:            // Edit on right, display on left.
                    grid.ColumnDefinitions[1].Width = GridLength.Auto;
                    grid.ColumnDefinitions[2].Width =
                            new GridLength(100, GridUnitType.Star);
                    Grid.SetColumn(txtbox, 2);
                    break;

                case Dock.Bottom:           // Edit on bottom, display on top.
                    grid.RowDefinitions[1].Height = GridLength.Auto;
                    grid.RowDefinitions[2].Height =
                            new GridLength(100, GridUnitType.Star);
                    Grid.SetRow(txtbox, 2);
                    break;
            }
        }
    }
}
```

The constructor of the *XamlCruncher* class also accesses the top-level Help menu item and adds a subitem of Help. This item displays a window that contains a short description of the program and the new menu items. In years gone by, this Help file might have been stored in the Rich Text Format (RTF) or that quaint but popular markup language, HTML.

However, let's demonstrate a commitment to new technologies and write the help file as a *FlowDocument* object, which is the type of object created by the *RichTextBox*. I hand-coded the following file in an early version of XAML Cruncher. It should be fairly self-explanatory because the elements are full words, such as *Paragraph*, *Bold*, and *Italic*.

XamlCruncherHelp.xaml

```
<!-- ====================================================
     XamlCruncherHelp.xaml (c) 2006 by Charles Petzold
     ==================================================== -->
<FlowDocument xmlns="http://schemas.microsoft.com/winfx/2006/xaml/presentation"
              xmlns:x="http://schemas.microsoft.com/winfx/2006/xaml"
              TextAlignment="Left">
```

```
<Paragraph TextAlignment="Center" FontSize="32" FontStyle="Italic"
        LineHeight="24">
    XAML Cruncher
</Paragraph>
<Paragraph TextAlignment="Center">
    &#x00A9; 2006 by Charles Petzold
</Paragraph>
<Paragraph FontSize="16pt" FontWeight="Bold" LineHeight="16">
    Introduction
</Paragraph>
<Paragraph>
    XAML Cruncher is a sample program from Charles Petzold's book
    <Italic>
        Applications = Code + Markup:
        A Guide to the Microsoft Windows Presentation Foundation
    </Italic>
    published by Microsoft Press in 2006.
    XAML Cruncher provides a convenient way to learn about and experiment
    with XAML, the Extensible Application Markup Language.
</Paragraph>
<Paragraph>
    XAML Cruncher consists of an Edit section (in which you enter and edit
    a XAML document) and a Display section that shows the object created
    from the XAML. If the XAML document has errors, the text is displayed
    in red and the status bar indicates the problem.
</Paragraph>
<Paragraph>
    Most of the interface and functionality of the edit section of
    XAML Cruncher is based on Windows Notepad.
    The <Bold>Xaml</Bold> menu provides additional features.
</Paragraph>
<Paragraph FontSize="16pt" FontWeight="Bold" LineHeight="16">
    Xaml Menu
</Paragraph>
<Paragraph>
    The <Bold>Orientation</Bold> menu item lets you choose whether you
    want the Edit and Display sections of XAML Cruncher arranged
    horizontally or vertically.
</Paragraph>
<Paragraph>
    The <Bold>Tab Spaces</Bold> menu item displays a dialog box that lets
    you choose the number of spaces you want inserted when you press the
    Tab key. Changing this item does not change any indentation
    already in the current document.
</Paragraph>
<Paragraph>
    There are times when your XAML document will be so complex that it
    takes a little while to convert it into an object. You may want to
    <Bold>Suspend Parsing</Bold> by checking this item on the
    <Bold>Xaml</Bold> menu.
</Paragraph>
```

```
    <Paragraph>
        If you've suspended parsing, or if you want to reparse the XAML file,
        select <Bold>Reparse</Bold> from the menu or press F6.
    </Paragraph>
    <Paragraph>
        If the root element of your XAML is <Italic>Window</Italic>,
        XAML Cruncher will not be able to display the <Italic>Window</Italic>
        object in its own window.
        Select the <Bold>Show Window</Bold> menu item or press F7 to view
        the window.
    </Paragraph>
    <Paragraph>
        When you start up XAML Cruncher (and whenever you select
        <Bold>New</Bold> from the <Bold>File</Bold> menu), the Edit window
        displays a simple startup document.
        If you want to use the current document as the startup document,
        select the <Bold>Save as Startup Document</Bold> item.
    </Paragraph>
</FlowDocument>
```

This file must be designated as a Resource in the XamlCruncher project in Microsoft Visual Studio. Visual Studio will want to make it a Page. It must be a Resource because that's how the *XamlCruncher* code treats it. The *HelpOnClick* event handler first obtains a URI object for the resource and creates a *Stream*:

```
Uri uri = new Uri("pack://application:,,,/XamlCruncherHelp.xaml");
Stream stream = Application.GetResourceStream(uri).Stream;
```

The method then creates a *Window*, sets the *Title*, and sets the *Content* property to the *Flow-Document* object that *XamlReader.Load* returns when passed the *Stream* object that references the resource:

```
Window win = new Window();
win.Title = "XAML Cruncher Help";
win.Content = XamlReader.Load(stream);
win.Show();
```

There are a couple of alternatives to this approach. One possibility is to create a *Frame* control and set its *Source* property directly to the *Uri* object:

```
Frame frame = new Frame();
frame.Source = new Uri("pack://application:,,/XamlCruncherHelp.xaml");
```

Now create the *Window* and set its content to the *Frame*:

```
Window win = new Window();
win.Title = "XAML Cruncher Help";
win.Content = frame;
win.Show();
```

A third approach: First, create a XAML file defining the Help window. Call it XamlHelpDialog.xaml, perhaps:

```
<Window xmlns="http://schemas.microsoft.com/winfx/2006/xaml/presentation"
        xmlns:x="http://schemas.microsoft.com/winfx/2006/xaml"
        Title="XAML Cruncher Help"
        x:Class="Petzold.XamlCruncher.XamlHelpDialog">
    <Frame Source="XamlCruncherHelp.xaml" />
</Window>
```

Notice the simplified syntax for setting the *Source* property of the *Frame* control. Now the *HelpOnClick* method reduces to the following three statements:

```
XamlHelpDialog win = new XamlHelpDialog();
win.InitializeComponent();
win.Show();
```

After creating the *XamlHelpDialog* object defined in the XAML, the method calls *InitializeComponent* (a job normally performed by a code-behind file) and then *Show*. One interesting aspect of this approach is that XamlCruncherHelp.xaml defining the *FlowDocument* can have a Build Action of either Resource or Page. In the latter case, the XAML file is stored in the .EXE file as a compiled BAML file.

Regardless of how you display the Help file, XAML Cruncher is now complete and ready to use. For much of this chapter and many of the chapters that follow I'll be showing you stand-alone XAML files that you can create and run in XAML Cruncher or any equivalent program.

Let's begin with the simple XAML file that XAML Cruncher creates by default:

```
<Button xmlns="http://schemas.microsoft.com/winfx/2006/xaml/presentation"
        xmlns:x="http://schemas.microsoft.com/winfx/2006/xaml>
    Hello, XAML!
</Button>
```

The static *XamlReader.Load* method parses this text and creates an object of type *Button*. For convenience, I will be referring to the *XamlReader.Load* method as the *parser* because it parses the XAML and creates one or more objects from it.

This first question that might occur to a programmer is this: How does the parser know which class to use to create this particular *Button* object? After all, there are three different *Button* classes in .NET. There's a *Button* in Windows Forms and another you use with ASP.NET (Active Server Pages). Although this XAML file contains two XML namespaces, it doesn't contain a Common Language Runtime namespace such as *System.Windows.Controls*. Nor does the XAML contain any references to the assembly PresentationFramework.dll in which the *System.Windows.Controls.Button* class resides. Why doesn't the parser require a fully qualified class name or something akin to a *using* directive?

One answer is that a WPF application probably doesn't have references to the Windows Forms assemblies or the ASP.NET assemblies in which the other *Button* classes reside, but it definitely has a reference to the PresentationFramework.dll assembly because that's where the *XamlReader* class is located. But even if a WPF application had references to System.Windows .Forms.dll or System.Web.dll, and these assemblies were loaded by the application, the parser *still* knows which *Button* class to use.

The solution to this mystery lies inside the PresentationFramework assembly. This assembly contains a number of custom attributes. (An application can interrogate these attributes by calling *GetCustomAttributes* on the *Assembly* object.) Several of these attributes are of type *XmlnsDefinitionAttribute*, and this class contains two properties of importance named *Xml-Namespace* and *ClrNamespace*. One of the *XmlnsDefinitionAttribute* objects in Presentation-Framework has its *XmlNamespace* set to the string "http://schemas.microsoft.com/winfx/ 2006/xaml/presentation" and its *ClrNamespace* property set to the string "System.Windows .Controls." The syntax looks like this:

```
[assembly:XmlnsDefinition
    ("http://schemas.microsoft.com/winfx/2006/xaml/presentation",
     "System.Windows.Controls")]
```

Other *XmlnsDefinition* attributes associate this same XML namespace with the CLR namespaces *System.Windows*, *System.Windows.Controls.Primitives*, *System.Windows.Input*, *System.Windows.Shapes*, and so forth.

The XAML parser examines the *XmlnsDefinition* attributes (if any) in all the assemblies loaded by the application. If any of the XML namespaces in these attributes match the XML namespace in the XAML file, the parser knows which CLR namespaces to assume when searching for a *Button* class in these assemblies.

The parser would certainly have a problem if the program referenced another assembly that contained a similar *XmlnsDefinition* attribute with the same XML namespace but a completely different *Button* class. But that really can't happen unless someone's created an assembly using Microsoft's XML namespace or somebody at Microsoft goofs up big time.

Let's give the button in XAML Cruncher an explicit width by setting the *Width* property:

```
<Button xmlns="http://schemas.microsoft.com/winfx/2006/xaml/presentation"
        xmlns:x="http://schemas.microsoft.com/winfx/2006/xaml"
        Width="144">
    Hello, XAML!
</Button>
```

The parser can determine from reflection that *Button* indeed has a *Width* property. The parser can also determine that this property is of type *double*, or the CLR type *System .Double*. However, as with every XML attribute, the value of the *Width* is a string. The parser must convert that string into an object of type *double*. This sounds fairly trivial. In fact, the *Double* structure includes a static *Parse* method for the express purpose of convert-ing strings to numbers.

In the general case, however, this conversion is not trivial, particularly considering that you can also specify that same width in inches like this:

```
Width="1.5in"
```

You can have a space between the number and the "in" string, and it can be spelled in uppercase or lowercase:

```
Width="1.5 IN"
```

Scientific notation is allowed:

```
Width="15e-1in"
```

So is specifying Not a Number (and case matters here):

```
Width="NaN"
```

Although not semantically proper for the *Width* property, some double attributes allow "Infinity" or "-Infinity." You can also go metric, of course:

```
Width="3.81cm"
```

Or, if you have a typographical background, you can use printer's points:

```
Width="108pt"
```

The *Double.Parse* method allows scientific notation, NaN, and Infinity, but not the "in," "cm," or "pt" strings. Those must be handled elsewhere.

When the XAML parser encounters a property of type *double*, it locates a class named *Double-Converter* from the *System.ComponentModel* namespace. This is one of many "converter" classes. They all derive from *TypeConverter* and include a method named *ConvertFromString* that ultimately (in this case) probably makes use of the *Double.Parse* method to perform conversion.

Similarly, when you set a *Margin* attribute (of type *Thickness*), the parser locates the *Thickness-Converter* class in the *System.Windows* namespace. This converter allows you to set a single value that applies to all four sides:

```
Margin="48"
```

or two values where the first applies to the left and right and the second applies to the top and bottom:

```
Margin="48 96"
```

You can separate these two numbers with a space or a comma. You can also use four numbers for the left, top, right, and bottom:

```
Margin="48 96 24 192"
```

If you want to use "in," or "cm," or "pt" here, there can't be a space between the number and the measurement string:

```
Margin="1.27cm 96 18pt 2in"
```

When you enter XAML in Visual Studio's editor, it applies some more stringent rules than the actual parser and displays warning messages if your XAML does not comply. For defining a *Thickness* object, Visual Studio prefers that commas separate the values.

For Boolean values, use "true" or "false" with whatever mix of case you want:

```
IsEnabled="FaLse"
```

Visual Studio, however, prefers "True" and "False."

For properties that you set to members of an enumeration, the *EnumConverter* class requires that you use the enumeration member by itself when setting the attribute:

```
HorizontalAlignment="Center"
```

As you'll recall, you set the *FontStretch*, *FontStyle*, and *FontWeight* properties not to enumeration members but to static properties of the *FontStretches*, *FontStyles*, and *FontWeights* classes. The *FontStretchConverter*, *FontStyleConverter*, and *FontWeightConverter* classes let you use those static properties directly. You set *FontFamily* to a string, and *FontSize* to a *double*:

```
FontFamily="Times New Roman"
FontSize="18pt"
FontWeight="Bold"
FontStyle="Italic"
```

Let's move on to something different. This is a XAML file named Star.xaml that is rendered as a five-pointed star:

```
Star.xaml
<!-- =====================================
        Star.xaml (c) 2006 by Charles Petzold
     ===================================== -->
<Polygon xmlns="http://schemas.microsoft.com/winfx/2006/xaml/presentation"
         xmlns:x="http://schemas.microsoft.com/winfx/2006/xaml"
         Points="144 48, 200 222, 53 114, 235 114, 88 222"
         Fill="Red"
         Stroke="Blue"
         StrokeThickness="5" />
```

Polygon contains a property named *Points* of type *PointCollection*. Fortunately a *PointCollection-Converter* exists that lets you specify the points as a series of alternating *X* and *Y* coordinates. The numbers can be separated with either spaces or commas. Some people put commas between the *X* and *Y* coordinates of each point and use spaces to separate the points. Others (including me) prefer using commas to separate the points.

The *BrushConverter* class lets you specify colors using static members of the *Brushes* class, of course, but you can also use hexadecimal RGB color values:

```
Fill="#FF0000"
```

The following is the same color but has an alpha channel of 128 (half transparent):

```
Fill="#80FF0000"
```

You can also use fractional red, green, and blue values in the scRGB color scheme, preceded by the alpha channel. This is half-transparent red:

```
Fill="sc#0.5,1,0,0"
```

Now instead of setting the *Fill* property to an object of type *SolidColorBrush*, let's set the *Fill* property to a *LinearGradientBrush*.

And suddenly we seem to hit a wall. How can you possibly represent an entire *LinearGradient-Brush* in a text string that you assign to the *Fill* property? The *SolidColorBrush* requires just one color value, while gradient brushes require at least two colors as well as gradient stops. The limitations of markup have now been revealed.

You can indeed specify a *LinearGradientBrush* in XAML, and to understand how it's done, let's first look at an alternative syntax for setting the *Fill* property to a solid red brush. First, replace the empty content tag of the *Polygon* object with an explicit end tag:

```
<Polygon xmlns="http://schemas.microsoft.com/winfx/2006/xaml/presentation"
         xmlns:x="http://schemas.microsoft.com/winfx/2006/xaml"
         Points="144 48, 200 222, 53 114, 235 114, 88 222"
         Fill="Red"
         Stroke="Blue"
         StrokeThickness="5">
</Polygon>
```

Now remove the *Fill* attribute from the *Polygon* tag and replace it with a child element named *Polygon.Fill*. The content of that element is the word "Red":

```
<Polygon xmlns="http://schemas.microsoft.com/winfx/2006/xaml/presentation"
         xmlns:x="http://schemas.microsoft.com/winfx/2006/xaml"
         Points="144 48, 200 222, 53 114, 235 114, 88 222"
         Stroke="Blue"
         StrokeThickness="5">
    <Polygon.Fill>
        Red
    </Polygon.Fill>
</Polygon>
```

Let's nail down some terminology. Many XAML elements refer to classes and structures and result in the creation of objects. These are known as *object elements*:

```
<Polygon ... />
```

Often the element contains attributes that set properties on these objects. These are known as *property attributes*:

```
Fill="Red"
```

It is also possible to specify a property with an alternative syntax that involves a child element. These are known as *property elements*:

```
<Polygon.Fill>
      Red
</Polygon.Fill>
```

The property element is characterized by a period between the name of the element and the name of the property. Property elements have no attributes. You will *never* see something like this:

```
<!-- Wrong Syntax! -->
<Polygon.Fill SomeAttribute="Whatever">
    ...
</Polygon.Fill>
```

Not even an XML namespace declaration can appear there. If you try to set an attribute on a property element in XAML Cruncher, you'll get the message "Cannot set properties on property elements," which is the message of the exception that *XamlReader.Load* throws when you try to do it.

The property element must contain content that is convertible to the type of the property. The *Polygon.Fill* property element refers to the *Fill* property, which is of type *Brush*, so the property element must have content that can be converted into a *Brush*:

```
<Polygon.Fill>
     Red
</Polygon.Fill>
```

This also works:

```
<Polygon.Fill>
     #FF0000
</Polygon.Fill>
```

You can make the content of *Polygon.Fill* more explicitly a *Brush* with the following (rather wordier) syntax:

```
<Polygon.Fill>
     <Brush>
          Red
     </Brush>
</Polygon.Fill>
```

Now the content of the *Polygon.Fill* property element is a *Brush* object element, the text string "Red." That content is actually convertible into an object of type *SolidColorBrush*, so you can write the *Polygon.Fill* property element like so:

```
<Polygon.Fill>
    <SolidColorBrush>
        Red
    </SolidColorBrush>
</Polygon.Fill>
```

SolidColorBrush has a property named *Color*, and the *ColorConverter* class allows the same conversions as the *Brush* converter, so you can set the *Color* property of *SolidColorBrush* with a property attribute:

```
<Polygon.Fill>
    <SolidColorBrush Color="Red">
    </SolidColorBrush>
</Polygon.Fill>
```

However, you cannot now substitute *Brush* for *SolidColorBrush* because *Brush* does not have a property named *Color*.

Since *SolidColorBrush* has no content, you can write the tag with the empty-element syntax:

```
<Polygon.Fill>
    <SolidColorBrush Color="Red" />
</Polygon.Fill>
```

Or, you can break out the *Color* property of *SolidColorBrush* with the property element syntax:

```
<Polygon.Fill>
    <SolidColorBrush>
        <SolidColorBrush.Color>
            Red
        </SolidColorBrush.Color>
    </SolidColorBrush>
</Polygon.Fill>
```

The *Color* property of the *SolidColorBrush* class is an object of type *Color*, so you can explicitly use an object element for the content of *SolidColorBrush.Color*:

```
<Polygon.Fill>
    <SolidColorBrush>
        <SolidColorBrush.Color>
            <Color>
                Red
            </Color>
        </SolidColorBrush.Color>
    </SolidColorBrush>
</Polygon.Fill>
```

As you'll recall, Color has properties named *A*, *R*, *G*, and *B*, of type *byte*. You can set those properties in the *Color* tag with either decimal or hexadecimal syntax:

```
<Polygon.Fill>
    <SolidColorBrush>
        <SolidColorBrush.Color>
            <Color A="255" R="#FF" G="0" B="0">
            </Color>
        </SolidColorBrush.Color>
    </SolidColorBrush>
</Polygon.Fill>
```

Keep in mind that you cannot set these four properties in the *SolidColorBrush.Color* tag because, as the exception message says, you "cannot set properties on property elements."

Because the *Color* element now has no content, you can write it with the empty-element syntax:

```
<Polygon.Fill>
    <SolidColorBrush>
        <SolidColorBrush.Color>
            <Color A="255" R="#FF" G="0" B="0" />
        </SolidColorBrush.Color>
    </SolidColorBrush>
</Polygon.Fill>
```

Or, you could break out one or more of the attributes of *Color*:

```
<Polygon.Fill>
    <SolidColorBrush>
        <SolidColorBrush.Color>
            <Color A="255" G="0" B="0">
                <Color.R>
                    #FF
                </Color.R>
            </Color>
        </SolidColorBrush.Color>
    </SolidColorBrush>
</Polygon.Fill>
```

The type of the *R* property in *Color* is *Byte*, a structure defined in the *System* namespace, and it's even possible to put a *Byte* element into the XAML to make the data type of *R* more explicit. However, the *System* namespace is not among the CLR namespaces associated with the two XML namespaces at the top of the XAML file. To refer to the *Byte* structure in a XAML file, you need another XML namespace declaration. Let's associate the *System* namespace with a prefix of *s*:

```
xmlns:s="clr-namespace:System;assembly=mscorlib"
```

Notice that the string in quotation marks begins with *clr-namespace* followed by a colon and a CLR namespace, just as if you were associating the prefix with a CLR namespace in your own program (as demonstrated in the UseCustomClass project in Chapter 19). Because the classes and structures in the *System* namespace are located in an external assembly, that information needs to follow. A semicolon follows the CLR namespace, with the word *assembly*, an equal sign, and the assembly name itself. Notice that a colon separates *clr-namespace* from the CLR namespace, but an equal sign separates *assembly* from the assembly name. The idea here is that the initial part of the string up through the colon is supposed to be analogous to the *http:* part of a conventional namespace declaration.

That declaration needs to go in the *Byte* element itself or a parent of the *Byte* element. Let's put it in the *Color* element (for reasons that will become apparent):

```
<Polygon.Fill>
    <SolidColorBrush>
        <SolidColorBrush.Color>
            <Color xmlns:s="clr-namespace:System;assembly=mscorlib"
                    A="255" G="0" B="0">
                <Color.R>
                    <s:Byte>
                        #FF
                    </s:Byte>
                </Color.R>
            </Color>
        </SolidColorBrush.Color>
    </SolidColorBrush>
</Polygon.Fill>
```

You can go to the extreme by breaking out all four properties of *Color*.

```
<Polygon.Fill>
    <SolidColorBrush>
        <SolidColorBrush.Color>
            <Color xmlns:s="clr-namespace:System;assembly=mscorlib">
                <Color.A>
                    <s:Byte>
                        255
                    </s:Byte>
                </Color.A>
                <Color.R>
                    <s:Byte>
                        255
                    </s:Byte>
                </Color.R>
                <Color.G>
                    <s:Byte>
                        0
                    </s:Byte>
                </Color.G>
                <Color.B>
                    <s:Byte>
                        0
                    </s:Byte>
                </Color.B>
            </Color>
        </SolidColorBrush.Color>
    </SolidColorBrush>
</Polygon.Fill>
```

This wouldn't have worked if the new namespace declaration appeared in the first *Byte* element. A namespace declaration applies to the element in which it appears and all *nested* elements.

I hope that's as far as you want to go, because we've reached the end of the line in making XAML much more verbose than it needs to be. What this syntax demonstrates, however, is an approach that is suitable for defining a gradient brush as the *Fill* property.

A *LinearGradientBrush* has two properties named *StartPoint* and *EndPoint*. By default, these properties are in a coordinate system relative to the object they're coloring. A third crucial property is named *GradientStops* of type *GradientStopCollection*, which is a collection of *GradientStop* objects that indicate the colors.

The *Polygon.Fill* property element must have content of type *Brush*. An object element of type *LinearGradientBrush* satisfies that criterion:

```
<Polygon.Fill>
    <LinearGradientBrush …>
        ...
    </LinearGradientBrush>
</Polygon.Fill>
```

The *StartPoint* and *EndPoint* properties are simple enough to be defined as attribute properties in the *LinearGradientBrush* start tag:

```
<Polygon.Fill>
    <LinearGradientBrush StartPoint="0 0" EndPoint="1 0">
        ...
    </LinearGradientBrush>
</Polygon.Fill>
```

However, the *GradientStops* property must become a property element:

```
<Polygon.Fill>
    <LinearGradientBrush StartPoint="0 0" EndPoint="1 0">
        <LinearGradientBrush.GradientStops>
            ...
        </LinearGradientBrush.GradientStops>
    </LinearGradientBrush>
</Polygon.Fill>
```

The *GradientStops* property is of type *GradientStopCollection*, so we can put in an object element for that class:

```
<Polygon.Fill>
    <LinearGradientBrush StartPoint="0 0" EndPoint="1 0">
        <LinearGradientBrush.GradientStops>
            <GradientStopCollection>
                ...
            </GradientStopCollection>
        </LinearGradientBrush.GradientStops>
    </LinearGradientBrush>
</Polygon.Fill>
```

The *GradientStopCollection* class implements the *IList* interface, and that's sufficient to allow its members to be written as simple children. Notice that each *GradientStop* element is most conveniently written with the empty-element syntax:

```
<Polygon.Fill>
    <LinearGradientBrush StartPoint="0 0" EndPoint="1 0">
        <GradientStopCollection>
            <GradientStop Offset="0" Color="Red" />
            <GradientStop Offset="0.5" Color="Green" />
            <GradientStop Offset="1" Color="Blue" />
        </GradientStopCollection>
    </LinearGradientBrush>
</Polygon.Fill>
```

This can actually be written a little simpler. It is not necessary for the *LinearGradientBrush. GradientStops* property element or the *GradientStopCollection* object element to be explicitly included. They can be removed:

```
<Polygon.Fill>
    <LinearGradientBrush StartPoint="0 0" EndPoint="1 0">
        <GradientStop Offset="0" Color="Red" />
        <GradientStop Offset="0.5" Color="Green" />
        <GradientStop Offset="1" Color="Blue" />
    </LinearGradientBrush>
</Polygon.Fill>
```

And that's it. The *Polygon.Fill* property is an object of type *LinearGradientBrush. LinearGradient-Brush* has properties *StartPoint*, *EndPoint*, and *GradientStops*. The *LinearGradientBrush* has a collection of three *GradientStop* objects. *GradientStop* has properties *Offset* and *Color*.

Here's a star with a *RadialGradientBrush*:

RadialGradientStar.cs

```
<!-- =======================================================
     RadialGradientStar.xaml (c) 2006 by Charles Petzold
     ======================================================= --><Polygon xmlns="http://
schemas.microsoft.com/winfx/2006/xaml/presentation"
        xmlns:x="http://schemas.microsoft.com/winfx/2006/xaml"
        Points="144 48, 200 222, 53 114, 235 114, 88 222"
        Stroke="Blue"
        StrokeThickness="5">
    <Polygon.Fill>
        <RadialGradientBrush>
            <RadialGradientBrush.GradientStops>
                <GradientStop Offset="0" Color="Blue" />
                <GradientStop Offset="1" Color="Red" />
            </RadialGradientBrush.GradientStops>
        </RadialGradientBrush>
    </Polygon.Fill>
</Polygon>
```

Let's go back to the *Button*. This XAML file shows three properties of *Button* set as attributes, including the *Content* property:

```
<Button xmlns="http://schemas.microsoft.com/winfx/2006/xaml/presentation"
        xmlns:x="http://schemas.microsoft.com/winfx/2006/xaml"
        Foreground="LightSeaGreen"
        FontSize="24 pt"
        Content="Hello, XAML!">
</Button>
```

You can make the *Foreground* attribute a property element like this:

```
<Button xmlns="http://schemas.microsoft.com/winfx/2006/xaml/presentation"
        xmlns:x="http://schemas.microsoft.com/winfx/2006/xaml"
        FontSize="24 pt"
        Content="Hello, XAML!">
    <Button.Foreground>
        LightSeaGreen
    </Button.Foreground>
</Button>
```

Or you can make the *FontSize* attribute a property element like this:

```
<Button xmlns="http://schemas.microsoft.com/winfx/2006/xaml/presentation"
        xmlns:x="http://schemas.microsoft.com/winfx/2006/xaml"
        Foreground="LightSeaGreen"
        Content="Hello, XAML!">
    <Button.FontSize>
        24 pt
    </Button.FontSize>
</Button>
```

Or both *Foreground* and *FontSize* can be property elements:

```
<Button xmlns="http://schemas.microsoft.com/winfx/2006/xaml/presentation"
        xmlns:x="http://schemas.microsoft.com/winfx/2006/xaml"
        Content="Hello, XAML!">
    <Button.Foreground>
        LightSeaGreen
    </Button.Foreground>
    <Button.FontSize>
        24 pt
    </Button.FontSize>
</Button>
```

It's also possible to make the *Content* property a property element:

```
<Button xmlns="http://schemas.microsoft.com/winfx/2006/xaml/presentation"
        xmlns:x="http://schemas.microsoft.com/winfx/2006/xaml"
        Foreground="LightSeaGreen"
        FontSize="24 pt">
    <Button.Content>
        Hello, XAML!
    </Button.Content>
</Button>
```

In this case, however, the *Button.Content* tags aren't required:

```
<Button xmlns="http://schemas.microsoft.com/winfx/2006/xaml/presentation"
        xmlns:x="http://schemas.microsoft.com/winfx/2006/xaml"
        Foreground="LightSeaGreen"
        FontSize="24 pt">
    Hello, XAML!
</Button>
```

And, in fact, you can mix that content with property elements. I've inserted a couple of blank lines in this XAML file just to make it more readable:

```
<Button xmlns="http://schemas.microsoft.com/winfx/2006/xaml/presentation"
        xmlns:x="http://schemas.microsoft.com/winfx/2006/xaml">

    <Button.Foreground>
        LightSeaGreen
    </Button.Foreground>

    Hello, XAML!

    <Button.FontSize>
        24 pt
    </Button.FontSize>

</Button>
```

For every property of *Button*, you either treat the property as an attribute that you set in the *Button* start tag, or you use a property element where the value is a child of the element—except for the *Content* property. The *Content* property is special because you can simply treat the value of the *Content* property as a child of the *Button* element without using property elements.

So what makes *Content* so special?

Every class that you can use with XAML potentially has one property that has been identified specifically as a *content property*. For *Button*, the content property is *Content*. A property is identified as the content property in the definition of the class with the *ContentPropertyAttribute* (defined in the *System.Windows.Serialization* namespace). The definition of the *Button* class in the PresentationFramework.dll source code possibly looks something like this:

```
[ContentProperty("Content")]
public class Button: ButtonBase
{
    ...
}
```

Or, *Button* simply inherits the setting of the *ContentProperty* attribute from *ContentControl*.

The *StackPanel*, on the other hand, is defined with a *ContentProperty* attribute that looks like this:

```
[ContentProperty("Children")]
public class StackPanel: Panel
{
    ...
}
```

That *ContentProperty* attribute makes it possible to include the children of *StackPanel* as children of the *StackPanel* element:

```
<StackPanel xmlns="http://schemas.microsoft.com/winfx/2006/xaml/presentation"
        xmlns:x="http://schemas.microsoft.com/winfx/2006/xaml">

    <Button HorizontalAlignment="Center">
        Button Number One
    </Button>

    <TextBlock HorizontalAlignment="Center">
        TextBlock in the middle
    </TextBlock>

    <Button HorizontalAlignment="Center">
        Button Number One
    </Button>

</StackPanel>
```

The content property of *LinearGradientBrush* and *radialGradientBrush* is *GradientStops*.

The content property of the *TextBlock* class is the *Inlines* collection, a collection of *Inline* objects. The *Run* class descends from *Inline*, and the content property of *Run* is *Text*, which is an object of type *string*. All of this combines to give you much freedom in defining the *TextBlock* content:

```
<TextBlock>
    This is <Italic>italic</Italic> text and this is <Bold>bold</Bold> text
</TextBlock>
```

The content properties of the *Italic* and *Bold* classes are both also *Inline*. This piece of XAML can alternatively be written by explicitly referencing the *Text* property that *Italic* and *Bold* both inherit from *Span*:

```
<TextBlock>
    This is <Italic Text="italic" /> text and this is <Bold Text="bold" /> text
</TextBlock>
```

Because the content property is important when writing XAML, you may be interested in getting a list of all the classes for which the *ContentProperty* attribute is defined and the content properties themselves. Here's a console program that provides this information.

```
DumpContentPropertyAttributes.cs
//-------------------------------------------------------------
// DumpContentPropertyAttributes.cs (c) 2006 by Charles Petzold
//-------------------------------------------------------------
using System;
using System.Collections.Generic;
using System.Reflection;
using System.Windows;
using System.Windows.Markup;
using System.Windows.Navigation;
```

```
public class DumpContentPropertyAttributes
{
    [STAThread]
    public static void Main()
    {
        // Make sure PresentationCore and PresentationFramework are loaded.
        UIElement dummy1 = new UIElement();
        FrameworkElement dummy2 = new FrameworkElement();

        // SortedList to store class and content property.
        SortedList<string, string> listClass = new SortedList<string, string>();

        // Formatting string.
        string strFormat = "{0,-35}{1}";

        // Loop through the loaded assemblies.
        foreach (AssemblyName asmblyname in
                  Assembly.GetExecutingAssembly().GetReferencedAssemblies())
        {
            // Loop through the types.
            foreach (Type type in Assembly.Load(asmblyname).GetTypes())
            {
                // Loop through the custom attributes.
                // (Set argument to 'false' for non-inherited only!)
                foreach (object obj in type.GetCustomAttributes(
                                  typeof(ContentPropertyAttribute), true))
                {
                    // Add to list if ContentPropertyAttribute.
                    if (type.IsPublic && obj as ContentPropertyAttribute != null)
                        listClass.Add(type.Name,
                                  (obj as ContentPropertyAttribute).Name);
                }
            }
        }
        // Display the results.
        Console.WriteLine(strFormat, "Class", "Content Property");
        Console.WriteLine(strFormat, "-----", "----------------");

        foreach (string strClass in listClass.Keys)
            Console.WriteLine(strFormat, strClass, listClass[strClass]);
    }
}
```

Some elements—mostly notably *DockPanel* and *Grid*—have attached properties that you use in C# code with syntax like this:

```
DockPanel.SetDock(btn, Dock.Top);
```

This code indicates that you want the *btn* control to be docked at the top of a *DockPanel*. The call has no effect if *btn* is not actually a child of a *DockPanel*. As you discovered in Chapter 8, the call to the static *SetDock* method is equivalent to:

```
btn.SetValue(DockPanel.DockProperty, Dock.Top);
```

In XAML, you use a syntax like this:

```
<Button DockPanel.Dock="Top" ... />
```

Here's a little stand-alone XAML file somewhat reminiscent of the DockAroundTheBlock program from Chapter 6 but not nearly as excessive.

AttachedPropertiesDemo.xaml

```
<!-- ========================================================
        AttachedPropertiesDemo.xaml (c) 2006 by Charles Petzold
     ======================================================== -->
<DockPanel xmlns="http://schemas.microsoft.com/winfx/2006/xaml/presentation"
           xmlns:x="http://schemas.microsoft.com/winfx/2006/xaml">
    <Button Content="Button No. 1" DockPanel.Dock="Left" />
    <Button Content="Button No. 2" DockPanel.Dock="Top" />
    <Button Content="Button No. 3" DockPanel.Dock="Right" />
    <Button Content="Button No. 4" DockPanel.Dock="Bottom" />
    <Button Content="Button No. 5" />
</DockPanel>
```

The *Grid* works particularly well in XAML because the row and column definitions aren't nearly as verbose as their C# equivalents. Each *RowDefinition* and *ColumnDefinition* can occupy a single line within *Grid.RowDefinitions* and *Grid.ColumnDefinitions* property elements. The following is another stand-alone XAML file.

SimpleGrid.xaml

```
<!-- ========================================================
        SimpleGrid.xaml (c) 2006 by Charles Petzold
     ======================================================== -->
<Grid xmlns="http://schemas.microsoft.com/winfx/2006/xaml/presentation"
      xmlns:x="http://schemas.microsoft.com/winfx/2006/xaml">
    <Grid.RowDefinitions>
        <RowDefinition Height="100" />
        <RowDefinition Height="Auto" />
        <RowDefinition Height="100*" />
    </Grid.RowDefinitions>
    <Grid.ColumnDefinitions>
        <ColumnDefinition Width="33*" />
        <ColumnDefinition Width="Auto" />
        <ColumnDefinition Width="67*" />
    </Grid.ColumnDefinitions>

    <Button Content="Button No. 1" Grid.Row="0" Grid.Column="0" />
    <Button Content="Button No. 2" Grid.Row="1" Grid.Column="0" />
    <Button Content="Button No. 3" Grid.Row="2" Grid.Column="0" />

    <GridSplitter HorizontalAlignment="Center" Width="6"
                  Grid.Row="0" Grid.Column="1" Grid.RowSpan="3" />

    <Button Content="Button No. 4" Grid.Row="0" Grid.Column="2" />
    <Button Content="Button No. 5" Grid.Row="1" Grid.Column="2" />
    <Button Content="Button No. 6" Grid.Row="2" Grid.Column="2" />

</Grid>
```

If you're satisfied with the default *Height* and *Width* of "1*" (to use the XAML syntax) you can even write *RowDefinition* and *ColumnDefinition* elements like this:

```
<RowDefinition />
```

Attached properties aren't the only attributes that can contain periods. You can also define an element's properties with attributes that contain a class name preceding the property name. The class name can be the same as the element in which the attribute appears, or an ancestor class, or a class that is also an owner of the same dependency property. For example, these are all valid attributes for a *Button* element:

```
Button.Foreground="Blue"
TextBlock.FontSize="24pt"
FrameworkElement.HorizontalAlignment="Center"
ButtonBase.VerticalAlignment="Center"
UIElement.Opacity="0.5"
```

In some cases, you can use an attribute containing a class name and a property in an element in which that property is not defined. Here's an example.

PropertyInheritance.xaml

```
<!-- =======================================================
        PropertyInheritance.xaml (c) 2006 by Charles Petzold
     ======================================================= -->
<StackPanel xmlns="http://schemas.microsoft.com/winfx/2006/xaml/presentation"
            HorizontalAlignment="Center"
            TextBlock.FontSize="16pt"
            TextBlock.Foreground="Blue" >
    <TextBlock>
        Just a TextBlock
    </TextBlock>
    <Button>
        Just a Button
    </Button>
</StackPanel>
```

This XAML file sets the *FontSize* and *Foreground* properties in the *StackPanel* element, a class that doesn't have these properties, so the properties must be prefaced by a class that does define the properties. These attributes result in both the *TextBlock* and the *Button* getting a font size of 16 points, but a mysterious quirk results in only the *TextBlock* getting a blue foreground.

You can also use an attribute with a class and event name to set a handler for a routed event. The handler affects all child elements. The RoutedEventDemo project contains two files, RoutedEventDemo.xaml and RoutedEventDemo.cs. The XAML file contains an attribute in the *ContextMenu* element of *MenuItem.Click*. This handler applies to the *MenuItem* elements that comprise the context menu of a *TextBlock*.

RoutedEventDemo.xaml

```xml
<!-- =================================================
         RoutedEventDemo.xaml (c) 2006 by Charles Petzold
     ================================================= -->
<Window xmlns="http://schemas.microsoft.com/winfx/2006/xaml/presentation"
        xmlns:x="http://schemas.microsoft.com/winfx/2006/xaml"
        x:Class="Petzold.RoutedEventDemo.RoutedEventDemo"
        Title="Routed Event Demo">
    <TextBlock Name="txtblk"
               FontSize="24pt"
               HorizontalAlignment="Center"
               VerticalAlignment="Center"
               ToolTip="Right click to display context menu">
        TextBlock with Context Menu
        <TextBlock.ContextMenu>
            <ContextMenu MenuItem.Click="MenuItemOnClick">
            <ContextMenu>
                <MenuItem Header="Red" />
                <MenuItem Header="Orange" />
                <MenuItem Header="Yellow" />
                <MenuItem Header="Greem" />
                <MenuItem Header="Blue" />
                <MenuItem Header="Indigo" />
                <MenuItem Header="Violet" />
            </ContextMenu>
        </TextBlock.ContextMenu>
    </TextBlock>
</Window>
```

The C# file contains a handler for that event. The *MenuItem* object that triggered the event is the *Source* property of the *RoutedEventArgs* object. Notice that the handler uses the static *ColorConverter.ConvertFromString* method to convert the *MenuItem* text to a *Color* object.

RoutedEventDemo.cs

```csharp
//-------------------------------------------------
// RoutedEventDemo.cs (c) 2006 by Charles Petzold
//-------------------------------------------------
using System;
using System.Windows;
using System.Windows.Controls;
using System.Windows.Input;
using System.Windows.Media;

namespace Petzold.RoutedEventDemo
{
    public partial class RoutedEventDemo : Window
    {
        [STAThread]
        public static void Main()
```

```
    {
        Application app = new Application();
        app.Run(new RoutedEventDemo());
    }
    public RoutedEventDemo()
    {
        InitializeComponent();
    }
    void MenuItemOnClick(object sender, RoutedEventArgs args)
    {
        string str = (args.Source as MenuItem).Header as string;
        Color clr = (Color)ColorConverter.ConvertFromString(str);
        txtblk.Foreground = new SolidColorBrush(clr);
    }
    }
}
```

You've now seen several cases where an element or an attribute can contain a period. Here's a summary:

If the element name doesn't contain a period, it's always the name of a class or a structure:

```
<Button ... />
```

If the element name contains a period, the element name consists of the name of a class or structure followed by a property in that class structure. It's a property element:

```
<Button.Background>
    ...
</Button.Background>
```

This particular element must appear as a child of a *Button* element, and the start tag never has attributes. This element must contain content that is convertible to the type of the property (for example, simply the text string "Red" or "#FF0000") or a child element of the same type as the property (for example, *Brush* or any class that derives from *Brush*).

Attribute names usually do not contain periods:

```
< ... Background="Red" ... >
```

These attributes correspond to properties of the element in which they appear. When an attribute contains a period, one possibility is that it's an attached property:

```
< ... DockPanel.Dock="Left" ... >
```

This particular attached property usually appears in a child of a *DockPanel*, but that's not a requirement. If this attached property appears in an element that is not a child of a *DockPanel*, it is simply ignored.

An attribute with a period can also be a routed input event:

```
< ... MenuItem.Click="MenuItemOnClick" ... >
```

It makes most sense for this attribute to appear not in a *MenuItem* element (because the attribute name could simply be *Click* in that case) but in an element of which multiple *MenuItem* elements are children. It's also possible for periods to appear in property definitions that are intended to be inherited by children:

```
< ... TextBlock.FontSize="24pt" ... >
```

I think you'll agree that in many cases XAML is more concise than equivalent C# code, and it better represents hierarchical structures such as those that arise in laying out a window with panels and controls. But markup in general is much more limited than procedural languages, mostly because there's no concept of flow control. Even the simple sharing of variables seems unlikely in XAML. As you'll begin to see in the next chapter, however, XAML has a number of features that compensate for these deficiencies.

Chapter 21
Resources

Suppose you're coding some XAML for a window or a dialog box, and you decide you'd like to use two different font sizes for the controls. Some controls in the window will get the larger font size and some will get the smaller. You probably know which controls will get which font size, but you're not quite sure yet what the actual font sizes will be. Perhaps you'd like to experiment first before settling on the final values.

The naive approach is to insert hard-coded *FontSize* values in the XAML, like so:

```
FontSize="14pt"
```

If you later decide that you actually want something a little larger or smaller, you could just perform a search-and-replace. Although search-and-replace may work on a small scale, as a programmer you know that it's not a general solution to problems of this sort. Suppose you were dealing with a complex gradient brush rather than a simple font size. You might begin by copying and pasting a gradient brush throughout the program, but if you ever need to tweak that brush, you'll need to do it in a bunch of places.

If you faced this problem in C#, you wouldn't duplicate the gradient brush code or hard-code the font size values. You'd define variables for these objects, or—to clarify your intentions and improve efficiency—you could define a couple of constant fields in the window class:

```
const double fontsizeLarge = 14 / 0.75;
const double fontsizeSmall = 11 / 0.75;
```

You could alternatively define them as static read-only values:

```
static readonly double fontsizeLarge = 14 / 0.75;
static readonly double fontsizeSmall = 11 / 0.75;
```

The difference is that constants are evaluated at compile time and the values substituted wherever they're used, while statics are evaluated at run time.

This technique is so common and so useful in procedural programming that an equivalent facility in XAML would be quite valuable. Fortunately, it exists. You can reuse objects in XAML by first defining them as *resources*.

The resources I'll be discussing in this chapter are quite different from resources discussed earlier in this book. I've previously shown you how to use Microsoft Visual Studio to indicate that certain files included in a project are to be compiled with a Build Action of Resource. These resources are perhaps more accurately termed *assembly resources*. Most often, assembly resources are binary files such as icons and bitmaps, but in Chapter 19 I also showed you how to use this technique with XML files. These assembly resources are stored in the assembly (the executable file or a dynamic-link library) and are accessible by defining a *Uri* object referencing the resource's original file name.

The resources in this chapter are sometimes referred to as *locally defined* resources because they are defined in XAML (or sometimes in C# code) and they are usually associated with an element, control, page, or window in the application. A particular resource is available only within the element in which the resource is defined and within the children of that element. You can think of these resources as the compensation XAML offers in place of C# static read-only fields. Like static read-only fields, resource objects are created once at run time and shared by elements that reference them.

Resources are stored in an object of type *ResourceDictionary*, and three very fundamental classes—*FrameworkElement*, *FrameworkContentElement*, and *Application*—all define a property named *Resources* of type *ResourceDictionary*. Each item in the *ResourceDictionary* is stored along with a key to identify the object. Generally these keys are just text strings. XAML defines an attribute of *x:Key* specifically for the purposes of defining resource keys.

Any element that derives from *FrameworkElement* can have a *Resources* collection. Almost always, the *Resources* section is defined with property element syntax at the very top of the element:

```
<StackPanel>
    <StackPanel.Resources>
        ...
    </StackPanel.Resources>
    ...
</StackPanel>
```

The resources defined within that *Resources* section can be used throughout the *StackPanel* and by any children of the *StackPanel*. Each resource in the *Resources* section has the following form:

```
<SomeType x:Key="mykey" ...>
    ...
</SomeType>
```

You can set properties of that object with either attribute syntax or property element syntax. XAML elements can then reference the resource with the key using a *markup extension*. As the term implies, a markup extension is a special keyword that has been defined for use in XAML. The particular markup extension you use with resources is named *StaticResource*.

I began this chapter describing a problem involving the use of two different font sizes. The following stand-alone XAML file shows how to define two font-size resources in the *Resources* collection of a *StackPanel* and then how to access those resources by child elements of the *StackPanel*.

FontSizeResources.xaml

```xml
<!-- ==================================================
     FontSizeResources.xaml (c) 2006 by Charles Petzold
     ================================================== -->
<StackPanel xmlns="http://schemas.microsoft.com/winfx/2006/xaml/presentation"
            xmlns:x="http://schemas.microsoft.com/winfx/2006/xaml"
            xmlns:s="clr-namespace:System;assembly=mscorlib">

    <StackPanel.Resources>
        <s:Double x:Key="fontsizeLarge">
            18.7
        </s:Double>
        <s:Double x:Key="fontsizeSmall">
            14.7
        </s:Double>
    </StackPanel.Resources>

    <Button HorizontalAlignment="Center"
            VerticalAlignment="Center"
            Margin="24">
        <Button.FontSize>
            <StaticResource ResourceKey="fontsizeLarge" />
        </Button.FontSize>
        Button with large FontSize
    </Button>

    <Button HorizontalAlignment="Center"
            VerticalAlignment="Center"
            Margin="24"
            FontSize="{StaticResource fontsizeSmall}" >
        Button with small FontSize
    </Button>

</StackPanel>
```

Notice that the *StackPanel* element tag defines an XML namespace prefix of *s* for the *System* namespace (*clr-namespace:System;assembly=mscorlib*), which allows referencing the *Double* structure in the *Resources* collection.

The *Resources* section of the *StackPanel* contains definitions of two *Double* objects with keys of "fontsizeLarge" and "fontsizeSmall." Within any particular *Resources* dictionary, the keys must be unique. The values of 18.7 and 14.7 are equivalent to 14 points and 11 points.

The *StackPanel* or child elements of the *StackPanel* can make use of these resources in one of two ways, both involving the *StaticResource* markup extension. The first *Button* accesses the resource using property element syntax for *FontSize* with an element of *StaticResource* and an attribute of *ResourceKey* to indicate the key of the item:

```xml
<Button.FontSize>
    <StaticResource ResourceKey="fontsizeLarge" />
</Button.FontSize>
```

The more common syntax is shown for the second *Button*. The *FontSize* attribute is set to a string with the words *StaticResource* and the key name all enclosed in curly brackets:

```
FontSize="{StaticResource fontsizeSmall}"
```

Take a close look at that syntax—you'll be seeing it a lot in this chapter, and again in Chapter 23 when I take on the subject of data binding. The curly brackets indicate that the expression inside is a markup extension. There is no *StaticResource* class. There is, however, a class named *StaticResourceExtension* that inherits from *MarkupExtension* and includes a property named *ResourceKey*. *StaticResource* is classified as a markup extension because it provides a way to do something in XAML that normally would only be possible in procedural code. The *StaticResourceExtension* class is essentially providing the value from the dictionary based on the specified key.

You'll be seeing two other markup extensions in this chapter: *x:Static* and *DynamicResource*, and they also will be enclosed in curly brackets. The curly brackets indicate to the XAML parser that a markup extension is present. No additional quotation marks are allowed within the curly brackets.

You might, on a rare occasion, need to begin a text string with some curly brackets that do not involve a markup extension:

```
<!-- Won't work right! -->
<TextBlock Text="{just a little text in here}" />
```

To prevent the XAML parser from searching for (and failing to find) a markup extension named *just*, insert an escape sequence in front consisting of a pair of empty curly brackets:

```
<!-- Works just fine! -->
<TextBlock Text="{}{just a little text in here}" />
```

The *Resources* section is almost always defined at the very top of an element because any resource must be defined earlier in the file than when it is referenced. Forward references of resources are not allowed.

Although all the keys in a particular *Resources* collection must be unique, the same keys can be used in two different *Resources* collections. When a resource must be located, the search begins with the *Resources* collection of the element referencing the resource and continues up through the tree until the key is found. The following stand-alone XAML file illustrates this process.

ResourceLookupDemo.xaml

```
<!-- ======================================================
        ResourceLookupDemo.xaml (c) 2006 by Charles Petzold
     ====================================================== -->
<StackPanel xmlns="http://schemas.microsoft.com/winfx/2006/xaml/presentation"
            xmlns:x="http://schemas.microsoft.com/winfx/2006/xaml"
            Orientation="Horizontal">
```

```
    <StackPanel.Resources>
        <SolidColorBrush x:Key="brushText" Color="Blue" />
    </StackPanel.Resources>

    <StackPanel>
        <StackPanel.Resources>
            <SolidColorBrush x:Key="brushText" Color="Red" />
        </StackPanel.Resources>

        <Button HorizontalAlignment="Center"
                VerticalAlignment="Center"
                Margin="24"
                Foreground="{StaticResource brushText}">
            Button with Red text
        </Button>
    </StackPanel>

    <StackPanel>
        <Button HorizontalAlignment="Center"
                VerticalAlignment="Center"
                Margin="24"
                Foreground="{StaticResource brushText}">
            Button with Blue text
        </Button>
    </StackPanel>

</StackPanel>
```

Three *StackPanel* elements are defined here. The first has a horizontal orientation; the other two *StackPanel* elements are children. For simplicity, each of these two *StackPanel* children contains just one button.

The parent *StackPanel* has a *Resources* collection defining a *SolidColorBrush* with a key of "brushText" and a color of blue. The first child *StackPanel* also has a *Resources* collection with another *SolidColorBrush* that also has a key of "brushText" but a color of red. Both buttons set their *Foreground* properties with a *StaticResource* extension referencing the "brushText" key. The first button (in the *StackPanel* with the red brush) has red text. The second button is in a *StackPanel* that has no resource named "brushText," so it uses the resource from the parent *StackPanel*. Its text is colored blue.

Defining resources with the same name is a powerful technique, particularly with *styles*, which I'll introduce in Chapter 24. Styles give you the ability to define properties used for multiple elements, and even to define how these elements react to particular events and property changes. In real-life WPF programs, most *Resources* collections are devoted to defining and redefining styles. Because styles are so important, I thought it best to introduce the topic of resources first to give you a good foundation for understanding these underlying concepts. Just keep in mind that if something appears to be missing from this chapter—mainly, the use of resources to define a bunch of properties for particular elements and controls—it's coming in Chapter 24.

Resources are shared. Only one object is created for each resource, and even that object won't be created if the resource isn't referenced.

You may wonder, "Can I define an element or control as a resource?" Yes, you can. For example, you can include the following in one of the *Resources* sections in ResourceLookupDemo.xaml:

```
<Button x:Key="btn"
        FontSize="24">
    Resource Button
</Button>
```

You can then use that *Button* as a child in the *StackPanel* (or a child *StackPanel*, depending where you've defined the resource) using the following syntax:

```
<StaticResource ResourceKey="btn" />
```

It works, but you can't do it twice. The *Button* object created as the resource is just one object, and if that *Button* is a child of a panel, it can't be another child of that same panel or a child of another panel. And notice you can't change anything about the *Button* when you reference it in the *StaticResource* element. You're not really gaining anything by making the *Button* a resource. So what's the point?

If you think you really have a need to define controls and other elements as resources, you're probably thinking about using the resource to define *some* properties of the element but not *all* the properties. It's very likely that what you really want is a style, and that you'll get in Chapter 24.

Although resources are almost always defined in XAML rather than procedural code, you can add an object to an element's *Resources* collection with C# code such as this:

```
stack.Resources.Add("brushText", new SolidColorBrush(Colors.Blue));
```

Here it's quite obvious that the resource is only a single object that's possibly shared among multiple elements or controls. The *Add* method is defined by *ResourceDictionary*. The first argument is the key and is defined as type *object*, but it's common to use strings. Each of the three main classes that define a *Resources* collection (*FrameworkElement*, *FrameworkContentElement*, and *Application*) also defines a method named *FindResource* that locates a resource with a particular key. This is the method that the *StaticResourceExtension* undoubtedly uses to locate a resource.

What's interesting is that calling the *FindResource* method for a particular element might find something from the element's *Resources* collection, but it won't stop there. It can also find a resource with the specified key from one of the element's ancestors in the element tree. I would guess that *FindResource* is implemented something like this:

```
public object FindResource(object key)
{
    object obj = Resources[key];
```

```
    if (obj != null)
        return obj;

    if (Parent != null)
        return Parent.FindResource(key);

    return Application.Current.FindResource(key);
}
```

The recursive search up the element tree is what makes *FindResource* much more valuable than simply indexing the *Resources* property with the key. Notice also that when the element tree is exhausted, *FindResource* checks the *Resources* dictionary in the *Application*. You can—and should—use the *Resources* collection of the *Application* object for application-wide settings, styles, and themes.

Up until now I've been recommending that you create empty projects in Visual Studio so that you have a better understanding of WPF itself without getting distracted by what Visual Studio provides for you. Now that you've been introduced to resources, it's probably safe to let Visual Studio impose its obstinate will on your programming style, at least experimentally.

Let's use Visual Studio to create a project of type Windows Presentation Foundation Application and give it a name of GradientBrushResourceDemo. Visual Studio creates a file named MyApp.xaml with a *Resources* section already defined and ready for your input:

MyApp.xaml
```
<Application x:Class="GradientBrushResourceDemo.MyApp"
    xmlns="http://schemas.microsoft.com/winfx/2006/xaml/presentation"
    xmlns:x="http://schemas.microsoft.com/winfx/2006/xaml"
    StartupUri="Window1.xaml"
    >
    <Application.Resources>

    </Application.Resources>
</Application>
```

That's how important this application-wide *Resources* section is considered to be in the context of WPF programming! Let's use that *Resources* section to define an application-wide gradient brush, so that MyApp.xaml now looks like this:

MyApp.xaml
```
<Application x:Class="GradientBrushResourceDemo.MyApp"
    xmlns="http://schemas.microsoft.com/winfx/2006/xaml/presentation"
    xmlns:x="http://schemas.microsoft.com/winfx/2006/xaml"
    StartupUri="Window1.xaml"
    >
    <Application.Resources>
        <LinearGradientBrush x:Key="brushGradient"
                             StartPoint="0, 0"
                             EndPoint="1, 1">
```

```
            <LinearGradientBrush.GradientStops>
                <GradientStop Offset="0" Color="Black" />
                <GradientStop Offset="0.5" Color="Green" />
                <GradientStop Offset="1" Color="Gold" />
            </LinearGradientBrush.GradientStops>
        </LinearGradientBrush>
    </Application.Resources>
</Application>
```

Visual Studio also creates a MyApp.xaml.cs code-behind file for MyApp.xaml, but this file doesn't do much. The Window1.xaml file that Visual Studio creates defines a *Window* element and a *Grid* by default.

Window1.xaml
```
<Window x:Class="GradientBrushResourceDemo.Window1"
    xmlns="http://schemas.microsoft.com/winfx/2006/xaml/presentation"
    xmlns:x="http://schemas.microsoft.com/winfx/2006/xaml"
    Title="GradientBrushResourceDemo" Height="300" Width="300"
    >
    <Grid>

    </Grid>
</Window>
```

The initial Window1.xaml.cs code-behind file simply contains a call to *InitializeComponent.*

Window1.xaml.cs
```
using System;
using System.Windows;
using System.Windows.Controls;
using System.Windows.Data;
using System.Windows.Documents;
using System.Windows.Media;
using System.Windows.Media.Imaging;
using System.Windows.Shapes;

namespace GradientBrushResourceDemo
{
    /// <summary>
    /// Interaction logic for Window1.xaml
    /// </summary>

    public partial class Window1 : Window
    {
        public Window1()
        {
            InitializeComponent();
        }
    }
}
```

To that code I added a resource to the window with one statement of C#.

Window1.xaml.cs

```csharp
using System;
using System.Windows;
using System.Windows.Controls;
using System.Windows.Data;
using System.Windows.Documents;
using System.Windows.Media;
using System.Windows.Media.Imaging;
using System.Windows.Shapes;

namespace GradientBrushResourceDemo
{
    /// <summary>
    /// Interaction logic for Window1.xaml
    /// </summary>

    public partial class Window1 : Window
    {
        public Window1()
        {
            Resources.Add("thicknessMargin", new Thickness(24, 12, 24, 23));

            InitializeComponent();
        }
    }
}
```

In the Window1.xaml file, a *StackPanel* can replace the *Grid*, and then four *TextBlock* elements can use the *LinearGradientBrush* resource and the *Thickness* resource.

Window1.xaml

```xml
<Window x:Class="GradientBrushResourceDemo.Window1"
    xmlns="http://schemas.microsoft.com/winfx/2006/xaml/presentation"
    xmlns:x="http://schemas.microsoft.com/winfx/2006/xaml"
    Title="GradientBrushResourceDemo" Height="300" Width="300"
    >
    <StackPanel>
        <TextBlock Margin="{StaticResource thicknessMargin}"
                Foreground="{StaticResource brushGradient}">
            Gradient text
        </TextBlock>
        <TextBlock Margin="{StaticResource thicknessMargin}"
                Foreground="{StaticResource brushGradient}">
            Of black, green, and gold
        </TextBlock>
        <TextBlock Margin="{StaticResource thicknessMargin}"
                Foreground="{StaticResource brushGradient}">
            Makes an app pretty,
        </TextBlock>
        <TextBlock Margin="{StaticResource thicknessMargin}"
```

```
                    Foreground="{StaticResource brushGradient}">
            Makes an app bold.
        </TextBlock>
    </StackPanel>
</Window>
```

It's no big secret that I don't like using the prefabricated Visual Studio projects in creating sample applications for my books. One problem is that I feel a need to rename everything so that my file names are more varied than MyApp and Window1. But now that you've seen what the *Application.Resource* tag means and how to use it, there's no problem if *you* want to use the Visual Studio projects and the XAML designer. (Just don't tell me about it.)

At the beginning of this chapter I described how you might define two different font sizes in a program as static read-only fields. Interestingly enough, XAML defines a markup extension named *x:Static* specifically to reference static properties or fields. It also works with enumeration members.

For example, suppose you want to set the *Content* property of a *Button* to a static property named *SomeStaticProp* from a class named *SomeClass*. The markup extension syntax is:

```
Content="{x:Static SomeClass:SomeStaticProp}"
```

Or, you can use an *x:Static* element within a property element syntax:

```
<Button.Content>
    <x:Static Member="SomeClass:SomeStaticProp" />
</Button.Content>
```

The type of the static field or property should match the type of the property you're setting, or there should exist a type converter to help the process. (Of course, the *Content* property is of type *object*, so anything goes.) For example, if you want to make a particular element the same height as the caption bar, you use:

```
Height="{x:Static SystemParameters.CaptionHeight}"
```

You aren't restricted to static properties or fields defined within the Windows Presentation Foundation, but if you access non-WPF classes, you'll need an XML namespace declaration for the CLR namespace in which those classes are found.

Here's a stand-alone XAML program that associates an XML prefix of *s* with the *System* namespace to display information from static properties in the *Environment* class.

EnvironmentInfo.xaml

```
<!-- =================================================
     EnvironmentInfo.xaml (c) 2006 by Charles Petzold
     ================================================= -->
<StackPanel xmlns="http://schemas.microsoft.com/winfx/2006/xaml/presentation"
            xmlns:x="http://schemas.microsoft.com/winfx/2006/xaml"
```

```
                 xmlns:s="clr-namespace:System;assembly=mscorlib">
    <TextBlock>
        <Label Content="Operating System Version: " />
        <Label Content="{x:Static s:Environment.OSVersion}" />
        <LineBreak />
        <Label Content=".NET Version: " />
        <Label Content="{x:Static s:Environment.Version}" />
        <LineBreak />
        <Label Content="Machine Name: " />
        <Label Content="{x:Static s:Environment.MachineName}" />
        <LineBreak />
        <Label Content="User Name: " />
        <Label Content="{x:Static s:Environment.UserName}" />
        <LineBreak />
        <Label Content="User Domain Name: " />
        <Label Content="{x:Static s:Environment.UserDomainName}" />
        <LineBreak />
        <Label Content="System Directory: " />
        <Label Content="{x:Static s:Environment.SystemDirectory}" />
        <LineBreak />
        <Label Content="Current Directory: " />
        <Label Content="{x:Static s:Environment.CurrentDirectory}" />
        <LineBreak />
        <Label Content="Command Line: " />
        <Label Content="{x:Static s:Environment.CommandLine}" />
    </TextBlock>
</StackPanel>
```

This program is only interested in displaying the text rendition of these properties. Most of these properties return strings, but two do not. *OSVersion*, which reveals the version of Microsoft Windows currently running, is of type *OperatingSystem*, and *Version* (which indicates the .NET version) is of type *Version*. The *ToString* methods of these classes fortunately format the information so that it's readable.

These two *x:Static* markup expressions couldn't simply be set to the *Text* properties of a *TextBlock* (for example). There is no automatic conversion of these non-*string* objects to *string*. Instead, I set the *x:Static* expressions to the *Content* properties of *Label* controls. The *Content* property, you'll recall, can be set to any object, and the object will be rendered with its *ToString* method. Making these *Label* elements the children of a *TextBlock* (in which case they actually become part of *InlineUIContainer* elements) allows interspersing *LineBreak* elements to separate the output into multiple lines.

Although you can run this file in XAML Cruncher or an equivalent program, it will not run in Internet Explorer. For all items except *OSVersion* and *Version*, the program requires security permissions not allowed when running XAML in Internet Explorer.

Another approach to using *x:Static* involves defining static fields or properties in your own C# source code and then accessing them from the project's XAML files. The next project I'll be showing you is named AccessStaticFields. The project contains an XAML file and a C# file that contribute to the same *Window* class as usual, but the project also contains a C# file named

Constants.cs with a class named *Constants* that contains three static read-only fields and properties. Here's that all-static class.

```
Constants.cs
//---------------------------------------
// Constants.cs (c) 2006 by Charles Petzold
//---------------------------------------
using System;
using System.Windows;
using System.Windows.Media;

namespace Petzold.AccessStaticFields
{
    public static class Constants
    {
        // Public static members.
        public static readonly FontFamily fntfam =
            new FontFamily("Times New Roman Italic");

        public static double FontSize
        {
            get { return 72 / 0.75; }
        }

        public static readonly LinearGradientBrush brush =
            new LinearGradientBrush(Colors.LightGray, Colors.DarkGray,
                                new Point(0, 0), new Point(1, 1));
    }
}
```

I've defined two of these items as static read-only fields and one as a static read-only property. That's just for variety; it doesn't really matter in this example. (Nor do they need to be read-only, but these fields can't be set from within an XAML file, so making them something other than read-only doesn't add any functionality.) Because these static fields and properties are defined as part of your own source code rather than the standard WPF assemblies, the XAML file needs an XML namespace declaration to define a prefix that is associated with the namespace of the class in which the fields or properties are located.

Here's the XAML file that associates the XML prefix *src* with the CLR namespace *Petzold.AccessStaticFields*. The file then uses the *x:Static* markup extension to access the static fields and properties. Two of these markup extensions use attribute syntax while the third uses property element syntax (again, just for variety).

```
AccessStaticFields.xaml
<!-- =================================================
        AccessStaticFields.xaml (c) 2006 by Charles Petzold
     ================================================= -->
<Window xmlns="http://schemas.microsoft.com/winfx/2006/xaml/presentation"
        xmlns:x="http://schemas.microsoft.com/winfx/2006/xaml"
```

```
        xmlns:src="clr-namespace:Petzold.AccessStaticFields"
        x:Class="Petzold.AccessStaticFields.AccessStaticFields"
        Title="Access Static Fields"
        SizeToContent="WidthAndHeight">
    <TextBlock  Background="{x:Static src:Constants.brush}"
                FontSize="{x:Static src:Constants.FontSize}"
                TextAlignment="Center">
        <TextBlock.FontFamily>
            <x:Static Member="src:Constants.fntfam" />
        </TextBlock.FontFamily>
            Properties from<LineBreak />Static Fields
        </TextBlock>
</Window>
```

The code-behind file is trivial.

AccessStaticFields.cs
```
//-------------------------------------------------
// AccessStaticFields.cs (c) 2006 by Charles Petzold
//-------------------------------------------------
using System;
using System.Windows;
using System.Windows.Controls;
using System.Windows.Input;
using System.Windows.Media;

namespace Petzold.AccessStaticFields
{
    public partial class AccessStaticFields : Window
    {
        [STAThread]
        public static void Main()
        {
            Application app = new Application();
            app.Run(new AccessStaticFields());
        }
        public AccessStaticFields()
        {
            InitializeComponent();
        }
    }
}
```

The static fields and properties don't have to be in their own file, of course. In an early version of this project I put them right into the C# part of the *AccessStaticFields* class, and the *x:Static* markup extensions referenced the *src:AccessStaticFields* class rather than the *src:Constants* class. But I rather liked the idea of devoting an entire static-only class to a bunch of constants used by the application.

You now know how to define objects as resources and reference those objects with the *StaticResource* markup extension. You also know how to reference static properties and fields of classes using *x:Static*. What's missing here is the ability to reference *instance* properties and fields of a particular object. That job requires specifying both an object and a property of that object, and the syntax goes beyond what *StaticResource* and *x:Static* can handle. It's a job for data binding, and you'll see how to do it in Chapter 23.

Here's another example of *x:Static*. This stand-alone XAML file sets both the *Content* and *Foreground* attributes of a *Label* control using *x:Static* expressions.

```
DisplayCurrentDateTime.xaml
<!-- ==========================================================
        DisplayCurrentDateTime.xaml (c) 2006 by Charles Petzold
     ========================================================== -->
<Label xmlns="http://schemas.microsoft.com/winfx/2006/xaml/presentation"
       xmlns:x="http://schemas.microsoft.com/winfx/2006/xaml"
       xmlns:s="clr-namespace:System;assembly=mscorlib"
       HorizontalAlignment="Center"
       VerticalAlignment="Center"
       FontSize="48"
       Content="{x:Static s:DateTime.Now}"
       Foreground="{x:Static SystemColors.ActiveCaptionBrush}" />
```

The *DateTime.Now* object is of type *DateTime* and the *Content* property displays the string returned from the structure's *ToString* method, so the result is nicely formatted. The last line in the XAML file sets the *Foreground* property to the *Brush* object from the static *SystemColors.ActiveCaptionBrush* property, so the text will be the same color as the window's caption bar.

I hope you're not expecting the time to be automatically updated with each passing second! If you're using XAML Cruncher (or an equivalent program) to run DisplayCurrentDateTime.xaml, the *DateTime.Now* property is accessed just once as the *Label* control is created. If you just type an innocuous space into the XAML file or press F6, XAML Cruncher will pass the "new" version to *XamlReader.Load* again and the time will be updated.

What do you suppose happens when system colors change? Do you think the program will automatically update the *Label* foreground color? Try it! Invoke the Display applet of Control Panel by right-clicking on the desktop and selecting Properties from the context menu. Click the Appearance tab and change the Color Scheme to something else. The default is Blue; the alternatives are Olive Green or Silver. Click Apply or OK. (With Microsoft Windows Vista, right-click the desktop and select Personalize from the context menu and then Desktop Colors from the list.)

As Windows applies the new system colors, you'll see the caption bars of all programs currently running under Windows change colors. The caption bar of XAML Cruncher changes color as well, but the color of the text displayed by the *Label* remains the same.

Are you disappointed? You probably shouldn't be surprised. It's the same situation as the date and time content. The static property *SystemColors.ActiveCaptionBrush* is accessed just once when the *Label* is being created and there's no automatic mechanism to update the control when that property changes. Of course, just as with the date and time, if you type an innocuous space into the DisplayCurrentDateTime.xaml file in XAML Cruncher or press F6, the file will be reparsed and the *Label* recreated with the new system color.

Would you like the *Label* foreground color to be automatically updated when system colors change? If so, it's certainly within your grasp.

The *SystemColors*, *SystemParameters*, and *SystemFonts* classes all have huge collections of static properties that an XAML file can access using the *x:Static* markup extension. If you've looked at these three classes, you may have noticed something quite odd: All the static properties exist in pairs. For every property named *Whatever*, there's also a property named *WhateverKey*. All properties ending with the word *Key* return objects of type *ResourceKey*.

The static *SystemColors.ActiveCaptionBrush* property returns an object of type *SolidColorBrush*, so it makes perfect sense that this object can be assigned to the *Foreground* property of *Label*, which requires an object of type *Brush*.

The *SystemColors.ActiveCaptionBrushKey* property returns an object of type *ResourceKey*. This *ResourceKey* object should also provide some way to access that same brush obtained from *SystemColors.ActionCaptionBrush*. The *ResourceKey* is a key into a dictionary, just like the keys that you can define in XAML resources using the *x:Key* attribute. The big difference with the *ResourceKey* object is that it includes a property of type *Assembly* so that the XAML parser knows the assembly in which the dictionary is stored.

It should be possible to access the brush using the *StaticResource* markup extension with the key returned by *SystemColors.ActiveCaptionBrushKey*. Perhaps something like this will work:

```
Foreground="{StaticResource SystemColors.ActiveCaptionBrushKey}"
```

Well, no. That doesn't work. If you try substituting this line for the *Foreground* attribute in DisplayCurrentDateTime.xaml, you'll get an error message that it can't find the resource. And this makes sense if you think about it. The parser is looking for a resource with a text key of "SystemColors.ActiveCaptionBrushKey." What we really want is the resource that's referenced by the key returned from the static property *SystemColors.ActiveCaptionBrushKey*.

It's not as elusive as it seems. Consider that this markup extension returns an object of type *SolidColorBrush*:

```
{x:Static SystemColors.ActiveCaptionBrush}
```

So this markup extension must return an object of type *ResourceKey*:

```
{x:Static SystemColors.ActiveCaptionBrushKey}
```

An object of type *ResourceKey* is exactly what *StaticResource* wants. So with a great leap of insight and daring, you try nesting an *x:Static* expression inside a *StaticResource* expression:

```
Foreground="{StaticResource {x:Static SystemColors.ActiveCaptionBrushKey}}"
```

And that works! Notice that one set of curly braces is nested within the other set so that the entire expression terminates with two right curly braces. This new *Foreground* setting is functionally equivalent to the original setting:

```
Foreground="{x:Static SystemColors.ActiveCaptionBrush}"
```

The resource referenced by *SystemColors.ActiveCaptionBrushKey* is a *SolidColorBrush* that is the same as the brush returned directly from *SystemColors.ActiveCaptionBrush*.

However, the alternative syntax seems to offer no benefits. If you run the new XAML file and change system colors, the foreground color of the *Label* does not automatically change.

Now let's make one little change to the alternative syntax. Let's change *StaticResource* to *DynamicResource*, which is the third and final markup extension I'll introduce in this chapter:

```
Foreground="{DynamicResource {x:Static SystemColors.ActiveCaptionBrushKey}}"
```

And it works! Now if you change the system colors, you'll see the *Label* text color change along with the caption bars.

Just for the sake of completeness, you might be interested in the property element syntax of *DynamicResource*. In DisplayCurrentDateTime.xaml, an end tag for *Label* needs to be added so that the *Foreground* property can appear as a property element:

```
<Label ... >
    <Label.Foreground>
        <DynamicResource>
            <DynamicResource.ResourceKey>
                <x:Static Member="SystemColors.ActiveCaptionBrushKey" />
            </DynamicResource.ResourceKey>
        </DynamicResource>
    </Label.Foreground>
</Label>
```

StaticResource and *DynamicResource* represent two different approaches to accessing resources. Both require keys and use those keys to access objects. With *StaticResource*, the key is used to access the object once, and the object is retained. When you use *DynamicResource*, the key is retained and the object is accessed when it's needed.

When a user changes system colors, Windows broadcasts a system-wide message that the colors have been changed. Applications customarily respond to this message by invalidating their windows. In WPF, this invalidation translates into an *InvalidateVisual* call, which means that every element gets a call to *OnRender*. At that time, if an element's *Foreground* property (for example) references a dynamic resource, the retained key is used to access the brush. It's not as if the whole element is being recreated, however. It's nowhere close. When you change system colors and the *Label* text color changes, the *Label* content remains the same: The date and time that the control displays is *not* updated.

The primary purpose of *DynamicResource* is to access system resources such as system colors. Don't try to overburden *DynamicResource* with too many expectations. There's no concept of notification when a resource has changed. If you need your controls and elements to update themselves based on property changes of other objects (and you probably will), you want to use data binding, which I cover in Chapter 23.

Normally you cannot make a forward reference to a resource. In other words, a resource referenced by a *StaticResource* markup extension must already have been defined in the file or in an ancestor element. But there might come a time when it's convenient to reference the resource before it's defined. For example, a panel start tag might contain a *Background* attribute referencing a resource that's defined in a *Resources* section that follows:

```
<StackPanel Background="{StaticResource mybrush}">
    <StackPanel.Resources>
        <SolidColorBrush x:Key="mybrush" ... />
    </StackPanel.Resources>
    ...
```

This won't work. You could remove the *Background* attribute from the start tag and use property element syntax instead:

```
<StackPanel>
    <StackPanel.Resources>
        <SolidColorBrush x:Key="mybrush" ... />
    </StackPanel.Resources>
    <StackPanel.Background>
        <StaticResource ResourceKey="mybrush" />
    </StackPanel.Background>
    ...
```

Or, you could change *StaticResource* to *DynamicResource*, in which case the access of the resource is deferred until the resource is actually needed to render the panel.

The brushes you create as resources can themselves be based on system colors. The following stand-alone XAML defines two brushes as resources. A *LinearGradientBrush* defines a gradient between the active caption color and the inactive caption color. The second brush is a *SolidColorBrush* that similarly uses *DynamicResource* with *SystemColors.ActiveCaptionColorKey*.

DynamicResourceDemo.xaml
```
<!-- ====================================================
        DynamicResourceDemo.xaml (c) 2006 by Charles Petzold
     ==================================================== -->
<StackPanel xmlns="http://schemas.microsoft.com/winfx/2006/xaml/presentation"
            xmlns:x="http://schemas.microsoft.com/winfx/2006/xaml"
            Background="{DynamicResource
```

```
                            {x:Static SystemColors.InactiveCaptionBrushKey}}">

    <StackPanel.Resources>
        <LinearGradientBrush x:Key="dynabrush1"
                             StartPoint="0 0" EndPoint="1 1">
            <LinearGradientBrush.GradientStops>

                <GradientStop Offset="0"
                    Color="{DynamicResource
                        {x:Static SystemColors.ActiveCaptionColorKey}}" />

                <GradientStop Offset="1"
                    Color="{DynamicResource
                        {x:Static SystemColors.InactiveCaptionColorKey}}" />

            </LinearGradientBrush.GradientStops>
        </LinearGradientBrush>

        <SolidColorBrush x:Key="dynabrush2"
                Color="{DynamicResource
                    {x:Static SystemColors.ActiveCaptionColorKey}}" />

    </StackPanel.Resources>

    <Label HorizontalAlignment="Center"
           FontSize="96"
           Content="Dynamic Resources"
           Background="{StaticResource dynabrush1}"
           Foreground="{StaticResource dynabrush2}" />

</StackPanel>
```

Notice that the two resources use *DynamicResource* to reference *SystemColors.ActiveCaptionColor-Key* and *SystemColors.InactiveCaptionColorKey*. These are keys (because they are used with *DynamicResource*), but the keys reference colors rather than brushes because they are used to set the *Color* property of the two *GradientStop* objects.

The program colors itself in three ways. Toward the top, you'll see that the background of the *StackPanel* is a *DynamicResource* based on *SystemColors.InactiveCaptionBrushKey*. The *Label* at the bottom uses the two locally defined resources to color its background and foreground. In this case, however, these two resource brushes are referenced as *static* resources.

When the system colors change, the two brushes defined as local resources also change by getting new *Color* properties. The *LinearGradientBrush* and *SolidColorBrush* objects are not replaced, however. They are the same objects. The *Label* element references these two objects, so when these objects change, the background and foreground properties of the *Label* reflects the change in system colors.

If you change the *Background* and *Foreground* attributes of *Label* to *DynamicResource*, the program stops responding to changes in system colors! The problem is that *DynamicResource* is expecting the object referenced by the key to be recreated. The brush objects are not being recreated, so *DynamicResource* doesn't bother with updating the *Foreground* and *Background* properties. (At least, that's the best explanation I can come up with.)

It's possible to use the keys associated with system colors and other system settings in your own resource definitions. In that case, the local resource definitions override the system settings unless a local resource cannot be found. This stand-alone XAML file is a variation of the ResourceLookupDemo.xaml program from earlier in this chapter.

```
AnotherResourceLookupDemo.xaml
<!-- ============================================================
        AnotherResourceLookupDemo.xaml (c) 2006 by Charles Petzold
     ============================================================ -->
<StackPanel xmlns="http://schemas.microsoft.com/winfx/2006/xaml/presentation"
            xmlns:x="http://schemas.microsoft.com/winfx/2006/xaml"
            Orientation="Horizontal">

    <StackPanel>
        <StackPanel.Resources>
            <SolidColorBrush
                x:Key="{x:Static SystemColors.ActiveCaptionBrushKey}"
                Color="Red" />
        </StackPanel.Resources>

        <Button HorizontalAlignment="Center"
                VerticalAlignment="Center"
                Margin="24"
                Foreground="{DynamicResource
                        {x:Static SystemColors.ActiveCaptionBrushKey}}">
            Button with Red text
        </Button>
    </StackPanel>

    <StackPanel>
        <Button HorizontalAlignment="Center"
                VerticalAlignment="Center"
                Margin="24"
                Foreground="{DynamicResource
                        {x:Static SystemColors.ActiveCaptionBrushKey}}">
            Button with Blue text
        </Button>
    </StackPanel>

</StackPanel>
```

Only the first embedded *StackPanel* includes a *Resources* section, which defines a red brush using the key obtained from *SystemColors.ActiveCaptionBrushKey*. The *Button* within that *StackPanel* gets that red brush, but the other *Button* gets the active caption brush and changes when the system colors change.

As you use resources more, there may come a time when you'd like to share resources among multiple applications. This is particularly true if you've developed a collection of custom styles that give your company's applications their unique look and feel.

Resources that you want to share among multiple projects can be collected in XAML files with a root element of *ResourceDictionary*. Each resource is a child of that root element. Here's a possible resource dictionary that has only one resource, although it could contain many.

MyResources1.xaml

```
<!-- ================================================
        MyResources1.xaml (c) 2006 by Charles Petzold
     ================================================ -->
<ResourceDictionary
        xmlns="http://schemas.microsoft.com/winfx/2006/xaml/presentation"
        xmlns:x="http://schemas.microsoft.com/winfx/2006/xaml">
    <LinearGradientBrush x:Key="brushLinear">
        <LinearGradientBrush.GradientStops>
            <GradientStop Color="Pink" Offset="0" />
            <GradientStop Color="Aqua" Offset="1" />
        </LinearGradientBrush.GradientStops>
    </LinearGradientBrush>
</ResourceDictionary>
```

Here's another resource dictionary that could also contain many resources but in this example has only one.

MyResources2.xaml.

```
<!-- ================================================
        MyResources2.xaml (c) 2006 by Charles Petzold
     ================================================ -->
<ResourceDictionary
        xmlns="http://schemas.microsoft.com/winfx/2006/xaml/presentation"
        xmlns:x="http://schemas.microsoft.com/winfx/2006/xaml">
    <RadialGradientBrush x:Key="brushRadial">
        <RadialGradientBrush.GradientStops>
            <GradientStop Color="Pink" Offset="0" />
            <GradientStop Color="Aqua" Offset="1" />
        </RadialGradientBrush.GradientStops>
    </RadialGradientBrush>
</ResourceDictionary>
```

You're now putting together a project named UseCommonResources, and you want to use the resources defined in MyResources1.xaml and MyResources2.xaml. You make those two files part of the project. They can have a Build Action of either Page or Resource. (Page is better because some preliminary processing occurs during compilation that turns the file from XAML into BAML.) In the application definition file for the project, you can have a *Resources* section with the syntax shown in the following file.

UseCommonResourcesApp.xaml

```
<!-- ========================================================
        UseCommonResourcesApp.xaml (c) 2006 by Charles Petzold
     ======================================================== -->
<Application xmlns="http://schemas.microsoft.com/winfx/2006/xaml/presentation"
             StartupUri="UseCommonResourcesWindow.xaml">
    <Application.Resources>
        <ResourceDictionary>
            <ResourceDictionary.MergedDictionaries>
                <ResourceDictionary Source="MyResources1.xaml" />
                <ResourceDictionary Source="MyResources2.xaml" />
            </ResourceDictionary.MergedDictionaries>
        </ResourceDictionary>
    </Application.Resources>
</Application>
```

Within the *Resources* section of the file is a *ResourceDictionary* element. *ResourceDictionary* defines a property named *MergedDictionaries*, which is a collection of other *ResourceDictionary* objects, and those objects are referenced by their file names. If you have only one resource dictionary, you can reference it in a single *ResourceDictionary* object without using the *ResourceDictionary.MergedDictionaries* property element.

The multiple resource dictionaries are truly merged. If you happen to use the same key in more than one file, the earlier resource with that key will be replaced by the later resource as the resource dictionaries are merged.

You can put the *ResourceDictionary* in the *Resources* section of a XAML file other than the application definition file, but the resources would be available only in that file and not throughout the application.

Finally, here's the *Window* element that makes use of the resources defined in the MyResources1.xaml and MyResources2.xaml files.

UseCommonResourcesWindow.xaml

```
<!-- ========================================================
        UseCommonResourcesWindow.xaml (c) 2006 by Charles Petzold
     ======================================================== -->
<Window xmlns="http://schemas.microsoft.com/winfx/2006/xaml/presentation"
        Title="Use Common Resources"
        Background="{StaticResource brushLinear}">
    <Button FontSize="96pt"
            HorizontalAlignment="Center"
            VerticalAlignment="Center"
            Background="{StaticResource brushRadial}">
        Button
    </Button>
</Window>
```

Approaching a new language like XAML can be accompanied by some anxiety. Has the language really been adequately defined so that we don't run into brick walls somewhere down the road? It's important for code to contain as little repetition as possible, and resources help achieve this goal. Not only can objects be defined once and reused throughout an application, but resources can also be stored in their own *ResourceDictionary* files to be reused in multiple applications.

Chapter 22
Windows, Pages, and Navigation

In the chapters ahead, I explore the many features and capabilities of XAML, mostly using just small, stand-alone XAML files. These XAML files demonstrate important techniques, of course, but in focusing exclusively on small files, it's easy to lose sight of the big picture. For that reason, I'd like to present in this chapter a complete program—with a menu and dialog boxes—that combines XAML and C# code.

Another reason to present this conventional WPF program is to immediately contrast it with WPF *navigation applications*. You can structure a WPF application (or part of an application) so that it functions more like the interconnected pages of a Web site. Rather than having a single, fixed application window that is acted on by user input and commands from menus and dialog boxes, navigation applications frequently change the contents of their window (or parts of the window) through hyperlinks. These types of applications are still client applications, but they act very much like Web applications.

This chapter also discusses the three file formats you can use for distributing a WPF application. The first, of course, is the traditional .exe format, and you've already seen numerous WPF applications that result in .exe files. At the other extreme is the stand-alone XAML file that can be developed in XAML Cruncher (or a similar program) and hosted in Microsoft Internet Explorer.

Between these two extremes is the XAML Browser Application, which has a file name extension of .xbap. As the name implies, these XAML Browser Applications are hosted in Internet Explorer just like stand-alone XAML files. Yet they generally consist of both XAML and C# code, and they are compiled. Because they're intended to run in the context of Internet Explorer, security restrictions limit what these applications can do. In short, they can't do anything that could harm the user's computer. Consequently, they can be run on a user's computer without asking for specific permission or causing undue anxiety.

Let's begin with a traditionally structured application that is distributable as an .exe file. The program I'll be discussing is built around an *InkCanvas* element, which collects and displays stylus input on the Tablet PC. The *InkCanvas* also responds to mouse input on both Tablet PCs and non-tablet computers, as you can readily determine by running this tiny, stand-alone XAML file.

JustAnInkCanvas.xaml

```
<!-- ================================================
        JustAnInkCanvas.xaml (c) 2006 by Charles Petzold
     ================================================ -->
<InkCanvas xmlns="http://schemas.microsoft.com/winfx/2006/xaml/presentation" />
```

My original intention was to display a window that resembled a small yellow legal pad so that the user could draw on multiple pages of the pad. When it became evident that I'd probably need a special file format for saving multiple pages, I decided to restrict the program to just *one* page. I'd originally chosen the name of YellowPad for the project, and even though the program saves only a single page, I liked the name and decided to keep it.

The YellowPadWindow.xaml file lays out the main application window. Most of this XAML file is devoted to defining the program's menu. Each menu item requires an element of type *MenuItem*, arranged in a hierarchy and all enclosed in a *Menu* element, which is docked at the top of a *DockPanel*. Notice that some of the menu items have their *Command* properties set to various static properties of the *ApplicationCommands* class, such as *New*, *Open*, and *Save*. Others have their *Click* events set.

YellowPadWindow.xaml

```
<!-- ================================================
        YellowPadWindow.xaml (c) 2006 by Charles Petzold
     ================================================ -->
<Window xmlns="http://schemas.microsoft.com/winfx/2006/xaml/presentation"
        xmlns:x="http://schemas.microsoft.com/winfx/2006/xaml"
        xmlns:src="clr-namespace:Petzold.YellowPad"
        x:Class="Petzold.YellowPad.YellowPadWindow"
        Title="Yellow Pad"
        SizeToContent="WidthAndHeight">

    <DockPanel>
        <Menu DockPanel.Dock="Top">

            <!-- File menu. -->
            <MenuItem Header="_File">
                <MenuItem Header="_New" Command="New" />
                <MenuItem Header="_Open..." Command="Open" />
                <MenuItem Header="_Save..." Command="Save" />
                <Separator />
                <MenuItem Header="E_xit" Command="Close" />
            </MenuItem>

            <!-- Edit menu. -->
            <MenuItem Header="_Edit" SubmenuOpened="EditOnOpened">
                <MenuItem Header="Cu_t" Command="Cut" />
                <MenuItem Header="_Copy" Command="Copy" />
                <MenuItem Header="_Paste" Command="Paste" />
                <MenuItem Header="_Delete" Command="Delete" />
                <Separator />
                <MenuItem Header="Select _All" Command="SelectAll" />
```

```
                    <MenuItem Header="_Format Selection..." Name="itemFormat"
                            Click="FormatOnClick"/>
            </MenuItem>

            <!-- Stylus-Mode menu. -->
            <MenuItem Header="_Stylus-Mode" SubmenuOpened="StylusModeOnOpened">
                <MenuItem Header="_Ink" Click="StylusModeOnClick"
                        Tag="{x:Static InkCanvasEditingMode.Ink}" />
                <MenuItem Header="Erase by _Point" Click="StylusModeOnClick"
                        Tag="{x:Static InkCanvasEditingMode.EraseByPoint}" />
                <MenuItem Header="_Erase by Stroke" Click="StylusModeOnClick"
                        Tag="{x:Static InkCanvasEditingMode.EraseByStroke}" />
                <MenuItem Header="_Select" Click="StylusModeOnClick"
                        Tag="{x:Static InkCanvasEditingMode.Select}" />
            </MenuItem>

            <!-- Eraser-Mode menu (hidden on non-tablet computers). -->
            <MenuItem Header="E_raser-Mode" SubmenuOpened="EraserModeOnOpened"
                    Name="menuEraserMode">
                <MenuItem Header="_Ink" Click="EraserModeOnClick"
                        Tag="{x:Static InkCanvasEditingMode.Ink}" />
                <MenuItem Header="Erase by _Point" Click="EraserModeOnClick"
                        Tag="{x:Static InkCanvasEditingMode.EraseByPoint}" />
                <MenuItem Header="_Erase by Stroke" Click="EraserModeOnClick"
                        Tag="{x:Static InkCanvasEditingMode.EraseByStroke}" />
                <MenuItem Header="_Select" Click="EraserModeOnClick"
                        Tag="{x:Static InkCanvasEditingMode.Select}" />
            </MenuItem>

            <!-- Tools menu. -->
            <MenuItem Header="_Tools">
                <MenuItem Header="_Stylus..." Click="StylusToolOnClick" />
                <MenuItem Header="_Eraser..." Click="EraserToolOnClick"/>
            </MenuItem>

            <!-- Help menu. -->
            <MenuItem Header="_Help">
                <MenuItem Header="_Help..." Command="Help" />
                <MenuItem Header="_About YellowPad..." Click="AboutOnClick"/>
            </MenuItem>
        </Menu>

        <!-- ScrollViewer encloses InkCanvas element. -->
        <ScrollViewer VerticalScrollBarVisibility="Auto" >
            <InkCanvas Name="inkcanv"
                        Width="{x:Static src:YellowPadWindow.widthCanvas}"
                        Height="{x:Static src:YellowPadWindow.heightCanvas}"
                        Background="LemonChiffon">
                <Line Stroke="Red" X1="0.875in" Y1="0" X2="0.875in"
                        Y2="{x:Static src:YellowPadWindow.heightCanvas}" />
                <Line Stroke="Red" X1="0.9375in" Y1="0" X2="0.9375in"
                        Y2="{x:Static src:YellowPadWindow.heightCanvas}" />
            </InkCanvas>
        </ScrollViewer>
    </DockPanel>
```

```
<!-- Accumulate all the CommandBinding objects. -->
<Window.CommandBindings>
    <CommandBinding Command="New" Executed="NewOnExecuted" />
    <CommandBinding Command="Open" Executed="OpenOnExecuted" />
    <CommandBinding Command="Save" Executed="SaveOnExecuted" />
    <CommandBinding Command="Close" Executed="CloseOnExecuted" />
    <CommandBinding Command="Cut" CanExecute="CutCanExecute"
                    Executed="CutOnExecuted" />
    <CommandBinding Command="Copy" CanExecute="CutCanExecute"
                    Executed="CopyOnExecuted" />
    <CommandBinding Command="Paste" CanExecute="PasteCanExecute"
                    Executed="PasteOnExecuted" />
    <CommandBinding Command="Delete" CanExecute="CutCanExecute"
                    Executed="DeleteOnExecuted" />
    <CommandBinding Command="SelectAll" Executed="SelectAllOnExecuted" />
    <CommandBinding Command="Help" Executed="HelpOnExecuted" />
</Window.CommandBindings>
</Window>
```

Following the definition of the menu, the XAML file sets the interior of the *DockPanel* to a *ScrollViewer* enclosing an *InkCanvas*. The *InkCanvas* is given a background of *LemonChiffon* and two red vertical lines. (The blue horizontal lines come later.) Notice that the file obtains the dimensions of the *InkCanvas* from static members of the *YellowPadWindow* class. (These are defined in the C# file coming up next.) The XAML file concludes with all the *CommandBinding* elements needed to bind the *Command* properties of many menu items with *CanExecute* and *OnExecuted* handlers.

I've divided the C# portion of the *YellowPadWindow* class into six small files. One is named YellowPadWindow.cs and the others are named after the top-level menu item each one supports, such as YellowPadWindow.File.cs.

The YellowPadWindow.cs file begins by defining the desired dimensions of the *InkCanvas* as public, static, read-only fields referred to in YellowPadWindow.xaml.

YellowPadWindow.cs

```
//----------------------------------------
// YellowPadWindow.cs (c) 2006 by Charles Petzold
//----------------------------------------
using System;
using System.Windows;
using System.Windows.Controls;
using System.Windows.Ink;
using System.Windows.Input;
using System.Windows.Media;
using System.Windows.Shapes;

namespace Petzold.YellowPad
{
    public partial class YellowPadWindow : Window
    {
        // Make the pad 5 inches by 7 inches.
```

```
public static readonly double widthCanvas = 5 * 96;
public static readonly double heightCanvas = 7 * 96;

[STAThread]
public static void Main()
{
    Application app = new Application();
    app.Run(new YellowPadWindow());
}
public YellowPadWindow()
{
    InitializeComponent();

    // Draw blue horizontal lines 1/4 inch apart.
    double y = 96;

    while (y < heightCanvas)
    {
        Line line = new Line();
        line.X1 = 0;
        line.Y1 = y;
        line.X2 = widthCanvas;
        line.Y2 = y;
        line.Stroke = Brushes.LightBlue;
        inkcanv.Children.Add(line);

        y += 24;
    }

    // Disable the Eraser-Mode menu item if there's no tablet present.
    if (Tablet.TabletDevices.Count == 0)
        menuEraserMode.Visibility = Visibility.Collapsed;
}
```

The *YellowPadWindow* constructor calls *InitializeComponent* (of course) but is also responsible for drawing the blue horizontal lines across the pad at one-quarter inch increments. I considered putting these *Line* elements in the XAML file, but I didn't like the idea of so much repetitive markup. I also realized that they'd need to be changed if the vertical dimension of the pad were ever changed.

The constructor concludes by disabling one of the top-level menu items if the program isn't running on a Tablet PC. Removing this menu item doesn't make the program any less functional on non-tablet computers.

As the user draws on the surface of the *InkCanvas* with the stylus or mouse, the *InkCanvas* stores the input in a property named *Strokes* of type *StrokeCollection*, a collection of *Stroke* objects. (Although *InkCanvas* is defined in the *System.Windows.Controls* namespace, *Stroke* and *StrokeCollection* are defined in *System.Windows.Ink.*) In the parlance of the Tablet PC, a *stroke* occurs when the user touches the stylus to the screen, moves it, and lifts it. When using a mouse, a stroke occurs when the user presses the left mouse button, moves the mouse, and releases the left mouse button. In either case, the *InkCanvas* tracks the movement of the stylus or mouse and renders a line on the screen.

In computer graphics terminology, a stroke is basically a *polyline*, a collection of short, connected lines defined by a series of points. Consequently, the *Stroke* object has a property named *StylusPoints* of type *StylusPointCollection*, which is a collection of *StylusPoint* objects. (*StylusPoint* and *StylusPointCollection* are defined in the *System.Windows.Input* namespace.) The *StylusPoint* structure contains *X* and *Y* properties indicating the coordinates of the point, as well as a *PressureFactor* property recording the pressure of the stylus on the screen. By default, *InkCanvas* draws wider lines when the pressure is higher. (This varying line width is absent when you use the mouse, of course.)

Tablet PCs of the future might record additional information about the stylus besides just position and pressure; this information is handled through the *Description* property of *StylusPoint*. See the static read-only fields of *StylusPointProperties* to get an idea of what other information might someday be recorded.

Besides the *StylusPoints* property, the *Stroke* class also defines a *DrawingAttributes* property. Each stroke can potentially have its own color, and this color is part of the *DrawingAttributes* object. *DrawingAttributes* also includes *Width* and *Height* properties that indicate the height and width of the line rendered by the stylus or mouse. These two values can be different, which can result in fancy, calligraphy-like effects. The shape of the stylus tip can be rectangular or elliptical, and it can even be rotated. The *InkCanvas* maintains a property named *DefaultDrawingAttributes*, which is the *DrawingAttributes* object applied to the current stroke and all future strokes until the property is changed.

StrokeCollection defines a *Save* method that saves the collection of strokes in the Ink Serialized Format (ISF), and a constructor that loads an ISF file. The Ink Serialized Format is also supported under version 1.7 of the Tablet PC Software Development Kit, so it's compatible with Tablet PC applications written for Windows Forms or the Win32 API.

The YellowPadWindow.File.cs portion of the YellowPadWindow class is responsible for all four items on the File menu. To keep the program reasonably short, I decided not to save the file name of the loaded file or to ask the user if it's all right to abandon a file that hasn't been saved. The Open and Save commands mostly implement file input and output using the Ink Serialized Format.

YellowPadWindow.File.cs

```
//-------------------------------------------------------
// YellowPadWindow.File.cs (c) 2006 by Charles Petzold
//-------------------------------------------------------
using Microsoft.Win32;
using System;
using System.IO;
using System.Windows;
```

```
using System.Windows.Ink;
using System.Windows.Input;
using System.Windows.Markup;
using System.Windows.Media;

namespace Petzold.YellowPad
{
    public partial class YellowPadWindow : Window
    {
        // File New command: just clear all the strokes.
        void NewOnExecuted(object sender, ExecutedRoutedEventArgs args)
        {
            inkcanv.Strokes.Clear();
        }
        // File Open command: display OpenFileDialog and load ISF file.
        void OpenOnExecuted(object sender, ExecutedRoutedEventArgs args)
        {
            OpenFileDialog dlg = new OpenFileDialog();
            dlg.CheckFileExists = true;
            dlg.Filter = "Ink Serialized Format (*.isf)|*.isf|" +
                    "All files (*.*)|*.*";

            if ((bool)dlg.ShowDialog(this))
            {
                try
                {
                    FileStream file = new FileStream(dlg.FileName,
                                        FileMode.Open, FileAccess.Read);
                    inkcanv.Strokes = new StrokeCollection(file);
                    file.Close();
                }
                catch (Exception exc)
                {
                    MessageBox.Show(exc.Message, Title);
                }
            }
        }
        // File Save command: display SaveFileDialog.
        void SaveOnExecuted(object sender, ExecutedRoutedEventArgs args)
        {
            SaveFileDialog dlg = new SaveFileDialog();
            dlg.Filter = "Ink Serialized Format (*.isf)|*.isf|" +
                    "XAML Drawing File (*.xaml)|*.xaml|" +
                    "All files (*.*)|*.*";

            if ((bool)dlg.ShowDialog(this))
            {
                try
                {
                    FileStream file = new FileStream(dlg.FileName,
                                        FileMode.Create, FileAccess.Write);

                    if (dlg.FilterIndex == 1 || dlg.FilterIndex == 3)
                        inkcanv.Strokes.Save(file);
```

```
        else
        {
            // Save strokes as DrawingGroup object.
            DrawingGroup drawgrp = new DrawingGroup();

            foreach (Stroke strk in inkcanv.Strokes)
            {
                Color clr = strk.DrawingAttributes.Color;

                if (strk.DrawingAttributes.IsHighlighter)
                    clr = Color.FromArgb(128, clr.R, clr.G, clr.B);

                drawgrp.Children.Add(
                    new GeometryDrawing(
                        new SolidColorBrush(clr),
                        null, strk.GetGeometry()));
            }
            XamlWriter.Save(drawgrp, file);
        }
        file.Close();
    }
    catch (Exception exc)
    {
        MessageBox.Show(exc.Message, Title);
    }
}
// File Exit item: just close window.
void CloseOnExecuted(object sender, ExecutedRoutedEventArgs args)
{
    Close();
}
```

As you'll note, the *SaveFileDialog* also includes an option to save the strokes as a "XAML Drawing File." This feature requires a bit more explanation.

One of the aspects of the Tablet PC that has always interested me is the potential for using stylus input in graphics programming. The *Stroke* class helps here because it defines a method named *GetGeometry* that returns an object of type *Geometry*. You'll learn about the *Geometry* object in Chapter 28; for now you should know that the most generalized kind of *Geometry* is quite similar to a traditional *graphics path*—a collection of connected and disconnected straight lines and curves. It pleased me a great deal to discover that the *Geometry* object returned from the *GetGeometry* method of *Stroke* is *not* simply the polyline that defines the stroke. It's actually the *outline* of the rendered stroke, taking into account the shape and dimensions of the stylus tip and the pressure of the stylus against the screen.

A *Geometry* is pure analytic geometry—points and lines and curves. A *Geometry* combined with an outline brush and a fill brush is an object of type *GeometryDrawing*, so the extra code in the *SaveOnExecuted* method uses the *DrawingAttributes* object for each *Stroke* to fill the geometry with that color. Each *GeometryDrawing* object corresponds to a *Stroke* object, and these are assembled in a *DrawingGroup* object, which is what the program saves to a file using the *XamlWriter.Save* method. (Both *GeometryDrawing* and *DrawingGroup* derive from the abstract *Drawing* class. I'll discuss these concepts in much more detail in Chapter 31.)

Now that you have a *DrawingGroup* object in a file, what can you do with it? From any object of type *Drawing* (named, perhaps, *drawing*) you can make a *DrawingImage* object:

```
DrawingImage drawimg = new DrawingImage(drawing);
```

Now it gets interesting, because *DrawingImage* derives from *ImageSource*, and *ImageSource* is the type of the *Source* property defined by *Image*, a class you first encountered in the ShowMyFace program in Chapter 3 of this book. While *Image* is normally employed to display bitmapped images, it can display vector images as well if these images are stored in objects of type *DrawingImage*.

So, whatever you draw in the YellowPad program, you can save in a format that is easily displayed as a WPF graphics object. I used this feature to save a copyright notice with my signature that appears in YellowPad's About box.

The next item on the top-level menu is Edit, but I want to skip that one for now and come back to it later. Two items appear after the Edit item—Stylus-Mode and Eraser-Mode. The stylus mode describes what happens when you draw on the screen with the stylus tip or the mouse, and it corresponds to the *EditingMode* property of *InkCanvas*. What I call the "eraser mode" is what happens when you turn the stylus upside down and use the eraser end on the screen. This option corresponds to the *EditingModeInverted* property of *InkCanvas*. Because this option makes no sense on a non-tablet computer, the Eraser-Mode item is present only when you run the program on a Tablet PC.

Both *EditingMode* and *EditingModeInverted* are set to members of the *InkCanvasEditingMode* enumeration. By default, *EditingMode* is set to *InkCanvasEditingMode.Ink* and *EditingModeInverted* is set to *InkCanvasEditingMode.EraseByStroke*, which means that an entire stroke is deleted when you erase part of it. For the sake of completeness—and to allow a mouse user to erase strokes—I put the same options on the Stylus-Mode and Eraser-Mode menus. Besides *Ink* and *EraseByStroke*, these menus let the user choose *EraseByPoint* (which cuts a stroke into two strokes rather than deleting an entire stroke) and *Selection*. The *Selection* option lets you select one or more strokes using a lasso-like object. I ignored the *InkCanvasEditingMode* members *GestureOnly*, *InkAndGesture*, and *None*.

The YellowPadWindow.Mode.cs file handles both the Stylus-Mode and Eraser-Mode menu items in very similar ways. When the submenu is opened, the code applies a checkmark to the item corresponding to the current property of the *InkCanvas* object. The *Click* handlers apply the selected item to the *InkCanvas*.

YellowPadWindow.Mode.cs

```
//-------------------------------------------------------
// YellowPadWindow.Mode.cs (c) 2006 by Charles Petzold
//-------------------------------------------------------
using System;
using System.Windows;
using System.Windows.Controls;

namespace Petzold.YellowPad
{
    public partial class YellowPadWindow : Window
    {
        // Stylus-Mode submenu opened: check one of the items.
        void StylusModeOnOpened(object sender, RoutedEventArgs args)
        {
            MenuItem item = sender as MenuItem;

            foreach (MenuItem child in item.Items)
                child.IsChecked = inkcanv.EditingMode ==
                                    (InkCanvasEditingMode)child.Tag;
        }
        // Set the EditingMode property from the selected item.
        void StylusModeOnClick(object sender, RoutedEventArgs args)
        {
            MenuItem item = sender as MenuItem;
            inkcanv.EditingMode = (InkCanvasEditingMode)item.Tag;
        }
        // Eraser-Mode submenu opened: check one of the items.
        void EraserModeOnOpened(object sender, RoutedEventArgs args)
        {
            MenuItem item = sender as MenuItem;

            foreach (MenuItem child in item.Items)
                child.IsChecked = inkcanv.EditingModeInverted ==
                                    (InkCanvasEditingMode)child.Tag;
        }
        // Set the EditingModeInverted property from the selected item.
        void EraserModeOnClick(object sender, RoutedEventArgs args)
        {
            MenuItem item = sender as MenuItem;
            inkcanv.EditingModeInverted = (InkCanvasEditingMode)item.Tag;
        }
    }
}
```

Checking the item based on the actual property of the *InkCanvas* is the safest approach here because the *EditingMode* can change without invoking this menu. For example, if the *Select* method of the *InkCanvas* is called, the *EditingMode* becomes *Select*.

I mentioned earlier that *InkCanvas* includes a property named *DefaultDrawingAttributes* of type *DrawingAttributes* that contains the color, stylus dimensions, and shape that apply to all future strokes. The *DrawingAttributes* class also includes two Boolean properties named

IgnorePressure and *IsHighlighter*. The first causes the *InkCanvas* to ignore stylus pressure when rendering strokes. The *IsHighlighter* property causes the selected color to be rendered with an alpha channel of 128, causing the color to be half transparent.

The eraser is less versatile. You can only change its shape and dimensions. The *EraserShape* property of *InkCanvas* is of type *StylusShape*, an abstract class that has *Height*, *Width*, and *Rotation* properties. From *StylusShape* descend the *EllipseStylusShape* and *RectangleStylusShape* classes.

Despite the differences in the way that the stylus and eraser are handled, I decided to implement interfaces to them both with the same basic dialog box. The program refers to the stylus and eraser collectively as "tools." The dialog box defined in the following XAML file has a title of "Stylus Tool" and it contains controls that correspond to most of the properties of *DrawingAttributes*.

StylusToolDialog.xaml

```
<!-- =====================================================
        StylusToolDialog.xaml (c) 2006 by Charles Petzold
     ===================================================== -->
<Window xmlns="http://schemas.microsoft.com/winfx/2006/xaml/presentation"
        xmlns:x="http://schemas.microsoft.com/winfx/2006/xaml"
        xmlns:color="clr-namespace:Petzold.ListColorsElegantly"
        x:Class="Petzold.YellowPad.StylusToolDialog"
        Title="Stylus Tool"
        ShowInTaskbar="False"
        WindowStartupLocation="CenterOwner"
        SizeToContent="WidthAndHeight"
        ResizeMode="NoResize">
    <Grid Margin="6">
        <Grid.ColumnDefinitions>
            <ColumnDefinition />
            <ColumnDefinition />
        </Grid.ColumnDefinitions>

        <Grid.RowDefinitions>
            <RowDefinition />
            <RowDefinition />
            <RowDefinition />
            <RowDefinition />
            <RowDefinition />
        </Grid.RowDefinitions>

        <!-- Three-by-three Grid displays three TextBox controls. -->
        <Grid Grid.Row="0" Grid.Column="0">
            <Grid.RowDefinitions>
                <RowDefinition />
                <RowDefinition />
                <RowDefinition />
            </Grid.RowDefinitions>

            <Grid.ColumnDefinitions>
                <ColumnDefinition />
```

```
                    <ColumnDefinition />
                    <ColumnDefinition />
                </Grid.ColumnDefinitions>

                <Label Content="_Width:" Grid.Row="0" Grid.Column="0"
                        Margin="6 6 0 6" />
                <TextBox Name="txtboxWidth" Grid.Row="0" Grid.Column="1"
                            Width="50" TextAlignment="Right" Margin="0 6 0 6" />
                <Label Content="points" Grid.Row="0" Grid.Column="2"
                        Margin="0 6 6 6" />

                <Label Content="_Height:" Grid.Row="1" Grid.Column="0"
                        Margin="6 6 0 6" />
                <TextBox Name="txtboxHeight" Grid.Row="1" Grid.Column="1"
                            Width="50" TextAlignment="Right" Margin="0 6 0 6" />
                <Label Content="points" Grid.Row="1" Grid.Column="2"
                        Margin="0 6 6 6" />

                <Label Content="_Rotation:" Grid.Row="2" Grid.Column="0"
                        Margin="6 6 0 6" />
                <TextBox Name="txtboxAngle" Grid.Row="2" Grid.Column="1"
                            Width="50" TextAlignment="Right" Margin="0 6 0 6" />
                <Label Content="degrees" Grid.Row="2" Grid.Column="2"
                        Margin="0 6 6 6" />
            </Grid>

            <!-- GroupBox has two RadioButton controls for stylus tip. -->
            <GroupBox Header="_Stylus Tip" Grid.Row="1" Grid.Column="0"
                    Margin="6">
                <StackPanel>
                    <RadioButton Name="radioEllipse" Content="Ellipse" Margin="6" />
                    <RadioButton Name="radioRect" Content="Rectangle" Margin="6" />
                </StackPanel>
            </GroupBox>

            <!-- Two CheckBox controls for pressure and highlighter flags. -->
            <CheckBox Name="chkboxPressure" Content="_Ignore pressure"
                    Grid.Row="2" Grid.Column="0" Margin="12 6 6 6" />
            <CheckBox Name="chkboxHighlighter" Content="_Highlighter"
                    Grid.Row="3" Grid.Column="0" Margin="12 6 6 6" />

            <!-- ColorListBox from ListColorsElegantly project. -->
            <color:ColorListBox x:Name="lstboxColor" Width="150" Height="200"
                            Grid.Row="0" Grid.Column="1" Grid.RowSpan="3"
                            Margin="6"/>

            <!-- OK and Cancel buttons. -->
            <UniformGrid Grid.Row="4" Grid.Column="0" Grid.ColumnSpan="2"
                        Columns="2">
                <Button Content="OK" Name="btnOk" Click="OkOnClick" IsDefault="True"
                        MinWidth="60" Margin="6" HorizontalAlignment="Center" />
                <Button Content="Cancel" IsCancel="True"
                        MinWidth="60" Margin="6" HorizontalAlignment="Center" />
            </UniformGrid>
        </Grid>
    </Window>
```

Notice that the *ColorListBox* control comes from the ListColorsElegantly program in Chapter 13, and the XAML file requires an XML namespace declaration for the namespace of that project.

The StylusToolDialog.cs file defines the remainder of the *StylusToolDialog* class. The *DrawingAttributes* property initializes the controls in its *set* accessor and creates a new *DrawingAttributes* object from the settings of its controls in its *get* accessor. The dialog displays the width and height of the tip in points (1/72 inch), so both the *set* and *get* accessor have conversion calculations.

StylusToolDialog.cs

```
//-------------------------------------------------
// StylusToolDialog.cs (c) 2006 by Charles Petzold
//-------------------------------------------------
using System;
using System.Windows;
using System.Windows.Controls;
using System.Windows.Ink;
using System.Windows.Media;

namespace Petzold.YellowPad
{
    public partial class StylusToolDialog : Window
    {
        // Constructor.
        public StylusToolDialog()
        {
            InitializeComponent();

            // Set event handlers to enable OK button.
            txtboxWidth.TextChanged += TextBoxOnTextChanged;
            txtboxHeight.TextChanged += TextBoxOnTextChanged;
            txtboxAngle.TextChanged += TextBoxOnTextChanged;

            txtboxWidth.Focus();
        }
        // Public property initializes controls and returns their values.
        public DrawingAttributes DrawingAttributes
        {
            set
            {
                txtboxHeight.Text = (0.75 * value.Height).ToString("F1");
                txtboxWidth.Text = (0.75 * value.Width).ToString("F1");
                txtboxAngle.Text =
                    (180 * Math.Acos(value.StylusTipTransform.M11) /
                                           Math.PI).ToString("F1");

                chkboxPressure.IsChecked = value.IgnorePressure;
                chkboxHighlighter.IsChecked = value.IsHighlighter;

                if (value.StylusTip == StylusTip.Ellipse)
                    radioEllipse.IsChecked = true;
```

```
                    else
                        radioRect.IsChecked = true;

                    lstboxColor.SelectedColor = value.Color;
                    lstboxColor.ScrollIntoView(lstboxColor.SelectedColor);
                }
                get
                {
                    DrawingAttributes drawattr = new DrawingAttributes();

                    drawattr.Height = Double.Parse(txtboxHeight.Text) / 0.75;
                    drawattr.Width = Double.Parse(txtboxWidth.Text) / 0.75;
                    drawattr.StylusTipTransform =
                        new RotateTransform(Double.Parse(txtboxAngle.Text)).Value;

                    drawattr.IgnorePressure = (bool)chkboxPressure.IsChecked;
                    drawattr.IsHighlighter = (bool)chkboxHighlighter.IsChecked;
                    drawattr.StylusTip =
                        (bool)radioEllipse.IsChecked ? StylusTip.Ellipse :
                                                       StylusTip.Rectangle;

                    drawattr.Color = lstboxColor.SelectedColor;
                    return drawattr;
                }
            }
            // Event handler enables OK button only if all fields are valid.
            void TextBoxOnTextChanged(object sender, TextChangedEventArgs args)
            {
                double width, height, angle;

                btnOk.IsEnabled = Double.TryParse(txtboxWidth.Text, out width) &&
                            width / 0.75 >= DrawingAttributes.MinWidth &&
                            width / 0.75 <= DrawingAttributes.MaxWidth &&
                            Double.TryParse(txtboxHeight.Text, out height) &&
                            height / 0.75 >= DrawingAttributes.MinHeight &&
                            height / 0.75 <= DrawingAttributes.MaxHeight &&
                            Double.TryParse(txtboxAngle.Text, out angle);
            }
            // OK button terminates dialog.
            void OkOnClick(object sender, RoutedEventArgs args)
            {
                DialogResult = true;
            }
        }
    }
```

The *get* accessor is able to call *Double.Parse* with impunity because the OK button of the dialog box isn't enabled unless all three *TextBox* controls contain valid *double* values. This logic occurs in the *TextChanged* event handler shared by all three *TextBox* controls.

The *EraserToolDialog* class inherits from *StylusToolDialog*. Its constructor applies a new *Title* property to the dialog and hides three controls with properties not supported for the eraser.

EraserToolDialog.cs

```
//-------------------------------------------------
// EraserToolDialog.cs (c) 2006 by Charles Petzold
//-------------------------------------------------
using System;
using System.Windows;
using System.Windows.Controls;
using System.Windows.Ink;

namespace Petzold.YellowPad
{
    public class EraserToolDialog : StylusToolDialog
    {
        // Constructor hides some irrelevant controls on StylusToolDialog.
        public EraserToolDialog()
        {
            Title = "Eraser Tool";
            chkboxPressure.Visibility = Visibility.Collapsed;
            chkboxHighlighter.Visibility = Visibility.Collapsed;
            lstboxColor.Visibility = Visibility.Collapsed;
        }
        // Public property initializes controls and returns their values.
        public StylusShape EraserShape
        {
            set
            {
                txtboxHeight.Text = (0.75 * value.Height).ToString("F1");
                txtboxWidth.Text = (0.75 * value.Width).ToString("F1");
                txtboxAngle.Text = value.Rotation.ToString();

                if (value is EllipseStylusShape)
                    radioEllipse.IsChecked = true;
                else
                    radioRect.IsChecked = true;
            }
            get
            {
                StylusShape eraser;
                double width = Double.Parse(txtboxWidth.Text) / 0.75;
                double height = Double.Parse(txtboxHeight.Text) / 0.75;
                double angle = Double.Parse(txtboxAngle.Text);

                if ((bool)radioEllipse.IsChecked)
                    eraser = new EllipseStylusShape(width, height, angle);
                else
                    eraser = new RectangleStylusShape(width, height, angle);

                return eraser;
            }
        }
    }
}
```

This class defines a new property named *EraserShape* of type *StylusShape* (the same as the *EraserShape* property defined by *InkCanvas*), and the code roughly parallels that of the *DrawingAttributes* property in *StylusToolDialog*, except that the two different shapes are represented by two different classes.

The Tools menu contains the two items Stylus and Eraser. The YellowPadWindow.Tools.cs file is responsible for displaying the *StylusToolDialog* and *EraserToolDialog* windows in response to these commands.

```
YellowPadWindow.Tools.cs
//------------------------------------------------------
// YellowPadWindow.Tools.cs (c) 2006 by Charles Petzold
//------------------------------------------------------
using System;
using System.Windows;
using System.Windows.Controls;

namespace Petzold.YellowPad
{
    public partial class YellowPadWindow : Window
    {
        // Display StylusToolDialog and use DrawingAttributes property.
        void StylusToolOnClick(object sender, RoutedEventArgs args)
        {
            StylusToolDialog dlg = new StylusToolDialog();
            dlg.Owner = this;
            dlg.DrawingAttributes = inkcanv.DefaultDrawingAttributes;

            if ((bool)dlg.ShowDialog().GetValueOrDefault())
            {
                inkcanv.DefaultDrawingAttributes = dlg.DrawingAttributes;
            }
        }
        // Display EraserToolDialog and use EraserShape property.
        void EraserToolOnClick(object sender, RoutedEventArgs args)
        {
            EraserToolDialog dlg = new EraserToolDialog();
            dlg.Owner = this;
            dlg.EraserShape = inkcanv.EraserShape;

            if ((bool)dlg.ShowDialog().GetValueOrDefault())
            {
                inkcanv.EraserShape = dlg.EraserShape;
            }
        }
    }
}
```

I want to go back to the Edit menu now. I mentioned earlier that you can choose Select from the Stylus-Mode menu and lasso one or more strokes. *InkCanvas* has *CopySelection* and *CutSelection* methods to copy the selected strokes to the clipboard. The *CutSelection* method also deletes the selected strokes from the strokes collection. *InkCanvas* also defines a *CanPaste* method that indicates if some ink is in the clipboard, and a *Paste* method that pastes that ink to the *InkCanvas*. The standard items on the Edit menu are thus fairly easy to implement, as the following file demonstrates.

YellowPadWindow.Edit.cs

```
//-------------------------------------------------------
// YellowPadWindow.Edit.cs (c) 2006 by Charles Petzold
//-------------------------------------------------------
using System;
using System.Windows;
using System.Windows.Controls;
using System.Windows.Ink;
using System.Windows.Input;

namespace Petzold.YellowPad
{
    public partial class YellowPadWindow : Window
    {
        // Enable Format item if strokes have been selected.
        void EditOnOpened(object sender, RoutedEventArgs args)
        {
            itemFormat.IsEnabled = inkcanv.GetSelectedStrokes().Count > 0;
        }
        // Enable Cut, Copy, Delete items if strokes have been selected.
        void CutCanExecute(object sender, CanExecuteRoutedEventArgs args)
        {
            args.CanExecute = inkcanv.GetSelectedStrokes().Count > 0;
        }
        // Implement Cut and Copy with methods in InkCanvas.
        void CutOnExecuted(object sender, ExecutedRoutedEventArgs args)
        {
            inkcanv.CutSelection();
        }
        void CopyOnExecuted(object sender, ExecutedRoutedEventArgs args)
        {
            inkcanv.CopySelection();
        }
        // Enable Paste item if the InkCanvas is cool with the clipboard.

        void PasteCanExecute(object sender, CanExecuteRoutedEventArgs args)
        {
            args.CanExecute = inkcanv.CanPaste();
        }
        // Implement Paste with method in InkCanvas.
        void PasteOnExecuted(object sender, ExecutedRoutedEventArgs args)
        {
            inkcanv.Paste();
        }
        // Implement Delete "manually."
        void DeleteOnExecuted(object sender, ExecutedRoutedEventArgs args)
        {
            foreach (Stroke strk in inkcanv.GetSelectedStrokes())
```

```
                        inkcanv.Strokes.Remove(strk);
        }
        // Select All item: select all the strokes.
        void SelectAllOnExecuted(object sender, ExecutedRoutedEventArgs args)
        {
            inkcanv.Select(inkcanv.Strokes);
        }
        // Format Selection item: invoke StylusToolDialog.
        void FormatOnClick(object sender, RoutedEventArgs args)
        {
            StylusToolDialog dlg = new StylusToolDialog();
            dlg.Owner = this;
            dlg.Title = "Format Selection";

            // Try getting the DrawingAttributes of the first selected stroke.
            StrokeCollection strokes = inkcanv.GetSelectedStrokes();

            if (strokes.Count > 0)
                dlg.DrawingAttributes = strokes[0].DrawingAttributes;
            else
                dlg.DrawingAttributes = inkcanv.DefaultDrawingAttributes;

            if ((bool)dlg.ShowDialog().GetValueOrDefault())
            {
                // Set the DrawingAttributes of all the selected strokes.
                foreach (Stroke strk in strokes)
                    strk.DrawingAttributes = dlg.DrawingAttributes;
            }
        }
    }
}
```

For enabling menu items that require strokes to be already selected, I use the *GetSelected-Strokes* method of *InkCanvas*, which returns an object of type *StrokeCollection*.

I was initially reluctant to implement an item to change the formatting of the selected strokes until I realized it could be handled largely by the *StylusToolDialog* with yet another *Title* property. The code at the bottom of the file initializes the dialog box from the *Drawing-Attributes* property of the first selected stroke, and then sets all the selected strokes from the new *DrawingAttributes* object created by the dialog box.

The YellowPadWindow.Help.cs file is responsible for the two items on the Help menu, both of which cause dialog boxes to be displayed. The Help item displays a modeless dialog box of type *YellowPadHelp*, while the About item displays a modal dialog of type *YellowPadAboutDialog*.

YellowPadWindow.Help.cs

```
//---------------------------------------------------
// YellowPadWindow.Help.cs (c) 2006 by Charles Petzold
//---------------------------------------------------
using System;
using System.Windows;
```

```
using System.Windows.Controls;
using System.Windows.Input;

namespace Petzold.YellowPad
{
    public partial class YellowPadWindow : Window
    {
        // Help command: display YellowPadHelp as modeless dialog.
        void HelpOnExecuted(object sender, ExecutedRoutedEventArgs args)
        {
            YellowPadHelp win = new YellowPadHelp();
            win.Owner = this;
            win.Show();
        }
        // About command: display YellowPadAboutDialog.
        void AboutOnClick(object sender, RoutedEventArgs args)
        {
            YellowPadAboutDialog dlg = new YellowPadAboutDialog();
            dlg.Owner = this;
            dlg.ShowDialog();
        }
    }
}
```

I'm going to hold off on showing you the *YellowPadHelp* class until later in this chapter when some necessary background has been illuminated. The following YellowPadAbout-Dialog.xaml file defines the layout of the About dialog.

YellowPadAboutDialog.xaml

```
<!-- =====================================================
        YellowPadAboutDialog.xaml (c) 2006 by Charles Petzold
     ===================================================== -->
<Window xmlns="http://schemas.microsoft.com/winfx/2006/xaml/presentation"
        xmlns:x="http://schemas.microsoft.com/winfx/2006/xaml"
        x:Class="Petzold.YellowPad.YellowPadAboutDialog"
        Title="About YellowPad"
        ShowInTaskbar="False"
        WindowStartupLocation="CenterOwner"
        SizeToContent="WidthAndHeight"
        ResizeMode="NoResize">
    <StackPanel>
        <!-- Program name. -->
        <TextBlock HorizontalAlignment="Center" Margin="12"
                   FontSize="48">
            <Italic>Yellow Pad</Italic>
        </TextBlock>

        <!-- Cover of the book the program is from. -->
        <Image Source="Images\BookCover.jpg" Stretch="None" Margin="12" />

        <!-- Another Image element for the copyright/signature file. -->
        <Image Name="imgSignature" Stretch="None" Margin="12" />
```

```
            <!-- Web Site link. -->
            <TextBlock HorizontalAlignment="Center" FontSize="20">
                <Hyperlink NavigateUri="http://www.charlespetzold.com"
                            RequestNavigate="LinkOnRequestNavigate">
                    www.charlespetzold.com
                </Hyperlink>
            </TextBlock>

            <!-- OK button is both default and cancel button. -->
            <Button HorizontalAlignment="Center" MinWidth="60" Margin="12"
                    IsDefault="True" IsCancel="True">
                OK
            </Button>
        </StackPanel>
</Window>
```

The file has two *Image* elements. The first loads a resource file from the Images directory of the project that is a bitmap image of the cover of this book. The second *Image* element has no *Source* property but does have a *Name* property of "imgSignature." The *Source* property for this element is set in C# code in the following file, YellowPadAboutDialog.cs. I created the Signature.xaml file from the YellowPad program by saving ink as a XAML Drawing File, and I made that file part of the YellowPad project with a build type of Resource. The code in the Yellow-PadAboutDialog constructor obtains a *Stream* for this resource and converts it into an object of type *Drawing* with *XamlReader.Load*. The *Source* of the second *Image* element in the XAML file is simply a *DrawingImage* object based on the *Drawing* object.

YellowPadAboutDialog.cs
```csharp
//---------------------------------------------------
// YellowPadAboutDialog.cs (c) 2006 by Charles Petzold
//---------------------------------------------------
using System;
using System.Diagnostics;            // for Process class.
using System.IO;
using System.Windows;
using System.Windows.Media;
using System.Windows.Markup;
using System.Windows.Navigation;     // for RequestNavigateEventArgs.

namespace Petzold.YellowPad
{
    public partial class YellowPadAboutDialog
    {
        public YellowPadAboutDialog()
        {
            InitializeComponent();

            // Load copyright/signature Drawing and set in Image element.
            Uri uri = new Uri("pack://application:,,,/Images/Signature.xaml");
            Stream stream = Application.GetResourceStream(uri).Stream;
            Drawing drawing = (Drawing)XamlReader.Load(stream);
            stream.Close();
```

```
            imgSignature.Source = new DrawingImage(drawing);
        }
        // when hyperlink is clicked, go to my web site.
        void LinkOnRequestNavigate(object sender, RequestNavigateEventArgs args)
        {
            Process.Start(args.Uri.OriginalString);
            args.Handled = true;
        }
    }
}
```

Let me also call your attention to the *Hyperlink* element in the YellowPadAboutDialog.xaml file. Clicking the link causes your default Web browser to display my Web site. You've seen this feature before. The *AboutDialog* class in the NotepadClone program from Chapter 18 defined a similar *Hyperlink* element but set its *Click* event to the following handler:

```
void LinkOnClick(object sender, RoutedEventArgs args)
{
    Process.Start("http://www.charlespetzold.com");
}
```

The YellowPadAboutDialog.xaml file instead assigns the *NavigateUri* property and the *RequestNavigate* event handler:

```
<Hyperlink NavigateUri="http://www.charlespetzold.com"
           RequestNavigate="LinkOnRequestNavigate">
    www.charlespetzold.com
</Hyperlink>
```

The *LinkOnRequestNavigate* handler in YellowPadAboutDialog.cs looks like this:

```
void LinkOnRequestNavigate(object sender, RequestNavigateEventArgs args)
{
    Process.Start(args.Uri.OriginalString);
    args.Handled = true;
}
```

The event handler is able to snag the URI assigned to the *NavigateUri* property for passing to *Process.Start*. That makes the code in the event handler a little more generalized, but otherwise it seems unnecessarily more verbose than the approach using our old friend *Click*.

Besides, it seems reasonable that if you give the *Hyperlink* element in the XAML the actual URI you want it to go to, *Hyperlink* should be able to go to that link by itself without any additional code. Yet if you remove the *RequestNavigate* event attribute from the *Hyperlink* element and recompile, nothing happens when you click the link. But what would you *like* to happen? Should *Hyperlink* launch your default Web browser as *Process.Start* does? Or should the desired Web page actually replace the entire content of the About box window?

If the latter approach appeals to you, you're in luck, for *Hyperlink* can do precisely that. All it needs is a proper home. Or rather, a window (or even just a frame).

Try this: In YellowPadAboutDialog.xaml, change both occurrences of *Window* to *Navigation-Window*, and enclose the *StackPanel* in a *NavigationWindow.Content* property element. *Navigation-Window* is the only class defined in the Windows Presentation Foundation that derives from *Window*. Now remove the *RequestNavigate* event attribute from the *Hyperlink* element (if you haven't already done so) and recompile.

Now when you invoke the About box, it appears in a slightly different kind of window. Two disabled buttons appear near the top, labeled with left and right arrows. These are Back and Forward buttons, and the horizontal strip they appear on is known as *navigation chrome*. When you click the link to my Web site, the Web site replaces the contents of the About box. Now the Back button has become enabled. Click it to go back to the About box.

Welcome to the world of WPF navigation applications. As you've discovered, the *Hyperlink* element normally doesn't work unless you install an event handler for it. However, if the *Hyperlink* is inside a *NavigationWindow* (or a *Frame* element), clicking the link automatically navigates to the page specified in the *NavigateUri* property. The *NavigateUri* property can reference a URI of a Web site, but it's more commonly the name of another XAML file in the program.

Taken to the extreme, the use of *NavigationWindow* and *Frame* lets you structure your entire WPF application much like a Web site, but without giving up any of the power of WPF elements, controls, and graphics.

The NavigationDemo project demonstrates some basic navigation techniques. The project has five XAML files and one C# file. The first XAML file is this application definition file.

```
NavigationDemoApp.xaml
<!-- =====================================================
        NavigationDemoApp.xaml (c) 2006 by Charles Petzold
     ===================================================== -->
<Application xmlns="http://schemas.microsoft.com/winfx/2006/xaml/presentation"
             xmlns:x="http://schemas.microsoft.com/winfx/2006/xaml"
             x:Class="Petzold.NavigationDemo.MyApp"
             StartupUri="NavigationDemoWindow.xaml" />
```

The *StartupUri* attribute indicates that the NavigationDemoWindow.xaml is to be loaded as the initial application window. The root element of NavigationDemoWindow.xaml is a *Navigation-Window*. The *NavigationWindow* element has its *Source* attribute set to yet another XAML file.

```
NavigationDemoWindow.xaml
<!-- =====================================================
        NavigationDemoWindow.xaml (c) 2006 by Charles Petzold
     ===================================================== -->
<NavigationWindow xmlns="http://schemas.microsoft.com/winfx/2006/xaml/presentation"
                  Title="Navigation Demo" FontSize="24"
                  Source="Page1.xaml" />
```

Source is one of several properties that *NavigationWindow* defines beyond the properties it inherits from *Window*. You'll recall that *Frame* also has a *Source* property. Both *NavigationWindow* and *Frame* derive from *ContentControl*, but if you set the *Content* of either element, that *Content* property will take precedence over the *Source* property. Generally you'll be using *NavigationWindow* or *Frame* to take advantage of their navigational abilities, so you'll want to focus on the *Source* property rather than on *Content*.

The *Source* property of the preceding *NavigationWindow* references the Page1.xaml file shown here.

```
Page1.xaml
<!-- ======================================
      Page1.xaml (c) 2006 by Charles Petzold
     ====================================== -->
<Page xmlns="http://schemas.microsoft.com/winfx/2006/xaml/presentation"
     Title="Page 1" WindowTitle="Navigation Demo: Page 1">
    <TextBlock HorizontalAlignment="Center"
               VerticalAlignment="Center">
        Go to
        <Hyperlink NavigateUri="Page2.xaml">Page 2</Hyperlink>.
    </TextBlock>
</Page>
```

It is not necessary for the *Source* property of *NavigationWindow* or *Frame* to be set to a XAML file with a root element of *Page*. (In code, it is not necessary to set the *Source* property to an object of type *Page*.) However, *Page* has several features that make it quite suitable for navigation applications. Two of these features are shown in Page1.xaml. The *Title* property is the text that appears in the lists of visited pages displayed by the Back and Forward buttons; these lists facilitate jumping to a previously navigated page. The *WindowTitle* property overrides the *Title* property of the *NavigationWindow*. (Here's another way you can tell that *Page* is specifically designed for navigation applications: A *Page* element can be a child only of a *NavigationWindow* or a *Frame*.)

Otherwise, Page1.xaml simply contains a *TextBlock* with an embedded *Hyperlink* element that has a *NavigateUri* of Page2.xaml. That's the file shown here.

```
Page2.xaml
<!-- ======================================
      Page2.xaml (c) 2006 by Charles Petzold
     ====================================== -->
<Page xmlns="http://schemas.microsoft.com/winfx/2006/xaml/presentation"
      xmlns:x="http://schemas.microsoft.com/winfx/2006/xaml"
      x:Class="Petzold.NavigationDemo.Page2"
      Title="Page 2" WindowTitle="Navigation Demo: Page 2">
    <Grid>
        <Grid.RowDefinitions>
            <RowDefinition Height="33*" />
            <RowDefinition Height="33*" />
```

```
                <RowDefinition Height="33*" />
            </Grid.RowDefinitions>
            <TextBlock Grid.Row="0" HorizontalAlignment="Center"
                                    VerticalAlignment="Center">
                RequestNavigate event handled for navigation to
                <Hyperlink NavigateUri="Page3.xaml"
                            RequestNavigate="HyperlinkOnRequestNavigate">
                    Page 3</Hyperlink>.
            </TextBlock>
            <Button Grid.Row="1" HorizontalAlignment="Center"
                                 VerticalAlignment="Center"
                    Click="ButtonOnClick">
                Click to go to Page 1
            </Button>
            <TextBlock Grid.Row="2" HorizontalAlignment="Center"
                                    VerticalAlignment="Center">
                Go to
                <Hyperlink NavigateUri="http://www.charlespetzold.com">
                    Petzold's Web site</Hyperlink>.
            </TextBlock>
        </Grid>
    </Page>
```

The *Page* element in the Page2.xaml file is a bit more complex than the first page. It has two *TextBlock* elements and one *Button*, all labeled as if they contained active links.

The first *TextBlock* has an embedded *Hyperlink* element that specifies a handler for its *Request-Navigate* event. The *Button* indicates a handler for its *Click* event. The third *Hyperlink* contains only a *NavigateUri* property, but it points to my Web site rather than to a local XAML page.

Page2.xaml requires a code-behind file for the two event handlers. That's why it includes an *x:Class* attribute, which Page1.xaml doesn't need. The code-behind file shown here includes a call to *InitializeComponent* in its constructor to wire up the event handlers, and the two event handlers themselves.

Page2.cs
```
//-------------------------------------
// Page2.cs (c) 2006 by Charles Petzold
//-------------------------------------
using System;
using System.Windows;
using System.Windows.Controls;
using System.Windows.Documents;
using System.Windows.Navigation;

namespace Petzold.NavigationDemo
{
    public partial class Page2
    {
        public Page2()
        {
            InitializeComponent();
        }
```

```
      void ButtonOnClick(object sender, RoutedEventArgs args)
      {
          NavigationService.Navigate(
                  new Uri("Page1.xaml", UriKind.Relative));
      }
      void HyperlinkOnRequestNavigate(object sender,
                                      RequestNavigateEventArgs args)
      {
          NavigationService.Navigate(args.Uri);
          args.Handled = true;
      }
    }
  }
```

The *ButtonOnClick* method needs to tell the *NavigationWindow* to navigate to the Page1.xaml file, and it can do this by calling the *Navigate* method defined by *NavigationWindow*. However, the *Page2* class doesn't have direct access to the *NavigationWindow* object with that crucial *Navigate* method. One approach to obtaining the *NavigationWindow* is through the static *Application.Current* property and then the *MainWindow* property of *Application*:

```
NavigationWindow navwin =
    (Application.Current.MainWindow as NavigationWindow);
```

You can then call the *Navigate* method of the *navwin* object to navigate to the file. However, the Page2.cs file demonstrates a somewhat easier approach. The *Page* class defines a property named *NavigationService* that itself has a *Navigate* method. The *NavigationService* object is accessible through the *Page* object and provides a conduit to the navigational abilities of the *NavigationWindow* of which the *Page* is a part. (The existence of this *NavigationService* property is another reason why *Page* is well suited for navigation applications. However, if you need to perform navigation in a class other than *Page*, you can obtain a *NavigationService* object from the static *NavigationService.GetNavigationService* method. The class calling *Navigate* still needs to be somewhere inside a *NavigationWindow* or *Frame*, however.)

The *Navigate* method requires a *Uri* or an object. In the *ButtonOnClick* method, the second argument of the *Uri* constructor indicates that the path given for the Page1.xaml file is relative to the path of the current XAML file, which is Page2.xaml.

The *RequestNavigate* event handler handles the navigation job similarly except that the *Uri* that the handler passes to the *Navigate* method is the one originally specified in the *Hyperlink* element of the Page2.xaml file. The event handler sets the *Handled* property to *true* to indicate that it has performed the navigation and nothing more needs to be done.

In this example, nothing is gained by taking over the call to *Navigate* in the event handler rather than having the *Hyperlink* perform it automatically. But you might have a need to examine a particular link as it's occurring.

The final Page3.xaml file that completes the NavigationDemo project is nearly as simple as Page1.xaml. It contains a *TextBox* at the top and a link at the bottom to navigate back to Page1.xaml.

```
Page3.xaml
<!-- =======================================
        Page3.xaml (c) 2006 by Charles Petzold
     ======================================= -->
<Page xmlns="http://schemas.microsoft.com/winfx/2006/xaml/presentation"
        Title="Page 3" WindowTitle="Navigation Demo: Page 3">
    <NavigationWindow.Content>
        <Grid>
            <Grid.RowDefinitions>
                <RowDefinition Height="50*" />
                <RowDefinition Height="50*" />
            </Grid.RowDefinitions>
            <TextBox Grid.Row="0" MinWidth="2in" Margin="48"
                        HorizontalAlignment="Center" VerticalAlignment="Top" />

            <TextBlock Grid.Row="2" Margin="48"
                        HorizontalAlignment="Right" VerticalAlignment="Bottom">
                Go back to
                <Hyperlink NavigateUri="Page1.xaml">
                    Page 1</Hyperlink>.
            </TextBlock>
        </Grid>
    </NavigationWindow.Content>
</Page>
```

As you navigate through this application, keep note of the Back and Forward buttons displayed at the top of the *NavigationWindow*. The *NavigationWindow* maintains a journal of the visited pages in two stacks corresponding to the two buttons. Whenever a program uses the *Navigate* method to navigate to a page, the page you navigated from is pushed onto the back stack and the forward stack is cleared. When you click the Back button, the current page is pushed onto the forward stack, and you navigate to the page popped from the back stack. When you click the Forward button, the current page is pushed onto the back stack, and you navigate to the page popped from the forward stack. You also have programmatic access to back and forward navigation, as you'll see later in this chapter.

Page3.xaml includes a *TextBox* at the top. While navigating, type something into it. If you navigate back to Page3.xaml again through hyperlinks, you'll find the *TextBox* empty. However, if you navigate to Page3.xaml through the Back or Forward buttons, you'll find the text you typed still there.

When you use *NavigationWindow*, the entire contents of the window change with each navigation. It could be that you only want to devote part of the window to navigation, or to perform independent navigation in several parts of the window. In those cases, you can use *Frame*.

The FrameNavigationDemo project has two files named FrameNavigationDemoApp.xaml and FrameNavigationWindow.xaml and also includes links to the four *Page* files from

NavigationDemo project. Because the *Page2* class has a namespace of *Petzold.NavigationDemo*, the FrameApplicationDemoApp.xaml application definition file defines that same namespace to make integration with the earlier code a bit easier.

FrameNavigationDemoApp.xaml

```
<!-- ======================================================
         FrameNavigationDemoApp.xaml (c) 2006 by Charles Petzold
     ====================================================== -->
<Application xmlns="http://schemas.microsoft.com/winfx/2006/xaml/presentation"
             xmlns:x="http://schemas.microsoft.com/winfx/2006/xaml"
             x:Class="Petzold.NavigationDemo.MyApp"
             StartupUri="FrameNavigationDemoWindow.xaml" />
```

The *StartupUri* attributes points to the next file, which is FrameApplicationDemoWindow .xaml.

FrameNavigationDemoWindow.xaml

```
<!-- ======================================================
         FrameNavigationDemoWindow.xaml (c) 2006 by Charles Petzold
     ====================================================== -->
<Window xmlns="http://schemas.microsoft.com/winfx/2006/xaml/presentation"
        Title="Frame Navigation Demo" FontSize="24">

    <Grid>
        <Grid.RowDefinitions>
            <RowDefinition />
            <RowDefinition />
        </Grid.RowDefinitions>

        <Frame Grid.Row="0" Background="Aqua"
               Source="Page1.xaml" />

        <Frame Grid.Row="1" Background="Pink"
               Source="Page2.xaml" />

    </Grid>
</Window>
```

The root element of this file is *Window*, but the window contains two *Frame* elements. They are given different colors so that you can tell them apart, and each points to a different *Page* file. When you compile and run this program, you'll note that each *Frame* has its own navigation chrome, but that chrome doesn't appear until the first time you navigate from the initial page.

As you can see, the navigation among the pages is entirely independent in the two *Frame* elements. But here's an interesting experiment: In FrameNavigationDemoWindow.xaml, change *Window* to *NavigationWindow* and recompile. Now there's only one piece of navigation chrome at the top of the window. However, both frames still navigate independently, and the Back and Forward buttons know which frame is which!

It is now time to return to the YellowPad project and create a Help system for it. The YellowPad project contains a directory named Help that contains ten XAML files and three PNG files with images of the program's dialog boxes. The XAML files are all fairly similar. They all have a root element of *Page* containing a *FlowDocument* inside a *FlowDocumentReader* with some help text and perhaps a link to one of the images or the other help files. Here's a typical file from the Help directory.

EraserToolDialog.xaml

```
<!-- ================================================
        EraserToolDialog.xaml (c) 2006 by Charles Petzold
     ================================================ -->
<Page xmlns="http://schemas.microsoft.com/winfx/2006/xaml/presentation"
      Title="The Eraser Tool Dialog">
    <FlowDocumentReader ViewingMode="Scroll">
        <FlowDocument>
            <Paragraph TextAlignment="Center"
                       FontSize="16pt">
                The Eraser Tool Dialog
            </Paragraph>
            <Paragraph>
                The <Bold>Eraser Tool</Bold> dialog lets you change the
                dimensions and shape of the eraser.
            </Paragraph>
            <BlockUIContainer>
                <Image Source="EraserToolDialog.png"
                       Stretch="None"/>
            </BlockUIContainer>
            <Paragraph>
                Use the <Bold>Width</Bold> and <Bold>Height</Bold> fields
                to specify the dimensions of the eraser in points
                (1/72<Run BaselineAlignment="Superscript">nd</Run> inch).
            </Paragraph>
            <Paragraph>
                Use the <Bold>Rotation</Bold> field to specify a
                rotation of the eraser. The rotation only makes sense
                when the horizontal and vertical dimensions of the eraser
                are unequal.
            </Paragraph>
        </FlowDocument>
    </FlowDocumentReader>
</Page>
```

The YellowPadHelp.xaml file contains the layout for the Help window. The root element is a *NavigationWindow* containing a three-column *Grid*.

YellowPadHelp.xaml

```
<!-- ================================================
        YellowPadHelp.xaml (c) 2006 by Charles Petzold
     ================================================ -->
<NavigationWindow
        xmlns="http://schemas.microsoft.com/winfx/2006/xaml/presentation"
        xmlns:x="http://schemas.microsoft.com/winfx/2006/xaml"
```

```xml
            x:Class="Petzold.YellowPad.YellowPadHelp"
            Title="YellowPad Help"
            Width="800" Height="600"
            ShowInTaskbar="False"
            WindowStartupLocation="CenterScreen">
    <NavigationWindow.Content>
        <Grid>
            <Grid.ColumnDefinitions>
                <ColumnDefinition Width="25*" />
                <ColumnDefinition Width="Auto" />
                <ColumnDefinition Width="75*" />
            </Grid.ColumnDefinitions>

            <TreeView Name="tree" FontSize="10pt"
                    SelectedItemChanged="HelpOnSelectedItemChanged">
                <TreeViewItem Header="Program Overview"
                            Tag="Help/Overview.xaml" />

                <TreeViewItem Header="Exploring the Menus">
                    <TreeViewItem Header="The File Menu"
                                Tag="Help/FileMenu.xaml" />

                    <TreeViewItem Header="The Edit Menu"
                                Tag="Help/EditMenu.xaml" />

                    <TreeViewItem Header="The Stylus-Mode Menu"
                                Tag="Help/StylusModeMenu.xaml" />

                    <TreeViewItem Header="The Eraser-Mode Menu"
                                Tag="Help/EraserModeMenu.xaml" />

                    <TreeViewItem Header="The Tools Menu"
                                Tag="Help/ToolsMenu.xaml">

                        <TreeViewItem Header="The Stylus Tool Dialog"
                                    Tag="Help/StylusToolDialog.xaml" />

                        <TreeViewItem Header="The Eraser Tool Dialog"
                                    Tag="Help/EraserToolDialog.xaml" />
                    </TreeViewItem>

                    <TreeViewItem Header="The Help Menu"
                                Tag="Help/HelpMenu.xaml" />
                </TreeViewItem>
                <TreeViewItem Header="Copyright Information"
                            Tag="Help/Copyright.xaml" />
            </TreeView>

            <GridSplitter Grid.Column="1" Width="6"
                        HorizontalAlignment="Center"
                        VerticalAlignment="Stretch" />

            <Frame Name="frame" Grid.Column="2" />
        </Grid>
    </NavigationWindow.Content>
</NavigationWindow>
```

The first column of the *Grid* contains a *TreeView* that serves as a contents list. I've set the all-purpose *Tag* property of each *TreeViewItem* to the XAML file associated with that item. On the right side of the *GridSplitter* is a *Frame* with the name of *frame*. The *SelectedItemChanged* event of the *TreeView* is assigned a handler that is implemented in the YellowPadHelp.cs code-behind file.

```
YellowPadHelp.cs
//--------------------------------------------
// YellowPadHelp.cs (c) 2006 by Charles Petzold
//--------------------------------------------
using System;
using System.Windows;
using System.Windows.Controls;

namespace Petzold.YellowPad
{
    public partial class YellowPadHelp
    {
        public YellowPadHelp()
        {
            InitializeComponent();

            // Select first item in TreeView and give it the focus.
            (tree.Items[0] as TreeViewItem).IsSelected = true;
            tree.Focus();
        }
        void HelpOnSelectedItemChanged(object sender,
                             RoutedPropertyChangedEventArgs<object> args)
        {
            TreeViewItem item = args.NewValue as TreeViewItem;

            if (item.Tag == null)
                return;

            // Navigate to the selected item's Tag property.
            frame.Navigate(new Uri(item.Tag as string, UriKind.Relative));
        }
    }
}
```

Whenever the user selects an item in the *TreeView* on the left, the event handler obtains the *Tag* property, converts it into a *Uri*, and passes it to the *Navigate* method of the *Frame*. The result is a fairly simple and elegant Help system. In Chapter 25 I'll show you a rather more generalized approach to displaying Help information.

The *NavigationWindow*, *Frame*, and *NavigationServices* classes all support several events that let you monitor the progress of a navigation and stop it if necessary. Obviously these are more important when you're loading pages over a network than when everything is on the user's hard drive.

One common type of navigation application is the *wizard*. A wizard is generally a series of pages occupying the same window that accumulate information. Each page of the wizard typically has buttons labeled Previous and Next, except for the first page and the last page and possibly the penultimate page. The Previous and Next buttons essentially navigate through the pages.

Because a wizard uses the Previous and Next buttons to perform navigation, a WPF wizard built inside a *NavigationWindow* or a *Frame* should *not* display the normal navigation chrome. (For *NavigationWindow*, set *ShowsNavigationUI* to *false*; for *Frame*, set *NavigationUIVisibility* to *Hidden*.) The program itself has to manage navigation in the *Click* event handlers for the Previous and Next buttons. Regardless of this "manual" handling of navigation, using WPF navigation facilities simplifies the job of writing wizards enormously. In short, you don't need to keep track of the user's journey forward and backward through the pages.

It is very desirable that the pages of a wizard do not lose information during navigation. A user who clicks a Previous button to return to an earlier page shouldn't find a blank page that requires filling in from scratch. A user who then clicks the Next button to return to a page previously visited shouldn't encounter a similar disregard for earlier work. We've all seen wizards—and, much more commonly, Web pages—that don't implement navigation well, and these programs are not to be emulated.

I'm going to show you a fairly simple wizard designed around the concept of a computer dating service. Don't let the 15 source code files in this project scare you! Each of the five pages of the wizard requires a XAML file and a C# file. One of the pages has an option to display another page, which requires another XAML file and C# file. The window that holds the whole thing together is yet another XAML file and another C# file.

The fifteenth file of the project is the one shown here. This is the file with public fields for all the information to be accumulated by the wizard.

Vitals.cs

```
//---------------------------------------
// Vitals.cs (c) 2006 by Charles Petzold
//---------------------------------------
using System;
using System.Windows;
using System.Windows.Controls;

namespace Petzold.ComputerDatingWizard
{
    public class Vitals
    {
        public string Name;
        public string Home;
        public string Gender;
        public string FavoriteOS;
        public string Directory;
        public string MomsMaidenName;
        public string Pet;
        public string Income;
```

```
        public static RadioButton GetCheckedRadioButton(GroupBox grpbox)
        {
            Panel pnl = grpbox.Content as Panel;

            if (pnl != null)
            {
                foreach (UIElement el in pnl.Children)
                {
                    RadioButton radio = el as RadioButton;

                    if (radio != null && (bool)radio.IsChecked)
                        return radio;
                }
            }
            return null;
        }
    }
}
```

These are the "vital statistics" that the wizard accumulates in its journey through the pages. The fields are *string* variables for reasons of simplicity, but some of these fields derive from *RadioButton* controls grouped in a *StackPanel* within a *GroupBox*. I have therefore included a static method that helps extract the checked *RadioButton* from the group.

During the entire time it's running, the Computer Dating Wizard program displays a single small window, which is based on the following XAML file.

ComputerDatingWizard.xaml

```
<!-- =======================================================
        ComputerDatingWizard.xaml (c) 2006 by Charles Petzold
     ======================================================= -->
<Window xmlns="http://schemas.microsoft.com/winfx/2006/xaml/presentation"
        xmlns:x="http://schemas.microsoft.com/winfx/2006/xaml"
        x:Class="Petzold.ComputerDatingWizard.ComputerDatingWizard"
        WindowStartupLocation="CenterScreen"
        Title="Computer Dating Wizard"
        Width="300" Height="300"
        ResizeMode="NoResize">
    <Grid>
        <Grid.RowDefinitions>
            <RowDefinition Height="Auto" />
            <RowDefinition Height="*" />
        </Grid.RowDefinitions>

        <TextBlock Grid.Row="0" Margin="12"
                   FontSize="16" FontStyle="Italic"
                   HorizontalAlignment="Center">
            Computer Dating Wizard
        </TextBlock>

        <Frame Grid.Row="1" Name="frame"
               NavigationUIVisibility="Hidden" Padding="6" />
    </Grid>
</Window>
```

The window has a fixed size, which is common for wizards. The client area is divided between the text "Computer Dating Wizard" and a *Frame* in which the various pages will appear. The text string simply symbolizes an area of the window that can remain the same throughout the wizard's existence. It doesn't need to be at the top, and it doesn't have to be text.

Notice that the *NavigationUIVisibility* property of the *Frame* is set to *Hidden*. You don't want the *Frame* to display its navigation chrome because the buttons on the various pages will be handling navigation instead.

The C# part of this class contains the *Main* method—I could have used an application definition file instead, of course—and a constructor that calls *InitializeComponent*.

```
ComputerDatingWizard.cs
//---------------------------------------------------------
// ComputerDatingWizard.cs (c) 2006 by Charles Petzold
//---------------------------------------------------------
using System;
using System.Windows;
using System.Windows.Controls;

namespace Petzold.ComputerDatingWizard
{
    public partial class ComputerDatingWizard
    {
        [STAThread]
        public static void Main()
        {
            Application app = new Application();
            app.Run(new ComputerDatingWizard());
        }
        public ComputerDatingWizard()
        {
            InitializeComponent();

            // Navigate to the greeting page.
            frame.Navigate(new WizardPage0());
        }
    }
}
```

The constructor concludes with an alternative form of the *Navigate* method that requires an object rather than a *Uri* instance. Although the argument to *Navigate* is defined as *object*, it's really the root element of a tree, so it corresponds closely to a XAML file specified as a URI. However, this form of *Navigate* is a little more versatile in some cases. Rather than passing the newly created object directly to *Navigate*, you might set some properties of the object. Or, you might create the object with a constructor that requires parameters. I'll be using this latter technique to pass an instance of the *Vitals* class through the various pages of the wizard.

The *ComputerDatingWizard* class is able to call *Navigate* directly on the *Frame* control because the *Frame* control is part of the class. Future pages won't have direct access to that *Frame* object, so they will have to use a *NavigationServices* object to perform navigation.

The *WizardPage0* class is simply an introductory message with a single button labeled Begin:

```
WizardPage0.xaml
<!-- =========================================
        WizardPage0.xaml (c) 2006 by Charles Petzold
     ========================================= -->
<Page xmlns="http://schemas.microsoft.com/winfx/2006/xaml/presentation"
      xmlns:x="http://schemas.microsoft.com/winfx/2006/xaml"
      x:Class="Petzold.ComputerDatingWizard.WizardPage0">
    <Grid>
        <Grid.RowDefinitions>
            <RowDefinition Height="Auto" />
            <RowDefinition Height="*" />
            <RowDefinition Height="Auto" />
        </Grid.RowDefinitions>

        <FlowDocumentScrollViewer Grid.Row="0" Margin="6"
                                  VerticalScrollBarVisibility="Hidden">
            <FlowDocument FontSize="10pt">
                <Paragraph>
                    Welcome to the Computer Dating Wizard.
                    This program probes the
                    <Italic>Inner You</Italic> to
                    match you with the mate of your dreams.
                </Paragraph>
                <Paragraph>
                    To begin, click the Begin button.
                </Paragraph>
            </FlowDocument>
        </FlowDocumentScrollViewer>

        <!-- Navigation button at bottom-right corner of page. -->
        <Grid Grid.Row="2">
            <Grid.ColumnDefinitions>
                <ColumnDefinition Width="*" />
                <ColumnDefinition Width="Auto" />
            </Grid.ColumnDefinitions>
            <Button Grid.Column="1" Click="BeginButtonOnClick"
                MinWidth="72" Margin="6"
                Content="Begin &gt;" />
        </Grid>
    </Grid>
</Page>
```

Keep in mind that the *Frame* in which this page appears is a fixed size, governed by the total size of the window set in ComputerDatingWizard.xaml minus the size of the *TextBlock* that appears in the window above the *Frame*. But the navigation buttons that appear in each page should be at the bottom of the client area. The *Grid* in WizardPage0.xaml defines three rows, the first and third with a size of *Auto* and the second occupying all leftover space. The *FlowDocumentScrollViewer* occupies the first row and the third row is occupied by a second *Grid* panel defined toward the bottom of the file. The second row is essentially unused but its existence serves to position the third row at the bottom. Similarly, the second *Grid* defines two columns, the first using all leftover space and the second having an *Auto* width. The first column is unused and the Begin button occupies the second column. The result is that the button is positioned at the far right of the window.

I use this technique throughout this project to keep the buttons in the same position relative to the window.

The code-behind file for *WizardPage0* has the event handler for the Begin button.

```
WizardPage0.cs
//-----------------------------------------------
// WizardPage0.cs (c) 2006 by Charles Petzold
//-----------------------------------------------
using System;
using System.Windows;
using System.Windows.Controls;

namespace Petzold.ComputerDatingWizard
{
    public partial class WizardPage0
    {
        public WizardPage0()
        {
            InitializeComponent();
        }
        void BeginButtonOnClick(object sender, RoutedEventArgs args)
        {
            if (NavigationService.CanGoForward)
                NavigationService.GoForward();
            else
            {
                Vitals vitals = new Vitals();
                WizardPage1 page = new WizardPage1(vitals);
                NavigationService.Navigate(page);
            }
        }
    }
}
```

There are two ways that a user can be looking at the *WizardPage0* page. The first way is when the program starts up. The second way is by clicking the Previous button on the next page (WizardPage1.xaml). Because this program is using the *Navigate* method to move from page to page, the pages are accumulated in the journal. The *NavigationWindow*, *Frame*, and *NavigationServices* classes all define two properties that indicate whether the journal contains an entry to go back to the previous page, or an entry to go forward to a previously visited page.

These properties are *CanGoBack* and *CanGoForward*, and the *NavigationWindow*, *Frame*, and *NavigationServices* classes also have *GoBack* and *GoForward* methods to actually navigate to those pages.

If the user starts up the wizard, clicks the Begin button on WizardPage0.xaml, clicks the Previous button on WizardPage1.xaml, and then clicks the Begin button on WizardPage0.xaml again, the *Click* handler for the Begin button knows what's happened because the *CanGoForward* property will be *true*. The *Click* handler can then call *GoForward* to navigate to WizardPage1.xaml. The advantage of calling *GoBack* and *GoFoward* (when they're available) is that the page has already been created, loaded, and perhaps modified by the user, and navigating with these methods preserves the user's input to the page.

If the *CanGoForward* property is *false*, the user is seeing WizardPage0.xaml for the first time. When the user clicks the Begin button, the *WizardPage0* class creates a new object of type *Vitals*. This single object will persist throughout the wizard. The handler next creates an object of type *WizardPage1*, passing the *Vitals* object to its constructor. It concludes by navigating to that page.

The *WizardPage1* class has a layout governed by this XAML file.

```
WizardPage1.xaml

<!-- =============================================
        WizardPage1.xaml (c) 2006 by Charles Petzold
     ============================================= -->
<Page xmlns="http://schemas.microsoft.com/winfx/2006/xaml/presentation"
      xmlns:x="http://schemas.microsoft.com/winfx/2006/xaml"
      x:Class="Petzold.ComputerDatingWizard.WizardPage1">
    <Grid>
        <Grid.RowDefinitions>
            <RowDefinition Height="Auto" />
            <RowDefinition Height="Auto" />
            <RowDefinition Height="*" />
            <RowDefinition Height="Auto" />
        </Grid.RowDefinitions>
        <Grid.ColumnDefinitions>
            <ColumnDefinition Width="50*" />
            <ColumnDefinition Width="50*" />
        </Grid.ColumnDefinitions>

        <!-- TextBox for Name. -->
        <StackPanel Orientation="Horizontal" Grid.ColumnSpan="2"
                    Margin="12">
            <Label>
                Name:
            </Label>
            <TextBox Name="txtboxName" Width="200" />
        </StackPanel>

        <!-- GroupBox for Home. -->
        <GroupBox Grid.Row="1" Grid.Column="0" Name="grpboxHome"
```

```
                    Header="Home" Margin="12">
        <StackPanel>
            <RadioButton Content="House" Margin="6" IsChecked="True" />
            <RadioButton Content="Apartment" Margin="6" />
            <RadioButton Content="Cave" Margin="6" />
        </StackPanel>
    </GroupBox>

    <!-- GroupBox for Gender. -->
    <GroupBox Grid.Row="1" Grid.Column="1" Name="grpboxGender"
                Header="Gender" Margin="12">
        <StackPanel>
            <RadioButton Content="Male" Margin="6" IsChecked="True" />
            <RadioButton Content="Female" Margin="6" />
            <RadioButton Content="Flexible" Margin="6" />
        </StackPanel>
    </GroupBox>

    <!-- Navigation buttons at bottom-right corner of page. -->
    <Grid Grid.Row="3" Grid.ColumnSpan="2">
        <Grid.ColumnDefinitions>
            <ColumnDefinition Width="*" />
            <ColumnDefinition Width="Auto" />
            <ColumnDefinition Width="Auto" />
        </Grid.ColumnDefinitions>
        <Button Grid.Column="1" Click="PreviousButtonOnClick"
            MinWidth="72" Margin="6"
            Content="&lt; Previous" />
        <Button Grid.Column="2" Click="NextButtonOnClick"
            MinWidth="72" Margin="6"
            Content="Next &gt;" />
    </Grid>
  </Grid>
</Page>
```

This page contains a *TextBox* and two *GroupBox* controls containing three *RadioButton* controls each. The two buttons at the bottom are labeled Previous and Next.

The code-behind file for the *WizardPage1* class has a single-parameter constructor. The *Vitals* object passed to the constructor is stored as a field. The constructor also needs to call *InitializeComponent*. (Alternatively, the code that creates the page can call *InitializeComponent* for the page.)

WizardPage1.cs

```
//------------------------------------------
// WizardPage1.cs (c) 2006 by Charles Petzold
//------------------------------------------
using System;
using System.Windows;
using System.Windows.Controls;

namespace Petzold.ComputerDatingWizard
```

```
{
    public partial class WizardPage1: Page
    {
        Vitals vitals;

        // Constructors.
        public WizardPage1(Vitals vitals)
        {
            InitializeComponent();
            this.vitals = vitals;
        }
        // Event handlers for Previous and Back buttons.
        void PreviousButtonOnClick(object sender, RoutedEventArgs args)
        {
            NavigationService.GoBack();
        }
        void NextButtonOnClick(object sender, RoutedEventArgs args)
        {
            vitals.Name = txtboxName.Text;
            vitals.Home =
                Vitals.GetCheckedRadioButton(grpboxHome).Content as string;
            vitals.Gender =
                Vitals.GetCheckedRadioButton(grpboxGender).Content as string;

            if (NavigationService.CanGoForward)
                NavigationService.GoForward();
            else
            {
                WizardPage2 page = new WizardPage2(vitals);
                NavigationService.Navigate(page);
            }
        }
    }
}
```

The Previous button is handled by a simple call to *GoBack*. The event handler is very sure that *GoBack* will always return to WizardPage0.xaml because that's the route taken to arrive at WizardPage1.xaml.

The event handler for the Next button obtains user input from the page and stores that information in the *Vitals* object. This event handler is the last opportunity to get this information directly from the page. It could be that the user will return to this page, but the only way to continue the wizard is to click the Next button again, at which time the event handler will store any updated items.

The Next handler then navigates to the *WizardPage2* class in the same way that *WizardPage0* navigated to *WizardPage1*. However, notice that the event handler can make some decisions here based on the inputted values. Perhaps there are separate routes through the wizard, depending on the user's selection in one of the groups of radio buttons.

The *WizardPage2* class begins with a XAML file, of course.

WizardPage2.xaml

```xml
<!-- =========================================
       WizardPage2.xaml (c) 2006 by Charles Petzold
     ========================================= -->
<Page xmlns="http://schemas.microsoft.com/winfx/2006/xaml/presentation"
      xmlns:x="http://schemas.microsoft.com/winfx/2006/xaml"
      x:Class="Petzold.ComputerDatingWizard.WizardPage2">
    <Grid>
        <Grid.RowDefinitions>
            <RowDefinition Height="Auto" />
            <RowDefinition Height="Auto" />
            <RowDefinition Height="Auto" />
            <RowDefinition Height="Auto" />
            <RowDefinition Height="Auto" />
            <RowDefinition Height="*" />
            <RowDefinition Height="Auto" />
        </Grid.RowDefinitions>

        <!-- TextBox for favorite operating system. -->
        <TextBlock Grid.Row="0" Margin="0, 12, 0, 0">
            Favorite operating system:
        </TextBlock>
        <TextBox Grid.Row="1" Name="txtboxFavoriteOS"
                 Text="Microsoft Windows Vista, of course!" />

        <!-- TextBox for favorite disk directory. -->
        <TextBlock Grid.Row="2" Margin="0, 12, 0, 0">
            Favorite disk directory:
        </TextBlock>
        <TextBox Grid.Row="3" Name="txtboxFavoriteDir"
                 Text="C:\"/>
        <Button Grid.Row="4" Click="BrowseButtonOnClick"
            HorizontalAlignment="Right"
            MinWidth="72" Margin="0, 2, 0, 0"
            Content="Browse..." />

        <!-- Navigation buttons at bottom-right corner of page. -->
        <Grid Grid.Row="6">
            <Grid.ColumnDefinitions>
                <ColumnDefinition Width="*" />
                <ColumnDefinition Width="Auto" />
                <ColumnDefinition Width="Auto" />
            </Grid.ColumnDefinitions>
            <Button Grid.Column="1" Click="PreviousButtonOnClick"
                MinWidth="72" Margin="6"
                Content="&lt; Previous" />
            <Button Grid.Column="2" Click="NextButtonOnClick"
                MinWidth="72" Margin="6"
                Content="Next &gt;" />
        </Grid>
    </Grid>
</Page>
```

This page is a little different. It has the normal Previous and Next buttons, but it also has a *TextBox* for the user's favorite disk directory together with a button labeled Browse. It's likely the user will surmise that clicking this Browse button will invoke a window or page containing a *TreeView* control. The user can then pick a favorite directory rather than laboriously typing it.

Clicking the Browse button is optional, so it functions as a little side excursion from the main journey through the wizard. The Browse button could be handled in one of two ways: You could display a modal dialog box that would appear as a separate window on top of the *ComputerDatingWizard* window, or you could implement it in a *Page* class that the program navigates to just like the regular wizard pages. I chose the latter approach.

The window or page invoked by the Browse button must return a value. In this case, a value of *DirectoryInfo* would be appropriate. The value must be returned to the code in *WizardPage2* so that *WizardPage2* can then fill in the *TextBox* with the selected disk directory. If you use a dialog box, you can define a property for this information and signal whether the user clicked OK or Cancel by setting the normal *DialogResult* property. You could also define a *Directory-Info* property in a *Page* class, of course, but returning from the page is a little more complicated. You want to remove this little side excursion from the journal so that clicking the Next button on WizardPage2.xaml doesn't execute a *GoForward* that puts the user back in the *TreeView* page selecting a favorite disk directory.

This process is facilitated by a class that derives from *Page* named *PageFunction* . The purpose of *PageFunction* is to display a page that returns a value. The class is generic: You define the type of the data the class returns in the definition of your *PageFunction* class. *PageFunction* also takes care of altering the journal so that the side excursion doesn't inadvertently repeat itself.

The class that I derived from *PageFunction* to display the *TreeView* is named *DirectoryPage* because it returns an object of type *DirectoryInfo*. Here's the DirectoryPage.xaml file.

DirectoryPage.xaml

```
<!-- =================================================
     DirectoryPage.xaml (c) 2006 by Charles Petzold
     ================================================= -->
<PageFunction xmlns="http://schemas.microsoft.com/winfx/2006/xaml/presentation"
              xmlns:x="http://schemas.microsoft.com/winfx/2006/xaml"
              xmlns:io="clr-namespace:System.IO;assembly=mscorlib"
              xmlns:tree="clr-namespace:Petzold.RecurseDirectoriesIncrementally"
              x:Class="Petzold.ComputerDatingWizard.DirectoryPage"
              x:TypeArguments="io:DirectoryInfo">
    <Grid>
        <Grid.RowDefinitions>
            <RowDefinition Height="Auto" />
            <RowDefinition Height="*" />
            <RowDefinition Height="Auto" />
```

```
        </Grid.RowDefinitions>

        <TextBlock Grid.Row="0" FontSize="16" FontStyle="Italic"
                   HorizontalAlignment="Center">
            Computer Dating Wizard
        </TextBlock>

        <tree:DirectoryTreeView x:Name="treevue" Grid.Row="1" />

        <!-- Buttons at bottom-right corner of page. -->
        <Grid Grid.Row="2">
            <Grid.ColumnDefinitions>
                <ColumnDefinition Width="*" />
                <ColumnDefinition Width="Auto" />
                <ColumnDefinition Width="Auto" />
            </Grid.ColumnDefinitions>
            <Button Grid.Column="1" Click="CancelButtonOnClick"
                    IsCancel="True" MinWidth="60" Margin="6">
                Cancel
            </Button>
            <Button Grid.Column="2" Name="btnOk" Click="OkButtonOnClick"
                    IsEnabled="False" IsDefault="True" MinWidth="60" Margin="6">
                OK
            </Button>
        </Grid>
    </Grid>
</PageFunction>
```

Notice that the *x:Class* attribute on the root element defines the name of the class as usual, but because *PageFunction* is a generic class, the root element also requires an *x:TypeArguments* attribute to indicate the generic type, in this case *DirectoryInfo*. A namespace declaration for *System.IO* (in which *DirectoryInfo* is defined) is required for the namespace prefix. Another namespace declaration associates the *tree* prefix with the namespace of the RecurseDirectories-Incrementally project from Chapter 16. That's where the *DirectoryTreeView* class comes from that forms the bulk of this page. The *PageFunction* concludes with buttons labeled "Cancel" and "OK."

Here's the DirectoryPage.cs file that completes the *DirectoryPage* class.

DirectoryPage.cs

```
//-------------------------------------------
// DirectoryPage.cs (c) 2006 by Charles Petzold
//-------------------------------------------
using Petzold.RecurseDirectoriesIncrementally;
using System;
using System.IO;
using System.Windows;
using System.Windows.Controls;
using System.Windows.Navigation;

namespace Petzold.ComputerDatingWizard
```

```
{
    public partial class DirectoryPage : PageFunction<DirectoryInfo>
    {
        // Constructor.
        public DirectoryPage()
        {
            InitializeComponent();
            treevue.SelectedItemChanged += TreeViewOnSelectedItemChanged;
        }
        // Event handler to enable OK button.
        void TreeViewOnSelectedItemChanged(object sender,
                        RoutedPropertyChangedEventArgs<object> args)
        {
            btnOk.IsEnabled = args.NewValue != null;
        }
        // Event handlers for Cancel and OK.
        void CancelButtonOnClick(object sender, RoutedEventArgs args)
        {
            OnReturn(new ReturnEventArgs<DirectoryInfo>());
        }
        void OkButtonOnClick(object sender, RoutedEventArgs args)
        {
            DirectoryInfo dirinfo =
                (treevue.SelectedItem as DirectoryTreeViewItem).DirectoryInfo;

            OnReturn(new ReturnEventArgs<DirectoryInfo>(dirinfo));
        }
    }
}
```

The constructor attaches a *SelectionChanged* event handler to the *DirectoryTreeView* control so that the OK button is enabled only if a disk directory has been selected. It would also be possible for the constructor to have an argument so that the *PageFunction* derivative could initialize itself based on information from the invoking page.

A class derived from *PageFunction* terminates by calling *OnReturn* with an argument of type *ReturnEventArgs*, another generic class that requires the type of object the *PageFunction* derivative is returning. The object itself is passed to the *ReturnEventArgs* constructor. Notice that the event handler for the Cancel button doesn't pass an argument to the *ReturnEventArgs* constructor. When the *PageFunction* is finished, it automatically removes itself from the journal, as indicated by the default *true* value of its *RemoveFromJournal* property.

The *WizardPage2* class has the *Click* event handler for the Browse button that navigates to the *DirectoryPage*, as shown in the WizardPage2.cs code-behind file.

WizardPage2.cs

```
//------------------------------------------
// WizardPage2.cs (c) 2006 by Charles Petzold
//------------------------------------------
using System;
using System.IO;
```

```
using System.Windows;
using System.Windows.Controls;
using System.Windows.Navigation;

namespace Petzold.ComputerDatingWizard
{
    public partial class WizardPage2
    {
        Vitals vitals;

        // Constructor.
        public WizardPage2(Vitals vitals)
        {
            InitializeComponent();
            this.vitals = vitals;
        }

        // Event handlers for optional Browse button.
        void BrowseButtonOnClick(object sender, RoutedEventArgs args)
        {
            DirectoryPage page = new DirectoryPage();
            page.Return += DirPageOnReturn;
            NavigationService.Navigate(page);
        }
        void DirPageOnReturn(object sender, ReturnEventArgs<DirectoryInfo> args)
        {
            if (args.Result != null)
                txtboxFavoriteDir.Text = args.Result.FullName;
        }
        // Event handlers for Previous and Back buttons.
        void PreviousButtonOnClick(object sender, RoutedEventArgs args)
        {
            NavigationService.GoBack();
        }
        void NextButtonOnClick(object sender, RoutedEventArgs args)
        {
            vitals.FavoriteOS = txtboxFavoriteOS.Text;
            vitals.Directory = txtboxFavoriteDir.Text;

            if (NavigationService.CanGoForward)
                NavigationService.GoForward();
            else
            {
                WizardPage3 page = new WizardPage3(vitals);
                NavigationService.Navigate(page);
            }
        }
    }
}
```

When the user clicks the *Browse* button, the event handler creates a *DirectoryPage* object, sets a handler for the *Return* event, and navigates to that page. The handler for the *Return* event obtains the value returned from the *PageFunction* from the *Result* property of the *Return-*

EventArgs argument to the handler. For the *PageFunction* derivative *DirectoryPage*, that *Result* property is an object of type *DirectoryInfo*. It will be *null* if the user ended the page by clicking Cancel; otherwise it indicates the user's favorite directory. The event handler transfers the directory name into the *TextBox*.

The remainder of WizardPage2.cs is normal. The handler for the Next button saves the user's input and goes on to WizardPage3.xaml.

The WizardPage3.xaml page is very much like WizardPage1.xaml except that the Next button is replaced by Finish, indicating that this is the last page of input. As usual, the XAML file defines the layout of controls and buttons.

WizardPage3.xaml

```xml
<!-- =============================================
        WizardPage3.xaml (c) 2006 by Charles Petzold
     ============================================= -->
<Page xmlns="http://schemas.microsoft.com/winfx/2006/xaml/presentation"
      xmlns:x="http://schemas.microsoft.com/winfx/2006/xaml"
      x:Class="Petzold.ComputerDatingWizard.WizardPage3">
    <Grid>
        <Grid.RowDefinitions>
            <RowDefinition Height="Auto" />
            <RowDefinition Height="Auto" />
            <RowDefinition Height="*" />
            <RowDefinition Height="Auto" />
        </Grid.RowDefinitions>
        <Grid.ColumnDefinitions>
            <ColumnDefinition Width="50*" />
            <ColumnDefinition Width="50*" />
        </Grid.ColumnDefinitions>

        <!-- TextBox for mother's maiden name. -->
        <StackPanel Orientation="Horizontal" Grid.ColumnSpan="2"
                    Margin="12">
            <Label>
                Mother's Maiden Name:
            </Label>
            <TextBox Name="txtboxMom" Width="100" />
        </StackPanel>

        <!-- GroupBox for pet. -->
        <GroupBox Grid.Row="1" Grid.Column="0" Name="grpboxPet"
                  Header="Favorite Pet" Margin="12">
            <StackPanel>
                <RadioButton Content="Dog" Margin="6" IsChecked="True" />
                <RadioButton Content="Cat" Margin="6" />
                <RadioButton Content="Iguana" Margin="6" />
            </StackPanel>
        </GroupBox>

        <!-- GroupBox for income level. -->
        <GroupBox Grid.Row="1" Grid.Column="1" Name="grpboxIncome"
```

```
                        Header="Income Level" Margin="12">
                <StackPanel>
                    <RadioButton Content="Rich" Margin="6" IsChecked="True" />
                    <RadioButton Content="So-so" Margin="6" />
                    <RadioButton Content="Freelancer" Margin="6" />
                </StackPanel>
            </GroupBox>

            <!-- Navigation buttons at bottom-right corner of page. -->
            <Grid Grid.Row="3" Grid.ColumnSpan="2">
                <Grid.ColumnDefinitions>
                    <ColumnDefinition Width="*" />
                    <ColumnDefinition Width="Auto" />
                    <ColumnDefinition Width="Auto" />
                </Grid.ColumnDefinitions>
                <Button Grid.Column="1" Click="PreviousButtonOnClick"
                    MinWidth="72" Margin="6"
                    Content="&lt; Previous" />
                <Button Grid.Column="2" Click="FinishButtonOnClick"
                    MinWidth="72" Margin="6"
                    Content="Finish &gt;" />
            </Grid>
        </Grid>
    </Grid>
</Page>
```

The code-behind file for *WizardPage3* is shown here.

WizardPage3.cs
```
//-------------------------------------------
// WizardPage3.cs (c) 2006 by Charles Petzold
//-------------------------------------------
using System;
using System.Windows;
using System.Windows.Controls;

namespace Petzold.ComputerDatingWizard
{
    public partial class WizardPage3: Page
    {
        Vitals vitals;

        // Constructor.
        public WizardPage3(Vitals vitals)
        {
            InitializeComponent();
            this.vitals = vitals;
        }
        // Event handlers for Previous and Finish buttons.
        void PreviousButtonOnClick(object sender, RoutedEventArgs args)
        {
            NavigationService.GoBack();
        }
        void FinishButtonOnClick(object sender, RoutedEventArgs args)
```

```
        {
            // Save information from this page.
            vitals.MomsMaidenName = txtboxMom.Text;
            vitals.Pet =
                Vitals.GetCheckedRadioButton(grpboxPet).Content as string;
            vitals.Income =
                Vitals.GetCheckedRadioButton(grpboxIncome).Content as string;

            // Always re-create the final page.
            WizardPage4 page = new WizardPage4(vitals);
            NavigationService.Navigate(page);
        }
    }
}
```

As usual, the event handler for the Next button (here called the Finish button) pulls user input from the page and stores it in the *Vitals* object. However, rather than determining whether it can call *GoForward* to navigate to the last page, this event handler always re-creates an object of type *WizardPage4* before navigating there. You'll see why shortly.

The last page is based on the *WizardPage4* class and simply displays all the information accumulated in the wizard. I choose a fairly simple approach to displaying textual information by defining a bunch of *Run* objects that are part of the same *TextBlock* element.

WizardPage4.xaml

```xml
<!-- ================================================
     WizardPage4.xaml (c) 2006 by Charles Petzold
     ================================================ -->
<Page xmlns="http://schemas.microsoft.com/winfx/2006/xaml/presentation"
      xmlns:x="http://schemas.microsoft.com/winfx/2006/xaml"
      x:Class="Petzold.ComputerDatingWizard.WizardPage4">

    <Grid>
        <Grid.RowDefinitions>
            <RowDefinition Height="Auto" />
            <RowDefinition Height="*" />
            <RowDefinition Height="Auto" />
        </Grid.RowDefinitions>

        <TextBlock Grid.Row="0">
            <LineBreak />
            <Run Text="Name: " />
            <Run Name="runName" />
            <LineBreak />
            <Run Text="Home: " />
            <Run Name="runHome" />
            <LineBreak />
            <Run Text="Gender: " />
            <Run Name="runGender" />
            <LineBreak />
            <Run Text="Favorite OS: " />
            <Run Name="runOS" />
```

```
                <LineBreak />
                <Run Text="Favorite Directory: " />
                <Run Name="runDirectory" />
                <LineBreak />
                <Run Text="Mother's Maiden Name: " />
                <Run Name="runMomsMaidenName" />
                <LineBreak />
                <Run Text="Favorite Pet: " />
                <Run Name="runPet" />
                <LineBreak />
                <Run Text="Income Level: " />
                <Run Name="runIncome" />
            </TextBlock>

            <!-- Navigation button at bottom-right corner of page. -->
            <Grid Grid.Row="2">
                <Grid.ColumnDefinitions>
                    <ColumnDefinition Width="*" />
                    <ColumnDefinition Width="Auto" />
                    <ColumnDefinition Width="Auto" />
                </Grid.ColumnDefinitions>
                <Button Grid.Column="1" Click="PreviousButtonOnClick"
                    MinWidth="72" Margin="6"
                    Content="&lt; Previous" />
                <Button Grid.Column="2" Click="SubmitButtonOnClick"
                    MinWidth="72" Margin="6"
                    Content="Submit!" />
            </Grid>
        </Grid>
    </Grid>
</Page>
```

The two buttons are now labeled "Previous" and "Submit." The user is allowed to go back and change something after viewing this information. The code-behind file completes the *WizardPage4* class.

WizardPage4.cs
```
//-------------------------------------------
// WizardPage4.cs (c) 2006 by Charles Petzold
//-------------------------------------------
using System;
using System.Windows;
using System.Windows.Controls;

namespace Petzold.ComputerDatingWizard
{
    public partial class WizardPage4: Page
    {
        // Constructor.
        public WizardPage4(Vitals vitals)
        {
            InitializeComponent();

            // Set text in the page.
```

```
            runName.Text = vitals.Name;
            runHome.Text = vitals.Home;
            runGender.Text = vitals.Gender;
            runOS.Text = vitals.FavoriteOS;
            runDirectory.Text = vitals.Directory;
            runMomsMaidenName.Text = vitals.MomsMaidenName;
            runPet.Text = vitals.Pet;
            runIncome.Text = vitals.Income;
        }
        // Event handlers for Previous and Submit buttons.
        void PreviousButtonOnClick(object sender, RoutedEventArgs args)
        {
            NavigationService.GoBack();
        }
        void SubmitButtonOnClick(object sender, RoutedEventArgs args)
        {
            MessageBox.Show("Thank you!\n\nYou will be contacted by email " +
                            "in four to six months.",
                            Application.Current.MainWindow.Title,
                            MessageBoxButton.OK, MessageBoxImage.Exclamation);
            Application.Current.Shutdown();
        }
    }
}
```

As you can see, the *WizardPage4* class uses its constructor to set all the *Run* objects on the page with the final results of the *Vitals* class. This is why the *WizardPage3* class re-creates the *WizardPage4* object whenever it navigates to it. If the user decides to click the Previous button and change something, the *WizardPage4* object must display the new information, and the most convenient place to do that is its constructor. (If you'd prefer, you can let the *Page* class be created only once and then set the information in the *Loaded* event handler, which is called whenever the page is displayed.)

Clicking Submit concludes the wizard (but doesn't get you a date).

Although wizards require significant code to accompany the XAML files, some navigation applications need no code at all. Using Windows Explorer, take a look at the BookReader directory of Chapter 22 of the companion content for this book. You'll find a collection of XAML files that include a few paragraphs from a few chapters of two books by Lewis Carroll. Launch the BookReaderPage.xaml file, which is shown here.

BookReaderPage.xaml

```
<!-- =====================
     BookReaderPage.xaml
     ===================== -->
<Page xmlns="http://schemas.microsoft.com/winfx/2006/xaml/presentation"
      WindowTitle="Book Reader">
    <Grid>
        <Grid.RowDefinitions>
            <RowDefinition Height="10*" />
```

```
                    <RowDefinition Height="Auto" />
                    <RowDefinition Height="90*" />
                </Grid.RowDefinitions>

                <!-- Frame for list of books. -->
                <Frame Grid.Row="0" Source="BookList.xaml" />

                <GridSplitter Grid.Row="1" Height="6"
                              HorizontalAlignment="Stretch"
                              VerticalAlignment="Center" />

                <Grid Grid.Row="2">
                    <Grid.ColumnDefinitions>
                        <ColumnDefinition Width="25*" />
                        <ColumnDefinition Width="Auto" />
                        <ColumnDefinition Width="75*" />
                    </Grid.ColumnDefinitions>

                    <!-- Frame for table of contents. -->
                    <Frame Grid.Column="0" Name="frameContents" />

                    <GridSplitter Grid.Column="1" Width="6"
                                  HorizontalAlignment="Center"
                                  VerticalAlignment="Stretch" />

                    <!-- Frame for the actual text. -->
                    <Frame Grid.Column="2" Name="frameChapter" />
                </Grid>
            </Grid>
        </Page>
```

When you launch this file, Internet Explorer displays the page. The two *Grid* panels divide the page into three areas separated by splitters. Each area is occupied by a *Frame* control. The *Frame* at the left has the name *frameContents*. The *Frame* at the right has the name *frame-Chapter*. The *Frame* at the top has its *Source* property set to BookList.xaml, which is the *Page* file shown here.

BookList.xaml

```
<!-- ================
        BookList.xaml
     ================ -->
<Page xmlns="http://schemas.microsoft.com/winfx/2006/xaml/presentation">
    <WrapPanel TextBlock.FontSize="10pt">
        <TextBlock Margin="12">
            <Hyperlink NavigateUri="AliceInWonderland.xaml"
                    TargetName="frameContents">
                <Italic>Alice's Adventures in Wonderland</Italic> by Lewis Carroll
            </Hyperlink>
        </TextBlock>
        <TextBlock Margin="12">
            <Hyperlink NavigateUri="ThroughTheLookingGlass.xaml"
                    TargetName="frameContents">
```

```
            <Italic>Through the Looking-Glass</Italic> by Lewis Carroll
        </Hyperlink>
      </TextBlock>
      <TextBlock Margin="12">
        ...
      </TextBlock>
    </WrapPanel>
  </Page>
```

The two *Hyperlink* elements contain not only *NavigateUri* attributes that reference two XAML files, but also *TargetName* attributes that reference the *Frame* at the left of the BookList.xaml page. This is how a *Hyperlink* can deposit a XAML page in another *Frame*.

The AliceInWonderland.xaml file and ThroughTheLookingGlass.xaml files are very similar. Here's the first:

AliceInWonderland.xaml

```
<!-- =======================
      AliceInWonderland.xaml
     ======================= -->
<Page xmlns="http://schemas.microsoft.com/winfx/2006/xaml/presentation"
      Title="Alice's Adventures in Wonderland">
    <StackPanel TextBlock.FontSize="10pt">
        <TextBlock Margin="12 12 12 6">
            <Hyperlink NavigateUri="AliceChapter01.xaml"
                        TargetName="frameChapter">
                Chapter I
            </Hyperlink>
        </TextBlock>
        <TextBlock Margin="12 6 12 6">
            <Hyperlink NavigateUri="AliceChapter02.xaml"
                        TargetName="frameChapter">
                Chapter II
            </Hyperlink>
        </TextBlock>
        <TextBlock Margin="12 6 12 6">
            <Hyperlink NavigateUri="AliceChapter03.xaml"
                        TargetName="frameChapter">
                Chapter III
            </Hyperlink>
        </TextBlock>
        <TextBlock Margin="12 6 12 6">
            ...
        </TextBlock>
    </StackPanel>
</Page>
```

This is another *Page* that contains several *Hyperlink* elements. The *NavigateUri* attributes reference individual chapters, and the *TargetName* indicates that they should be displayed by the *Frame* at the right of the original page. Here's AliceChapter01.xaml.

AliceChapter01.xaml

```xml
<!-- ====================
     AliceChapter01.xaml
     ==================== -->
<Page xmlns="http://schemas.microsoft.com/winfx/2006/xaml/presentation"
      Title="I. Down the Rabbit-Hole">
    <FlowDocumentReader>
        <FlowDocument>
            <Paragraph TextAlignment="Center" FontSize="16pt">
                Chapter I
            </Paragraph>
            <Paragraph TextAlignment="Center" FontSize="16pt">
                Down the Rabbit-Hole
            </Paragraph>
            <Paragraph TextIndent="24">
                Alice was beginning to get very tired of sitting by
                her sister on the bank, and of having nothing to do:
                once or twice she had peeped into the book her sister
                was reading, but it had no pictures or conversations
                in it, &#x201C;and what is the use of a book,&#x201D;
                thought Alice, &#x201C;without pictures or
                conversations?&#x201D;
            </Paragraph>
            <Paragraph TextIndent="24">
                So she was considering, in her own mind (as well as
                she could, for the hot day made her feel very sleepy
                and stupid), whether the pleasure of making a
                daisy-chain would be worth the trouble of getting up
                and picking the daisies, when suddenly a white
                Rabbit with pink eyes ran close by her.
            </Paragraph>
            <Paragraph TextIndent="24">
                There was nothing so <Italic>very</Italic>
                remarkable in that; nor did Alice think it so
                <Italic>very</Italic> much out of the way to hear the
                Rabbit say to itself &#x201C;Oh dear! Oh dear! I
                shall be too late!&#x201D; (when she thought it over
                afterwards, it occurred to her that she ought to have
                wondered at this, but at the time it all seemed quite
                natural); but, when the Rabbit actually <Italic>took
                a watch out of its waistcoat-pocket</Italic>, and
                looked at it, and then hurried on, Alice started to
                her feet, for it flashed across her mind that she
                had never seen a rabbit with either a waistcoat-pocket,
                or a watch to take out of it, and, burning with
                curiosity, she ran across the field after it, and was
                just in time to see it pop down a large rabbit-hole
                under the hedge.
            </Paragraph>
            <Paragraph TextIndent="24">
                In another moment down went Alice after it, never once
                considering how in the world she was to get out again.
            </Paragraph>
            <Paragraph TextIndent="24">
```

```
                ...
           </Paragraph>
         </FlowDocument>
      </FlowDocumentReader>
   </Page>
```

So, when you click one of the book titles in the top frame, the contents of that book are displayed in the left frame. When you click one of the chapters in the left frame, the contents of that chapter are displayed in the right frame.

This collection of XAML files also includes an example of fragment navigation, which is similar to HTML bookmarks. The first chapter of *Through the Looking-Glass* includes the poem "Jabberwocky." The title of the poem is its own paragraph, which appears in the LookingGlassChapter01.xaml file like this:

```
<Paragraph ... Name="Jabberwocky">
    Jabberwocky
</Paragraph>
```

The presence of the *Name* attribute allows navigation to that element within the page. The ThroughTheLookingGlass.xaml chapter list also includes an entry for "Jabberwocky" and navigates to that poem by separating the file name and the text in the *Name* attribute with a number sign:

```
<Hyperlink NavigateUri="LookingGlassChapter01.xaml#Jabberwocky"
           TargetName="frameChapter">
    "Jabberwocky"
</Hyperlink>
```

When organizing data into pages, some other controls might be useful. The *TabControl* derives from *Selector* and maintains a collection of *TabItem* controls. *TabItem* derives from *Headered-ContentControl* and the content of each *TabItem* occupies the same area of the page. The *Header* property is a tab, and the user selects which *TabItem* to view by clicking the tab. By default these tabs are arranged horizontally across the top, but that's changeable by the *TabStripPlacement* property. (I use *TabControl* in the TextGeometryDemo program in Chapter 28.

Another useful control of this sort is the *Expander*, which also derives from *HeaderedContent-Control*. In the case of the *Expander*, the content is toggled between visible and collapsed by clicking the header. Often the content contains hyperlinks much like the list of chapters in the AliceInWonderland.xaml file.

Although launching the BookReaderPage.xaml file successfully allows you to browse the various books and chapters that are part of the project, it only works because all the files are in the same directory and that's the current directory associated with Internet Explorer when you launch the BookReaderPage.xaml file. It might be preferable to package all the XAML files together into one executable, and of course that's certainly possible. The XAML files you've been looking at are part of a project named BookReader, and the project also contains the BookReaderApp.xaml application definition file.

BookReaderApp.xaml

```
<!-- =================================================
        BookReaderApp.xaml (c) 2006 by Charles Petzold
     ================================================= -->
<Application xmlns="http://schemas.microsoft.com/winfx/2006/xaml/presentation"
             StartupUri="BookReaderPage.xaml" />
```

This file simply starts the BookReaderPage.xaml file, which is the same file you launched from Windows Explorer.

The BookReader project is a normal WPF application project containing only XAML files, and when you build the project, you get a BookReader.exe file, and when you run that file you'll see a *NavigationWindow* hosting the XAML files. Where did that *NavigationWindow* come from? None of these XAML files makes any reference to a *NavigationWindow*. It turns out that when the application definition file has a *StartupUri* of a XAML file with a root element of *Page*, a *NavigationWindow* is automatically created to host the page.

So now you've seen how Internet Explorer can host the BookReaderPage.xaml file just by launching the XAML file from Windows Explorer, and how the XAML files can be compiled into BookReader.exe, which automatically creates a *NavigationWindow* to host BookReaderPage.xaml page.

There is a third option, and that's the XAML Browser Application. The easiest way to create a XAML Browser Application is with Visual Studio. In the collection of projects that comprise Chapter 22, I used Visual Studio to create a XAML Browser Application named BookReader2. I deleted the MyApp.xaml, MyApp.cs, Page1.xaml, and Page1.cs files that Visual Studio created for me and instead added links in the project for all the XAML files in BookReader, making sure to flag BookReaderApp.xaml as the application definition file.

The BookReader and BookReader2 projects contain all the same XAML source code files, but when you build the BookReader2 project, Visual Studio creates a file named BookReader2.xbap. The extension stands for XAML Browser Application. When Visual Studio launches this file, PresentationHost.exe takes over. This is the same program that lets Internet Explorer host stand-alone XAML files. Internet Explorer can host the XAML Browser Application as well, and it looks the same as when it hosts the individual XAML files. The *NavigationWindow* created by BookReader.exe is no longer present.

Although the file that launches the application is BookReader2.xbap, two other files must also be present: BookReader2.exe and BookReader2.exe.manifest. (The file with the extension of .exe is not a stand-alone executable, however.)

Because XAML Browser Applications are hosted in the Web browser, there are certain limitations to what they can do. These programs cannot create objects of type *Window* or *Navigation-Window*. They are essentially organized around *Page* objects. If necessary, they move from page to page through navigation. XAML Browser Applications can have menus, but they cannot create dialog boxes or objects of type *Popup*. These programs run with security permissions associated with the Internet zone. They cannot use the file system.

On the other hand, these applications are very easy to run from a Web site. To install a XAML Browser Application on your Web site, use Visual Studio to bring up the project properties, click the Publish tab on the left, and in the Publishing Location field, type the FTP address you normally use for copying files to your site. You'll probably include the directory that contains the HTML page you want to run the application from, and an additional directory named after the application. Click the Publish Now button. You'll be asked for your FTP user name and password as Visual Studio copies the various files to your Web site. Now you can include a link on a Web page to the .xbap file. Users who have the .NET Framework 3.0 installed who click that link will download and run the application without requiring any permissions. However, the application is not automatically installed on the user's computer.

It's probably best if you decide early on whether a particular application should be a full-fledged Windows application or a XAML Browser Application, because they tend to be structured very differently. XAML Browser Application can't use popups or dialog boxes, so they're usually structured as navigation applications. Although XAML Browser Applications are inherently limited in comparison to Windows applications, the navigational structure may suggest different types of program features. You may discover that what appear to be limitations may turn out to be opportunities.

The last program I want to show you in this chapter is a case in point. I decided to make a XAML Browser Application version of the PlayJeuDeTacquin program from Chapter 7. In the process of altering the original program to turn it into a XAML Browser Application, a feature came to mind that had never occurred to me before.

The new project is named simply JeuDeTacquin. It begins with an application definition file.

JeuDeTacquinApp.xaml

```
<!-- =================================================
        JeuDeTacquinApp.xaml (c) 2006 by Charles Petzold
     ================================================= -->
<Application xmlns="http://schemas.microsoft.com/winfx/2006/xaml/presentation"
             xmlns:x="http://schemas.microsoft.com/winfx/2006/xaml"
             x:Class="Petzold.JeuDeTacquin.JeuDeTacquinApp"
             StartupUri="JeuDeTacquin.xaml">
</Application>
```

The JeuDeTacquin.xaml file has a root element of *Page*, as is normal for XAML Browser Applications, and the file describes the layout of the page. I gave the program a big title, a *UniformGrid* object named *unigrid*, and two buttons labeled Scramble and Next Larger.

JeuDeTacquin.xaml

```
<!-- =================================================
        JeuDeTacquin.xaml (c) 2006 by Charles Petzold
     ================================================= -->
<Page xmlns="http://schemas.microsoft.com/winfx/2006/xaml/presentation"
      xmlns:x="http://schemas.microsoft.com/winfx/2006/xaml"
      x:Class="Petzold.JeuDeTacquin.JeuDeTacquin"
      WindowTitle="Jeu de Tacquin"
      Background="LightGray"
      Focusable="True"
      KeepAlive="True">
    <Grid HorizontalAlignment="Center" VerticalAlignment="Center"
          Background="LightGray">
        <Grid.RowDefinitions>
            <RowDefinition Height="Auto" />
            <RowDefinition Height="Auto" />
            <RowDefinition Height="Auto" />
            <RowDefinition Height="Auto" />
        </Grid.RowDefinitions>
        <TextBlock Grid.Row="0" FontFamily="Garamond"
                   FontSize="96" FontStyle="Italic" Margin="12">
            Jeu de Tacquin
        </TextBlock>
        <Border Grid.Row="1" BorderBrush="Black" BorderThickness = "1"
                HorizontalAlignment="Center" VerticalAlignment="Center">

            <UniformGrid Name="unigrid" />

        </Border>
        <Button Grid.Row="2" HorizontalAlignment="Left" Margin="12"
                MinWidth="1in" Click="ScrambleOnClick">
            Scramble
        </Button>
        <Button Grid.Row="2" HorizontalAlignment="Right" Margin="12"
                MinWidth="1in" Click="NextOnClick">
            Next Larger >>
        </Button>

        <TextBlock Grid.Row="3"
                   HorizontalAlignment="Center" VerticalAlignment="Center"
                   Margin="12">
            (c) 2006 by Charles Petzold
        </TextBlock>
    </Grid>
</Page>
```

The *JeuDeTacquin* class is completed with the following code-behind file. The two fields that indicate the number of rows and columns are no longer constants, and an additional field named *isLoaded* is defined. The constructor installs an event handler for the *Loaded* event and calls *InitializeComponent*. Recall that the *Loaded* event is fired whenever a *Page* appears as the subject of a navigation.

The *WindowOnLoaded* event handler initializes the *UniformGrid* with *Tile* objects and an *Empty* object. (This project includes links to Tile.cs and Empty.cs from the original PlayJeu-DeTacquin project.) Notice that it sets the *Title* property of the *Page* to the text "Jeu de Tacquin" with the number of rows and columns in parentheses. This is the text that appears in the Back and Forward journal lists. The *PageOnLoaded* event handler also sets the *isLoaded* field to *true* so that this initialization isn't performed again for the same *Page* object.

JeuDeTacquin.xaml.cs

```
//------------------------------------------
// JeuDeTacquin.cs (c) 2006 by Charles Petzold
//------------------------------------------
using Petzold.PlayJeuDeTacquin;
using System;
using System.Windows;
using System.Windows.Controls;
using System.Windows.Controls.Primitives;
using System.Windows.Input;
using System.Windows.Media;
using System.Windows.Threading;

namespace Petzold.JeuDeTacquin
{
    public partial class JeuDeTacquin : Page
    {
        public int NumberRows = 4;
        public int NumberCols = 4;
        bool isLoaded = false;

        int xEmpty, yEmpty, iCounter;
        Key[] keys = { Key.Left, Key.Right, Key.Up, Key.Down };
        Random rand;
        UIElement elEmptySpare = new Empty();

        public JeuDeTacquin()
        {
            Loaded += PageOnLoaded;
            InitializeComponent();
        }
        void PageOnLoaded(object sender, RoutedEventArgs args)
        {
            if (!isLoaded)
            {
                Title = String.Format("Jeu de Tacquin ({0}\x00D7{1})",
                                  NumberCols, NumberRows);

                unigrid.Rows = NumberRows;
                unigrid.Columns = NumberCols;
```

```
                    // Create Tile objects to fill all but one cell.
                    for (int i = 0; i < NumberRows * NumberCols - 1; i++)
                    {
                        Tile tile = new Tile();
                        tile.Text = (i + 1).ToString();
                        tile.MouseLeftButtonDown += TileOnMouseLeftButtonDown; ;
                        unigrid.Children.Add(tile);
                    }
                    // Create Empty object to fill the last cell.
                    unigrid.Children.Add(new Empty());
                    xEmpty = NumberCols - 1;
                    yEmpty = NumberRows - 1;

                    isLoaded = true;
                }
            Focus();
        }
        void TileOnMouseLeftButtonDown(object sender, MouseButtonEventArgs args)
        {
            Focus();

            Tile tile = sender as Tile;

            int iMove = unigrid.Children.IndexOf(tile);
            int xMove = iMove % NumberCols;
            int yMove = iMove / NumberCols;

            if (xMove == xEmpty)
                while (yMove != yEmpty)
                    MoveTile(xMove, yEmpty + (yMove - yEmpty) /
                                        Math.Abs(yMove - yEmpty));
            if (yMove == yEmpty)
                while (xMove != xEmpty)
                    MoveTile(xEmpty + (xMove - xEmpty) /
                                        Math.Abs(xMove - xEmpty), yMove);
            args.Handled = true;
        }
        protected override void OnKeyDown(KeyEventArgs args)
        {
            base.OnKeyDown(args);

            switch (args.Key)
            {
                case Key.Right: MoveTile(xEmpty - 1, yEmpty);  break;
                case Key.Left:  MoveTile(xEmpty + 1, yEmpty);  break;
                case Key.Down:  MoveTile(xEmpty, yEmpty - 1);  break;
                case Key.Up:    MoveTile(xEmpty, yEmpty + 1);  break;
                default:
                    return;
            }
            args.Handled = true;
        }
        void ScrambleOnClick(object sender, RoutedEventArgs args)
        {
            rand = new Random();
```

```csharp
            iCounter = 16 * NumberCols * NumberRows;

            DispatcherTimer tmr = new DispatcherTimer();
            tmr.Interval = TimeSpan.FromMilliseconds(10);
            tmr.Tick += TimerOnTick;
            tmr.Start();
        }
        void TimerOnTick(object sender, EventArgs args)
        {
            for (int i = 0; i < 5; i++)
            {
                MoveTile(xEmpty, yEmpty + rand.Next(3) - 1);
                MoveTile(xEmpty + rand.Next(3) - 1, yEmpty);
            }
            if (0 == iCounter--)
                (sender as DispatcherTimer).Stop();
        }
        void MoveTile(int xTile, int yTile)
        {
            if ((xTile == xEmpty && yTile == yEmpty) ||
                xTile < 0 || xTile >= NumberCols ||
                yTile < 0 || yTile >= NumberRows)
                return;

            int iTile = NumberCols * yTile + xTile;
            int iEmpty = NumberCols * yEmpty + xEmpty;

            UIElement elTile = unigrid.Children[iTile];
            UIElement elEmpty = unigrid.Children[iEmpty];

            unigrid.Children.RemoveAt(iTile);
            unigrid.Children.Insert(iTile, elEmptySpare);
            unigrid.Children.RemoveAt(iEmpty);
            unigrid.Children.Insert(iEmpty, elTile);

            xEmpty = xTile;
            yEmpty = yTile;
            elEmptySpare = elEmpty;
        }
        void NextOnClick(object sender, RoutedEventArgs args)
        {
            if (!NavigationService.CanGoForward)
            {
                JeuDeTacquin page = new JeuDeTacquin();
                page.NumberRows = NumberRows + 1;
                page.NumberCols = NumberCols + 1;

                NavigationService.Navigate(page);
            }
            else
                NavigationService.GoForward();
        }
    }
}
```

The new feature that came to mind when I was converting this program to a XAML Browser Application was the Next Larger button. This button is implemented by the event handler at the very bottom of the C# file. The first time you click that Next Larger button, the program creates a new object of type *JeuDeTacquin*, and sets the number of rows and columns to one greater than the existing grid for a dimension of five rows and five columns. A call to *NavigationService.Navigate* navigates to that new page. However, the previous game is retained and is accessible through the Back button, where the dimensions of the grid are identified. If you go back to that game and click Next Larger again, a new five-by-five game is not created, but you navigate to the one previously created. In this way, you can have multiple games going at once, each with a different dimension.

It would never have occurred to me to implement such a feature in the earlier version of the program. Certainly a menu option to set the number of rows and columns is an obvious feature, but not the ability to have several different games going at once. It would have been too awkward to manage. But with the WPF navigation facilities, such a feature becomes almost trivial.

Chapter 23
Data Binding

Data binding is the technique of connecting controls and elements to data, and if that definition seems a little vague, it only attests to the wide scope and versatility of these techniques. Data binding can be as simple as connecting a *CheckBox* control to a Boolean variable, or as massive as connecting a database to a data-entry panel.

Controls have always served the dual purpose of displaying data to the user and allowing the user to change that data. In modern application programming interfaces, however, many of the routine links between controls and data have become automated. In the past, a programmer would write code both to initialize a *CheckBox* from a Boolean variable, and to set the Boolean variable from the *CheckBox* after the user has finished with it. In today's modern programming environments, the programmer defines a binding between the *CheckBox* and the variable. This binding automatically performs both jobs.

Very often a data binding can replace an event handler, and that goes a long way to simplifying code, particularly if you're coding in XAML. Data bindings defined in XAML can eliminate the need for an event handler in the code-behind file and, in some cases, eliminate the code-behind file entirely. The result is code that I like to think of as having "no moving parts." Everything is initialization, and much less can go wrong. (Of course, the event handlers still exist, but they're behind the scenes, and presumably they come to us already debugged and robust enough for heavy lifting.)

Data bindings are considered to have a *source* and a *target*. Generally the source is some data and the target is a control. In actual practice you'll discover that the distinction between source and target sometimes gets a bit vague and sometimes the roles even seem to swap as a target supplies data to a source. Although the convenient terms do not describe a rigid mechanism, the distinction is important nonetheless.

Perhaps the simplest bindings are those that exist between two controls. For example, suppose you want to use a *Label* to view the *Value* property of a *ScrollBar*. You could install an event handler for the *ValueChanged* event of the *ScrollBar*, or you could define a data binding instead, as the following stand-alone XAML file demonstrates.

```
BindLabelToScrollBar.xaml
<!-- =======================================================
     BindLabelToScrollBar.xaml (c) 2006 by Charles Petzold
     ======================================================= -->
<StackPanel xmlns="http://schemas.microsoft.com/winfx/2006/xaml/presentation"
            xmlns:x="http://schemas.microsoft.com/winfx/2006/xaml">

    <!-- Binding Source. -->
```

```
    <ScrollBar Name="scroll"
               Orientation="Horizontal" Margin="24"
               Maximum="100" LargeChange="10" SmallChange="1" />

    <!-- Binding Target. -->

    <Label HorizontalAlignment="Center"
           Content="{Binding ElementName=scroll, Path=Value}" />

</StackPanel>
```

The binding itself is always set on the target of the binding. In this XAML file, the binding is set on the *Content* property of the *Label* control with this syntax:

```
Content="{Binding ElementName=scroll, Path=Value}"
```

Like *StaticResource* and *DynamicResource*, *Binding* is a markup extension. Curly braces surround the *Binding* definition. Both *ElementName* and *Path* are among several properties of the *Binding* class that can appear in this definition. In this particular *Binding* definition, the *ElementName* is set to *scroll*, which is the name given to the *ScrollBar* in its *Name* attribute. The *Path* property of *Binding* is set to *Value*, which in this context refers to the *Value* property of the *ScrollBar*. The *Content* property of the *Label*, then, is bound to the *Value* property of the *ScrollBar*. As you manipulate the *ScrollBar*, the *Label* shows the current value.

No matter how long you've been writing XAML, I can practically guarantee that you'll want to put quotation marks inside that *Binding* definition. *ElementName* and *Path* look so much like XML attributes that your fingers will want to type something like this:

```
Content="{Binding ElementName="scroll" Path="Value"}"
```

That's completely wrong! Within those curly braces, different rules apply. *ElementName* and *Path* are not XML attributes. The only attribute involved here is *Content*. Not only must there be no quotation marks within the curly braces, but the *ElementName* and *Path* items must also be separated by a comma.

On the other hand, if you really can't stop yourself from typing quotation marks in the *Binding* definition, perhaps you'd prefer the alternative property element syntax.

PropertyElementSyntax.xaml
```
<!-- ======================================================
        PropertyElementSyntax.xaml (c) 2006 by Charles Petzold
     ====================================================== -->
<StackPanel xmlns="http://schemas.microsoft.com/winfx/2006/xaml/presentation"
            xmlns:x="http://schemas.microsoft.com/winfx/2006/xaml">

    <!-- Binding Source. -->

    <ScrollBar Name="scroll"
```

```
                    Orientation="Horizontal" Margin="24"
                    Maximum="100" LargeChange="10" SmallChange="1" />

    <!-- Binding Target. -->

    <Label HorizontalAlignment="Center">
        <Label.Content>
            <Binding ElementName="scroll" Path="Value" />
        </Label.Content>
    </Label>

</StackPanel>
```

Now the *Binding* element appears within *Label.Content* start and end tags, and the *ElementName* and *Path* properties are treated as normal XML attributes. You may be tempted to remove the *Label.Content* tags under the assumption that they're not needed. They aren't needed under most circumstances, but they are needed here.

Regardless of how you do it, the control or element in which the *Binding* definition occurs is always the target of the binding. A binding target must derive from *DependencyObject*. The property on which the binding is set must be backed by a dependency property. In this particular case, therefore, it's necessary for *Label* to have a static public field of type *DependencyProperty* named *ContentProperty* (which, of course, it does).

The requirements for bindings are more evident when you examine a binding in C#. I'll assume you've created *ScrollBar* and *Label* controls and stored the objects as *scroll* and *lbl*. The code is:

```
Binding bind = new Binding();
bind.Source = scroll;
bind.Path = new PropertyPath(ScrollBar.ValueProperty);
lbl.SetBinding(Label.Content, bind);
```

This code is not the exact equivalent of the *Binding* definition in XAML because it sets the *Source* property of *Binding* to the *ScrollBar* object rather than setting the *ElementName* property to the string "scroll." But notice that the *SetBinding* method is called on the target of the binding. This method is defined by *FrameworkElement* and the first argument is *DependencyProperty*, so those two facts indicate that the binding target can't be just anything. The binding must be established on properties backed by dependency properties because controls and elements are designed to react to changes in their dependency properties.

Although not quite evident from this code, the requirements for a binding source are much looser. The bound property of the source need not be a dependency property. In the ideal case, the property should be associated with an event that indicates when the property changes, but some bindings can work even without that notification event.

Let's experiment a bit with the BindLabelToScrollBar.xaml file. Although the terms source and target seem to imply that changes in the source element (in this case, the *ScrollBar*) precipitate changes in the target element (the *Label*), that's only one of four possible binding modes. You specify the mode you want by using the *Mode* property and members of the *BindingMode* enumeration. This is the default:

```
Content="{Binding ElementName=scroll, Path=Value, Mode=OneWay}"
```

Notice that the setting of the *Mode* property is separated from the *Path* property setting by another comma, and that no quotation marks appear around the *BindingMode* enumeration member *OneWay*. If you prefer the property element syntax, you add it to the attributes in the *Binding* element:

```
<Label.Content>
    <Binding ElementName="scroll" Path="Value" Mode="OneWay" />
</Label.Content>
```

You can also set the mode to *TwoWay*:

```
Content="{Binding ElementName=scroll, Path=Value, Mode=TwoWay}"
```

In this program, the functionality is the same as *OneWay* but in theory, changes to the *Content* property of *Label* should now also be reflected in the *Value* property of the *ScrollBar*. Here's another possibility:

```
Content="{Binding ElementName=scroll, Path=Value, Mode=OneTime}"
```

The *OneTime* mode means that the target is initialized from the source but does not track changes in the source. In this program, the *Label* displays a value of 0 because that's the initial *Value* property of the *ScrollBar*, but changes in the *ScrollBar* cause no further changes in that displayed value. (You could explicitly set *Value* equal to 50 in the *ScrollBar* element; in that case the *Label* will display 50 because it is initialized with that value.)

The final option is:

```
Content="{Binding ElementName=scroll, Path=Value, Mode=OneWayToSource}"
```

This is the mind-boggler of the group because it's instructing the source to be updated from the target, which is the opposite of how we normally think about *source* and *target*. It's as if the bull's-eye wants to impale itself on the arrow. In this case, the target (the *Label*) is supposed to update the source (the *ScrollBar*), but the *Label* has no numeric data to give to the *ScrollBar*. The *Label* is blank and remains blank as you move the *ScrollBar*.

Although this *OneWayToSource* mode seems to violate fundamental laws of the universe, it turns out to be quite useful when you want to establish a binding between two properties but the target property isn't backed by a dependency property while the source property is. In that case, put the binding on the source, and set the *Mode* to *OneWayToSource*.

To explore these concepts a bit more, let's look at a similar XAML file in which the *ScrollBar* and *Label* controls have switched roles.

BindScrollBarToLabel.xaml

```
<!-- =======================================================
     BindScrollBarToLabel.xaml (c) 2006 by Charles Petzold
     ======================================================= -->
<StackPanel xmlns="http://schemas.microsoft.com/winfx/2006/xaml/presentation"
            xmlns:x="http://schemas.microsoft.com/winfx/2006/xaml">

    <!-- Binding Target. -->

    <ScrollBar Orientation="Horizontal" Margin="24"
               Maximum="100" LargeChange="10" SmallChange="1"
               Value="{Binding ElementName=lbl, Path=Content}" />

    <!-- Binding Source. -->

    <Label Name="lbl" Content="50"
           HorizontalAlignment="Center" />

</StackPanel>
```

Now the *Label* is the source and the *ScrollBar* is the target. As usual, the *Binding* definition appears on the target and binds the *Value* property of the *ScrollBar* with the *Content* property of the *Label*:

```
Value="{Binding ElementName=lbl, Path=Content}"
```

I've also given the *Label* control a *Content* of 50. When this program starts up, *Label* displays 50, and the *ScrollBar* thumb is poised in the center. As you move the *ScrollBar*, the *Label* is updated. Obviously a two-way binding has been established by default. It works the same way if you explicitly indicate that option:

```
Value="{Binding ElementName=lbl, Path=Content, Mode=TwoWay}"
```

However, it doesn't work when you change to a one-way mode:

```
Value="{Binding ElementName=lbl, Path=Content, Mode=OneWay}"
```

The *ScrollBar* is still initialized to its midpoint position because it is the target of the binding and the *Label* source indicates 50. But there are no further changes because the *ScrollBar* isn't getting any more numeric data from the *Label*. You'll get the same result with:

```
Value="{Binding ElementName=lbl, Path=Content, Mode=OneTime}"
```

But now try this one:

```
Value="{Binding ElementName=lbl, Path=Content, Mode=OneWayToSource}"
```

Now the *ScrollBar* target is governing the *Label* source. The *Label* is initialized to 0 because that's the initial *Value* of the *ScrollBar*. Thereafter, the *Label* dutifully reports changes in the *ScrollBar*.

The default *Mode* of a binding is governed by the property on which the binding is defined. This experimentation with BindScrollBarToLabel.xaml reveals that the *Value* property of *ScrollBar* has a default binding *Mode* of *TwoWay*. In theory, the *ValueProperty* dependency property of *ScrollBar* should have a *FrameworkPropertyMetadata* object with a *BindsTwoWayByDefault* property of *true*. However, the ExploreDependencyProperties program in Chapter 16 reveals that the scrollbar's *ValueProperty* has its metadata stored in a *PropertyMetadata* object rather than *FrameworkPropertyMetadata*.

For this reason, it's probably not a good idea to try to guess at the default binding modes of controls. This *Mode* property is one of the most important components of the binding, and it wouldn't hurt if you consider each binding carefully to determine what the proper *Mode* setting should be and then explicitly set it.

Some C# programs earlier in this book had some data bindings. These often made use of the *DataContext* property defined by *FrameworkElement*, which is an alternative way to denote the source object involved in the binding. Here's a little stand-alone file that shows how to set the *DataContext* in XAML:

```
BindingWithDataContext.xaml
<!-- ======================================================
        BindingWithDataContext.xaml (c) 2006 by Charles Petzold
     ====================================================== -->
<StackPanel xmlns="http://schemas.microsoft.com/winfx/2006/xaml/presentation"
            xmlns:x="http://schemas.microsoft.com/winfx/2006/xaml">

    <!-- Binding Source. -->

    <ScrollBar Name="scroll"
               Orientation="Horizontal" Margin="24"
               Maximum="100" LargeChange="10" SmallChange="1" />

    <!-- Binding Target. -->

    <Label HorizontalAlignment="Center"
           DataContext="{Binding ElementName=scroll}"
           Content="{Binding Path=Value}" />

</StackPanel>
```

Notice that both the *DataContext* and *Content* attributes of *Label* are set to a *Binding* definition, which has essentially been split up into two pieces. The first *Binding* definition indicates the *ElementName* and the second has the *Path*.

There's certainly no advantage to using the *DataContext* property in this example, but in some cases the *DataContext* property is extremely valuable. *DataContext* is inherited through the element tree, so if you set it for one element, it also applies to all the children of that element.

The TwoBindings.xaml file illustrates this technique. The *DataContext* is set once for the *StackPanel* element. Properties of both a *Label* and a *Button* are bound to the *ScrollBar*. For the *Label*, the bound property is just the *Content*, but for the *Button*, the bound property is *FontSize*. As you move the *ScrollBar* thumb, the text inside the *Button* gets larger and eventually so does the *Button* itself.

TwoBindings.xaml

```
<!-- ============================================
        TwoBindings.xaml (c) 2006 by Charles Petzold
     ============================================ -->
<StackPanel xmlns="http://schemas.microsoft.com/winfx/2006/xaml/presentation"
            xmlns:x="http://schemas.microsoft.com/winfx/2006/xaml"
            DataContext="{Binding ElementName=scroll}">

    <!-- Binding Source. -->

    <ScrollBar Name="scroll"
               Orientation="Horizontal" Margin="24"
               Minimum="1" Maximum="100" LargeChange="10" SmallChange="1" />

    <!-- Binding Targets. -->

    <Label HorizontalAlignment="Center"
           Content="{Binding Path=Value, Mode=OneWay}" />

    <Button HorizontalAlignment="Center" Margin="24"
            FontSize="{Binding Path=Value, Mode=OneWay}">
        Bound Button
    </Button>

</StackPanel>
```

Of course, we wouldn't have suffered much grief if we included the *ElementName* property in both *Binding* definitions. However, consider a panel in which many controls are bound to various properties of a particular type of object. By just setting the *DataContext* to a different object of that type, all the controls reflect the new object. In Chapter 26 you'll see an example of that technique.

Here's a little stand-alone file that uses data binding to display the current width and height of the program's client area:

WhatSize.xaml

```
<!-- ====================================
        WhatSize.xaml (c) 2006 by Charles Petzold
     ==================================== -->
<Grid xmlns="http://schemas.microsoft.com/winfx/2006/xaml/presentation"
      xmlns:x="http://schemas.microsoft.com/winfx/2006/xaml"
      Name="grid">
    <StackPanel Orientation="Horizontal"
                HorizontalAlignment="Center"
```

```
                        VerticalAlignment="Center">
        <TextBlock Text="{Binding ElementName=grid, Path=ActualWidth}" />
        <TextBlock Text=" &#x00D7; " />
        <TextBlock Text="{Binding ElementName=grid, Path=ActualHeight}" />
        <TextBlock Text=" device independent units" />
    </StackPanel>
</Grid>
```

The *StackPanel* has a horizontal orientation and contains four *TextBlock* elements that combine to form what appears to be a single line of text. Two of the *TextBlock* elements define bindings to the *ActualWidth* and *ActualHeight* properties of the *Grid*. These properties are read-only, so the binding mode can't be anything except one-way.

My first attempts at writing the WhatSize.xaml program weren't very successful. Rather than defining multiple *TextBlock* elements, I originally wanted to use a single *TextBlock* with multiple children of type *Run*. Two of these *Run* elements would have their *Text* properties bound to the *ActualWidth* and *ActualHeight* properties of the *Grid*. The markup looked like this:

```
<!-- This markup doesn't work! -->
<TextBlock>
    <Run Text="{Binding ElementName=grid, Path=ActualWidth}" />
    <Run Text=" &#x00D7; " />
    <Run Text="{Binding ElementName=grid, Path=ActualHeight}" />
    <Run Text=" device independent units" />
</TextBlock>
```

This chunk of XAML still looks fine to me, but it raised an exception that said "Object of type 'System.Windows.Data.Binding' cannot be converted to type 'System.String'", obviously referring to the type of the *Text* property. The message seemed very strange to me because it implied that the parser was ignoring the very nature of data bindings.

The solution to this mystery is very simple: The *Text* property defined by *TextBlock* is backed by the dependency property named *TextProperty*. The *Text* property defined by *Run* is *not* backed by a dependency property. The target of a data binding must be a dependency property. This little fact is much more obvious when you define the binding in C#: The first argument to *SetBinding* is of type *DependencyProperty*.

The binding source need not be a dependency property. All the data-binding examples so far have involved both targets and sources backed by dependency properties, but you'll see examples later in this chapter of binding sources that are plain old .NET properties. In the general case, a *OneWay* binding involves a continual transfer of information from the binding source to the target. For one-way bindings to be successful, the source must implement a mechanism of some sort to keep the target informed when the source property has changed.

When I say "a mechanism of some sort," do I mean an *event*? That's certainly one possibility, but not the only one. One of the primary incentives behind the invention of dependency properties was data binding, and the dependency property system has built-in notification support. The binding source doesn't have to be a dependency property, but it really helps if it is.

Here is a simple element. In fact, the class is named *SimpleElement* and it derives directly from *FrameworkElement*.

SimpleElement.cs

```
//---------------------------------------------
// SimpleElement.cs (c) 2006 by Charles Petzold
//---------------------------------------------
using System;
using System.Globalization;
using System.Windows;
using System.Windows.Media;

namespace Petzold.CustomElementBinding
{
    class SimpleElement : FrameworkElement
    {
        // Define DependencyProperty.
        public static DependencyProperty NumberProperty;

        // Create DependencyProperty in static constructor.
        static SimpleElement()
        {
            NumberProperty =
                DependencyProperty.Register("Number", typeof(double),
                                    typeof(SimpleElement),
                    new FrameworkPropertyMetadata(0.0,
                        FrameworkPropertyMetadataOptions.AffectsRender));
        }

        // Expose DependencyProperty as CLR property.
        public double Number
        {
            set { SetValue(NumberProperty, value); }
            get { return (double)GetValue(NumberProperty); }
        }

        // Hard-coded size for MeasureOverride.
        protected override Size MeasureOverride(Size sizeAvailable)
        {
            return new Size(200, 50);
        }

        // OnRender just displays Number property.
        protected override void OnRender(DrawingContext dc)
        {
            dc.DrawText(
                new FormattedText(Number.ToString(),
                        CultureInfo.CurrentCulture, FlowDirection.LeftToRight,
                        new Typeface("Times New Roman"), 12,
                        SystemColors.WindowTextBrush),
                new Point(0, 0));
        }
    }
}
```

This class defines a property named *Number* of type *double* that is backed by the *DependencyProperty* named (as is the convention) *NumberProperty*. The *FrameworkPropertyMetadata* indicates merely that the default value is 0, and that changes to the property should invalidate the visual and result in a call to *OnRender*. The *MeasureOverride* method takes a very simple approach to sizing and asks for a size of 200 by 50 device-independent units. The *OnRender* method simply displays the *Number* property.

I must confess that I was skeptical when I began assembling some markup that would let me explore bindings between *SimpleElement* and a *ScrollBar*. The application definition file is trivial as usual:

CustomElementBindingApp.xaml

```
<!-- =========================================================
        CustomElementBindingApp.xaml (c) 2006 by Charles Petzold
     ========================================================= -->
<Application xmlns="http://schemas.microsoft.com/winfx/2006/xaml/presentation"
             StartupUri="CustomElementBindingWindow.xaml">
</Application>
```

The *Window* element creates two *ScrollBar* controls and two *SimpleElement* elements and defines three bindings among them:

CustomElementBindingWindow.xaml

```
<!-- =========================================================
        CustomElementBindingWindow.xaml (c) 2006 by Charles Petzold
     ========================================================= -->
<Window xmlns="http://schemas.microsoft.com/winfx/2006/xaml/presentation"
        xmlns:x="http://schemas.microsoft.com/winfx/2006/xaml"
        xmlns:src="clr-namespace:Petzold.CustomElementBinding"
        Title="Custom Element Binding Demo">
    <StackPanel>
        <ScrollBar Orientation="Horizontal"
                   Margin="24"
                   Maximum="100"
                   LargeChange="10"
                   SmallChange="1"
                   Value="{Binding ElementName=simple, Path=Number,
                                   Mode=OneWayToSource}" />

        <src:SimpleElement x:Name="simple"
                           HorizontalAlignment="Center" />

        <ScrollBar Name="scroll"
                   Orientation="Horizontal"
                   Margin="24"
                   Maximum="100"
                   LargeChange="10"
                   SmallChange="1"
                   Value="{Binding ElementName=simple, Path=Number,
                                   Mode=TwoWay}" />
```

```
    <src:SimpleElement HorizontalAlignment="Center"
                    Number="{Binding ElementName=scroll, Path=Value,
                                    Mode=OneWay}" />
    </StackPanel>
</Window>
```

Notice the *x:Name* attribute on the first *SimpleElement* element. The *x:Name* attribute is intended for XAML elements that do not derive from *FrameworkElement* and hence have no *Name* property. However, using *Name* in this case generated an error message that said "Because 'SimpleElement' is implemented in the same assembly, you must set the x:Name attribute rather than the *Name* attribute." So I did.

The first *ScrollBar* defines a *OneWayToSource* binding with the *Number* property of the first *SimpleElement*. As you click on this *ScrollBar* and move its thumb, the first *SimpleElement* changes. This is the no-brainer: We all expect the first *ScrollBar* to successfully update the first *SimpleElement*.

The second *ScrollBar* defines a *TwoWay* binding with the *Number* property of the first *SimpleElement*, and you'll see that this one works as well. Although *SimpleElement* has no explicit notification mechanism, changes to the *Number* property as a result of manipulating the first *ScrollBar* are detected in this binding, and the second *ScrollBar* tracks the first *ScrollBar*. Because this is a *TwoWay* binding, you can manipulate the second *ScrollBar*, and *SimpleElement* also changes (although the first *ScrollBar* remains still).

The second *SimpleElement* element defines a *OneWay* data binding with the second *ScrollBar*. As the second *ScrollBar* moves—either through binding or directly by you—the second *SimpleElement* is updated with the new value.

The lesson is clear: Define a *DependencyProperty* and get a data binding notification for free.

Two metadata flags affect data binding. If you include the *FrameworkPropertyMetadataOptions.NotDataBindable* flag, other elements can still bind to the dependency property, but you can't define a binding on the dependency property itself. (In other words, a dependency property with this flag set can't be the target of a data binding.) The *FrameworkPropertyMetadataOptions.BindsTwoWayByDefault* flag affects only bindings defined where that dependency property is the target.

As you've seen, you set the *Path* property of *Binding* to a property of the source object. So why is it called *Path*? Why isn't it called *Property*?

It's called *Path* because it can be more than just a property. It can be a *series* of properties (possibly with indices) combined with periods, much like C# code but without the hassle of strong typing. Here's a stand-alone XAML program that has two *Path* properties with lengths a little past the comfort level.

LongBindingPath.xaml

```
<!-- ================================================
       LongBindingPath.xaml (c) 2006 by Charles Petzold
     ================================================ -->
<Page xmlns="http://schemas.microsoft.com/winfx/2006/xaml/presentation"
      xmlns:x="http://schemas.microsoft.com/winfx/2006/xaml"
      xmlns:s="clr-namespace:System;assembly=mscorlib"
      FontSize="12pt"
      Name="page">
    <StackPanel>
        <TextBlock HorizontalAlignment="Center">
            First element in StackPanel
        </TextBlock>

        <ListBox HorizontalAlignment="Center"
                 Margin="24">
            <ListBoxItem>First ListBox Item</ListBoxItem>
            <ListBoxItem>Second ListBox Item</ListBoxItem>
            <ListBoxItem>Third ListBoxItem</ListBoxItem>
            <ListBoxItem>Fourth ListBox Item</ListBoxItem>
            <ListBoxItem>Fifth ListBoxItem</ListBoxItem>
        </ListBox>

        <TextBlock HorizontalAlignment="Center">
            <Label Content="Number of characters in third ListBox item = " />
            <Label Content="{Binding ElementName=page,
                        Path=Content.Children[1].Items[2].Content.Length}" />
            <LineBreak />
            <Label Content="Number of characters in selected item = " />
            <Label Content="{Binding ElementName=page,
                        Path=Content.Children[1].SelectedItem.Content.Length}" />
        </TextBlock>
    </StackPanel>
</Page>
```

The only element that has a *Name* attribute is the root element. The *Page* contains a *StackPanel* that in turn contains two *TextBlock* elements surrounding a *ListBox*. The *ListBox* contains five *ListBoxItem* controls. The embedded *Label* controls inside that final *TextBlock* display the length of the text in the third item in the *ListBox* and the length of the text of the selected item. Here's the *Path* definition for the latter of those two:

```
Path=Content.Children[1].SelectedItem.Content.Length
```

Although this may look like a chain of nested properties in some C# code, keep in mind that it's just a string, and it is parsed as a string. The parser uses reflection to determine whether these items make sense, and if they don't make sense, the parsing is just abandoned without raising any objections or exceptions. Starting from the left, the *Path* consists of the *Content* of the *Page* (which is a *StackPanel*), the second item in the *Children* collection of the *StackPanel* (which is the *ListBox*), the *SelectedItem* of the *ListBox* (which is a *ListBoxItem*), the *Content* of the *ListBoxItem* (which is a *string*), and the *Length* property of that *string*.

What was your reaction the first time you dragged the thumb of one of the scrollbars earlier in this chapter and realized that the *Value* property was truly a double-precision floating-point number with a fractional value and 16-odd significant digits? I alternated between finding it very cool and deeply disturbing. But it's not just an aesthetic issue. The floating-point output of the *ScrollBar* is potentially a problem if you need to bind the *ScrollBar* with something expecting integers.

As data is transferred from a binding source to a target (and sometimes back) the data might need to be converted from one type to another. The *Binding* class includes a property named *Converter* that lets you specify a class that includes two methods named *Convert* and *ConvertBack* to perform this conversion.

The class performing the conversion must implement the *IValueConverter* interface and look something like this:

```
public class MyConverter: IValueConverter
{
    public object Convert(object value, Type typeTarget,
                          object param, CultureInfo culture)
    {
        ...
    }
    Public object ConvertBack(object value, Type typeTarget,
                              object param, CultureInfo culture)
    {
        ...
    }
}
```

The *value* parameter is the *object* to be converted, and *typeTarget* is the type that it's to be converted into. This is the type of the object that the method returns. If it can't return an object of that type, the method should return *null*. The third parameter is potentially an object specified by the *ConvertParameter* property of *Binding*, and the last parameter indicates the culture to assume when performing the conversion. (In many cases, it can be ignored.)

If you're creating a *Binding* in C#, you set the *Convert* property to an object of a class that implements the *IValueConverter* interface:

```
Binding bind = new Binding();
bind.Convert = new MyConverter();
```

You might also set the *ConvertParameter* property of *Binding* to an object that is passed as the *param* parameter to *Convert* and *ConvertBack* to control the conversion.

In XAML, getting that *MyConverter* class into the *Binding* definition is a little more round-about. You need to create an object of type *MyConverter* and then reference that object in markup. You learned how to do tasks like this in Chapter 21: You make it a resource.

So, in a *Resources* section in your XAML, you specify the class that implements *IValueConverter* and you associate it with a key:

```
<src:MyConverter x:Key="conv" />
```

MyConverter is prefaced with *src* because I assume it's in a C# source code for the project and you've included an XML namespace declaration associating *src* with the namespace of your project.

In the *Binding* definition, you use a *StaticResource* markup extension to reference the *MyConverter* object:

```
"{Binding ... Convert={StaticResource conv}, ... }"
```

You might also include a *ConverterParameter* property here. The conversion parameter lets you include additional information that affects the conversion. (You'll see an example shortly.) But that's not the only way to get additional information into the conversion class. The class must implement the *IValueConverter* interface but nothing prohibits it from defining public properties of its own. You can set these properties in XAML when the class is included in the *Resources* section of the XAML file:

```
<src:MyConverter Decimals="4" s:Key="conv" />
```

The following class provides a conversion from *double* to *decimal*. The conversion parameter is the number of decimal places to which the *decimal* result is rounded.

```csharp
DoubleToDecimalConverter.cs
//---------------------------------------------------------
// DoubleToDecimalConverter.cs (c) 2006 by Charles Petzold
//---------------------------------------------------------
using System;
using System.Globalization;
using System.Windows;
using System.Windows.Data;

namespace Petzold.DecimalScrollBar
{
    [ValueConversion(typeof(double), typeof(decimal))]
    public class DoubleToDecimalConverter : IValueConverter
    {
        public object Convert(object value, Type typeTarget,
                              object param, CultureInfo culture)
        {
            decimal num = new Decimal((double)value);

            if (param != null)
                num = Decimal.Round(num, Int32.Parse(param as string));

            return num;
        }
```

```
        public object ConvertBack(object value, Type typeTarget,
                                  object param, CultureInfo culture)
        {
            return Decimal.ToDouble((decimal)value);
        }
    }
}
```

The WPF documentation recommends that you include a *ValueConversion* attribute right before the class definition to alert development tools to the role this class plays. How bulletproof you make these conversion routines is really up to you. If you're using them in your own code, you can pretty much anticipate the types of the arguments. For example, the *Convert* method here assumes that the *param* argument is a string that can be safely parsed into an integer. It also assumes that the return value is a *Decimal* without checking the *typeTarget* parameter.

The *DoubleToDecimalConverter* class is part of the DecimalScrollBar project that also includes this *Window* definition.

```
DecimalScrollBarWindow.xaml
<!-- ===============================================================
        DecimalScrollBarWindow.xaml (c) 2006 by Charles Petzold
     =============================================================== -->
<Window xmlns="http://schemas.microsoft.com/winfx/2006/xaml/presentation"
        xmlns:x="http://schemas.microsoft.com/winfx/2006/xaml"
        xmlns:src="clr-namespace:Petzold.DecimalScrollBar"
        Title="Decimal ScrollBar">
    <Window.Resources>
        <src:DoubleToDecimalConverter x:Key="conv" />
    </Window.Resources>
    <StackPanel>

        <!-- Binding Source. -->

        <ScrollBar Name="scroll"
                   Orientation="Horizontal" Margin="24"
                   Maximum="100" LargeChange="10" SmallChange="1" />

        <!-- Binding Target. -->

        <Label HorizontalAlignment="Center"
               Content="{Binding ElementName=scroll, Path=Value,
                   Converter={StaticResource conv}, ConverterParameter=2}" />
    </StackPanel>
</Window>
```

The *Resources* section includes the *DoubleToDecimalConverter* class and associates it with the key "conv." The *Binding* definition in the *Label* element references the conversion class as a *StaticResource* and assigns the value "2" to the *ConverterParameter* property. (Obviously it's easy to assign a string to *ConverterParameter*. You can actually assign an object of any type to

ConverterParameter, but in that case the object must be a resource and referenced it as a *StaticResource*.) The application definition file rounds out the project.

DecimalScrollBarApp.xaml
```
<!-- ====================================================
        DecimalScrollBarApp.xaml (c) 2006 by Charles Petzold
     ==================================================== -->
<Application xmlns="http://schemas.microsoft.com/winfx/2006/xaml/presentation"
             StartupUri="DecimalScrollBarWindow.xaml">
</Application>
```

As you move the scrollbar in this program, the value is displayed with two decimal places.

One type of binding for which a conversion class is always required is the *multi-binding*. The multi-binding consolidates multiple objects from multiple sources into a single target object. The multi-binding converter must implement the *IMultiValueConverter* interface. The classic example of a multi-binding is combining red, green, and blue primaries into a single *Color* object.

The ColorScroll project is similar to ScrollCustomColors from Chapter 6, except that most of the functionality has been moved into XAML. As you might recall, ScrollCustomColors contains three scrollbars for the red, green, and blue primaries. The original program installed event handlers to construct a *SolidColorBrush* from the three primaries. The ColorScroll project uses binding. Here's the application definition file first:

ColorScrollApp.xaml
```
<!-- ====================================================
        ColorScrollAppDef.xaml (c) 2006 by Charles Petzold
     ==================================================== -->
<Application xmlns="http://schemas.microsoft.com/winfx/2006/xaml/presentation"
             StartupUri="ColorScrollPage.xaml">
</Application>
```

Just for variety, I've made the main XAML file a *Page* rather than a *Window*. The *Resources* section defines two conversion classes—the first to convert *double* values from the scrollbars to *byte* values for the labels, and the second to construct a *SolidColorBrush* from the three scrollbar values. As in the ScrollCustomColors project, the layout requires two *Grid* panels. The first has three columns. On the left is another *Grid* that contains the scrollbars and labels, on the right is a *Border* element used just to display the resultant color, and in between is a *GridSplitter*.

ColorScrollPage.xaml
```
<!-- ====================================================
        ColorScrollPage.xaml (c) 2006 by Charles Petzold
     ==================================================== -->
<Page xmlns="http://schemas.microsoft.com/winfx/2006/xaml/presentation"
      xmlns:x="http://schemas.microsoft.com/winfx/2006/xaml"
```

```
        xmlns:src="clr-namespace:Petzold.ColorScroll"
      WindowTitle="Color Scroll">
  <Page.Resources>
      <src:DoubleToByteConverter x:Key="convDoubleToByte" />
      <src:RgbToColorConverter x:Key="convRgbToColor" />
  </Page.Resources>

  <Grid>
      <Grid.ColumnDefinitions>
          <ColumnDefinition Width="*" />
          <ColumnDefinition Width="Auto" />
          <ColumnDefinition Width="*" />
      </Grid.ColumnDefinitions>

      <!-- Grid with ScrollBar and Label controls. -->

      <GridSplitter Grid.Row="0" Grid.Column="1" Width="6"
          <Grid.RowDefinitions>
              <RowDefinition Height="Auto" />
              <RowDefinition Height="100*" />
              <RowDefinition Height="Auto" />
          </Grid.RowDefinitions>

          <Grid.ColumnDefinitions>
              <ColumnDefinition Width="33*" />
              <ColumnDefinition Width="33*" />
              <ColumnDefinition Width="33*" />
          </Grid.ColumnDefinitions>

          <!-- Red. -->

          <Label Content="Red" Foreground="Red"
                 HorizontalAlignment="Center"
                 Grid.Row="0" Grid.Column="0" />

          <ScrollBar Name="scrRed" Background="Red" Value="128"
                     Minimum="0" Maximum="255" SmallChange="1" LargeChange="16"
                     Focusable="True" Grid.Row="1" Grid.Column="0" />

          <Label Content="{Binding ElementName=scrRed, Path=Value,
                  Mode=OneWay, Converter={StaticResource convDoubleToByte}}"
                 HorizontalAlignment="Center"
                 Grid.Row="2" Grid.Column="0" />

          <!-- Green. -->

          <Label Content="Green" Foreground="Green"
                 HorizontalAlignment="Center"
                 Grid.Row="0" Grid.Column="1" />

          <ScrollBar Name="scrGreen" Background="Green" Value="128"
                     Minimum="0" Maximum="255" SmallChange="1" LargeChange="16"
                     Focusable="True" Grid.Row="1" Grid.Column="1" />

          <Label Content="{Binding ElementName=scrGreen, Path=Value,
```

```
                              Mode=OneWay, Converter={StaticResource convDoubleToByte}}"
                        HorizontalAlignment="Center"
                        Grid.Row="2" Grid.Column="1" />


            <!-- Blue. -->

            <Label Content="Blue" Foreground="Blue"
                   HorizontalAlignment="Center"
                   Grid.Row="0" Grid.Column="2" />

            <ScrollBar Name="scrBlue" Background="Blue" Value="128"
                       Minimum="0" Maximum="255" SmallChange="1" LargeChange="16"
                       Focusable="True" Grid.Row="1" Grid.Column="2" />

            <Label Content="{Binding ElementName=scrBlue, Path=Value,
                             Mode=OneWay, Converter={StaticResource convDoubleToByte}}"
                   HorizontalAlignment="Center"
                   Grid.Row="2" Grid.Column="2" />
        </Grid>

        <GridSplitter Grid.Row="0" Grid.Column="1"
                      HorizontalAlignment="Center" VerticalAlignment="Stretch" />

        <Border Grid.Row="0" Grid.Column="2">
            <Border.Background>
                <MultiBinding Converter="{StaticResource convRgbToColor}">
                    <Binding ElementName="scrRed" Path="Value" Mode="OneWay" />
                    <Binding ElementName="scrGreen" Path="Value" Mode="OneWay" />
                    <Binding ElementName="scrBlue" Path="Value" Mode="OneWay" />
                </MultiBinding>
            </Border.Background>
        </Border>
    </Grid>
</Page>
```

The three *Label* controls that sit underneath the three scrollbars display the scrollbar values, and each has a data binding. Here's the *Binding* for the red primary that sets the *Content* property of the *Label* from the *Value* property of the *ScrollBar* (the element named "scrRed").

```
Content="{Binding ElementName=scrRed, Path=Value,
          Mode=OneWay, Converter={StaticResource convDoubleToByte}}"
```

The converter is a static resource with the key name "convDoubleToByte" that references the following class:

DoubleToByteConverter.xaml

```
//-------------------------------------------------------
// DoubleToByteConverter.cs (c) 2006 by Charles Petzold
//-------------------------------------------------------
using System;
using System.Globalization;
using System.Windows;
```

```
using System.Windows.Data;

namespace Petzold.ColorScroll
{
    [ValueConversion(typeof(double), typeof(byte))]
    public class DoubleToByteConverter : IValueConverter
    {
        public object Convert(object value, Type typeTarget,
                              object param, CultureInfo culture)
        {
            return (byte)(double)value;
        }
        public object ConvertBack(object value, Type typeTarget,
                                  object param, CultureInfo culture)
        {
            return (double)value;
        }
    }
}
```

Because the binding is one-way from source to target, the *ConvertBack* method doesn't come into play and could simply return *null*, but I've implemented it anyway. In *Convert*, it's necessary to cast the object first to a *double* and then to a *byte*, or a run-time exception will result when an object is converted directly into a *byte*.

The multi-binding occurs near the bottom of ColorScrollPage.xaml. The binding sets the *Background* property of the *Border* element:

```
<Border.Background>
    <MultiBinding Converter="{StaticResource convRgbToColor}">
        <Binding ElementName="scrRed" Path="Value" Mode="OneWay "/>
        <Binding ElementName="scrGreen" Path="Value" Mode="OneWay "/>
        <Binding ElementName="scrBlue" Path="Value" Mode="OneWay "/>
    </MultiBinding>
</Border.Background>
```

The *MultiBinding* element always contains one or more *Binding* elements as children. The converter defined in the *Resources* section of the file and referenced by the key name of "convRgbToColor" must take the three values from the three bindings and convert them into an object appropriate for the *Background* property of the *Border* control. Here's the class that implements the *IMultiValueConverter* interface.

RgbToColorConverter.xaml

```
//----------------------------------------------------
// RgbToColorConverter.cs (c) 2006 by Charles Petzold
//----------------------------------------------------
using System;
using System.Globalization;
using System.Windows;
using System.Windows.Data;
using System.Windows.Media;
```

```
namespace Petzold.ColorScroll
{
    public class RgbToColorConverter : IMultiValueConverter
    {
        public object Convert(object[] value, Type typeTarget,
                              object param, CultureInfo culture)
        {
            Color clr = Color.FromRgb((byte)(double)value[0],
                                      (byte)(double)value[1],
                                      (byte)(double)value[2]);

            if (typeTarget == typeof(Color))
                return clr;

            if (typeTarget == typeof(Brush))
                return new SolidColorBrush(clr);

            return null;
        }
        public object[] ConvertBack(object value, Type[] typeTarget,
                                    object param, CultureInfo culture)
        {
            Color clr;
            object[] primaries = new object[3];

            if (value is Color)
                clr = (Color) value;

            else if (value is SolidColorBrush)
                clr = (value as SolidColorBrush).Color;

            else
                return null;

            primaries[0] = clr.R;
            primaries[1] = clr.G;
            primaries[2] = clr.B;
            return primaries;
        }
    }
}
```

The first parameter to the *Convert* method is an array of objects. There will be one object for every *Binding* child of the *MultiBinding* element, and it need not be a fixed number. This particular converter knows that the array will contain three objects of type *double*, so it immediately casts those values into *byte* and constructs a *Color* object. I decided to make the routine just a *little* generalized by checking if the *typeTarget* parameter indicates *Color* or *Brush*.

Because this is a one-way binding, the *ConvertBack* method is never called and can simply return *null*, but I just couldn't resist breaking out the three primaries from the *Color* or *SolidColorBrush* argument and returning them as an array.

It is possible for the child *Binding* elements of a *MultiBinding* element to reference their own converters. In the ColorScroll program, for example, the individual *Binding* elements could have referenced the *DoubleToByteConveter* so that the values entering the *RgbToColorConverter* would be an array of bytes rather than an array of double-precision floating-point numbers.

All the bindings we've seen so far have updated the targets immediately from the source elements. Sometimes that's not necessarily desirable. Consequently, it's sometimes not the default operation.

Here's a stand-alone XAML file that contains three pairs of *TextBox* controls. Each pair has their *Text* properties connected in two-way bindings. The *TextBox* controls are arranged with the source of each pair on the left and the target on the right.

BindToTextBox.xaml

```xml
<!-- ===============================================
      BindToTextBox.xaml (c) 2006 by Charles Petzold
     =============================================== -->
<Grid xmlns="http://schemas.microsoft.com/winfx/2006/xaml/presentation"
      xmlns:x="http://schemas.microsoft.com/winfx/2006/xaml">

    <Grid.ColumnDefinitions>
        <ColumnDefinition Width="*" />
        <ColumnDefinition Width="*" />
    </Grid.ColumnDefinitions>

    <Grid.RowDefinitions>
        <RowDefinition Height="Auto" />
        <RowDefinition Height="Auto" />
        <RowDefinition Height="Auto" />
        <RowDefinition Height="Auto" />
    </Grid.RowDefinitions>

    <Label Grid.Row="0" Grid.Column="0"
           Margin="24 24 24 0"
           Content="Source TextBox Controls" />
    <Label Grid.Row="0" Grid.Column="1"
           Margin="24 24 24 0"
           Content="Target TextBox Controls" />

    <TextBox Grid.Row="1" Grid.Column="0" Name="txtbox1"
             Margin="24" />
    <TextBox Grid.Row="1" Grid.Column="1"
             Margin="24"
             Text="{Binding ElementName=txtbox1, Path=Text, Mode=TwoWay}" />

    <TextBox Grid.Row="2" Grid.Column="0" Name="txtbox2"
             Margin="24" />
    <TextBox Grid.Row="2" Grid.Column="1"
             Margin="24"
             Text="{Binding ElementName=txtbox2, Path=Text, Mode=TwoWay}" />

    <TextBox Grid.Row="3" Grid.Column="0" Name="txtbox3"
```

```
            Margin="24" />
    <TextBox Grid.Row="3" Grid.Column="1"
            Margin="24"
            Text="{Binding ElementName=txtbox3, Path=Text, Mode=TwoWay}" />

</Grid>
```

Give the upper-left *TextBox* the input focus by clicking on it. This is the source of a two-way binding. As you type something in, you'll see that what you type also appears in the bound target *TextBox* on the right. Now press the Tab key. Now the target *TextBox* on the right has input focus. Type something in. Although the text you type appears in the *TextBox* that has the focus, the binding source *TextBox* on the left isn't updated with the new text. Yet, the binding is explicitly a two-way binding.

Press the Tab key again. As the target *TextBox* on the right loses input focus, the entire contents of the target are now transferred to the bound source *TextBox* on the left. It is truly a two-way binding, except that the source isn't updated from the target until the target loses input focus. You can continue experimenting with this program by pressing the Tab key and entering text into each *TextBox*.

In the default case, when the *Text* property of a *TextBox* is a target property of a two-way binding, the binding source is not updated from the target until the target loses input focus. For this to make sense, consider the source *TextBox* controls on the left of the BindToTextBox program to be not *TextBox* controls at all, but actually some database that the program is interacting with. The *TextBox* controls on the right allow you to view and edit the underlying database. When something in the database changes, you want to see that change right away. That's why the *Text* property of a target *TextBox* is updated with every change in the source.

However, as you enter text into the *TextBox* to change a field in the underlying database, do you want the database to be updated with every keystroke you press, including all the mistakes and backspaces and cat-jumps-on-the-keyboard incidents? Probably not. Only when you're finished entering the text do you want the source to be updated, and the only simple way that the binding can determine when you're finished is when the *TextBox* loses input focus.

You can change this behavior by setting the *UpdateSourceTrigger* property of the *Binding*. You can set it to a member of the *UpdateSourceTrigger* enumeration, either *LostFocus* (the default for the *Text* property of a *TextBox*), *PropertyChanged* (which is normal for most properties), or *Explicit*, which requires special action by the program for the changes to be reflected in the source.

Try changing one of the bindings in BindToTextBox.xaml to this:

```
Text="{Binding ElementName=txtbox1, Path=Text, Mode=TwoWay,
                    UpdateSourceTrigger=PropertyChanged}"
```

Now the source *TextBox* changes with every keystroke typed in the target *TextBox*.

The *UpdateSourceTrigger.Explicit* option requires more work. A program using this option has to prepare by calling *GetBindingExpression* (a method defined by *FrameworkElement*) on the element on which you've defined the binding. The argument is the *DependencyProperty* involved in the binding:

```
BindingExpression bindexp =
            txtboxSource.GetBindingExpression(TextBox.TextProperty);
```

When you want to update the source from the target (perhaps upon pressing a button labeled "Update"), call

```
bindexp.UpdateSource();
```

This call can't override the binding mode. The binding mode must be *TwoWay* or *OneWayToSource* or the call will be ignored.

If we want to start thinking about data bindings in terms of databases and other external classes and objects, we need to move away from using the *ElementName* property. *ElementName* is great when you need to bind two elements, and you can have lots of fun doing so, but it's necessary to move beyond that limitation.

Instead of indicating the source of a binding with *ElementName*, most of the bindings in the remainder of this chapter will use the *Source* property. The *Source* property refers to an object, and *Path* continues to refer to a property (or a series of chained properties) of that object.

One possibility for *Source* is an *x:Static* markup extension. As you'll recall from Chapter 21, *x:Static* lets a XAML file reference a static field or property in a class. In some cases (such as with the static properties of the *Environment* class) you can use *x:Static* by itself to get those properties. However, it's possible that what you really need is a property of the object referenced by the static property. In that case, you need a binding.

For example, consider the *DayNames* property of the *DateTimeFormatInfo* class in the *System.Globalization* namespace. *DayNames* is an instance property that returns an array of seven strings for the seven days of the week. To access *DayNames* you need an object of type *DateTimeFormatInfo*, and the *DateTimeFormatInfo* class itself provides two static properties to obtain an instance of the class. The static *DateTimeFormatInfo.InvariantInfo* property returns an instance of *DateTimeFormatInfo* applicable for an "invariant" culture (that is, the culture that Microsoft Corporation is part of), while *DateTimeFormatInfo.CurrentInfo* returns an instance appropriate for the user's own culture.

In C#, the following code stores an array of strings with the days of the week in the current user's own language:

```
string[] strDayNames = DateTimeFormatInfo.CurrentInfo.DayNames;
```

In XAML, you must define a binding to get this information. The *Source* property is an *x:Static* markup extension for the static property *DateTimeFormatInfo.CurrentInfo*. The *Path* property of the binding is the string "DayNames." The XAML file also requires an XML namespace declaration to associate the *System.Globalization* namespace with a prefix (*g*, for example).

```xml
DaysOfWeek.xaml
<!-- ===============================================
        DaysOfWeek.xaml (c) 2006 by Charles Petzold
     =============================================== -->
<StackPanel xmlns="http://schemas.microsoft.com/winfx/2006/xaml/presentation"
            xmlns:x="http://schemas.microsoft.com/winfx/2006/xaml"
            xmlns:g="clr-namespace:System.Globalization;assembly=mscorlib">

    <!-- Bind ListBox ItemsSource to DayNames property of DateTimeFormatInfo. -->

    <ListBox Name="lstbox"
             HorizontalAlignment="Center"
             Margin="24"
             ItemsSource="{Binding
                          Source={x:Static g:DateTimeFormatInfo.CurrentInfo},
                          Path=DayNames,
                          Mode=OneTime}" />

    <!-- Bind TextBlock Text to SelectedItem property of ListBox. -->

    <TextBlock HorizontalAlignment="Center"
               Text="{Binding ElementName=lstbox,
                              Path=SelectedItem, Mode=OneWay}" />
</StackPanel>
```

The file actually has two bindings. The first obtains the *DayNames* array and assigns it to the *ItemsSource* property of a *ListBox*, thereby filling the *ListBox* with the days of the week. The second binding displays the currently selected item from the *ListBox* in a *TextBlock*.

The first binding in DaysOfWeek.xaml has its *Mode* property set to *OneTime*. It really can't be anything else because there's no way for the *DateTimeFormatInfo* class to issue a notification when the days of the week change. The file uses the *Binding* syntax to access a particular property, but it's only interested in getting that data just once.

Bindings generally involve a continual transfer of information from the binding source to the target, which requires that a mechanism exist to notify the target when the source property has changed. You get this mechanism for free when the source is a dependency property. Earlier in this chapter I showed you a class named *SimpleElement* that inherited from *FrameworkElement* and did little else beyond defining a dependency property named *Number*. This class was able to participate in data binding without any additional overhead.

It is not necessary to inherit from *FrameworkElement* to define dependency properties. If the source of your data is not a visual object, you can instead inherit from *DependencyObject*. That's the class that defines the *SetValue* and *GetValue* methods you need to implement dependency properties.

For example, suppose you wanted to write a little digital clock program. You want to do the visuals in XAML (of course) but a clock also requires a source of the current date and time, and a notification mechanism when the time changes. (We'll say every second to keep it simple.) Here's a class that inherits from *DependencyObject* and defines a property named *DateTime* backed by the dependency property *DateTimeProperty*.

ClockTicker1.cs

```
//----------------------------------------------
// ClockTicker1.cs (c) 2006 by Charles Petzold
//----------------------------------------------
using System;
using System.Windows;
using System.Windows.Threading;

namespace Petzold.DigitalClock
{
    public class ClockTicker1 : DependencyObject
    {
        // Define DependencyProperty.
        public static DependencyProperty DateTimeProperty =
                DependencyProperty.Register("DateTime", typeof(DateTime),
                                    typeof(ClockTicker1));

        // Expose DependencyProperty as CLR property.
        public DateTime DateTime
        {
            set { SetValue(DateTimeProperty, value); }
            get { return (DateTime) GetValue(DateTimeProperty); }
        }

        // Constructor sets timer.
        public ClockTicker1()
        {
            DispatcherTimer timer = new DispatcherTimer();
            timer.Tick += TimerOnTick;
            timer.Interval = TimeSpan.FromSeconds(1);
            timer.Start();
        }

        // Timer event handler sets DateTime property.
        void TimerOnTick(object sender, EventArgs args)
        {
            DateTime = DateTime.Now;
        }
    }
}
```

To me, the most interesting part of the *ClockTicker1* class is the event handler for *DispatcherTimer*. It merely sets its own *DateTime* property to *DateTime.Now*, and it does so with a confident assurance that a call to *SetValue* (for which is what setting the *DateTime* property precipitates) will have some kind of profound effect outside the class.

To see what that effect is, let's look at the XAML portions of the DigitalClock project. The application definition file is first.

DigitalClockApp.xaml
```
<!-- =================================================
        DigitalClockApp.xaml (c) 2006 by Charles Petzold
     ================================================= -->
<Application xmlns="http://schemas.microsoft.com/winfx/2006/xaml/presentation"
             StartupUri="DigitalClockWindow.xaml" />
```

To define the data binding, the *Window* file needs to reference the *ClockTicker1* class. *ClockTicker1* does not derive from *FrameworkElement*, so the *Binding* can't use the *ElementName* property. It must instead use *Source*. In this case, you want *Source* to reference an object of type *ClockTicker1*, and you already know how to reference an object in markup: You define the object in a *Resources* section and access it with *StaticResource*.

DigitalClockWindow.xaml
```
<!-- =================================================
        DigitalClockWindow.xaml (c) 2006 by Charles Petzold
     ================================================= -->
<Window xmlns="http://schemas.microsoft.com/winfx/2006/xaml/presentation"
        xmlns:x="http://schemas.microsoft.com/winfx/2006/xaml"
        xmlns:src="clr-namespace:Petzold.DigitalClock"
        Title="Digital Clock"
        SizeToContent="WidthAndHeight"
        ResizeMode="CanMinimize"
        FontFamily="Bookman Old Style"
        FontSize="36pt">
    <Window.Resources>
        <src:ClockTicker1 x:Key="clock" />
    </Window.Resources>
    <Window.Content>
        <Binding Source="{StaticResource clock}" Path="DateTime" />
    </Window.Content>
</Window>
```

The *Resources* section has a definition for *ClockTicker1* and associates it with a key of "clock." The *Content* property of the window is set to a *Binding* for which the *Source* property is the *StaticResource* named "clock" and the *Path* references the *DateTime* property in *ClockTicker1*.

The program displays the date and time in its default format, which will vary by regional preferences but only show the short version of the date and time. No seconds are displayed, so you'll have to wait up to a minute to assure yourself that *ClockTicker1* is actually doing sufficient work for the data binding to succeed.

Although defining a dependency property is probably the preferred way to enable a class to successfully serve as the source of a data binding, it's not the only approach. The more traditional approach is defining an event for the job. The trick is defining the event in such a way that the data-binding logic in WPF successfully locates it.

If you define a property named *Whatever* that you want to use as the source of a data binding, you can define an event named *WhateverChanged*, and WPF will successfully locate the event. You could modify the *ClockTicker2* class for such an event by first removing the *DateTimeProperty* dependency property. Then define a public event named *DateTimeChanged*:

```
public event EventHandler DateTimeChanged;
```

Change the definition of the *DateTime* property to this:

```
public DateTime DateTime
{
    get { return DateTime.Now; }
}
```

The constructor remains the same, but the *TimerOnTick* event handler is a little larger. It is responsible for firing the *DateTimeChanged* event:

```
void TimerOnTick(object sender, EventArgs args)
{
    if (DateTimeChanged != null)
        DateTimeChanged(this, new EventArgs());
}
```

And that's it.

The WPF data-binding logic will also successfully locate an event if it's defined in a class that implements the *INotifyPropertyChanged* interface. This interface requires the class to define an event named *PropertyChanged* based on the *PropertyChangedEventHandler* delegate:

```
public event PropertyChangedEventHandler PropertyChanged;
```

When the class fires the *PropertyChanged* event, the first argument is *this* (as usual) and the second argument is an object of type *PropertyChangedEventArgs*, which inherits from *EventArgs* and defines an additional property named *PropertyName* of type *string*. This *PropertyName* property identifies the property being changed. *PropertyChangedEventArgs* also defines a constructor with a *string* argument to set *PropertyName*.

So, if a class defines a property named *DateTime* and wants to fire the *PropertyChanged* event signaling that *DateTime* has changed, it can do so like this:

```
PropertyChanged(this, new PropertyChangedEventArgs("DateTime"));
```

This is a good approach for a class that has lots of changeable properties, because the single *PropertyChanged* event can handle them all. But it can also work for just one changeable property. This *ClockTicker2* class demonstrates how to use the *PropertyChanged* event to signal a change in the *DateTime* property.

```
ClockTicker2.cs
//---------------------------------------------
// ClockTicker2.cs (c) 2006 by Charles Petzold
//---------------------------------------------
using System;
using System.ComponentModel;
using System.Windows;
using System.Windows.Threading;

namespace Petzold.FormattedDigitalClock
{
    public class ClockTicker2 : INotifyPropertyChanged
    {
        // Event required by INotifyPropertyChanged interface.
        public event PropertyChangedEventHandler PropertyChanged;

        // Public property.
        public DateTime DateTime
        {
            get { return DateTime.Now; }
        }

        // Constructor sets timer.
        public ClockTicker2()
        {
            DispatcherTimer timer = new DispatcherTimer();
            timer.Tick += TimerOnTick;
            timer.Interval = TimeSpan.FromSeconds(1);
            timer.Start();
        }

        // Timer event handler triggers PropertyChanged event.
        void TimerOnTick(object sender, EventArgs args)
        {
            if (PropertyChanged != null)
                PropertyChanged(this,
                    new PropertyChangedEventArgs("DateTime"));
        }
    }
}
```

The *ClockTicker2* class is part of a new project named FormattedDigitalClock that not only has this alternative approach to signaling a change in the *DateTime* property but also gives the writer of the XAML code more flexibility in formatting the *DateTime* object.

The format of the date and time that the previous DigitalClock program displays is the result of calling *ToString* on the *DateTime* object. However, the *DateTime* class defines an overload of the *ToString* method that accepts a formatting string argument and can render the date and time in a variety of formats. (These are documented in the opening page of the *DateTimeFormatInfo* class.) For example, the string "T" displays the time with seconds, while the string "t" displays the time without seconds. When displaying a *DateTime* object with *Console.Write* or converting it into a string with *String.Format*, you can use one of these formatting strings in an individual format item—for example, "{2:T}" if the *DateTime* object is the third object to be formatted.

It would be nice to use these formatting strings directly in a XAML file, and that's the sole purpose of this *FormattedTextConverter* class. The class implements the *IValueConverter* interface so that you can use it for the *Converter* property in a data binding. The *ConverterParameter* property of the binding specifies the formatting string in the same way as if it were used in *String.Format*, because that's what the *Convert* method uses to convert the object to a string.

```
FormattedTextConverter.cs
//----------------------------------------------------------
// FormattedTextConverter.cs (c) 2006 by Charles Petzold
//----------------------------------------------------------
using System;
using System.Globalization;
using System.Windows;
using System.Windows.Data;

namespace Petzold.FormattedDigitalClock
{
    public class FormattedTextConverter : IValueConverter
    {
        public object Convert(object value, Type typeTarget,
                              object param, CultureInfo culture)
        {
            if (param is string)
                return String.Format(param as string, value);

            return value.ToString();
        }
        public object ConvertBack(object value, Type typeTarget,
                                  object param, CultureInfo culture)
        {
            return null;
        }
    }
}
```

You can use *FormattedTextConverter* with any type of object. It makes the most sense for those objects that have multiple formatting options (such as integers or floating-point numbers) but you can also use it to adorn the object with other text. For example, the *param* argument to *Convert* could be "-->{0}<--".

The FormattedDigitalClockWindow.xaml file sets the *ConverterParameter* property to "... {0:T} ..." so that the time with seconds is surrounded by ellipses.

```
FormattedDigitalClockWindow.xaml
<!-- =============================================================
        FormattedDigitalClockWindow.xaml (c) 2006 by Charles Petzold
     ============================================================= -->
<Window xmlns="http://schemas.microsoft.com/winfx/2006/xaml/presentation"
        xmlns:x="http://schemas.microsoft.com/winfx/2006/xaml"
        xmlns:src="clr-namespace:Petzold.FormattedDigitalClock"
        Title="Formatted Digital Clock"
        SizeToContent="WidthAndHeight"
        ResizeMode="CanMinimize"
        FontFamily="Bookman Old Style"
        FontSize="36pt">
    <Window.Resources>
        <src:ClockTicker2 x:Key="clock" />
        <src:FormattedTextConverter x:Key="conv" />
    </Window.Resources>
    <Window.Content>
        <Binding Source="{StaticResource clock}" Path="DateTime"
                 Converter="{StaticResource conv}"
                 ConverterParameter="... {0:T} ..." />
    </Window.Content>
</Window>
```

Watch out: The curly brackets used in the formatting specifications are the same curly brackets used to denote XAML markup extensions! You *cannot* set *ConveterParameter* property like this (without periods or spaces, unlike my previous example):

```
ConverterParameter="{0:T}"
```

If that's what you want, you must preface it with an escape sequence that consists of the left and right curly brackets together:

```
ConverterParameter="{}{0:T}"
```

Finally, here's the application definition file for the FormattedDigitalClock project.

```
FormattedDigitalClockApp.xaml
<!-- =============================================================
        FormattedDigitalClockApp.xaml (c) 2006 by Charles Petzold
     ============================================================= -->
<Application xmlns="http://schemas.microsoft.com/winfx/2006/xaml/presentation"
             StartupUri="FormattedDigitalClockWindow.xaml" />
```

Of course, if you're really enthusiastic about using .NET formatting strings in your XAML, you simply won't be satisfied with converting one object at a time because *Console.Write* and *String.Format* aren't limited in that way. It would be nice if you could format multiple objects into a single string.

This sounds like a job for *MultiBinding*. As you'll recall from the ColorScroll program, you can bind multiple sources into a single target by means of a converter class that implements the *IMultiValueConverter* interface. The class that follows assumes the parameter named *param* is a formatting string and the array of objects named *value* are the objects to be formatted. These are both just passed to *String.Format*.

FormattedMultiTextConverter.cs

```
//------------------------------------------------------------
// FormattedMultiTextConverter.cs (c) 2006 by Charles Petzold
//------------------------------------------------------------
using System;
using System.Globalization;
using System.Windows;
using System.Windows.Data;

namespace Petzold.EnvironmentInfo2
{
    public class FormattedMultiTextConverter : IMultiValueConverter
    {
        public object Convert(object[] value, Type typeTarget,
                              object param, CultureInfo culture)
        {
            return String.Format((string) param, value);
        }
        public object[] ConvertBack(object value, Type[] typeTarget,
                                    object param, CultureInfo culture)
        {
            return null;
        }
    }
}
```

To demonstrate how this works, let's revisit a problem from the previous chapter: formatting static properties from the *Environment* class. The earlier solution used a separate *TextBlock* for every little piece of text. The EnvironmentInfo2 program shown here uses a single *TextBlock* with its *Text* property bound to a *MultiBinding* object. The *Converter* property references the *FormattedMultiTextConverter* class, of course.

EnvironmentInfo2Window.xaml

```
<!-- ========================================================
        EnvironmentInfo2Window.xaml (c) 2006 by Charles Petzold
     ======================================================== -->
<Window xmlns="http://schemas.microsoft.com/winfx/2006/xaml/presentation"
        xmlns:x="http://schemas.microsoft.com/winfx/2006/xaml"
        xmlns:s="clr-namespace:System;assembly=mscorlib"
        xmlns:src="clr-namespace:Petzold.EnvironmentInfo2"
        Title="Environment Info">
    <Window.Resources>
        <src:FormattedMultiTextConverter x:Key="conv" />
```

```
    </Window.Resources>

    <TextBlock>
        <TextBlock.Text>
            <MultiBinding Converter="{StaticResource conv}"
                          ConverterParameter=
"Operating System Version: {0}
&#x000A;.NET Version: {1}
&#x000A;Machine Name: {2}
&#x000A;User Name: {3}
&#x000A;User Domain Name: {4}
&#x000A;System Directory: {5}
&#x000A;Current Directory: {6}
&#x000A;Command Line: {7}" >
                <Binding Source="{x:Static s:Environment.OSVersion}" />
                <Binding Source="{x:Static s:Environment.Version}" />
                <Binding Source="{x:Static s:Environment.MachineName}" />
                <Binding Source="{x:Static s:Environment.UserName}" />
                <Binding Source="{x:Static s:Environment.UserDomainName}" />
                <Binding Source="{x:Static s:Environment.SystemDirectory}" />
                <Binding Source="{x:Static s:Environment.CurrentDirectory}" />
                <Binding Source="{x:Static s:Environment.CommandLine}" />
            </MultiBinding>
        </TextBlock.Text>
    </TextBlock>
</Window>
```

The *ConverterParameter* is a long string that spills over onto multiple lines. To avoid excessive white space in this string, I aligned it against the left margin. Notice that line feeds are XML style ("
") rather than C# style, and they appear at the left margin, again to avoid white space from creeping into where it's not welcome.

Also notice that the *Binding* elements don't require *Path* attributes because we're interested in the *Source* itself rather than the property of the *Source*. Alternatively, you could specify the *Path* with an empty string:

```
Path=""
```

Here's the application definition file for the project.

EnvironmentInfo2App.xaml

```
<!-- ======================================================
     EnvironmentInfo2App.xaml (c) 2006 by Charles Petzold
     ====================================================== -->
<Application xmlns="http://schemas.microsoft.com/winfx/2006/xaml/presentation"
             StartupUri="EnvironmentInfo2Window.xaml" />
```

So far you've seen *Binding* markup using *ElementName* and *Source*. The only other alternative is *RelativeSource*, which lets you reference an ancestor element in the element tree, or the element itself. This RelativeSourceDemo.xaml file shows three bindings using *RelativeSource*.

RelativeSourceDemo.xaml

```
<!-- =====================================================
        RelativeSourceDemo.xaml (c) 2006 by Charles Petzold
     ===================================================== -->
<StackPanel xmlns="http://schemas.microsoft.com/winfx/2006/xaml/presentation"
            xmlns:x="http://schemas.microsoft.com/winfx/2006/xaml"
            TextBlock.FontSize="12" >

    <StackPanel Orientation="Horizontal"
                HorizontalAlignment="Center">
        <TextBlock Text="This TextBlock has a FontFamily of " />
        <TextBlock Text="{Binding RelativeSource={RelativeSource self},
                                  Path=FontFamily}" />
        <TextBlock Text=" and a FontSize of " />
        <TextBlock Text="{Binding RelativeSource={RelativeSource self},
                                  Path=FontSize}" />
    </StackPanel>

    <StackPanel Orientation="Horizontal"
                HorizontalAlignment="Center">
        <TextBlock Text="This TextBlock is inside a StackPanel with " />
        <TextBlock Text=
            "{Binding RelativeSource={RelativeSource
                            AncestorType={x:Type StackPanel}},
                    Path=Orientation}" />

        <TextBlock Text=" orientation" />
    </StackPanel>

    <StackPanel Orientation="Horizontal"
                HorizontalAlignment="Center">
        <TextBlock Text="The parent StackPanel has " />
        <TextBlock Text=
            "{Binding RelativeSource={RelativeSource
                            AncestorType={x:Type StackPanel}, AncestorLevel=2},
                    Path=Orientation}" />

        <TextBlock Text=" orientation" />
    </StackPanel>
</StackPanel>
```

Nothing in this file has a *Name* attribute. The first binding includes the *RelativeSource* markup extension that lets a binding reference the same element the binding occurs in:

```
RelativeSource={RelativeSource self}
```

In this example, the *TextBlock* displays its own font information. Later on in the program another *TextBlock* displays the *Orientation* property of the *StackPanel* it belongs to using a *RelativeSource* markup extension of

```
RelativeSource={RelativeSource AncestorType={x:Type StackPanel}}
```

However, that *StackPanel* is nested within another *StackPanel*. To get at another *StackPanel* further up the chain requires the *AncestorLevel* property, as the third binding demonstrates:

```
RelativeSource={RelativeSource AncestorType={x:Type StackPanel}, AncestorLevel=2}
```

This chapter has demonstrated several different manifestations of the *Binding* element and several ways you can use it. Data bindings also play an important role in programs that must display data from a database of some sort and in programs that let a user modify the data or enter new data. Chapter 26 explores the techniques you can use in writing such applications.

Chapter 24
Styles

Although the *Resources* sections of XAML files are useful for defining miscellaneous objects that you refer to in markup, many resource sections are used primarily for the definition of *Style* objects. Styles are essentially collections of property values that are applied to elements. Styles are partially the compensation for not being able to use loops in XAML to create multiple elements with identical properties.

For example, suppose your page contains a bunch of buttons. You want these buttons to share some common properties. You might want the same *Margin* property to apply to all these buttons, for example, or the same font. You can define these characteristics in a style, and then use that same style for multiple elements. In this way, styles are similar in purpose and functionality to style sheets in Microsoft Word and Cascading Style Sheets in HTML. But the WPF implementation of styles is more powerful because changes in properties can also be specified, which are triggered by changes in other properties, or by events.

The *Style* class is defined in *System.Windows*. It derives from *Object* and has no descendents. The most important property of *Style* is named *Setters*. The *Setters* property is of type *Setter-BaseCollection*, which is a collection of *SetterBase* objects. *SetterBase* is an abstract class from which *Setter* and *EventSetter* derive. These objects are called "setters" because they result in the setting of properties or event handlers.

Setter is the content property of *Style*, so *Setter* and *EventSetter* elements are children of the *Style* element:

```
<Style ...>
    <Setter ... />
    <EventSetter ... />
    <Setter ... />
</Style>
```

Within *Style* definitions, *Setter* objects typically show up much more often than *EventSetter* objects. A *Setter* basically associates a particular property with a value, and the two crucial properties of the *Setter* class are *Property* (of type *DependencyProperty*) and *Value* (of type *object*). In XAML, a *Setter* looks like this:

```
<Setter Property="Control.FontSize" Value="24" />
```

Although the *Property* attribute always references a dependency property, notice that the property is specified as *FontSize* rather than *FontSizeProperty*. The property name usually (but not always) needs to be preceded by the class in which the property is defined or inherited. In code, you need to use the actual dependency property name, and it's always preceded by a class name.

If you need to indicate a value of *null* for the *Value* attribute, use the markup extension *x:Null*:

```
Value="{x:Null}"
```

The *FrameworkElement* and *FrameworkContentElement* classes define a property named *Style* of type *Style*, so it's possible—but usually not particularly useful—to define a *Style* element that is local to an element to which the style applies. For example, the following stand-alone XAML file defines a *Style* local to a *Button* element.

```
ButtonWithLocalStyle.xaml
<!-- =======================================================
        ButtonWithLocalStyle.xaml (c) 2006 by Charles Petzold
     ======================================================= -->
<Button xmlns="http://schemas.microsoft.com/winfx/2006/xaml/presentation"
        HorizontalAlignment="Center" VerticalAlignment="Center"
        Foreground="Red">
    <Button.Style>
        <Style>
            <Setter Property="Button.FontSize" Value="18pt" />
            <Setter Property="Control.Foreground" Value="Blue" />
        </Style>
    </Button.Style>
    Button with Local Style
</Button>
```

The *Style* element here includes two *Setter* elements to define the button *FontSize* and *Foreground* properties. Notice that I've specified the first as *Button.FontSize* and the second as *Control.Foreground*. It doesn't really matter here which class name you use because *Button* inherits the *Foreground* property from *Control*. You could even use *TextBlock.FontSize* and *TextBlock.Foreground* and it would work the same. Even though there's no inheritance involved between *TextBlock* and *Button*, both *TextBlock* and *Control* define these two properties based on the original definitions in *TextElement*. (You can verify this by looking at the *Owner* class of these properties in the ExploreDependencyProperties program from Chapter 16.)

You'll also notice that the *Style* definition indicates that the *Foreground* property should be *Blue* but the *Foreground* property of the *Button* is assigned explicitly as *Red* near the top of the file. Which color is used? The button foreground is red because *local* settings—which is the term used for properties set directly on the element—take precedence over *Style* settings. But styles take precedence over properties inherited through the visual tree.

It is much more common for styles to be defined in resource sections so that they can be shared among multiple elements and controls. Like other resources, styles are identified and referenced by a text key, and they can potentially be used in any element lower in the visual tree. Styles defined in the *Resources* section of the *Application* object can be used throughout the application.

Here's a *StackPanel* that includes a *Resources* section with a *Style* definition. The *Style* is given a key name of "normal." The three buttons that are children of the *StackPanel* refer to this style with the *StaticResource* markup extension.

StyleWithMultipleButtons.xaml

```
<!-- ===========================================================
        StyleWithMultipleButtons.xaml (c) 2006 by Charles Petzold
     =========================================================== -->
<StackPanel xmlns="http://schemas.microsoft.com/winfx/2006/xaml/presentation"
            xmlns:x="http://schemas.microsoft.com/winfx/2006/xaml">
    <StackPanel.Resources>
        <Style x:Key="normal">
            <Setter Property="Control.FontSize" Value="24" />
            <Setter Property="Control.Foreground" Value="Blue" />
            <Setter Property="Control.HorizontalAlignment" Value="Center" />
            <Setter Property="Control.Margin" Value="24" />
            <Setter Property="Control.Padding" Value="20, 10, 20, 10" />
        </Style>
    </StackPanel.Resources>

    <Button Style="{StaticResource normal}">
        Button Number 1
    </Button>

    <Button Style="{StaticResource normal}">
        Button Number 2
    </Button>

    <Button Style="{StaticResource normal}">
        Button Number 3
    </Button>
</StackPanel>
```

Because elements and controls often share many of the same properties, you can define styles that are used for different types of elements. Here's a style that is shared by *Button* controls as well as a *TextBlock* element.

StyleWithMultipleElements.xaml

```
<!-- ===========================================================
        StyleWithMultipleElements.xaml (c) 2006 by Charles Petzold
     =========================================================== -->
<StackPanel xmlns="http://schemas.microsoft.com/winfx/2006/xaml/presentation"
            xmlns:x="http://schemas.microsoft.com/winfx/2006/xaml">
    <StackPanel.Resources>
        <Style x:Key="normal">
            <Setter Property="Control.FontSize" Value="24" />
            <Setter Property="Control.Foreground" Value="Blue" />
            <Setter Property="Control.HorizontalAlignment" Value="Center" />
            <Setter Property="Control.Margin" Value="24" />
            <Setter Property="Control.Padding" Value="20, 10, 20, 10" />
        </Style>
```

```
            </StackPanel.Resources>

            <Button Style="{StaticResource normal}">
                Button on top of the stack
            </Button>

            <TextBlock Style="{StaticResource normal}">
                TextBlock in the middle of the stack
            </TextBlock>

            <Button Style="{StaticResource normal}">
                Button on the bottom of the stack
            </Button>
        </StackPanel>
```

In fact, in this program you can even define a *Setter* for a property unique to the *Button*, like this one:

```
<Setter Property="Button.IsDefault" Value="true" />
```

The program still works. The *TextBlock* element just ignores that *Setter* because *TextBlock* doesn't have an *IsDefault* property.

As with other resources, you can use the same key for a *Style* definition in multiple resource sections. For any particular element, the applicable *Style* will be that which is first encountered going up the visual tree.

Here's a *Grid* that contains a *StackPanel* with three buttons. The *Grid* defines a style named "normal" with a *FontSize* of 24 and a *Foreground* of *Blue*. The *Resources* section of the *StackPanel* also contains a *Style* named "normal" with a *Foreground* of *Red*.

StylesWithSameKeys.xaml

```
<!-- ===================================================
        StylesWithSameKeys.xaml (c) 2006 by Charles Petzold
        =================================================== -->
<Grid xmlns="http://schemas.microsoft.com/winfx/2006/xaml/presentation"
      xmlns:x="http://schemas.microsoft.com/winfx/2006/xaml">
    <Grid.Resources>
        <Style TargetType="{x:Type Button}">
            <Setter Property="Control.FontSize" Value="24" />
            <Setter Property="Control.Foreground" Value="Blue" />
        </Style>
    </Grid.Resources>

    <StackPanel>
        <StackPanel.Resources>
            <Style TargetType="{x:Type Button}">
                <Setter Property="Control.Foreground" Value="Red" />
            </Style>
        </StackPanel.Resources>
        <Button>
```

```
            Button Number 1
        </Button>
        <Button>
            Button Number 2
        </Button>
        <Button>
            Button Number 3
        </Button>
    </StackPanel>
</Grid>
```

The buttons will use the style defined in the *StackPanel*. The foreground color is red and the *FontSize* is the default—not the *FontSize* defined in the earlier *Style*. Using the same name for multiple styles does *not* allow overriding selected properties while keeping the earlier definitions of others. (You'll see how to do that little trick shortly.) The choice here is between entire *Style* definitions.

If you can't express the value of a property with a text string in a *Setter*, you need to break out the *Value* property as a property element. The following XAML file has a *Setter* property for the *Background* property that requires a gradient brush.

StyleWithPropertyElement.xaml

```
<!-- ==========================================================
     StyleWithPropertyElement.xaml (c) 2006 by Charles Petzold
     ========================================================== -->
<StackPanel xmlns="http://schemas.microsoft.com/winfx/2006/xaml/presentation"
            xmlns:x="http://schemas.microsoft.com/winfx/2006/xaml">
    <StackPanel.Resources>
        <Style x:Key="normal">
            <Setter Property="Control.FontSize" Value="24" />
            <Setter Property="Control.HorizontalAlignment" Value="Center" />
            <Setter Property="Control.Margin" Value="24" />
            <Setter Property="Control.Background">
                <Setter.Value>
                    <LinearGradientBrush StartPoint="1,0" EndPoint="1,1">
                        <LinearGradientBrush.GradientStops>
                            <GradientStop Color="LightBlue" Offset="0" />
                            <GradientStop Color="Aquamarine" Offset="1" />
                        </LinearGradientBrush.GradientStops>
                    </LinearGradientBrush>
                </Setter.Value>
            </Setter>
        </Style>
    </StackPanel.Resources>

    <Button Style="{StaticResource normal}">
        Button Number 1
    </Button>

    <Button Style="{StaticResource normal}">
        Button Number 2
    </Button>
```

```
        <Button Style="{StaticResource normal}">
            Button Number 3
        </Button>
</StackPanel>
```

Another solution is to make that gradient brush a resource, and to refer to the resource in the *Style* definition using the *StaticResource* markup extension. As you learned in Chapter 21, the *Application*, *FrameworkElement*, and *FrameworkContentElement* classes all define a *Resources* property of type *ResourceDictionary*. *Style*, too, defines this same *Resources* property, so you can put the resources right in the *Style* definition. This is the architecturally preferable approach for resources not used anywhere else. The following XAML file shows an example.

StyleWithResource.xaml

```
<!-- =================================================
        StyleWithResource.xaml (c) 2006 by Charles Petzold
     ================================================= -->
<StackPanel xmlns="http://schemas.microsoft.com/winfx/2006/xaml/presentation"
            xmlns:x="http://schemas.microsoft.com/winfx/2006/xaml">
    <StackPanel.Resources>

        <Style x:Key="normal">

            <Style.Resources>
                <LinearGradientBrush x:Key="gradbrush"
                                     StartPoint="1,0" EndPoint="1,1">
                    <LinearGradientBrush.GradientStops>
                        <GradientStop Color="LightBlue" Offset="0" />
                        <GradientStop Color="Aquamarine" Offset="1" />
                    </LinearGradientBrush.GradientStops>
                </LinearGradientBrush>
            </Style.Resources>

            <Setter Property="Control.FontSize" Value="24" />
            <Setter Property="Control.HorizontalAlignment" Value="Center" />
            <Setter Property="Control.Margin" Value="24" />
            <Setter Property="Control.Background"
                    Value="{StaticResource gradbrush}" />
        </Style>
    </StackPanel.Resources>

    <Button Style="{StaticResource normal}">
        Button Number 1
    </Button>

    <Button Style="{StaticResource normal}">
        Button Number 2
    </Button>

    <Button Style="{StaticResource normal}">
        Button Number 3
    </Button>
</StackPanel>
```

The *Style* class defines only six properties, and you've already seen two of them (*Setters* and *Resources*). *Style* also defines a property named *TargetType* that lets you specify the type of the element you want the style to be applied to. The syntax requires the markup extension of *x:Type*, which is enclosed in curly brackets and followed by the name of the class whose type you want to reference:

```
<Style TargetType="{x:Type Button}" ...>
    ...
</Style>
```

You can think of *x:Type* as the XAML equivalent of *typeof* in C#. If you set the *TargetType*, you don't need to specify an *x:Key* value. A key is fabricated from the *TargetType*. Without an *x:Key*, the style shown in the preceding example applies to all *Button* controls in the element in which the *Style* is defined and all Button controls in any child elements. If that's not what you want, include an *x:Key* attribute as well and refer to that key in the *Button* elements.

When you use *TargetType* in the *Style*, the style will apply only to those elements that have the exact type. For example, you can't use *Control* in the *TargetType* and have the style apply to both *Button* controls and *Label* controls.

One advantage of using *TargetType* is that you don't need to fully qualify the property names within the *Setter* elements. Normally you need to use something like this:

```
<Setter Property="Button.FontSize" Value="24" />
```

When you use *TargetType* you can simplify that markup to this:

```
<Setter Property="FontSize" Value="24" />
```

This simplification may be worth adding the *TargetType* attribute even if you plan on also using an *x:Key* attribute in the style. The *TargetType* also clarifies your intentions to someone else looking at the file.

Here's a XAML file that defines two *Style* elements, the first with a *FontSize* of 24 and a *Foreground* of *Blue* that applies to *Button* objects, and the second with a *Foreground* of *Red* that applies to *TextBlock* objects. The *StackPanel* contains a *Button* with text content, a *TextBlock*, and a *Button* with *TextBlock* content. Can you anticipate the font size and foreground colors of these three elements?

StylesWithTargetTypes.xaml

```
<!-- ======================================================
        StylesWithTargetTypes.xaml (c) 2006 by Charles Petzold
     ====================================================== -->
<StackPanel xmlns="http://schemas.microsoft.com/winfx/2006/xaml/presentation"
            xmlns:x="http://schemas.microsoft.com/winfx/2006/xaml">
    <StackPanel.Resources>

        <Style TargetType="{x:Type Button}">
```

```
            <Setter Property="FontSize" Value="24" />
            <Setter Property="Foreground" Value="Blue" />
        </Style>

        <Style TargetType="{x:Type TextBlock}">
            <Setter Property="Foreground" Value="Red" />
        </Style>

    </StackPanel.Resources>

    <Button>
        Button with Text Content
    </Button>

    <TextBlock>
        TextBlock Text
    </TextBlock>

    <Button>
        <TextBlock>
            Button with TextBlock Content
        </TextBlock>
    </Button>
</StackPanel>
```

The first button gets the style with a *TargetType* of *Button*. The button displays blue text with a font size of 24. The *TextBlock* element gets the style with the *TargetType* of *TextBlock*. The text is red and the font size is the default. The bottom button gets the first style—a *Foreground* property of *Blue* and a *FontSize* of 24. However, the *TextBlock* inside the button gets the second style—a *Foreground* property of *Red*. Through normal property inheritance, the *TextBlock* inherits the *FontSize* property of its *Button* parent. The button displays red text with a font size of 24. The style normally takes precedence over property inheritance, but the *TextBlock* has no style setting for the font size, so it inherits the property from its visual parent.

If you have a bunch of dialog boxes in an application, and these dialog boxes have some radio buttons on stack panels within group boxes, you know you need to apply a *Margin* property to each *RadioButton to* make it look reasonably attractive. This is an excellent application of a *Style* with a *TargetType* of *RadioButton*.

You can define keys along with *TargetType* specifications. In that case, a particular element gets a particular style when the type of the element matches the *TargetType* of the style *and* the keys match. For multiple styles defined in any particular resource section, the keys must be unique.

For any particular element, only one *Style* applies. This is the *Style* encountered first when searching up the visual tree where the key matches, or the class of the element matches the *TargetType*, or both, if the *Style* has both. Obviously, sometimes you'll want to define a new *Style* that is based on an existing *Style* but has some different or additional property definitions. In such a case you can define a style with the *BasedOn* attribute referencing an existing style. Here's the stack of three buttons again, but notice that a *Style* with the key of "hotbtn" has been defined with a *Foreground* of *Red*. The *Button* in the middle uses this style rather than the "normal" style.

```
BasedOnStyle.xaml
<!-- =========================================
     BasedOnStyle.xaml (c) 2006 by Charles Petzold
     ========================================= -->
<StackPanel xmlns="http://schemas.microsoft.com/winfx/2006/xaml/presentation"
            xmlns:x="http://schemas.microsoft.com/winfx/2006/xaml">
    <StackPanel.Resources>

        <Style x:Key="normal">
            <Setter Property="Control.FontSize" Value="24" />
            <Setter Property="Control.Foreground" Value="Blue" />
            <Setter Property="Control.HorizontalAlignment" Value="Center" />
            <Setter Property="Control.Margin" Value="24" />
            <Setter Property="Control.Padding" Value="20, 10, 20, 10" />
        </Style>

        <Style x:Key="hotbtn" BasedOn="{StaticResource normal}">
            <Setter Property="Control.Foreground" Value="Red" />
        </Style>

    </StackPanel.Resources>

    <Button Style="{StaticResource normal}">
        Button Number 1
    </Button>

    <Button Style="{StaticResource hotbtn}">
        Button Number 2
    </Button>

    <Button Style="{StaticResource normal}">
        Button Number 3
    </Button>
</StackPanel>
```

The *BasedOn* syntax is the same as the syntax used in referencing a *Style* by an element, and the same rules apply: The new style is based on the first style encountered in the visual tree with a matching key.

It would not be entirely correct to say that the second button uses the properties defined by the "normal" style except when those properties are overridden by the "hotbtn" style. It is better to think of the second button as using the properties defined by the "hotbtn" style, where the "hotbtn" style is initialized with properties originally defined for the "normal" style. An element has at most only one *Style* object, and for the second button that *Style* is "hotbtn." When writing XAML, it's easy to forget that you're still dealing with properties and objects. *Style* is a property defined by *FrameworkElement*, the *Style* property is *null* by default, and the

Style object you set to this property has only one *Setters* collection that contains *Setter* objects for all the properties that the *Style* sets.

It is also possible to base a style on an existing style that has a *TargetType* attribute, but the *BasedOn* syntax is a bit messier:

```
BasedOn="{StaticResource {x:Type Button}}"
```

The new *Style* must also have a *TargetType* that is the same as the class the style is based on, or a derivative of that class. Here's an example where the *TargetType* properties of the two styles are the same.

BasedOnTargetType.cs

```
<!-- =================================================
        BasedOnTargetType.xaml (c) 2006 by Charles Petzold
     ================================================= -->
<StackPanel xmlns="http://schemas.microsoft.com/winfx/2006/xaml/presentation"
            xmlns:x="http://schemas.microsoft.com/winfx/2006/xaml">
    <StackPanel.Resources>

        <Style TargetType="{x:Type Button}">
            <Setter Property="Control.FontSize" Value="24" />
            <Setter Property="Control.Foreground" Value="Blue" />
            <Setter Property="Control.HorizontalAlignment" Value="Center" />
            <Setter Property="Control.Margin" Value="24" />
        </Style>

        <Style x:Key="hotbtn"
               TargetType="{x:Type Button}"
               BasedOn="{StaticResource {x:Type Button}}">
            <Setter Property="Control.Foreground" Value="Red" />
        </Style>

    </StackPanel.Resources>

    <Button>
        Button Number 1
    </Button>

    <Button Style="{StaticResource hotbtn}">
        Button Number 2
    </Button>

    <Button>
        Button Number 3
    </Button>
</StackPanel>
```

The second style definition requires an explicit *x:Key* attribute. Otherwise, there would be two conflicting styles.

However, try this: Change the *TargetType* of the first style to *Control*, and change the *BasedOn* of the second style to *Control* as well, but leave the *TargetType* of the second style as *Button*. This is valid. A style that combines a *BasedOn* property and a *TargetType* property can refer to the same class or a class it inherits from. Now the second style has a *TargetType* of *Button* and a *x:Key* of "hotbtn", so the second button uses that style. The first and third buttons get no style. If you eliminate the *x:Key* definition from the second style and the *Style* attribute from the second button, all three buttons get the second style.

If you're using *TargetType* so that particular types of elements always get a particular style, you can define a hierarchy of styles that parallel the hierarchy of classes. Here's an example.

TargetTypeDerivatives.xaml

```xml
<!-- =====================================================
      TargetTypeDerivatives.xaml (c) 2006 by Charles Petzold
     ===================================================== -->
<StackPanel xmlns="http://schemas.microsoft.com/winfx/2006/xaml/presentation"
            xmlns:x="http://schemas.microsoft.com/winfx/2006/xaml">
    <StackPanel.Resources>

        <Style TargetType="{x:Type Control}">
            <Setter Property="Control.FontSize" Value="24" />
            <Setter Property="Control.Foreground" Value="Blue" />
            <Setter Property="Control.HorizontalAlignment" Value="Center" />
            <Setter Property="Control.Margin" Value="24" />
        </Style>

        <Style TargetType="{x:Type Button}"
               BasedOn="{StaticResource {x:Type Control}}">
            <Setter Property="Control.Foreground" Value="Red" />
        </Style>

        <Style TargetType="{x:Type Label}"
               BasedOn="{StaticResource {x:Type Control}}">
            <Setter Property="Control.Foreground" Value="Green" />
        </Style>

        <Style TargetType="{x:Type TextBox}"
               BasedOn="{StaticResource {x:Type Control}}">
        </Style>
    </StackPanel.Resources>

    <Button>
        Button Control
    </Button>

    <Label>
        Label Control
    </Label>

    <TextBox>
        TextBox Control
    </TextBox>
</StackPanel>
```

The last *Style* element for the *TextBox* doesn't define any new properties, so the *TextBox* gets a *Foreground* of *Blue*. Of course, the latter *Style* elements can define properties specific to the individual control types.

Styles have certain inherent restrictions. For example, you might want to define a *Style* for a *StackPanel* so that it always contains several of the same types of elements:

```
<!-- This doesn't work! -->
<Style TargetType="{x:Type StackPanel}">
    <Setter Property="Children">
        <Setter.Value>
            ...
        </Setter.Value>
    </Setter>
</Style>
```

The main problem here is that the *Children* property defined by *Panel* is not backed by a dependency property; hence, you cannot use a *Style* to set that property. You might want to consider defining a new class derived from *StackPanel* for jobs of this nature, or perhaps a template (as discussed in the next chapter).

Here's a piece of XAML that attempts to define a style for a *Button* so that it always contains an *Image* object:

```
<!-- This doesn't work! -->
<Style TargetType="{x:Type Button}">
    <Setter Property="Content">
        <Setter.Value>
            <Image ... />
        </Setter.Value>
    </Setter>
</Style>
```

The problem—as the error message indicates—is that "*Setter* does not support values derived from *Visual* or *ContentElement*." Any object referred to in a particular *Style* is created only once to be part of that *Style*, and hence is shared among all elements that use that *Style*. An element like *Image*—and indeed, any element derived from *Visual* or *ContentElement*—can have only one parent, and that would not be the case if the *Style* object were shared. Again, consider a custom class or a template if you run into this problem.

The *Value* attribute of a *Setter* element can be a data binding, as the following XAML demonstrates.

SetterWithBinding.xaml
```
<!-- ====================================================
        SetterWithBinding.xaml (c) 2006 by Charles Petzold
     ==================================================== -->
<StackPanel xmlns="http://schemas.microsoft.com/winfx/2006/xaml/presentation"
            xmlns:x="http://schemas.microsoft.com/winfx/2006/xaml">
    <StackPanel.Resources>
```

```
        <Style TargetType="{x:Type Button}">

            <Setter Property="FontSize"
                Value="{Binding ElementName=scroll, Path=Value}" />

            <Setter Property="HorizontalAlignment" Value="Center" />
            <Setter Property="Margin" Value="24" />
        </Style>
    </StackPanel.Resources>

    <ScrollBar Name="scroll" Orientation="Horizontal" Margin="24"
            Minimum="11" Maximum="100" Value="24" />

    <Button>
        Button Number 1
    </Button>

    <Button>
        Button Number 2
    </Button>

    <Button>
        Button Number 3
    </Button>
</StackPanel>
```

The *Style* element for *Button* contains a *Setter* for the *FontSize* property in which the *Value* attribute is a *Binding* referencing the *Value* property of the *ScrollBar* named *scroll*. As you manipulate the scrollbar, the buttons get smaller and larger.

Although I've been demonstrating styles with simple controls and *TextBlock* elements, styles also play an important role in drawing graphics. Here's a XAML file that defines a *Style* with a *TargetType* of *Ellipse*. The *Style* defines the outline of each ellipse and its size, leaving the individual *Ellipse* elements to focus on the location and color.

GraphicsStyles.xaml
```
<!-- =================================================
     GraphicsStyles.xaml (c) 2006 by Charles Petzold
     ================================================= -->
<Canvas xmlns="http://schemas.microsoft.com/winfx/2006/xaml/presentation"
        xmlns:x="http://schemas.microsoft.com/winfx/2006/xaml">
    <Canvas.Resources>
        <Style TargetType="{x:Type Ellipse}">
            <Setter Property="Stroke" Value="Black" />
            <Setter Property="StrokeThickness" Value="3" />
            <Setter Property="Width" Value="96" />
            <Setter Property="Height" Value="96" />
        </Style>
    </Canvas.Resources>

    <Ellipse Canvas.Left="100" Canvas.Top="50" Fill="Blue" />
    <Ellipse Canvas.Left="150" Canvas.Top="100" Fill="Red" />
```

```
        <Ellipse Canvas.Left="200" Canvas.Top="150" Fill="Green" />
        <Ellipse Canvas.Left="250" Canvas.Top="100" Fill="Cyan" />
        <Ellipse Canvas.Left="300" Canvas.Top="50" Fill="Magenta" />
    </Canvas>
```

Suppose you need to draw a series of horizontal lines, perhaps similar to the ruled lines of the pad in the YellowPad program from Chapter 22. The *Style* element would include a *Setter* for the *Stroke* color, of course, and because each of the horizontal lines begins and ends at the same *X* coordinate, the *Style* could include *Setter* elements for both *X1* and *X2* as well.

```
<Style TargetType="Line">
    <Setter Property="Stroke" Value="Blue" />
    <Setter Property="X1" Value="100" />
    <Setter Property="X2" Value="300" />
</Style>
```

The individual *Line* elements could then be as simple as this:

```
<Line Y1="100" Y2="100" />
<Line Y1="125" Y2="125" />
<Line Y1="150" Y2="150" />
...
```

That's not too bad. But if you ever needed to alter the location of these lines—perhaps move them down by 12 units—you'd need to manually change the values of both *Y1* and *Y2*, which is about twice as much work as you probably want. Considering that these are horizontal lines, and the values of *Y1* and *Y2* are always the same, might there be a way to specify just one value in each *Line* element?

The solution is a *Binding* using *RelativeSource*, which I discussed toward the end of the previous chapter. You can define a *Setter* for the *Y2* property that indicates it should be the same as the *Y1* property:

```
<Setter Property="Y2"
        Value="{Binding RelativeSource={RelativeSource self}, Path=Y1}" />
```

You then need only specify the value *Y1* in the individual *Line* elements, and that value is also used for *Y2*.

The following XAML file uses this technique to draw a grid of horizontal and vertical lines. Both the "horz" and "vert" styles are based on a *Style* with an *x:Key* of "base" that defines the line colors.

DrawGrid.xaml

```
<!-- =========================================
     DrawGrid.xaml (c) 2006 by Charles Petzold
     ========================================= -->
<Canvas xmlns="http://schemas.microsoft.com/winfx/2006/xaml/presentation"
        xmlns:x="http://schemas.microsoft.com/winfx/2006/xaml">
```

```
        <Canvas.Resources>
            <Style x:Key="base" TargetType="Line">
                <Setter Property="Stroke" Value="Blue" />
            </Style>

            <Style x:Key="horz" TargetType="Line"
                   BasedOn="{StaticResource base}">
                <Setter Property="X1" Value="100" />
                <Setter Property="X2" Value="300" />
                <Setter Property="Y2"
                        Value="{Binding RelativeSource={RelativeSource self},
                                        Path=Y1}" />
            </Style>

            <Style x:Key="vert" TargetType="Line"
                   BasedOn="{StaticResource base}">
                <Setter Property="Y1" Value="100" />
                <Setter Property="Y2" Value="300" />
                <Setter Property="X2"
                        Value="{Binding RelativeSource={RelativeSource self},
                                        Path=X1}" />
            </Style>
        </Canvas.Resources>

        <Line Style="{StaticResource horz}" Y1="100" />
        <Line Style="{StaticResource horz}" Y1="125" />
        <Line Style="{StaticResource horz}" Y1="150" />
        <Line Style="{StaticResource horz}" Y1="175" />
        <Line Style="{StaticResource horz}" Y1="200" />
        <Line Style="{StaticResource horz}" Y1="225" />
        <Line Style="{StaticResource horz}" Y1="250" />
        <Line Style="{StaticResource horz}" Y1="275" />
        <Line Style="{StaticResource horz}" Y1="300" />

        <Line Style="{StaticResource vert}" X1="100" />
        <Line Style="{StaticResource vert}" X1="125" />
        <Line Style="{StaticResource vert}" X1="150" />
        <Line Style="{StaticResource vert}" X1="175" />
        <Line Style="{StaticResource vert}" X1="200" />
        <Line Style="{StaticResource vert}" X1="225" />
        <Line Style="{StaticResource vert}" X1="250" />
        <Line Style="{StaticResource vert}" X1="275" />
        <Line Style="{StaticResource vert}" X1="300" />
    </Canvas>
```

Although you should really consider a *for* loop in C# when drawing repetitive elements of this type, the numeric repetition in the individual elements has been reduced to such an extent that using XAML can almost be justified.

A *Style* property is defined not only for *FrameworkElement*, but also for *FrameworkContentElement*, which means that you can define styles for classes that derive from *TextElement*. This lets you define styles for use in formatting items in a *FlowDocument*. Here's the first paragraph from *Alice's Adventures in Wonderland*, with two *Paragraph* styles defined and referenced.

DocumentStyles.xaml

```
<!-- =====================================================
        DocumentStyles.xaml (c) 2006 by Charles Petzold
     ===================================================== -->
<Page xmlns="http://schemas.microsoft.com/winfx/2006/xaml/presentation"
      xmlns:x="http://schemas.microsoft.com/winfx/2006/xaml"
      Title="I. Down the Rabbit-Hole">
    <Page.Resources>

        <Style TargetType="{x:Type Paragraph}" x:Key="Normal">
            <Setter Property="TextIndent" Value="0.25in" />
        </Style>

        <Style TargetType="{x:Type Paragraph}" x:Key="ChapterHead">
            <Setter Property="TextAlignment" Value="Center" />
            <Setter Property="FontSize" Value="16pt" />
        </Style>

    </Page.Resources>
    <FlowDocumentReader>
        <FlowDocument>
            <Paragraph Style="{StaticResource ChapterHead}">
                Chapter I
            </Paragraph>
            <Paragraph Style="{StaticResource ChapterHead}">
                Down the Rabbit-Hole
            </Paragraph>
            <Paragraph Style="{StaticResource Normal}">
                Alice was beginning to get very tired of sitting by
                her sister on the bank, and of having nothing to do:
                once or twice she had peeped into the book her sister
                was reading, but it had no pictures or conversations
                in it, &#x201C;and what is the use of a book,&#x201D;
                thought Alice, &#x201C;without pictures or
                conversations?&#x201D;
            </Paragraph>
            <Paragraph Style="{StaticResource Normal}">
                ...
            </Paragraph>
        </FlowDocument>
    </FlowDocumentReader>
</Page>
```

Of course, you probably don't need convincing that text styles are quite valuable, as is the ability to base one style on another. Entire technologies (such as Cascading Style Sheets) are based on this premise.

Although *Setter* is the most common child of *Style*, you can also use the *EventSetter* element to set an event handler of a particular routed event. This is yet another way in which you can share an event handler among multiple elements. The EventSetterDemo project contains a XAML file and a C# file. The XAML file shown here contains a *Style* with an *EventSetter* element.

EventSetterDemo.xaml

```xml
<!-- ================================================
         EventSetterDemo.xaml (c) 2006 by Charles Petzold
     ================================================ -->
<Window xmlns="http://schemas.microsoft.com/winfx/2006/xaml/presentation"
        xmlns:x="http://schemas.microsoft.com/winfx/2006/xaml"
        x:Class="Petzold.EventSetterDemo.EventSetterDemo"
        Title="EventSetter Demo">
    <Window.Resources>
        <Style TargetType="{x:Type Button}">
            <Setter Property="FontSize" Value="24" />
            <Setter Property="HorizontalAlignment" Value="Center" />
            <Setter Property="Margin" Value="24" />
            <EventSetter Event="Click" Handler="ButtonOnClick" />
        </Style>
    </Window.Resources>

    <StackPanel>
        <Button>
            Button Number 1
        </Button>

        <Button>
            Button Number 2
        </Button>

        <Button>
            Button Number 3
        </Button>
    </StackPanel>
</Window>
```

The C# part of the *Window* class contains the event handler referred to in the *EventSetter* element.

EventSetterDemo.cs

```csharp
//-----------------------------------------------
// EventSetterDemo.cs (c) 2006 by Charles Petzold
//-----------------------------------------------
using System;
using System.Windows;
using System.Windows.Controls;
using System.Windows.Input;
using System.Windows.Media;

namespace Petzold.EventSetterDemo
{
    public partial class EventSetterDemo : Window
    {
        [STAThread]
        public static void Main()
```

```
        {
            Application app = new Application();
            app.Run(new EventSetterDemo());
        }
        public EventSetterDemo()
        {
            InitializeComponent();
        }
        void ButtonOnClick(object sender, RoutedEventArgs args)
        {
            Button btn = args.Source as Button;
            MessageBox.Show("The button labeled " + btn.Content +
                          " has been clicked", Title);
        }
    }
}
```

I mentioned earlier that *Style* defines six properties. I've now discussed *Setters*, *Resources*, *TargetType*, and *BasedOn*. The read-only *IsSealed* property becomes *true* when the *Seal* method is called, which happpens when the style is in use. The last property, named *Triggers*, lets you control how elements or controls respond to changes in properties of the element, or to changes in a data binding, or to events.

When first encountering setters and triggers, it is easy to become confused. Both setters and triggers generally involve properties being set. A *Setter* effectively sets properties when the element is first created. A *Trigger* sets properties only when something happens—that is, when something "triggers" the property to change.

The *Triggers* property of *Style* is of type *TriggerCollection*, which is a collection of objects of type *TriggerBase*. The classes that derive from the abstract *TriggerBase* class are shown here:

Object

    DispatcherObject (abstract)

        DependencyObject

            TriggerBase (abstract)

                DataTrigger

                EventTrigger

                MultiDataTrigger

                MultiTrigger

                Trigger

The class that I will not be discussing in this chapter is *EventTrigger*, which can cause a change to a control or element when a specified event occurs. Generally *EventTrigger* precipitates a graphical animation, so I cover this in Chapter 30. (You may have noticed that *FrameworkElement* itself defines a property named *Triggers*. I won't be discussing that property in this chapter because the only *Trigger* objects that can go in that collection are of type *EventTrigger*.)

The most common of the *TriggerBase* derivatives is *Trigger*, which specifies how a control or element should react to a particular property change. Very often, these properties involve user input, such as the property *IsMouseOver*. The *Trigger* reacts by changing some other property through a *Setter* definition. Here's a typical *Trigger* definition as it might appear within a *Style* element:

```
<Style.Triggers>
    <Trigger Property="Control.IsMouseOver" Value="True">
        <Setter Property="Control.FontStyle" Value="Italic" />
        <Setter Property="Control.Foreground" Value="Blue" />
    </Trigger>
</Style.Triggers>
```

Notice that the *Style.Triggers* property element is required within the *Style* definition. The *Property* and *Value* attributes of the *Trigger* element indicate that the *Trigger* will kick in when the *IsMouseOver* property becomes *true*. Although you aren't restricted to Boolean properties, they are certainly the most common. The property specified in a *Trigger* must be backed by a dependency property.

Like *Style*, *Trigger* has a property named *Setters*, and just like *Style*, this property is the content property of *Trigger*, and *Trigger* can contain more than one child *Setter* element. The two *Setter* objects in the *Trigger* element shown in the preceding example indicate that the control text is to be displayed with italics and in blue when the mouse is over the control. (*Trigger* also has a property named *SourceName*, but you don't use this property with styles. You use it with templates, which are covered in the next chapter.)

Here's the complete XAML file with two *Trigger* elements.

StyleWithTriggers.xaml

```
<!-- ================================================
        StyleWithTriggers.xaml (c) 2006 by Charles Petzold
     ================================================ -->
<StackPanel xmlns="http://schemas.microsoft.com/winfx/2006/xaml/presentation"
            xmlns:x="http://schemas.microsoft.com/winfx/2006/xaml">
    <StackPanel.Resources>
        <Style x:Key="normal">
            <Setter Property="Control.FontSize" Value="24" />
            <Setter Property="Control.HorizontalAlignment" Value="Center" />
            <Setter Property="Control.Margin" Value="24" />

            <Style.Triggers>
                <Trigger Property="Control.IsMouseOver" Value="true">
                    <Setter Property="Control.FontStyle" Value="Italic" />
                    <Setter Property="Control.Foreground" Value="Blue" />
                </Trigger>

                <Trigger Property="Button.IsPressed" Value="true">
```

```
                        <Setter Property="Control.Foreground" Value="Red" />
                </Trigger>
            </Style.Triggers>
        </Style>
    </StackPanel.Resources>

    <Button Style="{StaticResource normal}">
        Button Number 1
    </Button>

    <Button Style="{StaticResource normal}">
        Button Number 2
    </Button>

    <Button Style="{StaticResource normal}">
        Button Number 3
    </Button>
</StackPanel>
```

In addition to the *Trigger* based on the *IsMouseOver* property, another *Trigger* changes the *Foreground* color when the *IsPressed* property becomes *True*. In both cases, the properties return to their original states when the value of the property changes back.

In this particular case, the order of the two *Trigger* elements affects how the triggers work. If *Trigger* elements set the same properties, later *Trigger* elements override earlier *Trigger* elements. If you swap the two *Trigger* properties in the previous XAML file, the text never turns red because *IsPressed* is *true* only if *IsMouseOver* is also *true*, and the *Trigger* for *IsMouse-Over* has final say in setting the text blue.

If you can't get the order just right, you might consider using a *MultiTrigger*. The *MultiTrigger* is similar to the *Trigger* except that it only kicks in when two or more conditions hold. Here's an example.

MultiTriggerDemo.xaml

```
<!-- =================================================
     MultiTriggerDemo.xaml (c) 2006 by Charles Petzold
     ================================================= -->
<StackPanel xmlns="http://schemas.microsoft.com/winfx/2006/xaml/presentation"
            xmlns:x="http://schemas.microsoft.com/winfx/2006/xaml">
    <StackPanel.Resources>
        <Style x:Key="normal">
            <Setter Property="Control.FontSize" Value="24" />
            <Setter Property="Control.HorizontalAlignment" Value="Center" />
            <Setter Property="Control.Margin" Value="24" />

            <Style.Triggers>
                <Trigger Property="Button.IsPressed" Value="True">
                    <Setter Property="Control.Foreground" Value="Red" />
                </Trigger>

                <MultiTrigger>
```

```
                    <MultiTrigger.Conditions>
                        <Condition Property="Control.IsMouseOver" Value="True" />
                        <Condition Property="Button.IsPressed" Value="False" />
                    </MultiTrigger.Conditions>
                    <Setter Property="Control.FontStyle" Value="Italic" />
                    <Setter Property="Control.Foreground" Value="Blue" />
                </MultiTrigger>

            </Style.Triggers>
        </Style>
    </StackPanel.Resources>

    <Button Style="{StaticResource normal}">
        Button Number 1
    </Button>

    <Button Style="{StaticResource normal}">
        Button Number 2
    </Button>

    <Button Style="{StaticResource normal}">
        Button Number 3
    </Button>
</StackPanel>
```

The *Conditions* property of *MultiTrigger* is an object of type *ConditionCollection*. Each *Condition* element indicates a *Property* and a *Value*. The button text is blue when the mouse is over the button, and red when the button is clicked. The button text is italic only when the mouse is over the button but the button is not pressed, because that's part of the *MultiTrigger* with those conditions.

The *DataTrigger* class is similar to *Trigger* except that it substitutes *Binding* for *Property*. The *Binding* generally refers to another element. *DataTrigger* can set a property when this *Binding* has a particular value as demonstrated in the following file.

StyleWithDataTrigger.xaml

```
<!-- ==========================================================
     StyleWithDataTrigger.xaml (c) 2006 by Charles Petzold
     ========================================================== -->
<StackPanel xmlns="http://schemas.microsoft.com/winfx/2006/xaml/presentation"
            xmlns:x="http://schemas.microsoft.com/winfx/2006/xaml">
    <StackPanel.Resources>
        <Style TargetType="{x:Type Button}">
            <Setter Property="FontSize" Value="24" />
            <Setter Property="HorizontalAlignment" Value="Center" />
            <Setter Property="Margin" Value="24" />

            <Style.Triggers>
                <DataTrigger Binding="{Binding ElementName=txtbox,
                                               Path=Text.Length}"
                             Value="0">
                    <Setter Property="IsEnabled" Value="False" />
```

```
                </DataTrigger>
            </Style.Triggers>
        </Style>
    </StackPanel.Resources>

    <TextBox Name="txtbox" HorizontalAlignment="Center"
             Width="2in" Margin="24" />

    <Button>
        Button Number 1
    </Button>

    <Button>
        Button Number 2
    </Button>

    <Button>
        Button Number 3
    </Button>

</StackPanel>
```

The *DataTrigger* contains a binding with the *TextBox* element, referred to by its name of *txtbox*. The *Path* is *Text.Length*, which refers to the *Length* property of the *Text* property of the *TextBox*. When that value is 0, the *IsEnabled* property of the *Button* is set to *false*. The result is that the buttons are enabled only if there's some text in the *TextBox*. Dialog boxes commonly enable the OK button only when certain conditions are true, so this is an ideal application of a *DataTrigger*.

The *MultiDataTrigger* is to *DataTrigger* what *MultiTrigger* is to *Trigger*. The properties are set only when all binding conditions are met. Like *MultiTrigger*, *MultiDataTrigger* includes one or more *Condition* elements. The *Condition* class defines *Property*, *Binding*, and *Value* properties, perhaps suggesting that you can mix regular triggers and data triggers, but you can't. When defining a *MultiTrigger*, you use the *Property* and *Value* properties of *Condition*. When defining a *MultiDataTrigger*, you use the *Binding* and *Value* properties. Here's a XAML file in which the buttons are enabled only if two *CheckBox* controls are checked.

MultiDataTriggerDemo.xaml
```
<!-- =======================================================
     MultiDataTriggerDemo.xaml (c) 2006 by Charles Petzold
     ======================================================= -->
<StackPanel xmlns="http://schemas.microsoft.com/winfx/2006/xaml/presentation"
            xmlns:x="http://schemas.microsoft.com/winfx/2006/xaml">
    <StackPanel.Resources>
        <Style TargetType="{x:Type CheckBox}">
            <Setter Property="HorizontalAlignment" Value="Center" />
            <Setter Property="Margin" Value="12" />
        </Style>

        <Style TargetType="{x:Type Button}">
            <Setter Property="FontSize" Value="24" />
```

```
            <Setter Property="HorizontalAlignment" Value="Center" />
            <Setter Property="Margin" Value="12" />
            <Setter Property="IsEnabled" Value="False" />

            <Style.Triggers>
                <MultiDataTrigger>
                    <MultiDataTrigger.Conditions>
                        <Condition Binding="{Binding ElementName=chkbox1,
                                             Path=IsChecked}"
                                   Value="True" />
                        <Condition Binding="{Binding ElementName=chkbox2,
                                             Path=IsChecked}"
                                   Value="True" />
                    </MultiDataTrigger.Conditions>
                    <Setter Property="IsEnabled" Value="True" />
                </MultiDataTrigger>
            </Style.Triggers>
        </Style>
    </StackPanel.Resources>

    <CheckBox Name="chkbox1">
        Check 1
    </CheckBox>

    <CheckBox Name="chkbox2">
        Check 2
    </CheckBox>

    <Button>
        Button Number 1
    </Button>

    <Button>
        Button Number 2
    </Button>

    <Button>
        Button Number 3
    </Button>
</StackPanel>
```

As you've seen, styles give you the convenience of organizing the appearance of your controls in a very systematic way. Styles can be as simple as a few lines in a XAML file to reduce repetition among similar elements, or they can fill entire files and provide every control in your applications with a unique look. Whenever you're about to give two elements the same property value, use a style instead, and you'll be thankful if you ever need to change that value.

Chapter 25
Templates

Several programs in the first part of this book provided a little taste of templates. In Chapter 11, the BuildButtonFactory project showed how to create an object of type *ControlTemplate* and assign it to the *Template* property of a *Button*. This *ControlTemplate* object was essentially a complete description of the visual appearance of the button, including how its appearance changed when certain properties (such as *IsMouseOver* and *IsPressed*) changed values. All of the logic behind the button, and all of the event handling, remained intact.

The *ControlTemplate* is one important type of template supported by the Windows Presentation Foundation. As its name suggests, you use the *ControlTemplate* to define the visual appearance of a control. The *Control* class defines the *Template* property that you set to a *ControlTemplate* object.

Although styles and templates may seem to overlap, they really have quite different roles. An element or control does not have a default *Style* property, and consequently, the *Style* property of an element is normally *null*. You use the *Style* property to define property settings or triggers that you want associated with that element.

All controls defined within the Windows Presentation Foundation that have a visual appearance already have a *Template* property that is set to an object of type *ControlTemplate*. A *Button* looks like a *Button* and a *ScrollBar* looks like a *ScrollBar* as a direct result of these *ControlTemplate* objects. The *ControlTemplate* object defines the entire visual appearance of the control, and you have the power to replace that object. This is what is meant when the controls in the WPF are referred to (rather awkwardly) as "lookless" controls. They certainly have a "look" but it's not intrinsic to the functionality of the control and it can be replaced.

The ListColorsEvenElegantlier project in Chapter 13 introduced the *DataTemplate* object. The *ItemsControl* class (from which *ListBox* descends) defines a property named *ItemTemplate*, and you set a *DataTemplate* object to that property to govern how the control displays each of the items in the *ListBox*. As you might recall, the *DataTemplate* in the ListColorsEvenElegantlier program defined a visual tree that contained a *Rectangle* element and a *TextBlock* element to display each color in the *ListBox*.

Chapter 13 also presented two custom controls named *ColorGridBox* and *ColorWheel*, both of which were derived from *ListBox* but which presented the items in a completely different format from the *ListBox* default. This was made possible by the *ItemsPanel* property defined by *ItemsControl* that you can set to an object of type *ItemsPanelTemplate*. As the name suggests, this object defines the type of panel used for displaying the items within the *ListBox*.

Templates also made an appearance in several projects in Chapter 16. The ListSortedSystem-Parameters project and the *DependencyPropertyListView* control both used *ListView* controls, and both set the *View* property of the *ListView* control to a *GridView* object. The *GridView* object lets the *ListView* control display objects in columns. Whenever a column doesn't display quite what you want, you can create a *DataTemplate* that defines the appearance of the object in that column, and set this object to the *CellTemplate* property of the *GridViewColumn* object. Also in Chapter 16, the TemplateTheTree project created an object of type *HierarchicalDataTemplate* and set it to the *ItemTemplate* property of the *TreeViewItem* objects to control how the items of the tree obtained child objects.

The various types of template objects all derive from the abstract *FrameworkTemplate* class, as shown in the following class hierarchy:

Object

   FrameworkTemplate (abstract)

      ControlTemplate

      DataTemplate

         HierarchicalDataTemplate

      ItemsPanelTemplate

Obviously some practice is required before these different types of templates (and the properties you set them to) assume individual and familiar personalities. Here's a brief summary:

You create objects of type *ControlTemplate* to set to the *Template* property defined by *Control*. These *ControlTemplate* objects define the entire visual appearance of the control, including triggered changes to the visual appearance. Setting the *Template* property is quite powerful but also (of course) involves much responsibility.

You use objects of type *ItemsPanelTemplate* to set to the *ItemsPanel* property defined by *ItemsControl* to specify the type of panel used to display the multiple items in an *ItemsControl* (such as a *ListBox* or *ComboBox*). This is the simplest type of template.

All other templates are of type *DataTemplate*, and in actual practice are certainly the most common form of template. *DataTemplate* objects show up in all controls that derive from *ContentControl* and *ItemsControl* and let you govern how content and listed items are displayed.

The abstract *FrameworkTemplate* class defines only three properties. The read-only Boolean *IsSealed* property indicates whether the template can be altered. The *Resources* property of type *ResourceDictionary* lets you define resources that are accessible only within the template. The most important of the three properties is *VisualTree*, which defines the layout of elements that make up the visual appearance of the control (or the content of the control, or the listed items in the control).

VisualTree is of type *FrameworkElementFactory*, and if you look back at the projects that used templates in Part I of this book, you'll be reminded just how strange and unwieldy this *FrameworkElementFactory* was. This class allows you to define a hierarchy of elements (including properties and triggers) without actually creating those elements. The resultant code wasn't very pretty.

When you define templates in XAML, *FrameworkElementFactory* works entirely behind the scenes. The XAML syntax used in defining templates is the same as that which you use when defining a layout of elements and their properties, except that these elements aren't actually created until they're required.

The *ControlTemplate* class adds two properties to those defined by *FrameworkTemplate*: *TargetType* indicates the type of the control for which the template is intended; *Triggers* is a collection of *Trigger* objects.

The following stand-alone XAML file is quite similar to the *BuildButtonFactory* program from Chapter 11 except that it doesn't attach a *Click* event handler to the *Button*.

ButtonWithTemplate.xaml

```
<!-- =================================================
     ButtonWithTemplate.xaml (c) 2006 by Charles Petzold
     ================================================= -->
<Page xmlns="http://schemas.microsoft.com/winfx/2006/xaml/presentation"
      xmlns:x="http://schemas.microsoft.com/winfx/2006/xaml">

    <Button HorizontalAlignment="Center" VerticalAlignment="Center"
            FontSize="48" Padding="20">

        Button with Custom Template

        <Button.Template>
            <ControlTemplate>

                <!-- VisualTree property of ControlTemplate. -->

                <Border Name="border" BorderThickness="3" BorderBrush="Red"
                        Background="{DynamicResource
                            {x:Static SystemColors.ControlLightBrushKey}}">
                    <TextBlock
                        Name="txtblk"
                        FontStyle="Italic"
                        Text="{TemplateBinding ContentControl.Content}"
                        Margin="{TemplateBinding Control.Padding}" />
                </Border>

                <!-- Triggers property of ControlTemplate. -->

                <ControlTemplate.Triggers>
                    <Trigger Property="UIElement.IsMouseOver" Value="True">
                        <Setter TargetName="border"
```

```
                              Property="Border.CornerRadius" Value="24" />
                 <Setter TargetName="txtblk"
                              Property="TextBlock.FontWeight" Value="Bold" />
             </Trigger>

             <Trigger Property="Button.IsPressed" Value="True">
                 <Setter
                     TargetName="border"
                     Property="Border.Background"
                     Value="{DynamicResource
                              {x:Static SystemColors.ControlDarkBrushKey}}" />
             </Trigger>
         </ControlTemplate.Triggers>
        </ControlTemplate>
      </Button.Template>
    </Button>
</Page>
```

The *Button* definition begins normally by defining several properties (*HorizontalAlignment*, *VerticalAlignment*, *FontSize*, and *Padding*) and the button content, which is the text string "Button with Custom Template."

The *Button.Template* property element encloses the definition of the *Template* property of the button. This property is of type *ControlTemplate*. The content property of *FrameworkTemplate* and all its derivatives is *VisualTree*, so the layout of the control can begin immediately after the *ControlTemplate* start tag. The control begins with a single top-level element. Any additional elements are children of that element. Very often the *VisualTree* begins with a *Border* element, but it could also begin with a panel of some sort or even just a single element like *TextBlock*.

The *VisualTree* in ButtonWithTemplate.xaml begins with a *Border* that is given a 3-unit thickness and colored red. The *Background* property is a system color retrieved using the *DynamicResource* markup extension. Within the *Border* element is a *TextBlock* with a *FontStyle* initialized to *Italic*.

By using a *TextBlock*, I'm implicitly restricting this button to the display of text. I want the *Text* property of this *TextBlock* to be set to the *Content* property of the *Button*. The markup extension *TemplateBinding* is defined specifically for the purpose of linking a property in the template's visual tree with a property defined by the control. The syntax for binding the *Text* property of the *TextBlock* to the *Content* property of the *Button* is:

```
Text="{TemplateBinding ContentControl.Content}"
```

The argument of the *TemplateBinding* is really a dependency property, so it usually includes the class in which the property is defined or a class that inherits the property. You could use *Button.Content* here rather than *ContentControl.Content* and it would work the same way. Fortunately, the WPF template logic is flexible enough to allow a property of type *string* to have a *TemplateBinding* with a property of type *object*.

The next attribute in the *TextBlock* element is interesting:

```
Margin="{TemplateBinding Control.Padding}"
```

The margin around the *TextBlock* (that is, the space between the *TextBlock* and the *Border*) is bound to the *Padding* property of the *Button*, which is intended to be the space inside the button that surrounds the content. This particular *TemplateBinding* is typical for a *ContentControl*. Of course, the *Button* itself still has its own *Margin* property that defines the space around the button.

After you define the *VisualTree* in the template, an optional property element of *Control-Template.Triggers* defines triggers. This particular template has two triggers—one for the property *IsMouseOver* and one for the property *IsPressed*. In both cases, the *Trigger* comes into action when these properties are *true*. The *Setter* elements within these *Trigger* elements always affect a property of one of the elements of the *VisualTree*. That is why the two elements in the *VisualTree* were given names of *border* and *txtblk*. The *Setter* elements refer to these names with the *TargetName* attribute, and the *Property* and *Value* attributes work just as they do in styles.

It is possible to include a *TargetType* attribute in the *ControlTemplate* tag:

```
<ControlTemplate TargetType="{x:Type Button}">
```

In this case, you don't need to preface the dependency properties with class names in the *TemplateBinding* expressions, because the binding has the information it needs to reference these properties.

As ButtonWithTemplate.xaml demonstrates, you can define a *ControlTemplate* for just one control, and that's fine if all you want is one unique control. Generally you'll want to share templates, and one way to do that is by defining them as resources. Here's a stand-alone XAML file that contains a *ControlTemplate* defined as a resource with an *x:Key* of "btnCustom." I've used the *TargetType* attribute on *ControlTemplate* to avoid prefacing dependency properties and routed events with class names.

ResourceTemplate.xaml

```
<!-- =================================================
        ResourceTemplate.xaml (c) 2006 by Charles Petzold
     ================================================= -->
<Page xmlns="http://schemas.microsoft.com/winfx/2006/xaml/presentation"
      xmlns:x="http://schemas.microsoft.com/winfx/2006/xaml">
    <Page.Resources>
        <ControlTemplate x:Key="btnCustom" TargetType="{x:Type Button}">

            <!-- VisualTree property of ControlTemplate. -->

            <Border Name="border" BorderThickness="3" BorderBrush="Red"
                    Background="{TemplateBinding Foreground}">

                <TextBlock Name="txtblk"
```

```
                                FontStyle="Italic"
                                Text="{TemplateBinding Content}"
                                Margin="{TemplateBinding Padding}"
                                Foreground="{TemplateBinding Background}" />
            </Border>

            <!-- Triggers property of ControlTemplate. -->

            <ControlTemplate.Triggers>
                <Trigger Property="IsMouseOver" Value="True">
                    <Setter TargetName="border"
                            Property="CornerRadius" Value="12" />
                    <Setter TargetName="txtblk"
                            Property="FontWeight" Value="Bold" />
                </Trigger>

                <Trigger Property="IsPressed" Value="True">
                    <Setter TargetName="border"
                            Property="Background"
                            Value="{Binding Path=Background}" />
                    <Setter TargetName="txtblk"
                            Property="Foreground"
                            Value="{Binding Path=Foreground}" />
                </Trigger>
            </ControlTemplate.Triggers>
        </ControlTemplate>
    </Page.Resources>

    <StackPanel>
        <Button Template="{StaticResource btnCustom}"
                HorizontalAlignment="Center" Margin="24"
                FontSize="24" Padding="10"  >
            Button with Custom Template
        </Button>

        <Button HorizontalAlignment="Center" Margin="24"
                FontSize="24" Padding="10"  >
            Normal Button
        </Button>

        <Button Template="{StaticResource btnCustom}"
                HorizontalAlignment="Center" Margin="24"
                FontSize="24" Padding="10"  >
            Another Button with Custom Template
        </Button>
    </StackPanel>
</Page>
```

Toward the bottom of the file, a *StackPanel* contains three buttons, all with the same properties, except that the first and third buttons set their *Template* properties to the resource. This particular template switches around the meaning of the background and foreground colors. If you have your system colors set for a white background and black foreground, these two templated buttons display white text on a black background and then swap the colors when the buttons are pressed. This is not something you should normally do, but it suggests the type of flexibility you have.

You can combine a *Style* and a *ControlTemplate* in the same resource. The *Style* begins normally and then the *Template* property is set to an object of type *ControlTemplate*:

```
<Style ... >
    ...
    <Setter Property="Template">
        <Setter.Value>
            <ControlTemplate ...>
                ...
            </ControlTemplate>
        </Setter.Value>
    </Setter>
</Style>
```

That way, you can give a control both a style and a template just by setting the *Style* property.

The first two templates I've shown you in this chapter make the outrageous assumption that the *Content* property of the *Button* is set to a text string. If that's not the case, these templates would generate run-time errors. Even if you're entirely redesigning button visuals, you probably want the buttons to host more than just text.

It so happens that all classes that derive from *ContentControl* use an object of type *Content-Presenter* to display their content. *ContentPresenter* derives from *FrameworkElement*, and you can include a *ContentPresenter* object within the visual tree of the template. This is a *much* better approach than assuming that the content will always be text.

The CircledRadioButtons.xaml file defines a *ControlTemplate* resource for objects of type *RadioButton*. Notice the empty *ContentPresenter* element within the *Border* element.

```
CircledRadioButtons.xaml
<!-- =====================================================
        CircledRadioButtons.xaml (c) 2006 by Charles Petzold
    ===================================================== -->
<Page xmlns="http://schemas.microsoft.com/winfx/2006/xaml/presentation"
      xmlns:x="http://schemas.microsoft.com/winfx/2006/xaml">
    <Page.Resources>
        <ControlTemplate x:Key="newradio"
                        TargetType="{x:Type RadioButton}">
            <Border Name="border"
                    BorderBrush="{DynamicResource
                        {x:Static SystemColors.ControlTextBrushKey}}"
                    Padding="10"
                    CornerRadius="100">
                <ContentPresenter />
            </Border>

            <ControlTemplate.Triggers>
                <Trigger Property="IsChecked" Value="True">
```

```
                        <Setter TargetName="border"
                               Property="BorderThickness"
                               Value="1" />
                    </Trigger>
                </ControlTemplate.Triggers>
            </ControlTemplate>
        </Page.Resources>

        <GroupBox Header="Options" FontSize="12pt"
                  HorizontalAlignment="Center"
                  VerticalAlignment="Center">
            <StackPanel>
                <RadioButton Template="{StaticResource newradio}"
                             HorizontalAlignment="Center"
                             Content="RadioButton 1" />
                <RadioButton Template="{StaticResource newradio}"
                             HorizontalAlignment="Center"
                             Content="RadioButton 2"
                             IsChecked="True" />
                <RadioButton Template="{StaticResource newradio}"
                             HorizontalAlignment="Center"
                             Content="RadioButton 3" />
                <RadioButton Template="{StaticResource newradio}"
                             HorizontalAlignment="Center"
                             Content="RadioButton 4" />
            </StackPanel>
        </GroupBox>
    </Page>
```

You can bind the *Content* property of the *ContentPresenter* to the *Content* property of the control with markup like this:

```
<ContentPresenter Content="{TemplateBinding ContentControl.Content}" />
```

But this XAML file indicates that this binding occurs automatically. The *Border* element in the template defines a *CornerRadius* of 100, which should be sufficient to mimic an ellipse in most reasonably sized content of radio buttons. By default, the *BorderThickness* of a *Border* element is 0. The *Triggers* section of the template changes that to 1 only when the item is selected. The result is a *RadioButton* indicating that it is selected with an ellipse around the entire content, rather than with a little filled-in circle.

The following XAML file goes even further in redefining the appearance of a control. It uses the logic of a *CheckBox* but displays a little visual switch that flips a lever between the words Off and On.

ToggleSwitch.xaml
```
<!-- ===========================================
     ToggleSwitch.xaml (c) 2006 by Charles Petzold
     =========================================== -->
<Page xmlns="http://schemas.microsoft.com/winfx/2006/xaml/presentation"
      xmlns:x="http://schemas.microsoft.com/winfx/2006/xaml">
```

```
<Page.Resources>
    <ControlTemplate x:Key="switch" TargetType="{x:Type CheckBox}">
        <Grid>
            <Grid.RowDefinitions>
                <RowDefinition Height="Auto" />
                <RowDefinition Height="Auto" />
            </Grid.RowDefinitions>
            <Border Width="96" Height="48"
                    BorderBrush="Black" BorderThickness="1">
                <Canvas Background="LightGray">
                    <TextBlock Canvas.Left="0" Canvas.Top="0"
                            Foreground="Black"
                            Text="Off" Margin="2" />
                    <TextBlock Canvas.Right="0" Canvas.Top="0"
                            Foreground="Black"
                            Text="On" Margin="2" />
                    <Line Name="lineOff"
                            StrokeThickness="8" Stroke="Black"
                            X1="48" Y1="40" X2="20" Y2="16"
                            StrokeStartLineCap="Round"
                            StrokeEndLineCap="Round"  />
                    <Line Name="lineOn"
                            StrokeThickness="8" Stroke="Black"
                            X1="48" Y1="40" X2="76" Y2="16"
                            StrokeStartLineCap="Round"
                            StrokeEndLineCap="Round"
                            Visibility="Hidden"  />
                </Canvas>
            </Border>
            <ContentPresenter Grid.Row="1"
                            Content="{TemplateBinding Content}"
                            HorizontalAlignment="Center" />
        </Grid>
        <ControlTemplate.Triggers>
            <Trigger Property="IsChecked" Value="True">
                <Setter TargetName="lineOff" Property="Visibility"
                        Value="Hidden" />
                <Setter TargetName="lineOn" Property="Visibility"
                        Value="Visible" />
            </Trigger>
        </ControlTemplate.Triggers>
    </ControlTemplate>
</Page.Resources>

<CheckBox Template="{StaticResource switch}"
        Content="Master Switch"
        HorizontalAlignment="Center"
        VerticalAlignment="Center" />
</Page>
```

The visual tree begins with a two-row *Grid*. The bottom row is for the *ContentPresenter*. The top row is the graphical switch. It begins with a rectangle *Border* with a gray background containing a *Canvas*. The *Canvas* has two *TextBlock* elements for the Off and On labels and two thick lines with *Name* attributes of "lineOff" and "lineOn." Notice that the *lineOn Line* has its *Visibility* property initially set to *Hidden*.

The *Triggers* section contains a *Trigger* for the *IsChecked* property. When this property is *true*, the *Visibility* property of the *lineOff Line* changes to *Hidden* and the *Visiblity* property of *lineOn* changes to *Visible*, making it appear as if a line jumps between the two options.

I mentioned earlier that any control defined by the WPF that has a visual appearance already has its *Template* property set to an object of type *ControlTemplate*. When you set the *Template* property to a *ControlTemplate* of your own invention, you are essentially replacing the original template. If you want to create *ControlTemplate* objects that come up to the standards of the original templates, you'll want to examine those templates, and that's the entire purpose of the following program.

The DumpControlTemplate program has a top-level menu item labeled Control that displays all the public classes that derive from *Control* in a hierarchy that mimics the inheritance hierarchy. You select one of these controls, and the program creates an object of that type and displays it in the top part of a splitter-separated *Grid*. You then select the Template Property item from the Dump menu, and the program uses the bottom part of the *Grid* to display the *ControlTemplate* object in convenient XAML format. The XAML is displayed in a *TextBox*, so you can copy and paste it into Windows Notepad (or NotepadClone) for printing.

The DumpControlTemplate project has three source code files. The *ControlMenuItem* class inherits from *MenuItem* and constructs a menu containing all the classes that derive from *Control*. The *Header* of each item displays the name of the class; the *Tag* property stores the *Type* object for that class.

```
ControlMenuItem.cs
//-------------------------------------------------
// ControlMenuItem.cs (c) 2006 by Charles Petzold
//-------------------------------------------------
using System;
using System.Collections.Generic;
using System.Reflection;
using System.Windows;
using System.Windows.Controls;

namespace Petzold.DumpControlTemplate
{
    public class ControlMenuItem : MenuItem
    {
        public ControlMenuItem()
        {
            // Obtain the assembly in which the Control class is defined.
            Assembly asbly = Assembly.GetAssembly(typeof(Control));

            // This is an array of all the types in that class.
            Type[] atype = asbly.GetTypes();
```

```
              // We're going to store descendants of Control in a sorted list.
              SortedList<string, MenuItem> sortlst =
                                 new SortedList<string, MenuItem>();

              Header = "Control";
              Tag = typeof(Control);
              sortlst.Add("Control", this);

              // Enumerate all the types in the array.
              // For Control and its descendants, create menu items and
              //   add to the SortedList object.
              // Notice the menu item Tag property is the associated Type object.
              foreach (Type typ in atype)
              {
                  if (typ.IsPublic && (typ.IsSubclassOf(typeof(Control))))
                  {
                      MenuItem item = new MenuItem();
                      item.Header = typ.Name;
                      item.Tag = typ;
                      sortlst.Add(typ.Name, item);
                  }
              }

              // Go through the sorted list and set menu item parents.
              foreach (KeyValuePair<string, MenuItem> kvp in sortlst)
              {
                  if (kvp.Key != "Control")
                  {
                      string strParent = ((Type)kvp.Value.Tag).BaseType.Name;
                      MenuItem itemParent = sortlst[strParent];
                      itemParent.Items.Add(kvp.Value);
                  }
              }

              // Scan through again:
              //   If abstract and selectable, disable.
              //   If not abstract and not selectable, add a new item.
              foreach (KeyValuePair<string, MenuItem> kvp in sortlst)
              {
                  Type typ = (Type)kvp.Value.Tag;

                  if (typ.IsAbstract && kvp.Value.Items.Count == 0)
                      kvp.Value.IsEnabled = false;

                  if (!typ.IsAbstract && kvp.Value.Items.Count > 0)
                  {
                      MenuItem item = new MenuItem();
                      item.Header = kvp.Value.Header as string;
                      item.Tag = typ;
                      kvp.Value.Items.Insert(0, item);
                  }
              }
          }
      }
  }
}
```

The DumpControlTemplate.xaml file contains the layout of the program's window. Notice that the menu begins with the *ControlMenuItem* object, which is assigned a *Click* event handler for all items in the submenu. The Dump menu item has two items on its submenu: one to dump the *Template* property and the other to dump the *ItemsPanel* property. (The latter is applicable only for controls that derive from *ItemsControl*.) The file concludes with a *Grid* that occupies the rest of the program's window.

```
DumpControlTemplate.xaml

<!-- =====================================================
        DumpControlTemplate.xaml (c) 2006 by Charles Petzold
     ===================================================== -->
<Window xmlns="http://schemas.microsoft.com/winfx/2006/xaml/presentation"
        xmlns:x="http://schemas.microsoft.com/winfx/2006/xaml"
        xmlns:src="clr-namespace:Petzold.DumpControlTemplate"
        x:Class="Petzold.DumpControlTemplate.DumpControlTemplate"
        Title="Dump Control Template - no control">
    <DockPanel>
        <Menu DockPanel.Dock="Top">
            <src:ControlMenuItem MenuItem.Click="ControlItemOnClick"/>
            <MenuItem Header="Dump" SubmenuOpened="DumpOnOpened">
                <MenuItem Header="Template property (type ControlTemplate)"
                        Name="itemTemplate"
                        Click="DumpTemplateOnClick" />

                <MenuItem Header="ItemsPanel property (type ItemsPanelTemplate)"
                        Name="itemItemsPanel"
                        Click="DumpItemsPanelOnClick" />
            </MenuItem>
        </Menu>
        <Grid Name="grid">
            <Grid.RowDefinitions>
                <RowDefinition Height="2*" />
                <RowDefinition Height="Auto" />
                <RowDefinition Height="8*" />
            </Grid.RowDefinitions>
            <GridSplitter Grid.Row="1" Height="6"
                        HorizontalAlignment="Stretch"
                        VerticalAlignment="Center" />
            <TextBox Grid.Row="2"
                        Name="txtbox"
                        FontFamily="Lucida Console"
                        AcceptsReturn="True"
                        HorizontalScrollBarVisibility="Auto"
                        VerticalScrollBarVisibility="Auto" />
        </Grid>
    </DockPanel>
</Window>
```

The following DumpControlTemplate.cs file is mostly devoted to the *Click* handlers for the menu. The *ControlItemOnClick* handler creates a control of the selected type and puts it in the top cell of the *Grid*. (In my experience, the *Template* property only becomes non-*null* when the control has a parent.) The Dump menu items convert the object to XAML for display.

DumpControlTemplate.cs

```
//----------------------------------------------------
// DumpControlTemplate.cs (c) 2006 by Charles Petzold
//----------------------------------------------------
using System;
using System.Reflection;
using System.Text;
using System.Windows;
using System.Windows.Controls;
using System.Windows.Markup;
using System.Xml;

namespace Petzold.DumpControlTemplate
{
    public partial class DumpControlTemplate : Window
    {
        Control ctrl;

        [STAThread]
        public static void Main()
        {
            Application app = new Application();
            app.Run(new DumpControlTemplate());
        }
        public DumpControlTemplate()
        {
            InitializeComponent();
        }

        // Event handler for item clicked on Control menu.
        void ControlItemOnClick(object sender, RoutedEventArgs args)
        {
            // Remove any existing child from the first row of the Grid.
            for (int i = 0; i < grid.Children.Count; i++)
                if (Grid.GetRow(grid.Children[i]) == 0)
                {
                    grid.Children.Remove(grid.Children[i]);
                    break;
                }

            // Clear the TextBox.
            txtbox.Text = "";

            // Get the Control class of the clicked menu item.
            MenuItem item = args.Source as MenuItem;
            Type typ = (Type)item.Tag;

            // Prepare to create an object of that type.
            ConstructorInfo info = typ.GetConstructor(System.Type.EmptyTypes);

            // Try creating an object of that type.
            try
            {
                ctrl = (Control)info.Invoke(null);
```

```
        }
        catch (Exception exc)
        {
            MessageBox.Show(exc.Message, Title);
            return;
        }

        // Try putting it in the grid.
        // If that doesn't work, it's probably a Window.
        try
        {
            grid.Children.Add(ctrl);
        }
        catch
        {
            if (ctrl is Window)
                (ctrl as Window).Show();
            else
                return;
        }
        Title = Title.Remove(Title.IndexOf('-')) + "- " + typ.Name;
    }
    // When Dump menu is opened, enable items.
    void DumpOnOpened(object sender, RoutedEventArgs args)
    {
        itemTemplate.IsEnabled = ctrl != null;
        itemItemsPanel.IsEnabled = ctrl != null && ctrl is ItemsControl;
    }
    // Dump Template object attached to ControlTemplate property.
    void DumpTemplateOnClick(object sender, RoutedEventArgs args)
    {
        if (ctrl != null)
            Dump(ctrl.Template);
    }
    // Dump ItemsPanelTemplate object attached to ItemsPanel property.
    void DumpItemsPanelOnClick(object sender, RoutedEventArgs args)
    {
        if (ctrl != null && ctrl is ItemsControl)
            Dump((ctrl as ItemsControl).ItemsPanel);
    }
    // Dump the template.
    void Dump(FrameworkTemplate template)
    {
        if (template != null)
        {
            // Dump the XAML into the TextBox.
            XmlWriterSettings settings = new XmlWriterSettings();
            settings.Indent = true;
            settings.IndentChars = new string(' ', 4);
            settings.NewLineOnAttributes = true;

            StringBuilder strbuild = new StringBuilder();
            XmlWriter xmlwrite = XmlWriter.Create(strbuild, settings);

            try
```

```
            {
                XamlWriter.Save(template, xmlwrite);
                txtbox.Text = strbuild.ToString();
            }
            catch (Exception exc)
            {
                txtbox.Text = exc.Message;
            }
        }
        else
            txtbox.Text = "no template";
    }
  }
}
```

These templates provide a complete description of the visuals in every control defined by the Windows Presentation Foundation, including references to the *SystemParameters* and *SystemColors* classes. You can get lots of ideas about designing your own templates, and perhaps pick up a few tricks of the masters. It's the closest you can get to seeing actual WPF source code.

This is the general way in which the template draws small graphical objects, such as the *RadioButton* circle or the *CheckBox* square. You'll learn about the format of these strings in Chapter 28.

Some controls use other classes to render their visuals. The *Button* class makes extensive use of the *ButtonChrome* class defined in the *Microsoft.Windows.Themes* namespace. The *ScrollBar* class uses the *ScrollChrome* class defined there as well. The *TextBox* and *RichTextBox* controls have relatively simple templates because the controls are just *Border* elements enclosing *ScrollViewer* controls enclosing the actual editor, which is obviously implemented entirely in code.

So far in this chapter you've seen how you can set the *Template* property of a *Button* (or *RadioButton* or *CheckBox*) to an object of type *ControlTemplate* to completely redefine the visual appearance of the control. In most cases, this is probably a bigger job than you want to take on. More common, perhaps, will be a desire to monkey with the display of *content* in the control.

The *ContentPresenter* element is responsible for displaying content in all controls that derive from *ContentControl*. *ContentPresenter* divides the world into two types of objects: those that inherit from *UIElement* and those that don't. For those that don't, *ContentPresenter* uses the object's *ToString* method to display a text representation of the object. This feature allows controls that derive from *ContentControl* to be very versatile in displaying almost any type of content, but perhaps you'd like a bit more flexibility. Perhaps you'd like to set the content of a *ContentControl* to an object that does not derive from *UIElement*, but you want this object to be rendered in a way that's more sophisticated than *ToString*.

For example, consider the following class that defines a couple of simple properties that you might retain for each of your employees.

Employee.cs

```
//-----------------------------------------
// Employee.cs (c) 2006 by Charles Petzold
//-----------------------------------------
using System;

namespace Petzold.ContentTemplateDemo
{
    public class Employee
    {
        // Private fields.
        string name;
        string face;
        DateTime birthdate;
        bool lefthanded;

        // Parameterless constructor used in XAML.
        public Employee()
        {
        }
        // Constructor with parameter used in C# code.
        public Employee(string name, string face,
                        DateTime birthdate, bool lefthanded)
        {
            Name = name;
            Face = face;
            BirthDate = birthdate;
            LeftHanded = lefthanded;
        }

        // Public properties.
        public string Name
        {
            set { name = value; }
            get { return name; }
        }
        public string Face
        {
            set { face = value; }
            get { return face; }
        }
        public DateTime BirthDate
        {
            set { birthdate = value; }
            get { return birthdate; }
        }
```

```
        public bool LeftHanded
        {
            set { lefthanded = value; }
            get { return lefthanded; }
        }
    }
}
```

The *Face* property is defined as a *string* but it's actually a file name that references a bitmap file of the employee's face. Otherwise, these properties are fairly straightforward. (Why would you need to know if an employee is left-handed? Perhaps you run a factory where machines are designed to be operated by either a right-handed or left-handed person, and you need to pair the right employee with the right machine.)

Suppose you have several objects of type *Employee*, and you'd like to display those objects in buttons. Of course, you can simply set the *Content* property of the *Button* to the *Employee* object, but *Employee* doesn't even have a *ToString* method, so what you're going to get is the string "Petzold.ContentTemplateDemo.Employee", and that doesn't tell you much. (As the namespace declaration indicates, Employee.cs is the first file of a project named Content-TemplateDemo.)

You already know how to display a complex object in a *Button*. You first set the *Content* property of the *Button* to a panel of some sort. As children of this panel, you add other elements (probably *TextBlock* and *Image*, in this case) for the various properties of the *Employee* class. If you were doing this in C# code, you'd probably use this solution because everything can go in a *for* or *foreach* loop.

With XAML, however, you can take another approach. You can define a template specifically for the display of *Employee* objects and then just set the *Content* property of the *Button* to the *Employee* object.

As you know, *ContentControl* uses a *ContentPresenter* object to display content. *Content-Presenter* defines a property named *ContentTemplate* of type *DataTemplate* for defining a template used to display content. This *ContentTemplate* property is also exposed by *Content-Control* itself. By default, *ContentTemplate* is *null*.

You can define this *ContentTemplate* property in the actual *Button* element just as you define the *Template* property. Or, you can create a resource of type *DataTemplate* and assign that to the *ContentTemplate* property of the *Button*. Or, you can create a new class, named perhaps *EmployeeButton*, and define the *ContentTemplate* within that class, as is done here.

EmployeeButton.xaml

```
<!-- ================================================
        EmployeeButton.xaml (c) 2006 by Charles Petzold
     ================================================ -->
<Button xmlns="http://schemas.microsoft.com/winfx/2006/xaml/presentation"
        xmlns:x="http://schemas.microsoft.com/winfx/2006/xaml"
```

```
        xmlns:src="clr-namespace:Petzold.ContentTemplateDemo"
        x:Class="Petzold.ContentTemplateDemo.EmployeeButton">
    <Button.ContentTemplate>
        <DataTemplate DataType="{x:Type src:Employee}">
            <DockPanel>
                <Image DockPanel.Dock="Left" Stretch="None"
                        Source="{Binding Path=Face}" />
                <UniformGrid Rows="2" VerticalAlignment="Center" Margin="12">
                    <TextBlock FontSize="16pt" TextAlignment="Center"
                            Text="{Binding Path=Name}"/>
                    <StackPanel Orientation="Horizontal"
                                TextBlock.FontSize="12pt">
                        <TextBlock Text="{Binding Path=BirthDate.Month}" />
                        <TextBlock Text="/" />
                        <TextBlock Text="{Binding Path=BirthDate.Day}" />
                        <TextBlock Text="/" />
                        <TextBlock Text="{Binding Path=BirthDate.Year}" />
                    </StackPanel>
                </UniformGrid>
            </DockPanel>
        </DataTemplate>
    </Button.ContentTemplate>
</Button>
```

You can tell that this file defines a new class by the *x:Class* attribute in the root element. A *Button.ContentTemplate* property element surrounds a *DataTemplate* definition. The *DataType* of the object we're interested in displaying is *Employee*, which requires an XML namespace prefix of *src*.

As with *ControlTemplate* objects, the *DataTemplate* customarily begins with a visual tree. The tree in this case consists of a *DockPanel* with an *Image* element docked at the left and a *UniformGrid* occupying the interior. The *UniformGrid* has a *TextBlock* for the employee's name and then a *StackPanel* with six *TextBlock* elements that effectively format the employee's birth date.

In the *Image* and *TextBlock* elements, various properties of the *Employee* class are referenced with bindings. These bindings are the key to getting the information from an *Employee* object into the elements of the button's visual true in exactly the way you want. The *Image* element has the following attribute:

```
Source="{Binding Path=Face}"
```

Only the property name of *Face* is required here because the property will be accessed from the object set to the *Content* of the *Button*. The first part of the birth date display is a little more elaborate because it references a particular property of the *BirthDate* property:

```
<TextBlock Text="{Binding Path=BirthDate.Month}" />
```

The *EmployeeButton* class has the following code-behind file.

EmployeeButton.cs

```
//-------------------------------------------------
// EmployeeButton.cs (c) 2006 by Charles Petzold
//-------------------------------------------------
namespace Petzold.ContentTemplateDemo
{
    public partial class EmployeeButton
    {
        public EmployeeButton()
        {
            InitializeComponent();
        }
    }
}
```

Since EmployeeButton.xaml contains no *Name* attributes and no events, I'm not exactly sure why this file is needed, but I've included it for the best reason ever: The program doesn't work without it.

We are now ready to display some of our employees with these buttons. For the employee portraits, the ContentTemplateDemo project includes royalty-free image files obtained from the stock.xchng Web site (*www.sxc.hu*).

ContentTemplateDemo.xaml

```
<!-- ==================================================
        ContentTemplateDemo.xaml (c) 2006 by Charles Petzold
     ================================================== -->
<Window xmlns="http://schemas.microsoft.com/winfx/2006/xaml/presentation"
        xmlns:x="http://schemas.microsoft.com/winfx/2006/xaml"
        xmlns:src="clr-namespace:Petzold.ContentTemplateDemo"
        x:Class="Petzold.ContentTemplateDemo.ContentTemplateDemo"
        Title="ContentProperty Demo">
    <Window.Resources>
        <Style TargetType="{x:Type src:EmployeeButton}">
            <Setter Property="HorizontalAlignment" Value="Center" />
            <Setter Property="VerticalAlignment" Value="Center" />
            <Setter Property="Margin" Value="12" />
        </Style>
    </Window.Resources>

    <StackPanel Name="stack"
                Button.Click="EmployeeButtonOnClick">

        <src:EmployeeButton>
            <src:EmployeeButton.Content>
                <src:Employee Name="Betty"
                              BirthDate="8/31/1970"
                              Face="Betty.png"/>
            </src:EmployeeButton.Content>
        </src:EmployeeButton>
```

```
        <src:EmployeeButton>
            <src:EmployeeButton.Content>
                <src:Employee Name="Edgar"
                              BirthDate="2/2/1965"
                              Face="Edgar.png"/>
            </src:EmployeeButton.Content>
        </src:EmployeeButton>

        <src:EmployeeButton>
            <src:EmployeeButton.Content>
                <src:Employee Name="Sally"
                              BirthDate="7/12/1980"
                              Face="Sally.png"/>
            </src:EmployeeButton.Content>
        </src:EmployeeButton>
    </StackPanel>
</Window>
```

The *Content* property of *EmployeeButton* appears as the property element *EmployeeButton.Content*. The *Content* is set to an *Employee* object with three properties assigned. Because *EmployeeButton* includes a non-*null ContentTemplate* property, that template is used to display the *Employee* object. In reality, a program of this sort would probably access some database to obtain the employee information, so the following ContentTemplateDemo.cs code-behind file demonstrates the code that might be involved by adding another *EmployeeButton* to the *StackPanel*. The file also handles *Click* events from the button.

ContentTemplateDemo.cs

```
//-------------------------------------------------------
// ContentTemplateDemo.cs (c) 2006 by Charles Petzold
//-------------------------------------------------------
using System;
using System.Windows;
using System.Windows.Controls;
using System.Windows.Input;
using System.Windows.Media;

namespace Petzold.ContentTemplateDemo
{
    public partial class ContentTemplateDemo : Window
    {
        [STAThread]
        public static void Main()
        {
            Application app = new Application();
            app.Run(new ContentTemplateDemo());
        }
        public ContentTemplateDemo()
        {
            InitializeComponent();

            // Add another EmployeeButton just to demonstrate the code.
            EmployeeButton btn = new EmployeeButton();
```

```
            btn.Content = new Employee("Jim", "Jim.png",
                                     new DateTime(1975, 6, 15), false);
            stack.Children.Add(btn);
        }

        // Click event handler for button.
        void EmployeeButtonOnClick(object sender, RoutedEventArgs args)
        {
            Button btn = args.Source as Button;
            Employee emp = btn.Content as Employee;
            MessageBox.Show(emp.Name + " button clicked!", Title);
        }
    }
}
```

With any more than a few employees, you'll probably also want to put that *StackPanel* in the XAML file inside a *ScrollViewer*. In the next chapter, I'll show you some other techniques for accessing data and displaying it in controls.

Back in the EmployeeButton.xaml file, I set the *DataType* property of *DataTemplate* to the *Employee* class. It may have seemed as if this was necessary to match up the various properties of the bindings with the correct class, but that's not the case. You can actually remove the *DataType* attribute from the *DataTemplate* element and the program still runs fine.

Certainly the *DataType* attribute provides some helpful information for people who must examine the XAML file. But it actually works in reverse from what you might expect. It's actually used for *locating* a resource that matches the data type of a *Content* property.

The following stand-alone XAML file defines four *DataTemplate* objects as resources. Each of the templates has a different *DataType* (*Int32*, *Double*, *String*, and *DateTime*) and each of the templates indicates that particular data type when displaying data, so it's easy to determine which template is being used.

AutoTemplateSelection.xaml

```
<!-- ======================================================
        AutoTemplateSelection.xaml (c) 2006 by Charles Petzold
     ====================================================== -->
<Page xmlns="http://schemas.microsoft.com/winfx/2006/xaml/presentation"
      xmlns:x="http://schemas.microsoft.com/winfx/2006/xaml"
      xmlns:s="clr-namespace:System;assembly=mscorlib">
    <Page.Resources>

        <DataTemplate DataType="{x:Type s:Int32}">
            <StackPanel Orientation="Horizontal">
                <TextBlock Text="Integer: " />
                <TextBlock Text="{Binding}" />
            </StackPanel>
        </DataTemplate>

        <DataTemplate DataType="{x:Type s:Double}">
```

```xml
                <StackPanel Orientation="Horizontal">
                    <TextBlock Text="Double: " />
                    <TextBlock Text="{Binding}" />
                </StackPanel>
            </DataTemplate>

            <DataTemplate DataType="{x:Type s:String}">
                <StackPanel Orientation="Horizontal">
                    <TextBlock Text="String: " />
                    <TextBlock Text="{Binding}" />
                </StackPanel>
            </DataTemplate>

            <DataTemplate DataType="{x:Type s:DateTime}">
                <StackPanel Orientation="Horizontal">
                    <TextBlock Text="DateTime: " />
                    <TextBlock Text="{Binding Path=Month}" />
                    <TextBlock Text="/" />
                    <TextBlock Text="{Binding Path=Day}" />
                    <TextBlock Text="/" />
                    <TextBlock Text="{Binding Path=Year}" />
                </StackPanel>
            </DataTemplate>

            <Style TargetType="{x:Type Button}">
                <Setter Property="HorizontalAlignment" Value="Center" />
                <Setter Property="Margin" Value="12" />
                <Setter Property="FontSize" Value="12pt" />
                <Setter Property="Padding" Value="10" />
            </Style>

        </Page.Resources>

        <StackPanel>
            <Button>
                <s:Int32>
                    27
                </s:Int32>
            </Button>

            <Button>
                <s:Double>27.543</s:Double>
            </Button>

            <Button>
                27.543
            </Button>

            <Button>
                <x:Static Member="s:DateTime.Now" />
            </Button>
        </StackPanel>
</Page>
```

Toward the bottom of the file, four *Button* objects have four different types of *Content*. These are successfully matched up with the four *DataTemplate* objects stored as resources without any direct connections between the buttons and the resources. A *ContentControl* object automatically searches resources for a *DataTemplate* matching the type of its content, just as the *Button* itself searches for a *Style* that has a *TargetType* of *Button* defined.

That's one way to have different types of presentation of different types of content. A more flexible approach is provided by the *ContentTemplateSelector* property defined by *ContentControl*. This property is of type *DataTemplateSelector*, a class that contains a virtual method named *SelectTemplate*. You derive a class from *DataTemplateSelector* and override *SelectTemplate*. The first argument is the object being displayed by the *ContentControl*. The job of this method is to return an object of type *DataTemplate* for displaying the content.

The SelectDataTemplate project contains the following class that derives from *DataTemplate-Selector* and overrides *SelectTemplate*.

```
EmployeeTemplateSelector.cs
//-----------------------------------------------------------
// EmployeeTemplateSelector.cs (c) 2006 by Charles Petzold
//-----------------------------------------------------------
using Petzold.ContentTemplateDemo;
using System;
using System.Windows;
using System.Windows.Controls;

namespace Petzold.SelectDataTemplate
{
    public class EmployeeTemplateSelector : DataTemplateSelector
    {
        public override DataTemplate SelectTemplate(object item,
                                                DependencyObject container)
        {
            Employee emp = item as Employee;
            FrameworkElement el = container as FrameworkElement;

            return (DataTemplate) el.FindResource(
                emp.LeftHanded ? "templateLeft" : "templateRight");
        }
    }
}
```

In the context of this project, the first argument to *SelectTemplate* is an object of type *Employee*, and the second argument is an object of type *ContentPresenter*. The method uses *FindResource* to choose between templates with the keys of "templateLeft" and "templateRight" based in the *LeftHanded* property of *Employee*.

The following XAML file has a *Resources* section that associates the *EmployeeTemplateSelector* class with a key of "selectTemplate". The two templates are next, with keys of "templateRight" and "templateLeft". The templates are the same except that the *Image* is on the right side for right-handed employees and on the left side for left-handed employees.

SelectDataTemplate.xaml

```xml
<!-- ==================================================
        SelectDataTemplate.xaml (c) 2006 by Charles Petzold
     ================================================== -->
<Window xmlns="http://schemas.microsoft.com/winfx/2006/xaml/presentation"
        xmlns:x="http://schemas.microsoft.com/winfx/2006/xaml"
        xmlns:emp="clr-namespace:Petzold.ContentTemplateDemo"
        xmlns:src="clr-namespace:Petzold.SelectDataTemplate"
        x:Class="Petzold.SelectDataTemplate.SelectDataTemplate"
        Title="Select DataTemplate">
    <Window.Resources>
        <src:EmployeeTemplateSelector x:Key="selectTemplate" />

        <DataTemplate x:Key="templateRight">
            <DockPanel>
                <Image DockPanel.Dock="Right" Stretch="None"
                        Source="{Binding Path=Face}" />
                <UniformGrid Rows="2" VerticalAlignment="Center" Margin="12">
                    <TextBlock FontSize="16pt" TextAlignment="Center"
                            Text="{Binding Path=Name}"/>
                    <StackPanel Orientation="Horizontal"
                                TextBlock.FontSize="12pt">
                        <TextBlock Text="{Binding Path=BirthDate.Month}" />
                        <TextBlock Text="/" />
                        <TextBlock Text="{Binding Path=BirthDate.Day}" />
                        <TextBlock Text="/" />
                        <TextBlock Text="{Binding Path=BirthDate.Year}" />
                    </StackPanel>
                </UniformGrid>
            </DockPanel>
        </DataTemplate>

        <DataTemplate x:Key="templateLeft">
            <DockPanel>
                <Image DockPanel.Dock="Left" Stretch="None"
                        Source="{Binding Path=Face}" />
                <UniformGrid Rows="2" VerticalAlignment="Center" Margin="12">
                    <TextBlock FontSize="16pt" TextAlignment="Center"
                            Text="{Binding Path=Name}"/>
                    <StackPanel Orientation="Horizontal"
                                TextBlock.FontSize="12pt">
                        <TextBlock Text="{Binding Path=BirthDate.Month}" />
                        <TextBlock Text="/" />
                        <TextBlock Text="{Binding Path=BirthDate.Day}" />
                        <TextBlock Text="/" />
                        <TextBlock Text="{Binding Path=BirthDate.Year}" />
                    </StackPanel>
                </UniformGrid>
            </DockPanel>
        </DataTemplate>
```

```
            <Style TargetType="{x:Type Button}">
                <Setter Property="HorizontalAlignment" Value="Center" />
                <Setter Property="VerticalAlignment" Value="Center" />
                <Setter Property="Margin" Value="12" />
            </Style>
        </Window.Resources>

        <StackPanel>
            <Button ContentTemplateSelector="{StaticResource selectTemplate}">
                <Button.Content>
                    <emp:Employee Name="Betty"
                                  BirthDate="8/31/1970"
                                  Face="Betty.png"
                                  LeftHanded="False"/>
                </Button.Content>
            </Button>

            <Button ContentTemplateSelector="{StaticResource selectTemplate}">
                <Button.Content>
                    <emp:Employee Name="Edgar"
                                  BirthDate="2/2/1965"
                                  Face="Edgar.png"
                                  LeftHanded="True"/>
                </Button.Content>
            </Button>

            <Button ContentTemplateSelector="{StaticResource selectTemplate}">
                <Button.Content>
                    <emp:Employee Name="Sally"
                            BirthDate="7/12/1980"
                            Face="Sally.png"
                            LeftHanded="True"/>
                </Button.Content>
            </Button>

            <Button ContentTemplateSelector="{StaticResource selectTemplate}">
                <Button.Content>
                    <emp:Employee Name="Jim"
                                  BirthDate="6/15/1975"
                                  Face="Jim.png"
                                  LeftHanded="False"/>
                </Button.Content>
            </Button>
        </StackPanel>
    </Window>
```

The remainder of the XAML file defines the layout of the window. The four buttons require only that the *ContentTemplateSelector* be set to the "selectTemplate" resource (the *EmployeeTemplateSelector* object), which then indicates which template to use for displaying the content. The following file rounds out the project.

SelectDataTemplate.cs

```
//---------------------------------------------------
// SelectDataTemplate.cs (c) 2006 by Charles Petzold
//---------------------------------------------------
using System;
using System.Windows;

namespace Petzold.SelectDataTemplate
{
    public partial class SelectDataTemplate : Window
    {
        [STAThread]
        public static void Main()
        {
            Application app = new Application();
            app.Run(new SelectDataTemplate());
        }
        public SelectDataTemplate()
        {
            InitializeComponent();
        }
    }
}
```

Although the SelectDataTemplate project shows the most versatile approach for selecting templates used to display content, using the *ContentTemplateSelector* property isn't actually required for this particular job. The next project, called TriggerDataTemplate, shows an alternative approach. As with the previous project, the C# part of the *Window* class is fairly trivial.

TriggerDataTemplate.cs

```
//---------------------------------------------------------
// TriggerDataTemplate.cs (c) 2006 by Charles Petzold
//---------------------------------------------------------
using System;
using System.Windows;

namespace Petzold.TriggerDataTemplate
{
    public partial class TriggerDataTemplate : Window
    {
        [STAThread]
        public static void Main()
        {
            Application app = new Application();
            app.Run(new TriggerDataTemplate());
        }
        public TriggerDataTemplate()
        {
            InitializeComponent();
        }
    }
}
```

The following XAML file defines just one *DataTemplate*, which is given a key name of "template". The *Image* element is given a name of *img* and has its *DockPanel.Dock* property set to *Left*. This is the template for left-handed employees. The *DataTemplate* also includes a *Triggers* section with a *Binding* that references the *LeftHanded* property of the *Employee* object. When that value is *false* (indicating a right-handed employee), the *Setter* sets the *Dock-Panel.Dock* property of the *Image* object to a value of *Right*.

TriggerDataTemplate.xaml

```
<!-- =======================================================
        TriggerDataTemplate.xaml (c) 2006 by Charles Petzold
     ======================================================= -->
<Window xmlns="http://schemas.microsoft.com/winfx/2006/xaml/presentation"
        xmlns:x="http://schemas.microsoft.com/winfx/2006/xaml"
        xmlns:emp="clr-namespace:Petzold.ContentTemplateDemo"
        x:Class="Petzold.TriggerDataTemplate.TriggerDataTemplate"
        Title="Trigger DataTemplate">
    <Window.Resources>
        <DataTemplate x:Key="template">
            <DockPanel>
                <Image Name="img" DockPanel.Dock="Left"
                        Stretch="None" Source="{Binding Path=Face}" />
                <UniformGrid Rows="2" VerticalAlignment="Center" Margin="12">
                    <TextBlock FontSize="16pt" TextAlignment="Center"
                            Text="{Binding Path=Name}"/>
                    <StackPanel Orientation="Horizontal"
                                TextBlock.FontSize="12pt">
                        <TextBlock Text="{Binding Path=BirthDate.Month}" />
                        <TextBlock Text="/" />
                        <TextBlock Text="{Binding Path=BirthDate.Day}" />
                        <TextBlock Text="/" />
                        <TextBlock Text="{Binding Path=BirthDate.Year}" />
                    </StackPanel>
                </UniformGrid>
            </DockPanel>
            <DataTemplate.Triggers>
                <DataTrigger Binding="{Binding Path=LeftHanded}" Value="False">
                    <Setter TargetName="img"
                            Property="DockPanel.Dock" Value="Right" />
                </DataTrigger>
            </DataTemplate.Triggers>
        </DataTemplate>

        <Style TargetType="{x:Type Button}">
            <Setter Property="HorizontalAlignment" Value="Center" />
            <Setter Property="VerticalAlignment" Value="Center" />
            <Setter Property="Margin" Value="12" />
        </Style>
    </Window.Resources>

    <StackPanel>
        <Button ContentTemplate="{StaticResource template}">
            <Button.Content>
                <emp:Employee Name="Betty"
```

```
                                        BirthDate="8/31/1970"
                                        Face="Betty.png"
                                        LeftHanded="False"/>
                </Button.Content>
            </Button>

            <Button ContentTemplate="{StaticResource template}">
                <Button.Content>
                    <emp:Employee Name="Edgar"
                                  BirthDate="2/2/1965"
                                  Face="Edgar.png"
                                  LeftHanded="True"/>
                </Button.Content>
            </Button>

            <Button ContentTemplate="{StaticResource template}">
                <Button.Content>
                    <emp:Employee Name="Sally"
                            BirthDate="7/12/1980"
                            Face="Sally.png"
                            LeftHanded="True"/>
                </Button.Content>
            </Button>

            <Button ContentTemplate="{StaticResource template}">
                <Button.Content>
                    <emp:Employee Name="Jim"
                                  BirthDate="6/15/1975"
                                  Face="Jim.png"
                                  LeftHanded="False"/>
                </Button.Content>
            </Button>
        </StackPanel>
    </Window>
```

Keep in mind that you can use the *ContentTemplate* property to define a custom layout for any control that derives from *ContentControl*, which is certainly a significant proportion of WPF controls. After *ContentControl*, the *ItemsControl* class is the basis of the next most significant subset of controls. *ItemsControl* is the root of all classes that display multiple objects, including *MenuItem*, *TreeViewItem*, *ListBox*, *ComboBox*, and *ListView*.

The *ItemsControl* class inherits the normal *Template* property, of course. For *ListBox*, the *Template* property is fairly simple: a *Border* enclosing a *ScrollViewer* enclosing an *ItemsPresenter* that is responsible for displaying the items.

ItemsControl defines another template-related property, the *ItemsPanel* property, which is by far the simplest type of template. The property is of type *ItemsPanelTemplate*, and the entire visual tree must consist of only a single element that derives from *Panel*. You can use the DumpControlTemplate program described earlier in this chapter for examining the *ItemsPanel* property of *ItemsControl* and the classes that derive from *ItemsControl*. For most of these classes, the template is a *StackPanel*. For *Menu*, it's a *WrapPanel*. (That allows the top-level menu items to wrap from one line to the next.) For *StatusBar*, it's a *DockPanel*. For *ListBox* and *ListView*, it's a *VirtualizingStackPanel*, which is similar to the normal *StackPanel* but is optimized for large numbers of items.

It's fairly easy to replace the panel in a *ListBox* (or other class that derives from *ItemsControl*) with something else. Here's a simple example.

```
ListBoxWithItemsPanel.xaml
<!-- ========================================================
        ListBoxWithItemsPanel.xaml (c) 2006 by Charles Petzold
     ======================================================== -->
<Page xmlns="http://schemas.microsoft.com/winfx/2006/xaml/presentation"
      xmlns:x="http://schemas.microsoft.com/winfx/2006/xaml">

    <ListBox HorizontalAlignment="Center" VerticalAlignment="Center">

        <ListBox.ItemsPanel>
            <ItemsPanelTemplate>
                <UniformGrid />
            </ItemsPanelTemplate>
        </ListBox.ItemsPanel>

        <ListBoxItem>Whatever Item 1</ListBoxItem>
        <ListBoxItem>Whatever Item 2</ListBoxItem>
        <ListBoxItem>Whatever Item 3</ListBoxItem>
        <ListBoxItem>Whatever Item 4</ListBoxItem>
        <ListBoxItem>Whatever Item 5</ListBoxItem>
        <ListBoxItem>Whatever Item 6</ListBoxItem>
        <ListBoxItem>Whatever Item 7</ListBoxItem>
        <ListBoxItem>Whatever Item 8</ListBoxItem>
        <ListBoxItem>Whatever Item 9</ListBoxItem>

    </ListBox>
</Page>
```

All that's being done here is replacing the *VirtualizingStackPanel* normally used to display *ListBox* items with a *UniformGrid*. The *ListBox* still has a border, and if you make the page small enough, you'll see that the panel is enclosed in a *ScrollViewer*. All the selection logic is still intact.

Because the *ListBox* has nine items, the *UniformGrid* automatically determines that the number of rows and columns should both be three. You can override that in the *Uniform-Grid* element:

```
<UniformGrid Columns="2" />
```

A little problem with this *ListBox* is that all the items are smashed up against each other. Perhaps the best way to avoid that problem is to simply add a little *Style* to the *ListBoxItem* elements. You can include the following block of XAML within the *ListBox* element:

```
<ListBox.Resources>
    <Style TargetType="{x:Type ListBoxItem}">
        <Setter Property="Padding" Value="3" />
    </Style>
</ListBox.Resources>
```

You can use *Margin* here rather than *Padding*, but the effect is not quite as good. When an item is selected, the *Padding* is included in the selection but the *Margin* is not.

For displaying the individual items, *ItemsControl* defines a property named *ItemTemplate* of type *DataTemplate*. You use this property in a similar way that you use the *ContentTemplate* property defined by *ContentControl*, except that the *ItemTemplate* property governs the appearance of all items in the *ListBox*, and it references properties of the data stored in the *ListBox*.

You might recall the ListColorsEvenElegantlier project from Chapter 13 that defined a *DataTemplate* in code for displaying colors and their names in a *ListBox*. The ColorListBox-Template project coming up next is functionally equivalent to that program but does it all in XAML (except for the link to the *NamedBrush* class from the ListNamedBrushes project in Chapter 13). The project begins with the following application definition file.

ColorListBoxTemplateApp.xaml

```
<!-- =========================================================
        ColorListBoxTemplateApp.xaml (c) 2006 by Charles Petzold
     ========================================================= -->
<Application xmlns="http://schemas.microsoft.com/winfx/2006/xaml/presentation"
             StartupUri="ColorListBoxTemplateWindow.xaml" />
```

The XAML file for the program's window defines a *DataTemplate* in its *Resources* section. The *DataType* is the *NamedBrush* class. The visual tree is a horizontal *StackPanel* containing a *Rectangle* and a *TextBlock*. The *Fill* property of the *Rectangle* is bound to the *Brush* property of *NamedBrush*, and the *Text* property of the *TextBlock* is bound to the *Text* property of *Named-Brush*.

ColorListBoxTemplateWindow.xaml

```
<!-- =========================================================
        ColorListBoxTemplateWindow.xaml (c) 2006 by Charles Petzold
     ========================================================= -->
<Window xmlns="http://schemas.microsoft.com/winfx/2006/xaml/presentation"
        xmlns:x="http://schemas.microsoft.com/winfx/2006/xaml"
        xmlns:nb="clr-namespace:Petzold.ListNamedBrushes"
        Title="Color ListBox Template"
        Background="{Binding ElementName=lstbox, Path=SelectedValue}">
    <Window.Resources>
        <DataTemplate x:Key="clrlstbox" DataType="NamedBrush">
            <StackPanel Orientation="Horizontal">
                <Rectangle Width="16" Height="16" Margin="2"
                           Stroke="{DynamicResource
```

```
                                  {x:Static SystemColors.WindowTextBrushKey}}"
                          Fill="{Binding Path=Brush}" />
            <TextBlock VerticalAlignment="Center"
                          Text="{Binding Path=Name}" />
        </StackPanel>
    </DataTemplate>
</Window.Resources>

<ListBox Name="lstbox" ItemTemplate="{StaticResource clrlstbox}"
        ItemsSource="{x:Static nb:NamedBrush.All}"
        Width="150" Height="150"
        HorizontalAlignment="Center" VerticalAlignment="Center"
        SelectedValuePath="Brush" />
</Window>
```

The window contains a single *ListBox* with its *ItemTemplate* set to the *DataTemplate* defined as a resource. Each item in the *ListBox* will therefore be displayed as a horizontal *StackPanel* with a *Rectangle* and *TextBlock*. The *ItemsSource* property of *ListBox* is set to the static *All* property of *NamedBrush*, which is an array of all the *NamedBrush* objects generated from the *Brushes* class in *System.Windows.Media*.

Also notice that the *SelectedValuePath* property of *ListBox* is assigned to the *Brush* property of *NamedBrush*. This means that the *SelectedValue* property of *ListBox* will be the *Brush* property of the selected *NamedBrush*. The start tag of the *Window* element defines a *Binding* between that *SelectedValue* property and its own *Background* property.

While I was planning Chapter 26, I knew I wanted a *DatePicker* control, which the first release of the WPF doesn't have. It suddenly occurred to me that a calendar month could be displayed using a *ListBox* with a seven-column *UniformGrid* as its *ItemsPanelTemplate*. The *ListBox* would always contain 28, 29, 30, or 31 items, depending on the month, and the items themselves would just be numbers starting at 1. The *FirstColumn* property of *UniformGrid* is ideal for beginning the month on a day of the week other than Sunday, and actually seems designed for that very purpose.

The resultant *DatePicker* control displays a whole month and lets you click on one day of the month. The control also has repeat buttons for scrolling forward or back by month. But otherwise the control is fairly rudimentary. It isn't retractable into a single line, and it doesn't have much of a keyboard interface. You can't type numbers for the day, month, or year, for example. To compensate, I decided that the PageUp and PageDown keys would duplicate the repeat buttons, and that both the keys and the buttons would be affected by the Shift and Ctrl keys. When neither the Shift nor Ctrl key is pressed, the buttons and the PageUp and PageDown keys cause the calendar to go forward or backward by a month. With the Shift key down, the calendar goes forward or backward by a year. With the Ctrl key, it's by a decade, and with both Shift and Ctrl, it's by a century.

Here's the XAML portion of the *DatePicker* control. You'll notice the *x:Class* attribute in the root element that indicates a definition of a new class based on *UserControl*, which is essentially the same as *ControlControl*. The file begins with a *Resources* section containing a few *Style* definitions. The two *RepeatButton* controls get a style that makes the buttons square. The other two *Style* definitions are for *StatusBarItem* and *ListBoxItem*, neither of which explicitly appears in the XAML file. However, there is a *StatusBar* and there is a *ListBox*, so these styles apply to the items displayed by these controls.

Following the *Resources* section, the definition of the layout of the control begins. Overall, it's a four-row *Grid*. The first row displays the month and year with *RepeatButton* controls on each side. The second row shows the days of the week. The third row is the *ListBox* with the days of the month, and the fourth row is a *CheckBox* labeled "Not applicable." (More on this later.)

DatePicker.xaml

```xml
<!-- =========================================
        DatePicker.xaml (c) 2006 by Charles Petzold
     ========================================= -->
<UserControl xmlns="http://schemas.microsoft.com/winfx/2006/xaml/presentation"
             xmlns:x="http://schemas.microsoft.com/winfx/2006/xaml"
             xmlns:g="clr-namespace:System.Globalization;assembly=mscorlib"
             x:Class="Petzold.CreateDatePicker.DatePicker">
    <UserControl.Resources>

        <!-- Make the RepeatButton square. -->
        <Style TargetType="{x:Type RepeatButton}">
            <Setter Property="Width"
                    Value="{Binding RelativeSource={RelativeSource self},
                                    Path=ActualHeight}" />
            <Setter Property="Focusable" Value="False" />

            <Style.Triggers>
                <DataTrigger Binding="{Binding ElementName=chkboxNull,
                                               Path=IsChecked}"
                             Value="True">
                    <Setter Property="IsEnabled" Value="False" />
                </DataTrigger>
            </Style.Triggers>
        </Style>

        <!-- Styles for StatusBarItem (days of the week). -->
        <Style TargetType="{x:Type StatusBarItem}">
            <Setter Property="Margin" Value="1" />
            <Setter Property="HorizontalAlignment" Value="Center" />
            <Setter Property="VerticalAlignment" Value="Center" />
        </Style>

        <!-- Style for ListBoxItem (days of the month). -->
        <Style TargetType="{x:Type ListBoxItem}">
            <Setter Property="BorderThickness" Value="1" />
            <Setter Property="BorderBrush" Value="Transparent" />
            <Setter Property="Margin" Value="1" />
            <Setter Property="HorizontalContentAlignment" Value="Center" />
            <Style.Triggers>
                <MultiTrigger>
```

```xml
                    <MultiTrigger.Conditions>
                        <Condition Property="IsSelected" Value="True" />
                        <Condition Property="Selector.IsSelectionActive"
                                   Value="False" />
                    </MultiTrigger.Conditions>
                    <Setter Property="BorderBrush"
                            Value="{DynamicResource {x:Static
                                    SystemColors.ControlTextBrushKey}}" />
                </MultiTrigger>

                <DataTrigger Binding="{Binding ElementName=chkboxNull,
                                       Path=IsChecked}"
                             Value="True">
                    <Setter Property="IsEnabled" Value="False" />
                </DataTrigger>
            </Style.Triggers>
        </Style>
    </UserControl.Resources>

    <!-- Border contains main four-row Grid. -->
    <Border BorderThickness="1"
            BorderBrush="{DynamicResource {x:Static
                          SystemColors.WindowTextBrushKey}}">
        <Grid>
            <Grid.RowDefinitions>
                <RowDefinition Height="Auto" />
                <RowDefinition Height="Auto" />
                <RowDefinition Height="Auto" />
                <RowDefinition Height="Auto" />
            </Grid.RowDefinitions>

            <!-- Grid for Label and Buttons. -->
            <Grid Background="{DynamicResource
                              {x:Static SystemColors.ControlDarkDarkBrushKey}}"
                  TextBlock.Foreground="{DynamicResource
                              {x:Static SystemColors.ControlLightLightBrushKey}}">
                <Grid.ColumnDefinitions>
                    <ColumnDefinition Width="Auto" />
                    <ColumnDefinition Width="*" />
                    <ColumnDefinition Width="Auto" />
                </Grid.ColumnDefinitions>

                <RepeatButton Grid.Column="0" Content="&lt;" FontWeight="Bold"
                              Click="ButtonBackOnClick" />
                <TextBlock Name="txtblkMonthYear" Grid.Column="1"
                           HorizontalAlignment="Center"
                           VerticalAlignment="Center" Margin="3" />
                <RepeatButton Grid.Column="2" Content="&gt;" FontWeight="Bold"
                              Click="ButtonForwardOnClick" />
            </Grid>

            <!-- StatusBar with UniformGrid for days of the week. -->
            <StatusBar Grid.Row="1"
                       ItemsSource="{Binding Source={x:Static
                                     g:DateTimeFormatInfo.CurrentInfo},
```

```
                               Path=AbbreviatedDayNames}">
            <StatusBar.ItemsPanel>
                <ItemsPanelTemplate>
                    <UniformGrid Rows="1" />
                </ItemsPanelTemplate>
            </StatusBar.ItemsPanel>
        </StatusBar>

        <!-- ListBox with UniformGrid for days of the month. -->
        <Border Grid.Row="2"
                BorderThickness="0 1 0 1"
                BorderBrush="{DynamicResource {x:Static
                                SystemColors.WindowTextBrushKey}}">
            <ListBox Name="lstboxMonth"
                    SelectionChanged="ListBoxOnSelectionChanged">
                <ListBox.ItemsPanel>
                    <ItemsPanelTemplate>
                        <UniformGrid Name="unigridMonth"
                                     Columns="7" Rows="6"
                                     IsItemsHost="True"
                                Background="{DynamicResource {x:Static
                                    SystemColors.ControlLightBrushKey}}" />
                    </ItemsPanelTemplate>
                </ListBox.ItemsPanel>
                <ListBoxItem>dummy item</ListBoxItem>
            </ListBox>
        </Border>

        <!-- CheckBox for making Null dates. -->
        <CheckBox Name="chkboxNull" Grid.Row="3" Margin="3"
                HorizontalAlignment="Center"
                VerticalAlignment="Center"
                Checked="CheckBoxNullOnChecked"
                Unchecked="CheckBoxNullOnUnchecked">
            Not applicable
        </CheckBox>
      </Grid>
    </Border>
</UserControl>
```

The first row of the main *Grid* is another *Grid* with three columns containing the two *Repeat-Button* controls and a *TextBlock* for the month and year.

The second row of the main *Grid* displays the days of the week. I decided to use a *StatusBar* for this part of the calendar, mainly because a *StatusBar* displays multiple items but doesn't allow the items to be selected. Normally, the *StatusBar* uses a *DockPanel* for displaying its items, but I redefined the *ItemsPanel* of the *StatusBar* to be a seven-column *UniformGrid*. The *ItemsSource* is set to a *Binding* that references the *AbbreviatedDaysNames* property of the *DateTimeFormat-Info* class. This allows the days of the week to appear in the user's own language, but unfortunately, it doesn't work right for countries whose weeks don't begin with Sunday (like France). Accounting for those anomalies would require accessing the *FirstDayOfWeek* property of *DateTimeFormatInfo*, and making some manual adjustments (probably in C# code).

The third row of the main *Grid* is a *ListBox* with its *ItemsPanel* template set to another seven-column *UniformGrid*. This is for the days of the month, and is filled by C# code. For that reason, the *ListBox* has a *Name* attribute of *lstboxMonth*. As I mentioned earlier, C# code must also set the *FirstColumn* property of the *UniformGrid*, so the *UniformGrid* is given a *Name* attribute of *unigridMonth*.

The fourth and final row is a *CheckBox* control labeled "Not applicable." I wanted a way to have a *null* date, and for this particular *DatePicker* control, having such a *CheckBox* seemed to me the most simple and direct approach.

As you know, when you use XAML to define elements and controls normally in a window or page or on a panel, and you assign a string to the *Name* attribute of a particular element, that string becomes a variable name that you can use in the code portion of the class. However, *Name* attributes in templates don't work that way. These names do *not* automatically become variable names, mainly because the same template can be used in multiple controls. Instead, in the C# portion of the class, you must use the *FindName* method defined by *FrameworkTemplate* to find a particular named element within a template. *FindName* will return *null* if the element within the template has not yet been turned into an actual object. The process of creating objects from templates occurs when the control is being loaded and rendered. To ensure that *FindName* returns an actual value, you can preface calls to *FindName* with *ApplyTemplate*, a method defined by *FrameworkElement* that builds the visual tree.

At least that's the way ...it's supposed... to work. But the most problematic aspect of the *DatePicker* turned out to be the *UniformGrid* that displays the days of the month. This *UniformGrid* has a *Name* attribute (*unigridMonth*) but it's buried inside an *ItemsPanel* template in a *ListBox*. After trying a number of different approaches, I finally resorted to a recursive method that used *VisualTreeHelper* to find the *UniformGrid*. This code had to be delayed until the window hosting the control had been loaded.

DatePicker.cs is the code-behind file for *DatePicker*. The class defines a property named *Date* backed by the dependency property *DateProperty*. This property is a nullable *DateTime* object, where a *null* value indicates that the *DateTime* is inapplicable in a particular context. In the next chapter, I use the *DatePicker* on data-entry panels for people's birth dates and death dates. If the person is still alive, the death date is a *null* value.

Using a type of nullable *DateTime* rather than a simple *DateTime* presents some of its own difficulties. You can't simply access the properties of the nullable *DateTime* object. You must cast it to a regular *DateTime* first, and the cast will fail if the value is *null*.

DatePicker defines an event named *DateChanged* that is backed by the routed event *DateChangedEvent*. As the name suggests, this event is triggered when the *Date* property changes.

DatePicker.cs

```
//-------------------------------------------
// DatePicker.cs (c) 2006 by Charles Petzold
//-------------------------------------------
using System;
using System.Globalization;
using System.Windows;
using System.Windows.Controls;
using System.Windows.Controls.Primitives;
using System.Windows.Input;
using System.Windows.Media;

namespace Petzold.CreateDatePicker
{
    public partial class DatePicker
    {
        UniformGrid unigridMonth;
        DateTime datetimeSaved = DateTime.Now.Date;

        // Define DateProperty dependency property.
        public static readonly DependencyProperty DateProperty =
            DependencyProperty.Register("Date", typeof(DateTime?),
                typeof(DatePicker),
                new PropertyMetadata(new DateTime(), DateChangedCallback));

        // Define DateChangedEvent routed event.
        public static readonly RoutedEvent DateChangedEvent =
            EventManager.RegisterRoutedEvent("DateChanged",
                RoutingStrategy.Bubble,
                typeof(RoutedPropertyChangedEventHandler<DateTime?>),
                typeof(DatePicker));

        // Constructor.
        public DatePicker()
        {
            InitializeComponent();

            // Initialize Date property.
            Date = datetimeSaved;

            // Attach handler for Loaded event.
            Loaded += DatePickerOnLoaded;
        }
        // Handler for window Loaded event.
        void DatePickerOnLoaded(object sender, RoutedEventArgs args)
        {
            unigridMonth = FindUniGrid(lstboxMonth);

            if (Date != null)
            {
                DateTime dt = (DateTime)Date;
                unigridMonth.FirstColumn =
                    (int)(new DateTime(dt.Year, dt.Month, 1).DayOfWeek);
            }
        }
```

```
    // Recursive method to find UniformGrid.
    UniformGrid FindUniGrid(DependencyObject vis)
    {
        if (vis is UniformGrid)
            return vis as UniformGrid;

        for (int i = 0; i < VisualTreeHelper.GetChildrenCount(vis); i++)
        {
            Visual visReturn =
                FindUniGrid(VisualTreeHelper.GetChild(vis, i));
            if (visReturn != null)
                return visReturn as UniformGrid;
        }
        return null;
    }

    // Date property backed by DateProperty dependency property.
    public DateTime? Date
    {
        set { SetValue(DateProperty, value); }
        get { return (DateTime?)GetValue(DateProperty); }
    }

    // DateChanged event backed by DateChangedEvent routed event.
    public event RoutedPropertyChangedEventHandler<DateTime?> DateChanged
    {
        add { AddHandler(DateChangedEvent, value); }
        remove { RemoveHandler(DateChangedEvent, value); }
    }

    // Back and Forward repeat buttons.
    void ButtonBackOnClick(object sender, RoutedEventArgs args)
    {
        FlipPage(true);
    }
    void ButtonForwardOnClick(object sender, RoutedEventArgs args)
    {
        FlipPage(false);
    }

    // Buttons are duplicated by PageDown and PageUp keys.
    protected override void OnPreviewKeyDown(KeyEventArgs args)
    {
        base.OnKeyDown(args);

        if (args.Key == Key.PageDown)
        {
            FlipPage(true);
            args.Handled = true;
        }
        else if (args.Key == Key.PageUp)
        {
            FlipPage(false);
            args.Handled = false;
        }
    }
```

```csharp
        // Flip the page to the next month, year, decade, etc.
        void FlipPage(bool isBack)
        {
            if (Date == null)
                return;

            DateTime dt = (DateTime)Date;
            int numPages = isBack ? -1 : 1;

            // If Shift down, go by years.
            if (Keyboard.IsKeyDown(Key.LeftShift) ||
                Keyboard.IsKeyDown(Key.RightShift))
                    numPages *= 12;

            // If Ctrl down, go by decades.
            if (Keyboard.IsKeyDown(Key.LeftCtrl) ||
                Keyboard.IsKeyDown(Key.RightCtrl))
                    numPages = Math.Max(-1200, Math.Min(1200, 120 * numPages));

            // Calculate new DateTime.
            int year = dt.Year + numPages / 12;
            int month = dt.Month + numPages % 12;

            while (month < 1)
            {
                month += 12;
                year -= 1;
            }
            while (month > 12)
            {
                month -= 12;
                year += 1;
            }

            // Set Date property (generates DateChangedCallback).
            if (year < DateTime.MinValue.Year)
                Date = DateTime.MinValue.Date;
            else if (year > DateTime.MaxValue.Year)
                Date = DateTime.MaxValue.Date;
            else
                Date = new DateTime(year, month,
                    Math.Min(dt.Day, DateTime.DaysInMonth(year, month)));
        }

        // If CheckBox being checked, save the Date property and set to null.
        void CheckBoxNullOnChecked(object sender, RoutedEventArgs args)
        {
            if (Date != null)
            {
                datetimeSaved = (DateTime)Date;
                Date = null;
            }
        }

        // If CheckBox being unchecked, restore the Date property.
```

```
void CheckBoxNullOnUnchecked(object sender, RoutedEventArgs args)
{
    Date = datetimeSaved;
}

// For ListBox selection change, change the day of the month.
void ListBoxOnSelectionChanged(object sender,
                                SelectionChangedEventArgs args)
{
    if (Date == null)
        return;

    DateTime dt = (DateTime)Date;

    // Set new Date property (generates DateChangedCallback).
    if (lstboxMonth.SelectedIndex != -1)
        Date = new DateTime(dt.Year, dt.Month,
                    Int32.Parse(lstboxMonth.SelectedItem as string));
}

// This method is triggered by the DateProperty.
static void DateChangedCallback(DependencyObject obj,
                                DependencyPropertyChangedEventArgs args)
{
    // Call OnDateChange for the object being changed.
    (obj as DatePicker).OnDateChanged((DateTime?)args.OldValue,
                                (DateTime?)args.NewValue);
}

// OnDateChanged changes the visuals to match the new value of Date.
protected virtual void OnDateChanged(DateTime? dtOldValue,
                                DateTime? dtNewValue)
{
    chkboxNull.IsChecked = dtNewValue == null;

    if (dtNewValue != null)
    {
        DateTime dtNew = (DateTime)dtNewValue;

        // Set the month and year text.
        txtblkMonthYear.Text = dtNew.ToString(
                DateTimeFormatInfo.CurrentInfo.YearMonthPattern);

        // Set the first day of the month.
        if (unigridMonth != null)
            unigridMonth.FirstColumn =
                (int)(new DateTime(dtNew.Year,
                                dtNew.Month, 1).DayOfWeek);

        int iDaysInMonth = DateTime.DaysInMonth(dtNew.Year,
                                                dtNew.Month);

        // Fill up the ListBox if the number of days isn't right.
        if (iDaysInMonth != lstboxMonth.Items.Count)
        {
```

```
            lstboxMonth.BeginInit();
            lstboxMonth.Items.Clear();

            for (int i = 0; i < iDaysInMonth;  i++)
                lstboxMonth.Items.Add((i + 1).ToString());

            lstboxMonth.EndInit();
        }
        lstboxMonth.SelectedIndex = dtNew.Day - 1;
    }

    // Now trigger the DateChangedEvent.
    RoutedPropertyChangedEventArgs<DateTime?> args =
        new RoutedPropertyChangedEventArgs<DateTime?>(dtOldValue,
                        dtNewValue, DatePicker.DateChangedEvent);
    args.Source = this;
    RaiseEvent(args);
    }
  }
}
```

Following the constructor and the definitions of the *Date* property and *DateChanged* event, the DatePicker.cs file contains several methods for handling user input. Clicks on the *RepeatButton* controls and keyboard presses of the PageUp and PageDown keys all serve to move the calendar to a new month. The main logic occurs in the *FlipPage* method and concludes with setting a new *Date* property. The handler for the *SelectionChanged* event of the *ListBox* also changes the *Date* property.

The definition of the *DateProperty* dependency property at the beginning of the file indicates that the static *DateChangedCallback* method is called whenever the *Date* property changes. This method calls *OnDateChanged*, which is responsible for updating the visual display with the new date and firing the *DateChanged* routed event.

For testing the code, I constructed this small window. One *TextBlock* has a binding with the *Date* property of the *DatePicker* control. Another gets the value from a handler installed for the *DateChanged* event.

CreateDatePickerWindow.xaml

```
<!-- =========================================================
     CreateDatePickerWindow.xaml (c) 2006 by Charles Petzold
     ========================================================= -->
<Window xmlns="http://schemas.microsoft.com/winfx/2006/xaml/presentation"
        xmlns:x="http://schemas.microsoft.com/winfx/2006/xaml"
        xmlns:src="clr-namespace:Petzold.CreateDatePicker"
        x:Class="Petzold.CreateDatePicker.CreateDatePickerWindow"
        Title="Create DatePicker"
        SizeToContent="WidthAndHeight"
        ResizeMode="CanMinimize">
    <StackPanel>
        <src:DatePicker x:Name="datepick"
```

```
                            HorizontalAlignment="Center" Margin="12"
                            DateChanged="DatePickerOnDateChanged" />

            <StackPanel Orientation="Horizontal" Margin="12">
                <TextBlock Text="Bound value: " />
                <TextBlock Text="{Binding ElementName=datepick, Path=Date}" />
            </StackPanel>

            <StackPanel Orientation="Horizontal" Margin="12">
                <TextBlock Text="Event handler value: " />
                <TextBlock Name="txtblkDate" />
            </StackPanel>
        </StackPanel>
</Window>
```

The event handler is located in the code-behind file and updates the *TextBlock* with either a date or a blank indicating a null value.

CreateDatePickerWindow.cs

```
//------------------------------------------------------------
// CreateDatePickerWindow.cs (c) 2006 by Charles Petzold
//------------------------------------------------------------
using System;
using System.Windows;
using System.Windows.Controls;
using System.Windows.Input;
using System.Windows.Media;

namespace Petzold.CreateDatePicker
{
    public partial class CreateDatePickerWindow : Window
    {
        public CreateDatePickerWindow()
        {
            InitializeComponent();
        }

        // Handler for DatePicker DateChanged event.
        void DatePickerOnDateChanged(object sender,
                    RoutedPropertyChangedEventArgs<DateTime?> args)
        {
            if (args.NewValue != null)
            {
                DateTime dt = (DateTime)args.NewValue;
                txtblkDate.Text = dt.ToString("d");
            }
            else
                txtblkDate.Text = "";
        }
    }
}
```

The application definition file completes the project.

CreateDatePickerApp.xaml

```xml
<!-- =======================================================
        CreateDatePickerApp.xaml (c) 2006 by Charles Petzold
     ======================================================= -->
<Application xmlns="http://schemas.microsoft.com/winfx/2006/xaml/presentation"
             xmlns:x="http://schemas.microsoft.com/winfx/2006/xaml"
             x:Class="Petzold.CreateDatePicker.CreateDatePickerApp"
             StartupUri="CreateDatePickerWindow.xaml" />
```

Although the *DatePicker* control demonstrates that the *ListBox* can be put to unusual purposes, most often the *ListBox* displays data, and these days data frequently comes in the form of XML files. In the next chapter I'll show you how to create and flexibly view such files. For a little preview, let's assume that your six employees are stored in the following XML file. The goal of this exercise is to create a *ListBox* that displays these six employees.

Employees.xml

```xml
<!-- ======================================
        Employees.xml (c) 2006 by Charles Petzold
     ====================================== -->
<Employees xmlns="">
    <Employee Name="Betty">
        <BirthDate>8/31/1970</BirthDate>
        <Face>Betty.png</Face>
        <LeftHanded>False</LeftHanded>
    </Employee>
    <Employee Name="Edgar">
        <BirthDate>2/2/1965</BirthDate>
        <Face>Edgar.png</Face>
        <LeftHanded>True</LeftHanded>
    </Employee>
    <Employee Name="Sally">
        <BirthDate>7/12/1980</BirthDate>
        <Face>Sally.png</Face>
        <LeftHanded>True</LeftHanded>
    </Employee>
    <Employee Name="Jim">
        <BirthDate>6/15/1975</BirthDate>
        <Face>Jim.png</Face>
        <LeftHanded>False</LeftHanded>
    </Employee>
    <Employee Name="Anne">
        <BirthDate>4/7/1975</BirthDate>
        <Face>Anne.png</Face>
        <LeftHanded>True</LeftHanded>
    </Employee>
    <Employee Name="John">
        <BirthDate>12/2/1955</BirthDate>
        <Face>John.png</Face>
        <LeftHanded>False</LeftHanded>
    </Employee>
</Employees>
```

This file is part of a project named EmployeeWheel and has a Build Action of Resource. As you'll note, each *Employee* tag in this XML file contains the same information as the *Employee* class shown earlier in this chapter. However, that *Employee* class is not required in the EmployeeWheel project. The *ListBox* and its templates will get everything they need from the Employees.xml file.

The *ListBox* in the EmployeeWheel project will display these six employees in a circle using the *RadialPanel* class created in Chapter 12. The EmployeeWheel project requires the RadialButton.cs and RadialButtonOrientation.cs files from the CircleTheButtons project in that chapter.

You can access an XML file in the *Resources* section of a XAML file by defining an object of type *XmlDataProvider* with a *Source* attribute referencing the URI of the file:

```
<XmlDataProvider x:Key="emps" Source="Employees.xml" XPath="Employees" />
```

The *XPath* property is a string defined in XML Path Language as documented at *www.w3.org/ TR/xpath*, except that no functions are allowed.

You can alternatively embed the XML data directly in the XAML file by use of an XML data island, which is enclosed in an *x:XData* element, like so:

```
<XmlDataProvider x:Key="emps" XPath="Employees">
    <x:XData>
        <Employees xmlns="">
            ...
        </Employees>
    </x:XData>
</XmlDataProvider>
```

Either way, you can set the *ItemsSource* property of a *ListBox* to a *Binding* that references this resource:

```
ItemsSource="{Binding Source={StaticResource emps}, XPath=Employee}"
```

The *XPath* property here indicates that each item is an *Employee* node. The complete Employee-WheelWindow.xaml file using this technique is shown here.

EmployeeWheelWindow.xaml
```
<!-- =======================================================
        EmployeeWheelWindow.xaml (c) 2006 by Charles Petzold
     ======================================================= -->
<Window xmlns="http://schemas.microsoft.com/winfx/2006/xaml/presentation"
        xmlns:x="http://schemas.microsoft.com/winfx/2006/xaml"
        xmlns:rp="clr-namespace:Petzold.CircleTheButtons"
        x:Class="Petzold.EmployeeWheel.EmployeeWheel"
        Title="Employee Wheel">

    <Window.Resources>
        <XmlDataProvider x:Key="emps"
```

```
                              Source="Employees.xml" XPath="Employees" />
        </Window.Resources>

        <Grid>
            <ListBox Name="lstbox"
                    HorizontalAlignment="Center" VerticalAlignment="Center"
                    ItemsSource="{Binding Source={StaticResource emps},
                                          XPath=Employee}"
                    SelectedValuePath="Face">

                <!-- Panel used for displaying the items. -->
                <ListBox.ItemsPanel>
                    <ItemsPanelTemplate>
                        <rp:RadialPanel Orientation="ByHeight" />
                    </ItemsPanelTemplate>
                </ListBox.ItemsPanel>

                <!-- Template used for displaying each item. -->
                <ListBox.ItemTemplate>
                    <DataTemplate>
                        <DockPanel Margin="3">
                            <Image DockPanel.Dock="Right" Stretch="None"
                                    Source="{Binding XPath=Face}" />
                            <UniformGrid Rows="3" VerticalAlignment="Center"
                                        Margin="12">
                                <TextBlock FontSize="16pt" TextAlignment="Center"
                                        Text="{Binding XPath=@Name}"/>
                                <TextBlock FontSize="12pt" TextAlignment="Center"
                                        Text="{Binding XPath=BirthDate}" />
                                <TextBlock Name="txtblkHanded"
                                        FontSize="12pt" TextAlignment="Center"
                                        Text="Right-Handed" />
                            </UniformGrid>
                        </DockPanel>

                        <!-- DataTrigger to display "Left-Handed." -->
                        <DataTemplate.Triggers>
                            <DataTrigger Binding="{Binding XPath=LeftHanded}"
                                        Value="True">
                                <Setter TargetName="txtblkHanded" Property="Text"
                                        Value="Left-Handed" />
                            </DataTrigger>
                        </DataTemplate.Triggers>
                    </DataTemplate>
                </ListBox.ItemTemplate>
            </ListBox>

            <!-- Image in center shows selected item from ListBox. -->
            <Image HorizontalAlignment="Center" VerticalAlignment="Center"
                    Stretch="None"
                    Source="{Binding ElementName=lstbox, Path=SelectedValue}" />
        </Grid>
    </Window>
```

The resources section contains the *XmlDataProvider* object referencing the Employees.xml file with an *XPath* of *Employees*. The *ItemsSource* property of *ListBox* is a binding to that resource with an *XPath* of *Employee*. Following the *ListBox* start tag, the *ItemsPanel* property of *ListBox* defines the panel used for displaying the items. This is the *RadialPanel*.

The *ItemTemplate* property of the *ListBox* defines the way that each *Employee* node will be displayed. The *Source* property of the *Image* and the *Text* properties of each *TextBlock* are all assigned bindings whose definitions contain only *XPath* properties. For subnodes of the *Employee* node, the *XPath* property simply references the name of the node. Here's the binding for the *Image* element:

```
Source="{Binding XPath=Face}"
```

The Employees.xml file has subnodes for *BirthDate*, *Face*, and *LeftHanded*, but *Name* is an attribute of the *Employee* element. For referencing attributes of XML data, you must precede the attribute name with an @ symbol:

```
Text="{Binding XPath=@Name}"
```

I decided not to display the items in different formats based on the value of *LeftHanded*. Instead, each item displays the text "Right-Handed" or "Left-Handed." The *TextBlock* displays the text "Right-Handed" by default:

```
<TextBlock Name="txtblkHanded"
           FontSize="12pt" TextAlignment="Center"
           Text="Right-Handed" />
```

The *DataTemplate* also contains a *Triggers* section, and if the *LeftHanded* element is *true*, the *Text* property of the *TextBlock* is set to "Left-Handed":

```
<DataTrigger Binding="{Binding XPath=LeftHanded}"
             Value="True">
    <Setter TargetName="txtblkHanded" Property="Text"
            Value="Left-Handed" />
</DataTrigger>
```

The EmployeeWheelApp.xaml application definition file completes the EmployeeWheel project.

EmployeeWheelApp.xaml
```
<!-- ===================================================
        EmployeeWheelApp.xaml (c) 2006 by Charles Petzold
     =================================================== -->
<Application xmlns="http://schemas.microsoft.com/winfx/2006/xaml/presentation"
             xmlns:x="http://schemas.microsoft.com/winfx/2006/xaml"
             x:Class="Petzold.EmployeeWheel.EmployeeWheelApp"
             StartupUri="EmployeeWheelWindow.xaml" />
```

The only class that derives from *DataTemplate* is *HierarchicalDataTemplate*. As the name suggests, you use this class in conjunction with *Menu* or (more commonly) *TreeView* to display hierarchically arranged data. Earlier in this chapter, the AutoTemplateSelection.xaml file demonstrated that an element can access an appropriate *DataTemplate* by matching the type of data the element is displaying with the *DataType* property of the *DataTemplate* resources. This facility is key to using multiple *HierarchicalDataTemplate* definitions in displaying different types of data items.

The following stand-alone XAML file contains an XML data island that contains a few nineteenth-century British authors and their books. In this XML file, *Author* elements have *Name* attributes and children named *BirthDate*, *DeathDate*, and *Books*. The *Books* element contains multiple *Book* children. Each *Book* element has a *Title* attribute and a *PubDate* ("publication date") attribute. The goal is to display this data in a *TreeView* control.

HierarchicalTemplates.xaml

```xml
<!-- =======================================================
     HierarchicalTemplates.xaml (c) 2006 by Charles Petzold
     ======================================================= -->
<Page xmlns="http://schemas.microsoft.com/winfx/2006/xaml/presentation"
      xmlns:x="http://schemas.microsoft.com/winfx/2006/xaml"
      Title="Authors and Their Books">
    <Page.Resources>

        <!-- XML data. -->
        <XmlDataProvider x:Key="data" XPath="Authors">
            <x:XData>
                <Authors xmlns="">
                    <Author Name="Jane Austen">
                        <BirthDate>1775</BirthDate>
                        <DeathDate>1817</DeathDate>
                        <Books>
                            <Book Title="Sense and Sensibility">
                                <PubDate>1811</PubDate>
                            </Book>
                            <Book Title="Pride and Prejudice">
                                <PubDate>1813</PubDate>
                            </Book>
                        </Books>
                    </Author>
                    <Author Name="George Eliot">
                        <BirthDate>1819</BirthDate>
                        <DeathDate>1880</DeathDate>
                        <Books>
                            <Book Title="Adam Bede">
                                <PubDate>1859</PubDate>
                            </Book>
                        </Books>
                        <Books>
                            <Book Title="Middlemarch">
                                <PubDate>1872</PubDate>
                            </Book>
```

```
                        </Books>
                    </Author>
                    <Author Name="Anthony Trollope">
                        <BirthDate>1815</BirthDate>
                        <DeathDate>1882</DeathDate>
                        <Books>
                            <Book Title="Barchester Towers">
                                <PubDate>1857</PubDate>
                            </Book>
                            <Book Title="The Way We Live Now">
                                <PubDate>1875</PubDate>
                            </Book>
                        </Books>
                    </Author>
                </Authors>
            </x:XData>
        </XmlDataProvider>

        <!-- Template for Author elements. -->
        <HierarchicalDataTemplate DataType="Author"
                            ItemsSource="{Binding XPath=Books/Book}">
            <StackPanel Orientation="Horizontal"
                    TextBlock.FontSize="12pt">
                <TextBlock Text="{Binding XPath=@Name}" />
                <TextBlock Text=" (" />
                <TextBlock Text="{Binding XPath=BirthDate}" />
                <TextBlock Text="-" />
                <TextBlock Text="{Binding XPath=DeathDate}" />
                <TextBlock Text=")" />
            </StackPanel>
        </HierarchicalDataTemplate>

        <!-- Template for Book elements. -->
        <HierarchicalDataTemplate DataType="Book">
            <StackPanel Orientation="Horizontal"
                        TextBlock.FontSize="10pt">
                <TextBlock Text="{Binding XPath=@Title}" />
                <TextBlock Text=" (" />
                <TextBlock Text="{Binding XPath=PubDate}" />
                <TextBlock Text=")" />
            </StackPanel>
        </HierarchicalDataTemplate>
    </Page.Resources>

    <!-- The TreeView control. -->
    <TreeView ItemsSource="{Binding Source={StaticResource data},
                        XPath=Author}" />
</Page>
```

Let's begin examining this file at the bottom with the *TreeView* control. The *ItemsSource* property is a binding with the resource that has a key of "data." That's the *XmlDataProvider* object defined at the beginning of the resource section. The *XmlDataProvider* has an *XPath* property of *Authors*, and the *ItemsSource* binding of the *TreeView* has an *XPath* of *Author*.

Alternatively, you can define one of these *XPath* properties as *Authors/Author* and leave out the other. Whichever way you do it, the top-level items on the *TreeView* will be the three *Author* elements from the XML data.

How will these *Author* elements be displayed? The *TreeView* control searches the resources for a *DataTemplate* or *HierarchicalDataTemplate* with a *DataType* of *Author*, and it finds one—the first *HierarchicalDataTemplate* defined in the file's resources section. This template contains a visual tree describing how to display the items. Six *TextBlock* elements with a font size of 12 points display the *Name* attribute of the *Author* element, and the *BirthDate* and *DeathDate* elements surrounded by parentheses and separated by a dash. Keep in mind that you're specifying these elements and attributes using a *Binding*, so your template can include a reference to a data converter if you need one for proper formatting. Using such a data converter is probably a better approach to formatting dates, but I wanted to restrict this example to a single XAML file.

That first *HierarchicalDataTemplate* not only describes how to display the *Author* element, but the *ItemsSource* property indicates the *XPath* of the items to be displayed under each author. This *XPath* is *Books*/Book. Therefore, under each author in the *TreeView* will appear items for each of the author's books.

How are these *Book* elements to be displayed? The second *HierarchicalDataTemplate* has a *DataType* of *Book*, so that's the one. This time the visual tree contains four *TextBlock* elements to display the *Title* attribute and the *PubDate* element. The second *Hierarchical-DataTemplate* has no *ItemsSource* property, so the hierarchy ends here. But it could go much deeper.

Although it's convenient to define hierarchical data in XML, you can use objects as well. An *Author* class might have properties named *Name*, *BirthDate*, and *DeathDate*, and a *Books* property, perhaps of type *List<Book>*, referring to a *Book* class. The bindings are nearly the same, except that you use *Path* rather than *XPath*, and *ItemsSource* always refers to a collection.

Many real-life applications use a hierarchy in at least one area of the program, and that's the Help window. The Contents section of the Help window is very often a hierarchy of topics. The YellowPad program in Chapter 22 had a Help window that used navigation to display Help topics. I'd like to generalize that Help window a bit so that you can use it in your own applications, or enhance it if you'd like.

In any project in which you want to use this simple Help system, you use Visual Studio to create a directory named Help in the project. That directory must include a file named Help-Contents.xml with a Build Action of Resource. A sample HelpContents.xml file is shown here. This file and all files until the end of this chapter can be found in the FlowDocumentHelp project.

HelpContents.xml

```xml
<!-- ===============================================
        HelpContents.xml (c) 2006 by Charles Petzold
     =============================================== -->
<HelpContents xmlns="">
    <Topic Header="Copyright Information" Source="Help/Copyright.xaml" />
    <Topic Header="Program Overview" Source="Help/Overview.xaml" />
    <Topic Header="The Menu">
        <Topic Header="The File Menu" Source="Help/FileMenu.xaml" />
        <Topic Header="The Help Menu" Source="Help/HelpMenu.xaml" />
    </Topic>
</HelpContents>
```

The file consists of nested *Topic* elements with a required *Header* attribute and an optional *Source* attribute. Generally, the *Source* element is missing only from *Topic* elements that have child topics. Each *Source* element indicates a XAML file, also located in the Help directory. Here's a sample.

Overview.xaml

```xml
<!-- =======================================
        Overview.xaml (c) 2006 by Charles Petzold
     ======================================= -->
<Page xmlns="http://schemas.microsoft.com/winfx/2006/xaml/presentation"
      xmlns:x="http://schemas.microsoft.com/winfx/2006/xaml"
      Title="Program Overview">
    <FlowDocumentReader>
        <FlowDocument>
            <Paragraph Style="{StaticResource Header}">
                Program Overview
            </Paragraph>
            <Paragraph>
                This file presents an overview of the program.
            </Paragraph>
            <Paragraph>
                The description is probably several paragraphs in length.
                Perhaps it makes reference to the
                <Hyperlink NavigateUri="FileMenu.xaml">File Menu</Hyperlink>
                and
                <Hyperlink NavigateUri="HelpMenu.xaml">Help Menu</Hyperlink>.
            </Paragraph>
        </FlowDocument>
    </FlowDocumentReader>
</Page>
```

Each help topic is a file with a *Page* element containing a *FlowDocumentReader* and a *FlowDocument*. You'll notice that the first *Paragraph* element makes reference to a *Style* with a tag of "Header." The Help directory also contains a file named HelpStyles.xaml that you can make as simple or as elaborate as you want.

HelpStyles.xaml

```xml
<!-- =========================================
        HelpStyles.xaml (c) 2006 by Charles Petzold
        ========================================= -->
<ResourceDictionary
    xmlns="http://schemas.microsoft.com/winfx/2006/xaml/presentation"
    xmlns:x="http://schemas.microsoft.com/winfx/2006/xaml">

    <Style TargetType="{x:Type FlowDocumentReader}">
        <Setter Property="ViewingMode" Value="Scroll" />
    </Style>

    <Style x:Key="Center" TargetType="{x:Type Paragraph}">
        <Setter Property="TextAlignment" Value="Center" />
    </Style>

    <Style x:Key="ProgramName" TargetType="{x:Type Paragraph}"
           BasedOn="{StaticResource Center}">
        <Setter Property="FontSize" Value="32" />
        <Setter Property="FontStyle" Value="Italic" />
        <Setter Property="LineHeight" Value="24" />
    </Style>

    <Style x:Key="Header" TargetType="{x:Type Paragraph}">
        <Setter Property="FontSize" Value="20" />
        <Setter Property="FontWeight" Value="Bold" />
        <Setter Property="LineHeight" Value="16" />
    </Style>
</ResourceDictionary>
```

You reference this file in the *Resources* section of the application definition file, as shown in the following file for an application named Generic.

GenericApp.xaml

```xml
<!-- =========================================
        GenericApp.xaml (c) 2006 by Charles Petzold
        ========================================= -->
<Application xmlns="http://schemas.microsoft.com/winfx/2006/xaml/presentation"
             xmlns:x="http://schemas.microsoft.com/winfx/2006/xaml"
             x:Class="Petzold.Generic.GenericApp"
             StartupUri="GenericWindow.xaml">
    <Application.Resources>
        <ResourceDictionary>
            <ResourceDictionary.MergedDictionaries>
                <ResourceDictionary Source="Help/HelpStyles.xaml" />
            </ResourceDictionary.MergedDictionaries>
        </ResourceDictionary>
    </Application.Resources>
</Application>
```

Besides including the HelpStyles.xaml file as a resource, the application definition file also starts up the GenericWindow.xaml file, which lays out a simple window that includes a menu with a Help item.

GenericWindow.xaml

```xml
<!-- ===============================================
        GenericWindow.xaml (c) 2006 by Charles Petzold
     =============================================== -->
<Window xmlns="http://schemas.microsoft.com/winfx/2006/xaml/presentation"
        xmlns:x="http://schemas.microsoft.com/winfx/2006/xaml"
        x:Class="Petzold.Generic.GenericWindow"
        Title="Generic">
    <DockPanel>
        <Menu DockPanel.Dock="Top">
            <MenuItem Header="_Help">
                <MenuItem Header="_Help for Generic..."
                          Command="Help" />
            </MenuItem>
        </Menu>

        <TextBox AcceptsReturn="True" />
    </DockPanel>

    <Window.CommandBindings>
        <CommandBinding Command="Help" Executed="HelpOnExecuted" />
    </Window.CommandBindings>
</Window>
```

The *HelpOnExecuted* event handler for the Help menu item is located in the code-behind file for the window.

GenericWindow.cs

```csharp
//----------------------------------------------
// GenericWindow.cs (c) 2006 by Charles Petzold
//----------------------------------------------
using Petzold.FlowDocumentHelp;
using System;
using System.Windows;
using System.Windows.Controls;
using System.Windows.Input;
using System.Windows.Media;

namespace Petzold.Generic
{
    public partial class GenericWindow : Window
    {
        public GenericWindow()
        {
            InitializeComponent();
        }
        void HelpOnExecuted(object sender, ExecutedRoutedEventArgs args)
```

```
        {
            HelpWindow win = new HelpWindow();
            win.Owner = this;
            win.Title = "Help for Generic";
            win.Show();
        }
    }
}
```

And finally we reach the *HelpWindow* class, which displays the Help information. The Help-Window.xaml file makes reference to three image files, which are also located in the Help directory. These images are those commonly seen in Help tables of content. I obtained the images from the library included with Visual Studio, but I renamed them and in one case converted an image from an icon to a PNG file.

HelpWindow.xaml

```
<!-- =============================================
        HelpWindow.xaml (c) 2006 by Charles Petzold
     ============================================= -->
<Window xmlns="http://schemas.microsoft.com/winfx/2006/xaml/presentation"
        xmlns:x="http://schemas.microsoft.com/winfx/2006/xaml"
        x:Class="Petzold.FlowDocumentHelp.HelpWindow"
        Title="Help" Width="600" Height="500"
        WindowStartupLocation="CenterScreen"
        ShowInTaskbar="False">
    <Window.Resources>
        <XmlDataProvider x:Key="data"
                         Source="Help/HelpContents.xml"
                         XPath="HelpContents" />

        <HierarchicalDataTemplate DataType="Topic"
                                  ItemsSource="{Binding XPath=Topic}" >

            <!-- Each TreeViewItem is an Image and a TextBlock. -->
            <StackPanel Orientation="Horizontal">
                <Image Name="img"
                       Source="Help/HelpImageQuestionMark.png"
                       Margin="2"
                       Stretch="None" />
                <TextBlock Text="{Binding XPath=@Header}"
                           FontSize="10pt"
                           VerticalAlignment="Center" />
            </StackPanel>

            <HierarchicalDataTemplate.Triggers>

                <!-- Use closed-book image for items that have children. -->
                <DataTrigger Binding="{Binding RelativeSource={RelativeSource
                                       AncestorType={x:Type TreeViewItem}},
                                       Path=HasItems}"
                             Value="True">
```

```
                         <Setter TargetName="img"
                                 Property="Image.Source"
                                 Value="Help/HelpImageClosedBook.png" />
                     </DataTrigger>

                     <!-- Use open-book image for items that are expanded. -->
                     <DataTrigger Binding="{Binding RelativeSource={RelativeSource
                                     AncestorType={x:Type TreeViewItem}},
                                     Path=IsExpanded}"
                                  Value="True">
                         <Setter TargetName="img"
                                 Property="Image.Source"
                                 Value="Help/HelpImageOpenBook.png" />
                     </DataTrigger>
                 </HierarchicalDataTemplate.Triggers>
             </HierarchicalDataTemplate>
         </Window.Resources>

         <Grid>
             <Grid.ColumnDefinitions>
                 <ColumnDefinition Width="33*" />
                 <ColumnDefinition Width="Auto" />
                 <ColumnDefinition Width="67*" />
             </Grid.ColumnDefinitions>

             <!-- Contents TreeView on the left. -->
             <TreeView Name="treevue"
                       Grid.Column="0"
                       ItemsSource="{Binding Source={StaticResource data},
                                     XPath=Topic}"
                       SelectedValuePath="@Source"
                       SelectedItemChanged="TreeViewOnSelectedItemChanged" />

             <!-- GridSplitter in the middle. -->
             <GridSplitter Grid.Column="1" Width="6"
                           HorizontalAlignment="Center"
                           VerticalAlignment="Stretch" />

             <!-- Frame on the right. -->
             <Frame Name="frame" Grid.Column="2"
                    Navigated="FrameOnNavigated" />
         </Grid>
     </Window>
```

Approximately the first half of the file is devoted to a *Resources* section; the remainder is the layout of the *Window*, which is a three-column *Grid* with a *TreeView* on the left, a *Frame* on the right, and a *GridSplitter* in the middle.

The *Resources* section begins with an *XmlDataProvider* element that references the Help-Contents.xml file with a key of "data" and an *XPath* attribute of *HelpContents*, which is the root element of the HelpContents.xml file. Two *DataTrigger* elements select the proper images for the *TreeView* items.

Toward the bottom of the file, the *TreeView* control binds its *ItemsSource* property to this data and indicates that its *SelectedValuePath* is the *Source* attribute of the contents file. I originally bound the *Source* property of the *Frame* to the *SelectedValue* property of the *TreeView*, but it didn't quite provide the functionality I desired, so I decided to link the two controls in the code-behind file.

HelpWindow.cs

```
//-------------------------------------------
// HelpWindow.cs (c) 2006 by Charles Petzold
//-------------------------------------------
using System;
using System.Windows;
using System.Windows.Controls;
using System.Windows.Data;
using System.Windows.Input;
using System.Windows.Media;

namespace Petzold.FlowDocumentHelp
{
    public partial class HelpWindow
    {
        public HelpWindow()
        {
            InitializeComponent();
            treevue.Focus();
        }

        public HelpWindow(string strTopic): this()
        {
            if (strTopic != null)
                frame.Source = new Uri(strTopic, UriKind.Relative);
        }

        // When TreeView selected item changes, set the source of the Frame,
        void TreeViewOnSelectedItemChanged(object sender,
                            RoutedPropertyChangedEventArgs<object> args)
        {
            if (treevue.SelectedValue != null)
                frame.Source = new Uri(treevue.SelectedValue as string,
                                UriKind.Relative);
        }

        // When the Frame has navigated to a new source, synchronize TreeView.
        void FrameOnNavigated(object sender, NavigationEventArgs args)
        {
            if (args.Uri != null && args.Uri.OriginalString != null &&
                            args.Uri.OriginalString.Length > 0)
            {
                FindItemToSelect(treevue, args.Uri.OriginalString);
            }
        }
        // Search through items in TreeView to select one.
```

```
        bool FindItemToSelect(ItemsControl ctrl, string strSource)
        {
            foreach (object obj in ctrl.Items)
            {
                System.Xml.XmlElement xml = obj as System.Xml.XmlElement;
                string strAttribute = xml.GetAttribute("Source");
                TreeViewItem item = (TreeViewItem)
                    ctrl.ItemContainerGenerator.ContainerFromItem(obj);

                // If the TreeViewItem matches the Frame URI, select the item.
                if (strAttribute != null && strAttribute.Length > 0 &&
                                    strSource.EndsWith(strAttribute))
                {
                    if (item != null && !item.IsSelected)
                        item.IsSelected = true;

                    return true;
                }

                // Expand the item to search nested items.
                if (item != null)
                {
                    bool isExpanded = item.IsExpanded;
                    item.IsExpanded = true;

                    if (item.HasItems && FindItemToSelect(item, strSource))
                        return true;

                    item.IsExpanded = isExpanded;
                }
            }
            return false;
        }
    }
}
```

A second constructor allows a program using the *HelpWindow* class to initialize the *Frame* control with one of the documents. The handler for the *SelectedItemChanged* event obtains the selected value from the *TreeView* and sets it in the *Frame*. Getting the table of contents to synchronize with the document proved to be a little messy. Although *TreeView* defines *SelectedItem* and *SelectedValue* properties, they are read-only. To select an item in the *TreeView*, you must set the *IsSelected* property of the individual *TreeViewItem*. This required searching through all the items to find the one to select. Still, doing the job "manually" gave me a valuable feature, and I'm glad I did it. Bindings are powerful, but sometimes they're no substitute for actual code.

Despite the length of this chapter, the subject of templates is not yet exhausted. Toward the end of the next chapter, I'll show you how to group items in a *ListBox* and use templates to display headings on these groups.

Chapter 26
Data Entry, Data Views

For generations of programmers, one of the most common jobs has been the creation of programs that facilitate the entry, editing, and viewing of data. For such a program, generally you create a data-input form that has controls corresponding to the fields of the records in a database.

Let's assume you want to maintain a database of famous people (music composers, perhaps). For each person, you want to store the first name, middle name, last name, birth date, and date of death, which could be *null* if the person is still living. A good first step is to define a class containing public properties for all the items you want to maintain. As usual, these public properties provide a public interface to private fields.

It is very advantageous that such a class implement the *INotifyPropertyChanged* interface. Strictly speaking, the *INotifyPropertyChanged* interface requires only that the class have an event named *PropertyChanged* defined in accordance with the *PropertyChangedEventHandler* delegate. But such an event is worthless unless the properties of the class fire the event whenever the values of the properties change.

Here is such a class.

Person.cs
```
//----------------------------------------
// Person.cs (c) 2006 by Charles Petzold
//----------------------------------------
using System;
using System.ComponentModel;
using System.Xml.Serialization;

namespace Petzold.SingleRecordDataEntry
{
    public class Person: INotifyPropertyChanged
    {
        // PropertyChanged event definition.
        public event PropertyChangedEventHandler PropertyChanged;

        // Private fields.
        string strFirstName = "<first name>";
        string strMiddleName = "" ;
        string strLastName = "<last name>";
        DateTime? dtBirthDate = new DateTime(1800, 1, 1);
        DateTime? dtDeathDate = new DateTime(1900, 12, 31);
```

```
      // Public properties.
      public string FirstName
      {
          set
          {
              strFirstName = value;
              OnPropertyChanged("FirstName");
          }
          get { return strFirstName; }
      }
      public string MiddleName
      {
          set
          {
              strMiddleName = value;
              OnPropertyChanged("MiddleName");
          }
          get { return strMiddleName; }
      }
      public string LastName
      {
          set
          {
              strLastName = value;
              OnPropertyChanged("LastName");
          }
          get { return strLastName; }
      }

      [XmlElement(DataType="date")]
      public DateTime? BirthDate
      {
          set
          {
              dtBirthDate = value;
              OnPropertyChanged("BirthDate");
          }
          get { return dtBirthDate; }
      }

      [XmlElement(DataType = "date")]
      public DateTime? DeathDate
      {
          set
          {
              dtDeathDate = value;
              OnPropertyChanged("DeathDate");
          }
          get { return dtDeathDate; }
      }

      // Fire the PropertyChanged event.
      protected virtual void OnPropertyChanged(string strPropertyName)
```

```
        {
            if (PropertyChanged != null)
                PropertyChanged(this,
                    new PropertyChangedEventArgs(strPropertyName));
        }
    }
}
```

Implementing the *INotifyPropertyChanged* interface lets the properties of this class participate as sources in data bindings. They cannot be targets because they are not backed by dependency properties, but usually it's enough that they can be sources.

The *OnPropertyChanged* method is not required, but it provides a convenient place to fire the *PropertyChanged* event, and classes that implement the *INotifyPropertyChanged* interface usually include such a method. Some classes define the *OnPropertyChanged* method to have an argument of type *PropertyChangedEventArgs*, while other classes define it as I've done, which involves somewhat less code overall.

The next step is a data-input form. You could use a *Window* or a *Page* for this job, but the most flexible solution is a *Panel* of some sort. The following *PersonPanel* class uses a *Grid* to display three *TextBox* controls for the first, middle, and last names, and two *DatePicker* controls (from the CreateDatePicker project in the previous chapter) for the birth date and death date. *Label* controls identify each of the data-input controls.

PersonPanel.xaml

```
<!-- =================================================
        PersonPanel.xaml (c) 2006 by Charles Petzold
     ================================================= -->
<Grid xmlns="http://schemas.microsoft.com/winfx/2006/xaml/presentation"
      xmlns:x="http://schemas.microsoft.com/winfx/2006/xaml"
      xmlns:dp="clr-namespace:Petzold.CreateDatePicker"
      xmlns:src="clr-namespace:Petzold.SingleRecordDataEntry"
      x:Class="Petzold.SingleRecordDataEntry.PersonPanel" >

    <Grid.Resources>
        <Style TargetType="{x:Type Label}">
            <Setter Property="VerticalAlignment" Value="Center" />
            <Setter Property="Margin" Value="12" />
        </Style>

        <Style TargetType="{x:Type TextBox}">
            <Setter Property="Margin" Value="12" />
        </Style>

        <Style TargetType="{x:Type dp:DatePicker}">
            <Setter Property="Margin" Value="12" />
        </Style>
    </Grid.Resources>
```

```
<Grid.ColumnDefinitions>
    <ColumnDefinition Width="Auto" />
    <ColumnDefinition Width="Auto" />
</Grid.ColumnDefinitions>

<Grid.RowDefinitions>
    <RowDefinition Height="Auto" />
    <RowDefinition Height="Auto" />
    <RowDefinition Height="Auto" />
    <RowDefinition Height="Auto" />
    <RowDefinition Height="Auto" />
</Grid.RowDefinitions>

<Label Grid.Row="0" Grid.Column="0"
    Content="_First Name: " />

<TextBox Grid.Row="0" Grid.Column="1" Margin="12"
        Text="{Binding Path=FirstName,
                    Mode=TwoWay,
                    UpdateSourceTrigger=PropertyChanged}" />

<Label Grid.Row="1" Grid.Column="0"
    Content="_Middle Name: " />

<TextBox Grid.Row="1" Grid.Column="1" Margin="12"
        Text="{Binding Path=MiddleName,
                    Mode=TwoWay,
                    UpdateSourceTrigger=PropertyChanged}" />

<Label Grid.Row="2" Grid.Column="0"
    Content="_Last Name: " />

<TextBox Grid.Row="2" Grid.Column="1" Margin="12"
        Text="{Binding Path=LastName,
                    Mode=TwoWay,
                    UpdateSourceTrigger=PropertyChanged}" />

<Label Grid.Row="3" Grid.Column="0"
    Content="_Birth Date: " />

<dp:DatePicker Grid.Row="3" Grid.Column="1" Margin="12"
            HorizontalAlignment="Center"
            Date="{Binding Path=BirthDate, Mode=TwoWay}" />

<Label Grid.Row="4" Grid.Column="0"
    Content="_Death Date: " />

<dp:DatePicker Grid.Row="4" Grid.Column="1" Margin="12"
            HorizontalAlignment="Center"
            Date="{Binding Path=DeathDate, Mode=TwoWay}" />
</Grid>
```

Notice that the three *TextBox* controls contain bindings to their *Text* properties, and the two *DatePicker* controls contain bindings to their *Date* properties. Each of these bindings has a *Path* property that indicates a particular property of the *Person* class, and each of the bindings has an explicit *TwoWay* mode setting so that any change to the control will be reflected in the source data. In addition, the *TextBox* bindings have the *UpdateSourceTrigger* property set to *PropertyChanged* so that the source data is updated whenever the *Text* property changes and not (as is the default behavior) when the *TextBox* loses input focus.

These bindings are incomplete because they are missing a data source. Generally this source is given as the *Source* or *ElementName* property of the binding, but another way to provide a binding source is through the *DataContext* property defined by *FrameworkElement*.

The characteristic of *DataContext* that makes it so valuable is that it is inherited through the visual tree. The implications are simple and profound: If you set the *DataContext* property of a *PersonPanel* to an object of type *Person*, the *TextBox* and *DatePicker* controls will display the properties of that *Person* object, and any user input to those controls will be reflected in the *Person* object.

This is how one binding between an object and a panel's *DataContext* property becomes multiple bindings between properties of that object and controls on the panel.

The PersonPanel.cs code-behind file is trivial.

PersonPanel.cs
```
//----------------------------------------------
// PersonPanel.cs (c) 2006 by Charles Petzold
//----------------------------------------------
namespace Petzold.SingleRecordDataEntry
{
    public partial class PersonPanel
    {
        public PersonPanel()
        {
            InitializeComponent();
        }
    }
}
```

So that you can better grasp the mechanics of the binding between the *Person* object and the controls on the *PersonPanel*, the first project in this chapter loads and saves files containing only a single *Person* object. That's why the project is named SingleRecordDataEntry. Any database created from this program has only one record of type *Person*.

The next part of the SingleRecordDataEntry project is a *Window* containing the *PersonPanel* input panel. I've also included a menu with New, Open, and Save items.

SingleRecordDataEntry.xaml

```
<!-- =======================================================
     SingleRecordDataEntry.xaml (c) 2006 by Charles Petzold
     ======================================================= -->
<Window xmlns="http://schemas.microsoft.com/winfx/2006/xaml/presentation"
        xmlns:x="http://schemas.microsoft.com/winfx/2006/xaml"
        xmlns:pnl="clr-namespace:Petzold.SingleRecordDataEntry"
        x:Class="Petzold.SingleRecordDataEntry.SingleRecordDataEntry"
        Title="Single-Record Data Entry"
        SizeToContent="WidthAndHeight"
        ResizeMode="CanMinimize">
    <DockPanel Name="dock">
        <Menu DockPanel.Dock="Top">
            <MenuItem Header="_File">
                <MenuItem Header="_New" Command="New" />
                <MenuItem Header="_Open..." Command="Open" />
                <MenuItem Header="_Save..." Command="Save" />
            </MenuItem>
        </Menu>

        <!-- PersonPanel for entering information. -->
        <pnl:PersonPanel x:Name="pnlPerson" />
    </DockPanel>

    <Window.CommandBindings>
        <CommandBinding Command="New" Executed="NewOnExecuted" />
        <CommandBinding Command="Open" Executed="OpenOnExecuted" />
        <CommandBinding Command="Save" Executed="SaveOnExecuted" />
    </Window.CommandBindings>
</Window>
```

As you'll note, the three items on the File menu are associated with *Executed* handlers through command bindings. The *PersonPanel* object that occupies the interior of the *DockPanel* is given a name of *pnlPerson*.

The three *Executed* event handlers are located in the code-behind file that completes the SingleRecordDataEntry project.

SingleRecordDataEntry.cs

```
//----------------------------------------------------------
// SingleRecordDataEntry.cs (c) 2006 by Charles Petzold
//----------------------------------------------------------
using Microsoft.Win32;
using System;
using System.IO;
using System.Windows;
using System.Windows.Controls;
using System.Windows.Input;
using System.Xml.Serialization;
```

```
namespace Petzold.SingleRecordDataEntry
{
    public partial class SingleRecordDataEntry : Window
    {
        const string strFilter = "Person XML files (*.PersonXml)|" +
                                 "*.PersonXml|All files (*.*)|*.*";
        XmlSerializer xml = new XmlSerializer(typeof(Person));

        [STAThread]
        public static void Main()
        {
            Application app = new Application();
            app.Run(new SingleRecordDataEntry());
        }
        public SingleRecordDataEntry()
        {
            InitializeComponent();

            // Simulate File New command.
            ApplicationCommands.New.Execute(null, this);

            // Set focus to first TextBox in panel.
            pnlPerson.Children[1].Focus();
        }
        // Event handlers for menu items.
        void NewOnExecuted(object sender, ExecutedRoutedEventArgs args)
        {
            pnlPerson.DataContext = new Person();
        }
        void OpenOnExecuted(object sender, ExecutedRoutedEventArgs args)
        {
            OpenFileDialog dlg = new OpenFileDialog();
            dlg.Filter = strFilter;
            Person pers;

            if ((bool)dlg.ShowDialog(this))
            {
                try
                {
                    StreamReader reader = new StreamReader(dlg.FileName);
                    pers = (Person) xml.Deserialize(reader);
                    reader.Close();
                }
                catch (Exception exc)
                {
                    MessageBox.Show("Could not load file: " + exc.Message,
                                    Title, MessageBoxButton.OK,
                                    MessageBoxImage.Exclamation);
                    return;
                }
                pnlPerson.DataContext = pers;
            }
        }
    }
```

```
void SaveOnExecuted(object sender, ExecutedRoutedEventArgs args)
{
    SaveFileDialog dlg = new SaveFileDialog();
    dlg.Filter = strFilter;

    if ((bool)dlg.ShowDialog(this))
    {
        try
        {
            StreamWriter writer = new StreamWriter(dlg.FileName);
            xml.Serialize(writer, pnlPerson.DataContext);
            writer.Close();
        }
        catch (Exception exc)
        {
            MessageBox.Show("Could not save file: " + exc.Message,
                            Title, MessageBoxButton.OK,
                            MessageBoxImage.Exclamation);
            return;
        }
    }
}
```

The New command (which is also simulated in the constructor of the class) creates a new object of type *Person* and sets it to the *DataContext* property of the *PersonPanel*. When you start up the program, you'll see the default values defined in *Person* displayed in *PersonPanel*.

The Open and Save commands display *OpenFileDialog* and *SaveFileDialog* windows, respectively. These dialogs share the *strFilter* string defined at the top of the class and, by default, access files with the file name extension PersonXml. The *OpenOnExecuted* and *SaveOnExecuted* methods also make use of the same *XmlSerializer* object defined at the top of the class to store *Person* objects in XML format. The *SaveOnExecuted* method calls *Serialize* to convert the *Person* object currently stored as the *DataContext* property of the *PersonPanel* to an XML file. The *OpenOnExecuted* method loads a file saved earlier, calls *Deserialize* to convert it to a *Person* object, and then sets it to the *DataContext* property of the *PersonPanel*.

You can save multiple files with the SingleRecordDataEntry program, but each file contains only one *Person* object. A typical file looks like this:

```
<?xml version="1.0" encoding="utf-8"?>
<Person xmlns:xsi="http://www.w3.org/2001/XMLSchema-instance"
        xmlns:xsd="http://www.w3.org/2001/XMLSchema">
  <FirstName>Johannes</FirstName>
  <MiddleName />
  <LastName>Brahms</LastName>
  <BirthDate>1833-05-07</BirthDate>
  <DeathDate>1897-04-03</DeathDate>
</Person>
```

The next obvious job requires maintaining a collection of *Person* objects. The .NET Framework contains several classes that store collections of objects. I tend to use the generic *List* class when I want something simple. But when working with databases, it's often advantageous to use the generic *ObservableCollection* class defined in the *System.Collections.ObjectModel* namespace. You can define a collection of *Person* objects like this:

```
ObservableCollection<Person> people = new ObservableCollection<Person>();
```

Or you can derive a class (named *People*, perhaps) from the *ObservableCollection* class:

```
public class People : ObservableCollection<Person>
{
}
```

And then you can create an object of type *People*:

```
People people = new People();
```

One advantage of the latter approach is that you can put some methods in the *People* class that save *People* objects to files and later load them. (This is the approach I took in the upcoming MultiRecordDataEntry project.)

Because *ObservableCollection* is a generic class, you can add new objects of type *Person* to the collection without casting:

```
people.Add(new Person());
```

You can also index the collection and the result is an object of type *Person*:

```
Person person = people[5];
```

Beyond those two conveniences found in any generic collection class, *ObservableCollection* also defines two important events: *PropertyChanged* and *CollectionChanged*.

The *PropertyChanged* event is fired whenever a property of one of the members of the collection changes. Of course, this only works if the *ObservableCollection* object is based on a class that implements the *INotifyPropertyChanged* event and which fires its own *PropertyChanged* event when one of the properties changes. (Fortunately, the *Person* class qualifies.) Obviously, *ObservableCollection* attaches an event handler to the *PropertyChanged* event of each member of its collection and then fires its own *PropertyChanged* event in response.

The *CollectionChanged* event is fired whenever the collection as a whole changes, that is, whenever an item is added to the collection, removed from the collection, replaced, or moved within the collection.

The MultiRecordDataEntry project includes links to the files Person.cs, PersonPanel.xaml, and PersonPanel.cs from the SingleRecordDataEntry project, as well as the *DatePicker* files from the CreateDatePicker project in Chapter 25. The People.cs file is the first of three new files for this project. The file defines a *People* class that derives from *ObservableCollection* to maintain a collection of *Person* objects.

People.cs

```
//----------------------------------------
// People.cs (c) 2006 by Charles Petzold
//----------------------------------------
using Microsoft.Win32;
using Petzold.SingleRecordDataEntry;
using System;
using System.IO;
using System.Collections.ObjectModel;
using System.Windows;
using System.Xml.Serialization;

namespace Petzold.MultiRecordDataEntry
{
    public class People : ObservableCollection<Person>
    {
        const string strFilter = "People XML files (*.PeopleXml)|" +
                            "*.PeopleXml|All files (*.*)|*.*";

        public static People Load(Window win)
        {
            OpenFileDialog dlg = new OpenFileDialog();
            dlg.Filter = strFilter;
            People people = null;

            if ((bool)dlg.ShowDialog(win))
            {
                try
                {
                    StreamReader reader = new StreamReader(dlg.FileName);
                    XmlSerializer xml = new XmlSerializer(typeof(People));
                    people = (People)xml.Deserialize(reader);
                    reader.Close();
                }
                catch (Exception exc)
                {
                    MessageBox.Show("Could not load file: " + exc.Message,
                                win.Title, MessageBoxButton.OK,
                                MessageBoxImage.Exclamation);
                    people = null;
                }
            }
            return people;
        }
        public bool Save(Window win)
        {
            SaveFileDialog dlg = new SaveFileDialog();
            dlg.Filter = strFilter;
```

```
            if ((bool)dlg.ShowDialog(win))
            {
                try
                {
                    StreamWriter writer = new StreamWriter(dlg.FileName);
                    XmlSerializer xml = new XmlSerializer(GetType());
                    xml.Serialize(writer, this);
                    writer.Close();
                }
                catch (Exception exc)
                {
                    MessageBox.Show("Could not save file: " + exc.Message,
                                win.Title, MessageBoxButton.OK,
                                MessageBoxImage.Exclamation);
                    return false;
                }
            }
            return true;
        }
    }
}
```

I've also used this class for two methods named *Load* and *Save* that display the *OpenFileDialog* and *SaveFileDialog* windows and then use the *XmlSerializer* to load and save objects of type *People*. Notice that *Load* is a static method that returns an object of type *People*. Both *Load* and *Save* have arguments that you set to the parent *Window* object. The methods use this object to pass to the *ShowDialog* method and as a title in the two *MessageBox.Show* calls in case a problem is encountered with the file input or output. (Although putting the *XmlSerializer* code in the *People* class makes sense, normally I wouldn't also put the dialog boxes in there. There might be occasions when you'll want to load or save files without displaying dialog boxes. I've put the dialog boxes in the *People* class for convenience in simplifying the other programs in this chapter.)

The MultiRecordDataEntry program uses *PersonPanel* to display the information for one person, and yet it deals with a file containing multiple people. To accomplish this feat, the program must have some provision for navigating through the database. One approach is to keep track of a "current" record, and to have buttons for navigating to the next record and to the previous record, and to go to the first record and to the last record.

In the general case, you don't want to just view or edit the existing records of the file. You want to add new records and possibly delete records. In addition to the navigation buttons, you'll probably want to have buttons for Add New and Delete.

The following file, MultiRecordDataEntry.xaml, defines the layout of a window that includes a menu with the familiar New, Open, and Save commands. The remainder of the window has a *PersonPanel* and the six buttons I've described.

MultiRecordDataEntry.xaml

```xml
<!-- ========================================================
         MultiRecordDataEntry.xaml (c) 2006 by Charles Petzold
     ======================================================== -->
<Window xmlns="http://schemas.microsoft.com/winfx/2006/xaml/presentation"
        xmlns:x="http://schemas.microsoft.com/winfx/2006/xaml"
        xmlns:pnl="clr-namespace:Petzold.SingleRecordDataEntry"
        x:Class="Petzold.MultiRecordDataEntry.MultiRecordDataEntry"
        Title="Multi-Record Data Entry"
        SizeToContent="WidthAndHeight"
        ResizeMode="CanMinimize">
    <DockPanel Name="dock">
        <Menu DockPanel.Dock="Top">
            <MenuItem Header="_File">
                <MenuItem Header="_New" Command="New" />
                <MenuItem Header="_Open..." Command="Open" />
                <MenuItem Header="_Save..." Command="Save" />
            </MenuItem>
        </Menu>

        <StackPanel>
            <!-- PersonPanel to enter data. -->
            <pnl:PersonPanel x:Name="pnlPerson" />

            <!-- Buttons for navigation, adding, deleting. -->
            <UniformGrid Columns="6" HorizontalAlignment="Center">
                <UniformGrid.Resources>
                    <Style TargetType="{x:Type Button}">
                        <Setter Property="Margin" Value="6" />
                    </Style>
                </UniformGrid.Resources>
                <Button Name="btnFirst" Content="First" Click="FirstOnClick" />
                <Button Name="btnPrev" Content="Previous" Click="PrevOnClick" />
                <Button Name="btnNext" Content="Next" Click="NextOnClick" />
                <Button Name="btnLast" Content="Last" Click="LastOnClick" />
                <Button Name="btnAdd" Content="Add New" Click="AddOnClick" />
                <Button Name="btnDel" Content="Delete" Click="DelOnClick" />
            </UniformGrid>
        </StackPanel>
    </DockPanel>

    <Window.CommandBindings>
        <CommandBinding Command="New" Executed="NewOnExecuted" />
        <CommandBinding Command="Open" Executed="OpenOnExecuted" />
        <CommandBinding Command="Save" Executed="SaveOnExecuted" />
    </Window.CommandBindings>
</Window>
```

The following MultiRecordDataEntry.cs file completes the definition of the program's *Window* object with event handlers for the three menu items and the six buttons. This class maintains two fields: an object of type *People*, which is the file currently loaded, and an integer named *index*. This *index* variable is the index of the current record displayed in the *PersonPanel*. This value indexes the *People* object and is altered by the event handlers for the First, Previous, Next, and Last buttons.

With the *Load* and *Save* methods already defined in the *People* class, the three event handlers for the menu items are fairly simple. Both the New and Open items cause the creation of a new *People* object and a call to the *InitializeNewPeopleObject* method. This method sets the *index* variable to 0. If the *People* object has no records (which will be the case for the New command), this method creates a *Person* record and adds it to the collection. In either case, the *DataContext* of the *PersonPanel* is set to the first *Person* object in the *People* collection. A call to *EnableAndDisableButtons* enables the Previous button if the record being displayed is not the first record and enables the Next button if the record displayed is not the last record.

MultiRecordDataEntry.cs

```csharp
//--------------------------------------------------------
// MultiRecordDataEntry.cs (c) 2006 by Charles Petzold
//--------------------------------------------------------
using Petzold.SingleRecordDataEntry;
using System;
using System.Collections.Specialized;
using System.Windows;
using System.Windows.Controls;
using System.Windows.Input;
using System.Windows.Media;

namespace Petzold.MultiRecordDataEntry
{
    public partial class MultiRecordDataEntry
    {
        People people;
        int index;

        [STAThread]
        public static void Main()
        {
            Application app = new Application();
            app.Run(new MultiRecordDataEntry());
        }
        public MultiRecordDataEntry()
        {
            InitializeComponent();

            // Simulate File New command.
            ApplicationCommands.New.Execute(null, this);

            // Set focus to first TextBox in panel.
            pnlPerson.Children[1].Focus();
        }

        // Event handlers for menu items.
        void NewOnExecuted(object sender, ExecutedRoutedEventArgs args)
```

```
{
    people = new People();
    InitializeNewPeopleObject();
}
void OpenOnExecuted(object sender, ExecutedRoutedEventArgs args)
{
    people = People.Load(this);
    InitializeNewPeopleObject();
}
void SaveOnExecuted(object sender, ExecutedRoutedEventArgs args)
{
    people.Save(this);
}
void InitializeNewPeopleObject()
{
    index = 0;

    if (people.Count == 0)
        people.Insert(0, new Person());

    pnlPerson.DataContext = people[0];
    EnableAndDisableButtons();
}

// Event handlers for buttons.
void FirstOnClick(object sender, RoutedEventArgs args)
{
    pnlPerson.DataContext = people[index = 0];
    EnableAndDisableButtons();
}
void PrevOnClick(object sender, RoutedEventArgs args)
{
    pnlPerson.DataContext = people[index -= 1];
    EnableAndDisableButtons();
}
void NextOnClick(object sender, RoutedEventArgs args)
{
    pnlPerson.DataContext = people[index += 1];
    EnableAndDisableButtons();
}
void LastOnClick(object sender, RoutedEventArgs args)
{
    pnlPerson.DataContext = people[index = people.Count - 1];
    EnableAndDisableButtons();
}
void AddOnClick(object sender, RoutedEventArgs args)
{
    people.Insert(index = people.Count, new Person());
    pnlPerson.DataContext = people[index];
    EnableAndDisableButtons();
}
void DelOnClick(object sender, RoutedEventArgs args)
{
    people.RemoveAt(index);
```

```
        if (people.Count == 0)
            people.Insert(0, new Person());

        if (index > people.Count - 1)
            index--;

        pnlPerson.DataContext = people[index];
        EnableAndDisableButtons();
    }

    void EnableAndDisableButtons()
    {
        btnPrev.IsEnabled = index != 0;
        btnNext.IsEnabled = index < people.Count - 1;
        pnlPerson.Children[1].Focus();
    }
  }
 }
}
```

The event handlers for the six buttons are fairly straightforward. For the four navigation buttons, the event handler simply calculates a new value of *index*, uses that to index the *people* collection, and sets the *DataContext* property of the *PersonPanel* to that indexed *Person* object. The Add New button handler creates a new *Person* object and inserts it into the collection. The Delete button deletes the current record. If that results in an empty collection, a new *Person* object is added.

The MultiRecordDataEntry program saves and loads files that look like this:

```
<?xml version="1.0" encoding="utf-8"?>
<ArrayOfPerson xmlns:xsi="http://www.w3.org/2001/XMLSchema-instance"
               xmlns:xsd="http://www.w3.org/2001/XMLSchema">
  <Person>
    <FirstName>Franz</FirstName>
    <MiddleName />
    <LastName>Schubert</LastName>
    <BirthDate>1797-01-07</BirthDate>
    <DeathDate>1828-11-19</DeathDate>
  </Person>
  <Person>
    <FirstName>Johannes</FirstName>
    <MiddleName />
    <LastName>Brahms</LastName>
    <BirthDate>1833-05-07</BirthDate>
    <DeathDate>1897-04-03</DeathDate>
  </Person>
  <Person>
    <FirstName>John</FirstName>
    <MiddleName />
    <LastName>Adams</LastName>
    <BirthDate>1947-02-15</BirthDate>
    <DeathDate xsi:nil="true" />
  </Person>
</ArrayOfPerson>
```

Notice that the last *Person* element in this sample file is a living composer, so the *DeathDate* is *null*. This is indicated in XML using the *nil* attribute, as documented in the XML Schema specifications available at *http://www.w3.org/XML/Schema*.

The logic connected with using the *index* variable to indicate the current record is referred to as a *currency manager*. The *System.Windows.Data* namespace contains a class that itself implements a currency manager, and some other important features as well. This class is *CollectionView*, and much of the remainder of this chapter will focus on *CollectionView* and its important derivative, *ListCollectionView*.

As the names suggest, a *CollectionView* or *ListCollectionView* object is actually a *view* of a collection, which might be only part of the total collection or might be the total collection sorted or arranged in different ways. Changing the view does not change the underlying collection.

You can create a *CollectionView* object based on a collection of some sort using the *CollectionView* constructor:

```
CollectionView collview = new CollectionView(coll);
```

The *coll* argument must implement the *IEnumerable* interface. The *ListCollectionView* class has a similar constructor:

```
ListCollectionView lstcollview = new ListCollectionView(coll);
```

However, the *coll* argument to the *ListCollectionView* constructor must implement the *IList* interface, which encompasses *IEnumerable* and *ICollection* (which defines a *Count* property), and also defines an indexer and *Add* and *Remove* methods. The static *CollectionViewSource .GetDefaultView* method returns a *CollectionView* or a *ListCollectionView*, depending on the interfaces implemented by its argument. (*CollectionViewSource* is also handy for defining a *CollectionView* in XAML.) A *CollectionView* object cannot sort or group its collection; a *ListCollectionView* object can.

If you want to base a *CollectionView* object on an *ObservableCollection*, you can explicitly create a *ListCollectionView* because *ObservableCollection* implements the *IList* interface.

The currency manager in *CollectionView* is exposed through several properties and methods. The *Count*, *CurrentItem*, and *CurrentPosition* properties are all read-only. You change the current position using the methods *MoveCurrentTo*, *MoveCurrentToPosition*, *MoveCurrentToFirst*, *MoveCurrentToLast*, *MoveCurrentToPrevious*, and *MoveCurrentToNext*. The class will allow you to move to a position one less than the index of the first item, and one greater than the index of the last item, and the *IsCurrentBeforeFirst* and *IsCurrentAfterLast* properties will tell you if that's the case. *CollectionView* also defines events named *CollectionChanged*, *PropertyChanged*, *CurrentChanging*, and *CurrentChanged*.

In conjunction with using a *CollectionView* class, let's also reconsider the navigation interface. The .NET Framework 2.0 included a new Windows Forms control named *BindingNavigator* that displayed several graphical buttons to navigate through a database, and to add and delete records. I have attempted to duplicate the appearance of the Windows Forms *BindingNavigator* control in the following *NavigationBar* control.

NavigationBar.xaml

```xml
<!-- =================================================
      NavigationBar.xaml (c) 2006 by Charles Petzold
     ================================================= -->
<ToolBar xmlns="http://schemas.microsoft.com/winfx/2006/xaml/presentation"
        xmlns:x="http://schemas.microsoft.com/winfx/2006/xaml"
        x:Class="Petzold.DataEntry.NavigationBar">
    <Button Click="FirstOnClick" ToolTip="Move first">
        <Image Source="DataContainer_MoveFirstHS.png" Stretch="None" />
    </Button>
    <Button Name="btnPrev" Click="PreviousOnClick" ToolTip="Move previous">
        <Image Source="DataContainer_MovePreviousHS.png" Stretch="None" />
    </Button>
    <Separator />
    <TextBox Name="txtboxCurrent" Width="48" ToolTip="Current position"
            GotKeyboardFocus="TextBoxOnGotFocus"
            LostKeyboardFocus="TextBoxOnLostFocus"
            KeyDown="TextBoxOnKeyDown" />
    <TextBlock Text="of " VerticalAlignment="Center" />
    <TextBlock Name="txtblkTotal" Text="0" VerticalAlignment="Center"
            ToolTip="Total number of items"/>
    <Separator />
    <Button Name="btnNext" Click="NextOnClick" ToolTip="Move next">
        <Image Source="DataContainer_MoveNextHS.png" Stretch="None" />
    </Button>
    <Button Click="LastOnClick" ToolTip="Move last">
        <Image Source="DataContainer_MoveLastHS.png" Stretch="None" />
    </Button>
    <Separator />
    <Button Click="AddOnClick" ToolTip="Add new">
        <Image Source="DataContainer_NewRecordHS.png" Stretch="None" />
    </Button>
    <Button Name="btnDel" Click="DeleteOnClick" ToolTip="Delete">
        <Image Source="DeleteHS.png" Stretch="None" />
    </Button>
</ToolBar>
```

The PNG files were obtained from the image collection that comes with Visual Studio.

The code-behind file for the *NavigationBar* class defines two properties. The first property is named *Collection* of type *IList*. (It's anticipated that an *ObservableCollection* will be set to this property.) The *set* accessor uses the static *CollectionViewSource.GetDefaultView* method to create a *CollectionView* object, which will actually be a *ListCollectionView* object. The *set* accessor then sets event handlers to keep the navigation bar controls updated.

The second property is named *ItemType*, and it's the type of the item stored in the collection. The *NavigationBar* requires this type to implement the Add New button. Otherwise, most of the logic is similar to the navigation buttons shown earlier. In addition, the *NavigationBar* allows the user to type in a record number, and the three *TextBox* event handlers at the bottom of the file keep that number within proper bounds.

NavigationBar.cs

```
//----------------------------------------------
// NavigationBar.cs (c) 2006 by Charles Petzold
//----------------------------------------------
using System;
using System.Collections;                   // for IList.
using System.Collections.Specialized;       // for NotifyCollectionChangedEventArgs.
using System.ComponentModel;                // for ICollectionView.
using System.Reflection;                    // for ConstructorInfo.
using System.Windows;
using System.Windows.Controls;
using System.Windows.Data;
using System.Windows.Input;

namespace Petzold.DataEntry
{
    public partial class NavigationBar : ToolBar
    {
        IList coll;
        ICollectionView collview;
        Type typeItem;

        // Public constructor.
        public NavigationBar()
        {
            InitializeComponent();
        }

        // Public properties.
        public IList Collection
        {
            set
            {
                coll = value;

                // Create CollectionView and set event handlers.
                collview = CollectionViewSource.GetDefaultView(coll);
                collview.CurrentChanged += CollectionViewOnCurrentChanged;
                collview.CollectionChanged += CollectionViewOnCollectionChanged;

                // Call an event handler to initialize TextBox and Buttons.
                CollectionViewOnCurrentChanged(null, null);

                // Initialize TextBlock.
                txtblkTotal.Text = coll.Count.ToString();
            }
            get
```

```
        {
            return coll;
        }
    }

    // This is the type of the item in the collection.
    // It's used for the Add command.
    public Type ItemType
    {
        set { typeItem = value; }
        get { return typeItem; }
    }

    // Event handlers for CollectionView.
    void CollectionViewOnCollectionChanged(object sender,
                                NotifyCollectionChangedEventArgs args)
    {
        txtblkTotal.Text = coll.Count.ToString();
    }

    void CollectionViewOnCurrentChanged(object sender, EventArgs args)
    {
        txtboxCurrent.Text = (1 + collview.CurrentPosition).ToString();
        btnPrev.IsEnabled = collview.CurrentPosition > 0;
        btnNext.IsEnabled = collview.CurrentPosition < coll.Count - 1;
        btnDel.IsEnabled = coll.Count > 1;
    }

    // Event handlers for buttons.
    void FirstOnClick(object sender, RoutedEventArgs args)
    {
        collview.MoveCurrentToFirst();
    }
    void PreviousOnClick(object sender, RoutedEventArgs args)
    {
        collview.MoveCurrentToPrevious();
    }
    void NextOnClick(object sender, RoutedEventArgs args)
    {
        collview.MoveCurrentToNext();
    }
    void LastOnClick(object sender, RoutedEventArgs args)
    {
        collview.MoveCurrentToLast();
    }
    void AddOnClick(object sender, RoutedEventArgs args)
    {
        ConstructorInfo info =
            typeItem.GetConstructor(System.Type.EmptyTypes);
        coll.Add(info.Invoke(null));
        collview.MoveCurrentToLast();
    }
```

```
        void DeleteOnClick(object sender, RoutedEventArgs args)
        {
            coll.RemoveAt(collview.CurrentPosition);
        }


        // Event handlers for txtboxCurrent TextBox.
        string strOriginal;

        void TextBoxOnGotFocus(object sender,
                              KeyboardFocusChangedEventArgs args)
        {
            strOriginal = txtboxCurrent.Text;
        }
        void TextBoxOnLostFocus(object sender,
                               KeyboardFocusChangedEventArgs args)
        {
            int current;

            if (Int32.TryParse(txtboxCurrent.Text, out current))
                if (current > 0 && current <= coll.Count)
                    collview.MoveCurrentToPosition(current - 1);
            else
                txtboxCurrent.Text = strOriginal;
        }
        void TextBoxOnKeyDown(object sender, KeyEventArgs args)
        {
            if (args.Key == Key.Escape)
            {
                txtboxCurrent.Text = strOriginal;
                args.Handled = true;
            }
            else if (args.Key == Key.Enter)
            {
                args.Handled = true;
            }
            else
                return;

            MoveFocus(new TraversalRequest(FocusNavigationDirection.Right));
        }
    }
}
```

The two files that comprise the *NavigationBar* class and the required image files are part of a library project named Petzold.DataEntry that creates a dynamic-link library named Petzold.DataEntry.dll. That project and a project named DataEntryWithNavigation are the two projects in the DataEntryWithNavigation solution.

The DataEntryWithNavigation project has links to the Person.cs file, the People.cs file, the two files that make up the *PersonPanel* class, and the two files that make up the *DatePicker* class. The project also contains a XAML file and a C# file for the program's window.

The XAML file defines a *Window* with a *DockPanel*. The familiar menu is docked at the top, a *NavigationBar* is docked at the bottom, and a *PersonPanel* fills the interior.

DataEntryWithNavigation.xaml

```
<!-- ========================================================
        DataEntryWithNavigation.xaml (c) 2006 by Charles Petzold
     ======================================================== -->
<Window xmlns="http://schemas.microsoft.com/winfx/2006/xaml/presentation"
        xmlns:x="http://schemas.microsoft.com/winfx/2006/xaml"
        xmlns:pnl="clr-namespace:Petzold.SingleRecordDataEntry"
        xmlns:nav="clr-namespace:Petzold.DataEntry;assembly=Petzold.DataEntry"
        x:Class="Petzold.DataEntryWithNavigation.DataEntryWithNavigation"
        Title="Data Entry with Navigation"
        SizeToContent="WidthAndHeight"
        ResizeMode="CanMinimize">
    <DockPanel Name="dock">
        <Menu DockPanel.Dock="Top">
            <MenuItem Header="_File">
                <MenuItem Header="_New" Command="New" />
                <MenuItem Header="_Open..." Command="Open" />
                <MenuItem Header="_Save..." Command="Save" />
            </MenuItem>
        </Menu>

        <!-- NavigationBar for navigating. -->
        <nav:NavigationBar Name="navbar" DockPanel.Dock="Bottom" />

        <!-- PersonPanel for displaying and entering data. -->
        <pnl:PersonPanel x:Name="pnlPerson" />
    </DockPanel>

    <Window.CommandBindings>
        <CommandBinding Command="New" Executed="NewOnExecuted" />
        <CommandBinding Command="Open" Executed="OpenOnExecuted" />
        <CommandBinding Command="Save" Executed="SaveOnExecuted" />
    </Window.CommandBindings>
</Window>
```

The code-behind file becomes fairly trivial. Like the original SingleRecordDataEntry project, it need only implement event handlers for the three items on its menu. For both New and Open, the event handler calls the *InitializeNewPeopleObject* method to link the *People* object with the *PersonPanel* and the *NavigationBar*.

DataEntryWithNavigation.cs

```
//-----------------------------------------------------------
// DataEntryWithNavigation.cs (c) 2006 by Charles Petzold
//-----------------------------------------------------------
using Petzold.DataEntry;
using Petzold.MultiRecordDataEntry;
using Petzold.SingleRecordDataEntry;
using System;
```

```csharp
using System.Collections.Specialized;
using System.Windows;
using System.Windows.Controls;
using System.Windows.Input;
using System.Windows.Media;

namespace Petzold.DataEntryWithNavigation
{
    public partial class DataEntryWithNavigation
    {
        People people;

        [STAThread]
        public static void Main()
        {
            Application app = new Application();
            app.Run(new DataEntryWithNavigation());
        }
        public DataEntryWithNavigation()
        {
            InitializeComponent();

            // Simulate File New command.
            ApplicationCommands.New.Execute(null, this);

            // Set focus to first TextBox in panel.
            pnlPerson.Children[1].Focus();
        }

        // Event handlers for menu items.
        void NewOnExecuted(object sender, ExecutedRoutedEventArgs args)
        {
            people = new People();
            people.Add(new Person());
            InitializeNewPeopleObject();
        }
        void OpenOnExecuted(object sender, ExecutedRoutedEventArgs args)
        {
            people = People.Load(this);
            InitializeNewPeopleObject();
        }
        void SaveOnExecuted(object sender, ExecutedRoutedEventArgs args)
        {
            people.Save(this);
        }
        void InitializeNewPeopleObject()
        {
            navbar.Collection = people;
            navbar.ItemType = typeof(Person);
            pnlPerson.DataContext = people;
        }
    }
}
```

The *InitializeNewPeopleObject* method first assigns the *Collection* property of the *NavigationBar* to the newly created *People* object. This *Collection* property in *NavigationBar* creates a new object of type *ListCollectionView* and attaches event handlers to maintain the navigation bar. The second statement of *InitializeNewPeopleObject* assigns the *ItemType* property of *NavigationBar* so that *NavigationBar* can create new objects and add them to the collection when the user clicks the Add New button.

The last statement of *InitializeNewPeopleObject* assigns the *DataContext* of *PersonPanel* to the *People* object. This may seem strange. In previous programs, the *DataContext* property of *PersonPanel* has been assigned to a *Person* object so that the panel can display all the properties defined by the *Person* class. Assigning *DataContext* to a *People* object doesn't seem quite right, but it works. The *People* collection has been made the basis of a *ListCollectionView*, which is maintaining a current record, and that current record is what the *PersonPanel* actually displays.

Although the *NavigationBar* might be a good solution for some data-entry programs, it isn't quite adequate when you need a good view of the overall array of data in the database. You might wish you had a *ListBox* available to scroll through the database and select items to view or edit.

This approach is actually much easier than it sounds, and is demonstrated in the next project, which is called DataEntryWithListBox. The project requires the files contributing to the *Person*, *People*, *PersonPanel*, and *DatePicker* classes. The window is defined in the following XAML file and contains the familiar menu, a *ListBox*, and a *PersonPanel*.

DataEntryWithListBox.xaml

```xml
<!-- =====================================================
        DataEntryWithListBox.xaml (c) 2006 by Charles Petzold
     ===================================================== -->
<Window xmlns="http://schemas.microsoft.com/winfx/2006/xaml/presentation"
        xmlns:x="http://schemas.microsoft.com/winfx/2006/xaml"
        xmlns:pnl="clr-namespace:Petzold.SingleRecordDataEntry"
        x:Class="Petzold.DataEntryWithListBox.DataEntryWithListBox"
        Title="Data Entry With ListBox"
        SizeToContent="WidthAndHeight"
        ResizeMode="CanMinimize">
    <DockPanel Name="dock">
        <Menu DockPanel.Dock="Top">
            <MenuItem Header="_File">
                <MenuItem Header="_New" Command="New" />
                <MenuItem Header="_Open..." Command="Open" />
                <MenuItem Header="_Save..." Command="Save" />
            </MenuItem>
        </Menu>

        <Grid>
            <Grid.RowDefinitions>
                <RowDefinition Height="Auto" />
                <RowDefinition Height="Auto" />
            </Grid.RowDefinitions>
```

```xml
        <Grid.ColumnDefinitions>
            <ColumnDefinition Width="Auto" />
            <ColumnDefinition Width="Auto" />
        </Grid.ColumnDefinitions>

        <!-- ListBox to display and select items. -->
        <ListBox Name="lstbox" Grid.Column="0"
                Width="300" Height="300" Margin="24">
            <ListBox.ItemTemplate>
                <DataTemplate>
                    <StackPanel Orientation="Horizontal">
                        <TextBlock Text="{Binding Path=FirstName}" />
                        <TextBlock Text=" " />
                        <TextBlock Text="{Binding Path=MiddleName}" />
                        <TextBlock Text=" " Name="txtblkSpace"/>
                        <TextBlock Text="{Binding Path=LastName}" />
                        <TextBlock Text=" (" />
                        <TextBlock Text="{Binding Path=BirthDate.Year}" />
                        <TextBlock Text="-" />
                        <TextBlock Text="{Binding Path=DeathDate.Year}"
                                Name="txtblkDeath" />
                        <TextBlock Text=")" />
                    </StackPanel>
                    <DataTemplate.Triggers>
                        <DataTrigger Binding="{Binding Path=DeathDate}"
                                    Value="{x:Null}">
                            <Setter TargetName="txtblkDeath"
                                    Property="Text" Value="present" />
                        </DataTrigger>
                        <DataTrigger Binding="{Binding Path=MiddleName}"
                                    Value="">
                            <Setter TargetName="txtblkSpace"
                                    Property="Text" Value="" />
                        </DataTrigger>
                    </DataTemplate.Triggers>
                </DataTemplate>
            </ListBox.ItemTemplate>
        </ListBox>

        <!-- PersonPanel to enter and edit item. -->
        <pnl:PersonPanel x:Name="pnlPerson" Grid.Column="1" />

        <!-- Buttons to add and delete items. -->
        <StackPanel Orientation="Horizontal" Grid.Row="1" Grid.Column="1">
            <Button Margin="12" Click="AddOnClick">
                Add new item
            </Button>
            <Button Margin="12" Click="DeleteOnClick">
                Delete item
            </Button>
        </StackPanel>
    </Grid>
</DockPanel>
```

```xml
    <Window.CommandBindings>
        <CommandBinding Command="New" Executed="NewOnExecuted" />
        <CommandBinding Command="Open" Executed="OpenOnExecuted" />
        <CommandBinding Command="Save" Executed="SaveOnExecuted" />
    </Window.CommandBindings>
</Window>
```

The *ListBox* contains a definition of its *ItemTemplate* property under the assumption that the *ListBox* will be displaying items of type *Person*. A *StackPanel* with a horizontal orientation combines ten *TextBlock* elements that result in the display of items that look like this:

Franz Schubert (1797–1828)

The *StackPanel* is followed by a *DataTemplate.Triggers* section with two *DataTrigger* elements to fix two problems. First, if the *DeathDate* property is *null*, instead of displaying the *Year* property of the *DeathDate* I want to display the word "present" so that the entry looks like this:

John Adams (1947–present)

Without that *DataTrigger*, nothing would be displayed after the dash, which is also an acceptable way of displaying the information. The second *DataTrigger* fixes a problem that results if the composer doesn't have a middle name. Normally one space separates the first name from the middle name and another space separates the middle name from the last name. If there's no middle name, two blanks separate the first name from the last name. The second *DataTrigger* eliminates one of those blanks.

The window layout concludes with a *PersonPanel* and two buttons labeled "Add new item" and "Delete item." The navigation buttons aren't required because the *ListBox* allows scrolling through the items and selecting an item for viewing or editing.

Here's the code-behind file.

DataEntryWithListBox.cs

```csharp
//----------------------------------------------------
// DataEntryWithListBox.cs (c) 2006 by Charles Petzold
//----------------------------------------------------
using Petzold.MultiRecordDataEntry;
using Petzold.SingleRecordDataEntry;
using System;
using System.Collections.Specialized;
using System.ComponentModel;
using System.Windows;
using System.Windows.Controls;
using System.Windows.Data;
using System.Windows.Input;
using System.Windows.Media;
```

```
namespace Petzold.DataEntryWithListBox
{
    public partial class DataEntryWithListBox
    {
        ListCollectionView collview;
        People people;

        [STAThread]
        public static void Main()
        {
            Application app = new Application();
            app.Run(new DataEntryWithListBox());
        }
        public DataEntryWithListBox()
        {
            InitializeComponent();

            // Simulate File New command.
            ApplicationCommands.New.Execute(null, this);

            // Set focus to first TextBox in panel.
            pnlPerson.Children[1].Focus();
        }

        void NewOnExecuted(object sender, ExecutedRoutedEventArgs args)
        {
            people = new People();
            people.Add(new Person());
            InitializeNewPeopleObject();
        }
        void OpenOnExecuted(object sender, ExecutedRoutedEventArgs args)
        {
            people = People.Load(this);

            if (people != null)
                InitializeNewPeopleObject();
        }
        void SaveOnExecuted(object sender, ExecutedRoutedEventArgs args)
        {
            people.Save(this);
        }
        void InitializeNewPeopleObject()
        {
            // Create a ListCollectionView object based on the People object.
            collview = new ListCollectionView(people);

            // Define a property to sort the view.
            collview.SortDescriptions.Add(
                new SortDescription("LastName", ListSortDirection.Ascending));

            // Link the ListBox and PersonPanel through the ListCollectionView.
            lstbox.ItemsSource = collview;
            pnlPerson.DataContext = collview;
```

```
            // Set the selected index of the ListBox.
            if (lstbox.Items.Count > 0)
                lstbox.SelectedIndex = 0;
        }

        void AddOnClick(object sender, RoutedEventArgs args)
        {
            Person person = new Person();
            people.Add(person);
            lstbox.SelectedItem = person;
            pnlPerson.Children[1].Focus();
            collview.Refresh();
        }
        void DeleteOnClick(object sender, RoutedEventArgs args)
        {
            if (lstbox.SelectedItem != null)
            {
                people.Remove(lstbox.SelectedItem as Person);

                if (lstbox.Items.Count > 0)
                    lstbox.SelectedIndex = 0;
                else
                    AddOnClick(sender, args);
            }
        }
    }
}
```

Both the New and Open commands on the File menu result in a call to *InitializeNewPeople-Object*. This method creates a *ListCollectionView* based on the *People* object.

As I emphasized earlier, a *CollectionView* is a *view* of a collection. The *CollectionView* defines a way of arranging the items of a collection for viewing, but this view doesn't change anything in the underlying collection. The *CollectionView* supports three general ways in which the view can be altered:

- Sorting
- Filtering
- Grouping

You can sort the items based on one or more properties. Filtering is the restriction of the view to only those items that meet certain criteria. With grouping you arrange the items in groups, again based on certain criteria.

CollectionView supports three properties named *CanSort*, *CanFilter*, and *CanGroup*. The *CanSort* and *CanGroup* properties are *false* for a *CollectionView* object but *true* for a *ListCollectionView*.

To sort a *ListCollectionView* object, you create objects of type *SortDescription* and add those objects to the *SortDescriptions* property. Here's how the DataEntryWithListBox program sorts the *ListCollectionView* by the *LastName* property:

```
collview.SortDescriptions.Add(
            new SortDescription("LastName", ListSortDirection.Ascending));
```

The *SortDescriptions* collection can have multiple *SortDescription* objects. The second *Sort-Description* is used if two properties encountered by the first *SortDescription* are equal. The *SortDescriptions* property defined by *CollectionView* is of type *SortDescriptionCollection*, and it has methods named *SetItem*, *InsertItem*, *RemoveItem*, and *ClearItems* for manipulating the collection.

After defining a *SortDescription*, the *InitializeNewPeopleObject* method sets the *ItemsSource* property of the *ListBox* to this *ListCollectionView*:

```
lstbox.ItemsSource = collview;
```

The *ListBox* then displays all the items in the collection sorted by last name. That much should be obvious. But you also get a bonus. You are essentially linking the *ListBox* with the *CollectionView* so that the *CurrentItem* property of the *CollectionView* is set from the *Selected-Item* property of the *ListBox*. The *ListBox* becomes a means of navigating through the collection. This means that you set the *DataContext* property of the *PersonPanel* to this same *CollectionView*:

```
pnlPerson.DataContext = collview;
```

And now the *PersonPanel* displays the item selected in the *ListBox*, and you can use the *Person-Panel* to edit the item. The *PropertyChanged* events defined by *Person*, *ObservableCollection*, and *CollectionView* help the *ListView* update itself with every change.

The remainder of the program shouldn't be difficult to understand. The event handler for the Add button adds a new *Person* object to the *People* class. That new *Person* object automatically shows up in the *ListBox* at the bottom of the list. The event handler continues by selecting that new object in the *ListBox*, which causes the properties of the item to be displayed in the *PersonPanel*.

As you enter information in *PersonPanel*—and particularly as you enter the person's last name— the item will *not* automatically get a new position in the *ListBox* as a result of the sort descrip- tion. To re-sort the contents of the *CollectionView* based on new or altered items, a program must call *Refresh*. The particular place where you call *Refresh* will depend on the architecture of your program. Some data-entry programs allow a new item to be filled in and the Add button then adds that completed item to the collection. If you have such an Add button, you can add the new item to the collection and call *Refresh* at that time.

In the DataEntryWithListBox program, there is no button to signal that an item has been completed. Instead, the program calls *Refresh* at the end of the *AddOnClick* method to re-sort the collection with any previously added items. This also causes the newly created *Person* item to be moved to the top of the list because the default string of "<last name>" precedes any alphabetic characters.

Of course, you can add an interface to the program to sort by different fields. This is one way of facilitating searches for particular items. Another approach is called *filtering*. You restrict the *CollectionView* to only those items that satisfy particular criteria.

To filter a *CollectionView*, you must have a method defined in accordance with the *Predicate* delegate:

```
bool MyFilter(object obj)
{
    ...
}
```

The argument to the method is an object in the collection. The method returns *true* if the item is to be included in the view, and *false* if not. You set the *Filter* property of the *CollectionView* to this method:

```
collview.Filter = MyFilter;
```

If you look at the definition of the *Predicate* delegate, you'll discover that it's actually a generic delegate defined like this:

```
public delegate bool Predicate<T> (T obj)
```

This fact might lead you to believe that you could define the filter method with an argument of any type. However, the definition of the *Filter* property in *CollectionView* calls for a method of type *Predicate<Object>*, so the filter method must have an argument of type *object*.

The CollectionViewWithFilter program has links to the Person.cs and People.cs files and defines a window with XAML and C# files. The window includes three radio buttons that let you select whether you want to view living composers, dead composers, or all composers. Here's the XAML layout of the radio buttons and *ListBox*.

CollectionViewWithFilter.xaml
```
<!-- ====================================================
        CollectionViewWithFilter.xaml (c) 2006 by Charles Petzold
     ==================================================== -->
<Window xmlns="http://schemas.microsoft.com/winfx/2006/xaml/presentation"
        xmlns:x="http://schemas.microsoft.com/winfx/2006/xaml"
        x:Class="Petzold.CollectionViewWithFilter.CollectionViewWithFilter"
        Title="CollectionView with Filter"
        SizeToContent="WidthAndHeight"
        ResizeMode="CanMinimize">
```

```
<DockPanel Name="dock">
    <Menu DockPanel.Dock="Top">
        <MenuItem Header="_File">
            <MenuItem Header="_Open..." Command="Open" />
        </MenuItem>
    </Menu>

    <Grid>
        <Grid.RowDefinitions>
            <RowDefinition Height="Auto" />
            <RowDefinition Height="Auto" />
        </Grid.RowDefinitions>

        <!-- GroupBox with RadioButtons for filtering. -->
        <GroupBox Grid.Row="0" Margin="24" HorizontalAlignment="Center"
                Header="Criteria">
            <StackPanel>
                <RadioButton Name="radioLiving" Content="Living"
                        Checked="RadioOnChecked" Margin="6" />
                <RadioButton Name="radioDead" Content="Dead"
                        Checked="RadioOnChecked" Margin="6" />
                <RadioButton Name="radioAll" Content="All"
                        Checked="RadioOnChecked" Margin="6" />
            </StackPanel>
        </GroupBox>

        <!-- ListBox to display items. -->
        <ListBox Name="lstbox" Grid.Row="1" HorizontalAlignment="Center"
                Width="300" Height="300" Margin="24">
            <ListBox.ItemTemplate>
                <DataTemplate>
                    <StackPanel Orientation="Horizontal">
                        <TextBlock Text="{Binding Path=FirstName}" />
                        <TextBlock Text=" " />
                        <TextBlock Text="{Binding Path=MiddleName}" />
                        <TextBlock Text=" " Name="txtblkSpace"/>
                        <TextBlock Text="{Binding Path=LastName}" />
                        <TextBlock Text=" (" />
                        <TextBlock Text="{Binding Path=BirthDate.Year}" />
                        <TextBlock Text="-" />
                        <TextBlock Text="{Binding Path=DeathDate.Year}"
                                Name="txtblkDeath" />
                        <TextBlock Text=")" />
                    </StackPanel>
                    <DataTemplate.Triggers>
                        <DataTrigger Binding="{Binding Path=DeathDate}"
                                Value="{x:Null}">
                            <Setter TargetName="txtblkDeath"
                                    Property="Text" Value="present" />
                        </DataTrigger>
                        <DataTrigger Binding="{Binding Path=MiddleName}"
                                Value="">
                            <Setter TargetName="txtblkSpace"
                                    Property="Text" Value="" />
                        </DataTrigger>
```

```
                </DataTemplate.Triggers>
            </DataTemplate>
        </ListBox.ItemTemplate>
    </ListBox>
  </Grid>
</DockPanel>

<Window.CommandBindings>
    <CommandBinding Command="Open" Executed="OpenOnExecuted" />
</Window.CommandBindings>
</Window>
```

To keep this program relatively simple and focused, I didn't include a *PersonPanel* or buttons to add or delete items from the collection. The program simply lets you view an existing file based on the filter settings. You shouldn't assume from this program that once filtering enters the picture, you've lost the ability to enter new data. That's not the case.

The Chapter 26 directory of the companion content for this book includes a file named Composers.PeopleXml with which you can experiment in this program and the next two programs of this chapter.

The three *RadioButton* controls share the same event handler, which is located in the code-behind file. Based on the *Name* property of the three buttons, the handler sets the *Filter* property of the *CollectionView* to the *PersonIsLiving* method, the *PersonIsDead* method, or to *null*, which allows the display of all items.

CollectionViewWithFilter.cs

```
//-------------------------------------------------------
// CollectionViewWithFilter.cs (c) 2006 by Charles Petzold
//-------------------------------------------------------
using Petzold.SingleRecordDataEntry;
using Petzold.MultiRecordDataEntry;
using System;
using System.ComponentModel;
using System.Windows;
using System.Windows.Controls;
using System.Windows.Data;
using System.Windows.Input;
using System.Windows.Media;

namespace Petzold.CollectionViewWithFilter
{
    public partial class CollectionViewWithFilter : Window
    {
        ListCollectionView collview;

        [STAThread]
        public static void Main()
        {
            Application app = new Application();
```

```
        app.Run(new CollectionViewWithFilter());
}
public CollectionViewWithFilter()
{
    InitializeComponent();
}

void OpenOnExecuted(object sender, ExecutedRoutedEventArgs args)
{
    People people = People.Load(this);

    if (people != null)
    {
        collview = new ListCollectionView(people);

        collview.SortDescriptions.Add(
            new SortDescription("LastName",
                                 ListSortDirection.Ascending));

        lstbox.ItemsSource = collview;

        if (lstbox.Items.Count > 0)
            lstbox.SelectedIndex = 0;

        radioAll.IsChecked = true;
    }
}

// Event handlers for RadioButtons.
void RadioOnChecked(object sender, RoutedEventArgs args)
{
    if (collview == null)
        return;

    RadioButton radio = args.Source as RadioButton;

    switch (radio.Name)
    {
        case "radioLiving":
            collview.Filter = PersonIsLiving;
            break;

        case "radioDead":
            collview.Filter = PersonIsDead;
            break;

        case "radioAll":
            collview.Filter = null;
            break;
    }
}
bool PersonIsLiving(object obj)
{
    return (obj as Person).DeathDate == null;
}
```

```
        bool PersonIsDead(object obj)
        {
            return (obj as Person).DeathDate != null;
        }
    }
}
```

At any time, there can be only one method assigned to the *Filter* property of the *Collection-View*. If you want to filter based on multiple criteria, the best approach is probably *not* to have a whole bunch of different filter methods, but to have just *one* filter method that you assign just once to the *Filter* property. This single method examines the object against all the criteria and returns a verdict. Whenever there's a change to the criteria, the program can call *Refresh* on the *CollectionView* to force all the items to pass through the filter method once again.

One common use of filtering is a *TextBox* that lets the user type a letter or multiple letters. The *ListBox* then displays all the items in which the last name begins with those letters. This feature is easier to implement than it first seems. Here's a XAML file that resembles CollectionViewWithFilter.xaml except it has a *Label* and *TextBox* instead of a *GroupBox* and radio buttons. The *TextBox* has a *Name* property of *txtboxFilter* and a *TextChanged* event handler.

FilterWithText.xaml

```
<!-- =================================================
     FilterWithText.xaml (c) 2006 by Charles Petzold
     ================================================= -->
<Window xmlns="http://schemas.microsoft.com/winfx/2006/xaml/presentation"
        xmlns:x="http://schemas.microsoft.com/winfx/2006/xaml"
        x:Class="Petzold.FilterWithText.FilterWithText"
        Title="Filter with Text"
        SizeToContent="WidthAndHeight"
        ResizeMode="CanMinimize">
    <DockPanel Name="dock">
        <Menu DockPanel.Dock="Top">
            <MenuItem Header="_File">
                <MenuItem Header="_Open..." Command="Open" />
            </MenuItem>
        </Menu>

        <Grid>
            <Grid.RowDefinitions>
                <RowDefinition Height="Auto" />
                <RowDefinition Height="Auto" />
            </Grid.RowDefinitions>

            <!-- TextBox with Label. -->
            <StackPanel Grid.Row="0" Margin="24" Orientation="Horizontal"
                        HorizontalAlignment="Center">
                <Label Content="Search: " />
```

```
                        <TextBox Name="txtboxFilter" MinWidth="1in"
                                 TextChanged="TextBoxOnTextChanged" />
            </StackPanel>

            <!-- ListBox for displaying items. -->
            <ListBox Name="lstbox" Grid.Row="1" HorizontalAlignment="Center"
                     Width="300" Height="300" Margin="24">
                <ListBox.ItemTemplate>
                    <DataTemplate>
                        <StackPanel Orientation="Horizontal">
                            <TextBlock Text="{Binding Path=FirstName}" />
                            <TextBlock Text=" " />
                            <TextBlock Text="{Binding Path=MiddleName}" />
                            <TextBlock Text=" " Name="txtblkSpace"/>
                            <TextBlock Text="{Binding Path=LastName}" />
                            <TextBlock Text=" (" />
                            <TextBlock Text="{Binding Path=BirthDate.Year}" />
                            <TextBlock Text="-" />
                            <TextBlock Text="{Binding Path=DeathDate.Year}"
                                       Name="txtblkDeath" />
                            <TextBlock Text=")" />
                        </StackPanel>
                        <DataTemplate.Triggers>
                            <DataTrigger Binding="{Binding Path=DeathDate}"
                                         Value="{x:Null}">
                                <Setter TargetName="txtblkDeath"
                                        Property="Text" Value="present" />
                            </DataTrigger>
                            <DataTrigger Binding="{Binding Path=MiddleName}"
                                         Value="">
                                <Setter TargetName="txtblkSpace"
                                        Property="Text" Value="" />
                            </DataTrigger>
                        </DataTemplate.Triggers>
                    </DataTemplate>
                </ListBox.ItemTemplate>
            </ListBox>
        </Grid>
    </DockPanel>

    <Window.CommandBindings>
        <CommandBinding Command="Open" Executed="OpenOnExecuted" />
    </Window.CommandBindings>
</Window>
```

The code-behind file for the *FilterWithText* class prepares the window for a new *CollectionView* object by setting the *Text* property in the *TextBox* to an empty string, and assigning the *LastNameFilter* method to the *Filter* property:

```
txtboxFilter.Text = "";
collview.Filter = LastNameFilter;
```

The *LastNameFilter* method and the *TextChanged* event handler are both located toward the bottom of the code-behind file.

FilterWithText.cs

```
//-----------------------------------------------
// FilterWithText.cs (c) 2006 by Charles Petzold
//-----------------------------------------------
using Petzold.SingleRecordDataEntry;
using Petzold.MultiRecordDataEntry;
using System;
using System.ComponentModel;
using System.Windows;
using System.Windows.Controls;
using System.Windows.Data;
using System.Windows.Input;
using System.Windows.Media;

namespace Petzold.FilterWithText
{
    public partial class FilterWithText : Window
    {
        ListCollectionView collview;

        [STAThread]
        public static void Main()
        {
            Application app = new Application();
            app.Run(new FilterWithText());
        }
        public FilterWithText()
        {
            InitializeComponent();
        }

        void OpenOnExecuted(object sender, ExecutedRoutedEventArgs args)
        {
            People people = People.Load(this);

            if (people != null)
            {
                collview = new ListCollectionView(people);

                collview.SortDescriptions.Add(
                    new SortDescription("BirthDate",
                                ListSortDirection.Ascending));

                txtboxFilter.Text = "";
                collview.Filter = LastNameFilter;

                lstbox.ItemsSource = collview;

                if (lstbox.Items.Count > 0)
                    lstbox.SelectedIndex = 0;
            }
        }
        bool LastNameFilter(object obj)
        {
```

```
            return (obj as Person).LastName.StartsWith(txtboxFilter.Text,
                                    StringComparison.CurrentCultureIgnoreCase);
        }
        void TextBoxOnTextChanged(object sender, TextChangedEventArgs args)
        {
            if (collview == null)
                return;

            collview.Refresh();
        }
    }
}
```

The *LastNameFilter* method simply returns *true* if the *LastName* property of the *Person* object starts with the text in the *TextBox*, with case ignored. Any change in the *TextBox* causes a call to the *Refresh* method to re-evaluate all the items in the collection.

Besides sorting and filtering, a *CollectionView* can also group the items. The final program in this chapter will demonstrate this technique.

To group items, you supply a method that assigns a group name (actually an object) to each item in the collection. Within the *ListBox*, the items are grouped by this name, but you can also supply custom headers and panels to differentiate the groups.

CollectionView has a property named *GroupDescriptions* that is itself an *ObservableCollection*, and more specifically, of type *ObservableCollection<GroupDescription>*. *GroupDescription* is an abstract class with one derivative named *PropertyGroupDescription*, which you can use if you want to group items based on a property of the item. If this is not the case, you must define your own class that derives from *GroupDescription*. You are required to override the method named *GroupNameFromItem*.

I decided I wanted the composers in the sample file to be grouped by the musical period they are associated with. Generally and approximately, these periods are Baroque (1600-1750), Classical (1750-1820), Romantic (1820-1900), and Twentieth Century (after 1900), but I added other periods I called Pre-Baroque and Post-War. Because my file doesn't store information about when the composers were active, I based my criteria on their birth years.

Here's a class named *PeriodGroupDescription* that derives from *GroupDescription* and overrides the *GroupNameFromItem* method to return a text string for each item.

PeriodGroupDescription.cs
```
//----------------------------------------------------------
// PeriodGroupDescription.cs (c) 2006 by Charles Petzold
//----------------------------------------------------------
using Petzold.SingleRecordDataEntry;
using System;
using System.ComponentModel;
using System.Globalization;
```

```
namespace Petzold.ListBoxWithGroups
{
    public class PeriodGroupDescription : GroupDescription
    {
        public override object GroupNameFromItem(object item, int level,
                                                 CultureInfo culture)
        {
            Person person = item as Person;

            if (person.BirthDate == null)
                return "Unknown";

            int year = ((DateTime)person.BirthDate).Year;

            if (year < 1575)
                return "Pre-Baroque";

            if (year < 1725)
                return "Baroque";

            if (year < 1795)
                return "Classical";

            if (year < 1870)
                return "Romantic";

            if (year < 1910)
                return "20th Century";

            return "Post-War";
        }
    }
}
```

Let me show you the C# part of the window class first.

ListBoxWithGroups.cs

```
//-------------------------------------------------
// ListBoxWithGroups.cs (c) 2006 by Charles Petzold
//-------------------------------------------------
using Petzold.MultiRecordDataEntry;
using System;
using System.ComponentModel;
using System.Windows;
using System.Windows.Controls;
using System.Windows.Data;
using System.Windows.Input;
using System.Windows.Media;

namespace Petzold.ListBoxWithGroups
{
```

```
    public partial class ListBoxWithGroups : Window
    {
        ListCollectionView collview;

        [STAThread]
        public static void Main()
        {
            Application app = new Application();
            app.Run(new ListBoxWithGroups());
        }
        public ListBoxWithGroups()
        {
            InitializeComponent();
        }

        void OpenOnExecuted(object sender, ExecutedRoutedEventArgs args)
        {
            People people = People.Load(this);

            if (people != null)
            {
                collview = new ListCollectionView(people);

                collview.SortDescriptions.Add(
                    new SortDescription("BirthDate",
                                    ListSortDirection.Ascending));

                // Add PeriodGroupsDescription to GroupsDescriptions collection.
                collview.GroupDescriptions.Add(new PeriodGroupDescription());

                lstbox.ItemsSource = collview;

                if (lstbox.Items.Count > 0)
                    lstbox.SelectedIndex = 0;
            }
        }
    }
}
```

The *OpenOnExecuted* handler loads an existing *People* file, as usual, and creates a *ListCollectionView* object from it. The view is sorted by birth date, and a new object of type *PeriodGroupDescription* is added to the *GroupDescriptions* collections to group the items by the criteria in that class.

The XAML file for the program's window has the same *ListBox* you're accustomed to seeing, but also includes a property element for *ListBox.GroupStyle*.

ListBoxWithGroups.xaml
```
<!-- =================================================
     ListBoxWithGroups.xaml (c) 2006 by Charles Petzold
     ================================================= -->
<Window xmlns="http://schemas.microsoft.com/winfx/2006/xaml/presentation"
        xmlns:x="http://schemas.microsoft.com/winfx/2006/xaml"
        x:Class="Petzold.ListBoxWithGroups.ListBoxWithGroups"
```

```
            Title="ListBox with Groups"
        SizeToContent="WidthAndHeight"
        ResizeMode="CanMinimize">
<DockPanel Name="dock">
    <Menu DockPanel.Dock="Top">
        <MenuItem Header="_File">
            <MenuItem Header="_Open..." Command="Open" />
        </MenuItem>
    </Menu>

    <!-- ListBox to display items. -->
    <ListBox Name="lstbox" Grid.Row="1"
            HorizontalAlignment="Center" VerticalAlignment="Center"
            Width="300" Height="300" Margin="24">
        <ListBox.ItemTemplate>
            <DataTemplate>
                <StackPanel Orientation="Horizontal">
                    <TextBlock Text="{Binding Path=FirstName}" />
                    <TextBlock Text=" " />
                    <TextBlock Text="{Binding Path=MiddleName}" />
                    <TextBlock Text=" " Name="txtblkSpace"/>
                    <TextBlock Text="{Binding Path=LastName}" />
                    <TextBlock Text=" (" />
                    <TextBlock Text="{Binding Path=BirthDate.Year}" />
                    <TextBlock Text="-" />
                    <TextBlock Text="{Binding Path=DeathDate.Year}"
                                Name="txtblkDeath" />
                    <TextBlock Text=")" />
                </StackPanel>
                <DataTemplate.Triggers>
                    <DataTrigger Binding="{Binding Path=DeathDate.Year}"
                                Value="{x:Null}">
                        <Setter TargetName="txtblkDeath"
                                Property="Text" Value="present" />
                    </DataTrigger>
                    <DataTrigger Binding="{Binding Path=MiddleName}"
                                Value="">
                        <Setter TargetName="txtblkSpace"
                                Property="Text" Value="" />
                    </DataTrigger>
                </DataTemplate.Triggers>
            </DataTemplate>
        </ListBox.ItemTemplate>

        <!-- GroupStyle defines header for each group. -->
        <ListBox.GroupStyle>
            <GroupStyle>
                <GroupStyle.HeaderTemplate>
                    <DataTemplate>
                        <TextBlock Text="{Binding Path=Name}"
                                Foreground="White" Background="DarkGray"
                                FontWeight="Bold" FontSize="12pt"
                                Margin="6" />
                    </DataTemplate>
                </GroupStyle.HeaderTemplate>
```

```
                </GroupStyle>
            </ListBox.GroupStyle>
        </ListBox>
    </DockPanel>

    <Window.CommandBindings>
        <CommandBinding Command="Open" Executed="OpenOnExecuted" />
    </Window.CommandBindings>
</Window>
```

The *GroupStyle* property of *ListBox* is a collection of *GroupStyle* objects. If you have more than one *GroupStyle* object in the collection, you must also set the *GroupStyleSelector* property of *ListBox* to a method defined in accordance with the *GroupStyleSelector* delegate. This method gets a group name as an argument and returns a *GroupStyle* for that name.

If you have only one *GroupStyle*, it applies to all the groups displayed by the *ListBox*. Each group can have its own *Style* (which you set with the *ContainerStyle* property), its own type of panel for displaying the items in the group (which you set with the *Panel* property), and its own *HeaderTemplate*. This latter property is the only one I took advantage of. I used it to define a *TextBlock* that displays white text on a dark gray background. The *Text* itself is a binding to a property named *Name*, which is actually the group name. Thus, each group is preceded by a non-selectable header that identifies the period with which those composers are associated.

The grouping feature implemented by *ItemsControl* is very powerful and adds a whole other dimension to the data displayed in a *ListBox*. Not only can each item be displayed in a unique manner, but any consolidation of items can also have a unique identity within the control. It's one of those features that may not have an immediate application in your work. But on that day when a problem comes up that calls for *ListBox* groupings, you'll suddenly grow quite fond of this spectacular implementation.

Chapter 27
Graphical Shapes

The world of two-dimensional computer graphics is roughly divided between raster graphics (bitmaps) and vector graphics (lines, curves, and filled areas), but the key word in this statement is *roughly*. Considerable overlap exists between these two poles. When an ellipse is filled with a brush based on a bitmap, is that raster graphics or vector graphics? It's a little bit of both. When a bitmap is based on a vector drawing, is that raster graphics or vector graphics? Again, it's a little bit of both.

So far in this book, I've shown you how to use the *Image* element to display bitmaps and various classes from the *System.Windows.Shapes* namespace (also known as the Shapes library) to display vector graphics. These classes might be all that you'll ever need for applications that make only a modest use of graphics. However, these high-level classes are really just the tip of the graphics iceberg in the Windows Presentation Foundation. In the chapters ahead I will explore WPF graphics—including animation—in more detail, culminating with the merging of raster graphics and vector graphics in images, drawings, and brushes.

In this chapter, I want to examine the Shapes library more rigorously than I have in previous chapters. What makes the Shapes library convenient is that the classes derive from *FrameworkElement*, as shown in the following class hierarchy:

Object

    DispatcherObject (abstract)

        DependencyObject

            Visual (abstract)

                UIElement

                    FrameworkElement

                        Shape (abstract)

                            Ellipse

                            Line

                            Path

                            Polygon

                            Polyline

                            Rectangle

As a result of this illustrious ancestry, objects based on the *Shape* classes can render themselves on the screen and handle mouse, stylus, and keyboard input, much like regular controls.

The *Shape* class defines two properties of type *Brush*: *Stroke* and *Fill*. The *Stroke* property indicates the brush used for drawing lines (including the outlines of the *Ellipse*, *Rectangle*, and *Polygon*), while the *Fill* property is the brush that fills interiors. By default, both of these properties are *null*, and if you don't set one or the other you won't see the object.

Although it's not immediately obvious until you begin studying all of their properties, the classes that derive from *Shape* reveal two different rendering paradigms. The *Line*, *Path*, *Polygon*, and *Polyline* classes all include properties that let you define the object in terms of two-dimensional coordinate points—either *Point* objects or something equivalent. For example, *Line* contains properties named *X1*, *Y1*, *X2*, and *Y2* for the beginning and end points of the line.

However, *Ellipse* and *Rectangle* are different. You don't define these objects in terms of points. If you want these graphical objects to be a particular size, you use the *Width* and *Height* properties that these classes inherit from *FrameworkElement*. But you aren't required to set these properties. Very early in this book I demonstrated how to create an *Ellipse* object and set it as the content of a window so that the *Ellipse* fills the client area.

Getting a graphical object on the screen with the ease of *Ellipse* is certainly satisfying and convenient. But generally you want to combine several graphical objects into a composite image, probably with some overlap. To display multiple graphical objects you need a panel that can accommodate overlapping children. Panels such as *DockPanel*, *StackPanel*, *WrapPanel*, *Grid*, and *UniformGrid* are very good at keeping elements *separated* from each other, and for this reason, they're usually not quite adequate for generalized graphics programming.

The *Canvas* panel is excellent for displaying graphics because that's what it was made for. When displaying an *Ellipse* or a *Rectangle* object on a *Canvas* panel, you must set the *Width* and *Height* properties or the object will have a zero dimension and will not be visible. (Well, that's not entirely true. The *MinWidth* and *MinHeight* properties also suffice, and an object with zero dimensions might be visible if the *Stroke* property isn't *null* and the *StrokeThickness* is greater than 1. But you see the point.)

In addition to setting the *Width* and *Height* of the *Ellipse* or *Rectangle*, you'll probably want to set the attached properties *Canvas.Left* and *Canvas.Top*. These indicate the location of the upper-left corner of the *Ellipse* or *Rectangle* relative to the upper-left corner of the *Canvas*. Instead of *Canvas.Left* you can use *Canvas.Right* to indicate the location of the right side of the object relative to the right side of the *Canvas*. Rather than *Canvas.Top* you can use *Canvas.Bottom* to position the bottom of the object relative to the bottom of the *Canvas*.

With the other *Shape* derivatives—*Line*, *Path*, *Polygon*, and *Polyline*—it isn't necessary to set the *Canvas* attached properties because the coordinates of the object indicate its position on the *Canvas*. For example, here's a *Line* element in XAML:

```
<Line X1="100" Y1="50" X2="400" Y2="100" Stroke="Blue" />
```

The start of that line is the point (100, 50), and that means that the line begins 100 device-independent units from the left side of the *Canvas* and 50 units from the top. The end of the line is the point (400, 100), also relative to the top-left corner of the *Canvas*.

Although the *Canvas* attached properties aren't required on the *Line* element, you can include them. For example:

```
<Line X1="100" Y1="50" X2="400" Y2="100" Stroke="Blue"
      Canvas.Left="25" Canvas.Top="150" />
```

In effect, the *Canvas.Left* value is added to all the *X* coordinates of the line, and *Canvas.Top* is added to all the *Y* coordinates. The line is shifted 25 units to the right and 150 units down. It now begins at the point (125, 200) and ends at (425, 250) relative to the upper-left corner of the *Canvas*. The *Canvas.Left* and *Canvas.Top* properties can be negative to shift the element left and up.

If you set *Canvas.Right* rather than *Canvas.Left*, the rightmost point of the line will be shifted so that it is *Canvas.Right* units to the left of the right side of the *Canvas*. Set *Canvas.Right* to a negative value to shift the rightmost point of the object beyond the right side of the *Canvas*. The *Canvas.Bottom* property works similarly for positioning an element relative to the bottom of the *Canvas*.

Canvas is not the only type of panel that can accommodate children in the freeform manner required of most graphics programming. A single cell of a *Grid* panel can also host multiple children, and in some cases you might find a *Grid* cell convenient for this purpose. It's OK!

You can put multiple *Line*, *Path*, *Polygon*, and *Polyline* elements in a *Grid* cell, and their coordinates will position them relative to the upper-left corner of the cell. However, if you set *HorizontalAlignment* of any of these elements to *Right*, the object will be positioned at the right of the cell. If you set *HorizontalAlignment* to *Center*, the object will be positioned in the center of the cell. But not quite. The width of the object is calculated as the distance from 0 to the rightmost *X* coordinate. For example, the first *Line* element shown in the preceding example would be treated as if it had a width of 400, and that total width is what's centered, so the object itself will be somewhat to the right of center. Similar logic is used for *VerticalAlignment*.

Multiple *Ellipse* and *Rectangle* objects don't work very well in a *Grid* cell. You can set the *Width* and *Height* of these elements, and a *Margin* property as well, but you're really left with *HorizontalAlignment* and *VerticalAlignment* to position them, and that's just not very versatile.

Let's take a closer look at the *Polygon* and *Polyline* classes. (I'll save *Path* for the next chapter.) The *Polygon* and *Polyline* classes are very similar. Each has a *Points* property of type *PointCollection*. As you discovered in Chapter 20, in XAML you can supply an array of points by alternating *X* and *Y* coordinate values:

```
Points="100 50 200 50 200 150 100 150"
```

These are the four points of a square with an upper-left corner at (100, 50) and a lower-right corner at (200, 150). Of course, you can append a *px* to a number to more explicitly indicate device-independent coordinates, or you can use *cm* for centimeters, *in* for inches, or *pt* for points (1/72 inch).

You can use commas to separate the values or to separate the *X* and *Y* coordinates in each point, or to separate the points:

```
Points="100 50, 200 50, 200 150, 100 150"
```

If necessary, the string can run to multiple lines.

Although both *Polygon* and *Polyline* draw a series of straight lines, one common use of these classes is drawing curves. The trick is to make the individual lines very short and use plenty of them. Any curve that you can define mathematically you can draw using *Polygon* or *Polyline*. Don't hesitate to use hundreds or thousands of points. These classes were made for that purpose.

Of course, specifying thousands of points in a *Polyline* is only feasible in C# code. The following program draws a sine curve with a positive and negative amplitude of one inch and a period of four inches, with a total horizontal dimension of 2,000 device-independent units, and that's how many points there are.

SineWave.cs

```csharp
//----------------------------------------
// SineWave.cs (c) 2006 by Charles Petzold
//----------------------------------------
using System;
using System.Windows;
using System.Windows.Controls;
using System.Windows.Input;
using System.Windows.Media;
using System.Windows.Shapes;

namespace SineWave
{
    public class SineWave : Window
    {
        [STAThread]
        public static void Main()
        {
            Application app = new Application();
            app.Run(new SineWave());
        }
        public SineWave()
```

```
        {
            Title = "Sine Wave";

            // Make Polyline content of window.
            Polyline poly = new Polyline();
            poly.VerticalAlignment = VerticalAlignment.Center;
            poly.Stroke = SystemColors.WindowTextBrush;
            poly.StrokeThickness = 2;
            Content = poly;

            // Define the points.
            for (int i = 0; i < 2000; i++)
                poly.Points.Add(
                    new Point(i, 96 * (1 - Math.Sin(i * Math.PI / 192))));
        }
    }
}
```

Notice that the *Polyline* is set as the *Content* property of the *Window* and that vertical coordinates of the sine curve are scaled to range from 0 to 192. It's therefore possible for the *VerticalAlignment* property of *Polyline* to be set to *Center* to vertically center the sine curve in the window. If the vertical coordinates ranged from –96 to 96 (which can be accomplished by removing the 1 and the minus sign in front of *Math.Sin*), the curve is treated as if it had a vertical dimension of 96 rather than 192. In effect, negative coordinates are ignored in computing the height of the element for alignment purposes. The result is that the curve is actually positioned above the center of the window.

The SineWave program demonstrates one approach to filling up the *Points* property of *Polyline*. I suspect this isn't the most efficient approach. As more points are added, the *PointCollection* object undoubtedly needs to allocate more space. If you want to fill the *Points* property like this, it's preferable to indicate the number of points before the *for* loop begins:

```
poly.Points = new PointCollection(2000);
```

An altogether better approach to defining the *Points* property is demonstrated in the Spiral program, which uses parametric equations to draw a spiral. In this program, an array of *Point* objects is allocated, and that array becomes the argument to the *PointCollection* constructor.

Spiral.cs
```
//----------------------------------------
// Spiral.cs (c) 2006 by Charles Petzold
//----------------------------------------
using System;
using System.Windows;
using System.Windows.Controls;
using System.Windows.Input;
using System.Windows.Media;
using System.Windows.Shapes;

namespace Spiral
```

```
{
    public class Spiral : Window
    {
        const int revs = 20;
        const int numpts = 1000 * revs;
        Polyline poly;

        [STAThread]
        public static void Main()
        {
            Application app = new Application();
            app.Run(new Spiral());
        }
        public Spiral()
        {
            Title = "Spiral";

            // Make Canvas content of window.
            Canvas canv = new Canvas();
            canv.SizeChanged += CanvasOnSizeChanged;
            Content = canv;

            // Make Polyline child of Canvas.
            poly = new Polyline();
            poly.Stroke = SystemColors.WindowTextBrush;
            canv.Children.Add(poly);

            // Define the points.
            Point[] pts = new Point[numpts];

            for (int i = 0; i < numpts; i++)
            {
                double angle = i * 2 * Math.PI / (numpts / revs);
                double scale = 250 * (1 - (double) i / numpts);

                pts[i].X = scale * Math.Cos(angle);
                pts[i].Y = scale * Math.Sin(angle);
            }
            poly.Points = new PointCollection(pts);
        }
        void CanvasOnSizeChanged(object sender, SizeChangedEventArgs args)
        {
            Canvas.SetLeft(poly, args.NewSize.Width / 2);
            Canvas.SetTop(poly, args.NewSize.Height / 2);
        }
    }
}
```

The Spiral program also demonstrates a different approach to centering the object within the client area. The spiral is drawn on a *Canvas* but centered around the point (0, 0). Whenever the size of the *Canvas* changes, the *CanvasOnSizeChanged* event handler sets the *Left* and *Top* attached properties of the *Polyline* to the center of the *Canvas*, and the spiral is repositioned.

Polyline is intended to draw a series of connected straight lines and *Polygon* is intended to define a closed area for filling and possibly outlining. Yet the two classes are more similar than they might seem. Here's a *Polygon* element that includes two brushes to outline the object and fill it:

```
<Polygon Points="100 50, 200 50, 200 150, 100 150"
         Stroke="Red" Fill="Blue" />
```

You'll notice that the *Points* collection isn't explicitly closed. You could include a final point of (100, 50) but you don't need to. The *Polygon* class will automatically construct another line from the end point to the beginning point—in this case a line from (100, 150) to (100, 150)—so that it closes the square and defines an enclosed area. The lines defining the square (including the last added line) are colored with the *Stroke* brush, and the square is filled with the *Fill* brush.

Although the documentation for *Polyline* indicates that "setting the *Fill* property on a *Polyline* has no effect," this is not true. Given a non-*null Fill* property, *Polyline* will fill the same area as *Polygon*. The only real difference is that *Polyline* does not automatically add the last line that *Polygon* adds to the figure, although it fills the area as if it did.

Here's a XAML file that draws my portrait (if I actually happened to have an egg-shaped head) using a combination of *Ellipse*, *Polygon*, and *Line*.

SelfPortraitSansGlasses.xaml

```
<!-- ================================================================
        SelfPortraitSansGlasses.xaml (c) 2006 by Charles Petzold
     ================================================================ -->
<Canvas xmlns="http://schemas.microsoft.com/winfx/2006/xaml/presentation"
        xmlns:x="http://schemas.microsoft.com/winfx/2006/xaml">

    <!-- Head. -->
    <Ellipse Canvas.Left="96" Canvas.Top="96"
             Width="144" Height="240"
             Fill="PeachPuff" Stroke="Black" />

    <!-- Ears. -->
    <Polygon Points="100 192, 84 168, 84 240, 100 216"
             Fill="SandyBrown" Stroke="Black" />

    <Polygon Points="236 192, 252 168, 252 240, 236 216"
             Fill="SandyBrown" Stroke="Black" />

    <!-- Eyes. -->
    <Ellipse Canvas.Left="120" Canvas.Top="168"
             Width="36" Height="36"
             Fill="White" Stroke="Black" />

    <Ellipse Canvas.Left="180" Canvas.Top="168"
             Width="36" Height="36"
             Fill="White" Stroke="Black" />
```

```
<!-- Irises. -->
<Ellipse Canvas.Left="129" Canvas.Top="177"
         Width="18" Height="18"
         Fill="Brown" Stroke="Black" />

<Ellipse Canvas.Left="189" Canvas.Top="177"
         Width="18" Height="18"
         Fill="Brown" Stroke="Black" />

<!-- Nose. -->
<Polygon Points="168 192, 158 240, 178 240"
         Fill="Pink" Stroke="Black" />

<!-- Mouth. -->
<Ellipse Canvas.Left="120" Canvas.Top="260"
         Width="96" Height="24"
         Fill="White" Stroke="Red" StrokeThickness="8" />

<!-- Beard. -->
<Line X1="120" Y1="288" X2="120" Y2="336" Stroke="Black" StrokeThickness="2" />
<Line X1="126" Y1="290" X2="126" Y2="338" Stroke="Black" StrokeThickness="2" />
<Line X1="132" Y1="292" X2="132" Y2="340" Stroke="Black" StrokeThickness="2" />
<Line X1="138" Y1="294" X2="138" Y2="342" Stroke="Black" StrokeThickness="2" />
<Line X1="144" Y1="296" X2="144" Y2="344" Stroke="Black" StrokeThickness="2" />
<Line X1="150" Y1="297" X2="150" Y2="345" Stroke="Black" StrokeThickness="2" />
<Line X1="156" Y1="298" X2="156" Y2="346" Stroke="Black" StrokeThickness="2" />
<Line X1="162" Y1="299" X2="162" Y2="347" Stroke="Black" StrokeThickness="2" />
<Line X1="168" Y1="300" X2="168" Y2="348" Stroke="Black" StrokeThickness="2" />
<Line X1="174" Y1="299" X2="174" Y2="347" Stroke="Black" StrokeThickness="2" />
<Line X1="180" Y1="298" X2="180" Y2="346" Stroke="Black" StrokeThickness="2" />
<Line X1="186" Y1="297" X2="186" Y2="345" Stroke="Black" StrokeThickness="2" />
<Line X1="192" Y1="296" X2="192" Y2="344" Stroke="Black" StrokeThickness="2" />
<Line X1="198" Y1="294" X2="198" Y2="342" Stroke="Black" StrokeThickness="2" />
<Line X1="204" Y1="292" X2="204" Y2="340" Stroke="Black" StrokeThickness="2" />
<Line X1="210" Y1="290" X2="210" Y2="338" Stroke="Black" StrokeThickness="2" />
<Line X1="216" Y1="288" X2="216" Y2="336" Stroke="Black" StrokeThickness="2" />
</Canvas>
```

Because *Shape* derives from *FrameworkElement*, you can use *Style* elements to define common properties of these objects. For example, I could have eliminated the repetitious assignment of the *Stroke* and *StrokeThickness* attributes in the *Line* elements by including a *Style* like this:

```
<Style TargetType="{x:Type Line}">
    <Setter Property="Stroke" Value="Black" />
    <Setter Property="StrokeThickness" Value="2" />
</Style>
```

Unfortunately, styles probably wouldn't have reduced the overall length of this particular file, but I'll use styles in many of the upcoming programs in this chapter.

The image drawn by SelfPortraitSansGlasses.xaml has a fixed size. In some cases, you might want the size of a graphical image to scale itself up or down depending on the size of the program's window. You can easily accomplish this feat by putting a fixed-size *Canvas* inside a *Viewbox*. The *Viewbox* automatically resizes its content to its own size. The following rather simpler face demonstrates this technique.

ScalableFace.xaml

```
<!-- ==========================================
        ScalableFace.xaml (c) 2006 by Charles Petzold
     ========================================== -->
<Page xmlns="http://schemas.microsoft.com/winfx/2006/xaml/presentation"
      xmlns:x="http://schemas.microsoft.com/winfx/2006/xaml"
      Background="white">
    <Viewbox>
        <Canvas Width="100" Height="100">
            <Ellipse Canvas.Left="5" Canvas.Top="5"
                     Width="90" Height="90" Stroke="Black" />

            <!-- Eyes. -->
            <Ellipse Canvas.Left="25" Canvas.Top="30"
                     Width="10" Height="10" Stroke="Black" />
            <Ellipse Canvas.Right="25" Canvas.Top="30"
                     Width="10" Height="10" Stroke="Black" />

            <!-- Eyebrows. -->
            <Polyline Points="25 25, 30 20, 35 25" Stroke="Black" />
            <Polyline Points="65 25, 70 20, 75 25" Stroke="Black" />

            <!-- Nose. -->
            <Polyline Points="50 40, 45 60, 55 60, 50 40" Stroke="Black" />

            <!-- Mouth. -->
            <Polyline Points="25 70 50 80 75 70" Stroke="Black" />
        </Canvas>
    </Viewbox>
</Page>
```

Notice that *Viewbox* scales *everything* in the image up and down, including the width of the lines. When drawing such an image, you want to keep the overall size of the image and the line widths fairly consistent. You can use a very large or very small *Canvas* to draw the figure, but the overall image might look a bit strange unless you also set the *StrokeThickness* to a commensurate value.

By default, the *Viewbox* scales equally both horizontally and vertically so that no distortion of the image is introduced. If you don't mind a little distortion and prefer that the image occupy as much space as allowed for it, set the *Stretch* property to *Fill*.

Sometimes the lines defining a particular *Polyline* or *Polygon* overlap each other, and then issues arise about which enclosed areas are filled and which are not. Both *Polyline* and *Polygon* define a property named *FillRule* that indicates how enclosed areas are to be filled. The two options are the enumeration values *FillRule.EvenOdd* (the default) and *FillRule.NonZero*. The classic example to show the difference is a five-pointed star, and that's what the next XAML file displays.

To avoid a lot of repetition, the TwoStars.xaml file begins with a *Style* definition for the polygons that render the five-pointed star. The setters include the four *Polygon* properties *Points*, *Fill*, *Stroke*, and *StrokeThickness*. The coordinates used to define the star are based on a center at the point (0, 0) and a radius of one inch.

TwoStars.xaml

```xml
<!-- ==========================================
        TwoStars.xaml (c) 2006 by Charles Petzold
     ========================================== -->
<Canvas xmlns="http://schemas.microsoft.com/winfx/2006/xaml/presentation"
        xmlns:x="http://schemas.microsoft.com/winfx/2006/xaml"
        TextBlock.FontSize="16">
    <Canvas.Resources>

        <!-- Define properties common to both figures. -->

        <Style x:Key="star">
            <Setter Property="Polygon.Points"
                    Value="0 -96, 56, 78, -91 -30, 91 -30, -56 78" />
            <Setter Property="Polygon.Fill"
                    Value="Blue" />
            <Setter Property="Polygon.Stroke"
                    Value="Red" />
            <Setter Property="Polygon.StrokeThickness"
                    Value="3" />
        </Style>
    </Canvas.Resources>

    <!-- Draw first figure with "EvenOdd" FillRule. -->

    <TextBlock Canvas.Left="48" Canvas.Top="24"
               Text="FillRule = EvenOdd" />

    <Polygon Style="{StaticResource star}"
             FillRule="EvenOdd"
             Canvas.Left="120" Canvas.Top="168" />

    <!-- Draw second figure with "NonZero" FillRule. -->

    <TextBlock Canvas.Left="288" Canvas.Top="24"
               Text="FillRule = NonZero" />

    <Polygon Style="{StaticResource star}"
             FillRule="NonZero"
             Canvas.Left="360" Canvas.Top="168" />
</Canvas>
```

The file displays two *TextBlock* elements identifying the *FillRule* and two renditions of the five-pointed star using *Polygon* elements. (Notice that the start tag of the root element sets the *TextBlock.FontSize* property to 12 points.) The first five-pointed star has its *FillRule* set to "EvenOdd," and the second has *FillRule* set to "NonZero." The two stars are offset from the location implied by the *Points* collection using the *Canvas.Left* and *Canvas.Top* attached properties.

With the default *FillRule* of *EvenOdd*, you can imagine a line drawn from a point within an enclosed area to infinity. The enclosed area is filled only if that imaginary line crosses an odd number of boundary lines. That's why the points of the star are filled but the center is not.

That this algorithm really works is demonstrated a little more forcibly by the EvenOddDemo .xaml file. This file is very similar to TwoStars.xaml except that the figure it draws is a bit more elaborate and results in enclosed areas separated from infinity by up to six lines.

EvenOddDemo.xaml

```xml
<!-- =================================================
        EvenOddDemo.xaml (c) 2006 by Charles Petzold
     ================================================= -->
<Canvas xmlns="http://schemas.microsoft.com/winfx/2006/xaml/presentation"
        xmlns:x="http://schemas.microsoft.com/winfx/2006/xaml"
        TextBlock.FontSize="16">
    <Canvas.Resources>

        <!-- Define properties common to both figures. -->

        <Style x:Key="figure">
            <Setter Property="Polygon.Points"
                Value="  0    0,    0 144, 144 144,  144   24,
                        24   24,   24 168, 168 168,  168   48,
                        48   48,   48 192, 192 192,  192   72,
                        72   72,   72 216, 216 216,  216   96,
                        96   96,   96 240, 240 240,  240  120,
                       120  120,  120 264, 264 264,  264    0" />
            <Setter Property="Polygon.Fill"
                    Value="Blue" />
            <Setter Property="Polygon.Stroke"
                    Value="Red" />
            <Setter Property="Polygon.StrokeThickness"
                    Value="3" />
        </Style>
    </Canvas.Resources>

    <!-- Draw first figure with "EvenOdd" FillRule. -->

    <TextBlock Canvas.Left="48" Canvas.Top="24"
            Text="FillRule = EvenOdd" />

    <Polygon Style="{StaticResource figure}"
            FillRule="EvenOdd"
            Canvas.Left="48" Canvas.Top="72" />

    <!-- Draw second figure with "NonZero" FillRule. -->

    <TextBlock Canvas.Left="360" Canvas.Top="24"
            Text="FillRule = NonZero" />
```

```
    <Polygon Style="{StaticResource figure}"
             FillRule="NonZero"
             Canvas.Left="360" Canvas.Top="72" />
  </Canvas>
```

By now you might have concluded that the *NonZero* rule simply results in the filling of *all* enclosed areas. That's usually the case, but the algorithm is a bit more complex. Keep in mind that a polygon is defined by a series of connected points—*pt1*, *pt2*, *pt3*, *pt4*, and so forth—and these lines are conceptually drawn in a particular direction: from *pt1* to *pt2*, from *pt2* to *pt3*, from *pt3* to *pt4*, and so forth.

To determine whether an enclosed area is filled with the *NonZero* rule, you again imagine a line drawn from a point in that area to infinity. If the imaginary line crosses an odd number of boundary lines, that area is filled just as with the *EvenOdd* rule. But if the imaginary line crosses an even number of boundary lines, the area is filled only if the number of boundary lines going in one direction (relative to the imaginary line) is not equal to the number of boundary lines going in the other direction. In other words, an area is filled if the difference between the number of boundary lines going in one direction and the number of boundary lines going in the other direction is "nonzero," which is the name of the rule.

With a little thought, it's possible to come up with a simple figure that tests the rule, and here it is. The arrows show the direction in which the lines are drawn:

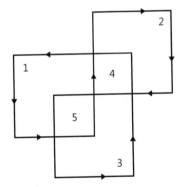

With both the *EvenOdd* and *NonZero* rules, the three L-shaped areas numbered 1 to 3 are always filled. The two smaller interior areas labeled 4 and 5 are not filled with the *EvenOdd* rule because an even number of boundary lines separate these areas from infinity. But with the *NonZero* rule, area number 5 is filled because you must cross two lines going in the same direction to get from the inside of that area to the outside of the figure. Area number 4 is not filled. You must again cross two lines, but the two lines go in opposite directions.

Here's a XAML file that draws two versions of that figure:

TwoFigures.xaml

```
<!-- ===============================================
        TwoFigures.xaml (c) 2006 by Charles Petzold
     =============================================== -->
<Canvas xmlns="http://schemas.microsoft.com/winfx/2006/xaml/presentation"
        xmlns:x="http://schemas.microsoft.com/winfx/2006/xaml"
        TextBlock.FontSize="16">
    <Canvas.Resources>

        <!-- Define properties common to both figures. -->

        <Style x:Key="figure">
            <Setter Property="Polygon.Points"
                    Value="0 48, 0 144, 96 144, 96 0, 192 0, 192 96,
                           48 96, 48 192, 144 192 144 48" />
            <Setter Property="Polygon.Fill"
                    Value="Blue" />
            <Setter Property="Polygon.Stroke"
                    Value="Red" />
            <Setter Property="Polygon.StrokeThickness"
                    Value="3" />
        </Style>
    </Canvas.Resources>

    <!-- Draw first figure with "EvenOdd" FillRule. -->

    <TextBlock Canvas.Left="48" Canvas.Top="24"
               Text="FillRule = EvenOdd" />

    <Polygon Style="{StaticResource figure}"
             FillRule="EvenOdd"
             Canvas.Left="48" Canvas.Top="72" />

    <!-- Draw second figure with "NonZero" FillRule. -->

    <TextBlock Canvas.Left="288" Canvas.Top="24"
               Text="FillRule = NonZero" />

    <Polygon Style="{StaticResource figure}"
             FillRule="NonZero"
             Canvas.Left="288" Canvas.Top="72" />
</Canvas>
```

When defining the appearances of the outlines of rectangles, ellipses, and polygons, so far I've been using only two *Shape* properties: The *Stroke* property to specify the brush used for coloring the lines, and *StrokeThickness* for the width of the lines.

The *System.Windows.Media* namespace includes a *Pen* class that defines eight properties related to drawing lines. Although the *Pen* is used elsewhere in WPF graphics, *Shape* does not define a *Pen* property. It obviously uses a *Pen* internally but *Shape* defines all its own properties—all beginning with the word *Stroke*—that parallel the *Pen* properties. Here's a chart of the *Pen* properties and corresponding *Shape* properties.

Pen Property	Type	*Shape* Property
Brush	Brush	Stroke
Thickness	Double	StrokeThickness
StartLineCap	PenLineCap	StrokeStartLineCap
EndLineCap	PenLineCap	StrokeEndLineCap
LineJoin	PenLineJoin	StrokeLineJoin
MiterLimit	Double	StrokeMiterLimit
DashStyle	DashStyle	StrokeDashArray (DoubleCollection)
		StrokeDashOffset (double)
DashCap	PenLineCap	StrokeDashCap

The definition of these properties by *Shape* obviously makes life easier for those of us who code XAML by hand. With the *Stroke* property defined by *Shape*, you can define a line color like this:

```
<Ellipse Stroke="Blue" ... />
```

If *Shape* instead defined a *Pen* property of type *Pen*, you'd have to do it like this:

```
<!-- Not the way we have to do it! -->
<Ellipse ... >
    <Ellipse.Pen>
        <Pen Brush="Blue" .../>
    </Ellipse.Pen>
</Ellipse>
```

The *StrokeThickness* property defined by *Shape* (corresponding to the *Thickness* property of the *Pen*) indicates the width of the line in device-independent units. As a line gets wider, the appearances of the two ends of the lines start to become more evident. By default, a thick line (shown in gray) straddles the geometric line that defines its start and end points (shown in black), and ends abruptly at those points:

The appearance of the beginning and end of the line is known as a *line cap* and is specified with members of the *PenLineCap* enumeration. The default is *PenLineCap.Flat*. The other options are *Square*, *Round*, and *Triangle*, all of which effectively increase the length of the line beyond its geometrical start and end points.

The following little stand-alone XAML file demonstrates the four line caps. As in the illustration, I've superimposed a thin black line that indicates the geometric start and end of the line.

LineCaps.xaml

```xml
<!-- =========================================
        LineCaps.xaml (c) 2006 by Charles Petzold
     ========================================= -->
<StackPanel xmlns="http://schemas.microsoft.com/winfx/2006/xaml/presentation"
            xmlns:x="http://schemas.microsoft.com/winfx/2006/xaml"
            Orientation="Horizontal">
    <StackPanel.Resources>
        <Style TargetType="{x:Type Canvas}">
            <Setter Property="Width" Value="150" />
            <Setter Property="Margin" Value="12" />
        </Style>

        <Style x:Key="thin">
            <Setter Property="Line.X1" Value="00" />
            <Setter Property="Line.Y1" Value="50" />
            <Setter Property="Line.X2" Value="100" />
            <Setter Property="Line.Y2" Value="50" />
            <Setter Property="Line.Stroke" Value="Black" />
        </Style>

        <Style x:Key="thick"
               BasedOn="{StaticResource thin}">
            <Setter Property="Line.Stroke" Value="LightGray" />
            <Setter Property="Line.StrokeThickness" Value="25" />
        </Style>
    </StackPanel.Resources>

    <!-- PenLineCap.Flat. -->
    <Canvas>
        <TextBlock Text="PenLineCap.Flat" />
        <Line Style="{StaticResource thick}"
              StrokeStartLineCap="Flat"
              StrokeEndLineCap="Flat" />
        <Line Style="{StaticResource thin}" />
    </Canvas>

    <!-- PenLineCap.Square. -->
    <Canvas>
        <TextBlock Text="PenLineCap.Square" />
        <Line Style="{StaticResource thick}"
              StrokeStartLineCap="Square"
              StrokeEndLineCap="Square" />
        <Line Style="{StaticResource thin}" />
    </Canvas>

    <!-- PenLineCap.Round. -->
    <Canvas>
        <TextBlock Text="PenLineCap.Round" />
        <Line Style="{StaticResource thick}"
              StrokeStartLineCap="Round"
```

```
                    StrokeEndLineCap="Round" />
            <Line Style="{StaticResource thin}" />
        </Canvas>

        <!-- PenLineCap.Triangle. -->
        <Canvas>
            <TextBlock Text="PenLineCap.Triangle" />
            <Line Style="{StaticResource thick}"
                  StrokeStartLineCap="Triangle"
                  StrokeEndLineCap="Triangle" />
            <Line Style="{StaticResource thin}" />
        </Canvas>

    </StackPanel>
```

A related issue exists for polylines and involves the juncture where one straight line joins another. This is known as a *line join*. You set the *StrokeLineJoin* property of the *Shape* object to a member of the *PenLineJoin* enumeration, which has members *Bevel*, *Miter*, and *Round*. Both the *Bevel* and the *Miter* joins imply that a union of two connected lines results in a sharp, arrow-like point. The *Bevel* join shaves off the point, while the *Miter* join does not (at least to a certain extent).

The *StrokeLineJoin* property affects *Rectangle* as well as *Polyline* and *Polygon*, as this stand-alone XAML program demonstrates.

LineJoins.xaml

```
<!-- =========================================
     LineJoins.xaml (c) 2006 by Charles Petzold
     ========================================= -->
<StackPanel xmlns="http://schemas.microsoft.com/winfx/2006/xaml/presentation"
            xmlns:x="http://schemas.microsoft.com/winfx/2006/xaml"
            Orientation="Horizontal">
    <StackPanel.Resources>
        <Style TargetType="{x:Type TextBlock}">
            <Setter Property="Canvas.Left" Value="25" />
        </Style>

        <Style TargetType="{x:Type Canvas}">
            <Setter Property="Width" Value="150" />
            <Setter Property="Margin" Value="12" />
        </Style>

        <Style TargetType="{x:Type Rectangle}">
            <Setter Property="Width" Value="100" />
            <Setter Property="Height" Value="100" />
            <Setter Property="Canvas.Top" Value="50" />
            <Setter Property="Canvas.Left" Value="25" />
            <Setter Property="Stroke" Value="Black" />
            <Setter Property="StrokeThickness" Value="25" />
        </Style>
    </StackPanel.Resources>
```

```
    <!-- PenLineJoin.Bevel. -->
    <Canvas>
        <TextBlock Text="PenLineJoin.Bevel" />
        <Rectangle StrokeLineJoin="Bevel" />
    </Canvas>

    <!-- PenLineJoin.Round. -->
    <Canvas>
        <TextBlock Text="PenLineJoin.Round" />
        <Rectangle StrokeLineJoin="Round" />
    </Canvas>

    <!-- PenLineJoin.Miter. -->
    <Canvas>
        <TextBlock Text="PenLineJoin.Miter" />
        <Rectangle StrokeLineJoin="Miter" />
    </Canvas>
</StackPanel>
```

There's a particular problem with the *Miter* join that's only revealed when the two lines join at a very small angle. To further explore these issues, you might want to experiment with the PenProperties.xaml file when setting line ends and joins.

PenProperties.xaml

```
<!-- ===============================================
        PenProperties.xaml (c) 2006 by Charles Petzold
     =============================================== -->
<Grid xmlns="http://schemas.microsoft.com/winfx/2006/xaml/presentation"
      xmlns:x="http://schemas.microsoft.com/winfx/2006/xaml">

    <!-- Draw the Polyline in the single-cell Grid. -->

    <Polyline Margin="0.5in, 1.5in, 0, 0"
              Points="0 0, 500 25, 0 50"
              VerticalAlignment="Center"
              Stroke="Blue"
              StrokeThickness="{Binding ElementName=sliderThickness,
                                        Path=Value }"
              StrokeStartLineCap="{Binding ElementName=lstboxStartLineCap,
                                           Path=SelectedItem.Content}"
              StrokeEndLineCap="{Binding ElementName=lstboxEndLineCap,
                                         Path=SelectedItem.Content}"
              StrokeLineJoin="{Binding ElementName=lstboxLineJoin,
                                       Path=SelectedItem.Content}"
              StrokeMiterLimit="{Binding ElementName=sliderMiterLimit,
                                         Path=Value }" />

    <!-- Create a horizontal StackPanel in the same cell of the Grid. -->

    <StackPanel Grid.Column="0"
                Margin="0, 12, 0, 0"
                Orientation="Horizontal" >

        <!-- Define a style for the five "user-interface" groups. -->
```

```
    <StackPanel.Resources>
        <Style x:Key="uigroup">
            <Setter Property="StackPanel.VerticalAlignment"
                    Value="Top" />
            <Setter Property="StackPanel.Width"
                    Value="100" />
            <Setter Property="StackPanel.Margin"
                    Value="12, 0, 12, 0" />
        </Style>
    </StackPanel.Resources>

    <!-- A Slider for the StrokeThickness property. -->

    <StackPanel Style="{StaticResource uigroup}">
        <Label Content="_Thickness" />
        <Slider Name="sliderThickness"
                Minimum="0"
                Maximum="100"
                Value="24" />
    </StackPanel>

    <!-- A ListBox for the StrokeStartLineCap property. -->

    <StackPanel Style="{StaticResource uigroup}">
        <Label Content="_StartLineCap" />
        <ListBox Name="lstboxStartLineCap">
            <ListBoxItem Content="{x:Static PenLineCap.Flat}" />
            <ListBoxItem Content="{x:Static PenLineCap.Square}" />
            <ListBoxItem Content="{x:Static PenLineCap.Round}" />
            <ListBoxItem Content="{x:Static PenLineCap.Triangle}" />
        </ListBox>
    </StackPanel>

    <!-- A ListBox for the StrokeEndLineCap property. -->

    <StackPanel Style="{StaticResource uigroup}">
        <Label Content="_EndLineCap" />
        <ListBox Name="lstboxEndLineCap">
            <ListBoxItem Content="{x:Static PenLineCap.Flat}" />
            <ListBoxItem Content="{x:Static PenLineCap.Square}" />
            <ListBoxItem Content="{x:Static PenLineCap.Round}" />
            <ListBoxItem Content="{x:Static PenLineCap.Triangle}" />
        </ListBox>
    </StackPanel>

    <!-- A ListBox for the StrokeLineJoin property. -->

    <StackPanel Style="{StaticResource uigroup}">
        <Label Content="_LineJoin" />
        <ListBox Name="lstboxLineJoin">
            <ListBoxItem Content="{x:Static PenLineJoin.Bevel}" />
            <ListBoxItem Content="{x:Static PenLineJoin.Round}" />
            <ListBoxItem Content="{x:Static PenLineJoin.Miter}" />
        </ListBox>
    </StackPanel>

    <!-- A Slider for the StrokeMiterLimit property. -->
```

```
        <StackPanel Style="{StaticResource uigroup}">
            <Label Content="_MiterLimit" />
            <Slider Name="sliderMiterLimit"
                    Minimum="0"
                    Maximum="100"
                    Value="10" />
        </StackPanel>
    </StackPanel>
</Grid>
```

The program draws a simple two-segment polyline that looks like an elongated greater than sign. It also creates *Slider* controls and *ListBox* controls that let you set five properties of the *Polyline*.

The *Polyline* is elongated to demonstrate a problem that could arise when you choose a *StrokeEndJoin* property of *LineEndJoin.Miter*. For example, a one-inch-thick polyline joined at an angle of 1 degree would have a miter join that extended more than 4.5 feet! (Let w be the width of the line and α be the join angle. It's easy to show that the extension of the miter tip past the actual join point is $(w/2)/\sin(\alpha/2)$.)

For this reason, a *StrokeMiterLimit* property is intended to limit the extent of a miter join by shaving off the tip. You can see the *StrokeMiterLimit* property kick in when you select a *Miter* join and increase the width of the line with the first *Slider* control. Past a certain point, the join is shaved off. You can increase the *StrokeMiterLimit* with the second *Slider* control.

The two remaining *Pen* properties in the preceding table are *DashStyle* and *DashCap*. These properties let you draw styled lines, which are lines composed of dots or dashes or combinations of dots and dashes. The *DashStyle* property is an object of type *DashStyle*, a class with two properties: *Dashes* (an object of type *DoubleCollection*) and *Offset* (a *Double*). The elements of the *Dashes* collection indicate an on/off pattern for drawing the line.

Shape, however, doesn't go anywhere near the *DashStyle* class and instead defines two properties that take its place named *StrokeDashArray* and *StrokeDashOffset*. This XAML file sets the *StrokeDashArray* property of a *Line* element to "1 2 2 1".

OneTwoTwoOne.xaml

```
<!-- =================================================
        OneTwoTwoOne.xaml (c) 2006 by Charles Petzold
     ================================================= -->
<Canvas xmlns="http://schemas.microsoft.com/winfx/2006/xaml/presentation"
        xmlns:x="http://schemas.microsoft.com/winfx/2006/xaml">
    <Line X1="48" Y1="48" X2="1000" Y2="48"
          Stroke="{DynamicResource {x:Static SystemColors.WindowTextBrushKey}}"
          StrokeThickness="12"
          StrokeDashArray="1 2 2 1" />
</Canvas>
```

When you execute this XAML file, you can see that the line begins with a dash the same length as the thickness of the line, followed by space that is twice the line thickness, then a dash that is twice the line thickness, and a space of the line thickness. The pattern repeats indefinitely.

The *StrokeDashOffset* value is an offset into the dash pattern. For example, in OneTwoTwo-One.xaml you can include an attribute to set *StrokeDashOffset* to 1:

```
StrokeDashOffset="1"
```

Now the line begins with the first two-unit space.

The *StrokeDashArray* in the OneTwoTwoOne.xaml file is actually problematic. The *Shape* class defines a *StrokeDashCap* property (corresponding to the *DashCap* property of *Pen*) of type *Pen-LineCap*, the same enumeration that you use with the *StrokeStartLineCap* and *StrokeEndLine-Cap* properties. The four members of the enumeration, you'll recall, are *Flat*, *Square*, *Round*, and *Triangle*. The default is *Flat*, which means that the dashes and spaces are precisely the lengths implied by the *StrokeDashArray* values. However, the other dash cap values effectively increase the length of the dashes. Try adding the following attribute to the XAML file to see the problem:

```
StrokeDashCap="Round"
```

Now the dots no longer look like dots—they look like little sausages. You'll probably want to change the *StrokeDashArray* to "0 3 1 2" to get something that looks similar to the earlier pattern.

The following stand-alone XAML program displays the four different dash caps using a *Stroke-DashArray* pattern of "2 2."

```
DashCaps.xaml
<!-- =======================================
     DashCaps.xaml (c) 2006 by Charles Petzold
     ======================================= -->
<Grid xmlns="http://schemas.microsoft.com/winfx/2006/xaml/presentation"
    xmlns:x="http://schemas.microsoft.com/winfx/2006/xaml">
    <Grid.Resources>
        <Style TargetType="{x:Type TextBlock}">
            <Setter Property="FontSize" Value="16" />
            <Setter Property="Margin" Value="24" />
            <Setter Property="VerticalAlignment" Value="Center" />
        </Style>

        <Style TargetType="{x:Type Line}">
            <Setter Property="Grid.Column" Value="1" />
            <Setter Property="Y1" Value="30" />
            <Setter Property="X2" Value="400" />
            <Setter Property="Y2" Value="30" />
            <Setter Property="StrokeThickness" Value="25" />
            <Setter Property="Stroke" Value="Black" />
            <Setter Property="StrokeDashArray" Value="2 2" />
```

```xml
            <Setter Property="StrokeStartLineCap"
                Value="{Binding RelativeSource={RelativeSource self},
                        Path=StrokeDashCap}" />

            <Setter Property="StrokeEndLineCap"
                Value="{Binding RelativeSource={RelativeSource self},
                        Path=StrokeDashCap}" />

        </Style>
    </Grid.Resources>

    <Grid.RowDefinitions>
        <RowDefinition Height="Auto" />
        <RowDefinition Height="Auto" />
        <RowDefinition Height="Auto" />
        <RowDefinition Height="Auto" />
    </Grid.RowDefinitions>

    <Grid.ColumnDefinitions>
        <ColumnDefinition Width="Auto" />
        <ColumnDefinition Width="Auto" />
    </Grid.ColumnDefinitions>

    <!-- PenLineCap.Flat. -->
    <TextBlock Grid.Row="0" Text="PenLineCap.Flat" />
    <Line Grid.Row="0" />

    <!-- PenLineCap.Square. -->
    <TextBlock Grid.Row="1" Text="PenLineCap.Square" />
    <Line Grid.Row="1" StrokeDashCap="Square" />

    <!-- PenLineCap.Round. -->
    <TextBlock Grid.Row="2" Text="PenLineCap.Round" />
    <Line Grid.Row="2" StrokeDashCap="Round" />

    <!-- Triangle.Triangle. -->
    <TextBlock Grid.Row="3" Text="PenLineCap.Triangle" />
    <Line Grid.Row="3" StrokeDashCap="Triangle" />
</Grid>
```

Notice that the *Style* definition for the *Line* defines a binding from the *StrokeDashCap* property to both the *StrokeStartLineCap* and *StrokeEndLineCap* properties. The lines really look the most "natural" when these three properties are set to the same value.

Only the *Flat* style appears to be alternating between a 2-unit dash and a 2-unit space. The others can also appear that way when the *StrokeDashArray* is set to "1 3."

The *System.Windows.Media* namespace includes both a *DashStyle* class (which has the properties *Dashes* and *Offset*) and a *DashStyles* class (notice the plural). The *DashStyles* class has five static properties named *Solid*, *Dot*, *Dash*, *DashDot*, and *DashDotDot* of type *DashStyle*. The following table shows the *Dashes* property for each of the static properties of *DashStyles*.

DashStyles Static Property	*Dashes* Property
Solid	
Dot	0 2
Dash	2 2
DashDot	2 2 0 2
DashDotDot	2 2 0 2 0 2

In the *Pen* class, the default *DashCap* property is *PenLineCap.Square*, which means that the dots and dashes are by default extended by half the thickness of the line. These various *Dashes* arrays have been chosen with that in mind. These values are *not* suitable when the *DashCap* property is *PenLineCap.Flat*, which is the default value of the *StrokeDashCap* property that *Shape* defines. If you set an attribute of

```
StrokeDashArray="0 2"
```

with the default *StrokeDashCap* property of *Flat*, you'll see no line at all because the dashes are 0 units long. My recommendation is that you manually set a *StrokeDashArray* property based on the *StrokeDashCap* property you choose.

If you set the *StrokeDashCap* to *Square*, *Round*, or *Triangle*, you can define a binding between *StrokeDashArray* and one of the static properties of the *DashStyles* class. The binding requires an *x:Static* markup extension to access the static property *DashStyles.Dot* (or whatever style you want to use) and a *Path* property referencing the *Dashes* property of *DashStyle*. Here's a program that uses such a binding to display a dotted line around an ellipse.

```
EllipseWithStyledLines.xaml
<!-- ========================================================
     EllipseWithStyledLines.xaml (c) 2006 by Charles Petzold
     ======================================================== -->
<Page xmlns="http://schemas.microsoft.com/winfx/2006/xaml/presentation"
      xmlns:x="http://schemas.microsoft.com/winfx/2006/xaml"
      WindowTitle="Ellipse with Styled Lines">
    <Ellipse Margin="0.5in"
             Fill="Blue"
             Stroke="Red"
             StrokeDashArray="{Binding Source={x:Static DashStyles.Dot},
                                       Path=Dashes,
                                       Mode=OneTime}"
             StrokeThickness="36pt"
             StrokeDashCap="Round">
    </Ellipse>
</Page>
```

The resultant image is actually quite interesting. Because the *StrokeDashCap* has been set to *Round*, the dots that comprise the line appear as actual dots and seem like a series of round balls that surround the ellipse. There's obviously been some special coding for this situation because there's no awkward point at which a partial dot appears.

In this chapter I have discussed all the classes that derive from *Shape* except *Path*. A graphics path is a collection of straight lines and curves. Beyond the properties defined by *Shape*, the *Path* class adds just one more: a property named *Data* of type *Geometry*, which opens a powerful array of graphics capabilities. Geometries and paths are the subject of the next chapter.

Chapter 28
Geometries and Paths

The classes that derive from *Shape* include the (by now) familiar *Rectangle, Ellipse, Line, Polyline,* and *Polygon.* The only other class that derives from *Shape* is named *Path,* and it's absolutely the most powerful of them all. It encompasses the functionality of the other *Shape* classes and does much more besides. *Path* could potentially be the only vector-drawing class you'll ever need. The only real drawback of *Path* is that it tends to be a little verbose in comparison with the other *Shape* classes. However, toward the end of this chapter I'll show you a shortcut that *Path* implements that lets you be quite concise.

The only property that *Path* defines is *Data,* which you set to an object of type *Geometry.* The *Geometry* class itself is abstract, but seven classes derive from *Geometry,* as shown in this class hierarchy:

Object

    DispatcherObject (abstract)

        DependencyObject

            Freezable (abstract)

                Animatable (abstract)

                    Geometry (abstract)

                        LineGeometry

                        RectangleGeometry

                        EllipseGeometry

                        GeometryGroup

                        CombinedGeometry

                        PathGeometry

                        StreamGeometry

I've arranged those *Geometry* derivatives in the order in which I'll discuss them in this chapter. These classes represent the closest that WPF graphics come to encapsulating pure analytic geometry. You specify a *Geometry* object with points and lengths. The *Geometry* object does not draw itself. You must use another class (most often *Path*) to render the geometric object with the desired fill brush and pen properties. The markup looks something like this:

```
<Path Stroke="Blue" StrokeThickness="3" Fill="Red">
    <Path.Data>
        <EllipseGeometry ... />
    </Path.Data>
</Path>
```

The *LineGeometry* class defines two properties: *StartPoint* and *EndPoint*. This stand-alone XAML file uses *LineGeometry* and *Path* to render two lines of different colors that cross each other.

LineGeometryDemo.xaml

```
<!-- =====================================================
        LineGeometryDemo.xaml (c) 2006 by Charles Petzold
     ===================================================== -->
<Canvas xmlns="http://schemas.microsoft.com/winfx/2006/xaml/presentation"
        xmlns:x="http://schemas.microsoft.com/winfx/2006/xaml">

    <Path Stroke="Blue" StrokeThickness="3">
        <Path.Data>
            <LineGeometry StartPoint="96 96"
                          EndPoint="192 192" />
        </Path.Data>
    </Path>

    <Path Stroke="Red" StrokeThickness="3">
        <Path.Data>
            <LineGeometry StartPoint="192 96"
                          EndPoint="96 192" />
        </Path.Data>
    </Path>

</Canvas>
```

Just as you can have multiple *Line* elements on the *Canvas*, you can have multiple *Path* elements, and each *Path* element can potentially have its own *Stroke* color and *StrokeThickness*.

The *RectangleGeometry* class defines a *Rect* property (of type *Rect*, of course) that indicates the location and size of the rectangle, and *RadiusX* and *RadiusY* properties for the curvature of the corners. In XAML, you can set a property of type *Rect* by a string containing four numbers: the *X* coordinate of the upper-left corner, the *Y* coordinate of the upper-left corner, the width, and the height.

RectangleGeometryDemo.xaml

```
<!-- =====================================================
        RectangleGeometryDemo.xaml (c) 2006 by Charles Petzold
     ===================================================== -->
<Canvas xmlns="http://schemas.microsoft.com/winfx/2006/xaml/presentation"
        xmlns:x="http://schemas.microsoft.com/winfx/2006/xaml">

    <Path Fill="Blue" Stroke="Red" StrokeThickness="3">
        <Path.Data>
            <RectangleGeometry Rect="96 48 288 192"
                               RadiusX="24" RadiusY="24" />
        </Path.Data>
    </Path>
</Canvas>
```

The *StartPoint* and *EndPoint* properties defined by *LineGeometry*—and the *Rect*, *RadiusX*, and *RadiusY* properties defined by *RectangleGeometry*—are all backed by dependency properties, which means that these properties can be animated (as you'll see in Chapter 30) and they can be targets of data bindings.

EllipseGeometry contains a constructor that lets you base the ellipse on a *Rect* object. However, this facility is not available when you define an *EllipseGeometry* in XAML. Instead, you specify the center of the ellipse with a *Center* property of type *Point* and the dimensions of the ellipse with *RadiusX* and *RadiusY* properties of type *double*. All three properties are backed by dependency properties.

EllipseGeometryDemo.xaml

```
<!-- ========================================================
        EllipseGeometryDemo.xaml (c) 2006 by Charles Petzold
     ======================================================== -->
<Canvas xmlns="http://schemas.microsoft.com/winfx/2006/xaml/presentation"
        xmlns:x="http://schemas.microsoft.com/winfx/2006/xaml">

    <Path Fill="Blue" Stroke="Red" StrokeThickness="3">
        <Path.Data>
            <EllipseGeometry Center="196, 144"
                             RadiusX="144" RadiusY="96" />
        </Path.Data>
    </Path>
</Canvas>
```

You might recall the DrawCircles program from Chapter 9 that lets you use the mouse to draw circles on a *Canvas*. The initial mouse click indicates the center of the circle and the later position of the mouse governs the radius. But that program uses an *Ellipse* element, which requires that the size of the ellipse be specified by its width and height. The location of the *Ellipse* on the *Canvas* is given by the *Left* and *Top* attached properties. When the DrawCircles program responds to mouse movements by expanding or contracting the circle, it needs to keep the ellipse centered on the same point, which requires moving the ellipse as well as increasing its size. If that program used *EllipseGeometry* instead, the logic would be simplified.

The *Path.Data* property element can have only one child of type *Geometry*. As you've seen, you can get around this limitation by using multiple *Path* elements. Or, you can mix *Path* elements with other elements such as *Rectangle*.

Another way to get around the limitation is to make a *GeometryGroup* object the child of *Path.Data*. *GeometryGroup* inherits from *Geometry* but has a property named *Children* of type *GeometryCollection*, which is a collection of *Geometry* objects. *GeometryGroup* can host multiple *Geometry* children. The markup might look something like this:

```
<Path Fill="Gold" Stroke="Pink" ...>
    <Path.Data>
```

```
    <GeometryGroup>
        <EllipseGeometry ... />
        <LineGeometry ... />
        <RectangleGeometry ... />
    </GeometryGroup>
  </Path.Data>
</Path>
```

Because all the *Geometry* objects in the *GeometryGroup* are part of the same *Path* element, they all have the same *Stroke* and *Fill* brushes. That's one major difference between using *GeometryGroup* rather than multiple *Path* elements.

The other major difference is illustrated in this XAML file. On the left are two overlapping rectangles rendered by two separate *Path* elements. On the right are two overlapping rectangles that are part of the same *GeometryGroup*.

OverlappingRectangles.xaml

```
<!-- =======================================================
        OverlappingRectangles.xaml (c) 2006 by Charles Petzold
     ======================================================= -->
<Canvas xmlns="http://schemas.microsoft.com/winfx/2006/xaml/presentation"
        xmlns:x="http://schemas.microsoft.com/winfx/2006/xaml">

    <Path Fill="Gold" Stroke="Red" StrokeThickness="3">
        <Path.Data>
            <RectangleGeometry Rect="96 96 192 192" />
        </Path.Data>
    </Path>

    <Path Fill="Gold" Stroke="Red" StrokeThickness="3">
        <Path.Data>
            <RectangleGeometry Rect="192 192 192 192" />
        </Path.Data>
    </Path>

    <Path Fill="Gold" Stroke="Red" StrokeThickness="3">
        <Path.Data>
            <GeometryGroup>
                <RectangleGeometry Rect="480 96 192 192" />
                <RectangleGeometry Rect="576 192 192 192" />
            </GeometryGroup>
        </Path.Data>
    </Path>

</Canvas>
```

With the first pair of rectangles, one rectangle simply sits on top of the other. But for the second pair of rectangles joined in a *GeometryGroup*, the area where they overlap is transparent. What's happening here is exactly what happens when a *Polygon* element has overlapping boundaries. *GeometryGroup* defines its own *FillRule* property, and the default value of *EvenOdd* doesn't fill enclosed areas separated from infinity by an even number of boundary lines. You can alternatively set the *FillRule* to *NonZero*, like this:

```
<GeometryGroup FillRule="NonZero">
```

In that case, the overlapping area will be filled, but the second pair of rectangles in the program still won't look like the first pair. With the first pair, the second rectangle obscures part of the first rectangle's border. With the second pair, all the borders are visible.

You can get some interesting effects by combining multiple geometries in the same *GeometryGroup*.

```
FourOverlappingCircles.cs
<!-- ============================================================
        FourOverlappingCircles.xaml (c) 2006 by Charles Petzold
     ============================================================ -->
<Canvas xmlns="http://schemas.microsoft.com/winfx/2006/xaml/presentation"
        xmlns:x="http://schemas.microsoft.com/winfx/2006/xaml">

    <Path Fill="Blue" Stroke="Red" StrokeThickness="3">
        <Path.Data>
            <GeometryGroup>
                <EllipseGeometry Center="150 150" RadiusX="100" RadiusY="100" />
                <EllipseGeometry Center="250 150" RadiusX="100" RadiusY="100" />
                <EllipseGeometry Center="150 250" RadiusX="100" RadiusY="100" />
                <EllipseGeometry Center="250 250" RadiusX="100" RadiusY="100" />
            </GeometryGroup>
        </Path.Data>
    </Path>
</Canvas>
```

That's the *GeometryGroup* class, and it's easy to confuse that class with another *Geometry* derivative named *CombinedGeometry*. But *CombinedGeometry* is quite different. First, it doesn't have a *Children* property. Instead, it has two properties named *Geometry1* and *Geometry2*. *CombinedGeometry* is a combination of two and only two other geometries.

The second difference between *GeometryGroup* and *CombinedGeometry* is that *CombinedGeometry* doesn't have a *FillRule* property. Instead it has a *GeometryCombineMode* property that you set to a member of the *GeometryCombineMode* enumeration: *Union*, *Intersect*, *Xor*, or *Exclude*. The first three options work like visual Venn diagrams; the *Exclude* option creates a geometry that consists of everything in *Geometry2* that's not also in *Geometry1*.

The following stand-alone XAML program demonstrates the four *GeometryCombineMode* options with two overlapping circles.

CombinedGeometryModes.xaml

```xml
<!-- =======================================================
         CombinedGeometryModes.xaml (c) 2006 by Charles Petzold
     ======================================================= -->
<UniformGrid xmlns="http://schemas.microsoft.com/winfx/2006/xaml/presentation"
             xmlns:x="http://schemas.microsoft.com/winfx/2006/xaml"
             Rows="2" Columns="2" TextBlock.FontSize="12pt">

    <UniformGrid.Resources>
        <Style TargetType="{x:Type Path}">
            <Setter Property="HorizontalAlignment" Value="Center" />
            <Setter Property="VerticalAlignment" Value="Center" />
            <Setter Property="Fill" Value="Blue" />
            <Setter Property="Stroke" Value="Red" />
            <Setter Property="StrokeThickness" Value="5" />
        </Style>
    </UniformGrid.Resources>

    <!-- GeometryCombineMode = "Union". -->

    <Grid>
        <TextBlock HorizontalAlignment="Center">
            GeometryCombineMode="Union"
        </TextBlock>
        <Path>
            <Path.Data>
                <CombinedGeometry GeometryCombineMode="Union">
                    <CombinedGeometry.Geometry1>
                        <EllipseGeometry Center="96 96"
                                         RadiusX="96" RadiusY="96" />
                    </CombinedGeometry.Geometry1>
                    <CombinedGeometry.Geometry2>
                        <EllipseGeometry Center="48 48"
                                         RadiusX="96" RadiusY="96" />
                    </CombinedGeometry.Geometry2>
                </CombinedGeometry>
            </Path.Data>
        </Path>
    </Grid>

    <!-- GeometryCombineMode = "Intersect". -->

    <Grid>
        <TextBlock HorizontalAlignment="Center">
            GeometryCombineMode="Intersect"
        </TextBlock>
        <Path>
            <Path.Data>
                <CombinedGeometry GeometryCombineMode="Intersect">
                    <CombinedGeometry.Geometry1>
                        <EllipseGeometry Center="96 96"
                                         RadiusX="96" RadiusY="96" />
                    </CombinedGeometry.Geometry1>
                    <CombinedGeometry.Geometry2>
```

```
                            <EllipseGeometry Center="48 48"
                                             RadiusX="96" RadiusY="96" />
                        </CombinedGeometry.Geometry2>
                    </CombinedGeometry>
                </Path.Data>
            </Path>
        </Grid>


        <!-- GeometryCombineMode = "Xor". -->

        <Grid>
            <TextBlock HorizontalAlignment="Center">
                GeometryCombineMode="Xor"
            </TextBlock>
            <Path>
                <Path.Data>
                    <CombinedGeometry GeometryCombineMode="Xor">
                        <CombinedGeometry.Geometry1>
                            <EllipseGeometry Center="96 96"
                                             RadiusX="96" RadiusY="96" />
                        </CombinedGeometry.Geometry1>
                        <CombinedGeometry.Geometry2>
                            <EllipseGeometry Center="48 48"
                                             RadiusX="96" RadiusY="96" />
                        </CombinedGeometry.Geometry2>
                    </CombinedGeometry>
                </Path.Data>
            </Path>
        </Grid>


        <!-- GeometryCombineMode = "Exclude". -->

        <Grid>
            <TextBlock HorizontalAlignment="Center">
                GeometryCombineMode="Exclude"
            </TextBlock>
            <Path>
                <Path.Data>
                    <CombinedGeometry GeometryCombineMode="Exclude">
                        <CombinedGeometry.Geometry1>
                            <EllipseGeometry Center="96 96"
                                             RadiusX="96" RadiusY="96" />
                        </CombinedGeometry.Geometry1>
                        <CombinedGeometry.Geometry2>
                            <EllipseGeometry Center="48 48"
                                             RadiusX="96" RadiusY="96" />
                        </CombinedGeometry.Geometry2>
                    </CombinedGeometry>
                </Path.Data>
            </Path>
        </Grid>

</UniformGrid>
```

Notice how different these images are from every other type of combination of objects you've seen so far. Even the *Union* option—which at first seems to offer no benefits over two simple overlapping figures—produces something different. The border of the combined circles goes around the composite object rather than the original objects. The *CombinedGeometry* can give you some effects that might otherwise be difficult. One example is this image of a dumbbell.

```
Dumbbell.xaml
<!-- ========================================
        Dumbbell.xaml (c) 2006 by Charles Petzold
     ======================================== -->
<Canvas xmlns="http://schemas.microsoft.com/winfx/2006/xaml/presentation"
        xmlns:x="http://schemas.microsoft.com/winfx/2006/xaml">

    <Path Fill="DarkGray" Stroke="Black" StrokeThickness="5">
        <Path.Data>
            <CombinedGeometry GeometryCombineMode="Union">
                <CombinedGeometry.Geometry1>
                    <CombinedGeometry GeometryCombineMode="Union">
                        <CombinedGeometry.Geometry1>
                            <EllipseGeometry Center="100 100"
                                             RadiusX="50" RadiusY="50" />
                        </CombinedGeometry.Geometry1>
                        <CombinedGeometry.Geometry2>
                            <RectangleGeometry Rect="100 75 200 50" />
                        </CombinedGeometry.Geometry2>
                    </CombinedGeometry>
                </CombinedGeometry.Geometry1>
                <CombinedGeometry.Geometry2>
                    <EllipseGeometry Center="300 100"
                                     RadiusX="50" RadiusY="50" />
                </CombinedGeometry.Geometry2>
            </CombinedGeometry>
        </Path.Data>
    </Path>
</Canvas>
```

This image makes use of two nested *CombinedGeometry* objects. The first combines an ellipse and a rectangle; the second combines that *CombinedGeometry* with another ellipse. All three objects are combined with the *Union* mode.

It is with the *Geometry* derivative named *PathGeometry* that we really get into the central focus of this whole geometry system. A graphics path is a collection of straight lines and curves, some of which might or might not be connected to each other. Any set of connected lines and curves within the path is known as a *subpath*, or—to use the synonymous term consistent with the WPF classes—a *figure*. Thus, a path is composed of zero or more figures.

Each figure can be either *open* or *closed*. A figure is closed if the end of the last line in the figure is connected to the beginning of the first line. Otherwise, the figure is open. (Traditionally, an open path cannot be filled with a brush; in the WPF, filling is independent of closure.)

Here's the brief rundown: A *PathGeometry* object is a collection of one or more *PathFigure* objects. Each *PathFigure* is a collection of connected *PathSegment* objects. A *PathSegment* is a single straight line or curve.

Now for the details. The *PathGeometry* class defines a *FillRule* property that governs how figures in the path are filled, and a *Figures* property of type *PathFigureCollection*, which is the collection of *PathFigure* objects.

PathFigure derives from *Animatable* and is sealed. (That is, no other classes derive from *Path-Figure*.) *PathFigure* defines two Boolean properties named *IsClosed* and *IsFilled*. By default, *IsClosed* is *false*. If you set the property to *true*, the figure will be automatically closed. A straight line will be automatically added from the last point of the figure to the start point if necessary to close the figure. The default value of *IsFilled* is *true* and governs whether internal areas are colored with a brush. An area is filled *as if* the area is closed even if the area is not closed. (You encountered a similar concept in Chapter 27 in the way that *Polyline* fills areas.)

Remember that a figure is a series of connected straight lines and curves. The figure has to start at some particular point, and that point is the *StartPoint* property of *PathFigure*. *PathFig-ure* also defines a property named *Segments* of type *PathSegmentCollection*, which is a collection of *PathSegment* objects. *PathSegment* is an abstract class with seven derivatives. The following class hierarchy shows all the path-related classes:

Object

    DispatcherObject (abstract)

        DependencyObject

            Freezable (abstract)

                Animatable (abstract)

                    PathFigure

                    PathFigureCollection

                    PathSegment (abstract)

                        ArcSegment

                        BezierSegment

                        LineSegment

                        PolyBezierSegment

                        PolyLineSegment

                        PolyQuadraticBezierSegment

                        QuadraticBezierSegment

                  PathSegmentCollection

In summary, the *PathGeometry* class has a *Figures* property of type *PathFigureCollection*. The *PathFigure* class has a *Segments* property of type *PathSegmentCollection*.

For readers who have been wondering where Bézier curves have been hidden in the WPF graphics system, here they are. They come in two varieties: the normal cubic form and a faster quadratic variation. Here also are *arcs*, which are curves on the circumference of an ellipse. These are the *only* classes in WPF that explicitly support Bézier curves and arcs. Even if you're drawing graphics at the *DrawingContext* level (either in an *OnRender* method or by creating a *DrawingVisual* object), you don't have explicit Bézier or arc-drawing methods. Instead, you must draw Bézier curves or arcs using the *DrawGeometry* method or (more remotely) the *DrawDrawing* method.

The classes that derive from *PathSegment* also provide you with the only way to create *Geometry* objects that describe arbitrary polygons. You might be able to patch polygons together using *CombinedGeometry* and rotation, but you'd probably go insane in the process.

In any figure, the *PathFigure* object indicates the starting point of the figure in the *StartPoint* property. The *LineSegment* class therefore has only a single *Point* property that you set to the end point of a line. Here's a trivial path that consists of a single straight line.

TrivialPath.xaml

```
<!-- ==========================================
        TrivialPath.xaml (c) 2006 by Charles Petzold
     ========================================== -->
<Canvas xmlns="http://schemas.microsoft.com/winfx/2006/xaml/presentation"
        xmlns:x="http://schemas.microsoft.com/winfx/2006/xaml">

    <Path Stroke="Blue" StrokeThickness="3">
        <Path.Data>
            <PathGeometry>
                <PathFigure StartPoint="96 96">
                    <LineSegment Point="384 192" />
                </PathFigure>
            </PathGeometry>
        </Path.Data>
    </Path>
</Canvas>
```

To draw multiple connected straight lines, you can use multiple *LineSegment* objects. Each *LineSegment* object continues the figure with another segment that starts at the end of the previous segment. Here's a small XAML file that draws a five-pointed star with four *LineSegment* objects.

MultipleLineSegments.xaml

```
<!-- ==========================================
        MultipleLineSegments.xaml (c) 2006 by Charles Petzold
     ========================================== -->
<Canvas xmlns="http://schemas.microsoft.com/winfx/2006/xaml/presentation"
        xmlns:x="http://schemas.microsoft.com/winfx/2006/xaml">
```

```
    <Path Fill="Aqua" Stroke="Maroon" StrokeThickness="3">
        <Path.Data>
            <PathGeometry>
                <PathFigure StartPoint="144 72">
                    <LineSegment Point="200 246" />
                    <LineSegment Point="53 138" />
                    <LineSegment Point="235 138" />
                    <LineSegment Point="88 246" />
                </PathFigure>
            </PathGeometry>
        </Path.Data>
    </Path>
</Canvas>
```

The star drawn by this markup might appear a little strange. The five points of the star are filled and the center is not filled—which we might expect from the default *FillRule* of *EvenOdd*—but the line from the lower-left point to the top point is missing. And sure enough, if you look at the markup, you'll see that the four *LineSegment* objects draw only four lines. You can fix this problem and make the star appear more normal by including a fifth *LineSegment* object with the same point specified in *PathFigure*:

```
<LineSegment Point="144 72" />
```

Or, you can set the *IsClosed* property of the *PathFigure* to *true*:

```
<PathFigure StartPoint="144 72" IsClosed="True">
```

Setting *IsClosed* to *true* automatically creates an additional straight line back to the starting point. The existence of this last line does *not* govern whether an internal area is filled. Whether areas are filled is based on the *IsFilled* property of *PathFigure* (which is *true* by default) and the *FillRule* of the *Path* element (which is *EvenOdd* by default).

Another approach to drawing a series of connected straight lines is the *PolyLineSegment*. The *Points* property defined by *PolyLineSegment* is an object of type *PointCollection*, and as with the *Points* property defined by the *Polyline* element, you can set it to a string of multiple points in XAML. In this file I've explicitly set the *IsClosed* property of *PathFigure* to *true*:

PolyLineSegmentDemo.xaml

```
<!-- =====================================================
        PolyLineSegmentDemo.xaml (c) 2006 by Charles Petzold
     ===================================================== -->
<Canvas xmlns="http://schemas.microsoft.com/winfx/2006/xaml/presentation"
        xmlns:x="http://schemas.microsoft.com/winfx/2006/xaml">

    <Path Fill="Aqua" Stroke="Maroon" StrokeThickness="3">
        <Path.Data>
            <PathGeometry>
                <PathFigure StartPoint="144 72" IsClosed="True">
                    <PolyLineSegment Points="200 246, 53 138, 235 138, 88 246" />
                </PathFigure>
```

```
                </PathGeometry>
            </Path.Data>
        </Path>
    </Canvas>
```

If this *PathFigure* contained an additional segment following the *PolyLineSegment*, it would continue from the last point of the *PolyLineSegment*. The *PathFigure* element always defines the start of the figure. Each segment contains one or more points that continue the figure from the last preceding point.

Five classes define a *FillRule* property. Both the *Polyline* and *Polygon* elements in the Shapes library define one, as well as *GeometryGroup*, *PathGeometry*, and *StreamGeometry* (which is conceptually similar to *PathGeometry*). With *PathGeometry*, the *FillRule* property also governs how overlapping multiple figures in the geometry are filled. Here's an example that combines two overlapping stars in the same *PathGeometry*.

OverlappingStars.xaml

```
<!-- ===================================================
     OverlappingStars.xaml (c) 2006 by Charles Petzold
     =================================================== -->
<Canvas xmlns="http://schemas.microsoft.com/winfx/2006/xaml/presentation"
        xmlns:x="http://schemas.microsoft.com/winfx/2006/xaml">

    <Path Fill="Aqua" Stroke="Maroon" StrokeThickness="3">
        <Path.Data>
            <PathGeometry>
                <PathFigure StartPoint="144 72" IsClosed="True">
                    <PolyLineSegment Points="200 246, 53 138, 235 138, 88 246" />
                </PathFigure>
                <PathFigure StartPoint="168 96" IsClosed="True">
                    <PolyLineSegment Points="224 260, 77 162, 259 162, 112 270" />
                </PathFigure>
            </PathGeometry>
        </Path.Data>
    </Path>
</Canvas>
```

The second star is offset from the first by one-quarter inch horizontally and one-quarter inch vertically. You'll see that the two stars are taken together to determine whether internal areas are filled based on the default *FillRule* of *EvenOdd*. If you enclose that *PathGeometry* in a *GeometryGroup*, the *FillRule* setting on the *GeometryGroup* takes precedence and the *FillRule* setting on the *PathGeometry* is ignored. Both stars will still be analyzed together to determine filling. If you need overlapping paths to be filled independently of each other, put them in separate *Path* elements.

The *ArcSegment* class defines a curved line on the circumference of an ellipse—a concept that turns out to be a little more complex than it first appears. Like *LineSegment*, the *ArcSegment* element defines just one point, and an arc is drawn from the last preceding point to the point specified in the *ArcSegment* element. However, some additional information is required in the *ArcSegment* element. The curve that connects the two points is an arc on the circumference of an ellipse, so the two radii of that ellipse need to be supplied. In the simplest case, the two radii are equal and the curve that connects the two points is actually an arc on the circumference of a circle. Still, in general there are four ways that an arc of that circle can connect the two points. Which one you get is governed by the *SweepDirection* property of *ArcSegment*, which you set to either *Clockwise* or *Counterclockwise* (the default) and the Boolean *IsLargeArc* property (*false* by default). The four possible arcs are demonstrated in the following program with different colors.

ArcPossibilities.xaml

```
<!-- ===================================================
        ArcPossibilities.xaml (c) 2006 by Charles Petzold
     =================================================== -->
<Canvas xmlns="http://schemas.microsoft.com/winfx/2006/xaml/presentation"
        xmlns:x="http://schemas.microsoft.com/winfx/2006/xaml">

    <!-- Counterclockwise (default), small arc (default) -->

    <Path Stroke="Red" StrokeThickness="3">
        <Path.Data>
            <PathGeometry>
                <PathFigure StartPoint="144 144">
                    <ArcSegment Point="240 240" Size="96 96" />
                </PathFigure>
            </PathGeometry>
        </Path.Data>
    </Path>

    <!-- Counterclockwise (default), IsLargeArc -->

    <Path Stroke="Blue" StrokeThickness="3">
        <Path.Data>
            <PathGeometry>
                <PathFigure StartPoint="144 144">
                    <ArcSegment Point="240 240" Size="96 96"
                                IsLargeArc="True" />
                </PathFigure>
            </PathGeometry>
        </Path.Data>
    </Path>

    <!-- Clockwise, small arc (default) -->

    <Path Stroke="Green" StrokeThickness="3">
        <Path.Data>
            <PathGeometry>
                <PathFigure StartPoint="144 144">
                    <ArcSegment Point="240 240" Size="96 96"
                                SweepDirection="Clockwise" />
                </PathFigure>
            </PathGeometry>
        </Path.Data>
```

```
        </Path>

    <!-- Clockwise, IsLargeArc -->

    <Path Stroke="Purple" StrokeThickness="3">
        <Path.Data>
            <PathGeometry>
                <PathFigure StartPoint="144 144">
                    <ArcSegment Point="240 240" Size="96 96"
                                SweepDirection="Clockwise"
                                IsLargeArc="True" />
                </PathFigure>
            </PathGeometry>
        </Path.Data>
    </Path>
</Canvas>
```

Each of the four *Path* elements uses the same starting point of (144, 144) and *ArcSegment*
point of (240, 240). In all four cases the points are connected with an arc on the circumference of a circle with a radius of 96. But the four combinations of *SweepDirection* and *IsLargeArc*
draw four different arcs in four different colors.

And if this isn't enough flexibility for you, *ArcSegment* defines another property named *Rota-
tionAngle* that indicates the clockwise rotation of the ellipse whose circumference connects the
points. The following program is identical to ArcPossibilities.xaml except that it uses an ellipse
with a horizontal radius of 144 and a vertical radius of 96, rotated clockwise by 45 degrees.

ArcPossibilities2.xaml
```
<!-- =================================================
     ArcPossibilities2.xaml (c) 2006 by Charles Petzold
     ================================================= -->
<Canvas xmlns="http://schemas.microsoft.com/winfx/2006/xaml/presentation"
        xmlns:x="http://schemas.microsoft.com/winfx/2006/xaml">

    <!-- Counterclockwise (default), small arc (default) -->

    <Path Stroke="Red" StrokeThickness="3">
        <Path.Data>
            <PathGeometry>
                <PathFigure StartPoint="144 144">
                    <ArcSegment Point="240 240" Size="144 96"
                                RotationAngle="45" />
                </PathFigure>
            </PathGeometry>
        </Path.Data>
    </Path>

    <!-- Counterclockwise (default), IsLargeArc -->

    <Path Stroke="Blue" StrokeThickness="3">
        <Path.Data>
            <PathGeometry>
```

```
                    <PathFigure StartPoint="144 144">
                        <ArcSegment Point="240 240" Size="144 96"
                                    RotationAngle="45"
                                    IsLargeArc="True" />
                    </PathFigure>
                </PathGeometry>
            </Path.Data>
        </Path>

        <!-- Clockwise, small arc (default) -->

        <Path Stroke="Green" StrokeThickness="3">
            <Path.Data>
                <PathGeometry>
                    <PathFigure StartPoint="144 144">
                        <ArcSegment Point="240 240" Size="144 96"
                                    RotationAngle="45"
                                    SweepDirection="ClockWise" />
                    </PathFigure>
                </PathGeometry>
            </Path.Data>
        </Path>

        <!-- Clockwise, IsLargeArc -->

        <Path Stroke="Purple" StrokeThickness="3">
            <Path.Data>
                <PathGeometry>
                    <PathFigure StartPoint="144 144">
                        <ArcSegment Point="240 240" Size="144 96"
                                    RotationAngle="45"
                                    SweepDirection="ClockWise"
                                    IsLargeArc="True" />
                    </PathFigure>
                </PathGeometry>
            </Path.Data>
        </Path>
</Canvas>
```

The following program is closer to one that you'd find in real life. It draws something that might be a piece of an imaginary machine—an outline consisting of straight lines and arcs, and also a hole comprising two arc segments.

FigureWithArcs.xaml

```
<!-- =================================================
     FigureWithArcs.xaml (c) 2006 by Charles Petzold
     ================================================= -->
<Canvas xmlns="http://schemas.microsoft.com/winfx/2006/xaml/presentation"
        xmlns:x="http://schemas.microsoft.com/winfx/2006/xaml">

    <Path Fill="Aqua" Stroke="Maroon" StrokeThickness="3">
        <Path.Data>
            <PathGeometry>
```

```
                    <PathFigure StartPoint="192 192">
                        <ArcSegment Point="192 288" Size="48 48" />
                        <LineSegment Point="480 288" />
                        <ArcSegment Point="480 192" Size="48 48" />
                        <LineSegment Point="384 192" />
                        <ArcSegment Point="288 192" Size="48 48" />
                        <LineSegment Point="192 192" />
                    </PathFigure>
                    <PathFigure StartPoint="336 200" IsClosed="True">
                        <ArcSegment Point="336 176" Size="12 12" />
                        <ArcSegment Point="336 200" Size="12 12" />
                    </PathFigure>
                </PathGeometry>
            </Path.Data>
        </Path>
    </Canvas>
```

The second *PathFigure* effectively draws a circle by connecting two semicircle arcs.

Most of the terminology used in computer graphics comes from geometry. But in one case, an actual person's name has been enshrined in the names of graphics drawing functions.

Pierre Etienne Bézier was born in Paris in 1910 into a family of engineers. He received a degree in mechanical engineering in 1930 and a second degree in electrical engineering the following year. In 1933 he began working at the French automotive company Renault, where he remained until 1975. During the 1950s, Bézier was responsible for implementing some of the first drilling and milling machines that operated under *NC*—that is, *numerical control* (a term rarely used these days).

Beginning in 1960, much of Bézier's work was centered around the UNISURF program, an early CAD/CAM system used at Renault for interactively designing automobile parts. Such a system required mathematical definitions of complex curves that designers could manipulate without knowing about the underlying mathematics. These curves could then be used in manufacturing processes. From this work came the curve that now bears Bézier's name. Pierre Bézier died in 1999.

The Bézier curve is a *spline*, which is a curve used to approximate discrete data with a smooth continuous function. A single cubic Bézier curve is uniquely defined by four points, which can be labeled p_0, p_1, p_2, and p_3. The curve begins at p_0 and ends at p_3. Often p_0 is referred to as the *start point* (or *begin point*) of the curve and p_3 is referred to as the *end point*, but sometimes both points are collectively called *end points*. The points p_1 and p_2 are called *control points*. These two control points seem to function like magnets in pulling the curve toward them. Here's a simple Bézier curve showing the two end points and two control points.

Notice that the curve begins at p_0 by heading toward p_1, but then abandons that trip and instead heads toward p_2. Without touching p_2 either, the curve ends at p_3. Here's another Bézier curve:

Only rarely does the Bézier curve pass through the two control points. However, if you position both control points between the end points, the Bézier curve becomes a straight line and passes through them:

At the other extreme, it's even possible to choose points that make the Bézier curve do a little loop:

To draw a single Bézier curve you need four points. In the context of a *PathFigure*, the first point (p_0 in the diagrams) is provided by the *StartPoint* property of the *PathFigure* object or the last point of the preceding segment. The two control points and the end point are provided by the *Point1*, *Point2*, and *Point3* properties of the *BezierSegment* class. The numbering of these three properties agrees with the numbering I've used in the preceding diagrams.

Here's a small XAML program that produces a figure similar to the first Bézier diagram on the previous page.

```
SingleBezier.xaml
<!-- ===============================================
        SingleBezier.xaml (c) 2006 by Charles Petzold
     =============================================== -->
<Canvas xmlns="http://schemas.microsoft.com/winfx/2006/xaml/presentation"
        xmlns:x="http://schemas.microsoft.com/winfx/2006/xaml">
    <Path Fill="Red" Stroke="Blue" StrokeThickness="3">
        <Path.Data>
            <GeometryGroup>
                <PathGeometry>
                    <PathFigure x:Name="fig"
                                StartPoint="50 150" IsFilled="False" >
                        <BezierSegment
                            Point1="25 25" Point2="400 300" Point3="450 150" />
                    </PathFigure>
                </PathGeometry>

                <EllipseGeometry Center="{Binding ElementName=fig,
                                                  Path=StartPoint}"
                                 RadiusX="5" RadiusY="5" />

                <EllipseGeometry Center="{Binding ElementName=fig,
                                                  Path=Segments[0].Point1}"
                                 RadiusX="5" RadiusY="5" />

                <EllipseGeometry Center="{Binding ElementName=fig,
                                                  Path=Segments[0].Point2}"
                                 RadiusX="5" RadiusY="5" />

                <EllipseGeometry Center="{Binding ElementName=fig,
                                                  Path=Segments[0].Point3}"
                                 RadiusX="5" RadiusY="5" />
            </GeometryGroup>
        </Path.Data>
    </Path>
</Canvas>
```

To the actual Bézier curve I've also added four *EllipseGeometry* objects with bindings to display the end points and control points.

The Bézier spline has achieved much prominence in graphics programming for several reasons, all of which become evident when you experiment with the curves a bit. That's the purpose of the following BezierExperimenter project, which consists of a XAML file and a C# file.

The XAML file lays out a *Canvas* beginning with four *EllipseGeometry* objects. These display the four points that define the Bézier curve and they are given *x:Name* attributes that become variable names that the C# file uses to actually set the points.

BezierExperimenter.xaml

```
<!-- ====================================================
        BezierExperimenter.xaml (c) 2006 by Charles Petzold
     ==================================================== -->
<Window xmlns="http://schemas.microsoft.com/winfx/2006/xaml/presentation"
        xmlns:x="http://schemas.microsoft.com/winfx/2006/xaml"
        x:Class="Petzold.BezierExperimenter.BezierExperimenter"
        Title="Bezier Experimenter">
    <Canvas Name="canvas">

        <!-- Draw the four points defining the curve. -->

        <Path Fill="{DynamicResource
                            {x:Static SystemColors.WindowTextBrushKey}}">
            <Path.Data>
                <GeometryGroup>
                    <EllipseGeometry x:Name="ptStart" RadiusX="2" RadiusY="2" />
                    <EllipseGeometry x:Name="ptCtrl1" RadiusX="2" RadiusY="2" />
                    <EllipseGeometry x:Name="ptCtrl2" RadiusX="2" RadiusY="2" />
                    <EllipseGeometry x:Name="ptEnd" RadiusX="2" RadiusY="2" />
                </GeometryGroup>
            </Path.Data>
        </Path>

        <!-- Draw the curve itself. -->

        <Path Stroke="{DynamicResource
                            {x:Static SystemColors.WindowTextBrushKey}}">
            <Path.Data>
                <PathGeometry>
                    <PathGeometry.Figures>
                        <PathFigure StartPoint="{Binding ElementName=ptStart,
                                                    Path=Center}">
                            <BezierSegment Point1="{Binding ElementName=ptCtrl1,
                                                    Path=Center}"
                                           Point2="{Binding ElementName=ptCtrl2,
                                                    Path=Center}"
                                           Point3="{Binding ElementName=ptEnd,
                                                    Path=Center}" />
                        </PathFigure>
                    </PathGeometry.Figures>
                </PathGeometry>
            </Path.Data>
        </Path>

        <!-- Draw gray lines connecting end points and control points. -->
```

```
            <Path Stroke="{DynamicResource
                            {x:Static SystemColors.GrayTextBrushKey}}">
                <Path.Data>
                    <GeometryGroup>
                        <LineGeometry StartPoint="{Binding ElementName=ptStart,
                                                    Path=Center}"
                                      EndPoint="{Binding ElementName=ptCtrl1,
                                                    Path=Center}" />
                        <LineGeometry StartPoint="{Binding ElementName=ptEnd,
                                                    Path=Center}"
                                      EndPoint="{Binding ElementName=ptCtrl2,
                                                    Path=Center}" />
                    </GeometryGroup>
                </Path.Data>
            </Path>

            <!-- Display some labels with the actual points. -->

            <Label Canvas.Left="{Binding ElementName=ptStart, Path=Center.X}"
                   Canvas.Top="{Binding ElementName=ptStart, Path=Center.Y}"
                   Content="{Binding ElementName=ptStart, Path=Center}" />

            <Label Canvas.Left="{Binding ElementName=ptCtrl1, Path=Center.X}"
                   Canvas.Top="{Binding ElementName=ptCtrl1, Path=Center.Y}"
                   Content="{Binding ElementName=ptCtrl1, Path=Center}" />

            <Label Canvas.Left="{Binding ElementName=ptCtrl2, Path=Center.X}"
                   Canvas.Top="{Binding ElementName=ptCtrl2, Path=Center.Y}"
                   Content="{Binding ElementName=ptCtrl2, Path=Center}" />

            <Label Canvas.Left="{Binding ElementName=ptEnd, Path=Center.X}"
                   Canvas.Top="{Binding ElementName=ptEnd, Path=Center.Y}"
                   Content="{Binding ElementName=ptEnd, Path=Center}" />
        </Canvas>
</Window>
```

The *Canvas* continues with a bunch of bindings, all of which reference the *Center* properties of the first four *EllipseGeometry* objects. A *PathSegment* draws the actual Bézier curve, and two gray lines connect the two end points with the two control points. (You'll see the rationale behind this shortly.) Finally, some labels print the actual values of the points, just in case you find a nice Bézier curve you want to reuse in some XAML markup.

The C# portion of the program resets the four points whenever the size of the window changes.

BezierExperimenter.cs
```
//---------------------------------------------------
// BezierExperimenter.cs (c) 2006 by Charles Petzold
//---------------------------------------------------
using System;
using System.Windows;
using System.Windows.Controls;
using System.Windows.Input;
```

```csharp
using System.Windows.Media;

namespace Petzold.BezierExperimenter
{
    public partial class BezierExperimenter : Window
    {
        [STAThread]
        public static void Main()
        {
            Application app = new Application();
            app.Run(new BezierExperimenter());
        }
        public BezierExperimenter()
        {
            InitializeComponent();
            canvas.SizeChanged += CanvasOnSizeChanged;
        }
        // When the Canvas size changes, reset the four points.
        protected virtual void CanvasOnSizeChanged(object sender,
                                    SizeChangedEventArgs args)
        {
            ptStart.Center = new Point(args.NewSize.Width / 4,
                                args.NewSize.Height / 2);
            ptCtrl1.Center = new Point(args.NewSize.Width / 2,
                                args.NewSize.Height / 4);
            ptCtrl2.Center = new Point(args.NewSize.Width / 2,
                                3 * args.NewSize.Height / 4);
            ptEnd.Center = new Point(3 * args.NewSize.Width / 4,
                                args.NewSize.Height / 2);
        }
        // Change the control points based on mouse clicks and moves.
        protected override void OnMouseDown(MouseButtonEventArgs args)
        {
            base.OnMouseDown(args);
            Point pt = args.GetPosition(canvas);

            if (args.ChangedButton == MouseButton.Left)
                ptCtrl1.Center = pt;

            if (args.ChangedButton == MouseButton.Right)
                ptCtrl2.Center = pt;
        }
        protected override void OnMouseMove(MouseEventArgs args)
        {
            base.OnMouseMove(args);
            Point pt = args.GetPosition(canvas);

            if (args.LeftButton == MouseButtonState.Pressed)
                ptCtrl1.Center = pt;

            if (args.RightButton == MouseButtonState.Pressed)
                ptCtrl2.Center = pt;
        }
    }
}
```

The two end points are always fixed relative to the window. The left mouse button controls the first control point, and the right mouse button controls the second control point. As you experiment with this program, you'll find that with a little practice you can manipulate the curve into something close to the shape you want.

The Bézier spline is very well controlled. Some splines don't pass through any of the points that define them. The Bézier spline is always anchored at the two end points. (As you'll see, this is one of the assumptions used to derive the Bézier formulas.) Some forms of splines have singularities where the curve veers off into infinity—an effect rarely desired in computer-design work. The Bézier spline is much better behaved. In fact, the Bézier curve is always bounded by a four-sided polygon (called a *convex hull*) that is formed by connecting the end points and the control points. (The way in which you connect the end points and the control points to form this convex hull depends on the particular curve.)

At the start point, the curve is always tangential to and in the same direction as a straight line drawn from the start point to the first control point. (This relationship is visually illustrated in the BezierExperimenter program.) At the end point, the curve is always tangential to and in the same direction as a straight line drawn from the second control point to the end point. These are actually two assumptions used to derive the Bézier formulas.

Apart from the mathematical characteristics, the Bézier curve is often aesthetically pleasing, which is the *primary* reason that it's found such extensive applications in computer-design work.

You can define multiple connected Bézier splines by setting the *Points* property of the *PolyBezierSegment* element. Although there are no restrictions on the number of points *PolyBezierSegment* is given, it really only makes sense if the number of points is a multiple of three. The first and second points are control points, and the third point is the end point. The third point is also the start point of the second Bézier curve (if any), and the fourth and fifth points are control points for that second Bézier.

Although connected Bézier curves share end points, it's possible that the point at which one curve ends and the next one begins won't be smooth. Mathematically, the composite curve is considered smooth only if the first derivative of the curve is continuous—that is, it doesn't make any sudden changes.

When you draw multiple Bézier curves, you might want the resultant composite curve to be smooth where one curve ends and the next one begins. Then again, you might not. It depends on what you're drawing. If you want two connected Bézier curves to join each other smoothly, the second control point of the first Bézier, the end point of the first Bézier (which is also the start point of the second Bézier), and the first control point of the second Bézier must be colinear—that is, lie on the same line.

Here's a little XAML file that demonstrates a standard technique to simulate a circle with four connected Bézier splines. These end points and control points have the colinearity required for a smooth curve.

SimulatedCircle.xaml

```
<!-- =================================================
        SimulatedCircle.xaml (c) 2006 by Charles Petzold
     ================================================= -->
<Canvas xmlns="http://schemas.microsoft.com/winfx/2006/xaml/presentation"
        xmlns:x="http://schemas.microsoft.com/winfx/2006/xaml">

    <Path Canvas.Left="150" Canvas.Top="150" Stroke="Black">
        <Path.Data>
            <PathGeometry>
                <PathGeometry.Figures>
                    <PathFigure StartPoint="0 100">
                        <PolyBezierSegment
                            Points="  55  100,  100   55,  100    0
                                     100  -55,   55 -100,    0 -100
                                     -55 -100, -100  -55, -100    0
                                    -100   55,  -55  100,    0  100" />
                    </PathFigure>
                </PathGeometry.Figures>
            </PathGeometry>
        </Path.Data>
    </Path>
</Canvas>
```

The simulated circle as defined by the *Points* array has a radius of 100 and is centered around the point (0, 0). The *Left* and *Top* attached properties of *Canvas* move the *Path* to a more visible location. The following program is a little variation of the simulated circle and draws an infinity sign with a linear gradient brush.

Infinity.xaml

```
<!-- =============================================
        Infinity.xaml (c) 2006 by Charles Petzold
     ============================================= -->
<Canvas xmlns="http://schemas.microsoft.com/winfx/2006/xaml/presentation"
        xmlns:x="http://schemas.microsoft.com/winfx/2006/xaml">

    <Path Canvas.Left="150" Canvas.Top="150" StrokeThickness="25">
        <Path.Stroke>
            <LinearGradientBrush>
                <LinearGradientBrush.GradientStops>
                    <GradientStop Offset="0.00" Color="Red" />
                    <GradientStop Offset="0.16" Color="Orange" />
                    <GradientStop Offset="0.33" Color="Yellow" />
                    <GradientStop Offset="0.50" Color="Green" />
                    <GradientStop Offset="0.67" Color="Blue" />
                    <GradientStop Offset="0.84" Color="Indigo" />
                    <GradientStop Offset="1.00" Color="Violet" />
                </LinearGradientBrush.GradientStops>
            </LinearGradientBrush>
        </Path.Stroke>
        <Path.Data>
            <PathGeometry>
```

```
                <PathGeometry.Figures>
                    <PathFigure StartPoint="0 -100">
                        <PolyBezierSegment
                            Points=" -55 -100, -100  -55, -100    0,
                                    -100   55,  -55  100,    0  100,
                                      55  100,  100   50,  150    0,
                                     200  -50,  245 -100,  300 -100,
                                     355 -100,  400  -55,  400    0,
                                     400   55,  355  100,  300  100,
                                     245  100,  200   50,  150    0,
                                     100  -50,   55 -100,    0 -100" />
                    </PathFigure>
                </PathGeometry.Figures>
            </PathGeometry>
        </Path.Data>
    </Path>
</Canvas>
```

It's sometimes helpful to know the underlying mathematics that a graphics system uses to render particular curves, and even to actually derive the curves, if only so that you don't think the formulas just fell out of the sky one day.

The cubic form of the Bézier spline is uniquely defined by four points, which I've called p_0 (the begin point), p_1 and p_2 (the two control points), and p_3 (the end point). These four points can also be denoted as (x_0, y_0), (x_1, y_1), (x_2, y_2), and (x_3, y_3).

The general parametric form of a cubic polynomial in two dimensions is:

$$x(t) = a_x \cdot t^3 + b_x \cdot t^2 + c_x \cdot t + d_x$$

$$y(t) = a_y \cdot t^3 + b_y \cdot t^2 + c_y \cdot t + d_y$$

where a_x, b_x, c_x, d_x, a_y, b_y, c_y, and d_y are constants, and t ranges from 0 to 1. Every Bézier spline is uniquely defined by these eight constants. The constants are dependent on the four points that define the curve. The object of this exercise is to derive the values of the eight constants in terms of the four points.

The first assumption is that the Bézier spline begins at the point (x_0, y_0) when t equals 0:

$$x(0) = x_0$$

$$y(0) = y_0$$

Even with this simple assumption we can make some headway in deriving the constants. If you put a 0 value for t in the parametric equations, you get:

$$x(0) = d_x$$

$$y(0) = d_y$$

That means that two of the constants are simply the coordinates of the start point:

$$d_x = x_0 \tag{1a}$$

$$d_y = y_0 \tag{1b}$$

The second assumption regarding the Bézier spline is that it ends at the point (x_3, y_3) when t equals 1:

$$x(1) = x_3$$

$$y(1) = y_3$$

Substituting a value of 1 for t in the parametric equations yields the following:

$$x(1) = a_x + b_x + c_x + d_x$$

$$y(1) = a_y + b_y + c_y + d_y$$

This means that the constants relate to the coordinate of the end point like so:

$$a_x + b_x + c_x + d_x = x_3 \tag{2a}$$

$$a_y + b_y + c_y + d_y = y_3 \tag{2b}$$

The remaining two assumptions involve the first derivative of the parametric equations, which describe the slope of the curve. The first derivatives of the generalized parametric equations of a cubic polynomial with respect to t are:

$$x'(t) = 3a_x t^2 + 2b_x t + c_x$$

$$y'(t) = 3a_y t^2 + 2b_y t + c_y$$

In particular we're interested in the slope of the curve at the two end points. At the start point the Bézier curve is tangential to and in the same direction as a straight line drawn from the start point to the first control point. That straight line would normally be defined by the parametric equations:

$$x(t) = (x_1 - x_0)t + x_0$$

$$y(t) = (y_1 - y_0)t + y_0$$

for t ranging from 0 to 1. However, another way of expressing this straight line would be the parametric equations:

$$x(t) = 3(x_1 - x_0)t + x_0$$

$$y(t) = 3(y_1 - y_0)t + y_0$$

where t ranges from 0 to 1/3. Why 1/3? Because the section of the Bézier curve that is tangential to and in the same direction as the straight line from p_0 to p_1 is roughly 1/3 of the total Bézier curve. Here are the first derivatives of those revised parametric equations:

$$x'(t) = 3(x_1 - x_0)$$

$$y'(t) = 3(y_1 - y_0)$$

We want these equations to represent the slope of the Bézier spline when t equals 0, so:

$$x'(0) = 3(x_1 - x_0)$$

$$y'(0) = 3(y_1 - y_0)$$

Substitute 0 for t in the generalized cube first derivatives and you get:

$$x'(0) = c_x$$

$$y'(0) = c_y$$

That means

$$c_x = 3(x_1 - x_0) \tag{3a}$$

$$c_y = 3(y_1 - y_0) \tag{3b}$$

The final assumption is that at the end points, the Bézier curve is tangential to and in the same direction as a straight line from the second control point to the end point. In other words

$$x'(1) = 3(x_3 - x_2)$$

$$y'(1) = 3(y_3 - y_2)$$

Since we know from the generalized formulas that

$$x'(1) = 3a_x + 2b_x + c_x$$

$$y'(1) = 3a_y + 2b_y + c_y$$

Then

$$3a_x + 2b_x + c_x = 3(x_3 - x_2) \tag{4a}$$

$$3a_y + 2b_y + c_y = 3(y_3 - y_2) \tag{4b}$$

Equations 1a, 2a, 3a, and 4a provide four equations and four unknowns that let you solve for a_x, b_x, c_x, and d_x in terms of x_0, x_1, x_2, and x_3. Go through the algebra and you'll find:

$$a_x = -x_0 + 3x_1 - 3x_2 + x_3$$

$$b_x = 3x_0 - 6x_1 + 3x_2$$

$$c_x = 3x_0 + 3x_1$$

$$d_x = x_0$$

Equations 1b, 2b, 3b, and 4b let us do the same for the y coefficients. We can then put the constants back into the generalized cubic parametric equations:

$$x(t) = (-x_0 + 3x_1 - 3x_2 + x_3)t^3 + (3x_0 - 6x_1 + 3x_2)t^2 + (3x_0 + 3x_1)t + x_0$$

$$y(t) = (-y_0 + 3y_1 - 3y_2 + y_3)t^3 + (3y_0 - 6y_1 + 3y_2)t^2 + (3y_0 + 3y_1)t + y_0$$

We're basically done. However, it's much more common for the terms to be rearranged to yield the more elegant and easier-to-use parametric equations:

$$x(t) = (1-t)^3 x_0 + 3t(1-t)^2 x_1 + 3t^2(1-t)x_2 + t^3 x_3$$

$$y(t) = (1-t)^3 y_0 + 3t(1-t)^2 y_1 + 3t^2(1-t)y_2 + t^3 xy_3$$

These equations are the customary form in which the Bézier spline is expressed. Each point on the curve is a weighted average of the four points that define the curve. It's fairly easy to demonstrate that the equations I've derived match the algorithm that the WPF uses. The BezierReproduce project includes both BezierExperimenter.xaml and BezierExperimenter.cs and the following file, which includes a class that inherits from BezierExperimenter to draw a blue *Polyline* with calculated points for the Bézier spline.

BezierReproduce.cs

```
//-----------------------------------------------
// BezierReproduce.cs (c) 2006 by Charles Petzold
//-----------------------------------------------
using System;
using System.Windows;
using System.Windows.Controls;
using System.Windows.Input;
using System.Windows.Media;
using System.Windows.Shapes;

namespace Petzold.BezierReproduce
{
    public class BezierReproduce : Petzold.BezierExperimenter.BezierExperimenter
    {
        Polyline bezier;
```

```
        [STAThread]
        public new static void Main()
        {
            Application app = new Application();
            app.Run(new BezierReproduce());
        }
        public BezierReproduce()
        {
            Title = "Bezier Reproduce";

            bezier = new Polyline();
            bezier.Stroke = Brushes.Blue;
            canvas.Children.Add(bezier);
        }
        protected override void CanvasOnSizeChanged(object sender,
                                    SizeChangedEventArgs args)
        {
            base.CanvasOnSizeChanged(sender, args);
            DrawBezierManually();
        }
        protected override void OnMouseDown(MouseButtonEventArgs args)
        {
            base.OnMouseDown(args);
            DrawBezierManually();
        }
        protected override void OnMouseMove(MouseEventArgs args)
        {
            base.OnMouseMove(args);
            DrawBezierManually();
        }
        void DrawBezierManually()
        {
            Point[] pts = new Point[10];

            for (int i = 0; i < pts.Length; i++)
            {
                double t = (double)i / (pts.Length - 1);

                double x = (1 - t) * (1 - t) * (1 - t) * ptStart.Center.X +
                           3 * t * (1 - t) * (1 - t) * ptCtrl1.Center.X +
                           3 * t * t * (1 - t) * ptCtrl2.Center.X +
                           t * t * t * ptEnd.Center.X;

                double y = (1 - t) * (1 - t) * (1 - t) * ptStart.Center.Y +
                           3 * t * (1 - t) * (1 - t) * ptCtrl1.Center.Y +
                           3 * t * t * (1 - t) * ptCtrl2.Center.Y +
                           t * t * t * ptEnd.Center.Y;

                pts[i] = new Point(x, y);
            }
            bezier.Points = new PointCollection(pts);
        }
    }
}
```

Although the blue *Polyline* has only ten points—it really looks more like a polyline than a curve—the match is very good.

The Windows Presentation Foundation also supports a so-called quadratic Bézier curve, which has one control point rather than two. When drawing many curves, the quadratic curve is more efficient than the cubic Bézier. The *QuadraticBezierSegment* class has a *Point1* property, which is the control point, and *Point2*, which is the end point. The *PolyQuadraticBezierSegment* class has a *Points* property that makes sense only when set to an even number of points—alternating control points and end points.

If the beginning point of the quadratic spline is (x_0, y_0), the control point is (x_1, y_1), and the end point is (x_2, y_2), the parametric formulas for the quadratic Bézier are

$$x(t) = (1-t)^2 x_0 + 2t(1-t)x_1 + t^2 x_2$$

$$y(t) = (1-t)^2 y_0 + 2t(1-t)y_1 + t^2 y_2$$

How different is this curve from a cubic Bézier when both control points of the cubic Bézier are the same and equal to the single control point of the quadratic Bézier? The quadratic Bézier is roughly the average between the cubic Bézier and a straight line connecting the end points. It's actually possible to convince yourself of this relationship without looking at any curves!

Consider a straight line between (x_0, y_0) and (x_2, y_2). What is the midpoint of that line? It's this:

$$x_{mid} = \frac{x_0}{2} + \frac{x_2}{2}$$

$$y_{mid} = \frac{y_0}{2} + \frac{y_2}{2}$$

What is the midpoint of the quadratic Bézier curve that begins and ends at the same point with a control point of (x_1, y_1)? Substitute 0.5 for t in the quadratic formulas and you get

$$x_{mid} = \frac{x_0}{4} + \frac{x_1}{2} + \frac{x_2}{4}$$

and similarly for y. It's a weighted average of the three points. Substitute 0.5 for t in the cubic Bézier formulas—and adjust the terminology so the two control points are both (x_1, y_1), and the end point is (x_2, y_2)—and you'll derive

$$x_{mid} = \frac{x_0}{8} + \frac{3x_1}{4} + \frac{x_2}{8}$$

The cubic Bézier places a greater weight on the control point and lesser weight on the end points than the quadratic curve. The average of the midpoint of the cubic Bézier and the straight line is

$$x_{mid} = \frac{5x_0}{16} + \frac{3x_1}{8} + \frac{5x_2}{16}$$

That's close to the midpoint of the quadratic curve.

Now that you have been introduced to all the *PathSegment* derivatives, it's time to unveil the *path mini-language* (more officially known as the *PathGeometry* Markup Syntax), which is a string encompassing all the types of path segments. You can set this string directly to the *Data* attribute of *Path* and any other property of type *Geometry* that you might encounter in other elements.

Let's look at a little example first.

```
PathMiniLanguage.xaml
<!-- =================================================
        PathMiniLanguage.xaml (c) 2006 by Charles Petzold
     ================================================= -->
<Canvas xmlns="http://schemas.microsoft.com/winfx/2006/xaml/presentation"
        xmlns:x="http://schemas.microsoft.com/winfx/2006/xaml">

    <Path Fill="Aqua" Stroke="Magenta" StrokeThickness="3"
          Data="M 50 75 L 250 75, 250 275, 50 275 Z" />

</Canvas>
```

The mini-language alternates letter commands with numeric parameters. The *M* stands for *move*, and it's the equivalent of the *StartPoint* property of *PathFigure*. The point is (50, 75). The *L* is *line*, of course—the three points that follow the *L* cause lines to be drawn from (50, 75) to (250, 75) to (250, 275) to (50, 275). The *Z* at the end doesn't stand for anything, except that as the last letter of the alphabet, it serves to close the figure (which is a 200-unit square). Another *M* command can follow to begin a new figure, or a new figure can implicitly begin at (50, 75), which is considered to be the last point of the figure after the figure is closed. New figures always begin with *M* or implicitly begin after a *Z*.

The *H* and *V* commands draw horizontal and vertical lines, respectively, to the specified coordinate. The same square could be drawn like this:

```
Data="M 50 75 H 250 V 275 H 50 Z"
```

Lowercase letters generally do the same thing as their uppercase counterparts, except relatively rather than absolutely. This string also creates the same square, but the numbers following *h* and *v* indicate lengths rather than coordinates:

```
Data="M 50 75 h 200 v 200 h -200 Z"
```

The line-drawing command also comes in a relative version:

```
Data="M 50 75 l 200 0, 0 200, -200 0 Z"
```

If you want to set the *FillRule* to *NonZero* rather than the default *EvenOdd*, you need to include an *F1* at the very beginning. (*F0* just means the default.)

The complete mini-language is described in the following table. In this table, the point (x_0, y_0) is the current point, which is initially the point set by the *move* command, and subsequently is the last point of the previous drawing command.

Command	Name	Description
$F\ i$	Fill Rule	$i=0$: EvenOdd.
		$i=1$: NonZero.
$M\ x\ y$	Move	Move to (x, y).
$m\ x\ y$	Relative move	Move to (x_0+x, y_0+y).
$L\ x\ y$	Line	Draw line to (x, y).
$l\ x\ y$	Relative line	Draw line to (x_0+x, y_0+y).
$H\ x$	Horizontal line	Draw line to (x, y_0).
$h\ x$	Relative horizontal line	Draw line to (x_0+x, y_0).
$V\ y$	Vertical line	Draw line to (x_0, y).
$v\ y$	Relative vertical line	Draw line to (x_0, y_0+y).
$A\ x_r\ y_r\ a\ i\ j\ x\ y$	Arc	Draw arc to (x, y) based on ellipse with radii (x_r, y_r) rotated a degrees. $i=1$: IsLargeArc. $j=1$: Clockwise.
$a\ x_r\ y_r\ a\ i\ j\ x\ y$	Relative arc	Draw arc to (x_0+x, y_0+y).
$C\ x_1\ y_1\ x_2\ y_2\ x_3\ y_3$	Cubic Bézier	Draw Bézier to (x_3, y_3) with control points (x_1, y_1) and (x_2, y_2).
$c\ x_1\ y_1\ x_2\ y_2\ x_3\ y_3$	Relative cubic Bézier	Draw Bézier to (x_0+x_3, y_0+y_3) with control points (x_0+x_1, y_0+y_1) and (x_0+x_2, y_0+y_2).
$S\ x_2\ y_2\ x_3\ y_3$	Smooth cubic Bézier	Draw Bézier to (x_3, y_3) with reflected control point and (x_2, y_2).
$s\ x_2\ y_2\ x_3\ y_3$	Relative smooth cubic Bézier	Draw Bézier to (x_0+x_3, y_0+y_3) with reflected control point and (x_0+x_2, y_0+y_2).
$Q\ x_1\ y_1\ x_2\ y_2$	Quadratic Bézier	Draw quadratic Bézier to (x_2, y_2) with control point (x_1, y_1).
$q\ x_1\ y_1\ x_2\ y_2$	Relative quadratic Bézier	Draw quadratic Bézier to (x_0+x_2, y_0+y_2) with control point (x_0+x_1, y_0+y_1).
Z	Close figure	
z		

The smooth cubic Bézier ensures that the curve is connected smoothly to the previous curve by calculating the first control point. Thus the start point of the Bézier curve is the midpoint of a straight line from the second control point of the previous Bézier curve to the calculated point. That's ideal for the infinity sign, as demonstrated here.

```
MiniLanguageInfinity.xaml
<!-- ====================================================
        MiniLanguageInfinity.xaml (c) 2006 by Charles Petzold
     ==================================================== -->
<Canvas xmlns="http://schemas.microsoft.com/winfx/2006/xaml/presentation"
        xmlns:x="http://schemas.microsoft.com/winfx/2006/xaml">

    <Path Canvas.Left="150" Canvas.Top="150" Stroke="Black"
        Data="M 0 -100
                C -55 -100, -100  -55, -100    0
                S -55  100,    0  100
                S 100   50,  150    0
                S 245 -100,  300 -100
                S 400  -55,  400    0
                S 355  100,  300  100
                S 200   50,  150    0
                S  55 -100,    0 -100" />
</Canvas>
```

You use geometries not only for drawing but for clipping. *UIElement* defines a property named *Clip* of type *Geometry* that you can set to any *Geometry* object, or you can set *Clip* directly to a path mini-language string directly in XAML. Any part of the geometry that would not normally be filled if the geometry were being drawn is not displayed by the element.

For example, the following XAML file sets the *Clip* property of a button to a mini-language string that defines four arcs. The first two effectively define an ellipse the width and height of the button, and the second defines a little circle within that ellipse.

```
ClippedButton.xaml
<!-- ===============================================
        ClippedButton.xaml (c) 2006 by Charles Petzold
     =============================================== -->
<Grid xmlns="http://schemas.microsoft.com/winfx/2006/xaml/presentation"
      xmlns:x="http://schemas.microsoft.com/winfx/2006/xaml">

    <Button HorizontalAlignment="Center" VerticalAlignment="Center"
            FontSize="24" Width="200" Height="100"
            Clip="M  0 50 A 100 50 0 0 0 200 50
                        A 100 50 0 0 0   0 50
                 M 90 50 A  10 10 0 0 0 110 50
                        A  10 10 0 0 0  90 50" >
        Clipped Button
    </Button>

</Grid>
```

The following program displays a famous image from the NASA Web site and clips it to an outline of a keyhole.

KeyholeOnTheMoon.xaml

```
<!-- =================================================
     KeyholeOnTheMoon.xaml (c) 2006 by Charles Petzold
     ================================================= -->
<Page xmlns="http://schemas.microsoft.com/winfx/2006/xaml/presentation"
      xmlns:x="http://schemas.microsoft.com/winfx/2006/xaml">

    <Image Source="http://images.jsc.nasa.gov/lores/AS11-40-5903.jpg"
           Clip="M 300 130 L 250 350 L 450 350 L 400 130 A 70 70 0 1 0 300 130"
           Stretch="None" />
</Page>
```

The outlines of the fonts that we use under Windows are defined by cubic and quadratic Bézier curves. Displayable font characters are created from these curves in a process called *rasterization*. These curves are not used blindly in this process, however. The font files contain "hints" so that rounding errors inherent in rasterization do not make the font characters unreadable at the small sizes common on video displays.

It's possible, however, to obtain font character outlines in the form of unhinted geometries. You can then use these outlines for certain graphical techniques that might not be possible otherwise.

You'll recall the *FormattedText* class, I hope. You use that class to prepare text for the *DrawText* method of the *DrawingContext* class. That class has a *BuildGeometry* method that returns an object of type *Geometry* containing the character outlines of the text. However, some problems exist with using the *FormattedText* class directly in XAML. You could certainly create a *FormattedText* object as a resource, but *BuildGeometry* is a method rather than a property, so it wouldn't be accessible by XAML elements.

Another approach you might consider is creating a class that derives from *Geometry*. Such a class could be used wherever any other *Geometry* derivative appears. This, too, is impossible. Not enough information is documented to successfully inherit from *Geometry* itself, and all the other classes that inherit from *Geometry* are sealed.

After encountering these obstacles I wrote the following simple class that has properties that parallel the arguments required for the *FormattedText* constructor, and another property named *Geometry* that calls the *BuildGeometry* method on the *FormattedText* object.

TextGeometry.cs

```
//-----------------------------------------------
// TextGeometry.cs (c) 2006 by Charles Petzold
//-----------------------------------------------
using System;
using System.Globalization;
using System.Windows;
using System.Windows.Media;
```

```
namespace Petzold.TextGeometryDemo
{
    public class TextGeometry
    {
        // Private fields backing public properties.
        string txt = "";
        FontFamily fntfam = new FontFamily();
        FontStyle fntstyle = FontStyles.Normal;
        FontWeight fntwt = FontWeights.Normal;
        FontStretch fntstr = FontStretches.Normal;
        double emsize = 24;
        Point ptOrigin = new Point(0, 0);

        // Public Properties.
        public string Text
        {
            set { txt = value; }
            get { return txt; }
        }
        public FontFamily FontFamily
        {
            set { fntfam = value; }
            get { return fntfam; }
        }
        public FontStyle FontStyle
        {
            set { fntstyle = value; }
            get { return fntstyle; }
        }
        public FontWeight FontWeight
        {
            set { fntwt = value; }
            get { return fntwt; }
        }
        public FontStretch FontStretch
        {
            set { fntstr = value; }
            get { return fntstr; }
        }
        public double FontSize
        {
            set { emsize = value; }
            get { return emsize; }
        }
        public Point Origin
        {
            set { ptOrigin = value; }
            get { return ptOrigin; }
        }

        // Public read-only property to return Geometry object.
        public Geometry Geometry
        {
            get
            {
```

```
                        FormattedText formtxt =
                            new FormattedText(Text, CultureInfo.CurrentCulture,
                                               FlowDirection.LeftToRight,
                                               new Typeface(FontFamily, FontStyle,
                                                            FontWeight, FontStretch),
                                               FontSize, Brushes.Black);

                        return formtxt.BuildGeometry(Origin);
                    }
                }

                // Required for animations using paths.
                public PathGeometry PathGeometry
                {
                    get
                    {
                        return PathGeometry.CreateFromGeometry(Geometry);
                    }
                }


            }
        }
```

This class certainly isn't very sophisticated. It doesn't have any dependency properties, but all I really wanted (for the moment) was something I could create as a resource and assign various properties. Then I could use the *Geometry* property as a one-time binding source.

The XAML file that makes use of this class is shown next. Sure enough, it creates two *TextGeometry* objects as resources. One contains the word "Hollow" and the other contains the word "Shadow," both with a 144-point Times New Roman Bold font.

TextGeometryWindow.xaml

```
<!-- ===================================================
         TextGeometryWindow.xaml (c) 2006 by Charles Petzold
     =================================================== -->
<Window xmlns="http://schemas.microsoft.com/winfx/2006/xaml/presentation"
        xmlns:x="http://schemas.microsoft.com/winfx/2006/xaml"
        xmlns:src="clr-namespace:Petzold.TextGeometryDemo"
        Title="TextGeometry Demo">
    <Window.Resources>
        <src:TextGeometry x:Key="txtHollow" Text="Hollow"
                          FontFamily="Times New Roman"
                          FontSize="192" FontWeight="Bold" />

        <src:TextGeometry x:Key="txtShadow" Text="Shadow"
                          FontFamily="Times New Roman"
                          FontSize="192" FontWeight="Bold" />
    </Window.Resources>


    <TabControl>
        <TabItem Header="Hollow">
            <Path Stroke="Blue" StrokeThickness="5"
```

```
                Data="{Binding Source={StaticResource txtHollow},
                              Path=Geometry}" />
     </TabItem>

     <TabItem Header="Dotted">
         <Path Stroke="Blue" StrokeThickness="5"
             StrokeDashArray="{Binding Source={x:Static DashStyles.Dot},
                                     Path=Dashes}"
             StrokeDashCap="Round"
             Data="{Binding Source={StaticResource txtHollow},
                           Path=Geometry}" />
     </TabItem>

     <TabItem Header="Shadow">
         <Canvas>
             <Path Fill="DarkGray"
                   Data="{Binding Source={StaticResource txtShadow},
                                 Path=Geometry}"
                   Canvas.Left="12" Canvas.Top="12" />
             <Path Stroke="Black" Fill="White"
                   Data="{Binding Source={StaticResource txtShadow},
                                 Path=Geometry}" />
         </Canvas>
     </TabItem>
   </TabControl>
</Window>
```

The window contains a *TabControl* with three tabs that reveal what the program does with the *Geometry* property of the *TextGeometry* objects. The first *TabItem* simply strokes the path with a blue brush. It sounds simple, but it creates outlined font characters, which as far as I know aren't available in WPF any other way.

The second *TabItem* does something similar but draws the outline with a dotted line. The third *TabItem* draws text with a drop shadow, but the foreground text has a white interior and is outlined with black. The following application-definition file completes the project.

TextGeometryApp.xaml

```
<!-- ===============================================
     TextGeometryApp.xaml (c) 2006 by Charles Petzold
     =============================================== -->
<Application xmlns="http://schemas.microsoft.com/winfx/2006/xaml/presentation"
             StartupUri="TextGeometryWindow.xaml" />
```

When you use these text outlines, it's important to keep the text reasonably large. Remember that these are only the bare, unhinted outlines, and they will degenerate considerably at smaller sizes.

Chapter 29
Graphics Transforms

In Chapter 27, I showed you a couple of XAML files that displayed the same *Polygon* figure with two different *FillMode* settings. Rather than having different sets of coordinate points in the two *Polygon* elements, I defined the coordinate points just once in a *Style* element. The two different figures were then displayed in two different parts of the *Canvas* with different *Canvas.Left* properties. These properties effectively provided offsets to the *X* and *Y* coordinates in the *Polygon*. Toward the end of Chapter 28 I did something similar for a program that applied a drop shadow to a text string.

While it's sometimes convenient to use *Canvas.Left* and *Canvas.Top* for this purpose, it's also beneficial to have a more generalized and systematic approach to changing all the coordinate points of a particular graphical object. These approaches are called *transforms*. Not only is it useful to *offset* coordinate points, but sometimes the need arises to make a figure larger or smaller, or even to rotate it, and the transforms do that as well.

Transforms are particularly useful when animation is involved. Suppose you want to move a *Polygon* from one location to another. Does it make more sense to animate all the coordinate points in the same way, or to animate only a translation factor that is applied to the whole figure? Certain techniques, particularly those involving rotation, are not easy at all without the help of transforms.

You can apply a transform to any object that derives from *UIElement*. *UIElement* defines a property named *RenderTransform* that you set to an object of type *Transform*. Search a little further and you'll find that *FrameworkElement* defines its own property of type *Transform*. This property is called *LayoutTransform*. One of the primary objectives of this chapter is to help you to understand the difference between *RenderTransform* and *LayoutTransform*, and when to use which.

The *RenderTransform* and *LayoutTransform* properties are similar in that they are both of type *Transform*. You can see the abstract *Transform* class and its derivatives in this class hierarchy:

Object

    DispatcherObject (abstract)

        DependencyObject

            Freezable (abstract)

                Animatable (abstract)

                    GeneralTransform (abstract)

                        GeneralTransformGroup

$$\textit{Transform (abstract)}$$

$$\textit{TranslateTransform}$$

$$\textit{ScaleTransform}$$

$$\textit{SkewTransform}$$

$$\textit{RotateTransform}$$

$$\textit{MatrixTransform}$$

$$\textit{TransformGroup}$$

I have arranged the derivatives of *Transform* in the order in which I cover them in this chapter. Also of great importance is the *Matrix* structure. *Matrix* will remain behind the scenes for much of this chapter, but eventually emerge as an important data structure in its own right.

Of the classes that derive from *Transform*, four are quite easy to use: *TranslateTransform*, *ScaleTransform*, *SkewTransform*, and *RotateTransform*. They provide an easy way to alter the location or appearance of an element, as this stand-alone XAML file demonstrates:

TransformedButtons.xaml

```
<!-- =====================================================
        TransformedButtons.xaml (c) 2006 by Charles Petzold
     ===================================================== -->
<Canvas xmlns="http://schemas.microsoft.com/winfx/2006/xaml/presentation"
        xmlns:x="http://schemas.microsoft.com/winfx/2006/xaml">

    <Button Canvas.Left="50" Canvas.Top="100">
        Untransformed
    </Button>

    <Button Canvas.Left="200" Canvas.Top="100">
        Translated
        <Button.RenderTransform>
            <TranslateTransform X="-100" Y="150" />
        </Button.RenderTransform>
    </Button>

    <Button Canvas.Left="350" Canvas.Top="100">
        Scaled
        <Button.RenderTransform>
            <ScaleTransform ScaleX="1.5" ScaleY="4" />
        </Button.RenderTransform>
    </Button>

    <Button Canvas.Left="500" Canvas.Top="100">
        Skewed
        <Button.RenderTransform>
            <SkewTransform AngleY="20" />
        </Button.RenderTransform>
    </Button>
```

```
    <Button Canvas.Left="650" Canvas.Top="100">
        Rotated
        <Button.RenderTransform>
            <RotateTransform Angle="-30" />
        </Button.RenderTransform>
    </Button>
</Canvas>
```

Without the transforms, these five buttons would sit in a simple row across the window. The second button has its *RenderTransform* property set to an object of type *TranslateTransform* that moves its location down and to the left. The third button is subjected to a *ScaleTransform* that enlarges its width by 1.5 and its height by a factor of 4. The fourth button is skewed along its vertical axis by 20 degrees, making it a parallelogram rather than a rectangle. The fifth button is rotated 30 degrees counterclockwise. All the buttons otherwise remain entirely functional.

In a C# program you can set the properties of the *Transform* classes just as in a XAML file, but these classes are all supplied with useful constructors as well, as the following C# program demonstrates. The program created from the following TransformedButtons.cs file is functionally equivalent to TransformedButtons.xaml.

TransformedButtons.cs

```
//----------------------------------------------------
// TransformedButtons.cs (c) 2006 by Charles Petzold
//----------------------------------------------------
using System;
using System.Windows;
using System.Windows.Controls;
using System.Windows.Input;
using System.Windows.Media;

namespace Petzold.TransformedButtons
{
    public class TransformedButtons : Window
    {
        [STAThread]
        public static void Main()
        {
            Application app = new Application();
            app.Run(new TransformedButtons());
        }
        public TransformedButtons()
        {
            Title = "Transformed Buttons";

            // Create Canvas as content of window.
            Canvas canv = new Canvas();
            Content = canv;

            // Untransformed button.
            Button btn = new Button();
            btn.Content = "Untransformed";
```

```
            canv.Children.Add(btn);
            Canvas.SetLeft(btn, 50);
            Canvas.SetTop(btn, 100);

            // Translated button.
            btn = new Button();
            btn.Content = "Translated";
            btn.RenderTransform = new TranslateTransform(-100, 150);
            canv.Children.Add(btn);
            Canvas.SetLeft(btn, 200);
            Canvas.SetTop(btn, 100);

            // Scaled button.
            btn = new Button();
            btn.Content = "Scaled";
            btn.RenderTransform = new ScaleTransform(1.5, 4);
            canv.Children.Add(btn);
            Canvas.SetLeft(btn, 350);
            Canvas.SetTop(btn, 100);

            // Skewed button.
            btn = new Button();
            btn.Content = "Skewed";
            btn.RenderTransform = new SkewTransform(0, 20);
            canv.Children.Add(btn);
            Canvas.SetLeft(btn, 500);
            Canvas.SetTop(btn, 100);

            // Rotated button.
            btn = new Button();
            btn.Content = "Rotated";
            btn.RenderTransform = new RotateTransform(-30);
            canv.Children.Add(btn);
            Canvas.SetLeft(btn, 650);
            Canvas.SetTop(btn, 100);
        }
    }
}
```

If you have experience with graphics transforms in other graphical programming environments (including Win32 or Windows Forms), you're going to find some differences in the way transforms are implemented in the Windows Presentation Foundation. In other graphical environments, transforms are properties of a drawing surface, and anything drawn on the surface is subjected to the current transform. In the WPF, transforms are properties of the elements themselves, and effectively transform the element relative to itself. Sometimes this difference in perspective is not noticeable, and sometimes it is.

The difference is most noticeable in the rotated button. All that has been specified here is an angle. In a conventional graphical environment, the rotation would be centered around the origin of the drawing surface—that is, the point (0, 0) on the *Canvas*. However, the WPF rotation is relative to the origin of the *Button* itself. The rotation occurs around the button's upper-left corner rather than the canvas's upper-left corner.

I mentioned that any class that derives from *FrameworkElement* has two properties of type *Transform*. These are *RenderTransform* and *LayoutTransform*, and both programs shown so far have focused on *RenderTransform*. In either the XAML file or the C# file you might want to globally replace *RenderTransform* with *LayoutTransform* and see the difference. You'll find that now the translated button isn't translated at all, but instead remains in its location at the point (200, 100). You'll also find that the rotated button is still rotated, but it has moved down a bit so that it really occupies the original area implied by the *Canvas.Left* and *Canvas.Top* attached properties. The reasons for these peculiarities will become evident as this chapter progresses.

I'd like to examine these various types of transforms in more detail with little XAML programs that you can experiment with. Let's begin with the simplest of these *Transform* derivatives, which is *TranslateTransform*. *TranslateTransform* defines two properties named *X* and *Y*. They are backed by dependency properties, so they are animatable and bindable.

The following stand-alone XAML file encloses within a *StackPanel* two *ScrollBar* controls labeled "X" and "Y" with their *Minimum* properties set to −300 and *Maximum* properties set to 1000. Two *TextBlock* elements are bound to the *Value* properties of the scrollbars to display the current scrollbar values. The last elements of the *StackPanel* are a *Canvas* panel containing two lines that intersect at the point (100, 100) relative to the upper-left corner of the *Canvas*, and a *Button*, which is positioned at the point (100, 100). Toward the bottom of the file, the *RenderTransform* property of the *Button* is assigned a *TranslateTransform* with the *X* and *Y* properties bound to the two scrollbars.

InteractiveTranslateTransform.xaml

```
<!-- ================================================================
        InteractiveTranslateTransform.xaml (c) 2006 by Charles Petzold
     ================================================================ -->
<StackPanel xmlns="http://schemas.microsoft.com/winfx/2006/xaml/presentation"
            xmlns:x="http://schemas.microsoft.com/winfx/2006/xaml">
    <Label Content="X" />
    <ScrollBar Name="xscroll" Orientation="Horizontal"
               Minimum="-300" Maximum="1000" />
    <TextBlock HorizontalAlignment="Center" Margin="12"
               Text="{Binding ElementName=xscroll, Path=Value}" />

    <Label Content="Y" />
    <ScrollBar Name="yscroll" Orientation="Horizontal"
               Minimum="-300" Maximum="1000" />
    <TextBlock HorizontalAlignment="Center" Margin="12"
               Text="{Binding ElementName=yscroll, Path=Value}" />

    <Canvas>
        <Line X1="100" Y1="0" X2="100" Y2="1000" Stroke="Black"/>
        <Line X1="0" Y1="100" X2="1000" Y2="100" Stroke="Black"/>

        <Button Content="Button" Canvas.Left="100" Canvas.Top="100">
            <Button.RenderTransform>
                <TranslateTransform
                    X="{Binding ElementName=xscroll, Path=Value}"
```

```
                        Y="{Binding ElementName=yscroll, Path=Value}" />
                </Button.RenderTransform>
            </Button>
        </Canvas>
    </StackPanel>
```

When the program begins, the upper-left corner of the Button is positioned at the point (100, 100). As you manipulate the two *ScrollBar* controls, the *Button* moves around the *Canvas*. The position of the upper-left corner of the button is obviously the original position plus the *X* and *Y* properties of the *TranslateTransform* object.

Let's try to formalize this process with convenient mathematical notation. The original position of the *Button* is (x, y) and the *X* and *Y* values of the *TranslateTransform* can be symbolized by d_x and d_y (where the *d* stands for *delta*, mathematically meaning *change*). The rendered position of the button is (x', y'). That rendered position can be expressed like so:

$$x' = x + d_x$$

$$y' = y + d_y$$

Notice that d_x and d_y can be negative. As you move the second scrollbar in the program to the left, you can even force the *Button* to escape the confines of the *Canvas* panel in which it is supposedly positioned and climb up over the scrollbars!

Now go into the XAML file and change the two occurrences of the property element *Button.RenderTransform* to *Button.LayoutTransform*. You'll find that the *Button* doesn't budge at all, no matter how ferociously you tug on the scrollbars. You may be disappointed, but the lesson you learned earlier is now reinforced: A *TranslateTransform* object applied to the *LayoutTransform* property has no effect on the location of the element.

The *ScaleTransform* class defines the four properties *ScaleX* and *ScaleY* (which both have default values of 1) and *CenterX* and *CenterY* (which both have default values of 0). These properties provide you with a means to increase or decrease the size of an element. The InteractiveScaleTransform.xaml file creates four scrollbars for these four properties and a *ScaleTransform* binds its properties to these scrollbar values.

InteractiveScaleTransform.xaml

```
<!-- =================================================================
        InteractiveScaleTransform.xaml (c) 2006 by Charles Petzold
     ================================================================= -->
<StackPanel xmlns="http://schemas.microsoft.com/winfx/2006/xaml/presentation"
            xmlns:x="http://schemas.microsoft.com/winfx/2006/xaml">

    <Label Content="ScaleX" />
    <ScrollBar Name="xscroll" Orientation="Horizontal"
               Value="1" Minimum="-20" Maximum="20" />
    <TextBlock HorizontalAlignment="Center" Margin="12"
```

```
                        Text="{Binding ElementName=xscroll, Path=Value}" />

        <Label Content="ScaleY" />
        <ScrollBar Name="yscroll" Orientation="Horizontal"
                   Value="1" Minimum="-20" Maximum="20" />
        <TextBlock HorizontalAlignment="Center" Margin="12"
                   Text="{Binding ElementName=yscroll, Path=Value}" />

        <Label Content="CenterX" />
        <ScrollBar Name="xcenter" Orientation="Horizontal"
                   Value="0" Minimum="-100" Maximum="100" />
        <TextBlock HorizontalAlignment="Center" Margin="12"
                   Text="{Binding ElementName=xcenter, Path=Value}" />

        <Label Content="CenterY" />
        <ScrollBar Name="ycenter" Orientation="Horizontal"
                   Value="0" Minimum="-100" Maximum="100" />
        <TextBlock HorizontalAlignment="Center" Margin="12"
                   Text="{Binding ElementName=ycenter, Path=Value}" />

        <Canvas>
            <Line X1="100" Y1="0" X2="100" Y2="1000" Stroke="Black"/>
            <Line X1="0" Y1="100" X2="1000" Y2="100" Stroke="Black"/>

            <Button Name="btn" Content="Button" Canvas.Left="100" Canvas.Top="100">
                <Button.RenderTransform>
                    <ScaleTransform
                        ScaleX="{Binding ElementName=xscroll, Path=Value}"
                        ScaleY="{Binding ElementName=yscroll, Path=Value}"
                        CenterX="{Binding ElementName=xcenter, Path=Value}"
                        CenterY="{Binding ElementName=ycenter, Path=Value}" />
                </Button.RenderTransform>
            </Button>

            <StackPanel Orientation="Horizontal">
                <TextBlock Text="{Binding ElementName=btn, Path=ActualWidth}" />
                <TextBlock Text="&#x00D7;" />
                <TextBlock Text="{Binding ElementName=btn, Path=ActualHeight}" />
            </StackPanel>
        </Canvas>
    </StackPanel>
</StackPanel>
```

You'll also notice that toward the bottom of the file, the *ActualWidth* and *ActualHeight* properties of the *Button* are displayed in the upper-left corner of the *Canvas*.

Try manipulating the *ScaleX* and *ScaleY* scrollbars first. These scrollbars increase or decrease the size of the *Button* by the scaling factor. For example, a *ScaleX* value of 2 doubles the width of the *Button*, while a *ScaleY* value of 0.5 halves the height. You can make *ScaleX* negative, in which case the *Button* flips around its left side, and the text of the button becomes a mirror image. You can also make *ScaleY* negative, and the *Button* flips around its top edge. Negative scaling is sometimes called *reflection*.

Notice that the *ActualWidth* and *ActualHeight* properties of the *Button* never change. Another property that doesn't change is *RenderSize*, which the element's *OnRender* method uses to draw the element. Transforms always occur *after* the element has rendered itself.

If the two scaling factors *ScaleX* and *ScaleY* are symbolized by s_x and s_y, the formulas that describe the scaling effect are:

$$x' = s_x \cdot x$$

$$y' = s_y \cdot y$$

And here let me emphasize again that both (x, y) and (x', y') are points relative to the upper-left corner of the untransformed *Button*. The point $(0, 0)$ is transformed to the point $(0, 0)$. That's why the upper-left corner of the button remains in the same place regardless of the *ScaleX* and *ScaleY* settings.

In some cases you might prefer that this not be the case. For example, you might want to double the size of an element, but you want the element to remain centered at the same spot. In other words, you don't want the element to expand just to the right and downward. You want the element to expand in all four directions.

This is the purpose of the *CenterX* and *CenterY* properties of *ScaleTransform*. Try setting the *CenterX* scrollbar to approximately half the width of the button and the *CenterY* scrollbar to approximately half the button height. (That's the second reason why the program displays the *ActualWidth* and *ActualHeight* properties of the *Button*.) Now when you increase the *ScaleX* and *ScaleY* properties, the *Button* expands in all four directions.

If you set *CenterX* to the *ActualWidth* of the *Button* and *CenterY* to 0, the right side of the *Button* will always occupy the same horizontal position. If you also set *CenterY* to the *ActualHeight* of the *Button*, the bottom right corner of the *Button* always remains in the same position.

If the *CenterX* and *CenterY* properties of the *ScaleTransform* are symbolized by cs_x and cs_y, the complete scaling formulas are actually

$$x' = s_x \cdot (x - cs_x) + cs_x$$

$$y' = s_y \cdot (y - cs_y) + cs_y$$

You can verify these formulas with an example or two. Suppose an element is 80 units wide and you set *CenterX* (that is, cs_x) to 40 and *ScaleX* (or s_x) to 3. All points of the form $(40, y)$, which is the horizontal center of the button, are transformed to $(40, y)$. The center of the button is unchanged. All points of the form $(80, y)$, which is the right side of the button, are transformed to $(160, y)$. All points of the form $(0, y)$, the left side of the button, are transformed to $(-80, y)$. The button is 240 units wide, which is 3 times the original width, but it's still centered at the same point.

It's actually a little better to write the complete scaling formulas like this:

$$x' = s_x \cdot x + (cs_x - s_x \cdot cs_x)$$

$$y' = s_y \cdot y + (cs_y - s_y \cdot cs_y)$$

This form clarifies that the complete transformation is actually just a single factor multiplied by the original coordinate combined with a translation.

If you edit InteractiveScaleTransform.xaml and change both occurrences of *Button.Render-Transform* to *Button.LayoutTransform*, you'll discover that the *ScaleX* and *ScaleY* scrollbars still function in making the button larger and smaller, even flipping it around its horizontal or vertical axis. However, the button always remains in the same place. The button is always just underneath and to the right of the point (100, 100) where those two lines cross. This is most noticeable when you give the button negative scaling factors. The button flips, but it remains in the same place. The *CenterX* and *CenterY* scrollbars have no effect on the *LayoutTransform* because those scrollbars essentially provide translation factors, and it's already been established that *LayoutTransform* ignores translation.

On to the *SkewTransform*. The *SkewTransform* defines four properties named *AngleX*, *AngleY*, *CenterX*, and *CenterY*, all of which have default values of 0. As the names imply, *AngleX* and *AngleY* are angles. Angles within the range −90 degrees to 90 degrees produce unique results; angles outside that range simply duplicate effects inside the range.

InteractiveSkewTransform.xaml

```
<!-- =============================================================
       InteractiveSkewTransform.xaml (c) 2006 by Charles Petzold
     ============================================================= -->
<StackPanel xmlns="http://schemas.microsoft.com/winfx/2006/xaml/presentation"
            xmlns:x="http://schemas.microsoft.com/winfx/2006/xaml">

    <Label Content="AngleX" />
    <ScrollBar Name="xscroll" Orientation="Horizontal"
            Value="0" Minimum="-90" Maximum="90" />
    <TextBlock HorizontalAlignment="Center" Margin="12"
            Text="{Binding ElementName=xscroll, Path=Value}" />

    <Label Content="AngleY" />
    <ScrollBar Name="yscroll" Orientation="Horizontal"
            Value="0" Minimum="-90" Maximum="90" />
    <TextBlock HorizontalAlignment="Center" Margin="12"
            Text="{Binding ElementName=yscroll, Path=Value}" />

    <Label Content="CenterX" />
    <ScrollBar Name="xcenter" Orientation="Horizontal"
            Value="0" Minimum="-100" Maximum="100" />
    <TextBlock HorizontalAlignment="Center" Margin="12"
            Text="{Binding ElementName=xcenter, Path=Value}" />
```

```
    <Label Content="CenterY" />
    <ScrollBar Name="ycenter" Orientation="Horizontal"
            Value="0" Minimum="-100" Maximum="100" />
    <TextBlock HorizontalAlignment="Center" Margin="12"
            Text="{Binding ElementName=ycenter, Path=Value}" />

    <Canvas>
        <Line X1="100" Y1="0" X2="100" Y2="1000" Stroke="Black"/>
        <Line X1="0" Y1="100" X2="1000" Y2="100" Stroke="Black"/>

        <Button Name="btn" Content="Button" Canvas.Left="100" Canvas.Top="100">
            <Button.RenderTransform>
                <SkewTransform
                    AngleX="{Binding ElementName=xscroll, Path=Value}"
                    AngleY="{Binding ElementName=yscroll, Path=Value}"
                    CenterX="{Binding ElementName=xcenter, Path=Value}"
                    CenterY="{Binding ElementName=ycenter, Path=Value}" />
            </Button.RenderTransform>
        </Button>

        <StackPanel Orientation="Horizontal">
            <TextBlock Text="{Binding ElementName=btn, Path=ActualWidth}" />
            <TextBlock Text="&#x00D7;" />
            <TextBlock Text="{Binding ElementName=btn, Path=ActualHeight}" />
        </StackPanel>
    </Canvas>
</StackPanel>
```

As you move the *AngleX* scrollbar, you'll see that the *Button* remains the same height, and the top of the button remains in the same place, but the bottom of the *Button* is shifted to the right for positive angles and to the left for negative angles. This is known as *horizontal skew* or *horizontal shear*. The button is distorted because it's no longer a rectangle. It's a parallelogram. Set *AngleX* back to 0. Now move the *AngleY* scrollbar. The *Button* remains the same width, and the left side of the button remains in the same place, but the right side of the button shifts down for positive angles and up for negative angles. This is *vertical skew*. In both cases, the upper-left corner of the button remains anchored at the point (100, 100).

If *AngleX* and *AngleY* are symbolized by α_x and α_y, the skewing formulas are:

$$x' = x + \tan(\alpha_x) \cdot y$$

$$y' = y + \tan(\alpha_y) \cdot x$$

Notice that both x' and y' are functions of both x and y. This is what makes the skewing formulas different from the translation formulas and the scaling formulas.

Let me convince you that these formulas are correct. In InteractiveSkewTransform.xaml, set the *AngleX* and *AngleY* scrollbars to 0. This is the default case. The tangent of 0 is 0, so x' equals x and y' equals y, and the button is entirely normal. Now change *AngleX* (symbolized by α_x in the formulas). You can see that the value you set on the scrollbar is the angle that the left side of the button makes with the vertical axis. Set the angle to 45 degrees. The tangent of 45 degrees is 1, so the formulas simplify to

$x' = x + y$

$y' = y$

The upper-left corner of the button is the point (0, 0), which has been transformed to (0, 0). If the width of the button is W, the upper-right corner of the button is (W, 0), which has been transformed to (W, 0). If the height of the button is H, the lower-left corner is (0, H). The skewing transform has shifted that corner right by an amount equal to the height of the button. It has become (H, H), and the skewing formulas have predicted that. The lower-right corner of the button is normally (W, H) and it has been transformed to (W + H, H), also predicted by the formulas.

As the angle gets very large, the button becomes skewed beyond the point of recognition. The tangent of 90 degrees is infinity and, fortunately, the transform doesn't "blow up" at that point, but it no longer makes any visual sense to display the button.

Now try this: Set the *AngleX* scrollbar to a positive number between 50 and 80. Set *AngleY* to the negative of that number. You'll see the button assume its normal rectangular shape. It will be larger than the original button and it will be rotated counterclockwise by *AngleX*, but it will no longer be distorted. Rotation, which is a combination of horizontal skew and vertical skew, is normally done in such a way as to preserve the original size.

As you've seen, changing the *AngleX* and *AngleY* properties always leaves the upper-left corner of the button in its original location. You can override that by changing the *CenterX* and *CenterY* properties. As with the same-named properties in the *ScaleTransform* class, these properties indicate the coordinates of the button that remains unaltered. But in practice these properties work a little differently for skew. If you're just setting horizontal skew (*AngleX*) to a non-default value, all points of the form (x, *CenterY*) remain unaffected by the skew. Similarly, for vertical skew used by itself, all points (*CenterX*, y) remain unaffected by changes in *AngleY*. For default 0 values of *AngleX* and *AngleY*, *CenterX* and *CenterY* do not affect the position of the element.

If *CenterX* and *CenterY* are represented by ck_x and ck_y (k stands for *skew* because s already stands for *scale*), the complete skewing formulas are

$x' = x + \tan(\alpha_x) \cdot (y - ck_x)$

$y' = y + \tan(\alpha_y) \cdot (x - ck_y)$

Once again, let's see how *LayoutTransform* is different. Edit InteractiveSkewTransform.xaml and replace *Button.RenderTransform* with *Button.LayoutTransform*. You might have predicted that *AngleX* and *AngleY* still skew the button, but the button always remains in the same area—below and to the right of the point (100, 100). *CenterX* and *CenterY* have no effect because the *LayoutTransform* doesn't respond to translation.

The *RotateTransform* class defines the familiar *CenterX* and *CenterY* properties, but unlike *SkewTransform*, *RotateTransform* defines just a single property named *Angle*.

InteractiveRotateTransform.xaml

```xml
<!-- ==========================================================
        InteractiveRotateTransform.xaml (c) 2006 by Charles Petzold
     ========================================================== -->
<StackPanel xmlns="http://schemas.microsoft.com/winfx/2006/xaml/presentation"
            xmlns:x="http://schemas.microsoft.com/winfx/2006/xaml">

    <Label Content="Angle" />
    <ScrollBar Name="angle" Orientation="Horizontal"
               Value="0" Minimum="0" Maximum="360" />
    <TextBlock HorizontalAlignment="Center" Margin="12"
               Text="{Binding ElementName=angle, Path=Value}" />

    <Label Content="CenterX" />
    <ScrollBar Name="xcenter" Orientation="Horizontal"
               Value="0" Minimum="-100" Maximum="100" />
    <TextBlock HorizontalAlignment="Center" Margin="12"
               Text="{Binding ElementName=xcenter, Path=Value}" />

    <Label Content="CenterY" />
    <ScrollBar Name="ycenter" Orientation="Horizontal"
               Value="0" Minimum="-100" Maximum="100" />
    <TextBlock HorizontalAlignment="Center" Margin="12"
               Text="{Binding ElementName=ycenter, Path=Value}" />

    <Canvas>
        <Line X1="100" Y1="0" X2="100" Y2="1000" Stroke="Black"/>
        <Line X1="0" Y1="100" X2="1000" Y2="100" Stroke="Black"/>

        <Button Name="btn" Content="Button" Canvas.Left="100" Canvas.Top="100">
            <Button.RenderTransform>
                <RotateTransform
                    Angle="{Binding ElementName=angle, Path=Value}"
                    CenterX="{Binding ElementName=xcenter, Path=Value}"
                    CenterY="{Binding ElementName=ycenter, Path=Value}" />
            </Button.RenderTransform>
        </Button>

        <StackPanel Orientation="Horizontal">
            <TextBlock Text="{Binding ElementName=btn, Path=ActualWidth}" />
            <TextBlock Text="&#x00D7;" />
            <TextBlock Text="{Binding ElementName=btn, Path=ActualHeight}" />
        </StackPanel>
    </Canvas>
</StackPanel>
```

I've set the range of the *Angle* scrollbar to a minimum of 0 and a maximum of 360 degrees, but negative angle values and angles outside that range are perfectly acceptable. The *Angle* value specifies a clockwise rotation and by default the rotation occurs around the upper-left corner of the element.

The *CenterX* and *CenterY* properties indicate the point relative to the upper-left corner of the element around which the rotation occurs. Set these properties to half the width and height of the element, and the rotation will occur around the element's center. The element always remains the same size.

Once again, edit the file and change *Button.RenderTransform* to *Button.LayoutTransform*. The button still rotates, but it remains below and to the right of the point (100, 100) where it was originally positioned.

The WPF graphics and layout system handles *RenderTransform* and *LayoutTransform* very differently. With *RenderTransform*, the system takes the image drawn by the element's *OnRender* method, applies the transform, and slaps the image on the screen. If that image happens to overlay some other control in the program (or be buried underneath), it doesn't matter. The element will be clipped to the border of the application's window, but it's otherwise free to roam.

Any change in an element's *LayoutTransform*, however, precipitates a new layout pass with calls to *MeasureOverride* and *ArrangeOverride* so that the transform can be respected when the element is accommodated in the layout. The *MeasureOverride*, *ArrangeOverride*, and *OnRender* methods don't need to know about the *LayoutTransform*, but certain values are finagled to account for layout. The *DesiredSize* property of an element's child reflects the *LayoutTransform*, for example, even though the child's *MeasureOverride* method doesn't take the transform into account.

The difference between *RenderTransform* and *LayoutTransform* is most obvious in a *StackPanel*, or in an auto-sized cell of a *Grid*, or in *UniformGrid*. The following stand-alone XAML program provides a dramatic illustration of that difference. The program assembles two three-by-three *UniformGrid* panels containing nine *Button* controls each. The center button in each grid is given a *RotateTransform* with an *Angle* property of 45 degrees. In the top *UniformGrid*, the *RotateTransform* is applied to the button's *RenderTransform* property. In the bottom grid, the *RotateTransform* is applied to *LayoutTransform*.

RenderTransformAndLayoutTransform.xaml

```
<!-- ========================================================
        RenderTransformAndLayoutTransform.xaml (c) 2006 by Charles Petzold
     ======================================================== -->
<StackPanel xmlns="http://schemas.microsoft.com/winfx/2006/xaml/presentation"
            xmlns:x="http://schemas.microsoft.com/winfx/2006/xaml"
            TextBlock.FontSize="18pt" >

    <!-- RenderTransform section. -->
```

```
    <TextBlock Margin="24">
        RenderTransform
    </TextBlock>
    <UniformGrid Rows="3" Columns="3">
        <Button Content="Button" />
        <Button Content="Button" />
        <Button Content="Button" />
        <Button Content="Button" />
        <Button Content="Button">
            <Button.RenderTransform>
                <RotateTransform Angle="45" />
            </Button.RenderTransform>
        </Button>
        <Button Content="Button" />
        <Button Content="Button" />
        <Button Content="Button" />
        <Button Content="Button" />
    </UniformGrid>

    <!-- LayoutTransform section. -->

    <TextBlock Margin="24">
        LayoutTransform
    </TextBlock>
    <UniformGrid Rows="3" Columns="3">
        <Button Content="Button" />
        <Button Content="Button" />
        <Button Content="Button" />
        <Button Content="Button" />
        <Button Content="Button" >
            <Button.LayoutTransform>
                <RotateTransform Angle="45" />
            </Button.LayoutTransform>
        </Button>
        <Button Content="Button" />
        <Button Content="Button" />
        <Button Content="Button" />
        <Button Content="Button" />
    </UniformGrid>
</StackPanel>
```

In the top grid, the rotated button doesn't affect anything else in the program. The *Uniform-Grid* is arranged as if the button weren't rotated at all. The button appears on top of elements created before it and behind elements created after it. In the bottom grid, however, the entire *UniformGrid* has been adjusted to accommodate the size that the rotated button requires in the cell.

You'll notice that the *Button* in the second *UniformGrid* is smaller than the other buttons in that grid. An element that is transformed is given the size it returns from *MeasureOverride*, rather than the size assigned to it by its parent's *ArrangeOverride* method.

You should run this little program whenever you momentarily forget about the difference between *RenderTransform* and *LayoutTransform*. (Chapter 30 has an animated version of this program that reveals the difference even more dramatically.)

If you are transforming an element in the context of a layout, and you want the transformed element to be reflected in that layout, you'll probably be using *LayoutTransform*. If the transform is set just once and doesn't change, there's really no performance difference between *RenderTransform* and *LayoutTransform*. However, if you're animating a transform or binding the transform to something that could change a lot, you'll probably want to use *RenderTransform* for the sake of efficiency.

Any translation applied to a *LayoutTransform* is ignored, so when you're setting a *LayoutTransform*, you needn't bother with translation or any *CenterX* or *CenterY* properties. The enlarged, skewed, or rotated element is always positioned in the space allocated for it during layout.

As you'll note, setting the *RenderTransform* property in the preceding XAML file causes the button to rotate around its top-left corner. You probably want the freedom to rotate the element around its center (for example). But to do that, you need to set the *CenterX* and *CenterY* properties of the *RotateTransform*. To set these properties to the center of the element, you need to know the element's size, and in the general case, that size is dependent on layout, which occurs during run time and which you, the XAML coder, cannot anticipate.

And that is why the WPF developers were both prescient and kind enough to include a property in *UIElement* named *RenderTransformOrigin*. You use this property as an alternative means to set an origin for the *RenderTransform*. The coordinates are fractions relative to the size of the element. (This scheme is similar to the default coordinate system for gradient brushes.)

For example, in the XAML program just shown, if you want the top button to be rotated around its center, include a *RenderTransformOrigin* attribute for that button. That top rotated button is currently the element that looks like this:

```
<Button Content="Button">
    <Button.RenderTransform>
        <RotateTransform Angle="45" />
    </Button.RenderTransform>
</Button>
```

Change that element to this:

```
<Button Content="Button" RenderTransformOrigin="0.5 0.5">
    <Button.RenderTransform>
        <RotateTransform Angle="45" />
    </Button.RenderTransform>
</Button>
```

Now the button is rotated around its center. Here's a program that uses *RenderTransformOrigin* to display one unrotated button and four buttons rotated around each of the button's corners.

RotatedButtons.xaml

```xml
<!-- ================================================
        RotatedButtons.xaml (c) 2006 by Charles Petzold
     ================================================ -->
<Grid xmlns="http://schemas.microsoft.com/winfx/2006/xaml/presentation"
      xmlns:x="http://schemas.microsoft.com/winfx/2006/xaml">

    <Grid.Resources>
        <Style TargetType="{x:Type Button}">
            <Setter Property="FontSize" Value="48" />
            <Setter Property="Content" Value="Button" />
            <Setter Property="HorizontalAlignment" Value="Center" />
            <Setter Property="VerticalAlignment" Value="Center" />
        </Style>
    </Grid.Resources>

    <Button />

    <Button RenderTransformOrigin="0 0">
        <Button.RenderTransform>
            <RotateTransform Angle="225" />
        </Button.RenderTransform>
    </Button>

    <Button RenderTransformOrigin="1 0">
        <Button.RenderTransform>
            <RotateTransform Angle="135" />
        </Button.RenderTransform>
    </Button>

    <Button RenderTransformOrigin="1 1">
        <Button.RenderTransform>
            <RotateTransform Angle="225" />
        </Button.RenderTransform>
    </Button>

    <Button RenderTransformOrigin="0 1">
        <Button.RenderTransform>
            <RotateTransform Angle="135" />
        </Button.RenderTransform>
    </Button>

</Grid>
```

To avoid a lot of repetition, a *Style* element defines properties for all five buttons, including *HorizontalAlignment* and *VerticalAlignment* values that position the buttons in the center of the *Grid* cell. The unrotated *Button* is just

```xml
<Button />
```

The other *Button* elements have both a *RenderTransformOrigin* and a *RenderTransform* set to rotate the element around one of its four corners.

When you're dealing with elements such as *Line*, *Path*, *Polygon*, and *Polyline* on a *Canvas*, you can probably set the *CenterX* and *CenterY* properties of the transform rather than rely on *RenderTransformOrigin* because you already know the size and locations of these objects. However, you should be aware of how these rotation origins work when you're dealing with elements with explicit coordinate points.

For example, consider the following element:

```
<Line Stroke="Black" X1="100" Y1="50" X2="500" Y2="100" />
```

If you apply a *RotateTransform* to the *RenderTransform* property of the element, by default the *CenterX* and *CenterY* properties are 0. The rotation will occur around the point (0, 0)—that is, the point 100 units to the left and 50 units above the starting point of the line. If you want the rotation to occur relative to the start point of the line, set *CenterX* to 100 and *CenterY* to 50. If you want the rotation to occur relative to the center of the line, set *CenterX* to 300 and *CenterY* to 75.

However, if you're intent on using *RenderTransformOrigin* to specify the rotation origin, you need to know that the element is considered to occupy the rectangle that stretches horizontally from 0 to 500 (the maximum *X* coordinate) and vertically from 0 to 100 (the maximum *Y* coordinate). The *RenderTransformOrigin* of (0, 0) corresponds to the point (0, 0), not to the leftmost coordinate of the line, which is the point (100, 50). A *RenderTransformOrigin* of (1, 0) corresponds to the coordinate point (500, 0).

The following C# program shows two different ways to rotate a bunch of lines so that they seem to form the spokes of a circle.

```
WheelAndSpokes.cs
//-----------------------------------------------
// WheelAndSpokes.cs (c) 2006 by Charles Petzold
//-----------------------------------------------
using System;
using System.Windows;
using System.Windows.Controls;
using System.Windows.Input;
using System.Windows.Media;
using System.Windows.Shapes;

namespace Petzold.WheelAndSpokes
{
    public class WheelAndSpokes : Window
    {
        [STAThread]
        public static void Main()
        {
            Application app = new Application();
            app.Run(new WheelAndSpokes());
        }
        public WheelAndSpokes()
```

```
{
    Title = "wheel and spokes";

    // Create Canvas for hosting graphics.
    Canvas canv = new Canvas();
    Content = canv;

    // Create Ellipse.
    Ellipse elips = new Ellipse();
    elips.Stroke = SystemColors.WindowTextBrush;
    elips.Width = 200;
    elips.Height = 200;
    canv.Children.Add(elips);
    Canvas.SetLeft(elips, 50);
    Canvas.SetTop(elips, 50);

    // Create Line objects.
    for (int i = 0; i < 72; i++)
    {
        // Draw horizontal line.
        Line line = new Line();
        line.Stroke = SystemColors.WindowTextBrush;
        line.X1 = 150;
        line.Y1 = 150;
        line.X2 = 250;
        line.Y2 = 150;

        // Rotate it around ellipse center (150, 150).
        line.RenderTransform = new RotateTransform(5 * i, 150, 150);
        canv.Children.Add(line);
    }

    // Create another Ellipse.
    elips = new Ellipse();
    elips.Stroke = SystemColors.WindowTextBrush;
    elips.Width = 200;
    elips.Height = 200;
    canv.Children.Add(elips);
    Canvas.SetLeft(elips, 300);
    Canvas.SetTop(elips, 50);

    // Create Line objects.
    for (int i = 0; i < 72; i++)
    {
        // Draw horizontal line.
        Line line = new Line();
        line.Stroke = SystemColors.WindowTextBrush;
        line.X1 = 0;
        line.Y1 = 0;
        line.X2 = 100;
        line.Y2 = 0;

        // Rotate it around (0, 0).
        line.RenderTransform = new RotateTransform(5 * i);
```

```
                    // Position the line in the center of the ellipse.
                    canv.Children.Add(line);
                    Canvas.SetLeft(line, 400);
                    Canvas.SetTop(line, 150);
                }
            }
        }
    }
```

In the wheel and spokes combination on the left, 72 *Line* elements are created starting at (150, 150), which is the center of the "wheel," and ending at (250, 150), which is the rightmost edge. These are all given a *RotateTransform*. The first argument of the *RotateTransform* constructor indicates the *Angle* property, and the second two arguments are *CenterX* and *CenterY*, which are set to (150, 150). Each line is rotated a different number of degrees around the point (150, 150).

The second rendition takes a different approach. Each *Line* element begins at (0, 0) and ends at (100, 0). The *RotateTransform* doesn't require *CenterX* and *CenterY* properties because the defaults of 0 indicate that line is to be rotated around the point (0, 0). However, the lines require *Canvas.SetLeft* and *Canvas.SetTop* properties to position the lines in the center of the second circle.

Of course, I could have written WheelAndSpokes as a XAML program rather than a C# program, but in that case, the file would have included 144 *Line* elements, and that seems contrary to my programming instincts. As programmers, we recognize the wisdom of keeping repetitive code to a minimum so that changes are as painless as possible. There's a reason why programming languages have loops such as *for*.

Still, at times you'll want to put several similar elements that differ only by a transform in a XAML file. As the RotatedButton.xaml file demonstrates, a *Style* element helps keep the repetition to a minimum. You'll also soon see some shortcuts in setting the transform itself on the individual elements, but it requires some further knowledge of the nature of these transforms.

If the *Angle* property of *RotateTransform* is symbolized by α without a subscript, the simple rotation formulas (without the influence of *CenterX* and *CenterY*) are

$$x' = \cos(\alpha) \cdot x - \sin(\alpha) \cdot y$$

$$y' = \sin(\alpha) \cdot x + \cos(\alpha) \cdot y$$

If the *CenterX* and *CenterY* properties are represented by cr_x and cr_y (the r stands for *rotate*), the complete rotation formulas are

$$x' = \cos(\alpha) \cdot (x - cr_x) - \sin(\alpha) \cdot (y - cr_y) + cr_x$$

$$y' = \sin(\alpha) \cdot (x - cr_x) + \cos(\alpha) \cdot (y - cr_y) + cr_y$$

The point (cr_x, cr_y) remains unchanged in these transforms.

Despite the seeming complexity of the final rotation formulas, all the transforms are of the general form

$$x' = s_x \cdot x + r_x \cdot y + d_x$$

$$y' = r_y \cdot x + s_y \cdot y + d_y$$

where s_x, s_y, r_x, r_y, d_x, and d_y are constants that define the particular transform. The s constants are scaling factors, the d constants are translation (delta) factors, and I've given the other two factors names of r_x and r_y to suggest rotation, but they are also responsible for skew.

These two formulas represent a two-dimensional *affine* transform, which is a transform that preserves colinearity. Although x' and y' are functions of both x and y, these formulas don't involve powers of x or y or anything like that. These transforms will always transform a straight line to another straight line. Straight lines never become curved. A pair of parallel lines will never be transformed to non-parallel lines. Objects that are the same size will be the same size under the same transformation. Parallelograms will always be transformed to parallelograms, ellipses will always be transformed to ellipses, and Bézier splines will always be transformed to Bézier splines.

For convenience in manipulating transforms, it is common to express the transform as a *matrix*, which is a rectangular array of numbers. Matrices always have a certain number of rows and columns. Here's a matrix with three columns and two rows:

$$\begin{vmatrix} 13 & -4 & 0 \\ -6 & 2 & 27 \end{vmatrix}$$

Matrices are usually symbolized by capital letters, so the following symbolizes a multiplication of two matrices:

$$A \times B = C$$

In a matrix multiplication, the number of columns in A must be equal to the number of rows in B. The product C has a number of rows equal to the number of rows in A, and a number of columns equal to the number of columns in B. The number in the ith row and jth column of C is equal to the sum of the products of the numbers in the ith row of A times the corresponding numbers in the jth column of B. Matrix multiplication is not commutative. The product $A \times B$ does not necessarily equal the product $B \times A$.

If we weren't dealing with translation, we could represent the transform as a 2 × 2 matrix:

$$\begin{vmatrix} s_x & r_y \\ r_x & s_y \end{vmatrix}$$

The transform calculation can then be shown by a 1 × 2 matrix containing the point (x, y) multiplied by the transform matrix to obtain another 1 × 2 matrix containing the point (x', y'):

$$\begin{vmatrix} x & y \end{vmatrix} \times \begin{vmatrix} s_x & r_y \\ r_x & s_y \end{vmatrix} = \begin{vmatrix} x' & y' \end{vmatrix}$$

Under the standard rules of matrix multiplication, that expression is equivalent to

$$x' = s_x \cdot x + r_x \cdot y$$

$$y' = r_y \cdot x + s_y \cdot y$$

Of course these formulas are not quite complete because they are missing the translation factor. To get the matrix multiplication to work properly with translation, the matrices containing (x, y) and (x', y') must be expanded to 1 × 3 matrices, and the transform itself to a 3 × 3 matrix:

$$\begin{vmatrix} x & y & 1 \end{vmatrix} \times \begin{vmatrix} s_x & r_y & 0 \\ r_x & s_y & 0 \\ d_x & d_y & 1 \end{vmatrix} = \begin{vmatrix} x' & y' & 1 \end{vmatrix}$$

Here are the resultant complete transform formulas, which are the same as those shown earlier:

$$x' = s_x \cdot x + r_x \cdot y + d_x$$

$$y' = r_y \cdot x + s_y \cdot y + d_y$$

The type of transform that can be represented by a matrix like this is often called a *matrix transform*. The default matrix transform doesn't do anything. It has scaling factors of 1 and rotation and translation factors of 0:

$$\begin{vmatrix} 1 & 0 & 0 \\ 0 & 1 & 0 \\ 0 & 0 & 1 \end{vmatrix}$$

This is called the *identity* matrix.

The transform matrix is encapsulated in a structure named *Matrix*. The *Matrix* structure has six read-write properties named *M11*, *M12*, *M21*, *M22*, *OffsetX*, and *OffsetY*, which correspond to the cells of the transform matrix like this:

$$\begin{vmatrix} M11 & M12 & 0 \\ M21 & M22 & 0 \\ OffsetX & OffsetY & 1 \end{vmatrix}$$

The values in the third column are fixed and cannot be changed. The *Transform* class–from which *TranslateTransform*, *ScaleTransform*, and the others derive–defines a read-only property named *Value* of type *Matrix*. This property indicates the transform matrix that results from the transform.

For example, suppose you set a *TranslateTransform* in code with this constructor:

```
TranslateTransform xform = new TranslateTransform(27, 55);
```

Or, you set it in XAML like so:

```
<TranslateTransform X="27" Y="55" />
```

In either case, the *Value* property of the *TranslateTransform* object will be this *Matrix* object:

$$\begin{vmatrix} 1 & 0 & 0 \\ 0 & 1 & 0 \\ 27 & 55 & 1 \end{vmatrix}$$

Similarly, you can create a *ScaleTransform* in code:

```
ScaleTransform xform = new ScaleTransform(5, 3);
```

Or you can do it in XAML:

```
<ScaleTransform ScaleX="5" ScaleY="3" />
```

Again, in either case, the *Value* property of the *ScaleTransform* object will reveal this equivalent *Matrix* object:

$$\begin{vmatrix} 5 & 0 & 0 \\ 0 & 3 & 0 \\ 0 & 0 & 1 \end{vmatrix}$$

These are the easy ones! As you've seen, you can also specify offset factors with the *ScaleTransform*. You do it in code like this:

```
ScaleTransform xform = new ScaleTransform(5, 3, 35, 12);
```

In XAML you set the *CenterX* and *CenterY* properties:

```
<ScaleTransform ScaleX="5" ScaleY="3" CenterX="35" CenterY="12" />
```

The matrix transform that results from these settings is actually a composite of three transforms. First, a translation moves the point (*CenterX, CenterY*) to the origin. Then the scaling is performed, followed by another translation that moves the origin back to the point (*CenterX, CenterY*). The composite transform is the product of these three matrices:

$$\begin{vmatrix} 1 & 0 & 0 \\ 0 & 1 & 0 \\ -35 & -12 & 1 \end{vmatrix} \times \begin{vmatrix} 5 & 0 & 0 \\ 0 & 3 & 0 \\ 0 & 0 & 1 \end{vmatrix} \times \begin{vmatrix} 1 & 0 & 0 \\ 0 & 1 & 0 \\ 35 & 12 & 1 \end{vmatrix}$$

Multiply the first two matrices together using the standard matrix multiplication rules:

$$\begin{vmatrix} 5 & 0 & 0 \\ 0 & 3 & 0 \\ -175 & -36 & 1 \end{vmatrix} \times \begin{vmatrix} 1 & 0 & 0 \\ 0 & 1 & 0 \\ 35 & 12 & 1 \end{vmatrix}$$

Then multiply those two matrices:

$$\begin{vmatrix} 5 & 0 & 0 \\ 0 & 3 & 0 \\ -140 & -24 & 1 \end{vmatrix}$$

That's the matrix corresponding to the *ScaleTransform* with *ScaleX* and *ScaleY* properties set to 5 and 3, and the *CenterX* and *CenterY* properties set to 35 and 12. If you're skeptical, you can go back to the InteractiveScaleTransform.xaml file and insert the following element at the very bottom of the *Canvas* element:

```
<Label Canvas.Right="0"
       Content="{Binding ElementName=btn, Path=RenderTransform.Value}" />
```

This *Label* displays the resultant *Value* property of the *RenderTransform* property of *Button*. It will appear as a string of six numbers in the order *M11, M12, M21, M22, OffsetX,* and *OffsetY*. Use the scrollbars to select the approximate values I've been discussing, and you'll see the resultant matrix.

Rotation by α degrees results in the following matrix:

$$\begin{vmatrix} \cos(\alpha) & \sin(\alpha) & 0 \\ -\sin(\alpha) & \cos(\alpha) & 0 \\ 0 & 0 & 1 \end{vmatrix}$$

If you set *CenterX* and *CenterY* to non-default values, a matrix multiplication is involved that is similar to the one shown earlier for scaling.

In the first program shown in this chapter—the TransformedButtons.xaml file—the rotated button had the following markup:

```
<Button Canvas.Left="650" Canvas.Top="100">
    Rotated
```

```
    <Button.RenderTransform>
        <RotateTransform Angle="-30" />
    </Button.RenderTransform>
</Button>
```

The cosine of −30 degrees is approximately 0.866 and the sine is −0.5, so the matrix that corresponds to this transform is

$$\begin{vmatrix} 0.866 & -0.5 & 0 \\ 0.5 & 0.866 & 0 \\ 0 & 0 & 1 \end{vmatrix}$$

Another class that derives from *Transform* is *MatrixTransform*. This class defines a property named *Matrix* of type *Matrix*, and if you know the values of the matrix you want, you can instead achieve the same transform with this markup:

```
<Button Canvas.Left="650" Canvas.Top="100">
    Rotated
    <Button.RenderTransform>
        <MatrixTransform>
            <MatrixTransform.Matrix>
                <Matrix M11="0.866" M12="-0.5" M21="0.5" M22="0.866" />
            </MatrixTransform.Matrix>
        </MatrixTransform>
    </Button.RenderTransform>
</Button>
```

My intuition tells me that unless you're a transform wizard from way back, you do not prefer this alternative to *RotateTransform*. However, there's a shortcut you can use. Instead of defining the *Matrix* element within a *MatrixTransform.Matrix* property element, you can set the *Matrix* property of *MatrixTransform* directly with a string containing the six values of the matrix starting with the top row:

```
<Button Canvas.Left="650" Canvas.Top="100">
    Rotated
    <Button.RenderTransform>
        <MatrixTransform Matrix="0.866 -0.5 0.5 0.866 0 0" />
    </Button.RenderTransform>
</Button>
```

But wait! It gets even better, for you can set the *RenderTransform* or *LayoutTransform* property directly to this string:

```
<Button Canvas.Left="650" Canvas.Top="100"
        RenderTransform="0.866 -0.5 0.5 0.866 0 0">
    Rotated
</Button>
```

And this form may be concise enough to entice you to use it for some simple transforms, particularly when you have several elements that are identical except for the transform. (Examples are coming up.)

The final class that derives from *Transform* is *TransformGroup*. The crucial property that *TransformGroup* defines is *Children*, which is a collection of other *Transform* objects. For example, suppose you want to scale a button to twice its size and also to rotate it 45 degrees. Here's the markup:

```
<Button.RenderTransform>
    <TransformGroup>
        <ScaleTransform ScaleX="2" ScaleY="2" />
        <RotateTransform Angle="45" />
    </TransformGroup>
</Button.RenderTransform>
```

In this particular case, the order of the *ScaleTransform* and *RotateTransform* doesn't matter, but in general it does. *TransformGroup* effectively performs a multiplication of the child transforms. However, this isn't a one-time-only deal. You can define a binding for *Angle* or you can animate *Angle*, and the composite transform will reflect that updated value.

The *Geometry* class defines a property named *Transform* of type *Transform*, so you can apply a transform directly to a geometry object. This is useful if you're using a *Geometry* object for clipping, for example. You can also set the transform even if the *Geometry* object is part of a *Path*. In effect, the geometry transform is applied before any possible *RenderTransform* or *LayoutTransform* of the *Path* itself. Because the geometry transform affects the coordinates and sizes that make up the *Path*, the transform will be reflected in layout.

Here's a program that shows two rectangles side by side. The first is a *Rectangle* element with a width and height of 10 units and a *RenderTransform* property that increases its size by a factor of 10. The second is a *Path* element that renders a *RectangleGeometry* object, also with a width and height of 10 and a *Transform* property that also increases its size by a factor of 10.

```
GeometryTransformDemo.xaml

<!-- ========================================================
        GeometryTransformDemo.xaml (c) 2006 by Charles Petzold
     ======================================================== -->
<Canvas xmlns="http://schemas.microsoft.com/winfx/2006/xaml/presentation"
        xmlns:x="http://schemas.microsoft.com/winfx/2006/xaml">

    <Rectangle Canvas.Left="100" Canvas.Top="100" Stroke="Red"
               Width="10" Height="10"
               RenderTransform="10 0 0 10 0 0" />

    <Path Canvas.Left="300" Canvas.Top="100" Stroke="Red">
        <Path.Data>
            <RectangleGeometry Rect="0 0 10 10"
                Transform="10 0 0 10 0 0" />
        </Path.Data>
    </Path>

</Canvas>
```

On the screen the two elements look very different in a way that you might not have anticipated. The red line that surrounds the *Rectangle* element is affected by the *RenderTransform* and is 10 units wide. The red line that surrounds the *Path* element is only one unit wide. A *Render Transform* or *LayoutTransform* applied to an element affects everything about the element— including the line widths. A *Transform* applied to a geometry object only affects the coordinates of that geometry. An untransformed line is then drawn on the transformed coordinates.

As you know from the previous chapter, you can define a *Canvas* of a particular size to use as a drawing surface. However, you might also prefer that the origin of this *Canvas*—the point (0, 0)—be not at the upper-left corner but perhaps somewhere else. Some graphics programmers prefer a drawing surface where the origin is the lower-left corner and increasing Y coordinates go up the screen. This scheme mimics the upper-right quadrant of a conventional Cartesian coordinate system. Some applications—for example, an analog clock—seem to cry out for a coordinate system in which the origin is in the center.

You can implement these alternative coordinate systems by setting the *RenderTransform* of the *Canvas* itself. If you want, that *Canvas* can go inside a *Viewbox* (as shown in the Scalable-Face.xaml program in Chapter 27) to make it stretchable.

The stand-alone CanvasModes.xaml file demonstrates four different *Canvas* coordinate systems.

CanvasModes.xaml

```
<!-- ===========================================
        CanvasModes.xaml (c) 2006 by Charles Petzold
     =========================================== -->
<Grid xmlns="http://schemas.microsoft.com/winfx/2006/xaml/presentation"
      xmlns:x="http://schemas.microsoft.com/winfx/2006/xaml">
    <Grid.ColumnDefinitions>
        <ColumnDefinition />
        <ColumnDefinition />
        <ColumnDefinition />
        <ColumnDefinition />
    </Grid.ColumnDefinitions>

    <Grid.Resources>
        <Style TargetType="{x:Type Canvas}">
            <Setter Property="Width" Value="100" />
            <Setter Property="Height" Value="100" />
            <Setter Property="HorizontalAlignment" Value="Center" />
            <Setter Property="VerticalAlignment" Value="Center" />
        </Style>

        <Style TargetType="{x:Type Path}">
            <Setter Property="Fill" Value="Red" />
            <Setter Property="Data">
                <Setter.Value>
                    <EllipseGeometry Center="0 0" RadiusX="5" RadiusY="5" />
                </Setter.Value>
            </Setter>
        </Style>
```

```xml
    </Grid.Resources>

    <!-- Normal: Origin at upper left. -->

    <Canvas Grid.Column="0">
        <Line X1="0" Y1="0" X2="100" Y2="100" Stroke="Black" />
        <Polyline Points="0 0 0 100 100 100 100 0 0 0" Stroke="Blue" />
        <Path />
    </Canvas>

    <!-- Origin at lower left. Y increases going up. -->

    <Canvas Grid.Column="1">
        <Canvas.RenderTransform>
            <TransformGroup>
                <ScaleTransform ScaleY="-1" />
                <TranslateTransform Y="100" />
            </TransformGroup>
        </Canvas.RenderTransform>

        <Line X1="0" Y1="0" X2="100" Y2="100" Stroke="Black" />

        <Polyline Points="0 0 0 100 100 100 100 0 0 0" Stroke="Blue" />
        <Path />
    </Canvas>

    <!-- Origin in center. Y increases going down. -->

    <Canvas Grid.Column="2">
        <Canvas.RenderTransform>
            <TransformGroup>
                <ScaleTransform ScaleY="1" />
                <TranslateTransform X="50" Y="50" />
            </TransformGroup>
        </Canvas.RenderTransform>

        <Line X1="0" Y1="0" X2="50" Y2="50" Stroke="Black" />
        <Polyline Points="-50 -50 50 -50 50 50 -50 50 -50 -50" Stroke="Blue" />
        <Path />
    </Canvas>

    <!-- Four-quadrant Cartesian coordinate system. -->

    <Canvas Grid.Column="3">
        <Canvas.RenderTransform>
            <TransformGroup>
                <ScaleTransform ScaleY="-1" />
                <TranslateTransform X="50" Y="50" />
            </TransformGroup>
        </Canvas.RenderTransform>

        <Line X1="0" Y1="0" X2="50" Y2="50" Stroke="Black" />
        <Polyline Points="-50 -50 50 -50 50 50 -50 50 -50 -50" Stroke="Blue" />
        <Path />
    </Canvas>
</Grid>
```

A *Style* for the *Canvas* sets the *Width* and *Height* to 100 units and *HorizontalAlignment* and *VerticalAlignment* to *Center*. Each of the four *Canvas* panels sits in the center of a cell of a four-column *Grid*.

The *Style* for the *Path* includes an *EllipseGeometry* centered around the point (0, 0) and colored red. Thus, the red dot always indicates the origin of the drawing surface. The *Polyline* outlines the 100-unit-square coordinate system. For the first two coordinate systems, in which the origin is in the corner, this outline begins at (0, 0) and extends to (100, 100). A black line is drawn from the origin to the point (100, 100). For the second two coordinate systems, the origin is in the center. The square outline begins at (−50, −50) and extends to (50, 50). The black line is drawn from the origin to the point (50, 50).

Watch out: Whenever you create a coordinate system in which values of *Y* increase going up, any text you display on the *Canvas* will be upside down! If that's not what you want, you'll have to compensate by setting a *ScaleTransform* on the element displaying the text. In addition, rotations based on positive angles are counterclockwise rather than clockwise.

Add another property to the *Canvas* style like this:

```
<Setter Property="Background" Value="Aqua" />
```

You may be a little shocked. For the second two transforms, it appears as if the drawing surface is mostly off the actual *Canvas*. The corner of the *Canvas* is always the point (0, 0), so the only way to make (0, 0) the center is to move the *Canvas* to one corner.

Let me assure you that this is OK. Because these transforms are applied to the *RenderTransform* property of the *Canvas*, the layout system still believes the *Canvas* to be located in the middle of the *Grid* cell, despite the *Canvas* not being rendered in that area.

If you want to use one of these alternative coordinate systems, you can set a matrix string directly to the *RenderTransform* attribute of the *Canvas*. For the second *Canvas* in the program where the origin is in the lower-left corner and increasing values of *Y* go up, the string is

```
RenderTransform="1 0 0 -1 0 100"
```

For an origin in the center where increasing values of *Y* go down, the string is

```
RenderTransform="1 0 0 1 50 50"
```

For the full-fledge Cartesian coordinate system, it's

```
RenderTransform="1 0 0 -1 50 50"
```

Keep in mind that these are all based on a total size of 100 units square. If you use something else, the offsets are increased proportionally. The following program, which draws a flower, uses a 200-unit-square *Canvas* within a *Viewbox*.

Flower.xaml

```xml
<!-- =====================================
     Flower.xaml (c) 2006 by Charles Petzold
     ===================================== -->
<Page xmlns="http://schemas.microsoft.com/winfx/2006/xaml/presentation"
      xmlns:x="http://schemas.microsoft.com/winfx/2006/xaml"
      Background="White">
    <Viewbox>

        <!-- Canvas is 200 units square with Cartesian coordinates. -->

        <Canvas Width="200" Height="200"
                RenderTransform="1 0 0 -1 100 100" >
            <Canvas.Resources>

                <!-- Style to avoid too much repetition in petals. -->

                <Style TargetType="{x:Type Path}" x:Key="petal">
                    <Setter Property="Stroke" Value="Black" />
                    <Setter Property="Fill" Value="Red" />
                    <Setter Property="Data"
                            Value="M 0 0 C 12.5 12.5, 47.5 12.5, 60 0
                                   C 47.5 -12.5, 12.5 -12.5, 0 0 Z" />
                </Style>
            </Canvas.Resources>

            <!-- The green stem. -->

            <Path Stroke="Green" StrokeThickness="5"
                  Data="M -100 -100 C -100 -50, -50 50, 0 0">
            </Path>

            <!-- Eight petals, many of them rotated. -->

            <Path Style="{StaticResource petal}" />

            <Path Style="{StaticResource petal}"
                  RenderTransform=".7 -.7 .7 .7 0 0" />

            <Path Style="{StaticResource petal}"
                  RenderTransform="0 -1 1 0 0 0" />

            <Path Style="{StaticResource petal}"
                  RenderTransform="-.7 -.7 .7 -.7 0 0" />

            <Path Style="{StaticResource petal}"
                  RenderTransform="-1 0 0 -1 0 0" />

            <Path Style="{StaticResource petal}"
                  RenderTransform="-.7 .7 -.7 -.7 0 0" />

            <Path Style="{StaticResource petal}"
                  RenderTransform="0 1 -1 0 0 0" />
```

```
            <Path Style="{StaticResource petal}"
                  RenderTransform=".7 .7 -.7 .7 0 0" />

            <!-- Put yellow circle in center to attract bees. -->

            <Path Fill="Yellow" Stroke="Black">
                <Path.Data>
                    <EllipseGeometry Center="0 0"
                                     RadiusX="15" RadiusY="15" />
                </Path.Data>
            </Path>
        </Canvas>
    </Viewbox>
</Page>
```

There are eight petals, each of which is based on two Bézier splines and rotated by a multiple of 45 degrees. To keep the markup bulk down, I've used matrix strings for each rotation. The values of 0.7 are gross approximations of half the square root of 2, but they seem to work fine.

One common application of *TranslateTransform* is the drop shadow. I did a drop shadow in the previous chapter by offsetting the shadow with the *Canvas* attached properties. Applying a *TranslateTransform* to the *RenderTransform* property is more versatile because you can do it in any type of panel. The following program displays a text drop shadow in a cell of a *Grid* panel.

TextDropShadow.xaml

```
<!-- =================================================
        TextDropShadow.xaml (c) 2006 by Charles Petzold
     ================================================= -->
<Grid xmlns="http://schemas.microsoft.com/winfx/2006/xaml/presentation"
      xmlns:x="http://schemas.microsoft.com/winfx/2006/xaml">
    <Grid.Resources>
        <Style TargetType="{x:Type TextBlock}">
            <Setter Property="Text" Value="Drop-Shadow" />
            <Setter Property="FontFamily" Value="Times New Roman Bold" />

            <Setter Property="FontSize" Value="96" />
            <Setter Property="HorizontalAlignment" Value="Center" />
            <Setter Property="VerticalAlignment" Value="Center" />
        </Style>
    </Grid.Resources>

    <!-- Shadow. -->

    <TextBlock Opacity="0.5" RenderTransform="1 0 0 1 5 5" />

    <!-- Foreground. -->

    <TextBlock />
</Grid>
```

Notice that the *Style* is so extensive that the foreground *TextBlock* is an empty element! The background shadow is offset by five units. Often shadows are made gray, but this one achieves its shadowy affect with a 50-percent opacity. The most important rule for shadows is to put them *behind* the text, not in front.

The following program shows a technique similar to a drop shadow but with a very different visual effect. The program displays gray text (actually *SystemColors.GrayTextBrush*) in the background and white text (actually *SystemColors.WindowBrush*) in the foreground with an offset of just two units.

EmbossAndEngrave.xaml

```
<!-- ====================================================
        EmbossAndEngrave.xaml (c) 2006 by Charles Petzold
     ==================================================== -->
<Grid xmlns="http://schemas.microsoft.com/winfx/2006/xaml/presentation"
      xmlns:x="http://schemas.microsoft.com/winfx/2006/xaml">
    <Grid.Resources>
        <Style TargetType="{x:Type TextBlock}">
            <Setter Property="FontFamily" Value="Times New Roman" />
            <Setter Property="FontSize" Value="144" />
            <Setter Property="HorizontalAlignment" Value="Center" />
            <Setter Property="VerticalAlignment" Value="Center" />
        </Style>
    </Grid.Resources>

    <Grid.RowDefinitions>
        <RowDefinition />
        <RowDefinition />
    </Grid.RowDefinitions>

    <!-- Shadow Text. -->

    <TextBlock Foreground="{DynamicResource
                    {x:Static SystemColors.GrayTextBrushKey}}">
        Emboss
        <TextBlock.RenderTransform>
            <TranslateTransform X="2" Y="2" />
        </TextBlock.RenderTransform>
    </TextBlock>

    <!-- Foreground Text. -->

    <TextBlock Foreground="{DynamicResource
                    {x:Static SystemColors.WindowBrushKey}}">
        Emboss
    </TextBlock>

    <!-- Shadow Text. -->

    <TextBlock Grid.Row="1"
            Foreground="{DynamicResource
                        {x:Static SystemColors.GrayTextBrushKey}}">
        Engrave
        <TextBlock.RenderTransform>
            <TranslateTransform X="-2" Y="-2" />
```

```
                </TextBlock.RenderTransform>
        </TextBlock>


        <!-- Foreground Text. -->

        <TextBlock Grid.Row="1"
                   Foreground="{DynamicResource
                                {x:Static SystemColors.WindowBrushKey}}">
            Engrave
        </TextBlock>

    </Grid>
```

The two effects are basically the same, except that the offset is negative in the second
example. Because we are accustomed to light sources that come from above, we interpret
an apparent shadow that appears on the bottom and right of the characters to be the
result of raised text. That's the "Emboss" string. A shadow on the top and left seems to
result from sunken text—the "Engrave" string.

If the shadow is skewed, the text appears to be standing on a surface like a floor. That's the
effect I tried to achieve in the following program.

EmpiricalTiltedTextShadow.xaml

```
<!-- ==========================================================
        EmpiricalTiltedTextShadow.xaml (c) 2006 by Charles Petzold
     ========================================================== -->
<Canvas xmlns="http://schemas.microsoft.com/winfx/2006/xaml/presentation"
        xmlns:x="http://schemas.microsoft.com/winfx/2006/xaml">
    <Canvas.Resources>
        <Style TargetType="{x:Type TextBlock}">
            <Setter Property="FontFamily" Value="Times New Roman" />
            <Setter Property="FontSize" Value="144" />
            <Setter Property="Text" Value="Shadow" />
            <Setter Property="Canvas.Left" Value="96" />
            <Setter Property="Canvas.Top" Value="192" />
        </Style>
    </Canvas.Resources>


    <!-- Shadow Text. -->

    <TextBlock Foreground="DarkGray">
        <TextBlock.RenderTransform>
            <TransformGroup>
                <ScaleTransform ScaleY="3" CenterY="100" />
                <SkewTransform AngleX="-45" CenterY="100" />
            </TransformGroup>
        </TextBlock.RenderTransform>
    </TextBlock>


    <!-- Foreground Text. -->

    <TextBlock />
</Canvas>
```

This XAML file applies both a *ScaleTransform* and a *SkewTransform* to the shadow. The *ScaleTransform* increases the shadow height by a factor of 3 while the *SkewTransform* tilts it right 45 degrees.

But if you run this program, it won't look right. The shadow is clearly behind the foreground text, but it doesn't seem to be in the correct position, and the more you look at it, the more you'll probably come to the conclusion that the baselines of the foreground and shadow text strings should be aligned.

You can fix that little problem by altering the values of the *CenterY* attributes for both the *ScaleTransform* and the *SkewTransform*. They should both be set to the same value, and you might want to experiment a bit trying to find what the value should be. (This program isn't called *Empirical*TiltedTextShadow.xaml because I like big words!) You want the shadow to align with the foreground text at the bottom of the *h* character. Portions of the other characters actually dip a bit below the baseline, so they're going to have slightly funny shadows anyway. Work at this a bit and you'll find that a value of 131 seems to achieve the best result.

What is that value of 131? It's the distance in device-independent units from the top of the text string to the baseline. That's the *Y* coordinate of the shadow that should be unaffected by the two transforms, so that's why it's set to the *CenterY* properties of the transforms.

Although you've now discovered a good value, of course it won't work for other font sizes. It won't even work for other font families, because every font apportions a different amount of its total height above and below the baseline. Try Arial, for example.

If you were coding this in C#, you'd calculate the value to use based on the *FontSize* property of the *TextBlock* and the *Baseline* property of the *FontFamily* class. The *Baseline* property is the distance from the top of the font characters to the baseline as a fraction of the font size. For a *FontFamily* object based on Times New Roman, for example, the *Baseline* property is approximately 0.91. Multiply that by the font size of 144 used in the EmpiricalTiltedText-Shadow.xaml program and you get 131.

Of course, that *Baseline* value of 0.91 isn't any good to a XAML programmer unless the *FontSize* is 1. You need to multiply the *Baseline* value by the *FontSize*, and there's no facility in XAML to perform a multiplication.

Or is there?

We've actually been performing multiplications and additions in XAML during this entire chapter. That's exactly what the transforms do, and you can use transforms to perform arbitrary calculations in a XAML file. Of course, these calculations won't be as clean and pretty as their equivalent C# code. In fact, they're appallingly convoluted. But if you're coding a stand-alone XAML program and you prefer that it not require any C# code just to do a calculation or two, transforms are definitely the solution.

For the particular task of calculating the baseline offset, you'll first want to define a *FontFamily* object as a resource:

```
<FontFamily x:Key="fntfam">
    Times New Roman
</FontFamily>
```

You'll also need a resource for the font size you want to use:

```
<s:Double x:Key="fntsize">
    144
</s:Double>
```

You'll also need a namespace declaration for the *System* namespace, of course. Following the definitions of the resources for the font family and font size, you define a resource for a *TransformGroup* containing two *ScaleTransform* objects:

```
<TransformGroup x:Key="xform">
    <ScaleTransform ScaleX="{Binding Source={StaticResource fntfam},
                                    Path=Baseline}" />
    <ScaleTransform ScaleX="{StaticResource fntsize}" />
</TransformGroup>
```

The *ScaleX* property of the first *ScaleTransform* is bound to the *Baseline* property of the *fntfam* resource. The second is simply the *fntsize* resource. The product of the two values ends up in the *xform* resource, but it's buried a bit. You'll recall that *TransformGroup* inherits a property named *Value* from *Transform*. The *Value* property is a *Matrix* object, and the *M11* property of this *Matrix* object will store the product of the font size and the *Baseline* property. You set the *CenterY* properties of the shadow's *ScaleTransform* and *SkewTransform* like this:

```
CenterY="{Binding Source={StaticResource xform}, Path=Value.M11}"
```

Here's the complete program.

TiltedTextShadow.xaml

```
<!-- =================================================
         TiltedTextShadow.xaml (c) 2006 by Charles Petzold
     ================================================= -->
<Canvas xmlns="http://schemas.microsoft.com/winfx/2006/xaml/presentation"
        xmlns:x="http://schemas.microsoft.com/winfx/2006/xaml"
        xmlns:s="clr-namespace:System;assembly=mscorlib" >
    <Canvas.Resources>
        <FontFamily x:Key="fntfam">
            Times New Roman
        </FontFamily>

        <s:Double x:Key="fntsize">
            144
        </s:Double>

        <TransformGroup x:Key="xform">
            <ScaleTransform ScaleX="{Binding Source={StaticResource fntfam},
                                           Path=Baseline}" />
```

```
                <ScaleTransform ScaleX="{StaticResource fntsize}" />
            </TransformGroup>

            <Style TargetType="{x:Type TextBlock}">
                <Setter Property="FontFamily" Value="{StaticResource fntfam}" />
                <Setter Property="FontSize" Value="{StaticResource fntsize}" />
                <Setter Property="Text" Value="Shadow" />
                <Setter Property="Canvas.Left" Value="96" />
                <Setter Property="Canvas.Top" Value="192" />
            </Style>
        </Canvas.Resources>

    <!-- Shadow Text. -->

    <TextBlock Foreground="DarkGray">
        <TextBlock.RenderTransform>
            <TransformGroup>
                <ScaleTransform ScaleY="3"
                    CenterY="{Binding Source={StaticResource xform},
                                      Path=Value.M11}" />
                <SkewTransform AngleX="-45"
                    CenterY="{Binding Source={StaticResource xform},
                                      Path=Value.M11}"/>
            </TransformGroup>
        </TextBlock.RenderTransform>
    </TextBlock>

    <!-- Foreground Text. -->

    <TextBlock />
</Canvas>
```

Notice that the *Style* for the *TextBlock* now references the font family and font size resources. If you want to change either value, just change it once toward the top of the *Resources* section and the change ripples through the rest of the code. (Just like a *real* program!)

The tilted drop shadow calculated with the *Baseline* property won't look quite right if the text you display has descenders. The *FontFamily* class also includes a property named *LineSpacing*, which is the suggested value to use for spacing successive lines of text as a fraction of the font size. *LineSpacing* is typically greater than 1 because the em size of a font is the approximate distance between the tops of the ascenders and the bottom of the descenders. Line spacing must also account for capital letters than contain diacritical marks.

The following program uses the *LineSpacing* property rather than *Baseline* for positioning the shadow for the word *quirky*. It comes close, but I don't think it works exactly.

TiltedTextShadow2.xaml

```
<!-- =================================================
        TiltedTextShadow2.xaml (c) 2006 by Charles Petzold
     ================================================= -->
<Canvas xmlns="http://schemas.microsoft.com/winfx/2006/xaml/presentation"
```

```
              xmlns:x="http://schemas.microsoft.com/winfx/2006/xaml"
              xmlns:s="clr-namespace:System;assembly=mscorlib" >
        <Canvas.Resources>
            <FontFamily x:Key="fntfam">
                Times New Roman
            </FontFamily>

            <s:Double x:Key="fntsize">
                144
            </s:Double>

            <TransformGroup x:Key="xform">
                <ScaleTransform ScaleX="{Binding Source={StaticResource fntfam},
                                                 Path=LineSpacing}" />
                <ScaleTransform ScaleX="{StaticResource fntsize}" />
            </TransformGroup>

            <Style TargetType="{x:Type TextBlock}">
                <Setter Property="FontFamily" Value="{StaticResource fntfam}" />
                <Setter Property="FontSize" Value="{StaticResource fntsize}" />
                <Setter Property="Text" Value="quirky" />
                <Setter Property="Canvas.Left" Value="96" />
                <Setter Property="Canvas.Top" Value="192" />
            </Style>
        </Canvas.Resources>

        <!-- Shadow Text. -->

        <TextBlock Foreground="DarkGray">
            <TextBlock.RenderTransform>
                <TransformGroup>
                    <ScaleTransform ScaleY="2.5"
                        CenterY="{Binding Source={StaticResource xform},
                                          Path=Value.M11}" />
                    <SkewTransform AngleX="-45"
                        CenterY="{Binding Source={StaticResource xform},
                                          Path=Value.M11}"/>
                </TransformGroup>
            </TextBlock.RenderTransform>
        </TextBlock>

        <!-- Foreground Text. -->

        <TextBlock />
    </Canvas>
```

You've already seen rotated buttons, so rotated text might not be as big a thrill as it once was. The following program rotates 18 *TextBlock* objects, each containing the same text, around a common point. Notice the use of *RenderTransformOrigin* set to the point (0, 0.5) to indicate the left edge of the *TextBlock* and the vertical center. The text itself is padded with four blank characters so that the initial letters aren't a complete jumble.

RotatedText.cs

```
//-------------------------------------------
// RotatedText.cs (c) 2006 by Charles Petzold
//-------------------------------------------
using System;
using System.Windows;
using System.Windows.Controls;
using System.Windows.Input;
using System.Windows.Media;

namespace Petzold.RotatedText
{
    public class RotatedText : Window
    {
        [STAThread]
        public static void Main()
        {
            Application app = new Application();
            app.Run(new RotatedText());
        }
        public RotatedText()
        {
            Title = "Rotated Text";

            // Make Canvas content of window.
            Canvas canv = new Canvas();
            Content = canv;

            // Display 18 rotated TextBlock elements.
            for (int angle = 0; angle < 360; angle += 20)
            {
                TextBlock txtblk = new TextBlock();
                txtblk.FontFamily = new FontFamily("Arial");
                txtblk.FontSize = 24;
                txtblk.Text = "     Rotated Text";
                txtblk.RenderTransformOrigin = new Point(0, 0.5);
                txtblk.RenderTransform = new RotateTransform(angle);

                canv.Children.Add(txtblk);
                Canvas.SetLeft(txtblk, 200);
                Canvas.SetTop(txtblk, 200);
            }
        }
    }
}
```

I wrote that program in C# because I felt reluctant to repeat an element 18 times that varied only by a transform. Let's go back to XAML for the following program, which displays the same text with four different combinations of horizontal and vertical scaling factors set to 1 and −1. These scaling values create reflected images, and the text string is reflected horizontally and vertically. As in TiltedTextShadow.xaml, this program multiplies the font size by the *Baseline* property of the *FontFamily* to set the *CenterY* property of two transforms.

ReflectedText.xaml

```xml
<!-- =============================================
        ReflectedText.xaml (c) 2006 by Charles Petzold
     ============================================= -->
<Canvas xmlns="http://schemas.microsoft.com/winfx/2006/xaml/presentation"
        xmlns:x="http://schemas.microsoft.com/winfx/2006/xaml"
        xmlns:s="clr-namespace:System;assembly=mscorlib">
    <Canvas.Resources>
        <FontFamily x:Key="fntfam">
            Times New Roman
        </FontFamily>

        <s:Double x:Key="fntsize">
            96
        </s:Double>

        <TransformGroup x:Key="xform">
            <ScaleTransform ScaleX="{Binding Source={StaticResource fntfam},
                                        Path=Baseline}" />
            <ScaleTransform ScaleX="{StaticResource fntsize}" />
        </TransformGroup>

        <Style TargetType="{x:Type TextBlock}">
            <Setter Property="FontFamily" Value="{StaticResource fntfam}" />
            <Setter Property="FontSize" Value="{StaticResource fntsize}" />
            <Setter Property="Text" Value="Reflect" />
            <Setter Property="Canvas.Left" Value="384" />
            <Setter Property="Canvas.Top" Value="48" />
        </Style>
    </Canvas.Resources>

    <TextBlock />

    <TextBlock>
        <TextBlock.RenderTransform>
            <ScaleTransform ScaleX="-1" />
        </TextBlock.RenderTransform>
    </TextBlock>

    <TextBlock>
        <TextBlock.RenderTransform>
            <ScaleTransform ScaleY="-1"
                CenterY="{Binding Source={StaticResource xform},
                            Path=Value.M11}" />
        </TextBlock.RenderTransform>
    </TextBlock>

    <TextBlock>
        <TextBlock.RenderTransform>
            <ScaleTransform ScaleX="-1" ScaleY="-1"
                CenterY="{Binding Source={StaticResource xform},
                            Path=Value.M11}" />
        </TextBlock.RenderTransform>
    </TextBlock>

</Canvas>
```

The following XAML is similar to the previous one except that it also rotates the reflected text by 45 degrees using a *RotateTransform* that's part of a *TransformGroup*.

RotateAndReflect.xaml

```xml
<!-- =================================================
        RotateAndReflect.xaml (c) 2006 by Charles Petzold
     ================================================= -->
<Canvas xmlns="http://schemas.microsoft.com/winfx/2006/xaml/presentation"
        xmlns:x="http://schemas.microsoft.com/winfx/2006/xaml"
        xmlns:s="clr-namespace:System;assembly=mscorlib">
    <Canvas.Resources>
        <FontFamily x:Key="fntfam">
            Times New Roman
        </FontFamily>

        <s:Double x:Key="fntsize">
            96
        </s:Double>

        <TransformGroup x:Key="xform">
            <ScaleTransform ScaleX="{Binding Source={StaticResource fntfam},
                                     Path=Baseline}" />
            <ScaleTransform ScaleX="{StaticResource fntsize}" />
        </TransformGroup>

        <Style TargetType="{x:Type TextBlock}">
            <Setter Property="FontFamily" Value="{StaticResource fntfam}" />
            <Setter Property="FontSize" Value="{StaticResource fntsize}" />
            <Setter Property="Text" Value="Reflect" />
            <Setter Property="Canvas.Left" Value="288" />
            <Setter Property="Canvas.Top" Value="192" />
        </Style>
    </Canvas.Resources>

    <TextBlock>
        <TextBlock.RenderTransform>
            <RotateTransform Angle="45"
                CenterY="{Binding Source={StaticResource xform},
                          Path=Value.M11}" />
        </TextBlock.RenderTransform>
    </TextBlock>

    <TextBlock>
        <TextBlock.RenderTransform>
            <TransformGroup>
                <ScaleTransform ScaleX="-1" />
                <RotateTransform Angle="45"
                    CenterY="{Binding Source={StaticResource xform},
                              Path=Value.M11}" />
            </TransformGroup>
        </TextBlock.RenderTransform>
    </TextBlock>

    <TextBlock>
        <TextBlock.RenderTransform>
```

```
                <TransformGroup>
                    <ScaleTransform ScaleY="-1"
                        CenterY="{Binding Source={StaticResource xform},
                                          Path=Value.M11}" />
                    <RotateTransform Angle="45"
                        CenterY="{Binding Source={StaticResource xform},
                                          Path=Value.M11}" />
                </TransformGroup>
            </TextBlock.RenderTransform>
        </TextBlock>

        <TextBlock>
            <TextBlock.RenderTransform>
                <TransformGroup>
                    <ScaleTransform ScaleX="-1" ScaleY="-1"
                        CenterY="{Binding Source={StaticResource xform},
                                          Path=Value.M11}" />
                    <RotateTransform Angle="45"
                        CenterY="{Binding Source={StaticResource xform},
                                          Path=Value.M11}" />
                </TransformGroup>
            </TextBlock.RenderTransform>
        </TextBlock>

    </Canvas>
```

Think about all the ways in which graphical objects have been manipulated in this chapter. I have just one sentence to tempt you to continue on to the next chapter:

Everything is animatable.

Chapter 30
Animation

Suppose you have a program with a button, and when the user clicks that button, you want the button to increase in size. You would prefer that the button not just jump from one size to a larger size. You want the button to increase in size smoothly. In other words, you want the increase in size to be animated. I'm sure there are some who would insist that buttons really shouldn't do such things, but their protests will be ignored in this chapter as the rest of us explore the animation facilities of the Microsoft Windows Presentation Foundation.

In the early chapters of this book, I showed you how to use *DispatcherTimer* to implement animation. Increasing the size of a button based on timer ticks is fairly easy.

```
EnlargeButtonWithTimer.cs
//-------------------------------------------------------
// EnlargeButtonWithTimer.cs (c) 2006 by Charles Petzold
//-------------------------------------------------------
using System;
using System.Windows;
using System.Windows.Controls;
using System.Windows.Input;
using System.Windows.Media;
using System.Windows.Threading;

namespace Petzold.EnlargeButtonWithTimer
{
    public class EnlargeButtonWithTimer : Window
    {
        const double initFontSize = 12;
        const double maxFontSize = 48;
        Button btn;

        [STAThread]
        public static void Main()
        {
            Application app = new Application();
            app.Run(new EnlargeButtonWithTimer());
        }
        public EnlargeButtonWithTimer()
        {
            Title = "Enlarge Button with Timer";

            btn = new Button();
            btn.Content = "Expanding Button";
            btn.FontSize = initFontSize;
            btn.HorizontalAlignment = HorizontalAlignment.Center;
```

```
            btn.VerticalAlignment = VerticalAlignment.Center;
            btn.Click += ButtonOnClick;
            Content = btn;
        }
        void ButtonOnClick(object sender, RoutedEventArgs args)
        {
            DispatcherTimer tmr = new DispatcherTimer();
            tmr.Interval = TimeSpan.FromSeconds(0.1);
            tmr.Tick += TimerOnTick;
            tmr.Start();
        }
        void TimerOnTick(object sender, EventArgs args)
        {
            btn.FontSize += 2;

            if (btn.FontSize >= maxFontSize)
            {
                btn.FontSize = initFontSize;
                (sender as DispatcherTimer).Stop();
            }
        }
    }
}
```

The button has an initial *FontSize* of 12 device-independent units. When clicked, the
event handler creates a *DispatcherTimer* that generates *Tick* events every tenth second. The
TimerOnTick method increases the *FontSize* by two units every tenth second until the size
reaches 48 units, at which point the button is restored to its original size and the timer is
stopped. It's easy to calculate that the whole process takes about 1.8 seconds: just multiply the
timer period by the difference in the initial and final *FontSize* values, divided by the increment
to the *FontSize* property.

What happens if you click the button a second time while it's expanding? The *Click* event
handler creates a second timer, so the button's size increases at twice the speed. When one of
the two timers increases the size to 48 units, that *Tick* handler restores the button's size and
stops that timer, but the other timer increases the button to 48 units again. Of course, such
behavior is easy to avoid if you set a Boolean variable when the timer is going and don't start
a second timer when that variable is set.

A couple of features of the WPF help make this animation a success. The retained graphics
system is designed so that visual objects can change size or position without flickering or
causing excessive redrawing. The dependency property system ensures that changing just the
FontSize property of the button will make the button larger to accommodate the new size.

Although you can always fall back on using *DispatcherTimer* if a particular animation requires
a lot of custom code, for many animations you can use the animation facilities built into the
WPF. Most of the animation-related classes are defined in the *System.Windows.Media.Animation*
namespace. Although this namespace contains almost 200 classes, very many of them fall into
just a few categories.

WPF animations always target dependency properties. The *System.Windows.Media.Animation* namespace has many classes because different classes exist for animating properties of various types. In alphabetical order, the 22 animatable types are *Boolean, Byte, Char, Color, Decimal, Double, Int16, Int32, Int64, Matrix, Object, Point, Point3D, Quaternion, Rect, Rotation3D, Single, Size, String, Thickness, Vector,* and *Vector3D*.

The *FontSize* property is of type *double,* so to animate the *FontSize* property, you can use a *double animation*—an animation that changes the size of a dependency property of type *double*. Properties of type double are very common throughout the WPF, and consequently, the double is probably the most common animated type.

There are actually three classes that implement *double* animations, as shown in the following partial class hierarchy:

Object

    DispatcherObject (abstract)

        DependencyObject

            Freezable (abstract)

                Animatable (abstract)

                    Timeline (abstract)

                        AnimationTimeline (abstract)

                            DoubleAnimationBase (abstract)

                                DoubleAnimation

                                DoubleAnimationUsingKeyFrames

                                DoubleAnimationUsingPath

For each of the 22 data types that you can animate, there exists an abstract class that begins with the data type followed by *AnimationBase,* such as *DoubleAnimationBase*. I'll refer to these classes collectively as *<Type>AnimationBase*. (But don't assume from my syntax that these classes are implemented as generics; they are not.) For all 22 data types, there also exists a *<Type>AnimationUsingKeyFrames* class. All but five types have a *<Type>Animation* class, and only three types have a *<Type>AnimationUsingPath* class. In total, there are 64 classes of *<Type>AnimationBase* and its derivatives.

The most straightforward of the classes that derive from *DoubleAnimationBase* is the *DoubleAnimation* class, which simply changes a property of type *double* linearly from one value to another. Here's a program that uses a *DoubleAnimation* object to mimic the behavior of the EnlargeButtonWithTimer program.

EnlargeButtonWithAnimation.cs

```
//---------------------------------------------------------
// EnlargeButtonWithAnimation.cs (c) 2006 by Charles Petzold
//---------------------------------------------------------
using System;
using System.Windows;
using System.Windows.Controls;
using System.Windows.Input;
using System.Windows.Media;
using System.Windows.Media.Animation;

namespace Petzold.EnlargeButtonWithAnimation
{
    public class EnlargeButtonWithAnimation : Window
    {
        const double initFontSize = 12;
        const double maxFontSize = 48;
        Button btn;

        [STAThread]
        public static void Main()
        {
            Application app = new Application();
            app.Run(new EnlargeButtonWithAnimation());
        }
        public EnlargeButtonWithAnimation()
        {
            Title = "Enlarge Button with Animation";

            btn = new Button();
            btn.Content = "Expanding Button";
            btn.FontSize = initFontSize;
            btn.HorizontalAlignment = HorizontalAlignment.Center;
            btn.VerticalAlignment = VerticalAlignment.Center;
            btn.Click += ButtonOnClick;
            Content = btn;
        }
        void ButtonOnClick(object sender, RoutedEventArgs args)
        {
            DoubleAnimation anima = new DoubleAnimation();
            anima.Duration = new Duration(TimeSpan.FromSeconds(2));
            anima.From = initFontSize;
            anima.To = maxFontSize;
            anima.FillBehavior = FillBehavior.Stop;

            btn.BeginAnimation(Button.FontSizeProperty, anima);
        }
    }
}
```

The constructor creates the *Button* object in the same way as the previous program, but the *Click* handler creates an object of type *DoubleAnimation*. Every animation has a duration, which you specify with a *Duration* structure, generally based on a *TimeSpan* object. In this case, the duration of the animation is set to two seconds.

The *ButtonOnClick* handler then sets the *From* and *To* properties of the *DoubleAnimation*, indicating that this animation will change a *double* property from an initial value of *initFontSize* (or 12) to a final value of *maxFontSize* (or 48). The animation essentially performs a linear interpolation between the two values to determine how large the *FontSize* of the button should be at any particular point in time during the animation.

Setting the *From* property isn't required in this example because the button's *FontSize* is initially 12 anyway. But if the *From* property indicated a value different from the value already set on the element being animated, the animation would begin by jumping to the value specified by the *From* property.

The *FillBehavior* property indicates what happens when the *double* reaches its value of 48 and the animation ends. The default value is *FillBehavior.HoldEnd*, which means that the value remains at 48. The *FillBehavior.Stop* option causes the *double* property to go back to its initial pre-animation value.

The *BeginAnimation* method is defined by *UIElement* (and a few other classes) and, of course, inherited by *Button*. The first argument is the dependency property being animated, and the second argument is the *DoubleAnimation* object to animate that property. Rather than calling the *BeginAnimation* method on the *Button* object, you could call *BeginAnimation* for the window:

```
BeginAnimation(Window.FontSizeProperty, anima);
```

This animation would change the *FontSize* of the *Window*, and the *Button* would then inherit that animated *FontSize* through normal property inheritance. Any other child of the window would also inherit that *FontSize*. In the complete scheme of dependency properties, animations have the highest priority in setting a property.

Rather than calling *BeginAnimation*, the program could kick off the animation with a call to *ApplyAnimationClock*, another method defined by *UIElement*:

```
btn.ApplyAnimationClock(Button.FontSizeProperty, anima.CreateClock());
```

Notice that the second argument is an object of type *AnimationClock* returned from the *CreateClock* method that is defined by *AnimationTimeline* and inherited by *DoubleAnimation*.

An object of type *Timeline* represents a period of time. This is the class that defines the *Duration* and *FillBehavior* properties, and some other time-related properties that I'll discuss shortly. The *AnimationTimeline* class derives from *Timeline* and defines the *CreateClock* method. The clock is the mechanism that paces the animation. The *DoubleAnimation* class itself defines the *From* and *To* properties, which are of type *double*.

The two C# programs shown so far begin the animation in response to a *Click* event from a *Button*. However, the animation could be started based on other criteria. For example, you could set a timer that checks the time of day and start an animation at the stroke of midnight. Or a program might use the *FileSystemWatcher* class to monitor the file system and start an animation whenever a new directory is created. Or a program might display an animation based on information obtained from a second thread of execution in the program.

Animations defined in XAML, however, are always associated with triggers. You are familiar with triggers and trigger collections from Chapters 24 and 25. The *Style*, *ControlTemplate*, and *DataTemplate* classes all define properties named *Triggers* that are collections of *TriggerBase* objects. In Chapter 24, I discussed four of the classes that derive from *TriggerBase*. These are *Trigger*, *MultiTrigger*, *DataTrigger*, and *MultiDataTrigger*. As you'll recall, these triggers have the power to change properties of elements based on changes in other properties or changes in data bindings.

Chapter 24 did not discuss the fifth class that derives from *TriggerBase*, which is *EventTrigger*, because this trigger is used mostly in connection with animations. (It can also trigger sounds.) This is the class you generally use in XAML in connection with animations, although you can also start an animation based on other types of triggers.

You might have discovered on your own that *FrameworkElement* defines a property named *Triggers* that is a collection of *Trigger* objects. I didn't discuss this *Triggers* collection in earlier chapters because it is very special. The *Triggers* collection defined by *FrameworkElement* can contain only *EventTrigger* objects, and you can't do much with *EventTrigger* objects except to trigger animations or play sounds.

EventTrigger defines three properties. The *SourceName* property is a *string* that refers to an element's *Name* or *x:Name* attribute. This is the element with the event that triggers the animation. (In common practice, the *SourceName* property is often implicitly defined by the context of *EventTrigger* and doesn't need to be explicitly specified.) The *RoutedEvent* property of *EventTrigger* is the particular triggering event. *EventTrigger* also defines an *Actions* property that indicates what happens when that event occurs. The *Actions* property is a collection of *TriggerAction* objects, and the most important class that derives from *TriggerAction* is *BeginStoryboard*.

A *Triggers* section of a *Button* control might look something like this:

```
<Button.Triggers>
    <EventTrigger RoutedEvent="Button.Click">
        <BeginStoryboard ... >
            ...
        </BeginStoryboard>
    </EventTrigger>
</Button.Triggers>
```

Animations in XAML always involve storyboards, which are objects that extend *Timeline* to provide information about property targeting. (You can also use storyboards in code, but as you've seen, you're not required to use them.) The child of *BeginStoryboard* is often a *Storyboard* element. Like *DoubleAnimation*, *Storyboard* derives from *Timeline*, as the following class hierarchy indicates:

Object

   DispatcherObject (abstract)

      Dependencyobject

         Freezable (abstract)

            Animatable (abstract)

               Timeline (abstract)

                  AnimationTimeline (abstract)

                     DoubleAnimationBase (abstract)

                        DoubleAnimation

                        DoubleAnimationUsingKeyFrames

                        DoubleAnimationUsingPath

                        ...

                     TimelineGroup (abstract)

                     ParallelTimeline

                     Storyboard

               MediaTimeline

The hierarchy is complete from *Timeline* on down, except for the ellipsis, which encompasses all of the various animation classes for all 22 animatable data types.

The *Storyboard* class has the ability to consolidate multiple timelines and also has attached properties to indicate the name and property of the element to which the animation applies. (Sometimes the element name is implied from the context.) The *TimelineGroup* class defines a *Children* property for a collection of timelines so that a *DoubleAnimation* can be a child of a *Storyboard*. Here's typical and more complete animation markup that goes all the way down to the *DoubleAnimation* object:

```
<Button.Triggers>
    <EventTrigger RoutedEvent="Button.Click">
        <BeginStoryboard ... >
            <Storyboard ... >
                <DoubleAnimation ... />
            </Storyboard>
        </BeginStoryboard>
    </EventTrigger>
</Button.Triggers>
```

These layers of markup might seem to form an excessively deep hole for the *DoubleAnimation* to reside in, but nothing is superfluous. The *Button.Triggers* section can have multiple *EventTrigger* elements. Often the trigger action is a *BeginStoryboard* object, but it can also be a *SoundPlayerAction* or a *ControllableStoryboardAction*. *BeginStoryboard* always has a *Storyboard* child, but that *Storyboard* can have multiple animations as children.

Here is the XAML equivalent of the animation that enlarges the button when you click it.

```
EnlargeButtonInXaml.xaml
<!-- =====================================================
        EnlargeButtonInXaml.xaml (c) 2006 by Charles Petzold
     ===================================================== -->
<Page xmlns="http://schemas.microsoft.com/winfx/2006/xaml/presentation"
      xmlns:x="http://schemas.microsoft.com/winfx/2006/xaml">

    <Button FontSize="12"
            HorizontalAlignment="Center" VerticalAlignment="Center">

        Expanding Button

        <Button.Triggers>
            <EventTrigger RoutedEvent="Button.Click">
                <BeginStoryboard>
                    <Storyboard TargetProperty="FontSize">
                        <DoubleAnimation From="12" To="48"
                                         Duration="0:0:2"
                                         FillBehavior="Stop" />
                    </Storyboard>
                </BeginStoryboard>
            </EventTrigger>
        </Button.Triggers>
    </Button>
</Page>
```

Notice that the *Triggers* section is part of the *Button* control, so the source element for the *EventTrigger* is implicitly the *Button* itself. The triggering event is *Click*. The *Storyboard* element refers to the *TargetProperty* of the animation. This is the property that the animation animates, and it must be a dependency property.

TargetProperty is more than just a property of *Storyboard*. It is an attached property of *Storyboard*, and the property alternatively can be moved to the *DoubleAnimation* element where it appears as *Storyboard.TargetProperty*:

```
<Storyboard>
    <DoubleAnimation Storyboard.TargetProperty="FontSize"
                 ... />
</Storyboard>
```

Storyboard also defines an attached property of *TargetName* so that different animations can target different elements in the XAML file. Both the *Storyboard.TargetName* and

Storyboard.TargetProperty attached properties are usually defined in children of the *Storyboard* element, but if all the child animations within a *Storyboard* have the same *TargetName* or *TargetProperty*, you can transfer the attribute to the *Storyboard* element, as I've done in the EnlargeButtonInXaml.xaml file.

Here's a variation of the previous XAML file that has two buttons in a *StackPanel*. They are given *Name* attributes of "btn1" and "btn2."

EnlargeButtonsInXaml.xaml

```xml
<!-- =====================================================
        EnlargeButtonsInXaml.xaml (c) 2006 by Charles Petzold
     ===================================================== -->
<Page xmlns="http://schemas.microsoft.com/winfx/2006/xaml/presentation"
      xmlns:x="http://schemas.microsoft.com/winfx/2006/xaml">

    <StackPanel HorizontalAlignment="Center" VerticalAlignment="Center">

        <Button Name="btn1" FontSize="12" Margin="12"
                HorizontalAlignment="Center">
            Expand Other Button
        </Button>

        <Button Name="btn2" FontSize="12" Margin="12"
                HorizontalAlignment="Center">
            Expand Other Button
        </Button>
    </StackPanel>

    <Page.Triggers>
        <EventTrigger SourceName="btn1" RoutedEvent="Button.Click">
            <BeginStoryboard>
                <Storyboard>
                    <DoubleAnimation Storyboard.TargetName="btn2"
                                     Storyboard.TargetProperty="FontSize"
                                     From="12" To="48"
                                     Duration="0:0:2"
                                     FillBehavior="Stop" />

                </Storyboard>
            </BeginStoryboard>
        </EventTrigger>

        <EventTrigger SourceName="btn2" RoutedEvent="Button.Click">
            <BeginStoryboard>
                <Storyboard>
                    <DoubleAnimation Storyboard.TargetName="btn1"
                                     Storyboard.TargetProperty="FontSize"
                                     From="12" To="48"
                                     Duration="0:0:2"
                                     FillBehavior="Stop" />

                </Storyboard>
            </BeginStoryboard>
        </EventTrigger>
    </Page.Triggers>
</Page>
```

Two *EventTrigger* elements are consolidated in the *Triggers* section of the *Page* rather than the *Triggers* section of the *Button*. Because these *EventTrigger* elements are actually concerned with *Button* events, they require a *SourceName* attribute to indicate the element generating the event. Each *DoubleAnimation* also has a *Storyboard.TargetName* attribute to indicate the control being animated. In an early version of this program, clicking a button caused that button to be enlarged, but I decided it was more interesting to switch the targets to that clicking a button causes the *other* button to expand.

The animation occurs over a period of time indicated by *Duration*, which commonly has a format of *hours:minutes:seconds*. Fractional seconds are allowed. For example, here's how you set the duration to 2.5 seconds:

```
Duration="0:0:2.5"
```

If you have long animations, you can simplify this syntax. The following attribute indicates three minutes:

```
Duration="0:3"
```

This next one is seven hours:

```
Duration="7"
```

Try it! (You don't have to let the animation continue to the end if you don't want to.) For durations of 24 hours or longer, you specify a number of days followed by a period, followed by the hours. The duration that follows is 4 days, 12 hours, and 7 minutes:

```
Duration="4.12:7"
```

If you leave out the *Duration* attribute or set it to the string "Automatic", the animation will run for one second. (In other contexts, it is also possible to set *Duration* to the string "Forever", but that option doesn't work in this particular context.)

The two XAML animations I've shown you change the *FontSize* property of the *Button* from a starting value to an ending value. The *From* and *To* attributes of *DoubleAnimation* indicate these values. If you leave out the *From* attribute, the animation will work pretty much the same because the *FontSize* of the *Button* is initially set to 12. (The difference occurs when you click the button in the middle of an animation. With the *From* attribute present, the animation begins again at 12; without this attribute, the animation continues from the value at the time you click the button.)

You can set the ending value to something less than the starting value:

```
From="48" To="12"
```

In this case, the animation begins by giving the button a *FontSize* of 48, which then decreases to 12.

An alternative to *To* is the *By* attribute:

`By="100"`

With *By*, the ending value is the starting value *plus* the *By* amount. If you use *By* by itself, the animation changes the button's font size from 12 to 112. The *To* and *By* attributes are mutually exclusive; if you include both, the *By* attribute is ignored.

This combination of attributes causes the *FontSize* to change from 50 to 100:

`From="50" To="100"`

With the following attributes, *FontSize* changes from 50 to 150:

`From="50" By="100"`

You can have a *From* attribute by itself with no *To* or *By* attributes:

`From="50"`

Now the animation changes the *FontSize* property from 50 to 12, which is the value specified in the *Button* element. If the *Button* element had no explicit *FontSize* attribute, the animation would change the property from 50 to the default *FontSize* value for the *Button* (typically 11).

If the animation includes *From* and *To* attributes, or *From* and *By* attributes, you can also include the *IsAdditive* attribute. Its default value is *false*; if you set it to *true*, the values specified in the *From*, *To*, and *By* attributes are added to the initial value of the target property. Here's an example:

`From="50" To="100" IsAdditive="True"`

If the initial value of *FontSize* is 12, the animation changes *FontSize* from 62 to 112. With the following markup with a *By* attribute instead of *To*, *FontSize* changes from 62 to 162:

`From="50" By="100" IsAdditive="True"`

So far, as you've seen, the *FontSize* snaps back to its starting value after the animation has completed. That's a result of setting the *FillBehavior* property to the enumeration value *FillBehavior.Stop*. The default value is *FillBehavior.HoldEnd*, which causes the *FontSize* to remain at the final value of the animation.

If you've been experimenting with either EnlargeButtonInXaml.xaml or EnlargeButtonsIn-Xaml.xaml, return to the file in its pristine state so that the *DoubleAnimation* element causes the *FontSize* to change from 12 to 48 over two seconds. You can set the *AutoReverse* property of *DoubleAnimation* to play the timeline in reverse after it's played forward:

`AutoReverse="True"`

Now the animation increases the *FontSize* from 12 to 48 over two seconds and then decreases *FontSize* from 48 back to 12 over two seconds. The *Duration* attribute indicates the time for just a single forward play of the *Timeline*.

So far, all the animations have run just once. You can change that by setting the *RepeatBehavior* attribute. Here's how you make the timeline play three times:

```
RepeatBehavior="3x"
```

This is called an *iteration* count. It indicates the total number of times the timeline is to play. (A value of 1x is the default.) The *Duration* attribute indicates the time for playing the timeline once. If you have the *Duration* attribute set to 0:0:2, *AutoReverse* set to *true*, and *RepeatBehavior* set to 3x, the entire animation lasts 12 seconds and the final *FontSize* value is 12. If you leave out the *AutoReverse* attribute or set it to *false*, the animation runs for six seconds, and the final value is 48 before the *FillBehavior* setting causes it to snap back to 12.

You can set *RepeatBehavior* to fractional iteration counts:

```
RepeatBehavior="1.5x"
```

If *AutoReverse* is *false*, the animation last three seconds, and the value when the animation ends is 30. (First the *FontSize* increases from 12 to 48, and then it begins increasing from 12 again but stops halfway through.) If *AutoReverse* is set to *true*, the animation lasts six seconds. The *FontSize* goes from 12 to 48 and then back to 12 (that's one iteration) and then from 12 to 48 (that's half of the second iteration).

Another approach is setting *RepeatBehavior* to a duration of time:

```
RepeatBehavior="0:0:10"
```

If *AutoReverse* is *false*, the animation changes the *FontSize* from 12 to 48 five times. If *Auto-Reverse* is *true*, the animation changes the *FontSize* from 12 to 48 and back to 12 twice, and then from 12 to 48. The duration specified in *RepeatBehavior* can be less than that in the *Duration* attribute, in which case the timeline doesn't finish playing once.

And then there is the ever-popular animation that continues forever or until boredom kicks in:

```
RepeatBehavior="Forever"
```

FillBehavior has no effect if *RepeatBehavior* is *Forever*.

When you set *RepeatBehavior* to play the timeline more than once, you can also set *IsCumulative* to *true*. Each iteration causes the values to accumulate. For example, consider the following markup:

```
<DoubleAnimation From="12" To="24"
                 Duration="0:0:2"
                 AutoReverse="true"
                 RepeatBehavior="3x"
                 IsCumulative="true" />
```

The first iteration goes from 12 to 24 and back to 12. The second iteration is from 24 to 36 and back to 24. The third iteration takes the values from 36 to 48 and back to 36.

If you want a delay between the event that triggers the animation and the time at which the timeline begins, you can specify that as the *BeginTime* attribute:

```
BeginTime="0:0:2"
```

Now there's a delay of two seconds before the timeline begins. After that, the *BeginTime* has no effect on repetitions and reversals. You can set *BeginTime* to a negative value to start the animation at a point beyond its actual beginning. For example, in the current examples, if you set *BeginTime* to −0:0:1, the animation begins with a *FontSize* of 30. You can also set *CutoffTime* to end an animation at a particular time. *CutoffTime* encompasses the duration you set in *BeginTime*.

Because an animation can last longer (or shorter) than the time you specify in the *Duration* property, I'll be using the term "total duration" to indicate the overall length of the animation as it's affected by *BeginTime*, *CutoffTime*, *RepeatBehavior*, and *AutoReverse*.

Storyboard derives from *TimelineGroup*, which defines a property named *Children* of type *Timeline*. This means that *Storyboard* can host multiple animations. All animations that share the same *Storyboard* are triggered by the same event.

The following stand-alone XAML file uses *Ellipse* to display a ball that is initially in the upper-left corner of a *Canvas* panel. The *EventTrigger* is based on the *MouseDown* event of the *Ellipse*. The *Storyboard* contains two *DoubleAnimation* objects. One animation changes the *Canvas.Left* attached property to make the ball move back and forth horizontally. The second animation changes the *Canvas.Top* attached property to make the ball move down and then back up. Notice that both *DoubleAnimation* elements include attributes for the *Storyboard. TargetProperty* attached property, and that the target properties of these two animations are themselves attached properties (*Canvas.Left* and *Canvas.Top*), so they must be enclosed in parentheses.

TwoAnimations.xaml

```
<!-- ===================================================
        TwoAnimations.xaml (c) 2006 by Charles Petzold
     =================================================== -->
<Canvas xmlns="http://schemas.microsoft.com/winfx/2006/xaml/presentation"
        xmlns:x="http://schemas.microsoft.com/winfx/2006/xaml">

    <Ellipse Width="48" Height="48" Fill="Red"
            Canvas.Left="0" Canvas.Top="0">

        <Ellipse.Triggers>
            <EventTrigger RoutedEvent="Ellipse.MouseDown">
                <BeginStoryboard>
                    <Storyboard>

                        <DoubleAnimation
                            Storyboard.TargetProperty="(Canvas.Left)"
                            From="0" To="288" Duration="0:0:1"
                            AutoReverse="True" />
```

```
                        <DoubleAnimation
                            Storyboard.TargetProperty="(Canvas.Top)"
                            From="0" To="480" Duration="0:0:5"
                            AutoReverse="True" />

                    </Storyboard>
                </BeginStoryboard>
            </EventTrigger>
        </Ellipse.Triggers>
    </Ellipse>
</Canvas>
```

Click the *Ellipse* to start the animation. The horizontal back-and-forth motion has a *Duration* setting of one second, whereas the up-and-down motion has a *Duration* of five seconds. Both have *AutoReverse* set to *true*. The total duration of the first animation is two seconds; the second is 10 seconds. These two animations begin at the same time. The composite animation has a total duration that is equal to the longest total duration of its components. That's 10 seconds.

What you'll see is the ball begin moving both down and to the right. After one second, the ball stops moving right and reverses itself to start moving left. When it reaches a horizontal position of 0, that first animation has concluded. The second animation continues moving the ball down and then back up.

If you want these two animations to have different *Duration* settings but to end at the same time, you need to set the *RepeatBehavior* property of the shorter animation. Here's a similar program, except that the horizontal motion has a *Duration* setting of one-fourth of a second. The vertical motion is five seconds. Both have *AutoReverse* set to *true*. For both animations to end at the same time, the first animation must have a *RepeatBehavior* setting of 20x.

WiggleWaggle.xaml

```
<!-- ================================================
        WiggleWaggle.xaml (c) 2006 by Charles Petzold
     ================================================ -->
<Canvas xmlns="http://schemas.microsoft.com/winfx/2006/xaml/presentation"
        xmlns:x="http://schemas.microsoft.com/winfx/2006/xaml">

    <Ellipse Width="48" Height="48" Fill="Red"
            Canvas.Left="0" Canvas.Top="0">

        <Ellipse.Triggers>
            <EventTrigger RoutedEvent="Ellipse.MouseDown">
                <BeginStoryboard>
                    <Storyboard>

                        <DoubleAnimation
                            Storyboard.TargetProperty="(Canvas.Left)"
                            From="0" To="288" Duration="0:0:0.25"
                            AutoReverse="True"
                            RepeatBehavior="20x" />
```

```
                                <DoubleAnimation
                                    Storyboard.TargetProperty="(Canvas.Top)"
                                    From="0" To="480" Duration="0:0:5"
                                    AutoReverse="True" />

                        </Storyboard>
                    </BeginStoryboard>
                </EventTrigger>
            </Ellipse.Triggers>
        </Ellipse>
    </Canvas>
```

Alternatively, you can set the *RepeatBehavior* of the first animation to a period of time. Because the second animation runs a total of 10 seconds, this would be as follows:

```
RepeatBehavior="0:0:10"
```

In either case, after the ball completes its 20 back-and-forth trips and its single up-and-down trip, the animation stops. If you want that show to run three times in a row, you can set the *RepeatBehavior* of the first animation to 60x and the *RepeatBehavior* of the second animation to 3x, or you can include a *RepeatBehavior* attribute right in the *Storyboard* element that applies to the two *DoubleAnimation* elements:

```
<Storyboard RepeatBehavior="3x">
```

You can also set that *RepeatBehavior* to *Forever*. Or you can leave out the *RepeatBehavior* in the *Storyboard* and set the *RepeatBehavior* to *Forever* in both *DoubleAnimation* elements.

If you decide that you'd like to speed up the animation by 50 percent, you don't need to change the *Duration* settings in the individual *DoubleAnimation* elements. You can just set the *SpeedRatio* property in the *Storyboard*:

```
<Storyboard SpeedRatio="1.5">
```

This feature is ideal for debugging animations, particularly when you are dealing with parallel animations. You can initially set *Duration* values so the animations run very slowly for debugging, and then you can eventually speed everything up by setting a *SpeedRatio* to apply to the composite animation.

All sibling animations begin at the same time. If that's not what you want, you need to use the *BeginTime* property to delay the start of an animation. In some cases, you might have a group of parallel animations that, when concluded, should be followed by another group of parallel animations. You can use the same *BeginTime* property on all the animations of the second group so that they follow the completion of the first group, or you can enclose the second group of animations in a *ParallelTimeline* element and set the *BeginTime* just for that element. Here's an example.

```
WiggleWaggleAndExplode.xaml
<!-- =======================================================
         WiggleWaggleAndExplode.xaml (c) 2006 by Charles Petzold
     ======================================================= -->
<Canvas xmlns="http://schemas.microsoft.com/winfx/2006/xaml/presentation"
        xmlns:x="http://schemas.microsoft.com/winfx/2006/xaml">

    <Ellipse Width="48" Height="48" Fill="Red"
             Canvas.Left="0" Canvas.Top="0">

        <Ellipse.Triggers>
            <EventTrigger RoutedEvent="Ellipse.MouseDown">
                <BeginStoryboard>
                    <Storyboard>

                        <DoubleAnimation
                            Storyboard.TargetProperty="(Canvas.Left)"
                            From="0" To="288" Duration="0:0:0.25"
                            AutoReverse="True"
                            RepeatBehavior="20x" />

                        <DoubleAnimation
                            Storyboard.TargetProperty="(Canvas.Top)"
                            From="0" To="480" Duration="0:0:5"
                            AutoReverse="True" />

                        <ParallelTimeline BeginTime="0:0:10"
                                          FillBehavior="Stop">
                            <DoubleAnimation
                                Storyboard.TargetProperty="Width"
                                From="48" To="480" Duration="0:0:1" />

                            <DoubleAnimation
                                Storyboard.TargetProperty="Height"
                                From="48" To="480" Duration="0:0:1" />
                        </ParallelTimeline>

                    </Storyboard>
                </BeginStoryboard>
            </EventTrigger>
        </Ellipse.Triggers>
    </Ellipse>
</Canvas>
```

The idea here is that after the ball returns to its original position, two *DoubleAnimation* elements quickly increase the *Width* and *Height* of the ball to 5 inches. Then the ball "explodes" and returns to its original size.

The two *DoubleAnimation* objects that increase the size are grouped in a *ParallelTimeline* element. This *ParallelTimeline* has a *BeginTime* of 10 seconds, which is the total duration of the first two animations. The *ParallelTimeline* element also sets the *FillBehavior* to *Stop*. Both the *BeginTime* and the *FillBehavior* apply to the two children of the *ParallelTimeline*. These two properties could have been included in both *DoubleAnimation* children, but consolidating them in the *ParallelTimeline* element makes the program easier to understand and change.

So far, most of the programs I've shown have altered an element or control in response to an event on that element or control. One element's events can also trigger animations in other elements. The following stand-alone XAML file displays a *Page* with three radio buttons labeled red, green, and blue. Clicking any button changes the background color of the *Page*.

This program uses *ColorAnimation* elements, which work pretty much the same as *Double-Animation* except that the *From*, *To*, and *By* properties are of type *Color*, and the *TargetProperty* must be of type *Color*.

ColorRadioButtons.xaml

```xaml
<!-- =====================================================
        ColorRadioButtons.xaml (c) 2006 by Charles Petzold
     ===================================================== -->
<Page xmlns="http://schemas.microsoft.com/winfx/2006/xaml/presentation"
      xmlns:x="http://schemas.microsoft.com/winfx/2006/xaml"
      Background="{x:Static SystemColors.WindowBrush}"
      Name="page">

    <Page.Resources>
        <Style TargetType="{x:Type RadioButton}">
            <Setter Property="Margin" Value="6" />
        </Style>
    </Page.Resources>

    <StackPanel HorizontalAlignment="Center"
                VerticalAlignment="Center"
                Background="{DynamicResource
                            {x:Static SystemColors.ControlBrushKey}}">

        <RadioButton Content="Red">
            <RadioButton.Triggers>
                <EventTrigger RoutedEvent="RadioButton.Checked">
                    <BeginStoryboard>
                        <Storyboard>
                            <ColorAnimation
                                Storyboard.TargetName="page"
                                Storyboard.TargetProperty="Background.Color"
                                To="Red" Duration="0:0:1" />
                        </Storyboard>
                    </BeginStoryboard>
                </EventTrigger>
            </RadioButton.Triggers>
        </RadioButton>

        <RadioButton Content="Green">
            <RadioButton.Triggers>
```

```
                    <EventTrigger RoutedEvent="RadioButton.Checked">
                        <BeginStoryboard>
                            <Storyboard>
                                <ColorAnimation
                                    Storyboard.TargetName="page"
                                    Storyboard.TargetProperty="Background.Color"
                                    To="Green" Duration="0:0:1" />
                            </Storyboard>
                        </BeginStoryboard>
                    </EventTrigger>
                </RadioButton.Triggers>
            </RadioButton>

            <RadioButton Content="Blue">
                <RadioButton.Triggers>
                    <EventTrigger RoutedEvent="RadioButton.Checked">
                        <BeginStoryboard>
                            <Storyboard>
                                <ColorAnimation
                                    Storyboard.TargetName="page"
                                    Storyboard.TargetProperty="Background.Color"
                                    To="Blue" Duration="0:0:1" />
                            </Storyboard>
                        </BeginStoryboard>
                    </EventTrigger>
                </RadioButton.Triggers>
            </RadioButton>
        </StackPanel>
    </Page>
```

The *Page* root element is assigned a *Name* property of *page*, and each of the *ColorAnimation* elements refers to that target. The *TargetProperty* is the *Color* property of the *Background* property of the *Page*, under the assumption that this *Background* property is a *SolidColorBrush* object, which is not normally the case. For this markup to work, the *Page* needs to be initialized with a *SolidColorBrush*, as it is in the root element. The animations have no *From* property, so the background color changes from the current color to the color specified as *To* over a period of one second.

The quantity of repetitious markup here will probably convince you to implement these radio buttons in code if you want to have more than just a couple of them.

Why didn't I use a *Style* to reduce the repetitious markup in ColorRadiusButtons.xaml? It is certainly possible to include animations in a *Triggers* section of a *Style* definition, but the animations in the *Style* cannot target an element other than the one being styled. Here's a stand-alone XAML file that includes a *Style* for *Button* elements. The *Style* includes a couple of *Setter* elements and, within the *Triggers* section, two *EventTrigger* elements. The first is triggered by the *MouseEnter* event, and the second by the *MouseLeave* event. Both start a *DoubleAnimation* that changes the *FontSize* of the *Button*.

FishEyeButtons1.xaml

```
<!-- =====================================================
        FishEyeButtons1.xaml (c) 2006 by Charles Petzold
     ===================================================== -->
<StackPanel xmlns="http://schemas.microsoft.com/winfx/2006/xaml/presentation"
            xmlns:x="http://schemas.microsoft.com/winfx/2006/xaml">

    <StackPanel.Resources>
        <Style TargetType="{x:Type Button}">
            <Setter Property="HorizontalAlignment" Value="Center" />
            <Setter Property="FontSize" Value="12" />
            <Style.Triggers>
                <EventTrigger RoutedEvent="Button.MouseEnter">
                    <BeginStoryboard>
                        <Storyboard>
                            <DoubleAnimation
                                Storyboard.TargetProperty="FontSize"
                                To="36" Duration="0:0:1" />
                        </Storyboard>
                    </BeginStoryboard>
                </EventTrigger>
                <EventTrigger RoutedEvent="Button.MouseLeave">
                    <BeginStoryboard>
                        <Storyboard>
                            <DoubleAnimation
                                Storyboard.TargetProperty="FontSize"
                                To="12" Duration="0:0:0.25" />
                        </Storyboard>
                    </BeginStoryboard>
                </EventTrigger>
            </Style.Triggers>
        </Style>
    </StackPanel.Resources>

    <Button>Button No. 1</Button>
    <Button>Button No. 2</Button>
    <Button>Button No. 3</Button>
    <Button>Button No. 4</Button>
    <Button>Button No. 5</Button>
    <Button>Button No. 6</Button>
    <Button>Button No. 7</Button>
    <Button>Button No. 8</Button>
    <Button>Button No. 9</Button>
</StackPanel>
```

These two *EventTrigger* elements cause the buttons to exhibit a "fish-eye" effect when the pointer passes over them. As the mouse pointer rests on a button, the button gradually grows to three times its normal size. When the pointer leaves, the button quickly returns to its normal size.

As you'll note, if you move the pointer over a button and then pull it away quickly, the button won't go to the full size of 36 specified in the first *DoubleAnimation*. This is a result of the default *HandoffBehavior* property defined by *BeginStoryboard*. This property governs the interaction of two different animations that affect the same property. The default setting for *HandoffBehavior* is the enumeration value *HandoffBehavior.SnapshotAndReplace*, which stops the previous animation, takes a "snapshot" of its current value, and then replaces the animation with the new one.

To see an alternative approach, change the *BeginStoryboard* element in the *MouseLeave* section to have a *HandoffBehavior* setting of *HandoffBehavior.Compose*:

```
<BeginStoryboard HandoffBehavior="Compose">
```

Also, change the *Duration* to one second. Now when you move the pointer over a button and then pull it away, the button continues to expand a bit before the second animation kicks in.

When you define an animation in an element, it needs to be triggered by an *EventTrigger* in the *Triggers* section of that element. In a *Style*, however, you don't need to trigger the animation with *EventTrigger*. Here's an alternative approach to the fish-eye buttons that triggers the animation with a regular *Trigger* for the property *IsMouseOver*.

FishEyeButtons2.xaml

```
<!-- ===================================================
        FishEyeButtons2.xaml (c) 2006 by Charles Petzold
     =================================================== -->
<StackPanel xmlns="http://schemas.microsoft.com/winfx/2006/xaml/presentation"
            xmlns:x="http://schemas.microsoft.com/winfx/2006/xaml">

    <StackPanel.Resources>
        <Style TargetType="{x:Type Button}">
            <Setter Property="HorizontalAlignment" Value="Center" />
            <Setter Property="FontSize" Value="12" />
            <Style.Triggers>
                <Trigger Property="IsMouseOver" Value="True">
                    <Trigger.EnterActions>
                        <BeginStoryboard>
                            <Storyboard>
                                <DoubleAnimation
                                    Storyboard.TargetProperty="FontSize"
                                    To="36" Duration="0:0:1" />
                            </Storyboard>
                        </BeginStoryboard>
                    </Trigger.EnterActions>

                    <Trigger.ExitActions>
                        <BeginStoryboard>
                            <Storyboard>
                                <DoubleAnimation
                                    Storyboard.TargetProperty="FontSize"
                                    To="12" Duration="0:0:0.25" />
                            </Storyboard>
                        </BeginStoryboard>
                    </Trigger.ExitActions>
```

```
                    </Trigger>
                </Style.Triggers>
            </Style>
        </StackPanel.Resources>

        <Button>Button No. 1</Button>
        <Button>Button No. 2</Button>
        <Button>Button No. 3</Button>
        <Button>Button No. 4</Button>
        <Button>Button No. 5</Button>
        <Button>Button No. 6</Button>
        <Button>Button No. 7</Button>
        <Button>Button No. 8</Button>
        <Button>Button No. 9</Button>
</StackPanel>
```

In this case, it's necessary for *BeginStoryboard* to be a child of the *EnterActions* and *ExitActions* collections that are defined by *TriggerBase*.

Changing the size of a *Button* by changing its *FontSize* is convenient, but it's not a general solution to changing the size of elements. In the general case, you'll probably want to set a transform for the element and then animate that transform. Animating transforms is particularly handy when you are implementing animated rotation. You may wonder about the propriety of a *Button* that rotates, but consider a program in which it might be useful to deliver a little feedback after a button click to assure the user that the program has recognized the click. You could, for example, use rotation to "shake" the button a bit.

When animating transforms, you can make the *TargetName* either the element that contains the transform, or the transform itself. Generally, you animate *RenderTransform* rather than *LayoutTransform*. The *TargetProperty* of the animation refers to a property of the *RenderTransform* of the element being animated. By default, the *RenderTransform* property is a *MatrixTransform* object, so if you don't want to animate individual properties of a *Matrix* structure, you must first set *RenderTransform* to a particular type of transform (for example, *RotateTransform*) and then animate a property of that transform.

The following XAML file defines a *Style* for a *Button*, where the *RenderTransform* property of the *Button* is set to a *RotateTransform* object with default settings (that is, no rotation). In addition, the *RenderTransformOrigin* is set to the value (0.5, 0.5), so any rotation occurs around the center of the button.

ShakingButton.xaml
```
<!-- =============================================
        ShakingButton.xaml (c) 2006 by Charles Petzold
     ============================================= -->
<StackPanel xmlns="http://schemas.microsoft.com/winfx/2006/xaml/presentation"
            xmlns:x="http://schemas.microsoft.com/winfx/2006/xaml">

    <StackPanel.Resources>
```

```
        <Style TargetType="{x:Type Button}">
            <Setter Property="HorizontalAlignment" Value="Center" />
            <Setter Property="Margin" Value="12" />
            <Setter Property="RenderTransformOrigin" Value="0.5 0.5" />
            <Setter Property="RenderTransform">
                <Setter.Value>
                    <RotateTransform />
                </Setter.Value>
            </Setter>
            <Style.Triggers>
                <EventTrigger RoutedEvent="Button.Click">
                    <BeginStoryboard>
                        <Storyboard TargetProperty="RenderTransform.Angle">
                            <DoubleAnimation
                                From="-5" To="5" Duration="0:0:0.05"
                                AutoReverse="True"
                                RepeatBehavior="3x"
                                FillBehavior="Stop" />
                        </Storyboard>
                    </BeginStoryboard>
                </EventTrigger>
            </Style.Triggers>
        </Style>
    </StackPanel.Resources>

    <Button>Button No. 1</Button>
    <Button>Button No. 2</Button>
    <Button>Button No. 3</Button>
    <Button>Button No. 4</Button>
    <Button>Button No. 5</Button>
</StackPanel>
```

The *TargetProperty* of the animation is *RenderTransform.Angle*, so obviously the animation is assuming that *RenderTransform* has already been set to an object of type *RotateTransform*. Over the course of 0.05 seconds, the rotation angle changes from –5 degrees to 5 degrees. It's then reversed and repeated twice more.

If you slowed down this animation, you would see that the button initially jumps from its normal position to a rotation of –5 degrees, and at the end jumps back. At high speeds, this is imperceptible, but in other cases, you might want to first animate the button from 0 degrees to –5 degrees, then move it repeatedly between –5 degrees and 5 degrees, and conclude with a third animation that moves it gracefully from –5 degrees back to 0 degrees. This is a job for a *key-frame* animation, which I'll discuss later in this chapter.

An animation can be controlled while in progress by making use of classes that derive from *ControllableStoryboardAction*. The following class hierarchy shows how these classes fit in with the other derivatives of *TriggerAction*.

Object

    DispatcherObject (abstract)

DependencyObject

 TriggerAction (abstract)

  SoundPlayerAction

  BeginStoryboard

  ControllableStoryboardAction (abstract)

   PauseStoryboard

   RemoveStoryboard

   ResumeStoryboard

   SeekStoryboard

   SetStoryboardSpeedRatio

   SkipStoryboardToFill

   StopStoryboard

To use these classes, you set up an animation normally with *BeginStoryboard*, and you assign *BeginStoryboard* a *Name* attribute. *ControllableStoryboardAction* defines a property named *BeginStoryboardName* that you use to refer to this name. Like *BeginStoryboard*, these derivatives of *ControllableStoryboardAction* are defined as part of a *TriggerAction* collection.

Here's a stand-alone XAML file with a *Rectangle* that has two *RotateTransform* objects defined—one centered around its lower-left corner and the other centered around its lower-right corner. The storyboard (defined normally except that the *BeginStoryboard* has its *Name* attribute defined) uses a *DoubleAnimation* to change the angle of the first *RotateTransform* from −90 degrees to 0 degrees, and then a second *DoubleAnimation* changes the angle of the second *RotateTransform* from 0 degrees to 90 degrees, making it appear as if the rectangle stands up, and then falls down in the other direction.

ControllingTheStoryboard.xaml

```
<!-- ========================================================
        ControllingTheStoryboard.xaml (c) 2006 by Charles Petzold
     ======================================================== -->
<Page xmlns="http://schemas.microsoft.com/winfx/2006/xaml/presentation"
      xmlns:x="http://schemas.microsoft.com/winfx/2006/xaml">
    <StackPanel>

        <!-- Canvas displaying animated rectangle. -->
        <Canvas Width="350" Height="200">
            <Rectangle Canvas.Left="150" Canvas.Top="50"
                       Stroke="Black" StrokeThickness="4" Fill="Aqua"
                       Width="50" Height="150">
```

```xml
                    <Rectangle.RenderTransform>
                        <TransformGroup>
                            <RotateTransform x:Name="xform1" Angle="-90"
                                             CenterX="0" CenterY="150" />
                            <RotateTransform x:Name="xform2"
                                             CenterX="50" CenterY="150" />
                        </TransformGroup>
                    </Rectangle.RenderTransform>
                </Rectangle>
            </Canvas>


            <!-- StackPanel with buttons to control animation. -->
            <StackPanel Orientation="Horizontal" HorizontalAlignment="Center">
                <Button Name="btnBegin" Content="Begin" Margin="12" />
                <Button Name="btnPause" Content="Pause" Margin="12" />
                <Button Name="btnResume" Content="Resume" Margin="12" />
                <Button Name="btnStop" Content="Stop" Margin="12" />
                <Button Name="btnSkip" Content="Skip to End" Margin="12" />
                <Button Name="btnCenter" Content="Skip to Center" Margin="12" />
            </StackPanel>


            <!-- Triggers section for button clicks. -->
            <StackPanel.Triggers>
                <EventTrigger SourceName="btnBegin" RoutedEvent="Button.Click">
                    <BeginStoryboard Name="storybrd">
                        <Storyboard >
                            <DoubleAnimation
                                Storyboard.TargetName="xform1"
                                Storyboard.TargetProperty="Angle"
                                From="-90" To="0" Duration="0:0:5" />

                            <DoubleAnimation
                                Storyboard.TargetName="xform2"
                                Storyboard.TargetProperty="Angle"
                                BeginTime="0:0:5"
                                From="0" To="90" Duration="0:0:5" />

                        </Storyboard>
                    </BeginStoryboard>
                </EventTrigger>

                <EventTrigger SourceName="btnPause" RoutedEvent="Button.Click">
                    <PauseStoryboard BeginStoryboardName="storybrd" />
                </EventTrigger>

                <EventTrigger SourceName="btnResume" RoutedEvent="Button.Click">
                    <ResumeStoryboard BeginStoryboardName="storybrd" />
                </EventTrigger>

                <EventTrigger SourceName="btnStop" RoutedEvent="Button.Click">
                    <StopStoryboard BeginStoryboardName="storybrd" />
                </EventTrigger>

                <EventTrigger SourceName="btnSkip" RoutedEvent="Button.Click">
                    <SkipStoryboardToFill BeginStoryboardName="storybrd" />
```

```
                </EventTrigger>

                <EventTrigger SourceName="btnCenter" RoutedEvent="Button.Click">
                    <SeekStoryboard BeginStoryboardName="storybrd"
                                    Offset="0:0:5" />
                </EventTrigger>

            </StackPanel.Triggers>
        </StackPanel>
    </Page>
```

Six buttons sit under the rectangle, each of which is given a *Name*. The *StackPanel.Triggers* section contains *EventTrigger* elements associated with the *Click* events for each of these buttons. The Begin button starts the animation like normal. The Pause button triggers the *PauseStoryboard* action, which pauses the animation. The Resume button resumes it. The Stop button returns the rectangle to its pre-animated state. The button labeled Skip To End triggers the *SkipStoryboardToFill* action, which skips to the end of the animation and whatever the *FillBehavior* has in store. The *SeekStoryboard* action can go to an arbitrary point in the animation. I chose to make it go to the middle.

I originally defined a *Triggers* section for each of the buttons and put the individual *EventTrigger* elements in these *Triggers* sections, but I couldn't get the program to work that way. Apparently, all the *EventTrigger* objects that begin and control the storyboard must be consolidated in the same *Triggers* section.

In many XAML demonstration programs, an animation begins as soon as the program is loaded and continues until the program is terminated. In these files, the *Loaded* event triggers the animation. This trigger can be the *Loaded* event for the element being animated or the *Loaded* event for another element, perhaps a *Panel* or the *Page*.

The following stand-alone XAML file is an animated version of the RenderTransformAndLayoutTransform.xaml file from the previous chapter. It demonstrates why you should usually animate *RenderTransform* to cause as little disruption to the element's environment as possible, unless you actually *want* the animated element to affect layout, in which case you should definitely animate *LayoutTransform*.

RenderTransformVersusLayoutTransform.xaml

```
<!-- =======================================================================
        RenderTransformVersusLayoutTransform.xaml (c) 2006 by Charles Petzold
     ======================================================================= -->
<StackPanel xmlns="http://schemas.microsoft.com/winfx/2006/xaml/presentation"
            xmlns:x="http://schemas.microsoft.com/winfx/2006/xaml"
            TextBlock.FontSize="18pt" >

    <!-- RenderTransform section. -->
    <TextBlock TextAlignment="Center"
               Margin="24">
        Animate <Italic>RenderTransform</Italic>
```

```xaml
        </TextBlock>
        <UniformGrid Rows="3" Columns="3">
            <Button Content="Button" />
            <Button Content="Button" />
            <Button Content="Button" />
            <Button Content="Button" />
            <Button Content="Button">
                <Button.RenderTransform>
                    <RotateTransform x:Name="xform1" />
                </Button.RenderTransform>
            </Button>
            <Button Content="Button" />
            <Button Content="Button" />
            <Button Content="Button" />
            <Button Content="Button" />
        </UniformGrid>

        <!-- LayoutTransform section. -->
        <TextBlock TextAlignment="Center"
                   Margin="24">
            Animate <Italic>LayoutTransform</Italic>
        </TextBlock>
        <UniformGrid Rows="3" Columns="3">
            <Button Content="Button" />
            <Button Content="Button" />
            <Button Content="Button" />
            <Button Content="Button" />
            <Button Content="Button" >
                <Button.LayoutTransform>
                    <RotateTransform x:Name="xform2" />
                </Button.LayoutTransform>
            </Button>
            <Button Content="Button" />
            <Button Content="Button" />
            <Button Content="Button" />
            <Button Content="Button" />
        </UniformGrid>

        <!-- Animations. -->
        <StackPanel.Triggers>
            <EventTrigger RoutedEvent="StackPanel.Loaded">
                <BeginStoryboard>
                    <Storyboard>
                        <DoubleAnimation Storyboard.TargetName="xform2"
                                         Storyboard.TargetProperty="Angle"
                                         Duration="0:0:10"
                                         From="0" To="360"
                                         RepeatBehavior="Forever" />

                        <DoubleAnimation Storyboard.TargetName="xform1"
                                         Storyboard.TargetProperty="Angle"
                                         Duration="0:0:10"
                                         From="0" To="360"
                                         RepeatBehavior="Forever" />
                    </Storyboard>
```

```
            </BeginStoryboard>
        </EventTrigger>
    </StackPanel.Triggers>
</StackPanel>
```

As you might recall from the nonanimated version of this program, two 3-by-3 *UniformGrid* panels are filled with buttons, and the middle button of each is rotated, the first with *RenderTransform* and the second with *LayoutTransform*. In this version, the two angles of rotation are animated.

The root element is a *StackPanel*, and the two animations are included in the *Triggers* section for the *StackPanel*, with a triggering event of *Loaded*. The target properties of the animations are the transforms themselves, which have both been given *x:Name* attributes. The *TargetProperty* is just *Angle*. The animations continue forever.

When you're using a program like XAML Cruncher to experiment with an animation triggered by a *Loaded* event, keep in mind that the animation begins anew when the file passes through the *XamlReader.Load* method and the elements are recreated. In XAML Cruncher, this happens with each editor keystroke that alters the text of the file. You might instead want to suspend automatic parsing and press F6 to parse manually and begin the animation.

Animations that start automatically and continue forever can be fun and educational as well. The following stand-alone XAML file defines a single *Path* based on two *EllipseGeometry* objects, the second of which is rotated by the animation. As the first circle meets up with the second circle, it provides a dramatic visual reminder of the default *FillRule* of *EvenOdd*.

TotalEclipseOfTheSun.xaml

```
<!-- ========================================================
     TotalEclipseOfTheSun.xaml (c) 2006 by Charles Petzold
     ======================================================== -->
<Canvas xmlns="http://schemas.microsoft.com/winfx/2006/xaml/presentation"
        xmlns:x="http://schemas.microsoft.com/winfx/2006/xaml">

    <Path Fill="Gray" Stroke="Black" StrokeThickness="3">
        <Path.Data>
            <GeometryGroup>
                <EllipseGeometry Center="96 288" RadiusX="48" RadiusY="48" />
                <EllipseGeometry Center="288 96" RadiusX="48" RadiusY="48">
                    <EllipseGeometry.Transform>
                        <RotateTransform x:Name="rotate"
                                         CenterX="288" CenterY="288" />
                    </EllipseGeometry.Transform>
                </EllipseGeometry>
            </GeometryGroup>
        </Path.Data>
    </Path>

    <Canvas.Triggers>
        <EventTrigger RoutedEvent="Canvas.Loaded">
```

```
                <BeginStoryboard>
                    <Storyboard>
                        <DoubleAnimation Storyboard.TargetName="rotate"
                                         Storyboard.TargetProperty="Angle"
                                         From="0" To="360" Duration="0:0:5"
                                         RepeatBehavior="Forever" />
                    </Storyboard>
                </BeginStoryboard>
            </EventTrigger>
        </Canvas.Triggers>
    </Canvas>
```

The following XAML program has a *TextBlock* with both a *ScaleTransform* and a *RotateTransform* defined in a *TransformGroup*. The *ScaleX* property of the *ScaleTransform* is animated between 1 and –1 to flip the text around the vertical axis, almost simulating text rotating in three dimensions around a vertical axis. The *RotateTransform* rotates the text around its center. The two animations have different durations and repeat forever for a mix of effects.

AnimatedTextTransform.xaml

```
<!-- =====================================================
        AnimatedTextTransform.xaml (c) 2006 by Charles Petzold
     ===================================================== -->
<Page xmlns="http://schemas.microsoft.com/winfx/2006/xaml/presentation"
      xmlns:x="http://schemas.microsoft.com/winfx/2006/xaml">

    <TextBlock Text="XAML" FontSize="144pt" FontFamily="Arial Black"
               HorizontalAlignment="Center" VerticalAlignment="Center"
               RenderTransformOrigin="0.5 0.5">

        <TextBlock.RenderTransform>
            <TransformGroup>
                <ScaleTransform x:Name="xformScale" />
                <RotateTransform x:Name="xformRotate" />
            </TransformGroup>
        </TextBlock.RenderTransform>

        <TextBlock.Triggers>
            <EventTrigger RoutedEvent="TextBlock.Loaded">
                <BeginStoryboard>
                    <Storyboard>
                        <DoubleAnimation Storyboard.TargetName="xformScale"
                                         Storyboard.TargetProperty="ScaleX"
                                         From="1" To="-1" Duration="0:0:3"
                                         AutoReverse="True"
                                         RepeatBehavior="Forever" />

                        <DoubleAnimation Storyboard.TargetName="xformRotate"
                                         Storyboard.TargetProperty="Angle"
                                         From="0" To="360" Duration="0:0:5"
                                         RepeatBehavior="Forever" />
                    </Storyboard>
                </BeginStoryboard>
```

```
                </EventTrigger>
            </TextBlock.Triggers>
        </TextBlock>
    </Page>
```

So far I've shown programs that use *DoubleAnimation* and *ColorAnimation*. Another common type of animation is *PointAnimation*, which is an animation between two *Point* objects. The following stand-alone XAML program defines a *Path* made of four *Bezier* splines.

SquaringTheCircle.xaml

```
<!-- ===================================================
        SquaringTheCircle.xaml (c) 2006 by Charles Petzold
     =================================================== -->
<Canvas xmlns="http://schemas.microsoft.com/winfx/2006/xaml/presentation"
        xmlns:x="http://schemas.microsoft.com/winfx/2006/xaml"
        RenderTransform="2 0 0 -2 300 300">

    <Path StrokeThickness="3" Stroke="Blue" Fill="AliceBlue">
        <Path.Data>
            <PathGeometry>
                <PathFigure x:Name="bez1" IsClosed="True">
                    <BezierSegment x:Name="bez2" />
                    <BezierSegment x:Name="bez3" />
                    <BezierSegment x:Name="bez4" />
                    <BezierSegment x:Name="bez5" />
                </PathFigure>
                <PathGeometry.Transform>
                    <RotateTransform Angle="45" />
                </PathGeometry.Transform>
            </PathGeometry>
        </Path.Data>
    </Path>

    <Canvas.Triggers>
        <EventTrigger RoutedEvent="Canvas.Loaded">
            <BeginStoryboard>
                <Storyboard RepeatBehavior="Forever" AutoReverse="True" >
                    <PointAnimation Storyboard.TargetName="bez1"
                            Storyboard.TargetProperty="StartPoint"
                            From="0 100" To="0 125" />

                    <PointAnimation Storyboard.TargetName="bez2"
                            Storyboard.TargetProperty="Point1"
                            From="55 100" To="62.5 62.5" />

                    <PointAnimation Storyboard.TargetName="bez2"
                            Storyboard.TargetProperty="Point2"
                            From="100 55" To="62.5 62.5" />

                    <PointAnimation Storyboard.TargetName="bez2"
                            Storyboard.TargetProperty="Point3"
                            From="100 0" To="125 0" />
```

```
                        <PointAnimation Storyboard.TargetName="bez3"
                                        Storyboard.TargetProperty="Point1"
                                        From="100 -55" To="62.5 -62.5" />

                        <PointAnimation Storyboard.TargetName="bez3"
                                        Storyboard.TargetProperty="Point2"
                                        From="55 -100" To="62.5 -62.5" />

                        <PointAnimation Storyboard.TargetName="bez3"
                                        Storyboard.TargetProperty="Point3"
                                        From="0 -100" To="0 -125" />

                        <PointAnimation Storyboard.TargetName="bez4"
                                        Storyboard.TargetProperty="Point1"
                                        From="-55 -100" To="-62.5 -62.5" />

                        <PointAnimation Storyboard.TargetName="bez4"
                                        Storyboard.TargetProperty="Point2"
                                        From="-100 -55" To="-62.5 -62.5" />

                        <PointAnimation Storyboard.TargetName="bez4"
                                        Storyboard.TargetProperty="Point3"
                                        From="-100 0" To="-125 0" />

                        <PointAnimation Storyboard.TargetName="bez5"
                                        Storyboard.TargetProperty="Point1"
                                        From="-100 55" To="-62.5 62.5" />

                        <PointAnimation Storyboard.TargetName="bez5"
                                        Storyboard.TargetProperty="Point2"
                                        From="-55 100" To="-62.5 62.5" />

                        <PointAnimation Storyboard.TargetName="bez5"
                                        Storyboard.TargetProperty="Point3"
                                        From="0 100" To="0 125" />

                </Storyboard>
            </BeginStoryboard>
        </EventTrigger>
    </Canvas.Triggers>
</Canvas>
```

The 13 *PointAnimation* objects change the 13 points that make up the figure. (The last point is the same as the first.) The *From* values define a circle centered on the point (0, 0), with a radius of 100. The *To* values define a square with sides of 177 units, so that the square occupies approximately the same area as the circle. The animation shifts between the circle and the square.

As defined by the *To* values, the corners of the square are at the left, top, right, and bottom, so the figure is more like a diamond shape. I decided I wanted the sides horizontal and vertical, but instead of changing all the coordinates, I simply added a *RotateTransform* to the *Path* to rotate the figure 45 degrees. The *RenderTransform* for the *Canvas* moves the origin to the point (300, 300) and doubles the size of the figure.

DrawingContext is the class you use for drawing when you override the *OnRender* method defined by *UIElement* and also when you create objects of type *DrawingVisual*. Many of the drawing methods defined by *DrawingContext* have overloads that include *AnimationClock* arguments. In this way you can define elements that intrinsically animate themselves, potentially forever. Here's an example of a class that derives from *FrameworkElement* and overrides *OnRender*.

AnimatedCircle.cs

```
//----------------------------------------------
// AnimatedCircle.cs (c) 2006 by Charles Petzold
//----------------------------------------------
using System;
using System.Windows;
using System.Windows.Media;
using System.Windows.Media.Animation;

namespace Petzold.RenderTheAnimation
{
    class AnimatedCircle : FrameworkElement
    {
        protected override void OnRender(DrawingContext dc)
        {
            DoubleAnimation anima = new DoubleAnimation();
            anima.From = 0;
            anima.To = 100;
            anima.Duration = new Duration(TimeSpan.FromSeconds(1));
            anima.AutoReverse = true;
            anima.RepeatBehavior = RepeatBehavior.Forever;
            AnimationClock clock = anima.CreateClock();

            dc.DrawEllipse(Brushes.Blue, new Pen(Brushes.Red, 3),
                new Point(125, 125), null, 0, clock, 0, clock);
        }
    }
}
```

You could put an instance of such a class in a XAML file or in code. I made it part of the following two-file project named RenderTheAnimation that also includes this C# file.

RenderTheAnimation.cs

```
//-----------------------------------------------------
// RenderTheAnimation.cs (c) 2006 by Charles Petzold
//-----------------------------------------------------
using System;
using System.Windows;

namespace Petzold.RenderTheAnimation
{
    class RenderTheAnimation : Window
    {
        [STAThread]
        public static void Main()
```

```
    {
        Application app = new Application();
        app.Run(new RenderTheAnimation());
    }
    public RenderTheAnimation()
    {
        Title = "Render the Animation";
        Content = new AnimatedCircle();
    }
}
}
}
```

The next stand-alone XAML file is an animation of an *Ellipse* that is triggered by the *Loaded* event of the *Ellipse* itself. The animation has a *TargetProperty* of *Width*, but the *Height* property is a *Binding* to the *Width* property, so both properties change in the same way.

Pulse.xaml

```
<!-- ======================================
        Pulsing.xaml (c) 2006 by Charles Petzold
     ====================================== -->
<Page xmlns="http://schemas.microsoft.com/winfx/2006/xaml/presentation"
      xmlns:x="http://schemas.microsoft.com/winfx/2006/xaml">

    <Ellipse HorizontalAlignment="Center" VerticalAlignment="Center"
             Width="48" Fill="Red"
             Height="{Binding RelativeSource={RelativeSource self},
                        Path=Width}">

        <Ellipse.Triggers>
            <EventTrigger RoutedEvent="Ellipse.Loaded">
                <BeginStoryboard>
                    <Storyboard TargetProperty="Width"
                            RepeatBehavior="Forever">
                        <DoubleAnimation From="48" To="288"
                                Duration="0:0:0.25"
                                BeginTime="0:0:1"
                                RepeatBehavior="2x"
                                FillBehavior="Stop" />
                    </Storyboard>
                </BeginStoryboard>
            </EventTrigger>
        </Ellipse.Triggers>
    </Ellipse>
</Page>
```

The *DoubleAnimation* has a *BeginTime* of one second, so the animation doesn't do anything during that time. The animation then increases the *Width* (and, through the binding, also the *Height*) quickly from one-half inch to three inches, snapping back to one-half inch. The *Repeat-Behavior* setting makes this happen twice.

The *Storyboard* itself also has a *RepeatBehavior* setting of *Forever* so that the *DoubleAnimation* is repeated indefinitely. For each repetition, the *BeginTime* delays the two pulses for one second, perhaps giving an overall effect of a heartbeat.

Here's an irritating little visual of a *Rectangle* that's animated in several ways. Two *DoubleAnimation* objects increase the *Width* and *Height* of the *Rectangle*. At the same time, two other *DoubleAnimation* objects decrease the *Canvas.Left* and *Canvas.Top* attached properties so that the *Rectangle* seems to stay in place. Two *PointAnimation* objects change the *Start-Point* and *EndPoint* properties of the *LinearGradientBrush*. These two points are initially the upper-left and lower-right corners of the rectangle, but they move to the upper-right and lower-left. Finally, two *ColorAnimation* objects swap the two colors used in the gradient brush.

PulsatingRectangle.xaml

```xml
<!-- ================================================
        PulsatingRectangle.xaml (c) 2006 by Charles Petzold
     ================================================ -->
<Canvas xmlns="http://schemas.microsoft.com/winfx/2006/xaml/presentation"
        xmlns:x="http://schemas.microsoft.com/winfx/2006/xaml">

    <Rectangle Name="rect"
               Canvas.Left="96" Canvas.Top="96"
               Width="192" Height="192"
               Stroke="Black">
        <Rectangle.Fill>
            <LinearGradientBrush x:Name="brush">
                <LinearGradientBrush.GradientStops>
                    <GradientStop Offset="0" Color="Red" />
                    <GradientStop Offset="1" Color="Blue" />
                </LinearGradientBrush.GradientStops>
            </LinearGradientBrush>
        </Rectangle.Fill>
    </Rectangle>

    <Canvas.Triggers>
        <EventTrigger RoutedEvent="Canvas.Loaded">
            <BeginStoryboard>
                <Storyboard>
                    <DoubleAnimation Storyboard.TargetName="rect"
                                     Storyboard.TargetProperty="Width"
                                     From="192" To="204" Duration="0:0:0.1"
                                     AutoReverse="True"
                                     RepeatBehavior="Forever" />

                    <DoubleAnimation Storyboard.TargetName="rect"
                                     Storyboard.TargetProperty="Height"
                                     From="192" To="204" Duration="0:0:0.1"
                                     AutoReverse="True"
                                     RepeatBehavior="Forever" />

                    <DoubleAnimation Storyboard.TargetName="rect"
                                     Storyboard.TargetProperty="(Canvas.Left)"
                                     From="96" To="90" Duration="0:0:0.1"
```

```
                                AutoReverse="True"
                                RepeatBehavior="Forever" />

                <DoubleAnimation Storyboard.TargetName="rect"
                                Storyboard.TargetProperty="(Canvas.Top)"
                                From="96" To="90" Duration="0:0:0.1"
                                AutoReverse="True"
                                RepeatBehavior="Forever" />

                <PointAnimation Storyboard.TargetName="brush"
                                Storyboard.TargetProperty="StartPoint"
                                From="0 0" To="1 0" Duration="0:0:5"
                                AutoReverse="True"
                                RepeatBehavior="Forever" />

                <PointAnimation Storyboard.TargetName="brush"
                                Storyboard.TargetProperty="EndPoint"
                                From="1 1" To="0 1" Duration="0:0:5"
                                AutoReverse="True"
                                RepeatBehavior="Forever" />

                <ColorAnimation
                    Storyboard.TargetName="brush"
                    Storyboard.TargetProperty="GradientStops[0].Color"
                    From="Red" To="Blue" Duration="0:0:1"
                    AutoReverse="True"
                    RepeatBehavior="Forever" />

                <ColorAnimation
                    Storyboard.TargetName="brush"
                    Storyboard.TargetProperty="GradientStops[1].Color"
                    From="Blue" To="Red" Duration="0:0:1"
                    AutoReverse="True"
                    RepeatBehavior="Forever" />
            </Storyboard>
        </BeginStoryboard>
    </EventTrigger>
  </Canvas.Triggers>
</Canvas>
```

These eight animation objects have three different *Duration* settings, and all have *RepeatBehavior* set to *Forever*. You might be tempted to set the *RepeatBehavior* for the *Storyboard* to *Forever* and to remove the individual *RepeatBehavior* attributes, but that wouldn't give the same effect. What would be repeated would be an animation that lasted 10 seconds (the total duration of the longest animation object taking *AutoReverse* into account). Animations with durations shorter than 10 seconds would occur only at the beginning of each 10-second period.

If you want all multiple animations to go on forever, you can move the *RepeatBehavior* setting of *Forever* to the *Storyboard* only if all the individual animations have the same total durations.

AutoReverse is very handy in animations that repeat forever because it helps avoid discontinuities when the animation repeats. But it's not the only way to make animations smooth. You can make nonreversing continuous animations smooth by making the ending position (or size or whatever) of one animated object coincide with the beginning position (or whatever) of another animated object.

The following XAML program uses five *EllipseGeometry* objects to define five concentric circles. (I used *EllipseGeometry* rather than *Ellipse* because it's easier to keep *EllipseGeometry* objects centered on the same point.) Ten *DoubleAnimation* objects increase the *RadiusX* and *RadiusY* of these five circles in a uniform way. All 10 *DoubleAnimation* objects have the *IsAdditive* property set to *true*, and all increase the dimension from 0 to 25. Because the radii of the five circles are 0, 25, 50, 75, and 100 units, each circle ends up at the initial size of the next-larger circle, making it seem as if all the circles are uniformly increasing in size.

To complete the illusion, special handling is required for the smallest circle and the largest circle. The smallest circle begins with a *RadiusX* and *RadiusY* of 0, and the first *DoubleAnimation* animates the *StrokeThickness* from 0 to the value specified in the *Path* element (12.5). Consequently, the smallest circle seems to arise out of nothingness. The final *DoubleAnimation* in the long list decreases the *Opacity* property of the largest circle, making it seem to fade away.

Because all the animations have the same *Duration*, the *RepeatBehavior* can be moved to the parent *Storyboard* in this program.

ExpandingCircles.xaml

```
<!-- ===================================================
     ExpandingCircles.xaml (c) 2006 by Charles Petzold
     =================================================== -->
<Page xmlns="http://schemas.microsoft.com/winfx/2006/xaml/presentation"
      xmlns:x="http://schemas.microsoft.com/winfx/2006/xaml"
      WindowTitle="Expanding Circles">
  <Canvas Width="400" Height="400"
          HorizontalAlignment="Center" VerticalAlignment="Center" >

    <!-- The inner circle. -->
    <Path Name="pathInner" Stroke="Red" StrokeThickness="12.5">
      <Path.Data>
          <EllipseGeometry x:Name="elips1"
                           Center="200 200" RadiusX="0" RadiusY="0" />
      </Path.Data>
    </Path>

    <!-- All circles except the inner and outer. circles -->
    <Path Stroke="Red" StrokeThickness="12.5">
      <Path.Data>
        <GeometryGroup>
          <EllipseGeometry x:Name="elips2"
                           Center="200 200" RadiusX="25" RadiusY="25" />
          <EllipseGeometry x:Name="elips3"
                           Center="200 200" RadiusX="50" RadiusY="50" />
          <EllipseGeometry x:Name="elips4"
                           Center="200 200" RadiusX="75" RadiusY="75" />
        </GeometryGroup>
```

```
        </Path.Data>
    </Path>

    <!-- The outer circle. -->
    <Path Name="pathOuter" Stroke="Red" StrokeThickness="12.5">
      <Path.Data>
          <EllipseGeometry x:Name="elips5"
                          Center="200 200" RadiusX="100" RadiusY="100" />
      </Path.Data>
    </Path>

    <Canvas.Triggers>
      <EventTrigger RoutedEvent="Canvas.Loaded">
        <BeginStoryboard>
          <Storyboard RepeatBehavior="Forever">
            <DoubleAnimation Storyboard.TargetName="pathInner"
                          Storyboard.TargetProperty="StrokeThickness"
                          From="0" Duration="0:0:5" />

            <DoubleAnimation Storyboard.TargetName="elips1"
                          Storyboard.TargetProperty="RadiusX"
                          From="0" To="25" IsAdditive="True"
                          Duration="0:0:5" />

            <DoubleAnimation Storyboard.TargetName="elips1"
                          Storyboard.TargetProperty="RadiusY"
                          From="0" To="25" IsAdditive="True"
                          Duration="0:0:5" />

            <DoubleAnimation Storyboard.TargetName="elips2"
                          Storyboard.TargetProperty="RadiusX"
                          From="0" To="25" IsAdditive="True"
                          Duration="0:0:5" />

            <DoubleAnimation Storyboard.TargetName="elips2"
                          Storyboard.TargetProperty="RadiusY"
                          From="0" To="25" IsAdditive="True"
                          Duration="0:0:5" />

            <DoubleAnimation Storyboard.TargetName="elips3"
                          Storyboard.TargetProperty="RadiusX"
                          From="0" To="25" IsAdditive="True"
                          Duration="0:0:5" />

            <DoubleAnimation Storyboard.TargetName="elips3"
                          Storyboard.TargetProperty="RadiusY"
                          From="0" To="25" IsAdditive="True"
                          Duration="0:0:5" />

            <DoubleAnimation Storyboard.TargetName="elips4"
                          Storyboard.TargetProperty="RadiusX"
                          From="0" To="25" IsAdditive="True"
                          Duration="0:0:5" />

            <DoubleAnimation Storyboard.TargetName="elips4"
```

```
                                Storyboard.TargetProperty="RadiusY"
                                From="0" To="25" IsAdditive="True"
                                Duration="0:0:5" />

        <DoubleAnimation Storyboard.TargetName="elips5"
                                Storyboard.TargetProperty="RadiusX"
                                From="0" To="25" IsAdditive="True"
                                Duration="0:0:5" />

        <DoubleAnimation Storyboard.TargetName="elips5"
                                Storyboard.TargetProperty="RadiusY"
                                From="0" To="25" IsAdditive="True"
                                Duration="0:0:5" />

        <DoubleAnimation Storyboard.TargetName="pathOuter"
                                Storyboard.TargetProperty="Opacity"
                                From="1" To="0" Duration="0:0:5" />
      </Storyboard>
    </BeginStoryboard>
   </EventTrigger>
  </Canvas.Triggers>
 </Canvas>
</Page>
```

Of course, I could have eliminated some of these *DoubleAnimation* objects with bindings between the *RadiusX* and *RadiusY* properties of the individual *EllipseGeometry* elements.

Sometimes you can replace a bunch of simultaneous animations with a single animation, but doing so might take some thought and perhaps even mathematics. The following program began with the Infinity.xaml file that I created in Chapter 28. In that file I used Bezier splines to draw an infinity sign colored with a *LinearGradientBrush* using the seven colors of the rainbow. For this chapter I decided I wanted to animate that brush by shifting to the right the colors that make up the gradient.

The following file has seven *DoubleAnimation* objects that animate the *Offset* properties of the seven *GradientStop* elements of the *Brush*. Each of these *DoubleAnimation* objects has the same *Duration* (seven seconds, but tripled in speed with a *SpeedRatio* setting of 3) and the same *From* and *To* values of 0 and 1, but each has a different *BeginTime*, from zero seconds to six seconds.

InfinityAnimation1.xaml

```
<!-- =====================================================
      InfinityAnimation1.xaml (c) 2006 by Charles Petzold
     ===================================================== -->
<Canvas xmlns="http://schemas.microsoft.com/winfx/2006/xaml/presentation"
        xmlns:x="http://schemas.microsoft.com/winfx/2006/xaml">

    <Path Canvas.Left="150" Canvas.Top="150" StrokeThickness="25">
        <Path.Data>
            <PathGeometry>
```

```
        <PathGeometry.Figures>
            <PathFigure StartPoint="0 -100">
                <PolyBezierSegment
                    Points=" -55 -100, -100  -55, -100    0,
                             -100   55,  -55  100,    0  100,
                               55  100,  100   50,  150    0,
                              200  -50,  245 -100,  300 -100,
                              355 -100,  400  -55,  400    0,
                              400   55,  355  100,  300  100,
                              245  100,  200   50,  150    0,
                              100  -50,   55 -100,    0 -100" />
            </PathFigure>
        </PathGeometry.Figures>
    </PathGeometry>
</Path.Data>
<Path.Stroke>
    <LinearGradientBrush x:Name="brush">
        <LinearGradientBrush.GradientStops>
            <GradientStop Color="Red" />
            <GradientStop Color="Orange" />
            <GradientStop Color="Yellow" />
            <GradientStop Color="Green" />
            <GradientStop Color="Blue" />
            <GradientStop Color="Indigo" />
            <GradientStop Color="Violet" />
        </LinearGradientBrush.GradientStops>
    </LinearGradientBrush>
</Path.Stroke>
<Path.Triggers>
    <EventTrigger RoutedEvent="Path.Loaded">
        <BeginStoryboard>
            <Storyboard TargetName="brush" SpeedRatio="3">
                <DoubleAnimation
                    Storyboard.TargetProperty="GradientStops[0].Offset"
                    From="0" To="1" Duration="0:0:7"
                    RepeatBehavior="Forever" />
                <DoubleAnimation
                    Storyboard.TargetProperty="GradientStops[1].Offset"
                    From="0" To="1"  Duration="0:0:7"
                    BeginTime="0:0:1" RepeatBehavior="Forever" />
                <DoubleAnimation
                    Storyboard.TargetProperty="GradientStops[2].Offset"
                    From="0" To="1" Duration="0:0:7"
                    BeginTime="0:0:2" RepeatBehavior="Forever" />
                <DoubleAnimation
                    Storyboard.TargetProperty="GradientStops[3].Offset"
                    From="0" To="1" Duration="0:0:7"
                    BeginTime="0:0:3" RepeatBehavior="Forever" />
                <DoubleAnimation
                    Storyboard.TargetProperty="GradientStops[4].Offset"
                    From="0" To="1" Duration="0:0:7"
                    BeginTime="0:0:4" RepeatBehavior="Forever" />
                <DoubleAnimation
                    Storyboard.TargetProperty="GradientStops[5].Offset"
                    From="0" To="1" Duration="0:0:7"
```

```
                              BeginTime="0:0:5" RepeatBehavior="Forever" />
                  <DoubleAnimation
                      Storyboard.TargetProperty="GradientStops[6].Offset"
                      From="0" To="1" Duration="0:0:7"
                      BeginTime="0:0:6" RepeatBehavior="Forever" />
              </Storyboard>
          </BeginStoryboard>
        </EventTrigger>
      </Path.Triggers>
    </Path>
  </Canvas>
```

When the program begins, all *GradientStop* objects have a default *Offset* property of 0. Normally that would result in the entire infinity sign being colored with the last *GradientStop* in the list, which is violet. However, the first *DoubleAnimation* begins immediately, assigning the first *GradientStop* a nonzero *Offset*, and the infinity sign turns red. A second later (actually a third of a second because of the *SpeedRatio* setting), the *Offset* of the first *GradientStop* is approximately 0.14, and the second *DoubleAnimation* kicks in, which colors the beginning of the infinity sign with orange. Each color progressively becomes active. Once all the *Double-Animation* objects have started, the cycling colors continue smoothly.

The program works, but I later realized that the *LinearGradientBrush* itself has a *Transform* property, and this property might serve to simplify the program considerably.

Sure enough. The following revised version of the program defines the *Offset* properties of the *GradientStop* objects explicitly but also includes a named *TranslateTransform* object for the brush.

InfinityAnimation2.xaml

```
<!-- ===================================================
     InfinityAnimation2.xaml (c) 2006 by Charles Petzold
     =================================================== -->
<Canvas xmlns="http://schemas.microsoft.com/winfx/2006/xaml/presentation"
        xmlns:x="http://schemas.microsoft.com/winfx/2006/xaml">

    <Path Canvas.Left="150" Canvas.Top="150" StrokeThickness="25"
        Data="M 0 -100
            C -55 -100, -100  -55, -100 0
            S -55  100,    0  100
            S 100   50,  150    0
            S 245 -100,  300 -100
            S 400  -55,  400    0
            S 355  100,  300  100
            S 200   50,  150    0
            S  55 -100,    0 -100">
        <Path.Stroke>
            <LinearGradientBrush SpreadMethod="Repeat">
                <LinearGradientBrush.Transform>
                    <TranslateTransform x:Name="xform" />
                </LinearGradientBrush.Transform>
```

```
                <LinearGradientBrush.GradientStops>
                    <GradientStop Offset="0.00" Color="Red" />
                    <GradientStop Offset="0.14" Color="Orange" />
                    <GradientStop Offset="0.28" Color="Yellow" />
                    <GradientStop Offset="0.42" Color="Green" />
                    <GradientStop Offset="0.56" Color="Blue" />
                    <GradientStop Offset="0.70" Color="Indigo" />
                    <GradientStop Offset="0.85" Color="Violet" />
                    <GradientStop Offset="1.00" Color="Red" />
                </LinearGradientBrush.GradientStops>
            </LinearGradientBrush>
        </Path.Stroke>
        <Path.Triggers>
            <EventTrigger RoutedEvent="Path.Loaded">
                <BeginStoryboard>
                    <Storyboard TargetName="xform" TargetProperty="X">
                        <DoubleAnimation From="0" To="621"
                                         Duration="0:0:2"
                                         RepeatBehavior="Forever" />
                    </Storyboard>
                </BeginStoryboard>
            </EventTrigger>
        </Path.Triggers>
    </Path>
</Canvas>
```

The single *DoubleAnimation* changes the *X* property of the *TranslateTransform* from 0 to 621, with a *Duration* of two seconds, repeated forever. By default the brush has a *WrapMode* of *Tile*, so the brush is essentially repeated beyond its bounds, and the transform shifts the brush with the same effect as in the earlier program.

So where does the 621 come from? You'll recall from diagrams in Chapter 2 that the default gradient of a *LinearGradientBrush* is from the upper-left to the lower-right of an element. Lines perpendicular to that diagonal line are colored the same. The InfinityAnimation2.xaml program defines eight *GradientStop* objects. The first and last are both red, and they have an offset of 0 and 1.0, respectively. The dashed lines in the following diagram symbolize the areas colored red.

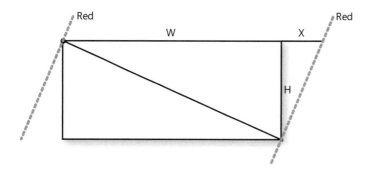

The element being colored is the infinity sign. It has a height of H and a width of W. Looking at the coordinates, one might conclude that H is 200 and W is 500, but the stroke thickness is 25, which extends the dimensions of the image 12.5 units on all four sides. H is actually 225, and W is 525.

The *TranslateTransform* shifts the brush right. When it shifts W plus X units, the brush appears the same as the unshifted version. What is X? Based on similar triangles, the ratio of X to H is the same as the ratio of H to W, so X can be easily calculated as approximately 96, so that W plus X equals 621.

And now I will confess that I originally derived this number empirically in XAML Cruncher by commenting out the animation and experimenting with the *X* property in the *Translate-Transform* element. I kept trying values until the brush remained the same with and without the translation factor.

One advantage of using the WPF animation facilities instead of *DispatcherTimer* is that animated values are calculated based on elapsed time. When using a timer, often animations are based solely on timer ticks, and if the program misses a few timer ticks because the system is over-loaded, the animation could be slowed down. That would be disastrous for a clock applica-tion, and that's why most clock applications obtain the actual time on each timer tick and update the clock hands from that.

The WPF animation facilities are designed to be accurate enough that you can use them to pace the hands of a clock, as in the XamlClock.xaml program that follows.

The following XAML file draws a clock. It uses a *Canvas* within a *Viewbox*, so the clock is as large or as small as the window that displays it. Take note of the two *Path* elements that draw the tick marks. These two elements display dotted lines in a circle with a radius of 90 units. The first element defines a *StrokeDashArray* of 0 and 3.14159 and a *StrokeThickness* of 3, which means that the dots are 3π units apart. The circumference of the circle is 180π, so the dotted line displays 60 small tick marks. The second element defines a *StrokeDashArray* of 0 and 7.854 (which is actually 2.5π) and a *StrokeThickness* of 6, so the dots are 15π units apart, which means that 12 large dots are displayed in the circle.

Following the definition of the tick marks, three additional *Path* elements draw the hands of the clock. All three clock hands point straight up. Each hand is associated with a *RotateTrans-form* that has an *xName* attribute set. The three *DoubleAnimation* elements change the angles of the transforms from 0 degrees to 360 degrees, with a *Duration* of 12 hours for the hour hand, one hour for the minute hand, and one minute for the second hand.

XamlClock.xaml

```
<!-- =========================================
     XamlClock.xaml (c) 2006 by Charles Petzold
     ========================================= -->
<Window xmlns="http://schemas.microsoft.com/winfx/2006/xaml/presentation"
        xmlns:x="http://schemas.microsoft.com/winfx/2006/xaml"
```

```
        x:Class="Petzold.XamlClock.XamlClock"
        Title="XAML Clock">
<Window.Resources>
    <!-- Every drawn object is a Path, so this style affects all of them. -->
    <Style TargetType="{x:Type Path}">
        <Setter Property="Stroke"
                Value="{DynamicResource
                            {x:Static SystemColors.WindowTextBrushKey}}" />
        <Setter Property="StrokeThickness" Value="2" />
        <Setter Property="StrokeStartLineCap" Value="Round" />
        <Setter Property="StrokeEndLineCap" Value="Round" />
        <Setter Property="StrokeLineJoin" Value="Round" />
        <Setter Property="StrokeDashCap" Value="Round" />
    </Style>
</Window.Resources>

<Viewbox>
    <!-- Draw clock on canvas, with center at (0, 0). -->
    <Canvas Width="200" Height="200">
        <Canvas.RenderTransform>
            <TranslateTransform X="100" Y="100" />
        </Canvas.RenderTransform>

        <!-- Tick marks (small and large). -->
        <Path Data="M 0 -90 A 90 90 0 1 1 -0.01 -90"
            StrokeDashArray="0 3.14159"
            StrokeThickness="3" />

        <Path Data="M 0 -90 A 90 90 0 1 1 -0.01 -90"
            StrokeDashArray="0 7.854"
            StrokeThickness="6" />

        <!-- Hour hand pointing up. -->
        <Path Data="M 0 15 L 10 0, 0 -60, -10 0 Z"
            Fill="{DynamicResource
                        {x:Static SystemColors.ControlDarkBrushKey}}">
            <Path.RenderTransform>
                <RotateTransform x:Name="xformHour" />
            </Path.RenderTransform>
        </Path>

        <!-- Minute hand pointing up. -->
        <Path Data="M 0 20 L 5 0 0 -80 -5 0 Z"
            Fill="{DynamicResource
                        {x:Static SystemColors.ControlLightBrushKey}}">
            <Path.RenderTransform>
                <RotateTransform x:Name="xformMinute" />
            </Path.RenderTransform>
        </Path>

        <!-- Second hand pointing up. -->
        <Path Data="M 0 10 L 0 -80">
            <Path.RenderTransform>
                <RotateTransform x:Name="xformSecond" />
```

```
                </Path.RenderTransform>
            </Path>
        </Canvas>
    </Viewbox>

    <!-- All animations. -->
    <Window.Triggers>
        <EventTrigger RoutedEvent="Canvas.Loaded">
            <BeginStoryboard>
                <Storyboard Name="storyboard">
                    <DoubleAnimation Storyboard.TargetName="xformHour"
                                     Storyboard.TargetProperty="Angle"
                                     From="0" To="360" Duration="12:0:0"
                                     RepeatBehavior="Forever" />

                    <DoubleAnimation Storyboard.TargetName="xformMinute"
                                     Storyboard.TargetProperty="Angle"
                                     From="0" To="360" Duration="1:0:0"
                                     RepeatBehavior="Forever" />

                    <DoubleAnimation Storyboard.TargetName="xformSecond"
                                     Storyboard.TargetProperty="Angle"
                                     From="0" To="360" Duration="0:1:0"
                                     RepeatBehavior="Forever" />
                </Storyboard>
            </BeginStoryboard>
        </EventTrigger>
    </Window.Triggers>
</Window>
```

You can load this XAML file into XAML Cruncher, remove the *x:Class* attribute near the top, and precisely at noon or the stroke of midnight, press F7 to open the window. You then have a clock that will keep the correct time (until daylight-saving time starts or ends, of course).

Are you not quite happy about the inconvenience of starting the program at noon or midnight? Okay then, just before you press F7, check the current time. Perhaps it's 4:38. In the *Storyboard* element, set the *BeginTime* property to the negative of that time:

```
<Storyboard Name="storyboard" BeginTime="-4:38">
```

Now if you launch the window, you will see that the clock is set correctly. You're essentially saying, "I want the animation to begin 4 hours and 38 minutes ago, which means I want all hands pointing straight up 4 hours and 38 minutes ago."

As you've probably figured out, XamlClock.xaml is part of a project named XamlClock, and the *Storyboard* element has a *Name* attribute set for a reason. A little bit of C# code is all that's necessary to initialize the *BeginTime* property to the negative of the current time.

```
XamlClock.cs
//------------------------------------------
// XamlClock.cs (c) 2006 by Charles Petzold
//------------------------------------------
using System;
using System.Windows;
using System.Windows.Controls;
using System.Windows.Input;
using System.Windows.Media;

namespace Petzold.XamlClock
{
    public partial class XamlClock : Window
    {
        [STAThread]
        public static void Main()
        {
            Application app = new Application();
            app.Run(new XamlClock());
        }
        public XamlClock()
        {
            InitializeComponent();

            // Initialize Storyboard to display current time.
            storyboard.BeginTime = -DateTime.Now.TimeOfDay;
        }
    }
}
```

The *TimeOfDay* property of *DateTime* returns an object of type *TimeSpan*, which is the type of the *BeginTime* property.

In the previous chapter, I developed a technique that put transforms to work performing calculations in XAML. Might it be possible to use this technique to create a clock *entirely* in XAML? Yes, it *is* possible, and the following stand-alone XAML file demonstrates it. The *Resources* section of the *Page* begins with a *FrameworkElement* whose *Tag* is set to the current *DateTime*. I thought it would be wise to obtain the current *DateTime* just once rather than several times and avoid the risk of the time changing between accesses.

Three *TransformGroup* objects perform all the necessary calculations. For example, the initial angle of the hour hand must be set to the sum of 30 degrees times the hour and 0.5 degrees times the minute. (For 3:30, that's 105 degrees, halfway between the 3 and 4.) That's accomplished by setting the *X* and *Y* offsets of a *TranslateTransform* to the hour and minute values, and multiplying by a matrix with *M11* set to 30 and *M21* set to 0.5. The product has an *OffsetX* property equal to 30 times the hour plus 0.5 times the minute. The *RotateTransform* for the hour hand initializes the *Angle* property to this value. The *DoubleAnimation* elements all have the *IsAdditive* property set to *true* to add to these initial values the animated values from 0 degrees to 360 degrees.

In addition, I've used Bezier splines to make the hour hand and minute hand just a little fancier.

AllXamlClock.xaml

```xml
<!-- =============================================
       AllXamlClock.xaml (c) 2006 by Charles Petzold
     ============================================= -->
<Page xmlns="http://schemas.microsoft.com/winfx/2006/xaml/presentation"
      xmlns:x="http://schemas.microsoft.com/winfx/2006/xaml"
      xmlns:s="clr-namespace:System;assembly=mscorlib">

    <Page.Resources>
        <!-- Get the current DateTime just once and stash it in
                a Tag property of an arbitrary FrameworkElement. -->
        <FrameworkElement x:Key="dt" Tag="{x:Static s:DateTime.Now}" />

        <!-- Multiply Hour by 30 degrees and Minute by 0.5 degrees
                and add. Result is stored in angleHour.Value.OffsetX. -->
        <TransformGroup x:Key="angleHour">
            <TranslateTransform
                X="{Binding Source={StaticResource dt}, Path=Tag.Hour}"
                Y="{Binding Source={StaticResource dt}, Path=Tag.Minute}" />
            <MatrixTransform Matrix="30 0 0.5 1 0 0" />
        </TransformGroup>

        <!-- Multiply Minute by 6 degrees and Second by 0.1 degrees
                and add. Result is stored in angleMinute.Value.OffsetX. -->
        <TransformGroup x:Key="angleMinute">
            <TranslateTransform
                X="{Binding Source={StaticResource dt}, Path=Tag.Minute}"
                Y="{Binding Source={StaticResource dt}, Path=Tag.Second}" />
            <MatrixTransform Matrix="6 0 0.1 1 0 0" />
        </TransformGroup>

        <!-- Multiply Second by 6 degrees. Result is angleSecond.Value.M11. -->
        <TransformGroup x:Key="angleSecond">
            <ScaleTransform
                ScaleX="{Binding Source={StaticResource dt}, Path=Tag.Second}" />
            <ScaleTransform ScaleX="6" />
        </TransformGroup>

        <!-- Every drawn object is a Path, so this style affects all of them. -->
        <Style TargetType="{x:Type Path}">
            <Setter Property="Stroke"
                    Value="{DynamicResource
                                {x:Static SystemColors.WindowTextBrushKey}}" />
            <Setter Property="StrokeThickness" Value="2" />
            <Setter Property="StrokeStartLineCap" Value="Round" />
            <Setter Property="StrokeEndLineCap" Value="Round" />
            <Setter Property="StrokeLineJoin" Value="Round" />
            <Setter Property="StrokeDashCap" Value="Round" />
        </Style>
    </Page.Resources>

    <Viewbox>
        <!-- Draw clock on canvas, with center at (0, 0). -->
        <Canvas Width="200" Height="200">
```

```xml
            <Canvas.RenderTransform>
                <TranslateTransform X="100" Y="100" />
            </Canvas.RenderTransform>

            <!-- Tick marks (small and large). -->
            <Path Data="M 0 -90 A 90 90 0 1 1 -0.01 -90"
                    StrokeDashArray="0 3.14159"
                    StrokeThickness="3" />

            <Path Data="M 0 -90 A 90 90 0 1 1 -0.01 -90"
                    StrokeDashArray="0 7.854"
                    StrokeThickness="6" />

            <!-- Hour hand pointing up. -->
            <Path Data="M 0 -60 C 0 -30, 20 -30, 5 -20 L 5 0
                                C 5 7.5, -5 7.5, -5 0 L -5 -20
                                C -20 -30, 0 -30 0 -60"
                    Fill="{DynamicResource
                                {x:Static SystemColors.ControlDarkBrushKey}}">
                <Path.RenderTransform>
                    <RotateTransform x:Name="xformHour"
                        Angle="{Binding Source={StaticResource angleHour},
                                        Path=Value.OffsetX}" />
                </Path.RenderTransform>
            </Path>

            <!-- Minute hand pointing up. -->
            <Path Data="M 0 -80 C 0 -75, 0 -70, 2.5 -60 L 2.5 0
                                C 2.5 5, -2.5 5, -2.5 0 L -2.5 -60
                                C 0 -70, 0 -75, 0 -80"
                    Fill="{DynamicResource
                                {x:Static SystemColors.ControlLightBrushKey}}">
                <Path.RenderTransform>
                    <RotateTransform x:Name="xformMinute"
                        Angle="{Binding Source={StaticResource angleMinute},
                                        Path=Value.OffsetX}" />
                </Path.RenderTransform>
            </Path>

            <!-- Second hand pointing up. -->
            <Path Data="M 0 10 L 0 -80">
                <Path.RenderTransform>
                    <RotateTransform x:Name="xformSecond"
                        Angle="{Binding Source={StaticResource angleSecond},
                                        Path=Value.M11}" />
                </Path.RenderTransform>
            </Path>
        </Canvas>
    </Viewbox>

    <!-- All animations. -->
    <Page.Triggers>
        <EventTrigger RoutedEvent="Canvas.Loaded">
            <BeginStoryboard>
                <Storyboard>
```

```
                          <DoubleAnimation Storyboard.TargetName="xformHour"
                                           Storyboard.TargetProperty="Angle"
                                           From="0" To="360" Duration="12:0:0"
                                           IsAdditive="True"
                                           RepeatBehavior="Forever" />

                          <DoubleAnimation Storyboard.TargetName="xformMinute"
                                           Storyboard.TargetProperty="Angle"
                                           From="0" To="360" Duration="1:0:0"
                                           IsAdditive="True"
                                           RepeatBehavior="Forever" />

                          <DoubleAnimation Storyboard.TargetName="xformSecond"
                                           Storyboard.TargetProperty="Angle"
                                           From="0" To="360" Duration="0:1:0"
                                           IsAdditive="True"
                                           RepeatBehavior="Forever" />
                      </Storyboard>
                  </BeginStoryboard>
              </EventTrigger>
          </Page.Triggers>
      </Page>
```

I wanted to have a ball bounce between the midpoints of the four sides of its container. Notice that the animation in the following stand-alone XAML file is triggered on the *SizeChanged* event of the *Canvas*, so it starts anew whenever the window holding the *Canvas* changes size.

FourSidedBounce1.xaml

```
<!-- =================================================
        FourSidedBounce1.xaml (c) 2006 by Charles Petzold
     ================================================= -->
<Canvas xmlns="http://schemas.microsoft.com/winfx/2006/xaml/presentation"
        xmlns:x="http://schemas.microsoft.com/winfx/2006/xaml"
        Name="canv">

    <Ellipse Name="elips" Fill="Blue" Width="48" Height="48" />

    <Canvas.Triggers>
        <EventTrigger RoutedEvent="Canvas.SizeChanged">
            <BeginStoryboard>
                <Storyboard TargetName="elips">
                    <DoubleAnimation Storyboard.TargetProperty="(Canvas.Left)"
                        BeginTime="-0:0:1"
                        Duration="0:0:2"
                        RepeatBehavior="Forever" AutoReverse="True"
                        From="0" To="{Binding ElementName=canv,
                                               Path=ActualWidth}" />

                    <DoubleAnimation Storyboard.TargetProperty="(Canvas.Top)"
                        Duration="0:0:2"
                        RepeatBehavior="Forever" AutoReverse="True"
                        From="0" To="{Binding ElementName=canv,
                                               Path=ActualHeight}" />
```

```
                </Storyboard>
            </BeginStoryboard>
        </EventTrigger>
    </Canvas.Triggers>
</Canvas>
```

The first *DoubleAnimation* changes the horizontal location of the ball between 0 and the *ActualWidth* of the canvas, whereas the second *DoubleAnimation* changes the vertical location between 0 and *ActualHeight*, both with *AutoReverse* turned on. Normally, this would cause the ball to bounce between the upper-left corner and the lower-right corner, but the first *DoubleAnimation* has a *BeginTime* set to the negative of half the *Duration*, so the initial position of the ball is at the middle of the top of the canvas.

Everything works fine except that the ball goes *beyond* the right side and bottom of the container. The *Canvas.Left* property can't change from 0 to the *ActualWidth* of the canvas; it has to change from 0 to *ActualWidth* minus the diameter of the ball. I could have used a similar technique as in AllXamlClock to perform this calculation, but I figured it was easier to put the ball in the upper-left quadrant of a four-cell *Grid*, where the rightmost column and bottom row were given the same dimensions as the ball, as shown in the following program.

FourSidedBounce2.xaml

```xaml
<!-- ===================================================
        FourSidedBounce1.xaml (c) 2006 by Charles Petzold
     =================================================== -->
<Page xmlns="http://schemas.microsoft.com/winfx/2006/xaml/presentation"
      xmlns:x="http://schemas.microsoft.com/winfx/2006/xaml">
    <Grid>
        <Grid.RowDefinitions>
            <RowDefinition />
            <RowDefinition Height="48" />
        </Grid.RowDefinitions>

        <Grid.ColumnDefinitions>
            <ColumnDefinition />
            <ColumnDefinition Width="48" />
        </Grid.ColumnDefinitions>

        <Canvas Name="canv">

            <Ellipse Name="elips" Fill="Blue" Width="48" Height="48" />

            <Canvas.Triggers>
                <EventTrigger RoutedEvent="Canvas.SizeChanged">
                    <BeginStoryboard>
                        <Storyboard TargetName="elips">

                            <DoubleAnimation
                                Storyboard.TargetProperty="(Canvas.Left)"
                                BeginTime="-0:0:1"
                                Duration="0:0:2"
```

```
                                        RepeatBehavior="Forever" AutoReverse="True"
                                        From="0" To="{Binding ElementName=canv,
                        '                                    Path=ActualWidth}" />
                            <DoubleAnimation
                                Storyboard.TargetProperty="(Canvas.Top)"
                                Duration="0:0:2"
                                RepeatBehavior="Forever" AutoReverse="True"
                                From="0" To="{Binding ElementName=canv,
                                                    Path=ActualHeight}" />
                        </Storyboard>
                    </BeginStoryboard>
                </EventTrigger>
            </Canvas.Triggers>
        </Canvas>
    </Grid>
</Page>
```

The following stand-alone XAML file is intended to simulate a ball bouncing on a floor. The floor is a horizontal *Line* element. The animation varies the *Canvas.Top* property of the ball between 96 and 480 units over the course of a second, with *AutoReverse* turned on, of course, and repeating forever. Because the maximum *Canvas.Top* property is 480, the *Height* of the ellipse is 24, and *StrokeThickness* of the floor is 5, I set the *Y* coordinate of the *Line* element that defines the floor to 480 plus 24 plus 2 (about half the *StrokeThickess*).

BouncingBall.xaml

```
<!-- =========================================
        BouncingBall.xaml (c) 2006 by Charles Petzold
     ========================================= -->
<Canvas xmlns="http://schemas.microsoft.com/winfx/2006/xaml/presentation"
        xmlns:x="http://schemas.microsoft.com/winfx/2006/xaml"
        xmlns:s="clr-namespace:System;assembly=mscorlib">

    <Line X1="0" Y1="506" X2="1000" Y2="506" Stroke="Black" StrokeThickness="5" />

    <Ellipse Name="elips" Width="24" Height="24" Fill="Red"
            Canvas.Left="96">

        <Ellipse.Triggers>
            <EventTrigger RoutedEvent="Ellipse.Loaded">
                <BeginStoryboard>
                    <Storyboard TargetName="elips" RepeatBehavior="Forever">
                        <DoubleAnimation
                                Storyboard.TargetProperty="(Canvas.Top)"
                                From="96" To="480" Duration="0:0:1"
                                AutoReverse="True" />
                    </Storyboard>
                </BeginStoryboard>
            </EventTrigger>
        </Ellipse.Triggers>
    </Ellipse>
</Canvas>
```

This animation has many problems that prevent it from looking realistic. Of course, by repeating forever, it violates physical laws, but even that might be forgiven if only the speed of the ball weren't quite so consistent. The ball should speed up as it drops and slow down as it rises.

You can vary the speed of an animation with the *AccelerationRatio* and *DecelerationRatio* attributes. By default these are both 0. You can set them to values between 0 and 1, but the sum must not exceed 1. An *AccelerationRatio* of 0.25 means that the animation speeds up during the first 25 percent of its *Duration* time. The *DecelerationRatio* similarly slows down the animation at the end of the *Duration*.

To more closely simulate a bouncing ball, insert the following attribute into the *DoubleAnimation* element:

```
AccelerationRatio="1"
```

This setting speeds up the animation during its entire duration so it's moving fastest as the ball hits the floor. When the animation reverses, the same *AccelerationRatio* causes the ball to slow down as it reaches its peak.

To see a different effect, set the *DecelerationRatio*:

```
DecelerationRatio="1"
```

Now it looks like a ball suspended from a spring and bouncing up and down. Set both attributes to 0.5 to achieve an effect where the ball travels fastest midway in its journey up or down, much like a pendulum.

The following BetterBouncingBall.xaml file has an *AccelerationRatio* set and also attempts to make the ball flatten out a bit as it strikes the floor.

```
BetterBouncingBall.xaml
<!-- ===================================================
        BetterBouncingBall.xaml (c) 2006 by Charles Petzold
     =================================================== -->
<Canvas xmlns="http://schemas.microsoft.com/winfx/2006/xaml/presentation"
        xmlns:x="http://schemas.microsoft.com/winfx/2006/xaml"
        xmlns:s="clr-namespace:System;assembly=mscorlib">

    <Line X1="0" Y1="506" X2="1000" Y2="506" Stroke="Black" StrokeThickness="5" />

    <Ellipse Name="elips" Width="24" Height="24" Fill="Red"
             Canvas.Left="96">

        <Ellipse.Triggers>
            <EventTrigger RoutedEvent="Ellipse.Loaded">
                <BeginStoryboard>
                    <Storyboard TargetName="elips" RepeatBehavior="Forever">
                        <DoubleAnimation
                            Storyboard.TargetProperty="(Canvas.Top)"
```

```
                             From="96" To="490" Duration="0:0:1"
                             AutoReverse="True"
                             AccelerationRatio="1" />

                 <ParallelTimeline BeginTime="0:0:0.98"
                                   AutoReverse="True">

                     <DoubleAnimation Storyboard.TargetProperty="Width"
                                      To="32" Duration="0:0:0.02" />

                     <DoubleAnimation Storyboard.TargetProperty="Height"
                                      To="16" Duration="0:0:0.02" />

                     <DoubleAnimation
                             Storyboard.TargetProperty="(Canvas.Left)"
                             From="0" To="-4"  Duration="0:0:0.02"
                             IsAdditive="True" />
                 </ParallelTimeline>
             </Storyboard>
         </BeginStoryboard>
        </EventTrigger>
      </Ellipse.Triggers>
    </Ellipse>
</Canvas>
```

A pendulum should accelerate as it approaches the midpoint of its arc, and then it should decelerate, so both the acceleration and the deceleration ratios can be set to 0.5. The following stand-alone XAML file constructs a pendulum from a *Line* element and a *Button* that (rather perversely) displays the date and time at which the program was loaded. To keep both the *Line* and *Button* swinging together, I assembled them on a *StackPanel*, gave the panel a *RotateTransform*, and animated the *Angle* property between –30 degrees and 30 degrees.

PendulumButton.xaml

```
<!-- ==================================================
     PendulumButton.xaml (c) 2006 by Charles Petzold
     ================================================== -->
<Page xmlns="http://schemas.microsoft.com/winfx/2006/xaml/presentation"
      xmlns:x="http://schemas.microsoft.com/winfx/2006/xaml"
      xmlns:s="clr-namespace:System;assembly=mscorlib">
    <StackPanel Width="200">
        <Line X1="100" X2="100" Y2="200"
              StrokeThickness="3" Stroke="Black" />

        <Button Content="{x:Static s:DateTime.Now}"
                HorizontalAlignment="Center" />

        <StackPanel.RenderTransform>
            <RotateTransform x:Name="xform" CenterX="100" />
        </StackPanel.RenderTransform>
    </StackPanel.RenderTransform>
```

```
        <StackPanel.Triggers>
            <EventTrigger RoutedEvent="StackPanel.Loaded">
                <BeginStoryboard>
                    <Storyboard TargetName="xform" TargetProperty="Angle">
                        <DoubleAnimation From="-30" To="30" Duration="0:0:1"
                            AccelerationRatio="0.5" DecelerationRatio="0.5"
                            AutoReverse="True" RepeatBehavior="Forever" />
                    </Storyboard>
                </BeginStoryboard>
            </EventTrigger>
        </StackPanel.Triggers>
    </StackPanel>
</Page>
```

Although *AccelerationRatio* and *DecelerationRatio* are handy, you have no control over the rate at which the animation speeds up or slows down. If you need that control—or if you want to create an animation that is more complex than a linear change from one value to another—you'll want to explore the *key-frame* animation.

To animate a property of type *double* by using key frames, you use a *DoubleAnimationUsing-KeyFrames* element rather than *DoubleAnimation*. *DoubleAnimationUsingKeyFrames* contains a property named *KeyFrames*, of type *DoubleKeyFrameCollection*. This collection consists of elements of type *DiscreteDoubleKeyFrame* (to jump to discrete values), *LinearDoubleKey-Frame* (to linearly change a value), and *SplineDoubleKeyFrame* (to change a value at a non-linear rate based on a Bezier spline). These children of *DoubleAnimationUsingKeyFrames* are all derived from the abstract *DoubleKeyFrame* class, as shown in the following class hierarchy:

Object

    DispatcherObject (abstract)

        DependencyObject

            Freezable (abstract)

                DoubleKeyFrame (abstract)

                    DiscreteDoubleKeyFrame

                    LinearDoubleKeyFrame

                    SplineDoubleKeyFrame

                    DoubleKeyFrameCollection

A *<Type>KeyFrame* class and a *<Type>KeyFrameCollection* class exist for all 22 animatable types. All 22 types have a *Discrete<Type>KeyFrame* class; all but five types have *Linear<Type>KeyFrame* and *Spline<Type>KeyFrame* classes. The total number of classes involved here is 100.

The following table summarizes the types of animations supported for the 22 animatable types.

Type	<Type>Animation	<Type>Animation-UsingPath	<Type>AnimationUsingKeyFrames		
			Discrete	Linear	Spline
Boolean			✓		
Byte	✓		✓	✓	✓
Char			✓		
Color	✓		✓	✓	✓
Decimal	✓		✓	✓	✓
Double	✓	✓	✓	✓	✓
Int16	✓		✓	✓	✓
Int32	✓		✓	✓	✓
Int64	✓		✓	✓	✓
Matrix		✓	✓		
Object			✓		
Point	✓	✓	✓	✓	✓
Point3D	✓		✓	✓	✓
Quaternion	✓		✓	✓	✓
Rect	✓		✓	✓	✓
Rotation3D	✓		✓	✓	✓
Single	✓		✓	✓	✓
Size	✓		✓	✓	✓
String			✓		
Thickness	✓		✓	✓	✓
Vector	✓		✓	✓	✓
Vector3D	✓		✓	✓	✓

Five of these types—specifically *Boolean*, *Char*, *Matrix*, *Object*, and *String*—can only take on discrete values. You can't interpolate between two values of these types. (Although *Char* can be interpolated in theory, it probably doesn't make much sense for an animation to animate from one Unicode character to another. Objects of type *Matrix* can be interpolated in theory, but the results might not be quite meaningful.) I'll discuss *<Type>AnimationUsingPath* toward the end of this chapter.

The abstract *DoubleKeyFrame* class defines two properties named *KeyTime* (of type *KeyTime*) and *Value*. Neither *DiscreteDoubleKeyFrame* nor *LinearDoubleKeyFrame* defines any additional properties. Each key frame element essentially indicates the value of the animated property at a particular time. The key frame elements must be specified in the order in which they take effect.

Here's a simple example using two elements of type *LinearDoubleKeyFrame* and two elements of type *DiscreteDoubleKeyFrame*.

```
SimpleKeyFrameAnimation.xaml

<!-- ========================================================
     SimpleKeyFrameAnimation.xaml (c) 2006 by Charles Petzold
     ======================================================== -->
<Canvas xmlns="http://schemas.microsoft.com/winfx/2006/xaml/presentation"
        xmlns:x="http://schemas.microsoft.com/winfx/2006/xaml">

    <Ellipse Name="elips"
             Width="48" Height="48" Fill="Red"
             Canvas.Left="480" Canvas.Top="96" />

    <Canvas.Triggers>
        <EventTrigger RoutedEvent="Canvas.Loaded">
            <BeginStoryboard>
                <Storyboard TargetName="elips" TargetProperty="(Canvas.Left)">
                    <DoubleAnimationUsingKeyFrames RepeatBehavior="Forever"
                                                   Duration="0:0:10">
                        <LinearDoubleKeyFrame KeyTime="0:0:5" Value="0" />
                        <LinearDoubleKeyFrame KeyTime="0:0:5.5" Value="48" />
                        <DiscreteDoubleKeyFrame KeyTime="0:0:6" Value="144" />
                        <DiscreteDoubleKeyFrame KeyTime="0:0:7" Value="240" />
                    </DoubleAnimationUsingKeyFrames>
                </Storyboard>
            </BeginStoryboard>
        </EventTrigger>
    </Canvas.Triggers>
</Canvas>
```

The ball begins at the location (480, 96), as specified with the *Canvas.Left* and *Canvas.Top* attached properties in the *Ellipse* element. The animation changes the *Canvas.Left* property. For the first five seconds of the animation, that property changes from 480 to 0. As the first *LinearDoubleKeyFrame* indicates, at time 0:0:5, the value of *Canvas.Left* should equal 0. The second *LinearDoubleKeyFrame* element indicates that at time 0:0:5.5, the value of *Canvas.Left* should equal 48. Therefore, over the next half second, the ball moves right because *Canvas.Left* changes from 0 to 48.

A half second later—when the time from the beginning of the animation is six seconds—the ball jumps to a position of 144. A second later it jumps to 240.

The key frames are finished, but the *DoubleAnimationUsingKeyFrames* element indicates that the total duration of the animation is 10 seconds, so the ball sits at the position (240, 96) for three seconds. The *DoubleAnimationUsingKeyFrames* element also indicates a *RepeatBehavior* of *Forever*, so at the end of the 10 seconds, the ball jumps back to its initial position of (480, 96), and the animation begins again.

With both *DiscreteDoubleKeyFrame* and *LinearDoubleKeyFrame*, the value of the animated property at the time indicated by *KeyTime* is the value given as *Value*. With *DiscreteDoubleKeyFrame*, the animated value jumps to *Value* at *KeyTime*. With *LinearDoubleKeyFrame*, the animated value changes linearly from its previous value to the *Value* at *KeyTime*. How fast it appears to change depends on the previous *Value* and the previous *KeyTime*.

Here's a program that uses four elements of type *DiscretePointKeyFrame*.

DiscretePointJumps.xaml

```
<!-- =====================================================
        DiscretePointJumps.xaml (c) 2006 by Charles Petzold
     ===================================================== -->
<Canvas xmlns="http://schemas.microsoft.com/winfx/2006/xaml/presentation"
        xmlns:x="http://schemas.microsoft.com/winfx/2006/xaml">

    <Path Fill="Red">
        <Path.Data>
            <EllipseGeometry x:Name="elips" RadiusX="24" RadiusY="24" />
        </Path.Data>
    </Path>

    <Canvas.Triggers>
        <EventTrigger RoutedEvent="Canvas.Loaded">
            <BeginStoryboard>
                <Storyboard TargetName="elips" TargetProperty="Center">
                    <PointAnimationUsingKeyFrames Duration="0:0:4"
                                                  RepeatBehavior="Forever">
                        <DiscretePointKeyFrame KeyTime="0:0:0" Value="288 96" />
                        <DiscretePointKeyFrame KeyTime="0:0:1" Value="480 288" />
                        <DiscretePointKeyFrame KeyTime="0:0:2" Value="288 480" />
                        <DiscretePointKeyFrame KeyTime="0:0:3" Value="96 288" />
                    </PointAnimationUsingKeyFrames>
                </Storyboard>
            </BeginStoryboard>
        </EventTrigger>
    </Canvas.Triggers>
</Canvas>
```

Without the animation, the ellipse would be centered at the point (0, 0), but the first *Discrete-PointKeyFrame* element indicates it should be located at the point (288, 96) at the key time of 0. If you look closely, you might be able to see the ellipse jump from (0, 0) to (288, 96) as the program loads. The ellipse remains at (288, 96) for one second until the key time of one second in the second *DiscretePointKeyFrame* element.

When three seconds have elapsed from the time the program was loaded, the ellipse is moved to point (96, 288). That's the last *DiscretePointKeyFrame* element, but the *PointAnimationUsingKey-*

Frames element indicates that the total *Duration* of the animation is four seconds, so the ellipse sits at the point (96, 288) for the last of those four seconds.

If you leave out the *Duration* attribute, the last key time governs the total length of the animation. In this example, that's three seconds, so the animation ends at the same time the last *Discrete-PointKeyFrame* is supposed to take effect. You won't even see it. The ellipse will seem to jump directly from the bottom position at (288, 480) to the top position at (288, 96).

The following file uses *LinearPointKeyFrame* to move a ball between four points, seemingly bouncing between the four sides of a rectangle.

```
KeyFramePointAnimation.xaml
<!-- ========================================================
        KeyFramePointAnimation.xaml (c) 2006 by Charles Petzold
     ======================================================== -->
<Canvas xmlns="http://schemas.microsoft.com/winfx/2006/xaml/presentation"
        xmlns:x="http://schemas.microsoft.com/winfx/2006/xaml">

    <Rectangle Stroke="Black" Width="480" Height="480" />

    <Path Fill="Aqua" Stroke="Chocolate" StrokeThickness="3">
        <Path.Data>
            <EllipseGeometry x:Name="elips"
                             Center="240 50" RadiusX="48" RadiusY="48" />
        </Path.Data>
    </Path>
    <Canvas.Triggers>
        <EventTrigger RoutedEvent="Canvas.Loaded">
            <BeginStoryboard>
                <Storyboard TargetName="elips" TargetProperty="Center">
                    <PointAnimationUsingKeyFrames Duration="0:0:4"
                                                  RepeatBehavior="Forever">
                        <LinearPointKeyFrame Value="430 240" KeyTime="0:0:1" />
                        <LinearPointKeyFrame Value="240 430" KeyTime="0:0:2" />
                        <LinearPointKeyFrame Value="50 240" KeyTime="0:0:3" />
                        <LinearPointKeyFrame Value="240 50" KeyTime="0:0:4" />
                    </PointAnimationUsingKeyFrames>
                </Storyboard>
            </BeginStoryboard>
        </EventTrigger>
    </Canvas.Triggers>
</Canvas>
```

If the *KeyTime* properties are not present, the default is the static property *KeyTime.Uniform*, which means that every key frame has the same length of time. The *Duration* indicated for the overall animation is apportioned equally. If there is no *Duration* attribute, a default of one second is assumed.

If you remove all the *KeyTime* attributes from the previous XAML file, it will work the same way.

Another option is to specify a *KeyTime* as a percentage of the *Duration*. Such percentages must consecutively increase. If you replace the *LinearPointKeyFrame* elements in the previous program with the following markup, the program runs the same way:

```
<LinearPointKeyFrame Value="430 240" KeyTime="25%" />
<LinearPointKeyFrame Value="240 430" KeyTime="50%" />
<LinearPointKeyFrame Value="50 240" KeyTime="75%" />
<LinearPointKeyFrame Value="240 50" KeyTime="100%" />
```

The final option is *KeyTime.Paced*, which allocates the time among the key frames so that the overall rate of change is constant. For example, if one *LinearDoubleKeyFrame* changes a *double* from 0 to 500, and another changes a *double* from 500 to 750, twice as much time is allocated to the first than to the second. Here's an example.

```
PacedAnimation.xaml
<!-- =================================================
        PacedAnimation.xaml (c) 2006 by Charles Petzold
     ================================================= -->
<Canvas xmlns="http://schemas.microsoft.com/winfx/2006/xaml/presentation"
        xmlns:x="http://schemas.microsoft.com/winfx/2006/xaml">

    <Path Fill="Aqua" Stroke="Chocolate" StrokeThickness="3">
        <Path.Data>
            <EllipseGeometry x:Name="elips" RadiusX="24" RadiusY="24" />
        </Path.Data>
    </Path>
    <Canvas.Triggers>
        <EventTrigger RoutedEvent="Canvas.Loaded">
            <BeginStoryboard>
                <Storyboard TargetName="elips" TargetProperty="Center">
                    <PointAnimationUsingKeyFrames Duration="0:0:5"
                                                  RepeatBehavior="Forever">
                        <LinearPointKeyFrame Value="48 48" KeyTime="Paced" />
                        <LinearPointKeyFrame Value="480 240" KeyTime="Paced" />
                        <LinearPointKeyFrame Value="480 48" KeyTime="Paced" />
                        <LinearPointKeyFrame Value="48 240" KeyTime="Paced" />
                        <LinearPointKeyFrame Value="48 48" KeyTime="Paced" />
                    </PointAnimationUsingKeyFrames>
                </Storyboard>
            </BeginStoryboard>
        </EventTrigger>
    </Canvas.Triggers>
</Canvas>
```

The ball moves in a bow tie pattern, but each leg of the trip gets enough time so that the overall speed is constant.

The clock programs I showed earlier moved the second hand continuously in a smooth motion. You might prefer a second hand that makes discrete jumps between the seconds. (Or, better yet, you might prefer giving your users the option to change the clock's second hand to suit their own preference.)

Here's a little program that shows two second hands without anything else. The first has the *Angle* property of its *RotateTransform* animated with *DoubleAnimation* from 0 to 360 degrees, with a *Duration* of one minute, just as in the earlier clock programs.

The right-hand second hand uses *DoubleAnimationUsingKeyFrames* with a single child of *DiscreteDoubleKeyFrame*. The *KeyTime* for the key frame is one second and the *Value* is 6, meaning 6 degrees. However, the *IsCumulative* property on the *DoubleAnimationUsingKeyFrames* element is set to *true*, so those 6-degree values are accumulated.

SecondHandSteps.xaml

```xml
<!-- ==================================================
        SecondHandSteps.xaml (c) 2006 by Charles Petzold
     ================================================== -->
<Canvas xmlns="http://schemas.microsoft.com/winfx/2006/xaml/presentation"
        xmlns:x="http://schemas.microsoft.com/winfx/2006/xaml">

    <Line Stroke="Black" StrokeThickness="3"
          X1="0" Y1="0" X2="0" Y2="-100"
          Canvas.Left="150" Canvas.Top="150">
        <Line.RenderTransform>
            <RotateTransform x:Name="xform1" />
        </Line.RenderTransform>
    </Line>

    <Line Stroke="Black" StrokeThickness="3"
          X1="0" Y1="0" X2="0" Y2="-100"
          Canvas.Left="450" Canvas.Top="150">
        <Line.RenderTransform>
            <RotateTransform x:Name="xform2" />
        </Line.RenderTransform>
    </Line>

    <Canvas.Triggers>
        <EventTrigger RoutedEvent="Canvas.Loaded">
            <BeginStoryboard>
                <Storyboard>
                    <DoubleAnimation Storyboard.TargetName="xform1"
                                     Storyboard.TargetProperty="Angle"
                                     From="0" To="360" Duration="0:1"
                                     RepeatBehavior="Forever" />

                    <DoubleAnimationUsingKeyFrames
                                Storyboard.TargetName="xform2"
                                Storyboard.TargetProperty="Angle"
                                RepeatBehavior="Forever"
                                IsCumulative="True">
                        <DiscreteDoubleKeyFrame KeyTime="0:0:1" Value="6" />
                    </DoubleAnimationUsingKeyFrames>

                </Storyboard>
            </BeginStoryboard>
        </EventTrigger>
    </Canvas.Triggers>
</Canvas>
```

The following XAML file has two simultaneous *DoubleAnimationUsingKeyFrames* elements, each containing two *DiscreteDoubleKeyFrame* elements that alternate between values of 0 and 1. The *TargetProperty* is the *Opacity* property of a *TextBlock*. The two *TextBlock* elements display the words "EAT" and "HERE", and as the *Opacity* properties change values, the two words alternate on the screen, much like the neon sign on a diner.

```
Diner1.xaml
<!-- =======================================
     Diner1.xaml (c) 2006 by Charles Petzold
     ======================================= -->
<Page xmlns="http://schemas.microsoft.com/winfx/2006/xaml/presentation"
    xmlns:x="http://schemas.microsoft.com/winfx/2006/xaml">
    <Grid TextBlock.FontSize="192">
        <TextBlock Name="eat" Text="EAT" Foreground="Red"
                   HorizontalAlignment="Center"
                   VerticalAlignment="Center" />
        <TextBlock Name="here" Text="HERE" Foreground="Blue"
                   Opacity="0"
                   HorizontalAlignment="Center"
                   VerticalAlignment="Center" />
    </Grid>
    <Page.Triggers>
        <EventTrigger RoutedEvent="Canvas.Loaded">
            <BeginStoryboard>
                <Storyboard TargetProperty="Opacity" RepeatBehavior="Forever">

                    <DoubleAnimationUsingKeyFrames Storyboard.TargetName="eat">
                        <DiscreteDoubleKeyFrame KeyTime="0:0:1" Value="0" />
                        <DiscreteDoubleKeyFrame KeyTime="0:0:2" Value="1" />
                    </DoubleAnimationUsingKeyFrames>

                    <DoubleAnimationUsingKeyFrames Storyboard.TargetName="here">
                        <DiscreteDoubleKeyFrame KeyTime="0:0:1" Value="1" />
                        <DiscreteDoubleKeyFrame KeyTime="0:0:2" Value="0" />
                    </DoubleAnimationUsingKeyFrames>
                </Storyboard>
            </BeginStoryboard>
        </EventTrigger>
    </Page.Triggers>
</Page>
```

The highest value of *KeyTime* in this example is two seconds, which is the length of the animation. The two *TextBlock* elements have initial *Opacity* values of 1 and 0. At the *KeyTime* of one second, they are changed to values of 0 and 1, respectively. The second *DiscreteDouble-KeyFrame* in each group changes the values back to their initial values at the end of the animation. The animation then repeats. If you set a *Duration* property of 0:0:2 in the *Storyboard* element, you can remove the second *DiscreteDoubleKeyFrame* in each collection.

As usual with XAML animations (or programming in general), you can build the diner sign in several different ways. Here's a version with just one *TextBlock* element.

Diner2.xaml

```
<!-- =====================================
     Diner2.xaml (c) 2006 by Charles Petzold
     ===================================== -->
<Page xmlns="http://schemas.microsoft.com/winfx/2006/xaml/presentation"
      xmlns:x="http://schemas.microsoft.com/winfx/2006/xaml">
    <Grid TextBlock.FontSize="192">
        <TextBlock Name="txtblk" Foreground="Black"
                   HorizontalAlignment="Center" VerticalAlignment="Center" />
    </Grid>

    <Page.Triggers>
        <EventTrigger RoutedEvent="Canvas.Loaded">
            <BeginStoryboard>
                <Storyboard TargetName="txtblk" Duration="0:0:2"
                            RepeatBehavior="Forever">

                    <StringAnimationUsingKeyFrames
                            Storyboard.TargetProperty="Text">
                        <DiscreteStringKeyFrame KeyTime="0:0:0" Value="EAT" />
                        <DiscreteStringKeyFrame KeyTime="0:0:1" Value="HERE" />
                    </StringAnimationUsingKeyFrames>

                    <ColorAnimationUsingKeyFrames
                            Storyboard.TargetProperty="Foreground.Color">
                        <DiscreteColorKeyFrame KeyTime="0:0:0" Value="Red" />
                        <DiscreteColorKeyFrame KeyTime="0:0:1" Value="Blue" />
                    </ColorAnimationUsingKeyFrames>
                </Storyboard>
            </BeginStoryboard>
        </EventTrigger>
    </Page.Triggers>
</Page>
```

This single *TextBlock* element has no *Text* property set, and the *Foreground* property exists solely to ensure that a *SolidColorBrush* exists. The *StringAnimationUsingKeyFrames* alternates the *Text* property between EAT and HERE. The *ColorAnimationUsingKeyFrames* alternates the *Color* property of *Foreground* between *Red* and *Blue*. In each case, the first key frame has a *Key-Time* of zero seconds to specify the initial values (the word "EAT" in red), and the second key frame has a *KeyTime* of one second to change the values of the word "HERE" in blue. The *Story-board* indicates a *Duration* of two seconds.

The following XAML file has eight *LinearColorKeyFrame* elements that change the background of the *Canvas* to each of the colors of the rainbow. The animation lasts as long as the highest *KeyTime*, which is seven seconds. At the beginning of the animation, the color is set to red and immediately starts changing to orange. Between second six and second seven, the color changes from violet to red, so when the animation begins again after those seven seconds have elapsed, there's no discontinuity as the color starts again at red.

ColorAnimation.xaml

```
<!-- ================================================
     ColorAnimation.xaml (c) 2006 by Charles Petzold
     ================================================ -->
<Canvas xmlns="http://schemas.microsoft.com/winfx/2006/xaml/presentation"
        xmlns:x="http://schemas.microsoft.com/winfx/2006/xaml"
        Background="Red">
    <Canvas.Triggers>
        <EventTrigger RoutedEvent="Canvas.Loaded">
            <BeginStoryboard>
                <Storyboard TargetProperty="Background.Color">
                    <ColorAnimationUsingKeyFrames RepeatBehavior="Forever">
                        <LinearColorKeyFrame KeyTime="0:0:0" Value="Red" />
                        <LinearColorKeyFrame KeyTime="0:0:1" Value="Orange" />
                        <LinearColorKeyFrame KeyTime="0:0:2" Value="Yellow" />
                        <LinearColorKeyFrame KeyTime="0:0:3" Value="Green" />
                        <LinearColorKeyFrame KeyTime="0:0:4" Value="Blue" />
                        <LinearColorKeyFrame KeyTime="0:0:5" Value="Indigo" />
                        <LinearColorKeyFrame KeyTime="0:0:6" Value="Violet" />
                        <LinearColorKeyFrame KeyTime="0:0:7" Value="Red" />
                    </ColorAnimationUsingKeyFrames>
                </Storyboard>
            </BeginStoryboard>
        </EventTrigger>
    </Canvas.Triggers>
</Canvas>
```

I've discussed *Discrete<Type>KeyFrame* and *Linear<Type>KeyFrame* but not yet the third possibility for key frame elements, which is *Spline<Type>KeyFrame*. The *Spline<Type>Key-Frame* interpolates between the starting and ending values based on a spline rather than a straight line. Using this key frame, you can get effects similar to the *Acceleration* and *Deceleration* properties but with much more control.

The *Spline<Type>KeyFrame* classes inherit the *KeyTime* and *Value* properties and define just one additional property named *KeySpline*, which consists of just two control points of a Bezier curve. The Bezier curve is assumed to begin at the point (0, 0) and end at the point (1, 1). The two points specified in the *KeySpline* must have *X* and *Y* coordinates not less than 0 or greater than 1. With the values of the control points restricted in this way, it's not possible for the Bezier curve to loop. The resultant curve defines a relationship between time (the *X* axis) and the value of the animation (the *Y* axis).

For example, suppose you're animating a *double* between the values of 100 and 200 over a period of 10 seconds. What is the value of the *double* at five seconds? With a plain *Double-Animation* or *LinearDoubleKeyFrame*, the value is obviously 150. With a *SplineDoubleKey-Frame*, the value depends on the spline you've defined. The time of five seconds is the halfway point between 0 and 10 seconds, so it corresponds to an *X* coordinate of 0.5. If the *Y* coordinate of the spline at that point is 0.75, the value of the *double* is 75 percent of the amount between 100 and 200, or 175.

Here's an example of applying *SplineDoubleKeyFrame* to the bouncing ball problem.

```
AnotherBouncingBall.xaml
<!-- ================================================
       AnotherBouncingBall.xaml (c) 2006 by Charles Petzold
     ================================================ -->
<Canvas xmlns="http://schemas.microsoft.com/winfx/2006/xaml/presentation"
        xmlns:x="http://schemas.microsoft.com/winfx/2006/xaml"
        xmlns:s="clr-namespace:System;assembly=mscorlib">

    <Line X1="0" Y1="506" X2="1000" Y2="506" Stroke="Black" StrokeThickness="5" />

    <Ellipse Name="elips" Width="24" Height="24" Fill="Red" Canvas.Left="96">

        <Ellipse.Triggers>
            <EventTrigger RoutedEvent="Ellipse.Loaded">
                <BeginStoryboard>
                    <Storyboard TargetName="elips"
                                TargetProperty="(Canvas.Top)"
                                RepeatBehavior="Forever">
                        <DoubleAnimationUsingKeyFrames>
                            <DiscreteDoubleKeyFrame KeyTime="0:0:0" Value="96" />
                            <SplineDoubleKeyFrame KeyTime="0:0:1" Value="480"
                                                  KeySpline="0.25 0, 0.6 0.2" />
                            <SplineDoubleKeyFrame KeyTime="0:0:2" Value="96"
                                                  KeySpline="0.75 1, 0.4 0.8" />
                        </DoubleAnimationUsingKeyFrames>
                    </Storyboard>
                </BeginStoryboard>
            </EventTrigger>
        </Ellipse.Triggers>
    </Ellipse>
</Canvas>
```

The *Canvas.Top* attached property is set to 96 by the initial *DiscreteDoubleKeyFrame* element. It is animated to 480 by the first *SplineDoubleKeyFrame* and back to 96 by the second. Each *SplineDoubleKeyFrame* element sets the *KeySpline* property to a string consisting of two points.

How did I derive the points I used for the *KeySpline* values? I created a program, named SplineKeyFrameExperiment, that allows me to experiment with the control points. The program consists of a XAML file that lays out the window as well as the following C# file that defines several properties and event handlers.

```
SplineKeyFrameExperiment.cs
//-----------------------------------------------------------
// SplineKeyFrameExperiment.cs (c) 2006 by Charles Petzold
//-----------------------------------------------------------
using System;
using System.Windows;
using System.Windows.Controls;
using System.Windows.Input;
```

```
using System.Windows.Media;
using System.Windows.Shapes;

namespace Petzold.SplineKeyFrameExperiment
{
    public partial class SplineKeyFrameExperiment : Window
    {
        // Two dependency properties for ControlPoint1 and ControlPoint2
        public static DependencyProperty ControlPoint1Property =
            DependencyProperty.Register("ControlPoint1", typeof(Point),
                typeof(SplineKeyFrameExperiment),
                new PropertyMetadata(new Point(0, 0), ControlPointOnChanged));

        public static DependencyProperty ControlPoint2Property =
            DependencyProperty.Register("ControlPoint2", typeof(Point),
                typeof(SplineKeyFrameExperiment),
                new PropertyMetadata(new Point(1, 1), ControlPointOnChanged));

        [STAThread]
        public static void Main()
        {
            Application app = new Application();
            app.Run(new SplineKeyFrameExperiment());
        }

        // Constructor: Mostly draws tick marks too numerous for XAML
        public SplineKeyFrameExperiment()
        {
            InitializeComponent();

            for (int i = 0; i <= 10; i++)
            {
                // Horizontal text and lines
                TextBlock txtblk = new TextBlock();
                txtblk.Text = (i / 10m).ToString("N1");
                canvMain.Children.Add(txtblk);
                Canvas.SetLeft(txtblk, 40 + 48 * i);
                Canvas.SetTop(txtblk, 14);

                Line line = new Line();
                line.X1 = 48 * (i + 1);
                line.Y1 = 30;
                line.X2 = line.X1;
                line.Y2 = 528;
                line.Stroke = Brushes.Black;
                canvMain.Children.Add(line);

                // Vertical text and lines
                txtblk = new TextBlock();
                txtblk.Text = (i / 10m).ToString("N1");
                canvMain.Children.Add(txtblk);
                Canvas.SetLeft(txtblk, 5);
                Canvas.SetTop(txtblk, 40 + 48 * i);

                line = new Line();
                line.X1 = 30;
```

```
                        line.Y1 = 48 * (i + 1);
                        line.X2 = 528;
                        line.Y2 = line.Y1;
                        line.Stroke = Brushes.Black;
                        canvMain.Children.Add(line);
                    }
                    UpdateLabel();
                }


                // ControlPoint1 and ControlPoint2 properties.
                public Point ControlPoint1
                {
                    set { SetValue(ControlPoint1Property, value); }
                    get { return (Point)GetValue(ControlPoint1Property); }
                }
                public Point ControlPoint2
                {
                    set { SetValue(ControlPoint2Property, value); }
                    get { return (Point)GetValue(ControlPoint2Property); }
                }


                // Called whenever one of the ControlPoint properties changes.
                static void ControlPointOnChanged(DependencyObject obj,
                                          DependencyPropertyChangedEventArgs args)
                {
                    SplineKeyFrameExperiment win = obj as SplineKeyFrameExperiment;

                    // Set KeySpline element in XAML animation.
                    if (args.Property == ControlPoint1Property)
                        win.spline.ControlPoint1 = (Point)args.NewValue;

                    else if (args.Property == ControlPoint2Property)
                        win.spline.ControlPoint2 = (Point)args.NewValue;
                }
                // Handles MouseDown and MouseMove events.
                void CanvasOnMouse(object sender, MouseEventArgs args)
                {
                    Canvas canv = sender as Canvas;
                    Point ptMouse = args.GetPosition(canv);
                    ptMouse.X = Math.Min(1, Math.Max(0, ptMouse.X / canv.ActualWidth));
                    ptMouse.Y = Math.Min(1, Math.Max(0, ptMouse.Y / canv.ActualHeight));

                    // Set ControlPoint properties.
                    if (args.LeftButton == MouseButtonState.Pressed)
                        ControlPoint1 = ptMouse;

                    if (args.RightButton == MouseButtonState.Pressed)
                        ControlPoint2 = ptMouse;

                    // Update the label showing ControlPoint properties.
                    if (args.LeftButton == MouseButtonState.Pressed ||
                        args.RightButton == MouseButtonState.Pressed)
                            UpdateLabel();
                }
                // Set content of XAML Label.
                void UpdateLabel()
```

```
            {
                lblInfo.Content = String.Format(
                    "Left mouse button changes ControlPoint1 = ({0:F2})\n" +
                    "Right mouse button changes ControlPoint2 = ({1:F2})",
                    ControlPoint1, ControlPoint2);
            }
        }
    }
}
```

This file defines two properties named *ControlPoint1* and *ControlPoint2* that are backed by dependency properties. These are the two control points for the Bezier curve used in the animation. Whenever one of these properties changes, the static *ControlPointOnChanged* method in the class is called, setting the properties of a *KeySpline* object defined in the XAML portion of the window (coming up).

The C# code also has an event handler for *MouseDown* and *MouseMove* events that sets *ControlPoint1* and *ControlPoint2* based on mouse coordinates. The last method of the file sets the content of a *Label* (also defined in the XAML file) with the values of *ControlPoint1* and *ControlPoint2*.

Here's the XAML file. The light-gray *Canvas* displays a surface whose upper-left corner is the point (0, 0) and lower-right corner is the point (1, 1). The window constructor in the C# portion of the program draws lines marking every 0.1 units. This *Canvas* also displays a Bezier curve between the two corners whose two control points are the *ControlPoint1* and *ControlPoint2* properties of the *Window* object. You change these points by clicking and dragging on the surface of the *Canvas*.

SplineKeyFrameExperiment.xaml

```xml
<!-- ===============================================================
        SplineKeyFrameExperiment.xaml (c) 2006 by Charles Petzold
     =============================================================== -->
<Window xmlns="http://schemas.microsoft.com/winfx/2006/xaml/presentation"
        xmlns:x="http://schemas.microsoft.com/winfx/2006/xaml"
        xmlns:src="clr-namespace:Petzold.SplineKeyFrameExperiment"
        x:Class="Petzold.SplineKeyFrameExperiment.SplineKeyFrameExperiment"
        Title="SplineKeyFrame Experiment"
        Name="window">
    <Canvas>
        <!-- Canvas with gray box and axes with tick marks. -->
        <Canvas Name="canvMain" Canvas.Left="24" Canvas.Top="24" >

            <!-- Horizontal axis header. -->
            <Line X1="0.5in" Y1="0.08in" X2="2.75in" Y2="0.08in"
                    Stroke="{DynamicResource {x:Static
                                    SystemColors.WindowTextBrushKey}}" />
            <TextBlock Text="Time" Canvas.Left="2.85in" Canvas.Top="0in" />
            <Line X1="3.25in" Y1="0.08in" X2="5.5in" Y2="0.08in"
                    Stroke="{DynamicResource {x:Static
                                    SystemColors.WindowTextBrushKey}}" />
```

```
<!-- Gray box for displaying grid. -->
<Canvas Canvas.Left="48" Canvas.Top="48" Width="480" Height="480"
        Background="LightGray"
        MouseDown="CanvasOnMouse" MouseMove="CanvasOnMouse">

    <!-- The Bezier curve formed by the control points. -->
    <Path Stroke="Black" StrokeThickness="0.005">
        <Path.Data>
            <PathGeometry>
                <PathFigure StartPoint="0 0">
                    <BezierSegment
                        Point1="{Binding ElementName=window,
                                         Path=ControlPoint1}"
                        Point2="{Binding ElementName=window,
                                         Path=ControlPoint2}"
                        Point3="1 1" />
                </PathFigure>
            </PathGeometry>
        </Path.Data>
        <Path.RenderTransform>
            <ScaleTransform ScaleX="480" ScaleY="480" />
        </Path.RenderTransform>
    </Path>

    <!-- Line between (0, 0) and first control point. -->
    <Line Stroke="DarkGray" StrokeThickness="0.005" X1="0" Y1="0"
        X2="{Binding ElementName=window, Path=ControlPoint1.X}"
        Y2="{Binding ElementName=window, Path=ControlPoint1.Y}">
        <Line.RenderTransform>
            <ScaleTransform ScaleX="480" ScaleY="480" />
        </Line.RenderTransform>
    </Line>

    <!-- Line between second control point and (1, 1). -->
    <Line Stroke="DarkGray" StrokeThickness="0.005" X1="1" Y1="1"
        X2="{Binding ElementName=window, Path=ControlPoint2.X}"
        Y2="{Binding ElementName=window, Path=ControlPoint2.Y}">
        <Line.RenderTransform>
            <ScaleTransform ScaleX="480" ScaleY="480" />
        </Line.RenderTransform>
    </Line>
</Canvas>
</Canvas>

<!-- Ball showing elapsing time (changed by animation). -->
<Path Name="time" Fill="Blue">
    <Path.Data>
        <EllipseGeometry Center="72 556" RadiusX="6" RadiusY="6" />
    </Path.Data>
</Path>

<!-- Ball showing changing value (changed by animation). -->
<Path Name="value" Fill="Blue">
    <Path.Data>
        <EllipseGeometry Center="556 72" RadiusX="6" RadiusY="6" />
```

```xml
                </Path.Data>
        </Path>

        <!-- Line showing elapsing time. -->
        <Line Stroke="Blue"
            X1="{Binding ElementName=time, Path=Data.Center.X}"
            Y1="{Binding ElementName=value, Path=Data.Center.Y}"
            X2="{Binding ElementName=time, Path=Data.Center.X}"
            Y2="556" />

        <!-- Line showing changing value. -->
        <Line Stroke="Blue"
            X1="{Binding ElementName=time, Path=Data.Center.X}"
            Y1="{Binding ElementName=value, Path=Data.Center.Y}"
            X2="556"
            Y2="{Binding ElementName=value, Path=Data.Center.Y}" />

        <!-- Label showing control points (set from code). -->
        <Label Name="lblInfo" Canvas.Left="38" Canvas.Top="580"  />

        <!-- Go button. -->
        <Button Canvas.Left="450" Canvas.Top="580" MinWidth="72" Content="Go!">
            <Button.Triggers>
                <EventTrigger RoutedEvent="Button.Click">
                    <BeginStoryboard>
                        <Storyboard>
                            <!-- Show time elapsing linearly. -->
                            <PointAnimation
                                Storyboard.TargetName="time"
                                Storyboard.TargetProperty="Data.Center"
                                From="72 556" To="552 556"
                                Duration="0:0:5" />

                            <!-- Show value changing by spline. -->
                            <PointAnimationUsingKeyFrames
                                    Storyboard.TargetName="value"
                                    Storyboard.TargetProperty="Data.Center">
                                <DiscretePointKeyFrame KeyTime="0:0:0"
                                                    Value="556 72" />

                                <SplinePointKeyFrame KeyTime="0:0:5"
                                                    Value="556 552">
                                <!-- KeySpline set from code. -->
                                <SplinePointKeyFrame.KeySpline>
                                    <KeySpline x:Name="spline" />
                                </SplinePointKeyFrame.KeySpline>
                                </SplinePointKeyFrame>
                            </PointAnimationUsingKeyFrames>
                        </Storyboard>
                    </BeginStoryboard>
                </EventTrigger>
            </Button.Triggers>
        </Button>
    </Canvas>
</Window>
```

At the lower-right corner of the window is a *Button* labeled "Go!" When you click this *Button*, two animations are triggered. A *PointAnimation* moves a little ball with a target name of "time" at a linear rate across the bottom of the grid to represent the passing of time. A *PointAnimation-UsingKeyFrames* moves a little ball with a target name of "value" down the right side of the grid to represent changing values based on a *SplinePointKeyFrame* with a *KeySpline* set from the Bezier spline you've specified.

In this way you can experiment with control points to get the effect you want. If both control points are values of (0.1, 0.9), the animated property changes very quickly at first and then slows down. If both control points are (0.9, 0.1), the opposite happens: the animation starts off slow but then speeds up.

If the first control point is (0.1, 0.9) and the second is (0.9, 0.1), the animation starts up fast, then slows down, then speeds up again. Switch the two to get the opposite effect: the animation starts slowly, then speeds up, and then slows down again. If you need something more elaborate, use multiple *Spline<Type>KeyFrame* elements in a row.

An object in free fall covers a distance proportional to the square of the time. To mimic this effect with a *KeySpline*, you'll want a curve that maps a time of 0.1 to a value of 0.01, a time of 0.2 to a value of 0.04, a time of 0.3 to a value of 0.09, and so forth. You won't be able to get the beginning of the curve quite right, but the rest of it is well approximated with a first control point of (0.25, 0) and a second of (0.6, 0.2). That's what I used in the AnotherBouncing-Ball.xaml program for the fall. I used the mirror image of the curve—the points (0.75, 1) and (0.4, 0.8)—for the bounce back up.

I use those same values for the movement of the five suspended balls in the physics apparatus (and executive toy) known as Newton's Cradle.

NewtonsCradle.xaml

```
<!-- ===============================================
     NewtonsCradle.xaml (c) 2006 by Charles Petzold
     =============================================== -->
<Page xmlns="http://schemas.microsoft.com/winfx/2006/xaml/presentation"
      xmlns:x="http://schemas.microsoft.com/winfx/2006/xaml"
      Title="Newton's Cradle"
      WindowTitle="Newton's Cradle by Charles Petzold">
    <Canvas>
        <Canvas.Resources>
            <Style TargetType="{x:Type Path}">
                <Setter Property="Stroke" Value="Black" />
                <Setter Property="StrokeThickness" Value="3" />
                <Setter Property="Fill" Value="Silver" />
                <Setter Property="Data"
                        Value="M 0 0 V 300 A 25 25 0 1 1 0 350
                                            A 25 25 0 1 1 0 300" />
            </Style>
        </Canvas.Resources>
```

```
<Path>
    <Path.RenderTransform>
        <TransformGroup>
            <RotateTransform x:Name="xform1" Angle="30" />
            <TranslateTransform X="200" />
        </TransformGroup>
    </Path.RenderTransform>
</Path>

<Path>
    <Path.RenderTransform>
        <TransformGroup>
            <RotateTransform x:Name="xform2" Angle="30" />
            <TranslateTransform X="252" />
        </TransformGroup>
    </Path.RenderTransform>
</Path>

<Path>
    <Path.RenderTransform>
        <TransformGroup>
            <RotateTransform x:Name="xform3" Angle="30" />
            <TranslateTransform X="304" />
        </TransformGroup>
    </Path.RenderTransform>
</Path>

<Path>
    <Path.RenderTransform>
        <TransformGroup>
            <RotateTransform x:Name="xform4" />
            <TranslateTransform X="356" />
        </TransformGroup>
    </Path.RenderTransform>
</Path>

<Path>
    <Path.RenderTransform>
        <TransformGroup>
            <RotateTransform x:Name="xform5" />
            <TranslateTransform X="408" />
        </TransformGroup>
    </Path.RenderTransform>
</Path>

<Canvas.Triggers>
    <EventTrigger RoutedEvent="Page.Loaded">
        <BeginStoryboard>
            <Storyboard TargetProperty="Angle" RepeatBehavior="Forever">
                <DoubleAnimationUsingKeyFrames
                        Storyboard.TargetName="xform1">
                    <DiscreteDoubleKeyFrame KeyTime="0:0:0" Value="30"/>
                    <SplineDoubleKeyFrame KeyTime="0:0:1" Value="0"
                                        KeySpline="0.25 0, 0.6 0.2" />
                    <DiscreteDoubleKeyFrame KeyTime="0:0:3" Value="0" />
```

```
                        <SplineDoubleKeyFrame KeyTime="0:0:4" Value="30"
                                        KeySpline="0.75 1, 0.4 0.8" />
                    </DoubleAnimationUsingKeyFrames>

                    <DoubleAnimationUsingKeyFrames
                            Storyboard.TargetName="xform2">
                        <DiscreteDoubleKeyFrame KeyTime="0:0:0" Value="30"/>
                        <SplineDoubleKeyFrame KeyTime="0:0:1" Value="0"
                                        KeySpline="0.25 0, 0.6 0.2" />
                        <DiscreteDoubleKeyFrame KeyTime="0:0:3" Value="0" />
                        <SplineDoubleKeyFrame KeyTime="0:0:4" Value="30"
                                        KeySpline="0.75 1, 0.4 0.8" />
                    </DoubleAnimationUsingKeyFrames>

                    <DoubleAnimationUsingKeyFrames
                            Storyboard.TargetName="xform3">
                        <DiscreteDoubleKeyFrame KeyTime="0:0:0" Value="30"/>
                        <SplineDoubleKeyFrame KeyTime="0:0:1" Value="0"
                                        KeySpline="0.25 0, 0.6 0.2" />
                        <SplineDoubleKeyFrame KeyTime="0:0:2" Value="-30"
                                        KeySpline="0.75 1, 0.4 0.8" />
                        <SplineDoubleKeyFrame KeyTime="0:0:3" Value="0"
                                        KeySpline="0.25 0, 0.6 0.2" />
                        <SplineDoubleKeyFrame KeyTime="0:0:4" Value="30"
                                        KeySpline="0.75 1, 0.4 0.8" />
                    </DoubleAnimationUsingKeyFrames>

                    <DoubleAnimationUsingKeyFrames
                            Storyboard.TargetName="xform4">
                        <DiscreteDoubleKeyFrame KeyTime="0:0:0" Value="0" />
                        <DiscreteDoubleKeyFrame KeyTime="0:0:1" Value="0" />
                        <SplineDoubleKeyFrame KeyTime="0:0:2" Value="-30"
                                        KeySpline="0.75 1, 0.4 0.8" />
                        <SplineDoubleKeyFrame KeyTime="0:0:3" Value="0"
                                        KeySpline="0.25 0, 0.6 0.2" />
                    </DoubleAnimationUsingKeyFrames>

                    <DoubleAnimationUsingKeyFrames
                            Storyboard.TargetName="xform5">
                        <DiscreteDoubleKeyFrame KeyTime="0:0:0" Value="0" />
                        <DiscreteDoubleKeyFrame KeyTime="0:0:1" Value="0" />
                        <SplineDoubleKeyFrame KeyTime="0:0:2" Value="-30"
                                        KeySpline="0.75 1, 0.4 0.8" />
                        <SplineDoubleKeyFrame KeyTime="0:0:3" Value="0"
                                        KeySpline="0.25 0, 0.6 0.2" />
                    </DoubleAnimationUsingKeyFrames>
                </Storyboard>
            </BeginStoryboard>
        </EventTrigger>
    </Canvas.Triggers>
  </Canvas>
</Page>
```

A *DoubleAnimationUsingKeyFrames* element is associated with each of the five suspended balls. Each collection of key frames is a combination of *DiscreteDoubleKeyFrame* and *Spline-DoubleKeyFrame*. The two balls on each side stop in the center; the one in the middle does not.

All animations described so far either set a property to a specified value (*Discrete<Type>Key-Frame*) or perform an interpolation between two values. The interpolated value is always somewhere along the straight line that connects the starting value and the ending value. The difference between *Linear<Type>KeyFrame* and *Spline<Type>KeyFrame* is how the interpolation calculation treats time—linearly or as an *X* coordinate of a spline. But in neither case does the interpolated value deviate from that straight line between the starting and ending values.

This does not imply that you can't move an animated object in anything other than a straight line. You've seen how to animate the *Angle* property of a *Rotate* transform to make an object move in circles. But how would you like a general approach to moving an object along an arbitrary path? That's the purpose of the final category of animation classes, which is restricted to just three classes: *DoubleAnimationUsingPath*, *PointAnimationUsingPath*, and *MatrixAnimation-UsingPath*. Each of these classes defines *IsAdditive* and *IsCumulative* properties and, most importantly, a *PathGeometry* property that you set to a graphics path.

Here's an example of a *PointAnimationUsingPath* that sets the *PathGeometry* property to a Bezier curve that makes a little loop. The target of the animation is the center of a little ball (what else?), such that the ball moves back and forth along the Bezier curve.

```
SimplePathAnimation.xaml
<!-- =====================================================
     SimplePathAnimation.xaml (c) 2006 by Charles Petzold
     ===================================================== -->
<Canvas xmlns="http://schemas.microsoft.com/winfx/2006/xaml/presentation"
        xmlns:x="http://schemas.microsoft.com/winfx/2006/xaml">

    <Path Fill="Blue">
        <Path.Data>
            <EllipseGeometry x:Name="elips"
                             RadiusX="12" RadiusY="12" />
        </Path.Data>

        <Path.Triggers>
            <EventTrigger RoutedEvent="Path.Loaded">
                <BeginStoryboard>
                    <Storyboard TargetName="elips" TargetProperty="Center">
                        <PointAnimationUsingPath Duration="0:0:2.5"
                                                 AutoReverse="True"
                                                 RepeatBehavior="Forever">
                            <PointAnimationUsingPath.PathGeometry>
                                <PathGeometry
                                    Figures="M 96 288 C 576 0, 0 0, 480 288" />
                            </PointAnimationUsingPath.PathGeometry>
                        </PointAnimationUsingPath>
                    </Storyboard>
```

```
                    </BeginStoryboard>
                </EventTrigger>
            </Path.Triggers>
        </Path>
    </Canvas>
```

To actually see the *PathGeometry* that's controlling the movement of the ball, you can include another *Path* element right after the *Canvas* start tag:

```
<Path Stroke="Black" Data="M 96 288 C 576 0, 0 0, 480 288" />
```

The center of the ball tracks this path exactly. *PointAnimationUsingPath* animates a property of type *Point* by forcing the property to take on values defined by a graphics path, in this case a Bezier curve. The path can alternatively be a rectangle, ellipse, arc, or any combination of those figures.

PointAnimationUsingPath is very different from *SplinePointKeyFrame*, which it might be confused with because Bezier splines are often (but not exclusively) used with *PointAnimation-UsingPath* and Bezier splines are always (but in a restricted way) used with *SplinePointKeyFrame*. It's important to distinguish between these two classes.

With *SplinePointKeyFrame*, the interpolated point always lies on the straight line between a starting point and an ending point. Elapsed time is used to calculate an *X* coordinate of the spline (between 0 and 1), and the *Y* coordinate of the spline (also between 0 and 1) is then used to calculate the interpolated value.

With *PointAnimationUsingPath*, time is allocated based on the *total length* of the path you've set to the *PathGeometry* property. For example, if the animation has a *Duration* of four seconds, and one second has elapsed, the animation determines the *X* and *Y* coordinates of the path one-quarter of the distance from the beginning to the end. These become the *Point* value of the animation.

What if you want to move an object along a path and the element does not have a *Point* property? Perhaps you want to move a *Button* along a path. You position a *Button* object on a *Canvas* panel by specifying the *Left* and *Right* attached properties. To move the *Button*, you must animate these properties.

To move any arbitrary object (such as a *Button*) along a path, you can mimic *PointAnimation-UsingPath* with two *DoubleAnimationUsingPath* objects. One animation controls the *X* coordinate, and the other controls the *Y* coordinate. *DoubleAnimationUsingPath* defines a *Source* property specifically for this purpose. You set this property to a member of the *PathAnimation-Source* enumeration—*X*, *Y*, or *Angle*. (More on the *Angle* option shortly.)

Here's a XAML file that defines a Bezier curve in a *PathGeometry* as a resource. It uses this resource both to draw the Bezier curve with the *Path* element and also to set the *PathGeometry* in two *DoubleAnimationUsingPath* elements, the first controlling the *Canvas.Left* property of the *Button* by setting *Source* to *X*, and the second controlling the *Canvas.Top* property by setting *Source* to *Y*.

PathAnimatedButton.xaml

```xml
<!-- =====================================================
        PathAnimatedButton.xaml (c) 2006 by Charles Petzold
     ===================================================== -->
<Canvas xmlns="http://schemas.microsoft.com/winfx/2006/xaml/presentation"
        xmlns:x="http://schemas.microsoft.com/winfx/2006/xaml">

    <Canvas.Resources>
        <PathGeometry x:Key="path"
                      Figures="M 96 192 C 288 0, 384 384, 576 192" />
    </Canvas.Resources>

    <Path Stroke="Black" Data="{StaticResource path}" />

    <Button Name="btn">
        Button
    </Button>

    <Canvas.Triggers>
        <EventTrigger RoutedEvent="Canvas.Loaded">
            <BeginStoryboard>
                <Storyboard TargetName="btn">

                    <DoubleAnimationUsingPath
                        Storyboard.TargetProperty="(Canvas.Left)"
                        Duration="0:0:2.5"
                        AutoReverse="True"
                        RepeatBehavior="Forever"
                        PathGeometry="{StaticResource path}"
                        Source="X" />

                    <DoubleAnimationUsingPath
                        Storyboard.TargetProperty="(Canvas.Top)"
                        Duration="0:0:2.5"
                        AutoReverse="True"
                        RepeatBehavior="Forever"
                        PathGeometry="{StaticResource path}"
                        Source="Y" />
                </Storyboard>
            </BeginStoryboard>
        </EventTrigger>
    </Canvas.Triggers>
</Canvas>
```

You can also set the *Source* property of *DoubleAnimationUsingPath* to *PathAnimationSource .Angle*, and when you specify that member, *DoubleAnimationUsingPath* animates a property based on the slope of the path in degrees. Typically, you would then use this *DoubleAnimationUsingPath* to animate the *Angle* property of a *RotateTransform*.

The following program demonstrates this technique. It is very similar to the previous XAML file, except that the *PathGeometry* is a bit more elaborate and defines a continuous curved line based on two Bezier curves. The *Button* element now includes a *RotateTransform* that is set to its *RenderTransform* property. A third *DoubleAnimationUsingPath* animates the *Angle* property of this transform with the same Bezier curve and *Source* set to *Angle*.

PathAngleAnimatedButton.xaml

```
<!-- =======================================================
        PathAngleAnimatedButton.xaml (c) 2006 by Charles Petzold
     ======================================================= -->
<Canvas xmlns="http://schemas.microsoft.com/winfx/2006/xaml/presentation"
        xmlns:x="http://schemas.microsoft.com/winfx/2006/xaml">

    <Canvas.Resources>
        <PathGeometry x:Key="path"
                      Figures="M 96 192 C 288 0, 384 384, 576 192
                               S 662 192 576 576 S 384 576 96 192" />
    </Canvas.Resources>

    <Path Stroke="Black" Data="{StaticResource path}" />

    <Button Name="btn">
        Button
        <Button.RenderTransform>
            <RotateTransform x:Name="xform" />
        </Button.RenderTransform>
    </Button>

    <Canvas.Triggers>
        <EventTrigger RoutedEvent="Canvas.Loaded">
            <BeginStoryboard>
                <Storyboard RepeatBehavior="Forever">

                    <DoubleAnimationUsingPath
                        Storyboard.TargetName="btn"
                        Storyboard.TargetProperty="(Canvas.Left)"
                        Duration="0:0:10"
                        PathGeometry="{StaticResource path}"
                        Source="X" />

                    <DoubleAnimationUsingPath
                        Storyboard.TargetName="btn"
                        Storyboard.TargetProperty="(Canvas.Top)"
                        Duration="0:0:10"
                        PathGeometry="{StaticResource path}"
                        Source="Y" />

                    <DoubleAnimationUsingPath
                        Storyboard.TargetName="xform"
                        Storyboard.TargetProperty="Angle"
                        Duration="0:0:10"
                        PathGeometry="{StaticResource path}"
                        Source="Angle" />
```

```
                    </Storyboard>
                </BeginStoryboard>
            </EventTrigger>
        </Canvas.Triggers>
    </Canvas>
```

Run this program and you'll see the upper-left corner of the button tracing the Bezier curve as you might expect, but the rotation of the button also traces the curve so that the top of the button is always parallel to the curve.

Keep in mind that although it seems natural to animate the horizontal position of an element by setting *Source* to *X*, to animate the vertical position by setting *Source* to *Y*, and to animate the *Angle* of rotation by setting *Source* to *Angle*, you're not restricted to those options. For example, the following program animates the *Opacity* property of a *TextBlock* by using a path constructed from three straight lines that if graphed form a rectangle.

RectangularOpacity.xaml

```
<!-- =======================================================
     RectangularOpacity.xaml (c) 2006 by Charles Petzold
     ======================================================= -->
<Page xmlns="http://schemas.microsoft.com/winfx/2006/xaml/presentation"
      xmlns:x="http://schemas.microsoft.com/winfx/2006/xaml">

    <TextBlock x:Name="txtblk" Text="XAML"
               FontSize="144pt" FontFamily="Arial Black"
               HorizontalAlignment="Center" VerticalAlignment="Center">

        <TextBlock.Triggers>
            <EventTrigger RoutedEvent="TextBlock.Loaded">
                <BeginStoryboard>
                    <Storyboard TargetName="txtblk"
                                TargetProperty="Opacity"
                                RepeatBehavior="Forever">
                        <DoubleAnimationUsingPath Duration="0:0:4"
                                                  Source="Y">
                            <DoubleAnimationUsingPath.PathGeometry>
                                <PathGeometry>
                                    <PathGeometry.Figures>
                                        <PathFigure StartPoint="0 0">
                                            <LineSegment Point="0 1" />
                                            <LineSegment Point="2 1" />
                                            <LineSegment Point="2 0" />
                                        </PathFigure>
                                    </PathGeometry.Figures>
                                </PathGeometry>
                            </DoubleAnimationUsingPath.PathGeometry>
                        </DoubleAnimationUsingPath>
                    </Storyboard>
                </BeginStoryboard>
            </EventTrigger>
        </TextBlock.Triggers>
    </TextBlock>
</Page>
```

The *DoubleAnimationUsingPath* element has a *Source* property set to *Y*, which means the *Y* values of the path will be used to animate the *Opacity* property of the *TextBlock*. (These *Y* values should be between 0 and 1.) The path is a series of straight lines from (0, 0) to (0, 1) to (2, 1) to (2, 0). The total length of this path is 4 units. The first line is from the point (0, 0) to (0, 1). That's 1 unit in length, so it will govern the first quarter of the duration of the animation. The animation is conveniently four seconds in duration, so over the first second of the animation, the *Y* coordinate of the path (and the *Opacity* of the *TextBlock*) changes from 0 to 1. The next line in the path is (0, 1) to (2, 1), a distance of two units, so over the next two seconds, the *Y* coordinate (and the *Opacity*) remains at 1. The final line is from (2, 1) to (2, 0), a distance of 1 unit, which brings the *Y* coordinate and *Opacity* back to 0 over the final second. (Of course, you can easily do something similar with a combination of *LinearDoubleKeyFrame* and *DiscreteDoubleKeyFrame*.)

If you use three *DoubleAnimationUsingPath* elements (or one *PointAnimationUsingPath* and one *DoubleAnimationUsingPath*) to animate horizontal and vertical position and rotation angle, you can replace those elements with a single *MatrixAnimationUsingPath* element. This element animates a *Matrix* object. The *X* and *Y* coordinates of the path become the *OffsetX* and *OffsetY* properties of the transform matrix; the remainder of the matrix optionally defines a rotation based on the tangent angle of the path. (You need to set *DoesRotateWithTangent* to *true* to get the rotation.)

The visuals of the MatrixAnimatedButton.xaml file are identical to those of the previous PathAngleAnimatedButton.xaml..

MatrixAnimatedButton.xaml

```
<!-- =====================================================
        MatrixAnimatedButton.xaml (c) 2006 by Charles Petzold
     ===================================================== -->
<Canvas xmlns="http://schemas.microsoft.com/winfx/2006/xaml/presentation"
        xmlns:x="http://schemas.microsoft.com/winfx/2006/xaml">

    <Canvas.Resources>
        <PathGeometry x:Key="path"
                      Figures="M 96 192 C 288 0, 384 384, 576 192
                               S 662 192 576 576 S 384 576 96 192" />
    </Canvas.Resources>

    <Path Stroke="Black" Data="{StaticResource path}" />

    <Button>
        Button
        <Button.RenderTransform>
            <MatrixTransform x:Name="xform" />
        </Button.RenderTransform>
    </Button>

    <Canvas.Triggers>
        <EventTrigger RoutedEvent="Canvas.Loaded">
            <BeginStoryboard>
                <Storyboard RepeatBehavior="Forever">
```

```
                    <MatrixAnimationUsingPath
                        Storyboard.TargetName="xform"
                        Storyboard.TargetProperty="Matrix"
                        Duration="0:0:10"
                        PathGeometry="{StaticResource path}"
                        DoesRotateWithTangent="True" />

            </Storyboard>
        </BeginStoryboard>
    </EventTrigger>
 </Canvas.Triggers>
</Canvas>
```

I will freely admit that applications involving moving and rotating a button along a path don't arise very frequently. However, one common application of path animations is the unicycle-man cyborg, who must navigate a treacherous path over the hills of Bezier Boulevard.

UnicycleMan.xaml
```
<!-- ===============================================
      UnicycleMan.xaml (c) 2006 by Charles Petzold
     =============================================== -->
<Canvas xmlns="http://schemas.microsoft.com/winfx/2006/xaml/presentation"
        xmlns:x="http://schemas.microsoft.com/winfx/2006/xaml">

    <Canvas.Resources>
        <PathGeometry x:Key="path"
                      Figures="M 200   200
                               C 300     0,  500 400, 700 200
                               C 900     0, 1000 200, 900 300
                               C 100  1100, 1200 800, 400 500
                               C 100   400,  100 400, 200 200" />
        <Style TargetType="{x:Type Path}">
            <Setter Property="Stroke"
                    Value="{DynamicResource {x:Static
                                SystemColors.WindowTextBrushKey}}" />
        </Style>
    </Canvas.Resources>

    <!-- Draw the path. -->
    <Path Data="{StaticResource path}" />

    <!-- Draw the unicycle-man. -->
    <Path>
        <Path.Data>
            <GeometryGroup>
                <!-- Wheel. -->
                <EllipseGeometry Center="0 -25" RadiusX="25" RadiusY="25" />

                <!-- Spokes -->
                <GeometryGroup>
                    <LineGeometry StartPoint="0 0" EndPoint="0 -50" />
                    <LineGeometry StartPoint="-25 -25" EndPoint="25 -25" />
                    <LineGeometry StartPoint="-18 -7" EndPoint="18 -43" />
```

```
                <LineGeometry StartPoint="18 -7" EndPoint="-18 -43" />
              <GeometryGroup.Transform>
                  <RotateTransform x:Name="xformSpokes"
                                    CenterX="0" CenterY="-25" />
              </GeometryGroup.Transform>
          </GeometryGroup>

          <!-- Body, head, and arms. -->
          <LineGeometry StartPoint="0 -25" EndPoint="0 -80" />
          <EllipseGeometry Center="0 -90" RadiusX="10" RadiusY="10" />
          <LineGeometry StartPoint="9 -85" EndPoint="0 -90" />
          <LineGeometry StartPoint="-35 -70" EndPoint="35 -70">
              <LineGeometry.Transform>
                  <RotateTransform x:Name="xformArm"
                                    CenterX="0" CenterY="-70" />
              </LineGeometry.Transform>
          </LineGeometry>

      </GeometryGroup>
    </Path.Data>
    <Path.RenderTransform>
        <MatrixTransform x:Name="xformUnicycleMan" />
    </Path.RenderTransform>
</Path>

<Canvas.Triggers>
    <EventTrigger RoutedEvent="Canvas.Loaded">
        <BeginStoryboard>
            <Storyboard SpeedRatio="0.5">
                <!-- Move the unicycle-man along the path. -->
                <MatrixAnimationUsingPath
                    Storyboard.TargetName="xformUnicycleMan"
                    Storyboard.TargetProperty="Matrix"
                    Duration="0:0:12"
                    PathGeometry="{StaticResource path}"
                    DoesRotateWithTangent="True"
                    RepeatBehavior="Forever" />

                <!-- Rotate the spokes of the wheel. -->
                <DoubleAnimation
                    Storyboard.TargetName="xformSpokes"
                    Storyboard.TargetProperty="Angle"
                    Duration="0:0:1"
                    RepeatBehavior="Forever"
                    From="0" To="360" />

                <!-- Move the arms for balance. -->
                <DoubleAnimation
                    Storyboard.TargetName="xformArm"
                    Storyboard.TargetProperty="Angle"
                    Duration="0:0:0.2"
                    RepeatBehavior="Forever"
                    AutoReverse="True"
                    From="-20" To="20" />
            </Storyboard>
```

```
            </BeginStoryboard>
        </EventTrigger>
    </Canvas.Triggers>
</Canvas>
```

Notice that the unicycle-man is a single *Path* object that has its *RenderTransform* set to a *MatrixTransform* with a name of "xformUnicycleMan." This is the transform subjected to the *MatrixAnimationUsingPath* element.

The point (0, 0) of the object animated with *MatrixAnimationUsingPath* (or *PointAnimation-UsingPath*) traces the path exactly. For paths drawn from left to right on the screen, positive *Y* coordinates of the object appear below the path, and negative *Y* coordinates appear above the path. That's why the unicycle-man is drawn with negative *Y* coordinates (and why the *Button* in previous programs hangs below the initial portion of the path).

Two other components of the unicycle-man are also animated. The spokes of the wheel are a series of *Line* elements in a *GeometryGroup*, and this *GeometryGroup* has its own animated *RotateTransform* named "xformSpokes." The arms are a single *Line* element with an animated *RotateTransform* named "xformArm." These animations occur within the context of the complete unicycle-man, who is moved and rotated along the path.

The TextGeometryDemo program in Chapter 28 demonstrates how to obtain a *Geometry* object that describes the outlines of text characters and how to put that *Geometry* to use in graphics programming. It's also possible to use those *Geometry* objects in animations. The companion content for this chapter includes a project named AnimatedTextGeometry that demonstrates animations based on the outlines of text characters.

A program in which unicycle-man travels up, down, across, and through text characters is an exercise left to the reader.

Chapter 31

Bitmaps, Brushes, and Drawings

Computer graphics has traditionally been divided into the two opposing domains of raster graphics and vector graphics. Raster graphics involves bitmaps, which often encode real-world images, whereas vector graphics involves lines, curves, and filled areas. The two classes that derive from *FrameworkElement* most frequently used to display graphics objects seem to parallel this division. The *Image* class (which I first introduced in Chapter 3) is generally enlisted to display a bitmap, whereas the derivatives of the *Shape* class (which I also introduced in Chapter 3 but explored in more detail in Chapter 27) offer the most straightforward approach to displaying vector graphics. For most basic graphics requirements, *Image* and the *Shape* derivatives are really all you need.

However, the graphics capabilities of the Microsoft Windows Presentation Foundation (WPF) are really not so clearly divided between raster graphics and vector graphics. It's true that the *Image* class is used mostly to display bitmaps, but the class is not restricted to bitmaps. You can also use *Image* to display objects of type *DrawingImage*; you got a little taste of this capability in the About box in the YellowPad program in Chapter 22, which uses *DrawingImage* to display my signature. A *DrawingImage* object is always based on a *Drawing* object, and the word *drawing* usually refers to a picture composed of vector graphics elements, but *Drawing* is not restricted to vector graphics. A *Drawing* object can actually be a mix of vector graphics, raster graphics, and video.

This chapter sorts out the various ways in which raster graphics and vector graphics intermingle in the WPF, and it also finishes a discussion about brushes that began in Chapter 2. In that early chapter, I demonstrated how you can create solid and gradient brushes. But you can also base brushes on *Drawing* objects, bitmaps, or objects of type *Visual*. Because *UIElement* derives from *Visual*, you can base a brush on elements such as *TextBlock* and controls such as *Button*, making for some interesting effects.

Let's begin with bitmaps. Bitmaps in the WPF are supported by the abstract *BitmapSource* class and its descendants. Both *BitmapSource* and *DrawingImage* (which is generally but not always used to display vector graphics) directly descend from *ImageSource*, as shown in the following class hierarchy:

Object

   DispatcherObject (abstract)

    DependencyObject

Freezable (abstract)

   Animatable (abstract)

      ImageSource (abstract)

         BitmapSource (abstract)

            BitmapFrame (abstract)

            BitmapImage

            CachedBitmap

            ColorConvertedBitmap

            CroppedBitmap

            FormatConvertedBitmap

            RenderTargetBitmap

            TransformedBitmap

         DrawingImage

You generally use an *Image* element to display one of these objects by setting the *Source* property of *Image* to an object of type *ImageSource*. The *ImageSource* class defines read-only *Height* and *Width* properties in device-independent units.

BitmapSource is the first class in the hierarchy that is unambiguously a bitmap. It defines read-only *PixelWidth* and *PixelHeight* properties, read-only *DpiX* and *DpiY* properties indicating the image resolution, and a read-only *Format* property of type *PixelFormat*. Unless the bitmap is very strange, the *Format* property is set to one of the 26 static read-only properties of the *PixelFormats* class. For example, a value of *PixelFormats.Bgr32* indicates 32 bits per pixel, with 1-byte blue, green, and red values (in that order) and 1 unused byte per pixel. *PixelFormats* .*Gray8* indicates 8 bits per pixel, encoding a gray shade. *PixelFormats.Indexed8* indicates 8 bits per pixel, where the values index a color palette table. If the bitmap contains a color table, that is available from the *Palette* property of *BitmapSource*. The *Palette* property is of type *BitmapPalette*, which has a *Colors* property of type *IList<Color>*.

Of the classes that inherit from *BitmapSource*, the most frequently used is undoubtedly *BitmapImage*, mainly because it has a constructor that accepts a *Uri* object. That constructor (and a property named *UriSource*) lets you load a bitmap from a local file, a file on the network, or a file embedded in the application. File types BMP, JPEG, GIF, TIFF, and PNG are supported.

The ShowMyFace program in Chapter 3 contained the following code to create a *BitmapImage* object from a file on my Web site and then to display it with the *Image* element:

```
Uri uri = new Uri("http://www.charlespetzold.com/PetzoldTattoo.jpg");
BitmapImage bitmap = new BitmapImage(uri);
Image img = new Image();
img.Source = bitmap;
```

In XAML you simply set the *Source* property of *Image* to the URI string:

```
<Image Source="http://www.charlespetzold.com/PetzoldTattoo.jpg" />
```

Obviously, the XAML implementation gets a lot of help from *ImageSourceConverter*.

In code, you can alternatively create a *BitmapImage* using a parameterless constructor and then load the image by setting the *UriSource* or *StreamSource* property. Use whichever property is convenient, but enclose the code to set the property within calls to *BeginInit* and *EndInit*:

```
BitmapImage bitmap = new BitmapImage();
bitmap.BeginInit();
bitmap.UriSource = uri;
bitmap.EndInit();
```

Yes, there is an advantage to this approach because you can also rotate the bitmap in increments of 90 degrees as it's being loaded:

```
BitmapImage bitmap = new BitmapImage();
bitmap.BeginInit();
bitmap.UriSource = uri;
bitmap.Rotation = Rotation.Rotate90;
bitmap.EndInit();
```

In XAML, you can rotate a *BitmapImage* by breaking out the *Source* property of *Image* as a property element that encloses a *BitmapImage* element:

```
<Image>
    <Image.Source>
        <BitmapImage UriSource="http://www.charlespetzold.com/PetzoldTattoo.jpg"
                     Rotation="Rotate90" />
    </Image.Source>
</Image>
```

You can also set the *SourceRect* property of *BitmapImage* to use only a subset of the entire image:

```
<Image>
    <Image.Source>
        <BitmapImage UriSource="http://www.charlespetzold.com/PetzoldTattoo.jpg"
                     SourceRect="150 100 200 200" />
    </Image.Source>
</Image>
```

Besides loading an existing bitmap into memory, you can also create new bitmaps in code, and you can put images on those bitmaps. There are two distinct ways to put images on bitmaps that you create. You can draw on the bitmap, or you can define the actual bitmap bits that make up the image. To save a bitmap that you create in this way, use the *Save* method of one of the classes that derive from *BitmapEncoder*.

If you want to create a bitmap whose image consists of graphics objects that your program draws on the bitmap, you first create an object of type *RenderTargetBitmap*:

```
RenderTargetBitmap renderbitmap =
    new RenderTargetBitmap(width, height, 96, 96, PixelFormats.Default);
```

The first two arguments are the pixel width and height of the bitmap. The second two arguments are the horizontal and vertical resolutions in dots per inch (which you can set to whatever you want). The last argument indicates the format of the pixels. With *RenderTarget-Bitmap*, you must use either *PixelFormats.Default* or *PixelFormats.Pbgra32*, which stands for "premultiplied blue-green-red-alpha 32 bits." Each pixel requires 4 bytes, which are in the order blue, green, red, and alpha channel. The values of the three primary colors for each pixel have been premultiplied by the transparency indicated by the alpha channel.

When you first create the *RenderTargetBitmap*, the image is entirely transparent. The *RenderTarget-Bitmap* class has a method named *Render* that has an argument of type *Visual*, so you can draw on this bitmap in the same way you draw on a printer page. You can call *Render* multiple times. To clear the bitmap of images and restore it to its pristine state, call the *Clear* method.

Here's a program that uses *RenderTargetBitmap* to create a bitmap that is 100 pixels square. It then draws a rounded rectangle on the bitmap. The window's background is colored khaki so you can see that the corners of the bitmap remain transparent.

```
DrawGraphicsOnBitmap.cs
//-------------------------------------------------------
// DrawGraphicsOnBitmap.cs (c) 2006 by Charles Petzold
//-------------------------------------------------------
using System;
using System.Windows;
using System.Windows.Controls;
using System.Windows.Input;
using System.Windows.Media;
using System.Windows.Media.Imaging;

namespace Petzold.DrawGraphicsOnBitmap
{
    public class DrawGraphicsOnBitmap : Window
    {
        [STAThread]
        public static void Main()
        {
            Application app = new Application();
            app.Run(new DrawGraphicsOnBitmap());
        }
```

```
        public DrawGraphicsOnBitmap()
        {
            Title = "Draw Graphics on Bitmap";

            // Set background to demonstrate transparency of bitmap.
            Background = Brushes.Khaki;

            // Create the RenderTargetBitmap object.
            RenderTargetBitmap renderbitmap =
                new RenderTargetBitmap(100, 100, 96, 96, PixelFormats.Default);

            // Create a DrawingVisual object.
            DrawingVisual drawvis = new DrawingVisual();
            DrawingContext dc = drawvis.RenderOpen();
            dc.DrawRoundedRectangle(Brushes.Blue, new Pen(Brushes.Red, 10),
                                new Rect(25, 25, 50, 50), 10, 10);
            dc.Close();

            // Render the DrawingVisual on the RenderTargetBitmap.
            renderbitmap.Render(drawvis);

            // Create an Image object and set its Source to the bitmap.
            Image img = new Image();
            img.Source = renderbitmap;

            // Make the Image object the content of the window.
            Content = img;
        }
    }
}
```

By default, the *Image* element stretches the bitmap to fill the available area while preserving the aspect ratio. When a bitmap is stretched by *Image*, the colors of the pixels are interpolated to avoid a boxy look. Images with sharp edges (such as this one) seem blurry. To force *Image* to display the bitmap in its natural size, set the *Stretch* property:

```
img.Stretch = Stretch.None;
```

Just as you can display elements such as panels and controls on the printer page, you can display elements on a bitmap. The following program creates a *UniformGrid* and puts 32 *ToggleButton* objects on its surface. The buttons have no content, but notice that some of the buttons have their *IsChecked* property set, which results in a slightly darker background color. The darker buttons seem to form another rounded rectangle.

DrawButtonsOnBitmap.cs

```
//-------------------------------------------------
// DrawButtonsOnBitmap.cs (c) 2006 by Charles Petzold
//-------------------------------------------------
using System;
using System.Windows;
using System.Windows.Controls;
```

```
using System.Windows.Controls.Primitives;
using System.Windows.Input;
using System.Windows.Media;
using System.Windows.Media.Imaging;

namespace Petzold.DrawButtonsOnBitmap
{
    public class DrawButtonsOnBitmap : Window
    {
        [STAThread]
        public static void Main()
        {
            Application app = new Application();
            app.Run(new DrawButtonsOnBitmap());
        }
        public DrawButtonsOnBitmap()
        {
            Title = "Draw Buttons on Bitmap";

            // Create a UniformGrid for hosting buttons.
            UniformGrid unigrid = new UniformGrid();
            unigrid.Columns = 4;

            // Create 32 ToggleButton objects on UniformGrid.
            for (int i = 0; i < 32; i++)
            {
                ToggleButton btn = new ToggleButton();
                btn.Width = 96;
                btn.Height = 24;
                btn.IsChecked = (i < 4 | i > 27) ^ (i % 4 == 0 | i % 4 == 3);
                unigrid.Children.Add(btn);
            }

            // Size the UniformGrid.
            unigrid.Measure(new Size(Double.PositiveInfinity,
                                     Double.PositiveInfinity));

            Size szGrid = unigrid.DesiredSize;

            // Arrange the UniformGrid.
            unigrid.Arrange(new Rect(new Point(0, 0), szGrid));

            // Create the RenderTargetBitmap object.
            RenderTargetBitmap renderbitmap =
                new RenderTargetBitmap((int)Math.Ceiling(szGrid.Width),
                                       (int)Math.Ceiling(szGrid.Height),
                                       96, 96, PixelFormats.Default);

            // Render the UniformGrid on the RenderTargetBitmap.
            renderbitmap.Render(unigrid);

            // Create an Image object and set its Source to the bitmap.
            Image img = new Image();
            img.Source = renderbitmap;
```

```
            // Make the Image object the content of the window.
            Content = img;
        }
    }
}
```

When you display elements and controls on the printer page, it is essential that you call *Measure* and *Arrange* on the parent element so it doesn't have a size of 0.

The other approach to creating bitmaps in code involves setting the actual bitmap bits. To create a bitmap from the bitmap bits, you use a static *Create* method of *BitmapSource*:

```
BitmapSource bitmap =
    BitmapSource.Create(width, height, 96, 96, pixformat, palette, array, stride);
```

An alternative form of the *BitmapSource.Create* method has an *IntPtr* argument. The first two arguments indicate the desired pixel width and height of the bitmap. You set the second two arguments to the horizontal and vertical resolution in dots per inch. The fifth argument is generally a static property of the *PixelFormats* class.

For bitmap formats that require a color table—specifically, bitmaps created using static properties of *PixelFormats* beginning with the word *Indexed*—the next argument is an object of type *BitmapPalette*, which is a collection of *Color* objects. This collection can have fewer than the number of entries implied by the format. For example, *PixelFormats.Indexed4* means that each pixel is encoded as 4 bits, so the *BitmapPalette* collection can have a maximum of 16 colors. It doesn't make sense for it to have as few as four colors, because then you can use *PixelFormats.Indexed2* and encode each pixel with 2 bits. Before you create your own *Bitmap-Palette* object, take a look at the precreated *BitmapPalette* objects available as static properties of the *BitmapPalettes* class. For formats that don't require a color table, set this argument to *null*.

Regardless of the pixel format of the bitmap, each row of pixels in the bitmap consists of a whole number of bytes. For example, suppose you create a bitmap with a width of 5 pixels and a format of *PixelFormats.Indexed4*, which means that each pixel requires 4 bits. Multiply 5 pixels by 4 bits and you get 20 bits, or 2.5 bytes. Each row requires a whole number of bytes, and that whole number is 3. The first byte stores the first and second pixels of the row (the first pixel in the most significant 4 bits of the byte, and the second pixel in the least significant 4 bits); the second byte stores the third and fourth pixels; and the third byte stores the fifth pixel. The least significant 4 bits of the third byte in each row are ignored.

Another example: You're creating a bitmap with a width of 5 pixels and a format of *PixelFormats .Rgb24*. Each pixel requires 3 bytes (red first, then green, then blue), and the number of bytes required for each row is 15.

You generally set the last argument of *BitmapSource.Create*, called *stride*, to the whole number of bytes required for each row. That's a value of 3 for the first example and 15 for the second example. However, you can optionally set the *stride* argument to a larger integer than the calculated value. (In some earlier Windows graphical programming environments, *stride* values were required to be a multiple of 4 to improve the efficiency of rendering bitmaps on 32-bit microprocessors. This is not a requirement for the WPF.)

The array argument you pass as the seventh argument to *BitmapSource.Create* is a single-dimension numeric array. If this is a *byte* array, the number of elements in the array is equal to the *stride* value times the pixel height of the bitmap. (In essence, the *stride* value informs *BitmapSource.Create* how to access the array.) You can also use a *short*, *ushort*, *int*, or *uint* array for this purpose, in which case the number of elements in the array can be halved or quartered. The least significant byte in multibyte numeric elements corresponds to the leftmost pixel. If the *stride* is not an even number, a particular element of a *ushort* array, for example, will contain information for the end of one row and the beginning of the next row. This is allowed. The only thing that's not allowed is for a single byte to contain data that straddles two rows.

The following program creates a bitmap with a *PixelFormats.Indexed8* format. The color table contains 256 entries, which are various combinations of red and blue. The 256-pixel square bitmap contains one-byte pixels that index this color table to display the various red and blue combinations in a pattern, with black at the upper-left corner and magenta at the lower-right corner.

```
CreateIndexedBitmap.cs
//-----------------------------------------------------
// CreateIndexedBitmap.cs (c) 2006 by Charles Petzold
//-----------------------------------------------------
using System;
using System.Collections.Generic;
using System.Windows;
using System.Windows.Controls;
using System.Windows.Input;
using System.Windows.Media;
using System.Windows.Media.Imaging;

namespace Petzold.CreateIndexedBitmap
{
    public class CreateIndexedBitmap : Window
    {
        [STAThread]
        public static void Main()
        {
            Application app = new Application();
            app.Run(new CreateIndexedBitmap());
        }
        public CreateIndexedBitmap()
        {
            Title = "Create Indexed Bitmap";

            // Create palette with 256 colors, combining red and blue.
            List<Color> colors = new List<Color>();
```

```
            for (int r = 0; r < 256; r += 17)
            for (int b = 0; b < 256; b += 17)
                colors.Add(Color.FromRgb((byte)r, 0, (byte)b));

            BitmapPalette palette = new BitmapPalette(colors);

            // Create bitmap bit array.
            byte[] array = new byte[256 * 256];

            for (int x = 0; x < 256; x++)
            for (int y = 0; y < 256; y++)
                array[256 * y + x] = (byte)(((int)Math.Round(y / 17.0) << 4) |
                                             (int)Math.Round(x / 17.0));
            // Create bitmap.
            BitmapSource bitmap =
                BitmapSource.Create(256, 256, 96, 96, PixelFormats.Indexed8,
                                    palette, array, 256);

            // Create an Image object and set its Source to the bitmap.
            Image img = new Image();
            img.Source = bitmap;

            // Make the Image object the content of the window.
            Content = img;
        }
    }
}
```

The following program displays a similar image but with much finer gradation because it uses a bitmap format of *PixelFormats.Bgr32*. Each pixel requires 4 bytes, so for convenience the program defines an *int* array for storing the pixel values. The upper byte of each 4-byte value is not used with this pixel format.

CreateFullColorBitmap.cs

```
//-----------------------------------------------------
// CreateFullColorBitmap.cs (c) 2006 by Charles Petzold
//-----------------------------------------------------
using System;
using System.Windows;
using System.Windows.Controls;
using System.Windows.Input;
using System.Windows.Media;
using System.Windows.Media.Imaging;

namespace Petzold.CreateFullColorBitmap
{
    public class CreateFullColorBitmap : Window
    {
        [STAThread]
        public static void Main()
        {
            Application app = new Application();
            app.Run(new CreateFullColorBitmap());
        }
```

```
        public CreateFullColorBitmap()
        {
            Title = "Create Full-Color Bitmap";

            // Create bitmap bit array.
            int[] array = new int[256 * 256];

            for (int x = 0; x < 256; x++)
            for (int y = 0; y < 256; y++)
            {
                int b = x;
                int g = 0;
                int r = y;

                array[256 * y + x] = b | (g << 8) | (r << 16);
            }

            // Create bitmap.
            BitmapSource bitmap =
                BitmapSource.Create(256, 256, 96, 96, PixelFormats.Bgr32,
                                    null, array, 256 * 4);

            // Create an Image object and set its Source to the bitmap.
            Image img = new Image();
            img.Source = bitmap;

            // Make the Image object the content of the window.
            Content = img;
        }
    }
}
```

Many of the other classes that derive from *BitmapSource* create new bitmaps from existing bitmaps. You can often use these classes in XAML. For example, the following stand-alone XAML program uses *CroppedBitmap* to load an image from my Web site and crop it to the dimensions indicated in the *SourceRect* property. This bitmap becomes the source for *Format-ConvertedBitmap*, which converts it to a 2-bit-per-pixel gray shade format. The result is a source for *TransformedBitmap*, which rotates the image 90 degrees. Finally, *Image* displays the resultant cropped, converted, and transformed image.

ConvertedBitmapChain.xaml

```
<!-- =======================================================
        ConvertedBitmapChain.xaml (c) 2006 by Charles Petzold
     ======================================================= -->
<Page xmlns="http://schemas.microsoft.com/winfx/2006/xaml/presentation"
      xmlns:x="http://schemas.microsoft.com/winfx/2006/xaml">
    <Image>
        <Image.Source>
            <TransformedBitmap>
                <TransformedBitmap.Transform>
                    <RotateTransform Angle="90" />
                </TransformedBitmap.Transform>
```

```
                <TransformedBitmap.Source>
                    <FormatConvertedBitmap DestinationFormat="Gray2">
                        <FormatConvertedBitmap.Source>
                            <CroppedBitmap Source=
                                "http://www.charlespetzold.com/PetzoldTattoo.jpg"
                                          SourceRect="120 80 220 200" />
                        </FormatConvertedBitmap.Source>
                    </FormatConvertedBitmap>
                </TransformedBitmap.Source>
            </TransformedBitmap>
        </Image.Source>
    </Image>
</Page>
```

The first class hierarchy I showed you in this chapter focused on *ImageSource*, which is the type of the object you set to the *Source* property of *Image*. Here's that class hierarchy again with an ellipsis in place of all the bitmap-related classes that derive from *BitmapSource*:

Object

  DispatcherObject (abstract)

   DependencyObject

    Freezable (abstract)

     Animatable (abstract)

      ImageSource (abstract)

       BitmapSource (abstract)

        ...

       DrawingImage

This class hierarchy implies that you can also set the *Source* property of *Image* to an object of type *DrawingImage*. That word "drawing" in the class name seems to imply vector graphics, and that's usually (but not always) the case. In general, a *DrawingImage* is a composite of vector graphics, bitmaps, and video.

DrawingImage has a rather exalted position in the class hierarchy. It seems to be positioned as the vector equivalent to bitmaps, which might imply that *DrawingImage* is being groomed to become an interchange medium for vector graphics—perhaps the XAML equivalent of graphics metafiles. There is no indication that Microsoft has such big plans for *DrawingImage*, but if you want to think of *DrawingImage* as a graphics metafile, you won't be too far off.

The concept of *Image* displaying a chunk of vector graphics may be a little startling at first, so let me begin by showing you a simple example.

ImageDisplaysVectorGraphics.xaml

```
<!-- =============================================================
        ImageDisplaysVectorGraphics.xaml (c) 2006 by Charles Petzold
     ============================================================= -->
<Page xmlns="http://schemas.microsoft.com/winfx/2006/xaml/presentation"
      xmlns:x="http://schemas.microsoft.com/winfx/2006/xaml">
    <Image Stretch="None">
        <Image.Source>
            <DrawingImage>
                <DrawingImage.Drawing>
                    <GeometryDrawing Brush="Blue">

                        <GeometryDrawing.Pen>
                            <Pen Brush="Red" Thickness="5" />
                        </GeometryDrawing.Pen>

                        <GeometryDrawing.Geometry>
                            <EllipseGeometry Center="0,0" RadiusX="50"
                                                          RadiusY="50" />
                        </GeometryDrawing.Geometry>

                    </GeometryDrawing>
                </DrawingImage.Drawing>
            </DrawingImage>
        </Image.Source>
    </Image>
</Page>
```

The *Source* property of *Image* is broken out as the property element *Image.Source*. This is set to an object of type *DrawingImage*. *DrawingImage* has only one modifiable property—a property named *Drawing* of type *Drawing*. One class that derives from *Drawing* is *GeometryDrawing*. A *GeometryDrawing* is a *Geometry* object—which, as you learned in Chapter 28 combines the closest that the WPF comes to pure analytic geometry—with a *Brush* and a *Pen* used to render that object. In this example, the *Geometry* property of *GeometryDrawing* is set to an *EllipseGeometry* object.

You don't need to break out the *Geometry* property of *GeometryDrawing* as a property element. You can instead use the geometry markup syntax. The following markup describes a triangle right in the *GeometryDrawing* start tag.

```
<GeometryDrawing Brush="Blue" Geometry="M 0 0 L 100 0 L 0 100 Z">
```

It's useful to examine the ImageDisplaysVectorGraphics.xaml file starting with the most nested element and working out: The file begins with a *Geometry* object, specifically of type *EllipseGeometry*. A geometry is really just coordinate points. That geometry, along with a *Brush* and *Pen*, becomes a *GeometryDrawing*. The *GeometryDrawing* has gone beyond pure analytic geometry and now has real colors and pen dimensions. As you'll see shortly, the *Geometry-Drawing* class derives from *Drawing*. A *DrawingImage* object is always based on a *Drawing* object. *DrawingImage* has a constructor that accepts a *Drawing* object and a property named

Drawing of type *Drawing*. From *ImageSource*, *DrawingImage* inherits two read-only properties named *Width* and *Height* that provide the width and height of the *Drawing* in device-independent units. In this example, those *Width* and *Height* properties would both indicate 105 units, which is the diameter of the ellipse plus 2.5 units of pen thickness on each side.

The *Image* element has its *Stretch* property set to *None*. This causes the ellipse to be displayed in its actual size of 105 units square. Remove that *Stretch* attribute and the ellipse becomes as large as the area allowed for it while still maintaining its correct aspect ratio. You have to set *Stretch* to *Fill* to persuade *Image* to ignore the aspect ratio of the drawing.

GeometryDrawing is one of five classes that derive from *Drawing*, as the following class hierarchy shows:

Object

  DispatcherObject (abstract)

   DependencyObject

    Freezable (abstract)

     Animatable (abstract)

      Drawing (abstract)

       DrawingGroup

       GeometryDrawing

       GlyphRunDrawing

       ImageDrawing

       VideoDrawing

The *DrawingGroup* class is very important. It defines a *Children* property that stores a collection of other *Drawing* objects. This is how you combine vector graphics and bitmaps into one composite drawing. Very often, when WPF documentation refers to an object of type *Drawing*, in reality that object will be of type *DrawingGroup*, so it's potentially a mix of different types of graphics objects.

The other four classes that derive from *Drawing* are more specific. As you saw in the previous XAML file, the *GeometryDrawing* object combines a *Geometry* object with *Brush* and *Pen*.

The *GlyphRunDrawing* class combines a *GlyphRun* object with a foreground brush. A *Glyph-Run* is a series of characters in a particular font and size, but this class is very difficult to use, and I won't be discussing it here.

An *ImageDrawing* object generally references a bitmap, which you set to the *ImageSource* property. You must also set the *Rect* property of *ImageDrawing* to give this bitmap a specific size.

The *VideoDrawing* class has a *Player* property of type *MediaPlayer* and a *Rect* property to give it a specific size. I won't be demonstrating this class.

For the last several paragraphs, I've been discussing a class named *DrawingImage*, and now I've just introduced a new class called *ImageDrawing*. Not only are the class names very similar but you can set a *DrawingImage* object to the *ImageSource* property of an *ImageDrawing* object, and you can set an *ImageDrawing* object to the *Drawing* property of a *DrawingImage* object. Here's a little chart that may or may not add to your confusion.

Class	Derives From	Contains Property Named	Of Type
DrawingImage	*ImageSource*	*Drawing*	*Drawing*
ImageDrawing	*Drawing*	*ImageSource*	*ImageSource*

Of course, a big part of this confusion is that we prefer to keep raster graphics and vector graphics separate, but both classes combine the words "image" (which suggests raster graphics) and "drawing" (which suggests vector graphics). Perhaps you can think of *DrawingImage* as a drawing that can be treated the same way as an image; that is, you can display it using the *Image* element. *ImageDrawing* is generally an image that is treated as a drawing, which means that it can be combined with other drawings into a *DrawingGroup*.

Here's a stand-alone XAML file that uses both *DrawingImage* and *ImageDrawing* in the ways they were intended to be used, rather than in the various ways implied by the circular nature of the property definitions. This XAML file contains an *Image* element whose *Source* property has been set to an object of type *DrawingImage*. The *Drawing* property of this *DrawingImage* is set to a *DrawingGroup* object whose children include an *ImageDrawing* object referencing a bitmap, three *GeometryDrawing* objects that draw a frame around the bitmap, and a wire to hang the frame on the wall.

PictureAndFrame.xaml

```
<!-- =================================================
     PictureAndFrame.xaml (c) 2006 by Charles Petzold
     ================================================= -->
<Page xmlns="http://schemas.microsoft.com/winfx/2006/xaml/presentation"
      xmlns:x="http://schemas.microsoft.com/winfx/2006/xaml">

    <Image Stretch="None">
        <Image.Source>
            <DrawingImage>
                <DrawingImage.Drawing>
                    <DrawingGroup>

                        <!-- Bitmap image of fixed size. -->
                        <ImageDrawing Rect="5 5 200 240"
                                      ImageSource=
```

```
                                "http://www.charlespetzold.com/PetzoldTattoo.jpg" />

                    <!-- Dotted pen for scalloped pattern effect. -->
                    <GeometryDrawing>
                        <GeometryDrawing.Pen>
                            <Pen Brush="DodgerBlue" Thickness="10"
                                                    DashCap="Round">
                                <Pen.DashStyle>
                                    <DashStyle Dashes="0 1" />
                                </Pen.DashStyle>
                            </Pen>
                        </GeometryDrawing.Pen>

                        <GeometryDrawing.Geometry>
                            <RectangleGeometry Rect="5 5 200 240" />
                        </GeometryDrawing.Geometry>
                    </GeometryDrawing>

                    <!-- Solid pen to hide half the dotted pen. -->
                    <GeometryDrawing>
                        <GeometryDrawing.Pen>
                            <Pen Brush="DodgerBlue" Thickness="5" />
                        </GeometryDrawing.Pen>

                        <GeometryDrawing.Geometry>
                            <RectangleGeometry Rect="2.5 2.5 205 245" />
                        </GeometryDrawing.Geometry>
                    </GeometryDrawing>

                    <!-- Wire to hang the frame on the wall. -->
                    <GeometryDrawing Geometry="M 10 0 L 105 -50 L 200 0" >
                        <GeometryDrawing.Pen>
                            <Pen Brush="Black" />
                        </GeometryDrawing.Pen>
                    </GeometryDrawing>

                </DrawingGroup>
            </DrawingImage.Drawing>
        </DrawingImage>
    </Image.Source>
  </Image>
</Page>
```

DrawingGroup is intended for assembling composite images, which in practice come mostly from *ImageDrawing* objects (generally bitmaps) and *GeometryDrawing* objects. *GeometryDrawing* objects are based on geometries, so they already have specific coordinates and sizes. A bitmap always has a metrical size as well, which is implied by its pixel dimensions and resolution. But a way to position that bitmap relative to other graphical objects is also required here. That's the purpose of the *Rect* property defined by *ImageDrawing*. It not only gives the bitmap a specific size but it also positions that bitmap within a two-dimensional coordinate space.

Notice that a separate *GeometryDrawing* object is required for each *Brush* or *Pen* object you use for coloring the geometries. If you have several *Geometry* objects that are to be colored with the same brush and pen, you can combine them into a *GeometryGroup* and use that as the basis for the *GeometryDrawing*.

The *DrawingGroup* class doesn't restrict itself to defining a *Children* property that lets you assemble a composite drawing; the class also defines several properties that let you alter that composite drawing.

To set a clipping region for the composite drawing, you set the *ClipGeometry* property of *DrawingGroup* to a *Geometry* object. You can put this markup in PictureAndFrame.xaml to cut a corner off the portrait:

```
<DrawingGroup ClipGeometry="M 0 -50 L 210 -50 L 210 120 L 0 250 z" >
```

To make the drawing partially transparent, you can set the *Opacity* or *OpacityMask* properties. For example, this change to the *DrawingGroup* start tag makes the entire drawing 50 percent transparent:

```
<DrawingGroup Opacity="0.5">
```

You set the *OpacityMask* property to a *Brush* object. All the colors of the *Brush* are ignored except for the alpha channel of each color, which is used to set the transparency of the *DrawingGroup*. You can put the following markup anywhere within the *DrawingGroup* start and end tags but not within another property element or child of *DrawingGroup*:

```
<DrawingGroup.OpacityMask>
    <RadialGradientBrush>
        <GradientStop Offset="0" Color="White" />
        <GradientStop Offset="1" Color="Transparent" />
    </RadialGradientBrush>
</DrawingGroup.OpacityMask>
```

The drawing remains opaque in the center but fades near the boundaries. An *OpacityMask* property is also defined by *UIElement* so you can use this technique with any element.

Another property defined by both *UIElement* and *DrawingGroup* is *BitmapEffect*, which lets you use classes defined in the *System.Windows.Media.Effects* namespace for applying common visual effects to items. For example, try this:

```
<DrawingGroup.BitmapEffect>
    <DropShadowBitmapEffect />
</DrawingGroup.BitmapEffect>
```

This applies a drop shadow to the lower right of the picture frame. You can control the color, size, and other aspects of this drop shadow with properties defined by *DropShadowBitmapEffect*. This one makes the whole thing seem a bit radioactive:

```
<DrawingGroup.BitmapEffect>
    <OuterGlowBitmapEffect GlowColor="Red" />
</DrawingGroup.BitmapEffect>
```

And don't worry about your eyesight when you try this one:

```
<DrawingGroup.BitmapEffect>
    <BlurBitmapEffect />
</DrawingGroup.BitmapEffect>
```

The *DrawingGroup* class also defines a *Transform* property that lets you apply a transform to the entire drawing, perhaps if you've discovered that it's really much larger than you'd prefer:

```
<DrawingGroup.Transform>
    <ScaleTransform ScaleX="0.25" ScaleY="0.25" />
</DrawingGroup.Transform>
```

Because *Image* is effectively centering the composite drawing within the *Page*, any translation transforms are ignored. To "swing" the picture on its nail, you can animate the *RenderTransform* of the *Image* object itself. This markup can go right after the *Image* start tag:

```
<Image.RenderTransform>
    <RotateTransform x:Name="xform" />
</Image.RenderTransform>

<Image.RenderTransformOrigin>
    <Point X="0.5" Y="0" />
</Image.RenderTransformOrigin>

<Image.Triggers>
    <EventTrigger RoutedEvent="Image.Loaded">
        <BeginStoryboard>
            <Storyboard TargetName="xform" TargetProperty="Angle">
                <DoubleAnimation From="-10" To="10" AutoReverse="True"
                                 RepeatBehavior="Forever"
                                 AccelerationRatio="0.5"
                                 DecelerationRatio="0.5" />
            </Storyboard>
        </BeginStoryboard>
    </EventTrigger>
</Image.Triggers>
```

Along with exploring the power of high-level drawing classes, it's also helpful to be familiar with the low-level drawing facilities, if only to get a sense of the overall capabilities and limitations of the system. The lowest-level drawing methods you can use and still call yourself a full-fledged Windows Presentation Foundation application are those defined by the *DrawingContext* class.

As you'll recall, a class that derives from *UIElement* or *FrameworkElement* can override the *OnRender* method to draw the element. The single parameter to *OnRender* is an object of type *DrawingContext*. It is also possible to create an object of type *DrawingVisual* and to use the

RenderOpen method to obtain a *DrawingContext* object. You then call methods of the *Drawing-Context* class to draw on this object, and you conclude by calling *Close*. You're left with a *DrawingVisual* object that stores the graphics. This is the technique you use when printing and when displaying graphics on a bitmap of type *RenderTargetBitmap*.

If you think of *DrawingContext* as the class that defines all the capabilities and limitations of the WPF graphics system, it has surprisingly few drawing methods. In the following statements, *dc* is an object of type *DrawingContext*, *brush* is a *Brush*, *pen* is a *Pen*, *rect* is a *Rect*, anything that begins with *pt* is a *Point*, and anything that begins with *x* or *y* is a *double*.

Of course, *DrawingContext* has a method to draw a single line between two points:

```
dc.DrawLine(pen, pt1, pt2);
```

DrawingContext also includes a version of *DrawLine* that has two arguments of type *Animation-Clock*:

```
dc.DrawLine(pen, pt1, anima1, pt2, anima2);
```

An *OnRender* method can create one or two *AnimationClock* objects to animate the two points. So, with one *DrawLine* call, *OnRender* can display a graphic that changes over time without further intervention. I demonstrated animation in an *OnRender* method in the RenderThe-Animation program in the previous chapter.

The next method in *DrawingContext* draws a rectangle:

```
dc.DrawRectangle(brush, pen, rect);
```

The *Rect* structure indicates the location of the upper-left corner of the rectangle, and its width and height. The *Brush* or *Pen* arguments can be set to *null* to suppress the drawing of the rectangle's interior or perimeter. There is also a version of *DrawRectangle* that includes an *AnimationClock* argument that animates the *Rect* object.

The *DrawRoundedRectangle* method draws a rectangle with rounded corners. The extent of the rounding is governed by the last two arguments:

```
dc.DrawRoundedRectangle(brush, pen, rect, xRadius, yRadius);
```

A version of *DrawRoundedRectangle* with three *AnimationClock* objects can animate the rectangle or either of the two radii.

You can use *DrawRoundedRectangle* to draw an ellipse by calculating the last two arguments based on the *Rect* argument:

```
dc.DrawRoundedRectangle(brush, pen. rect, rect.Width / 2, rect.Height / 2);
```

Or you can use the *DrawEllipse* method for that purpose:

```
dc.DrawEllipse(brush, pen, ptCenter, xRadius, yRadius);
```

Notice that this method is a little different from *DrawRectangle* because you specify the center of the figure. A second version of *DrawEllipse* has three *AnimationClock* arguments for the center and the two radii.

You'll remember the *DrawText* method that requires an argument of type *FormattedText*:

```
dc.DrawText(formtxt, ptOrigin);
```

Another method defined by *DrawingContext* requires a *GlyphRun*, which is a collection of characters at precise locations:

```
dc.DrawGlyphRun(brush, glyphrun);
```

In the following method, the *media* argument is an instance of *MediaPlayer*, a class that can play movies and sound files by referencing the URI of a local or remote media file:

```
dc.DrawVideo(media, rect);
```

The final three drawing methods handle generalized vector graphics, raster graphics, and a combination of the two. To render a *Geometry* object on the screen, you must supply a *Brush* and *Pen* in this *DrawingContext* method call:

```
dc.DrawGeometry(brush, pen, geometry);
```

At the other extreme is the method that renders a bitmap. The first argument is of type *Image-Source*, which (as you know now) also encompasses the *DrawingImage* class as well as *Bitmap-Source* class and its derivatives:

```
dc.DrawImage(imgsrc, rect);
```

If you haven't already guessed, the final drawing method accepts a *Drawing* argument:

```
dc.DrawDrawing(drawing);
```

DrawingContext also includes a few methods to set clipping, opacity, and transforms. These all take the form of methods that push the attribute on a stack so it applies to all future drawing calls until *Pop* removes it from the stack. The *PushClip* method takes an argument of type *Geometry* and sets a clipping region. The *PushOpacity* method takes a *double* argument that ranges from 0 (transparent) to 1 (opaque), and a second version of *PushOpacity* includes an *AnimationClock*. The *PushTransform* method takes an argument of type *Transform*.

Just how important is *Drawing* in the whole scheme of WPF graphics? When you create a *DrawingVisual* object and then call *RenderOpen* to obtain a *DrawingContext*, when you're finished drawing on the *DrawingContext* object, the *DrawingVisual* stores all the graphics you've drawn. It stores these graphics as a read-only property named *Drawing* that returns an object of type *DrawingGroup*.

I tackled the subject of brushes in the second chapter in this book, but that chapter didn't include all the available types of brushes. It is now time to explore those other brushes. Here's the complete *Brush* class hierarchy:

Object

   DispatcherObject (abstract)

    DependencyObject

     Freezable (abstract)

      Animatable (abstract)

       Brush (abstract)

        GradientBrush (abstract)

         LinearGradientBrush

         RadialGradientBrush

        SolidColorBrush

        TileBrush (abstract)

         DrawingBrush

         ImageBrush

         VisualBrush

Note the three classes that derive from *TileBrush*. These brushes are based on other graphical objects. The *DrawingBrush* has a *Drawing* property. Often this will be a *GeometryDrawing* object (which means the brush will display some vector graphics), but the *Drawing* could include bitmaps or media players. The *ImageBrush* has an *ImageSource* property. Often this will be a *BitmapImage* object, but it could be a *DrawingImage* object and include various graphics objects. The *VisualBrush* has a *Visual* property. That could be a *DrawingVisual* object created by drawing on a *DrawingContext*, but recall that *UIElement* and *FrameworkElement* also derive from *Visual*. *VisualBrush* is often used to display controls or other parts of the user interface, perhaps as a shadow or reflection.

The three types of brushes that derive from *TileBrush* all work in fundamentally the same way. A surface is covered with a drawing, an image, or a visual. However, you have lots of options for how the drawing (or image or visual) is stretched or tiled over the surface. These options are all controlled through eight properties defined by *TileBrush* and inherited by the other three brushes. Mastery of these eight properties of *TileBrush* governs how effectively you use these three types of brushes.

Here's a simple *ImageBrush* example that uses the default settings of those eight *TileBrush* properties and sets the *ImageSource* property of the brush to a bitmap from my Web site. The brush is set to the *Background* property of a *Page*.

SimpleImageBrush.xaml
```
<!-- =====================================================
        SimpleImageBrush.xaml (c) 2006 by Charles Petzold
     ===================================================== -->
<Page xmlns="http://schemas.microsoft.com/winfx/2006/xaml/presentation"
      xmlns:x="http://schemas.microsoft.com/winfx/2006/xaml">
    <Page.Background>
        <ImageBrush
            ImageSource="http://www.charlespetzold.com/PetzoldTattoo.jpg">
        </ImageBrush>
    </Page.Background>
</Page>
```

When you run this program in XAML Cruncher, you'll see that the bitmap is stretched to fill the page's entire background. If the aspect ratio of the page doesn't match the aspect ratio of the bitmap, the image is distorted. This is *not* the default approach that *Image* takes in displaying bitmaps, but it's more appropriate when you're using a bitmap as a brush. You want that bitmap to emcompass the entire area that the brush covers—in this case, the entire *Page*.

Here's a simple *VisualBrush* example with the same overall structure as SimpleImage Brush.xaml.

SimpleVisualBrush.xaml
```
<!-- =================================================
        SimpleVisualBrush.xaml (c) 2006 by Charles Petzold
     ================================================= -->
<Page xmlns="http://schemas.microsoft.com/winfx/2006/xaml/presentation"
      xmlns:x="http://schemas.microsoft.com/winfx/2006/xaml">
    <Page.Background>
        <VisualBrush>
            <VisualBrush.Visual>
                <Button Content="Button?" />
            </VisualBrush.Visual>
        </VisualBrush>
    </Page.Background>
</Page>
```

The *Visual* property of *VisualBrush* is broken out as a property element. That *Visual* property is set to a *Button* element, and that's what the brush looks like—a big button. The *Button* displays the text "Button?" because it's not really a button. It doesn't respond to the mouse or keyboard. It's the *visual image* of a button, stretched to fill the entire background of the page without regard to the original aspect ratio. Again, if using a button image as a brush is what you want, this is good default behavior.

To complete the package, here's a simple *DrawingBrush* example.

SimpleDrawingBrush.xaml

```
<!-- =================================================
     SimpleDrawingBrush.xaml (c) 2006 by Charles Petzold
     ================================================= -->
<Page xmlns="http://schemas.microsoft.com/winfx/2006/xaml/presentation"
      xmlns:x="http://schemas.microsoft.com/winfx/2006/xaml">
    <Page.Background>
        <DrawingBrush>
            <DrawingBrush.Drawing>
                <GeometryDrawing Brush="Red">

                    <GeometryDrawing.Pen>
                        <Pen Brush="Blue" />
                    </GeometryDrawing.Pen>

                    <GeometryDrawing.Geometry>
                        <EllipseGeometry Center="0,0" RadiusX="10"
                                                      RadiusY="10" />
                    </GeometryDrawing.Geometry>

                </GeometryDrawing>
            </DrawingBrush.Drawing>
        </DrawingBrush>
    </Page.Background>
</Page>
```

This is an ellipse centered at the point (0, 0), with a blue outline and a red interior. The entire ellipse is stretched to fill the background of the page, and the width of the blue pen is stretched proportionally. Because the ellipse radii are so small (10 units), the 1-unit default thickness of the blue line around the circumference probably appears quite thick.

Here's a more extensive *DrawingBrush* object, which is intended to resemble interlocked blue and pink fish swimming in opposite directions.

FishBrush.xaml

```
<!-- =========================================
     FishBrush.xaml (c) 2006 by Charles Petzold
     ========================================= -->
<Page xmlns="http://schemas.microsoft.com/winfx/2006/xaml/presentation"
      xmlns:x="http://schemas.microsoft.com/winfx/2006/xaml">
    <Page.Background>
        <DrawingBrush>
            <DrawingBrush.Drawing>
                <DrawingGroup>

                    <!-- Fill the background with pink. -->
                    <GeometryDrawing Brush="Pink">
                        <GeometryDrawing.Geometry>
                            <RectangleGeometry Rect="0 0 200 100" />
```

```
                </GeometryDrawing.Geometry>
            </GeometryDrawing>

            <GeometryDrawing Brush="Aqua">
                <GeometryDrawing.Pen>
                    <Pen Brush="Blue" Thickness="2" />
                </GeometryDrawing.Pen>

                <GeometryDrawing.Geometry>
                    <GeometryGroup>

                        <!-- Draw the outline of the blue fish. -->
                        <PathGeometry>
                            <PathFigure StartPoint="200 0"
                                        IsClosed="True"
                                        IsFilled="True">

                                <BezierSegment Point1="150 100"
                                               Point2="50 -50"
                                               Point3="0 50" />

                                <BezierSegment Point1="50 150"
                                               Point2="150 0"
                                               Point3="200 100" />
                            </PathFigure>
                        </PathGeometry>

                        <!-- Draw the fish eyes. -->
                        <EllipseGeometry Center="35 35"
                                         RadiusX="5" RadiusY="5" />
                        <EllipseGeometry Center="165 85"
                                         RadiusX="5" RadiusY="5" />
                    </GeometryGroup>
                </GeometryDrawing.Geometry>
            </GeometryDrawing>
        </DrawingGroup>
        </DrawingBrush.Drawing>
      </DrawingBrush>
    </Page.Background>
</Page>
```

The XAML here looks rather deeply nested, but the overall structure is the same as in the previous examples. The file defines a *Page* with its *Background* property set to a *DrawingBrush*. The *Drawing* property of the *DrawingBrush* is set to a *DrawingGroup* containing two *Geometry-Drawing* objects. The first object defines a rectangle 200 units wide and 100 units high. The second contains a *PathGeometry* that draws the outline of a fish and contains two *EllipseGeometry* elements that draw the fish eyes.

When you run this program in XAML Cruncher, you'll see the figure fill up the page. In the center is a blue fish swimming left. On the bottom is half a pink fish swimming right, and on the top is another pink half fish swimming right. Obviously this drawing was designed for tiling, but that's not something that happens by default.

Based on the coordinates of the various *Geometry* objects in FishBrush.xaml, it's easy to determine that the figure is 200 units wide and 100 units high. But as a result of the physical thickness of the pen and the default *LineJoin* property of *Miter*, the *Drawing* object is actually a little larger that those dimensions. To determine the actual dimensions of the *Drawing* object, you can give the *DrawingGroup* element a name:

```
<DrawingGroup x:Name="drawgrp">
```

You can then insert this *Label* control right before the *Page* end tag:

```
<Label Content="{Binding ElementName=drawgrp, Path=Bounds}" />
```

The drawing is closer to 202 units wide and 108 units high. In XAML Cruncher you can actually see a white perimeter around the pink rectangle where the blue pen extends. You can reduce that white perimeter considerably by giving the pen a *LineJoin* property of *Bevel*:

```
<Pen Brush="Blue" Thickness="2" LineJoin="Bevel" />
```

And you might start fiddling with some coordinates so that the *Drawing* is really 200 units wide by 100 units high, but don't bother. The white perimeter will be annoying at first, but eventually you'll see a way to make it disappear.

So you now have XAML files containing *ImageBrush*, *VisualBrush*, and *DrawingBrush* objects. Each of these brushes is based on an object that has a distinct metrical size. For the bitmap in the *ImageBrush*, that metrical size is calculated by dividing the pixel dimensions of the bitmap by the resolution in dots per inch. For the *Button* in the *VisualBrush*, that metrical size is the size of the *Button* as determined by its *MeasureOverride* method. For the *Drawing* object in the *DrawingBrush*, the metrical size is available from the *Bounds* property of the *Drawing* object. In all cases, that metrical size and aspect ratio is ignored, and the object is stretched to fill the area covered by the brush.

Let's start playing. All the properties I'll be describing in this discussion of brushes are defined by *TileBrush*, so you can set these properties in the *ImageBrush*, *VisualBrush*, or *DrawingBrush* elements of the four XAML files that use these brushes.

The default stretching behavior is governed by the property defined by the *TileBrush* named *Stretch*, which you set to a member of the *Stretch* enumeration. The default is *Stretch.Fill*, which stretches without regard to aspect ratio.

You might try the other *Stretch* options in either (or all) of the XAML files. Try this in Simple-ImageBrush.xaml:

```
<ImageBrush Stretch="Uniform" ...
```

Or try this in SimpleVisualBrush.xaml:

```
<VisualBrush Stretch="Uniform">
```

Or try this in SimpleDrawingBrush.xaml or FishBrush.xaml:

```
<DrawingBrush Stretch="Uniform">
```

In all cases, you'll see the image (or visual or drawing) assume its correct aspect ratio. The brush still covers the entire background of the page, but the image on the brush does not. The bitmap, button, or drawing fills the background in one dimension but not the other. In the other dimension, the brush is transparent on both sides of the bitmap, button, or drawing.

If you set *Stretch* to *Uniform*, and the image occupies the full height of the page, you can move it to the left or right side of the brush by setting the *AlignmentX* property defined by *TileBrush* to the *Left* or *Right* members of the *AlignmentX* enumeration. The default is *Center*. Similarly, if the image occupies the full width of the page, you can move it to the top or bottom side by setting *AlignmentY* to *Top* or *Bottom*.

Another option for *Stretch* is *UniformFill*. In this case the image (or visual or drawing) has a correct aspect ratio, but it fills the background anyway through truncation. By default, the image is centered in the brush. If the image fits within the height of the page, and parts of the left and right side are truncated, you can set *AlignmentX* to *Left* to truncate only the right side. Similarly, if parts of the top and bottom are truncated and you set *AlignmentY* to *Top*, you truncate only the bottom part of the image.

The final option for *Stretch* is *None*, which makes the image (or visual or drawing) become its metrical size and sit in the center of the brush. You can move it to one of the sides or corners with a combination of *AlignmentX* and *AlignmentY*.

One important option of the classes that derive from *TileBrush* is, of course, tiling, which means that the image (or visual or drawing) repeats itself in the horizontal and vertical dimensions. You control tiling (in part) with the *TileMode* property, which you set to a member of the *TileMode* enumeration. The default *TileMode* setting is *TileMode.None*. To enable tiling, you usually set the *TileMode* property to *TileMode.Tile*.

By itself, setting *TileMode* to *TileMode.Tile* doesn't seem to do anything. By default, the size of each tile is assumed to be the same as the size of the brush, so each tile is the size of the page, and that means you're seeing only one tile.

To get multiple tiles, you must set the *Viewport* and *ViewportUnits* properties. But first you must make a decision about these tiles. Do you want to fix the *number* of tiles that comprise the brush? Or do you want to fix the metrical *size* of the tiles?

Suppose you want an *ImageBrush* to always have 10 tiles horizontally and 5 tiles vertically, regardless of the size of the brush. The implication is that you want the width of each tile to be one-tenth of the total width of the brush and the height of each tile to be one-fifth (or 20 percent) of the total height of the brush. You set the *Viewport* property to indicate those dimensions:

```
<ImageBrush TileMode="Tile" Viewport="0 0 0.1 0.2" …
```

By default, the coordinate system associated with the *Viewport* property is based on the total size of the brush, just like the points you specify for gradient brushes. The *Viewport* property is of type *Rect*, but the *Left* and *Right* properties of *Rect* (the first two numbers in the string you set to the *Viewport* property) are ignored here. The *Width* and *Height* properties of *Rect* indicate the width and height of the tile as a fraction of the width and height of the brush. The default *Viewport* is equivalent to the string "0 0 1 1", which makes the tile the same size as the brush.

With the *VisualBrush* example, here's how you make an array of 10 buttons horizontally and 10 buttons vertically:

```
<VisualBrush TileMode="Tile" Viewport="0 0 0.1 0.1">
```

In FishBrush.xaml, you can make 25 tiles horizontally and 33.33 tiles vertically with this markup:

```
<DrawingBrush TileMode="Tile" Viewport="0 0 0.04 0.03">
```

Here the white space around each tile will seem quite unpleasant and will interfere with the tiled effect. But please be patient.

When you use *Viewport* in its default mode, the dimension of each tile is based on the dimension of the brush and the *Viewport* dimensions, so the image in each tile will (in general) be distorted. If you want to fix the number of horizontal and vertical tiles, but you also want to preserve the aspect ratio of the original image, you can set *Stretch* to *Uniform* (in which case there will be some blank space on the sides) or *UniformToFill* (which will truncate part of the image). But don't set *Stretch* to *None*, because that causes the image to be displayed in its metrical size. It's likely that the tile will be smaller than the unstretched image and thus will contain only a little part of that image.

If you want each tile to be a fixed size, you will probably set that size proportional to the metrical size of the image so the aspect ratio is preserved. You can use device-independent units in the *Viewport* property if you set the *ViewportUnits* property to the enumeration value *Brush-MappingMode.Absolute*. (The default is *BrushMappingMode.RelativeToBoundingBox*.) This is the same enumeration you use to set the *MappingMode* property defined by *GradientBrush*.

The image displayed by the SimpleImageBrush.xaml file has an aspect ratio of approximately 1:1.19, so the following markup sets each tile to a width of about one-half inch and a height about 19 percent greater:

```
<ImageBrush TileMode="Tile" Viewport="0 0 50 60" ViewportUnits="Absolute" …
```

When setting *ViewportUnits* to *Absolute*, the first two numbers of *Viewport* make a difference in how the tile at the upper-left corner of the brush is displayed. With values set to 0 and 0, the upper-left corner of the upper-left tile is positioned at the upper-left corner of the brush. But try values of 25 and 30:

```
<ImageBrush TileMode="Tile" Viewport="25 30 50 60" ViewportUnits="Absolute" …
```

The tiles are the same size, but the whole array of tiles is shifted 25 units left and 30 units up, so you see only the lower-right quadrant of the tile at the upper-left corner of the brush.

The drawing displayed by FishBrush.xaml has an aspect ratio of 2:1, so it's easy to size the tile appropriately:

```
<DrawingBrush TileMode="Tile" Viewport="0 0 60 30" ViewportUnits="Absolute">
```

TileBrush defines two properties similar to *Viewport* and *ViewportUnits*, called *Viewbox* and *ViewboxUnits*. The *Viewbox* specifies a rectangle within the image (or drawing or visual) that is used for tiling. By default, you specify it in coordinates relative to the bounding box. Here's some markup for SimpleImageBrush.xaml:

```
<ImageBrush TileMode="Tile" Viewport="0 0 50 60" ViewportUnits="Absolute"
            Viewbox="0.3 0.05 0.4 0.6" …
```

In this case, only 40 percent of the width of the bitmap is used for tiling, starting 30 percent from the left side. Only 60 percent of the height of the bitmap is used, starting 5 percent from the top. You can use negative values for the first two numbers, or values greater than 1 for the second two numbers, which both have the effect of creating some transparent areas around the image.

Using *Viewbox* in *Absolute* mode lets you eliminate the blank areas around the FishBrush.xaml tiles caused by the finite pen width:

```
<DrawingBrush TileMode="Tile" Viewport="0 0 60 30" ViewportUnits="Absolute"
              Viewbox="0 0 200 100" ViewboxUnits="Absolute">
```

I've already discussed the two members of the *TileMode* enumeration named *None* and *Tile*. The enumeration has three additional members. The *FlipX* option causes every other column of tiles to be flipped around its vertical axis, like a mirror image. The *FlipY* option causes every other row of tiles to be flipped upside down. Combine the effects by using *FlipXY*. Sometimes you can turn an otherwise normal image into an almost abstract design. Try this use of *FlipXY* in SimpleImageBrush.xaml:

```
<ImageBrush TileMode="FlipXY" Viewport="0 0 50 60" ViewportUnits="Absolute"
            Viewbox="0.3 0.10 0.4 0.6" …
```

One interesting application of a *VisualBrush* is in decorating a user interface with a shadow or a reflection of controls and elements. The following stand-alone XAML file creates a *StackPanel* containing two *TextBlock* elements and three *CheckBox* controls. Another *StackPanel* is colored with a *VisualBrush* background that shows a reflection of those controls. Notice the *Visual* property of the *VisualBrush* is set to a binding of the *StackPanel* containing the controls. An *OpacityMask* that's based on a *LinearGradientBrush* that make the image fade near the bottom.

ReflectedControls.xaml

```xml
<!-- =================================================
     ReflectedControls.xaml (c) 2006 by Charles Petzold
     ================================================= -->
<Page xmlns="http://schemas.microsoft.com/winfx/2006/xaml/presentation"
      xmlns:x="http://schemas.microsoft.com/winfx/2006/xaml">
    <Page.Resources>
        <Style TargetType="{x:Type TextBlock}">
            <Setter Property="VerticalAlignment" Value="Bottom" />
            <Setter Property="FontFamily" Value="Lucida Calligraphy" />
            <Setter Property="FontSize" Value="36" />
        </Style>

        <Style TargetType="{x:Type CheckBox}">
            <Setter Property="FontSize" Value="24" />
            <Setter Property="Margin" Value="12" />
        </Style>
    </Page.Resources>

    <!-- StackPanel for controls and their reflections. -->
    <StackPanel>

        <!-- StackPanel for controls. -->
        <StackPanel Name="pnlControls" Orientation="Horizontal"
                    HorizontalAlignment="Center">

            <TextBlock Text="Check..." />

            <StackPanel HorizontalAlignment="Center">
                <CheckBox Content="CheckBox 1" />
                <CheckBox Content="CheckBox 2" />
                <CheckBox Content="CheckBox 3" />
            </StackPanel>

            <TextBlock Text="...Boxes" />

        </StackPanel>

        <!-- StackPanel for reflection. -->
        <StackPanel Height="{Binding ElementName=pnlControls,
                                     Path=ActualHeight}">

            <!-- VisualBrush inverts image of controls. -->
            <StackPanel.Background>
                <VisualBrush Visual="{Binding ElementName=pnlControls}"
                             Stretch="None">
                    <VisualBrush.RelativeTransform>
                        <TransformGroup>
                            <ScaleTransform ScaleX="1" ScaleY="-1" />
                            <TranslateTransform Y="1" />
                        </TransformGroup>
                    </VisualBrush.RelativeTransform>
                </VisualBrush>
            </StackPanel.Background>
        </StackPanel>
```

```
            <!-- OpacityMask makes it fade. -->
            <StackPanel.OpacityMask>
                <LinearGradientBrush StartPoint="0 0" EndPoint="0 1">
                    <GradientStop Offset="0" Color="#80000000" />
                    <GradientStop Offset="1" Color="#00000000" />
                </LinearGradientBrush>
            </StackPanel.OpacityMask>
        </StackPanel>
    </StackPanel>
</Page>
```

Although the *CheckBox* buttons in the *VisualBrush* are nonfunctional, they dynamically change their appearance when the real *CheckBox* buttons are checked.

You can animate a *Geometry* that is the basis of a *DrawingBrush*, although this next little program might persuade you not to do so.

AnimatedDrawingBrush.xaml

```
<!-- ======================================================
     AnimatedDrawingBrush.xaml (c) 2006 by Charles Petzold
     ====================================================== -->
<Page xmlns="http://schemas.microsoft.com/winfx/2006/xaml/presentation"
      xmlns:x="http://schemas.microsoft.com/winfx/2006/xaml">
    <Page.Background>
        <DrawingBrush TileMode="Tile" Stretch="None"
                      Viewport="0 0 12 12" ViewportUnits="Absolute">
            <DrawingBrush.Drawing>
                <GeometryDrawing Brush="Blue">
                    <GeometryDrawing.Geometry>
                        <EllipseGeometry x:Name="elipsgeo" Center="0 0" />
                    </GeometryDrawing.Geometry>
                </GeometryDrawing>
            </DrawingBrush.Drawing>
        </DrawingBrush>
    </Page.Background>

    <Page.Triggers>
        <EventTrigger RoutedEvent="Page.Loaded">
            <BeginStoryboard>
                <Storyboard TargetName="elipsgeo" RepeatBehavior="Forever">
                    <DoubleAnimation Storyboard.TargetProperty="RadiusX"
                                     From="4" To="6" Duration="0:0:0.25"
                                     AutoReverse="True" />
                    <DoubleAnimation Storyboard.TargetProperty="RadiusY"
                                     From="6" To="4" Duration="0:0:0.25"
                                     AutoReverse="True" />
                </Storyboard>
            </BeginStoryboard>
        </EventTrigger>
    </Page.Triggers>
</Page>
```

The final program in this book doesn't animate a *DrawingBrush*, but it does animate an *Ellipse* element filled with a *DrawingBrush*. It is a program I call HybridClock, and it's compiled as a XAML Browser Application. The clock contains a round face like a normal analog clock, but it has only one hand that sweeps around the clock to indicate the seconds. The clock hand itself is a digital clock of sorts because it displays a text string that provides the current date and time. A context menu lets you pick a preferred date and time format.

The following class provides the clock with the current date and time formatted in a string. The class implements the *INotifyPropertyChanged* interface and provides a *PropertyChanged* event for the *DateTime* property, so this class can be a source in a data binding. This is how the date and time displayed by the clock's hand is updated.

ClockTicker.cs

```
//-------------------------------------------
// ClockTicker.cs (c) 2006 by Charles Petzold
//-------------------------------------------
using System;
using System.ComponentModel;
using System.Windows.Threading;

namespace Petzold.HybridClock
{
    public class ClockTicker : INotifyPropertyChanged
    {
        string strFormat = "F";

        // Event required for interface.
        public event PropertyChangedEventHandler PropertyChanged;

        // Public property.
        public string DateTime
        {
            get { return System.DateTime.Now.ToString(strFormat); }
        }

        public string Format
        {
            set { strFormat = value; }
            get { return strFormat; }
        }

        // Constructor.
        public ClockTicker()
        {
            DispatcherTimer timer = new DispatcherTimer();
            timer.Tick += TimerOnTick;
            timer.Interval = TimeSpan.FromSeconds(0.10);
            timer.Start();
        }

        // Timer event handler triggers PropertyChanged event.
        void TimerOnTick(object sender, EventArgs args)
```

```
        {
            if (PropertyChanged != null)
                PropertyChanged(this,
                    new PropertyChangedEventArgs("DateTime"));
        }
    }
}
```

The HybridClock project includes a small application definition file that simply references the only other XAML file in the project.

HybridClockApp.xaml
```
<!-- ================================================
        HybridClockApp.xaml (c) 2006 by Charles Petzold
     ================================================ -->
<Application x:Class="Petzold.HybridClock.HybridClockApp"
    xmlns="http://schemas.microsoft.com/winfx/2006/xaml/presentation"
    xmlns:x="http://schemas.microsoft.com/winfx/2006/xaml"
    StartupUri="HybridClockPage.xaml" />
```

When considering how this clock would work, I knew that I wanted to enclose the whole thing in a *Viewbox* so it would get larger and smaller as the user changed the window size. But I also recognized that the text string that formed the clock's single hand would cause scaling problems. If the user selected a date and time format that included the text month, the length of the string would change as the month changed. The length of the string would also change when the time went from 12:59 to 1:00 or when the date advanced from the ninth of the month to the tenth. For the most part, I wanted the XAML file to compensate for these changes.

The total clock contains no fewer than eight *TextBlock* elements, each of which displays the same date and time string. The first of these eight *TextBlock* elements contains a binding to the *ClockTicker* object; the others contain a binding to the *Text* property of that first *TextBlock*. Each *TextBlock* exists in a side-by-side pair with another *TextBlock*. One pair is used to set the horizontal size of the clock face, and another pair is used to set the vertical size. These four *TextBlock* elements are on a transparent panel. The two other pairs rotate in unison around their mutual centers. Only one *TextBlock* is visible at any time. When the hand is straight up or straight down, an animation causes one to fade out and another to fade in so that the text is never upside down.

HybridClockPage.xaml
```
<!-- ================================================
        HybridClockPage.xaml (c) 2006 by Charles Petzold
     ================================================ -->
<Page x:Class="Petzold.HybridClock.HybridClockPage"
    xmlns="http://schemas.microsoft.com/winfx/2006/xaml/presentation"
    xmlns:x="http://schemas.microsoft.com/winfx/2006/xaml"
    xmlns:src="clr-namespace:Petzold.HybridClock"
```

```
          WindowTitle="Hybrid Analog/Digital Clock"
          Title="Hybrid Analog/Digital Clock"
          Background="Pink">

    <!-- Resource for class that provides current time. -->
    <Page.Resources>
        <src:ClockTicker x:Key="clock" />
    </Page.Resources>

    <!-- ToolTip has program copyright notice. -->
    <Page.ToolTip>
        <TextBlock TextAlignment="Center">
            Hybrid Analog/Digital Clock
            <LineBreak />&#x00A9; 2006 by Charles Petzold
            <LineBreak />www.charlespetzold.com
        </TextBlock>
    </Page.ToolTip>

    <Viewbox>
        <!-- Outer single-cell grid encompasses the whole clock face. -->
        <Grid>
            <Ellipse>
                <Ellipse.Fill>
                    <SolidColorBrush Color="{x:Static
                        src:HybridClockPage.clrBackground}" />

                    <!-- Unfortunately, this radial brush hurt performance. -->
                    <!-- RadialGradientBrush GradientOrigin="0.4, 0.4">
                        <RadialGradientBrush.GradientStops>
                            <GradientStop Offset="0" Color="White" />
                            <GradientStop Offset="1"
                                Color="{x:Static
                                src:HybridClockPage.clrBackground}" />
                        </RadialGradientBrush.GradientStops>
                    </RadialGradientBrush -->

                </Ellipse.Fill>
            </Ellipse>

            <!-- This inner single-cell Grid is sized by the text width. -->
            <Grid Name="grd" Margin="12">

                <!-- Make two invisible horizontal date/time strings. -->
                <StackPanel Orientation="Horizontal" Opacity="0"
                        VerticalAlignment="Center">
                    <TextBlock Name="datetime"
                            Text="{Binding Source={StaticResource clock},
                                        Path=DateTime}" />
                    <TextBlock Text="{Binding ElementName=datetime,
                                        Path=Text}" />
                </StackPanel>

                <!-- Make two invisible vertical date/time strings. -->
                <StackPanel Orientation="Horizontal" Opacity="0"
                        HorizontalAlignment="Center">
```

```xml
            <TextBlock Text="{Binding ElementName=datetime,
                                      Path=Text}" />
            <TextBlock Text="{Binding ElementName=datetime,
                                      Path=Text}" />
            <StackPanel.LayoutTransform>
                <RotateTransform Angle="90" />
            </StackPanel.LayoutTransform>
        </StackPanel>

        <!-- Make two rotatable date/time strings. -->
        <StackPanel Orientation="Horizontal"
                    HorizontalAlignment="Center"
                    VerticalAlignment="Center"
                    StackPanel.RenderTransformOrigin="0.5 0.5">
            <TextBlock Text="{Binding ElementName=datetime, Path=Text}"
                    Opacity="0" />
            <TextBlock Text="{Binding ElementName=datetime, Path=Text}"
                    Name="txt1" Opacity="0.5"/>

            <StackPanel.RenderTransform>
                <RotateTransform x:Name="xform1"/>
            </StackPanel.RenderTransform>
        </StackPanel>

        <!-- Make two more rotatable date/time strings. -->
        <StackPanel Orientation="Horizontal"
                    HorizontalAlignment="Center"
                    VerticalAlignment="Center"
                    RenderTransformOrigin="0.5 0.5">
            <TextBlock Text="{Binding ElementName=datetime, Path=Text}"
                    Name="txt2"
                    Opacity="0.5" />
            <TextBlock Text="{Binding ElementName=datetime, Path=Text}"
                    Opacity="0" />

            <StackPanel.RenderTransform>
                <RotateTransform x:Name="xform2"/>
            </StackPanel.RenderTransform>
        </StackPanel>
    </Grid>

    <!-- Rotatable mask (defined in code). -->
    <Ellipse Name="mask"
             RenderTransformOrigin="0.5 0.5" >
        <Ellipse.RenderTransform>
            <RotateTransform x:Name="xform3"/>
        </Ellipse.RenderTransform>
    </Ellipse>
    </Grid>
</Viewbox>

<Page.Triggers>
    <EventTrigger RoutedEvent="Page.Loaded">
        <BeginStoryboard>
            <Storyboard x:Name="storyboard">
```

```
                                   <!-- Double animations turn the text and opacity mask. -->
                                   <DoubleAnimation Storyboard.TargetName="xform1"
                                               Storyboard.TargetProperty="Angle"
                                               From="-90" To="270" Duration="0:1:0"
                                               RepeatBehavior="Forever" />

                                   <DoubleAnimation Storyboard.TargetName="xform2"
                                               Storyboard.TargetProperty="Angle"
                                               From="-270" To="90" Duration="0:1:0"
                                               RepeatBehavior="Forever" />

                                   <DoubleAnimation Storyboard.TargetName="xform3"
                                               Storyboard.TargetProperty="Angle"
                                               From="-90" To="270" Duration="0:1:0"
                                               RepeatBehavior="Forever" />

                                   <!-- Key frame animations do fades. -->
                                   <DoubleAnimationUsingKeyFrames
                                           Storyboard.TargetName="txt1"
                                           Storyboard.TargetProperty="Opacity"
                                           Duration="0:1:0" RepeatBehavior="Forever">
                                       <LinearDoubleKeyFrame Value="1" KeyTime="0:0:0.5" />
                                       <DiscreteDoubleKeyFrame Value="1" KeyTime="0:0:29.5" />
                                       <LinearDoubleKeyFrame Value="0" KeyTime="0:0:30.5" />
                                       <DiscreteDoubleKeyFrame Value="0" KeyTime="0:0:59.5" />
                                       <LinearDoubleKeyFrame Value="0.5" KeyTime="0:1:0" />
                                   </DoubleAnimationUsingKeyFrames>

                                   <DoubleAnimationUsingKeyFrames
                                           Storyboard.TargetName="txt2"
                                           Storyboard.TargetProperty="Opacity"
                                           Duration="0:1:0" RepeatBehavior="Forever">
                                       <LinearDoubleKeyFrame Value="0" KeyTime="0:0:0.5" />
                                       <DiscreteDoubleKeyFrame Value="0" KeyTime="0:0:29.5" />
                                       <LinearDoubleKeyFrame Value="1" KeyTime="0:0:30.5" />
                                       <DiscreteDoubleKeyFrame Value="1" KeyTime="0:0:59.5" />
                                       <LinearDoubleKeyFrame Value="0.5" KeyTime="0:1:0" />
                                   </DoubleAnimationUsingKeyFrames>
                               </Storyboard>
                           </BeginStoryboard>
                       </EventTrigger>
                   </Page.Triggers>
               </Page>
```

Because the size of the clock face is based on the length of the text displayed by the clock hand, any changes to the length of text (for example, when one month ends and another starts) results in a change to the size of the clock face. However, the clock face is inside a *Viewbox*, and the *Viewbox* immediately adjusts its contents so it appears to maintain the same size. What seems to change is the font size of the text relative to the size of the clock face. (You can see this more dramatically if you right-click the clock and select a much shorter or longer date and time format.)

These dramatic changes in the actual size of the clock face prevented me from including the clock ticks in the XAML file. I decided to do those in code and to change them whenever the length of the text string changed. I also included a rotating ellipse in the XAML—this is the ellipse that's rotated with the third *DoubleAnimation* object—filled with a brush with a varying amount of transparency. This brush seems to make the tick marks pop into view as the hand approaches them and then to slowly fade out. This brush had to be recalculated in code whenever the text length changed.

Here's the code part of the HybridClock project. Besides handling the tick marks and the partially transparent ellipse, it also manages the context menu.

HybridClockPage.xaml.cs

```
//--------------------------------------------------------
// HybridClockPage.xaml.cs (c) 2006 by Charles Petzold
//--------------------------------------------------------
using System;
using System.Windows;
using System.Windows.Controls;
using System.Windows.Input;
using System.Windows.Media;
using System.Windows.Media.Imaging;
using System.Windows.Shapes;

namespace Petzold.HybridClock
{
    public partial class HybridClockPage : Page
    {
        // Initialize colors for XAML access.
        public static readonly Color clrBackground = Colors.Aqua;
        public static readonly Brush brushBackground = Brushes.Aqua;

        // Save transforms for clock ticks.
        TranslateTransform[] xform = new TranslateTransform[60];

        public HybridClockPage()
        {
            InitializeComponent();

            // Set the Storyboard BeginTime property.
            storyboard.BeginTime = -DateTime.Now.TimeOfDay;

            // Set handler for context menu Opened event.
            ContextMenu menu = new ContextMenu();
            menu.Opened += ContextMenuOnOpened;
            ContextMenu = menu;

            // Set handler for Loaded event.
            Loaded += WindowOnLoaded;
        }

        void WindowOnLoaded(object sender, EventArgs args)
```

```
{
    // Create tick marks around clock.
    for (int i = 0; i < 60; i++)
    {
        Ellipse elips = new Ellipse();
        elips.HorizontalAlignment = HorizontalAlignment.Center;
        elips.VerticalAlignment = VerticalAlignment.Center;
        elips.Fill = Brushes.Blue;
        elips.Width =
        elips.Height = i % 5 == 0 ? 6 : 2;

        TransformGroup group = new TransformGroup();
        group.Children.Add(xform[i] =
            new TranslateTransform(datetime.ActualWidth, 0));
        group.Children.Add(
            new TranslateTransform(grd.Margin.Left / 2, 0));
        group.Children.Add(
            new TranslateTransform(-elips.Width / 2, -elips.Height /2));
        group.Children.Add(
            new RotateTransform(i * 6));
        group.Children.Add(
            new TranslateTransform(elips.Width / 2, elips.Height /2));

        elips.RenderTransform = group;
        grd.Children.Add(elips);
    }
    // Make the opacity mask.
    MakeMask();

    // Set event handler for change in size of the date/time string.
    datetime.SizeChanged += DateTimeOnSizeChanged;
}
// Date/time string changes: Recalculate transforms and mask.
void DateTimeOnSizeChanged(object sender, SizeChangedEventArgs args)
{
    if (args.WidthChanged)
    {
        for (int i = 0; i < 60; i++)
            xform[i].X = datetime.ActualWidth;

        MakeMask();
    }
}
// Make the opacity mask.
void MakeMask()
{
    DrawingGroup group = new DrawingGroup();
    Point ptCenter = new Point(datetime.ActualWidth + grd.Margin.Left,
                               datetime.ActualWidth + grd.Margin.Left);

    // Calculate 256 wedges around circle.
    for (int i = 0; i < 256; i++)
    {
        Point ptInner1 =
            new Point(ptCenter.X + datetime.ActualWidth *
```

```
                                    Math.Cos(i * 2 * Math.PI / 256),
                        ptCenter.Y + datetime.ActualWidth *
                            Math.Sin(i * 2 * Math.PI / 256));

            Point ptInner2 =
                new Point(ptCenter.X + datetime.ActualWidth *
                            Math.Cos((i + 2) * 2 * Math.PI / 256),
                        ptCenter.Y + datetime.ActualWidth *
                            Math.Sin((i + 2) * 2 * Math.PI / 256));

            Point ptOuter1 =
                new Point(ptCenter.X +
                        (datetime.ActualWidth + grd.Margin.Left) *
                            Math.Cos(i * 2 * Math.PI / 256),
                        ptCenter.Y +
                        (datetime.ActualWidth + grd.Margin.Left) *
                            Math.Sin(i * 2 * Math.PI / 256));

            Point ptOuter2 =
                new Point(ptCenter.X +
                        (datetime.ActualWidth + grd.Margin.Left) *
                            Math.Cos((i + 2) * 2 * Math.PI / 256),
                        ptCenter.Y +
                        (datetime.ActualWidth + grd.Margin.Left) *
                            Math.Sin((i + 2) * 2 * Math.PI / 256));

            PathSegmentCollection segcoll = new PathSegmentCollection();
            segcoll.Add(new LineSegment(ptInner2, false));
            segcoll.Add(new LineSegment(ptOuter2, false));
            segcoll.Add(new LineSegment(ptOuter1, false));
            segcoll.Add(new LineSegment(ptInner1, false));

            PathFigure fig = new PathFigure(ptInner1, segcoll, true);

            PathFigureCollection figcoll = new PathFigureCollection();
            figcoll.Add(fig);

            PathGeometry path = new PathGeometry(figcoll);
            byte byOpacity = (byte)Math.Min(255, 512 - 2 * i);

            SolidColorBrush br = new SolidColorBrush(
                Color.FromArgb(byOpacity, clrBackground.R,
                            clrBackground.G, clrBackground.B));

            GeometryDrawing draw =
                new GeometryDrawing(br, new Pen(br, 2), path);
            group.Children.Add(draw);
        }

        DrawingBrush brush = new DrawingBrush(group);
        mask.Fill = brush;
    }

    // Initialize context menu for date/time format.
    void ContextMenuOnOpened(object sender, RoutedEventArgs args)
```

```
        {
            ContextMenu menu = sender as ContextMenu;
            menu.Items.Clear();

            string[] strFormats = { "d", "D", "f", "F", "g", "G", "M",
                                    "R", "s", "t", "T", "u", "U", "Y" };

            foreach (string strFormat in strFormats)
            {
                MenuItem item = new MenuItem();
                item.Header = DateTime.Now.ToString(strFormat);
                item.Tag = strFormat;
                item.IsChecked = strFormat ==
                    (Resources["clock"] as ClockTicker).Format;
                item.Click += MenuItemOnClick;
                menu.Items.Add(item);
            }
        }
        // Process clicked item on context menu.
        void MenuItemOnClick(object sender, RoutedEventArgs args)
        {
            MenuItem item = (sender as MenuItem);
            (Resources["clock"] as ClockTicker).Format = item.Tag as string;
        }
    }
}
```

The *MakeMask* method is easily the most complex part of this job. It is responsible for making the *DrawingBrush* object that is used to set the *Fill* property of the *Ellipse* element identified in the XAML file with the name "mask." This *DrawingBrush* object is mostly transparent except for wedges around the circumference of a circle. These wedges coincide with the tick marks displayed by the clock. The wedges are colored the same as the background of the clock face and are gradated in transparency. The result is that only half the tick marks behind the *Ellipse* are visible, and those that are visible range from fully visible to fully transparent.

The real magic occurs when this *Ellipse* is rotated and the individual tick marks seem to suddenly pop into view and then fade away. An alternative (perhaps practical only if there were much fewer tick marks) would be to animate the *Opacity* property of each one independently. But I rather prefer my solution.

HybridClock is built mostly from elements that are hidden from view. These invisible elements provide structure to the visible elements, and sometimes (as with the clock hand as it passes 6:00 and 12:00) the visible and invisible change roles, mutually offering support for the sake of an overall effect.

Index

Symbols & Number

Charles Petzold

Charles Petzold has been writing about personal computer programming for two decades. His class book *Programming Windows*, now in its fifth edition, has influenced a generation of programmers and is one of the best-selling programming books of all time. He is also the author of *Code: The Hidden Language of Computer Hardware and Software*, the critically acclaimed narrative on the inner life of smart machines. Charles is also a Microsoft MVP for Client Application Development. His Web site is *www.charlespetzold.com*.

Additional Resources for Developers: Advanced Topics and Best Practices

Published and Forthcoming Titles from Microsoft Press

Code Complete, Second Edition
Steve McConnell • ISBN 0-7356-1967-0

For more than a decade, Steve McConnell, one of the premier authors and voices in the software community, has helped change the way developers write code—and produce better software. Now his classic book, *Code Complete*, has been fully updated and revised with best practices in the art and science of constructing software. Topics include design, applying good techniques to construction, eliminating errors, planning, managing construction activities, and relating personal character to superior software. This new edition features fully updated information on programming techniques, including the emergence of Web-style programming, and integrated coverage of object-oriented design. You'll also find new code examples—both good and bad—in C++, Microsoft® Visual Basic®, C#, and Java, although the focus is squarely on techniques and practices.

More About Software Requirements: Thorny Issues and Practical Advice
Karl E. Wiegers • ISBN 0-7356-2267-1

Have you ever delivered software that satisfied all of the project specifications, but failed to meet any of the customers expectations? Without formal, verifiable requirements—and a system for managing them—the result is often a gap between what developers think they're supposed to build and what customers think they're going to get. Too often, lessons about software requirements engineering processes are formal or academic, and not of value to real-world, professional development teams. In this follow-up guide to *Software Requirements*, Second Edition, you will discover even more practical techniques for gathering and managing software requirements that help you deliver software that meets project and customer specifications. Succinct and immediately useful, this book is a must-have for developers and architects.

Software Estimation: Demystifying the Black Art
Steve McConnell • ISBN 0-7356-0535-1

Often referred to as the "black art" because of its complexity and uncertainty, software estimation is not as hard or mysterious as people think. However, the art of how to create effective cost and schedule estimates has not been very well publicized. *Software Estimation* provides a proven set of procedures and heuristics that software developers, technical leads, and project managers can apply to their projects. Instead of arcane treatises and rigid modeling techniques, award-winning author Steve McConnell gives practical guidance to help organizations achieve basic estimation proficiency and lay the groundwork to continue improving project cost estimates. This book does not avoid the more complex mathematical estimation approaches, but the non-mathematical reader will find plenty of useful guidelines without getting bogged down in complex formulas.

Debugging, Tuning, and Testing Microsoft .NET 2.0 Applications
John Robbins • ISBN 0-7356-2202-7

Making an application the best it can be has long been a time-consuming task best accomplished with specialized and costly tools. With Microsoft Visual Studio® 2005, developers have available a new range of built-in functionality that enables them to debug their code quickly and efficiently, tune it to optimum performance, and test applications to ensure compatibility and trouble-free operation. In this accessible and hands-on book, debugging expert John Robbins shows developers how to use the tools and functions in Visual Studio to their full advantage to ensure high-quality applications.

The Security Development Lifecycle
Michael Howard and Steve Lipner • ISBN 0-7356-2214-0

Adapted from Microsoft's standard development process, the Security Development Lifecycle (SDL) is a methodology that helps reduce the number of security defects in code at every stage of the development process, from design to release. This book details each stage of the SDL methodology and discusses its implementation across a range of Microsoft software, including Microsoft Windows Server™ 2003, Microsoft SQL Server™ 2000 Service Pack 3, and Microsoft Exchange Server 2003 Service Pack 1, to help measurably improve security features. You get direct access to insights from Microsoft's security team and lessons that are applicable to software development processes worldwide, whether on a small-scale or a large-scale. This book includes a CD featuring videos of developer training classes.

Software Requirements, Second Edition
Karl E. Wiegers • ISBN 0-7356-1879-8

Writing Secure Code, Second Edition
Michael Howard and David LeBlanc • ISBN 0-7356-1722-8

CLR via C#, Second Edition
Jeffrey Richter • ISBN 0-7356-2163-2

For more information about Microsoft Press® books and other learning products, visit: **www.microsoft.com/mspress** *and* **www.microsoft.com/learning**

Additional Resources for Web Developers

Published and Forthcoming Titles from Microsoft Press

Microsoft® Visual Web Developer™ 2005 Express Edition: Build a Web Site Now!
Jim Buyens • ISBN 0-7356-2212-4

With this lively, eye-opening, and hands-on book, all you need is a computer and the desire to learn how to create Web pages now using Visual Web Developer Express Edition! Featuring a full working edition of the software, this fun and highly visual guide walks you through a complete Web page project from set-up to launch. You'll get an introduction to the Microsoft Visual Studio® environment and learn how to put the light-weight, easy-to-use tools in Visual Web Developer Express to work right away—building your first, dynamic Web pages with Microsoft ASP.NET 2.0. You'll get expert tips, coaching, and visual examples at each step of the way, along with pointers to additional learning resources.

Microsoft ASP.NET 2.0 Programming
Step by Step
George Shepherd • ISBN 0-7356-2201-9

With dramatic improvements in performance, productivity, and security features, Visual Studio 2005 and ASP.NET 2.0 deliver a simplified, high-performance, and powerful Web development experience. ASP.NET 2.0 features a new set of controls and infrastructure that simplify Web-based data access and include functionality that facilitates code reuse, visual consistency, and aesthetic appeal. Now you can teach yourself the essentials of working with ASP.NET 2.0 in the Visual Studio environment—one step at a time. With *Step by Step*, you work at your own pace through hands-on, learn-by-doing exercises. Whether you're a beginning programmer or new to this version of the technology, you'll understand the core capabilities and fundamental techniques for ASP.NET 2.0. Each chapter puts you to work, showing you how, when, and why to use specific features of the ASP.NET 2.0 rapid application development environment and guiding you as you create actual components and working applications for the Web, including advanced features such as personalization.

Programming Microsoft ASP.NET 2.0
Core Reference
Dino Esposito • ISBN 0-7356-2176-4

Delve into the core topics for ASP.NET 2.0 programming, mastering the essential skills and capabilities needed to build high-performance Web applications successfully. Well-known ASP.NET author Dino Esposito deftly builds your expertise with Web forms, Visual Studio, core controls, master pages, data access, data binding, state management, security services, and other must-know topics—combining definitive reference with practical, hands-on programming instruction. Packed with expert guidance and pragmatic examples, this *Core Reference* delivers the key resources that you need to develop professional-level Web programming skills.

Programming Microsoft ASP.NET 2.0
Applications: *Advanced Topics*
Dino Esposito • ISBN 0-7356-2177-2

Master advanced topics in ASP.NET 2.0 programming—gaining the essential insights and in-depth understanding that you need to build sophisticated, highly functional Web applications successfully. Topics include Web forms, Visual Studio 2005, core controls, master pages, data access, data binding, state management, and security considerations. Developers often discover that the more they use ASP.NET, the more they need to know. With expert guidance from ASP.NET authority Dino Esposito, you get the in-depth, comprehensive information that leads to full mastery of the technology.

Programming Microsoft Windows® Forms
Charles Petzold • ISBN 0-7356-2153-5

Programming Microsoft Web Forms
Douglas J. Reilly • ISBN 0-7356-2179-9

CLR via C++
Jeffrey Richter with Stanley B. Lippman
ISBN 0-7356-2248-5

Debugging, Tuning, and Testing Microsoft .NET 2.0 Applications
John Robbins • ISBN 0-7356-2202-7

CLR via C#, Second Edition
Jeffrey Richter • ISBN 0-7356-2163-2

For more information about Microsoft Press® books and other learning products, visit: **www.microsoft.com/books** *and* **www.microsoft.com/learning**

What do you think of this book?
We want to hear from you!

Do you have a few minutes to participate in a brief online survey? Microsoft is interested in hearing your feedback about this publication so that we can continually improve our books and learning resources for you.

To participate in our survey, please visit:

www.microsoft.com/learning/booksurvey

And enter this book's ISBN, 0-7356-1957-3. As a thank-you to survey participants in the United States and Canada, each month we'll randomly select five respondents to win one of five $100 gift certificates from a leading online merchant.* At the conclusion of the survey, you can enter the drawing by providing your e-mail address, which will be used for prize notification *only*.

Thanks in advance for your input. Your opinion counts!

Sincerely,

Microsoft Learning

Microsoft | Learning

Learn More. Go Further.